*The* DECLARATION *of* INDEPENDENCE *in*

HISTORICAL CONTEXT

# *The* DECLARATION *of* INDEPENDENCE *in* HISTORICAL CONTEXT

*American State Papers, Petitions, Proclamations,*

*& Letters of the Delegates to the First National Congresses*

*Compiled, Edited, and Introduced by*

BARRY ALAN SHAIN

LIBERTY FUND/INDIANAPOLIS

This book is published by Liberty Fund, Inc., a foundation established to
encourage study of the ideal of a society of free and responsible individuals.

𒂼𒄄

The cuneiform inscription that serves as our logo is the earliest-known
appearance of the word "freedom" (*amagi*), or "liberty." It is
taken from a clay document written about 2300 B.C.
in the Sumerian city-state of Lagash.

Published with assistance from the foundation established
in memory of Amasa Stone Mather of the Class of 1907, Yale College.

Designed by Mary Valencia.
Set in Minion type by Westchester Book Group.
Printed in the United States of America.

Library of Congress Cataloging-in-Publication Data

The Declaration of Independence in historical context:
American state papers, petitions, proclamations, and letters
of the delegates to the first national congresses
compiled, edited, and introduced by Barry Alan Shain.
[Liberty Fund paperback edition].
pages       cm
Includes bibliographical references and index.
ISBN 978-0-86597-889-8 (pbk.: alk. paper)
1. United States. Declaration of Independence.
2. United States—History—Revolution, 1775–1783—Causes—Sources.
3. United States—Politics and government—1775–1783—Sources.
I. Shain, Barry Alan, 1950– editor of compilation.
E221.D38 2015
973.3'13—dc23                    2014003579

Liberty Fund, Inc.
8335 Allison Pointe Trail, Suite 300
Indianapolis, Indiana 46250-1684

This paper meets the requirements of ANSI/NISO Z39.48–1992 (Permanence
of Paper).

10  9  8  7  6  5  4  3  2  1

*To my wife,*
*Carolyn Nagase Shain,*
*whose support,*
*in innumerable ways,*
*made the completion of this work possible*

# CONTENTS

CONTENTS

CONTENTS

CONTENTS

CONTENTS

CONTENTS

# CONTENTS

CONTENTS

CONTENTS

# ACKNOWLEDGMENTS

Like most scholarly works, this volume highlights the efforts of an author or editor—for good and bad—while leaving in the background those individuals and organizations whose assistance and emotional or financial support made the work possible. With such assistance in mind, I must begin by thanking Vanessa N. Persico, recently graduated from the University of California's Hastings School of Law and currently attorney-advisor to the Honorable Thomas M. Burke in the U.S. Department of Labor Office of Administrative Law Judges, for her invaluable help in the preparation of this collection. Over the course of four summers beginning in 2006, while I read through thousands of pages of documents and letters and chose among them, Ms. Persico, at the time a Colgate University undergraduate, tracked down, if needed typed, and formatted those documents that we decided on using. In addition, she researched the circumstances under which each was written and began the process of putting together documentary introductions. In short, this volume, along with another already completed and published (and yet another still in process), would have never been completed without Ms. Persico's wonderfully able assistance. Although she deserves the lion's share of the credit for aiding me with the demanding editorial tasks of putting this volume together, other Colgate University students also served for a semester as research assistants, among them Adam Zimmermann, Emily Bradley, Katie Esteves, David Gelman, Grace Seery, and Leigh Herzog. Over the past two academic years, Sebastian Kooyman, Claire Littlefield, and, most recently, Anna Phipps have helped greatly in completing all manner of last-minute tasks. To all of them and, again, most especially to Ms. Persico, I owe a great deal.

My work with these students was made possible by funding from the Colgate University Research Council, which allowed me to hire Ms. Persico for three summers, and Mr. Gelman and Ms. Herzog each for one summer (and Ms. Littlefield as well, though she worked with me mostly on a different project and was funded by the Division of the Social Sciences). In addition, Research Council funding permitted me to hire the research assistants named above during the academic year. In each of the summers from 2009 to 2011, either in addition to or in lieu of Colgate funding, I was awarded grants from the Earhart Foundation with which to hire a summer research assistant. I wish, accordingly, to extend my thanks to the Colgate University Research Council; its two past chairs, Professors Nina Moore and Judith Oliver; the current chair, Lynn Staley; the board of directors of the Earhart Foundation; and its program director, Dr. Montgomery Brown, for their much-needed support.

A number of my colleagues, too, deserve recognition for the assistance they have provided. Among them, three have helped shape my research over the years—indeed, in each instance for twenty or more years. Here, I would like to thank Professors Daniel L. Dreisbach of American University, Philip Hamburger of Columbia University Law School, and Rogers M. Smith of the University of Pennsylvania. Although not directly involved in this project, each of them has read my past work, provided needed and valuable guidance, and offered me his friendship. Professor Smith has been doing this and so much more for far longer than either of us would wish (or soon will be able) to remember. I would also like to thank two Colgate colleagues, Professors Jay Swain and Robert Kraynak, who, as fellow members of a summer reading group in which part of the manuscript for this volume was read, offered me important and unexpected feedback, that is, that eighteenth-century American materials are more difficult to read than one might have expected, which guided me in my revisions. Drafts of the general introduction, in particular, were read by Professor Swain, Dr. Emilio Pacheco of the Liberty Fund, and Professor George W. Carey of Georgetown University, and the final version is, I believe, much improved from their having done so. Finally, it is hard to know what to write in order to express my gratitude for the dozens of e-mail exchanges, usually ones of respectful disagreement, between me and Professor Craig Yirush of the University of California at Los Angeles, who critically read the entire manuscript, at least once, before using it twice in one of his classes. No doubt there are far fewer errors, overblown statements, and unneeded modifiers in this work as a result of his meticulous reading of the manuscript. Still there is much about which we can continue to disagree. I hope that our challenging conversations will last into the future far longer than the current ones have during the recent past.

I wish also to thank our departmental administrative assistant, Cindy Terrier, for her help with whatever I asked of her, most particularly the formatting of tricky matters. Similarly, I owe much to William Frucht, executive editor at Yale University Press, and his assistant, Jaya Chatterjee. Mr. Frucht was enthusiastically and genuinely supportive of the project from the get-go and exceptionally patient during any number of unforeseen delays. Ms. Chatterjee was consistently unselfish with her time and counsel, both of which I greatly relied upon. Ash Lago, too, of Yale University Press, helped out with formatting demands that had left me stumped. More deserving of my thanks is the copy editor assigned to this project by Yale's manuscript editor, Susan Laity. As most readers will recognize, many of my claims of gratitude, although genuine, are much to be expected. My debt to Kip Keller, the copy editor for this book, is far more than this. In ways utterly unexpected and in a manner far more than anyone could reasonably demand, he deleted innumerable redundancies, turned my too frequently turgid prose into something at times even approaching the artful, and, most importantly, caught mistaken statements, dates, and documentary errors that had eluded my own countless efforts. In truth, anything infelicitous in the text is due to my stubborn refusal to accept all of Mr. Keller's ever-helpful suggestions. Thank you, Kip.

Yale solicited a number of reports that proved instructive. One report signed by Professor George McKenna of the City College of the City University of New York, along with an anonymous one, provided insightful understandings of my project that helped me in making my revisions; another anonymous report, of some sixteen pages, led to a great reduction in the number of errors in this volume. All three readers were most generous with their time, and for this and their evaluations of the manuscript, I owe them my heartfelt thanks.

Finally, I wish to thank my wife, Dr. Carolyn Nagase Shain, to whom this volume is dedicated. Everything I put in print is greatly improved by her editing and her critical scrutiny. In the fall semester of 2010, Carolyn consented to my accepting from Colgate a semester of unpaid leave, and it was during this time that I wrote initial drafts of the introductory materials offered in this book. For her generosity of spirit and willingness to live rather simply during that semester and for so much else, I owe her my love and far more than can be adequately expressed here.

# DOCUMENT CHRONOLOGY

Metropolitan British documents listed below are bolded to assist readers in getting a sense of the tit-for-tat nature of the persistent, even tragic pattern of the deteriorating imperial relationship between the colonies and Great Britain. Displaying this graphically helps, in part, to dispel the too-common assumption that the congressional delegates consistently directed events toward an outcome they uniformly sought and understood, guided by an agreed-upon philosophy that would support the emergence of republican polities outside the British Empire. Instead, the reactive nature of the colonists' developing positions is readily mapped out in their responses to misguided British policies. Only the most significant British documents have been included in this volume; many more could have been added.

1754:   July 9, the Albany Plan of Union
1764:   October 18, New York Petitions to the King and House of Commons
        November 3, Petition from the Massachusetts House of Representatives to the
                House of Commons
        December 18, Virginia Petitions to the King and Parliament
1765:   June–December, Resolves of Virginia, Pennsylvania, Maryland, Connecticut,
                Massachusetts, South Carolina, New Jersey, and New York
        October 8–18(?), Report of the Committee to Whom Was Referred the
                Considerations of the Rights of the British Colonies
        October 19–21, Declarations of the Stamp Act Congress; Petitions to the
                King and Parliament
        December 1765–March 1766, Statements of the Sons of Liberty
1766:   **February 13, Examination of Benjamin Franklin in the House of Commons**
        **March 18, An Act Repealing the Stamp Act; Declaratory Act**
        December 11, Samuel Adams to Christopher Gadsden

# NOTE TO THE READER

In a possibly unusual way, the structure of this work has been shaped by the highly contested interpretive issues surrounding the years of American Revolutionary and early national history. Different interpretive schools choose from widely divergent sources, often by a difficult-to-avoid cherry-picking from a universe of documents that stretches across fifty years, in support of a particular thesis. By contrast, this collection predominantly draws on a circumscribed but rich subset of materials in an effort to reduce the problem of selection bias while offering heightened interpretive authority. Accordingly, almost all the documents in this collection were drawn from, or found ultimate expression in, one of the three continental (more accurately, intercolonial) congresses, which took place in 1765 and 1774–77, rather than primarily from potentially idiosyncratic municipal or provincial bodies such as the Boston Town Meeting or the Massachusetts General Court; second, all (or almost all) the theoretically relevant documents (that is, those concerned with political organization, collective moral ends, constitutional matters, or imperial issues) from those gatherings have been included in this collection; and third, the documents offered below retain their original language and spelling and most of their formatting, only occasionally being cut for excessive length.

Additionally, the design and goals of this volume, something of a hybrid, challenge the traditional division between historical monographs, with clearly delineated theses, and putatively nondiscursive documentary collections. This approach was taken because it seemed unlikely that an additional history book with carefully selected evidence, no matter how well done, would necessarily do much either to advance our understanding of the place of the Declaration of Independence in Revolutionary-era political thought or, possibly still more critically, to help in adjudicating between the varying schools of interpretation described below in the Introduction. Put more starkly, a traditional history book on the Declaration of Independence, with carefully selected but not inclusive documentary evidence (for example, one building on an earlier essay of mine on the rights claims of the Declaration, which I intended to expand into a full-length monograph)[1] would be unlikely to convince anyone not already sympathetic to its interpretive outlook.

Similarly, yet another collection of sundry material drawing upon documents from individual actors, municipal and provincial state papers, and periodical editorials, and lacking any special warrant or interpretive authority such as that provided by congressional "state papers," almost all of which enjoyed intercolonial or continental standing, is, no matter how carefully done, unlikely to help resolve the by now too deeply entrenched lines of debate regarding how best to understand the Declaration of Independence and, more broadly, the nature of early American political thought. This volume, therefore, makes the somewhat unorthodox choice of placing directly before the reader not carefully selected citations, no matter how abundant, nor longer snippets of documents, no matter how carefully selected, but almost all the theoretically rich documents (that is, those not concerning personal or military matters) from these three bodies in their entirety. With the addition of pointed, comprehensive introductions to the minimally edited documents, it is hoped that this collection will allow readers to place the Declaration of Independence in its proper imperial historical context more clearly than they might have done from reading either a traditional focused monograph or a broader-gauged documentary collection.

Every effort has been made to include in this volume as many as possible of the congressional proclamations, petitions, resolutions, and accompanying letters from the period under examination, that is, first from the beginning years of the Imperial Crisis (1764–66) and then from the years immediately before and after the colonies declared their independence and put forward their first national plan of government (1774–77). I hope that this will provide the reader with a higher level of confidence in the integrity of the selection process followed here than would necessarily have been the case if documents had been chosen from a more extensive assortment of newspaper editorials, pamphlets, and public documents from municipal and provincial bodies and spread over fifty years, and sometimes even longer (think, in particular, of the frequently cited "Detached Memoranda" of James Madison, written sometime between 1817 and 1832). This is not meant to demean the fine work of others who have used different selection criteria from those offered here, for example, Jack Greene or Charles Hyneman and Donald Lutz, but only to draw attention to the overlooked merits of using a more delimited set of materials, in particular that doing so greatly reduces editorial discretion in choosing documents.[2] The benefits of such a procedure and the hoped-for resulting increase in interpretive authority, I believe, may be available only when almost all relevant materials are included and, at best, lightly edited—as has been done here.

This procedure meant excluding provincial colonial materials produced during the middle years of the Imperial Crisis, 1767–70, since they lacked a continental congress for their expression and thus fell outside the principal selection rule used for this volume.[3] Although these documents would surely have enhanced the comprehensive historical character of the book, they would have added little theoretical novelty, and they would have fallen outside the "naturally" circumscribed universe of materials to be considered in this work.

Most of the documents are complete, so readers will be able to come to their own conclusions regarding the dominant political visions advanced in them and in early America, the relationship between the documents and the Declaration of Independence, and thus the degree to which the Declaration should be viewed as broadly representative of American political thought of the period. Yet an explanation is still needed why—no matter how inclusive the selection process—some documents were included but not others.

There were three criteria used in selecting documents and letters. Well-known documents or those generally understood to form a significant part of the historical record were included. Second, long documents with limited or no political theoretical interest (for example, draft military or economic treaties) were not included. And third, those materials not broadly recognized as an essential part of the historical record were included only if they met a relatively modest standard of theoretical richness or, more likely, helped make sense of the principal congressional state papers included in the collection. Since there are around 5,000 printed pages alone of letters from congressional delegates for the period of the First Congress and the early years of the Second (1774 until the end of 1777), little else could be done if the volume were to be kept to a manageable length.[4]

Doubts might remain that a different but equally inclusive collection of documents would have told a different story in support of one or another of the alternative schools of interpretation discussed below in the Introduction. As with any scholarly work, readers will, in the end, have to judge for themselves whether the selection of documents seems unbiased. All I can promise here is that every congressional document and delegate letter that I read and that met the criteria for inclusion—that is, it had historical relevance for the period or continuing theoretical interest, no matter whose line of interpretation it might be viewed as supporting—was chosen for this volume. If readers are convinced of the same, as I hope they will be, they should be prepared to begin exploring the dominant political ideas of these bodies' delegates and the comparative standing of the Declaration of Independence within the political aspirations and goals of the American colonists during the years leading to America's declaring its independence, 1764–76, and the especially revealing year that followed its issuance. Thus prepared, readers should be able to assess the strengths and weaknesses of contending theories of interpretation of the founding movement to which the Declaration of Independence gave voice, and of its place in early American political thought.

Finally, let me offer a few comments on the documents themselves. I avoided introducing potentially intrusive notes into the text that might, even if ever so subtly, influence a reader's understanding of the documents. Such commentary is limited to my introductions or, at most, to an explanatory comment in a headnote. In addition, although not facsimiles or drawn directly from archival materials, almost all the documents retain their original eighteenth-century spelling and punctuation, in all its variety (often an indicator of an author's socioeconomic status), along with the original formatting and underlining or italicization (both printed as *italics*). If most of a document was underlined, however, that formatting was silently removed. Very occasionally, when source materials regarding an original document differ, silent corrections were made to any apparent typographical errors in a reprinted edition. Ellipsis points in the documents indicate where material was omitted by an editor, whereas suspension points present in the source texts themselves are enclosed in square brackets [ . . . ]. Parallel lines in materials taken from the *Journals of the Continental Congress* were added by the editor, W. C. Ford, to indicate that the text enclosed within the lines was taken from the "Corrected Journal" (which began on September 5, 1775), not the original manuscript *Journal*. Finally, in those letters taken from Paul H. Smith's superbly edited *Letters of Delegates to Congress,* I have retained a number of his editing conventions: conjectural readings for missing text are bracketed in roman font [roman], editorial insertions are bracketed in italics [*italics*], and matter that was crossed out in the manuscript but later restored by the author is in parentheses and italics (*italics*).

*The* DECLARATION *of* INDEPENDENCE *in*

HISTORICAL CONTEXT

# INTRODUCTION

## THREE CONGRESSES, ANGLO-AMERICAN CONSTITUTIONALISM, AND BRITISH IMPERIALISM AND MONARCHY

*In Search of a New/Old Approach to Understanding
American Revolutionary-Era History*

Over the past century, the American Declaration of Independence and the movement it gave voice to, a separation of the major North American continental colonies from Great Britain and the creation of thirteen independent republican governments, have not lacked for interpreters. Most importantly, as pointed out by Alan Gibson, intellectual historians and political theorists have made every effort to use the Declaration's theoretically rich second paragraph as the foundation of all manner of American political thought and creeds while tying it to, or contrasting it with, European schools of thought.[1] Indeed, there are, at a minimum, seven competing schools of interpretation: four are text-based ones that turn to earlier European philosophical and theological treatises in search of the most powerful formative influences on America's independence movement, and three of them turn to more varied material for sources to explore.

Most important among those schools of interpretation derived from the work of antecedent European political thinkers is that which holds that Revolutionary-era Americans were committed adherents of a certain political philosophy, often loosely described as Enlightenment liberalism, that is most often associated with the seventeenth-century English philosopher and political activist John Locke. This Lockean (liberal) philosophy is generally taken to hold that all men enjoy equal civil standing and unalienable universal natural rights, that they are "motivated primarily by the pursuit of their passions and interests," and that "governors derive their just powers from the consent of the governed."[2] Indeed, much here seems to coincide with the rich, though sparse, claims advanced in the Declaration's famous second paragraph.

During the second half of the past century, this understanding of the dominant philosophy of the American Founders was challenged by intellectual historians who argued that two other predominantly text-based traditions, both of them more communal and concerned with directly promoting private and public virtue than does Lockean liberalism, had shaped the thinking of soon-to-be Americans and had led them to separate from Britain and to embark on an experiment in republican government. The second school of philosophically derived thought, republicanism, includes the treatises of seventeenth- and early eighteenth-century radical and Whig English republican or commonwealth authors, with some scholars emphasizing incarnations of republicanism from the Renaissance Italian (civic humanism) or ancient Roman (classical republican) worlds.[3] Proponents of this school of thought emphasize corporate concerns and a robust understanding of the public good and political virtue (*virtu*), and show a diminished concern with narrowly understood individual well-being. A third tradition, also offered as a challenge to the dominance of Lockean liberalism, looks to Scottish moral or commonsense thinking, of which Francis Hutcheson is seen as the progenitor.[4] Here again, the individualistic or selfish understanding of human nature is discounted among its adherents, then and now, in comparison with that commonly associated with early-modern and classical liberalism. Accordingly, moral-sense theories highlight "perfectionist" strategies for achieving public and private virtue.

Late in the twentieth century, a small number of scholars challenged the philosophical-republican take on the American founding. This group focused on treatises also, but in this case, on theological and ecclesiological rather than philosophical ones. They argued that the most important formative influence on the political thought and institutions of late eighteenth-century Americans—often with scant attention paid to the Declaration of Independence, not something that went unnoticed—was Reformed Protestantism.[5] Adherents of this school of interpretation might be described, then, as defenders of something in many ways akin to Calvinism as formative in the shaping of American political thought. They hold that it, most especially in the New England colonies, which served a leading—perhaps dominant—role, both intellectually and still more politically, in the movement toward independence, had been deeply shaped by norms such as the pervasive character of original sin and human depravity, and the consequent need for all men, even the most elevated, to live in close-knit communities in which each person watched and helped his fellow citizens approach a more godly and virtuous manner of living. In this tradition, to the degree that monarchy might be seen to compete with God for the role of true sovereign, republicanism long enjoyed a certain privileging.

They also argue that Reformed Protestantism, in particular an American variant that defends the idea of a national covenant between all the colonists (believers or not) and God, helps make sense of the idea of America as a unitary moral community in which people were held to demanding, even intrusive, public standards, regardless of the likelihood of individual salvation. Supporting this view, they point to the numerous days of fasting and prayer proclaimed by the Continental Congresses, in which citizens were to repair to their houses of worship and seek the forgiveness of Christ and the intervention of the Holy Spirit for help in overcoming their "manifold sinfulness" (see documents 17.2, 28.1, and 40.1). In contrast with these invasive characteristics, Reformed Protestant ecclesiology, with its relatively egalitarian ethos and deeply localistic patterns of church governance, pushed toward a decentralized control of moral policing—thus, along with its pro-republican propensity in New England, this provided for a certain radical edge.[6] Not surprisingly, some scholars have argued that an amalgamation, in some form or other, of these four text-based traditions principally shaped the American mind that produced the Declaration of Independence and the closely associated American War of Independence.[7]

Scholars defending the predominantly political philosophical and theological traditions, most importantly Lockean liberalism and some form of republicanism (assuming—a matter open to question—that they significantly differ), share several common features. First, they are idealist in suggesting that well-developed high-level abstract political theories—derived from European thinkers, colonial or British pamphleteers, patriot statesmen, or Protestant theologians—served as the principal guides in directing North American colonists to resist British parliamentary imperial governance, to declare independence, and to set up thirteen independent republican state governments. Second, and possibly of greatest importance, they frequently view the second paragraph of the Declaration of Independence as a stand-alone piece of political philosophy that uniquely gives full expression to the American mind circa 1776 while additionally providing the nation's founding and perpetual creed. Third, these interpreters often characterize the Founders as temporally, socially, and geographically unified, as if despite being dispersed across 1,500 miles of coastline, enduring twenty-five years of wars and revolution (or even when writing thirty years later in their dotage), and inhabiting distinct social, professional, and sectional groupings, they can be described as believing and writing in a unitary fashion.

Fourth, defenders of liberal and republican historiography often assume, without much argument, that the colonial and later American characterizations of the twenty-year British Imperial Crisis (1763–83) are factually accurate, unbiased, and normatively unchallengeable in comparison with largely ignored British metropolitan views. Thus, it is rare to encounter learned American accounts that highlight a British perspective, including those that view the British Empire and its imperial agents as defenders of cosmopolitanism (in opposition to colonial parochialism), Native Americans, and French Roman Catholics while serving in a certain sense as emancipators of African

American (and soon-to-be liberators of Afro-Caribbean) slaves. In short, few empha-size that the British were as progressive as the colonists, or even more so, in their defense of an ethnically, linguistically, religiously, and racially pluralistic polity; thus, it may have been the colonists who in certain senses were the more reactionary of the two populations.[8]

Not surprisingly, given the prevalence of such one-sided accounting, a fifth charac-teristic of the treatise-based line of argument is that the putatively unchanging political thinking defended by a select number of prominent colonial figures is deserving of continued national, even international, approbation and emulation for its uplifting morality.[9] In sum, following these accounts, the colonists, in gaining inde-pendence, were successful in achieving their original aspirations, philosophically and morally elevated in comparison with their British opponents, consciously and confi-dently directed, and possessed of a remarkably high level of consistency and integrity, so much so that their independence movement can be fairly viewed as an outgrowth of a certain measure of genius. Indeed, it is too often difficult to distinguish patriotic embellishment, even apotheosis, from scholarly analysis of the period in the work of too many interpreters.[10]

Not all twentieth-century interpreters, though, turned to high-level political philosophical or theological treatises in trying to make sense of the Declaration of Independence and the independence movement to which it formally gave birth. Most importantly, three schools of historiography, two with roots early in the last century and a third that was more a product of late last century, looked beyond narrowly political-philosophical or theological treatises in making sense of the decades sur-rounding the North American continental colonies' quest for independence. Those from the early twentieth century include the Progressives and later neo-Progressives, which focus on economics and class or social divisions, and another, difficult-to-define tradition that finds its roots in the 1920s and 1930s and has enjoyed a contemporary renaissance.[11] This later tradition of scholarly interpretation of the Revolutionary era, the Imperial school, understands much of what others believe to be exceptional, enlightened, or universal in the colonies to be, in truth, a parochial product of British political, legal, religious, and broadly cultural antecedents.[12] Similarly, the difficulties that led to the War of Independence resulted from the inability of the colonists and the British Parliament to resolve intractable constitutional dilemmas, not from the colonists being moved by inherited or novel liberal or republican theoretical aspira-tions. Finally, the third extratextually based school of interpretation (and the seventh overall) includes the diverse approaches that make up the school of American social history, in which social and economic formations, not political discourse, are empha-sized in explaining much of American political behavior.[13]

Of particular importance to this volume are the claims of the Imperial school. Most especially this is because, in keeping with the documents to follow, the original adherents of this tradition and their later followers explain that the crisis that led to the War of Independence was concerned primarily with British corporate, not individual, rights, and was viewed by the majority of the colonists through the lens of British constitutional, not abstract natural, rights.[14] The war, moreover, from this tradition's perspective was the product of failed Anglo-American imperial relations and the inability of legislative majorities on either side to advance a mutually acceptable imperial-federal constitution, rather than the result of innovative republican political theorizing or liberal constitutionalism.[15]

More surprising still is the insistence of a number of these authors—again, much in keeping with the documents collected here—on the anachronistic promonarchical commitments of the colonists, to the point that the colonial position in important ways was more royalist than general attitudes in late eighteenth-century Britain and at times verged on embracing elements of seventeenth-century Stuart absolutism. Thus, one contemporary scholar writes that the all-encompassing royalism of colonial America "has been gradually wiped from out national memory. Royalism, it has seemed to the general public and most American scholars, had never really taken deep root in colonial society."[16] These contemporary scholars and their early twentieth-century predecessors are not alone in their suspicions, for in the eighteenth century, according to Lord North, it was the king's friends and ministers who "'contended for the rights of parliament, while the Americans talked of their belonging to the crown. Their language therefore was that of toryism.'"[17] By emphasizing the essentially imperial character of the crisis that led to the War of Independence, and the centrality of monarchy for more than a decade to the colonial opposition position and, in the long-term, to American political institutions, contemporary adherents of the Imperial school are effectively challenging the republican historiography of the late 1960s and early 1970s, which in turn challenged several earlier generations of Progressive and liberal-consensus historians such as Cecelia Kenyon, who asserted with authority that "the Americans were not republican in either a formal or an ideological sense before 1776."[18]

This tradition of interpretation, though, is not without substantial controversies; most important among them is the question whether the American colonial constitutional position should, from any number of perspectives, be viewed as reasonable. Staking out opposing positions on the historical accuracy of the colonial American historical account and implicitly on the defensibility of the colonists' position were Charles McIlwain in 1923 and Robert Schuyler in 1929, with Barbara Black serving in 1976 as arbiter between them.[19] Still, controversies notwithstanding, this early twentieth-century school of thought arose during a time of unusual openness, when professional history briefly separated itself from Whiggish and uniquely patriot-centered historiography, and thus it is well worth the renewed attention it has recently received.[20]

Each group of scholars, in its effort to understand the Declaration of Independence and the American War of Independence, has its preferred resources to which it turns for insight and for evidence of the accuracy of its interpretation. Not surprisingly, scholars who are adherents of the three mostly European treatise-based traditions look to the works of those authors believed to be most influential and then to one, two, or even numerous American documents or publications for language that they believe drew on the European theorists for inspiration.[21] In addition, those who believe that Reformed Protestantism was especially influential in shaping American political institutions and thought are most likely to consider America's several hundred Revolutionary-era, theoretically rich election and other political sermons; scores of proclamations and religiously intolerant and intrusive Reformed Protestant codes of law from across the seventeenth and eighteenth centuries; a century of theological writings; and, still more importantly, ecclesiological commentary emanating from a transnational community of Reformed Protestant pastors and theologians.[22]

Among the three schools of interpretation in which scholars are less narrowly influenced by extant treatise-based approaches, Progressives and neo-Progressives find inspiration in widely varied sources, but have been "profoundly skeptical of relying on the professed beliefs of historical actors for understanding their motives" and therefore have frequently turned to "empirical studies" while downplaying the influence of high-level European political treatises.[23] Social historians, too, have generally shied away from a wholesale reliance on textual antecedents, both European and American, and instead have sought to explain the political behavior of American colonists of the period by examining town and city political behavior, voting studies, legislative behavior, gender relationships, the nature and formation of social and economic classes and their conflicts, and the commercial and material world of the eighteenth century broadly understood.[24]

In general, adherents of the Imperial school are neither narrowly treatise-based nor materialist and thus have regularly used a variety of materials in advancing their interpretation. Their sources have included British and colonial state papers and governmental records in both Britain and the colonies. At the same time, of particular relevance are the divisive politics regularly found in legislative bodies and metropolitan executive offices. Possibly of greatest importance to these scholars are the divergent constitutional arguments found in municipal, provincial, continental, and imperial state papers put forward by each side during the British Imperial Crisis that began in 1763–64.[25] It is these arguments that the documents and letters reproduced in this volume, at the continental or intercolonial level, seem most fully to reflect. It is the Imperial school, too, that emphasizes that the principal question confronted by North American colonists was a relatively simple one to characterize though not necessarily to solve: whether Parliament had the right to legislate for and to tax the colonists for revenue. Moreover, according to those drawing on this school of interpretation, both sides relied on contrasting understandings of the British and imperial constitution (and possibly, too, an older English one), especially regarding the proper relationships between the British realm and the Crown's or king's dominions, in arguing their cases.

The scholars of these different interpretative schools, as one would expect, have explained the meaning of America's 1776 Declaration of Independence, both its words and the role it played in America's separation from Britain, in different ways. Some have explored its draftsman's (that is, Thomas Jefferson's) sparse published record, along with his copious personal correspondence and public statements; many others have investigated the thought of prominent seventeenth- and eighteenth-century European political thinkers and activists who may have influenced Jefferson; and most recently and successfully, prominent scholars have attempted to make sense of the Declaration by comparing it to other contemporaneous declarations and thus examining how it was understood, both domestically and internationally, in the eighteenth and nineteenth centuries.[26] There is, of course, much to be said for each of these approaches and the materials their adherents explore. But what may be the most essential materials needed to understand the Declaration and the American independence movement to which it gave birth, I would suggest, have not as yet been examined in a methodologically systematic and defensible manner. This is, then, the goal of this work and the documents it contains.

What I have in mind is an effort to understand the Declaration and the War of Independence against the background provided by the hundreds of continental-level congressional state papers—declarations, petitions, resolutions, and proclamations— and the debates and correspondence of those in attendance at the three continental or intercolonial congresses of 1765 and 1774–77, years that spanned the formative period of the Imperial Crisis that led to the colonies' declaring independence and the consequent war that followed. It was the men in attendance at those congresses who gave voice to the continental—not the individual, provincial, or sectional—aspirations that led to the July 4 Declaration of Independence and, on November 15, 1777, to America's first national constitution, the Articles of Confederation and Perpetual Union.[27] For this reason—if for no other, and there are more (as discussed at greater length in the "Note to the Reader")—these men and the congressional state papers to which they gave birth deserve careful consideration for the insight they can provide on the static or, more likely, changing goals and reasons that led to the colonies declaring their independence.

Possibly providing an even more compelling reason for examining these materials with unusual care is that those in attendance at the Second Continental Congress were the very men who vetted and voted to approve—after carefully considering and excising nearly a third of it—Jefferson's committee draft of the Declaration of Independence. But long before, as well as after, many of these same men approved scores of petitions, resolves, and declarations that, when taken together, provide readers with a far more detailed and complete picture of the political thought, goals, practices, and consistency (or inconsistency) of the delegates than even the most careful line-by-line close reading, or exegesis, of the second paragraph of the Declaration of Independence can offer, especially when it is read in isolation and understood as a stand-alone treatise in political philosophy (in which a nation's essence is then, too, to be found).[28] Even as it gave birth to thirteen newly independent states, the Declaration was still more the culmination of a twelve-year struggle in which three intercolonial or continental congresses penned dozens of allied petitions, resolves, and declarations. These works, when taken as an extended text, should help readers understand the place of the Declaration of Independence—as will be seen in the following documents, in many ways a rather marginal one—in the continental-level political thought of the twelve years preceding its creation.[29] Nearly a century ago, McIlwain ended his path-breaking study, *The American Revolution,* with an arresting conclusion: "The Declaration of Independence is a totally different kind of document from any of its predecessors. For the first time the grievances it voices are grievances against the King, and not against Parliament. It is addressed to the world, not to Great Britain, and naturally the ground of such a protest will be one understood by a world that knows little of the British constitution and cares less: it will be based on the law of nature instead of the constitution of the British Empire."[30] The readings that follow, I believe, will offer copious and compelling support for McIlwain's conclusion.

Thus, by exploring the continental congressional state papers collected in this volume that are antecedent to Congress' declaring the American colonies independent, readers should be reasonably well positioned to adjudicate between the contrasting and divergent schools of interpretation described above, and to find many of them wanting. Of course, no single collection of materials can hope to end seemingly interminable and intractable debates, but by examining the critical documents and letters reproduced herein, readers should be able to move toward an informed understanding of the dominant thought of congressional delegates in the years 1765–77 and thereby to be able to put in historical context the Declaration of Independence. The state papers of the three early continental or intercolonial congresses offer a far more authoritative view of colonial or early national political thought against which to view the Declaration of Independence than does a paragraph from the same document, even when read alongside ancillary materials with impressive provincial pedigrees, editorials selected from hundreds of newspaper pieces, pamphlets from half a dozen national figures (out of several hundred, and sometimes several decades after the period in question), or long-dead or distant European authors.[31] With such varied materials, the temptation to select materials consistent with one interpretation or another may be hard, even impossible, to resist.

With such preparation, readers will be able to assess whether the Declaration of Independence, especially its celebrated second paragraph, accurately gives voice to the political and constitutional theorizing and agitation of the preceding twelve years[32] or to the dominant thinking in Congress during the postindependence year that followed, in which America's first national constitution, the Articles of Confederation and Perpetual Union, was slowly and fitfully agreed upon. Importantly, during 1777, Congress, in responding to a number of issues, helps us understand its delegates' surprisingly narrow and anything but expansive understanding of the words in the Declaration. This is most readily apparent in congressional recommendations to local extralegal bodies to arrest suspected deserters and to evict Quakers from Pennsylvania, both actions wholly lacking any semblance of due process; in the widespread forced seizure of agricultural products in and around Valley Forge; or, most glaringly of all, in the explicit rejection of the rights language of the Declaration in Congress' denial of the petition for statehood of the residents of the New Hampshire Grants, what would soon come to be called Vermont.

This volume's effort to view the Declaration of Independence in a broad, continent-wide historical and imperial context deserves its standing because unlike many other collections of source materials, the state papers of these three congresses embodied the goals and intentions of continental constituencies—not individual authors, particular cities or colonies, or even regional groupings, for example, the most boisterous of them, the widely disseminated views of the New England colonies. For this reason, the continental congressional state papers taken as a whole—with little pruning or tendentious selection—ought to enjoy a higher level of interpretative authority than almost all other imaginable source materials or collections. This is not to suggest that the state papers, declarations, and recorded debates of these three continental congresses perfectly reveal the thinking of all colonists engaged in twelve years of intermittent resistance to imperial British edicts, or the goals of all parties, or the intentions of all congressional delegates regarding various pronouncements, including that of independence. But these documents are more revealing, and less subject to selection bias, than collections that include difficult-to-assess materials sometimes drawn from across a hundred-year period or longer and from multiple continents, and that fail to give due recognition to contemporaneous congressional state papers that enjoyed intercolonial standing.

The collected continental documents offered here, in giving voice to the congressional delegates that in a narrowly legal sense "wrote" the Declaration of Independence not only help us better understand the contemporary standing of the Declaration of Independence when set against other congressional state papers, but also challenge a number of well-received ideas about the colonial movement toward independence and republican government. Possibly most striking, the vast majority of the documents dispute whether the failed colonial movement for reconciliation with George III that culminated in the colonies' declaring independence was, in fact, the result of a well-planned and theoretically sophisticated American democratic project for republican government or, as seems more likely, the result of British parliamentary misjudgment, internal British political struggles, and parliamentary and Crown intransigence and pride, most particularly from mid-1775 through early 1776.[33]

If so, the end reached in the Declaration of Independence during the summer of 1776 is less a product of careful orchestration, even by conductors of colonial resistance such as Samuel Adams and Richard Henry Lee, than of necessity resulting from persistent British failure to handle properly an intransigent colonial situation (most especially in one colony, Massachusetts). Indeed, the documents suggest that there is reason to believe that the fragile majority in Congress that ultimately supported independence could well have been dissuaded or, at least, delayed from doing so, by a properly constructed British conciliatory offer. If Lord Howe had arrived off the coast of Staten Island ten days earlier in July 1776, the potential for negotiations would likely have changed. Congressional radicals, afraid of that very possibility, smartly pushed the Declaration through Congress before Howe's arrival with his woefully inadequate commission to bring the king's peace to his colonies.

Another idea challenged by these documents is that of unified or unitary continental congresses.[34] This is most especially true because at least for the First and the early years of the Second Congress, these bodies were deeply divided between two distinct political visions and approaches to the conflict.[35] On one side were congressional radicals—mostly men of New England and Virginia—who moved more quickly than others away from the colonists' dutiful adherence to, and even love of, the king and inclusion in the British Empire.[36] On the other side were congressional moderates (and, early on, conservatives, who would in the end remain loyal to the king)—most importantly, men of the mid-Atlantic colonies—who were far more cautious about distancing themselves from Crown and empire and far more hopeful, up to the beginning of 1776, of achieving a just and constitutional reconciliation with Great Britain that would leave the colonists under the rule of their British monarch and still within the British Empire.[37]

It was the congressional radicals' view that, in the end, rightly described the outcome of the Imperial Crisis, but the too often underappreciated or ignored moderate view was dominant in the First Congress and the beginning months of the Second Congress; indeed, it held a majority in Congress until six to twelve months before the colonies declared independence, and remained a force to be reckoned with well into the spring of 1776.[38] Such findings stand in contrast to common hagiographic portraits of the American colonial elites—loyalists excepted—as having acted with unanimity in a deliberate and well thought-through fashion and as having been consistently guided by a well-developed democratic political philosophy resting on individual, universal, natural rights.[39]

Notably, too, many of the same moderate men from the mid-Atlantic colonies who long resisted the break with Britain were among those who later pushed most strenuously for the adoption of the Constitution in 1787–88.[40] This, too, suggests that an important division existed in the world of the Founders between the likes of Samuel Adams and Richard Henry Lee, older men who deserve an inordinate share of the responsibility for the colonies' break with Great Britain, and a mostly younger generation, men like James Madison (twenty-five in 1776), Gouverneur Morris (twenty-four), and Alexander Hamilton (nineteen), who in 1787 played such prominent roles in replacing one short-lived national constitutional order by another that was more (or less) to their liking.[41]

Approaching the Declaration and the movement that culminated in the War of Independence from the perspective of a twelve-year history of mostly continental congressional state papers also challenges the view of this movement as having been guided principally by a long-dominant colonial radicalism derived from the progressive aspirations of earlier British progressive political or religious thinkers.[42] Most particularly, a decade of continental congressional documents puts in question the enduring interpretation of this period offered by the most famous student of the Declaration of Independence, Carl L. Becker, and the many scholars and interpreters who have followed his lead. For Becker, America's Declaration, the war that it reflected, and the thought of most colonial Americans were deeply indebted to a Lockean liberal political philosophy that has much in common with other ideas of the European Enlightenment (assuming, mistakenly, the existence of a unitary Enlightenment consensus) and, ultimately, the goals, even if greatly attenuated, of the French Revolution.[43]

This interpretation is difficult to sustain in light of the dogged commitment of the majority of congressional delegates to remain within the British Empire; to preserve the sanctity of English or British constitutionalism, customs, laws, traditions, and explicitly corporate (and only in the background, individual) English rights; and, what is still more difficult to understand today, to defend British constitutional monarchy—indeed, even more strongly royalist in important ways than was true of many "Old" Whigs in Britain who remained wary of resurgent royal power and were dedicated to upholding Parliamentary supremacy, which they believed followed the Glorious Revolution of 1688.[44] These commitments (of the majority of delegates in three congresses), so readily discovered in the documents below, stand in sharp contrast with the universal natural rights and popular-consent theorizing associated with Lockean liberalism and the Declaration of Independence. Additionally, the persistent record, revealed here, of the colonists' denial or narrow restriction of the rights of Roman Catholic Canadians, Native Americans, African Americans, loyalists, Quakers, and, to lesser degrees, other British colonials in Ireland, the West Indies, and elsewhere necessarily places in question the centrality of the soaring, liberal, universal rhetoric of the Declaration. Indeed, in almost every instance, British imperial agents, in trying to serve the interests of metropolitan Britons and others in a diverse empire with distinct and clashing interests, were far more protective of the rights of each of these populations (the Irish excepted) than were the colonists. The latter, in fact, viewed the British efforts to protect the rights of subordinate peoples as grievances, which they complained of in the Declaration of Independence, including, most importantly, the freeing of Virginia's slaves by Lord Dunmore.[45]

Finally, congressional documents challenge the view that the colonists aggressively sought to create a republican and democratic plan of government free of monarchical influence.[46] In fact, the representatives of most of the colonies' legislative or extralegal legislative executive bodies, with no British ministerial or Crown encouragement or any manner of reward for their ill-fated efforts, intermittently for twelve years sought reconciliation with Britain and the intercession of the British king in the colonies' struggles with Parliament, as well as the continuation of mixed monarchical government (with representatives from one or two of the nonroyal colonies, most famously Benjamin Franklin, seeking in the late 1760s to come under the king's direct governance) and membership in the British Empire.

As will become apparent, the majority of congressional delegates sought to strengthen—not weaken—the king's prerogative powers while denying Parliament's right to oversee the king's activities in the colonies. In the minds of many Britons, the colonists sought to resurrect in the king powers that British Whigs had spent the past century fighting to diminish. Britons and many influential Continental Europeans—such as Montesquieu, the author most cited by Americans—celebrated the outcome of this legislative constraint over potentially arbitrary executive power as a unique British development and advanced form of liberty.[47] The republican governments, as declared in 1776 and long celebrated by popular interpreters of this period as the goal of the colonial opposition movement, were in fact not the openly stated goal of any of the delegates in 1765 or 1774, and by mid-1775 it was the admitted goal of only a minority, mostly from Reformed Protestant New England or deeply indebted Virginia. The limited desire for independence and republican government among a group of, at best, reluctant revolutionaries is, especially outside the circle of professional historians, too little appreciated.[48]

In light of these misconceptions, the Declaration may more accurately be seen as the unintended and undesired culmination of a process of resistance in which the majority of the colonists believed they were defending customary and traditional British constitutional institutions and historical political rights against misguided ministerial and parliamentary innovations;[49] as tied to the ascendancy of localist and relatively democratic forces in the colonies over centralizing and relatively more elitist factions; as the moment of birth of a new republican political and popular cultural order in which inherited English corporate political rights previously limited to select populations were replanted in a different soil, also largely English and inherited from the seventeenth and early eighteenth centuries, of universal individual natural rights; and as the end of what can only be viewed an intimate relationship between the colonies and their king after his rejection of one set of his "children" (the North American colonists) and his privileging of another (the metropolitan British).

This clear moment of regime change, however, exercised a surprisingly limited theoretical influence on the political actions of the members of Congress as they moved ahead with managing an extremely difficult war and trying to give birth to a yet-unborn new nation. For such efforts, the potent rights language of the Declaration was largely ignored, even denied, in Congress in the year following its issuance. And thus the year 1777 is particularly valuable for placing the Declaration in its proper historical context, because the universalistic rhetoric of the Declaration—as authorized by nearly the same body of men—was then absent from Congress' numerous resolutions and its most important product, the Articles of Confederation and Perpetual Union. The individualistic, rights-based concerns and absolutist republican theories of popular consent that one might have expected to be emphasized in that momentous year are absent from Congress' actions and state papers. The omission is most glaring in Congress' rejection of the request of the residents of the New Hampshire Grants (the future Vermont) for admission to Congress: congressional delegates openly rejected the universal language of Congress' own declarations of May 15 and July 4, 1776. It is similarly absent from congressional adjudications of former colonial land claims, in which Congress promptly turned not to any universal code of abstract rights but to the colonies' English charters and the dictates of the British common law.

The congressional and associated documents found in this volume should help readers understand the constitutional issues at the center of the Imperial Crisis: intractable ones that made the crisis, from the perspective of both sides, even when acting in good faith, so difficult to resolve.[50] In particular, the documents should help clarify why the American opposition movement, when advancing prominent lines of argument, was viewed as so threatening to British constitutional arrangements by Whig factions in Parliament. That is, the colonists' refusal to accept parliamentary oversight and dominance while continuing to support enthusiastically their ties to the British Crown—even going so far as to be willing to provide the king with requisitions uncontrolled by Parliament—seemed to threaten the revolutionary ascendancy of the British Parliament since the Glorious Revolution of 1688, in short, eighteenth-century British constitutional government. The frightening character of the American threat makes more understandable—even if not defensible—the stubborn resistance of the vast majority in Parliament to compromise on the matter of its sovereign rights. Most, even among the "king's friends," feared that without such power, parliamentary control over the king's prerogatives might be lost. From the colonial perspective, and rightly so, Parliament's taxing of the colonists and, even more troubling, its legislating for their internal affairs—without extending representation to the property holders of the colonies—abrogated, along with Parliament's limiting the reach of common-law juries, long-cherished inherited English corporate political rights.

On both sides, the practical consequences of often-negligible taxes were less seriously at stake than the rights of Parliament (which, from the American perspective, was Britain's, not the colonies', legislature) versus those of the colonists' legislative bodies, their parliaments. The controversy was about the rights of competing legislatures and thus was difficult to reconcile. As a modern commentator observed, "The conflict between Great Britain and her Colonies was a tragedy in the classic sense; it was a conflict of rights."[51] (Thus, I have chosen to divide this work into "acts," as in a dramatic tragedy.) Among congressional delegates, the king's extensive governmental role in the colonies was, until near the end of the crisis in the spring of 1776, never at issue. Of course, the same couldn't be claimed for truly radical elements "out of doors" (that is, not in Congress or Parliament) in the colonies and, possibly less expected, in Britain too.

Put differently, the basic constitutional issue separating the colonists and Parliament was whether the colonies were dominions of the Crown or king and, if the former, whether Parliament enjoyed supremacy over them: this seemingly trivial definitional issue was anything but.[52] If, as may have been true when many of the colonies were planted in the seventeenth century, they were held by the king not as crown territories but as his personal holdings, then being located outside the British dominions would have rendered them free from parliamentary oversight, like certain of the Channel Islands.[53] If, however, they had always been held under the king as crown territories or if, as declared in 1649 by Parliament and later in 1688 and in subsequent legislation, the king's North American colonies had been absorbed into the British nation, then Parliament, as the supreme sovereign body, enjoyed legislative oversight over them, as over the rest of the nation. This, along with a number of arcane legal and constitutional complexities, was at the heart of the impasse between Parliament and the colonies. The intractability of this issue and the unwillingness (or inability) of both sides to compromise, and not the widespread embrace of some theoretically rich political theory, led most in Congress to declare independence.[54] The exploration of this issue should be, then, at the heart of general studies of the American Revolution. It was the focus of the Imperial school historians of the early twentieth century and is central to some of their early twenty-first-century intellectual descendants, and to this volume.[55]

Unfortunately, the dominant eighteenth-century Anglo-American Whig political perspective was adapted with difficulty to responsible party politics, in which the executive branch and the legislature work in tandem rather than in opposition. Instead, many Old Whigs continued to hang on tenaciously to outdated features of the 1688 revolutionary settlement that were already being displaced by George III during his reign as he worked closely with "his friends in Parliament"—something close to anathema for many old-fashioned Whigs.[56] Similarly, Whig political thought, in its devotion to parliamentary supremacy, even if not parliamentary absolutism in the case of men like Chatham (William Pitt the elder), lacked a model or understanding of how to incorporate multiple federal parliaments into a matrix of shared imperial sovereignty.[57] Accordingly, with several types of Whigs predominant on both sides of the Atlantic (to many in Britain, in fact, the colonists in their embrace of royal prerogatives and their rejection of parliamentary dominance appeared to be as much Tory as Whig), there were relatively few who could envision or support a novel constitutional solution.[58] An exception was Joseph Galloway, a former speaker of the Pennsylvania assembly, close confidant and protégé of Benjamin Franklin, and future loyalist whose proposed solution was stricken from the records of the First Continental Congress (see document 10.1). With the exception of Franklin too, in his similarly rejected 1775 Articles of Confederation (see document 44.1), no other prominent colonial thinker offered a similarly viable solution.[59]

Instead, what the American colonial spokesmen came to embrace was an early seventeenth-century vision of the English Constitution in which the king's colonial holdings could be governed without parliamentary involvement (and in which Parliament was additionally constrained by fundamental law) or, in a number of alternative prescriptions, the king ruled his personal dominions independent of the British Parliament, whose authority stopped at the edge of the British realm.[60] The colonists' constitutional theory thus would have likely been more at home in pre–Civil War seventeenth-century England, late seventeenth-century Scotland, the last decade of eighteenth-century Ireland, or the king's holdings in Hanover, Germany, than in late eighteenth-century Britain or in its empire.[61]

The documents below suggest that the colonists never fully appreciated the king's constitutional role in the British and imperial constitutions or his inability to act independently of a parliamentary majority—even if he had wished to circumvent one he did so much to create and to direct, which he adamantly didn't—in trying to fulfill colonial requests for protection against parliamentary oversight. One must keep in mind that the last British monarchical veto was in 1707. No doubt, if George III had tried to act in accord with the colonists' often despairing, yet consistently affectionate and deferential, petitions (see, for example, documents 15.1 and 19.1)—thus acting truly tyrannically, in distinction to the false accusations leveled against him in the Declaration—he would have, at a minimum, lost support in Parliament and likely would have provoked a constitutional crisis.[62] As a limited constitutional monarch and as head of the British Empire, even a clever one learning to manipulate the reins of an emerging party government, he sought to remain true to the eighteenth-century British Constitution and a Parliament that exercised, at minimum, co-sovereignty over the empire.[63] The colonists' failure to appreciate the difficulties of his position led them to take on the role of a spurned lover or, still more accurately, of the forsaken and disfavored son of a much-loved father.

In fairness, it should be added that only a minority of members of Parliament—whose majority was content with a system of colonial dependence that privileged British commerce, manufacturing, and shipping—were interested in finding an equitable solution to the imperial constitutional conundrum that Britain and its colonists faced: how, within the British Empire, to protect the corporate British political rights of the colonists—which were understood by most on both sides as being potentially subject to violation by Parliament—while maintaining Parliament's supremacy in Britain. Most in Britain believed that the American colonies had served as a rich resource over the previous century and had done much to produce Britain's rapidly increasing national wealth; however, few members of Parliament, even as late as 1778 for some, as seen in the instructions to the Carlisle Peace Commission (see document 47.1), were willing, any more than they had been in 1766 in the Declaratory Act (see document 8.2), to limit constitutionally parliamentary oversight over the colonies.[64] Political control that had been exercised jointly by British imperial officers in Britain and the colonies, and colonial legislatures, even if of long-standing practice, was difficult to enshrine in the language of constitutional right in a manner that would have been acceptable to two difficult-to-satisfy populations of legislators.

At best, friends of the colonies in Parliament such as Edmund Burke and Lord Camden argued that one must avoid invoking constitutional theory and parliamentary rights and colonial prerogatives; Chatham, another supporter, held that a bright-line (even if impossible to ascertain) distinction should be maintained between raising revenue through taxation and other forms of parliamentary legislation.[65] Few members of Parliament, and not many more outside it, were able to envision an adequate constitutional solution to the problem of how to provide the colonists with entrenched British political liberties while keeping them within the British Empire under a sovereign Parliament.[66] An adequate solution in Britain would have to wait for a new century and for forms of imperial federalism to develop within the British Commonwealth. The proposed solutions offered by prominent colonial thinkers and political actors failed too in tackling these and other difficult constitutional issues. Their inability to resolve this issue, in the end, led the colonists' delegates to declare independence and thus to put off the question of how constitutionally (they already knew how to do so practically and had done so, in some instances, for over a century) to organize a federal polity in which sovereignty is shared between widely dispersed subordinate polities and a superordinate central one.

Looked at with the future in mind, America's Declaration of Independence and the closely linked War of Independence failed to address or provide a solution to a second, closely related constitutional dilemma that the Imperial Crisis had also exposed: the proper balance of power or sovereignty between subordinate units, colonies or states, and some manner of American intercolonial government. This was an issue that colonial representatives, at least from some of the colonies, had begun exploring at the Albany Congress in 1754 (see document 10.5) and that others would continue to wrestle with during the following thirty-plus years.[67] What will be seen from the documents herein is that this issue did not invite novel theorizing and that the solutions offered by several incarnations of the Articles of Confederation and Perpetual Union were not expressions of an increasingly sophisticated constitutionalism.[68] Instead, solutions arose as they enjoyed the support of opposed political constellations—most particularly, at first a predominantly localist one and then a slower to develop (or better said, redevelop) centralizing variant that borrowed much from the aspirations of an earlier generation of British imperial agents.[69]

Two overlapping and close to indistinguishable constitutional questions of how to arrange a federal union, imperial or national, that colonial thinkers addressed initially without success were closely allied with something still more purely the stuff of both political theory and lived politics, that is, which social groupings were to control the new state governments. To answer "the people" was of limited help when there was declining agreement, following independence, regarding who should be legitimately included among "the people."[70] This question arose rather quickly in the spring of 1776, when it appeared likely that the colonies were not going to stay within the British Empire but declare their independence as newly republican governments. Accordingly, the issue of how popular the new governments were going to be, without the weight of the Crown to arbitrate between contending factions, rapidly became relevant. Put differently, should the state governments remain relatively select in awarding suffrage and continue to be controlled by elite coastal populations (from which came almost all the delegates selected for service in the Continental Congresses), as had been true before the war, or, as increasingly came to be the case after the war, should the states extend the franchise more widely to all or almost all white males, with increased representation too of inland areas?[71]

The above questions were tightly interlocked during the 1770s, and it is far from clear in the documents here that politically active Americans approached them primarily as theoretical or constitutional questions rather than as political ones to be resolved in favor of whichever group enjoyed superior political power. Readers may be surprised, but likely shouldn't be, to discover that the controversies that most roiled Congress during the framing of the Articles of Confederation—representation in Congress, the state foundation upon which to apportion national expenses, and treatment of the unoccupied (at least by European Americans) western lands (see documents 34.1, 38.1, and 42.1)—are of limited theoretical interest and were decided by political jockeying, not by anything that can be described as innovative theorizing, liberal or republican, reflecting the powerful rights discourse of the Declaration of Independence.

The materials collected in this volume suggest that Americans, like other peoples in a revolutionary context, ended their struggle in a position that the majority of their representatives had repeatedly denied was their intention, and indebted to the generous support of an interested foreign great power. The alternative to accepting that the majority of delegates and their constituents had in 1776 fundamentally transformed the goals of their resistance is to conclude that they had consistently lied to themselves and others in the numerous petitions, resolutions, declarations, and letters in which they affirmed their deep loyalty and affection for the king and their commitment to remain British. The likelihood that the colonists consistently lied, though, is not supported by the documents offered below. A far more credible conclusion is that a majority of the colonists, and certainly most of their elected delegates, had begun their resistance against parliamentary legislation in 1764–65 by hoping to achieve a just reconciliation through a newly empowered monarchy and an entrenched imperial constitution based on long-established British norms, laws, practices, and constitutional rights. It was in spite of such intentions that a decade later the majority of colonial delegates awkwardly found themselves declaring independence for their colonies from that same king while setting up thirteen separate republican governments and claiming that they did so based on a universal right to self-government.

The declarations, petitions, resolutions, and letters of those in Congress point toward the conclusion that the independence that thirteen colonies declared in July 1776 (as will be seen, the actual date was not the fourth) was not the product of a liberal political theoretical breakthrough, a commitment among most delegates to republican government, a radical attachment to a yet-to-be born nineteenth-century individualism,[72] a unified elite, or even a "done deal" at the end. Rather, declaring independence was something that the colonists had sought to avoid doing, or even contemplating, during the previous twelve years, and it was still viewed by many in 1776—likely a majority in the mid-Atlantic colonies—with great suspicion. Most colonists were reluctantly brought to independence by the provocations of the pious Protestant republicans of the New England colonies, the dogmatic inflexibility of Parliament and a monarch overly committed to fulfilling his strictly constitutional roles, and the intractability of the constitutional problems confronting Britons on both sides of the Atlantic.

But if a careful reading of these documents leads the reader to such a conclusion, one must necessarily ask why the dominant understanding of the Declaration of Independence asserts that congressional delegates broke with Britain in defense of a self-assured liberalism and a novel and popular republicanism while seeking to put in place universal individual abstract natural rights. How is it that many people of intelligence, insight, and goodwill have seemingly gotten so much wrong? In part, the answer turns on legitimately different frames of reference. For the documents in this volume, the period of central interest is the decade or so leading up to the Declaration of Independence and the year following it, during which Congress adopted a government for the thirteen new republics—that is, 1764–1777. For many students of the Revolutionary and early national eras, however, the point of departure is July 1776, and therefore much that precedes that date is of peripheral interest. Still others focus on the writings of particular individuals or corporate groups, men and women of a far more radical turn than any of the congressional delegates—even the most radical among them, such as Samuel Adams or Christopher Gadsden.[73] These factors surely explain some of the differences.

Still, such reasons by themselves cannot account for what Jack Greene, one of the most accomplished students of this period, who has been working on it for fifty years, recently noted was the "almost total neglect of this point of view [the constitutionalist perspective, similar to that captured in the documents below] by mainstream historians" and even less by political theorists, as evidenced by Alan Gibson's relegating such a perspective to a peripheral status, along with Native American influences on American constitutionalism. Accordingly, Greene urges that this puzzle may "be an interesting subject for speculation in itself." He writes that in the work of the leading contemporary expositor of this approach, the legal historian John Phillip Reid, the American independence movement is portrayed as "a British revolution that has to be understood as an episode in British imperial history and not as the first step in the creation of the American nation," and that such an argument "runs powerfully against the grain of revolutionary scholarship since the late 1960s," which is much associated with republicanism.[74] But this explanation, insightful as it is, still does not go far enough. Isn't it still more likely that an account that diminishes the exceptionalist character of the American independence movement would be viewed critically by diverse groups of commentators who, in varying ways, are invested in a heroic view of American success, genius, and uniqueness?[75]

Understanding the independence movement of thirteen settler colonies—technically, plantations where what was to be planted was settlers—to be, well, not all that different from other such independence movements would suggest that American colonists had much in common with other colonial communities, that they may have been as much backward as forward looking, and that their sometimes confused and often frustrated leaders were not all brilliant demigods. In short, although differing time frames may explain some of the preeminence given to the liberal and republican interpretations of the Declaration of Independence and its role in the American independence movement, the continuing hunger for flattering historical accounts that make the American experience seem unlike any other likely explains still more.[76]

Finally, if this period were simply of antiquarian interest, it might not matter whether the dominant creation narratives that Americans tell of their forebears' separation from Britain ignore much of the materials reproduced here, which emphasize a colonial independence movement that inadvertently arose from irreconcilable interpretations of the eighteenth-century British and imperial constitutions. But it does matter, for the Revolutionary era continues to serve as a common inheritance to which contemporary American public policy advocates and political commentators turn when defending their preferred goals, both foreign and domestic. The nation's colonial past, even if often treated as more mythical than historical, continues to shape what is publicly possible to defend (or even what can be widely thought or suggested) in a number of policy arenas.[77] Thus, allowing for the possibility that the most widely disseminated accounts of the movement toward independence and the place of the Declaration of Independence in that movement are at odds with key features of the historical record found in the state papers of America's first three continental congresses makes an exploration of the documents that follow fully defensible, even crucial. And however much a more textured historical account of the movement of the colonies toward independence might add to Americans' self-understanding, such an account is likely to add more, in a comparative political context, to our understanding of revolutionary politics, colonial opposition movements for independence, and national formation.[78] America's eighteenth century may, in truth, prove far less exceptional and far more interesting than is often imagined.

# ACT I

## THE STAMP ACT CRISIS, 1764–1766

For North American colonists, the most important outcome of the 1754–63 war (commonly confused with an interconnected war in Germany and called, in spite of its lasting nine years, the Seven Years' War) and the Treaty of Paris was possibly the French decision to cede Canada (New France) to Britain rather than two of its lucrative sugar islands, Guadeloupe and Martinique. Accordingly, for the first time in the eighteenth century, the North American British colonists no longer had to fear a hostile neighbor to their north. This made a war of independence, formerly unthinkable, now far more imaginable—as the French may well have understood. In February 1763, with the Treaty of Paris and the end of the Seven Years' War, Great Britain was in possession of new territories worldwide. For its North American colonists, the new possessions included the formerly French colony of Quebec (present-day Quebec and Ontario), much of the north-central United States east of the Mississippi and west of the Appalachian Mountains (also formerly under French control), and the formerly Spanish colonies of East and West Florida (present-day Florida and large parts of the South), along with the island of Grenada. In September, the Earl of Hillsborough, the president of the Board of Trade and Plantations and a future secretary of state for the colonies, took over the task of formulating a policy for integrating these new territories into the British Empire and improving Britain's strained relationship with Native American populations. With these goals in mind, the king issued a proclamation in October 1763 that was to govern this vast new area.

In what might be understood as Canada's first constitution, George III sought to protect Native American hunting grounds from colonial predation and to begin building a relationship of trust, and to make some effort to accommodate his French subjects while also encouraging additional British immigration to the newly ceded lands.

To the dismay both of American colonists in the older English colonies and of metropolitan British land speculators, with the 1763 proclamation the king closed the frontier west of the colonies to new settlement and private land purchases and ordered the removal of colonial settlements in that area. Shortly before the issuance of the proclamation, as if to add credence to the Crown's position, several Native American nations or tribes under Pontiac, chief of the Ottawa, attacked and destroyed every British post west of the Niagara River except Detroit. Beyond attempting to accommodate Native Americans, the king also took into consideration the appropriate model of government for the former French populations and promised, "as soon as the state and circumstances of the said colonies will admit," to set up representative assemblies and to introduce the use of English law. Those promises went unfulfilled and, in fact, were retracted in the Quebec Act of 1774, which went further still in its accommodation of French residents by retaining the rule of a centralized administrator and allowing for the free use of the French language, customs, civil law, and Roman Catholicism—including the right of the clergy to collect tithes. Those two pieces of liberally inclusive British imperial policy, in spite of, or more likely because of, their protection of Native Americans and French Catholic Canadians from the intrusion, even depredation, of North American Protestant colonists served as additional sparks helping ignite the impending Imperial Crisis.

In 1764, at the opening of Parliament in March, metropolitan British relations with the colonists began to spiral downward with the presentation of a bill by the administration of George Grenville (first minister and leader of the House of Commons, April 1763–July 1765)—in response to a British national debt that had doubled as a result of nearly a decade of worldwide war—that sought to raise revenues in the North American colonies for use there, primarily to benefit the newly added areas. This act, the American Revenue Act, better known as the Sugar Act of April 1764, extended the 1733 Molasses Act duties (lowering some and raising others) on molasses and raw and foreign refined sugar. It placed new or higher import duties on non-British textiles, coffee, and indigo, and on Madeira and Canary wines imported directly into the colonies; and it doubled the duties on foreign goods reshipped from England to the colonies. Finally, it added iron, hides, whale fins, raw silk, potash, and pearl ash to the enumerated list (that is, products grown or extracted from the colonies that could be shipped only to Britain or other British colonies) and banned the import into the colonies of foreign rum and French wines.

In addition, the Grenville administration passed at the same time the Currency Act of 1764, which banned all further North American colonial emissions of paper currencies, extending to the other colonies what had been in effect in New England since 1751 while preventing the extension of the recall dates of all paper currencies already in circulation. The act nullified all contrary colonial laws and provided for a fine of £1,000 and dismissal from office for any colonial governor failing to veto opposed colonial legislation. At the same time that Grenville introduced these bills, he also laid before Parliament his plans to have Parliament impose on the colonies the following year stamp duties that would be similar to those in force in England (and earlier in Holland), which had been instituted in 1694 and have continued to this day.

For the New England colonies, of greater significance than the new duties was Grenville's including in a companion measure new regulations that would make it easier to enforce the new trade laws and older ones by revamping the imperial customs service. This was to be done by establishing at Halifax (in present-day Nova Scotia) a new vice-admiralty court with jurisdiction over all the American colonies; that way, customs agents could try suits in Halifax rather than being limited to bringing cases before potentially hostile local colonial courts. Additionally, the right of colonists to sue customs agents for trespass and illegal seizure was stricken; the burden of proof was placed on the accused, who would be forced to post bond for the cost of the trial in advance; and stricter registration and bonding procedures were put in place for cargo. Possibly most troubling, to colonists involved in mercantile affairs and to British customs officers, these officials were required to live in the colonies whose customs duties they were to collect.

The response in the colonies, particularly in Massachusetts, was swift; the Boston Town Meeting denounced the Sugar and Currency Acts and by the end of May 1764 had pushed the Massachusetts House to form a committee of correspondence, which was to communicate with other North American British colonies. By the fall, limited forms of nonimportation agreements—most importantly, ones restricting the importation and use of elaborate English-style mourning dress—had been adopted in Boston and New York. In short order eight of the colonial assemblies, as exemplified in the first three documents offered below, wrote strongly worded petitions in which they condemned Parliament for the passage of the Sugar and Currency Acts and appealed for reconsideration of the pending Stamp Act, on both principled political and practical economic grounds.

In 1765, Parliament passed yet another troublesome law. This act, the First Quartering Act, with a second in 1766 and a third in 1774 (the last one was part of the Coercive Acts), created still deeper concerns about the postwar direction of parliamentary legislation. The first of the Quartering Acts required colonial authorities to provide housing and supplies to British regulars stationed in their colonies. By January 1766, this had led to a standoff in New York between General Thomas Gage—the British commander in chief in the colonies—who was headquartered there, and the assembly, which refused to fully satisfy his request for supplies. By December, the assembly had wholly refused to appropriate funds for Gage's army, and so it was prorogued (that is, suspended for a time). Parliament then voted to dissolve the assembly, but before the order could be carried out, and unknown to Parliament, in June 1767 the assembly voted to supply the British troops' needs; the temporary dissolution was subsequently revoked.

Unquestionably, though, the dominant event in this period's British colonial politics was Parliament's passage of the Stamp Act. The legislation was among the first to levy a direct—that is, internal—tax on the colonists (earlier ones, such as those involving postage, had proved uncontroversial). Like the 1764 duties, it was unusual in being explicitly intended to raise revenue rather than incidentally doing so as a by-product of regulating trade or providing a service. The legislation was not designed to raise revenue for use in Britain but, along with the 1764 duties, to help offset the cost of administering and maintaining a military establishment in the North American colonies, mostly in the newly acquired ones. In the most optimistic scenario, Grenville estimated that the returns from both measures might come close to meeting one-third of Britain's costs for its North American colonial presence. The Stamp Act, like similar laws in England, raised revenue through the distribution and sale of required stamped (that is, embossed) paper, vellum, or parchment used for newspapers, almanacs, pamphlets and broadsides, legal documents of all types, insurance policies, ship's papers, licenses, and even dice and playing cards. Grenville intended, through this legislation, to confirm by practice and explicit law Parliament's uncertain right to legislate for and tax the colonies. It was exactly this, the law's intention, that almost all North American colonists in the older colonies strongly resented.

The colonial response was immediate. It transcended region and, to some degree, class and political divisions. In fact, by targeting articulate colonial elites—lawyers, landowners, speculators, college graduates, and newspapers editors, all of whom would be affected by its taxation of legal documents—the law unintentionally encouraged their reconsideration of the undefined constitutional relationship between the colonies and Parliament. Again, as with the legislation from a year earlier, the colonial protest focused on three issues: the unconstitutional character of Parliament (effectively, a foreign body in which the colonists were unrepresented) attempting to govern their internal affairs and to tax them without representation of their property interests; the extended jurisdiction granted to vice-admiralty courts and the consequent decrease in the domain of jury trials; and the pragmatic economic concern that additional taxation, during a time of financial difficulty, simply could not be borne by the colonists and would lead to a consequent loss of orders placed with British manufacturers and wholesalers.

The colonial assemblies responded by petitioning the king and Parliament for redress of their grievances (see documents 4.1–4.11), but in a number of towns, secret extralegal groups sought, generally through violence and the threat of it, to force those who were to distribute the stamped paper, generally well-to-do colonists, to resign their posts. These groups worked also to prevent the landing of the stamped paper (see documents 6.1–6.5). Following the lead of James Otis, Jr., of Massachusetts, and a resolution of the Massachusetts General Court of June 6, 1765, a circular letter sent to the colonial assemblies proposed a continental gathering in New York City to petition the king and Parliament for relief. Six colonies (Massachusetts, Connecticut, Rhode Island, Pennsylvania, Maryland, and South Carolina) sent official delegations to what would come to be called the Stamp Act Congress; New Jersey, Delaware, and New York sent delegations as well, though they were not formally approved by their colonial governments. In total, when this first congress met on October 7, 1765, it seated twenty-seven delegates from nine colonies. Before adjourning on October 25, this first of three continental congresses produced a declaration of colonial rights, along with petitions to the king and both houses of Parliament (see documents 5.1–5.3) that covered much of the same ground as the nearly contemporaneous resolves issued by the individual colonial assemblies. The difference between the documents produced by the Stamp Act Congress and the colonial assemblies lay in the moderate language used in the continental or intercolonial appeals and the lack of any hint of revolutionary zeal. In general, that moderation remained true of continental congressional state papers until the spring of 1776.

Of much greater practical importance: immediately after the close of the Stamp Act Congress, 200 New York City merchants signed a nonimportation agreement committing them to not import British goods until the Stamp Act was repealed and the trade regulations of 1764 were modified. Similar agreements were reached in November by 400 Philadelphia merchants and in December by 250 Boston merchants. When the Stamp Act officially went into effect on November 1, 1765, the almost uniform refusal of North American colonists to use the stamped paper for official transactions substantially disrupted colonial life—administrative, mercantile, and judicial. But before the end of the year, matters had returned almost to normal because of widespread violations of the act and the ongoing use of unstamped paper for commercial and legal transactions. Even if the colonies' resolves and petitions failed to have a positive effect—in fact, they went unread by the king, often at the behest of the colonies' supporters in Parliament who feared that they would give offense to MPs and the king because of the provocative invocation of colonial rights—the nonimportation agreements took a toll on British exports to the colonies, which dropped "from £2,249,710 in 1764 to £1,944,108 in 1765."[1]

With the collapse in 1765 of the Grenville administration because of unrelated matters, George Grenville was replaced as first minister by the Marquess of Rockingham, who, under pressure from metropolitan British merchants, manufactures, and shipping interests, sought to undo the handiwork of his predecessor. When Parliament met on January 14, 1766, its members were determined to put an end to the violation of the Stamp Act in the continental "English" colonies, the violent intimidation there of Crown officials, and the unpunished destruction of private property and leveling of personal threats. Almost all members of Parliament agreed that something had to be done, but exactly what to do was less clear. Grenville and others like him believed that British army units needed to be stationed strategically throughout the North American colonies to enforce the duties imposed by Parliament; others, such as William Pitt the elder and Lord Camden, commended the colonists for their resistance to unconstitutional taxes; and still others supporting the government, including Edmund Burke, sought some kind of compromise. Burke in particular hoped to end the unfortunate contest over rights—that of the colonial legislatures versus that of Parliament regarding which was sovereign in the colonies—without creating a theoretically clear constitutional hierarchy and order. For most members, Parliament constitutionally had the right to legislate for and tax the colonies, but for members like Burke, it was a right that should never be put into use or even discussed.[2]

Burke's view didn't enjoy majority support. Thus, the compromise that the Rockingham administration brought before Parliament, for which Burke was the foremost political thinker and parliamentary spokesman, sought to satisfy both the mercantile community's wish to regain its best colonial customers, and the MPs who insisted that, whatever else was to be done, Parliament had to confirm its supremacy and boldly defend its sovereign right to legislate for the colonies. Its sovereign supremacy did not necessarily mean, though, that Parliament had the right to tax the colonies; for some members, direct taxation was a far more delicate issue, and Parliament, even if it were in important senses sovereign and absolute, could not impose it on the colonists. Accordingly, the administration brought forward two bills: one to repeal the Stamp Act, that is, to remove the offending internal and intentional duties, with the implied promise that no others would be forthcoming; and a second bill, in which Parliament stipulated its sovereign rights and supremacy over the colonies. Both bills were signed on March 18, 1766 (see documents 8.1 and 8.2), and went into effect on May 1.

Later in the year the colonial supporter William Pitt the elder, having taken over as first minister and having been elevated as the Earl of Chatham, led Parliament into going further by removing those duties that had led to the first eruption of the Imperial Crisis a year earlier, by revoking the duties on foreign molasses imported into the colonies in favor of a uniform nominal tax on all imported molasses, British as well as foreign. Similarly, export duties on British West Indian sugar shipped to the colonies were removed. The colonists responded to these measures by immediately abandoning their nonimportation schemes, and most felt, in their relief, a hope for a future untainted by such constitutionally threatening measures. As suggested, though, in Samuel Adams' letter to Christopher Gadsden (document 8.3), not all the colonists were either relieved or looking forward to a calm and peaceful future.

## DOCUMENT SUMMARY

In the first three sets of documents, colonial objections to new and proposed parliamentary legislation are developed by the lower houses of New York, Massachusetts, and Virginia in late-fall or early-winter petitions to the king and Parliament. The petitions seek a redress of grievances under which, according to the petitioners, their constituents were suffering because of the Sugar and Currency Acts of 1764. In the first, from New York, the assembly, in writing to the king, defends its traditional practice of meeting the financial needs of his colonial government and describes this as one of its most important British liberties, privileges, or civil rights, one that the colonists shared equally with the king's subjects in Great Britain. In writing to the House of Commons, though, the assembly insists on defending this hallowed practice as a right, not a privilege, and even claims that denial of it would be an infringement of a natural right of mankind, resting this most striking assertion on the solid and stable foundation of British constitutionalism. Indeed, the assembly wanted Parliament to understand, in spite of its bold language, that it wasn't challenging Parliament's right to regulate imperial commercial relations but "only" its right to tax the colonists, whether by an internal or external variety. The assembly concludes by objecting to Parliament's extension of the jurisdiction of vice-admiralty courts, the consequent limitation on trials by juries, and the difficulties that Parliament's ban on paper monies would impose on imperial commerce.

The Massachusetts petition, although it forgoes describing the long-standing colonial practice of raising taxes by means of local legislatures as a right, makes nearly the same arguments as the New York petitions. Interestingly, the Massachusetts petitioners point out that the extra costs imposed on the colonists by parliamentary commercial regulations meant that they were already paying as much to support the king's administration as they would in the future because of additional duties such as those placed on molasses and other products, or those proposed by the Stamp Act. Virginia's petitions add two concerns that soon resonated throughout all the other colonies: Parliament not only was unable constitutionally to tax the colonists but, at least as importantly, also could not constitutionally enact legislation respecting the internal affairs of any colony; and Virginians had no desire to be represented in the British Parliament. Virginia claimed that its residents had their own "parliament," where their property holders' interests were represented, and they needed no other. Also of significance was Virginia's claim that its initial colonial settlers came "not as Vagabonds or Fugitives, but [were] licensed and encouraged by their Prince and animated with a laudable Desire of enlarging the *British* Dominion." In short, according to these resolves, Virginia had been settled with the British Crown's guidance and permission, not by sovereign-less, "free" individuals.

The fourth set of documents begins with the Virginia resolves advanced by Patrick Henry in late May 1765. Four of his resolves were approved, and they were little different from the petitions approved by Virginia six months earlier. In some ways, his approved resolves may have been more modest than the earlier petitions, since his focused on less assertive "privileges" and "liberties" rather than on bolder "rights" and made no mention of the colony being uninterested in sending delegates to Parliament. Much again is made of Parliament's legal inability to legislate regarding the colonies' domestic affairs. Virginia's resolves, accordingly, insisted on "the inestimable Right of being governed by such Laws, respecting their internal Polity and Taxation, as are derived from their own Consent, with the Approbation of their Sovereign, or his Substitute." Other colonies, however, mistakenly thinking (because of misreporting in newspapers) that Virginia had acted with greater boldness than it in fact had, included in their own lists resolves that Virginia had not accepted—for example, Rhode Island promised to indemnify provincial officers who refused to levy Stamp Act duties. Such a resolve, of course, provocatively urged colonial officials to disobey explicit parliamentary legislation.

While the resolves of Massachusetts and, less so, Pennsylvania made active use of abstract universal-rights language in defense of the colonists' right to raise their own taxes through colonial legislatures, none of the other colonies—including Maryland, Connecticut, South Carolina, or New Jersey—followed their lead, not even New York, whose boldly universal language of six months earlier is entirely absent from its 1765 resolves. Of interest too is that many of the resolves placed far greater emphasis on the English rather than on the British origins of their rights, suggesting that the older rights in place when many of the colonies were settled were, somehow, viewed as more trustworthy than later British ones tied to an ascendant Parliament.

All the 1765 resolves made much of the North American colonists' commitment and loyalty to their king, George III, and his family. Additionally, they all emphasized three aspects of political equality: the king's subjects in his North American dominions were equal in status to his subjects living in the realm (that is, Great Britain); the colonists therefore were entitled to the same rights as subjects living in England; and the colonists had done nothing to forfeit this shared equality. Also of great significance to the colonists was the need to protect the hallowed English right to a jury trial, which was threatened by the extension of the jurisdiction of vice-admiralty courts, which operated under Roman law. Other colonies, like Virginia in its 1764 petition, insisted that their landowners were fully represented in their local assemblies and that they could not be effectively represented in the British Parliament; thus, none of them sought to have Parliament extend representation to their residents. Finally, most petitions and resolves lamented the grievous financial harm that the Stamp Act duties would cause to the commercial interests of both colonists and metropolitan Britons.

The fifth set of readings includes the Declaration of Rights and the Petition to the House of Commons, both issued by the Stamp Act Congress in October 1765. That meeting, at which twenty-seven delegates representing nine colonies convened in New York, came close to a full intercolonial representation of colonial interests and concerns. Not surprisingly, many of the themes rehearsed in the contemporaneous colonial resolves are identical to those advanced in the declaration—most importantly, two essential rights of the colonists and their core English birthright: taxes could be imposed only by colonial legislatures in which the colonists' property was represented, and a subject could be tried only by a jury of his peers. Congress reiterated that the colonists enjoyed all the same rights and liberties as the king's subjects living in Britain; that the colonists' property holders could not be represented in the British Parliament; and that the economic effects of the Stamp Act would be destructive for all concerned.

In a number of ways, this moderate continental body made an effort to be somewhat more deferential to Parliament, even if only vaguely and rhetorically so, than most colonial assemblies had been in their resolves. Thus, in the Declaration of Rights, written by John Dickinson of Pennsylvania after drawing liberally from the committee report of William Samuel Johnson of Connecticut, Congress writes of owing "all due Subordination to that August Body, the Parliament of *Great-Britain*." In the Petition to the House of Commons, Congress holds that the colonists "shall always retain the most grateful Sense of their [the Crown's and Parliament's] Assistance and Protection." By the end of the 1760s, one would be hard pressed to find a colonial statement acknowledging, let alone thanking, Parliament for its assistance in settling the colonies. In the Petition to the House, Congress goes so far as to accept, hypothetically, that even if Parliament "virtually" represented the colonists' interests, indeed even those of the whole world, there would still be good, prudential reasons for repealing the Stamp Act and the Sugar and Currency Acts because of their deleterious economic effects.

The sixth set of readings, statements of the Sons of Liberty from December 1765 to March 1766, are of particular interest from having been written, in some cases (as evidenced by less regular spelling and grammar), by provincial colonists who were not lawyers, merchants, or large landowners, groups that made up nearly three-fourths of congressional delegates from all three congresses. This is likely true of the statement by the Sons of Liberty from New London, Connecticut, which, of all the documents in this collection, is possibly the most radical, the most hostile to the British Crown, and the most prorepublican, perhaps as much so as the Declaration of Independence. Most of the other statements, including popular statements from North Carolina and Virginia, and even that cowritten by Connecticut and New York Sons of Liberty, were more moderate in tone.

These statements sought to commit the members of these secret bodies to oppose, by all lawful means (a condition more often observed in the breach than not), the implementation of the Stamp Act and to come to the aid, when called upon, of Sons of Liberty in neighboring towns or provinces "in preventing entirely the Operation of the Stamp-Act." Despite the fervent claims of loyalty to the king made in these documents, what might have made their statements and consequent actions worrisome to many considering taking on the duty of distributing stamped paper was the Sons' view that "whoever is concerned, directly or indirectly, in using or causing to be used, in any way or manner whatever, within this colony . . . those detestable papers called the

Stamps, shall be deemed, to all intents and purposes, an enemy to his country, and by the Sons of Liberty treated accordingly." In ways too often overlooked, such threats would come to be acted upon and thus were to be taken seriously.

The seventh reading is the celebrated testimony of Benjamin Franklin before the British House of Commons in February 1766.[3] Here, under examination by a Rockingham administration intent upon repealing the Stamp Act, Franklin put before Parliament a favorable but realistic portrait of the colonists and their views of the Stamp Act. Thus, Franklin did his best to characterize the colonists as loyal to both king and Parliament, noting that the colonists had long admired and looked to Parliament for succor in the colonial legislatures' traditionally testy relationship with the king and his imperial ministers. Of particular relevance, Franklin noted that the colonists had always been willing, when properly requisitioned by his imperial officers, to support the king's government in the colonies. He accordingly made every effort to avoid any mention of rights, knowing that it was a subject, in particular regarding the right of Parliament to legislate for the colonies, of great sensitivity to the members.

Among those less favorable matters that honesty forced him to make note of, however, were the following: the colonists viewed the recent war as having been fought primarily in defense of Britain's, not the colonies', interests; and the colonists, no matter how it might be packaged, would always refuse the imposition of taxes by Parliament, particularly internal ones like the Stamp Act duties. The series of questions and answers that were likely most troubling to his auditors began with Franklin being asked whether the colonists knew of the Declaration of Rights of 1689 (later the Bill of Rights), which made it unconstitutional for the king to raise revenues without Parliament's approval. And if the colonists were familiar with this act, whether they still thought that they could constitutionally send the king monies without Parliament's having first authorized such requisitions. To those questions, Franklin responded that the colonists were well acquainted with the English Bill of Rights but believed that the particular stipulation applied only to those subjects living inside the realm, not those living in one of the king's (overseas) dominions. Accordingly, he believed that the colonists felt themselves at full liberty to give and grant aid to the king without Parliament's authorization. No doubt his response left a deep and disturbing impression on the members in attendance, for there is little else that he might have said that would have proved less congenial to the mind of a post-1688 Whig MP.

On a far more positive note, Franklin correctly predicted that the colonists would be little concerned if the Stamp Act were to be repealed on grounds merely of convenience rather than as part of the sought-after recognition of colonial rights. But when Parliament imposed new external taxes for revenue in the 1767 Townshend Acts, many of the most articulate colonists rapidly came to insist on the need for a permanent framing of the constitutional relationship between the colonies and Great Britain, in effect, a new, more carefully considered and entrenched imperial constitution. Only after the repeal of the Stamp Act and then the passage of the Townshend Acts would most colonists begin to distrust Parliament and come to doubt that it was acting in pursuit of their common interests.

The final two paired documents in this section were passed by Parliament and approved by the king on March 18, 1766: An Act Repealing the Stamp Act and the Declaratory Act, which asserted Parliament's unlimited right to legislate for the colonists "in all cases whatsoever." It is worth noting that Parliament framed the repeal of the Stamp Act as a matter of convenience while simultaneously asserting its absolute sovereignty and supremacy over the colonies as a matter of right. Clearly, members understood the different grounding they were assigning to each. Still, largely because of the influence of William Pitt the elder, the Declaratory Act says nothing about Parliament's right to tax (which Pitt and his followers thought illegitimate), and that omission, without Parliament's subsequent passage of additional tax measures, might have offered some kind of constitutional victory to the colonial position.

## THEORETICAL ISSUES

In this section's documents, in spite of Parliament's persistent pattern of provocation, the North American colonists consistently demonstrate their loyalty to the British monarch and the empire, a due recognition of the king's prerogative rights, and a steadfast wish to return to the imperial British constitution circa 1763. The colonists thus were far from advancing any manner of radical republican claims, but instead adamantly embraced both governance by the British Crown and the status quo ante. Nonetheless, they can also be seen coming to challenge Parliament's constitutional role in the colonies' internal life, most particularly regarding taxation. They were to reject far more slowly—even as the grounding became increasingly contested—Parliament's traditional role in shaping imperial commercial regulations. The colonists were reluctant to deny Parliament's right to do so even while recognizing and accepting that Parliament had consistently done so in a manner that unfairly benefited the merchants, shippers, sailors, and manufacturers of metropolitan Great Britain. Regarding all manner of grievances, American intercolonial or continental spokesmen consistently defended their claims by invoking British constitutional norms and charter rights rather than by turning to universal norms and international rights. As will be seen, particular constituencies, most especially New Englanders and their delegates in Congress, were keen to employ universal norms far earlier than Congress as a whole, which began doing so only in late 1775.

Beyond steadfastly rejecting Parliament's right to a share in colonial governance, while bolstering and glorifying the king's, the colonists can be seen regularly demanding that they be treated, by both king and Parliament, as the equals of their fellow subjects in Great Britain (the equality of other British subjects is, surprisingly, rarely mentioned or defended—see documents 14.1 and 22.1). As the colonists frequently asked, why should one of the king's peoples, those living in the British realm, be permitted to tax another of the king's peoples, those living in the king's North American dominions? Not unreasonably, they expected that those who enjoyed actual parliamentary representation would try to lighten their own tax burden by shifting it onto others. The colonists' insistence on their equality with the king's subjects in Great Britain led them to emphasize that they shared the same English birthright as the king's subjects in the realm.

Among these fundamental rights were two that the colonial assemblies believed Parliament had violated: first, in particular because of the Stamp Act's open intention of using taxation to raise revenues rather than to control shipping or manufacturing in the colonies, was the right of property owners to participate in raising the taxes that they would have to pay—that is, the inherited English right not to be taxed by a body in which property holders enjoyed no representation. Second, they resented new restrictions on the English right to be tried only by juries using common law rather than by judges in admiralty courts using Roman or civil law. On a more practical level, the assemblies complained of financial duress resulting from the heavy, war-induced debt burden under which they labored, which would only be exacerbated by additional taxes. Similarly, they complained of the near impossibility of managing their economies without the use of paper currencies. That problem, they believed, would be made worse by the Currency Act. Last, they argued that because of the heavy premium paid by colonists on British goods and the burdensome commercial and shipping regulations imposed on them by Parliament, they were already effectively contributing as much as the king's English subjects to the British Crown, and far more than would ever be raised through direct taxation.

The colonists tried to persuade both king and Parliament—in their Stamp Act petitions, the colonists addressed Parliament directly, which they wouldn't do a decade later after declaring that Parliament had no right to legislate for them—that any disruption to imperial commercial relations would harm merchants and manufacturers in Britain as much as or more than the North American colonists. Colonists were willing to defend their inherited constitutional-monarchical government and its provincial legislative assemblies not only by invoking English and British constitutional and charter rights, but also by asserting prudential economic grounds and, occasionally, more abstract ones too. Thus, by claiming their constitutional rights to self-government through colonial legislatures operating under monarchical oversight, an assumed equality between the king's British and North American subjects, and manifest economic needs, the colonists insisted that Parliament could not constitutionally legislate for or tax them, and all such legislation from 1764–65 had to be repealed.

As Franklin rightly predicted, most of the colonists (though not all, Samuel Adams being one of those little satisfied) were little troubled by the fragile prudential rather than rights-based grounds upon which the Stamp Act repeal rested or by the aggressive stance taken by Parliament in defense of its absolute rights as declaimed in the language of the Declaratory Act. The colonists may have taken note of the language in both acts but still hoped that, as in the case of the Irish, who were governed under their own Declaratory Act of 1719/20, Parliament would forgo ever again trying to levy taxes for revenue on them. If Parliament had been so forbearing, the colonists might have been able to get by without demanding a fundamental restructuring of the British imperial constitution. Of course, all such conjectures must remain matters of speculation, for a little over a year later, Parliament, under an administration headed by Pitt the elder (by then Lord Chatham), with Charles Townshend serving as chancellor of the exchequer, put forward a new round of taxes with which to confirm its sovereign power over the colonies. These "external" (that is, imposed outside the colonies) taxes, the colonists quickly discovered, were no more palatable when imposed by another people and a foreign legislature than had been the "internal" Stamp Act duties of 1765, which they had fought so vigorously (and successfully) to have repealed.

## 1. NEW YORK PETITIONS OPPOSING THE SUGAR, CURRENCY, AND STAMP ACTS, OCTOBER 18, 1764

These petitions, along with those issued by Rhode Island, Connecticut, Virginia, North Carolina, South Carolina, and Massachusetts, opposed the Sugar Act of 1764 (the American Revenue Act of April 5, generally known as the Sugar Act), the Currency Act (also of 1764), and the proposed Stamp Act of 1765.[4] They were the product of a committee appointed by the New York Assembly on September 19, 1764, which was likely chaired by William Bayard, a distinguished merchant who had extensive landholdings in present-day Hoboken, New Jersey, and personal and familial ties to the British army and the British East India Company.[5] Its members included the New York triumvirate of William Smith, Jr., William Livingston, and John Morin Scott, who each wrote one of the petitions. The first and most provocative, to the House of Commons, was written by Smith, the future loyalist, and was reported on October 4; those to the king and the House of Lords were penned by Scott and Livingston respectively and approved on October 11.[6]

In these petitions, the otherwise aristocratic-leaning New York Assembly, made up principally of large landowners, proved to be the first colony-wide body to deny Parliament's right to tax the colonies, either internally or externally, in order to raise revenue. Little apparently came of its articulate challenge, for as Edmund S. Morgan notes, "It is doubtful that the petitions had any positive effect in England, because Robert Charles, the agent [that is, the colony's hired lobbyist in Britain], was unable to get any member of Parliament to present them."[7] In truth, given the fate of the Stamp Act Congress' petitions (documents 5.2 and 5.3) and the Rockingham ministry's effort to keep the colonists' petitions hidden from the view of other MPs, it was likely to the colonists' benefit that this and other petitions went largely unread.

In the assembly's petition to the king, Smith asks that "their civil Rights and Liberties as individuals . . . [be held] in a State of perfect Equality with their fellow

Subjects in *Great-Britain*" and, more broadly, that the same be awarded to them as a political body, namely, that their "Right of Taxing Themselves" be equally respected. The right of exclusively taxing themselves, the assembly claimed, was one that the king's predecessors had allowed English settlers to carry with them to the colonies and thereafter enjoy, as did the Irish and foreign Protestants. The petitioners argued that a subject of the king, "by the Laws of our happy Constitution, carries with him his Allegiance to the most distant Corners of the Earth, and that the Protection of his constitutional Rights and Privileges, is the true Reason of that Allegiance"; they further understood that the king "acquiesced in the transfer of those Rights and Privileges, to this distant Part of [his] Dominions, to be enjoyed by them, on the same Tenure of Subjection by which they held them at Home." For them, clearly, the English king had authorized emigration from England to North America and in doing so had permitted the transfer of English rights and privileges with the initial settlers. Here, though, the particular history of New York—the only conquered colony among the thirteen and thus one without any internationally recognized claims to English common-law rights—is conveniently overlooked.[8]

New York not only defended its right to tax itself, but claimed under British law covering municipal and corporate charters that it had always exercised the right of self-taxation responsibly and thus that there was no legal grounds for forfeiture.[9] Almost every one of America's congressional state papers over the next twelve years continued to claim that the colonists had, under British law, done nothing to forfeit their charter rights—for those colonies with charters—to self-government and taxation.

Moreover, according to the petitioners, their concerns were not ones in which the king's prerogative powers would, either way, be affected—that is, whether they raised taxes on themselves or Parliament did so, the king's rights were left untouched. Accordingly, the petitioners begged for the intervention of the king "as the common Father of all his People" to protect equally "the Interests of his *British* and *American* Subjects." Again, they argued that the right of self-taxation, with the king's assent, even if it could be forfeited by abuse, was one that New York had always used responsibly, and thus it was unconscionable that "any Part of a Community . . . [could], as individuals, claim the Right of taxing the whole." Here, New York portrays members of Parliaments as nothing more than "individuals" lacking the legal standing to claim a right to tax the colonies. Depriving the colonists of the right to tax themselves, the petitioners claimed, would render them effectively not much different from slaves. It was exactly their constitutional status in the empire, as equals of the British people, and their colony's relationship to Parliament that were at issue.

The assembly then reminded the king that there were mutually beneficial commercial interests at stake and that if the Sugar and Currency Acts were not repealed, the colonies and Great Britain would both suffer. In particular, a legislatively sanctioned inequality between the king's subjects in America and Britain added to the difficulties faced by colonists living in a frontier region and might cause immigration to the colonies to decrease, even reverse, with a consequent loss of the country's population and prosperity, and the king's international standing and power. The petition hammers home that the legislation will harm the king's subjects in North American and Britain while benefiting only the opulent planters, fellow subjects, in the king's West Indian sugar colonies.

Foreshadowing a grievance appearing in almost all American congressional state papers, one of nearly equal importance to the colonists as the right of self-taxation, New York strongly opposed the enlarged jurisdiction of vice-admiralty courts, with their Roman-law jurisprudence and the consequent limitation of the role of juries, the "antient Badge of *English* Liberty." The assembly feared too the dire effects that would follow from the colony's need to suspend the issuance of paper monies, for "the Want of a Paper Currency, [w]as the last, though not the least Evil, to which the Colonies, are unhappily made Subject, by an Act of Parliament lately passed for that Purpose." In regard to these judicial and commercial issues, as well as taxation, the New York Assembly humbly sought the king to interpose his will on Parliament and redress his (American) subjects' grievances.

1.1

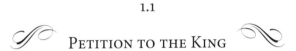 PETITION TO THE KING

*Journal of the Votes and Proceedings of the General Assembly of the Colony of New York.
Began on the 8th Day of November, 1743; and Ended the 23rd of December, 1765*
(New York: Hugh Gaine, 1766), 2:769–75.

PETITION TO THE KING

Die Jovis, 9 bo. A.M. Oct. 18, 1764.

THE ingrossed Representation and Petition to the King's most excellent Majesty; was read, and approved of by the House.

*Ordered,* That Mr. Speaker sign the said Representation and Petition in Behalf of the House; and is in the Words following, viz.

To the KING's most excellent Majesty. The humble Petition and Representation of the Representatives of your Majesty's loyal Colony of New-York.

Permit, most gracious Sovereign, your faithful Representatives for your Majesty's loyal Subjects, the Freemen and Freeholders of your Colony of *New-York,* to approach the Throne, with a submissive Tender of the most firm and unshaken Allegiance. And as they shall ever esteem it a peculiar Mark of the royal Favour, in behalf of themselves and their Constituents, to be indulged in renewing their Demonstrations of the most inviolable Fidelity to their Prince, may they be allowed, at a Juncture so critical, to the Rights and Liberties of those whom the[y] represent, with all Humility to shew,

That your Majesty's royal Predecessors, sensible that the Subject, by the Laws of our happy Constitution, carries with him his Allegiance to the most distant Corners of the Earth, and that the Protection of his constitutional Rights and Privileges, is the true Reason of that Allegiance, not only authorized the Emigration of their Subjects, but acquiesced in the transfer of those Rights and Privileges, to this distant Part of your Dominions, to be enjoyed by them, on the same Tenure of Subjection by which they held them at Home.

That hence so soon after the first Planting of this Colony, as in the Year 1683, a political Frame was erected, in the nearest possible Resemblance to that of our Mother Country; of which the constituent Parts were a Governor and a Council, in the royal Appointment, and a Representation of the People by their own free Election.

That in these three Branches was lodged the legislative Authority of the Colony, and particularly the Power of taxing it's inhabitants for the Support of Government. And in the uninterrupted Enjoyment of this Constitution has your Majesty's Colony of *New-York* continued, from that Period down to the present Day.

That under the Influence of this happy Imitation of the political Frame of our Mother Country, we are, by the numerous Emigrations from your Majesty's Kingdoms of *Great-Britain* and *Ireland,* and the Accession of foreign Protestants, become a Dominion filled with Subjects, who esteem themselves happy in the firmest Attachment to your royal Person, Family and Government; the more happy, as under this Allegiance, they have had the highest Reason, from the hitherto uninterrupted Enjoyment of their civil Rights and Liberties as individuals, to consider themselves, in a State of perfect Equality with their fellow Subjects in *Great-Britain,* and as a political Body, enjoying, like the Inhabitants of that Country, the exclusive Right of Taxing themselves; a Right, which with the most profound Submission be it spoken, whether inherent in the People, or sprung from any other Cause, has received the royal Sanction, is at the Basis of our Colony State, and become venerable by long Usage.

Your Majesty's faithful Representatives for this your Colony of *New-York,* cannot, therefore, without the strongest Demonstrations of Grief, express their Sentiments on the late Intimation of a Design, to impose Taxes on your Majesty's Colonists, by Laws to be passed in *Great-Britain.* On a Subject so interesting to us, we have the peculiar Felicity of observing, that the royal Prerogative, by our tender Regard to which, we shall ever be ready to evince our unfeigned Obedience to our Prince, is not in the least interested: For we humbly conceive that, whether the Aids, which the Support of your Majesty's Government require from this People, be raised by ourselves, or our fellow Subjects, will neither heighten or diminish the Lustre of the imperial Diadem, but as one or other of those Modes of Taxation will, either prove advancive or destructive of the publick Weal.

Permit us, therefore, most gracious Sovereign, in behalf of ourselves and our Constituents, to supplicate our Prince as the common Father of all his People, who sees with equal Eye, and regards with undiscriminating Tenderness and Concern, the Interests of his *British* and *American* Subjects; who by our happy Constitution, is armed with the Power to negative every unconstitutional Law: and whose princely Goodness, we account ourselves happy in the Reflection, will ever direct the Execution of his Authority.

That the Power of taxing ourselves has been fundamentally interwoven in our Constitution, we flatter ourselves will not be denied; that we have uninterruptedly enjoyed this Power, the numerous Acts we have passed for the Support of Government, in the Enacting of which, the Crown has always participated, will fully evince; and that we have not abused this Power, our strenuous Exertions, upon every publick Emergency, will we humbly hope, most fully demonstrate. Many indeed are our Testimonials on this Subject, furnished by the Speeches of our Governors under your Majesty and your royal Ancestors, and recorded in our Acts of Assembly, for a long and uninterrupted series of Years.

But we flatter ourselves, that this People has given your Majesty, the most recent Proofs, of their Zeal for the Glory of their Sovereign, of their Readiness to bleed at every Vein in his Service, and of that uncommon Alacrity with which they have in the late War, so glorious to your Majesty, and your royal Grandfather, even out of their Poverty so liberally contributed to the common Cause: Proofs which, with the fullest Conviction have reached the Breasts of those, who through the most groundless Misrepresentations are now moved, to destroy the Power which furnished them. For we conceive that those frequent parliamentary Provisions, to lighten the heavy Taxes, with which we voluntarily burthened ourselves, for the national Weal, could have been dictated by nothing less, than the fullest Conviction, that in exercising the Power of Taxing ourselves, your Majesty's Service, and the publick Welfare were our invariable Objects.

May we not therefore humbly hope, for your Majesty's royal Approbation of our Unwillingness to part with a Right, which the Authority of the Prince, in the Infancy of this Colony, thought proper to put into its Hands, as the Birth Right of the Subject, a Right which we have ever since undisturbedly possessed; a Right to which even could it be forfeited by Abuse, we have secured our Title by the best Improvement of it. May we not also, while the Liberty of the Subject has ever been the greatest Glory, of the illustrious House of *Hanover,* with full Assurance of Acceptance lay at your Majesty's Feet, our Jealousies upon every Invasion of our Rights? We value ourselves in being the free Subjects of a glorious Prince, who tenderly regards the Liberties of his People, and who will ever maintain that excellent Constitution, which with all others, that the Wisdom of Man has hitherto contrived, forbids, that any Part of a Community shall, as individuals, claim the Right of taxing the whole. And these our Jealousies we bring recommended with an Argument, which we trust will ever have the greatest Weight with our Sovereign.

For besides, that involuntary Taxes and Impositions, are absolutely and necessarily excluded from a State of Liberty; that it would be the basest Vassalage, to be taxed at the Pleasure of a Fellow Subject; that all real Property is lost, whensoever it becomes subordinate to Laws, in the making of which, the Proprietor does not participate; and that thus to treat us, would be to sink us into a Subjugation, infinitely below the ignominious Rank of the most tributary States: Besides all this, we have the Welfare of the Nation, that most powerful Advocate with a wise King, to plead our Cause before your Majesty, and by this we are encouraged to observe,

That your Majesty's *North-American* Colonies, in the extensive Tracts of Country they contain, furnish Room for an endless increase of Inhabitants. And as Numbers are the most athletic Sinew of national Power, the Strength of *Great-Britain,* which can never grow from this Cause at Home, must gain continual and never ending Accessions in her Colonies. That the Consumption of *British* Manufactures, originally made necessary by the Nature of our Climate, will continually Increase with our Numbers, and by this Means, the Trade and Maritime Power of the Nation, will grow daily more dreaded, unrivalled and irresistable; and your Majesty and your royal Descendants, become more conspicuously, as your Majesty in Truth is, the most powerful Princes in *Europe.*

These, we presume, are the happy Effects, which can flow only from the Increase and Prosperity of the Colonies; and for which, the Mother Country, being long e'er now arrived at the fullest Maturity, can afford no Room.

But as Liberty is at the Bottom of all our Enjoyments, as your Majesty's Subjects can neither be happy nor rich, but in the independent Fruition of their Property; can your Majesty, we ask it with Submission, conceive, that a Discrimation of Privileges between the Mother Country and the Colonies, will be attended with a Consequence, less fatal than the Decrease of the Latter? While the Subject, can enter the nearer Protection of the Crown, enjoy the largest Portions of Liberty, and the greatest Accummulations of Privileges that a free People can even wish for, the more inhospitable Climes of *America,* more inhospitable for our Vicinity to a Barbarian, and irreconcilable Foe, will furnish no Temptations to emigrate. Actuated by the same Principles, which will prevent all future Emigrations, great Numbers of our present Inhabitants will transplant themselves into the Mother Country; where they may enjoy their Property with the fullest Security, and a perfect Equality with their fellow Subjects. Thus will our Colonies decrease, and with them the Strength, the Glory, the Lustre of the *British* Empire.

These, permit us, with the deepest Concern for the Honour of our King, and the Prosperity of the Nation, to assure your Majesty, will be the fatal, yet unavoidable Consequences, of a Method of Taxation for the Colonies, so inconsistent with the Genius of the *British* Constitution, so destructive of that Right of taxing ourselves, which in common with our fellow Subjects in *Great-Britain,* we have hitherto uninterruptedly enjoyed; and which, it is hoped, we may with the strictest Justice say, have been secured against a Forfeiture, as far as the most invaluable Rights can, by the best Improvement of them, be secured.

May we not therefore, most gracious Sovereign, with a Measure of Confidence hope, that an Evil, so great, so extensive, will by your Majesty's wise and princely Interposition be prevented? An Evil, which no Instance in the whole Tenor of our Conduct, can possibly make necessary; for what Period, we ask it with all Humility, can be assigned, in which even our Backwardness, much less our Refusal, to exercise the Right of Taxation, for the Benefit of ourselves, or the national Weal was manifested? We have ever been a People, zealous for the Honour of our Sovereign, sanguine in the publick Cause, ready to strain every Nerve, upon every Occasion; we have supported the whole Weight of Savage and *Canadian* Fury, for near a Century; been as liberal of our Blood, as our Treasure; and even anticipated the Demands of our Sovereign, on every Occasion of public Emergency. So conspicuous indeed, was our willingness, to exercise this invaluable Right in the national Cause, that at a Juncture, when a Failure of the Military Chest, suspended your Majesty's important Operations, for the Conquest of *Canada* (the most luminous Event, that ever adorned the Page of *English* History) your Majesty's Commander in Chief betook himself to the Legislature of this Colony, for Relief. And on that momentous Occasion, how chearfully did they load the Colony with a Sum, immensely beyond the Abilities of a poor People to bear, upon no other Security for a Reimbursement, than the Merit of the Service.

Next to the Right of taxing ourselves, for the Support of your Majesty's Government, we beg leave, humbly, to recommend to the gracious Consideration of our Sovereign, the present ruinous State of our Commerce. If the Trade of *Great-Britain,* is her chief Glory, if she is to excel her Neighbours in commercial Arts, we speak from our present woful Experience, the Prosperity of our Trade, is absolutely necessary for the Support of hers. This Country can, at best, afford a very incompetent Supply of immediate Remittances, for those prodigious Quantities of her Manufactures, which we daily consume. Our Staple is calculated, principally, for the *West-India* Markets; and their Produce is the best Return we can possibly make for her Commodities. And as our Communication with the foreign Islands, would, besides a Vent for our own Staple, open a wide Door for the Sale of *British* Manufactures, the Trade of *Great-Britain,* would by this Means, be immensely increased; while on the other Hand, your Majesty's Sugar Colonies, afford a very inadequate Market for *British* Wares, and the Staple of our Country; and by such a Restriction, our Trade, and of Course the Trade of *Great-Britain,* is reduced to the most scanty Limits. It is therefore with a Concern, that equally embraces our Mother Country, as well as our Colony Interests, that we received the late Act of Parliament, by which all commercial Intercourse between these Colonies, and the foreign *West-India* Settlements is at an end; the Duties thereby imposed being equal to a Prohibition. And we have too great Reason, from the present Decay of our Commerce to conclude, that this Measure, which can only be serviceable to a very inconsiderate Part of the *British* Empire, will be attended with Consequences, destructive to the general Interest, of your Majesty's Realm and Dominions.

Our Demands for Linen Manufactures, which till the passing of the late Act, we have been permitted freely to supply, by Importations from your Majesty's Kingdom of *Ireland,* must remain, in a great Measure, unsatisfied, by the Prohibition laid on our Exportation of Lumber to that Kingdom. As we humbly conceive, that no national Advantage can arise, from this Restriction; we flatter ourselves with the Hopes, of your Majesty's most gracious and powerful Interposition, in this Instance, for our Relief.

It is with the deepest Distress, that our Duty to our Constituents, constrains us to observe to our Prince, that this, and many others of the Acts of trade, have diverted the publick Stream of Justice, from their antient Course. The Wisdom of our Ancestors shines in nothing more brightly, than in the Institution of Juries, for the Decision of all Controversies, that concern the Lives, Liberties, and Property of the Subject; and if we are emboldened, with equal Earnestness and Humility, to supplicate your Majesty's royal Favour and Countenance, in this important Point, we have that conspicuous Tenderness for the Rights of the Subject, which is one of the most distinguished Graces of your Majesty's illustrious House, to plead our Excuse. Your Majesty's unexampled Goodness will, therefore, pardon the Bitterness of our Grief, at the gradual, though not the less dangerous Diminution, of this antient Badge of *English* Liberty. For though we could, with the most becoming Alacrity, submit our Lives and Property, and what we hold dearer than both, that inestimable Liberty with which our Ancestors have set us free, to your Majesty's royal Clemency, and princely Discretion; yet the unavoidable Delegations of the royal Authority, which necessarily expose us to the rapacious Designs of wicked Men, leave us, neither Rest nor Security, while a Custom-house Officer may wantonly seize, what a Judge of your Majesty's Court of Vice-Admiralty, may condemn in his Discretion; or at best restore to the honest Proprietor, without the Possibility of a Restitution for the Injury. Shall we not therefore be allowed, with the most lowly Reverence, and upon the Arms of the most firm and unshaken Fidelity, to tender our humble Petitions to the Throne, that this great, this growing, this mighty Evil may be removed from among us?

Permit us, most gracious Sovereign, to observe on the Want of a Paper Currency, as the last, though not the least Evil, to which the Colonies, are unhappily made Subject, by an Act of Parliament lately passed for that Purpose. Our Commerce affords us so small a Return of Specie, that without a Paper Currency, supported on the Credit of the Colony, our Trade, and the Commutation of Property, must necessarily fail. The Want of Money will disable us to pay our internal Taxes, and effectually prevent our Exertions in the common Cause; ever on the most interesting, and alarming Occasions. In the Use of this Means for Supplying our political Wants, we have been continually indulged, ever since the Reign of your Majesty's glorious Predecessor, King *William* the Third. And what Use we have made of it, we appeal to past Occurrences for Proof; your Majesty's poor Subjects in the Colonies, are unable to bear the Weight of a heavy, and immediate Tax: And no other Expedient can possibly be devised, to acquit them in the Discharge of public Duties, in momentuous and pressing Occasions, than an Emission of Paper Money, to be sunk at a distant, though certain Period, by Taxes gradually and annually imposed. Had the immense Sums this loyal Colony has contributed, to promote your Majesty's Service, during the late War, been immediately imposed; besides the absolute Impossibility of supplying them, the whole Colony must have sunk under so intolerable a Burden. Had we then been deprived of this easy Method, of raising a Sum for immediate Use, we should have lost the Opportunity of testifying our Love and Loyalty to our Sovereign, when his General made Requisition of the prodigious Sum of, *One Hundred and Fifty Thousand Pounds,* without which, the important Operations, of the most eventful Campaign, must at least unavoidably have stagnated, if not miscarried. These, Sire, were the good Uses that we made of this political Engine; and we may safely defy the World, to produce an Instance, in which, by neglecting, to sink our Emissions of Paper Currency, in due Season, we suffered it either to depreciate, or fall into discredit. May the Consideration of our past faithful Services, and a sincere Tender of our Readiness, on all future Occasions, have their proper Weight with your Majesty; and produce a Repeal of that Law, which has deprived this People, of the most effectual Means, to demonstrate their Fidelity and Affection to their Prince.

These, may it please your Majesty, are the important Points, upon which your faithful Representatives for your loyal Colony of *New-York,* have in behalf of their Constituents, and with the most humble Submission, presumed to approach the Throne; assuring your Majesty, that one of the principal Blessings they have to expect, from a Continuence of their exclusive Right to tax themselves, the Restoration and Extension of their Commerce, the Execution of Law, in the antient and ordinary Method, and the Continuance of their Bills of Credit, will be, their Capacity to do the most faithful and ready Services, to their King and Country, upon every Occasion.

The Inhabitants of this your Majesty's loyal Colony of *New-York,* have the highest Sense of the Wisdom, Justice, Integrity and Impartiality, of both your Majesty's Houses of Parliament; and are therefore fully convinced, that Measures so destructive of our, and the publick Emolument, must be grounded, on the Misrepresentation of those, who, by opposing the Interests of the Colonies, strike at the Well-being of the nation in general. It is extremely difficult, for those highly honourable Houses, at so great a Distance, to preserve from Polution, the Channel of Intelligence. But your Majesty, being representatively present, by your Governors, and Councils, who, doubtless, will be ready, to give their truest Intelligence, when commanded by their Sovereign, may, by this infalliable Method, discover our truly deplorable Circumstances; and provide such Redress, for this, and your other loyal and distressed *North American* Colonies, as to your Majesty, in your princely Wisdom and Goodness, shall seem meet.

That Almighty God, in whose Hand are the Hearts of Princes, may direct the Counsels of our most gracious Sovereign, for the Welfare, even of his most distant Subjects; that the Imperial Diadem of *Great-Britain,* may sit long and easy, on his royal Head; that he may be conspicuously blest, among the Princes of the Earth, in his sacred Person, illustrious Family, and auspicious Government; that the *British* Scepter may never depart, from his august House, nor his faithful Subjects, throughout his extensive Kingdoms and Dominions, want Hearts, on every Occasion, to testify the most unshaken Fidelity, the most ardent Affection, and the most chearful and unreserved Obedience, to a Prince of his royal Lineage, while Sun and Moon endure, are the sincere, the ardent, the unremitted Prayers, of your Majesty's most dutiful, most loyal, and most devoted Subjects, the Representatives of your Majesty's Colony of *New-York*.

By Order of the General Assembly,

William Nicoll, *Speaker.*

Assembly-Chamber,
City of New-York,
Oct. 18, 1764.

1.2

 PETITION TO THE HOUSE OF COMMONS

The assembly's Petition to the House of Commons begins by claiming that the colony was settled by Protestant emigrants from, in the main, Great Britain and Ireland and then notes that its constitution "was originally modelled with the Intervention of the Crown, and not excepted to by the Realm of *England* before, nor by *Great-Britain*, since the Union, [and] the Planters and Settlers conceived the strongest Hopes, that the Colony had gained a civil Constitution, which, so far at least as the Rights and Privileges of the People were concerned, would remain permanent." In short, continued use and acceptance had led them to believe that their constitution was no longer subject to revision by the British Crown, and thus they were taken by surprise when Parliament attempted to collect internal taxes for revenue in the colonies.[10] The consequences of Parliament's action, the assembly predicted, could only be tragic. Next, the petition notes that if exemption from Parliament-imposed taxes was a privilege, then New York had done nothing to deserve its forfeiture, most importantly because of its generous contributions to the king for his military needs in the colonies.

The Petition to the House is emphatic in defending the colonists' corporate right to self-taxation. While this power was characterized in the Petition to the King as a privilege, a liberty, or a constitutional civil right, in the Petition to the House of Commons the New York Assembly's tone, in the surprisingly bold language of the future loyalist William Smith, asserts that a people's right to self-taxation is not a privilege but a "natural Right of Mankind," and accordingly, the petitioners "nobly disdain the thought of claiming that Exemption as a Privilege . . . and glory in it as their Right." Liberties, rights, privileges, and franchises were legally distinct concepts in British law, though often intermingled, with liberties and privileges being less secure than rights as bases for claiming exemption from some general restriction or governmental demand. The petitioners' grounds for defending their exemption as a right, not a privilege, rested, though, not on natural rights but on the precedent of "their Ancestors [having] enjoyed [the right] in *Great-Britain* and *Ireland,*" and on the wish that "their Descendants returning to those Kingdoms" would "enjoy it again."[11]

In short, although the right of self-taxation is a natural one, the New York Assembly rested its defense on customary "antient Rights" and, still more emphatically, on an equality of rights between the king's metropolitan and colonial peoples. Accordingly, the petitioners found that "no History can furnish an Instance of a Constitution to permit one Part of a Dominion to be taxed by another, and that too in Effect, but by a Branch of that other Part; who in all Bills for public Aids, suffer not the least Alteration" from their action. For the New York Assembly, the idea that the legislature of one part of the empire, Britain's Parliament, was able to tax those living in another part, the North American colonies, was "absurd and unequal." Similarly, the assembly defended the equality of "their Love and Loyalty" toward the king with that of his British and Irish subjects. The central claims of an equality enjoyed by all the king's people and the affectionate loyalty of his American subjects toward the king strikingly persisted throughout the Imperial Crisis.

Still, the assembly asked the House of Commons to understand that none of its claims should be taken as a challenge either to the constitutionality of Parliament's restrictions on colonial trade and manufacturing or to other maritime laws. Although the colonists rightly understood those laws as greatly advantaging Britain, that understanding did not lead them to "a Desire of Independency upon the supreme Power of the Parliament": "Of so extravagant a Disregard to our own Interests we cannot be guilty.—From what other Quarter can we hope for Protection? We reject the Thought with the utmost Abhorrence." The assembly claimed, accordingly, that it had no intention of invading the "Rights of Great Britain," specifically the right of Parliament to regulate imperial commercial matters for the benefit of Great Britain. Parliament was still viewed as enjoying commercial rights "naturally founded upon her Superiority." And in according that right to Britain, the New York Assembly, like many Britons, found little or no meaningful distinction between internal and external taxes or duties. The assembly ended, like other colonial legislatures, by complaining of the extension of vice-admiralty courts in the colonies and the prohibition of paper money by the Sugar and Currency Acts.

*Journal of the Votes and Proceedings of the General Assembly of the Colony of New York. Began on the 8th Day of November, 1743; and Ended the 23rd of December, 1765* (New York: Hugh Gaine, 1766), 2:776–79. The New York State Assembly also sent a Petition to the House of Lords, but it is omitted here because of the overlap in content between it and this document.

## PETITION TO THE HOUSE OF COMMONS

To the Honourable the Knights, Citizens and Burgesses, representing the Commons of Great-Britain, in Parliament assembled.

The Representation and Petition of the General-Assembly of the Colony of New York.

Most humbly Shew,

That from the Year 1683, to this Day, there have been three Legislative Branches in this Colony; consisting of the Governor and Council appointed by the Crown, and the Representatives chosen by the People, who, besides the Power of making Laws for the Colony, have enjoyed the Right of Taxing the Subject for the Support of the Government.

Under this Political Frame, the Colony was settled by Protestant Emigrants from several Parts of *Europe,* and more especially from *Great-Britain* and *Ireland:* And as it was originally modelled with the Intervention of the Crown, and not excepted to by the Realm of *England* before, nor by *Great-Britain,* since the Union, the Planters and Settlers conceived the strongest Hopes, that the Colony had gained a civil Constitution, which, so far at least as the Rights and Privileges of the People were concerned, would remain permanent, and be transmitted to their latest Posterity.

It is therefore with equal Concern and Surprize, that they have received Intimations of certain Designs lately formed, if possible, to induce the Parliament of *Great-Britain,* to impose Taxes upon the Subjects *here,* by Laws to be passed *there;* and as we who have the Honour to represent them, conceive that this Innovation, will greatly affect the Interest of the Crown and the Nation, and reduce the Colony to absolute Ruin; it became our indispensable Duty, to trouble you with a seasonable Representation of the Claim of our Constituents, to an Exemption from the Burthen of all Taxes not granted by themselves, and their Foresight of the tragical Consequences of an Adoption of the contrary Principle, to the Crown, the Mother Country, themselves and their Posterity.

Had the Freedom from all Taxes not granted by ourselves been enjoyed as a *Privilege,* we are confident the Wisdom and Justice of the *British* Parliament, would rather establish than destroy it, unless by our abuse of it, the Forfeiture was justly incurred; but his Majesty's Colony of *New-York,* can not only defy the whole World to impeach their Fidelity, but appeal to all the Records of their past Transactions, as well for the fullest Proof of their steady Affection to the Mother Country, as for their strenuous Efforts to support the Government, and advance the general Interest of the whole *British* Empire.

It has been their particular Misfortune, to be always most exposed to the Incursions of the *Canadians,* and the more barbarous Irruptions of the Savages of the Desart, as may appear by all the Maps of this Country; and in many Wars we have suffered an immense Loss both of Blood and Treasure, to repel the Foe, and maintain a valuable Dependency upon the *British* Crown.

On no Occasion can we be justly reproached for with-holding a necessary Supply, our Taxes have been equal to our Abilities, and confessed to be so by the Crown; for Proof of which we refer to the Speeches of our Governors in all Times of War; and though we remember with great Gratitude, that in those grand and united Struggles, which were lately directed for the Conquest of *Canada,* Part of our Expences was reimbursed, yet we cannot suppress the Remark, that our Contribution surpassed our Strength, even in the Opinion of the Parliament, who under that Conviction, thought it but just to take off Part of the Burthen, to which we had loyally and voluntarily submitted; in a Word, if there is any Merit in facilitating on all Occasions, the publick Measures in the remote Extremes of the national Dominion, and in preserving untainted Loyalty and chearful Obedience, it is ours; and (with Submission) unabused, nay more, well improved Privileges cannot, ought not, to be taken away from any People.

But an Exemption from the Burthen of ungranted, involuntary Taxes, must be the grand Principle of every free State.—Without such a Right vested in themselves, exclusive of all others, there can be no Liberty, no Happiness, no Security; it is inseparable from the very Idea of Property, for who can call that his own, which may be taken away at the Pleasure of another? And so evidently does this appear to be the natural Right of Mankind, that even conquered tributary States, though subject to the Payment of a fixed periodical Tribute, never were reduced so abject and forlorn a Condition, as to yield to all the Burthens which their Conquerors might at any future Time think fit to impose. The Tribute paid, the Debt was discharged; and the Remainder they could call their own.

And if conquered Vassals upon the Principle even of *natural Justice,* may claim a Freedom from Assessments unbounded and unassented to, without which they would sustain the Loss of every Thing, and Life itself become intolerable, with how much Propriety and Boldness may we proceed to inform the Commons of *Great-Britain,* who, to their distinguished Honour, have in all Ages asserted the Liberties of Mankind, that the People of this Colony, inspired by the Genius of their Mother Country, nobly disdain the thought of claiming that Exemption as a *Privilege.*—They found it on a Basis more honourable, solid and stable; they challenge it, and glory in it as their Right. That Right their Ancestors enjoyed in *Great-Britain* and *Ireland;* their Descendants returning to those Kingdoms, enjoy it again: And that it may be exercised by his Majesty's Subjects at Home, and justly denied to those who submitted to Poverty, Barbarian Wars, Loss of Blood, Loss of Money, personal Fatigues, and ten Thousand unutterable Hardships, to enlarge the Trade, Wealth, and Dominion of the Nation; or, to speak with the most unexceptionable Modesty, that when *as Subjects,* all have equal Merit; a Fatal, nay the most odious Discrimination should nevertheless be made between them, no Sophistry can recommend to the Sober, impartial Decision of common Sense.

Our Constituents exult in that glorious Model of Government, of which your Hon. House is so essential a Part; and earnestly pray the Almighty Governor of all, long to support the due Distribution of the Power of the Nation in the three great Legislative Branches. But the Advocates for divesting us of the Right to tax ourselves, would by the Success of their Machination, render the Devolution of all civil Power upon the *Crown alone,* a Government more favourable, and therefore more eligible to these *American* Dependences. The supreme Ruler in a Monarchy, even in a despotic Monarchy, will naturally consider his Relation to be, what it is, equal to all his good Subjects: And equal

Dispensation of Favours will be the natural Consequence of those Views; and the Increase of mutual Affection must be productive of an Increase of the Felicity of *all*. But no History can furnish an Instance of a Constitution to permit one Part of a Dominion to be taxed by another, and that too in Effect, but by a Branch of that other Part; who in all Bills for public Aids, suffer not the least Alteration.—And if such an absurd and unequal Constitution should be adopted, who, that considers the natural Reluctance of Mankind to burthens, and their Inclination to cast them upon the Shoulders of others, cannot foresee, that while the People on one Side of the *Atlantic,* enjoy an Exemption from the Load, those on the other, must submit to the most unsupportable Oppression and Tyranny.

Against these Evils, the Indulgence of the present Parliament, of which we have had such large Experience, cannot provide, if the grand Right to tax ourselves is invaded. Depressed by the Prospect of an endless Train of the most distressing Mischiefs, naturally attendant upon such an Innovation, his Majesty's *American* Subjects, will think it no inconsiderable Augmentation of their Misery, that the Measure itself implies the most severe and unmerited Censure, and is urged, as far as they are acquainted, by no good Reasons of State.

They are unconscious of any Conduct that brings the least Imputation upon their Love and Loyalty, and whoever has accused them, has abused both the Colonies and their Mother Country; more faithful Subjects his Majesty has not, in any Part of his Dominions, nor *Britain* more submissive and affectionate Sons.

And if our Contributions to the Support of the Government upon this Continent, or for the Maintenance of an Army, to awe and subdue the Savages should be thought necessary, why shall it be presumed, without a Trial, that we more than others, will refuse to hearken to a just Requisition from the Crown? To Requisitions for Aids salutary to our own Interests? Or why should a more incorrigible and unreasonable Spirit be imputed to us, than to the Parliament of *Ireland,* or any other of his Majesty's Subjects?

Left to the Enjoyment of our antient Rights, the Government will be truly informed when a Tax is necessary, and of the Abilities of the People; and there will be an equitable Partition of the Burthen. And as the publick Charges will necessarily increase with the Increase of the Country, and the Augmentation or Reduction of the Force kept up, be regulated by the Power and Temper of our barbarian Enemy, the Necessity for continuing the present Model must appear to be most strongly inforced.—At the remote Distance of the *British* Commons from the sequestered Shades of the interior Parts of this Desart, false Intelligence of the State of the *Indians* may be given; whereas the Vicinity of the Colonies will enable them, not only, to detect all false Alarms, and check all fraudulent Accounts, but urge them by the never failing Motive of Self-Preservation, to oppose any hostile Attempts upon their Borders.

Nor will the Candour of the Commons of *Great-Britain,* construe our Earnestness to maintain this Plea, to arise from a Desire of Independency upon the supreme Power of the Parliament. Of so extravagant a Disregard to our own Interests we cannot be guilty.—

From what other Quarter can we hope for Protection? We reject the Thought with the utmost Abhorrence; and a perfect Knowledge of this Country will afford the fullest Proof, that nothing in our Temper can give the least Ground for such a Jealousy.

The peaceable and invariable Submission of the Colonies, for a Century past, forbids the Imputation, or proves it a Calumny.—What can be more apparent, than that the State which exercises a Sovereignty in Commerce, can draw all the Wealth of its Colonies into its own Stock? And has not the whole Trade of *North-America,* that growing Magazine of Wealth, been, from the Beginning, directed, restrained, and prohibited at the sole Pleasure of the Parliament? And whatever some may pretend, his Majesty's American Subjects are far from a Desire to invade the just Rights of *Great-Britain,* in all commercial Regulations. They humbly conceive, that a very manifest Distinction presents itself, which, while it leaves to the Mother Country an incontestable Power, to give Laws for the Advancement of her own Commerce, will, at the same Time, do no Violence to the Rights of the Plantations.

The Authority of the Parliament of *Great-Britain,* to model the Trade of the whole Empire, so as to subserve the Interest of her own, we are ready to recognize in the most extensive and positive Terms. Such a Preference is naturally founded upon her Superiority, and indissolubly connected with the Principle of Self-Preservation.—And therefore, to assign one Instance, instead of many, the Colonies cannot, would not ask for a Licence to import woolen Manufactures from *France;* or to go into the most lucrative Branches of Commerce, in the least Degree incompatible with the Trade and Interest of *Great-Britain.*

But a Freedom to drive all Kinds of Traffick in a Subordination to, and not inconsistent with, the *British* Trade; and an Exemption from all Duties in such a Course of Commerce, is humbly claimed by the Colonies, as the most essential of all the Rights to which they are intitled, as Colonists from, and connected, in the common Bond of Liberty, with the unenslaved Sons of *Great-Britain.*

For, with Submission, since all Impositions, whether they be internal Taxes, or Duties paid, for what we consume, equally diminish the Estates upon which they are charged; what avails it to any People, by which of them they are impoverished? Every Thing will be given up to preserve Life; and though there is a Diversity in the Means, yet, the whole Wealth of a Country may be as effectually drawn off, by the Exaction of Duties, as by any other Tax upon their Estates.

And therefore, the General Assembly of *New-York,* in Fidelity to their Constituents, cannot but express the most earnest Supplication, that the Parliament will charge our Commerce with no other Duties, than a necessary Regard to the particular Trade of *Great-Britain,* evidently demands; but leave it to the legislative Power of the Colony, to impose all other Burthens upon it's own People, which the publick Exigences may require.

Latterly, the Laws of Trade seem to have been framed without an Attention to this fundamental Claim.

Permit us, also, in Defence of our Attachment to the Mother Country, to add, what your Merchants (to whom we boldly make the Appeal) know to be an undoubted Truth; that this Continent contains some of the *most useful* of her Subjects.—Such is the Nature of our Produce, that all we acquire is less than sufficient to purchase what we want of your Manufactures; and, be the Policy of your Commerce what it will, all our Riches must flow into *Great-Britain.*—Immense have been our Contributions to the National Stock.—Our Staple, Industry, Trade and Wealth, all conduce to the particular Advantage of our fellow Subjects there.—The natural State of this Country, necessarily forms the Ballance of Trade in her Favour.—Her growing Opulence must elevate her above all Fear and Jealousy of these Dependences. How much stronger then the Reasons for leaving us free from ungranted Impositions? Whoever will give full Scope to his Meditations on this Topic, will see it the Interest of *Great-Britain,* to adopt the Maxim, that her own Happiness is most intimately connected with the Freedom, Ease and Prosperity of her Colonies: The more extensive our Traffick, the Greater her Gains; we carry all to her Hive, and consume the Returns; and we are content with any constitutional Regulation that inriches her, though it impoverishes ourselves. But a fuller Display of these Principles, being prepared by our Merchants, to be laid before the honorable House, at the last Sitting, we shall only beg Leave to add, that any Information, repugnant to this Account of the low State of our Traffick, must proceed from partial, or incompetent Witnesses; who may have formed their Estimate of the Wealth of the Colony, during the late War, when the *French* and *Spanish West-Indies,* were laid open to our Trade, and those immense Profits acquired there, for the Manufactures of *Great-Britain* and *Ireland,* flowed into the Colonies, and Luxury advanced upon us slower than our Gains.—But Trade being now confined to it's old Channels, and indeed still more restricted, and the late acquired Cash, remitted home for necessary Cloathing, other very indifferent Appearances begin to take place, and the *British* Merchants are, or will soon be convinced to their Sorrow, that our Splendor was not supported by solid Riches.

The honourable House will permit us to observe next, that the Act of the last Session of Parliament, inhibiting all Intercourse between the Continent and the foreign Sugar Colonies, will prove equally detrimental to us and *Great-Britain.*—*That* Trade, gave a value to a vast, but now alas unsaleable Staple, which being there converted into Cash and Merchandize, made necessary Remittances for the *British* Manufactures we consumed:—The same Law contains a Clause unfriendly to the Linen Manufactory in *Ireland,* for the Restraint upon the Exportation of Lumber to that Kingdom, prevents even our dunnaging the Flax-Seed Casks sent there with Staves.—And when we consider the Wisdom of our Ancestors in contriving Trials by Juries, we cannot stifle our Regret, that the Laws of Trade in general, change the Current of Justice from the common Law, and subject Controversies of the utmost Importance to the Decisions of the Vice-Admiralty Courts, who proceed not according the old wholesome Laws of the Land, nor are always filled with Judges of approved Knowledge and Integrity.—To this Objection, the aforementioned Statute will at first View appear to be so evidently open, that we shall content ourselves with barely suggesting, that the amazing Confidence it reposes in the Judges, gives great Grief to his Majesty's *American* Subjects; and pass on to a few Remarks on that other Law of the same Session, which renders our Paper Money no legal Tender.

The Use of this Sort of Currency in procuring a speedy Supply on Emergences, all the Colonies have often experienced.—We have had Recourse to this Expedient in every War, since the Reign of King *William* the Third; and without it we could not have co-operated so vigorously in the Reduction of *Canada,* that grand stroke which secured to *Great-Britain,* the immense Dominion of the Continent of *North-America.* We had no other Alternative but *that,* or the taking up Money upon Loan, Lenders could not have been easily found, and if they were, the Interest upon all the Sums raised in that Way, would have exceeded our Ability now to discharge. Happy for us, therefore, that we fell upon the Project of giving a Credit to Paper, which was always supported by seasonable Taxes on our Estates; the Currency of the Bills being prolonged only till we were able to burn up the Quantity from Time to Time emitted.—Our Laws, or the Copies transmitted to the Plantation Office, will evince that of the numerous Emissions we have made since the first, which was on the 8th of *June,* 1709, all were for the urgent Service of the Crown.—One Instance is so recent, and shews the Necessity of the Continuation of such a Power in the Colonies, in so striking a Point of Light, that it deserves more particular Notice. The Operations of the Year 1759, were nearly at a Stand for want of Money. The military Chest being exhausted, the General was alarmed, and seeing no other Method to ward of[f] the impending Disaster, was obliged to ask the Colony for a Loan of *One Hundred and Fifty Thousand Pounds:* We immediately gratified his Request,—Such was our Concern for the publick Weal! We wish his Majesty's Service may suffer no Impediment, by this new Restraint in an Article which has been of so much Utility.—The Traffick of the Colony certainly will, for want of a competent Medium; and on that Account, and in behalf of those miserable Debtors, whose Estates, through the Scarcity of legal Cash, must be extended by Executions, and hastily sold beneath their true Value, to the Ruin of many Families, permit us to implore your tender Commiseration.

The General Assembly of this Colony have no desire to derogate from the Power of the Parliament of *Great-Britain;* but they cannot avoid deprecating the Loss of such Rights as they have hitherto enjoyed, Rights established in the first Dawn of our Constitution, founded upon the most substantial Reasons, confirmed by invariable Usage, conducive to the best Ends; never abused to bad Purposes, and with the Loss of which Liberty, Property, and all the Benefits of Life, tumble into Insecurity and Ruin: Rights, the Deprivation of which, will dispirit the People, abate their Industry, discourage Trade, introduce Discord, Poverty and Slavery; or, by depopulating the Colonies, turn a vast, fertile, prosperous Region, into a dreary Wilderness: impoverish *Great-Britain,* and shake the Power and Independency of the most opulent and flourishing Empire in the World.

All which your Petitioners (who repose the highest Confidence in your Wisdom and Justice) humbly pray, may be now taken into your seasonable Consideration, and such Measures pursued, as the Event may prove to have been concerted for the Common-Weal, of all the Subjects of *Great-Britain,* both at home and abroad.

By Order of the General Assembly,

Wm. Nicoll, *Speaker.*

Assembly-Chamber,
*City of* New-York,
Oct. 18, 1764.

## 2. A MASSACHUSETTS PROTEST AGAINST THE SUGAR ACT, NOVEMBER 3, 1764

Meeting in a special October session, the Massachusetts House of Representatives chose a committee of eleven to register its opposition to the Sugar Act and to "draf[t] an Address to the King and Parliament claiming exemption from any kind of colonial taxes for revenue levied by Parliament."[12] The Speaker of the House, Samuel White, headed the committee, which included Oxenbridge Thacher, an established progressive Massachusetts attorney who had represented Boston merchants in opposing the renewal of general writs of assistance. Thacher drafted the petition—addressed to the king and Parliament—but it was rejected by the Massachusetts Council (effectively, the upper house) for being too brash. As a consequence, a twenty-one-member committee drawn from both houses and chaired also by White was formed. It included Thacher, Thomas Cushing, and James Otis, Jr., from the House, and Thomas Hutchinson and James Bowdoin from the Council.

Hutchinson, a descendant of the religious dissenter Anne Hutchinson, was a wealthy and urbane merchant who served, among a large number of other posts—often consecutively—as lieutenant governor from 1758 until 1771, when he was named governor. He had been an influential delegate to the first continental or intercolonial meeting of seven American colonies, the Albany Congress of 1754, and became a focus of anti-British animosity in Massachusetts before choosing to remain loyal to the king. He was, in 1764, serving as lieutenant governor and chief justice of the Massachusetts General Court. The most powerful opponent of Thacher's draft, he successfully moved the final petition in a more moderate direction.[13]

Bowdoin, a well-off amateur scientist with close family ties to members of the British imperial administration, was less wedded to the king's government than Hutchinson; he later served as president of the Massachusetts Revolutionary Council and presided over the state's constitutional convention in 1780.[14] Speaker White also, like most other colonists, differed with Hutchinson over his articulate defense of Parliament's supremacy and its legal right to legislate in all matters for the king's dominions.[15] When White was placed on the Council in 1766, Otis, a prominent lawyer and radical, was chosen to replace him as Speaker. Governor Francis Bernard, however, rejected his nomination.[16] Otis, although known by then for having written a widely read pamphlet condemning parliamentary taxation of the colonies on the basis of the English Constitution of the seventeenth century, with its incorporation of natural law into English law,[17] later became well-known, like Hutchinson, for his unpopular defense of Parliament's sovereignty over all matters colonial.[18] After Otis' rejection, the House chose Cushing, a man of moderation from a family of wealthy merchants. Later as a delegate to the First Continental Congress in 1774, Cushing, like most in attendance, was a strong proponent of colonial rights but, in the end, a reluctant supporter of colonial independence; in 1776, he was maneuvered out of the Second Congress by radical members of the Massachusetts delegation and replaced by a younger man, Elbridge Gerry, who was a far stronger advocate of American independence.[19]

The petition produced by the second joint committee, unlike Thacher's original House draft, was addressed solely to the House of Commons. By the time of the next continental or intercolonial gathering of delegates, in 1774, Congress no longer found it appropriate to address its petitions to Parliament. Doing so would have implied that Parliament had authority to legislate for the colonies. The petition begins with a vigorous protest against the trade restrictions resulting from the Sugar Act, which American colonists believed to benefit mainly the wealthy British West Indian plantation owners. The petition argues that the legislation would do great harm to the commercial interests of the colonies, in particular to the fisheries, which netted large quantities of low-quality fish that couldn't be sold in Europe but that French planters bartered sugar or molasses for, for consumption by their slaves. Since the French allowed American fishing boats to trade only if they bartered for sugar or molasses, and since the Sugar Act forbade Americans from acquiring sugar or molasses from French West Indian planters, the fishermen would subsequently lack a way to profit from their low-quality fish, which would have to be discarded. The petitioners also draw attention to the enforcement provisions outlined in the legislation, with the extension of the jurisdiction of vice-admiralty courts, the protection of customs officers from common-law civil suits, and the consequent limitation on the role of jury trials, "one of the most valuable of English liberties."

The petitioners, looking ahead to the proposed Stamp Act, argued, as did almost every other American colonial author or body during the next twelve years, that taxing the colonies for revenues, that is, imposing taxes to be paid in the colonies, was unconstitutional and that such taxes could be legally raised only by the colonial legislatures—not by, effectively, a foreign legislature, the British Parliament. By implication, however, the petitioners seemed to suggest that Parliament-imposed taxes designed to control imperial trade, that is, external taxes, might be viewed in the colonies as constitutional and, thus, acceptable.[20] Of course, when such external taxation was imposed by Parliament with the explicit and declared goal of raising revenues in the colonies, even if restricted to use in the colonies, by the Townshend Duties of 1767, American colonists found such taxation no more acceptable than they had the internal variety levied by George Grenville in 1764 and 1765, which was the focus of colonial opposition in this document.

As a result of the opposition of the more conservative members of the committee, in particular Hutchinson, the petitioners were careful to use the term *humbly* as frequently as possible and to describe their traditional colonial exemptions from internal taxation by Parliament as "liberties" or "privileges," not as "rights." As John Adams notes, "It was by their [Governor Hutchinson and Andrew Oliver's] influence that the two houses were induced to wave the word *rights* and an express denial of the right of parliament to tax us, to the great grief and distress of the friends of liberty in both houses."[21] Still, even a petition as deferential as this one holds that the colonists, by residing outside the realm, were still "more beneficial to the nation than they would be if they should be removed to Britain and there held to a full proportion of the national taxes and duties of every kind." This line of argument became a consistent refrain during the next twelve years as members of Congress offered either to guarantee the colonial payment of imperial taxes or to entrench the limitations imposed by commercial disabilities for the foreseeable future, just not both (see documents 5.2 and 23.4).

2.1

 PETITION TO THE HOUSE OF COMMONS

Alden Bradford, ed., *Speeches of the Governors of Massachusetts from 1765 to 1775: And the answers of the House of Representatives to the same; With their resolutions and addresses for that period and other public papers relating to the dispute between this country and Great Britain which led to the independence of the United States* (Boston: Russell and Gardner, 1818). http://avalon.law.yale.edu/18th_century/petition_mass_1764.asp.

NOVEMBER 3, 1764

The petition of the Council and House of Representatives of his Majesty's Province of Massachusetts Bay, Most humbly showeth:

That the Act passed in the last session of Parliament, entitled "An act for granting certain duties in the British colonies and plantations in America," etc., must necessarily bring many burdens upon the inhabitants of these colonies and plantations, which your petitioners conceive would not have been imposed if a full representation of the state of the colonies had been made to your honourable House. That the duties laid upon foreign sugars and molasses by a former Act of Parliament entitled "an Act for the better securing and encouraging the trade of his Majesty's sugar colonies in America," if the Act had been executed with rigour, must have had the effect of an absolute prohibition.

That the duties laid on those articles by the present Act still remain so great that, however otherwise intended, they must undoubtedly have the same effect. That the importation of foreign molasses into this province in particular is of the greatest importance, and a prohibition will be prejudicial to many branches of its trade and will lessen the consumption of the manufactures of Great Britain. That this importance does not arise merely, nor principally, from the necessity of foreign molasses in order to its being consumed or distilled within the province. That if the trade for many years carried on for foreign molasses can be no longer continued, a vent cannot be found for more than one half the fish of inferior quality which are caught and cured by the inhabitants of the province, the French not permitting fish to be carried by foreigners to any of their islands, unless it be bartered or exchanged for molasses.

That if there be no sale of fish of inferior quality it will be impossible to continue the fishery, the fish usually sent to Europe will then cost so dear that the French will be able to undersell the English at all the European markets; and by this means one of the most valuable returns to Great Britain will be utterly lost, and that great nursery of seamen destroyed.

That the restraints laid upon the exportation of timber, boards, staves, and other lumber from the colonies to Ireland and other parts of Europe, except Great Britain, must greatly affect the trade of this province and discourage the clearing and improving of the lands which are yet uncultivated.

That the powers given by the late Act to the court of vice-admiralty, instituted over all America, are so expressed as to leave it doubtful, whether goods seized for illicit importation in any one of the colonies may not be removed, in order to trial, to any other colony where the judge may reside, although at many hundred miles distance from the place of seizure.

That if this construction should be admitted, many persons, however legally they goods may have been imported, must lose their property, merely from an inability of following after it, and making that defence which they might do if the trial had been in the colony where the goods were seized.

That this construction would be so much the more grievous, seeing that in America the officers by this Act are indemnified in case of seizure whenever the judge of admiralty shall certify that there was probable cause; and the claimant can neither have costs nor maintain an action against the person seizing, how much soever he may have expended in defence of his property.

That the extension of the powers of courts of vice-admiralty has, so far as the jurisdiction of the said courts hath been extended, deprived the colonies of one of the' most valuable of English liberties, trials by juries.

That every Act of Parliament, which in this respect distinguishes his Majesty's subjects in the colonies from their fellow subjects in Great Britain, must create a very sensible concern and grief.

That there have been communicated to your petitioners sundry resolutions of the House of Commons in their last session for imposing stamp duties or taxes upon the inhabitants of the colonies, the consideration whereof was referred to the next session. That your petitioners acknowledge with all gratitude the tenderness of the legislature of Great Britain of the liberties of the subjects in the colonies, who have always judged by their representatives both of the way and manner in which internal taxes should be raised within their respective governments, and of the ability of the inhabitants to pay them.

That they humbly hope the colonies in general have so demeaned themselves, more especially during the late war, as still to deserve the continuance of all those liberties which they have hitherto enjoyed.

That although during the war the taxes upon the colonies were greater than they have been since the conclusion of it, yet the sources by which the inhabitants were enabled to pay their taxes having ceased, and their trade being decayed, they are not so able to pay the taxes they are subjected to in time of peace as they were the greater taxes in time of war.

That one principal difficulty which has ever attended the trade of the colonies, proceeds from the scarcity of money, which scarcity is caused by the balance of trade with Great Britain, which has been continually against the colonies. That the drawing sums of money from the colonies from time to time must distress the trade to that degree that eventually Great Britain may lose more by the diminution of the consumption of her manufactures than all the sums which it is possible for the colonies thus to pay can countervail.

That they humbly conceive if the taxes which the inhabitants of this province are obliged annually to pay towards the support of the internal government, the restraint they are under in their trade for the benefit of Great Britain, and the consumption thereby occasioned of British manufactures, be all considered and have their due weight it must appear that the subjects of this province are as fully burdened as their fellow subjects in Britain, and that they are, whilst in America, more beneficial to the nation than they would be if they should be removed to Britain and there held to a full proportion of the national taxes and duties of every kind.

Your petitioners, therefore, most humbly pray that they may be relieved from the burdens which, they have humbly represented to have been brought upon them by the late Act of Parliament, as to the wisdom of the honourable House shall seem meet, that the privileges of the colonies relative to their internal taxes which they have so longed enjoyed, may still be referred, until your petitioners, in conjunction with the other governments, can have opportunity to make a more full representation of the state and the condition of the colonies and the interest of Great Britain with regard to them.

## 3. VIRGINIA PETITIONS TO THE KING AND PARLIAMENT, DECEMBER 18, 1764

These petitions were produced in the House of Burgesses (the Virginia lower house) under the speakership of John Robinson, who, until his death in 1766 (he was subsequently disgraced), wielded great power in the colony as treasurer and, since 1738, as Speaker. The committee chosen to draft the petitions was chaired by Peyton Randolph, a wealthy attorney from a well-established Virginia family, who would become the Continental Congress' first president in 1774. It included Richard Bland, Benjamin Harrison, Edmund Pendleton, Richard Henry Lee, John Fleming, Landon Carter, George Wythe, and Archibald Cary.[22] The committee was divided between radical and more moderate delegates. The moderates opposed Parliament's right to legislate for and tax the colonies but believed that important benefits accrued from a close imperial relationship. Most significantly, they accepted Parliament's right or responsibility to enact imperial commercial legislation. Radicals were beginning to question the colonies' role within the empire and to challenge Parliament's constitutional authority to pass commercial and maritime legislation—and indeed to question the overarching motives of the British imperial government.

Among the moderates was Bland, a wealthy planter and man of letters who "hoped to avoid the need for colonial independence," and did so from a perspective informed by his being one of Virginia's foremost authorities on colonial legal history.[23] Indeed, Thomas Jefferson remembered him as "the most learned and logical man of those who took [a] prominent lead in public affairs."[24] Harrison, a wealthy planter who was a prominent member of the House of Burgesses and would be elected governor in 1781, was lukewarm in his support of radicals like Patrick Henry.[25] Pendleton, a self-educated lawyer, after being elected to the House of Burgesses in 1752, quickly came to be called "Moderation."[26] Landon Carter was a planter, county court justice, legislator, and extensive diarist, and he too opposed any efforts to radicalize the resistance to Parliament. Randolph, the author of the Memorial to the House of Lords, though a staunch opponent of Parliament's pretensions to legislate for the colonies, battled those who wanted to use still bolder language in the petitions.[27]

There were radical-leaning members too, though at this time they were in the minority, even in Virginia. The boldest among them was Richard Henry Lee, an aristocratic planter and the most successful radical among a group of brothers closely aligned in Virginia with Patrick Henry and in Massachusetts with Samuel Adams. Lee long urged the creation of committees of correspondences; in March 1773 he finally helped establish and chair one in Virginia.[28] Others on the drafting committee who veered toward a radical view of imperial relations included Fleming, a lawyer who later worked with Henry on his famous resolves, and Wythe, an intimate of Jefferson who quickly became a bold opponent of Parliament and, in 1779, America's first professor of law.

In these petitions there is much that is similar to those of New York and Massachusetts. Like other American colonists, the Virginians implored the king to protect the "People of this Colony in the Enjoyment of their ancient and inestimable Right of being governed by such Laws respecting their internal Polity and Taxation as are derived from their own Consent, with the Approbation of their Sovereign or his Substitute." Similarly, when turning to the House of Lords, Virginians besought the Lords to protect them in "their just and undoubted Rights as *Britons,*" rights and privileges that their ancestors had brought with them from Britain and that "their Descendants may conclude they cannot be deprived of . . . without Injustice." The petition goes into some detail in grounding Virginians' right to self-taxation by rehearsing earlier statutes, even those from "the Reign of Charles II." In short, it was their rights as British subjects that they sought the Commons and the Lords to protect.

Along with the assemblies of New York and Massachusetts, Virginians complained of how deeply in debt they were, of their lack of specie, and vaguely of the "late Restrictions upon the Trade of the Colonies." They announced that, following their contributions to the recent war, they were financially strapped and that any additional taxes would render them unable to purchase British manufactured goods, to the great detriment of Britain and its commercial and laboring classes. Still, there are differences between these petitions and the somewhat earlier ones of New York and Massachusetts. For example, Virginia is more strident than the others in declaring that "the Colonies cannot be represented" in Parliament. Additionally, there is no explicit mention of the hardships to be imposed by the Sugar and Currency Acts: lacking a merchant class,[29] Virginians were more concerned with the proposed Stamp Act taxes. Similarly, without a port city, Virginians had no immediate concern with the imposition of vice-admiralty courts and the diminution of common-law jury trials. Still, many of the main lines of argument that would eventually be turned on the king himself are here being advanced by the colonies against Parliament.

3.1

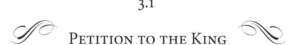

PETITION TO THE KING

J. P. Kennedy, ed., *Journals of the House of Burgesses of Virginia, 1761–1765*
(Richmond, 1907), 302.

To the King's Most Excellent Majesty.
Most gracious Sovereign.
We your Majesty's dutiful and loyal Subjects, the Council and Burgesses of your ancient Colony and Dominion of *Virginia,* now met in General Assembly, beg Leave to

assure your Majesty of our firm and inviolable Attachment to your sacred Person and Government; and as your faithful Subjects here have at all Times been zealous to demonstrate this Truth, by a ready Compliance with the Royal Requisitions during the late War, by which a heavy and oppressive Debt of near Half a Million hath been incurred, so at this Time they implore Permission to approach the Throne with humble Confidence, and to intreat that your Majesty will be graciously pleased to protect your People of this Colony in the Enjoyment of their ancient and inestimable Right of being governed by such Laws respecting their internal Polity and Taxation as are derived from their own Consent, with the Approbation of their Sovereign or his Substitute: A Right which as Men, and Descendents of *Britons,* they have ever quietly possessed since first by Royal Permission and Encouragement they left the Mother Kingdom to extend its Commerce and Dominion.

Your Majesty's dutiful Subjects of *Virginia* most humbly and unanimously hope that this invaluable Birthright descended to them from their Ancestors, and in which they have been protected by your Royal Predecessors, will not be suffered to receive an Injury under the Reign of your Sacred Majesty, already so illustriously distinguished by your gracious Attention to the Liberties of the People.

That your Majesty may long live to make Nations happy is the ardent Prayer of your faithful Subjects, the Council and Burgesses of *Virginia.*

## 3.2

 Memorial to the House of Lords

J. P. Kennedy, ed., *Journals of the House of Burgesses of Virginia, 1761–1765* (Richmond, 1907), 302.

To the Right Honourable the Lords Spiritual and Temporal in Parliament assembled:

The Memorial of the council and Burgesses of *Virginia,* now met in General Assembly, Humbly represents,

That your Memorialists hope on Application to your Lordships, the fixed and hereditary Guardians of *British* Liberty, will not be thought improper at this Time, when Measures are proposed subversive, as they conceive, of that Freedom which all Men, especially those who derive their Constitution from *Britain,* have a Right to enjoy; and they flatter themselves that your Lordships will not look upon them as Objects so unworthy your Attention as to regard any Impropriety in the Form or Manner of their Application, for your Lordships Protection of their just and undoubted Rights as *Britons.*

It cannot be Presumption in your Memorialists to call themselves by this distinguished Name, since they are descended from *Britons* who left their native Country to extend its Territory and Dominion, and who happily for *Britain,* and as your Memorialists once thought for themselves too, effected this Purpose. As our Ancestors brought with them every Right and Privilege they could with Justice claim in their Mother Kingdom, their Descendants may conclude they cannot be deprived of those Rights without Injustice.

Your Memorialists conceive it to be a fundamental Principle of the *British* Constitution, without which Freedom can no Where exist, that the People are not subject to any Taxes but such as are laid on them by their own Consent, or by those who are legally appointed to represent them: Property must become too precarious for the Genius of a free People which can be taken from them at the Will of others, who cannot know what Taxes such People can bear, or the easiest Mode of raising them; and who are not under that Restraint, which is the greatest Security against a burthensome Taxation, when the Representatives themselves must be affected by every Tax imposed on the People.

Your Memorialists are therefore led into an humble Confidence that your Lordships will not think any Reason sufficient to support such a Power in the *British* Parliament, where the Colonies cannot be represented; a Power never before constitutionally assumed, and which if they have a Right to exercise on any Occasion must necessarily establish this melancholy Truth, that the Inhabitants of the Colonies are the Slaves of *Britons,* from whom they are descended, and from whom they might expect every Indulgence that the Obligations of Interest and Affection can entitle them to.

Your Memorialists have been invested with the Right of taxing their own People from the first Establishment of a regular Government in the Colony, and Requisitions have been constantly made to them by their Sovereigns on all Occasions when the Assistance of the Colony was thought necessary to preserve the *British* Interest in America; from whence they must conclude they cannot now be deprived of a Right they have so long enjoyed, and which they have never forfeited.

The Expenses incurred during the last War, in Compliance with the Demands on this Colony by our late and present most gracious Sovereigns, have involved us in a Debt of near Half a Million; a Debt not likely to decrease under the continued Expense we are at in providing for the Security of the People against the Incursions of our savage Neighbours, at a Time when the low state of our Stable Commodity, the total Want of Specie, and the late Restrictions upon the Trade of the Colonies, render the circumstances of the People extremely distressful, and which, if Taxes are accumulated upon them by the *British* Parliament, will make them truly deplorable.

Your Memorialists cannot suggest to themselves any Reason why they should not still be trusted with the Property of their People, with whose Abilities, and the least burthensome Mode of taxing (with great Deference to the superior Wisdom of Parliament) they must be best acquainted.

Your Memorialists hope they shall not be suspected of being actuated on this Occasion by any Principles but those of the purest Loyalty and Affection as they always endeavoured by their Conduct to demonstrate that they consider their connexions with *Great Britain,* the Seat of Liberty, as their greatest Happiness.

The Duty they owe to themselves and their Posterity lays your Memorialists under the Necessity of endeavouring to establish their Constitution upon its proper Foundation; and they do most humbly pray your Lordships to take this Subject into your Consideration with the Attention that is due to the Well being of the Colonies, on which the Prosperity of *Great Britain* does in a great Measure depend.

## 3.3

 REMONSTRANCE TO THE HOUSE OF COMMONS

J. P. Kennedy, ed., *Journals of the House of Burgesses of Virginia, 1761–1765*
(Richmond, 1907), 303–4.

To the Honourable the Knights, Citizens, and Burgesses of *Great Britain,* in Parliament assembled:

The Remonstrance of the Council and Burgesses of *Virginia.*

It appearing by the printed Votes of the House of Commons of *Great Britain* in Parliament assembled that in a Committee of the whole House, the 17th Day of *March* last, it was resolved that towards defending, protecting, and securing the *British* Colonies and Plantations in *America,* it may be proper to charge certain Stamp Duties in the said Colonies and Plantations; and it being apprehended that the same Subject, which was then declined, may be resumed and further pursued in a succeeding Session, the Council and Burgesses of *Virginia,* met in General Assembly, judge it their indispensable Duty, in a respectful Manner, but with decent Firmness, to remonstrate against such a Measure, that at least a cession of those Rights, which in their Opinion must be infringed by that Procedure, may not be inferred from their Silence, at so important a Crisis.

They conceive it is essential to *British* Liberty that Laws imposing Taxes on the People ought not to be made without the consent of Representatives chosen by themselves; who, at the same time that they are acquainted with the Circumstances of their Constituents, sustain a Proportion of the Burthen laid on them. This Privilege, inherent in the Persons who discovered and settled these Regions, could not be renounced or forfeited by their Removal hither, not as Vagabonds or Fugitives, but licensed and encouraged by their Prince and animated with a laudable Desire of enlarging the *British* Dominion, and extending its Commerce: On the contrary, it was secured to them and their Descendants, with all other Rights and Immunities of *British* Subjects, by a Royal Charter, which hath been invariably recognised and confirmed by his Majesty and his Predecessors in their Commissions to the several Governours, granting a Power, and prescribing a Form of Legislation; according to which, Laws for the Administration of Justice, and for the Welfare and good Government of the Colony, have been hitherto enacted by the Governour, Council, and General Assembly, and to them Requisitions and Applications for Supplies have been directed by the Crown. As an Instance of the Opinion which former Sovereigns entertained of these Rights and Privileges, we beg Leave to refer to three Acts of the General Assembly passed in the 32d Year of the Reign of King Charles II (one of which is entitled *An Act for raising a Publick Revenue for the better Support of the Government of his Majesty's Colony of* Virginia, imposing several Duties for that Purpose) which they thought absolutely necessary, were prepared in *England,* and sent over by their then Governour, the Lord *Culpeper,* to be passed by the General Assembly, with a full Power to give the Royal Assent thereto; and which were accordingly passed, after several Amendments were made to them here: Thus tender was his Majesty of the Rights of his *American* Subjects; and the Remonstrants do not discern by what Distinction they can be deprived of that sacred Birthright and most valuable Inheritance by their Fellow Subjects, nor with what Propriety they can be taxed or affected in their Estates by the Parliament, wherein they are not, and indeed cannot, constitutionally be represented.

And if it were proper for the Parliament to impose Taxes on the Colonies at all, which the Remonstrants take Leave to think would be inconsistent with the fundamental Principles of the Constitution, the Exercise of that Power at this Time would be ruinous to *Virginia,* who exerted herself in the late War it is feared beyond her Strength, insomuch that to redeem the Money granted for that Exigence her People are taxed for several Years to come: This, with the large Expenses incurred for defending the Frontiers against the restless *Indians,* who have infested her as much since the Peace as before, is so grievous that an Increase of the Burthen will be intolerable; especially as the People are very greatly distressed already from the Scarcity of circulating Cash amongst them, and from the little Value of their Staple at the *British* Markets.

And it is presumed that adding to that Load which the Colony now labours under will not be more oppressive to her People than destructive of the Interests of *Great Britain:* For the Plantation Trade, confined as it is to the Mother Country, hath been a principal Means of multiplying and enriching her Inhabitants; and, if not too much discouraged, may prove an inexhaustible Source of Treasure to the Nation. For Satisfaction in this Point, let the present State of the *British* Fleets and Trade be compared with what they were before the Settlement of the Colonies; and let it be considered that whilst Property in Land may be acquired on very easy Terms, in the vast uncultivated Territory of *North America,* the Colonists will be mostly, if not wholly, employed in Agriculture; whereby the Exportation of their Commodities of *Great Britain,* and the Consumption of their

Manufactures supplied from thence, will be daily increasing. But this most desirable connexion between *Great Britain* and her Colonies, supported by such a happy Intercourse of reciprocal Benefits as is continually advancing the Prosperity of both, must be interrupted, if the People of the latter, reduced to extreme Poverty, should be compelled to manufacture those Articles they have been hitherto furnished with from the former.

From these Considerations, it is hoped that the Honourable House of Commons will not prosecute a Measure which those who may suffer under it cannot but look upon as fitter for Exiles driven from their native Country after ignominiously forfeiting her Favours and Protection, than for the Prosperity of *Britons* who have at all Times been forward to demonstrate all due Reverence to the Mother Kingdom, and are so instrumental in promoting her Glory and Felicity; and that *British* Patriots will never consent to the Exercise of anticonstitutional Power, which even in this remote Corner may be dangerous in its Example to the interiour Parts of the *British* Empire, and will certainly be detrimental to its Commerce.

## 4. COLONIAL RESOLVES OPPOSING THE STAMP ACT, JUNE–DECEMBER 1765

The most celebrated and yet curiously the tamest of the colonial resolves opposing the Stamp Act were those of Virginia that Patrick Henry proposed. A former storekeeper and ambitious young lawyer from Hanover County, Henry was first elected to the House of Burgesses in 1764, when he was already famous for a speech he had made in 1763 during Virginia's Parson's Cause, which some thought treasonous even then. He became still more famous for his "Give Me Liberty or Give Me Death" speech in March 1775; he served as Virginia's governor in 1776 and again in 1784. Henry introduced what became Virginia's resolves at the very end of the legislative session in 1765, when most members had left for home and only 39 out of 116 delegates were present. Yet even the rump House, under its powerful Speaker John Robinson, refused to go as far as Henry had hoped, and three of his boldest resolutions failed to be introduced or to pass.

His proposed resolutions included one, the fifth, that likely was first accepted and then, the next day, rejected. It declared that the Virginia General Assembly, "along with His Majesty or his Substitutes," possessed "the *only and sole exclusive* Right and Power to lay Taxes and Impositions upon the Inhabitants" of Virginia. Two still more radical resolutions, the sixth and the seventh, were never introduced. The sixth resolution is believed to have held that "the Inhabitants of this Colony, are not bound to yield Obedience to any" illegal parliamentary law imposing taxes on them, and the seventh, in one version, stated that anyone upholding the power of any agency other than the General Assembly or the king to tax the colony would "be deemed an Enemy to this his Majesty's Colony." Almost all the other colonies included one or more of his resolutions that hadn't been introduced or that Virginia had refused to endorse. Accordingly, most of the other sets of resolves went further than Virginia's in opposing the proposed changes to the colonial judicial system and the "fatal" economic consequences sure to follow passage of the Stamp Act. For example, the final resolve of Rhode Island promised colonial officials that the assembly would "indemnify and save harmless all the said Officers" who followed the colony's resolutions and disobeyed those of Parliament.

The four resolutions that the burgesses agreed upon echoed themes articulated by the same body in its petitions of six months earlier. The burgesses reiterated, first, that the settlers' ancestors had brought with them all the same and equal liberties, privileges, franchises, and immunities—rights are not mentioned in the 1764 petition— "possessed, by the people of *Great Britain.*" Next, Virginia claimed that under two royal charters, they were "entitled to all Liberties, Privileges, and Immunities of Denizens . . . as if abiding and born within the Realm of *England.*" Third, Virginia then moderately explained that self-taxation is "the distinguishing Characteristic of British Freedom, without which the ancient Constitution cannot exist." Finally, the colony held that "his Majesty's liege people" have ever enjoyed without forfeit "the inestimable Right of being governed by such Laws, respecting their internal Polity [or in later versions, "police"] and Taxation, as are derived from their own Consent, with the Approbation of their Sovereign, or his Substitute." In sum, the resolutions, in keeping with the earlier petitions of 1764, provided a moderate template for the colonial resolves opposing the Stamp Act that were passed by eight of the other twelve continental British colonies.[30]

Because the conservative editor of the *Virginia Gazette* refused to print the resolves, other colonial assemblies were forced to look elsewhere for them, most often in newspapers published by more radical opponents of Parliament. The published accounts regularly included one or more of Henry's resolutions that either had not been introduced or had been rejected by the Virginia General Assembly and, in many instances, others as well. This confusion led to other colonies believing that "the Virginia Burgesses appeared much bolder than they had actually been, and their supposed example stirred up other assemblies to a degree of emulation which sometimes surpassed the original."[31] Not surprisingly, the first colony to imitate and then go beyond Virginia was Rhode Island, where the resolves were first published in the *Newport Mercury* on August 19, 1765. The *Mercury* printed not only three of the four approved by Virginia (deleting the third), but also the more radical fifth, sixth, and seventh, which had failed to be introduced or passed by Virginia. The same pattern, in which the other colonies' resolves went beyond those of Virginia in a misguided attempt at emulation, quickly became the norm.[32]

John Dickinson, a moderate lawyer, wrote Pennsylvania's resolves.[33] A Quaker born into a family of wealth, he later, as a representative of Pennsylvania, attended the First and Second Continental Congresses (and later still, the Constitutional Convention in Philadelphia), where he fought against parliamentary taxation of the colonies and changes in the judiciary system while strenuously opposing colonial independence and a separation from king and empire.[34] In spite of his moderation, his celebrated *Letters from a Farmer in Pennsylvania to the Inhabitants of the British Colony* (1768) was the third most widely published colonial pamphlet in the years leading up to independence; it guided many in their opposition to parliamentary claims of supremacy.[35] Like earlier petitions and resolves, Virginia's being an exception, Pennsylvania's objected to the extension of vice-admiralty courts and new commercial regulations. A more surprising difference is that Dickinson included a resolution (the third) modeled on Virginia's first, but going beyond it in its universalism by holding that "the Constitution of Government in this Province is founded on the natural Rights of Mankind, and the Noble Principles of *English* Liberty." What is hard for a contemporary reader to discern is whether his argument reflects a seventeenth-century understanding of English law and constitutionalism resting on natural law, or a more radical understanding that was then far more common, even if still impotent, in Britain and that appealed to a new, abstract understanding of natural rights and law, seeing them "no longer as a part of the British constitution, but as the rights of man in general."[36] In the colonies, it was almost surely the former. Either way, such arguments were sure to inflame the Whig minds of most members of Parliament, who would have found the first interpretation, a seventeenth-century understanding, of limited appeal after the Glorious Revolution, and the second, a more radical possibility, one with which they were more familiar than the colonists, troubling for its shared ideology with British radicalism and offensive for its implications pointing toward independence from Britain and the absence of a common sovereign (a position that it is hard to imagine Dickinson could have intended). (Note: In the Pennsylvania resolutions and others, the abbreviation "NCD" stands for the Latin phrase "nemine contradicente," "with no one speaking against.")

Massachusetts, a colony very different from Pennsylvania and unusually radical in its words and deeds, also made much in its resolves of October 19, 1765, of a language that even more closely paralleled the separatist Declaration of Independence in holding that "the Inhabitants of this Province are *unalienably* entitled to those [certain] essential Rights in common with all Men: And that no Law of Society can consistent with the Law of God and Nature divest them of those Rights."[37] Still, Massachusetts went on to appeal to support from diverse British sources, including the Magna Carta, "an Act of Parliament," the royal charter, "Principles of their *British Ancestors*," and British antecedent constitutional claims "consistent with a Subordination [of Massachusetts] to the supreme Power of *Great Britain*." Nonetheless, its universalist language pushing for an identity between natural and civil rights is striking and precocious.[38] Although also discoverable in some of the provincial petitions, like that of the Connecticut Sons of Liberty, such language was notably absent from the remaining provincial resolves of 1765 and still more so from the state papers of the First Continental Congress, with only intermittent use in the Second.

Maryland, in its resolves, unanimously passed by the colony's assembly on September 28, 1765, makes no mention of universal natural law or rights, instead relying solely on British constitutional ones.[39] Indeed, it goes to great length to rest its opposition to the Stamp Act taxes on its 1632 royal charter. The resolves of South Carolina (passed on November 29) and New Jersey (passed on November 30) similarly limit their use of rights language to "the undoubted Right of Englishmen" and the "Right of the British Subjects in this Province, to petition the King or either House of Parliament." Instead, both colonies concentrated on the economic burdens they expected to follow from the imposition of Stamp Act duties. In the New Jersey resolves, two additional concerns are of interest. First, the colony complains that parliamentary taxation would render it subject "to the Taxation of two Legislatures, a grievance unprecedented" (of course, essential to federalism and today perfectly acceptable); and second, it uniquely points to the dangers to the liberty of the press from the duties (possibly from the cost of stamped paper).

The resolves of Connecticut passed on October 25.[40] While making much of its charter rights—surprisingly, given the claims of its New London Sons of Liberty and the general political radicalism of New England in its Protestant republicanism—Connecticut rested its opposition to the Stamp Act duties on British constitutional grounds and most emphatically on the colonists' equal rights as Englishmen. Connecticut too noted its citizens' loyalty to the king as "Part of his Majesty's Dominions" or his "British American Dominions," with the clear implication that the dominions were neither part of the British realm nor subordinate to Parliament.

Perhaps more surprisingly still, given its petition of 1764 (document 1.2), New York's resolves (passed on December 18) argue that the colonists "owe Obedience to all Acts of Parliament not inconsistent with the essential Rights and Liberties of *Englishmen*"—not men in the abstract—and due "submission to the Supreme Legislative Power." Like every other colony, New York emphasized that the colonists "are intitled to the same Rights and Liberties which his Majesty's *English* Subjects both within and without the Realm have ever enjoyed," and the inconsistency of assuming that "the honourable House of commons of *Great-Britain,* can without divesting the Inhabitants of this Colony of their own most essential Rights, grant to the Crown their, or any Part of their Estates for any Purpose whatsoever." No mention was made this time of natural rights, only English ones. For whatever reason, something had changed in the New York Assembly's approach to the emerging crisis.

Following Virginia's resolves of 1764, every colony except Pennsylvania explicitly rejected the possibility of any manner of colonial representation in Parliament. Each colony demonstrated an affectionate reverence for the king, along with an opposition to Parliament's claimed right to pass legislation regarding internal colonial affairs. With the exception of Virginia, every colony opposed Parliament's effort to deprive them of common-law jury trials and to put in their place admiralty or vice-admiralty courts, and most complained of new commercial regulations "affecting the Trade of the Colonies." Accordingly, one might reasonably find that "together with the declaration and petitions of the Stamp Act Congress [of October 19, 1765]," these colonial resolves "offer the most carefully formulated and most widely approved statements of the American position in 1765." The colonies' grievances continued to multiply during the next eleven years.[41]

4.1

 # VIRGINIA RESOLVES IN GOVERNOR FAUQUIER'S ACCOUNT, JUNE 5, 1765

J. P. Kennedy, ed., *Journals of the House of Burgesses of Virginia, 1761–1765*
(Richmond, 1907), lxvii–lxviii.

Williamsburg, June 5th, 1765

My Lords,

On *Saturday* the 1st instant I dissolved the Assembly after passing all the Bills, except one, which were ready for my assent. The four Resolutions which I have now the honor to inclose to your Lordships, will shew Your Lordships the reason of my conduct, and I hope justify it. I will relate the whole proceeding to your Lordships in as concise a manner as I am able.

On *Wednesday* the 29th of May, just at the end of the Session when most of the members had left the town, there being but 39 present out of 116 of which the House of Burgesses now consists, a motion was made to take into consideration the Stamp Act, a copy of which had crept into the House, and in a Committee of the whole House five resolutions were proposed and agreed to, all by very small majorities. On *Thursday* the 30th they were reported & agreed to by the House, the numbers being as before in the Committee; the greatest majority being 22 to 17; for the 5th Resolution, 20 to 19 only. On *Friday* the 31st there having happened a small alteration in the House there was an attempt to strike all the Resolutions off the Journals. The 5th which was thought the most offensive was accordingly struck off, but it did not succeed as to the other four. I am informed the gentlemen had two more resolutions in their pocket, but finding the difficulty they had in carrying the 5th which was by a single voice, and knowing them to be more virulent and inflammatory; they did not produce them. The most strenuous opposers of this rash heat were the late Speaker, the King's Attorney and Mr. *Wythe;* but they were overpowered by the young hot and giddy members. In the course of the debates I have heard that very indecent language was used by a Mr. *Henry* a young lawyer who had not been a month a Member of the House; who carryed all the young Members with him; so that I hope I am authorised in saying there is cause at least to doubt whether this would have been the sense of the Colony if more of their Representatives had done their duty by attending the end of the Session. . . .

. . . And as there is, with me, a great doubt whether the elections in the New Assembly to be called will fall on cool reasonable men, and consequently a doubt whether Mr *Robinson* will be re-chosen Speaker. I should be glad to know your Lordships sentiments whether I should agree to the appointment of any gentleman to be Treasurer who shall be chosen Speaker, whether I should refuse all indiscriminately or shew this favor to Mr *Robinson* particularly, who has deserved so well.

I am with the greatest regard

My Lords

Your Lordships most obed.t

And devoted Serv.t

FRAN. FAUQUIER

### 4.2

 Virginia Resolves as Printed in the *Journal*  of the *House of Burgesses*, June 1765

J. P. Kennedy, ed., *Journals of the House of Burgesses of Virginia, 1761–1765* (Richmond, 1907), 359–60.

Mr *Attorney,* from the Committee of the whole House, reported, according to Order, that the Committee had considered of the Steps necessary to be taken in Consequence of the Resolutions of the House of Commons of *Great Britain* relative to the charging Stamp Duties in the Colonies and Plantations in *America,* and that they had come to several Resolutions thereon; which he read in his Place, and then delivered in at the Table, where they were again twice read, and agreed to by the House, with some Amendments, and are as follow:

*Resolved,* That the first Adventurers and Settlers of this his Majesty's Colony and Dominion of *Virginia* brought with them, and transmitted to their Posterity, and all other his Majesty's Subjects since inhabiting in this his Majesty's said Colony, all the

Liberties, Privileges, Franchises, and Immunities, that have at any Time been held, enjoyed, and possessed, by the people of *Great Britain.*

*Resolved,* That by two royal Charters, granted by King *James* the First, the Colonists aforesaid are declared entitled to all Liberties, Privileges, and Immunities of Denizens and natural Subjects, to all Intents and Purposes, as if they had been abiding and born within the Realm of *England.*

*Resolved,* That the Taxation of the People by themselves, or by Persons chosen by themselves to represent them, who can only know what Taxes the People are able to bear, or the easiest Method of raising them, and must themselves be affected by every Tax laid on the People, is the only Security against a burthensome Taxation, and the distinguishing Characteristick of *British* Freedom, without which the ancient Constitution cannot exist.

*Resolved,* That his Majesty's liege People of this his most ancient and loyal Colony have without Interruption enjoyed the inestimable Right of being governed by such Laws, respecting their internal Polity and Taxation, as are derived from their own Consent, with the Approbation of their Sovereign, or his Substitute; and that the same hath never been forfeited or yielded up, but hath been constantly recognized by the Kings and People of *Great Britain.*

## 4.3

 Virginia Resolves as Recalled by Patrick Henry, June 1765

Edmund S. Morgan, ed., *Prologue to Revolution: Sources and Documents on the Stamp Act Crisis, 1764–1766* (Chapel Hill: University of North Carolina Press, 1959), 48.

Resolved

That the first Adventurers and Settlers of this his Majesties Colony and Dominion brought with them and transmitted to their Posterity and all other his Majesties Subjects since inhabiting in this his Majestie's said Colony all the Priviledges, Franchises and Immunities that have at any Time been held, enjoyed, and possessed by the People of Great Britain.

Resolved

That by two royal Charters granted by King James the first the Colonists aforesaid are declared intituled to all the Priviledges, Liberties and Immunities of Denizens and natural born Subjects to all Intents and Purposes as if they had been abiding and born within the Realm of England.

Resolved

That the Taxation of the People by themselves or by Persons chosen by themselves to represent them who can only know what Taxes the People are able to bear and the easiest Mode of raising them and are equally affected by such Taxes Themselves is the distinguishing Characteristick of British Freedom and without which the ancient Constitution cannot subsist.

Resolved

That his Majestie's liege People of his most ancient Colony have uninterruptedly enjoyed the Right of being thus governed by their own assembly in the Article of their Taxes and internal Police and that the same hath never been forfeited or any other Way given up but hath been constantly recognized by the Kings and People of Great Britain.

Resolved

Therefore that the General Assembly of this Colony have the *only and sole exclusive* Right and Power to lay Taxes and Impositions upon the Inhabitants of this Colony and that every attempt to vest such Power in any Person or Persons whatsoever other than the General Assembly aforesaid has a manifest Tendency to destroy British as well as American Freedom.

## 4.4

 VIRGINIA RESOLVES AS PRINTED BY THE
*NEWPORT MERCURY*, JUNE 24, 1765

Edmund S. Morgan, ed., *Prologue to Revolution: Sources and Documents on the Stamp Act Crisis, 1764–1766* (Chapel Hill: University of North Carolina Press, 1959), 49.

WHEREAS the Hon. House of Commons, in England, have of late drawn into Question, how far the General Assembly of this Colony hath Power to enact Laws for laying of Taxes and imposing Duties, payable by the People of this his Majesty's most antient Colony: For settling and ascertaining the same to all future Times, the House of Burgesses of this present General Assembly have come to the following Resolves:—

*Resolved*, That the first Adventurers, Settlers of this his Majesty's Colony and Dominion of Virginia, brought with them and transmitted to their Posterity, and all other his Majesty's Subjects since inhabiting in this his Majesty's Colony, all the Privileges and Immunities that have at any Time been held, enjoyed and possessed by the People of Great-Britain.

*Resolved,* That by two Royal Charters, granted by King *James* the First, the Colony aforesaid are declared and entitled to all Privileges and Immunities of natural born Subjects, to all Intents and Purposes, as if they had been abiding and born within the Realm of England.

*Resolved,* That his Majesty's liege People of this his antient Colony have enjoy'd the Right of being thus govern'd, by their own Assembly, in the Article of Taxes and internal Police; and that the same have never been forfeited, or any other Way yielded up, but have been constantly recogniz'd by the King and People of Britain.

*Resolved,* therefore, That the General Assembly of this Colony, together with his Majesty or his Substitutes, have, in their representative Capacity, the only exclusive Right and Power to lay Taxes and Imposts upon the Inhabitants of this Colony: And that every Attempt to vest such Power in any other Person or Persons whatever, than the General Assembly aforesaid, is illegal, unconstitutional and unjust, and have a manifest Tendency to destroy British as well as American Liberty.

*Resolved,* That his Majesty's liege People, the Inhabitants of this Colony, are not bound to yield Obedience to any Law or Ordinance whatever, designed to impose any Taxation whatsoever upon them, other than the Laws or Ordinances of the General Assembly aforesaid.

*Resolved,* That any Person who shall, by speaking or writing, assert or maintain, that any Person or Persons, other than the General Assembly of this Colony, have any Right or Power to impose or lay any Taxation on the People here, shall be deemed an Enemy to this his Majesty's Colony.

## 4.5

 PENNSYLVANIA RESOLVES, SEPTEMBER 21, 1765

"Resolves of the Pennsylvania Assembly on the Stamp Act, September 21, 1765," http://avalon.law.yale.edu/18th_century/penn_assembly_1765.asp.

The House taking into Consideration, that an Act of Parliament has lately passed in England, for imposing certain Stamp Duties, and other Duties, on his Majesty's Subjects in America, whereby they conceive some of their most essential and valuable Rights, as British Subjects, to be deeply affected, think it a Duty they owe to themselves, and their Posterity, to come to the following Resolutions, viz.

Resolved, N. C. D. 1. That the Assemblies of this Province have, from Time to Time, whenever Requisitions have been made by his Majesty, for carrying on military

Operations, for the Defence of America, most chearfully and liberally contributed their full Proportion of Men and Money for those Services.

Resolved, N. C. D. 2. That whenever his Majesty's Service shall, for the future, require the Aids of the Inhabitants of this Province, and they shall be called upon for that Purpose in a constitutional Way, it will be their indispensable Duty most chearfully and liberally to grant to his Majesty their Proportion of Men and Money for the Defence, Security, and other public services of the British American Colonies.

Resolved, N. C. D. 3. That the inhabitants of this Province are entitled to all the Liberties, Rights and Privileges of his Majesty's Subjects in Great-Britain, or elsewhere, and that the Constitution of Government in this Province is founded on the natural Rights of Mankind, and the noble Principles of English Liberty, and therefore is, or ought to be, perfectly free.

Resolved, N. C. D. 4. That it is the inherent Birth-right, and indubitable Privilege, of every British Subject, to be taxed only by his own Consent, or that of his legal Representatives, in Conjunction with his Majesty, or his Substitutes.

Resolved, N. C. D. 5. That the only legal Representatives of the Inhabitants of this Province are the Persons they annually elect to serve as Members of Assembly.

Resolved, therefore, N. C. D. 6. That the Taxation of the People of this Province by any other Persons whatsoever than such their Representatives in Assembly, is unconstitutional, and subversive of their most valuable Rights.

Resolved, N. C. D. 7. That the laying Taxes upon the Inhabitants of this Province in any other Manner, being manifestly subversive of public Liberty, must, of necessary Consequence, be utterly destructive of public Happiness.

Resolved, N. C. D. 8. That the vesting and Authority in the Courts of Admiralty to decide in Suits relating to the Stamp Duty, and other Matters, foreign to their proper Jurisdiction, is highly dangerous to the Liberties of his Majesty's American Subjects, contrary to Magna Charta, the great Charter and Fountain of English Liberty, and destructive of one of their most darling and acknowledged Rights, that of Trials by Juries.

Resolved, N. C. D. 9. That it is the Opinion of this House, that the Restraints imposed by several late Acts of Parliament on the Trade of this Province, at a Time when the People labour under an enormous Load of Debt, must of Necessity be attended with the most fatal Consequences, not only to this Province, but to the Trade of our Mother Country.

Resolved, N. C. D. 10. That this House think it their Duty thus firmly to assert, with Modesty and Decency, their inherent Rights, that their Posterity may learn and know, that it was not with their Consent and Acquiescence, that any Taxes should be levied on them by any Persons but their own Representatives; and are desirous that these their Resolves should remain on their Minutes, as a Testimony of the Zeal and ardent Desire of the present House of Assembly to preserve their inestimable Rights, which, as Englishmen, they have possessed ever since this Province was settled, and to transmit them to their latest Posterity.

## 4.6

 MARYLAND RESOLVES, SEPTEMBER 28, 1765

J. Hall Pleasants, ed. *Archives of Maryland 59: Proceedings and Acts of the General Assembly of Maryland, 1764–1765* (Baltimore: Maryland Historical Society, 1942), 30–32. http://aomol.net/megafile/msa/speccol/sc2900/sc2908/000001/000059/html/am59—30.html.

1:st Resolved Unanimously that the first Adventurers and Setlers of this Province of Maryland brought with them and transmitted to their posterity and all other his Majestys Subjects since Inhabiting in the province all the Liberties privileges Franchises and Immunities that any time have been held enjoyed and possessed by the People of Great Britain

2.d Resolved Unanimously that it was Granted by the Magna Charta and other the Good Laws and Statutes of England and Confirmed by the Petition and Bill of Rights that the Subject should not be Compelled to Contribute to any Tax Tallage Aid or other like Charge not set by common Consent of Parliament

3:d Resolved Unanimously that by a Royal Charter Granted by his Majesty King Charles the first in the eighth year of his Reign And in the Year of our Lord One thousand Six hundred and thirty two to Caecilius then Lord Baltimore it was for the Encouragement for People to Transport themselves and families in this Province amongst other things Covenanted and Granted by his said Majesty for himself his heirs and Successors as followeth And we will also and for our more Special Grace for us our heirs and Successors we do strictly enjoin Constitute Ordain and Command that the said Province shall be of our Allegiance and that all and Singular the Subjects and liege People of us our heirs and Successors transported or to be Transported into the said Province and the Children of them and of such as shall descend from them there already born or hereafter to be born be and shall be Denizens and lieges of us our heirs and Successors of our Kingdoms of England and Ireland and be in all things held treated reputed and esteemed as the liege faith full People of our heirs and Successors born within our Kingdom of England and likewise any Lands Tenements Revenues Services and other Hereditaments whatsoever within our Kingdom of England and other our Dominions may inherit or otherwise purchase receive take have hold buy and possess and them may Occupy and enjoy give Sell Alien and bequeath as likewise all Liberties Franchises and privileges of this our Kingdom of England freely quietly and peacably have and possess Occupy and enjoy as our liege people born or to be born within our said Kingdom of England without the Let Molestation Vexation trouble or Grievance of us our heirs and Successors Any Statute Act Ordinance or provision to the Contrary thereof Notwithstanding

And further our pleasure is and by these presents for us our heirs and Successors We do Covenant and Grant to and with the said now Lord Baltimore his heirs and Assigns that we our heirs and Successors shall at no time hereafter Set or make or cause to be Set any Imposition Custom or other Taxation Rate or Contribution whatsoever in or upon the Dwellers and Inhabitants of the aforesaid Province for their Lands Tenements Goods or Chattels within the said Province or in or upon any Goods or Merchandizes within the said Province to be laden or unladen within any the Ports or Harbours of the said Province And our Pleasure is and for us our heirs and Successors We Charge and Command that this our Declaration shall be hence forward from time to time received and allowed in all our Courts and before all the Judges of us our heirs and Successors for a Sufficient and lawfull Discharge Payment and Acquittance commanding all and Singular our Officers and Ministers of us our heirs and Successors and enjoyning them upon pain of our high Displeasure that they do not presume at any time to Attempt any thing to the Contrary of the Premisses or that they do in any Sort withstand the same but that they be at all times Aiding and Assisting as is fitting unto the said now Lord Baltimore and his heirs and to the Inhabitants and Merchants of Maryland aforesaid their Servants Ministers factors and Assigns in the full use and Fruition of the Benefit of this our Charter

4:th Resolved that it is the Unanimous Opinion of this House that the said Charter is Declaratory of the Constitutional Rights and Privileges of the Freemen of this Province

5:th Resolved Unanimously That Tryals by Juries is the Grand Bulwark of Liberty the undoubted Birthright of every Englishman and Consequently of every British Subject in America and that the Erecting other Jurisdictions for the Tryal of Matters of fact is unconstitutional and renders the Subject insecure in his Liberty and Property

6:th Resolved That it is the Unanimous Opinion of this House that it cannot with any truth or Propriety be said that the Freemen of this Province of Maryland are Represented in the British Parliament

7:th Resolved Unanimously that his Majestys liege People of this Ancient Province have always enjoyed the Right of being Governed by Laws to which they themselves have consented in the Articles of Taxes and internal Polity and that the same hath never been forfeited or any other way Yielded up but hath been Constantly recognized by the King and People of Great Britain

8:th Resolved that it is the Unanimous Opinion of this House that the Representatives of the Freemen of this Province in their Legislative Capacity together with the other part of the Legislature have the Sole Right to lay Taxes and Impositions on the Inhabitants of this Province or their Property and effects And that laying imposing levying or Collecting any Tax on or from the Inhabitants of Maryland under Colour of any other Authority is Unconstitutional and a Direct Violation of the Rights of the Freemen of this Province.

## 4.7

 CONNECTICUT RESOLVES, OCTOBER 25, 1765

Charles J. Hoadly, ed., *The Public Records of the Colony of Connecticut from May, 1762, to October, 1767, Inclusive* (Hartford: Case, Lockwood, and Brainard, 1881), 421–25.

The House of Representatives of his Majesty's Colony of Connecticut in New England, in general Court assembled, taking into their serious consideration, that an act of the Parliament of Great Britain has been lately past, for granting and applying certain stamp-duties &c. in the British Colonies and Plantations in America, find ourselves distressed with the most alarming apprehensions, when we observe, that grand legislature to entertain sentiments so different from ours respecting what we ever, reckoned among our most important and essential rights as Englishmen. The constitution of the British government we esteem the happiest in the world, founded on maxims of consummate wisdom, and in the best manner calculated to secure the prerogatives of the crown, while it maintains the just rights and liberties of the subject. By virtue of which constitution, and the royal grant and charter of his Majesty King Charles the second, the inhabitants of this Colony have enjoyed great and inestimable liberties and priviledges, of a civil and religious nature, for more than a century past, and more especially under the auspicious government of the illustrious House of Hanover. That royal house have ever held sacred and inviolable, those rights and priviledges of their loyal subjects in this Colony, derived to them as aforesaid. In return for which, the princes of that exalted line have ever had from this people their ardent desires of all happiness to their persons, and glory to their empire. Inspired with the warmest sentiments of affectionate loyalty and duty, the colonists have been ever ready to sacrifice their lives and fortunes, to the service of their King and country; and believing that his Majesty's interest in this Colony cannot be more firmly established and perfectly secured, nor the happiness of the British nation more effectually promoted by us, than in our full possession and priviledges of the British constitution, which we have not forfeited, but ought to hold as Englishmen, and which are, if possible, rendered more sacred and indefeasible by the royal grant and charter aforesaid, which we conceive to stand upon the same basis with the grand charters and fountains of English liberty. And as the aforesaid act tends, (as we conceive,) to deprive us of the most interesting, important, and essential of those rights, which we hold most dear and cannot on any possible considerations be induced willingly to part with, we are, therefore, filled with the most sensible grief and concern, and think it a duty we owe to his Majesty, to the Nation, to Ourselves and to Posterity, to express and declare the sense we have respecting the rights and priviledges which we may justly claim, and humbly hope to enjoy, under his Majesty's gracious protection and government; and do therefore declare and make it known, in the following Declarations and Resolves.

1. In the first Place, we do most expressly declare, recognize and acknowledge his Majesty King George the third to be lawful and rightful King of Great Britain and all other the dominions and countries thereto belonging, and that it is the indispensable duty of the people of this Colony, as being part of his Majesty's dominions, always to bear faithful and true allegiance to his Majesty, and him to defend to the utmost of their power against all attempts against his person, crown and dignity.

2. That, this Colony, or the greatest part thereof, was purchased and obtained for great and valuable considerations, and some other part thereof gained by conquest, with much difficulty, and at the only endeavours, expences and charges of our forefathers; and that thereby considerable addition was made to his Majesty's dominions and interest; and that in consideration of such purchase &c. as aforesaid, his Majesty King Charles the second in the fourteenth year of his reign did for himself, his heirs and successors, ordain, declare and grant, unto the Governor and Company of this Colony and their successors, that all and every of the subjects of him, his heirs and successors, which should go to inhabit within the said Colony, and every of their children, which should be born there or on the sea in going thither or returning from thence, should have and enjoy all liberties and immunities of free and natural subjects within any of the dominions of the said King, his heirs or successors, to all intents, constructions and purposes whatsoever, as if they and every of them were born within the realm of England.

3. That the free natural subjects of Great Britain born within the realm of England have a property in their own estate, and are to be taxed only by their own consent, given in person or by their representatives, and are not to be disseized of their liberties or free customs, sentenced or condemned, but by lawful judgment of their peers; and that the said rights and immunities were granted to and conferred on the inhabitants of this Colony by the royal grant and charter aforesaid, and therefore are their rights to all intents, constructions and purposes whatsoever.

4. That the consent of the inhabitants of this Colony was not given to the said act of Parliament, personally or by representation, actual or virtual, in any sense or degree that at all comports with the true intendment, spirit, or equitable construction of the British constitution.

5. That his Majesty's liege subjects of this colony have enjoyed the right and privi-ledge of being governed by their General Assembly in the article of taxing and internal police, agreeable to the powers and priviledges granted and contained in the royal char-ter aforesaid, for more than a century past; and that the same have never been forfeited or any way yielded up, but have been constantly recognized by the King and Parliament of Great Britain.

6. That, in the opinion of this House, an act for raising money by duties or taxes differs from other acts of legislation, in that it is always considered as a free gift of the people made by their legal and elected representatives; and that we cannot conceive that the people of Great Britain, or their representatives, have right to dispose of our property.

7. That the only legal representatives of the inhabitants of this Colony are the persons they elect to serve as members of the General Assembly thereof.

8. That the vesting an authority in the courts of admiralty, as in said act is pro-vided, to judge and determine in suits relating to the duties and forfeitures contained in said act, and other matters foreign to their accustomed and established jurisdic-tion, is in the opinion of this House highly dangerous to the liberties of his Majesty's American subjects, contrary to the great charter of English liberty, and destructive of one of their most darling rights, that of tryal by juries, which is justly esteemed one chief excellence of the British constitution and principle bulwark of English liberty.

9. That it is the opinion of this House, that the said act for granting and applying certain stamp-duties &c., as aforesaid, is unprecedented and unconstitutional.

10. That whenever his Majesty's service shall require the aid of the inhabitants of this Colony, the same fixed principles of loyalty, as well as self preservation, which have hitherto induced us fully to comply with his Majesty's requisitions, will, together with the deep sense we have of its being our indispensable duty, (in the opinion of this House,) ever hold us under the strongest obligations which can be given or desired, most cheerfully to grant his Majesty from time to time our further proportion of men and money for the defence, security, and other services of the British-American Dominions.

11. That we look upon the well being and greatest security of this Colony to depend (under God) on our connections with Great Britain, which we ardently wish may con-tinue to the latest posterity; and that it is the humble opinion of this House, that the constitution of this Colony being understood and practiced upon as it has been ever since it existed is the surest band of union, confidence and mutual prosperity of our mother country and us, and the best foundation on which to build the good of the whole, whether considered in a civil, military or mercantile light; and of the truth of this opinion we are the more confident, as it is not founded on speculation only, but has been verified in fact, and by long experience found to produce, according to our extent

and other circumstances, as many loyal, virtuous, industrious and well-governed subjects, as any part of his Majesty's dominions, and as truly zealous, and as warmly engaged to promote the best good and real glory of the grand whole, which constitutes the British Empire.

## 4.8

 MASSACHUSETTS RESOLVES, OCTOBER 29, 1765

*Journal of the Honourable House of Representatives, at a Great and General Court or Assembly for His Majesty's Province of the Massachusetts-Bay in New-England: Begun and held at Boston, in the County of Suffolk, on Wednesday the Twenty-ninth Day of May, Annoque Domini, 1765* (Boston, 1765), 151–53.

Whereas the just Rights of His Majesty's Subjects of this Province, derived to them from the *British Constitution,* as well as the *Royal Charter,* have been lately drawn into Question: In order to ascertain the same, this House do UNANIMOUSLY come into the following Resolves.

1. *Resolved,* That there are certain essential Rights of the *British* Constitution of Government, which are founded in the Law of God and Nature, and are the common Rights of Mankind—Therefore

2. *Resolved,* That the Inhabitants of this Province are *unalienably* entitled to those essential Rights in common with all Men: And that no Law of Society can consistent with the Law of God and Nature divest them of those Rights.

3. *Resolved,* That no Man can justly take the Property of another without his Consent: And that upon this *original* Principle the Right of Representation in the same Body, which exercises the Power of making Laws for levying Taxes, which is one of the main Pillars of the British Constitution, is evidently founded.

4. *Resolved,* That this *inherent* Right, together with all other, essential Rights, Liberties, Privileges and Immunities of the People of *Great Britain,* have been fully confirmed to them by *Magna Charta,* and by former and later Acts of Parliament.

5. *Resolved,* That His Majesty's subjects in *America,* are in Reason and Common Sense, entitled to the same Extent of Liberty with His Majesty's Subjects in *Britain.*

6. *Resolved,* That by the Declaration of the Royal Charter of this Province the Inhabitants are entitled, to all the Rights, Liberties, and Immunities of free and natural Subjects of *Great-Britain,* to all Intents, Purposes and Constructions whatever.

7. *Resolved,* That the Inhabitants of this Province appear to be entitled to all the Rights aforementioned, by an Act of Parliament, 13th of *Geo.* 2d.

8. *Resolved,* That those Rights do belong to the Inhabitants of this Province, upon Principles of *common Justice;* their Ancestors having settled this Country at their *sole Expence;* and *their* Posterity, having constantly approved themselves most loyal and faithful Subjects of *Great-Britain.*

9. *Resolved,* That every Individual in the Colonies is as advantageous to *Great-Britain,* as if he were in *Great-Britain,* and held to pay his full Proportion of Taxes there: And as the Inhabitants of this Province pay their full Proportion of Taxes, for the Support of his Majesty's Government *here,* it is unreasonable for them to be called upon, to pay any Part of the Charges of the Government *there.*

10. *Resolved,* That the Inhabitants of this Province are not, and have never been, represented in the Parliament of *Great-Britain;* And that such a Representation *there,* as the Subjects in *Britain* do actually and rightfully enjoy, is *impracticable* for the subjects *in America:*—And further, That in the Opinion of this House, the several subordinate Powers of Legislation in *America,* were constituted, upon the Apprehensions of this *Impracticability.*

11. *Resolved,* That the *only* Method, whereby the constitutional Rights of the Subjects of this Province can be secure, consistent with a Subordination to the supreme Power of *Great-Britain,* is by the continued Exercise of such Powers of Government as are granted in the royal Charter, and a firm Adherence to the Privileges of the same.

12. *Resolved,* As a just Conclusion from some of the foregoing Resolves, That all Acts made, by any Power whatever, other than the General Assembly of this Province, imposing Taxes on the Inhabitants are Infringements of our *inherent* and *unalienable* Rights, as *Men* and *British Subjects:* and render void the most valuable Declarations of our *Charter.*

13. *Resolved,* That the Extension of the Powers of the Court of Admiralty within this Province, is a most violent Infraction of the Right of Trials by Juries.—A Right, which this House upon the Principles of their *British Ancestors,* hold most dear and sacred; it being the only Security of the Lives, Liberties and Properties of his Majesty's Subjects here.

14. *Resolved,* That this House owe the strictest Allegiance to his Most Sacred Majesty King GEORGE the Third: That they have the greatest Veneration for the Parliament: And that they will, after the Example of *all* their Predecessors, from the Settlement of this Country, exert themselves to their utmost, in supporting his Majesty's Authority in the Province,—in promoting the true Happiness of his Subjects: and in enlarging the Extent of his Dominion.

*Ordered,* That all the foregoing Resolves be kept in the Records of this House; that a just Sense of Liberty, and the firm Sentiments of Loyalty may be transmitted to Posterity.

4.9

 SOUTH CAROLINA RESOLVES, NOVEMBER 29, 1765

Edmund S. Morgan, ed., *Prologue to Revolution: Sources and Documents on the Stamp Act Crisis, 1764–1766* (Chapel Hill: University of North Carolina Press, 1959), 57–59.

THIS HOUSE, Sincerely devoted, with the warmest Sentiments of Affection and Duty to His Majesty's Person and Government, inviolably attached to the present happy Establishment of the Protestant Succession; and with minds deeply impressed by a sense of the present and impending Misfortunes of the People of this Province; esteem it their indispensable Duty to their Constituents, to themselves, and to Posterity, to come to the following RESOLUTIONS, respecting their most essential Rights and Liberties, and the Grievances under which they labour, by reason of several late Acts of Parliament.

1st. RESOLVED, That His Majesty's Subjects in this Province owe the same Allegiance to the Crown of Great Britain, that is due from His Subjects born there.

2d. THAT His Majesty's Liege Subjects in this Province, are intitled to all the inherent Rights and Liberties of His natural born subjects with the Kingdom of Great Britain.

3d. THAT the Inhabitants of this Province appear also to be confirmed in all the rights aforementioned, not only by their Charter, but by an Act of Parliament of the 13th George 2d.

4th. THAT it is inseperably essential to the Freedom of a People, and the undoubted Right of Englishmen, that no Taxes be imposed on them, but with their own Consent, given personally, or by their representatives.

5th. THAT the People of this Province are not, and, from their local Circumstances, cannot be, represented, in the House of commons of Great Britain, And farther, That, in the Opinion of this House, the several Powers of Legislation in America were constituted, in some Measure, upon the Apprehension of this Impracticability.

6th. THAT the only Representatives of the People of this Province are Persons chosen therein by themselves; and that no Taxes ever have been, or can be, constitutionally imposed on them, but by the Legislature of this Province.

7th. THAT all Supplies to the Crown being free Gifts of the People, it is unreasonable and inconsistent with the Principles and Spirit of the British Constitution, for the People of Great Britain to grant to His Majesty the Property of the People of this Province.

8th. THAT Trial by Jury, is the inherent and invaluable right of every British subject in this Province.

9th. THAT the late Act of Parliament, intituled, "an Act for granting and applying certain Stamp Duties and other Duties on the British colonies and Plantations in America," &c. by imposing Taxes on the Inhabitants of this Province; and the said Act and several other Acts, by extending the Jurisdiction of the Courts of Admiralty, beyond its ancient Limits, have a Manifest Tendency to subvert the Rights and Liberties of the People of this Province.

10th. THAT the Duties imposed, by several late Acts of Parliament, on the People of this Province, will be extreamly burthensome and grievous, and, from the Scarcity of Gold and Silver, the Payment of them absolutely impracticable.

11th. THAT, as the Profits of the Trade of the People of this Province ultimately center in Great Britain, to pay for the Manufactures which they are obliged to take from thence, they eventually contribute very largely to all the Supplies granted there to the Crown; And besides, as every Individual in this Province, is as advantageous at least to Great Britain, as if he were in Great Britain; and as they pay their full Proportion of Taxes for the Support of His Majesty's Government here (which Taxes are equal, or more, in Proportion to our Estates, than those paid by our Fellow Subjects in Great Britain upon theirs); it is unreasonable, for them to be called upon, to pay any farther part of the Charges of the Government there.

12th. THAT the Assemblies of this Province have, from Time to Time, whenever Requisitions have been made by His Majesty, for carrying on Military Operations, either for the Defence of themselves, or that of America in general, most chearfully and liberally contributed their full Proportion, of Men and Money, for these Services.

13th. THAT, though the Representatives of the People of this Province had equal Assurances and reasons, with those of the other Provinces, to expect a proportional Reimbursement, of those immense Charges they had been at, for His Majesty's Service, in the late War, out of the several Parliamentary Grants for the use of America; yet, they have obtained only their Proportion of the first of those Grants; and the small Sum of Two Hundred and Eighty five Pounds Sterling received since.

14th. THAT notwithstanding, whenever His Majesty's Service shall, for the future, require the Aids of the Inhabitants of this Province, and they shall be called upon for that Purpose in a Constitutional Way, it shall be their indispensable Duty, most chearfully and liberally, to grant to His Majesty, their Proportion, according to their ability, of Men and Money, for the Defence, Security, and other public Services of the British American Colonies.

15th. THAT the Restrictions on the Trade of the People of this Province, together with the late Duties and Taxes, imposed on them by Acts of Parliament, must necessarily greatly lessen the Consumption of British Manufactures amongst them.

16th. THAT the Increase, Prosperity, and Happiness of the People of this Province, depend on the full and free Enjoyment of their Rights and Liberties, and an affectionate Intercourse with Great Britain.

17th. THAT the Readiness of the Colonies to comply with His Majestys Requisitions, as well as their Inability to bear any additional Taxes, beyond what is laid on them by their respective Legislatures, is apparent, from the several Grants of Parliament, to reimburse them Part of the heavy Expences they were at in the late War in America.

18th. THAT it is the Right of the British Subjects in this Province, to petition the King or either House of Parliament.

ORDERED that these VOTES AND RESOLUTIONS, be Signed by the Speaker, and be Printed, and made Public that a just Sense of Liberty, and a firm Sentiments of the Loyalty, of the Representatives of the People of this Province, may be known to their Constituents, and transmitted to Posterity.

## 4.10

 NEW JERSEY RESOLVES, NOVEMBER 30, 1765

Edmund S. Morgan, ed., *Prologue to Revolution: Sources and Documents on the Stamp Act Crisis, 1764–1766* (Chapel Hill: University of North Carolina Press, 1959), 59–60.

Whereas the late Act of Parliament called the Stamp Act, is found to be utterly subversive of Privileges inherent in and originally secured by, Grants and Confirmations from the Crown of Great-Britain to the Settlers of this Colony: In Duty therefore to ourselves, our Constituents, and Posterity, this House think it absolutely necessary to leave the following Resolves in our Minutes.

1. Resolved, N. C. D. That his Majesty's Subjects Inhabiting this Province are, from the strongest Motives of Duty, Fidelity and Gratitude, inviolably attached to his Royal Person and Government, and have ever shewn, and we doubt not ever will, their utmost Readiness and Alacrity in, acceding to the constitutional Requisitions of the Crown, as they have been from time to time made to this colony.

2. Resolved, N. C. D. That his Majesty's liege Subjects in this Colony, are entituled to all the inherent Rights and Liberties of his natural born Subjects within the Kingdom of Great-Britain.

3. Resolved, N. C. D. That it is inseparably essential to the Freedom of a People, and the undoubted right of Englishmen, that no Taxes be imposed on them but with their own Consent, given personally, or by their Representatives.

4. Resolved, N. C. D. That the People of this Colony are not, and from their remote situations cannot be, represented in the Parliament of Great-Britain. And if the Principle of taxing the Colonies without their own Consent should be adopted, the People here would be subjected to the Taxation of two Legislatures, a grievance unprecedented, and not to be thought of without the greatest Anxiety.

5. Resolved, N. C. D. That the only Representatives of the People of this Colony are Persons chosen by themselves, and that no Taxes ever have been, or can be imposed on them, agreeable to the constitution of this Province, granted and confirmed by his Majesty's most gracious Predecessors, but by their own Legislature.

6. Resolved, N. C. D. That all Supplies being free Gifts, for the People of Great-Britain to grant his Majesty the Property of the People of this Colony, without their Consent, and being represented, would be unreasonable, and render useless Legislation in this Colony, in the most essential Point.

7. Resolved, N. C. D. That the Profits of Trade arising from this Colony, centering in Great Britain, eventually contribute to the supplies granted there to the Crown.

8. Resolved, N. C. D. That the giving unlimited Power to any Subject or Subjects, to impose what Taxes they please in the Colonies, under the Mode of regulating the Prices of stamped Vellum, Parchment and Paper, appears to us unconstitutional, contrary to the Rights of the Subject, and apparently dangerous in its Consequences.

9. Resolved, N. C. D. That any Incumbrances which, in Effect, restrains the Liberty of the Press in America, is an infringement upon the Subjects' Liberty.

10. Resolved, N. C. D. That the Extension of the Powers of the Court of Admiralty within this Province, beyond its antient Limits, is a violent Innovation of the Right of trials by Jury, a Right which this House, upon the Principles of their British Ancestors, hold most dear and invaluable.

11. Resolved, N. C. D. That as the Tranquility of this Colony hath been interrupted, through Fear of the dreadful Consequences of the Stamp Act, that therefore the Officers of the Government, who go on in their Offices for the Good and Peace of the Province, in the accustomed Manner, while Things are in their present unsettled Situation, will, in the Opinion of this House, be intitled to the Countenance of the Legislature. And it is recommended to our Constituents, to use what Endeavours lie in their Power, to preserve the Peace, Quiet, Harmony, and good Order of the Government; that no Heats, Disorders or Animosities, may in the least obstruct the united Endeavours that are now strongly engaged, for the Repealing the Act above mentioned, and other Acts affecting the Trade of the Colonies.

## 4.11

 New York Resolves, December 18, 1765

Edmund S. Morgan, ed., *Prologue to Revolution: Sources and Documents on the Stamp Act Crisis, 1764–1766* (Chapel Hill: University of North Carolina Press, 1959), 60–62.

Die Mercurij, 9 bo. A. M. Dec. 18, 1765

The General Assembly of the Colony of New York, taking into their most serious Consideration, several Acts of Parliament lately passed, granting Stamp, and other Duties to his Majesty, and restricting the Trade of this Colony, apprehending an Abolition of that Constitution under which they have so long and happily enjoyed the Rights and

Liberties of Englishmen, and being clearly of Opinion that it is the Interest of Great Britain, a Dependence on which they esteem their felicity, to confirm them in the Enjoyment of those rights, think it their indispensable Duty to make a Declaration of their Faith and Allegiance to his Majesty King George the Third, of their Submission to the Supreme Legislative Power; and at the same Time to shew that the Rights claimed by them are in no Manner inconsistent with either; For which Purpose they are come to the following Resolutions, that is to say:

Resolved, Nemine Contradicente,

That the People of this Colony owe the same Faith and Allegiance to his Majesty King George the Third, that are due to him from his Subjects in Great-Britain.

Resolved, Nemine Contradicente,

That they owe Obedience to all Acts of Parliament not inconsistent with the essential Rights and Liberties of Englishmen, and are entitled to the same Rights and Liberties which his Majesty's English Subjects both within and without the Realm have ever enjoyed.

Resolved, Nemine Contradicente,

That his Majesty's Subjects in England, are secured in the superior Advantages they enjoy principally, by the Privilege of an Exemption from Taxes not of their own Grant, and their Right to Trials by their Peers. The First secures the People collectively from unreasonable Impositions; and without the Second, Individuals are at the arbitrary Disposition of the executive Powers.

Resolved, Nemine Contradicente,

That the Colonists did not forfeit these essential Rights by their Emigration; because this was by the Permission and Encouragement of the Crown; and that they rather merit Favour, than a Deprivation of those Rights, by giving an almost boundless Extent to the British Empire, expanding its Trade, increasing its wealth, and augmenting that Power which renders it so formidable to all Europe.

Resolved, Nemine Contradicente,

That the Acts of Trade giving a Right of Jurisdiction to the Admiralty courts, in Prosecutions for Penalties and Forfeitures, manifestly infringes the Right of Trials by Jury; and that the late Act for granting Stamp Duties, not only exposes the American Subjects to an intolerable Inconvenience and Expence, by compelling them to a Defence at a great Distance from Home; but, by imposing a Tax, utterly deprives them of the essential Right of being the sole Disposers of their own Property.

Resolved, Nemine Contradicente,

That all Aids to the Crown, in Great-Britain, are Gifts of the People by their Representatives in Parliament, as appears from the Preamble of every Money Bill, in which the Commons are said to give and grant to his Majesty.

Resolved, Nemine Contradicente,

That it involves the greatest Inconsistency with the known Principles of the English Constitution, to suppose that the honourable House of Commons of Great-Britain, can without diverting the Inhabitants of this Colony of their own most essential Rights, grant to the Crown their, or any Part of their Estates for any Purpose whatsoever.

Resolved, Nemine Contradicente,

That from the first Settlement of the Colonies, it has been the Sense of the Government at Home, that such Grants could not be constitutionally made; and therefore Applications for the Support of Government, and other Public Exigencies, have always been made to the Representatives of the People of this Colony; and frequently during the late War by immediate Orders from the Crown, upon which they exerted themselves with so much Liberality, that the Parliament thought proper to contribute to their Reimbursement.

Resolved, Nemine Contradicente,

That if the People of this Colony should be deprived of the sole Right of Taxing themselves, or presenting such Sums as the public Exigencies require, they would be laid under the greatest Disadvantages, as the united Interest of the Electors, or Elected, which constitute the Security of his Majesty's Subjects in Great-Britain, will operate strongly against them.

Resolved, Nemine Contradicente,

That the Impracticability of inducing the colonies to grant Aids in an equal Manner, proportioned to their several Abilities, does by no Means induce a Necessity of divesting the Colonies of their essential Rights.

Resolved, Nemine Contradicente,

That it is the Duty of every Friend to Great-Britain, and this Colony to cultivate a hearty Union between them.

Resolved, Nemine Contradicente,

That if the honourable House of Commons insist on their Power of Taxing this Colony, and by that Means deprive its Inhabitants of what they have always looked upon as an undoubted Right, though this Power should be exerted in the mildest Manner, it will teach them to consider the People of Great-Britain, as vested with absolute Power to dispose of all their Property, and tend to weaken that Affection for the Mother Country, which this Colony ever had, and is extremely desirous of retaining.

Resolved, Nemine Contradicente,

That in order to keep the Colonies in due Subjection to, in Dependence on Great-Britain, it is not necessary to deprive them of the Right they have long enjoyed, of Taxing themselves; since the same Right has been enjoyed by the Clergy within the Realm, and by all the Subjects of Great-Britain without the Realm, until the late Innovation.

Resolved, Nemine Contradicente,

That the Duties lately imposed by Act of Parliament on the Trade of this Colony, are very grievous and burthensome; and in the Apprehension of this House, impossible to be paid: Have already greatly diminished the advantageous Traffic heretofore carried on with the foreign Islands in the West-Indies; and in consequence, must render us unable to purchase the Manufactures of Great-Britain.

## 5. STATEMENTS OF THE STAMP ACT CONGRESS, OCTOBER 1765

On June 8, 1765, the Massachusetts House of Representatives, following a motion of James Otis, Jr., sent a circular letter to the mainland British North American colonies (the Canadian and West Indian colonies were not invited), asking them to join Massachusetts in a general congress to meet the following October in New York City to "implore Relief" from the anticipated effects of the Stamp Act.[42] What came to be called the Stamp Act Congress, the first or second intercolonial congress (after that in Albany in 1754, which representatives from seven colonies attended), convened on October 7, 1765. Twenty-seven delegates from nine colonies took part—the governors of five colonies (Delaware, New Jersey, Virginia, North Carolina, and Georgia) had prevented their legislatures from electing delegates; nonetheless, Delaware and New Jersey sent them. The delegates included James Otis, Oliver Partridge (a delegate to the earlier Albany Congress), and Timothy Ruggles of Massachusetts; Eliphalet Dyer (later a Continental Congress delegate), William Samuel Johnson, and David Rowland of Connecticut; George Bryan, John Dickinson, and John Morton (the second and third future Continental Congress delegates) from Pennsylvania; Thomas McKean and Caesar Rodney (both future Continental Congress delegates) from Delaware; and in the impressive delegation from South Carolina, Christopher Gadsden, Thomas Lynch, Sr., and John Rutledge, all future Continental Congress delegates.[43] New Hampshire declined to attend, but later formally approved the proceedings. The New York Assembly's Committee of Correspondence nominated itself to attend and sent William Bayard, John Cruger, Leonard Lispenard, Philip Livingston, and Robert R. Livingston, Jr. (the Livingstons were later delegates to the Continental Congress, with Philip having attended the Albany congress a decade earlier). Rhode Island, New Jersey, and Maryland also sent delegates; Edward Tilghman from Maryland later became a Continental Congress delegate as well.

The congress was chaired by Ruggles, a lawyer, chief justice of the court of common pleas in Worcester County, conservative delegate from Massachusetts, and future leading loyalist, who was selected by a one-vote margin over Otis, his fellow delegate from Massachusetts, a brilliant lawyer who was viewed by many as radical or, more accurately, as highly unpredictable in his political stances.[44] In spite of such differences regarding their choice of leadership, the delegates were unanimous, as were the provincial resolves found above, in their opposition to Parliament's claimed right to tax them for revenue.[45] Far more controversial, as it would be for much of the next eleven years, was how to characterize Parliament's traditional practice of regulating

American commercial activity and imperial trade, in most instances—and rarely contested—for the benefit of metropolitan Britain.

When the congress finally began work on Monday, October 7, the delegates picked John Cotton, a thirty-seven-year old Massachusetts resident and Harvard graduate, to be secretary for the meetings, though he was not a delegate himself. Robert R. Livingston, Jr., McKean, and Rutledge were chosen to serve on a committee of inspection that would oversee the minutes and publication of the proceedings of the congress.[46] Livingston, the son of Judge Robert R. Livingston, was a scion of a wealthy and powerful New York family and a prominent lawyer; he was later selected to serve on the committee drafting the Declaration of Independence, though he did not support or sign it.[47] McKean came from a relatively modest background before pursuing a career in law; active in the politics of three colonies, he was a fervent opponent of Parliament's pretensions. Rutledge came from a wealthy planter family, maintained a lucrative law career, and ran a number of plantations. He, like many with numerous commercial interests, opposed a precipitous movement toward colonial independence.[48]

The first major issue that the congress confronted was the hugely consequential question of how to structure its voting: either by the population or relative wealth of each colony or by an equal vote of all the colonies. With the strong insistence of the delegates from tiny Rhode Island—the politically prominent Henry Ward and Metcalf Bowler, a rich merchant who, it seems, worked as a paid informer for the British administration in 1776—each colony was awarded an equal vote.[49] This, not surprisingly, remained a persistent point of contention until the so-called Connecticut Compromise was finally struck on July 16, 1787, in the Philadelphia Constitutional Convention; that agreement led, under the proposed U.S. Constitution, to different systems of state representation, proportional and equal, in the U.S. House and Senate.[50]

For more than two weeks, Congress worked on the logic and wording of the Declaration of Rights. In the end Dickinson, the man described, for good reason, as the penman of the American Revolution,[51] wrote three drafts of the Declaration of Rights. In them, he tried to find the most carefully limited, but still respectful, characterization of the colonies' subordination to Parliament. In the first draft, Dickinson wrote that "all Acts of Parliament not inconsistent with the Rights and Liberties of the Colonists are obligatory upon them"; in the second, "all Acts of Parliament not inconsistent with the Principles of Freedom are obligatory upon the Colonists"; in the final one, following the language in Johnson's report (see document 5.4), he began with the colonists owing "all due Subordination to that August Body the Parliament of *Great-Britain*," a phrase repeated in the petitions to each house of Parliament.[52] Such ambiguous language satisfied men with varying levels of impatience with Parliament—a model akin to that found in the rights language of the Declaration of Independence.[53]

The Declaration of Rights and Grievances, which passed on October 19, 1765, sets out, much like the moderate colonial resolves written nearly contemporaneously, the fundamental elements of the colonial position. Congress begins with a declaration of allegiance to the king and an avowal of the colonies' subordination to Parliament before declaring the equality of American and British subjects and affirming, according to their common rights as Englishmen, that taxes can be imposed on them only in person or by elected representatives. Because the colonists "cannot be represented in the House of Commons," taxation could be raised only "by their respective Legislatures." Next, the declaration objects to the extended jurisdiction of admiralty courts, which, with their lack of juries, had a "manifest Tendency to subvert the Rights and Liberties of the Colonists."

The congress reminded the readers of its declaration that "as the Profits of the Trade of these Colonies ultimately centre in *Great-Britain,* to pay for the Manufactures which they are obliged to take from thence," the colonists in fact already "contribute very largely to all Supplies granted there to the Crown." Like most of the colonial resolves except Virginia's, the declaration closes by reminding British officials of the painful commercial consequences that both sides would suffer from the Sugar, Currency, and Stamp Acts barring immediate repeal. Finally, the congress asserted "the Right of the *British* subjects in these Colonies, to Petition the King, or either House of Parliament." This essential declaration, along with the congress' petitions, are lacking in the radical, universal-rights language and popular republicanism regularly found in New England provincial documents or in the Declaration of Independence. The majority of the delegates from regions other than New England in these gatherings clearly understood the disruptive affect of such language and, particularly, when not to use it.

In addition, on October 21, the Stamp Act Congress issued petitions to the king and to each house of Parliament—the last ones that the colonies acting collectively would address to Parliament during the ensuing crisis—before adjourning five days later. In the Petition to the King, following again the colonial resolves, the congress makes clear "that these Colonies were Originally Planted by Subjects of the *British* Crown . . . [and] have happily added these vast and valuable Dominions to the Empire of *Great-Britain.*" Next, it recalls that the colonies' and much of Great Britain's growth resulted from the colonists, after a dangerous voyage, expending their own blood and treasure in expanding the empire. The delegates next noted, with a particular emphasis on the English character of their rights' inheritance, that their structure of government was based on the "Principles of the *English Constitution*"—a reference to the British Constitution might have implied Scottish antecedents too.[54] As they reiterated several times, these principles included the right to grant the king "such Aids as are required," by which "they are secured from unreasonable Impositions," and the right to "trials by their Peers" and "the wise Rules of the Common Law, the Birthright of *Englishmen,*" by which they are secured "from Arbitrary Decisions of the executive Power." And with Parliament's invasion of both rights, the prosperous future of the British Empire, with the colonies as "a boundless Source of Wealth and Naval Strength," would be jeopardized. The essential English rights to self-taxation and legislation, and the constitutional right to jury trials, were confirmed by the "Great CHARTER of *English* Liberty," and the right to self-taxation was enjoyed by all the king's "*English* Subjects, both within and without the Realm."

The petitions to the House of Lords (not reproduced below) and the Commons largely avoid the contentious issue of Parliament's claimed right to legislate for all the nation, including the colonies, and begin by arguing that the novel duties and taxes would "be attended with Consequences very Injurious to the Commercial Interest of *Great-Britain* and her Colonies" and the "Eventual Ruin of the latter." The congress rejected anything smacking of independence or universalism by staying within a distinctly English ambit and holding that "it is from and under the *English* Constitution [that] we derive all our Civil and Religious Rights and Liberties." The congress respectfully reminded the House of Commons that the colonies could not be represented in that body and that, accordingly, Parliament, could not constitutionally tax them, Ireland, "or any other of the Subjects without the Realm." And borrowing from the counterfactual supposition in Johnson's report, the petition argues that even if one were to accept that the colonists could be virtually represented in Parliament, there remained strong practical reasons for Parliament to repeal its recent acts imposing duties and taxes and extending the jurisdiction of admiralty courts beyond their ancient limits. Such reasons included the scarcity of specie, the heavy debt burden found in the colonies, and an almost certain reduction in the ability of the colonists to purchase British manufactured goods, which "eventually contribute very largely to the Revenues of the Crown."

After listing its reasons, the petition carefully inquires "whether there be not a material Distinction in Reason and sound Policy, at least, between the necessary Exercise of Parliamentary Jurisdiction in general Acts, for the Amendment of the Common Law, and the Regulation of Trade and Commerce through the whole Empire, and the Exercise of that Jurisdiction, by imposing Taxes on the Colonies." In effect, the congress drew a distinction between, on the one hand, Parliament's accepted right to legislate for continental American concerns and imperial commercial ones, and, on the other, its lack of legitimacy to pass laws regarding local colonial matters or, most particularly, to tax the colonists for revenue. The petition closes by reminding the Commons that "the People here, as everywhere else, retain a great Fondness for their old Customs and Usages . . . [and] that we esteem our Connections with, and Dependance upon *Great-Britain,* as one of our greatest Blessings." While it is hard to imagine a more moderate petition than this one, which could in fact be seen as deeply conservative, the president of the congress, Ruggles, along with Robert Ogden of New Jersey, a large landowner and Speaker of the New Jersey Assembly, nonetheless refused to sign it "because of the omission of any precise acknowledgement of Parliament's authority" to regulate imperial commerce, a matter of controversy that again divided congressional delegates—moderate and radical—a decade later.[55]

### 5.1

 ## DECLARATION OF RIGHTS AND GRIEVANCES,  OCTOBER 19, 1765

Stamp Act Congress, *Proceedings of the Congress at New-York* (Annapolis, 1766), 15–16.

The Congress met according to Adjournment, and Resumed, &c. as Yesterday. And upon mature Deliberation, agreed to the following Declaration of the Rights and Grievances of the Colonists, in America, which were Ordered to be inserted.

The Members of this Congress, sincerely devoted, with the warmest Sentiments of Affection and Duty to his Majesty's Person and Government, inviolably attached to the present happy Establishment of the Protestant Succession, and with Minds deeply impressed by a Sense of the present and impending Misfortunes of the *British* Colonies on this Continent; having considered as maturely as Time would permit, the Circumstances of said Colonies, esteem it our indispensable Duty, to make the following Declarations of our humble Opinion, respecting the most Essential Rights and Liberties of the Colonists, and of the Grievances under which they labour, by Reason of several late Acts of Parliament.

I. That his Majesty's Subjects in these Colonies, owe the same Allegiance to the Crown of *Great-Britain,* that is owing from his Subjects born within the Realm, and all due Subordination to that August Body, the Parliament of *Great-Britain.*

II. That his Majesty's Liege Subjects in these Colonies are entitled to all the inherent Rights and Liberties of his Natural born Subjects within the Kingdom of *Great-Britain.*

III. That it is inseparably essential to the Freedom of a People, and the undoubted Right of *Englishmen,* that no Taxes should be imposed on them, but with their own Consent, given personally, or by their Representatives.

IV. That the People of these Colonies are not, and from their local Circumstances cannot be, Represented in the House of Commons in *Great-Britain.*

V. That the only Representatives of the People of these Colonies, are Persons chosen therein by themselves, and that no Taxes ever have been, or can be Constitutionally imposed on them, but by their respective Legislatures.

VI. That all Supplies to the Crown, being free Gifts of the People, it is unreasonable and inconsistent with the Principles and Spirit of the *British* Constitution, for the People of *Great-Britain* to grant to his Majesty the Property of the Colonists.

VII. That Trial by Jury is the inherent and invaluable Right of every *British* Subject in these colonies.

VIII. That the late Act of Parliament entitled, *An Act for granting and applying certain Stamp Duties, and other Duties in the* British *Colonies and Plantations in* America, *&c.*, by imposing Taxes on the Inhabitants of these Colonies, and the said Act, and several other Acts, by extending the Jurisdiction of the Courts of Admiralty beyond its ancient Limits, have a manifest Tendency to subvert the Rights and Liberties of the Colonists.

IX. That the Duties imposed by several late Acts of Parliament, from the peculiar Circumstances of these Colonies, will be extremely Burthensome and Grievous, and from the scarcity of Specie, the Payment of them absolutely impracticable.

X. That as the Profits of the Trade of these Colonies ultimately centre in *Great-Britain*, to pay for the Manufactures which they are obliged to take from thence, they eventually contribute very largely to all Supplies granted there to the Crown.

XI. That the Restrictions imposed by several late Acts of Parliament, on the Trade of these Colonies, will render them unable to purchase the Manufactures of *Great-Britain*.

XII. That the Increase, Prosperity, and Happiness of these Colonies, depend on the full and free Enjoyment of their Rights and Liberties, and an Intercourse, with *Great-Britain* mutually Affectionate and Advantageous.

XIII. That it is the Right of the *British* subjects in these Colonies, to Petition the King, or either House of Parliament.

*Lastly,* That it is the indispensable Duty of these Colonies, to the best of Sovereigns, to the Mother Country, and to themselves, to endeavour, by a loyal and dutiful Address to his Majesty, and humble Application to both Houses of Parliament, to procure the Repeal of the Act for granting and applying certain Stamp Duties, of all Clauses of any other Acts of Parliament, whereby the Jurisdiction of the Admiralty is extended as aforesaid, and of the other late Acts for the Restriction of the *American* Commerce.

## 5.2

 PETITION TO THE KING, OCTOBER 21, 1765

Stamp Act Congress, *Proceedings of the Congress at New-York* (Annapolis, 1766), 17–19. The colonies of South Carolina, New York, and Connecticut did not authorize their delegates to sign the petitions issued by the congress, and so those colonies do not appear as petitioners in documents 5.2 and 5.3.

To the King's most Excellent Majesty.

The PETITION of the Freeholders and other Inhabitants of the *Massachusetts-Bay, Rhode-Island,* and *Providence* Plantations, *New-Jersey, Pennsylvania,* the Government of the Counties of *New-Castle, Kent,* and *Sussex,* upon *Delaware,* Province of *Maryland,* Most humbly Sheweth,

THAT the Inhabitants of these Colonies, Unanimously devoted with the warmest Sentiments of Duty and Affection to your Majesty's Sacred Person and Government, Inviolably attached to the present Happy Establishment of the Protestant Succession in your Illustrious House, and deeply sensible of your royal Attention to their Prosperity and Happiness, humbly beg Leave to approach the Throne, by representing to your Majesty, That these Colonies were Originally Planted by Subjects of the *British* Crown, who, animated with the Spirit of Liberty, encouraged by your Majesty's Royal Predecessors, and confiding in the Public Faith for the Enjoyment of all the Rights and Liberties essential to Freedom, emigrated from their Native Country to this Continent, and by their successful Perseverance in the midst of innumerable Dangers and Difficulties, together with a Profusion of their Blood and Treasure, have happily added these vast and valuable Dominions to the Empire of *Great-Britain.* That for the Enjoyment of these Rights and Liberties, several Governments were early formed in the said Colonies, with full Power of Legislation, agreeable to the Principles of the *English* Constitution.

That under those Governments, these Liberties, thus vested in their Ancestors, and transmitted to their Posterity, have been exercised and enjoyed, and by the inestimable Blessings thereof (under the Favour of Almighty GOD), the inhospitable Desarts of *America* have been converted into Flourishing Countries; Science, Humanity, and the Knowledge of Divine Truths, diffused through Remote Regions of Ignorance, Infidelity, and Barbarism; the Number of *British* Subjects wonderfully Increased, and the Wealth and Power of *Great-Britain* proportionably Augmented.

That by Means of these Settlements, and the unparalleled Success of your Majesty's Arms, a Foundation is now laid for rendering the *British* Empire the most Extensive and Powerful of any Recorded in History. Our Connection with this Empire, we esteem our greatest Happiness and Security, and humbly conceive it may now be so established by your Royal Wisdom, as to endure to the latest Period of Time; This with most humble Submission to your Majesty, we apprehend will be most effectually Accomplished, by fixing the Pillars thereof on Liberty and Justice, and securing the inherent Rights and Liberties of your Subjects here, upon the Principles of the *English* Constitution. To this Constitution these Two Principles are essential, the Right of your faithful Subjects, freely to grant to your Majesty, such Aids as are required for the Support of your Government over them, and other Public Exigencies, and Trials by their Peers: By the One they are secured from unreasonable Impositions; and by the Other from Arbitrary Decisions of the executive Power.

The Continuation of these Liberties to the Inhabitants of *America* we ardently Implore, as absolutely necessary to Unite the several Parts of your wide extended Dominions, in that Harmony so essential to the Preservation and Happiness of the Whole. Protected in these Liberties, the Emoluments *Great-Britain* receives from us, however great at present, are inconsiderable, compared with those she has the fairest Prospect of acquiring. By this Protection she will for ever secure to herself the Advantage of conveying to all *Europe,* the Merchandizes which *America* furnishes, and of Supplying through the same Channel whatever is wanted from thence. Here opens a boundless Source of Wealth and Naval Strength; yet these immence Advantages, by the Abridgment of those invaluable Rights and Liberties, by which our Growth has been Nourished, are in Danger of being for ever Lost; and our subordinate Legislatures, in Effect, rendered useless, by the late Acts of Parliament imposing Duties and Taxes on these Colonies, and extending the Jurisdiction of the Courts of Admiralty here, beyond its antient Limits: Statutes by which your majesty's Commons in *Britain* undertake, absolutely to dispose of the Property of their Fellow Subjects in *America,* without their Consent, and for the enforcing whereof, they are subjected to the Determination of a single Judge in a Court unrestrained by the wise Rules of the Common Law, the Birthright of *Englishmen,* and the Safeguard of their Persons and Properties.

The invaluable Rights of Taxing ourselves, and Trial by our Peers, of which we implore your Majesty's Protection, are not, we most humbly conceive Unconstitutional; but confirmed by the Great CHARTER of *English* Liberty. On the First of these Rights the Honourable the House of Commons Found their Practice of Originating Money Bills, a Right enjoyed by the Kingdom of *Ireland,* by the Clergy of *England,* until relinquished by themselves, a Right, in fine, which all other your Majesty's *English* Subjects, both within, and without the Realm, have hitherto enjoyed.

With Hearts therefore impressed with the most indelible characters of Gratitude to your Majesty, and to the Memory of the Kings of your Illustrious House, whose Reigns have been Signally distinguished by their Auspicious Influence on the Prosperity of the *British* Dominions, and convinced by the most affecting Proofs of your Majesty's Paternal Love to all your People, however distant, and your unceasing and benevolent Desires to promote their Happiness, We most humbly beseech your Majesty, that you will be graciously pleased to take into your Royal Consideration, the Distresses of your faithful Subjects on this Continent, and to lay the same before your Majesty's Parliament, and to afford them such Relief, as in your Royal Wisdom their unhappy Circumstances shall be judged to require.

And your Petitioners as in Duty bound will pray.

## 5.3

 Petition to the House of Commons,
October 21, 1765

Stamp Act Congress, *Proceedings of the Congress at New-York* (Annapolis, 1766), 21–24.

To the Honourable the Knights, Citizens, and Burgesses of Great-Britain, in Parliament assembled.

The PETITION, of his Majesty's dutiful and loyal Subjects, the Freeholders and other Inhabitants of the Colonies of the *Massachusetts-Bay, Rhode-Island,* and *Providence* Plantations, *New-Jersey, Pennsylvania,* the Government of the Counties of *New-Castle, Kent,* and *Sussex,* upon *Delaware,* Province of *Maryland,*

Most humbly Sheweth,

That the several late Acts of Parliament imposing divers Duties and Taxes on the Colonies, and laying the Trade and Commerce thereof under very Burthensome Restrictions, but above all the Act for granting and applying certain Stamp Duties, &c. in *America,* have fill'd them with the deepest Concern and Surprize; and they humbly conceive the Execution of them will be attended with Consequences very Injurious to the Commercial Interest of *Great-Britain* and her Colonies, and must terminate in the Eventual Ruin of the latter.

Your Petitioners therefore most ardently implore the Attention of the Honourable House, to the united and dutiful Representation of their circumstances, and to their earnest Supplications for Relief, from those Regulations which have already involv'd this Continent in Anxiety, Confusion and Distress.

We most sincerely recognize our Allegiance to the Crown, and acknowledge all due Subordination to the Parliament of *Great-Britain,* and shall always retain the most grateful Sense of their Assistance and Protection. It is from and under the *English* Constitution, we derive all our Civil and Religious Rights and Liberties: We Glory in being Subjects of the best of Kings, and having been Born under the most perfect Form of Government; but it is with most ineffable and humiliating Sorrow, that we find ourselves, of late, deprived of the Right of Granting our own Property for his Majesty's Service, to which our Lives and Fortunes are entirely devoted, and to which, on his royal Requisitions, we have ever been ready to contribute to the utmost of our Abilities.

We have also the Misfortune to find, that all the Penalties and Forfeitures mentioned in the Stamp Act, and in divers late Acts of Trade extending to the Plantations, are, at the Election of the Informer, Recoverable in any Court of Admiralty in *America.* This, as the newly erected Court of Admiralty has a general jurisdiction over all *British America,* renders his Majesty's Subjects in these Colonies, liable to be carried, at an immense Expence, from one End of the Continent, to the other.

It gives us also great Pain, to see a manifest Distinction made therein, between the Subjects of our Mother Country, and those in the Colonies, in that the like Penalties and Forfeitures recoverable there only in his Majesty's Courts of Record, are made cognizable here by a Court of Admiralty: By these Means we seem to be, in Effect, unhappily deprived of Two Privileges essential to Freedom, and which all *Englishmen* have ever considered as their best Birthrights, that of being free from all Taxes but such as they have consented to in Person, or by their Representatives, and of Trial by their Peers.

Your Petitioners further shew, That the remote Situation, and other Circumstances of the Colonies, render it impracticable that they should be Represented, but in their respective subordinate Legislature; and they humbly conceive, that the Parliament, adhering strictly to the Principles of the Constitution, have never hitherto Tax'd any, but those who were actually therein Represented; for this Reason, we humbly apprehend, they never have Tax'd *Ireland,* or any other of the Subjects without the Realm.

But were it ever so clear, that the Colonies might in Law, be reasonably deem'd to be Represented in the Honourable House of Commons, yet we conceive, that very good Reasons, from Inconvenience, from the Principles of true Policy, and from the Spirit of the *British* Constitution, may be adduced to shew, that it would be for the real Interest of *Great-Britain,* as well as her Colonies, that the late Regulations should be rescinded, and the several Acts of Parliament imposing Duties and Taxes on the Colonies, and extending the Jurisdiction of the Courts of Admiralty here, beyond their ancient Limits, should be Repeal'd.

We shall not Attempt a minute Detail of all the Reasons which the Wisdom of the Honourable House may suggest, on this Occasion, but would humbly submit the following Particulars to their Consideration.

That Money is already become very scarce in these Colonies, and is still decreasing by the necessary Exportation of specie from the Continent, for the Discharge of our Debts to *British* Merchants.

That an immensely heavy Debt is yet due from the Colonies for *British* Manufactures, and that they are still heavily burthen'd with Taxes to discharge the Arrearages due for Aids granted by them in the late War.

That the Balance of Trade will ever be much against the Colonies, and in Favour of *Great-Britain,* whilst we consume her Manufactures, the Demand for which must ever Increase in Proportion to the Number of Inhabitants settled here, with the Means of Purchasing them. We therefore humbly conceive it to be the Interest of *Great-Britain,* to increase, rather than diminish, those Means, as the Profits of all the Trade of the Colonies ultimately center there to pay for her Manufactures, as we are not allowed to purchase elsewhere; and by the Consumption of which, at the advanced Prices the British Taxes oblige the Makers and Venders to set on them, we eventually contribute very largely to the Revenue of the Crown.

That from the Nature of *American* Business, the Multiplicity of Suits and Papers used in Matters of small Value, in a Country where Freeholds are so minutely divided, and Property so frequently transferr'd, a Stamp Duty must ever be very Burthensome and Unequal.

That it is extremely improbable that the Honourable House of Commons, shou'd at all Times, be thoroughly acquainted with our Condition, and all Facts requisite to a just and equal Taxation of the Colonies.

It is also humbly submitted, Whether there be not a material Distinction in Reason and sound Policy, at least, between the necessary Exercise of Parliamentary Jurisdiction in general Acts, for the Amendment of the Common Law, and the Regulation of Trade and Commerce through the whole Empire, and the Exercise of that Jurisdiction, by imposing Taxes on the Colonies.

That the several subordinate Provincial Legislatures have been moulded into Forms, as nearly resembling that of their Mother Country, as by his Majesty's Royal Predecessors was thought convenient; and their Legislatures seem to have been wisely and graciously established, that the Subjects in the Colonies might, under the due Administration thereof, enjoy the happy Fruits of the *British* Government, which in their present Circumstances, they cannot be so fully and clearly availed of, any other way under these Forms of Government we and our Ancestors have been Born or Settled, and have had our Lives, Liberties, and Properties, protected. The People here, as everywhere else, retain a great Fondness for their old Customs and Usages, and we trust that his Majesty's Service, and the Interest of the Nation, so far from being obstructed, have been vastly promoted by the Provincial Legislatures.

That we esteem our Connections with, and Dependance upon *Great-Britain,* as one of our greatest Blessings, and apprehend, the latter will appear to be sufficiently secure, when it is considered, that the Inhabitants in the Colonies have the most unbounded Affection for his Majesty's Person, Family, and Government, as well as for the Mother country, and that their Subordination to the Parliament, is universally acknowledged.

We therefore most humbly entreat, That the Honourable House would be pleased to hear our Counsel in Support of this Petition, and take our distressed and deplorable Case into their serious Consideration, and that the Acts and Clauses of Acts, so grievously restraining our Trade and Commerce, imposing Duties and Taxes on our Property, and extending the Jurisdiction of the Court of Admiralty beyond its ancient Limits, may be repeal'd; or that the Honourable House would otherwise relieve your Petitioners, as in your great Wisdom and Goodness shall seem meet.

And your Petitioners as in Duty bound shall ever pray.

5.4

## Report of the Committee to Whom Was Referred the Considerations of the Rights of the British Colonies, October 8–18(?), 1765

One of the Stamp Act Congress' more influential delegates was William Samuel Johnson, the son of a prominent Anglican minister in overwhelmingly Congregationalist Connecticut and a highly successful lawyer in his own right. He had close ties to Crown officials and refused in the end to take sides in the Imperial Crisis. He was nonetheless, as can be seen below, adamant in his opposition to parliamentary taxation of the colonies. He declined to serve in the next two Continental Congresses and sat out the war, though he later served in the Confederation Congress and took over the presidency of Columbia University (like his father before him) before playing an active role in drafting the U.S. Constitution. Serving in the Stamp Act Congress led to Johnson's forming a close friendship with John Dickinson and, still more surprising, with the radical South Carolina merchant Christopher Gadsden and the hard-to-predict, brilliant (and soon to be insane) James Otis.

He wrote the following report, in which he and his colleagues began outlining the rights and duties of the colonies and Parliament in their imperial constitutional relationship, which was never to be adequately defined or agreed upon. It was the very lack of agreement regarding the imperial relationship, along with unfounded fears on both sides, that led to the imperial controversy then confronting them.[56] The British feared that the colonists sought freedom from disadvantageous commercial regulations and, ultimately, independence, which they believed would do grievous harm to Britain's export-led prosperity (both concerns were erroneous); the American colonists feared that Parliament was planning to tax and oppress them into slavery (similarly, almost certainly wrong).

Johnson begins his report by rehearsing, in a manner not regularly found in congressional state papers, "the natural Rights of Englishmen . . . the [individual] Rights of personal Security, personal Liberty, and Private Property" and then goes on to assert that the British Constitution does not allow a man's property to be taken without his consent and "that the Common Law of England and the grand leading Principles of the British Constitution have their foundation in the Laws of Nature [and] universal reason."[57] In his view, royal charters awarded British subjects in the king's North American dominions "all the Rights and Privileges of natural born Subjects within the Realm." Accordingly, the British Parliament could not constitutionally grant the colonists' monies for the king's use—only the colonists were able to do so—and thus it was particularly onerous that they were not "allowed the Honor of making a free Gift and Grant of their own for his Majesty's Service."

Next, while admitting that "Parliament, collectively Considered as consisting of King, Lords and Commons, are the Supreme Legislature of the whole Empire, and as such have an undoubted Jurisdiction over the Colonies so far as is Consistent with our Essential Rights of which also they are and must be the final Judges," Johnson nonetheless disputes whether any of the colonists can be represented in Parliament, virtually or otherwise. He distinguishes between North American colonies and certain British cities that, while "send[ing] no Members to Parliament," do in fact "return Members" as part of British counties, concluding that such examples are not "reasonable Precedents for Taxing all America" without actual representation in Parliament. Accordingly, for the colonists to enjoy rights and privileges comparable to those of subjects residing in the realm, "several Colony Jurisdictions should be Erected, all of them however, subordinate to and controllable by the Supreme Power of Great Britain." And it was "under these subordinate Jurisdictions" that the colonists had enjoyed "a full and free Legislative Power in Levying Taxes . . . till very lately." Johnson then explains the intimate British relationship between property in land and the right to be represented in legislatures authorized to tax, noting that the colonists' property, without representation in Parliament, would be necessarily insecure.

Even if Parliament—in a line of argument copied in the Stamp Act Congress' Petition to the House of Commons—could, through virtual representation, legislate for all the dominions, indeed for the entire world, Johnson argues that Parliament should still forgo doing so on practical grounds, including the shortage of money in the colonies, the existence of a heavy debt burden, and the certainty that "no British Freeholder[,] Manufacturer or Merchant who knows his own Interest can wish to see" North American colonists being forced into manufacturing for themselves. In the fourth proposition, Johnson describes, in language that Dickinson borrowed, the "due subordination of the Colonies to the Crown and Parliament, and the dependency of the Colonies on Great Britain" as a condition that every intelligent American desires. But that dependency had limits: Parliament's legitimate jurisdiction over "general Acts for the Amendment [of] the Common Law, or even in general Regulation of Trade and Commerce through the Empire" should not be extended to "the actual Exercise of that Jurisdiction in levying External and Internal Duties and Taxes on the Colonists while they neither are nor can be represented in Parliament."[58] His rejection of internal and external taxation, well before the Townshend duties of 1767, is worthy of note, but the colonists' theory of total independence from Parliament was clearly still in development.

Close to the end of his remarks, Johnson reminds his readers that as a result of the Trade and Navigation Acts, the British North American colonists paid prices 50 percent higher than did the king's subjects in Britain for manufactured goods, and thus the colonists already paid their "full proportion to every branch of our Sovereign's revenues as now Established and Collected at home." A full decade later, in 1775, Benjamin Franklin took a similar position (see document 23.4).

Text taken from a handwritten manuscript in the William Samuel Johnson Papers, 1753–1802, Library of Congress, number 79027961. All ampersands have been replaced by "and," and paragraph breaks have been introduced.

The Comm. to whom was referred the Consideration of the Rights of the British Colonies—Report, as their opinion, that the primary, absolute, natural Rights of Englishmen as frequently Declared, in Acts of Parliament from Magna Charta to this day, are the Rights of personal Security, personal Liberty and Private Property. It is a Fundamental principle of the British Constitution that the Supreme Power cannot take from any Man any part of his Property without his Consent in person or by representation that is Taxes are not to be laid on the People but by their consent in person or by Deputy. It seems to be agreed on all hands that the Common Law of England and the grand leading Principles of the British Constitution have their foundation in the Laws of Nature [and] universal reason.

It is also certain that the British American Subjects by charters from the Crown and other Royal Instruments are declared Entitled to all the Rights and Privileges of natural born Subjects within The Realm. To all Intents Constructions and Purposes, this is also the voice of the Common Law and agreeable to the decisions of the Judges Ancient and Modern. By the 13 Geo. 2nd, even Foreigners having resided seven years in the Colonies on taking the Oath of Allegiance, etc. are declared to be his Majesty's natural born Subjects of the Kingdom of Great Britain, to all Intents Constr. and purposes as if any of them had been Born within the Kingdom. The Preamble of that act runs thus "Whereas the increase of the People is the means of advancing the Wealth and Strength of any Nation and Country and that many Foreigners ~~may~~ and Strangers, from the purity of our Religion, the benefit of our Laws, the advantages of our Trade, and the security of our property, might be induced to come and settle in some of his Majesty's Colonies in America if they were made partakers of the advantages the natural born Subjects there Enjoy." The Colonists are by this act considered as natural born Subjects and Entitled to all essential Rights of Such, unless it could be supposed, that Foreigners naturalized by this Act are Entitled to more than the Natives, for Foreigners so Naturalized ~~they~~ are to all Intents, Constructions, and Purposes declared to be Natural Born Subjects, as if Born within the Realm and consequently Entitled to personal Security, personal Liberty, and the free Disposal of their private Property, the Grand security of all which is that the last shall not be taken away without the Consent of the owner.

The House of Commons have long claimed and exercised a Right of originating all Money Bills; hence it is plain the Commons of Great Britain are in Effect the sole Judges in person or by their Representatives [of] what part of their Property shall be appropriated to the Service of the public. It is remarkable that the Stamp Act for America has this Clause, viz. "We your Majesty's most Dutiful and Loyal Subjects the Commons of Great Britain in Parliament assembled have Resolved to Give and Grant unto your Majesty the several Rates and Duties following etc. Is this a Gift of the Property of the Members of the House of Commons and of their Constituents, or of that ~~Property~~ of the Colonists? If the latter, it seems hard that they should not be allowed the Honor of making a free Gift and Grant of their own for his Majesty's Service.

It is also observable that in the Act of James II wherein the Parliament Recognized their most constant Faith Obedience and Loyalty to his Majesty [and] his Royal Progeny as in that high Court of Parliament where all the whole body of the Realm and every particular Member thereof either in person or by representation upon of their own free Election are by the Laws of this Realm deemed to be personally present, there is not a Word of any Virtual Representation of Ireland or any other of the Dominions, nor is there in the Bill of Rights, and yet as no Man can doubt but that all the Dominions were bound by those Acts and that King James and King William were Kings *De Jure* as well in the Dominions as well as in the Realm, so it is equally clear that the Declaration of the Ancient indubitable Rights and Liberties of the Subject mentioned and confirmed in the last Act are also the Essential Rights and Privileges of the Subject in the British Dominions. It is also observable that the Clause cited from the Act of James II first shows how Equitable and reasonable it is, that all the Subjects within the Realm, should be deemed to be present in Parliament because they are in fact all there as the Act expresses it in person or by representation upon their own free Election. Can it be said that the Colonists or any of them, are thus there while this whole Continent containing Millions of his Majesty's subjects have neither the Return of one Member of Parliament nor a single Vote in the Election of one? Are the Cases of Birmingham, Manchester and a few other Towns places who send no Members to Parliament, reasonable Precedents for Taxing all America especially when it is considered that all Counties return Members and all Freeholders have a Vote in their Election? There is not one Act or Resolution of Parliament nor any Law Book that we have seen that declares the Colonists to be in any sense represented in the House of Commons. Yet it is acknowledged that the Parliament, collectively Considered as consisting of King, Lords and Commons, are the Supreme Legislature of the whole Empire, and as such have an undoubted Jurisdiction over the Colonies so far as is Consistent with our Essential Rights of which also they are and must be the final Judges, and even the Applications and Petitions to the King and Parliament to implore Relief in our present difficulties will be an ample Recognition of our Subjection to and dependence on that Legislature.

It is to be apprehended that an undue Bias may some Time or other take place in the House of Commons were it only from the Single Consideration that they must ever lighten their own Taxes in proportion as they are pleased to give and Grant to his Majesty Taxes on our Freeholds and other Property. It seems Evident from these and other obvious Considerations that the British American Colonies are well entitled to all the Essential Rights and Privileges of natural born Subjects within the Realm. The whole might may be reduced to this single Question—How can they be availed of the actual Enjoyment of those rights and Privileges especially in the great article of Taxation at their distance from the Mother Country. Their various Circumstances have rendered it necessary for the Enjoyment of those Rights and Privileges that Several Colony Jurisdictions should be Erected all of them however subordinate to and controllable by the Supreme Power of Great Britain so far as is consistent with Civil Liberty and Happiness.

The Wisdom of Ages has dictated this practice hitherto, what requires that it should be now so Essentially altered, is hard to Conceive.

Under these subordinate Jurisdictions and with an idea of being at least as free in America as they or their Forefathers were at any Time in Europe, the British Colonists have settled the finest part of America with little or no assistance from the Crown till the late War. Some of these Colonies have been settled more than a Century and an Half; they have from the beginning Exercised a full and free Legislative Power, in the Levying Taxes and Impositions on their own Property uncontrolled and unquestioned by the Parliament till very lately. The Conduct of the Crown and of the Parliament towards the Colonies particularly in the late War strongly Imply an Exclusive Right of Taxation here. The requisitions of the Crown for Aids of Men and Money seem always to have been made on this principle. The Governors of the several Colonies were directed from time to time to use their Interest and Influence with the Several Assemblies to Grant such aids as were required; this must have been on the supposition that the Power and Liberty of Granting or refusing was vested in those Assemblies. The Several Acts of Parliament for granting to the King sums of Money to enable him to reimburse to his faithful Colonies part of their Expenses (which paternal favours are held in grateful Remembrance) suppose that those aids so granted by the Colonies were voluntary and free Gifts and that the right of Granting them was vested in the several Provincial Legislatures. It is certain the Colonies made very strenuous efforts in the Common Cause during the late War and some of them are now deeply in arrears for Debts contracted in that War which was not so much a dispute about Boundaries as a Contest between Great Britain and France for the Empire of North America and the Commerce of one half the world.

This constant Exercise of the Right of Taxation as it is the best Security of Property that a People can have has been one great Inducement to the Inhabitants to settle on this Continent, and has been ever Conceived by them to be an Essential part of the Compact betw or social Tie between Great Britain and her Colonies. The Tenures of our Lands are as free here as in England and Land being the most valuable and permanent Property, and the Possession that most firmly attaches the owner to the Interest of the Country in which it lies a share of the Legislative Authority has been always annexed to this kind of Property and great regard has ever been had the Freehold. On this Principle the Constitution of England appears to have been founded it being Evident that the Parliament in its original Form consisted only of the greater Barons who that held Lands. Many of the Baronies being afterwards divided into lesser ones in process of Time the Number of those lesser Barons became so great that they could not all assemble with Convenience; that they therefore chose some of their Body to represent them. The Extension of Commerce and the increase of Wealth at length rendered it necessary to admit those who carried it on to a representation and share in the national Councils, though they were not Entirely Entitled to it by holding Lands. Thus no person can at this day Vote for the Election of Members of Parliament in Great Britain unless he is qualified by virtue of some Franchise Freehold or other Estate held in that Kingdom; and it is worthy of Remark that for the preservation of the original Constitution, it has been found necessary to recur and adhere to its first Principle by providing that none can be legally chosen Members of Parliament even by those who do not Vote as Land holders, unless the Persons chosen are Entitled to considerable Estates in Lands. The Power of Imposing Taxes upon a people without their consent, must in the End deprive them of their Liberty be such Power in the hands of One, the Few, or the Many; an absolute Power had as good be in, nay in the opinion of some, had better be in the hands of one than of Many.

But after all supposeing we may be rightly Deemed to be Virtually represented in the House of Commons and that they represent not only the Commons of the Realm but those of all Dominions as they would the Inhabitants of the whole globe should the Empire ever be Extended all over as it now is all round the World. Let it also be believed that their Property is none of ours but that all ours is theirs to Give and Grant to his Majesty, Freehold and all at pleasure. Yet it [is] humbly conceived that very strong Reasons from Inconvenience, from the principles of true Policy, and the real Interests of Great Britain as such, may be adduced to show that the late Regulations should be rescinded and the late Acts imposing Duties and Taxes in America imposing repealed.

1st    First Money is already become very scarce in America and is every day decreasing by the Exportation of specie from this Continent to Great Britain to discharge our Debts to the Merchants there.

2ly    An Immensely heavy Debt is yet due from the Colonies for her Manufactures imported in larger Quantities than usual during the War by reason of the Money then Circulating here for a few years, and the Extraordinary Credit obtained thereby at home.

3ly    The Balance of Trade as it ever has been so it probably will ever continue against America and in favor of Britain unless the Necessities of the People arising from Regulations similar to those now complained of shall prevent the Colonists from purchasing the Manufactures of Britain and force them to make for themselves, an Event that no British Freeholder Manufacturer or Merchant who knows his own Interest can wish to see.

4ly    Although the due Subordination of the Colony to the Crown and Parliament and the dependency of the Colonies on Great Britain are what every Intelligent American may wish; as under this system Established with the Protestant Succession in his Majesty's Royal Person and Family we derive our greatest Temporal Blessings, the Security of our Privileges, Civil and Religious; in consideration of which our Lives and Fortunes are and ever have been devoted to his Majesty's service in every Constitutional way. Yet it is most humbly conceived that this subordination and dependency is sufficiently provided for secured by the Common Law, by our Allegiance, by the Negative of our the Crown on the Laws of most of the Provinces, but above all by the general superintending Power and Authority of the whole Empire indisputably lodged in that

August Body the Parliament of Great Britain which Authority is clearly admitted here so far as ~~in~~ our Circumstances is consistent with the Enjoyment of our Essential Rights as Freemen and British Subjects, and we further humbly Conceive that by the Constitution it is no further admissible in Great Britain itself. It is also submitted whether there is not a vast difference between the Exercise of Parliamentary Jurisdiction in general Acts for the Amendment of the Common Law, or even in general Regulations of Trade and Commerce through the Empire and the actual Exercise of that Jurisdiction in levying External and Internal ~~taxes~~ Duties and Taxes on the Colonists while they neither are nor can be represented in Parliament. The former may very well consist with a reasonable Measure of Civil Liberty in the Colonies but we must ~~say~~ beg leave to say that how the latter is consistent with any degree of Freedom we are wholly at a loss how to Comprehend. Be that as it may while the Restrictions on the Trade, Commerce, and Manufacturers of America are every Day increasing, that Duties and Taxes External or Internal should be required of us seems to be a case of singular hardship.

5ly    From the Nature of American Business, Circumstances of our Affairs, the multiplicity of Suits and Papers ~~the circumstances of our Affairs~~ used in a Country where Freeholds are so minutely divided, a Stamp Duty especially as this Act is constructed must be so very unequal and burdensome.

6ly    All the Penalties and Forfeitures mentioned in this and other late Acts are determinable in a Court of Admiralty at the mere Election of an Informer and so at his will and pleasure the Subject may be deprived of the inestimable privilege of being Tried by his Peers which the Common Law considers as one of the best Birthrights of an Englishman. ~~For~~ This is not all, for by the Constitution of the newly Erected Court of Admiralty with a general Jurisdiction over all his Majesty's Dominions in America the Subject according to the residence of the Judge which has hitherto been at Halifax, in Nova Scotia may be carried from one End of a Continent of 2000 miles Extent to the other.

7ly    We think it much in favor of the Colonies that as it is a well grounded general maxim in this Doctrine of Taxes that the Consumer ultimately pays them and all the Riches of America are as naturally Pouring into Britain as the Rivers into the Sea, and all Manufactures must by the Acts of Trade and Navigation come to us from them, as we are allowed to go no where else for them and that at an advanced price ~~from~~ it is said 50 percent above what they otherwise might be, by reason of the heavy Duties and Taxes, at home It is clear to a Demonstration that as America takes off and Consumes one half the British manufactures that we eventually Pay our full proportion to every branch of our Sovereign's revenues as now Established and Collected at home.

8ly    And lastly the high Honours and Lucrative Places and Employments for which every good and loyal Subject at home is or may be a Candidate if his abilities will admit of it, the Colonists and their Posterity must by their great Distance from their Prince the fountain be ever Excluded from any reasonable hopes of. We neither ask nor desire more than what every ordinary Commoner and Freeholder in Britain boasts of, viz. quiet Possession and free Disposal of our Property being ever ready freely and cheerfully as our Duty and Loyalty require to Contribute [two words scratched out] to the utmost of our abilities to the Support of the Common Cause ~~when~~ and his Majesty's Service when his just Requisitions as heretofore shall be made known.

## 6. STATEMENTS OF THE SONS OF LIBERTY, DECEMBER 1765–MARCH 1766

During the summer of 1765, secret organizations of men formed in colonial towns to oppose the Stamp Act. They described themselves as the "Sons of Liberty" or, in some cases, "The True Sons of Liberty." Most likely, they were inspired to take this name after a powerful speech in the House of Commons by Isaac Barré in February 1765.[59] He was a member of Parliament and a follower of William Pitt who, like others in Pitt's "party," strongly opposed parliamentary taxation of the colonies.[60] The Sons of Liberty were often socially diverse; on occasion, they were led by well-off shopkeepers, lawyers, and merchants, who directed the violence and the destruction of private property by less affluent members, who, according to General Gage, "had taken a good deal of prodding before they could be brought to act."[61] Indeed, a Boston mob that began under the direction of the "Loyal Nine" and comprised urban workers, sailors, and other lower-class residents who were directly responsible for the violence (burnings in effigy, physical attacks on persons and property) was organized by members of the professional classes, who directed and, importantly, were the greatest beneficiaries of "popular" action. As Clinton Weslager notes, "The [Stamp] tax fell most heavily on those who dealt with newspapers, almanacs, and legal documents in their daily affairs, namely, editors and publishers, lawyers, judges, and clergymen, and merchants and ships' masters. . . . The ordinary colonist might have accepted the tax with only mild protest if he had not been aroused by the propaganda devised by editors, lawyers, and merchants."[62] While some prominent families, such as the Livingstons in New York, opposed the sometimes out-of-control violence that led to the resignation of the stamp masters in the major continental colonies (though not in some other North American British colonies), other leading colonists, such as Christopher Gadsden, a wealthy merchant from South Carolina and himself a Son of Liberty, were openly supportive of it.[63]

Throughout the colonies, the Sons of Liberty responded with organized violence to reports that Parliament planned on "cramming stamps down American throats."[64] Their stated purpose was to force, through intimidation and threatened or realized violence, agents to resign, courts to refuse to use stamped paper, or merchants to refuse commercial transactions with stamped paper. The groups published statements in which they outlined the grounds of their opposition to the Stamp Act; this action was facilitated by a number of their members being newspapers publishers. In stark contrast to the moderation of the declaration and petitions of the Stamp Act Congress and the state papers produced by the First Continental Congress and those from the first year of the Second, even while at war, the statements of these urban groups from late 1765 to early 1766 make frequent use of radical language of a sort found often in newspaper editorials and similar to that found in the Massachusetts Resolves (document 4.8) and the Declaration of Independence. The statements contain radical references to "those privileges and immunities, which God and Nature seem to have intended us," though commonly followed by persistent claims of devotion to George III and promises that the signatories would "at all times faithfully adhere to his royal Person, and just government, and heartily defend him from every attempt to injure his person, crown, or dignity."

One of the statements is remarkable for its lack of any reference to inherited English rights, royal charters, the British Constitution, or devotion and loyalty to the king. It is the first of them of December 1765, from republican Connecticut (in its words, politics, and congregational church governance, Connecticut often outstripped Massachusetts in the vehemence of its republicanism). It drips with seventeenth-century, Civil War–era English republican zeal of a sort found in none of the other statements and still less in any of the intercolonial congressional state papers until the Declaration of Independence, which it anticipates with remarkable prescience.[65] In its unusual character, the document highlights how the Declaration was out of step with most of the congressional state papers issued before the spring of 1776, but not with the more extreme republican language found in newspapers and elsewhere.

Here, the Sons of Liberty hold that "the Boundaries set by the People in all Constitutions, are the only Limits within which any Officer can lawfully exercise Authority. . . . That whenever those Bounds are exceeded, the People have a Right to resume the exercise of that Authority which by Nature they had, before they delegated it to Individuals. . . . That every Tax imposed upon English Subjects without Consent, is against the natural Rights and the Bounds prescribed by the English Constitution."[66] Only at the end of the Imperial Crisis in the summer of 1776, and even then only briefly, did such mostly off-stage republican language of unconstrained popular sovereignty move from anonymous newspaper editorials, pamphlets, and coffeehouse chatter to seminal congressional documents—most famously, the Declaration of Independence. After independence, such language largely returned again to newspaper editorials, radical pamphlets, and coffeehouses as Congress sought to manage the difficult-to-control, absolute understanding of popular sovereignty; for an example, see Congress' firm rejection of the residents of the New Hampshire Grants, the future state of Vermont, and their claimed right to self-government (document 39.1).[67]

Strikingly, the other Sons of Liberty statements are more in keeping with continental congressional state papers in their claims of loyalty to the king and in resting their defense of the right of self-taxation on inherited British historical rights and the British or English Constitution. For example, the joint statement of Connecticut and New York declares that the Sons "bear the most unshaken faith and true allegiance to his majesty King *George* the Third—that they are most affectionately and zealously attached to his royal person and family, and are fully determined to the utmost of their power, to maintain and support his crown and dignity . . . and with the greatest cheerfulness they submit to his government, according to the known and just principles of the BRITISH CONSTITUTION." Indeed, the Sons regularly assert that their goals are to preserve, not change, their "accustomed rights as British subjects . . . not in the least desiring any alteration or innovation in the grand bulwark of their liberties and the wisdom of ages."

North Carolina and Virginia Sons of Liberty were even more conservative in eschewing the use of rights language at all, even regarding British rights. The North Carolina Sons described the Stamp Act duties as "subversive of the Liberties and Charters of North America" handed down to them from their ancestors before noting their detestation of rebellion. Similarly, Virginia's Sons of Liberty, without ever mentioning nature or rights, described their desire, very much in keeping with contemporary continental statements, to "preserve inviolate to posterity, those inestimable privileges of all free-born British subjects, of being taxed by none but representatives of their own choosing, and of being tried only by a jury of their own Peers." Clearly, even in 1766, there were already at least two lines of discourse within popular bodies opposed to Parliament's transgressions—a radically republican one, found mostly in New England and emphasizing natural rights and unlimited popular sovereignty, and another, concentrated in the mid-Atlantic colonies outside the two relatively populous cities (20,000–30,000 inhabitants), stressing particular British constitutional rights and loyalty to the king.[68]

6.1

## STATEMENT OF THE SONS OF LIBERTY OF NEW LONDON, CONNECTICUT, DECEMBER 10, 1765

Edmund S. Morgan, ed., *Prologue to Revolution: Sources and Documents on the Stamp Act Crisis, 1764–1766* (Chapel Hill: University of North Carolina Press, 1959), 114–15.

At a Meeting of a large Assembly of the respectable Populace in New-London, the 10th of Dec. 1765, the following Resolves were unanimously come into.

Resolved 1st. That every Form of Government rightfully founded, originates from the Consent of the People.

2d. That the Boundaries set by the People in all Constitutions, are the only Limits within which any Officer can lawfully exercise Authority.

3d. That whenever those Bounds are exceeded, the People have a Right to resume the exercise of that Authority which by Nature they had, before they delegated it to Individuals.

4th. That every Tax imposed upon English Subjects without Consent, is against the natural Rights and the Bounds prescribed by the English Constitution.

5th. That the Stamp-Act in special, is a Tax imposed on the Colonies without their Consent.

6th. That it is the Duty of every Person in the Colonies, to oppose by every lawful Means, the Execution of those Acts imposed on them,—and if they can in no other Way be relieved to reassume their natural Rights, and the Authority the Laws of Nature and of God have vested them with.

And in order effectually to prevent the Execution thereof it is recommended,

1st. That every Officer in this Colony duly execute the Trust reposed in him, agreeable to the true Spirit of the English Constitution and the Laws of this Colony.

2nd. That every Officer neglecting the Exercise of his Office, may justly expect the Resentment of the People; and those who proceed may depend on their Protection.

3rd. It is presumed no Person will publickly, in the Pulpit or otherwise, inculcate the Doctrine of passive Obedience, or any other Doctrine tending to quiet the Minds of the People in a tame Submission to any unjust Impositions.

4th. We fully concur with the respectable Body of the Populace in all their Resolves made at Windham the 26th November, 1765, and published in the New-London Gazette.

## 6.2

 Union in Arms, December 25, 1765

"Sons of Liberty Agreement, New London, Conn., Dec. 25, 1765," in *The History of the Rise, Progress, and Establishment of the Independence of the United States of America,* ed. William Gordon (London, 1788), 1:195–98.

Certain reciprocal and mutual agreements, concessions and associations made, concluded and agreed upon by and between the sons of liberty of the colony of *New York* of the one part, and the sons of liberty of the colony of *Connecticut* on the other part, this twenty-fifth day of December, in the sixth year of the reign of our sovereign Lord *George* the Third, by the grace of God, of *Great Britain, France* and *Ireland* king, defender of the faith, and in the year of our Lord one thousand seven hundred and sixty-five.

The aforesaid parties taking into their most serious consideration the melancholy and unsettled state of *Great Britain* and her *North American colonies,* proceeding as they are fully persuaded, from a design in her most insidious and inveterate enemies, to alienate the affections of his majesty's most loyal and faithful subjects of *North America* from his person and government—Therefore to prevent as much as in us lies the dissolution of so inestimable a union, they do, in the presence of *Almighty God,* declare that they bear the most unshaken faith and true allegiance to his majesty King *George* the Third—that they are most affectionately and zealously attached to his royal person and family, and are fully determined to the utmost of their power, to maintain and support his crown and dignity, and the succession as by law established; and with the greatest cheerfulness they submit to his government, according to the known and just principles of the BRITISH CONSTITUTION, which they conceive to be founded on the eternal and immutable principles of justice and equity, and that every attempt to violate or wrest it, or any part of it from them, under whatever pretence, colour or authority, is an heinous sin against God, and the most daring contempt of the people, from whom (under God) all just government springs. From a sacred regard to all which, and a just sense of the impending evils that might befal them, in consequence of such a dreadful dissolution, They do hereby voluntarily, and of their own free will, as well for the support of his majesty's just prerogative and the British constitution as their own mutual security and preservation, agree and concede to associate, advise, protect, and defend each other in the peaceable, full and just enjoyment of their inherent and accustomed rights as British subjects of their respective *colonies,* not in the least desiring any alteration or innovation in the grand bulwark of their liberties and the wisdom of ages, but only to preserve it inviolate from the corrupt hands of its implacable enemies—And whereas a certain pamphlet has appeared in America in the form of an act of parliament, called and known by the name of the *Stamp-Act,* but has never been legally published or introduced, neither can it, as it would immediately deprive them of the most invaluable part of the British constitution, viz. the trial by juries, and the most just mode of taxation in the world, that is, of taxing themselves, rights that every British subject becomes heir to as soon as born. For the preservation of which, and every part of the British constitution, they do reciprocally resolve and determine to march with the utmost dispatch, at their own proper costs and expence, on the first proper notice, (which must be signified to them by at least six of the sons of liberty) with their whole force if required, and it can be spared, to the relief of those that shall, are, or may be in danger from the *stamp-act,* or its promoters and abettors, or any thing relative to it, on account of any thing that may have been done in opposition to its obtaining— And they do mutually and most fervently recommend it to each other to be vigilant in watching all those who, from the nature of their offices, vocations or dispositions, may be the most likely to introduce the use of stamped papers, to the total subversion of the British constitution and American liberty; and the same, when discovered, immediately to advise each other of, let them be of what rank or condition soever; and they do agree, that they will mutually, and to the utmost of their power, by all just ways and means, endeavour to bring all such betrayers of their country to the most condign punishment—And further, they do mutually resolve to defend the liberty of the press in their respective colonies from all unlawful violations and impediments whatever, on account of the said act, as the only means (under divine Providence) of preserving their lives, liberties and fortunes, and the same in regard to the judges, clerks, attornies, &c. that shall proceed without any regard to the *stamp-act,* from all pains, fines, mulcts, penalties, or any molestation whatever—And finally, that they will, to the utmost of their power, endeavour to bring about, accomplish, and perfect the like *association* with all the *colonies* on the continent for the like salutary purposes and no other."

## 6.3

## Statement of the Sons of Liberty of North Carolina, February 18, 1766

Edmund S. Morgan, ed., *Prologue to Revolution: Sources and Documents on the Stamp Act Crisis, 1764–1766* (Chapel Hill: University of North Carolina Press, 1959), 117.

We the Subscribers, free and natural-born Subjects of George the Third, true and lawful King of Great-Britain, and all its Dependencies, (whom God preserve) whose sacred Person, Crown, and Dignity, we are ready and willing, at the Expence of our Lives and Fortunes, to defend, being fully convinced of the oppressive and arbitrary Tendency of a late Act of Parliament, imposing Stamp Duties on the Inhabitants of this Province, and fundamentally subversive of the Liberties and Charters of North-America; truly sensible of the inestimable Blessings of a free Constitution, gloriously handed down to us by our brave Forefathers, detesting Rebellion, yet preferring Death to Slavery, do with all Loyalty to our most gracious Sovereign, with all deference to the just Laws of our Country, and with a proper and necessary Regard to Ourselves and Posterity, hereby mutually and solemnly plight our Faith and Honour that we will, at any Risk whatever, and whenever called upon, unite, and truly and faithfully assist each other, to the best of our Power, in preventing entirely the Operation of the Stamp-Act.

Witness our Hands this 18th Day of Feb. 1766.

## 6.4

 STATEMENT OF THE SONS OF LIBERTY OF NEW
BRUNSWICK, NEW JERSEY, FEBRUARY 25, 1766

Edmund S. Morgan, ed., *Prologue to Revolution: Sources and Documents on the Stamp Act Crisis, 1764–1766* (Chapel Hill: University of North Carolina Press, 1959), 115–16.

At a meeting of the Sons of Liberty of the city of New-Brunswick, in the county of Middlesex, and province of New-Jersey, the 25th of February, 1766, it was resolved;

1. That we will chearfully embark our lives and fortunes in the defence of our liberties and privileges.

2. That we will resist, as far as in us lies, all illegal attempts to deprive us of our indubitable rights; and for that reason, will, to the last extremity, oppose the exercise of the Stamp Act in the colony.

3. That we will contribute all in our power to preserve the public tranquility, so far as it may be preserved, consistent with the principles already professed.

4. That we will do our utmost to support and defend the officers of government in this colony, who shall act agreeable to the above resolves.

5. That we shall always be ready with hearts and hands, to assist the neighbouring provinces, in opposing every attempt that may be made to deprive them and us, of those privileges and immunities, which God and Nature seem to have intended us.

And lastly, That we do bear his Majesty King George the Third, true Allegiance, and will at all times faithfully adhere to his royal Person, and just government, and heartily defend him from every attempt to injure his person, crown or dignity.

## 6.5

 STATEMENT OF THE SONS OF LIBERTY OF NORFOLK,
VIRGINIA, MARCH 31, 1766

"Proceedings of the Sons of Liberty at Norfolk," *Southern Literary Messenger* 1, no. 7 (1835): 355–56. When this statement was published, the *Southern Literary Messenger* was edited by Edgar Allan Poe.

At a meeting of a considerable number of inhabitants of the town and county of Norfolk, and others, Sons of Liberty, at the court-house of the said county, in the colony of Virginia, on Monday, the 31st of March, 1766—

Having taken into consideration the evil tendency of that oppressive and unconstitutional act of Parliament, commonly called the stamp act, and being desirous that our sentiments should be known to posterity, and recollecting that we are a part of that colony who first in general assembly, openly expressed their detestation to the said act, (which is pregnant with ruin, and productive of the most pernicious consequences,) and unwilling to rivet the shackles of slavery and oppression on ourselves and millions yet unborn, have unanimously come to the following resolutions—

1. *Resolved,* That we acknowledge our sovereign lord and king George the Third to be our rightful and lawful king, and that we will at all times, to the utmost of our power and ability, support and defend his most sacred person, crown and dignity; and will be always ready, when constitutionally called upon, to assist his majesty with our lives and fortunes, and defend all his just rights and prerogatives.

2. *Resolved,* That we will, by all lawful ways and means which Divine Providence hath put into our hands, defend ourselves in the full enjoyment of, and preserve inviolate to posterity, those inestimable privileges of all free born British subjects, of being taxed by none but representatives of their own choosing, and of being tried only by a jury of their peers; for if we quietly submit to the execution of the said stamp act, all our claims to civil liberty will be lost, and we and our posterity become absolute slaves.

3. *Resolved,* That we will, on any future occasion, sacrifice our lives and fortunes, in concurrence with the other Sons of Liberty in the American provinces, to defend and preserve our invaluable blessings transmitted us by our ancestors.

4. *Resolved,* That whoever is concerned, directly or indirectly, in using or causing to be used, in any way or manner whatsoever, within this colony, unless authorized by the general assembly thereof, those detestable papers called stamps, shall be deemed to all intents and purposes, an enemy to his country, and by the Sons of Liberty treated accordingly.

5. *Resolved,* That a committee be appointed to present the thanks of the Sons of Liberty to Colonel Richard Bland, for his treatise, entitled "An Inquiry into the Rights of the British Colonies."

6. *Resolved,* That a committee be appointed, who shall make public the above resolutions, and correspond, as they shall see occasion, with the associated Sons of, and Friends to Liberty, in the British colonies in America.

## 7. BENJAMIN FRANKLIN DEFENDS THE COLONIES BEFORE
## PARLIAMENT, FEBRUARY 1766

In 1764, the Boston-born printer, scientist, and emerging world celebrity Benjamin Franklin went to London to represent one of the Pennsylvania Quaker factions—working with his close ally and protégé in such matters, the future loyalist Joseph Galloway—in petitioning the king and Parliament to revoke Pennsylvania's proprietary charter and to make it a Crown colony with a governor appointed directly by the king.[69] It was under those circumstances that Franklin found himself pressed into testifying as a procolonial witness by a friendly Rockingham ministry opposed to the Stamp Act. Franklin was an agent (something like a lobbyist) for the colony of Pennsylvania; by 1770, he was representing also Georgia, New Jersey, and Massachusetts in London.

In July 1765, the king had dismissed the Grenville administration, under whose leadership Parliament had attempted, unsuccessfully, to limit British expenditures in the colonies by raising taxes, and had appointed the Marquess of Rockingham to head his new government. Franklin, along with other witnesses, was called by Lord Rockingham to the bar of the House of Commons to provide a firsthand account of American sentiments concerning the Stamp Act. Rockingham and his Whig followers, sympathetic to the colonies, had summoned thirty British merchants and North American colonists residing in Britain to report on the ill consequences, on both sides of the Atlantic, of the prior administration's Stamp Act. Rockingham hoped, through this testimony, to move Parliament's attention away from "the declarations and petitions of the Stamp Act Congress"—those very statements of colonial rights and the American understanding of British constitutionalism that colonial delegates had painstakingly drafted (documents 5.1–5.3)—to less controversial issues of common commercial interests so that Parliament might act rapidly to avert the economic storm that had begun forming since the Stamp Act took effect on November 1, 1765.[70] During his appearance before the Commons, Franklin took note of his examiners and, in the main, described each as "Friend" or "Adversary." In some instances, though, he recorded their names, including the former first minister, George Grenville, first lord of the treasury and chancellor of the exchequer; Grey Cooper, the secretary of the treasury; and Charles Townshend, paymaster and soon to be, under a new administration, chancellor of the exchequer.[71]

In "Franklin's Examination before Parliament," here presented in a somewhat abbreviated form, readers get a sense not only of important positions likely held by many in the colonies, but also of the positions taken by prominent members of Parliament. (Additionally, Franklin's testimony reveals something of his sense of humor, which resulted in his witty testimony becoming one of the most popular pamphlets in the colonies, being reprinted no less than six times, including in a German edition.)[72] Among the critical issues discussed were whether American colonists were lightly or heavily taxed; whether, if taxed lightly, they shouldn't bear a larger share of the empire's debt burden; and where and how the revenues from stamp duties would be spent. (According to Franklin, they would be paid by the established colonies and spent in the newly acquired ones, that is, Quebec, the Floridas, and some of the islands.) And when explicitly asked "What was the temper of America towards Great Britain before the year 1763?" he famously responded:

The best in the world. They submitted willingly to the government of the crown, and paid, in all their courts, obedience to the acts of Parliament. . . . They were governed by this country at the expence only of a little pen, ink, and paper. They were led by a thread. They had not only a respect, but an affection for Great Britain; for its laws, its customs and manners, and even a fondness for its fashions, that greatly increased the commerce. . . . To be an Old-England man was, of itself, a character of some respect, and gave a kind of rank among us.

When subsequently asked "What is their temper now?" he responded, "O, very much altered."

Parliament also explored with Franklin the nature of the commercial relationship between the colonies and Britain, along with the character and size of the balance of trade between them. Concerning Parliament's role in shaping those commercial relations, Franklin was asked whether he had ever heard of "the authority of Parliament to make laws for America questioned till lately," to which Franklin responded, "The authority of Parliament was allowed to be valid in all laws, except such as should lay internal taxes," and most particularly, "It was never disputed in laying duties to regulate commerce." That response led to an examination of the differences, if any, between internal taxes and external duties, a distinction that Franklin sought to defend but, when confronting the difficulty of consistently doing so, eventually conceded, with typical Franklin humor, that "many arguments have been lately used here to shew them [the colonists] that there is no difference, and . . . at present they do not reason so, but in time they may possibly be convinced by these arguments."

Another consequential discussion concerned the views of the colonists and the British regarding the primary beneficiaries of the Seven Years' War and, thus, whether the North American colonists should be asked to pay off part of the accumulated British debt (of course, colonists were largely already responsible for provincial debt). Questions by the members of Parliament suggest that they viewed the war to have been fought to benefit the colonists. For Franklin and, one must suppose, many in the colonies, however, "the war, as it commenced for the defence of territories of the crown, the property of no American, and for the defence of a trade purely British, was really a British war." Here was yet another issue that both sides had already come to view through different prisms. Such revenue concerns were linked to the Stamp Act, and when asked, several times and in various ways, whether the colonists "would submit to the Stamp Act, if it was modified, the obnoxious parts taken out, and the duty reduced to some particulars, of small moment," Franklin consistently answered no: "They will never submit to it." And when asked what would follow from not repealing the Stamp Act, he responded, "A total loss of the respect and affection the people of America bear to this country, and of all the commerce that depends upon that respect and affection." Here, he didn't mince words.

When further asked about the colonists' traditional view of Parliament, he replied with a standard post-1688 Whig response: "They considered the parliament as the great bulwark and security of their liberties and privileges, and always spoke of it with the utmost respect and veneration. Arbitrary ministers, they thought, might possibly, at times, attempt to oppress them; but they relied on it, that the Parliament, on application, would always give redress." Yet Parliament's claimed right to legislate for and tax them had so changed the colonists' perception of the relationship that now Parliament, not the king, had become the feared source of arbitrarily exercised power. The issue of Parliament's right to legislate for the colonies, though, was one that Franklin tried to finesse rather than address directly. He could not escape it entirely, and when asked "Have not you heard of the resolution of this House, and of the House of Lords, asserting the right of parliament relating to America, including a power to tax the people there?" he answered, "Yes, I have heard of such resolutions." And when pushed regarding "the opinion of the Americans on those resolutions," he responded without the slightest embellishment, "They will think them unconstitutional and unjust." Franklin, however, made no mention of countervailing, legislative rights, describing the colonists as possessing only "the common rights of Englishmen, as declared by Magna Charta, and the Petition of Right"—nothing universal or natural that might challenge British sovereignty.

When asked, though, whether the colonists, in an attempt to resolve the emerging crisis, would be dissatisfied without a clear renunciation by Parliament of its claimed sovereign right to tax and legislate for them, Franklin rightly predicted: "Resolutions of [parliamentary] right will give them very little concern, if they are never attempted to be carried into practice. The colonies will probably consider themselves in the same situation, in that respect, with Ireland; they know you claim the same right with regard to Ireland [in the Declaratory Act of 1719/20], but you never exercise it." Later, he counseled that repealing the Stamp Act on grounds of inexpediency rather than of right would be a matter of indifference to most colonists. American colonists, he predicted, would be satisfied with a de facto resolution of the incipient crisis without needing an answer to the constitutional question. That position changed over the next several years as colonial distrust of Parliament steadily mounted. In February 1775, when Parliament included in Lord North's peace proposal a statement that it would forgo taxing its North American colonists (see document 23.1), the achievement of that long-cherished goal proved inadequate: Congress demanded in addition a well-defined constitutional plan in which Parliament's rights to legislate domestically for the colonies and directly tax them would be renounced and then, somehow, made permanent.

Where Franklin may have shown less discretion, though no less honesty, was when he was asked "Do you think the assemblies have a right to levy money on the subject there, to grant to the crown?" and responded, "I certainly think so; they have always done it." He was next asked a most momentous question: were the colonists "acquainted with the Declaration of Rights; and do they know that by that statute, money is not to be raised on the subject but by consent of Parliament?" He replied that of course they were familiar with it. In response to the logical follow-up question, "How then can they think they have a right to levy money for the crown, or for any other than local purposes?" Franklin pointed up a distinction between colonists and metropolitan Britons: "They understand that clause to relate to subjects only within the realm." Here, two of the most difficult and controversial constitutional issues were joined—whether the colonies could directly raise tax receipts for the Crown without parliamentary approval, and what exactly was the colonies' constitutional status vis-à-vis the King's dominions and the British realm. Franklin was provocatively next asked, "Suppose the King should require the colonies to grant a revenue, and the parliament should be against their doing it, do they think they can grant a revenue to the King, without the consent of the parliament of Great Britain?" Franklin dodged giving a general answer to that "deep question" and spoke personally instead: "As to my own opinion, I should think myself at liberty to do it, and should do it, if I liked the occasion." These were, for most members of Parliament, fighting words.

It is hard to imagine a response that would have cut closer to the marrow of British Whig political thought and would have been certain to alienate those who believed that only the Commons' close control of taxation and finances had reined in the king during the previous century and continued to prevent him from acting arbitrarily, thereby creating Britain's much vaunted liberty.[73] Indeed, parliamentary control over the Crown might have been the most essential element of Britain's post-1688 Whig constitutional settlement and its highly regarded balance of power.[74] Franklin's unsettling response, like the colonists' threatening and, at times, curiously reactionary, almost Stuart-like constitutionalism, pushed the majority in Parliament toward defending that body's sovereign rights all the more tenaciously, even irrationally, in light of its other preeminent goal of maintaining commercial advantages for British merchants and manufacturers through maritime regulation of the colonies.[75]

7.1

 EXAMINATION OF FRANKLIN IN THE HOUSE OF COMMONS, FEBRUARY 13, 1766

*The Works of Benjamin Franklin,* ed. Jared Sparks (Boston: Hilliard, Gray, 1840), 4:161–98.

Q. WHAT is your name, and place of abode?
A. Franklin, of Philadelphia.
Q. Do the Americans pay any considerable taxes among themselves?
A. Certainly many, and very heavy taxes.
Q. What are the present taxes in Pennsylvania, laid by the laws of the colony?

A. There are taxes on all estates real and personal, a poll tax, a tax on all offices, professions, trades, and businesses, according to their profits; an excise on all wine, rum, and other spirits; and a duty of ten pounds per head on all negroes imported, with some other duties.

Q. For what purposes are those taxes laid?

A. For the support of the civil and military establishments of the country, and to discharge the heavy debt contracted in the last war.

Q. How long are those taxes to continue?

A. Those for discharging the debt are to continue till 1772, and longer, if the debt should not be then all discharged. The others must always continue.

Q. Was it not expected that the debt would have been sooner discharged?

A. It was, when the peace was made with France and Spain; but a fresh war breaking out with the Indians, a fresh load of debt was incurred; and the taxes, of course, continued longer by a new law.

Q. Are not all the people very able to pay those taxes?

A. No. The frontier counties, all along the continent, having been frequently ravaged by the enemy and greatly impoverished, are able to pay very little tax. And therefore, in consideration of their distresses, our late tax laws do expressly favor those counties, excusing the sufferers; and I suppose the same is done in other governments.

Q. Are you not concerned in the management of the post-office in America?

A. Yes. I am deputy-postmaster-general of North America.

Q. Don't you think the distribution of stamps by post to all the inhabitants very practicable, if there was no opposition?

A. The posts only go along the seacoasts; they do not, except in a few instances, go back into the country; and if they did, sending for stamps by post would occasion an expence of postage, amounting in many cases to much more than that of the stamps themselves. . . .

Q. Are not the colonies, from their circumstances, very able to pay the stamp duty?

A. In my opinion, there is not gold and silver enough in the colonies to pay the stamp duty for one year.

Q. Don't you know that the money arising from the stamps was all to be laid out in America?

A. I know it is appropriated by the act to the American service; but it will be spent in the conquered colonies, where the soldiers are; not in the colonies that pay it.

Q. Is there not a balance of trade due from the colonies where the troops are posted, that will bring back the money to the old colonies?

A. I think not. I believe very little would come back. I know of no trade likely to bring it back. I think it would come, from the colonies where it was spent, directly to England; for I have always observed, that in every colony the more plenty of means of remittance to England, the more goods are sent for, and the more trade with England carried on.

Q. What number of white inhabitants do you think there are in Pennsylvania?

A. I suppose there may be about one hundred and sixty thousand.

Q. What number of them are Quakers?

A. Perhaps a third.

Q. What number of Germans?

A. Perhaps another third; but I cannot speak with certainty.

Q. Have any number of the Germans seen service, as soldiers, in Europe?

A. Yes, many of them, both in Europe and America.

Q. Are they as much dissatisfied with the stamp duty as the English?

A. Yes, and more; and with reason, as their stamps are, in many cases, to be double.

Q. How many white men do you suppose there are in North America?

A. About three hundred thousand, from sixteen to sixty years of age.

Q. What may be the amount of one year's imports into Pennsylvania from Britain?

A. I have been informed that our merchants compute the imports from Britain to be above five hundred thousand pounds.

Q. What may be the amount of the produce of your province exported to Britain?

A. It must be small, as we produce little that is wanted in Britain. I suppose it cannot exceed forty thousand pounds

Q. How then do you pay the balance?

A. The balance is paid by our produce carried to the West Indies, and sold in our own islands, or to the French, Spaniards, Danes, and Dutch; by the same produce carried to other colonies in North America, as to New England, Nova Scotia, Newfoundland, Carolina, and Georgia; by the same, carried to different parts of Europe, as Spain, Portugal, and Italy. In all of which places we receive either money, bills of exchange, or commodities that suit for remittance to Britain; which, together with all the profits on the industry of our merchants and mariners, arising in those circuitous voyages, and the freights made by their ships, centre finally in Britain to discharge the balance, and pay for British manufactures continually used in the province, or sold to foreigners by our traders.

Q. Have you heard of any difficulties lately laid on the Spanish trade?

A. Yes, I have heard that it has been greatly obstructed by some new regulations, and by the English men-of-war and cutters stationed all along the coast in America.

Q. Do you think it right that America should be protected by this country and pay no part of the expence?

A. That is not the case. The colonies raised, clothed, and paid, during the last war, near twenty-five thousand men, and spent many millions.

Q. Were you not reimbursed by Parliament?

A. We were only reimbursed what, in your opinion, we had advanced beyond our proportion, or beyond what might reasonably be expected from us; and it was a very small part of what we spent. Pennsylvania, in particular, disbursed about five hundred thousand pounds, and the reimbursements, in the whole, did not exceed sixty thousand pounds.

Q. You have said that you pay heavy taxes in Pennsylvania; what do they amount to in the pound?

A. The tax on all estates, real and personal, is eighteen pence in the pound, fully rated; and the tax on the profits of trades and professions, with other taxes, do, I suppose, make full half a crown in the pound.

Q. Do you know anything of the rate of exchange in Pennsylvania, and whether it has fallen lately?

A. It is commonly from one hundred and seventy to one hundred and seventy-five. I have heard, that it has fallen lately from one hundred and seventy-five to one hundred and sixty-two and a half; owing, I suppose, to their lessening their orders for goods; and, when their debts to this country are paid, I think the exchange will probably be at par.

Q. Do not you think the people of America would submit to pay the stamp duty, if it was moderated?

A. No, never, unless compelled by force of arms.

Q. Are not the taxes in Pennsylvania laid on unequally, in order to burden the English trade; particularly the tax on professions and business?

A. It is not more burdensome in proportion than the tax on lands. It is intended and supposed to take an equal proportion of profits.

Q. How is the assembly composed? Of what kinds of people are the members; landholders or traders?

A. It is composed of landholders, merchants, and artificers.

Q. Are not the majority landholders?

A. I believe they are.

Q. Do not they, as much as possible, shift the tax off from the land, to ease that, and lay the burden heavier on trade?

A. I have never understood it so. I never heard such a thing suggested. And indeed an attempt of that kind could answer no purpose. The merchant or trader is always skilled in figures, and ready with his pen and ink. If unequal burdens are laid on his trade, he puts an additional price on his goods; and the consumers, who are chiefly landowners, finally pay the greatest part, if not the whole.

Q. What was the temper of America towards Great Britain before the year 1763?

A. The best in the world. They submitted willingly to the government of the crown, and paid, in their courts, obedience to the acts of Parliament. Numerous as the people are in the several old provinces, they cost you nothing in forts, citadels, garrisons, or armies, to keep them in subjection. They were governed by this country at the expence only of a little pen, ink, and paper. They were led by a thread. They had not only a respect, but an affection for Great Britain; for its laws, its customs and manners, and even a fondness for its fashions, that greatly increased the commerce. Natives of Britain were always treated with particular regard; to be an Old-England man was, of itself, a character of some respect, and gave a kind of rank among us.

Q. And what is their temper now?

A. O, very much altered.

Q. Did you ever hear the authority of Parliament to make laws for America questioned till lately?

A. The authority of Parliament was allowed to be valid in all laws, except such as should lay internal taxes. It was never disputed in laying duties to regulate commerce.

Q. In what proportion hath population increased in America?

A. I think the inhabitants of all the provinces together, taken at a medium, double in about twenty-five years. But their demand for British manufactures increases much faster; as the consumption is not merely in proportion to their numbers, but grows with the growing abilities of the same numbers to pay for them. In 1723, the whole importation from Britain to Pennsylvania was about fifteen thousand pounds sterling; it is now near half a million.

Q. In what light did the people of America use to consider the Parliament of Great Britain?

A. They considered the Parliament as the great bulwark and security of their liberties and privileges, and always spoke of it with the utmost respect and veneration. Arbitrary ministers, they thought, might possibly, at times, attempt to oppress them; but they relied on it, that the Parliament, on application, would always give redress. They remembered, with gratitude, a strong instance of this, when a bill was brought into Parliament, with a clause, to make royal instructions laws in the colonies, which the House of Commons would not pass, and it was thrown out.

Q. And have they not still the same respect for Parliament?

A. No; it is greatly lessened.

Q. To what cause is that owing?

A. To a concurrence of causes; the restraints lately laid on their trade, by which the bringing of foreign gold and silver into the colonies was prevented; the prohibition of making paper money among themselves, and then demanding a new and heavy tax by stamps, taking away, at the same, trials by juries, and refusing to receive and hear their humble petitions.

Q. Don't you think they would submit to the Stamp Act, if it was modified, the obnoxious parts taken out, and the duty reduced to some particulars, of small moment?

A. No, they will never submit to it.

Q. What do you think is the reason that the people of America increase faster than in England?

A. Because they marry younger, and more generally.

Q. Why so?

A. Because any young couple, that are industrious, may easily obtain land of their own, on which they can raise a family.

Q. Are not the lower ranks of people more at their ease in America than in England?

A. They may be so, if they are sober and diligent, as they are better paid for their labor.

Q. What is your opinion of a future tax, imposed on the same principle with that of the Stamp Act? How would the Americans receive it?

A. Just as they do this. They would not pay it.

Q. Have not you heard of the resolutions of this House, and of the House of Lords, asserting the right of Parliament relating to America, including a power to tax the people there?

A. Yes, I have heard of such resolutions.

Q. What will be the opinion of the Americans on those resolutions?

A. They will think them unconstitutional and unjust.

Q. Was it an opinion in America before 1763, that the Parliament had no right to lay taxes and duties there?

A. I had never heard any objection to the right of laying duties to regulate commerce; but a right to lay internal taxes was never supposed to be in Parliament, as we are not represented there.

Q. On what do you found your opinion, that the people in America made any such distinction?

A. I know that whenever the subject has occurred in conversation where I have been present, it has appeared to be the opinion of every one, that we could not be taxed by a Parliament wherein we were not represented. But the payment of duties laid by an act of Parliament, as regulations of commerce, was never disputed.

Q. But can you name any act of assembly, or public act of any of your governments, that made such distinction?

A. I do not know that there was any; I think there was never an occasion to make any such act, till now that you have attempted to tax us; that has occasioned resolutions of assembly, declaring the distinction, in which I think every assembly on the continent, and every member in every assembly, have been unanimous.

Q. What, then, could occasion conversations on that subject before that time?

A. There was, in 1754, a proposition made, (I think it came from hence,) that in case of a war, which was then apprehended, the governors of the colonies should meet, and order the levying of troops, building of forts, and taking every other necessary measure for the general defence; and should draw on the treasury here for the sums expended, which were afterwards to be raised in the colonies by a general tax, to be laid on them by *act of Parliament*. This occasioned a good deal of conversation on the subject, and the general opinion was, that the Parliament neither would, nor could lay any tax on us, till we were duly represented in Parliament; because it was not just, nor agreeable to the nature of an English constitution.

Q. Don't you know there was a time in New York, when it was under consideration to make an application to Parliament to lay taxes on that colony, upon a deficiency arising from the assembly's refusing or neglecting to raise the necessary supplies for the support of the civil government?

A. I never heard of it.

Q. There was such an application under consideration in New York; and do you apprehend that they could suppose the right of Parliament to lay a tax in America was only local, and confined to the case of a deficiency in a particular colony, by a refusal of its assembly to raise the necessary supplies?

A. They could not suppose such a case, as that the assembly would not raise the necessary supplies to support its own government. An assembly that would refuse it must want common sense; which cannot be supposed. I think there was never any such case at New York, and that it must be a misrepresentation, or the fact must be misunderstood. I know there have been some attempts, by ministerial instructions from hence, to oblige the assemblies to settle permanent salaries on governors, which they wisely refused to do; but I believe no assembly of New York, or any other colony, ever refused duly to support government by proper allowances, from time to time, to public officers.

Q. But in case a governor, acting by instruction, should call on an assembly to raise the necessary supplies, and the assembly should refuse to do it, do you not think it would then be for the good of the people of the colony, as well as necessary to government, that the Parliament should tax them?

A. I do not think it would be necessary. If an assembly could possibly be so absurd, as to refuse raising the supplies requisite for the maintenance of government among them, they could not long remain in such a situation; the disorders and confusion occasioned by it must soon bring them to reason.

Q. If it should not, ought not the right to be in Great Britain of applying a remedy?

A. A right, only to be used in such a case, I should have no objection to; supposing it to be used merely for the good of the people of the colony.

Q. But who is to judge of that, Britain or the colony?

A. Those that feel can best judge.

Q. You say the colonies have always submitted to external taxes, and object to the right of Parliament only in laying internal taxes; now can you show, that there is any kind of difference between the two taxes to the colony on which they may be laid?

A. I think the difference is very great. An *external* tax is a duty laid on commodities imported; that duty is added to the first cost and other charges on the commodity, and, when it is offered to sale, makes a part of the price. If the people do not like it at that price, they refuse it; they are not obliged to pay it. But an *internal* tax is forced from the people without their consent, if not laid by their own representatives. The Stamp Act says, we shall have no commerce, make no exchange of property with each other, neither purchase, nor grant, nor recover debts; we shall neither marry nor make our wills, unless we pay such and such sums; and thus it is intended to extort our money from us, or ruin us by the consequences of refusing to pay for it.

Q. But supposing the external tax or duty to be laid on the necessaries of life, imported into your colony, will not that be the same thing in its effects as an internal tax?

A. I do not know a single article imported into the northern colonies, but what they can either do without or make themselves. . . .

Q. Considering the resolution of Parliament, *as to the right,* do you think, if the Stamp Act is repealed, that the North Americans will be satisfied?

A. I believe they will.

Q. Why do you think so?

A. I think the resolutions of *right* will give them very little concern, if they are never attempted to be carried into practice. The colonies will probably consider themselves in the same situation, in that respect, with Ireland; they know you claim the same right with regard to Ireland, but you never exercise it, and they may believe you never will exercise it in the colonies, any more than in Ireland, unless on some very extraordinary occasion.

Q. But who are to be the judges of that extraordinary occasion? Is not the Parliament?

A. Though the Parliament may judge of the occasion, the people will think it can never exercise such right, till representatives from the colonies are admitted into Parliament, and that, whenever the occasion arises, representatives *will* be ordered. . . .

Q. Did the Americans ever dispute the controlling power of Parliament to regulate the commerce?

A. No.

Q. Can any thing less than a military force carry the Stamp Act into execution?

A. I do not see how a military force can be applied to that purpose.

Q. Why may it not?

A. Suppose a military force sent into America, they will find nobody in arms; what are they then to do? They cannot force a man to take stamps who chooses to do without them. They will not find a rebellion; they may indeed make one.

Q. If the act is not repealed, what do you think will be the consequences?

A. A total loss of the respect and affection the people of America bear to this country, and of all the commerce that depends upon that respect and affection.

Q. How can the commerce be affected?

A. You will find, that if the act is not repealed, they will take very little of your manufactures in a short time.

Q. Is it in their power to do without them?

A. I think they may very well do without them.

Q. Is it their interest not to take them?

A. The goods they take from Britain are either necessaries, mere conveniences, or superfluities. The first, as cloth, &c., with a little industry they can make at home; the second they can do without, till they are able to provide them among themselves; and the last, which are much the greatest part, they will strike off immediately. They are mere articles of fashion, purchased and consumed, because the fashion in a respected country; but will now be detested and rejected. The people have already struck off, by general agreement, the use of all goods fashionable in mournings, and many thousand pounds' worth are sent back as unsalable.

Q. Is it their interest to make cloth at home?

A. I think they may at present get it cheaper from Britain; I mean, of the same fineness and neatness of workmanship; but, when one considers other circumstances, the restraints on their trade, and the difficulty of making remittances, it is their interest to make every thing.

Q. Suppose an act of internal regulations connected with a tax; how would they receive it?

A. I think it would be objected to.

Q. Then no regulation with a tax would be submitted to?

A. Their opinion is, that, when aids to the crown are wanted, they are to be asked of the several assemblies, according to the old established usage; who will, as they have always done, grant them freely. And that their money ought not to be given away, without their consent, by persons at a distance, unacquainted with their circumstances and abilities. The granting aids to the crown is the only means they have of recommending themselves to their sovereign; and they think it extremely hard and unjust, that a body of men, in which they have no representatives, should make a merit to itself of giving and granting what is not its own, but theirs; and deprive them of a right they esteem of the utmost value and importance, as it is the security of all their other rights.

Q. But is not the post-office, which they have long received, a tax as well as a regulation?

A. No; the money paid for the postage of a letter is not of the nature of a tax; it is merely a *quantum meruit* for a service done; no person is compellable to pay the money if he does not choose to receive the service. A man may still, as before the act, send his letter by a servant, a special messenger, or a friend, if he thinks it cheaper or safer.

Q. But do they not consider the regulations of the post-office, by the act of last year, as a tax?

A. By the regulations of last year the rate of postage was generally abated near thirty per cent through all America; they certainly cannot consider such an abatement *as a tax*.

Q. If an excise was laid by Parliament, which they might likewise avoid paying, by not consuming the articles excised, would they then not object to it?

A. They would certainly object to it, as an excise is unconnected with any service done, and is merely an aid, which they think ought to be asked of them, and granted by them, if they are to pay it; and can be granted for them by no others whatsoever, whom they have not empowered for that purpose.

Q. You say they do not object to the right of Parliament, in laying duties on goods to be paid on their importation; now, is there any kind of difference between a duty on the importation of goods, and an excise on their consumption?

A. Yes, a very material one; an excise, for the reasons I have just mentioned, they think you can have no right to lay within their country. But the sea is yours; you maintain, by your fleets, the safety of navigation in it, and keep it clear of pirates; you may have, therefore, a natural and equitable right to some toll or duty on merchandises carried through that part of your dominions, towards defraying the expense you are at in ships to maintain the safety of that carriage.

Q. Does this reasoning hold in the case of a duty laid on the produce of their lands exported? And would they not then object to such a duty?

A. If it tended to make the produce so much dearer abroad, as to lessen the demand for it, to be sure they would object to such a duty; not to your right of laying it, but they would complain of it as a burden, and petition you to lighten it. . . .

Q. What are the body of the people in the colonies?

A. They are farmers, husbandmen, or planters.

Q. Would they suffer the produce of their lands to rot?

A. No; but they would not raise so much. They would manufacture more, and plough less.

Q. Would they live without the administration of justice in civil matters, and suffer all the inconveniencies of such a situation for any considerable time, rather than take the stamps, supposing the stamps were protected by a sufficient force, where every one might have them?

A. I think the supposition impracticable, that the stamps should be so protected as that every one might have them. The act requires sub-distributors to be appointed in every county town, district, and village, and they would be necessary. But the principal distributors, who were to have had a considerable profit on the whole, have not thought it worth while to continue in the office; and I think it impossible to find sub-distributors fit to be trusted, who, for the trifling profit that must come to their share, would incur the odium, and run the hazard, that would attend it; and, if they could be found, I think it impracticable to protect the stamps in so many distant and remote places.

Q. But in places where they could be protected, would not the people use them, rather than remain in such a situation, unable to obtain any right, or recover by law any debt?

A. It is hard to say what they would do. I can only judge what other people will think, and how they will act, by what I feel within myself. I have a great many debts due to me in America, and I had rather they should remain unrecoverable by any law, than submit to the Stamp Act. They will be debts of honor. It is my opinion the people will either continue in that situation, or find some way to extricate themselves; perhaps by generally agreeing to proceed in the courts without stamps. . . .

Q. If the Stamp Act should be repealed, would not the Americans think they could oblige the Parliament to repeal every external tax law now in force?

A. It is hard to answer questions of what people at such a distance will think.

Q. But what do you imagine they will think were the motives of repealing the act?

A. I suppose they will think, that it was repealed from a conviction of its inexpediency; and they will rely upon it, that, while the same inexpediency subsists, you will never attempt to make such another.

Q. What do you mean by its inexpediency?

A. I mean its inexpediency on several accounts; the poverty and inability of those who were to pay the tax, the general discontent it has occasioned, and the impracticability of enforcing it.

Q. If the Act should be repealed, and the legislature should show its resentment of the opposers of the Stamp Act, would the colonies acquiesce in the authority of the legislature? What is your opinion they would do?

A. I don't doubt at all, that if the legislature repeal the Stamp Act, the colonies will acquiesce in the authority. . . .

Q. But suppose Great Britain should be engaged in a war in Europe, would North America contribute to the support of it?

A. I do think they would as far as their circumstances would permit. They consider themselves as a part of the British empire, and as having one common interest with it; they may be looked on here as foreigners, but they do not consider themselves as such. They are zealous for the honor and prosperity of this nation; and while they are well used, will always be ready to support it, as far as their little power goes. In 1739 they were called upon to assist in the expedition against Carthagena, and they sent three thousand men to join your army. It is true, Carthagena is in America, but as remote from the northern colonies, as if it had been in Europe. They make no distinction of wars, as to their duty of assisting in them.

I know the last war is commonly spoke of here, as entered into for the defence, or for the sake, of the people of America. I think it is quite misunderstood. It began about the limits between Canada and Nova Scotia; about territories to which the *crown* indeed laid claim, but which were not claimed by any British *colony;* none of the lands had been granted to any colonist; we had therefore no particular concern or interest in that dispute. As to the Ohio, the contest there began about your right of trading in the Indian country, a right you had by the treaty of Utrecht, which the French infringed; they seized the traders and their goods, which were your manufactures; they took a fort which a company of your merchants, and their factors, and correspondents, had erected there to secure that trade. Braddock was sent with an army to retake that fort, (which was looked on here as another encroachment on the King's territory,) and to protect your trade. It was not till after his defeat, that the colonies were attacked. They were before in perfect peace with both French and Indians; the troops were not, therefore, sent for their defence.

The trade with the Indians, though carried on in America, is not an American interest. The people of America are chiefly farmers and planters; scarce any thing that they raise or produce is an article of commerce with the Indians. The Indian trade is a British interest; it is carried on with British manufactures, for the profit of British merchants and manufacturers; therefore the war, as it commenced for the defence of territories of the crown (the property of no American), and for the defence of a trade purely British, was really a British war, and yet the people of America made no scruple of contributing their utmost towards carrying it on, and bringing it to a happy conclusion.

Q. Do you think, then, that the taking possession of the King's territorial rights, and strengthening the frontiers, is not an American interest?

A. Not particularly, but conjointly a British and an American interest.

Q. You will not deny, that the preceding war, the war with Spain, was entered into for the sake of America; was it not occasioned by captures made in the American seas?

A. Yes; captures of ships carrying on the British trade there, with British manufactures. . . .

Q. Do you think the assemblies have a right to levy money on the subject there, to grant to the crown?

A. I certainly think so; they have always done it.

Q. Are they acquainted with the declaration of rights? And do they know, that, by that statute, money is not to be raised on the subject but by consent of Parliament?

A. They are very well acquainted with it.

Q. How then can they think they have a right to levy money for the crown, or for any other than local purposes?

A. They understand that clause to relate to subjects only within the realm; that no money can be levied on them for the crown, but by consent of Parliament. The colonies are not supposed to be within the realm; they have assemblies of their own, which are their parliaments, and they are, in that respect, in the same situation with Ireland. When money is to be raised for the crown upon the subject in Ireland, or in the colonies, the consent is given in the Parliament of Ireland, or in the assemblies of the colonies. They think the Parliament of Great Britain cannot properly give that consent, till it has representatives from America; for the petition of right expressly says, it is to be by common consent in Parliament; and the people of America have no representatives in Parliament, to make a part of that common consent.

Q. If the Stamp Act should be repealed, and an act should pass, ordering the assemblies of the colonies to indemnify the sufferers by the riots, would they obey it?

A. That is a question I cannot answer.

Q. Suppose the King should require the colonies to grant a revenue, and the Parliament should be against their doing it, do they think they can grant a revenue to the King, without the consent of the Parliament of Great Britain?

A. That is a deep question. As to my own opinion, I should think myself at liberty to do it, and should do it, if I liked the occasion. . . .

Q. Did the Secretary of State ever write for money for the crown?

A. The requisitions have been to raise, clothe, and pay men, which cannot be done without money.

Q. Would they grant money alone, if called on?

A. In my opinion they would, money as well as men, when they have money, or can make it.

Q. If the Parliament should repeal the Stamp Act, will the assembly of Pennsylvania rescind their resolutions?

A. I think not.

Q. Before there was any thought of the Stamp Act, did they wish for a representation in Parliament?

A. No.

Q. Don't you know, that there is, in the Pennsylvania charter, an express reservation of the right of Parliament to lay taxes there?

A. I know there is a clause in the charter, by which the King grants, that he will levy no taxes on the inhabitants, unless it be with the consent of the assembly, or by an act of Parliament.

Q. How, then, could the assembly of Pennsylvania assert, that laying a tax on them by the Stamp Act was an infringement of their rights?

A. They understand it thus; by the same charter, and otherwise, they are entitled to all the privileges and liberties of Englishmen; they find in the Great Charters, and the Petition and Declaration of Rights, that one of the privileges of English subjects is, that they are not to be taxed but by their common consent; they have therefore relied upon it, from the first settlement of the province, that the Parliament never would, nor could, by color of that clause in the charter, assume a right of taxing them, till it had qualified itself to exercise such right, by admitting representatives from the people to be taxed, who ought to make a part of that common consent.

Q. Are there any words in the charter that justify that construction?

A. "The common rights of Englishmen," as declared by *Magna Charta,* and the Petition of Right, all justify it.

Q. Does the distinction between internal and external taxes exist in the words of the charter?

A. No, I believe not.

Q. Then may they not, by the same interpretation, object to the Parliament's right of external taxation?

A. They never have hitherto. Many arguments have been lately used here to show them, that there is no difference, and that, if you have no right to tax them internally, you have no right to tax them externally, or make any other law to bind them. At present they do not reason so; but in time they may possibly be convinced by these arguments.

Q. Do not the resolutions of the Pennsylvania assemblies say, "all taxes"?

A. If they do, they mean only internal taxes; the same words have not always the same meaning here and in the colonies. By taxes, they mean internal taxes; by duties, they mean customs; these are the ideas of the language . . .

Q. What used to be the pride of the Americans?
A. To indulge in the fashions and manufactures of Great Britain.
Q. What is now their pride?
A. To wear their old clothes over again, till they can make new ones.
Withdrew.

## 8. PARLIAMENT'S IMMEDIATE RESOLUTION OF THE IMPERIAL CRISIS, MARCH 1766

On January 14, 1766, a highly animated debate began in Parliament on whether to repeal the Stamp Act. It was two-pronged in nature, for while the act itself had produced serious financial losses on both sides of the Atlantic, most members of Parliament resolutely refused either to give in to the colonies and the mob violence perpetrated against British customs agents and would-be stamp agents or, even more staunchly, to concede to the constitutional claims of the colonial assemblies or the Stamp Act Congress regarding three closely related matters: that Parliament had no right to tax the colonies, or to replace common-law jury trials with admiralty courts that operated without juries and under civil (Roman) law, or to legislate for the colonies regarding matters internal to each of them.[76] All in all, what was at stake for the British was Parliament's conjoined sovereignty over the empire; for the colonists, the proper relationship between the king and the colonies, with a limited imperial role, if any, for Parliament. Accordingly, and not altogether surprisingly, Parliament was willing to go to war to defend the post-1688 settlement and its ascendancy over both king and colonies—in essence, to defend the British Constitution and even the nation. The colonists, even if inadvertently, had ratcheted up tensions and made the situation far less tractable, with their petitions embodying rights claims of various kinds.[77] Making repeal of the Stamp Act still more difficult was the fragility of the Rockingham administration's (ultimately short-lived) coalition, made up in part of vestiges of the last two administrations and a sometimes-divided group of supporters.[78]

One way out of the quandary for the government was to repeal the disliked Stamp Act on economic and prudential grounds while simultaneously passing legislation that would affirm the sovereignty of Parliament and its legitimate power to legislate for the North American colonies, while making that power a matter of right. The language in regard to taxation was intentionally vague because of Pitt and his supporters' concern regarding the unconstitutionality of Parliament's taxation of the colonists (though not of its ability to legislate more generally), and because Parliament's claimed right to legislate was more essential than its right to levy direct taxes and would be the right that Parliament refused to surrender long after taxation no longer was an issue.[79] Thus, the Repealing Act explained the need to rescind the Stamp Act: "said act would be attended with many inconveniencies, and may be productive of consequences greatly detrimental to the commercial interests of these kingdoms." In the Declaratory Act, however, Parliament provocatively reminded the colonists that it "had, hath, and of right ought to have, full power and authority to make laws and statutes of sufficient force and validity to bind the colonies and people of *America,* subjects of the crown of *Great Britain,* in all cases whatsoever." Those words would, over the next ten years, come to enjoy a certain infamy.

In spite of the colonies' similarly acute concern about asserting and protecting their constitutional rights, Franklin had accurately predicted their attitude in his parliamentary testimony: "Resolutions of [parliamentary] right will give them very little concern, if they are never [again] attempted to be carried into practice. The colonies will probably consider themselves in the same situation, in that respect, with Ireland; they know you [Parliament] claim the same right with regard to Ireland, but you never exercise it." Parliament too had Ireland in mind, for it had a precedent to which to turn, the Declaratory Act of 1719/20, in which Parliament had also enunciated its absolute right to legislate for all British dominions, including its colonies. The Declaratory Act of 1766 was a near-verbatim copy of the earlier Irish one, with each meant to bind as subordinate a particular British colony under a sovereign, even if purportedly benign, British Parliament. The most significant difference between the two acts was that Ireland was labeled as subordinate "unto and dependent upon the imperial crown of *Great Britain,*" while the North American colonies were considered "subordinate unto, and dependent upon the imperial crown and parliament of *Great Britain.*" Parliament, clearly, in the intervening forty years had come to see itself as at least equal to, and possibly superior to, the British Crown.[80]

In its Declaratory Act, Parliament concludes that "all resolutions, votes, orders, and proceedings, in any of the said colonies or plantations, whereby the power and authority of the parliament of *Great Britain* to make laws and statutes as aforesaid, is denied, or drawn into question, are, and are hereby declared to be, utterly null and void to all intents and purposes whatsoever." This was, needless to say, an emphatic statement of Parliament's sovereign powers. Americans wrongly dismissed the claims as face-saving window dressing, but as Samuel Adams suggested in a letter of December 1766 (document 8.3), not all of them misunderstood how important this issue was to the British parliamentary majority.

## 8.1

 AN ACT REPEALING THE STAMP ACT, MARCH 18, 1766

Danby Pickering, ed., *The Statutes at Large from the Magna Charta to the End of the Eleventh Parliament of Great Britain* (Cambridge: John Archdeacon, 1775), 27:19.

*An act to repeal an act made in the last session of parliament, intituled,* An act for granting and applying certain stamp duties, and other duties, in the *British* colonies and plantations in *America,* towards further defraying the expences of defending, protecting, and securing the same; and for amending such parts of the several acts of parliament relating to the trade and revenues of the said colonies and plantations, as direct the manner of determining and recovering the penalties and forfeitures therein mentioned.

WHEREAS *an act was passed in the last session of Parliament, intitled,* An act for granting and applying certain stamp duties, and other duties in the *British* colonies and plantations in *America,* towards further defraying the expences of defending, protecting, and securing the same; and for amending such parts of the several acts of parliament relating to the trade and revenues of the said colonies and plantations, as direct the manner of determining and recovering the penalties and forfeitures therein mentioned: *and whereas the continuance of the said act would be attended with many inconveniencies, and may be productive of consequences greatly detrimental to the commercial interests of these kingdoms;* may it therefore please your most excellent Majesty, that it may be enacted; and be it enacted by the King's most excellent majesty, by and with the advice and consent of the lords spiritual and temporal, and commons, in this present parliament assembled, and by the authority of the same, That from and after the first day of *May,* one thousand seven hundred and sixty six, the above-mentioned act, and the several matters and things therein contained, shall be, and is and are hereby repealed and made void to all intents and purposes whatsoever.

## 8.2

 DECLARATORY ACT, MARCH 18, 1766

Danby Pickering, ed., *The Statutes at Large from the Magna Charta to the End of the Eleventh Parliament of Great Britain* (Cambridge: John Archdeacon, 1775), 27:19–20.

An act for the better securing the dependency of his Majesty's dominions in America upon the crown and parliament of Great Britain.

WHEREAS several of the houses of representatives in his Majesty's colonies and plantations in America, have of late, against law, claimed to themselves, or to the general assemblies of the same, the sole and exclusive right of imposing duties and taxes upon his Majesty's subjects in the said colonies and plantations; and have, in pursuance of such claim, passed certain votes, resolutions, and orders, derogatory to the legislative authority of parliament, and inconsistent with the dependency of the said colonies and plantations upon the crown of Great Britain: may it therefore please your most excellent Majesty, that it may be declared; and be it declared by the King's most excellent majesty, by and with the advice and consent of the lords spiritual and temporal, and commons, in this present parliament assembled, and by the authority of the same, That the said colonies and plantations in America have been, are, and of right ought to be, subordinate unto, and dependent upon the imperial crown and Parliament of Great Britain; and that the King's majesty, by and with the advice and consent of the lords spiritual and temporal, and commons of Great Britain, in parliament assembled, had, hath, and of right ought to have, full power and authority to make laws and statutes of sufficient force and validity to bind the colonies and people of America, subjects of the crown of Great Britain, in all cases whatsoever.

II. And be it further declared and enacted by the authority aforesaid, That all resolutions, votes, orders, and proceedings, in any of the said colonies or plantations, whereby the power and authority of the parliament of *Great Britain*, to make laws and statutes as aforesaid, is denied, or drawn into question, are, and are hereby declared to be, utterly null and void to all intents and purposes whatsoever.

## 8.3

 SAMUEL ADAMS TO CHRISTOPHER GADSDEN,
DECEMBER 11, 1766

In 1765, shortly before the death of Oxenbridge Thacher, the Massachusetts attorney who drafted the original address in opposition to the Sugar Act of 1764, Samuel Adams was selected to be his replacement as one of Boston's delegates to the Massachusetts lower house, the General Court. Adams, who was born to a successful brewing and merchant family, was a distant cousin of John Adams, the second president of the United States.[81] He himself, however, was a failed businessman and tax collector who found his true calling as a political activist and the father, and even mastermind, of the opposition movement that culminated in war and independence. Adams was on good terms with the Loyal Nine of Boston, which was to become the Sons of Liberty, but he was not a member himself. The recipient of the following letter, Gadsden, was a prominent, influential, and comparably radical South Carolina merchant who, with reason, future historians would label the "Samuel Adams of the South."[82] Their common friend, the Boston radical James Otis, Jr., described Gadsden as "a zealous Assertor of the most important Cause in which the British Colonys were then struggling."

Adams and Gadsden looked favorably on independence earlier than most. They believed that they confronted a ministerial conspiracy and thus welcomed the Stamp Act, for by helping foster opposition movements among the colonists, it began the process of unifying otherwise politically separate, even frequently feuding, colonies. Indeed, Gadsden, after returning from the Stamp Act Congress, wrote to Charles Garth, the South Carolina agent in London, that "there ought to be no New England men, no New Yorker, etc., known on the Continent, but all of us Americans."[83] And unlike most who had reacted to the Repealing and Declaratory Acts, as Franklin had predicted, by celebrating the first and ignoring the second, Adams continued to be apprehensive. Regarding the fragile distinction between external and internal taxes, to say nothing of that between taxation and legislation more broadly, he presciently laid out a troubling scenario: if "some time hereafter under the Pretext of Regulating Trade only, a revenue should be designd to be raisd out of the Colonys, would it signify any thing whether it be called a Stamp Act or an Act for the Regulation of the Trade of America"? Similarly, again with foresight, he warned of "an Act of Parliamt [the Quartering Acts of 1765–66] I have lately seen, wherein the Govr & Council of any Province where any of his Majestys Troops may happen to be are enjoyned to make certain Provision for them at the Expense of the People of such Province. Tell me Sir whether this is not taxing the Colonys as effectually as the Stamp Act." Indeed, as New York discovered between 1766 and 1768, it was a tax that could lead to the suspension of a colonial legislature. Adams may have been too right in suggesting that "either we have complaind without Reason, or we have still reason to complain." Possibly, ironically, both may have been true.

*The Writings of Samuel Adams,* ed. Harry Alonzo Cushing (New York and London: G. P. Putnam's Sons, 1904–8), 1:108–11.

BOSTON Decr 11 1766

SIR

I have no other Apology for writing a familiar Epistle to a Gentleman perfectly a Stranger to me than to gratify the request of my good Friend Mr John Hurd who has promisd to deliver this Letter with his own hand—to him I must refer you, & beg you candidly to receive the best Excuse he can make. I have indeed often heard, another of my valuable friends mention you with great Respect: This Gentleman, Mr Otis, had the pleasure of sitting with you in the late Congress at New York, & he has frequently told me that you were a zealous Assertor of the most important Cause in which the British Colonys were then struggling. Happy was it for us that a Union was then formd, upon which in my humble Opinion the Fate of the Colonys turnd. What a Blessing to us has the Stamp Act eventually, or to use a trifling word virtually provd, which was calculated to enslave & ruin us. When the Colonys saw the common Danger they at the same time saw their mutual Dependence & naturally calld in the Assistance of each other, & I dare say such Friendships & Connections are establishd between them, as shall for the future deter the most virulent Enemy from making another open Attempt upon their Rights as Men & Subjects. But is there no Reason to fear that the Libertys of the Colonys may be infringd in a less observable manner? The Stamp Act was like the sword that Nero wishd for, to have decollated the Roman People at a stroke, or like Jobs Sea monster in the heightned Language of Young, "who sinks a River, & who thirsts again." The Sight of such an Enemy at a distance is formidable, while the lurking Serpent lies conceald, & not noticd by the unwary Passenger, darts its fatal Venom. It is necessary then that each Colony should be awake & upon its Guard—you may ask me what is the Danger—I answer none from His present Majesty & the Parliamt, in their Intention—yet such is human Frailty that "the best may err sometimes"—and consider Sir we are remote from the national Parliamt, & unrepresented. You are sensible that what are called Acts of Trade sensibly affect the Colonys. May not such Acts be made thro the Inadvertency of our friends or for want of suitable Intelligence from the Colonys, as may not only injure their Trade but wound their Libertys—suppose for Instance that some time hereafter under the Pretext of Regulating Trade only, a revenue should be designd to be raisd out of the Colonys, would it signify any thing whether it be called a Stamp Act or an Act for the Regulation of the Trade of America. I wish there was a Union and a Correspondence kept up among the merchts thro'out the Continent, but I am still upon the Libertys of the Colonys. I should tell you what perhaps you know already was I to mention an Act of Parliamt I have lately seen, wherein the Govr & Council of any Province where any of his Majestys Troops may happen to be are enjoyned to make certain Provision for them at the Expense of the People of such Province. Tell me Sir whether this is not taxing the Colonys as effectually as the Stamp Act & if so, either we have complaind without Reason, or we have still reason to complain. I have heard that George Grenville was told to his face that he missd it in his politicks, for he should have stationd a sufficient number of Troops in America before he sent the Stamp Act among them. Had that been the Case it is possible your Congress mt have been turnd out of Doors. New York has had regular troops among them for some months. I never could hear a reason given to my Satisfaction why they were orderd at least to remain there so long; perhaps I am captious—however I always lookd upon a standing Army especially in a time of peace not only a Disturbance but in every respect dangerous to civil Community. Surely then we cannot consent to their quartering among us, & how hard is it for us to be obligd to pay our money to subsist them. If a number shd happen to come into a Province thro

Necessity & stand in Need of Supplys, as is the Case at present here, is it not a Disgrace to us to suppose we should be so wanting in humanity, or in regard to our Sovereign as to refuse to grant him the aid with our free Consent?

I feel a Disposition to hint many things more; but I am at present very much streightened for time & besides I am affraid you will think me a very troublesome Correspondent. I shall therefore write no more till I am encouragd by a Letter from you which will very much oblige

Sr yr hume Servt

# ACT II

## RESPONSE TO THE COERCIVE ACTS, 1774

After the repeal on March 18, 1766, of the Stamp Act and the passage of the Declaratory Act, and with the modification of other trade laws later that year, the Imperial Crisis ebbed and flowed during the next seven years without the perceived need in most of the colonies, until 1774, for calling another intercolonial or continental congress (many in Massachusetts disagreed). The dominant event in the colonial-British relationship during those years was the passage in June 1767 of the Townshend Acts under the administration headed by Lord Chatham, with Charles Townshend serving as his chancellor of the exchequer. Townshend was concerned, as his predecessor, George Grenville, had been, to establish beyond constitutional and practical question Parliament's sovereign right to legislate for and raise revenues in the colonies. Accordingly, in keeping with a distinction that some colonists themselves had emphasized during the Stamp Act crisis, namely, the distinction between "external" (offshore) and "internal" (domestic) taxation, Townshend proposed a series of new taxes with the declared goal of raising revenues that would all be "external," most importantly on colonial imports of glass, lead, paint, paper, and tea.

These tax revenues were to be used in the colonies—including those newly acquired—for defense and for "defraying the charge of the administration of justice, and the support of civil government." Additionally, to provide for more efficient collection of the new duties, Townshend's legislation provided that superior or supreme court justices would be permitted to issue writs of assistance; established additional vice-admiralty courts; and created the American Board of Commissioners of the Customs in Boston, which would be directly responsible to the British Treasury Board. Resistance to the legislation through nonimportation agreements, followed by the substantial repeal of the law in 1770, and the subsequent collapse of the nonimportation plans during the following year, dominated imperial relations over the next several years, 1767–71.

Thus, by the end of 1767, after receipt of the news of the passage of the Townshend Acts on June 29, 1767, the capital and port cities of New England adopted nonimportation agreements. John Dickinson had, in November, begun publishing what would become one of the best-selling pamphlets of the period, his *Letters from a Farmer in Pennsylvania,* in the *Pennsylvania Chronicle.* Resistance ramped up still more in 1768 with Samuel Adams' authoring a circular letter to be distributed throughout the colonies under the auspices of the Massachusetts General Court. The missive was condemned by the British secretary of state for the colonies, Lord Hillsborough, who demanded that if the Massachusetts General Court did not rescind it, the governor, Francis Bernard, was to dissolve the General Court—which he did on July 1. Continued agitation in Boston, including mob assaults on British customs agents at home and work, and on seized shipping, led in October 1768 to two regiments of British regulars being stationed in Boston. By early 1769, in almost every major port city in the colonies, merchants had adopted nonimportation agreements to be kept in place until the Townshend Acts were repealed.

In May 1769, the other hotbed of opposition, Virginia, adopted a stinging resolve asserting that the sole right of taxing Virginians lay with the governor and colony's provincial legislature while also castigating the British ministry for its attempt to quash the Massachusetts and Virginia circular letters from the previous year. Additionally, the Virginia legislature condemned the parliamentary proposal that would have permitted North American colonists to be brought to Great Britain for trial under an antiquated act of Henry VIII. Of possibly more importance for the next Continental Congress, which met five years later, Virginia adopted a frequently copied model of association that banned the importation of duty-laden British goods, slaves, and certain luxury items. Within a few months, most of the southern colonies had adopted their own associations or endorsed that of Virginia. Thus, by the end of 1769, nonimportation agreements, or associations, had been entered into by the merchants or subjects in every colony except New Hampshire, Pennsylvania (in particular the merchants of Philadelphia), and New Jersey. The effects on British trade were sizable, with colonial imports from Britain falling "from £2,157,218 in 1768 to £1,336,122 in 1769."[1]

By 1770, these economic pressures began to take their toll on the British government, led by the Duke of Grafton. He was replaced as the king's first minister by Lord North, who served in that position until 1782 and the end of the American crisis. It was clear to North and his administration that enforcing the Townshend duties was an unsustainable proposition, at least without going to war, which the British government was not in any manner prepared to do. Jack Greene observes that fears of a continuing crisis, which might lead to a questioning of the very structure of the imperial constitution, prompted North to resist "the impulse to take sweeping coercive measures against the colonies during the crisis over the Townshend Acts."[2] Still, the North government feared that a repeal of the Townshend taxes would be interpreted in the colonies as a sign of weakness, as many members of Parliament believed had been true of the repeal of the Stamp Act. He thus urged only a partial repeal, along with a promise that Parliament would issue no new taxes. On April 12, 1770, the king assented to the repeal of all the Townshend duties except that on tea, and when the news of this reached the colonies, in all of them except Massachusetts, there was a general and collective sigh of relief and an abandonment of nonimportation agreements and associations.[3]

But well before news of the repeal reached the colonies, tensions were running high between activists in Boston and British soldiers stationed there. On March 5, a scuffle broke out that quickly worsened into something approaching a riot. Finally, around nine that night, a sentry under duress called others to his aid, and the responding body of troops, attacked by the mob with rocks, pavement stones, and balls of ice, fired into it, killing three outright and wounding two others, who later died. The event became known as the Boston Massacre. In the end, six soldiers were indicted; four were acquitted and two found guilty of manslaughter, branded on the hand, and released.

All in all, though, a general calm returned to the colonies for three years after repeal of almost all the Townshend duties, with only tea and sugar continuing to be lightly taxed. As Greene suggests, "Parliament's repeal of most of the Townshend duties in 1770 and the rapid subsidence of overt colonial opposition to Parliament over the next three years provided dramatic testimony to the" shared hope on both sides of the Atlantic for reconciliation.[4]

The heightened tensions between the British Parliament and the colonies that had so disturbed imperial relations during the previous six years fell into a temporary hiatus, and the colonial-British relationship returned to something closer to a traditional pattern of bickering "over the relative balance between [the] prerogative power" vested in the king's servants—the royal governors and his Privy Council—and the colonies' rights advanced by their legislatures. Conflicts between royal prerogatives and colonial rights, which "had been an endemic feature of metropolitan-colonial relations ever since the middle of the seventeenth century," returned to the fore after having "been subordinated to the new and more pressing debate over the extent of Parliament's colonial authority" in the previous six years.[5] Such differences were particularly acute in Massachusetts, where the British ministry had begun paying the salaries of Superior Court judges from customs revenues and where the American-born royal governor, Thomas Hutchinson, battled Boston radicals, in particular James Otis,

Jr., Samuel Adams, and Joseph Warren. Late in 1772, Adams began to resurrect Massachusetts' committees of correspondence and printed, during this period of quiescence and a personal loss of popularity, "A State of the Rights of the Colonists," in which Adams fanned the dying embers of opposition to the British administration by defending colonial rights—as was rarely done—on naturalistic grounds.[6]

Adams' efforts bore fruit, and by the end of 1773 committees of correspondence in Massachusetts and in other colonies had begun to organize. Virginia's efforts were spearheaded by Patrick Henry and Richard Henry Lee, two southerners who shared Adams' republican sympathies, though not his Reformed Protestant, New England perspective. Their efforts, which continued over the next three years, were facilitated by a Parliament that never failed to accommodate the radicals' organizing needs. Passage on April 27, 1773, of the Tea Act (to take effect on May 10), by which Parliament tried to assist the nearly bankrupt East India Company, allowed for the remission of British duties on tea exported by the East India Company from Britain to the American colonies. Although the old Townshend tea duty of three pence per pound was still in force, the act allowed the company's agents or consignees in the colonies, with their newly awarded "drawback" on British duties, to undersell other colonial merchants, who might be forced out of this line of trade, and to undercut even well-established smugglers, men like John Hancock, who bought their tea from illegal sources, frequently in Holland. In sum, the renewed imperial tensions resulted not from additional taxes—those in effect were six years old—but from Britain having effectively reduced taxes on East India Company tea in transit and from the continued use of the older tax.

It was the intrusive character of this parliamentary legislation that raised colonial ire, especially among merchants in Boston, New York, Philadelphia, and Charleston, cities where half a million pounds of tea was to be delivered. The new crisis, which rapidly returned the conflict between the British Parliament and the colonies to center stage, took a decisive turn in early December when a standoff developed between Governor Hutchinson and radical forces in Boston (Samuel Adams and friends). Adams and the Sons of Liberty wanted to force the first of three cargo ships, the *Dartmouth,* to return to England without having paid the Townshend duties owed on its shipment of tea and, thus, without having unloaded its tea. On December 16, 1773, the tea aboard the *Dartmouth* became liable to seizure for nonpayment of duties, and that evening, after being informed of Hutchinson's refusal to allow the ship to depart, Adams directed a group of men disguised as Mohawk Native Americans (except for one man, Dr. Thomas Young) to board the three ships (the *Eleanor* and the *Beaver* arrived after the *Dartmouth*) and, working through the night, to dump all of their tea (342 chests of it) into Boston Harbor. The protest came to be called the Boston Tea Party. In a series of events in which action led to reaction, the Imperial Crisis entered its final phase: radical colonists and recalcitrant, proud, and dogmatic majorities in

Parliament inadvertently worked together to render ultimately unsolvable the difficult constitutional issues separating Britain and her major continental North American colonies.

In 1774, additional tea shipments to New York were similarly consigned to the sea, again by colonists disguised as Native Americans. Many members of Parliament became convinced that they had been overly indulgent with the colonists, in particular by yielding to public pressure and repealing the Stamp Act. Thus, when Parliament met on March 7, 1774, a rising tide of anger and resentment led to the passage of the four Coercive Acts, which did so much to shape imperial relations over the next several years and, ultimately, to independence being declared. In particular, Parliament sought to punish Massachusetts and, especially, Boston for their roles in the Tea Party, but still more for Samuel Adams and colleagues' continual fueling of the Imperial Crisis over the past decade.

Accordingly, by the end of March the first of four Coercive Acts, the Boston Port Bill, which moved the Customs House to Salem and closed the Port of Boston to most shipping until the East India Company was compensated for the destroyed tea, had been approved. In May, Parliament passed two related acts. The Massachusetts Government Act annulled much of the Massachusetts Charter of 1691. All members of the Council (the upper house), previously chosen by the lower house, were thenceforth to be appointed by the king. Additionally, the governor was to appoint the attorney general, inferior court judges, sheriffs, and justices of the peace, and to nominate the chief justice and Superior Court judges, who were then to be selected by the king. Of particular importance, juries were to be summoned by royally appointed sheriffs rather than chosen by town selectmen. This threatened to change the makeup of grand and petit juries, which had been so protective of Boston radicals and smugglers. Finally, the act provided that town meetings were to be prohibited except for the annual ones at which legislative representatives were to be chosen. The Administration of Justice Act, also passed in May 1774, protected crown officials from prosecution before hostile juries in Massachusetts. Upon the sworn statement of the governor that an official had been indicted for performing an act attendant upon putting down a riot or collecting treasury revenues, trials could be transferred to another colony or to Britain. In June, Parliament passed the fourth of the coercive measures, the Quartering Act, which made it mandatory for all colonial assemblies to provide housing and supplies for British regulars (which colonists in Boston were beginning to see as an occupying force)—an earlier quartering act had been allowed to lapse in 1770. Colonial legislatures were, thus, again to provide British troops with prescribed provisions and to quarter them at their expense in taverns and deserted buildings—but now in occupied dwellings as well.[7]

A third act approved in late May, the Quebec Act, was regarded, inaccurately, by the colonists as a fifth "Intolerable" Act. Building upon the king's Proclamation

Concerning America (October 7, 1763), it provided for a permanent civil government in Canada, which had been ruled by improvised measures since the end of the Seven Years' War. In keeping with extant French legal and political traditions in Canada, legislative authority was to be centralized and vested in a council appointed by the king; its acts were, like those in the "English" colonies, subject to royal veto. Most matters that extended beyond a narrow range of local concerns were to be referred to Parliament. In keeping with the French legal tradition (civil or Roman law), as with the admiralty, military, ecclesiastical, and equity courts in Britain, cases were to be tried without a jury. Far more troubling to the residents in the "English" colonies, Roman Catholics were to be tolerated, and their church and its priests protected; that was not the case in other colonies or Britain. Even less acceptable to future Americans was the extension of Quebec's borders down to the Mississippi and Ohio Rivers, areas where land speculators from Massachusetts, Connecticut, and Virginia possessed massive land claims, often of questionable legality. The border extensions, along with the prohibition of further colonial intrusion into Native American lands, were designed to protect northern tribes. In part, Britain was doing so in gratitude for their support during the Seven Years' War. These twin features, Parliament's provocative tolerance of Roman Catholicism and protection of Native American lands, were viewed by many colonists as among the most resented features of parliamentary legislation.[8]

Many American colonists by early in the summer of 1774 were looking for an intercolonial or continental response. Moderates, too, supported such a move, in the hope that they could control events, in particular by moderating Massachusetts and urban radicals elsewhere. Ultimately, all of the colonies except Georgia, mostly in provincial congresses or county conventions, chose delegates to attend a continental congress scheduled to convene in September in Philadelphia. The congress—an extragovernmental diplomatic body whose delegates could pass resolutions that would then be offered as recommendations to the participating "governments"—met on September 5. One hundred thirty delegates took part in congressional deliberations during its first three years. They elected Peyton Randolph of Virginia president and, although strongly opposed by a fellow Pennsylvanian, Joseph Galloway, Charles Thomson of Pennsylvania was elected secretary, a post he held until 1789, when he retired to work on a new translation of the Bible. Early on, a decision with long-lasting repercussions was made to provide each of the colonies with one vote. After adopting a pledge of secrecy, Congress chose members to serve on a grand committee charged with enunciating the nature of British and American constitutional rights and articulating how the latter had been infringed by Parliament.

Many of the colonists' grievances from the previous ten years were similar to those described by the Stamp Act Congress in 1765: Parliament had unconstitutionally raised taxes for revenue in the colonies, whose citizens were and could not be represented in

Parliament; Parliament had altered judicial proceedings so that in certain instances colonists were to be tried before admiralty or vice-admiralty courts, without the benefit of juries or the common law; and Parliament had extended additional powers to customs officers. Of greater concern—indeed, the specific reason for Congress having been called—were the punitive measures Parliament recently imposed on Massachusetts for its inhabitants' destruction of East India Company tea. Congress complained also of some long-standing tensions that had arisen between royal governors and colonial legislatures—for example, over judges' tenures, the creation of a civil list to be funded by customs duties, and the proroguing of colonial legislatures by governors in regard to a wide range of matters. In short, although Congress was focused on cataloguing parliamentary trespasses and imploring the king to intercede on the colonists' behalf, it had not completely put aside perceived grievances of an executive nature—issues to which Congress powerfully returned in 1776, when it finally declared the colonies' independent of the British Crown.

## DOCUMENT SUMMARY

The readings begin with the Suffolk resolves (September 17), in which that county's committee of correspondence, led by Dr. Joseph Warren, who worked in tandem with the Massachusetts Congressional delegation and Samuel Adams, asked the Continental Congress to declare Parliament's Coercive Acts unconstitutional and to support a number of radical, bellicose, and republican-leaning proposals. These included the forced resignation of royal officials in Massachusetts, a remodeling of the colony's militia, the arrest of British officials, an immediate continental cessation of "all commercial intercourse with Great Britain," and the formation of a new republican government in the Massachusetts Bay Colony. Congress responded, without specifically supporting any of the county's radical aims, with a vote of shared sympathy.

In the second principal reading, the Speaker of the Pennsylvania House and a close ally of Benjamin Franklin, Joseph Galloway, attempted to avert a rupture between Great Britain and its colonies by offering an imperial federal plan of union able to encompass, as well, colonial peoples beyond those of continental North America. While protecting colonial provincial autonomy, the plan addressed two of the central constitutional dilemmas driving the crisis: how to organize the empire on uniformly shared British political principles of legislative representation of property owners and of jury trials, and how to create a central government in the colonies with the power to coordinate action around common colonial needs—for example, for defense, as proposed in 1754 in Albany. In essence, his plan would have created a president-general and a grand council that, in conjunction with the British Parliament, would have legislated in all matters regarding "the general affairs of America." Appropriate measures could have originated in either body, with the consent of the other being required before a measure could become law. The plan failed to enjoy the support of those fearful of a more prominent role in colonial life for Parliament as well as those fearful of any system of central government. It was defeated in a close procedural vote (6–5) and expunged from the congressional record.

In the next principal reading, the Continental Congress, in the first document to be signed by the delegates, committed its member colonies to a concerted plan of breaking off commercial relations with Great Britain, Ireland, and the West Indies. The plan built on earlier successful colonial nonimportation agreements of 1765 and 1767–1769; in particular, it was modeled on a Virginia plan of association from May 1769. It should be remembered that the nonimportation movement of 1765 had been especially effective in inducing Parliament in 1766 to repeal the Stamp Act. Congress' Continental Association additionally created an unusually demanding moral code that included the banning "of every species of extravagance and dissipation, especially all horse racing, and all kinds of gaming, cock-fighting, exhibitions of shews, plays, and other expensive diversions." The code was to be enforced by extralegal Committees of Safety and Correspondence working directly with a body that had, as yet, no legal authority to direct them. Large numbers of likely recalcitrant fellow subjects were to be under the scrutiny of these committees of questionable legality. Nonetheless, by April 1775 the Association was in operation in twelve colonies.

In the next, paired readings, the Continental Congress addressed its fellow subjects in Great Britain and its colonial constituents. It began by making clear to both audiences that a constitutional reconciliation was possible only if Parliament were to abandon its claimed sovereign right to legislate for the colonies—its right to taxation had in 1770 already been largely surrendered and would be wholly so in Lord North's Peace Proposal of February 1775 (see document 23.1). In addressing the people of Britain, Congress remarkably—one wonders how well the delegates understood the character of their own position—raised the dangers of a king freed from parliamentary control and enjoying American tax receipts in a manner reminiscent of James II in England (a menace that Whig members of Parliament accused them of fostering), and the grave danger represented by Parliament's intolerable toleration of Roman Catholicism in Quebec. Yet Congress still demonstrated, while warning of impending doom to British freedoms, its persistent commitment to reconciliation and its loyalty to the king.

The single most important state paper produced by the First Continental Congress was the bill of rights from late October 1774, which is the fifth principal reading. Here, Congress criticizes thirteen parliamentary acts passed since 1763 that had imposed taxes on the colonies, extended the jurisdiction of admiralty and vice-admiralty courts, dissolved colonial assemblies, and maintained a standing army in colonial towns in peacetime. The bill of rights defends both the colonists' right to resist those unconstitutional actions and the provincial legislatures' exclusive right to legislate "in all cases of taxation and internal polity," subject only to the royal veto (that is, in crown colonies, by the governor, the upper house of the legislature, and then the king's

Privy Council in Britain). The bill further claims for the colonists the right to "life, liberty, and property" and, more critically, asserts that "they have never ceded to any sovereign power whatever, a right to dispose of either without their consent." While resting its claims almost wholly on either English constitutional grounds or charter or common-law rights, Congress provocatively included a brief mention of natural law as an additional foundation. The grounding of colonial rights and the question of whether any extraconstitutional right should be included, along with formulating the colonists' consent to parliamentary commercial legislation as a matter of goodwill rather than parliamentary right, proved sufficiently controversial to consume Congress for almost its entire first meeting, from September 5 to October 26, 1774.

In the sixth principal reading, "A Letter to the Inhabitants of the Province of Quebec" (October 22), the Continental Congress attempted to distance the Canadians from the British administration or, even more ambitiously, to entice them into joining the American opposition movement. What makes the document of such interest is that in it Congress outlined its understanding of the essential nature of British liberty—public freedom from arbitrary power—while highlighting the five fundamental rights that the Canadians would obtain by joining the other continental colonists in opposition: a popular share in self-government, trial by jury, habeas corpus, land tenure by easy rents, and freedom of the press. The letter emphasizes the benefits of English constitutional liberty that Congress believed the Canadians had been promised in the royal proclamation of 1763 but that the British government had failed to provide, in particular as a result of the recent passage of the Quebec Act. Congress wished also to persuade its neighbors that the British tolerance of Roman Catholicism couldn't be trusted, whereas the forbearance of their still more fervent and intolerant Protestant North American neighbors could. In any number of other congressional documents, however, the colonists revealed their truer colors: an almost phobic fear of and hostility to Roman Catholicism, which was embodied in legal prohibitions in all the colonies except one. (With the suppression of legal government, however, most such interdictions were suspended, allowing one Catholic to become a member of the Continental Congress.)

The last principal reading of this section, the Petition to the King of October 26 (the First Continental Congress' final state paper), begins by listing grievances, some long enduring, that were more executive than legislative in nature. Thus, even during the all-absorbing crisis with Parliament, differences of a less critical nature with the Crown weren't completely ignored. Necessarily more central, though, were objections to parliamentary legislation, with the Quebec Act again highlighted because of its dangerous tolerance of Roman Catholics to the north "of the free protestant English settlements." Also revealing here are Congress' appeal to the king to intervene "as the loving father of . . . [his] whole people" in protecting the colonists from Parliament's unconstitutional overreach, and its proud defense once again of the king's prerogative rights to rule his North American colonies without parliamentary intrusion.

## THEORETICAL ISSUES

The First Continental Congress, during its short duration, successfully laid out its views on governmental rights. The colonies remained committed to sharing in governance with the king, who enjoyed the right to veto legislation and to appoint governors and hybrid legislative-executive upper councils; however, Parliament's perceived right to share in the same had diminished considerably from the already limited role defined by the Stamp Act Congress nearly a decade earlier. If there was one issue that had fueled the conflict between Britain and its North American colonies over the previous ten years, this was it—whether Parliament had the sovereign right to legislate for and tax the colonies. The right was one that almost no member of Parliament—even friends of the colonies in the opposition—was prepared, in principle, to surrender. Still, notwithstanding that intractable difference, Congress made clear that the principal goal of its delegates was to keep the colonies in the British Empire and to find a constitutional means to reconcile with Parliament, in large measure by appealing to the king to intercede with Parliament on the colonists' behalf.

Thus, Congress consistently emphasizes in the following documents that Americans were a people who enjoyed equal rights with the king's subjects in Great Britain, though little attention is paid to the plight of British colonists elsewhere in Ireland or the West Indies. The central argument underlying its position, what might be called the "dominion theory," was that the North American colonies were located outside the British realm and therefore could and should not be represented in Parliament. They were therefore constitutionally independent of its jurisdiction, though still part of the king's dominions—something like his ancestral lands in Hanover, Germany; like Scotland before union with Britain in 1707; or like Ireland or the Channel Islands. Parliament, committed to the core teachings of Whig political theory and its own supremacy, refused to concede the constitutionality of the colonies being independent of its sovereign jurisdiction or of the colonists' right to send financial requisitions directly to the king, without parliamentary oversight.[9] Neither side, over a fifteen-year period, showed any willingness to accommodate the other concerning that core constitutional difference, an intractability exacerbated, oddly enough, by their common adherence to Whig political theory as variously interpreted by each side.

In an important sense, the first two principal documents, the Suffolk resolves and Galloway's "Plan of Union," point not to the matters about which all members of the First Continental Congress agreed upon, but to those that divided the provincial delegations in the congress into different factions: one radical and leaning forward against parliamentary oversight and possibly, too, against central government of any kind, and the other more moderate in its response to what Americans on all sides understood to be Parliament's unconstitutional (though possibly legal—they were different standards) attempts to tax the colonists for revenue and to legislate for them.[10] In most instances, radical delegates from the New England colonies and

Virginia pushed Congress toward taking actions sure to be viewed as provocations by Parliament. The New England delegates' radicalism resulted from long-held republican sympathies and practices, and Reformed Protestant religiosity, all of which were viewed with enduring suspicion by most other delegates. Virginia's radical delegates, with their debt-ridden and self-assured aristocratic slave-owning republicanism, came from a world without a port, merchants, or an urban working class (mechanics) and were thus relatively free from otherwise ubiquitous class tensions. Their republicanism may, in truth, have been rather different from that of the pious New Englanders. The mid-Atlantic colonies were the center of moderation, and their delegates worked to delay radical initiatives while ensuring that if they couldn't stop their passage, they would be joined to others of a more clearly conciliatory tone that accorded with the instructions provided to all of the delegates.

One of the more theoretically rich examples of this persistent split, at least until July 1776, is found in the debate recorded by John Adams on September 8, 1774 (document 13.3) in the "great committee on rights," that is, the body responsible for preparing a list of colonial rights that Congress believed Parliament had unconstitutionally infringed. Here, the split among the delegates is readily visible, with radicals insisting on including a claim in defense of colonial rights that looked to nature for its foundation, while moderates were just as adamantly opposed to the inclusion of any such language. A few delegates took a pragmatic view, believing that such a grounding might prove useful in the near future. Other issues, including the nature of monarchical prerogatives, rights associated with emigration, the right of imposing law on conquered lands, and, possibly most importantly, the nature of the colonial obligation to obey parliamentary commercial regulations, also divided the committee. But what distinguished the two sides most sharply was the question whether to make any mention of natural law or natural rights.

In the end, a single four-word mention appeared in the bill of rights passed in October 1774, which was the only mention of natural law or natural rights in the state papers of the First Continental Congress. The implication suggested by such language—that the colonies were in some manner without a recognized sovereign and thus were in a state of nature—was, for many delegates, too dangerous to invoke and still more difficult to control. Their fears derived from concerns regarding internal matters, including who would rule at home, and external ones focused on the standing of the royal prerogative. Of course, the second issue was put to rest by the Declaration of Independence. That question regarding who should rule at home took far longer to resolve, if indeed it has even yet been permanently settled.

## 9. MASSACHUSETTS OPPOSITION TO THE DECLARATORY ACT
### AND THE COERCIVE ACTS, SEPTEMBER 1774

These resolves, a document that helped define the vision of radicals in the First Continental Congress and the early years of the Second, were a product of Suffolk

County, Massachusetts, which includes the city of Boston, referred to as the "center of revolutionary activity," for good reason.[11] They were written by Dr. Joseph Warren, introduced to the Suffolk County Committee of Correspondence on September 6, 1774—in a banned public meeting—and, after being debated, adopted on September 9. They were then delivered to Congress by Paul Revere on September 16 and given to the Massachusetts delegation. On September 17, Congress responded with two brief resolutions of its own before ordering both sets published.[12] While almost all of the First Continental Congress' business was kept secret, the Suffolk and congressional resolutions were made public.

The Suffolk resolves, unlike similar documents found in the first section of this collection, do not focus only on Parliament's attempt to raise revenues in 1764–65 (or later in 1767). Instead, by claiming to rest on an inheritance found in nature—a controversial matter in Congress, as John Adams recorded in his notes—the British Constitution, and the Massachusetts Charter, the resolves take on new concerns. Most particularly, along with continued opposition to the Declaratory Act (see document 8.2), the author of the resolves castigates the Coercive Acts (Americans regularly described them as the "Intolerable Acts"), which were passed in Parliament with the intention of punishing the residents of Boston and Massachusetts for their wanton destruction of private property, particularly during the Boston Tea Party.

In spite of a focus on newer parliamentary legislation (passed in reaction to colonial responses to previous parliamentary legislation, a pattern that would continue for the next two years of the crisis), not all the nineteen Suffolk resolves were novel in character. Indeed, many advanced claims analogous to the more radical ones issued in response to the Stamp Act Crisis of 1764–66: no obedience was due to unconstitutional laws, public officials who refused to obey unconstitutional parliamentary legislation would be indemnified, colonial governmental officials appointed under provisions of the new legislation would have to resign immediately, those who acted in accord with the new parliamentary laws would be viewed as "incorrigible enemies to this country," and commercial intercourse with Great Britain and other colonies in the British Empire would be suspended. The purported goal, too, was claimed to be the same as that of resolves drawn up in opposition to the Sugar and Stamp Acts: "renewing that harmony and union between Great-Britain and the colonies, so earnestly wished for by all good men." Much that is advanced in the resolves, however, raised questions regarding the believability of their enunciated goals.

Not all the resolutions, then, looked back to the relative moderation of the era of the Stamp Act. Indeed, some sought to inflame the smoldering Imperial Crisis, which had been reignited by Parliament's passage of the Tea Act (May 10, 1773) after three years of relative quiescence. In the more incendiary resolves, the political activists of Suffolk County demanded that the colonists begin acquainting themselves with the arts of war and forming a defensive network of correspondence to call forth military assistance from one town to another. In the event that any colonist was apprehended, efforts were to be made to "seize and keep in safe custody, every servant of the present tyrannical and unconstitutional government throughout the county." In addition, Suffolk County urged that a Massachusetts provincial congress be called—in effect, an appeal for a parallel government to that legally constituted by the Crown. It seems as if some in Massachusetts were ready in 1774, as their ancestors likely had been for a century or more, to begin moving North American politics in a radically republican direction.[13]

In response, the First Continental Congress, made up mostly of men far more moderate than those of Suffolk County, dedicated constitutional monarchists still far removed from embracing republicanism, committed the colonies only to two relatively modest resolves: objecting, with their fellow subjects in Massachusetts, to their suffering at the hands of an oppressive Parliament—with no mention of the king or a putative "agreeable compact"—while recommending that Massachusetts maintain a temperate stance, and seeking continued "contributions from all the colonies for supplying the necessities, and alleviating the distresses of our brethren at Boston." Radical voices, such as the Adams cousins of Massachusetts, claimed that they had won with the congressional resolutions a great victory, and moderate delegates viewed them as a great defeat; yet both sides seem to have exaggerated the measured stance and limited action taken by Congress in its first public statement. Still, as Joseph Galloway of Pennsylvania rightly noted, by not openly rejecting the Suffolk resolves, Congress in September 1774 seemed to leave open the possibility of later—in truth, only eighteen months or so later—embracing independence and a radical republican agenda.

The Suffolk resolves' author, Joseph Warren, a leading voice in the Boston area and a close ally of Samuel and John Adams, was fearful of a ministerial conspiracy, and possibly straining toward republican independence. Before preparing the resolves, Warren had led the Massachusetts Committee of Safety, served as president of the Massachusetts Provincial Congress, and helped draft in 1770 the hyperbolic *Short Narrative of the Horrid Massacre in Boston*. An even more important figure in moving the debate, and the driving force behind the first meeting of the Continental Congress itself, was Samuel Adams. It was with such a gathering in mind that he had presented, on June 17, 1774, a resolution to the Massachusetts House. In language similar to that of the Suffolk resolves, he urged that the colonies be invited to send delegates to meet for the purpose of organizing "the recovery and establishment of the just rights and liberties, civil and religious" of the colonies while considering, too, how best to restore "the union and harmony between Great Britain and the colonies." Of course, such moderate ends enjoyed broad, almost universal support in the colonies and in Britain.

Yet in Congress, Adams used the Suffolk resolves, which he had helped draft, to begin moving opinion, ever so slowly and carefully, away from the announced end of a constitutional reconciliation with Britain—the position favored by a large majority of congressional delegates, who responded positively to Adams' announced purpose—and toward the independence he soon came to seek.[14] It took almost two years for Adams' goal to be realized, and his success critically depended on the consistent help of the Crown and Parliament, whose actions, even more than the wily ways of Adams, proved decisive in alienating moderate delegates and their constituents from their allegiance to king and country. Adams, who in 1764 had written Boston's instructions for the Massachusetts legislature to defend American rights against Grenville's and Parliament's plans to raise future revenue by means of stamp taxes, was also responsible for setting up the committees of correspondence, first in Massachusetts and then, while working with Richard Henry Lee of Virginia, throughout the colonies. He worked tirelessly, remarkably effectively, and almost always secretively in defense of colonial rights and, ultimately, for American independence.[15] If there were one man disproportionately responsible for the colonies declaring independence on July 2, 1776, it is surely Samuel Adams, who was a failure at everything he tried except for the one thing that he seemed born to accomplish: transforming recalcitrant British North American constitutional monarchists from loyal British subjects to independence-seeking republicans.[16] His campaign to achieve this may well have started with this document and Congress' refusal to reject it.

9.1

 SUFFOLK RESOLVES, SEPTEMBER 17, 1774

*Journals of the Continental Congress, 1774–1789*, ed. Worthington Chauncey Ford et al. (Washington, D.C.: Government Printing Office, 1904–37), 1:31–40.

[SATURDAY, SEPTEMBER 17, 1774, A.M.]

The Resolutions entered into by the delegates from the several towns and districts in the county of Suffolk, in the province of the Massachusetts-bay, on tuesday the 6th instant, and their address to his excellency Govr. Gage, dated the 9th instant, were laid before the congress, and are as follows:

At a meeting of the delegates of every town & district in the county of Suffolk, on tuesday the 6th of Septr., at the house of Mr. Richard Woodward, of Deadham, & by adjournment, at the house of Mr. [Daniel] Vose, of Milton, on Friday the 9th instant, Joseph Palmer, esq. being chosen moderator, and William Thompson, esq. clerk, a committee was chosen to bring in a report to the convention, and the following being several times read, and put paragraph by paragraph, was unanimously voted, viz.

Whereas the power but not the justice, the vengeance but not the wisdom of Great-Britain, which of old persecuted, scourged, and exiled our fugitive parents from their native shores, now pursues us, their guiltless children, with unrelenting severity: And whereas, this, then savage and uncultivated desart, was purchased by the toil and treasure, or acquired by the blood and valor of those our venerable progenitors; to us they bequeathed the dearbought inheritance, to our care and protection they consigned it, and the most sacred obligations are upon us to transmit the glorious purchase, unfettered by power, unclogged with shackles, to our innocent and beloved offspring. On the fortitude, on the wisdom and on the exertions of this important day, is suspended the fate of this new world, and of unborn millions. If a boundless extent of continent, swarming with millions, will tamely submit to live, move and have their being at the arbitrary will of a licentious minister, they basely yield to voluntary slavery, and future generations shall load their memories with incessant execrations.—On the other hand, if we arrest the hand which would ransack our pockets, if we disarm the parricide which points the dagger to our bosoms, if we nobly defeat that fatal edict which proclaims a power to frame laws for us in all cases whatsoever, thereby entailing the endless and numberless curses of slavery upon us, our heirs and their heirs forever; if we successfully resist that unparalleled usurpation of unconstitutional power, whereby our capital is robbed of the means of life; whereby the streets of Boston are thronged with military executioners; whereby our coasts are lined and harbours crouded with ships of war; whereby the charter of the colony, that sacred barrier against the encroachments of tyranny, is mutilated and, in effect, annihilated; whereby a murderous law is framed to shelter villains from the hands of justice; whereby the unalienable and inestimable inheritance, which we derived from nature, the constitution of Britain, and the privileges warranted to us in the charter of the province, is totally wrecked, annulled, and vacated, posterity will acknowledge that virtue which preserved them free and happy; and while we enjoy the rewards and blessings of the faithful, the torrent of panegyrists will roll our reputations to that latest period, when the streams of time shall be absorbed in the abyss of eternity.—Therefore, we have resolved, and do *resolve*,

1. That whereas his majesty, George the Third, is the rightful successor to the throne of Great-Britain, and justly entitled to the allegiance of the British realm, and agreeable to compact, of the English colonies in America—therefore, we, the heirs and successors of the first planters of this colony, do cheerfully acknowledge the said George the Third to be our rightful sovereign, and that said covenant is the tenure and claim on which are founded our allegiance and submission.

2. That it is an indispensable duty which we owe to God, our country, ourselves and posterity, by all lawful ways and means in our power to maintain, defend and preserve those civil and religious rights and liberties, for which many of our fathers fought, bled and died, and to hand them down entire to future generations.

3. That the late acts of the British parliament for blocking up the harbour of Boston, for altering the established form of government in this colony, and for screening the most flagitious violators of the laws of the province from a legal trial, are gross infractions of those rights to which we are justly entitled by the laws of nature, the British constitution, and the charter of the province.

4. That no obedience is due from this province to either or any part of the acts abovementioned, but that they be rejected as the attempts of a wicked administration to enslave America.

5. That so long as the justices of our superior court of judicature, court of assize, &c. and inferior court of common pleas in this county are appointed, or hold their places, by any other tenure than that which the charter and the laws of the province direct, they must be considered as under undue influence, and are therefore unconstitutional officers, and, as such, no regard ought to be paid to them by the people of this county.

6. That if the justices of the superior court of judicature, assize, &c. justices of the court of common pleas, or of the general sessions of the peace, shall sit and act during their present disqualified state, this county will support, and bear harmless, all sheriffs and their deputies, constables, jurors and other officers who shall refuse to carry into execution the orders of said courts; and, as far as possible, to prevent the many inconveniencies which must be occasioned by a suspension of the courts of justice, we do most earnestly recommend it to all creditors, that they shew all reasonable and even generous forbearance to their debtors; and to all debtors, to pay their just debts with all possible speed, and if any disputes relative to debts or trespasses shall arise, which cannot be settled by the parties, we recommend it to them to submit all such causes to arbitration; and it is our opinion that the contending parties or either of them, who shall refuse so to do, ought to be considered as co-operating with the enemies of this country.

7. That it be recommended to the collectors of taxes, constables and all other officers, who have public monies in their hands, to retain the same, and not to make any payment thereof to the provincial county treasurer until the civil government of the province is placed upon a constitutional foundation, or until it shall otherwise be ordered by the proposed provincial Congress.

8. That the persons who have accepted seats at the council board, by virtue of a mandamus from the King, in conformity to the late act of the British parliament, entitled, an act for the regulating the government of the Massachusetts-Bay, have acted in direct violation of the duty they owe to their country, and have thereby given great and just offence to this people; therefore, resolved, that this county do recommend it to all persons, who have so highly offended by accepting said departments, and have not already publicly resigned their seats at the council board, to make public resignations of their places at said board, on or before the 20th day of this instant, September; and that all persons refusing so to do, shall, from and after said day, be considered by this county as obstinate and incorrigible enemies to this country.

9. That the fortifications begun and now carrying on upon Boston Neck, are justly alarming to this county, and gives us reason to apprehend some hostile intention against that town, more especially as the commander in chief has, in a very extraordinary manner, removed the powder from the magazine at Charlestown, and has also forbidden the keeper of the magazine at Boston, to deliver out to the owners, the powder, which they had lodged in said magazine.

10. That the late act of parliament for establishing the Roman Catholic religion and the French laws in that extensive country, now called Canada, is dangerous in an extreme degree to the Protestant religion and to the civil rights and liberties of all Amer-

ica; and, therefore, as men and Protestant Christians, we are indispensably obliged to take all proper measures for our security.

11. That whereas our enemies have flattered themselves that they shall make an easy prey of this numerous, brave and hardy people, from an apprehension that they are unacquainted with military discipline; we, therefore, for the honour, defence and security of this county and province, advise, as it has been recommended to take away all commissions from the officers of the militia, that those who now hold commissions, or such other persons, be elected in each town as officers in the militia, as shall be judged of sufficient capacity for that purpose, and who have evidenced themselves the inflexible friends to the rights of the people; and that the inhabitants of those towns and districts, who are qualified, do use their utmost diligence to acquaint themselves with the art of war as soon as possible, and do, for that purpose, appear under arms at least once every week.

12. That during the present hostile appearances on the part of Great-Britain, notwithstanding the many insults and oppressions which we most sensibly resent, yet, nevertheless, from our affection to his majesty, which we have at all times evidenced, we are determined to act merely upon the defensive, so long as such conduct may be vindicated by reason and the principles of self-preservation, but no longer.

13. That, as we understand it has been in contemplation to apprehend sundry persons of this county, who have rendered themselves conspicuous in contending for the violated rights and liberties of their countrymen; we do recommend, should such an audacious measure be put in practice, to seize and keep in safe custody, every servant of the present tyrannical and unconstitutional government throughout the county and province, until the persons so apprehended be liberated from the bands of our adversaries, and restored safe and uninjured to their respective friends and families.

14. That until our rights are fully restored to us, we will, to the utmost of our power, and we recommend the same to the other counties, to withhold all commercial intercourse with Great-Britain, Ireland, and the West-Indies, and abstain from the consumption of British merchandise and manufactures, and especially of East-India teas and piece goods, with such additions, alterations, and exceptions only, as the General Congress of the colonies may agree to.

15. That under our present circumstances, it is incumbent on us to encourage arts and manufactures amongst us, by all means in our power, and that be and are hereby appointed a committee, to consider of the best ways and means to promote and establish the same, and to report to this convention as soon as may be.

16. That the exigencies of our public affairs, demand that a provincial Congress be called to consult such measures as may be adopted, and vigorously executed by the whole people; and we do recommend it to the several towns in this county, to chuse members for such a provincial Congress, to be holden at Concord, on the second Tuesday of October, next ensuing.

17. That this county, confiding in the wisdom and integrity of the continental Congress, now sitting at Philadelphia, pay all due respect and submission to such

measures as may be recommended by them to the colonies, for the restoration and establishment of our just rights, civil and religious, and for renewing that harmony and union between Great-Britain and the colonies, so earnestly wished for by all good men.

18. That whereas the universal uneasiness which prevails among all orders of men, arising from the wicked and oppressive measures of the present administration, may influence some unthinking persons to commit outrage upon private property; we would heartily recommend to all persons of this community, not to engage in any routs, riots, or licentious attacks upon the properties of any person whatsoever, as being subversive of all order and government; but, by a steady, manly, uniform, and persevering opposition, to convince our enemies, that in a contest so important, in a cause so solemn, our conduct shall be such as to merit the approbation of the wise, and the admiration of the brave and free of every age and of every country.

19. That should our enemies, by any sudden manoeuvres, render it necessary to ask the aid and assistance of our brethren in the country, some one of the committee of correspondence, or a select man of such town, or the town adjoining, where such hostilities shall commence, or shall be expected to commence, shall despatch couriers with written messages to the select men, or committees of correspondence, of the several towns in the vicinity, with a written account of such matter, who shall despatch others to committees more remote, until proper and sufficient assistance be obtained, and that the expense of said couriers be defrayed by the county, until it shall be otherwise ordered by the provincial Congress.

At a meeting of delegates from the several towns and districts in the county of Suffolk, held at Milton, on Friday, the 9th day of September, 1774—*Voted,*

That Dr. Joseph Warren, of Boston, &c. be a committee to wait on his excellency the governor, to inform him, that this county are alarmed at the fortifications making on Boston Neck, and to remonstrate against the same, and the repeated insults offered by the soldiery, to persons passing and repassing into that town, and to confer with him upon those subjects.

Attest, WILLIAM THOMPSON, *Clerk....*

### SATURDAY, SEPTEMBER 18, 1774.

The Congress, taking the foregoing into consideration,

*Resolved unan,* That this assembly deeply feels the suffering of their countrymen in the Massachusetts-Bay, under the operation of the late unjust, cruel, and oppressive acts of the British Parliament—that they most thoroughly approve the wisdom and fortitude, with which opposition to these wicked ministerial measures has hitherto been conducted, and they earnestly recommend to their brethren, a perseverance in the same firm and temperate conduct as expressed in the resolutions determined upon, at a [*late*] meeting of the delegates for the county of Suffolk, on Tuesday, the 6th

instant, trusting that the effect[s] of the united efforts of North America in their behalf, will carry such conviction to the British nation, of the unwise, unjust, and ruinous policy of the present administration, as quickly to introduce better men and
wiser measures.

*Resolved unan,* That contributions from all the colonies for supplying the necessities,
and alleviating the distresses of our brethren at Boston, ought to be continued, in such
manner, and so long as their occasions may require.

*Ordered,* That a copy of the above resolutions be transmitted to Boston by the president.

*Ordered,* That these resolutions, together with the resolutions of the County of Suffolk, be published in the newspapers.

9.2

 JOHN ADAMS, DIARY ENTRY, SEPTEMBER 17, 1774

John Adams, the son of a farmer, was born in Braintree, Massachusetts, attended
Harvard College, developed a flourishing law practice, and served in both Continental Congresses. He spent a year in France as a diplomatic commissioner, served
as an envoy to Holland and as the first American minister to Great Britain, became
President George Washington's vice president, and in 1796 was elected president in
his own right. His diary entries and personal letters are vast in number, and given
his desire that his views of this pivotal period in American history outlast him, he
saved an inordinate number of them (unlike his secretive cousin Samuel). In this
passage, his approval of the actions of his fellow congressional delegates is evident.
Adams, like a handful of mostly New England and Virginia congressional radicals,
harbored anti-imperial sentiments from the Continental Congress' earliest days,
perhaps even well before.[17] This set them apart from most of their more moderate
colleagues—for example, "the old, grave, pacific Quakers of Pennsylvania," who, like
most delegates, sincerely hoped to find a constitutional means of achieving a just
reconciliation with Great Britain while remaining loyal to their king and inside the
British Empire. Such views, as Adams later recounted, led to his being enormously
disliked (though not because of this alone), even if, for many of the same reasons,
he remained difficult to best in debate.

*The Works of John Adams,* ed. Charles Francis Adams (Boston: Little, Brown, 1851–65),
   2:380. In an extended note, C. F. Adams, the editor, adds: "On this day the celebrated
   resolutions of Suffolk County, in Massachusetts, had been laid before Congress, and
   resolutions were adopted by the Congress expressive of sympathy and support. See the

*Journals.*" He then included an excerpt from a letter John Adams wrote to Abigail Adams on September 18: "The proceedings of the Congress are all a profound secret as yet, except two votes which were passed yesterday, and ordered to be printed. You will see them from every quarter. These votes were passed in full Congress with perfect unanimity. The esteem, the affection, the admiration for the people of Boston and the Massachusetts, which were expressed yesterday, and the fixed determination that they should be supported, were enough to melt a heart of stone. I saw the tears gush into the eyes of the old, grave, pacific Quakers of Pennsylvania."

[September] 17. Saturday. This was one of the happiest days of my life. In Congress we had generous, noble sentiments, and manly eloquence. This day convinced me that America will support the Massachusetts or perish with her.

## 9.3

SAMUEL ADAMS TO JOSEPH WARREN,
SEPTEMBER 25, 1774

Samuel Adams' letter to Dr. Joseph Warren, who was back in Boston, helps capture some of the tensions between the congressional delegations. In particular, Adams describes the distrust directed against the Massachusetts delegation because of what others already suspected—a quest for independence, potentially including from the other colonies as well. Thus, he writes Warren and ponders "whether they [his fellow delegates] will ever be prevailed upon to think it necessary for you [Massachusetts] to set up another form of government [that is a republican one]," and answers that this he "very much" questions. By June 1775, his too cautious estimate had proved wrong as Congress then supported his Colony's request to set up, even if only temporarily at that time, a new republican form of government (see document 17.1).

*Writings of Samuel Adams,* ed. Harry Alonzo Cushing (New York and London: G. P. Putnam's Sons, 1904–8), 3:157–59.

PHILADELPHIA, September 25, 1774.
MY DEAR SIR,—I wrote you yesterday by the post. A frequent communication at this critical conjuncture is necessary. As the all-important American cause so much depends upon each colony's acting agreeably to the sentiments of the whole, it must be useful to you to know the sentiments which are entertained here of the temper and con-

duct of our province. Heretofore we have been accounted by many, intemperate and rash; but now we are universally applauded as cool and judicious, as well as spirited and brave. This is the character we sustain in congress. There is, however, a certain degree of jealousy in the minds of some, that we aim at a total independency, not only of the mother-country, but of the colonies too; and that, as we are a hardy and brave people, we shall in time overrun them all. However groundless this jealousy may be, it ought to be attended to, and is of weight in your deliberations of the subject of your last letter. I spent yesterday afternoon and evening with Mr. Dickinson. He is a true Bostonian. It is his opinion, that, if Boston can safely remain on the defensive, the liberties of America, which that town has so nobly contended for, will be secured. The congress have, in their resolve of the 17th instant, given their sanction to the resolutions of the county of Suffolk, one of which is to act merely on the defensive, so long as such conduct may be justified by reason and the principles of self-preservation, but NO LONGER. They have great dependence upon your tried patience and fortitude. They suppose you mean to defend your civil constitution. They strongly recommend perseverance in a firm and temperate conduct, and give you a full pledge of their united efforts in your behalf. They have not yet come to final resolutions. It becomes them to be deliberate. I have been assured, in private conversation with individuals, that, if you should be driven to the necessity of acting in the defence of your lives or liberty, you would be justified by their constituents, and openly supported by all the means in their power; but whether they will ever be prevailed upon to think it necessary for you to set up another form of government, I very much question, for the reason I have before suggested. It is of the greatest importance, that the American opposition should be united, and that it should be conducted so as to concur with the opposition of our friends in England. Adieu,

9.4

 JOHN ADAMS TO WILLIAM TUDOR
SEPTEMBER 29, 1774

John Adams' exuberance of twelve days earlier had somewhat abated (and soon vanished for the next eighteen months), to be replaced by frustration with congressional debate. In this letter to William Tudor, a student whom Adams had been instructing in the law since 1769, Adams reveals the need of the radicals in the Massachusetts delegation to act with stealth and "to insinuate our Sentiments, Designs and Desires by means of other Persons, Sometimes of one Province and Sometime of another."

Paul H. Smith, ed., *Letters of Delegates to Congress, 1774–1789* (Washington, D.C.: Library of Congress, 1976–93), 1:129–31. The Latin tag can be translated as "Sweet and fitting it is to die for one's country" (Horace, *Odes,* bk. 3, no. 2). The verse is from *The Judgment of Hercules,* by Robert Lowth.

Dear Sir,                                                    Philadelphia Septr. 29. 1774.

I wish it was in my Power, to write you any Thing for the Relief of our Anxiety, under the Pressure of those Calamities which now distress our beloved Town of Boston and Province of Massachusetts. The Sentiments expressed in your last to me, are Such as would do honour to the best of Citizens, in the Minds of the Virtuous and worthy of any Age or Country in the worst of Times.

Dulce et decorum est pro Patria mori.

Wouldst thou receive thy Countrys loud Applause,
Lov'd as her Father, as her God ador'd,
Be thou the bold Asserter of her Cause,
Her Voice in Council, in the Fight her Sword.

You can have no adequate Idea of the Pleasures or of the Difficulties of the Errand I am now upon. The Congress is Such an Assembly as never before came together on a Sudden, in any Part of the World. Here are Fortunes, Abilities, Learning, Eloquence, Acuteness equal to any I ever met with my Life. Here is a Diversity of Religions, Educations, Manners, Interests, Such as it would Seem almost impossible to unite in any one Plan of Conduct.

Every Question is discussed with a Moderation, and an Acuteness and a minuteness equal to that of Queen Elizabeths privy Council.

This occasions infinite Delays. We are under obligations of Secrecy in every Thing except the Single Vote which you have Seen approving the Resolutions of the County of Suffolk. What Effect this Vote may have with you is uncertain. What you will do, God knows. You Say you look up to the Congress. It is well you Should: but I hope you will not expect too much from Us.

The Delegates here are not Sufficiently acquainted with our Pr[ovince] and with the Circumstances you are in, to form a Judgment [of] what Course it is proper for you to take. They Start at one Thought of taking up the old Charter. They Shudder at the Prospect of Blood. Yet they are unanimously and unalterably against your Submission, to any of the Acts for a Single Moment.

You See by this What they are for-vizt, that you Stand Stock Still, and live without Government, or Law. At least for the present and as long as you can. I have represented to them, whenever I see them, the Utter Impossibility, of four hundred Thousand People existing long with [ou]t a Legislature or Courts of Justice. They all Seem to acknowledge it: Yet nothing can be as yet accomplished.

We hear, perpetually, the most figurative Panegyricks upon our Wisdom Fortitude and Temperance: The most fervent Exhortations to perseverance, But nothing more is done.

I may venture to tell you, that I believe We Shall agree to N. Imp., N. Consumption, and Non Exportation, but not to commence so soon as I could wish.

Indeed all this would be insufficient, for our Purpose—a more adequate Support, and Relief to the Massachusetts Should be adopted—But I tremble for fear, We should fail of obtaining it.

There is however a most laudable Zeal, and an excellent Spirit, which every Day increases, especially in this City. The Quakers had a General Meeting here last Sunday, and are deeply affected with the Complexion of the Times. They have recommended it to all their People to renounce Tea, and indeed the People of this City of all Denominations have laid it generally aside Since our Arrival here. The are about Setting up Companys of Cadets, voluntarily. &c &c &c.

It is the universal opinion here that the General, Gage, is in the Horrors, and that he means only to act upon the Defensive. How well this opinion is founded you, can judge better than I.

I must beseech you to Shew this Letter to no Man, in whom you have not the most perfect Confidence. It may do a great deal of Mischief.

We have had numberless Prejudices to remove here. We have been obliged to act, with great Delicacy and Caution. We have been obliged to keep ourselves out of Sight, and to feel Pulses, and Sound the Depths—to insinuate our Sentiments, Designs and Desires by means of other Persons, Sometimes of one Province and Sometime of another—a future opportunity I hope in Conversations will make you acquainted with all. Adieu John Adams.

## 10. A DESIGN FOR UNIFYING THE COLONIES WITHIN THE EMPIRE, SEPTEMBER 1774

Joseph Galloway of Philadelphia, a friend and longtime ally of Benjamin Franklin, joined him in trying to find a means of unifying the colonies, first in a federal union and then with Britain in an imperial one. He ultimately remained loyal to the king, and in 1778 left the colonies for England, where he became "one of the most prominent figures in the pamphlet literature during the last five years of the conflict."[18] But in 1774, as a congressional delegate from Pennsylvania and still Speaker of its House, he remained vigorously engaged in colonial affairs while seeking to maintain both colonial and parliamentary rights, which, like the firmest of the colonies' friends in Parliament—the Whig factions led by Lord Chatham and Lord Rockingham—he wished to see equally protected.

10.1

# Joseph Galloway, "Plan of Union," September 28, 1774

Eleven days after the Suffolk resolves were partially endorsed, Joseph Galloway brought in his "Plan of Union," with which he hoped to unify the disparate colonies and to heal the growing rift between the colonies and Britain. In the resolutions introducing the plan, Galloway points out that a governmental plan for colonization had never been properly developed or later properly incorporated into the British Constitution, and thus, however admirable the constitution was when applied to Britain alone, it was defective when extended to the plantations and colonies and was thus greatly in need of amendment. And since most colonists fervently wished to remain loyal to their king and to stay within the empire, but were unable to be adequately represented in the British/Imperial Parliament, where they could protect their rights and liberties, a new plan of American national or imperial governance was sorely needed. Accordingly, as Henry Steele Commager rightly explained, Galloway offered an elegant solution to "the problem of colonial home rule by a plan which would give to the American colonies something approaching dominion status."[19]

Galloway calls for a Crown-appointed executive (president-general), who would have veto power over the legislative branch (Grand Council), which would contain delegations from the colonies, chosen in proportion to, most likely, wealth or population—that provision, of course, did nothing to win over the support of small colonies, which at the time enjoyed equal standing in the Continental Congress. Legislators would have three-year terms and would elect their own Speaker. Crucial to Galloway's vision of union was that the American central government was to be "an inferior and distinct branch of the British legislature, united and incorporated with it, for the aforesaid general purposes; and that any of the said general regulations may originate and be formed and digested, either in the Parliament of Great Britain, or in the said Grand Council . . . and that the assent of both shall be requisite to the validity of all such general acts," except "in a time of war" those concerning "all bills for granting aid to the crown" will not need "the assent of the British Parliament." Importantly, each American colony was to retain both its charter and its individual autonomy or sovereignty regarding all matters of internal policy (or "police"). That innovative proposal anticipated the Articles of Confederation, which in places was copied verbatim from Galloway's plan; it looked forward to Franklin's plan of the following year (document 44.1) and the U.S. Constitution; and it anticipated key elements of the British Commonwealth of the nineteenth and twentieth centuries. Galloway thus offered a solution that would have satisfied the corporate-rights claims of the colonists and partially those of Parliament by creating an American national legislature that would "'hold and exercise all the like rights, liberties, and privileges, as are held and exercised by and in the House of Commons of Great-Britain.'"[20]

After an initial consideration of Galloway's plan on September 28, Congress voted on whether it "should be entered in the proceedings of Congress, or be referred to further consideration." On a vote of six colonies to five, with one divided, the plan was deferred for further consideration until a later date. When Congress returned on October 21 to consider it, it was dismissed and its record expunged from the congressional *Journal*.[21] Had the plan been given full consideration and then adopted, the future of the North American British colonies likely would have been strikingly different. During the initial procedural vote, the difference between two contrasting futures for the colonies came down to the vote of one colony.[22] The vote of that delegation determined that a plausible solution to the colonies' two perplexing constitutional conundrums—how to structure and divide sovereignty between the colonies and Great Britain (a question that the Declaration rendered moot), and how to structure and divide sovereignty between the colonies and some form of unified central government (which the Articles of Confederation inadequately attempted to solve)—was not given fair or serious consideration. Without adequate documentation, we are ultimately left to speculate on the causes for the plan's not being given full consideration.

We do know that, like similar proposals offered by Benjamin Franklin in the summer of 1754 and again on July 21, 1775 (see document 44.1), Galloway's plan died without further action. Most probably, the squabbling and disparate colonies and their representatives and delegates were far too possessive of local autonomy to surrender it to a federal union, be it British or American.[23] Radical delegates, possibly already beginning to look forward to republican independence, were unwilling to support Galloway's plan for at least two reasons: it would have created an intercolonial government detrimental to provincial autonomy, and it would have legitimated parliamentary involvement in colonial affairs and made the imperial framework more defensible. Like John Dickinson's original draft of the Articles of Confederation in 1776, but unlike the document eventually adopted by the Continental Congress, Galloway's plan gave significant power to the central government, as did the centralizing federalism of the U.S. Constitution.[24] In 1774 and 1775, defenders of customary colonial localism refused to countenance either parliamentary or centralized national oversight, for "the foremost colonial leaders still cherished the belief that they were fighting to smash the fetters of all central government, thus freeing each colony for local self-rule."[25] Accordingly, the record of Galloway's plan was expunged, and a year later Franklin's was largely ignored.

Not surprisingly, when members of Parliament learned from New Jersey's royal governor, William Franklin, and several other sources of Galloway's plan in late

December 1774,[26] it did little to bolster their confidence in Congress' claimed moderation when they learned later that body had expunged it from its *Journal*.[27] Finding a constitutional means of meeting the colonies' and Parliament's almost incompatible claims to corporate rights would have taken men of unusual breadth of vision and goodwill on both sides of the Atlantic. Finding such men would have been most difficult; as Neil York observes, "There could be no federal restructuring because there were never enough politicians on either side of the Atlantic who concurred on the same plan at the same time."[28] A few men might have met the test, such as Galloway and Franklin on the American side, and Thomas Crowley and John Cartwright on the British side, but they were far too few and almost always too late in offering conciliatory proposals that might have been accepted by both sides.[29]

Worthington Chauncey Ford et al., eds., *Journals of the Continental Congress, 1774–1789* (Washington, D.C.: Government Printing Office, 1904–37), 1:48–51. The first two paragraphs below are from Galloway's *Historical and Political Reflections on the Rise and Progress of the American Rebellion* (1780); they were inserted into the *Journals* by Ford, the editor. "Governor Franklin" refers to William Franklin, the last colonial governor of New Jersey.

The introductory motion being seconded, the Plan was presented and read. Warm and long debates immediately ensued on the question, Whether it should be entered in the proceedings of Congress, or be referred to further consideration. All the men of property, and most of the ablest speakers, supported the motion, while the republican party strenuously opposed it.

The question was at length carried by a majority of one Colony.

*Governor Franklin's version.*

*Resolved,* That there is a manifest *Defect* in the Constitution of the British Empire in respect to the Government of the Colonies upon those principles of Liberty which form an essential Part of that Constitution; and that such Defect has arisen from the circumstance of Colonization which was not included in the System of the British Government at the Time of its Institution, nor has been provided for since.

*Resolved,* That the Colonists hold in Abhorance the Idea of being considered Independent Communities on the British Government, and most ardently desire the Establishment of a Political Union not only among themselves but with the Mother State upon those principles of Safety and Freedom which are Essential in the Constitution of all free Governments and particularly that of the British Legislature, and Therefore,

*Resolved,* As the Colonies from their local & other circumstances cannot be represented in the British Parliament, the Congress do most Earnestly recommend (as a Measure of the Greatest Importance in reconciling the Difference between G. Britain and her Colonies, and restoring them to a permanent Union & Harmony) to the consideration of the several Continental American Assemblies the following Plan of Government to be by them humbly proposed to his Majesty and his two Houses of Parliament under which the whole Empire may be drawn together on every Emergency, the Interest of both Countries advanced and the Rights and Liberties of America secured: vizt— . . .

*A Plan of a proposed Union between Great Britain and the Colonies.*

That a British and American legislature, for regulating the administration of the general affairs of America, be proposed and established in America, including all the said colonies; within, and under which government, each colony shall retain its present constitution, and powers of regulating and governing its own internal police, in all cases what[*so*]ever.

That the said government be administered by a President General, to be appointed by the King, and a grand Council, to be chosen by the Representatives of the people of the several colonies, in their respective assemblies, once in every three years.

That the several assemblies shall choose members for the grand council in the following proportions, viz.

| | |
|---|---|
| New Hampshire. | Delaware Counties. |
| Massachusetts-Bay. | Maryland. |
| Rhode Island. | Virginia. |
| Connecticut. | North Carolina. |
| New-York. | South-Carolina. |
| New-Jersey. | Georgia. |
| Pennsylvania. | |

Who shall meet at the city of      for the first time, being called by the President-General, as soon as conveniently may be after his appointment.

That there shall be a new election of members for the Grand Council every three years; and on the death, removal or resignation of any member, his place shall be supplied by a new choice, at the next sitting of Assembly of the Colony he represented.

That the Grand Council shall meet once in every year, if they shall think it necessary, and oftener, if occasions shall require, at such time and place as they shall adjourn to, at the last preceding meeting, or as they shall be called to meet at, by the President-General, on any emergency.

That the grand Council shall have power to choose their Speaker, and shall hold and exercise all the like rights, liberties and privileges, as are held and exercised by and in the House of Commons of Great-Britain.

That the President-General shall hold his office during the pleasure of the King, and his assent shall be requisite to all acts of the Grand Council, and it shall be his office and duty to cause them to be carried into execution.

That the President-General, by and with the advice and consent of the Grand-Council, hold and exercise all the legislative rights, powers, and authorities, necessary for regulating and administering all the general police and affairs of the colonies, in which Great-Britain and the colonies, or any of them, the colonies in general, or more than one colony, are in any manner concerned, as well civil and criminal as commercial.

That the said President-General and the Grand Council, be an inferior and distinct branch of the British legislature, united and incorporated with it, for the aforesaid general purposes; and that any of the said general regulations may originate and be formed and digested, either in the Parliament of Great Britain, or in the said Grand Council, and being prepared, transmitted to the other for their approbation or dissent; and that the assent of both shall be requisite to the validity of all such general acts or statutes.

That in time of war, all bills for granting aid to the crown, prepared by the Grand Council, and approved by the President General, shall be valid and passed into a law, without the assent of the British Parliament.

10.2

JOSEPH GALLOWAY, STATEMENT ON HIS
"PLAN OF UNION" (BEGINNING), SEPTEMBER 28, 1774

Galloway's statement (documents 10.2 and 10.3) provides an insightful, though clearly opinionated and critical, view of the Continental Congress' first month and ends with an advertisement for his plan for a federal union of the colonies and Britain. He begins his statement by reminding his readers that all the colonies' instructions to their delegates committed them to seeking reconciliation, but nonetheless two parties had immediately formed in Congress: one that sought to remain within their limited mandate, and a second that desired to move the colonies toward some measure of independence, though of a rather limited character.[30] Those of the second party, Galloway suggests, were motivated either by Reformed Protestant religiosity and long-held republican political principles—clearly, these were the New Englanders—or by fear of bankruptcy because of the enormous debts they had accumulated— meaning, no doubt, the Virginians, who owed nearly £2,500,000, about half the colonies' total commercial debt to British merchants.[31] He also corroborates that the Adams cousins were right in their assessment that New Englanders needed to be secretive if they were to achieve their radical goals, as the history of the next two years bore out. Indeed, he both praises and condemns Samuel Adams for his political brilliance: whatever he wished "to promote . . . in Congress, Mr. Adams advised and directed to be done [back in Massachusetts]; and when done, it was dispatched by express to Congress," as had recently occurred with the Suffolk resolves.

Galloway next reviews the Suffolk resolves. In opposition to John Adams, who was frustrated by the lack of more aggressive action taken by Congress, Galloway concludes that what had been done already approached a "complete declaration of war against Great Britain." Certainly, if the totality of the resolves had been endorsed by Congress, which the two brief congressional resolutions did not do, his assessment would have been more justified. Nonetheless, the future proved his fears prescient. By taking both the Suffolk resolves and Galloway's "Plan of Union" (document 10.1) into account, we have a valuable window onto the visions of the two factions in Congress and their intended futures for the colonies.[32] In a certain sense, each found fulfillment: the Suffolk resolves succeeded far more fully and rapidly by hastening the colonies' separation in 1776 from Great Britain; with a federal plan of government, the Constitution, reflecting key aspects of Galloway's Plan and in many cases being supported by the same men representing the same interests, his vision came to fruition in September 1788. The document reprinted here, although based on contemporaneous notes, was written several years after the events described. It originally appeared in Galloway's *Historical and Political Reflections on the Rise and Progress of the American Rebellion* (London, 1780).

Paul H. Smith, ed., *Letters of Delegates to Congress, 1774–1789* (Washington, D.C.: Library of Congress, 1976–93), 1:119–22.

The Congress met at Philadelphia in September, 1774. They brought with them their appointments and instructions. The latter plainly discover the dispositions of the assemblies, and of the people who gave them, and demonstrate their aversion to every thing which might tend to a seditious or illegal opposition to Government. They strictly enjoined their delegates to "pursue *proper, prudent, and lawful measures,* and to adopt a plan for obtaining a redress of American grievances, ascertaining American rights upon the most solid and *constitutional* principles, and for establishing that union and harmony between Great Britain and the Colonies, *which is indispensably necessary to the welfare and happiness of both.*" Under these instructions, it was the general expectation that decent petitions would be presented to Parliament, explicitly pointing out the measures by which its authority over the colonies might be rendered more constitutional, and the grievances complained of might be redressed; because this was nothing more than the reasonable duty of subjects, and it was the sincere wish of the people.

Upon the meeting of Congress, two parties were immediately formed, with different views, and determined to act upon different principles. One intended candidly and clearly to define American rights, and explicitly and dutifully to petition for the remedy which would redress the grievances justly complained of—to form a more solid and constitutional union between the two countries, and to avoid every measure which tended to sedition, or acts of violent opposition. The other consisted of persons, whose design, from the beginning of their opposition to the Stamp Act, was to throw off all subordination and connexion with Great-Britain; who meant by every fiction, false hood and fraud, to delude the people from their due allegiance, to throw the subsisting Governments into anarchy, to incite the ignorant and vulgar to arms, and with those arms to establish American Independence. The one were men of loyal principles, and possessed the greatest fortunes in America; the other were congregational and presbyterian republicans, or men of bankrupt fortunes, overwhelmed in debt to the British merchants. The first suspected the designs of the last, and were therefore cautious; but as they meant to do nothing but what was reasonable and just, they were open and ingenuous. The second, fearing the opposition of the first, were secret and hypocritical, and left no art, no falsehood, no fraud unessayed to conceal their intentions. The loyalists rested, for the most part, on the defensive, and opposed, with success, every measure which tended to violent opposition. Motions were made, debated and rejected, and nothing was carried by either.

While the two parties in Congress remained thus during three weeks on an equal balance, the republicans were calling to their assistance the aid of their factions without. Continual expresses were employed between Philadelphia and Boston. These were under the management of Samuel Adams—a man, who though by no means remarkable for brilliant abilities, yet is equal to most men in popular intrigue, and the management of a faction. He eats little, drinks little, sleeps little, thinks much, and is most decisive and indefatigable in the pursuit of his objects. It was this man, who by his superior application managed at once the faction in Congress at Philadelphia, and the factions in New England. Whatever these patriots in Congress wished to have done by their colleagues without, to induce General Gage, then at the head of his Majesty's army at Boston, to give them a pretext for violent opposition, or to promote their measures in Congress, Mr. Adams advised and directed to be done; and when done, it was dispatched by express to Congress. By one of these expresses came the inflammatory resolves of the county of Suffolk, which contained a complete declaration of war against Great-Britain. By these resolves it is declared, "that no obedience is due to acts of Parliament affecting Boston:"

That "the justices of the superior courts of judicature, court of assize, &c. are unconstitutional officers, and that no *regard ought to be paid to them by the people*:"

That "the county will support and bear harmless all sheriffs and their deputies, constables, jurors and other officers, who shall *refuse to carry into execution the orders of the said courts*:"

That "the collectors of taxes, constables and other officers, retain in their hands *all public monies,* and not make any payment thereof to the provincial county treasurer:"

And that "the persons who had accepted seats at the council board, *by virtue of a mandamus from the King,* should be considered as *obstinate and incorrigible enemies to their country.*"

They advise the people "to elect the officers of militia, and to use their *utmost diligence to acquaint themselves with the art of war* as soon as possible, and for that purpose to appear under arms once in every week:"

And to carry these and other measures into execution; among many other things equally treasonable, they recommend it to the several towns to "chuse a Provincial Congress."

Upon these resolves being read, a motion was made that the Congress should give them their sanction. Long and warm debates ensued between the parties. At this time the republican faction in Congress had provided a mob, ready to execute their secret orders. The cruel practice of tarring and feathering had been long since introduced. This lessened the firmness of some of the loyalists; the vote was put and carried. Two of the dissenting members presumed to offer their protest against it in writing, which was negatived. They next insisted that the tender of their protest and its negative should be entered on the minutes; this was also rejected.

By this treasonable vote the foundation of military resistance throughout America was effectually laid. The example was now set by the people of Suffolk, and the measure was approved of by those who called themselves the *representatives of all America*. The loyal party, although they knew a great majority of the colonists were averse to the measure, perceived the improbability of stemming the torrent. They had no authority, no means in their own power to resist it; they saw those who held the powers of Government inactive spectators, and either shrinking from their duty, or uniting in the measures of sedition; they saw the flame of rebellion spreading with more rapidity in a province under the eye of his Majesty's army than in any other; and that no effectual measures were taking by Government in Britain to suppress it; and yet, as a petition to his Majesty had been ordered to be brought in, they resolved to continue their exertions. They hoped to prevail in stating the rights of America on just and constitutional principles; in proposing a plan for uniting the two countries on those principles, and in a clear, definitive and decent prayer, to ask for what a majority of the colonies wished to obtain; and as they had no reason to doubt the success of this measure in a British Parliament, they further hoped, that it would stop the effusion of blood and the ruin of their country.

With this view, as well as to probe the ultimate design of the republicans, and to know with certainty whether any proposal, short of the absolute independence of the Colonies, would satisfy them, a plan of union was drawn by a member of the loyal party [that is, by Joseph Galloway], and approved by the rest. It was so formed as to leave no room for any reasonable objection on the part of the republicans, if they meant to be united to Great Britain on any grounds whatever. It included a restoration of all their rights, and a redress of all their grievances, on constitutional principles; and it accorded with all the instructions given to them as members of Congress.

10.3

JOSEPH GALLOWAY, STATEMENT ON HIS
"PLAN OF UNION" (CONTINUED), SEPTEMBER 28, 1774

Like John Adams, Galloway reminded his congressional audience that most of September had been spent in "fruitless debates on equivocal and indecisive propositions," that is, not on those that he believed would lead to a constitutionally legitimate reconciliation. With stark clarity, Galloway rejected the two alternative strategies then before Congress for seeking redress: returning matters to the pre-1764 status quo or imposing a trade embargo. The first, he argued, rightly, would not get to the heart of the major issue confronting the empire: the existence of at least two incompatible understandings of the British imperial constitution. A trade embargo would, Galloway believed, be illegal and would lead, as it did, to Parliament's prohibiting the colonies from trading with anyone (see document 29.2). Accordingly, Galloway proposed to lay before Congress "the facts" of the current situation. He began by castigating the colonies for their selfish behavior during the worldwide Seven Years' War. He pointedly reminded them that some "Colonies gave nothing during the war; none gave equitably in proportion to their wealth, and all that did give were actuated by partial and self-interested motives, and gave only in proportion to the approach or remoteness of the danger" confronting them. Because of the lack of equity and accountability in the colonies for the enormous war debt that Britain had taken on, Galloway argued that Parliament had found it necessary to pass the Stamp Act, and because the colonies in petitions and declarations had denied Parliament's sovereign authority, it had been forced in 1766 to pass the Declaratory Act.

Galloway assessed the incompatible and contrasting constitutional claims of the colonies and Parliament, and after asserting that sovereignty demands "one supreme legislative head in every civil society" and, moreover, that allegiance and protection are reciprocal, he declares in favor of Parliament's supremacy, a position not commonly encountered in the colonies, with the curious exception of an early-1764 pamphlet by James Otis, Jr., of Massachusetts.[33] In support of his position, Galloway explained that Parliament had continuously exercised authority over the colonies, so its mid-1760s taxation of them was not unprecedented.[34] (In this, his position resembled that of Thomas Hutchinson, the former governor of Massachusetts.) Still, Galloway had to concede that Parliament's taxation of the colonies for revenue, even if within its sovereign rights and not wholly unprecedented, was "not perfectly constitutional in respect to the Colonies." "We know," he admitted, "that the whole landed interest of Britain is represented in that body, while neither the land nor the people of America hold the least participation in the legislative authority of the State. Representation, or a participation in the supreme councils of the State, is the great principle upon which the freedom of the British Government is established and secured." Keep in mind that this was argued by a man of a conservative temperament who would ultimately remain loyal to the king, not by a member of the radical faction in Congress.

With this principle settled, Galloway urged that "the right to participate in the supreme councils of the State [should be] extended, in some form, not only to America, but to all the British dominions." Indeed, it is striking how rarely, if at all, proponents of American colonial rights, while defending the equality of American subjects' rights with those of metropolitan Britons, demonstrated a comparable concern that the same rights be extended to Canadians, Irishmen, or colonists in the West or East Indies. Apparently, American essayists and delegates were concerned only with the equality between Englishmen in America and those Englishmen still living in the realm. Galloway was a refreshing exception. He insightfully went on to argue that "it is want of constitutional principle" that "is the source of American grievances," and that what was needed to repair that lack was a new structure "fixed on solid constitutional principles." And since the colonists did "not approve of a representation in Parliament," he asked "for a participation in the freedom and power of the English constitution in some other mode of incorporation." That involvement could have been accomplished by an imperial federal union of the sort that Galloway proposed to Congress, one that could have incorporated other colonists too in a constitutionally defensible political formation with the king's metropolitan British subjects.

Galloway's "Plan of Union," might have solved the constitutional conundrum facing Parliament and its colonies and might have extended equal corporate political rights throughout the empire. Still, his own understanding or defense of the antecedents that had led to the impasse was anachronistic, failing to take account of the ways that the British and imperial constitutions had changed over the course of 150 years. Thus, in writing that "the Colonists have ever sworn allegiance to the British State," he skirted around the different meanings of that state: in the mid-seventeenth century, well before the creation of Great Britain, the head of state was the king in council, and in the mid-eighteenth century it was the king in Parliament. Just as almost all American colonists were guilty of ignoring the lived reality of the eighteenth-century British Constitution, with its core commitment to Parliamentary supremacy and the post-1688 (Protestant) settlement, which tamed the monarchical prerogatives of the king and committed the country to a Protestant succession, Galloway was guilty of having moved that constitutional arrangement back into the seventeenth century, a time before Parliament gained ascendancy over the king and before his royal, rather than Crown, dominions were absorbed, as early as 1649, into those of the English Commonwealth.[35]

Paul H. Smith, ed., *Letters of Delegates to Congress, 1774–1789* (Washington, D.C.: Library of Congress, 1976–93), 1:122–27. Galloway refers to himself in the third person here.

Introductory to his motion which led to this plan, the author of it made, in substance, the following speech, which is taken from his short notes: "He told Congress that he came with instructions to propose some mode, by which the harmony between Great-Britain and the Colonies might be restored on constitutional principles: that this appeared to be the genuine sense of all the instructions brought into Congress by the Delegates of the several Colonies. He had long waited with great patience under an expectation of hearing some proposition which should tend to that salutary and important purpose; but, to his great mortification and distress, a month had been spent in fruitless debates on equivocal and indecisive propositions, which tended to inflame rather than reconcile—to produce war instead of peace between the two countries. In this disagreeable situation of things he thought it his incumbent duty to speak plainly, and to give his sentiments without the least reserve.

"There are," says he, "two propositions before the Congress for restoring the wished-for harmony: one, that Parliament should be requested to place the Colonies in the state they were in in the year 1763; the other, that a non-exportation and non-importation agreement should be adopted. I will consider these propositions, and venture to reject them both; the first, as indecisive, tending to mislead both countries, and to lay a foundation for further discontent and quarrel; the other, as illegal, and ruinous to America.

"The first proposition is indecisive, because it points out no ground of complaint—asks for a restoration of no right, settles no principle, and proposes no plan for accommodating the dispute. There is no statute which has been passed to tax or bind the Colonies since the year 1763, which was not founded on precedents and statutes of a similar nature before that period; and therefore the proposition, while it expressly denies the right of Parliament, confesses it by the strongest implication. In short, it is nugatory, and without meaning; and however it may serve, when rejected by Parliament, as it certainly will be, to form a charge of injustice upon, and to deceive and inflame the minds of the people hereafter, it cannot possibly answer any other purpose.

"The second proposition is undutiful and illegal: it is an insult on the supreme authority of the State; it cannot fail to draw on the Colonies the united resentment of the Mother Country. If we will not trade with Great Britain, she will not suffer us to trade at all. Our ports will be blocked up by British men of war, and troops will be sent to reduce us to reason and obedience. A total and sudden stagnation of commerce is what no country can bear: it must bring ruin on the Colonies: the produce of labour must perish on their hands and not only the progress of industry be stopped, but industry and labour will cease, and the country itself be thrown into anarchy and tumult. I must therefore reject both the propositions; the first as indecisive, and the other as inadmissible upon any principle of prudence or policy.

"If we sincerely mean to accommodate the difference between the two countries, and to establish their union on more firm and constitutional principles, we must take into consideration a number of facts which led the Parliament to pass the acts complained of, since the year 1763, and the real state of the Colonies. A clear and perfect knowledge of these matters only can lead us to the ground of substantial redress and permanent harmony. I will therefore call your recollection to the dangerous situation of the Colonies from the intrigues of France, and the incursions of the Canadians and their Indian allies, at the commencement of the last war. None of us can be ignorant of the just sense they then entertained of that danger, and of their incapacity to defend themselves against it, nor of the supplications made to the Parent State for its assistance, nor of the cheerfulness with which Great-Britain sent over her fleets and armies for their protection, of the millions she expended in that protection, and of the happy consequences which attended it.

"In this state of the Colonies it was not unreasonable to expect that Parliament would have levied a tax on them proportionate to their wealth, and the sums raised in Great Britain. Her ancient right, so often exercised, and never controverted, enabled her, and the occasion invited her, to do it. And yet, not knowing their wealth, a generous tenderness arising from the fear of doing them injustice, induced Parliament to forbear to levy aids upon them—It left the Colonies to do justice to themselves and to the nation. And moreover, in order to allure them to a discharge of their duty, it offered to reimburse those Colonies which should generously grant the aids that were necessary to their own safety. But what was the conduct of the Colonies on this occasion, in which their own existence was immediately concerned? However painful it may be for me to repeat, or you to hear, I must remind you of it. You all know there were Colonies which at some times granted liberal aids, and at others nothing; other Colonies gave nothing during the war; none gave equitably in proportion to their wealth, and all that did give were actuated by partial and self-interested motives, and gave only in proportion to the approach or remoteness of the danger. These delinquencies were occasioned by the want of the exercise of some supreme power to ascertain, with equity, their proportions of aids, and to over-rule the particular passions, prejudices, and interests, of the several Colonies.

"To remedy these mischiefs, Parliament was naturally led to exercise the power which had been, by its predecessors, so often exercised over the Colonies, and to pass the Stamp Act. Against this act, the Colonies petitioned Parliament, and denied its authority. Instead of proposing some remedy, by which that authority should be rendered more equitable and more constitutional over the Colonies, the petitions rested in a declaration that the Colonies could not be represented in that body. This justly alarmed the British Senate. It was thought and called by the ablest men and Britain, a clear and explicit declaration of American Independence, and compelled the Parliament to pass the Declaratory Act, in order to save its ancient and incontrovertible right of supremacy over all the parts of the empire. By this injudicious step the cause of our complaints became fixed, and instead of obtaining a constitutional reformation of the authority of Parliament over the Colonies, it brought on an explicit declaration of a right in Parliament to exercise absolute and unparticipated power over them. Nothing now can be wanting to convince us, that the Assemblies have pursued measures which have produced no relief, and answered no purpose but a bad one. I therefore hope that the collected wisdom of Congress will perceive and avoid former mistakes; that they will candidly and thoroughly examine the real merits of our dispute with the Mother Country, and take such ground as shall firmly unite us under one system of polity, and make us one people.

"In order to establish those principles, upon which alone American relief ought, in reason and policy, to be founded, I will take a brief view of the arguments on both sides of the great question between the two countries—a question in its magnitude and importance exceeded by none that has been ever agitated in the councils of any nation. The advocates for the supremacy of Parliament over the Colonies contend, that there must be one supreme legislative head in every civil society, whose authority must extend to the regulation and final decision of every matter susceptible of human direction; and that every member of the society, whether political, official, or individual must be subordinate to its supreme will, signified in its laws: that this supremacy and subordination are essential in the constitution of all States, whatever may be their forms; that no society ever did or could exist, without it; and that these truths are solidly established in the practice of all governments, and confirmed by the concurrent authority of all writers on the subject of civil society.

"These advocates also assert, what we cannot deny—That the discovery of the Colonies was made under a commission granted by the supreme authority of the British State, that they have been settled under that authority, and therefore are truly the property of that State. Parliamentary jurisdiction has been constantly exercised over them from their first settlement; its executive authority has ever run through all their inferior political systems: the Colonists have ever sworn allegiance to the British State, and have been considered, both by the State and by themselves, as subjects of the British Government. Protection and allegiance are reciprocal duties; the one cannot exist without the other. The Colonies cannot claim the protection of Britain upon any principle of reason or law, while they deny its supreme authority. Upon this ground the authority of Parliament stands too firm to be shaken by any arguments whatever; and therefore to deny that authority, and at the same time to declare their incapacity to be represented, amounts to a full and explicit declaration of independence.

"In regard to the political state of the Colonies, you must know that they are so many inferior societies, disunited and unconnected in polity. That while they deny the authority of Parliament, they are, in respect to each other, in a perfect state of nature, destitute of any supreme direction or decision whatever, and incompetent to the grant of national aids, or any other general measure whatever, even to the settlement of differences among themselves. This they have repeatedly acknowledged, and particularly by their delegates in Congress in the beginning of the last war; and the aids granted by them since that period, for their own protection, are a proof of the truth of that acknowledgment.

"You also knew that the seeds of discord are plentifully sowed in the constitution of the Colonies; that they are already grown to maturity, and have more than once broke out into open hostilities. They are at this moment only suppressed by the authority of the Parent State; and should that authority be weakened or annulled, many subjects of unsettled disputes, and which in that case, can only be settled by an appeal to the sword, must involve us in all the horrors of civil war. You will now consider whether you wish to be destitute of the protection of Great Britain, or to see a renewal of the claims of France upon America; or to remain in our present disunited state, the weak exposed to the force of the strong. I am sure no honest man can entertain wishes so ruinous to his country.

"Having thus briefly stated the arguments in favour of parliamentary authority, and considered the state of the Colonies, I am free to confess that the exercise of that authority is not perfectly constitutional in respect to the Colonies. We know that the whole landed interest of Britain is represented in that body, while neither the land nor the people of America hold the least participation in the legislative authority of the State. Representation, or a participation in the supreme councils of the State, is the great principle upon which the freedom of the British Government is established and secured. I also acknowledge, that that territory whose people have no enjoyment of this privilege, are subject to an authority unrestrained and absolute; and if the liberty of the subject were not essentially concerned in it, I should reject a distinction so odious between members of the same state, so long as it shall be continued. I wish to see it exploded, and the right to participate in the supreme councils of the State extended, in some form, not only to America, but to all the British dominions; otherwise I fear that profound and excellent fabrick of civil polity will, ere long, crumble to pieces.

"The case of the Colonies is not a new one. It was formerly the very situation of Wales, Durham and Chester.

"As to the tax, it is neither unjust or oppressive, it being rather a relief than a burthen; but it is want of constitutional principle in the authority that passed it, which is the ground for complaint. This, and this only, is the source of American grievances. Here, and here only, is the defect; and if this defect were removed, a foundation would be laid for the relief of every American complaint; the obnoxious statutes would of course be repealed, and others would be made, with the assent of the Colonies, to answer the same and better purposes; the mischiefs arising from the disunion of the Colonies would be removed; their freedom would be established, and their subordination fixed on solid constitutional principles.

"Desirous as I am to promote the freedom of the Colonies, and to prevent the mischiefs which will attend a military contest with Great-Britain, I must intreat you to desert the measures which have been so injudiciously and ineffectually pursued by antecedent Assemblies. Let us thoroughly investigate the subject matter in dispute, and endeavour to find from that investigation the means of perfect and permanent redress. In whatever we do, let us be particular and explicit, and not wander in general allegations. These will lead us to no point, nor can produce any relief; they are besides dishonourable and insidious. I would therefore acknowledge the necessity of the supreme authority of Parliament over the Colonies, because it is a proposition which we cannot deny without manifest contradiction, while we confess that we are subjects of the British Government; and if we do not approve of a representation in Parliament, let us ask for a participation in the freedom and power of the English constitution in some other mode of incorporation: for I am convinced, by long attention to the subject, that let us deliberate, and try what other expedients we may, we shall find none that can give to the Colonies substantial freedom, but some such incorporation. I therefore beseech you, by the respect you are bound to pay to the instructions of your constituents, by the regard you have for the honour and safety of your country, and as you wish to avoid a war with Great-Britain, which must terminate, at all events in the ruin of America, not to rely on a denial of the authority of Parliament, a refusal to be represented, and on a non-importation agreement; because whatever protestations, in that case, may be made to the contrary, it will prove to the world that we intend to throw off our allegiance to the State, and to involve the two countries in all the horrors of a civil war." . . .

10.4

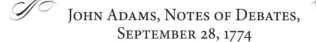

JOHN ADAMS, NOTES OF DEBATES,
SEPTEMBER 28, 1774

Like Benjamin Franklin of Pennsylvania and Thomas Hutchinson of Massachusetts twenty years earlier at the Albany Congress (see document 10.5) and Franklin a year later in drawing up articles of confederation (see document 44.1), we find Galloway, in Adams' record of his remarks and the debate they spawned, drawing attention to the need for an imperial federal plan of government with two classes of law: one purely domestic, which would concern the local "police" of a particular colony, and the second national or imperial, which would demand the assent of both the colonial central government and Parliament. The moderates in the First Continental Congress are on display in this debate, men such as James Duane and John Jay of New York and Edward Rutledge of South Carolina, giving their full support to Galloway along with their recognition of the need for a domestic central government for the otherwise wholly separate colonies, with legal and governmental affiliation with the British Crown but without any between one another. Indeed, such men would continue to press their case for a central government connecting states and nation until they achieved success some fifteen years later with the Constitution. Their defense and support of Galloway's plan rested as much on their belief that the colonies needed some form of national center—an enduring constitutional issue—as it did on their commitment to maintaining their heartfelt ties to the king and a close relationship with Great Britain.

How to conceive of the inequitable commercial relationship between the colonies and Britain continued to separate moderates and radicals as it had at the Stamp Act Congress (see document 5.1). In particular, Duane, a New York delegate to the First and Second Continental Congresses, the son of a wealthy merchant, a well-established lawyer, a staunch supporter of Galloway's plan, and in 1776 a most reticent supporter of independence, insisted that Congress "expressly ceed to Parliament the Right of regulating trade." Jay, a lawyer born into a wealthy family of Huguenot descent and later the first chief justice of the U.S. Supreme Court, demanded much the same. Edward Rutledge, the younger brother of John, a wealthy lawyer from Charleston, and at twenty-five the youngest member of the congress, was decidedly opposed to the radicals and described Galloway's proposal as "almost a perfect Plan." In large measure, Galloway and his colleagues recognized that there was "no American Constitution" connecting the colonies, so they were "totally independent of each other." That want of affiliation, the supporters of Galloway's plan believed, should not be allowed to continue, for "there is a Necessity that an American Legislature should be set up, or else that We should give the Power to Parliament or King."

Those on the other side, including Richard Henry Lee and Patrick Henry, both Virginia radicals, opposed Galloway's plan because they seemed uninterested—as such men no doubt would have been in 1754 at Albany and were in 1787 in Philadelphia—in seeing their colony cede power to a distant central government, whether in the colonies or in London.[36] Lee, one of a family of famous brothers including Arthur, Francis Lightfoot, and Thomas Ludwell, was a wealthy planter who from 1766 worked with great success in organizing Virginia's opposition to Parliament and in 1776 to king and empire. As the opponents of Galloway's plan make understandable, their two sets of concerns regarding a proposed central government were easily joined. Additionally, as Henry suggested, anticipating a powerful line of argument, Parliament should be able to tax the colonists or control their trade, but not both. As he noted, "Before We are obliged to pay Taxes as they do, let us be as free as they. Let us have our trade open with all the World." Led by Lee and Henry in Virginia, as well as by John and Samuel Adams from Massachusetts—rarely did such men hail from the well-born of the mid-Atlantic region—the congressional radicals opposed central governmental oversight—be it imperial or national.

Paul H. Smith, ed., *Letters of Delegates to Congress, 1774–1789* (Washington, D.C.: Library of Congress, 1976–93), 1:109–12.

Mr. Galloway. The Proposal I intended to make having been opposed, I have waited to hear a more effectual one. A general Non Importation from G. Britain and Ireland has been adopted, but I think this will be too gradual in its Operation for the Relief of Boston.

A General Non Exportation, I have ever looked on as an indigested Proposition. It is impossible America can exist, under a total Non Exportation. We in this Province should have tens of Thousands of People thrown upon the cold Hand of Charity. Our Ships would lie by the Walls, our Seamen would be thrown out of Bread, our Shipwrights &c. out of Employ and it would affect the landed Interest. It would weaken us in another Struggle which I fear is too near.

To explain my Plan I must state a Number of facts relative to Great Britain, and relative to America.

I hope no facts which I shall state will be disagreable.

In the last War, America was in the greatest Danger of Destruction. This was held up by the Massa[chusetts] and by the Congress in 1754. They said We are disunited among ourselves. Their is no indifferent Arbiter between us.

Requisitions came over. A No. of the Colonies gave most extensively and liberally, other[s] gave nothing, or late. Pensylvania gave nothing or late. Pensylvania gave late not for Want of Zeal or Loyalty, but owing to their Disputes, with Proprietors—their disunited State.

These Delinquencies were handed up to the Parent State, and these gave Occasion to the Stamp Act.

America with the greatest Reason and Justice complained of the Stamp Act.

Had they proposed some Plan of Policy—some Negociation but set afoot, it would have terminated in the most happy Harmony between the two Countries.

They repealed the Stamp Act, but they passed the declaratory Act.

Without some Supream Legislature, some common Arbiter, you are not, say they, part of the State.

I am as much a friend of Liberty [as] exists—and No Man shall go further, in Point of Fortune, or in Point of Blood, than the Man who now addresses you.

Burlamaqui, Grotius, Puffendorf, Hooker. There must be an Union of Wills and Strength. Distinction between a State and a Multitude. A State is animated by one Soul.

As We are not within the Circle of the Supream Jurisdiction of the Parliament, We are independent States. The Law of Great Britain dont bind us in any Case whatever.

We want the Aid and Assistance and Protection of the Arm of our Mother Country. Protection And Allegiance are reciprocal Duties. Can We lay claim to the Money and Protection of G. Britain upon any Principles of Honour or Conscience? Can We wish to become Aliens to the Mother State.

We must come upon Terms with G. Britain.

Some Gentlemen are not for Negociation. I wish I could hear some Reason against it.

The Minister must be at 20, or 30 millions to inforce his Measures.

I propose this Proposition. The Plan. 2 Classes of Laws. 1. Laws of Internal Policy. 2. Laws in which more than one Colony were concerned, raising Money for War. No one Act can be done, without the Assent of Great Britain. No one without the Assent of America. A British American Legislature.

Mr. Duane. As I mean to second this Motion, I think myself bound to lay before the Congress my Reasons. N. York thought it necessary to have a Congress for the Relief of Boston and Mass. And to do more, to lay a Plan for a lasting Accommodation with G. Britain.

Whatever may have been the Motive for departing from the first Plan of the Congress, I am unhappy that We have departed from it. The Post Office Act was before the Year 1763. Can we expect lasting Tranquility. I have given my full Assent to a Non Im and Exportation Agreement.

The Right of regulating Trade, from the local Circumstances of the Colonies, and their Disconnection with each other, cannot be exercised by the Colonies.

Mass. disputed the Navigation Act, because not represented, but made a Law of their own, to inforce that Act.

Virginia did the same nearly.

I think Justice requires that we should expressly ceed to Parliament the Right of regulating Trade.

In the Congress in 1754 which consisted of the greatest and best Men in the Colonies, this was considered as indispensable.

A civil War with America, would involve a national Bankruptcy.

Coll. Lee. How did We go on for 160 Years before the Year 1763? We flourished and grew.

This Plan would make such Changes in the Legislatures of the Colonies that I could not agree to it, without consulting my Constituents.

Mr. Jay. I am led to adopt this Plan.

It is objected that this Plan will alter our Constitutions and therefore cannot be adopted without consulting Constituents.

Does this Plan give up any one Liberty?—or interfere with any one Right.

Mr. Henry. The original Constitution of the Colonies, was founded on the broadest and most generous Base.

The Regulation of Our Trade, was Compensation enough for all the Protection we ever experienced from her.

We shall liberate our Constituents from a corrupt House of Commons, but thro them into the Arms of an American Legislature that may be bribed by that Nation which avows in the Face of the World, that Bribery is a Part of her System of Government.

Before We are obliged to pay Taxes as they do, let us be as free as they. Let us have our Trade open with all the World.

We are not to consent by the Representatives of Representatives.

I am inclined to think the present Measures lead to War.

Mr. Ed. Rutledge. I came with an Idea of getting a Bill of Rights, and a Plan of permanent Relief.

I think the Plan may be freed from almost every objection. I think it almost a perfect Plan.

Mr. Galloway. In every Govennment, Patriarchal, Monarchical, Aristocratical or democratical, there must be a Supream Legislature.

I know of no American Constitution. A Virginia Constitution, a Pensylvanian Constitution We have. We are totally independent of each other.

Every Gentleman here thinks, that Parliament ought to have the Power over Trade, because Britain protects it and us.

Why then will we not declare it.

Because Parliament and Ministry is wicked, and corrupt and will take Advantage of such Declaration to tax us—and will also Reason from this Acknowledgment, to further Power over us.

Answer. We shall not be bound further than We acknowledge it.

Is it not necessary that the Trade of the Empire should be regulated by some Power or other? Can the Empire hold together, without it. No. Who shall regulate it? Shall the Legislature of Nova Scotia, or Georgia, regulate it? Mass. or Virginia? Pensylvania or N. York. It cant be pretended. Our Legislative Powers extend no farther than the Limits of our Governments. Where then shall it be placed. There is a Necessity that an American Legislature should be set up, or else that We should give the Power to Parliament or King.

Protection. Acquiescence. Mass. Virginia.

Advantages derived from our Commerce.

10.5

 ALBANY PLAN OF UNION, JULY 9, 1754

Galloway's "Plan of Union" was not the first serious effort to connect in some way most the colonies; that honor belongs to the intercolonial or continental congress that gathered on June 19, 1754, when twenty-four commissioners representing seven colonies (New Jersey and Virginia refused to send delegates, and a number of the southern colonies were not invited) met at the invitation of the British Lords of Trade (the principal British ministerial committee then overseeing colonial matters).[37] They did so at the Albany City Hall with their northern Native American allies to devise a concerted plan of defense but also, at least as envisioned by the forward-looking delegation from Massachusetts, to enter "'into articles of Union and Confederation with the aforesaid Governments.'"[38] At a minimum, the delegates hoped that the meeting would repair the colonies' difficult relationship with the Six Nations of the Iroquois Confederation.

The large Massachusetts delegation included John Chandler, Thomas Hutchinson, Samuel Welles, John Worthington, and Oliver Partridge, who, eleven years later, would attend the Stamp Act Congress. From Rhode Island came Stephen Hopkins and Martin Howard, Jr.; from New Hampshire, Theodore Atkinson, Henry Sherburne, Jr., Meshec Weare, and Richard Wibbird; and from Connecticut, William Pitkin, Elisha Williams, and Roger Wolcott. From Maryland there were Abraham Barnes and Benjamin Tasker; from Pennsylvania, the already celebrated Benjamin Franklin, and Isaac Norris and John Penn; and from New York, although not officially commissioned to attend, came John Chambers, William Johnson,

Joseph Murray, Philip Livingston (also a delegate to the Stamp Act Congress), and William Smith.[39] Hopkins and Franklin would be the two oldest delegates in the Continental Congress in 1775 and, with Philip Livingston, the only Albany delegates to sign the Declaration of Independence, with Franklin being on hand, most remarkably, to sign as well the Constitution in 1787. The "Albany Plan of Union," like Galloway's plan, was rejected by the colonies long before it reached Britain because colonial legislatures had no intention of seeing their own power limited by another layer of government.[40] The colonies may, in fact, have preferred to rely on the British administration to coordinate their joint activities and, in some instances, to shoulder much of the burden for their common defense.[41]

The plan was based, in the main, on Franklin's "Short Hints," but included elements of Hutchinson's "New England Plan."[42] It presented a federal structure that addressed both the colonies' imperial relationship with Parliament and the lack of a relationship among the colonies. The plan contributed later to Galloway's "Plan of Union," including some verbatim language, a common structure, a fully federal protection of internal police powers within each colony, and the creation of a president-general and a Grand Council. Where they most differed, however, concerned two matters: their primary foci, and the relationship between the continental American legislature and Parliament. In the Albany Plan, the focus is primarily military, though ancillary issues such as taxation were also necessarily incorporated, and there is no mention of Parliament—it was to "the King in Council" to which all laws would be sent for his approbation, not to the king in Parliament. Still, in both plans the president-general, as the king's representative, would enjoy the traditional royal power of an absolute veto over legislation. Nonetheless, in contradistinction to later American claims to the contrary, it was to Parliament that Franklin had looked for permission to act, for he had written that "humble application be made for an act of the Parliament of Great Britain by virtue of which one General Government may be formed in America including all the said Colonies within & under which Government each Colony may retain its present constitution."[43]

The Galloway plan was not limited to military concerns, and more importantly, under it all "general" legislation—it is unclear whether this was only for intercolonial matters or also for broader imperial ones affecting Britain itself—had to be passed by both the American General Council and Parliament before becoming law. Galloway's plan, the Albany Plan, and Franklin's proposal of July 1775 (document 44.1) served as models of an American federal union well into the future.[44]

Robert C. Newbold, *The Albany Congress and Plan of Union of 1754* (New York: Vantage, 1955), 184–87.

Plan of a proposed Union of the Several Colonies of Massachusetts Bay, New Hampshire, Connecticut, Rhode Island, New York, New Jersey, Pensilvania, Maryland, North

Carolina, and South Carolina, for their mutual defence & Security & for the Extending the British Settlements in North America.

That humble application be made for an act of the Parliament of Great Britain by virtue of which one General Government may be formed in America including all the said Colonies within & under which Government each Colony may retain its present constitution except in the Perticulars wherein a Change may be directed by the said act as Hereafter follow.—

That the said General Government be administered by a President General to be appointed & supported by the Crown, & a Grand Council to be chosen by the Representatives of the People of the several Colonies met in their respective Assemblies.

That within        Months after the passing of such act, the House of Representatives in the several Assemblies that happens to be sitting within that time or that shall be especially for that purpose convened may & Shall chuse Members for the Grand Council in the following proportions that is to say.

| | | | |
|---|---|---|---|
| Massachusetts Bay | 7 | Pensilvania | 6 |
| New Hampshire | 2 | Maryland | 4 |
| Connecticut | 5 | Virginia | 7 |
| Rhode Island | 2 | North Carolina | 4 |
| New York | 4 | South Carolina | 4 |
| New Jersey | 3 | | 48 |

Who shall meet for the first time at the City of Philadelphia in Pensilvania being called by the President General as soon as conveniently may be after his Appointment.

That there shall be a new Election of members for the Grand Council every three Years, & on the Death or resignation of any Member, his place shall be Supplyed by a new choice at the next sitting of the Assembly of the Colony he represented.

That after the first three years when the proportion of Money arising out of each Colony, to the General Treasury can be known, the Number of Members to be chosen for each Colony shall from time to time in all Ensuing Elections be regulated by that proportion yet so as that the Number to be chosen by any one Province be not more than Seven nor less than two.

That the Grand Council shall meet once in every year and oftener if occasion require at such time & place as they shall adjourn to at the last preceding meeting or as they shall be called to meet at by the President General on any Emergency he having first obtained in Writing the consent of Seven of the Members to such a Call, & sent due & timely notice to the whole.

That the Grand Council have power to chuse their Speaker & shall neither be dissolved, prorogued, nor continue Sitting longer than Six Weeks at one time, without the[ir] own consent or the Special Command of the Crown.

That the Members of the Grand Council shall be allowed for their Service ten Shillings Sterling per diem during their Sessions and Journey to & from the place of meeting; twenty Miles to be reckoned a Days Journey.

That the assent of the President General be requisite to all Acts of the Grand Council, & that it be his Office & duty to cause them to be Carried into Execution.

That the President General with the advice of the Grand Council hold or direct all Indian Treaties in which the General Interest or Welfare of the Colonies be concerned, & to make Peace or declare War with Indian Nations. That they make such Laws as they judge necessary for regulating all Indian Trade. That they make all purchases from Indians for the Crown, of Lands now not within the bounds of particular Colonies or that Shall not be within their Bounds when some of them are reduced to more Convenient Dimensions. That they make New Settlements on such Purchases by Granting Lands in the Kings name reserving a Quit Rent to the Crown for the use of the General Treasury. That they make Laws for Regulating & Governing such new Settlements till the Crown shall think fit to form them into particular Governments. That they may raise & pay Soldiers, and build Forts for the Defense of any of the Colonies, & equip Vessels of force to guard the Coast and protect the Trade on the Ocean Lakes or great Rivers, but they shall not impress men in any Colony without the consent of its Legislature—That for these Purposes they have power to make Laws, & lay, & levy such General Dutys Imposts or Taxes as to themselves appear most equal & just considering the ability & other Circumstances of the Inhabitants in the Several Colonies, & such as may be collected with the least Inconvenience to the People, rather discourageing Luxury, than loading Industry with unnecessary Burthens—that they may appoint a general Treasurer, and perticular Treasurer in each Government when necessary and from time to time may order the Sums in the Treasuries of each Government into the General Treasury, or draw on them for special Payments as they find most convenient, Yet no money to Issue but by joint orders of the President General and Grand Council except when Sums have been appropriated to perticular purposes, and the President General is previously impowered by an Act to draw for Such Sums—That the General Accounts shall be yearly settled & reported to the Several Assemblies.—that a Quorom of the Grand Counsil, impowered to Act with the President General do consist of Twenty Five Members among who there shall be one or more from a Majority of the Colonies.—That the Laws made by them for the purposes aforesaid shall not be repugnant but as near as may be agreeable to the Laws of England and shall be transmitted to the King in Council for approbation as soon as may be after their passing and if not disapproved within three years after presentation to remain in force.—That in case of the Death of the President General the Speaker of the Grand Council for the time being shall Succeed and be vested with the same power and authorities & continue till the Kings pleasure be known.

That all Military Commission Officers whether for land or Sea Service to act under this General Constitution Shall be nominated by the President General, but the approbation of the General Council is to be obtained before they receive their Commissions And all civil Officers are to be nominated by the General Council, and to receive the President Generals approbation before they officiate But in case of Vacancy by Death or removal of any Officer civil or Military under this Constitution, the Governor of the

Provinces in which such Vacancy happens may appoint till the Pleasure of the President General and Grand Council be known.—That the perticular Military as well as civil Establishments in each Colony remain in their present State, this General Constitution notwithstanding; and that on Sudden Emergencys any Colony may defend itself, and lay the Accounts of Expence Thence arisen before the President General and Grand Council, who may allow and order payment of the same as far as they judge such Accounts just and reasonable.

## 11. COLONIAL BOYCOTTS OF BRITISH GOODS,
### SEPTEMBER–OCTOBER 1774

The authorship of the late-September resolutions made by the Continental Congress remains uncertain, but it is believed that John Adams may have written them. The motion to prohibit the importation of British and Irish goods was made by Richard Henry Lee of Virginia, and it passed unanimously.[45] The motion to prohibit colonial exports was more contentious, and it faced opposition from a number of southern delegates, including those of Virginia and South Carolina; it was claimed that the exemption resulted from an effort "not to injure . . . fellow-subjects in Great Britain, Ireland, or the West Indies." Congress, in the end, committed its member colonies to cease importation of British and Irish goods and to end exportation to Great Britain, Ireland, and the West Indies "unless the grievances of America are redressed before that time." Congress did not really consider the financial difficulties that their fellow colonists in Ireland and the West Indies would experience as a result of these measures, or the suffering, even famine, that the loss of continental foodstuffs might inflict on African slaves in the British and French West Indies. A committee was appointed to "bring in a plan for carrying into effect, the non-importation, non-consumption, and non-exportation resolved on."

The agreed-upon Continental Association of course wasn't the first attempt by American colonists to put economic pressure on British commercial interests in an effort to impel Parliament to rescind taxes or punitive legislation, or to change policy. Beginning in October 1765, New York merchants—at about the same time that the Stamp Act Congress was breaking up—had agreed to boycott English imports, and during the next two months, Philadelphia and Boston merchants did the same. Those embargoes did much to encourage Parliament to repeal the Stamp Act, certainly more than off-putting petitions to the king and Parliament had done.[46] Similar actions frequently occurred during the years 1767–70, but in most instances at the provincial level.[47] The Continental Congress reasonably might have believed that comparable resolutions would work once more in bringing British merchants to their defense. This time, they did not achieve their goal.[48]

Curiously, the precise authorship of the Association is unknown, most likely because "it was not one of the more glamorous state papers produced by Congress and rival claimants did not step forward in the years following the Revolution to boast of its paternity."[49] Yet it is likely one of the first "national" (more accurately, continental) governmental acts passed by Congress, even though there was as yet no American national state and Congress lacked the legal authority to tax or pass binding legislation. The committee, appointed on September 30, consisted of Thomas Mifflin of Pennsylvania, Thomas Johnson of Maryland, Richard Henry Lee of Virginia, Thomas Cushing of Massachusetts, and Isaac Low of New York. Among them, Mifflin and Lee leaned toward independence. Cushing was a leading Boston merchant and politician who played an ever-more active role in opposition to the Stamp Act and the Townshend Acts. Still, he refused to support the colonies' strongly worded declarations or, ultimately, the Declaration of Independence.[50] Low, too, was a successful and leading New York City merchant and banker who exemplified, even more than Cushing, those who went to the brink of separatism before, at the last minute, refusing to support it. He later joined the ranks of loyalists, and in 1783 left New York City with the fleet and sailed to Great Britain.[51]

As on most congressional committees, as well as in Congress itself, membership was divided between those dedicated to protecting colonial rights while earnestly searching for a means to restore, constitutionally, imperial relations with Britain, and those pushing, more or less incrementally, even if in ways not always obvious to themselves, toward independence. On October 12 the committee brought in its report; it was debated on October 15 and 17; and "after sundry amendments," it was adopted on October 18 and "ordered to be transcribed, that it may be signed by the several members."[52] It was the first, though possibly the least famous, document to be signed by the congressional delegates.

To put into effect the nonimportation, nonconsumption, and nonexportation resolutions, Congress appointed a committee to formulate a plan. The plan, the Continental Association, followed that of earlier colonial boycotts, most particularly Virginia's in 1769 (which had been adopted by others as well) and again in August 1774. The nonimportation of British and Irish goods, along with the cessation of the slave trade, was to begin on December 1, 1774, and the nonconsumption of specified goods on March 1, 1775. Nonexportation, again, was, "at the insistence of the southern staple colonies," put off until September 10, 1775.[53] According to Merrill Jensen, the Association had a powerful economic impact: British imports to the North American colonies dropped by ninety percent between 1774 and 1775.[54] But of possibly equal importance, the Association was the first measure to extend intercolonial governance into the colonies themselves. In addition, this unusually muscular congressional measure forced colonists to choose sides in the intensifying conflict with Britain.

The Association begins by attesting to the colonists' "allegiance to his majesty" and their "affection and regard for our fellow-subjects in Great-Britain and elsewhere." It next explains that the colonists were filled with the "most alarming apprehensions, at those grievances and distresses, with which his Majesty's American subjects are oppressed," concluding that "the present unhappy situation of our affairs is occasioned by a ruinous system of colony administration, adopted by the British ministry about the year 1763." Following this are details of the colonists' grievances, including the by-now perfunctory ones against parliamentary taxation and its limitation of jury trials in the colonies, and newer ones against the Coercive Acts, including the Quebec Act. One should take note, in the religiously motivated protest against the Quebec Act, of the delegates' description of themselves as members of "free Protestant colonies."

Congress then claimed that "to obtain redress of these grievances, which threaten destruction to the lives, liberty, and property of his majesty's subjects, in North America," it adopted "a non-importation, non-consumption, and non-exportation agreement" that, when "faithfully adhered to, will prove the most speedy, effectual, and peaceable measure" to put an end to the difficulties. Congress pledged to increase the number and quality of sheep in the colonies, to implement colony-wide price controls, and to put in place a set of intrusive moral strictures similar to those one might have found in England a century earlier during the Civil War. This last component, although serving an important economic function, was also reflective of a certain kind of Reformed Protestant moralism widespread in America.[55] While encouraging "frugality, economy, and industry," it declared that all Americans should make every effort to "discountenance and discourage every species of extravagance and dissipation, especially all horse-racing, and all kinds of gaming, cock-fighting, exhibitions of shews, plays, and other expensive diversions and entertainments." And for those who "take advantage of the scarcity of goods" by raising prices, Congress stipulated that "no person ought, nor will any of us deal with any such person."

More threateningly, the Association stipulates that "a committee be chosen . . . whose business it shall be attentively to observe the conduct of all persons touching this association," and if "any person within the limits of their appointment has violated this association," his name was to be published so "that all such foes to the rights of British-America may be publicly known, and universally contemned as the enemies of American liberty." Similarly, committees of correspondence, at Congress' urging and without the approval of still-legal provincial governments, were to "inspect the entries of their custom-houses, and inform each other, from time to time, of the true state thereof, and of every other material circumstance that may occur relative to this association." A conservative observer of Congress at the time compared the Association to "the Spanish Inquisition," calling it "subversive of, inconsistent with, the wholesome laws of our happy Constitution; it abrogates or suspends many of them essential to the peace and order of Government." As Janice Potter further observes, "There was, on the surface at least, a most blatant contradiction between Patriot rhetoric about liberty and their intolerance of opposing views and willingness to violate others' freedom of conscience."[56] Of course, much the same could be said of Congress' overall treatment of any group lacking in appropriate patriotic enthusiasm.

Though the Association was not exactly freedom enhancing, John Adams was likely right in viewing it "as the commencement of the American Union," and John H. Powell in thinking that it was "the first act binding on the American people generally of a constituted American authority larger than" their colonial governments.[57] But it was not a particularly liberal beginning to truly national government. As the historian Lynn Montross observes: "This phase abounded in ugly incidents. At their worst the committees of safety were composed of petty tyrants, addicted to snooping, who made it their business to supervise the moral conduct as well as the patriotism of their communities. Publicity and social ostracism were potent enough weapons, but too often the village Cromwells did not hesitate to sanction such reprisals as tarring and feathering."[58] Given the extralegal status of Congress and the lack of a legally constituted continental government with the authority to order such action, such intrusiveness was all the more remarkable, and suggestive of anything but an individualistic and freedom-enhancing beginning to the first actions of what was to become an American national state.[59]

## 11.1

 NONIMPORTATION, NONCONSUMPTION, AND NONEXPORTATION RESOLUTIONS, SEPTEMBER 27 AND 30, 1774

Worthington Chauncey Ford et al. eds., *Journals of the Continental Congress, 1774–1789* (Washington, D.C.: Government Printing Office, 1904–37), 1:43, 51–53.

TUESDAY, SEPTR. 27, 1774, AM

The Congress met according to adjournment, and resuming the consideration of the means most proper to be used for a restoration of American rights,

*Resolved unanimously,* That from and after the first day of December next, there be no importation into British America from Great Britain or Ireland, of any goods, wares or merchandizes whatsoever, or from any other place, of any such goods, wares or merchandizes, as shall have been exported from Great-Britain or Ireland; and that no such goods, wares or merchandizes, imported after the said first day of December next, be used or purchased.

Adjourned till to-morrow.

[FRIDAY, SEPTEMBER 30, 1774]

Wednesday and Thursday being taken up in the consideration and debates on the means, &c., the Congress met on

FRIDAY, SEPTR. 30

and upon the question,

*Resolved,* That from and after the 10th day of Septr., 1775, the exportation of all merchandize and every commodity whatsoever to Great Britain, Ireland and the West Indies, ought to cease, unless the grievances of America are redressed before that time.

*Agreed,* That Mr. [Thomas] Cushing, Mr. [Isaac] Low, Mr. [Thomas] Mifflin, Mr. [Richard Henry] Lee, and Mr. [Thomas] Johnson, be a committee to bring in a plan for carrying into effect, the non-importation, non-consumption, and non-exportation resolved on.

11.2

 CONTINENTAL ASSOCIATION, OCTOBER 20, 1774

Worthington Chauncey Ford et al., eds., *Journals of the Continental Congress, 1774–1789* (Washington, D.C.: Government Printing Office, 1904–37), 1:75–81. Note: In the resolution on nonimportation, "paneles" refers to unpurified brown sugar.

THURSDAY, OCTOBER 20, 1774.

The Congress met.

The association being copied, was read and signed at the table, and is as follows:—
Here insert the Association.

WE, his majesty's most loyal subjects, the delegates of the several colonies of New-Hampshire, Massachusetts-Bay, Rhode-Island, Connecticut, New-York, New-Jersey, Pennsylvania, the three lower counties of New-Castle, Kent and Sussex, on Delaware, Maryland, Virginia, North-Carolina, and South-Carolina, deputed to represent them in a continental Congress, held in the city of Philadelphia, on the 5th day of September, 1774, avowing our allegiance to his majesty, our affection and regard for our fellow-subjects in Great-Britain and elsewhere, affected with the deepest anxiety, and most alarming apprehensions, at those grievances and distresses, with which his Majesty's American subjects are oppressed; and having taken under our most serious deliberation, the state of the whole continent, find, that the present unhappy situation of our affairs is occasioned by a ruinous system of colony administration, adopted by the British ministry about the year 1763, evidently calculated for inslaving these colonies, and, with them, the British empire. In prosecution of which system, various acts of parliament have been passed, for raising a revenue in America, for depriving the American subjects, in many instances, of the constitutional trial by jury, exposing their lives to danger, by directing a new and illegal trial beyond the seas, for crimes alleged to have been committed in America: and in prosecution of the same system, several late, cruel, and oppressive acts have been passed, respecting the town of Boston and the Massachusetts-Bay, and also an act for extending the province of Quebec, so as to border on the western frontiers of these colonies, establishing an arbitrary government therein, and discouraging the settlement of British subjects in that wide extended country; thus, by the influence of civil principles and ancient prejudices, to dispose the inhabitants to act with hostility against the free Protestant colonies, whenever a wicked ministry shall chuse so to direct them.

To obtain redress of these grievances, which threaten destruction to the lives, liberty, and property of his majesty's subjects, in North America, we are of opinion, that a non-importation, non-consumption, and non-exportation agreement, faithfully adhered to, will prove the most speedy, effectual, and peaceable measure: and, therefore, we do, for ourselves, and the inhabitants of the several colonies, whom we represent, firmly agree and associate, under the sacred ties of virtue, honour and love of our country, as follows:

1. That from and after the first day of December next, we will not import, into British America, from Great-Britain or Ireland, any goods, wares, or merchandise whatsoever, or from any other place, any such goods, wares, or merchandise, as shall have been exported from Great-Britain or Ireland; nor will we, after that day, import any East-India tea from any part of the world; nor any molasses, syrups, paneles, coffee, or pimento, from the British plantations or from Dominica; nor wines from Madeira, or the Western Islands; nor foreign indigo.

2. We will neither import nor purchase, any slave imported after the first day of December next; after which time, we will wholly discontinue the slave trade, and will neither be concerned in it ourselves, nor will we hire our vessels, nor sell our commodities or manufactures to those who are concerned in it.

3. As a non-consumption agreement, strictly adhered to, will be an effectual security for the observation of the non-importation, we, as above, solemnly agree and associate, that, from this day, we will not purchase or use any tea, imported on account of the East-India company, or any on which a duty hath been or shall be paid; and from and after the first day of March next, we will not purchase or use any East-India tea whatever; nor will we, nor shall any person for or under us, purchase or use any of those goods, wares, or merchandise, we have agreed not to import, which we shall know, or have cause to suspect, were imported after the first day of December, except such as come under the rules and directions of the tenth article hereafter mentioned.

4. The earnest desire we have, not to injure our fellow-subjects in Great-Britain, Ireland, or the West-Indies, induces us to suspend a non-exportation, until the tenth day of September, 1775; at which time, if the said acts and parts of acts of the British parliament herein after mentioned are not repealed, we will not, directly or indirectly, export any merchandise or commodity whatsoever to Great-Britain, Ireland, or the West-Indies, except rice to Europe.

5. Such as are merchants, and use the British and Irish trade, will give orders, as soon as possible, to their factors, agents and correspondents, in Great-Britain and Ireland, not to ship any goods to them, on any pretence whatsoever, as they cannot be received in America; and if any merchant, residing in Great-Britain or Ireland, shall directly or

indirectly ship any goods, wares or merchandise, for America, in order to break the said non-importation agreement, or in any manner contravene the same, on such unworthy conduct being well attested, it ought to be made public; and, on the same being so done, we will not, from thenceforth, have any commercial connexion with such merchant.

6. That such as are owners of vessels will give positive orders to their captains, or masters, not to receive on board their vessels any goods prohibited by the said non-importation agreement, on pain of immediate dismission from their service.

7. We will use our utmost endeavours to improve the breed of sheep, and increase their number to the greatest extent; and to that end, we will kill them as seldom as may be, especially those of the most profitable kind; nor will we export any to the West-Indies or elsewhere; and those of us, who are or may become overstocked with, or can conveniently spare any sheep, will dispose of them to our neighbours, especially to the poorer sort, on moderate terms.

8. We will, in our several stations, encourage frugality, economy, and industry, and promote agriculture, arts and the manufactures of this country, especially that of wool; and will discountenance and discourage every species of extravagance and dissipation, especially all horse-racing, and all kinds of gaming, cock-fighting, exhibitions of shews, plays, and other expensive diversions and entertainments; and on the death of any relation or friend, none of us, or any of our families, will go into any further mourning-dress, than a black crape or ribbon on the arm or hat, for gentlemen, and a black ribbon and necklace for ladies, and we will discontinue the giving of gloves and scarves at funerals.

9. Such as are venders of goods or merchandise will not take advantage of the scarcity of goods, that may be occasioned by this association, but will sell the same at the rates we have been respectively accustomed to do, for twelve months last past.—And if any vender of goods or merchandise shall sell any such goods on higher terms, or shall, in any manner, or by any device whatsoever violate or depart from this agreement, no person ought, nor will any of us deal with any such person, or his or her factor or agent, at any time thereafter, for any commodity whatever.

10. In case any merchant, trader, or other person, shall import any goods or merchandise, after the first day of December, and before the first day of February next, the same ought forthwith, at the election of the owner, to be either re-shipped or delivered up to the committee of the county or town, wherein they shall be imported, to be stored at the risque of the importer, until the non-importation agreement shall cease, or be sold under the direction of the committee aforesaid; and in the last-mentioned case, the owner or owners of such goods shall be reimbursed out of the sales, the first cost and charges, the profit, if any, to be applied towards relieving and employing such poor inhabitants of the town of Boston, as are immediate sufferers by the Boston port-bill; and a particular account of all goods so returned, stored, or sold, to be inserted in the public papers; and if any goods or merchandises shall be imported after the said first day of February, the same ought forthwith to be sent back again, without breaking any of the packages thereof.

11. That a committee be chosen in every county, city, and town, by those who are qualified to vote for representatives in the legislature, whose business it shall be attentively to observe the conduct of all persons touching this association; and when it shall be made to appear, to the satisfaction of a majority of any such committee, that any person within the limits of their appointment has violated this association, that such majority do forthwith cause the truth of the case to be published in the gazette; to the end, that all such foes to the rights of British-America may be publicly known, and universally contemned as the enemies of American liberty; and thenceforth we respectively will break off all dealings with him or her.

12. That the committee of correspondence, in the respective colonies, do frequently inspect the entries of their custom-houses, and inform each other, from time to time, of the true state thereof, and of every other material circumstance that may occur relative to this association.

13. That all manufactures of this country be sold at reasonable prices, so that no undue advantage be taken of a future scarcity of goods.

14. And we do further agree and resolve, that we will have no trade, commerce, dealings or intercourse whatsoever, with any colony or province, in North-America, which shall not accede to, or which shall hereafter violate this association, but will hold them as unworthy of the rights of freemen, and as inimical to the liberties of their country.

And we do solemnly bind ourselves and our constituents, under the ties aforesaid, to adhere to this association, until such parts of the several acts of parliament passed since the close of the last war, as impose or continue duties on tea, wine, molasses, syrups, paneles, coffee, sugar, pimento, indigo, foreign paper, glass, and painters' colours, imported into America, and extend the powers of the admiralty courts beyond their ancient limits, deprive the American subject of trial by jury, authorize the judge's certificate to indemnify the prosecutor from damages, that he might otherwise be liable to from a trial by his peers, require oppressive security from a claimant of ships or goods seized, before he shall be allowed to defend his property, are repealed.—And until that part of the act of the 12 G. 3. ch. 24, entitled "An act for the better securing his majesty's dock-yards, magazines, ships, ammunition, and stores," by which any persons charged with committing any of the offences therein described, in America, may be tried in any shire or county within the realm, is repealed—and until the four acts, passed the last session of parliament, viz. that for stopping the port and blocking up the harbour of Boston—that for altering the charter and government of the Massachusetts-Bay—and that which is entitled "An act for the better administration of justice, &c."—and that "for extending the limits of Quebec, &c." are repealed. And we recommend it to the provincial conventions, and to the committees in the respective colonies, to establish such farther regulations as they may think proper, for carrying into execution this association.

The foregoing association being determined upon by the Congress, was ordered to be subscribed by the several members thereof; and thereupon, we have hereunto set our respective names accordingly.

In Congress, Philadelphia, *October 20, 1774.*

Signed,                                                                    Peyton Randolph, *President.*

| New Hampshire | { Jno. Sullivan<br>{ Nathel. Folsom | | { J. Kinsey<br>{ Wil: Livingston |
| Massachusetts<br>Bay | ⎧ Thomas Cushing<br>⎨ Saml. Adams<br>⎨ John Adams<br>⎩ Robt. Treat Paine | New Jersey | { Stepn. Crane<br>{ Richd. Smith<br>{ John De Hart |
| Rhode Island | { Step. Hopkins<br>{ Sam: Ward | Pennsylvania | ⎧ Jos. Galloway<br>⎨ John Dickinson<br>⎨ Cha Humphreys<br>⎨ Thomas Mifflin<br>⎨ E. Biddle<br>⎨ John Morton<br>⎩ Geo: Ross |
| Connecticut | ⎧ Elipht Dyer<br>⎨ Roger Sherman<br>⎩ Silas Deane | | |
| New York | ⎧ Isaac Low<br>⎨ John Alsop<br>⎨ John Jay<br>⎨ Jas. Duane<br>⎨ Phil. Livingston<br>⎨ Wm. Floyd<br>⎨ Henry Wisner<br>⎩ S: Boerum | The Lower Counties<br>New Castle | { Cæsar Rodney<br>{ Tho. M: Kean<br>{ Geo: Read |
| | | Maryland | ⎧ Mat Tilghman<br>⎨ Ths. Johnson Junr.<br>⎨ Wm. Paca<br>⎩ Samuel Chase |
| Virginia | ⎧ Richard Henry Lee<br>⎨ Go. Washington<br>⎨ P. Henry Jr.<br>⎨ Richard Bland<br>⎨ Benja. Harrison<br>⎩ Edmd. Pendleton | South Carolina | ⎧ Henry Middleton<br>⎨ Tho Lynch<br>⎨ Christ Gadsden<br>⎨ J Rutledge<br>⎩ Edward Rutledge |
| North Carolina | ⎧ Will Hooper<br>⎨ Joseph Hewes<br>⎩ Rd. Caswell | | |

Ordered, that this association be committed to the press, and that one hundred & twenty copies be struck off.

11.3

 John Adams, Proposed Resolutions,
September 30, 1774

The following resolutions, along with ones that Congress later put forward
(see document 11.4), help illuminate the interplay between the pressing demands

of the Massachusetts delegation for ever-more radical measures and those of the majority in Congress for continued moderation, in hopes of an eventual reconciliation. John Adams' resolutions sought, unsuccessfully, an immediate cessation of trade upon the advent of British military activity. Like the Suffolk resolves (document 9.1), Adams urges that colonial imperial officials be taken into custody if resistance leaders in Massachusetts (most likely the Adams cousins and like-minded colleagues) are arrested. He even goes so far as to insist that such official actions be considered "a Declaration of War and a Commencement of Hostilities against all the Colonies and that Reprisals ought to be made in all the Colonies." Some of his sentiments later found more nuanced expression in the resolves of Congress issued a week or so later.

Paul H. Smith, ed., *Letters of Delegates to Congress, 1774–1789* (Washington, D.C.: Library of Congress, 1976–93), 1:131–32.

Resolved, That the Province of the Massachusetts Bay, and the Town of Boston are now Suffering and Struggling in the common Cause of American Freedom and therefore that it is the indispensible Duty of all the Colonies, to Support them by every necessary Means, and to the last Extremity.

Whereas Hostilities have been already been commenced against the Province of Massachusetts-Bay and through them against all the Colonies, and whereas this congress have already advised the People of that Province by no Means to Submit to the late Act of Parliament for altering their Government,

Resolved, that in Case Hostilities should be further pursued against that Province, and Submission be attempted to be compelled by Force of Arms, that as soon as Intelligence of this shall be communicated to the several Colonies, they ought immediately to cease all Exportations of Goods Wares & Merchandise to Great Britain, Ireland and the West Indies.

Resolved, That, in Case any Person or Persons, Should be arrested, in the Massachusetts Bay, or any other Colony, by General Gage or any other Person, in order to be sent to Great Britain to be there tryed for any Crime whatsoever, committed in America, under Pretence of Authority of the Statute of Henry the Eighth or that of the present Reign, that this ought to be considered, as a Declaration of War and a Commencement of Hostilities against all the Colonies and that Reprisals ought to be made in all the Colonies, and held as Hostages for the Security of the Person or Persons so arrested, and all Exportations of Merchandise to Great Britain Ireland and the West Indies ought immediately to cease.

*(Whereas the Debts and Taxes, the Luxury and Venality prevalent in Great Britain prove too clearly that Americans have can have little well grounded Hope of Defence, Protection or Security from anything but their own wisdom, & Valour, Frugality and Industry, in Times to come,*

*Resolved that it be recommended to all the Colonies, to establish by Provincial Laws, where it can be done, a regular well furnished, and disciplined Militia, and where it cannot be done by Law, by voluntary Associations, and private Agreements.*

*Resolved that it be recommended to all the Colonies, to encourage Arts Manufactures and Agriculture, by all Means in their Power, and for this End to establish in each Colony a distinct Society.)*

11.4

  CONGRESSIONAL RESOLUTIONS, OCTOBER 7–11, 1774

On October 7, Congress discussed a letter from the Boston Committee of Correspondence of September 29 (it, along with the Suffolk resolves, was the only correspondence officially received by Congress). The Boston Committee complained of General Gage's building fortifications and asked for Congress' advice: "If the Congress advise to quit the town,—they obey—if it is judged that by maintaining their ground they can better serve the public cause, they will not shrink from hardship & danger."[60] Congress appointed a committee of three to write General Gage to impress upon him, along the lines sketched out by John Adams in his resolves, that Boston's suffering was that of the colonies. Thomas Lynch of South Carolina, Samuel Adams of Massachusetts, and Edmund Pendleton of Virginia were appointed to the committee.

The resolution of October 8 fell far short of the hoped-for or threatened declaration of war proposed by John Adams. Congress simply announced that if Massachusetts were to be attacked, "all America ought to support them." Still, even this mild statement was strongly opposed by Galloway and Duane as treasonous; indeed, they sought to have their protests entered into the congressional record, and when that was refused, Galloway tried to persuade Duane to join him in boycotting Congress.[61] The resolutions of October 10 again disappointed the Boston Committee of Correspondence by advising Bostonians against abandoning the city and encouraging them "to submit to a suspension of the administration of Justice"; Richard Henry Lee opposed the measure as being insufficiently aggressive. More to Boston's and, no doubt, Adams' and Lee's liking was the last resolution on the 10th, which held those who "act under any commission or authority, in any wise derived from the act passed in the last session of parliament, changing the form of government, and violating the charter of the province of Massachusetts-bay, ought to be held in detestation and abhorrence by all good men." Finally, on October 11, the people of Boston were advised to "conduct themselves peaceably towards his excellency General Gage . . . [while] avoiding & discountenancing every violation of his Majesty's property, or any insult to his troops." Congress, still a predominantly moderate body, was not yet ready to be led into declaring war (or even less so, independence) by its radical New England members.

Worthington Chauncey Ford et al., eds., *Journals of the Continental Congress, 1774–1789* (Washington, D.C.: Government Printing Office, 1904–37), 1:57–62.

FRIDAY, OCTOBER 7, 1774

The Congress resumed the consideration of the letter from the committee of correspondence in Boston [dated September 29], & after some debate,

*Resolved,* That a committee be appointed to prepare a letter to his excellency General Gage, representing "that the town of Boston, & province of Massachusetts-bay, are considered by all America, as suffering in the common cause, for their noble and spirited opposition to oppressive acts of parliament, calculated to deprive us of our most sacred rights and privileges." . . .

To entreat his excellency, from the assurance we have of the peaceable disposition of the inhabitants of the town of Boston and the province of the Massachusetts-bay, to discontinue his fortifications, and that a free and safe communication be restored and continued between the town of Boston & the country, and prevent all injuries on the part of the troops, until his Majesty's pleasure shall be known, after the measures now adopting shall have been laid before him.

Mr. [Thomas] Lynch, Mr. S. Adams, and Mr. [Edmund] Pendleton, are appointed the committee to prepare a letter agreeable to the foregoing resolution.

SATURDAY, OCTOBER 8, 1774

The Congress resumed consideration of the letter from Boston, and upon motion,

*Resolved,* That this Congress approve of the opposition by the Inhabitants of the Massachusetts-bay, to the execution of the late acts of Parliament; and if the same shall be attempted to be carryed into execution by force, in such case, all America ought to support them in their opposition.

MONDAY, OCTOBER 10, 1774

The Congress resuming the consideration of the letter of Boston,

*Resolved unamimously,* That it is the opinion of this body, that the removal of the people of Boston into the country, would be not only extremely difficult in the execution, but so important in its consequences, as to require the utmost deliberation before it is adopted; but, in case the provincial meeting of that Colony should judge it absolutely necessary, it is the opinion of the Congress, that all America ought to contribute towards recompensing them for the injury they may thereby sustain; and it will be recommended accordingly.

*Resolved,* That the Congress recommend to the inhabitants of the colony of Massachusetts-bay, to submit to a suspension of the administration of Justice, where it cannot be procured in a legal & peaceable manner, under the rules of their present charter, and the laws of the colony founded thereon.

*Resolved unanimously,* That every person and persons whatsoever, who shall take, accept, or act under any commission or authority, in any wise derived from the act passed in the last session of parliament, changing the form of government, and violating the charter of the province of Massachusetts-bay, ought to be held in detestation and abhorrence by all good men, and considered as the wicked tools of that despotism, which is preparing to destroy those rights, which God, nature, and compact, have given to America. . . .

TUESDAY, OCTOBER 11, 1774

A copy of the letter to general Gage, was brought in to Congress . . .

As the Congress have given general Gage an assurance of the peaceable disposition of the people of Boston and the Massachusetts-bay,

*Resolved unanimously,* That they be advised still to conduct themselves peaceably towards his excellency General Gage, and his majesty's troops now stationed in the town of Boston, as far as can possibly be consistent with their immediate safety, and the security of the town; avoiding & discountenancing every violation of his Majesty's property, or any insult to his troops, and that they peaceably and firmly persevere in the line they are now conducting themselves, on the defensive.

*Ordered,* That a copy of the foregoing resolve, & of that passed on Saturday and the three passed yesterday, be made out, and that the President enclose them in a letter to the committee of correspondence for the town of Boston, being the sentiments of the Congress on the matters referred to them by the Committee, in their letter of the 29th of Septr. last.

*Resolved, unanimously,* That a memorial be prepared to the people of British America, stating to them the necessity of a firm, united, and invariable observation of the measures recommended by the Congress, as they tender the invaluable rights and liberties derived to them from the laws and constitution of their country.

Also an address to the people of Great Britain.

Mr. [Richard Henry] Lee, Mr. [William] Livingston, and Mr. [John] Jay are appointed a committee to prepare a draught of the memorial & address.

## 12. CONGRESS DEFENDS ITSELF TO METROPOLITAN BRITONS AND CONTINENTAL COLONISTS, OCTOBER 21, 1774

The Library of Congress' James Hutson writes that "to explain its actions to its two most important audiences, Congress on October 11, 1774, resolved to prepare an 'Address to the People of Great Britain' and a 'Memorial to the Inhabitants of British America.' Richard Henry Lee of Virginia, John Jay of New York, and William Livingston of New Jersey were appointed a committee to draft both documents."[62] While Jay is widely accepted as the author of the address, based on his own statement and that of Thomas Jefferson, an additional draft that differs considerably from the version approved by Congress has been recently identified among Richard Henry Lee's papers. Jay remains, nonetheless, the likely author of the address, with Lee instead probably having been asked to write the first draft of the "Memorial to the Inhabitants of British America." With Jay, the committee included a moderate; with Lee, a radical; and with Livingston, something of a bridge between them, though leaning in the moderate direction. (John Adams viewed him as a staunch opponent of independence; see document 33.6.) Livingston was a prominent lawyer who urged his fellow colonists, first in New York and then in New Jersey after relocating there in 1772, to become politically active. He served on New Jersey's congressional delegation until 1776, when he was elected the state's first governor.[63] The committee returned to Congress with a draft of the address on October 18 and a draft of the memorial the next day. After being debated and amended over several days, both were approved on October 21 and "immediately committed to the press."[64]

The address, like almost all congressional state papers, defends the equality of the colonists with the king's English subjects and insists that a foreign legislature— Parliament—could not legitimately tax them: "we are and ought to be, as free as our fellow-subjects in Britain, and that no power on earth has a right to take our property from us without our consent." Consistent with colonial claims of the previous decade, they rhetorically ask their fellow subjects whether "the Proprietors of the soil of America [are] less Lords of their property than you are of yours, or why should they submit it to the disposal of your Parliament, or any other Parliament, or Council in the world, not of their election." The colonists claim to possess "all the benefits secured to the subject by the English constitution, and particularly that inestimable one of trial by jury," and reaffirm that Parliament is gravely mistaken in claiming that it has "a right to bind us in all cases without exception, whether we consent or not."

Added to an already well-developed list of grievances are those that followed from Parliament's imposition of the Coercive Acts of 1774. Given special emphasis is that these punitive measures imposed wholesale punishment on the residents of Boston and Massachusetts rather than prosecuting only those individuals guilty of trespass. The innocent, accordingly, were involved "in one common punishment with the guilty, and for the act of thirty or forty," Parliament brought "poverty, distress and calamity on thirty thousand souls, and those not your enemies, but your friends, brethren, and fellow subjects." Such grievances were reiterated again and again until Congress declared the colonies independent in 1776.

The address emphasizes a heightened hostility toward the Roman Catholicism of French Canadians, a new item in Congress' litany of grievances. Parliament is castigated for establishing "a religion, fraught with sanguinary and impious tenets" and for extending the dominion of Canada, since "Catholic emigrants from Europe . . . might become formidable to us, and on occasion, be fit instruments in the hands of power, to reduce the ancient free Protestant Colonies to the same state of slavery with themselves." Congress was astonished by Parliament's actions and hoped that metropolitan Britons would be also taken aback "that a British Parliament should ever consent to establish in that country a religion that has deluged your island in blood, and dispersed impiety, bigotry, persecution, murder and rebellion through every part of the world." In the address and the memorial, Congress attempted to build solidarity with Americans' fellow British subjects and among the colonists themselves by highlighting their shared Protestant heritage, while also trying to raise the specter of Roman Catholicism as a common threat, one especially of concern to Anglo-American Whigs (see also document 13.1).[65]

Perhaps this was to be expected; far less so was the threat that Congress wanted their fellow subjects to consider, namely, that the king, with an uncontrolled flow of American monies, might soon be freed from parliamentary oversight as: "The quit-rents reserved to the Crown, from the numberless grants of this vast continent, will pour large streams of wealth into the royal coffers, and if to this be added the power of taxing America at pleasure, the Crown will be rendered independent on you for supplies, and will possess more treasure than may be necessary to purchase the *remains of* Liberty in your Island." Of course, in this traditional parliamentary charge against the Crown, Congress showed its long-practiced familiarity with Whig rhetoric, but also an unexpected measure of confusion in reverting back to a familiar language that had been put aside during its opposition to parliamentary legislation and taxation of the colonies.[66] By raising the specter of an out-of-control Crown engorged with colonial tax receipts, Congress effectively sides with Parliament against its own—in truth, Tory-like—support of an increase in royal prerogative. Congress did so again the following July (see document 23.1). Of course, that position was identical to the one taken by the Rockingham Whigs in Parliament in opposing the colonies' constitutional vision of their being governed solely by the king (see, for example, Franklin's testimony in document 7.1). In short, Congress here strangely argued against the legitimacy of colonial requisitions to the king made without parliamentary oversight—which was at the center of their own constitutional theory. The oddly Tory-like character of the colonial position was, it seems, hard even for Congress to adhere to consistently.

Congress concluded by asking that their fellow British subjects permit the colonists to be as free as themselves, but warned: "If you are determined that your Ministers shall wantonly sport with the rights of Mankind—If neither the voice of justice, the dictates of the law, the principles of the constitution, or the suggestions of humanity can restrain your hands from shedding human blood in such an impious cause, we must then tell you, that we will never submit to be hewers of wood or drawers of water for any ministry or nation in the world." Congress hoped, though, that in upcoming elections "the magnanimity and justice of the British Nation will furnish a Parliament of such wisdom, independence and public spirit, as may save the violated rights of the whole empire from the devices of wicked Ministers and evil Counsellors." Such hopes went unfulfilled.

## 12.1

 ADDRESS TO THE PEOPLE OF GREAT BRITAIN

Worthington Chauncey Ford et al., eds., *Journals of the Continental Congress, 1774–1789* (Washington, D.C.: Government Printing Office, 1904–37), 1:81–90.

FRIDAY, OCTOBER 21, 1774.

The address to the people of Great-Britain being brought in, and the amendments directed being made, the same was approved, and is as follows:

Here insert the address to the people of Great-Britain.

*To the people of Great-Britain, from the delegates appointed by the several English colonies of New-Hampshire, Massachusetts-Bay, Rhode-Island and Providence Plantations, Connecticut, New-York, New-Jersey, Pennsylvania, the lower counties on Delaware, Maryland, Virginia, North-Carolina, and South-Carolina, to consider of their grievances in general Congress, at Philadelphia, September 5th, 1774.*

FRIENDS AND FELLOW SUBJECTS,

WHEN a Nation, led to greatness by the hand of Liberty, and possessed of all the glory that heroism, munificence, and humanity can bestow, descends to the ungrateful task of forging chains for her Friends and Children, and instead of giving support to Freedom, turns advocate for Slavery and Oppression, there is reason to suspect she has either ceased to be virtuous, or been extremely negligent in the appointment of her rulers.

In almost every age, in repeated conflicts, in long and bloody wars, as well civil as foreign, against many and powerful nations, against the open assaults of enemies, and the more dangerous treachery of friends, have the inhabitants of your island, your great and glorious ancestors, maintained their independence and transmitted the rights of men, and the blessings of liberty to you their posterity.

Be not surprized therefore, that we, who are descended from the same common ancestors; that we, whose forefathers participated in all the rights, the liberties, and the constitution, you so justly boast [of], and who have carefully conveyed the same fair inheritance to us, guarantied by the plighted faith of government and the most solemn compacts with British Sovereigns, should refuse to surrender them to men, who found their claims on no principles of reason, and who prosecute them with a design, that by having our lives and property in their power, they may with the greater facility enslave you.

The cause of America is now the object of universal attention: it has at length become very serious. This unhappy country has not only been oppressed, but abused and misrepresented; and the duty we owe to ourselves and posterity, to your interest, and the general welfare of the British empire, leads us to address you on this very important subject.

*Know then,* That we consider ourselves, and do insist, that we are and ought to be, as free as our fellow-subjects in Britain, and that no power on earth has a right to take our property from us without our consent.

That we claim all the benefits secured to the subject by the English constitution, and particularly that inestimable one of trial by jury.

That we hold it essential to English Liberty, that no man be condemned unheard, or punished for supposed offences, without having an opportunity of making his defence.

That we think the Legislature of Great-Britain is not authorized by the constitution to establish a religion, fraught with sanguinary and impious tenets, or, to erect an arbitrary form of government, in any quarter of the globe. These rights, we, as well as you, deem sacred. And yet sacred as they are, they have, with many others, been repeatedly and flagrantly violated.

Are not the Proprietors of the soil of Great-Britain Lords of their own property? can it be taken from them without their consent? will they yield it to the arbitrary disposal of any man, or number of men whatever?—You know they will not.

Why then are the Proprietors of the soil of America less Lords of their property than you are of yours, or why should they submit it to the disposal of your Parliament, or any other Parliament, or Council in the world, not of their election? Can the intervention of the sea that divides us, cause disparity in rights, or can any reason be given, why English subjects, who live three thousand miles from the royal palace, should enjoy less liberty than those who are three hundred miles distant from it?

Reason looks with indignation on such distinctions, and freemen can never perceive their propriety. And yet, however chimerical and unjust such discriminations are, the Parliament assert, that they have a right to bind us in all cases without exception, whether we consent or not; that they may take and use our property when and in what manner they please; that we are pensioners on their bounty for all that we possess, and can hold it no longer than they vouchsafe to permit. Such declarations we consider as heresies in English polities, and which can no more operate to deprive us of our property, than the interdicts of the Pope can divest Kings of scepters which the laws of the land and the voice of the people have placed in their hands.

At the conclusion of the late war—a war rendered glorious by the abilities and integrity of a Minister, to whose efforts the British empire owes its safety and its fame: At the conclusion of this war, which was succeeded by an inglorious peace, formed under the auspices of a Minister of principles, and of a family unfriendly to the protestant cause, and inimical to liberty.—We say at this period, and under the influence of that man, a plan for enslaving your fellow subjects in America was concerted, and has ever since been pertinaciously carrying into execution.

Prior to this æra you were content with drawing from us the wealth produced by our commerce. You restrained our trade in every way that could conduce to your emolument.

You exercised unbounded sovereignty over the sea. You named the ports and nations to which alone our merchandise should be carried, and with whom alone we should trade; and though some of these restrictions were grievous, we nevertheless did not complain; we looked up to you as to our parent state, to which we were bound by the strongest ties: And were happy in being instrumental to your prosperity and your grandeur.

We call upon you yourselves, to witness our loyalty and attachment to the common interest of the whole empire: Did we not, in the last war, add all the strength of this vast continent to the force which repelled our common enemy? Did we not leave our native shores, and meet disease and death, to promote the success of British arms in foreign climates? Did you not thank us for our zeal, and even reimburse us large sums of money, which, you confessed, we had advanced beyond our proportion and far beyond our abilities? You did.

To what causes, then, are we to attribute the sudden change of treatment, and that system of slavery which was prepared for us at the restoration of peace?

Before we had recovered from the distresses which ever attend war, an attempt was made to drain this country of all its money, by the oppressive Stamp-Act. Paint, Glass, and other commodities, which you would not permit us to purchase of other nations, were taxed; nay, although no wine is made in any country, subject to the British state, you prohibited our procuring it of foreigners, without paying a tax, imposed by your parliament, on all we imported. These and many other impositions were laid upon us most unjustly and unconstitutionally, for the express purpose of raising a Revenue.—In order to silence complaint, it was, indeed, provided, that this revenue should be expended in America for its protection and defence.—These exactions, however, can receive no justification from a pretended necessity of protecting and defending us. They are lavishly squandered on court favorites and ministerial dependents, generally avowed enemies to America and employing themselves, by partial representations, to traduce and embroil the Colonies. For the necessary support of government here, we ever were and ever shall be ready to provide. And whenever the exigencies of the state may require it, we shall, as we have heretofore done, cheerfully contribute our full proportion of men and money. To enforce this unconstitutional and unjust scheme of taxation, every fence that the wisdom of our British ancestors had carefully erected against arbitrary power, has been violently thrown down in America, and the inestimable right of trial by jury taken away in cases that touch both life and property.—It was ordained, that whenever offences should be committed in the colonies against particular Acts imposing various duties and restrictions upon trade, the prosecutor might bring his action for the penalties in the Courts of Admiralty; by which means the subject lost the advantage of being tried by an honest uninfluenced jury of the vicinage, and was subjected to the sad necessity of being judged by a single man, a creature of the Crown, and according to the course of a law which exempts the prosecutor from the trouble of proving his accusation, and obliges the defendant either to evince his innocence or to suffer. To give this new judicatory the greater importance, and as, if with design to protect false accusers, it is further provided, that the Judge's certificate of there having been probable causes of seizure and prosecution, shall protect the prosecutor from actions at common law for recovery of damages.

By the course of our law, offences committed in such of the British dominions in which courts are established and justice duely and regularly administered, shall be there tried by a jury of the vicinage. There the offenders and the witnesses are known, and the degree of credibility to be given to their testimony, can be ascertained.

In all these Colonies, justice is regularly and impartially administered, and yet by the construction of some, and the direction of other Acts of Parliament, offenders are to be taken by force, together with all such persons as may be pointed out as witnesses, and carried to England, there to be tried in a distant land, by a *jury* of strangers, and subject to all the disadvantages that result from want of friends, want of witnesses, and want of money.

When the design of raising a revenue from the duties imposed on the importation of tea into America had in great measure been rendered abortive by our ceasing to import that commodity, a scheme was concerted by the Ministry with the East-India Company, and an Act passed enabling and encouraging them to transport and vend it in the colonies. Aware of the danger of giving success to this insidious manœuvre, and of permitting a precedent of taxation thus to be established among us, various methods were adopted to elude the stroke. The people of Boston, then ruled by a Governor, whom, as well as his predecessor Sir Francis Bernard, all America considers as her enemy, were exceedingly embarrassed. The ships which had arrived with the tea were by his management prevented from returning.—The duties would have been paid; the cargoes landed and exposed to sale; a Governor's influence would have procured and protected many purchasers. While the town was suspended by deliberations on this important subject, the tea was destroyed. Even supposing a trespass was thereby committed, and the Proprietors of the tea entitled to damages.—The Courts of Law were open, and Judges appointed by the Crown presided in them.—The East India Company however did not think proper to commence any suits, nor did they even demand satisfaction, either from individuals or from the community in general. The Ministry, it seems, officiously made the case their own, and the great Council of the nation descended to intermeddle with a dispute about private property.—Divers papers, letters, and other unauthenticated ex parte evidence were laid before them; neither the persons who destroyed the Tea, or the people of Boston, were called upon to answer the complaint. The Ministry, incensed by being disappointed in a favourite scheme, were determined to recur from the little arts of finesse, to open force and unmanly violence. The port of Boston was blocked up by a fleet, and an army placed in the town. Their trade was to be suspended, and thousands reduced to the necessity of gaining subsistance from charity, till they should submit to pass under the yoke, and consent to become slaves, by confessing the omnipotence of Parliament, and acquiescing in whatever disposition they might think proper to make of their lives and property.

Let justice and humanity cease to be the boast of your nation! consult your history, examine your records of former transactions, nay turn to the annals of the many arbitrary states and kingdoms that surround you, and shew us a single instance of men being condemned to suffer for imputed crimes, unheard, unquestioned, and without even the specious formality of a trial; and that too by laws made expres[s]ly for the purpose, and which had no existence at the time of the fact committed. If it be difficult to reconcile these proceedings to the genius and temper of your laws and constitution, the task will become more arduous when we call upon our ministerial enemies to justify, not only condemning men untried and by hearsay, but involving the innocent in one common punishment with the guilty, and for the act of thirty or forty, to bring poverty, distress and calamity on thirty thousand souls, and those not your enemies, but your friends, brethren, and fellow subjects.

It would be some consolation to us, if the catalogue of American oppressions ended here. It gives us pain to be reduced to the necessity of reminding you, that under the confidence reposed in the faith of government, pledged in a royal charter from a British Sovereign, the fore-fathers of the present inhabitants of the Massachusetts-Bay left their former habitations, and established that great, flourishing, and loyal Colony. Without incurring or being charged with a forfeiture of their rights, without being heard, without being tried, without law, and without justice, by an Act of Parliament, their charter is destroyed, their liberties violated, their constitution and form of government changed: And all this upon no better pretence, than because in one of their towns a trespass was committed on some merchandize, said to belong to one of the Companies, and because the Ministry were of opinion, that such high political regulations were necessary to compel due subordination and obedience to their mandates.

Nor are these the only capital grievances under which we labor. We might tell of dissolute, weak and wicked Governors having been set over us; of Legislatures being suspended for asserting the rights of British subjects—of needy and ignorant dependents on great men, advanced to the seats of justice and to other places of trust and importance;—of hard restrictions on commerce, and a great variety of lesser evils, the recollection of which is almost lost under the weight and pressure of greater and more poignant calamities.

Now mark the progression of the ministerial plan for inslaving us.

Well aware that such hardy attempts to take our property from us; to deprive us of that valuable right of trial by jury; to seize our persons, and carry us for trial to Great-Britain; to blockade our ports; to destroy our Charters, and change our forms of government, would occasion, and had already occasioned, great discontent in all the Colonies, which might produce opposition to these measures: An Act was passed to protect, indemnify, and screen from punishment such as might be guilty even of murder, in endeavoring to carry their oppressive edicts into execution; And by another Act the dominion of Canada is to be so extended, modelled, and governed, as that by being disunited from us, detached from our interests, by civil as well as religious prejudices, that by their numbers daily swelling with Catholic emigrants from Europe, and by their devotion to Administration, so friendly to their religion, they might become formidable to us, and on occasion, be fit instruments in the hands of power, to reduce the ancient free Protestant Colonies to the same state of slavery with themselves.

This was evidently the object of the Act:—And in this view, being extremely dangerous to our liberty and quiet, we cannot forebear complaining of it, as hostile to British America.—Superadded to these considerations, we cannot help deploring the unhappy condition to which it has reduced the many English settlers, who, encouraged by the Royal Proclamation, promising the enjoyment of all their rights, have purchased estates in that country.—They are now the subjects of an arbitrary government, deprived of trial by jury, and when imprisoned cannot claim the benefit of the habeas corpus Act, that great bulwark and palladium of English liberty:—Nor can we suppress our astonishment, that a British Parliament should ever consent to establish in that country a religion that has deluged your island in blood, and dispersed impiety, bigotry, persecution, murder and rebellion through every part of the world.

This being a true state of facts, let us beseech you to consider to what end they lead.

Admit that the Ministry, by the powers of Britain, and the aid of our Roman Catholic neighbors, should be able to carry the point of taxation, and reduce us to a state of perfect humiliation and slavery. Such an enterprize would doubtless make some addition to your national debt, which already presses down your liberties, and fills you with Pensioners and Placemen.—We presume, also, that your commerce will somewhat be diminished. However, suppose you should prove victorious—in what condition will you then be? What advantages or what laurels will you reap from such a conquest?

May not a Ministry with the same armies inslave you—It may be said, you will cease to pay them—but remember the taxes from America, the wealth, and we may add, the men, and particularly the Roman Catholics of this vast continent will then be in the power of your enemies—nor will you have any reason to expect, that after making slaves of us, many among us should refuse to assist in reducing you to the same abject state.

Do not treat this as chimerical—Know that in less than half a century, the quit-rents reserved to the Crown, from the numberless grants of this vast continent, will pour large streams of wealth into the royal coffers, and if to this be added the power of taxing America at pleasure, the Crown will be rendered independent on [of] you for supplies, and will possess more treasure than may be necessary to purchase the *remains of* Liberty in your Island.—In a word, take care that you do not fall into the pit that is preparing for us.

We believe there is yet much virtue, much justice, and much public spirit in the English nation—To that justice we now appeal. You have been told that we are seditious, impatient of government and desirous of independence. Be assured that these are not facts, but calumnies.—Permit us to be as free as yourselves, and we shall ever esteem a union with you to be our greatest glory and our greatest happiness, we shall ever be ready to contribute all in our power to the welfare of the Empire—we shall consider your enemies as our enemies, and your interest as our own.

But if you are determined that your Ministers shall wantonly sport with the rights of Mankind—If neither the voice of justice, the dictates of the law, the principles of the constitution, or the suggestions of humanity can restrain your hands from shedding human blood in such an impious cause, we must then tell you, that we will never submit to be hewers of wood or drawers of water for any ministry or nation in the world.

Place us in the same situation that we were at the close of the last war, and our former harmony will be restored.

But lest the same supineness and the same inattention to our common interest, which you have for several years shewn, should continue, we think it prudent to anticipate the consequences.

By the destruction of the trade of Boston, the Ministry have endeavored to induce submission to their measures.—The like fate may befall us all, we will endeavor therefore to live without trade, and recur for subsistence to the fertility and bounty of our native soil, which will afford us all the necessaries and some of the conveniences of life.—We have suspended our importation from Great Britain and Ireland; and in less than a year's time, unless our grievances should be redressed, shall discontinue our exports to those kingdoms and the West-Indies.

It is with the utmost regret, however, that we find ourselves compelled by the overruling principles of self-preservation, to adopt measures detrimental in their consequences to numbers of our fellow subjects in Great Britain and Ireland. But we hope, that the magnanimity and justice of the British Nation will furnish a Parliament of such wisdom, independence and public spirit, as may save the violated rights of the whole empire from the devices of wicked Ministers and evil Counsellors whether in or out of office, and thereby restore that harmony, friendship and fraternal affection between all the Inhabitants of his Majesty's kingdoms and territories, so ardently wished for by every true and honest American.

## 12.2

## Memorial to the Inhabitants of British America

The following memorial has been traditionally attributed to Richard Henry Lee. In 1969, however, a seventeen-page draft by John Dickinson of Pennsylvania was uncovered, and it is nearly identical to the version Congress adopted. This discovery raises the possibility that the committee, when first appointed on October 11, appealed to Dickinson to write the memorial; or alternatively, that Congress was dissatisfied with Lee's original effort and pressed Dickinson into service a few days before the memorial was accepted, most likely on October 19, 1774.[67] Dickinson, however, did not take his seat in Congress until October 17, leading Hutson to suggest that since "his reputation as a penman was so formidable, since his authority with the delegates was so great, and since he may have been privy to what was occurring in Congress," he might have been asked to assist the committee in making revisions or even in writing the memorial before he joined Congress.[68]

Dickinson was a well-known London-trained lawyer, born in Maryland and, at different times, a prominent member of the Delaware and Pennsylvania Assemblies; he became one of the most articulate and impressive of the moderate delegates. He was also a member of the Pennsylvania delegation to the Stamp Act Congress, and he participated in the Constitutional Convention before supporting the Constitution's ratification. Though he refused to support independence or to sign the Declaration of Independence, Dickinson was a firm opponent of the Sugar Act, the Stamp Act, and the Townshend Acts, which he had attacked in 1768 in an unusually influential series of essays, *Letters from a Farmer in Pennsylvania.* He wrote the initial draft of the Articles of Confederation (July 12, 1776) and vigorously fought on the patriot side during the war.[69]

The memorial, which has been edited for length and ease of reading, begins, like the Declaration, by explaining those facts that must be judged impartially. In particular, the memorial focuses on the parliamentary revenue and trade acts of 1764–67 and certain administrative acts from 1768—with little concern with more recent events. Parliament, it points out, had made "a remarkable distinction between the subjects in Great-Britain and those in America," especially by claiming that Parliament enjoyed the "power of *taxing* us" and by extending "the jurisdiction of the courts of *Admiralty* and *Vice-Admiralty* . . . to matters arising within the body of a county," that is, to nonmaritime cases in the colonies. Congress here objected not only to the substance of the Stamp Act, but to the grounds upon which it was repealed, that is, convenience rather than the absence of a constitutional right in Parliament to tax or legislate for the colonies. The Declaratory Act's hubris in claiming to bind the colonies "IN ALL CASES WHATSOEVER" was thus duly condemned.

Congress then explained that "after the repeal of the Stamp-Act, having again resigned ourselves to our ancient unsuspicious affections for the parent state, and anxious to avoid any controversy with her, in hopes of a favorable alteration in sentiments and measures towards us, we did not press our objections against the . . . Statutes made subsequent to that repeal." The colonists' reserved behavior, Congress contends, was not rewarded, and "by a Statute commonly called the *Glass, Paper* and *Tea Act,* made fifteen months after the repeal of the *Stamp-Act,* the Commons of Great-Britain resumed their former language, and again undertook to '*give and grant* rates and duties to be paid in these Colonies,' for the express purpose of '*raising a revenue.*'" Congress reasonably drew attention to the fact that the Townshend duties had "revived the apprehensions and discontents that had entirely subsided on the repeal of the Stamp-Act."

In short, according to Congress, it was Parliament's insistence on making explicit its claimed right to tax the colonies for revenue that had led to the present difficulties. The first section of the memorial ends by concluding that "the immediate tendency of these statutes is, to subvert the right of having a share in legislation, by rendering Assemblies useless; the right of property, by taking the money of the Colonists without their consent; the right of trial by jury," by replacing common-law courts with civil-law ones. Nothing here was new, nor would these preeminent concerns change over the next twenty months.

After listing Parliament's persistence in undermining traditional British rights, Congress impressed on its constituents that in 1768, based on letters from Governor Bernard, Massachusetts had done everything in its power to bring the impending crisis to a just resolution. The memorial declares that "severe as the Acts of *Parliament* before mentioned are, yet the conduct of *Administration* hath been equally injurious, and irritating to this devoted country," for "under pretence of governing them, so many new institutions, uniformly rigid and dangerous, have been introduced, as could only be expected from incensed masters, for collecting the tribute or rather the plunder of conquered provinces." The administration, not only Parliament, is being taken to task. In particular, Congress complained that "expensive and oppressive offices have been multiplied" and that "humble and reasonable petitions from the Representatives of the people have been frequently treated with contempt; and Assemblies have been repeatedly and arbitrarily dissolved."

Still, in spite of these executive provocations, the memorial mentions petitioning the king and beseeching him to intervene on behalf of his American subjects, whose social bond with their fellow subjects they "ardently wish *may never* be dissolved, and which *cannot* be dissolved, until their minds shall become *indisputably hostile* . . . [to] the colonists." Although such a dissolution might prove necessary (as it later did), they had "not yet reached that fatal point," and so "a hearty reconciliation with our fellow-citizens on the other side of the Atlantic" was still to be sought. Most especially, Congress, as in its companion address to the people of Great Britain, expressed the hope that Britain would soon elect a new Parliament, one ready to demonstrate that the British would not "take part against their affectionate protestant brethren in the colonies, in favour of *our open* and *their own secret* enemies." And as for Americans, the memorial closes by asking that the colonists humble themselves "and implore the favour of almighty God."

Worthington Chauncey Ford et al., eds., *Journals of the Continental Congress, 1774–1789* (Washington, D.C.: Government Printing Office, 1904–37), 1:90–101.

The Congress then resumed the consideration of the memorial to the inhabitants of the British Colonies, and the same being gone through and debated by paragraphs [and amended] was approved, and is as follows:

Here insert the Memorial &c.

*To the inhabitants of the colonies of New-Hampshire, Massachusetts-Bay, Rhode Island and Providence Plantations, Connecticut, New-York, New-Jersey, Pennsylvania, the counties of New Castle, Kent and Sussex, on Delaware, Maryland, Virginia, North-Carolina and South-Carolina:*

FRIENDS AND FELLOW COUNTRYMEN,

We, the Delegates appointed by the good people of the above Colonies to meet at Philadelphia in September last, for the purposes mentioned by our respective Constituents, have in pursuance of the trust reposed in us, assembled, and taken into our most serious consideration the important matters recommended to the Congress. Our resolutions thereupon will be herewith communicated to you. But as the situation of public affairs grows daily more and more alarming; and as it may be more satisfactory to you to be informed by us in a collective body, than in any other manner, of those sentiments that have been approved, upon a full and free discussion by the Representatives of so great a part of America, we esteem ourselves obliged to add this Address to these Resolutions.

In every case of opposition by a people to their rulers, or of one state to another, duty to Almighty God, the creator of all, requires that a true and impartial judgment be formed of the measures leading to such opposition; and of the causes by which it has been provoked, or can in any degree be justified: That neither affection on the one hand, nor resentment on the other, being permitted to give a wrong bias to reason, it may be enabled to take a dispassionate view of all circumstances, and settle the public conduct on the solid foundations of wisdom and justice.

From Councils thus tempered arise the surest hopes of the divine favor, the firmest encouragement to the parties engaged and the strongest recommendation of their cause to the rest of mankind.

With minds deeply impressed by a sense of these truths, we have diligently, deliberately and calmly enquired into and considered those exertions, both of the legislative and executive power of Great-Britain, which have excited so much uneasiness in America, and have with equal fidelity and attention considered the conduct of the Colonies. Upon the whole, we find ourselves reduced to the disagreeable alternative, of being silent and betraying the innocent, or of speaking out and censuring those we wish to revere.—In making our choice of these distressing difficulties, we prefer the course dictated by honesty, and a regard for the welfare of our country.

Soon after the conclusion of the late war, there commenced a memorable change in the treatment of these Colonies. By a statute made in the fourth year of the present reign, a time of *profound peace,* alledging, "the expediency of new provisions and regulations for extending the commerce between Great-Britain and his majesty's dominions in America, and the *necessity* of *raising a Revenue* in the said dominions for defraying the expenses of *defending,* protecting and securing the same," the *Commons of Great-Britain* undertook to *give* and *grant* to his Majesty many rates and duties, to be paid in these Colonies. To enforce the observance of this Act, it prescribes a great number of severe penalties and forfeitures; and in two sections makes a remarkable distinction between the subjects in Great-Britain and those in America. By the one, the penalties and forfeitures incurred *there* are to be recovered in any of the King's Courts of Record, at Westminster, or in the Court of Exchequer in Scotland; and by the other, the penalties and forfeitures incurred *here* are to be recovered in any Court of Record, or in any Court of *Admiralty, or Vice-Admiralty, at the election of the informer or prosecutor.*

The Inhabitants of these Colonies confiding in the justice of Great-Britain, were scarcely allowed *sufficient* time to receive and consider this Act, before another, well known by the name of the *Stamp Act,* and passed in the fifth year of this reign, engrossed their whole attention. By this statute the British Parliament exercised, in the most explicit manner a power of *taxing* us, and extending the jurisdiction of the courts of *Admiralty* and *Vice-Admiralty* in the Colonies, to matters arising within the body of a county, directed the numerous penalties and forfeitures, thereby inflicted, to be recovered in the said courts.

In the same year a tax was imposed upon us, by an Act, establishing several new fees in the customs. In the next year, the Stamp-Act was repealed; not because it was founded in an erroneous principle, but as the repealing Act recites, because "the continuance thereof would be attended with many inconveniences, and might be productive of consequences greatly detrimental to the commercial interest of Great-Britain."

In the same year, and by a subsequent Act, it was declared, "that his Majesty in Parliament, of right, had power to bind the people of these Colonies, BY STATUTES, IN ALL CASES WHATSOEVER."

In the same year, another Act was passed, for imposing rates and duties payable in these Colonies. In this Statute the Commons avoiding the terms of *giving* and *granting,* "humbly besought his Majesty, that it might be enacted, &c." But from a declaration in the preamble, that the rates and duties were "in lieu of" several others granted by the Statute first before mentioned *for raising a revenue* and from some other expressions it appears, that these duties were intended *for that purpose.*

In the next year, (1767) an Act was made "to enable his Majesty to put the customs, and *other duties* in America, under the management of Commissioners, &c." and the King thereupon erected the present expensive Board of Commissioners, for the express purpose of carrying into execution the several Acts relating to the *revenue* and trade in *America.*

After the repeal of the Stamp-Act, having again resigned ourselves to our antient unsuspicious affections for the parent state, and anxious to avoid any controversy with her, in hopes of a favourable alteration in sentiments and measures towards us, we did not press our objections against the above mentioned Statutes made subsequent to that repeal.

Administration attributing to trifling causes, a conduct that really proceeded from generous motives, were encouraged in the same year (1767) to make a bolder experiment on the patience of America.

By a Statute commonly called the *Glass, Paper* and *Tea Act,* made fifteen months after the repeal of the *Stamp-Act,* the Commons of Great-Britain resumed their former language, and again undertook to *"give* and *grant* rates and duties to be paid in these Colonies," for the express purpose of *"raising a revenue,* to defray the charges of the *administration of justice,* the support of *civil government,* and *defending* the King's dominions," on this continent. The penalties and forfeitures, incurred under this Statute, are to be recovered *in the same manner,* with those mentioned in the foregoing Acts."

To this Statute, so naturally tending to disturb the tranquillity then universal throughout the Colonies, Parliament, in the same session, added another no less extraordinary.

Ever since the making the present peace, a standing army has been kept in these Colonies. From respect for the mother country, the innovation was not only tolerated, but the provincial Legislatures generally made provision for supplying the troops.

The Assembly of the province of New York, having passed an Act of this kind, but differing in some articles, from the directions of the Act of Parliament made in the *fifth* year of this reign, the House of Representatives in that Colony was prohibited by a Statute made in the session last mentioned, from making any bill, order, resolution or vote, except for adjourning or chusing a Speaker, until provision should be made by the said Assembly for furnishing the troops, within that province, not only with all such necessaries as were required by the Statute *which they were charged with disobeying,* but also with those required by two other *subsequent* Statutes, which were declared to be in force until the twenty fourth day of March 1769.

These Statutes of the year 1767 revived the apprehensions and discontents, that had entirely subsided on the repeal of the *Stamp-Act;* and amidst the just fears and jealousies thereby occasioned, a Statute was made in the next year (1768) to establish Courts of *Admiralty* and *Vice-Admiralty* on a new model, expressly for the end of more *effectually* recovering of the *penalties* and *forfeitures* inflicted by Acts of Parliament, framed for the purpose of *raising a revenue* in America, &c.

The immediate tendency of these statutes is, to subvert the right of having a share in legislation, by rendering Assemblies useless; the right of property, by taking the money of the Colonists without their consent; the right of trial by jury, by substituting in their place trials in Admiralty and Vice-Admiralty courts, where single Judges preside, holding their Commissions during pleasure; and unduly to influence the Courts of common law, by rendering the Judges thereof totally dependant on the Crown for their salaries. . . .

These circumstances and the following extracts from Governor Bernard's letters in 1768, to the Earl of Shelburne, Secretary of State, clearly shew, with what grateful tenderness they strove to bury in oblivion the unhappy occasion of the late discords, and with what respectful reluctance they endeavoured to escape other subjects of future controversy. "The House, (says the Governor) from the time of opening the session to this day, has shewn a disposition to *avoid* all dispute with me; every thing having passed with as much good humour as I could desire, except only their continuing to act in *ad-*

*dressing* the King, *remonstrating* to the Secretary of State, and *employing* a separate agent. It is the *importance of this innovation,* without any wilfulness of my own, which induces me to make this remonstrance at a time when I have a fair prospect of having, *in all other business,* nothing but good to say of the proceedings of the House."

"They have acted *in all things,* even in their remonstrance *with temper and moderation;* they have *avoided* some subjects of dispute, and have laid a foundation for *removing* some causes of former altercation."

"I shall make such a prudent and proper use of this Letter as, I hope, will perfectly restore the peace and tranquillity of this province, for which purpose *considerable steps have been made by the House of Representatives.*"

The vindication of the province of Massachusetts-Bay contained in these Letters will have greater force, if it be considered, that they were written several months after the fresh alarm given to the colonies by the statutes passed in the preceding year.

In this place it seems proper to take notice of the insinuation in one of these statutes, that the interference of Parliament was *necessary* to provide for "defraying the charge of the *administration of justice,* the support of *civil government,* and defending the King's dominions 'in America.'"

As to the two first articles of expense, every colony had made such provision, as by their respective Assemblies, the best judges on such occasions, was thought expedient, and suitable to their several circumstances. Respecting the last, it is well known to all men, the least acquainted with American affairs, that the colonies were established, and have generally defended themselves, without the least assistance from Great-Britain; and, that at the time of her *taxing* them by the statutes before mentioned, most of them were labouring under very heavy debts contracted in the last war. So far were they from sparing their money, when their Sovereign, constitutionally, asked their aids, that during the course of that war, Parliament repeatedly made them compensations for the expences of those strenuous efforts, which, consulting their zeal rather than their strength, they had chearfully incurred.

Severe as the Acts of *Parliament* before mentioned are, yet the conduct of *Administration* hath been equally injurious, and irritating to this devoted country.

Under pretence of governing them, so many new institutions, uniformly rigid and dangerous, have been introduced, as could only be expected from incensed masters, for collecting the tribute or rather the plunder of conquered provinces.

By an order of the King, the authority of the Commander in chief, and under him, of the Brigadiers general, *in time of peace,* is rendered *supreme* in all the civil governments, in *America;* and thus an uncontroulable military power is vested in officers not known to the constitution of these colonies.

A large body of troops and a considerable armament of ships of war, have been sent to assist in taking their money without their consent.

Expensive and oppressive offices have been multiplied, and the acts of corruption industriously practiced to divide and destroy.

The Judges of the Admiralty and Vice-Admiralty Courts are impowered to receive their salaries and fees from the effects to be condemned by themselves; the Commissioners of the customs are impowered to break open and enter houses without the authority of any civil magistrate founded on legal information.

Judges of Courts of Common Law have been made entirely dependent on the Crown for their commissions and salaries.

A court has been established at Rhode-Island, for the purposes of taking Colonists to England to be tried.

Humble and reasonable petitions from the Representatives of the people have been frequently treated with contempt; and Assemblies have been repeatedly and arbitrarily dissolved.

From some few instances it will sufficiently appear, on what presences of justice those dissolutions have been founded.

The tranquillity of the colonies having been again disturbed, as has been mentioned, by the statutes of the year 1767, the Earl of Hillsborough, Secretary of State, in a letter to Governor Bernard, dated April 22, 1768, censures the *"presumption"* of the House of Representatives for "resolving upon a measure of so inflammatory a nature *as that of writing to the other colonies, on the subject of their intended representations against some late Acts of Parliament,"* then declares that "his Majesty considers this step as evidently tending to create unwarrantable combinations to excite an unjustifiable opposition to the constitutional authority of Parliament:"—and afterwards adds,—"It is the *King's pleasure,* that as soon as the General Court is again assembled, at the time prescribed by the Charter, you should require of the House of Representatives, in his Majesty's name, to *rescind* the resolution which gave birth to the circular letter from the Speaker, and to declare their disapprobation of, and dissent to that rash and hasty proceeding."

"If the new Assembly should refuse to comply with his Majesty's reasonable expectation, it is the King's pleasure, that you should immediately dissolve them."

This letter being laid before the House, and the resolution not being rescinded according to the order, the Assembly was dissolved. A letter of a similar nature was sent to other Governors to procure resolutions approving the conduct of the Representatives of Massachusetts-Bay, to be *rescinded* also; and the Houses of Representatives in other colonies refusing to comply Assemblies were dissolved . . .

At this unhappy period, we have been authorized and directed to meet and consult together for the welfare of our common country. We accepted the important trust with diffidence, but have endeavored to discharge it with integrity. Though the state of these colonies would certainly justify other measures than we have advised, yet weighty reasons determined us to prefer those which we have adopted. In the first place, it appeared to us a conduct becoming the character, these colonies have ever sustained, to perform, even in the midst of the unnatural distresses and imminent dangers that surround them, every act of loyalty; and therefore, we were induced to offer once more to his Majesty the petitions of his faithful and oppressed subjects in America. Secondly, regarding with the tender affection, which we knew to be so universal among our countrymen, the people of the kingdom, from which we derive our original, we could not forbear to regulate our steps by an expectation of receiving full conviction, that the colonists are equally dear to them. Between these provinces and that body, subsists the social band, which we ardently wish *may never* be dissolved, and which *cannot* be dissolved, until their minds shall become *indisputably hostile,* or their *inattention* shall permit those who are thus hostile to persist in prosecuting with the powers of the realm the destructive measures already operating against the colonists; and in either case, shall reduce the latter to such a situation, that they shall be compelled to renounce every regard, but that of self-preservation. Notwithstanding the vehemence with which affairs have been impelled, they have not yet reached that fatal point. We do not incline to accelerate their motion, already alarmingly rapid; we have chosen a method of opposition, that does not preclude a hearty reconciliation with our fellow-citizens on the other side of the Atlantic. We deeply deplore the urgent necessity that presses us to an immediate interruption of commerce, that may prove injurious to them. We trust they will acquit us of any unkind intentions towards them, by reflecting, that we subject ourselves to similar inconveniences; that we are driven by the hands of violence into unexperienced and unexpected public convulsions, and that we are contending for freedom, so often contended for by our ancestors.

The people of England will soon have an opportunity of declaring their sentiments concerning our cause. In their piety, generosity, and good sense, we repose high confidence; and cannot, upon a review of past events, be persuaded that *they,* the defenders of true religion, and the assertors of the rights of mankind, will take part against their affectionate protestant brethren in the colonies, in favour of *our open* and *their own secret* enemies; whose intrigues, for several years past, have been wholly exercised in sapping the foundations of civil and religious liberty.

Another reason, that engaged us to prefer the commercial mode of opposition, arose from an assurance, that the mode will prove efficacious, if it be persisted in with fidelity and virtue; and that your conduct will be influenced by these laudable principles, cannot be questioned. Your own salvation, and that of your posterity, now depends upon yourselves. You have already shewn that you entertain a proper sense of the blessings you are striving to retain. Against the temporary inconveniences you may suffer from a stoppage of trade, you will weigh in the opposite balance, the endless miseries you and your descendants must endure from an established arbitrary power. You will not forget the honour of your country, that must from your behavior take its title in the estimation of the world, to glory, or to shame; and you will, with the deepest attention, reflect, that if the peaceable mode of opposition recommended by us, be broken and rendered ineffectual, as your cruel and haughty ministerial enemies, from a contemptuous opinion of your firmness, insolently predict will be the case, you must inevitably be reduced to chuse, either a more dangerous contest, or a final, ruinous, and infamous submission.

Motives thus cogent, arising from the emergency of your unhappy condition, must excite your utmost diligence and zeal, to give all possible strength and energy to the pacific measures calculated for your relief: But we think ourselves bound in duty to observe to you that the schemes agitated against these colonies have been so conducted, as to render it prudent, that you should extend your views to the most mournful events, and be in all respects prepared for every contingency. Above all things we earnestly intreat you, with devotion of spirit, penitence of heart, and amendment of life, to humble your-selves, and implore the favour of almighty God: and we fervently beseech his divine goodness, to take you into his gracious protection.

*Ordered,* That the Address to the people of Great Britain and the memorial to the inhabitants of the British colonies be immediately committed to the press & that no more than one hundred and twenty copies of each be struck off without further orders from the Congress.

## 13. A STATEMENT OF PRINCIPLES AND COMPLAINTS, OCTOBER 1774

On the second day that the First Continental Congress met, September 6, 1774, it resolved to appoint delegates to a grand committee to examine the colonies' rights and to compile a list of grievances. The following day, Congress elected two prominent delegates from each of the colonies: from Massachusetts, Samuel and John Adams; from Rhode Island, Stephen Hopkins and Samuel Ward; from Connecticut, Eliphalet Dyer and Roger Sherman; from New York, James Duane and John Jay; from New Jersey, William Livingston and John De Hart; from Pennsylvania, Joseph Galloway and Edward Biddle; from Delaware, Caesar Rodney and Thomas McKean; from Maryland, Thomas Johnson and Robert Goldsborough; from Virginia, Richard Henry Lee and Edmund Pendleton; and from South Carolina, Thomas Lynch and John Rutledge. On September 19, Thomas Cushing of Massachusetts, Patrick Henry of Virginia, and Thomas Mifflin of Pennsylvania—in response to the concerns of the large Colonies that their numbers weren't adequately represented—were added.[70] According to John Adams, in order to more easily draft Congress' stance, the unusually large committee was whittled down to a smaller subcommittee.[71]

The entire committee presented "a report of the Rights" on September 22 and "a report of the infringements and violations" of those rights on September 24. These reports were not discussed until October 12, and then "were debated until October 14, when tentative agreement was apparently reached on them." Although most sources place the final adoption on that date, the Library of Congress' Hutson convincingly argues that "we do not know when a fair copy finally issued from the committee of which Adams was a member or when Congress approved it."[72] While we know that

John Adams prepared a clean copy of the document, the identity of the author of the declaration that combined the two drafts is still contested. Based, however, on an analysis of the handwriting of what is errantly described in the *Journal* as the "Sullivan Draught," Hutson concludes that John Dickinson, once again, was the author of this critically important state paper.

As with the "Memorial to the People of British America," discussed above, two possibilities exist to explain Dickinson's involvement: first, he was the most famous essayist among colonial authors and, accordingly, had been asked to write it even before being seated in Congress. Alternatively, and according to Hutson the more likely explanation, Congress had great difficulty in agreeing on the wording of the bill of rights and continued working on it until almost immediately before adjourning on October 26, well after Dickinson had taken his seat on the 17th. Hutson supports the second scenario with a number of observations, including that the document was "not published until October 27, 1774 in the *Extracts from the Votes and Proceedings . . . [of]* *Congress*."[73] Whenever it was ultimately approved, it was certainly the most important state paper of the First Continental Congress.

As in most of Congress' documents, this one begins (and ends) with a listing of stock colonial grievances: parliamentary taxation of the colonies, extending the jurisdiction of admiralty courts, and the Coercive Acts, in particular the one that established "the Roman Catholic religion in the province of Quebec . . . to the great danger, from so total a dissimilarity of religion, law, and government to the neighboring British colonies" (see document 14.2, in which the opposite is disingenuously claimed by Congress). Congress added that assemblies, such as New York's in 1766–70, "have been frequently dissolved" and that "their dutiful, humble, loyal and reasonable petitions to the crown for redress, have been repeatedly treated with contempt by his Majesty's ministers of state." At the end of the document, other parliamentary acts are similarly condemned, including the Post Office Act of 1765, which lowered rates in the colonies, and the Dockyards Act of 1772, which declared that any person who set fire to or otherwise destroyed a British ship of war was guilty of a capital crime.

Congress asserted that its purpose was "to obtain such establishment, as that their religion, laws, and liberties may not be subverted," and then declared that the delegates were acting "as Englishmen" and offered the comprehensive grounds upon which their rights rested, "the immutable laws of nature, the principles of the English constitution, and the several charters or compacts." Ten resolutions follow. As is clear from Adams' record of the debate during the committee's first meeting, the inclusion of "laws of nature"—which was in the Suffolk resolves also but here was for the first time among the grounds offered for American colonial rights by a continental congress—was a matter of great controversy because of the radical implications suggested by listing it separately from, rather than as part of, the English Constitution and English rights.[74] Of course, such language in the not too distant future of July 1776, as Adams rightly predicted, would prove necessary.[75]

After declaring that the colonists were, like all Englishmen, "entitled to life, liberty, and property," Congress emphasized that the colonists, acting corporately, had "never ceded to any sovereign power whatever, a right to dispose of [those entitlements] without their consent." Near the end, the document returns to this central theme: Congress' "constituents, do claim, demand, and insist on [the rights listed in resolutions 2–10], as their indubitable rights and liberties; which cannot be legally taken from them, altered or abridged by any power whatever, without their own consent, by their representatives in their several provincial legislatures." Importantly, this claim to the expansive power of their own legislatures begins and ends the list of rights and, like the list of grievances, is repeated twice. Its meaning is clear: Parliament had no right to legislate for American colonists—that could be done only by their legislatures. There is, however, no similar restriction on their legislatures' power to enact such legislation, for example, if one of them wished to protect individual rights against majoritarian intrusion or, contrariwise, if they wished to enforce the opposite. These sorts of modifications came later.

In the list of resolutions, Congress rests its rights claims on English legal and constitutional precedents and nothing else—the laws of nature, once mentioned, are never referred to again.[76] The document declares that the colonists' ancestors came to America with the same rights as those possessed by other Englishmen, rights confirmed in their charters and the English Bill of Rights, in particular the right to be tried by a jury of one's peers, and that the American colonists had done nothing to forfeit them. The all-important fourth resolution asserts that the rights of Englishmen include the "right in the people to participate in their legislative council," which means that only provincial legislatures, in which property was represented, could tax and pass laws affecting the internal life of the colonists, "subject only to the negative of their sovereign."

But then, importantly, following Duane's propositions (document 13.2), Congress declared that Americans would "cheerfully consent to the operation of such acts of the British parliament, as are bona fide, restrained to the regulation of our external commerce . . . excluding every idea of taxation internal or external." Congress denied that Parliament had any constitutional right to legislate for the colonies, even regarding commercial regulation, but for convenience' sake, Congress would consent to Parliament's continuing to manage imperial commercial relations, and even to its giving the advantage to metropolitan Britons when doing so. Such language, however, did little to help Parliament, given its absolute commitment to protecting its sovereign rights, find a mutually satisfactory compromise with the colonists. The final resolution, the tenth, defends the necessity of independence between legislative branches while condemning the appointment by the Crown, not Parliament, of the upper houses in several colonies. In directing this grievance at the king, of course, Congress was again pointing toward concerns that had long predated those with Parliament.

Much here follows from earlier documents, and much here was repeated in later ones. Like almost all congressional state papers, the Bill of Rights and List of Grievances explains "that the course pursued by Congress was rendered necessary by specified instances of British aggression, coercion, on infringement of what were believed to be undoubted rights," but in the hope of bringing about a just and prompt reconciliation, Congress would limit its focus only to those "measures as have been adopted since the last war," that is, after 1763. Put somewhat differently, "the causal origin of every important resolution or series of resolutions affecting the continental concerns may be found in some previous British action."[77] This would be true up to and including the Declaration of Independence.

What had to change, though, before independence could be declared is that the source of rights had to move from an almost entirely English grounding to something more natural and universal, and the king—not only Parliament and the king's ministers—had to be held singularly culpable for the most serious transgressions. Through a series of speeches and pronouncements beginning in late 1774—and made largely in response to the First Continental Congress' productions, the state papers presented here—and throughout 1775, the king alienated even relatively moderate members of Congress. With the American Prohibitory Act of December 1775 (document 29.2), in which he announced that he had hired foreign mercenaries to attack his North American continental subjects, whom he had declared outside his protection, he went a long way in relieving his colonial subjects of their reciprocal duty of loyalty and allegiance. In July 1776, shortly after the colonists had learned that the king had rejected a final petition for reconciliation from the mayor of London (document 32.3), many of them were able to find him guilty of the wrongs that they had suffered over the previous twelve years and that had been, in the main, charged against Parliament and the Crown's ministers.

13.1

 BILL OF RIGHTS AND LIST OF GRIEVANCES,
OCTOBER 18–26, 1774

James Hutson, *A Decent Respect to the Opinions of Mankind: Congressional State Papers, 1774-1776* (Washington, D.C.: Library of Congress, 1975), 52–56.

WHEREAS, since the close of the last war, the British parliament claiming a power, of right to bind the people of America, by statute in all cases whatsoever, hath in some acts expressly imposed taxes on them, and in others under various pretences, but in fact for the purpose of raising a revenue, hath imposed rates and duties payable in these colonies, established a board of commissioners with unconstitutional powers, and extended the jurisdiction of courts of admiralty, not only for collecting the said duties, but for the trial of causes merely arising within the body of a county.

AND whereas in consequence of other statutes, judges, who before held only estates at will in their offices, have been made dependant on the crown alone for their salaries, and standing armies kept in time of peace. And it has lately been resolved in parliament, that by force of a statute, made in the thirty-fifth year of the reign of King Henry the eighth, colonists may be transported to England and tried there upon accusations for treasons and misprisions, or concealments of treasons committed in the colonies; and by a late statute, such trials have been directed in cases therein mentioned.

AND whereas in the last session of parliament, three statutes were made: one entitled, "An act to discontinue in such manner, and for such time as are therein mentioned, the landing and discharging, lading or shipping of goods, wares and merchandize, at the town, and within the harbour of Boston, in the province of Massachusetts-Bay, in North-America." Another entitled, "An act for the better regulating the government of the province of the Massachusetts-Bay, in New-England." And another entitled, "An act for the impartial administration of justice, in the cases of persons questioned for any act done by them in the execution of the law, or for the suppression of riots and tumults, in the province of the Massachusetts-Bay, in New-England." And another statute was then made, "for making more effectual provision for the government of the province of Quebec, &c." All which statutes are impolitic, unjust, and cruel, as well as unconstitutional, and most dangerous and destructive of American rights.

AND whereas, assemblies have been frequently dissolved, contrary to the rights of the people, when they attempted to deliberate on grievances; and their dutiful, humble, loyal and reasonable petitions to the crown for redress, have been repeatedly treated with contempt by his Majesty's ministers of state.

THE good people of the several colonies of New-Hampshire, Massachusetts-Bay, Rhode-Island and Providence plantations, Connecticut, New-York, New-Jersey, Pennsylvania, New-Castle Kent and Sussex on Delaware, Maryland, Virginia, North-Carolina, and South-Carolina, justly alarmed at these arbitrary proceedings of parliament and administration, have severally elected, constituted, and appointed deputies to meet and sit in general congress in the city of Philadelphia, in order to obtain such establishment, as that their religion, laws, and liberties may not be subverted: Whereupon the deputies so appointed being now assembled, in a full and free representation of these colonies, taking into their most serious consideration the best means of attaining the ends aforesaid, do in the first place, as Englishmen, their ancestors in like cases have usually done, for asserting and vindicating their rights and liberties, DECLARE,

THAT the inhabitants of the English colonies in North-America, by the immutable laws of nature, the principles of the English constitution, and the several charters or compacts, have the following RIGHTS.—

*Resolved, N. C. D.* 1. THAT they are entitled to life, liberty, and property: and they have never ceded to any sovereign power whatever, a right to dispose of either without their consent.

*Resolved, N. C. D.* 2. THAT our ancestors, who first settled these colonies, were at the time of their emigration from the mother country, entitled to all the rights, liberties, and immunities of free and natural born subjects, within the realm of England.

*Resolved, N. C. D.* 3. THAT by such emigration they by no means forfeited, surrendered, or lost any of those rights, but that they were, and their descendants now are, entitled to the exercise and enjoyment of all such of them, as their local and other circumstances enable them to exercise and enjoy.

*Resolved,* 4. THAT the foundation of English liberty and of all free government, is a right in the people to participate in their legislative council: and as the English colonists are not represented, and from their local and other circumstances cannot properly be represented in the British parliament, they are entitled to a free and exclusive power of legislation in their several provincial Legislatures, where their right of representation can alone be preserved, in all cases of taxation and internal polity, subject only to the negative of their sovereign, in such manner as has been heretofore used and accustomed: But from the necessity of the case, and a regard to the mutual interests of both countries, we cheerfully consent to the operation of such acts of the British parliament, as are bona fide, restrained to the regulation of our external commerce, for the purpose of securing the commercial advantages of the whole empire to the mother country, and the commercial benefits of its respective members, excluding every idea of taxation internal or external, for raising a revenue on the subjects in America without their consent.

*Resolved, N. C. D.* 5. THAT the respective colonies are entitled to the common law of England, and more especially to the great and inestimable priviledge of being tried by their peers of the vicinage, according to the course of that law.

*Resolved,* 6. THAT they are entitled to the benefit of such of the English statutes, as existed at the time of their colonization; and which they have, by experience, respectively found to be applicable to their several local and other circumstances.

*Resolved, N. C. D.* 7. THAT these, his Majesty's, colonies are likewise entitled to all the immunities and privileges granted and confirmed to, them by royal charters, or secured by their several codes of provincial laws.

*Resolved, N. C. D.* 8. THAT they have a right peaceably to assemble, consider of their grievances, and petition the King; and that all prosecutions, prohibitory proclamations, and commitments for the same, are illegal.

*Resolved, N. C. D.* 9. THAT the keeping a standing army in these colonies, in times of peace, without the consent of the legislature of that colony in which such army is kept, is against law.

*Resolved, N. C. D.* 10. IT is indispensibly necessary to good government, and rendered essential by the English constitution, that the constituent branches of the legislature be independent of each other; that, therefore, the exercise of legislative power in several colonies, by a council appointed, during pleasure, by the crown, is unconstitutional, dangerous, and destructive to the freedom of American legislation.

ALL and each of which, the aforesaid deputies in behalf of themselves, and their constituents, do claim, demand, and insist on, as their indubitable rights and liberties; which cannot be legally taken from them, altered or abridged by any power whatever, without their own consent, by their representatives in their several provincial legislatures.

IN the course of our inquiry, we find many infringements and violations of the foregoing rights; which, from an ardent desire that harmony and mutual intercourse of affection and interest may be restored, we pass over for the present, and proceed to state such acts and measures as have been adopted since the last war, which demonstrate a system formed to enslave America.

*Resolved, N. C. D.* THAT the following acts of parliament are infringements and violations of the rights of the colonists; and that the repeal of them is essentially necessary, in order to restore harmony between Great-Britain and the American colonies, viz.

THE several acts of 4 Geo. III, ch. 15. and ch. 34.—5 Geo. III, ch. 25.—6 Geo. III. ch. 52.—7 Geo. III. ch. 41. and ch. 46.—8 Geo. III. ch. 22. which impose duties for the purpose of raising a revenue in America, extend the powers of the admiralty courts beyond their ancient limits, deprive the American subject of trial by jury, authorise the judges [to issue] certificate[s] to indemnify the prosecutor from damages, that he might otherwise be liable to, requiring oppressive security from a claimant of ships and goods seized, before he shall be allowed to defend his property, and are subversive of American rights.

ALSO 12 Geo. III. ch. 24. intituled, "An act for the better securing his Majesty's dock-yards, magazines, ships, ammunition and Stores." Which declares a new offence in America, and deprives the American subject of a constitutional trial by jury of the vicinage, by authorising the trial of any person charged with the committing any offence described in the said act out of the realm, to be indicted and tried for the same in any shire or county within the realm.

ALSO the three acts passed in the last session of parliament, for stopping the port and blocking up the harbour of Boston, for altering the charter and government of Massachusetts-Bay, and that which is intituled, "An act for the better administration of justice," &c.

ALSO the act passed in the same session for establishing the Roman catholic religion in the province of Quebec, abolishing the equitable system of English laws, and erecting a tyranny there, to the great danger, from so total a dissimularity of religion, law, and government to the neighbouring British colonies, by the assistance of whose blood and treasure the said country was conquered from France.

ALSO the act passed in the same session for the better providing suitable quarters for officers and soldiers in his Majesty's service in North-America.

ALSO, that the keeping a standing army in several of these colonies, in time of peace, without the consent of the legislature of that colony in which such army is kept, is against law.

13.2

⚜ JAMES DUANE, PROPOSITIONS BEFORE THE
COMMITTEE ON RIGHTS, SEPTEMBER 7–22, 1774 ⚜

It is unclear when exactly James Duane presented these propositions to the grand Committee on Rights, yet he implies here that he did so over time, beginning with the appointment of delegates on September 7 and ending with the committee's presentation of a draft report on rights to Congress on September 22. In the first section of his remarks, Duane explores the rights of the king, Parliament, and the colonies, and in the second section, those resolves that he believed followed from these rights properly understood. Accordingly, he begins by declaring that the king deserves the same allegiance and enjoys the same prerogatives (that is, rights) in the colonies as he does in the realm of England.

Next, Duane examines the rights of the British nation—effectively, Parliament—and divides them into two branches: those relating to commercial and manufacturing rights, and those based on Britain's defense of the empire. He admits that the central question concerning the first, which affected all imperial matters, was how to recognize that Parliament had the constitutional right to regulate imperial trade without also granting it the same right to legislate for or tax the colonies. Duane's solution, given that all the colonies had "submitted to and acquiesed in its Authority for more than a Century," was that they should continue to cede to Parliament the authority to regulate imperial trade, not as a matter of right but "upon the footing of a Compact," that is, as a voluntary agreement of long standing. That arrangement would not have satisfied Parliament, for it was committed to protecting its practices as constitutional rights, not simply long-enjoyed traditional privileges. Duane's offer, in truth, was exactly opposite to Parliament's understanding, that is, that the colonies should be permitted to continue to enjoy long-practiced customary privileges and Parliament its fully entrenched sovereign rights.[78]

In regard to defense, Duane readily admits that a more equitable and dependable system of support must be fashioned, and he recommends something analogous to the plan proposed ten years earlier by the Albany Congress and soon to be submitted again by Lord North and Chatham in Parliament (see documents 23.1 and 23.3). Duane proposes that "Deputies from each respective House of Assembly shoud be authorized by provincial Laws, when calld Upon by the Crown, to meet it's Commissionr in a (*Congress*) general Continental Council and adjust the several Quotas and their determination to be declard decisive and binding upon each Colony." For the moderates, such mechanisms might have accommodated Parliament's desire to pay for colonial defense through increased colonial tax revenues rather than by adding to Britain's staggering war debt, without either side ceding their claimed rights.

And for the colonies' rights, which rested on the common law of England, their respective charters, and their individual codes of law, nothing more would be required than to restrict *"legislation in each Colony respecting Taxation and internal Polity,"* to each colony, "Subject only to the Negative of the Crown." Note that Duane's concern, which was shared by almost all his colleagues, was with the constitutionally questionable nature of parliamentary legislation and oversight, not with the king's power exercised through his colonial governors and his Privy Council, with their absolute royal vetoes over colonial legislation. Although that relationship was far from irenic for most of the eighteenth century as colonial legislatures battled the Crown and its imperial agents, it was rarely contested in congressional state papers until the spring of 1776.[79]

In the second half of the document, Duane turns to those resolutions that should be included in the Bill of Rights—the focus of the committee. The resolutions in which Duane defended the royal prerogative, regular and dedicated tax revenues to support colonial governance, and colonial contributions to imperial defense proved unacceptable to the majority of his colleagues and thus were not included in the Bill of Rights. Others, for example, the second and sixth resolutions, regarding the rights and duties of Parliament and the colonial legislatures, were incorporated almost verbatim into the fourth resolution of the approved Bill of Rights. As was the fifth resolution, which founded colonial rights on the laws of England. It holds that "his Majesty's Colonies are Lik[ewise] entitled to all the Immunities and Priviledges granted to them by the royal Charter and Confirmed and secured by their several Codes of provincial Laws," and that those "Rights cannot be altered or abridged by any other Authority than that of their respective Legislatures." Such rights were not declared inviolable—in fact, they were subject to being changed by colonial legislatures—but were nonetheless immune from parliamentary oversight.

Paul H. Smith, ed., *Letters of Delegates to Congress, 1774–1789* (Washington, D.C.: Library of Congress, 1976–93), 1:38–43. Words and phrases shown in parentheses were crossed out in the original manuscript but then restored in the official record. Two paragraphs at the end of the second resolution are omitted here because they simply restate the resolution. The bracketed additions in the fifth resolution were made by Edmund Pendleton, one other (unidentified) member of the committee, and William Paca, who was not a member of the committee.

A firm Union between the Parent State and her Colonies ought to be the great object of this Congress. It is this alone which can ensure the permanent Stability of the british Empire & the mutual Happiness of its' respective Members. In the Resolves therefore to be adopted the Prerogatives of the Crown, the Interest of Great

Britain and the Rights of the Colonies ought each to have their proper Influence, & our proceedings to be tempered not only with a Regard to justice but a desire of Reconciliation.

I. The Supremacy of the Crown will be secured upon the Principle that the King is entitled to the same Allegiance and to the like royal Prerogatives in the respective Colonies as are due from his Subjects and appertains to his Sovereignty within the Realm of England.

II. The Rights of the british Nation.

These may be divided into two Branches.

(1)  The Advantages of Commerce.
(2)  Aids from the Colonists for the Defence of the Empire.

(1) The Advantages of Commerce

These arise

a. By furnishing the present State in preference to every other (*Nation*) Country with so much of the Produce of the Colonies as they can spare and she may require.

b. By receiving from her exclusively every Commodity which she may raise or Manufacture, & of which we stand in need.

3. By admitting only her ships navigated with her Subjects to an commercial intercourse with the respective Colonies.

4. By Yielding Up to her the Power of regulating the general Trade of the Empire to answer these purposes, and to preserve a uniform System in this respect among the several Colonies.

The difficulty is to establish a Principle upon which we can submit this Authority to Parliament without the Danger of (*a hurtful Precedent*) their pleading a Right *to bind us in all Cases whatsoever.*

I think a solid Distinction may be taken.

It has hitherto been a receivd Maxim that we brought over as our Birth right the Common Law of England, and such Statutes, applicable to our locale Circumstances, as existed at the Time of our Colonization; and that these, with our Charter Rights, and provincial Codes, form our Colony Constitutions. This principle seems indisputable: because every Charter comprehends a prohibitory Clause against the enacting any Laws repugant to those of England; which necessarily implies that the latter must originally have extended and been the Basis of our Constitution.

*Some* of the Colonies have been planted since the navigation Act passed in the Reign of King Charles the Second which explicitly asserts claims and reserves for the people of England the Commercial Advantages we have enumerated. In such Colonies therefore this Statute is a part of the Law of the Land. *Others* have adopted or extended it by positive Law. *All* have submitted to and acquiesed in its Authority for more than a Century. By all therefore the Regulation of Trade may be yielded to Parliament upon the footing of a Compact, reasonable in itself, & essentiel to the well-being of the whole Empire as a Commercial People.

The Principle from which our (*internal*) exclusive Colony Legislation with respect to Taxation and internal Polity is derived, will not be crossed by such a Concession & this is the point to be guarded.

(2) Aids from the Colonists for the Defence of the Empire.

These are founded in Justice, due for Protection, and necessary for common Preservation.

The Difficulty of drawing together the Strength, and the Just Contributions, of so many seperate Branches of the Empire, and the Danger of leaving it to the discretion of each, is the great Basis on which the Reasonableness of parliamentary Interposition is built. Nothing coud be more conciliatory than to obviate this Objection. For that Purpose it is proper

1. That each Colony shoud engage to provide a Competent and honourable Support for the administration of Government & Justice within its own Limits.

2. That considering the present perilous state of the Nation'l Funds, & the protection we constantly derive from it's Fleets, a present Supply be recommended in Lieu of the Mony extorted from Us under the fallacious Idea of regulating the Trade.

3. That a Plan be offered for ascertaining the Quotas and securing the Aids of every Colony in Case of future Emergency.

1st. The first we Justly consider as a priviledge instead of a Burthen.

2. To *a present Supply is* objected the Danger of it's being employed as a Means of Corruption: but this might be prevented by a specific Application: to the Support, for Instance, of a certain Number of the royal Navy on an American Establishment, the Funds to be raised by the Authority & on the Inhabitants of each Colony in such proportion as might be agreed upon in genrl. Congress.

3. The Plan for securing the Aids of the Colonies, in future Emergencies can only be established by the mutual Consent of the Crown & the respective Colony Assemblies. Would it not be sufficient for this purpose if Deputies from each respective House of Assembly shoud be authorized by provincial Laws, when calld Upon by the Crown, to meet it's Commissionr in a (*Congress*) general Continental Council and adjust the several Quotas and their determination to be declard decisive and binding upon each Colony.

I do not know that the Dutch States have any other Bond of Union; or at least that one Province has by the Terms of the Confederacy coercive Authority over the other. Common Interest, which, is the only Cement of such States, will prove a sufficient obligation.

III. The Rights of the Colonies. These as has been already intimated are derived

1. From the Common Law of England and such antient Statutes, applicable to our local Circumstances, as existed at the time of our Colonization which are fundamentals in our Constitution. 2. From our respective Charters confirming those Rights. 3. From our several Codes of provincial Laws.

Nothing seems necessary for the preservation of those Rights but *an exclusive provincial Legislation in each Colony respecting Taxation and internal Polity, &* comprehending the Dispensation of Justice both civil and criminal; & Subject only to the Negative of the Crown where that negative has not been ceded by royal Charter.

If these Ideas are Just, and properly arranged, then the Resolves of the Congress may be to the following Effect.

I. That his Majesty is entitled to the same Allegiance and to the like royal Prerogatives in these his loyal Colonies as are due from his Subjects and constitute his Sovereignty within the Realm of England.

II. That the Acts of Navigation, & for the Encouragement of Trade, passed in the reign of King Charles the second tho' in some Respects extremely burthensome to the Colonies do in their general Tendency establish wise and Salutary (*Laws*) Regulations, on which the Wealth Strength and Safety of the whole british Empire greatly depend; and having taken place before the Settlement of some Of the Colonies; and been adopted (*and extended*) in others in their Infancy by positive provincial Law; and in all having been submitted to and acquiesced in for more than a Century ought to be considered in the Light of a Compact between the Parent Kingdom and these Colonies which has reserved to the british Parliament (*an exclusive Authority*) the Supreme direction & superintendance proper over the general Trade of all his Majesty's Dominions, And that this Authority interwoven with our Establishments from their first Rise ought not to be drawn into Question provided that it is bona fide restrained to the regulation of our Trade. . . .

And this Authority exercised bona fide for the purposes of securing the Commercial Advantages of the whole Empire to Great Britain with a Just Regard to the Interest of its respective Members ought not to be Questioned. But in this declaration we absolutely exclude every Idea of Taxation internal & external for raising a Revenue on the Subjects of America without their Consent. . . .

III. That it is the Duty of the several Colonies *not only to* provide a Competent and honourable Support for the Administration of his Majesty's Government and the Dispensation of Justice within their respective Limits: but also to grant a present and annual Supply towards defraying the Expence of the royal Navy from which we derive the great Blessings of Protection in Common with the rest of our Fellow Subjects throughout the Empire.

IV. That it is the Duty of the several Colonies on every Emergency that may threaten the Security (*of any part*) of the Empire to contribute their Aids of Men and money in the common Cause, according to their several Abilities And that this Congress is firmly perswaded that the respective Legislatures of the Colonies will agree to any reasonable Plan which shall be recommended by his Majesty for drawing forth the united Strength and Aids of these Branches of his royal Dominions Whenever it shall be found necessary.

V. That the Colonies are (*bound by and*) entitled to the benefits of, the common Law of England and such of the Statutes of that Realm, [& from Experience have been found] applicable to [their respective] local Circumstances, as existed at the time of our Colonization. We do not however admit but absolutely reject the Authority of the

Statutes of 26th King Henry 8th [Ch. 13th] and King Edward 6 respecting [the trials for] Treasons and Misprisions [or Concealmts] of Treasons [committd out of the Realm as applied to Us by a late Constructn. which would effectually destroy all Security of the Lives, Liberties & Properties of the Colonists] which can not, nor were intended to be of force where (*Justice is duly administered*) [Tribunals are Established For the due Administration of Justice] according to the Laws of England, but only in remote and foreign parts where offenders for want of (*proper*) such Tribunals cannot be brought to legal Trial. That these his Majesty's Colonies are Lik[ewise] entitled to all the Immunities and Priviledges granted to them by the royal Charter and Confirmed and secured by their several Codes of provincial Laws; And that these respective Rights cannot be altered or abridged by any other Authority than that of their respective Legislatures.

VI. That the Colonists within their several Colonies are respectively entitled to a free and exclusive power of Legislation in all Cases of Taxation and internal Polity, Subject only to the negative of the Crown when that Negative has not been ceded by royal Charter. And that to the Representatives of the people in General Assembly constitute a fundamental indispensable Branch in such Legislation.

13.3

## JOHN ADAMS, NOTES OF DEBATES, SEPTEMBER 8, 1774

In the remarkable exchange recorded in this, one of the most theoretically rich documents in this collection, one learns that, according to John Adams, the debate in the Committee on Rights focused for almost a month on two questions: "whether We should recur to Law of Nature, as well as to the British Constitution and our American Charters and Grant," and "what Authority We should conceed to Parliament: whether We should deny the Authority of Parliament in all Cases: whether We should allow any Authority to it, in our internal Affairs: or whether We should allow it to regulate the Trade of the Empire, with or without any restrictions." Concerning the first question, Adams was "very strenuous for retaining and insisting on it [the law of nature], as a Resource to which We might be driven, by Parliament much sooner that We were aware."[80] John Rutledge of South Carolina, James Duane, and Joseph Galloway, however, argued forcefully against resting American rights on a natural or universal grounding. As Rutledge noted, "Our Claims I think are well founded on the british Constitution, and not on the Law of Nature." Duane, too, argued for "grounding our Rights on the Laws and Constitution of the Country from whence We sprung, and Charters, without recurring to the Law of Nature—because this will be a feeble Support."

Galloway claimed, "I never could find the Rights of Americans, in the Distinctions between Taxation and Legislation, nor in the Distinction between Laws for Revenue and for the Regulation of Trade. I have looked for our Rights in the Laws of Nature—but could not find them in a State of Nature, but always in a State of political Society." The deeply conservative Galloway, soon to join the ranks of loyalists, concluded that the English Constitution had always rested on the right of landholders to consent to the laws that bind them, and in a manner that succinctly captures the essence of the imperial debate, he found that the colonists might reduce their "Rights to one": "An exemption from all Laws made by British Parliament, made since the Emigration of our Ancestors." The logical implication was "that all Acts of Parliament made since, are Violations of our Rights." But Galloway surprisingly admitted, "My Arguments tend to an Independency of the Colonies," something that, nevertheless, he resisted. In sum, almost no one in the colonies—even those who would remain loyal—found Parliament's actions constitutional, while almost everyone equally accepted the king's right to rule as a constitutional monarch.

Others, however, including Richard Henry Lee, Roger Sherman of Connecticut, and, far more surprisingly, the young John Jay of New York (who rarely found himself in agreement with the radical faction in Congress), were in favor of recurring to the laws of nature. Lee could not "see why We should not lay our Rights upon the broadest Bottom, the Ground of Nature;" after all, "Our Ancestors found here no Government." In essence, Lee undercut the English Crown's prerogative right to grant charters and maintain the need for allegiance. He rightly drew attention to the weakness of charter rights, arguing, "We shall rest our Rights on a feeble foundation, if we rest em only on Charters." His remarks were not immediately met with rebuttal; instead, the moderate William Livingston of New Jersey reminded his colleagues that as English corporations with the power only to create bylaws (and thus, not sovereign binding law), the colonies could not "make a Corporation," even though "Charter governments have done it." Since America should not rest its rights claims "wholly on the Laws of England"—doing so would make for bad law—there was a need for some more essential foundation. For some, including possibly John Adams, turning to a naturalistic foundation may have been less a matter of principle than, in part, a defensive measure.

The debate struck another deep vein of difference. The pertinent issue was the rights associated with emigration and the grounds used by Lee, Jay, Jefferson, and others in defending a republicanism that undercut the monarchical character of the colonists' constitutional ties to Britain. They envisioned their relationship to the king, in the language of radical English republican discourse, as a fully voluntary compact between equal parties.[81] When Jay claimed that "Emigrants have a Right, to erect what Government they please," John Rutledge immediately replied, with greater historical accuracy, "An Emigrant would not have a Right to set up what constitution they please. A Subject could not alienate his Allegiance." One of the leaders of the moderate faction in Virginia, Edmund Pendleton, then brought the issue home: if such a natural right did exist, then could the British or the colonists legitimately prevent the Canadians from creating any form of government, including a Catholic-dominated one, that they might like against the wishes of Britain or, still more strenuously, the colonies? Later, the radical Connecticut delegate Eliphalet Dyer clarified that Canada, as a conquered land, possessed no such rights under international or Roman law, and thus the king could impose "what law he pleases." The authoritative William Blackstone, in a manner little countenanced by radical delegates, held that the same applied to the American colonies.[82]

The radical delegate Roger Sherman ignored Pendleton's aside and went still further down the road toward republicanism: "The Colonies [are] not bound to the King or Crown by the Act of Settlement, but by their consent to it." He advocated that "the Colonies adopt the common Law, not as the common Law, but as the highest Reason," that is, as a universal norm. Lee, not surprisingly, pushed the radically republican line of argument still further, anticipating the end reached by some in the colonies eighteen months later when he suggested that civil and natural liberty may be indistinguishable: "Life and Liberty, which is necessary for the Security of Life, cannot be given up when We enter into Society." In 1809, Edmund Randolph, a U.S. attorney general and secretary of state, noted that such arguments, if strictly observed in a slave-owning society, might have proved far more revolutionary than even the aristocratic Lee could have anticipated.[83]

Rutledge remained unmoved by Lee's radical assertion, responding that "the first Emigrants could not be considered as in a State of Nature—they had no Right to elect a new King." Here, in this wonderfully rich and deeply divided debate, is clearly articulated the close connection in colonial thought between rights of emigration and the legal conditions, charter or some kind of compact, under which it occurred, voluntary or circumscribed by duties and allegiance to the Crown—along with much else of what was and would be closely contested in the American movement toward independence.[84] As noted by Adams, much of the debate centered on whether any recurrence to nature should be made. In the end, the First Continental Congress made a brief mention of it in the Bill of Rights—along with dozens of references to English law—and then not in any other of its state papers. Each side may have viewed itself as the victor.

Paul H. Smith, ed., *Letters of Delegates to Congress, 1774–1789* (Washington, D.C.: Library of Congress, 1976–93), 1:46–49.

Septr. 8. Thursday. [1774]
In the Committee for States Rights, Grievances and Means of Redress.
Coll. Lee. The Rights are built on a fourfold foundation—on Nature, on the british Constitution, on Charters, and on immemorial Usage. The Navigation Act, a Capital Violation.

Mr. Jay. It is necessary to recur to the Law of Nature, and the british Constitution to ascertain our Rights.

The Constitution of G.B. will not apply to some of the Charter Rights.

A Mother Country surcharged with Inhabitants, they have a Right to emigrate. It may be said, if We leave our Country, We cannot leave our Allegiance. But there is no Allegiance without Protection. And Emigrants have a Right, to erect what Government they please.

Mr. J. Rutledge. An Emigrant would not have a Right to set up what constitution they please. A Subject could not alienate his Allegiance.

Lee. Cant see why We should not lay our Rights upon the broadest Bottom, the Ground of Nature. Our Ancestors found here no Government.

Mr. Pendleton. Consider how far We have a Right to interfere, with Regard to the Canada Constitution.

If the Majority of the People there should be pleased with the new Constitution, would not the People of America and of England have a Right to oppose it, and prevent such a Constitution being established in our Neighbourhood.

Lee. It is contended that the Crown had no Right to grant such Charters as it has to the Colonies—and therefore We shall rest our Rights on a feeble foundation, if we rest em only on Charters—nor will it weaken our Objections to the Canada Bill.

Mr. Rutledge. Our Claims I think are well founded on the british Constitution, and not on the Law of Nature.

Coll. Dyer. Part of the Country within the Canada Bill, is a conquered Country, and part not. It is said to be a Rule that the King can give a Conquered Country what Law he pleases.

Mr. Jay. I cant think the british Constitution inseperably attached to the Person of every Subject. Whence did the Constitution derive i[t]s Authority? From compact. Might not that Authority be given up by Compact.

Mr. Wm. Livingston. A Corporation cannot make a Corporation. Charter Governments have done it. K[ing] cant appoint a Person to make a Justice of Peace. All Governors do it. Therefore it will not do for America to rest wholly on the Laws of England.

Mr. Sherman. The Ministry contend, that the Colonies are only like Corporations in England, and therefore subordinate to the Legislature of the Kingdom. The Colonies not bound to the King or Crown by the Act of Settlement, but by their consent to it.

There is no other Legislative over the Colonies but their respective Assemblies.

The Colonies adopt the common Law, not as the common Law, but as the highest Reason.

Mr. Duane. Upon the whole for grounding our Rights on the Laws and Constitution of the Country from whence We sprung, and Charters, without recurring to the Law of Nature—because this will be a feeble Support. Charters are Compacts between the Crown and the People and I think on this foundation the Charter Governments stand firm.

England is Governed by a limited Monarchy and free Constitution.

Priviledges of Englishmen were inherent, their Birthright and Inheritance, and cannot be deprived of them, without their Consent.

Objection. That all the Rights of Englishmen will make us independent.

I hope a Line may be drawn to obviate this Objection.

James was against Parliaments interfering with the Colonies. In the Reign of Charles 2d. the Sentiments of the Crown seem to have been changed. The Navigation Act was made. Massachusetts denied the Authority—but made a Law to inforce it in the Colony.

Lee. Life and Liberty, which is necessary for the Security of Life, cannot be given up when We enter into Society.

Mr. Rutledge. The first Emigrants could not be considered as in a State of Nature—they had no Right to elect a new King.

Mr. Jay. I have always withheld my Assent from the Position that every Subject discovering Land [*does so*] for the State to which they belong.

Mr. Galloway. I never could find the Rights of Americans, in the Distinctions between Taxation and Legislation, nor in the Distinction between Laws for Revenue and for the Regulation of Trade. I have looked for our Rights in the Laws of Nature—but could not find them in a State of Nature, but always in a State of political Society.

I have looked for them in the Constitution of the English Government, and there found them. We may draw them from this Soursce securely.

Power results from the Real Property, of the Society.

The States of Greece, Macedon, Rome, were founded on this Plan. None but Landholders could vote in the Comitia, or stand for Offices.

English Constitution founded on the same Principle. Among the Saxons the Landholders were obliged to attend and shared among them the Power. In the Norman Period the same. When the Land holders could not all attend, the Representation of the freeholders, came in. Before the Reign of H[enry] 4., an Attempt was made to give the Tenants in Capite a Right to vote. Magna Charta. Archbishops, Bishops, Abbots, Earls and Barons and Tenants in Capite held all the Lands in England.

It is of the Essence of the English Constitution, that no Law shall be binding, but such as are made by the Consent of the Proprietors in England.

How then did it stand with our Ancestors, when they came over here? They could not be bound by any Laws made by the British Parliament—excepting those made before. I never could see any Reason to allow that we are bound to any Law made since—nor could I ever make any Distinction between the Sorts of Laws.

I have ever thought We might reduce our Rights to one. An Exemption from all Laws made by British Parliament, made since the Emigration of our Ancestors. It follows therefore that all the Acts of Parliament made since, are Violations of our Rights.

These Claims are all defensible upon the Principles even of our Enemies—Ld. North himself when he shall inform himself of the true Principles of the Constitution, &c.

I am well aware that my Arguments tend to an Independency of the Colonies, and militate against the Maxim that there must be some absolute Power to draw together all the Wills and strength of the Empire.

13.4

## SILAS DEANE TO THOMAS MUMFORD, OCTOBER 16, 1774

Silas Deane, a delegate to Congress from Connecticut, had a reputation for creating stealthy schemes. He would make use of such talents while serving with Benjamin Franklin and Arthur Lee as congressional representatives in France before being accused of financial irregularities and recalled by Congress. Deane was also accused of being a traitor after the British published letters in which he argued at length for the need for reconciliation. In this letter to Thomas Mumford, a merchant from Groton, Connecticut, member of the Connecticut Assembly, and agent for the Secret Committee of Congress, Deane nicely summarizes the goals, accomplishments, and difficulties of the First Continental Congress. Its goals were simple: to produce a bill of rights, to list American grievances, and to suggest measures of redress. Its accomplishments, he argues, were many—most importantly, creating a consensus and harmonization among men otherwise "from infancy, habituated to different modes, of Treating Subjects." In discussing these issues, Deane claims that "the whole British Constitution, its rise, progress, & completion, has been reveiwed minutely" in Congress' debates.

Paul H. Smith, ed., *Letters of Delegates to Congress, 1774–1789* (Washington, D.C.: Library of Congress, 1976–93), 1:201–3.

Dear Sir                                                    Philadelphia Octr 16th 1774

I little Thought when I left Home on the 22d of August last That I should be detained, in this City, untill the 16th of October, but so it has happened, that We are even Now but within View, as I may say, of, not The End of Our Business, but of this Sitting of the Congress, for it seems a Matter pretty much concluded on that it will be most prudent to adjourn. It is probable that This Week will go near to close The Affairs immediately before Us, as the General Heads are agreed on, and Committees appointed to make the Draughts. No Resolution of any Consequence, and I dare say, you will judge, some of them so, has been pass'd in the Congress, but with an Unanimous Voice, though they have many of them taken up Days in close, & at Times, warm debate. Three capital, &, general Objects were in View From The First—A Bill of American Rights,—A List of American Greivances,—And Measures For Redress. You will easily consider the First the most important Subject that could possibly be taken up by Us, as on the Fixing them rightly, with precision, yet sufficiently explicit, & on a certain, and durable Basis, such as the Reason & Nature of things, the Natural Rights of Mankind, The Rights of British Subjects, in general, and the particular, & local privileges, Rights, & immunities of British American Subjects, considered in degree distinct, yet connected with the Empire at large. On This I say, all the Consistency at least, of Our future proceedings, in America depends, and in a great degree, the peace, & Liberty, of the American Colonies. In doing this, We have proceeded with the Utmost Caution knowing how critical and important an undertaking it was, & how fatal a misstep must be, not to Ourselves only but to all posterity. Consequently the whole British Constitution, its rise, progress, & completion, has been reviewed minutely,— All the Statutes respecting it, or affecting the Colonies attended To and considered— when You add to This, The Time necessarily spent as well as Difficulty to be encountered at last, To bring Men, From infancy, habituated to different modes, of Treating Subjects, perfectly to harmonize, You will set down no small portion of Our Time to this Head of Business. Our Greivances You will say are evident To all, and may be enumerated in one Day as well as in a Month,—on second Thought You will perhaps be willing to give Us longer Time on that part—For a Greivance deserving the Notice of the United Continent must not only be a real, but one so general, That a Stand must be made against it, and Our measures for redress, be persevered in, untill it is removed. To enumerate as greivances, matters of lesser Moment, would be below the dignity, & lessen the weight of this Continental Council, here again, We have recourse To the Statutes, the Usages, & Customs of both Countries to direct Us, as Well as to their, & Our Bill of Rights. The Measures to be pursued for, or mode of obtaining Redress is a delicate, yet important Subject. These Three Subjects have taken up the Cheif of Our Time. We meet at Nine, & set untill half past Three, then adjourn untill the Next Morning, this brings Us to Dinner at Four or afterwards, which being generally in parties, on invitation out, or at Our Lodgings concludes the Day, and though We have sat, now, Six Weeks, We have not had One day's respite. Two Expresses from Boston, have taken up part of Our Time, by one of them I wrote largely, the substance of which You have doubtless seen. The Assembly of this province met Yesterday and chose Mr. Biddle Speaker, and appointed *Mr. Dickinson* an additional Member, to represent this Province in Congress, so that We may expect his Company Tomorrow in *Carpenters Hall*. . . .

. . . Connecticut stands in a reputable, and important point of View, with the other Colonies The more so as We have not been silent on their History, and police, as well as on their other Connections, & their Manners. The Cause of Boston You have already seen is made by Us a Common Cause, & You must not be surprized at a Resolution, of all the Colonies, here represented, made Unanimously, to stand by, & support them to the last with Life, & Fortune, and that Resolution published on the housetop at West-minster. I hope We shall be at New Haven before the Assembly rises. It is quite uncertain whither I shall be able to procure a place for Your Son, as No Mercht. in this City will give any Answer to a Question respecting future Business untill he hears, the Report, of the doings of this Congress, but I have spoke to several kind, & worthy Freinds on the subject, who have promised to make thorough inquiry. I should prefer this City, To any place on the Continent for a Lad to serve his Time in. The Manners are simple, & pure, and their industry and Oeconomy, exceeding any thing to be expected in so populous a City. I mean by simple & pure only comparatively, for here are *Debauchees, Whores, & Rogues* as well as in other places, but not so Numerous. I have spoke for Four places, & may possibly obtain Them, if so I can provide for You and Your Brothers Sons. I am determined to fix a Brother, & Soninlaw of mine here, if possible. I pray that a Regulation of the Connecticut Militia may be attended to in earnest, much, perhaps all Depends on it there & throughout America. I have neither Time, nor Room to write at large, in a Word if You go on making Colonels &c in the Common old Way All is over as to a Militia. While all America is about to exhibit proofs of Virtue, let Those old Field Officers never more than Nominally so, at least sacrifice a Sound to a Reality. Compliments to Freinds.

Yours                                                                                          Silas Deane

[*P.S.*] Shew this to Col. Saltonstall, & others as You please.

## 14. MESSAGES TO OTHER BRITISH COLONIES, OCTOBER 1774

On October 21, Congress resolved to prepare a message to the people of Quebec, St. John's, Nova Scotia, Georgia, and East and West Florida (that is, to the other continental British colonies, along with Georgia, which had not yet been represented in Congress). The committee was made up of Thomas Cushing of Massachusetts, John Dickinson of Pennsylvania, and Richard Henry Lee of Virginia.[85] Cushing, a wealthy merchant, was rather conservative for a delegate from New England and, consequently, was not elected to attend the Second Continental Congress. The message approved by Congress urged that "the measures contained in the enclosed papers . . . be adopted [by the other colonies] with all the earnestness, that a well directed zeal for American liberty can prompt." Only such an opposition to British measures, it was suggested, could prevent the loss of "their ancient, just, and constitutional liberty."

## 14.1

 Messages to the Colonies of St. John's, Nova Scotia, Georgia, East Florida, and West Florida, October 22, 1774

Worthington Chauncey Ford et al., eds., *Journals of the Continental Congress, 1774–1789* (Washington, D.C.: Government Printing Office, 1904–37), 1:102–3.

The committee appointed to prepare a letter to the colonies of St. John's, &c. reported a draught, which was read, and being amended, the same was approved, and is as follows:

PHILADELPHIA, *October 22, 1774.*

GENTLEMEN,

The present critical and truly alarming state of American affairs, having been considered in a general Congress of deputies, from the colonies of New-hampshire, Massachusetts-bay, Rhode-island, Connecticut, New-York, New-Jersey, Pennsylvania, the lower counties on Delaware, Maryland, Virginia, North-Carolina, and South-Carolina, with that attention and mature deliberation, which the important nature of the case demands, they have determined, for themselves and the colonies they represent, on the measures contained in the enclosed papers; which measures they recommend to your colony to be adopted with all the earnestness, that a well directed zeal for American liberty can prompt. So rapidly violent and unjust has been the late conduct of the British Administration against the colonies, that either a base and slavish submission, under the loss of their ancient, just, and constitutional liberty, must quickly take place, or an adequate Opposition be formed.

We pray God to take you under his protection, and to preserve the freedom and happiness of the whole British empire. We are as

[By order of the Congress,

HENRY MIDDLETON, *President.*]

## 14.2

 "To the Inhabitants of the Province of Quebec," October 26, 1774

The first draft of "To the Inhabitants of the Province of Quebec," when presented to Congress on October 24, was found wanting and thus recommitted. The revised

draft was accepted two days later, and then translated into French by Pierre du Simitière, a Swiss-born resident of Philadelphia, before being sent to Quebec for distribution.[86] James Hutson and others report that, yet again, the author was John Dickinson, and the letter apparently "had some influence in promoting the efforts of the British residents of Montreal to send delegates to the Second Continental Congress."[87]

The letter serves as a useful guide to those rights most valued by Congress in its effort to win Canadians over to its cause. Indeed, according to Richard Perry, "of the addresses prepared by Congress, none more clearly demonstrates the opinions of its members regarding the essential rights of the colonists than the one approved October 26 to the inhabitants of Quebec."[88] The primary focus of the document was not on natural or individual rights, but rather on the right of the conquered inhabitants of Quebec to a government founded on those English rights guaranteed by the British Constitution. And what according to Congress was the essence of British liberty? It was "that to live by the will of one man, or sett of men, is the production of misery to all men. . . . On the solid foundation of this principle, Englishmen reared up the fabrick of their constitution."

The first celebrated right is "that of the people having a share in their own government by their representatives chosen by themselves"; that right should be considered the "bulwark surrounding and defending their property," that is, popular participation in defense of property. And the right extends further: if their money is sought by oppressive rulers, the people enjoy the right of withholding it until "their grievances are redressed." As might be expected, the second essential right highlighted in the letter is that of trial by jury; no one can be deprived of life, liberty, or property until fairly judged by "twelve of his unexceptionable countrymen and peers of his vicinage, who from that neighborhood may reasonably be supposed to be acquainted with his character." According to Congress, as rehearsed in document after document, those were the two most important rights of the English and British Constitutions, which the colonists believed themselves defending, as had their English ancestors. It should be noted that the right to trial by a jury of one's peers who are familiar with one's character could potentially be threatening to a strict understanding of the rule of law and of individual rights.[89]

Three other ancillary rights were included as part of the colonists' vaunted English inheritance. They included the right to habeas corpus, which "relates merely to the liberty of the person"; the holding of lands through easy rents rather than personal service; and freedom of the press, "whereby oppressive officers are shamed or intimidated, into more honourable and just modes of conducting affairs." Congress claimed that the Canadians were "entitled to and ought at this moment in perfection, to exercise" these five rights, which the king in his proclamation of 1763 had promised them but which Parliament in the Quebec Act of 1774 had failed to extend to them—for what Parliament and many of the French in Quebec believed were good reasons, most particularly the lack of familiarity with self-government.[90] According to Charles Ritcheson, with the governmental structure put in place by the Quebec Act, "no longer would a handful of English merchants and fur traders, constituting a 'representative Assembly,' rule a population who outnumbered them a hundred-fold."[91]

In addition, following Montesquieu's celebrated but too theoretical understanding of the British Constitution, Congress made much of the necessity of a separation of powers and pointed out to the residents of Quebec that for them, "the *legislative, executive* and *judging* powers are *all* moved by the nods of a Minister." In sum, Congress challenged the Canadians "to discover a single circumstance, promising from any quarter the faintest hope of liberty to you or your posterity, but from an entire adoption into the union of these Colonies." In effect, Congress asked them to join the colonies in opposing Parliament and thereby to enjoy all the rights of "English freemen." There is no mention by Congress of personal rights inviolate before a people or a legislature, and only one mention of natural rights, with all other references to the importance of English rights resting on a legitimate and promised English constitutional foundation.

It is worth noting too that the invitation to join the Second Continental Congress may have been well intentioned; Congress may have been in earnest when it wrote that it never would "desert or betray you." But when viewed alongside other congressional publications, such as its Address to the People of Great Britain and the Bill of Rights and List of Grievances (documents 12.1 and 13.1), in which the Roman Catholicism of the French residents was highlighted as a grave cause for concern, along with the military attacks on the border and into Canada then being formulated in Congress (to begin six months later and to continue for over a year), it is difficult to accept the offer at anything close to face value. Congress' sincerity was questionable when it reassured the Canadians, using the example of Catholic and Protestant Switzerland, that it was impossible that a "difference of religion will prejudice you against a hearty amity with us," because "the transcendent nature of freedom elevates those, who unite in her cause, above all such low-minded infirmities." Of course, over much of the next hundred and fifty years, the colonists turned Americans regularly made substantially different claims regarding their view of the dangerous and invidious character of Roman Catholicism and the need to limit the freedoms of its adherents.[92]

Worthington Chauncey Ford et al., eds., *Journals of the Continental Congress, 1774–1789* (Washington, D.C.: Government Printing Office, 1904–37), 1:105–13.

*To the Inhabitants of the Province of Quebec.*

*Friends and fellow-subjects,*

WE, the Delegates of the Colonies of New-Hampshire, Massachusetts-Bay, Rhode-Island and Providence Plantations, Connecticut, New-York, New-Jersey, Pennsylvania, the Counties of Newcastle Kent and Sussex on Delaware, Maryland, Virginia, North-Carolina and South-Carolina, deputed by the inhabitants of the said Colonies, to represent them in a General Congress at Philadelphia, in the province of Pennsylvania, to consult together concerning the best methods to obtain redress of our afflicting grievances, having accordingly assembled, and taken into our most serious consideration the state of public affairs on this continent, have thought proper to address your province, as a member therein deeply interested.

When the fortune of war, after a gallant and glorious resistance, had incorporated you with the body of English subjects, we rejoiced in the truly valuable addition, both on our own and your account; expecting, as courage and generosity are naturally united, our brave enemies would become our hearty friends, and that the Divine Being would bless to you the dispensations of his over-ruling providence, by securing to you and your latest posterity the inestimable advantages of a free English constitution of government, which it is the privilege of all English subjects to enjoy.

These hopes were confirmed by the King's proclamation, issued in the year 1763, plighting the public faith for your full enjoyment of those advantages.

Little did we imagine that any succeeding Ministers would so audaciously and cruelly abuse the royal authority, as to with-hold from you the fruition of the irrevocable rights, to which you were thus justly entitled.

But since we have lived to see the unexpected time, when Ministers of this flagitious temper, have dared to violate the most sacred compacts and obligations, and as you, educated under another form of government, have artfully been kept from discovering the unspeakable worth of *that* form you are now undoubtedly entitled to, we esteem it our duty, for the weighty reasons herein after mentioned, to explain to you some of its most important branches.

"In every human society," says the celebrated Marquis *Beccaria,* "there is an *effort, continually tending* to confer on one part the heighth of power and happiness, and to reduce the other to the extreme of weakness and misery. The intent of good laws is to *oppose this effort,* and to diffuse their influence *universally* and *equally.*"

Rulers stimulated by this pernicious "effort," and subjects animated by the just "intent of opposing good laws against it," have occasioned that vast variety of events, that fill the histories of so many nations. All these histories demonstrate the truth of this simple position, that to live by the will of one man, or sett of men, is the production of misery to all men.

On the solid foundation of this principle, Englishmen reared up the fabrick of their constitution with such a strength, as for ages to defy time, tyranny, treachery, internal and foreign wars: And, as an illustrious author of your nation, hereafter mentioned, observes,—"They gave the people of their Colonies, the form of their own government, and this government carrying prosperity along with it, they have grown great nations in the forests they were sent to inhabit."

In this form, the first grand right, is that of the people having a share in their own government by their representatives chosen by themselves, and, in consequence, of being ruled by *laws,* which they themselves approve, not by *edicts* of *men* over whom they have no controul. This is a bulwark surrounding and defending their property, which by their honest cares and labours they have acquired, so that no portions of it can legally be taken from them, but with their own full and free consent, when they in their judgment deem it just and necessary to give them for public service, and precisely direct the easiest, cheapest, and most equal methods, in which they shall be collected.

The influence of this right extends still farther. If money is wanted by Rulers, who have in any manner oppressed the people, they may retain it, until their grievances are redressed; and thus peaceably procure relief, without trusting to despised petitions, or disturbing the public tranquillity.

The next great right is that of trial by jury. This provides, that neither life, liberty nor property, can be taken from the possessor, until twelve of his unexceptionable countrymen and peers of his vicinage, who from that neighbourhood may reasonably be supposed to be acquainted with his character, and the characters of the witnesses, upon a fair trial, and full enquiry, face to face, in open Court, before as many of the people as chuse to attend, shall pass their sentence upon oath against him; a sentence that cannot injure him, without injuring their own reputation, and probably their interest also; as the question may turn on points, that, in some degree, concern the general welfare; and if it does not, their verdict may form a precedent, that, on a similar trial of their own, may militate against themselves.

Another right relates merely to the liberty of the person. If a subject is seized and imprisoned, tho' by order of Government, he may, by virtue of this right, immediately obtain a writ, termed a Habeas Corpus, from a Judge, whose sworn duty it is to grant it, and thereupon procure any illegal restraint to be quickly enquired into and redressed.

A fourth right, is that of holding lands by the tenure of easy rents, and not by rigorous and oppressive services, frequently forcing the possessors from their families and their business, to perform what ought to be done, in all well regulated states, by men hired for the purpose.

The last right we shall mention, regards the freedom of the press. The importance of this consists, besides the advancement of truth, science, morality, and arts in general, in its diffusion of liberal sentiments on the administration of Government, its ready communication of thoughts between subjects, and its consequential promotion of union among them, whereby oppressive officers are shamed or intimidated, into more honourable and just modes of conducting affairs.

These are the invaluable rights, that form a considerable part of our mild system of government; that, sending its equitable energy through all ranks and classes of men, defends the poor from the rich, the weak from the powerful, the industrious from the rapacious, the peaceable from the violent, the tenants from the lords, and all from their superiors.

These are the rights, without which a people cannot be free and happy, and under the protecting and encouraging influence of which, these colonies have hitherto so amazingly flourished and increased. These are the rights, a profligate Ministry are now striving, by force of arms, to ravish from us, and which we are, with one mind, resolved never to resign but with our lives.

These are the rights *you* are entitled to and ought at this moment in perfection, to exercise. And what is offered to you by the late Act of Parliament in their place? Liberty of conscience in your religion? No. God gave it to you; and the temporal powers with which you have been and are connected, firmly stipulated for your enjoyment of it. If laws, divine and human, could secure it against the despotic caprices of wicked men, it was secured before. Are the French laws in *civil* cases restored? *It seems so.* But observe the cautious kindness of the Ministers, who pretend to be your benefactors. The words of the statute are—that those "laws shall be the rule, until they shall be *varied* or *altered* by any ordinances of the Governor and Council." Is the "certainty and lenity of the *criminal* law of England, and its benefits and advantages," commended in the said statute, and said to "have been sensibly felt by you," secured to you and your descendants? No. They too are subjected to arbitrary "*alterations*" by the Governor and Council; and a power is expressly reserved of appointing "such courts of *criminal, civil,* and *ecclesiastical* jurisdiction, as shall be thought proper." Such is the precarious tenure of mere *will,* by which you hold your lives and religion. The Crown and its Ministers are impowered, as far as they could be by Parliament, to establish even the *Inquisition* itself among you. Have you an Assembly composed of worthy men, elected by yourselves, and in whom you can confide, to make laws for you, to watch over your welfare, and to direct in what quantity, and in what manner, your money shall be taken from you? No. The power of making laws for you is lodged in the governor and council, all of them dependent upon, and removable at, the *pleasure* of a Minister. Besides, another late statute, made without your consent, has subjected you to the impositions of *Excise,* the horror of all free states; thus wresting your property from you by the most odious of taxes, and laying open to insolent tax-gatherers, houses, the scenes of domestic peace and comfort, and called the castles of English subjects in the books of their law. And in the very act for altering your government, and intended to flatter you, you are not authorized to "assess, levy, or apply any *rates* and *taxes,* but for the inferior purposes of *making roads,* and erecting and repairing *public buildings,* or for other *local* conveniences, within your respective towns and districts." Why this degrading distinction? Ought not the property, honestly acquired by *Canadians,* to be held as sacred as that of *Englishmen?* Have not Canadians sense enough to attend to any other public affairs, than gathering stones from one place, and piling them up in another? Unhappy people! who are not only injured, but insulted. Nay more!—With such a superlative contempt of your understanding and spirit, has an insolent Ministry presumed to think of you, our respectable fellow-subjects, according to the information we have received, as firmly to perswade themselves that your gratitude, for the injuries and insults they have recently offered to you, will engage you to take up arms, and render yourselves the ridicule and detestation of the world, by becoming tools, in their hands, to assist them in taking that freedom from *us*, which they have treacherously denied to *you;* the unavoidable consequence of which attempt, if successful, would be the extinction of all hopes of you or your posterity being ever restored to freedom: For idiocy itself cannot believe, that, when their drudgery is performed, they will treat you with less cruelty than they have us, who are of the same blood with themselves.

What would your countryman, the immortal *Montesquieu,* have said to such a plan of domination, as has been framed for you? Hear his words, with an intenseness of thought suited to the importance of the subject.—"In a free state, every man, who is supposed a free agent, *ought to be concerned in his own government:* Therefore the *legislative* should reside in the whole body of the *people,* or their *representatives."*—"The political liberty of the subject is *a tranquillity of mind,* arising from the opinion each person has of his *safety.* In order to have this liberty, it is requisite the government be so constituted, as that one man need not be *afraid* of another. When the power of *making* laws, and the power of *executing* them, are *united* in the same person, or in the same body of Magistrates, *there can be no liberty;* because apprehensions may arise, lest the same *Monarch* or *Senate,* should *enact* tyrannical laws, to *execute* them in a tyrannical manner."

"The power of *judging* should be exercised by persons taken from the *body of the people,* at certain times of the year, and pursuant to a form and manner prescribed by law. *There is no liberty,* if the power of *judging* be not *separated* from the *legislative* and *executive* powers."

"Military men belong to a profession, which *may be* useful, but *is often* dangerous."— "The enjoyment of liberty, and even its support and preservation, consists in every man's being allowed to speak his thoughts, and lay open his sentiments."

Apply these decisive maxims, sanctified by the authority of a name which all Europe reveres, to your own state. You have a Governor, it may be urged, vested with the *executive* powers, or the powers of *administration:* In him, and in your Council, is lodged the power of *making laws.* You have *Judges,* who are *to decide* every cause affecting your lives, liberty or property. Here is, indeed, an appearance of the several powers being *separated* and *distributed* into *different* hands, for checks one upon another, the only effectual mode ever invented by the wit of men, to promote their freedom and prosperity. But scorning to be illuded by a tinsel'd outside, and exerting the natural sagacity of Frenchmen, examine the specious device, and you will find it, to use an expression of holy writ, "a whited sepulchre," for burying your lives, liberty and property.

Your *Judges,* and your *Legislative Council,* as it is called, are *dependant* on your *Governor,* and *he* is *dependant* on the servant of the Crown, in Great-Britain. The *legislative, executive* and *judging* powers are *all* moved by the nods of a Minister. Privileges and immunities last no longer than his smiles. When he frowns, their feeble forms dissolve. Such a treacherous ingenuity has been exerted in drawing up the code lately offered you, that every sentence, beginning with a benevolent pretension, concludes with a destructive power; and the substance of the whole, divested of its smooth words, is—that the Crown and its Ministers shall be as absolute throughout your extended province, as the despots of Asia or Africa. What can protect your property from taxing edicts, and the rapacity of necessitous and cruel masters? your persons from Letters de Cachet, goals, dungeons, and oppressive services? your lives and general liberty from arbitrary and unfeeling rulers? We defy you, casting your view upon every side, to discover a single circumstance, promising from any quarter the faintest hope of liberty to you or your posterity, but from an entire adoption into the union of these Colonies.

What advice would the truly great man before-mentioned, that advocate of freedom and humanity, give you, was he now living, and knew that we, your numerous and powerful neighbours, animated by a just love of our invaded rights, and united by the indissoluble bands of affection and interest, called upon you, by every obligation of regard for yourselves and your children, as we now do, to join us in our righteous contest, to make common cause with us therein, and take a noble chance for emerging from a humiliating subjection under Governors, Intendants, and Military Tyrants, into the firm rank and condition of English freemen, whose custom it is, derived from their ancestors, to make those tremble, who dare to think of making them miserable?

Would not this be the purport of his address? "Seize the opportunity presented to you by Providence itself. You have been conquered into liberty, if you act as you ought. This work is not of man. You are a small people, compared to those who with open arms invite you into a fellowship. A moment's reflection should convince you which will be most for your interest and happiness, to have all the rest of North-America your unalterable friends, or your inveterate enemies. The injuries of Boston have roused and associated every colony, from Nova-Scotia to Georgia. Your province is the only link wanting, to compleat the bright and strong chain of union. Nature has joined your country to theirs. Do you join your political interests. For their own sakes, they never will desert or betray you. Be assured, that the happiness of a people inevitably depends on their liberty, and their spirit to assert it. The value and extent of the advantages tendered to you are immense. Heaven grant you may not discover them to be blessings after they have bid you an eternal adieu."

We are too well acquainted with the liberality of sentiment distinguishing your nation, to imagine, that difference of religion will prejudice you against a hearty amity with us. You know, that the transcendent nature of freedom elevates those, who unite in her cause, above all such low-minded infirmities. The Swiss Cantons furnish a memorable proof of this truth. Their union is composed of Roman Catholic and Protestant States, living in the utmost concord and peace with one another, and thereby enabled, ever since they bravely vindicated their freedom, to defy and defeat every tyrant that has invaded them.

Should there be any among you, as there generally are in all societies, who prefer the favours of Ministers, and their own private interests, to the welfare of their country, the temper of such selfish persons will render them incredibly active in opposing all public-spirited measures, from an expectation of being well rewarded for their sordid industry, by their superiors; but we doubt not you will be upon your guard against such men, and not sacrifice the liberty and happiness of the whole Canadian people and their posterity, to gratify the avarice and ambition of individuals.

We do not ask you, by this address, to commence acts of hostility against the government of our common Sovereign. We only invite you to consult your own glory and welfare, and not to suffer yourselves to be inveigled or intimidated by infamous ministers so far, as to become the instruments of their cruelty and despotism, but to unite with us in one social compact, formed on the generous principles of equal liberty, and cemented by such an exchange of beneficial and endearing offices as to render it perpetual. In order to complete this highly desirable union, we submit it to your consideration, whether it may not be expedient for you to meet together in your several towns and districts, and elect Deputies, who afterwards meeting in a provincial Congress, may chuse Delegates, to represent your province in the continental Congress to be held at Philadelphia on the tenth day of May, 1775.

In this present Congress, beginning on the fifth of the last month, and continued to this day, it has been, with universal pleasure and an unanimous vote, resolved, That we should consider the violation of your rights, by the act for altering the government of your province, as a violation of our own, and that you should be invited to accede to our confederation, which has no other objects than the perfect security of the natural and civil rights of all the constituent members, according to their respective circumstances, and the preservation of a happy and lasting connection with Great-Britain, on the salutary and constitutional principles herein before mentioned. For effecting these purposes, we have addressed an humble and loyal petition to his Majesty, praying relief of our and your grievances; and have associated to stop all importations from Great-Britain and Ireland, after the first day of December, and all exportations to those Kingdoms and the West-Indies, after the tenth day of next September, unless the said grievances are redressed.

That Almighty God may incline your minds to approve our equitable and necessary measures, to add yourselves to us, to put your fate, whenever you suffer injuries which you are determined to oppose, not on the small influence of your single province, but on the consolidated powers of North-America, and may grant to our joint exertions an

event as happy as our cause is just, is the fervent prayer of us, your sincere and affectionate friends and fellow-subjects.

By order of the Congress,

HENRY MIDDLETON, *President.*

## 15. CONGRESS PLEADS WITH GEORGE III, OCTOBER 1774

In Congress' continuing effort to find a path toward reconciliation with Britain and a
redress of grievances, a committee was appointed on October 1 to draft a petition to the
king. The committee included three unusually radical, given the document to be written,
delegates—John Adams, Patrick Henry, and Richard Henry Lee. The committee included
two moderate delegates as well, Thomas Johnson of Maryland and John Rutledge of South
Carolina.[93] Johnson was a southern lawyer from Maryland who had opposed parliamentary actions from the early days of the Stamp Act and went on to serve as the first
governor of Maryland before beginning his judicial career in 1790. The most moderate of
the committee's members was Rutledge, who was nonetheless one of the leading figures
in South Carolina's resistance movement. At the same time that Congress took under
consideration the committee's instructions, it was debating whether an offer should be
made to pay for the tea destroyed in Boston and whether some mention might be made of
the colonies' defensive capabilities in the petition to the king. Neither matter, in the end,
was included in the committee's instructions (see documents 15.2 and 15.3).

A draft delivered to Congress on October 21 was viewed as unacceptable—not
entirely surprising given the committee's composition—so John Dickinson, a man
well known for his moderation and able pen, was added to the committee. A new draft
was presented on October 24 and approved a day later.[94] As convincingly argued by
Edwin Wolf, Dickinson was again the author of another of the First Continental
Congress' most important documents.[95] The petition was printed and signed by all of
the members—the second such document, after the Association, to carry that sanction. Two copies were sent to Benjamin Franklin, who was then in London serving as
agent for three of the colonies; Franklin in turn transmitted it to the secretary of state
for the American colonies, Lord Dartmouth, who promised to present it to the king.
He could not properly do so until Parliament next sat (about a month later, during the
third week of January 1775). Franklin had been advised not to make the petition public
until then, but it was leaked to the press and published in mid-January 1775. By
January 18, the petition had been published in the Philadelphia papers also.[96]

The petition begins with a relatively unfamiliar list of grievances advanced by
Congress, ones directed against the king's executive functions in the colonies and not
the legislative actions of Parliament. Congress complained that a standing army was
maintained in the colonies in peacetime, that the commander in chief of the British

forces had been appointed governor of a colony, that charges for imperial offices had been greatly increased, that assemblies had been frequently dissolved, and that a number of administrative posts had taken on legislative authority. Of course, those and many other long-standing concerns became still more prominent when the colonies' relationship to the king was severed in 1776. Following these administrative or executive concerns are grievances more commonly advanced by Congress: parliamentary legislation and unconstitutional taxation of the colonies, legislative changes made to the colonial judicial system, and the passage of the Coercive Acts, including the Quebec Act, which, is described as an act that forced "great numbers of British freemen" in Canada to live under "an absolute government and the Roman Catholick religion throughout those vast regions, that border on the westerly and northerly boundaries of the free protestant English settlements"—not exactly the sentiments contemporaneously expressed by Congress in "To the Inhabitants of Quebec."

Rejecting any and all charges that the colonists, in advancing a secret desire for independence, had produced the "unhappy differences between Great-Britain and these colonies," Congress wrote that if such charges were in any measure true, American colonists "should merit the opprobrious terms frequently bestowed upon us, by those we revere." In fact, the petition asserts that Congress wished for no "diminution of the prerogative, nor do we solicit the grant of any new right in our favour." The colonists' loyalty to the Crown remained undiminished: "Your royal authority over us and our connexion with Great-Britain, we shall always carefully and zealously endeavour to support and maintain"; the colonists "much more willingly would bleed in your majesty's service" than oppose his government; congressional opposition to parliamentary taxation, at least in part, stemmed from a desire to provide aid to the king directly, without intermediation, for "yielding to no British subjects, in affectionate attachment to your majesty's person, family and government, we too dearly prize the privilege of expressing that attachment" by bestowing such gifts. For the majority of delegates, all that was probably still true—independence was not the goal of their resistance. But attitudes changed over the next twenty months with the failure of their petitions and appeals for reconciliation, and with the king's and Parliament's refusal to compromise in their assertion of Parliament's sovereign right to legislate for the North American colonies.

What Congress hoped for, in effect, was for the king to take a stand in opposition to his own government and Parliament as if they were not integral components of his administration, but rather foreign impositions on him. The petition asks the king, "as the loving father of your whole people, connected by the same bands of law, loyalty, faith and blood, though dwelling in various countries," to prevent "the transcendent relation formed by these ties to be farther violated" and to rein in "those designing and dangerous men . . . interposing themselves between your royal person and your faithful subjects." This was a clear demonstration of Congress' flawed understanding of the eighteenth-century British Constitution as viewed by the king to whom they were appealing and, of course, by the majority in Parliament.[97]

The conundrum confronting both the colonists and the king was that the colonists' constitutional theory was closer to that of early seventeenth-century England, in which, as part of the king's dominions, they had been subordinate to him but not to Parliament. If the late eighteenth-century king, reigning under the auspices of a fundamentally different British Constitution, had embraced Congress' theory, it would have triggered a constitutional crisis. As Charles Ritcheson convincingly argues, the American colonial position was "in British eyes indefensible," even absurd, in its denial of "the fundamentals of the Glorious Revolution" and its attempt "to re-establish the royal power after it had been finally defeated in Great Britain."[98] Fifty years of turmoil, death, and destruction in Britain had led to the king becoming an integral part of parliamentary governance—something which George III seemed to embrace—rather than being Parliament's adversary, as in the atavistic thinking of some Whigs.[99] Scotland before 1707 and the king's ancestral lands in Hanover were not sufficiently similar to Britain in the eighteenth century to provide meaningful support for the colonial position with the Crown or in Parliament.[100]

In closing, Congress highlighted its loyalty as well as a continued adherence to its contested constitutional theory by wishing that the king's "descendants may inherit [his] prosperity and dominions 'til time shall be no more," suggesting that the dominions were personally his to bequeath. At the end of the First Continental Congress, the majority of delegates in Congress were still committed constitutional monarchists hoping the king could resolve the colonies' differences with Parliament.

15.1

 PETITION TO THE KING, OCTOBER 26, 1774

Worthington Chauncey Ford et al., eds., *Journals of the Continental Congress, 1774–1789* (Washington, D.C.: Government Printing Office, 1904–37), 1:115–22.

*The Petition of Congress.*

*To the Kings most excellent majesty*

Most gracious Sovereign

We your majestys faithful subjects of the colonies of Newhampshire, Massachusetts-bay, Rhode-island and Providence Plantations, Connecticut, New-York, New-Jersey, Pennsylvania, the counties of New-Castle Kent and Sussex on Delaware, Maryland, Virginia, North-Carolina, and South Carolina, in behalf of ourselves and the inhabitants of these colonies who have deputed us to represent them in General Congress, by this our humble petition, beg leave to lay our grievances before the throne.

A standing army has been kept in these colonies, ever since the conclusion of the late war, without the consent of our assemblies; and this army with a considerable naval armament has been employed to enforce the collection of taxes.

The Authority of the commander in chief, and, under him, of the brigadiers general has in time of peace, been rendered supreme in all the civil governments in America.

The commander in chief of all your majesty's forces in North-America has, in time of peace, been appointed governor of a colony.

The charges of usual offices have been greatly increased; and, new, expensive and oppressive offices have been multiplied.

The judges of admiralty and vice-admiralty courts are empowered to receive their salaries and fees from the effects condemned by themselves. The officers of the customs are empowered to break open and enter houses without the authority of any civil magistrate founded on legal information.

The judges of courts of common law have been made entirely dependant on one part of the legislature for their salaries, as well as for the duration of their commissions.

Councellors holding their commissions, during pleasure, exercise legislative authority.

Humble and reasonable petitions from the representatives of the people have been fruitless.

The agents of the people have been discountenanced and governors have been instructed to prevent the payment of their salaries.

Assemblies have been repeatedly and injuriously dissolved.

Commerce has been burthened with many useless and oppressive restrictions.

By several acts of parliament made in the fourth, fifth, sixth, seventh, and eighth years of your majestys reign, duties are imposed on us, for the purpose of raising a revenue, and the powers of admiralty and vice-admiralty courts are extended beyond their ancient limits, whereby our property is taken from us without our consent, the trial by jury in many civil cases is abolished, enormous forfeitures are incurred for slight offences, vexatious informers are exempted from paying damages, to which they are justly liable, and oppressive security is required from owners before they are allowed to defend their right.

Both houses of parliament have resolved that colonists may be tried in England, for offences alledged to have been committed in America, by virtue of a statute passed in the thirty fifth year of Henry the eighth; and in consequence thereof, attempts have been made to enforce that statute. A statute was passed in the twelfth year of your majesty's reign, directing, that persons charged with committing any offence therein described, in any place out of the realm, may be indicted and tried for the same, in any shire or county within the realm, whereby inhabitants of these colonies may, in sundry cases by that statute made capital, be deprived of a trial by their peers of the vicinage.

In the last sessions of parliament, an act was passed for blocking up the harbour of Boston; another, empowering the governor of the Massachusetts-bay to send persons indicted for murder in that province to another colony or even to Great Britain for trial whereby such offenders may escape legal punishment; a third, for altering the chartered constitution of government in that province; and a fourth for extending the limits of Quebec, abolishing the English and restoring the French laws, whereby great numbers of British freemen are subjected to the latter, and establishing an absolute government and the Roman Catholick religion throughout those vast regions, that border on the westerly and northerly boundaries of the free protestant English settlements; and a fifth for the better providing suitable quarters for officers and soldiers in his majesty's service in North America.

To a sovereign, who "glories in the name of Briton" the bare recital of these acts must we presume, justify the loyal subjects, who fly to the foot of his throne and implore his clemency for protection against them.

From this destructive system of colony administration adopted since the conclusion of the last war, have flowed those distresses, dangers, fears and jealousies, that overwhelm your majesty's dutiful colonists with affliction; and we defy our most subtle and inveterate enemies, to trace the unhappy differences between Great-Britain and these colonies, from an earlier period or from other causes than we have assigned. Had they proceeded on our part from a restless levity of temper, unjust impulses of ambition, or artful suggestions of seditious persons, we should merit the opprobrious terms frequently bestowed upon us, by those we revere. But so far from promoting innovations, we have only opposed them; and can be charged with no offence, unless it be one, to receive injuries and be sensible of them.

Had our creator been pleased to give us existence in a land of slavery, the sense of our condition might have been mitigated by ignorance and habit. But thanks be to his adoreable goodness, we were born the heirs of freedom, and ever enjoyed our right under the auspices of your royal ancestors, whose family was seated on the British throne, to rescue and secure a pious and gallant nation from the popery and despotism of a superstitious and inexorable tyrant. Your majesty, we are confident, justly rejoices, that your title to the crown is thus founded on the title of your people to liberty; and therefore we doubt not, but your royal wisdom must approve the sensibility, that teaches your subjects anxiously to guard the blessings, they received from divine providence, and thereby to prove the performance of that compact, which elevated the illustrious house of Brunswick to the imperial dignity it now possesses.

The apprehension of being degraded into a state of servitude from the pre-eminent rank of English freemen, while our minds retain the strongest love of liberty, and clearly foresee the miseries preparing for us and our posterity, excites emotions in our breasts, which though we cannot describe, we should not wish to conceal. Feeling as men, and thinking as subjects, in the manner we do, silence would be disloyalty. By giving this faithful information, we do all in our power, to promote the great objects of your royal cares, the tranquillity of your government, and the welfare of your people.

Duty to your majesty and regard for the preservation of ourselves and our posterity, the primary obligations of nature and society command us to entreat your royal attention; and as your majesty enjoys the signal distinction of reigning over freemen, we apprehend the language of freemen can not be displeasing. Your royal indignation, we hope, will rather fall on those designing and dangerous men, who daringly interposing themselves between your royal person and your faithful subjects, and for several years past incessantly employed to dissolve the bonds of society, by abusing your majesty's authority, misrepresenting your American subjects and prosecuting the most desperate and irritating projects of oppression, have at length compelled us, by the force of accumulated injuries too severe to be any longer tolerable, to disturb your majesty's repose by our complaints.

These sentiments are extorted from hearts, that much more willingly would bleed in your majesty's service. Yet so greatly have we been misrepresented, that a necessity has been alledged of taking our property from us without our consent "to defray the charge of the administration of justice, the support of civil government, and the defence protection and security of the colonies." But we beg leave to assure your majesty, that such provision has been and will be made for defraying the two first articles, as has been and shall be judged, by the legislatures of the several colonies, just and suitable to their respective circumstances: And for the defence protection and security of the colonies, their militias, if properly regulated, as they earnestly desire may immediately be done, would be fully sufficient, at least in times of peace; and in case of war, your faithful colonists will be ready and willing, as they ever have been when constitutionally required, to demonstrate their loyalty to your majesty, by exerting their most strenuous efforts in granting supplies and raising forces. Yielding to no British subjects, in affectionate attachment to your majesty's person, family and government, we too dearly prize the privilege of expressing that attachment by those proofs, that are honourable to the prince who receives them, and to the people who give them, ever to resign it to any body of men upon earth.

Had we been permitted to enjoy in quiet the inheritance left us by our forefathers, we should at this time have been peaceably, cheerfully and usefully employed in recommending ourselves by every testimony of devotion to your majesty, and of veneration to the state, from which we derive our origin. But though now exposed to unexpected and unnatural scenes of distress by a contention with that nation, in whose parental guidance on all important affairs we have hitherto with filial reverence constantly trusted, and therefore can derive no instruction in our present unhappy and perplexing circumstances from any former experience, yet we doubt not, the purity of our intention and the integrity of our conduct will justify us at that grand tribunal, before which all mankind must submit to judgment.

We ask but for peace, liberty, and safety. We wish not a diminution of the prerogative, nor do we solicit the grant of any new right in our favour. Your royal authority over us and our connexion with Great-Britain, we shall always carefully and zealously endeavour to support and maintain.

Filled with sentiments of duty to your majesty, and of affection to our parent state, deeply impressed by our education and strongly confirmed by our reason, and anxious to evince the sincerity of these dispositions, we present this petition only to obtain redress of grievances and relief from fears and jealousies occasioned by the system of statutes and regulations adopted since the close of the late war, for raising a revenue in America—

extending the powers of courts of admiralty and vice-admiralty—trying persons in Great Britain for offences alledged to be committed in America—affecting the province of Massachusetts-bay, and altering the government and extending the limits of Quebec; by the abolition of which system, the harmony between Great-Britain and these colonies so necessary to the happiness of both and so ardently desired by the latter, and the usual inter-courses will be immediately restored. In the magnanimity and justice of your majesty and parliament we confide, for a redress of our other grievances, trusting, that when the causes of our apprehensions are removed, our future conduct will prove us not unworthy of the regard, we have been accustomed, in our happier days, to enjoy. For appealing to that being who searches thoroughly the hearts of his creatures, we solemnly profess, that our councils have been influenced by no other motive, than a dread of impending destruction.

Permit us then, most gracious sovereign, in the name of all your faithful people in America, with the utmost humility to implore you, for the honour of Almighty God, whose pure religion our enemies are undermining; for your glory, which can be ad-vanced only by rendering your subjects happy and keeping them united; for the inter-ests of your family depending on an adherence to the principles that enthroned it; for the safety and welfare of your kingdoms and dominions threatened with almost un-avoidable dangers and distresses; that your majesty, as the loving father of your whole people, connected by the same bands of law, loyalty, faith and blood, though dwelling in various countries, will not suffer the transcendant relation formed by these ties to be farther violated, in uncertain expectation of effects, that, if attained, never can com-pensate for the calamities, through which they must be gained.

We therefore most earnestly beseech your majesty, that your royal authority and in-terposition may be used for our relief; and that a gracious answer may be given to this petition.

That your majesty may enjoy every felicity through a long and glorious reign over loyal and happy subjects, and that your descendants may inherit your prosperity and domin-ions 'til time shall be no more, is and always will be our sincere and fervent prayer.

Henry Middleton
Jno Sullivan
Nathl Folsom
Thomas Cushing
Samuel Adams
John Adams
Robt. Treat Paine
Step Hopkins
Sam: Ward
Elipht Dyer
Roger Sherman
Silas Deane

John Dickinson
John Morton
Thomas Mifflin
George Ross
Chas Humphreys
Cæsar Rodney
Thos M: Kean
Geo: Read
Mat. Tilghman
Ths. Johnson Junr
Wm. Paca
Samuel Chase

Phil. Livingston

John Alsop

Isaac Low

Jas. Duane

John Jay

Wm. Floyd

Henry Wisner

S: Bœrum

Wil: Livingston

John De Hart

Stepn. Crane

Richd. Smith

E Biddle

J: Galloway

Richard Henry Lee

Patrick Henry

Go. Washington

Edmund Pendleton

Richd. Bland

Benjn Harrison

Will Hooper

Joseph Hewes

Rd. Caswell

Tho Lynch

Christ Gadsden

J. Rutledge

Edward Rutledge

Agents to whom the Address to the King is to be sent for

New Hampshire, Paul Wentworth Esqr.

Massachusetts bay,

⎧ William Bollan Esqr,
⎨ Doctr. Benj: Franklin
⎩ Doctr. Arthur Lee.

Rhode Island, none

Connecticut, Thomas Life, Esqr.

New Jersey, Doctr Benj. Franklin

Pensylvania,                                        ditto

New York, Edmund Burke

Delaware, Maryland ⎫
Virginia, N. Carolina ⎬ none
                      ⎭

South Carolina, Charles Garth, Esqr

15.2

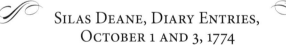

# SILAS DEANE, DIARY ENTRIES, OCTOBER 1 AND 3, 1774

Deane recorded in his diary the debate in Congress regarding the instructions to be issued to the committee appointed to prepare the petition to the king. The focus of the debate on October 1 was whether Congress should include in the instructions a proposal for paying for the tea destroyed in Boston's famous Tea Party. As one might expect, Congress was divided over this issue, though far from evenly. The proposal was made by John Jay and seconded by Isaac Low, a future loyalist, both of

New York. It was supported by James Duane, also of New York, Edmund Pendleton of Virginia, and George Ross of Pennsylvania—all moderates hoping for a just reconciliation with Britain. It was opposed by Richard Henry Lee and Patrick Henry, both of Virginia; John Adams; Samuel Ward of Rhode Island; Robert Goldsborough of Maryland; and, more surprisingly, almost the entire South Carolina delegation. In the end, "the question put carried Unanimously in the Negative." Congress, and even some of its more moderate delegates, was unwilling to appear apologetic when it believed the colonies to have been wronged in Parliament's unconstitutional attack on the colonists' rights.

The diary entry of October 3 records Congress' debate of an amendment proposed by Lee to be added to a proposal made by James Duane that would be largely incorporated in Congress' October 3 resolution (see document 15.3). Lee's rejected amendment had urged Congress to include in its instructions that since "North America is able, willing, and under Providence, determined to defend, protect, and secure itself, . . . Congress do most earnestly recommend to the several colonies, that a militia be forthwith appointed and well disciplined, and that it be well provided with ammunition and proper arms."[101] A majority in Congress opposed the amendment. Among those supporting the proposal, in addition to Lee, were other congressional radicals: Roger Sherman and Eliphalet Dyer of Connecticut, Patrick Henry, and Thomas Lynch of South Carolina. Arguing in opposition was a more moderate faction: the Rutledges of South Carolina; Benjamin Harrison, Edmund Pendleton, and Richard Bland of Virginia; Isaac Low, John Jay, and James Duane of New York; and William Hooper of North Carolina. As Harrison noted, the language of the amendment would "tend only to irritate, whereas Our Business is to reconcile." Henry responded unambiguously: "Arms are a Resource to which We shall be forced, a Resource afforded Us by God & Nature, & why in the Name of both are We to hesitate to providing them Now whilst in Our power." In the end, the original motion by Duane, without Lee's provocative amendment, was carried unanimously.

Paul H. Smith, ed., *Letters of Delegates to Congress, 1774–1789* (Washington, D.C.: Library of Congress, 1976–93), 1:133–34, 138–40. James Duane's motion can be found in *Letters of Delegates to Congress,* ed. Smith, 1:134; Lee's proposed amendment is in *Journals of the Continental Congress,* ed. Ford, 1:54.

[October 1, 1774]

Moved, that the proposal for paying for the Tea be added to the Instructions. Motion for this made by Mr. Jay, Seconded by Mr. Low—supported by Mr. Pendleton—opposed by Mr. Lee, Mr. Gadsden, Mr. Lynch. Mr. Ross rather in favor of it. Mr. Lee against it. Mr. Jno. Rutledge against it—spoke long & well. Mr. Pendleton again for it. His principle is, that We expressly justify the Town of Boston for destroying the Tea, & offer to pay for the Tea, on Condition, that the Town of Boston be instantly relieved and at the same time We resolve never hereafter to Use E India Commodities more untill the E India Company refund the Money.

Mr. Henry, against it intirely. Forcible, & spirited in his harangue.

Mr. Jno Adams against it.

Mr. Low again for it, his Reason that it will take away the Ostensible Reason for the Act. Govr. Ward against it.

Mr. Low again for the Motion.

Mr. Goldsborou[gh] long Against it.

Mr. Duane lengthy in favor of it.

Mr. Rutledge Junr. long against it. The question put carried Unanimously in the Negative.

Mr. Duane made a Long speech & then a Motion. See the Journal. Mr. Adams, & Mr. Rutledge for postponing it to Monday.

Col. Lee proposes to extend it, to raising also, a Militia, & arming them, for Our defence. Mr. Duane resents it.

Col. Lee, & Mr. Mifflin defend it. Postponed untill Monday.

Motion for Nonex[portatio]n of Flaxseed & Lumber to commence instantly. Spoke against by Mr. Ross that it is quarreling with Ireland before We begin with G Brittain.

Adjd half past Three.

Two Motions lye for Monday, one for instant Nonexportation of Flaxseed, the other respecting Administration of Justice.

[October 3, 1774]

Monday Congress opened.

3d Octo. The president in the Chair. Ten o Clock—both Motions read. Col. Lee makes a Motion for Amendment. See the Motion Seconded by Col. Lee.

Opposed by Mr. Rutledge as being out of Line of Our Business, and in degree, a Declaration of Warr, which if intended, no other Measure ought to be taken up, but that We should he says speak out at Once. Col. Lee opposes him & defends his Motion—that it is the Duty of the Congress to put the Americans on defending themselves.

Mr. Roger Sherman, for it, confusedly enough though *miss'd the Question & sat down.* Col. Harrison against it, that it will tend, only to irritate, whereas Our Business is to reconcile—that we are unable to defend Ourselves. Mr. Henry for it. Says that a preparation for Warr is Necessary to obtain peace—That America is not Now in a State of peace—That all the Bulwarks, of Our Safety, of Our Constitn. are thrown down, That We are Now in a State of Nature—that We ought to ask Ourselves the Question should the plans of Nonim[portatio]n & Nonexp[ortatio]n fail of success—in that Case Arms are Necessary, & if then, it is Necessary Now. Arms are a Resource to which We shall be forced, a Resource afforded Us by God & Nature, & why in the Name of both are We to hesitate providing them Now whilst in Our power.

Mr. Rutledge again moving to postpone this and to take it up here after that it is out of Order and is a New Motion.

Mr. Henry corrects him.

Mr. Rutledge again.

Col. Lee in the same Way.

Mr. Duane in support of his First Motion that he is not for Warr, nor are his people.

Mr. Rutledge again to Order.

Mr. Pendleton declares it to be in Order but that it is exceptionable and proposes it to be amended.

Mr. Rutledge junr. against it.

Col Dyar for it at large.

Mr. Low against it.

Col. Bland against it.

Mr. Henry again lengthy & zealous for it.

Mr. Hooper against it as a most impolitic measure at this Time & if pursued will defeat its design. North Carolina has a Militia Law. South Carolina also has such a Law. Virginia has had one for a Century, but N. Carolinas is a Temporary one pass'd at the express desire of the Governor. General Gage is now besieged, & is dependant on our Lenity. That N. Carolina is able to defend itself.

Mr. Duane again.

Mr. Lynch for it and Lengthy says We have already adopted much the same thing—That all Europe can not subdue it, &c but proposes a different Bill which Col. Lee agrees to.

Mr. Jay says he would be for it were it as innocent as it is wise.

Col. Bland against it. The Motion was again altered & amended and the Question being put was carried Unanimously. Mr. Lynch moved respecting the Regulations of Trade or Acts of Charles the Second should be considered as obligatory.

After long debating put off the Question untill Tomorrow & adjd.

Supp'd at Evening at Mr. Mifflins.

## 15.3

### CONGRESSIONAL RESOLUTIONS, OCTOBER 3 AND 5, 1774

In the resolution of October 3, Congress issued its first of two sets of instructions to the committee appointed to prepare the petition to the king. Congress largely follows the proposal offered by James Duane of New York on October 1 (as discussed above in Deane's diary entry for the same day) in asking the committee to "assure his Majesty, that the colonies have, or will make ample provision for defraying all the necessary expenses of supporting government, and the due administration of Justice in the respective colonies." Left out of the instructions was the still more conciliatory language proposed by John Jay of New York but not accepted by his colleagues, along with the still more provocative and bellicose language proposed by Richard Henry Lee of Virginia.[102]

On October 5, Congress issued its second set of instructions and asked that the committee assure the king "that in case the colonies shall be restored to the state they were in, at the close of the late war," with the removal of all manner of offensive legislation passed subsequently, "the jealousies, which have been occasioned by such acts and regulations of parliament, will be removed and commerce again restored." Not the most conciliatory language imaginable, but it was free from the intentional provocations that had been sought by Lee and others radical delegates in Congress.

Worthington Chauncey Ford et al., eds., *Journals of the Continental Congress, 1774–1789* (Washington, D.C.: Government Printing Office, 1904–37), 1:53–55.

MONDAY, OCTOBER 3, 1774.

The Congress met, according, to adjournment, and after some debate,

*Resolved unanimously,* That it be an instruction to the committee, who are appointed to draw up an address to the King: "Whereas parliamentary taxes on America have been laid, on pretence of defraying the expenses of government, and supporting the administration of justice, and defending, protecting, and securing the Colonies," that they do assure his Majesty, that the colonies have, or will make ample provision for defraying all the necessary expenses of supporting government, and the due administration of Justice in the respective colonies; that the militia, if put upon a proper footing, would be amply sufficient for their defence in time of peace; that they are desirous to put it on such a footing immediately; and that in case of war, the colonists are ready to grant supplies for raising any further forces that may be necessary.

The remainder of this day and the day following, was taken up in deliberating and debating on matters proper to be contained in the address to his majesty.

WEDNESDAY, OCTOBER 5, 1774, A. M.

The congress resumed the consideration of the subject in debate yesterday, and after some time spent thereon,

*Resolved,* That the committee appointed to prepare an address to his majesty, be instructed to assure his majesty, that in case the colonies shall be restored to the state they were in, at the close of the late war, by abolishing the system of laws and regulations—for raising a revenue in America—for extending the powers of the courts of Admiralty—for the trial of persons beyond the sea for crimes committed in America—for affecting the colony of the Massachusetts bay—and for altering the government, and extending the limits of Canada, the jealousies, which have been occasioned by such acts and regulations of parliament, will be removed and commerce again restored.

## 15.4

 PATRICK HENRY, DRAFT PETITION TO THE KING,
OCTOBER 21, 1774

Patrick Henry, famed for having introduced the resolutions that led to the Virginia resolves of 1765 and for his still more famous speech of March 1775 in which he is reported to have asked for liberty or death, was one of the most ardent defenders of the colonies' rights. At times his intemperance approached a treasonous contempt for the Crown, as in the "Parson's Cause" case of 1763, in which he argued that the king had violated his compact with the people and thus had forfeited his claim to his subjects' loyalty. Yet in his draft petition to the king, Henry claimed that the colonists sought nothing more than to return to the relationship they had enjoyed with Britain in 1763 at the end of the Seven Years' War and, ironically, the end of the French-Canadian threat to their west and north (and thus the end of the need for British protection). Henry's petition, like the one adopted by Congress, urges the king to intercede on behalf of the colonists—"We most earnestly entreat you Royal Sire to interpose your Royal Influence to procure us Redress of these our Greivances"—and supports fully his traditional prerogative rights to rule them.

Where Henry may have even gone beyond the position taken by Congress in its petition to the king is in his concern with the harmful effects of the Quebec Act. Henry claimed that because "the Religion of Rome bloody Idolatrous & strongly inimical to Protestantism will ever stimulate its Votarys to attempts fatal to those who differ from them in Religious & Civil Policy," the colonists needed to "strengthen the Protestant interest & the cause of Liberty." Parliament's tolerance of Canadian Roman Catholicism was viewed with fervent hostility among the more religiously dogmatic colonists, who were often the more republican ones as well.[103] All and all, though, there is little that distinguishes Henry's appeal (or the draft by the equally radical Richard Henry Lee) from the version adopted by Congress. It seems, then, that even the most radical of the delegates were, when called on to do so at the end of 1774, willing to defend the goal of reconciliation, constitutional monarchy, and continued membership in the British Empire.

Paul H. Smith, ed., *Letters of Delegates to Congress, 1774–1789* (Washington, D.C.: Library of Congress, 1976–93), 1:222–25.

May it please your most excellent Majesty

Graciously to receive the humble & dutifull address of your Majestys most loyal subjects the Representatives of all the American Colonys Situated between Nova Scotia & Georgia now met in general Congress. When we present ourselves before the Throne with hearts deeply impressed with a Sense of that Duty affection & Loyalty which we owe & Cordially tender to the person of your most sacred Majesty, we lament the necessity by which we are compelled to complain of injurys of the most alarming nature. These Complaints are not the Voice of Faction, but the United Sense of North America.

Several Acts & Resolutions of Parliament made since the begining of the year 1763 have violated the dearest rights & most essential privileges which belong to us as freemen & British Subjects. We mean the Acts made for raising a Revenue in America—for extending the Jurisdiction of the Courts of Admiralty beyond the ancient limits—The Resolutions of the two houses of Parliamt. & the Act declaring that persons who commit certain Crimes in America shall be tryed beyond the Seas—& The several Acts passed last session of Parliamt. respecting the Town of Boston & Province of Massachusetts Bay & that for altering the Govermt. & extending the Limits of Canada.

These Acts & proceedings are fraught with mischief & destruction to America. Some of them take from us the power of giving & granting our own money because taxes are thereby imposed for raising a Revenue in America, and as the pretence for such interposition of Parliament is to provide a Fund for supporting the Goverment & the Administration of Justice therein, & for defending securing & protecting the Colonys, We do assure your Majesty that the Colony assemblys have made or are willing to make ample provision for defraying all the necessary expences of supporting Goverment & the administration of Justice in their respective Colonys: That our Militia if put upon a proper footing, which we are willng & desirous should be immediately done, would be sufficient for our defense in time of peace. And in case your Majesty should at any time be engaged in war, your Colonies are ready to grant supplys for raising any other forces that may be necessary.

By other Acts & extrajudicial Resolutions the parliament has attempted to take from us the darling privilege of Tryal by Jurys of the Vicinage & to send us far away from our Native Land to encounter a series of sufferings & Distress too great to be borne. How deplorable must be the Condition of that man who seized & shackled in America, must bid adieu to his native Country & embark for a distant one when the pains & sufferings of a tedious Imprisonment will not be alleviated by the assistance of Friends or the hope that Innocence will be acquitted. On the Contrary the unhappy sufferer far removed from the possibility of proving his innocence & from all that can minister to his Necessitys or soften his Distresses must Sink under the accumulated Misery & find no Asylum but in Death.

The Town of Boston & Province of Massachusetts Bay present to our View a most alarming Example of Parliamentary Vengeance. With Greif & astonishment we behold those powers of Goverment which so long harmonized with America now formed into dangerous Efforts for her destruction. Judge Royal Sir what must be our feelings when we see our fellow subjects of that Town & Colony suffering a Severity of punishment of which the British History gives no Example, & the Annals of Tyranny can scarcely equal. And when we see in the Fate of this our sister Colony that which awaits us, we are filled with the most terrible apprehensions—Apprehensions which are heighten'd & increased almost to Despair, when we turn our Attention to the Quebec Act.

In vain do your Majestys faithfull Subjects look around them for a ground to hope that they or their Posterity can be safe free or happy in the neighbourhood of a Goverment so much at variance with the true Spirit of English liberty. The Religion of Rome bloody Idolatrous & strongly inimical to Protestantism will ever stimulate its Votarys to attempts fatal to those who differ from them in Religious & Civil Policy. Strongly impressed with these Sentiments we chearfully contributed our blood & treasure to the conquest of that country in the late war confident that we should thereby change a dangerous & hostile neighbour into a British Province & strengthen the Protestant interest & the cause of Liberty. Our amazement therefore is indeed extreme to see these well-grounded hopes disappointed, & that Popery & the Laws of France have found Establishment & Patronage in a British Parliament. The local extent assigned for the Operation of this fatal scheme of Goverment is an additional Circumstance to make it dangerous & alarming to the ancient British Colonys.

Thus encompassed with Injurys apprehensions & Dangers, your faithfull American Subjects look up to your Majesty for Assistance & Releif. We most earnestly entreat you Royal Sire to interpose your Royal Influence to procure us Redress of these our Greivances. We are distressed with the most Poignant feelings, by that prospect which the present System adopted by Parliament holds up to our view. Unworthy submission, or unjust Resistance are Equally far from us & abhorrent to our Ideas. Either would render unfit objects of yr. Majestys Paternal regards—Drive us not to Despair—Urge us not to the last extremity most gracious Sovereign. We can never submit to the Encroachments of the British Parliament. Compell us not therefore to that Situation in which All is Gloom & horror, & from whence no Ray of Peace or Comfort can be discern'd. All we ask is that we may be restored to that State in which America stood at the Close of the last War. We desire no new privileges. Restore us royal Sir our Ancient & indubitable rights & we are contented. We shall then return with Joy & Gladness to that friendly intercourse & mutually beneficial commerce so much to be desired by the mother Country & the Colonys, but which has of late been so unhappily disturbed.

Thus restored to peace & tranquility we shall bless the royal hand that was held forth for our Deliverance. We shall rejoice under the Dominion of a Prince to whom Allegiance Affection & Gratitude shall concur to bind us by their most sacred ties. Your Majestys faithfull Americans will ever be ready to offer their blood & treasure to Support your

Majestys illustrious house. And we trust that no length of Time no distance of Situation or change of Circumstances shall ever efface the remembrance of that Signal interposition of yr. Majesty upon which we rely for Deliverance from the wicked Attempts of those Ministers whose Designs are fatal to the true interests of yr. Majesty & destructive to all that is dear to us.

# ACT III

## THE FIGHTING BEGINS, 1775

*Resolved, that it be recommended to the congress aforesd. To persevere the more vigorously in preparing for their defence, as it is very uncertain whether the earnest endeavours of the Congress to accommodate the unhappy differences between G. Britain and the colonies by conciliatory Measures will be successful.*

—*Journals of the Continental Congress,* May 26, 1775

T he year in which the Second Continental Congress began, 1775, was marked by a descent into war between Great Britain and the colonies (France, Spain, and the Netherlands, in the years to come, joined in the battle against Britain) and an even more violent civil war between colonial patriots (or rebels) and loyalists (or Tories).[1] The year ended disastrously for the colonists. But there was not a straight trajectory to war or defeat, for on February 1, Lord Chatham introduced in the House of Lords a Bill for Settling the Troubles in America (document 23.3), which would have committed Parliament, under reasonable conditions, to cease taxing the colonies and would have repealed all of Parliament's offending legislation from the period 1764–74. The bill, however, was defeated in the Lords by a 2–1 margin. Several weeks later, on February 27, the first minister, Lord North, proved more successful in seeing through Parliament his conciliatory peace proposal (see document 23.1), which also committed Parliament to forgo taxing the colonists. With that concession, the colonists gained what is often assumed to be the most important goal of their decade-long opposition to parliamentary actions, namely, the ability of each colony's property holders, through representatives in colonial assemblies, to enjoy the sole authority to tax their residents for provincial needs. Congress, in large measure because of Parliament's unwillingness to repeal the Declaratory Act and other offending legislation, and after a considerable delay, rejected as unacceptable Parliament's peace proposal at the end of July.

Adding considerably to the tension early in 1775 was Parliament's consideration of another punitive measure—the stick to the peace proposal's carrot—the New England Restraining Act. This legislation prevented the New England colonies, after July 1, from trading with any country other than Great Britain and the British West Indies. In addition, in possibly an even more crippling blow, it prohibited residents of the New England colonies from fishing in the North Atlantic cod banks after July 20, 1775. The bill was a tit-for-tat retaliation to the First Continental Congress' state papers from late October 1774, which were laid before Parliament in late January at its opening; those papers included the Continental Association, which banned imports and exports between the colonies and Britain. The New England Restraining Act was approved on March 30 (document 18.3), and after news reached Parliament of several additional colonies ratifying the Association, was extended on April 13 in a second act to New Jersey, Pennsylvania, Maryland, Virginia, and South Carolina.

The confrontation that gave an immediate face to the worsening imperial relations was the fighting between British and colonial forces that took place in Lexington and Concord, Massachusetts, on April 19, 1775. General Gage, the commander of the British forces as of April 14, was under orders from Lord Dartmouth, secretary of state for the colonies, to use force, even if it led to bloodshed, when administering particular parliamentary measures, including the Coercive Acts, and to hinder colonial militias from organizing further resistance to them. Since Concord was a major supply depot of military materiel for the Massachusetts militia, it was natural that Gage, under his new orders, viewed it as an appropriate military target. Accordingly, on April 19, he sent an expeditionary force of seven hundred British soldiers to destroy the ammunition and other supplies stored there.

In Lexington, early in the morning, they were met by a group of seventy minutemen, whom they engaged. There are conflicting accounts of who fired the first shot, but eight colonists were killed and nineteen wounded. The British forces continued to Concord, where they destroyed the designated stores. Upon their return to Boston, the British forces were persistently attacked by militiamen lining the roads and shooting from behind cover, and were able to make it back only because of the arrival of reinforcements. The British suffered more than 275 casualties; of the nearly 4,000 Massachusetts militiamen who saw action that day, fewer than 100 were killed, wounded, or missing.[2] The colonial forces followed the British troops back to Boston and began a siege that lasted until March 1776. In effect, the War of American Independence, long feared by many and excitedly anticipated by others, had begun—and with it, a possibly still more savage civil war.[3]

In May, forces from what would become Vermont and some from Massachusetts, under the command of Ethan Allen and Benedict Arnold, moved across Lake Champlain and took the lightly garrisoned British forts at Ticonderoga and Crown Point. Those attacks on British forces exacerbated an already-explosive situation and, when reported to Parliament, further inflamed sentiment. On May 16, the Provincial

Congress of Massachusetts, working closely with its congressional delegation, requested from Congress guidance in reinstituting its royal charter of 1691. On May 31, in Mecklenburg County, North Carolina, a county committee, based on the actions of Parliament from the previous February, went still further by explicitly vacating its formal allegiance to the king and suspending "the former civil Constitution of these Colonies," the first corporate body in the colonies to do so.[4]

At nearly the same time that the New England forces were taking the offense in attacking British forces near Canada, the Second Continental Congress met on May 10, though without some of the more outspoken conservative delegates from the previous Congress, men such as Joseph Galloway of Pennsylvania, who had requested to be excused from further service. Those men had done much to moderate the First Continental Congress. On May 26, Congress elected a new president, John Hancock of Massachusetts (the day after President Peyton Randolph's departure), after reviewing delegates' credentials and instructions and provocatively putting the colonies into a defensive posture (see document 16.2). On May 29, Congress approved its second letter of friendship to the Canadians (document 16.1). It did so a month before agreeing on June 27 to attack the two major Canadian cities. Indeed, most of Congress' war efforts for the next year were directed against Canada and, in the end, resulted in America's first major military defeat.

To add to the colonies' already substantial war footing, Congress resolved on June 10 to organize the Continental Army, and on June 14 it requested "that six companies of expert riflemen, be immediately raised in Pennsylvania, two in Maryland, and two in Virginia . . . [and] that each company, as soon as completed, shall march and join the army near Boston." The next day, Congress resolved "that a General be appointed to command the continental forces, raised, or to be raised, for the defence of American liberty"; it then chose George Washington of Virginia, who, on being formally notified the next day, accepted his commission while rejecting any payment for his services.[5] He arrived in Cambridge, Massachusetts, on July 3 and formally took command of an army of 14,500 men besieging the British forces occupying Boston.

Before Washington's arrival, the first major military engagement of what became, truly, the War of Independence, the Battle of Bunker Hill and Breed's Hill, took place on June 17, 1775. In May, after the April confrontation that began in Concord and Lexington, both the British and the colonial forces surrounding them had taken on reinforcements. In June, having learned that General Gage hoped to take Dorchester Heights on the eighteenth, the Boston Committee of Safety decided to take preemptive action by capturing Bunker Hill, which overlooks the city. On the evening of June 16, colonial forces began building a redoubt on Breed's Hill, which was closer to the city than Bunker Hill. On the morning of the seventeenth, their work discovered, the colonial forces came under British fire from warships anchored in the harbor. The bombardment was followed by three direct British frontal assaults on the American position; the colonists, running low on ammunition, finally gave way. Bunker Hill too was taken as the Americans retreated. The British victory, though, was enormously expensive: "1,054 casualties, a high proportion of them officers." American losses, "almost all of which were suffered after the fall of the redoubt," were about a third of the British total: "100 dead (including Joseph Warren), 267 wounded, 30 taken prisoner."[6] The battle may have been the closest thing to a real massacre in Boston. Britain's North American colonists, at least those in Massachusetts, were clearly in revolt, as the king reasonably concluded on learning of the taking of Fort Ticonderoga in May and the costly British "victory" at the Battle of Bunker Hill.

At nearly the same time as the Battle of Bunker Hill, Congress began deliberation on two addresses. The first, A Declaration on Taking Arms (document 18.1), explained the need for what the colonists understood to be defensive military actions, as evidenced in its offensive attacks on British positions and in Canada and Boston. The second one, of a very different nature, was truly a humble address to the king, the Olive Branch Petition (document 19.1), which again sought his intercession to help stop the bloodletting and resolve the outstanding constitutional differences between the colonies and Parliament. Both documents were written by John Dickinson, after a draft of the first written by the newly arrived delegate Thomas Jefferson of Virginia had been rejected (small parts of his draft were retained by Dickinson). These were two of the last three essential congressional state papers known to be written by Dickinson (the Articles of Confederation were still to come), who served as the colonists' most important author for ten years and in three congresses. Although Jefferson's draft was rejected, the document he drafted a month later, the Report on Lord North's Peace Proposal (document 23.1), Congress approved. A year before the Declaration of Independence, in a country at war and with commercial life grievously threatened by bans imposed by both congressional and parliamentary acts, much had changed from the situation faced by the First Continental Congress on its close in late October 1774.

The Second Continental Congress' adjournment, August 2–September 12, did nothing to stop the fighting, in part because before leaving, on June 27, Congress had authorized attacks on Canadian locations that might prove threatening to the "English" colonies to the south and east (as distinct from the newly acquired ones to the north and west). Colonial forces lay siege to St. John's; it fell on November 2. On November 13, colonial forces under General Richard Montgomery took and occupied Montreal. From there, Montgomery marched on Quebec with part of his forces and on December 3 joined forces there with Benedict Arnold and his 650 men, who had been recruited outside Boston from Washington's main army.

During the campaign against Canadian targets, Congress reconvened on September 13—it had tried to do so on September 5 but lacked a quorum—with thirteen colonies in attendance, Georgia having finally agreed to send a delegation representing the entire colony. Throughout September and October, Congress' focus was almost entirely on war preparations: appointing a secret committee to purchase military stores, making plans to intercept British shipping, deciding on October 13 to form the Continental navy, appointing an overseer of military hospitals, and resolving to allow colonial exports in exchange for arms. At the end of October, Congress received word that the king had declared the colonies to be in open rebellion in his Proclamation for Suppressing Rebellion and Sedition of August 23 (document 25.2). Given the siege of Boston, the creation of the Continental Army and Navy, the offensive attacks on Canadian cities and earlier on British forts, and Congress' war planning, the king seemingly reacted with good reason. Additionally, immediately before being presented Congress' Olive Branch Petition of July 8, the king had, unfortunately, received news of the deadly cost of the Battle of Bunker Hill. He made the reasonable but unfortunate choice to refuse to receive Congress' petition formally for consideration on the throne—a disappointment Congress learned of two months later, at the end of October.

In November and December, with colonial attacks against Canadian cities continuing—and initially meeting with success—Congress made additional war plans: promoting the production of saltpeter, enlisting the first two battalions of marines, creating and adopting rules and regulations for the Continental Army and Navy, adopting regulations for the selling of British ships seized (as prizes), authorizing the construction of thirteen ships for the Continental navy, and planning an attack on the British forces in Boston. In addition, Congress took into consideration requests by three colonies to institute new provincial republican governments without Crown participation, at least until the current war and colonial-parliamentary differences were resolved. On November 7, Lord Dunmore placed Virginia under martial law while continuing to recruit loyalist troops. On November 17, he freed all African slaves willing to fight against their former owners, thereby, as one might imagine, effectively alienating their owners, who were fighting for political rather than, like the former slaves, personal freedom. In late November, a congressional committee was formed to begin looking abroad for friendly countries willing to help the American cause with supplies, arms, and financial support.

In early December, Congress answered the king's proclamation of August 23 (document 25.1) by denying that the colonists had any intention of abandoning either their loyalty or their duties to him, but again repeating that Parliament lacked any right to govern them. Finally, on December 31, the congressionally approved assault on Canada came to a disastrous end when the commander, General Montgomery, was killed, and 400 soldiers (most from New England) were killed, wounded, or captured. Thus, 1775, a year of war and preparation for more war, much of it initiated by the American colonists against British positions in or near Canada, ended on anything but a positive note.

## DOCUMENT SUMMARY

The first state paper produced by the Second Continental Congress was the letter "To the Oppressed Inhabitants of Canada," completed on May 29, 1775. It is similar to

"To the Inhabitants of the Province of Quebec" of 1774 (document 14.2): for example, Congress appeals to Canadians' pride as Frenchmen and tries to impress on them, rather nonsensically, that it is Parliament that is threatening their right to practice Roman Catholicism. In contrast to the earlier letter, the vast preponderance of whose argument rests on English or British foundations, the appeal here rests—though still not consistently so—on a natural-rights foundation. Additionally, Congress had to explain the colonists' unprovoked attacks on Ticonderoga and Crown Point; it incredibly suggested that they were acts of self-preservation or that they were needed to facilitate better communication between the Canadians and the American "English" colonists. Congress reassured its northern neighbors of its good intentions: "We hope it [the two attacks] has given you no uneasiness, and you may rely on our assurances, that these colonies will pursue no measures whatever, but such as friendship and a regard for our mutual safety and interest may suggest." It is hard to know how Congress, in light of that promise, viewed its decision a month later, on June 27, to attack and lay siege to Canada's two principal cities, Montreal and Quebec—not exactly what one thinks of as still more friendly gestures.

The next principal document produced by Congress was its Response to Massachusetts Bay's Request for Instructions on Forming a New Government on June 9. Here, once again responding to Massachusetts' prodding—a pattern developed in the First Continental Congress—Congress granted the colony's request of May 16 to be allowed to form a new government until the king appointed a governor who would abide by Massachusetts' royal charter of 1691. A similar sequence was repeated in November and December as instructions were granted to three other royal colonies, New Hampshire, South Carolina, and Virginia, to create new governments. Of course, such actions were seen by Parliament as confirming in its members' minds that the colonies were steadily moving toward independence—something that even as late as the first part of 1776, many in Congress continued to deny vehemently.

The third and fourth principal readings of this Section are Congress' Declaration on Taking Arms (July 6) and its Olive Branch Petition to the king (July 8). Although Thomas Jefferson wrote a draft of the declaration, John Dickinson penned the approved version, as he did the petition, the second and final formal congressional petition to the king—Congress had stopped petitioning Parliament a decade earlier. In July 1775, with the commercial bite of the New England Restraining Act (document 18.3) beginning to be felt and those of the Association soon to take effect, war and commercial distress pushed the delegates, and most likely American subjects at large, even many in the moderate mid-Atlantic colonies, in a more bellicose and less conciliatory direction.

In the declaration, Congress laments the by now well-rehearsed grievances of the past eleven years, paying particular attention to the Declaratory Act of 1766 and additionally noting that "several threatening expressions against the colonies were inserted in his Majesty's speech" at the opening of Parliament on November 30, 1774 (see document 18.2). Also attracting Congress' disdain were Lord North's peace proposal, which was viewed as an invidious attempt to divide the colonies into auctioning off their rights; the events at Concord; and the fear, soon to be realized, that British officials might begin freeing slaves to fight against the colonists. In the second document, the final formal petition to the king, Congress refuses to rehearse its grievances, out of deference, but urges him to propose a means for direct negotiation with the colonies. It is hard to imagine Parliament concurring with this, and if Parliament had participated, the colonists were unlikely to have agreed to do so.

In the fifth principal reading, Congress' second address to the inhabitants of Great Britain, dated July 8 (for the first one, on October 21, 1774, see document 12.1), Congress appeals to the common ties that bind the two English peoples and their long shared history, before launching into a well-developed list of grievances. Yet the address makes it clear that the colonists were still ready to "consent to the Operation of such Acts of the *British* Parliament, as shall be restrained to the Regulation of our external Commerce, for the Purpose of securing the commercial Advantages of the whole Empire to the Mother Country." Reiterating a position it had held for over a decade, Congress argued that "it is a fundamental Principle of the *British* Constitution that every Man should have at least a Representative Share in the Formation of those Laws, by which he is bound." Accordingly, Congress could not accept Lord North's peace proposal (see document 23.1), for although promising that Parliament would no longer tax the colonies, it retained for Parliament the right to intervene in the internal affairs of the colonists, a position utterly unacceptable to Congress.

The sixth principal document is Congress' Speech to the Six Confederate Native-American Nations of July 13. Its purpose is clear: to persuade the allied nations of the Iroquois Confederation to not participate, especially on the side of the British, in what Congress describes as a coming civil war between a people who are like two brothers, the English colonists and their brethren in England; the congressional effort was largely unsuccessful. What makes the speech of interest, in spite of its condescension in addressing Native Americans, are three things: Congress' description of the colonists as heavily burdened by parliamentary taxes; its psychologically clarifying view of the colonists as the unloved sons of the king, who favored his other children back in England; and the defense of its position by consistent references to charters and English or British constitutionalism rather than more universal claims. There is little defensible in Congress' claim of being already heavily taxed by the British, given the removal of most of the Townshend duties and reductions in earlier taxes.[7] As for the second claim, it provides unexpected insight into how the colonists viewed themselves—as being unfairly and unequally subject to legislation and taxation in comparison with the king's favored children in his realm of Great Britain.

Congress' address to the people of Ireland of July 18 is included less for what it claims than for what it doesn't. Boldly resting its claims solely on the "rights of mankind" and "the universal, the divine law of self-preservation," Congress somewhat tediously rehearses the grievances under which the colonists suffered for the past decade, including, again, the feared freeing of African slaves, with the "expected horrors of domestic insurrections," which Congress describes as a form of "parental cruelty, at which the genius of Britain must blush." One must wonder how this objection to limited British emancipation of African slaves in the colonies is consistent with Congress' simultaneous appeal, here and elsewhere, to the "rights of mankind." In addition, the address apologizes, though not convincingly, for Congress' need to ban imports from and (soon) exports to Ireland, along with those from and to Britain and their fellow colonists in the West Indies. Surprisingly relegated to a couple of sentences at the end of the address is Congress' attempt to find common ground with the Irish: "We know that *you* are not without your grievances. We sympathize with you in your distress, and are pleased to find that the design of subjugating us, has persuaded administration to dispense to Ireland, some vagrant rays of ministerial sunshine." Toward another people who were part of the British Empire and the king's dominions and largely subject to the sovereign impositions of Parliament—even under its own Declaratory Act—one might have expected something more.

Possibly the most important nonevent of the Second Continental Congress was its rejection of Lord North's peace proposal of February 20 in its report on the same (July 31), which was passed the day before Congress adjourned for six weeks. In North's proposal, the colonists finally received the written promise that they had been demanding for a decade: Parliament would no longer tax them, internally or externally, for revenue. (In practice, Parliament had largely abandoned colonial taxation in 1770 with the repeal of almost all the Townshend duties.) Remarkably, almost unbelievably, this essential concession produced almost no response among the congressional delegates. Congress asked Thomas Jefferson to draft its response, as he had done for Virginia immediately before taking his seat in Congress.

Of particular interest in it is the unusual concern, which was advanced too in October 1774 by the First Continental Congress (see document 12.1), about the dangers posed by the king if freed, by means of colonial requisitions, from "an important barrier against the undue exertion of prerogative." Of course, that worry had long been one of the central concerns of British Whigs in Parliament. Also of interest is Congress' first explicit offer, more fully developed in Benjamin Franklin's remarks (see document 23.4), to pay higher taxes, along with the rest of the empire, if freed from Parliament's unequal commercial regulations, or to continue paying lower taxes while being disadvantaged by Parliament's commercial regulations, but not both.

The ninth set of documents is similar to the first document from the second set (document 17.1) in that three more colonies request "instructions on forming a new government." Congress completed work on them in November and December 1775. Each Colony was given instructions similar to those offered to Massachusetts six months earlier. But unlike Massachusetts, which demanded an adherence to its royal charter, New Hampshire, South Carolina, and Virginia were to form more or less republican governments, even if only for a limited duration. Although this was a measure of some success for congressional radicals, men like John Adams really wanted for the same instructions to be extended to the mid-Atlantic colonies so that insurrections might be encouraged there and moderate governments replaced by more radical ones. Adams was too early in his desire. Congress, even with a weakened moderate faction, remained too divided to support Adams' proposal. The mid-Atlantic delegations still hoped, even if ever more remotely, for reconciliation; Adams had to wait another six months, until May 15 (see document 31.2) for his prayers to come true.

This section's final document cluster concerns Congress's answer to the king's Proclamation for Suppressing Rebellion and Sedition of December 6, 1775. For strong reasons—the Continental Association's ban of British imports and impending ban of exports from the colonies to Britain; the capture of Ticonderoga and Crown Point; and the slaughter of British troops at the Battle of Bunker Hill—the king in late August had concluded that his North American subjects were in revolt. He additionally believed that they were being aided by radicals in Britain—thus the concern with sedition.[8] In its answer, Congress claims that the colonists had not in any manner rebelled against any constitutional mandates imposed upon them, and regarding allegiance to the king, the colonists had "ever avowed it," and Congress' "conduct had ever been consistent with it."

Moreover, Congress continued to claim that the colonists had consistently fulfilled their duties to the king under the British Constitution—one of a dwindling number of such references in the state papers of the Second Continental Congress—even as they attempted to protect their rights. And in what might pass for a pledge of loyalty, Congress' answer claims that the colonists "will not, on our part, lose the distinction between the King and his Ministers: happy would it have been for some former Princes, had it been always preserved on that part of the Crown." Congress ends by issuing an ominous and anything but humble warning: "Whatever punishment shall be inflicted upon any persons in the power of our enemies for favouring, aiding, or abetting the cause of American liberty, shall be retaliated in the same kind, and the same degree upon those in our power, who have favoured, aided, or abetted, or shall favour, aid, or abet the system of ministerial oppression." Protestations of loyalty notwithstanding, little in the tone of the answer brings to mind the humble and deferential formal Petition to the King of only five months earlier.

## THEORETICAL ISSUES

When the Second Continental Congress opened its session on May 10, 1775, active warfare raged in several of the colonies. Yet much remained the same: the delegates continued to reject Parliament's interference in their internal affairs, to insist on their loyalty to the king, and to express a desire for reconciliation. Until the end of 1775, if even then, there was no talk in Congress or in most delegates' private correspondence of a desire for independence. With decreasing frequency, the delegates continued to draw the attention of their fellow subjects in England and in other North American colonies to the high costs, both commercial and, potentially, political, that attended the putatively unconstitutional actions of Parliament.

But there was also much in 1775 that was new. Possibly most significant was the presence of war—between the colonists and the British, and, still more frequently though usually less lethally, between groups of colonists—throughout the summer. There was almost continual continental preparation in the fall and winter of 1775 for more. Also changed, in keeping with Congress' war posture, was the language advanced in defense of the colonists' claims to the right, with the king's continued participation, to self-government. Strikingly, in all of 1775 there was still no challenge to the right of the king to participate actively in colonial government; there was, however, far less emphasis than before on all colonial rights resting principally on British or English foundations. Five congressional state papers from 1775 make some reference to natural or universal rights, whereas only one or two congressional documents had done so, ever so briefly, in 1774. Congress seemed to be preparing, even if only very subtly, the way forward toward independence and the need for an explanatory language that didn't rest on an English foundation. Also important in this regard were the requests of Massachusetts Bay, New Hampshire, South Carolina, and Virginia for instructions on forming new governments. In each instance there was a certain tentativeness on the part of Congress, since it insisted on including a reservation that any new institutions would last only until the crisis was resolved, and that the colonies needed some authority greater than their own assemblies or even of their people to authorize some actions. Yet it is equally clear, especially in retrospect, that these instructions were among the first tentative steps toward independence.

Similarly, some of this section's documents, anticipating the Declaration of Independence, put an increased emphasis on appealing to world—not just British—opinion, principally that of particular European powers. This is apparent in Congress' Declaration on Taking Arms of July 6, 1775, written by John Dickinson. A month later, in its Report on Lord North's Peace Proposal, Congress endorsed Jefferson's handiwork, which unyieldingly rejected Parliament's reasonable peace proposal from February, in which it agreed to forgo further efforts to tax the colonists, and, even more boldly, Jefferson's challenge of monarchical prerogative. With Jefferson's arrival in Congress, Parliament's ending of much of colonial commercial life on July 1 with the Restraining Acts, and Jefferson's "Report," Congress' tone became noticeably steelier than previously, and the confidence of its once-dominant moderate faction began to atrophy.

Finally, in a persistent pattern that continued unabated until independence, each important step that the delegates took was preceded by an alienating act passed by Parliament or by a speech or proclamation made by the king. Both king and Parliament did much to undermine the link between the king's protection of his North American subjects and their duty and allegiance to obey him. The majority of colonial delegates, rather than marching toward independence, seem rather to have been largely forced into it, as they so frequently claimed, by the politically misguided, even if wholly understandable under the British constitutions, actions of their king. Of course, the British might well have claimed the same or more, since the king and Parliament were forced by persistent, ever-more belligerent and bold colonial military actions against British and Canadian interests to take the stances that, in turn, led to additional colonial responses and, ultimately, to Britain's loss of the commercially and psychologically most important part of the empire, an outcome that men of goodwill on both sides so much wished to prevent. What remains rather extraordinary, and possibly disappointing, is the colonists' inability or refusal to recognize that the king was boxed in by the eighteenth-century British Constitution, which permitted little or no alternative action on his part than his spirited and open defense of Parliament's rights.

## 16. CONGRESS JUSTIFIES ITSELF TO CANADIAN AND AMERICAN COLONISTS, MAY 1775

When the Second Continental Congress convened on May 10, 1775, as scheduled, circumstances were far more threatening than they had been when the First Continental Congress adjourned on the previous October 26. On April 19, 1775, open warfare had broken out between the colonists and British military forces in and around the Massachusetts towns of Lexington and Concord. An immediate reconciliation became ever less likely. In addition, as John Brown, a member of the Boston Committee of Correspondence, reported before Congress, the British governor of Canada, General Guy Carleton, had ordered the creation of a Canadian military force to aid the British administration in putting down what the king soon described as open rebellion in some of his North American colonies.

In response to Carleton's efforts, on May 26, 1775, Congress chose Silas Deane, John Jay, and Samuel Adams to write a letter with which it hoped to woo French Canadians to side with the older "English" (that is, formerly neither French nor Spanish) North American colonists (this was Congress' second such attempt; for the first, see document 14.2).[9] The next day the committee reported a draft; Congress rejected it. Another draft, written by John Jay, was submitted and approved on May 29. John Dickinson and Thomas Mifflin, both of Pennsylvania, had the letter translated into French and a thousand copies printed.[10] James Price, a Montreal merchant and a supporter of the colonies, agreed to distribute them there.[11] On June 12, 1775, an English version of the letter was distributed in Canada. It was first published in the lower, "English" colonies on June 14 in the *Pennsylvania Journal* and the *Pennsylvania Gazette*.[12]

Congress ardently sought, both in this letter and its earlier one, the support of the Canadians by highlighting the oppressive character of British parliamentary governance and, possibly, that of future kings, even going so far as to suggest that under the present government, "you and your wives and your children are made slaves." Congress also appealed to their pride as Frenchmen: "We can never believe that the present race of Canadians are so degenerated as to possess neither the spirit, the gallantry, nor the courage of their ancestors." Similarly, the letter emphasizes that the colonists were the Canadians' friends and that the taking of Ticonderoga, Crown Point, and St. John's earlier in the month, and the placing of "armed vessels on the lake [Champlain], was dictated by the great law of self-preservation"—and so no need for any concern. Shortly before ordering assaults on the two principal Canadian cities, Congress made its neighbors this promise: "We hope it has given you no uneasiness, and you may rely on our assurances, that these colonies will pursue no measures whatever, but such as friendship and a regard for our mutual safety and interest may suggest." How amicably Canadians might have viewed the six-month siege of Quebec is not hard to imagine. The Canadians' true enemy, according to Congress, was "a licentious Ministry" running "riot in the ruins of the rights of Mankind." In claiming that "rights, bestowed by the almighty," not those bestowed on British subjects by the British Constitution, were being violated, the language in this first state paper of the Second Continental Congress marks a significant shift from the "Letter to the Inhabitants of the Province of Quebec," sent seven months earlier, and, more generally, from the language of English or British rights used in the state papers of the previous Congress.

More in keeping with the earlier letter, Congress again warned the French Canadians of the threat posed to their Roman Catholicism by Parliament—"Your priests are exposed to expulsion, banishment, and ruin, whenever their wealth and possessions furnish sufficient temptation"—the very body that with the Quebec Act had done much to protect French Catholicism. It was the colonists, by contrast, who considered the act one of the Coercive Acts and thus repeatedly listed it as one of their grievances. The First Continental Congress had highlighted for North American colonists and the British people that the presence of Roman Catholics in Canada posed a grave danger to the English Protestant colonies, to the Protestant succession in Britain, and even to Protestantism in general (see documents 12.1, 12.2, and 15.3). In short, Congress was playing it both ways. In urging the residents of Quebec to join its cause, it claimed that religious differences were of little importance and that the colonists' "perceived the fate of the protestant [American] and catholic [Canadian] colonies to be strongly linked together." When addressing their fellow Protestant colonists and subjects in Britain, the delegates stressed the religious differences and the great threat posed by parliamentary support of Roman Catholicism in Canada.[13]

16.1

## "TO THE OPPRESSED INHABITANTS OF CANADA," MAY 29, 1775

Worthington Chauncey Ford et al., eds., *Journals of the Continental Congress, 1774–1789* (Washington, D.C.: Government Printing Office, 1904–37), 2:68–70. The letter's mention of the Canadians being "called upon to waste your lives in a contest with us" refers to General Carleton's efforts to raise a Canadian army.

*To the oppressed Inhabitants of Canada.*

FRIENDS AND COUNTRYMEN,

Alarmed by the designs of an arbitrary Ministry, to extirpate the Rights and liberties of all America, a sense of common danger conspired with the dictates of humanity, in urging us to call your attention, by our late address, to this very important object.

Since the conclusion of the late war, we have been happy in considering you as fellow-subjects, and from the commencement of the present plan for subjugating the continent, we have viewed you as fellow-sufferers with us. As we were both entitled by the bounty of an indulgent creator to freedom, and being both devoted by the cruel edicts of a despotic administration, to common ruin, we perceived the fate of the protestant and catholic colonies to be strongly linked together, and therefore invited you to join with us in resolving to be free, and in rejecting, with disdain, the fetters of slavery, however artfully polished.

We most sincerely condole with you on the arrival of that day, in the course of which, the sun could not shine on a single freeman in all your extensive dominion. Be assured, that your unmerited degradation has engaged the most unfeigned pity of your sister colonies; and we flatter ourselves you will not, by tamely bearing the yoke, suffer that pity to be supplanted by contempt.

When hardy attempts are made to deprive men of rights, bestowed by the almighty, when avenues are cut thro' the most solemn compacts for the admission of despotism, when the plighted faith of government ceases to give security to loyal and dutiful subjects, and when the insidious stratagems and manœuvres of peace become more terrible than the sanguinary operations of war, it is high time for them to assert those rights, and, with honest indignation, oppose the torrent of oppression rushing in upon them.

By the introduction of your present form of government, or rather present form of tyranny, you and your wives and your children are made slaves. You have nothing that you can call your own, and all the fruits of your labour and industry may be taken from you, whenever an avaritious governor and a rapacious council may incline to demand them. You are liable by their edicts to be transported into foreign countries to fight

Battles in which you have no interest, and to spill your blood in conflicts from which neither honor nor emolument can be derived: Nay, the enjoyment of your very religion, on the present system, depends on a legislature in which you have no share, and over which you have no control, and your priests are exposed to expulsion, banishment, and ruin, whenever their wealth and possessions furnish sufficient temptation. They cannot be sure that a virtuous prince will always fill the throne, and should a wicked or a careless king concur with a wicked ministry in extracting the treasure and strength of your country, it is impossible to conceive to what variety and to what extremes of wretchedness you may, under the present establishment, be reduced.

We are informed you have already been called upon to waste your lives in a contest with us. Should you, by complying in this instance, assent to your new establishment, and a war break out with France, your wealth and your sons may be sent to perish in expeditions against their islands in the West indies.

It cannot be presumed that these considerations will have no weight with you, or that you are so lost to all sense of honor. We can never believe that the present race of Canadians are so degenerated as to possess neither the spirit, the gallantry, nor the courage of their ancestors. You certainly will not permit the infamy and disgrace of such pusillanimity to rest on your own heads, and the consequences of it on your children forever.

We, for our parts, are determined to live free, or not at all; and are resolved, that posterity shall never reproach us with having brought slaves into the world.

Permit us again to repeat that we are your friends, not your enemies, and be not imposed upon by those who may endeavour to create animosities. The taking the fort and military stores at Ticonderoga and Crown-Point, and the armed vessels on the lake, was dictated by the great law of self-preservation. They were intended to annoy us, and to cut off that friendly intercourse and communication, which has hitherto subsisted between you and us. We hope it has given you no uneasiness, and you may rely on our assurances, that these colonies will pursue no measures whatever, but such as friendship and a regard for our mutual safety and interest may suggest.

As our concern for your welfare entitles us to your friendship, we presume you will not, by doing us injury, reduce us to the disagreeable necessity of treating you as enemies.

We yet entertain hopes of your uniting with us in the defence of our common liberty, and there is yet reason to believe, that should we join in imploring the attention of our sovereign, to the unmerited and unparalleled oppressions of his American subjects, he will at length be undeceived, and forbid a licentious Ministry any longer to riot in the ruins of the rights of Mankind.

## 16.2

 CERTAIN RESOLUTIONS RESPECTING THE
STATE OF AMERICA, MAY 26, 1775

In these four resolutions passed early in the session, the continuing divisions in Congress are still visible, even if the moderate stance had become more difficult to defend. Indeed, the difference between the first two resolutions and the last two reflects something of this split personality. In the first resolution, Congress still refuses to blame the king for Parliament's attacks on "his Majesty's most faithful subjects" and the "laying of taxes in America . . . [and] changing the constitution and internal police of some of the colonies." Instead, blame continues to be placed on "the british Ministry" and "several unconstitutional and oppressive acts of the british Parliament." Language probably inspired by congressional radicals claimed that Parliament had violated not only the rights of the colonists as English or British subjects, but also "the natural and civil rights of the colonists."[14] (At the time, civil rights, those remaining after entering society, were analogous to English ones.) Here and in "To the Oppressed Inhabitants of Canada," Congress employed, with greater freedom than before, the language of natural rights made famous in the Declaration of 1776. Also, surely pleasing to the radical faction was the second resolution, which highlights the military threats encountered in and around Boston in order to support its claim that the colonies needed to "be immediately put into a state of defence."

The last two resolutions, of a decidedly more conciliatory tone, were moved by the moderate New Yorker James Duane and led to "a warm debate of two days."[15] They committed Congress to sending an additional humble petition to the king, seeking a means to achieve "this most desirable reconciliation" through "a Negotiation, in order to accommodate the unhappy disputes subsisting between Great Britain and these colonies." This Continental Congress, like the previous one, remained torn between, on the one hand, its allegiance to Great Britain and loyalty to the king, and, on the other, its unwillingness to accept the eighteenth-century British Constitution, in which Parliament exercised supremacy over most of the Crown's widespread and subordinate dominions. Unfortunately for any chance of reconciliation, the king and almost all the members of Parliament were as steadfast in their commitment to the extant British Constitution as the colonists were to an alternate version of it. Of course, the colonists' Whiggish defense of British legislative supremacy—only later did concerns regarding legislative tyranny in America develop—had helped shape Americans' divided thinking on the subject.[16]

Worthington Chauncey Ford et al., eds., *Journals of the Continental Congress, 1774–1789* (Washington, D.C.: Government Printing Office, 1904–37), 2:64–66.

The Congress then resolved themselves into a committee of the whole, to take into consideration the state of America; after some time spent therein, the president resumed the chair, and Mr. [Samuel] Ward reported from the committee, that they had come to certain resolutions respecting the state of America, which he was desired to report, but not having finished the business referred to them desired him to move for leave to sit again.

The report from the committee being read, the Congress came into the following Resolutions:

*Resolved unanimously,* 1, That his Majesty's most faithful subjects, in these colonies, are reduced to a dangerous and critical situation, by the attempts of the british Ministry to carry into execution, by force of arms, several unconstitutional and oppressive acts of the british parliament for laying taxes in America; to enforce the collection of those taxes, and for altering and changing the constitution and internal police of some of these colonies, in violation of the natural and civil rights of the colonists.

*Unanimously* 2. Hostilities being actually commenced in the Massachusetts bay, by the British troops, under the command of General Gage, and the lives of a number of the inhabitants of that colony destroyed, the town of Boston having not only been long occupied as a garrisoned town in an enemy's country, but the inhabitants thereof treated with a severity and cruelty not to be justifyed even towards declared enemies; large reinforcements too being ordered and soon expected, for the declared purpose of compelling these colonies to submit to the operation of the sd acts; *Resolved,* therefore, that for the express purpose of securing and defending these colonies, and preserving them in safety against all attempts to carry the sd acts into execution by force of arms, these colonies be immediately put into a state of defence.

*Unanimously* 3. But, as we most ardently wish for a restoration of the harmony formerly subsisting between our Mother country and these colonies, the interruption of which must, at all events, be exceedingly injurious to both countries, *Resolved,* that with a sincere design of contributing by all the means in our power, not incompatible with a just regard for the undoubted rights and true interests of these colonies, to the promotion of this most desirable reconciliation, an humble and dutiful petition be presented to his Majesty.

4. *Resolved,* That measures be entered into for opening a Negotiation, in order to accommodate the unhappy disputes subsisting between Great Britain and these colonies, and that this be made a part of the petition to the King.

## 17. POLITICAL RECOMMENDATIONS FOR MASSACHUSETTS AND RELIGIOUS RECOMMENDATIONS FOR THE COLONIES, JUNE 1775

In a letter written on May 16, 1775—the third such letter received in Congress from Massachusetts (see documents 9.1 and 11.3)—and read and debated in Congress on June 2, Massachusetts representatives deferentially requested that Congress, a body "composed of men, who through time must in every land of freedom be revered among the most faithful assertors of the essential rights of human nature," invite them to form a new government and for Congress to take control of the growing army forming around Boston "for the general defence of the right of America" (with Congress, too, being urged to assume financial responsibility for the troops).[17] Massachusetts argued that because its citizens had been "denied the exercise of civil government according to . . . [their] charter, or the fundamental principles of the English constitution," the colony sought from Congress its "most explicit advice respecting the taking up and exercising the powers of civil government." The letter was signed by Dr. Joseph Warren, the president pro tempore of the Massachusetts Provincial Convention and a man who, as noted previously, worked closely with the Adams cousins in moving Congress, as quickly as the recalcitrance of the majority of the delegates and colonies would permit, toward declaring the independence of the American continental colonies from Britain.[18] Strikingly, though, even Massachusetts was unwilling to act without authorization or support from a body or authority above itself.

On June 3, Congress appointed five delegates to prepare a response. The committee included John Rutledge of South Carolina, Thomas Johnson of Maryland, John Jay of New York, James Wilson of Pennsylvania, and Richard Henry Lee of Virginia. Wilson, the likely author of the response, was born, bred, and educated in Scotland and arrived in the colonies in 1765 at age twenty-two. He was an eminent lawyer and an early and unusually powerful defender of popular sovereignty in Congress and, later, in the Constitutional Convention. Concerning the question of independence, however, he was among the moderates. The other three moderates on the committee (that is, everyone but Lee) remained committed until well into the spring of 1776 to finding a just and constitutional means of bringing the crisis to a close.

On June 9, Congress took bold but not radical action. It urged the Massachusetts Provincial Congress to invite its towns to elect members for a new assembly. Congress insisted, however, that the new government of Massachusetts "conform, as near as may be, to the spirit and substance of the charter," that is, the colony's royal charter of 1691, and that the provisional government continue only "until a Governor, of his Majesty's appointment, will consent to govern the colony according to its charter" rather than under the Massachusetts Government Act, one of the Coercive Acts. Massachusetts, thus, was not free to experiment in designing a popular government. Massachusetts was the first colony to request such instructions from Congress; by the end of the year, three other royal colonies, New Hampshire, South Carolina, and Virginia, would ask Congress for similar, indeed bolder, instructions to form new governments. Lacking the constraint of an earlier charter, those governments looked increasingly republican in their openness to "such a form of government, as, in their judgment, will best produce the happiness of the people" (see document 24.1).

17.1

## Response to Massachusetts Bay's Request for Instructions on Forming a New Government, June 2, 3, and 9, 1775

Worthington Chauncey Ford et al., eds., *Journals of the Continental Congress, 1774–1789*
(Washington, D.C.: Government Printing Office, 1904–37), 2:76–79, 83–84.

FRIDAY, JUNE 2, 1775

The Congress met according to adjournment.

The president laid before the Congress a letter from the prov: Convention of Massachusetts, wch. was read and is as follows:

IN PROV. CONGRESS, *Watertown, May 16, 1775.*

*Resolved,* That Doctr. Benjamin Church be ordered to go immediately to Philada. and deliver to the president of the Honble. American Congress there now sitting, the following application to be by him communicated to the members thereof: and the sd. Church is also directed to confer with the sd. Congress, respecting such other matters as may be necessary to the defence of this colony and particularly the state of the army therein.

May it please yr Honours.

That system of colony administration, which in the most firm, dutiful and loyal manner has been in vain remonstrated against by the representative body of the united colonies, seems still, unless speedily and vigorously opposed by the collected wisdom and force of all America to threaten ruin and destruction to this continent.

For a long time past, this colony has, by a corrupt administration in Great Britain and here, been deprived of the exercise of those powers of Government, without which a people can be neither rich, happy or secure. The whole continent saw the blow pending, which if not warded off, must inevitably have subverted the freedom and happiness of each colony; the principles of self defence, roused in the breasts of freemen by the dread of impending slavery, caused to be collected the wisdom of America, in a Congress composed of men, who through time must in every land of freedom be revered among the most faithful assertors of the essential rights of human nature.

This colony was then reduced to great difficulties, being denied the exercise of civil government according to our charter, or the fundamental principles of the English constitution and a formidable navy and army (not only inimical to our safety, but flattered with the prospect of enjoying the fruit of our industry) were stationed for that purpose in our Metropolis. The prospect of deciding the question between our Mother country and us, by the sword, gave us the greatest pain and anxiety; but we have made all the preparation for our necessary defence that our confused state would admit of; and as the question equally affected our sister colonies and us, we have declined though urged thereto by the most pressing necessity to assume the reins of civil government, without their advice and consent; but have hitherto borne the many difficulties and distressing embarrassments necessarily resulting from a want thereof.

We are now compelled to raise an Army, which with the assistance of the other colonies, we hope under the smiles of heaven, will be able to defend us and all America from the further butcheries and devastations of our implacable enemies.—But as the sword should in all free states be subservient to the civil powers and as it is the duty of the Magistrates to support it for the peoples necessary defence, we tremble at having an army (although consisting of our countrymen) established here without a civil power to provide for and controul them.

We are happy in having an opportunity of laying our distressed state before the representative body of the continent, and humbly hope you will favour us with your most explicit advice respecting the taking up and exercising the powers of civil government, wch. we think absolutely necessary for the Salvation of our country and we shall readily submit to such a general plan as you may direct for the colonies, or make it our great study to establish such a form of government here, as shall not only most promote our advantage but the union and interest of all America.

As the Army now collecting from different colonies is for the general defence of the right of America, we wd. beg leave to suggest to yr. consideration the propriety of yr. taking the regulation and general direction of it, that the operations may more effectually answer the purposes designed.

Signed,      Jos: WARREN<br>President P. T.

Ordered to lye on the table.

The above letter referring to Doct. Church, on motion, agreed that he be introduced.

After he withdrew, an express arriving from Massachusetts bay, the president laid before the Congress Letters from the conventions of Massachusetts bay, and New Hampshire, also a letter from Govr. Trumbull, all which were read. . . .

[SATURDAY, JUNE 3, 1775]

Upon motion *Resolved,* That a committee of five persons be chosen to take into consideration the letter from the Convention of Massachusetts bay, dated the 16 of May, and report to this Congress what in their opinion is the proper Advice to be given to that Convention.

The following persons were chosen by ballot, to compose that committee, viz. Mr. J[ohn] Rutledge, Mr. [Thomas] Johnson, Mr. [John] Jay, Mr. [James] Wilson, and Mr. [Richard Henry] Lee. . . .

FRIDAY, JUNE 9, 1775

The Congress met according to adjournment.

~~Agreeable to the order of the day~~

The report of the committee, on the Letter from the convention of Massachusetts bay, being again read, Congress came to the following resolution:

*Resolved,* That no obedience being due to the Act of parliament for altering the charter of the Colony of Massachusetts bay, nor to a Governor, or a lieutenant-Governor, who will not observe the directions of, but endeavour to subvert that charter, the govr. and lieutenant-govr. of that Colony are to be considered as absent, and these offices vacant; and as there is no council there, and the inconveniences, arising from the suspension of the powers of Government, are intollerable, especially at a time when Genl. Gage hath actually levied war, and is carrying on hostilities, against his Majesty's peaceable and loyal subjects of that Colony; that, in order to conform, as near as may be, to the spirit and substance of the charter, it be recommended to the provincial Convention, to write letters to the inhabitants of the several places, which are intituled to representation in Assembly, requesting them to chuse such representatives, and that the Assembly, when chosen, do elect counsellors; which assembly and council should exercise the powers of Government, until a Governor, of his Majesty's appointment, will consent to govern the colony according to its charter.

*Ordered,* that the president transmit a copy of the above to the convention of Massachusetts bay.

17.2

## First Proclamation for a Day of Humiliation, Fasting, and Prayer, June 12, 1775

On June 7, 1775, Congress created a committee to organize its first Day of Humiliation, Fasting, and Prayer; it included William Hooper of North Carolina and John Adams and Robert Treat Paine of Massachusetts. They brought in the proclamation on June 12. In explaining its action, Congress noted that communal devotion paid to God was "our indispensable duty," especially "in times of impending danger and public calamity, to reverence and adore his immutable justice, as well as to implore his merciful interposition for our deliverance." Hooper and Paine were sons of ministers, Episcopal and Congregational, respectively, and Paine had served as a clergyman. On June 19, the *Pennsylvania Packet* printed the proclamation, and on July 20, 1775, the date set aside by Congress, the delegates attended, en masse, "Reverend Duché's Episcopalian Church in the morning and Dr. Francis Allison's Presbyterian Church in the afternoon."[19] The choice of congregations was in keeping with the Reformed Protestant affiliations of the vast majority of the delegates—Congregationalists and Presbyterians in the north and middle colonies, and Anglicans in the South[20]—as was the felt need to seek communally Christ's intervention and assistance to help achieve "a reconciliation with the parent state, on terms constitutional and honorable to both" and to secure "civil and religious priviledges . . . to the latest posterity."

The proclamation asked members of Congress and their constituents, in the midst of a time of economic and political dislocations, to confess their many sins and to bless their "rightful sovereign, King George the third." It was recommended—for Congress had no power to legislate for the colonies—that "the inhabitants of all the English colonies . . . assemble for public worship" and "abstain from servile labour and recreation" on the day Congress had set aside. Congress went further, hoping "that virtue and true religion may revive and flourish throughout our land; And that all America may soon behold a gracious interposition of Heaven, for the redress of her many grievances, the restoration of her invaded rights, a reconciliation with the parent state, on terms constitutional and honorable to both." The proclamation was one of dozens, both at the continental and provincial level, that urged the colonists gather for collective humiliation before God and to fast and pray in common for his forgiveness.[21] (Many of the later ones were legal requirements rather than recommendations.) By the time of the second one, in March 1776, Congress was no longer asking that George III be blessed or that colonists pray for a just reconciliation of the crisis—times had changed.

Besides reflecting the ills that the colonists believed themselves suffering, the first proclamation was a product of their collective guilt at having fallen away from the strict path of religious devotion and piety followed by their ancestors, most especially in New England. Jack Greene, who is not known to focus unnecessarily on either New England or America's Protestant ways, nonetheless insists there was a popular view that "Parliament, and now the British Army were the agencies of God's punishment for the colonists' impiety and moral degeneration." Accordingly, the proclamation demanded "humiliation before God, acknowledgement of sins, and a sincere determination to inaugurate and carry through a moral reformation" so that on behalf of the colonists "God would intervene to help in removing the source of the afflictions."[22] For many, resistance to Parliament's unjust actions required primarily political organization, but the crisis was seen also in a moral and religious light that demanded moral and religious reformation and renewal, surrender to Christ, and the intervention of the Holy Spirit.[23]

Worthington Chauncey Ford et al., eds., *Journals of the Continental Congress, 1774–1789* (Washington, D.C.: Government Printing Office, 1904–37), 2:87–88.

MONDAY, JUNE 12, 1775

The Congress met according to adjournment.

The committee, appointed for preparing a resolve for a fast, brought in a report, which, being read, was agreed to as follows:

As the great Governor of the World, by his supreme and universal Providence, not only conducts the course of nature with unerring wisdom and rectitude, but frequently influences the minds of men to serve the wise and gracious purposes of his providential government; and it being, at all times, our indispensible duty devoutly to acknowledge his superintending providence, especially in times of impending danger and public calamity, to reverence and adore his immutable justice as well as to implore his merciful interposition for our deliverance:

This Congress, therefore, considering the present critical, alarming and calamitous state of these colonies, do earnestly recommend that Thursday, the 20th day of July next, be observed, by the inhabitants of all the English colonies on this continent, as a day of public humiliation, fasting and prayer; that we may, with united hearts and voices, unfeignedly confess and deplore our many sins; and offer up our joint supplications to the all-wise, omnipotent, and merciful Disposer of all events; humbly beseeching him to forgive our iniquities, to remove our present calamities, to avert those desolating judgments, with which we are threatned, and to bless our rightful sovereign, King George the third, and [to] inspire him with wisdom to discern and pursue the true interest of all his subjects, that a speedy end may be put to the civil discord between Great Britain and the American colonies, without farther effusion of blood: And that the British nation may be influenced to regard the things that belong to her peace, before they are hid from her eyes: That these colonies may be ever under the care and protection of a kind Providence, and be prospered in all their interests; That the divine blessing may descend and rest upon all our civil rulers, and upon the representatives of the people, in their several assemblies and conventions, that they may be directed to wise and effectual measures for preserving the union, and securing the just rights and priviledges of the colonies; That virtue and true religion may revive and flourish throughout our land; And that all America may soon behold a gracious interposition of Heaven, for the redress of her many grievances, the restoration of her invaded rights, a reconciliation with the parent state, on terms constitutional and honorable to both; And that her civil and religious priviledges may be secured to the latest posterity.

And it is recommended to Christians, of all denominations, to assemble for public worship, and to abstain from servile labour and recreations on said day.

*Ordered,* That a copy of the above be signed by the president and attested by the Secy and published in the newspapers, and in hand bills.

## 18. CONGRESS PLANS FOR WAR, JULY 1775

On June 23, 1775, Congress selected a committee of mainly moderate delegates—John Rutledge (South Carolina), William Livingston (New Jersey), John Jay (New York), and Thomas Johnson (Maryland)—and one considerably less so, Benjamin Franklin (Pennsylvania), to write a declaration explaining America's reluctantly accepted need to begin organizing militarily while simultaneously offering encouragement to what would become the Continental Army. On June 17, 1775, those troops had engaged in the first pitched battle of the war, during which British forces suffered over a thousand casualties in their successful effort to dislodge American forces (with over three hundred casualties) from Breed's Hill and Bunker Hill outside Boston. The first draft of the declaration, originally to have been published by George Washington upon his arrival outside Boston, was written by Rutledge.[24] His draft, though, was returned to the committee after it had been reinforced by the addition of two of America's most eloquent penmen, John Dickinson and Thomas Jefferson.[25]

Although the two men soon strongly disagreed regarding the desirability of American independence, they worked together on this declaration. The final product was written by Dickinson, Congress having retained only the last four paragraphs of the draft written by Jefferson.[26] Even in Jefferson's contribution, it is the king's ministers and Parliament that are held culpable, not the king himself. Jefferson humbly appeals to the king to find a constitutional solution to the impasse between the colonies and Parliament, thereby "stopping the further effusion of blood" and "averting the impending calamities that threaten the British Empire." Congress claimed, or at least its majority did, that it had no desire for independence and no interest in abandoning its constitutional-monarchical form of government.

This declaration sits "midway in time and principle between the Declaration and Resolves of the First Continental Congress and the Declaration of Independence" (see documents 13.1 and 33.1). The three declarations "were concerned with obtaining recognition of the rights of the people" to enjoy joint colonial legislative—and, in the first two documents, monarchical—governance. The first declaration sought to achieve that through the use of "the trade restrictions of the Association"; this, the second one, through still-hesitant steps toward "armed resistance"; and the last and most famous through a separation from Great Britain.[27] As well, with Dickinson relinquishing the role of chief congressional penman to Jefferson, the second declaration represents a symbolic, even if far from complete, transition in the leadership of Congress.

Congress approved the declaration on July 6. Rather than having Washington publish this declaration upon his arrival outside Boston, Congress decided to send it in tandem—perhaps reflecting Congress' internal division—to Britain with Dickinson's conciliatory Olive Branch Petition to the king and a second address to the people of Great Britain (see document 19.1 for the first, document 20.1 for the second). On July 9, 1775, Richard Penn, "a staunch loyalist" and a "respected former governor of Pennsylvania," as well as a descendant of Pennsylvania's founder, William Penn, set sail for London with the three documents.[28] On orders from Congress, Penn was to publish the declaration and address in the London papers as soon and as widely as possible; by August 17, 1775, he had done so.[29]

The declaration begins by explaining that Parliament, driven by "an inordinate passion for power," had abandoned "the very constitution of that kingdom," and so

Congress, out "of respect to the rest of the world"—a phrase repeated in the Declaration of 1776—had to "make known the justice" of its cause. In opposition to the factually loose language initially used by Jefferson—wherein he writes that "possessing all, what is inherent in all, the full and perfect powers of legislation . . . they arranged themselves by charters of compact under the same one common king"—Dickinson wrote that "societies or governments, vested with perfect legislatures, were formed under charters from the crown, and an harmonious intercourse was established between the colonies and the kingdom from which they derived their origin." It is hard to make too much of the differences between Jefferson's rejected language and Dickinson's approved version. Yet language similar to that employed by Jefferson here was accepted by Congress one year later when it endorsed his call for republican government based on a radical theory of voluntary compact between a people and its government, to replace a hierarchical one between a king and his people.[30]

The declaration rehashes Congress' by now standard list of grievances, beginning, as the colonists had since 1764, with Parliament having "undertaken to give and grant our money without our consent" and having denied the colonists "the accustomed and inestimable privilege of trial by jury." Next, Congress objects to Parliament's retaliation against colonial resistance in Massachusetts and to parliamentary impositions regarding the quartering of troops in New York—in short, to the Declaratory and Coercive Acts—while insisting that the American colonists remained "a virtuous, loyal, and affectionate people" of their king.

Adding to its growing list of grievances, Congress claimed that "several threatening expressions against the colonies" had been inserted in the king's speech of November 30, 1774 (document 18.2)—note that he was not responsible for this—and that its petition to the king in 1774 had been "huddled into both houses amongst a bundle of American papers, and there neglected." Moreover, Parliament had regrettably pressured the British monarch to "take the most effectual measures to enforce due obedience to the laws and authority of the supreme legislature," and had gone on to prevent the New England colonies from trading with other nations and benefiting from the critically important North Atlantic fisheries. Congress censured as well the peace proposal put forward by Lord North on February 27, 1775, which Congress soon rejected (see document 23.1), for as Congress claims here, Parliament had "adopted an insidious manoeuvre calculated to divide us, to establish a perpetual auction of taxations where colony should bid against colony . . . and thus to extort from us, at the point of the bayonet, the unknown sums that should be sufficient to gratify, if possible to gratify, ministerial rapacity."

Congress lamented the beginning of active hostilities: British troops under General Gage "murdered eight of the inhabitants" of Lexington, and Gage subsequently imposed martial law. As in the Declaration of Independence, Congress complains here of efforts to recruit Canadians and Native Americans, along with the slaves of Virginia freed by the British, to fight against the colonists. The colonists, therefore, were "reduced to the alternative of chusing an unconditional submission to the tyranny of irritated ministers, or resistance by force," the latter being their obvious, though undesired, choice.

We learn too that the colonists' "cause is just," their union perfect, and that in support of their resistance, Congress expects divine favor and possibly future foreign assistance. But in an expression of loyalty to the Empire—surprisingly, drawn from Jefferson's draft—Congress assures its readers "that we mean not to dissolve that Union which has so long and so happily subsisted between us, and which we sincerely wish to see restored.—Necessity has not yet driven us into that desperate measure," and "we have not raised armies with ambitious designs of separating from Great Britain, and establishing independent states." Again drawing from Jefferson, the declaration closes by affirming that the colonists had taken up arms only "in defence of the freedom that is our birth-right . . . for the protection of our property, acquired solely by the honest industry of our fore-fathers and ourselves." Still more unexpectedly, Congress followed Jefferson in a prayer for reconciliation: "With an humble confidence in the mercies of the supreme and impartial Judge and Ruler of the universe, we most devoutly implore his divine goodness to protect us happily through this great conflict, to dispose our adversaries to reconciliation on reasonable terms, and thereby to relieve the empire from the calamities of civil war." Writing for Congress in July 1775, Jefferson made this wish exactly a year before famously appealing in 1776 for something quite different.

## 18.1

 DECLARATION ON TAKING ARMS, JULY 6, 1775

Worthington Chauncey Ford et al., eds., *Journals of the Continental Congress, 1774–1789* (Washington, D.C.: Government Printing Office, 1904–37), 2:140–57. Both John Dickinson's draft and the final form adopted are included in the *Journals,* but only the final version is printed below.

A declaration by the Representatives of the United Colonies of North America, now met in General Congress at Philadelphia, setting forth the causes and necessity of their taking up arms.

If it was possible for men, who exercise their reason, to believe, that the Divine Author of our existence intended a part of the human race to hold an absolute property in, and an unbounded power over others, marked out by his infinite goodness and wisdom, as the objects of a legal domination never rightfully resistible, however severe and oppressive, the Inhabitants of these Colonies might at least require from the Parliament of Great Britain some evidence, that this dreadful authority over them, has been granted to that body. But a reverence for our great Creator, principles of humanity, and the dictates of common sense, must convince all those who reflect upon the subject, that government was instituted to promote the welfare of mankind, and ought to be administered for the attainment of that end. The legislature of Great Britain, however, stimulated by an inordinate passion for a power, not only unjustifiable, but which they know to be peculiarly reprobated by the very constitution of that kingdom, and desperate of success in any mode of contest, where regard should be had to truth, law, or right, have at length, deserting those, attempted to effect their cruel and impolitic purpose of enslaving these Colonies by violence, and have thereby rendered it necessary for us to close with their last appeal from Reason to Arms.—Yet, however blinded that assembly may be, by their intemperate rage for unlimited domination, so to slight justice and the opinion of mankind, we esteem ourselves bound, by obligations of respect to the rest of the world, to make known the justice of our cause.

Our forefathers, inhabitants of the island of Great Britain, left their native land, to seek on these shores a residence for civil and religious freedom. At the expence of their blood, at the hazard of their fortunes, without the least charge to the country from which they removed, by unceasing labor, and an unconquerable spirit, they effected settlements in the distant and inhospitable wilds of America, then filled with numerous and warlike nations of barbarians. Societies or governments, vested with perfect legislatures, were formed under charters from the crown, and an harmonious intercourse was established between the colonies and the kingdom from which they derived their origin. The mutual benefits of this union became in a short time so extraordinary, as to excite astonishment. It is universally confessed, that the amazing increase of the wealth, strength, and navigation of the realm, arose from this source; and the minister, who so wisely and successfully directed the measures of Great Britain in the late war, publicly declared, that these colonies enabled her to triumph over her enemies.—Towards the conclusion of that war, it pleased our sovereign to make a change in his counsels.— From that fatal moment, the affairs of the British empire began to fall into confusion, and gradually sliding from the summit of glorious prosperity, to which they had been advanced by the virtues and abilities of one man, are at length distracted by the convulsions, that now shake it to its deepest foundations. The new ministry finding the brave foes of Britain, though frequently defeated, yet still contending, took up the unfortunate idea of granting them a hasty peace, and of then subduing her faithful friends.

These devoted colonies were judged to be in such a state, as to present victories without bloodshed, and all the easy emoluments of statuteable plunder.—The uninterrupted tenor of their peaceable and respectful behaviour from the beginning of colonization, their dutiful, zealous, and useful services during the war, though so recently and amply acknowledged in the most honorable manner by his majesty, by the late king, and by Parliament, could not save them from the meditated innovations.—Parliament was influenced to adopt the pernicious project, and assuming a new power over them, have, in the course of eleven years, given such decisive specimens of the spirit and consequences attending this power, as to leave no doubt concerning the effects of acquiescence under it. They have undertaken to give and grant our money without our consent, though we have ever exercised an exclusive right to dispose of our own property; statutes have been passed for extending the jurisdiction of courts of Admiralty and Vice-Admiralty beyond their ancient limits; for depriving us of the accustomed and inestimable privilege of trial by jury, in cases affecting both life and property; for suspending the legislature of one of the colonies; for interdicting all commerce to the capital of another; and for altering fundamentally the form of government established by charter, and secured by acts of its own legislature solemnly confirmed by the crown; for exempting the "murderers" of colonists from legal trial, and in effect, from punishment; for erecting in a neighboring province, acquired by the joint arms of Great Britain and America, a despotism dangerous to our very existence; and for quartering soldiers upon the colonists in time of profound peace. It has also been resolved in parliament, that colonists charged with committing certain offences, shall be transported to England to be tried.

But why should we enumerate our injuries in detail? By one statute it is declared, that parliament can "of right make laws to bind us IN ALL CASES WHATSOEVER." What is to defend us against so enormous, so unlimited a power? Not a single man of those who assume it, is chosen by us; or is subject to our controul or influence; but, on the contrary, they are all of them exempt from the operation of such laws, and an American revenue, if not diverted from the ostensible purposes for which it is raised, would actually lighten their own burdens in proportion as they increase ours. We saw the misery to which such despotism would reduce us. We for ten years incessantly and ineffectually besieged the Throne as supplicants; we reasoned, we remonstrated with parliament, in the most mild and decent language. But Administration, sensible that we should regard these oppressive measures as freemen ought to do, sent over fleets and armies to enforce them. The indignation of the Americans was roused, it is true; but it was the indignation of a virtuous, loyal, and affectionate people. A Congress of Delegates from the United Colonies was assembled at Philadelphia, on the fifth day of last September. We resolved again to offer an humble and dutiful petition to the King, and also addressed our fellow-subjects of Great Britain. We have pursued every temperate, every respectful measure: we have even proceeded to break off our commercial intercourse with our fellow-subjects, as the last peaceable admonition, that our attachment to no nation upon earth should supplant our attachment to liberty.—This, we flattered ourselves, was the ultimate step of the controversy: But subsequent events have shewn, how vain was this hope of finding moderation in our enemies.

Several threatening expressions against the colonies were inserted in his Majesty's speech; our petition, though we were told it was a decent one, and that his Majesty had been pleased to receive it graciously, and to promise laying it before his Parliament, was huddled into both houses amongst a bundle of American papers, and there neglected. The Lords and Commons in their address, in the month of February, said, that "a rebellion at that time actually existed within the province of Massachusetts bay; and that those concerned in it, had been countenanced and encouraged by unlawful combinations and engagements, entered into by his Majesty's subjects in several of the other colonies; and therefore they besought his Majesty, that he would take the most effectual measures to enforce due obedience to the laws and authority of the supreme legislature."— Soon after, the commercial intercourse of whole colonies, with foreign countries, and with each other, was cut off by an act of Parliament; by another, several of them were entirely prohibited from the fisheries in the seas near their coasts, on which they always depended for their sustenance; and large re-inforcements of ships and troops were immediately sent over to General Gage.

Fruitless were all the entreaties, arguments, and eloquence of an illustrious band of the most distinguished Peers, and Commoners, who nobly and strenuously asserted the justice of our cause, to stay, or even to mitigate the heedless fury with which these accumulated and unexampled outrages were hurried on.—Equally fruitless was the interference of the city of London, of Bristol, and many other respectable towns in our favour. Parliament adopted an insidious manœuvre calculated to divide us, to establish a perpetual auction of taxations where colony should bid against colony, all of them uninformed what ransom would redeem their lives; and thus to extort from us, at the point of the bayonet, the unknown sums that should be sufficient to gratify, if possible to gratify, ministerial rapacity, with the miserable indulgence left to us of raising, in our own mode, the prescribed tribute. What terms more rigid and humiliating could have been dictated by remorseless victors to conquered enemies? In our circumstances to accept them, would be to deserve them.

Soon after the intelligence of these proceedings arrived on this continent, General Gage, who in the course of the last year had taken possession of the town of Boston, in the province of Massachusetts Bay, and still occupied it as a garrison, on the 19th day of April, sent out from that place a large detachment of his army, who made an unprovoked assault on the inhabitants of the said province, at the town of Lexington, as appears by the affidavits of a great number of persons, some of whom were officers and soldiers of that detachment, murdered eight of the inhabitants, and wounded many others. From thence the troops proceeded in warlike array to the town of Concord, where they set upon another party of the inhabitants of the same province, killing several and wounding more, until compelled to retreat by the country people suddenly assembled to repel this cruel aggression. Hostilities, thus commenced by the British troops, have been since prosecuted by them without regard to faith or reputation.—The inhabitants of Boston being confined within that town by the General their Governor, and having, in order to procure their dismission, entered into a treaty with him, it was stipulated that the said inhabitants having deposited their arms with their own magistrates, should have liberty to depart, taking with them their other effects. They accordingly delivered up their arms, but in open violation of honor, in defiance of the obligation of treaties, which even savage nations esteemed sacred, the Governor ordered the arms deposited as aforesaid, that they might be preserved for their owners, to be seized by a body of soldiers; detained the greatest part of the inhabitants in the town, and compelled the few who were permitted to retire, to leave their most valuable effects behind.

By this perfidy wives are separated from their husbands, children from their parents, the aged and the sick from their relations and friends, who wish to attend and comfort them; and those who have been used to live in plenty and even elegance, are reduced to deplorable distress.

The General, further emulating his ministerial masters, by a proclamation bearing date on the 12th day of June, after venting the grossest falsehoods and calumnies against the good people of these colonies, proceeds to "declare them all, either by name or description, to be rebels and traitors, to supersede the course of the common law, and instead thereof to publish and order the use and exercise of the law martial."—His troops have butchered our countrymen, have wantonly burnt Charles-Town, besides a considerable number of houses in other places; our ships and vessels are seized; the necessary supplies of provisions are intercepted, and he is exerting his utmost power to spread destruction and devastation around him.

We have received certain intelligence that General Carleton, the Governor of Canada, is instigating the people of that province and the Indians to fall upon us; and we have but too much reason to apprehend, that schemes have been formed to excite domestic enemies against us. In brief, a part of these colonies now feels, and all of them are sure of feeling, as far as the vengance of administration can inflict them, the complicated calamities of fire, sword, and famine.—We are reduced to the alternative of chusing an unconditional submission to the tyranny of irritated ministers, or resistance by force.—The latter is our choice.—We have counted the cost of this contest, and find nothing so dreadful as voluntary slavery.—Honor, justice, and humanity, forbid us tamely to surrender that freedom which we received from our gallant ancestors, and which our innocent posterity have a right to receive from us. We cannot endure the infamy and guilt of resigning succeeding generations to that wretchedness which inevitably awaits them, if we basely entail hereditary bondage upon them.

Our cause is just. Our union is perfect. Our internal resources are great, and, if necessary, foreign assistance is undoubtedly attainable.—We gratefully acknowledge, as signal instances of the Divine favour towards us, that his Providence would not permit us to be called into this severe controversy, until we were grown up to our present strength, had been previously exercised in warlike operation, and possessed of the means of defending ourselves.—With hearts fortified with these animating reflections, we most solemnly, before God and the world, declare, that, exerting the utmost energy of those powers, which our beneficent Creator hath graciously bestowed upon us, the arms we have been compelled by our enemies to assume, we will, in defiance of every hazard, with unabating firmness and perseverance, employ for the presevation of our liberties; being with our [one] mind resolved to dye Free-men rather than live Slaves.

Lest this declaration should disquiet the minds of our friends and fellow-subjects in any part of the empire, we assure them that we mean not to dissolve that Union which has so long and so happily subsisted between us, and which we sincerely wish to see restored.—Necessity has not yet driven us into that desperate measure, or induced us to excite any other nation to war against them.—We have not raised armies with ambitious designs of separating from Great Britain, and establishing independent states. We fight not for glory or for conquest. We exhibit to mankind the remarkable spectacle of a people attacked by unprovoked enemies, without any imputation or even suspicion of offence. They boast of their privileges and civilization, and yet proffer no milder conditions than servitude or death.

In our own native land, in defence of the freedom that is our birth-right, and which we ever enjoyed till the late violation of it—for the protection of our property, acquired solely by the honest industry of our fore-fathers and ourselves, against violence actually offered, we have taken up arms. We shall lay them down when hostilities shall cease on the part of the aggressors, and all danger of their being renewed shall be removed, and not before.

With an humble confidence in the mercies of the supreme and impartial Judge and Ruler of the universe, we most devoutly implore his divine goodness to protect us happily through this great conflict, to dispose our adversaries to reconciliation on reasonable terms, and thereby to relieve the empire from the calamities of civil war.

By order of Congress,

JOHN HANCOCK,
*President.*

Attested,

CHARLES THOMSON,
*Secretary.*
*Philadelphia, July 6th, 1775.*

18.2

## GEORGE III, SPEECH FROM THE THRONE AT THE OPENING OF PARLIAMENT, NOVEMBER 30, 1774

After petitioning the king to rescind the Coercive Acts of 1774 and to provide for what the majority of colonists viewed as a proper constitutional relationship between the colonies and Parliament, Congress saw its efforts come to naught. It was persistently rebuffed by a constitutionally constrained and unimaginative king and a shortsighted and chauvinistic Parliament.[31] The king's unwillingness and, regardless of his inclination, inability to meet the colonists' central demand that he reject Parliament's constitutional claim to supremacy over its subordinate colonies are evident in his speech to Parliament at the opening of its autumn session in 1774. He declared, in language hard to misunderstand, the right of Parliament to rule over his dominions and his intention to "withstand every attempt to weaken or impair the supreme authority of this Legislature over all the Dominions of my crown, the maintenance of which I consider as essential to the dignity, the safety, and the welfare of the British Empire." Accordingly, it was necessary that his people in all parts of his Dominions "be taught by your [Parliament's] example to have a due reverence for the laws, and a just sense of the blessings of our excellent Constitution." His response, in light of the dominant strain of British constitutionalism in the mid-eighteenth century, which placed him in a subordinate role (one that he accepted), should have been predictable. The colonists, though, thought that they might be able—against considerable odds—to persuade him otherwise.

In his speech, he singled out Massachusetts Bay for its "most daring spirit of resistance and disobedience to the law" and its "fresh violences of a very criminal nature." Among the deeds that might have caused the king to view his Massachusetts subjects in this harsh light were the well-known and unpunished Stamp Act riots of 1765, the Boston Tea Party of 1773 (and further instances in 1774), the formation in September 1774 of the first ranks of minutemen in Worcester County, and, of course, attacks on the king's imperial officers and supports by Massachusetts radicals intent on undermining royal government.[32] The king seemed also particularly concerned about the damaging effects of the Continental Association on British commerce, in which "unwarrantable attempts have been made to obstruct the Commerce of this Kingdom, by unlawful combinations," and so he had "taken such measures, and given such orders . . . for the protection and security of the Commerce of my subjects." Still, even putting aside the unusual provocations from the republican-leaning Reformed Protestants of Massachusetts, the empire's basic problems went well beyond the difficulties of governing one colony. Indeed, the King was constitutionally prohibited from satisfying the colonists' claim to independence from parliamentary legislation while being still subject to the Crown's direct oversight.

Peter Force, ed., *American Archives,* 4th series (Washington, D.C.: M. St. Clair Clarke and Peter Force, 1839), 1:1465.

*My Lords and Gentlemen:*

It gives me much concern that I am obliged, at the opening of this Parliament, to inform you that a most daring spirit of resistance and disobedience to the law still unhappily prevails in the Province of the *Massachusetts Bay,* and has in divers parts of it broke forth in fresh violences of a very criminal nature. These proceedings have been countenanced and encouraged in other of my Colonies, and unwarrantable attempts have been made to obstruct the Commerce of this Kingdom, by unlawful combinations. I have taken such measures, and given such orders as I judged most proper and effectual for carrying into execution the laws which were passed in the last session of the late Parliament, for the protection and security of the Commerce of my subjects, and for the restoring and preserving peace, order, and good Government in the Province of the *Massachusetts Bay.* And you may depend on my firm and steadfast resolution to withstand every attempt to weaken or impair the supreme authority of this Legislature over all the Dominions of my crown, the maintenance of which I consider as essential to the dignity, the safety, and the welfare of the *British* Empire, assuring myself that, while I act upon these principles, I shall never fail to receive your assistance and support.

I have the greatest satisfaction in being able to inform you that a treaty of peace is concluded between *Russia* and the *Porte.* By this happy event the troubles which have so long prevailed in one part of *Europe,* are composed, and the general tranquillity rendered complete. It shall be my constant aim and endeavour to prevent the breaking out of fresh disturbances, and I cannot but flatter myself I shall succeed, as I continue to receive the strongest assurances from other Powers of their being equally disposed to preserve the peace.

*Gentlemen of the House of Commons:*

I have ordered the proper Estimates for the service of the ensuing year to be laid before you; and I doubt not but that, in this House of Commons, I shall meet with the same affectionate confidence, and the same proofs of zeal and attachment to my person and Government, which I have always, during the course of my reign, received from my faithful Commons.

*My Lords and Gentlemen:*

Let me particularly recommend to you, at this time, to proceed with temper in your deliberations, and with unanimity in your resolutions. Let my people, in every part of my Dominions, be taught by your example to have a due reverence for the laws, and a just sense of the blessings of our excellent Constitution. They may be assured that, on my part, I have nothing so much at heart as the real prosperity and lasting happiness of all my subjects.

18.3

 NEW ENGLAND RESTRAINING ACT,
MARCH 30, 1775

In response both to the king's concerns and to the First Continental Congress' issuance of the Continental Association and the nonimportation, nonconsumption, and nonexportation resolutions (documents 11.1 and 11.2), the British ministry introduced in Parliament on February 27, 1775, the New England Restraining Act, which forbade the New England colonies, after July 1, from trading with any nation other than Britain, Ireland, or the British West Indies. The act further damaged New England commercial interests by barring New Englanders, after July 20, from entering the North Atlantic fisheries.[33] Remember, under the Continental Association, a ban on the importation of all goods from Britain into the colonies began on

December 1, 1774. It was to be followed, on September 10, 1775, by a ban on the exportation of colonial goods to Britain, Ireland, and the West Indies. The combination of the two enactments came close to ending, by July 1775, North American commerce and shipping, all of which, even coastal shipping, would in fact be legally ended on March 1, 1776, by the American Prohibitory Act of December 22, 1775 (see document 29.2). In short, both sides created increasingly unsustainable circumstances that were sure to exacerbate the already warlike crisis while leading both sides away from the mutually agreed-upon goal of reconciliation.

After getting news that the Continental Association had been ratified by a number of additional colonies, Parliament, not content with the ample ammunition it had provided the radicals in Congress, further enflamed the situation by extending, in a Second Restraining Act of April 13, 1775, the same commercial restrictions (though not regarding the fisheries) to Pennsylvania, New Jersey, Maryland, Virginia, and South Carolina. Six days later, with the Battles of Lexington and Concord and "the shot heard around the world," the tensions between the colonies and Great Britain, and between differing groups of colonists, reached the point of active hostilities, quite likely a point of no return.

Danby Pickering, ed., *The Statutes at Large from the Magna Charta to the End of the Eleventh Parliament of Great Britain* (Cambridge: John Archdeacon, 1775), 31:4–8.

An Act of Parliament in the fifteenth year of King George the III's reign
CAP. X
*An act to restrain the trade and commerce of the provinces of* Massachuset's Bay *and* New Hampshire, *and colonies of* Connecticut *and* Rhode Island, *and* Providence Plantation, *in* North America, *to* Great Britain, Ireland, *and the* British islands *in the* West Indies; *and to prohibit such provinces and colonies from carrying on any fishery on the banks of* Newfoundland, *or other places therein mentioned, under certain conditions and limitations.*

WHEREAS . . . *[d]uring the continuance of the combinations and disorders, which at this time prevail within the provinces of* Massachuset's Bay *and* New Hampshire, *and the colonies of* Connecticut *and* Rhode Island, *to the obstruction of the commerce of these kingdoms, and other his Majesty's dominions, and in breach and violation of the laws of this realm, it is highly unfit that the inhabitants of the said provinces and colonies should enjoy the same privileges of trade, and the same benefits and advantages to which his Majesty's faithful and obedient subjects are intitled;* be it therefore enacted by the King's most excellent majesty, by and with the advice and consent of the lords spiritual and temporal, and commons, in this present parliament assembled, and by the authority of the same, That from and after the first day of *July,* one thousand seven hundred and seventy-five, and during the continuance of this act, no goods, wares, or merchandises, which are particularly enumerated in, and by the said act made in the twelfth year of king *Charles* the Second or any other act, being the growth, product, or manufacture of the provinces of *Massachuset's Bay,* or *New Hampshire,* or colonies of *Connecticut, Rhode Island,* or *Providence Plantation,* in *North America,* or any or either of them, are to be brought to some other *British* colony, or to *Great Britain;* or any such enumerated goods, wares, or merchandise, which shall at any time or times have been imported or brought into the said provinces or colonies, or any or either of them, shall be shipped, carried, conveyed, or transported, from any of the said provinces or colonies respectively, to any land, island, territory, dominion, port, or place whatsoever, other than to *Great Britain,* or some of the *British* islands in the *West Indies,* to be laid on shore there; and that no other goods, wares, or merchandise whatsoever, of the growth, product, or manufacture of the provinces or colonies herein-before mentioned, or which shall at any time or times have been imported or brought into the same, shall, from and after the said first day of *July,* and during the continuance of this act, be shipped, carried, conveyed, or transported, from any of the said provinces or colonies respectively, to any other land, island, territory, dominion, port, or place whatsoever, except to the kingdoms of *Great Britain* or *Ireland,* or to some of the *British* islands in the *West Indies,* to be laid on shore there; any law, custom, or usage, to the contrary notwithstanding. . . .

IV. And it is hereby further enacted by the authority aforesaid, That from and after the first day of *September,* one thousand seven hundred and seventy-five, and during the continuance of this act, no sort of wines, salt, or any goods or commodities whatsoever, (except horses, victual, and linen cloth, the produce and manufacture of *Ireland,* imported directly from thence), shall be imported into any of the said colonies or provinces hereinbefore respectively mentioned, upon any pretence whatsoever, unless such goods shall be *bona fide* and without fraud laden and shipped in *Great Britain,* and carried directly from thence, upon forfeiture thereof, and of the ship or vessel on board which such goods shall be laden; and it shall be lawful for any admiral, chief commander, or commissioned officer, of his Majesty's fleet, or ship of war, or any officer of his Majesty's customs, to seize any ship or vessel arriving at any of the said provinces or colonies before-mentioned, or which shall be discovered within two leagues of any shore thereof, having such goods on board, and the goods laden thereon, (except as before excepted), for which the master, or other person taking charge of such ship or vessel, shall not produce a cocket or clearance from the collector, or proper officer of his Majesty's customs, certifying that the said goods were laden on board the said ship or vessel, in some port of *Great Britain;* any law, custom, or usage, to the contrary notwithstanding. . . .

VII. And it is hereby further enacted by the authority aforesaid, That if any ship or vessel, being the property of the subjects of *Great Britain,* not belonging to and fitted out from *Great Britain* or *Ireland,* or the islands of *Guernsey, Jersey, Sark, Alderney,* or *Man,* shall be found, after the twentieth day of *July,* one thousand seven hundred and seventy-five, carrying on any fishery, of what nature or kind soever, upon the banks of *Newfoundland,* the coast of *Labrador,* or within the river or gulf of *Saint Lawrence,* or upon the coast of *Cape Breton,* or *Nova Scotia,* or any other part of the coast of *North*

*America,* or having on board materials for carrying on any such fishery, every such ship or vessel, with her guns, ammunition, tackle, apparel, and furniture, together with the fish, if any shall be found on board, shall be forfeited, unless the master, or other person, having the charge of such ship or vessel, do produce to the commander of any of his Majesty's ships of war, stationed for the protection and superintendence of the *British* fisheries in *America,* a certificate, under the hand and seal of the governor or commander in chief, of any of the colonies of plantations of *Quebec, Newfoundland, Saint John, Nova Scotia, New York, New Jersey, Pensylvania, Maryland, Virginia, North Carolina, South Carolina, Georgia, East Florida, West Florida, Bahamas,* and *Bermudas,* setting forth, that such ship or vessel, expressing her name, and the name of her master, and describing her built and burthen, hath fitted and cleared out, from some one of the said colonies or plantations, in order to proceed upon the said fishery, and that she actually and *bona fide* belongs to and is the whole and entire property of his Majesty's subjects, inhabitants of the said colony or plantation, which certificates such governors, or commanders in chief respectively, are hereby authorised and required to grant.

VIII. *And to the end that the foregoing prohibitions, restrictions, and regulations, may be more effectually carried into execution,* it is hereby further enacted by the authority aforesaid, That it shall and may be lawful to and for all or any of the commanders of his Majesty's ships or vessels of war, stationed and appointed for the regulation and protection of the *British* fishery upon the coasts of *North America,* or to and for the commanders of any other of his Majesty's ships or vessels employed at sea, and they and every of them are hereby required and enjoined to examine, search, and visit all ships and vessels suspected to be carrying on the said fisheries; and to seize, arrest, and prosecute, in manner herein-after directed, all and every such ships and vessels as shall be found to be carrying on the said fisheries, not belonging to and fitted out from *Great Britain* or *Ireland,* or the islands of *Guernsey, Jersey, Alderney, Sark,* or *Man,* which shall not have on board the certificate herein-before required.

## 19. CONGRESS ISSUES A FINAL PLEA FOR PEACE, JULY 1775

In an environment of active hostilities, the possibility of finding common ground with Parliament became ever less likely. Nonetheless, Congress formed a committee on June 3, 1775, to draft a second (and final) petition to the king seeking his intercession in resolving the conflict before additional fraternal blood was shed. Appropriately, Congress appointed a largely conservative group that did not include any congressional radicals. It was made up of John Dickinson and Benjamin Franklin (who by now was no longer a proponent of reconciliation), Thomas Johnson, John Rutledge, and John Jay.[34] Jay was to be the lead author, yet after Congress reviewed his draft on June 19, it was sent back to committee and Dickinson, once again, took over the writing of yet another congressional state paper.[35]

Congress began deliberation on the petition on June 19, 1775—two days after the bloody Battle of Bunker (or Breed's) Hill, and after heated discussion—not all in Congress were as willing as Jefferson to accommodate Dickinson and his party of moderates—Congress approved it on July 5.[36] On July 8, it was signed—the third document to be signed by all the members of Congress—and entrusted to Richard Penn to take to England, along with a second address to the people of Great Britain, and the Declaration on Taking Arms. Penn, along with Arthur Lee, brought the three documents to the American Department on August 21, 1775, and then presented them personally on September 1 to Lord Dartmouth, the generally sympathetic secretary of state for the American colonies, for presentation to the king.[37]

But the king, after being informed of the grievous losses suffered by British forces in their costly victory at Bunker Hill and the taking in May of Fort Ticonderoga by colonial forces, had already concluded that his North American continental colonists were in revolt. His response was to commit his administration, in his proclamation of August 23, to the suppression of rebellion and sedition in the colonies (see document 25.2).[38] Given those circumstances, it is unsurprising that he refused to accept Congress' personally deferential, but unfortunately timed and provocative, petition.[39] On September 4, Lee and Penn published the petition to the king in the London newspapers. As a matter of propriety, Congress had delayed publishing it in the colonies until it had had time to reach the king, and so it did not appear in the colonies until, with remarkable timing, it was published by the *Pennsylvania Packet* on August 21, 1775, the very same day that Penn and Lee had presented it to the secretary of state for the American colonies.[40]

The petition begins by rehearsing the highly salutary relationship of the colonies and Britain, then describes the colonies' active participation in the recent war with France, which led to "an enlargement of the dominions of the Crown." Unfortunately, the lamentable parliamentary and ministerial actions that followed the close of the war led the colonists to perceive "domestic dangers, in their judgment, of a more dreadful kind" than even the late war. In addition, the colonists drew to the king's attention that the effects of this system of administration "were more immediately felt by them, yet its influence appeared to be" as least as "injurious to the commerce and prosperity of Great Britain," perhaps even more so. Out of deference to the king's sensibilities, Congress declined to enumerate fully the grievous actions of Parliament and his ministers.

The petition emphasizes the loyalty of the colonists, who were led into "a controversy so peculiarly abhorrent to the affections of your still faithful colonists." It further assures the king that the colonists "not only most ardently desire the former harmony between her and these colonies may be restored, but that a concord may be established between them upon so firm a basis as to perpetuate its blessings, uninterrupted by any future dissentions, to succeeding generations in both countries." This meant to them some form of permanent constitutional arrangement that would protect the colonies' rights so that they would not be dependent on the temporary and changeable good graces of Parliament. Congress again confirmed that while defending the right of colonial legislatures to participate in raising taxes in the Colonies, it would not resist the (unspecified) rights of Britain.

Seeking relief as a supplicant, Congress begged the king "to procure us relief from our afflicting fears and jealousies" and to organize negotiations between him and his American subjects "by which the united applications of your faithful colonists to the throne, in pursuance of their common councils, may be improved into a happy and permanent reconciliation." Although no direct negotiations, ones that might have helped resolve the crisis, ever took place, that Congress humbly sought such a resolution, offers compelling testimony that finding a permanent constitutional solution to the crisis was still in the summer of 1775 the outstanding goal of a majority, or close to it, of congressional delegates. Indeed, as Dickinson explained in a subsequent letter, Congress had intentionally avoided any mention, in the petition, of rights, British or natural, in order to project the appropriate level of deference. That concern with protocol, however, did not prevent the colonists from provocatively once again making clear that they were subjects of the king but not of Parliament.

In fact, the deferential tone of the petition frustrated radical delegates like John Adams, who wrote, referring to Dickinson, that "a certain great fortune and piddling genius, whose fame has been trumpeted so loudly, has given a silly cast to our whole doing. We are between a hawk and buzzard."[41] Such comments by Adams, however, proved rather embarrassing, most especially after the letter containing them was intercepted by the British and published for Dickinson, other members of Congress, and the rest of the world to read.[42] Nor were his views as yet representative of the majority in Congress, which still hoped for a "most desirable reconciliation."[43] Congress, instead of holding the king responsible—as it finally did in the spring of 1776 and still more famously that summer in the Declaration of Independence— continued to pray that the king would understand the colonists' awkward predicament: according to Congress, most colonists remained loyal and committed to their constitutional monarch, but had been compelled to take up arms in self-defense "against those artful and cruel enemies [in Parliament and the king's ministry], who abuse your royal confidence and authority, for the purpose of effecting our destruction."[44] Congress closed the petition by praying that the king would "enjoy a long and prosperous reign" and that his descendants would govern his "dominions with honor to themselves and happiness to their subjects."

## 19.1

 ## OLIVE BRANCH PETITION TO THE KING, JULY 8, 1775

Worthington Chauncey Ford et al., eds., *Journals of the Continental Congress, 1774–1789* (Washington, D.C.: Government Printing Office, 1904–37), 2:158–62.

SATURDAY, JULY 8, 1775

The Congress met according to adjournment.

The Petition to the King being engrossed, was compared, and signed by the several members.

*To the king's most excellent Majesty:*

MOST GRACIOUS SOVEREIGN,

We, your Majesty's faithful subjects of the colonies of new Hampshire, Massachusetts bay, Rhode island and Providence Plantations, Connecticut, New York, New Jersey, Pennsylvania, the counties of New Castle, Kent, and Sussex, on Delaware, Maryland, Virginia, North Carolina, and South Carolina, in behalf of ourselves, and the inhabitants of these colonies, who have deputed us to represent them in general Congress, entreat your Majesty's gracious attention to this our humble petition.

The union between our Mother country and these colonies, and the energy of mild and just government, produced benefits so remarkably important, and afforded such an assurance of their permanency and increase, that the wonder and envy of other Nations were excited, while they beheld Great Britain riseing to a power the most extraordinary the world had ever known.

Her rivals, observing that there was no probability of this happy connexion being broken by civil dissensions, and apprehending its future effects, if left any longer undisturbed, resolved to prevent her receiving such continual and formidable accessions of wealth and strength, by checking the growth of these settlements from which they were to be derived.

In the prosecution of this attempt, events so unfavourable to the design took place, that every friend to the interests of Great Britain and these colonies, entertained pleasing and reasonable expectations of seeing an additional force and extention immediately given to the operations of the union hitherto experienced, by an enlargement of the dominions of the Crown, and the removal of ancient and warlike enemies to a greater distance.

At the conclusion, therefore, of the late war, the most glorious and advantageous that ever had been carried on by British arms, your loyal colonists having contributed to its success, by such repeated and strenuous exertions, as frequently procured them the distinguished approbation of your Majesty, of the late king, and of parliament, doubted not but that they should be permitted, with the rest of the empire, to share in the blessings of peace, and the emoluments of victory and conquest. While these recent and honorable acknowledgments of their merits remained on record in the journals and acts of that august legislature, the Parliament, undefaced by the imputation or even the suspicion of any offence, they were alarmed by a new system of statutes and regulations adopted for the administration of the colonies, that filled their minds with the most painful fears and jealousies; and, to their inexpressible astonishment, perceived the dangers of a foreign quarrel quickly succeeded by domestic dangers, in their judgment, of a more dreadful kind.

Nor were their anxieties alleviated by any tendency in this system to promote the welfare of the Mother country. For tho' its effects were more immediately felt by them, yet its influence appeared to be injurious to the commerce and prosperity of Great Britain.

We shall decline the ungrateful task of describing the irksome variety of artifices, practised by many of your Majesty's Ministers, the delusive pretences, fruitless terrors, and unavailing severities, that have, from time to time, been dealt out by them, in their attempts to execute this impolitic plan, or of traceing, thro' a series of years past, the progress of the unhappy differences between Great Britain and these colonies, which have flowed from this fatal source.

Your Majesty's Ministers, persevering in their measures, and proceeding to open hostilities for enforcing them, have compelled us to arm in our own defence, and have engaged us in a controversy so peculiarly abhorrent to the affections of your still faithful colonists, that when we consider whom we must oppose in this contest, and if it continues, what may be the consequences, our own particular misfortunes are accounted by us only as parts of our distress.

Knowing to what violent resentments and incurable animosities, civil discords are apt to exasperate and inflame the contending parties, we think ourselves required by indispensable obligations to Almighty God, to your Majesty, to our fellow subjects, and to ourselves, immediately to use all the means in our power, not incompatible with our safety, for stopping the further effusion of blood, and for averting the impending calamities that threaten the British Empire.

Thus called upon to address your Majesty on affairs of such moment to America, and probably to all your dominions, we are earnestly desirous of performing this office, with the utmost deference for your Majesty; and we therefore pray, that your royal magnanimity and benevolence may make the most favourable construction of our expressions on so uncommon an occasion. Could we represent in their full force, the sentiments that agitate the minds of us your dutiful subjects, we are persuaded your Majesty would ascribe any seeming deviation from reverence in our language, and even in our conduct, not to any reprehensible intention, but to the impossibility of reconciling the usual appearances of respect, with a just attention to our own preservation against those artful and cruel enemies, who abuse your royal confidence and authority, for the purpose of effecting our destruction.

Attached to your Majesty's person, family, and government, with all devotion that principle and affection can inspire, connected with Great Britain by the strongest ties that can unite societies, and deploring every event that tends in any degree to weaken them, we solemnly assure your Majesty, that we not only most ardently desire the former harmony between her and these colonies may be restored, but that a concord may be established between them upon so firm a basis as to perpetuate its blessings, uninterrupted by any future dissentions, to succeeding generations in both countries, and to transmit your Majesty's Name to posterity, adorned with that signal and lasting glory, that has attended the memory of those illustrious personages, whose virtues and abilities have extricated states from dangerous convulsions, and, by securing happiness to others, have erected the most noble and durable monuments to their own fame.

We beg leave further to assure your Majesty, that notwithstanding the sufferings of your loyal colonists, during the course of the present controversy, our breasts retain too tender a regard for the kingdom from which we derive our origin, to request such a reconciliation as might in any manner be inconsistent with her dignity or her welfare. These, related as we are to her, honor and duty, as well as inclination, induce us to support and advance; and the apprehensions that now oppress our hearts with unspeakable grief, being once removed, your Majesty will find your faithful subjects on this continent ready and willing at all times, as they ever have been, with their lives and fortunes, to assert and maintain the rights and interests of your Majesty, and of our Mother country.

We, therefore, beseech your Majesty, that your royal authority and influence may be graciously interposed to procure us relief from our afflicting fears and jealousies, occasioned by the system before mentioned, and to settle peace through every part of your dominions, with all humility submitting to your Majesty's wise consideration whether it may not be expedient for facilitating those important purposes, that your Majesty be pleased to direct some mode, by which the united applications of your faithful colonists to the throne, in pursuance of their common councils, may be improved into a happy and permanent reconciliation; and that, in the mean time, measures may be taken for preventing the further destruction of the lives of your Majesty's subjects; and that such statutes as more immediately distress any of your Majesty's colonies may be repealed.

For by such arrangements as your Majesty's wisdom can form, for collecting the united sense of your American people, we are convinced your Majesty would receive such satisfactory proofs of the disposition of the colonists towards their sovereign and parent state, that the wished for opportunity would soon be restored to them, of evincing the sincerity of their professions, by every testimony of devotion becoming the most dutiful subjects, and the most affectionate colonists.

That your Majesty may enjoy a long and prosperous reign, and that your descendants may govern your dominions with honor to themselves and happiness to their subjects, is our sincere and fervent prayer.

John Hancock

colony of New hampshire
  John Langdon
colony of Massachusetts bay
  Thomas Cushing
  Saml Adams
  John Adams
  Robt Treat Paine
colony of Rhode-island and
providence plantations
  Step Hopkins
  Sam: Ward
colony of Connecticut
  Elipht Dyer
  Roger Sherman
  Silas Deane
colony of New York
  Phil. Livingston
  Jas Duane
  John Alsop
  Frans. Lewis
  John Jay
  Robt R Livingston junr
  Lewis Morris
  Wm Floyd
  Henry Wisner
New Jersey
  Wil: Livingston
  John De Hart
  Richd Smith
Pennsylvania
  John Dickinson

B Franklin
Geo: Ross
James Wilson
Chas Humphreys
Edwd Biddle
counties of New Castle Kent and
Sussex on delawar
  Caesar Rodney
  Thos Mc. Kean
  Geo: Read
Maryland
  Mat. Tilghman
  Ths Johnson Junr
  Wm Paca
  Samuel Chase
  Thos Stone
colony of Virginia
  P. Henry Jr
  Richard Henry Lee
  Edmund Pendleton
  Benja Harrison
  Th: Jefferson
North Carolina
  Will Hooper
  Joseph Hewes
South Carolina
  Henry Middleton
  Tho Lynch
  Christ Gadsden
  J. Rutledge
  Edward Rutledge

## 19.2

 JOHN DICKINSON TO ARTHUR LEE, JULY 1775

Shortly after the members of Congress signed the so-called Olive Branch Petition, Dickinson wrote to Arthur Lee, one of Richard Henry Lee's brothers (along with Francis Lightfoot, William, and Thomas Ludwell), a physician and lawyer living in London, a radical supporter of John Wilkes (a relentless critic of ministerial domination and a champion of American colonial rights), a severe critic of the British monarchy, and a close ally of Samuel Adams.[45] Lee provided information to Congress' Committee of Secret Correspondence and, later, served on the diplomatic mission to France with Silas Deane and Benjamin Franklin, in which role his disruptive and paranoid personality likely did more harm than good. As was typical of Congress in so many instances, it initially split between those supporting the moderate Deane and those supporting the radical Lee. Ultimately, in 1779, Congress dismissed both, leaving the canny Franklin as its sole official minister in Paris, after having its independence recognized and having signed treaties in mid-1778 with France.

In this letter, Dickinson revealingly explains to this radical agent for Massachusetts why Congress in the petition makes "no *Claim*, and mention[s] no *Right*": Congress wished to appear duly humble "in an address [to] the Throne" so as to provide the administration with no excuse for rejecting a proper and "unexceptional Petition, praying for [an] Accommodation." Clearly, as shown in the recorded debate regarding the terms to be used in the Bill of Rights and List of Grievances (see document 13.1), rights claims were invariably provocative. They carried particular meanings that, though not always used with care, were understood at the time, but are too often lost on readers today. Congress, as Dickinson suggests here, used rights claims thoughtfully, and so any increase in references to natural rights, as is found in the state papers of the Second Continental Congress, likely signaled a shifting consensus in the body away from an agreed-upon sovereign, George III, and the preeminence of English or British common-law or constitutional (that is, civil) rights, and toward independence.

Paul H. Smith, ed., *Letters of Delegates to Congress, 1774–1789* (Washington, D.C.: Library of Congress, 1976–93), 1:688. Smith notes that the letter is in Dickinson's hand, but that his signature was inked out.

Dear Sir,                                                                      Fairhill July [? 1775]

Before this comes to Hand, You will have receiv'd, I presume, the Petition to the King. You will perhaps at first be surpriz'd, that We make no *Claim*, and mention no

*Right.* But I hope [on] considering all Circumstances, You will be [of] opinion, that this Humility in an address [to] the Throne is at present proper.

Our Rights [have] been already stated—our Claims made—[War] is actually begun, and We are carrying it on Vigor[ously.] This Conduct & our other Publications will shew, [that our] spirits are not lowered. If Administration [be] desirious of stopping the Effusion of British [blood] the opportunity is now offered to them [by this] unexceptionable Petition, praying for [an] Accommodation. If they reject this appl[ication] with Contempt, the more humble it is, [the more] such Treatment will confirm the Minds of [our] Countrymen, to endure all the Misfortunes [that] may attend the Contest.

I do not know what [is] thought in London of the several Engagements near Boston. But this You may be assured [of] everyone of them has been favorable to Us—& particularly that of Bunker's Hill on [the] 17th of last month, when a mere Carnage was [made] of the Royalists—tho they gained our Intrench[ments.]

I am Sir, your very affectionate hble [servant.]

(*John Dickinson*)

## 20. CONGRESS APPEALS TO BRITONS, JULY 8, 1775

Like their predecessors in the First Continental Congress, those in the Second determined to send, along with their petition to the king, a second address to their fellow British subjects. Thus, on June 3, 1775, the same day that a committee was appointed to write the petition, Congress selected a separate committee to draft an address to the king's British subjects. This committee was made up of Richard Henry Lee (Virginia), Edmund Pendleton (Virginia), and Robert R. Livingston, Jr. (New York).[46] Lee had been on the committee that wrote the "Address to the People of Great Britain" in 1774, along with Robert R. Livingston's cousin, William Livingston. The Livingston family, wealthy and politically influential, contained a number of Roberts who played prominent political roles in New York and New Jersey. Robert R. Livingston, Sr., was, like William, a New York City lawyer and wealthy landowner. He later became a judge and served on the New York Supreme Court. His son, Robert R. Jr., also a lawyer and a partner of John Jay, was sufficiently well regarded to be chosen to serve on the committee that drafted the Declaration of Independence, though like many from New York, he opposed its passage—thinking the time not yet ripe—and declined to vote for it. Although he initially became a leader of the Federalists in New York while strongly supporting the Constitution, he broke with them and joined forces with the Republicans (and the Clinton family faction) before being appointed by President Jefferson to help negotiate the Louisiana Purchase. Pendleton was a Virginian moderate, in stark contrast to some of the more radical members of the Virginia delegation, particularly Patrick Henry and Richard Henry Lee.

The initial draft was submitted to Congress on June 27, 1775, debated, and returned to the committee on July 6. On July 7, the committee provided Congress with a second draft, which was discussed and approved on July 8. Lee may have written the first draft, but which member of the committee wrote the document approved by Congress is still unknown.[47] This address, along with the Olive Branch Petition and the Declaration on Taking Arms, was given to Richard Penn, who departed for London on July 9. The address must have been printed with great dispatch, almost overnight, by the Bradfords, a Philadelphia family that printed, with sympathy, radical works during the colonies' struggles with Great Britain, so that Penn could take a copy with him on the ninth.[48]

The address opens by appealing to the common ties that bind American colonists to their brethren in Great Britain before rehearsing the by now familiar list of grievances (though in new and bold ways): unconstitutional parliamentary legislation, replacement of common-law courts by Roman-law ones, and a number of coercive measures imposed by Parliament on the colonies. Congress does not mention taxes, an omission highlighting a shift of focus from its earlier concern to its opposition to Parliament's more inclusive right of legislating for the colonists. (In truth, taxation was not an issue after Congress received Lord North's peace proposal, which abandoned Parliament's claim to tax the colonies; see document 23.1.) The contested right of Parliament to legislate for the colonists and of the colonists' right to trial by jury were the issues that, over and over again for twelve years, Congress considered the nub of the crisis.

In addition, Congress also condemned the Restraining Acts (for the New England Restraining Act, see document 18.3), which, conjoined to the Continental Association, ended American shipping and most commerce. It also was concerned with the threat of foreign soldiers being recruited to be used in the conflict, leaving the colonists prey "to the lawless Ravages of a merciless Soldiery," and with the imposition of military law in Boston: "Without Law, without Right, Powers are assumed unknown to the Constitution. Private Property is unjustly invaded." In short, it seemed to Congress that the British ministry's aim was "the reduction of these Colonies to Slavery and Ruin." Although the claim was certainly a gross exaggeration, the evident aim of Parliament and the ministry was, at minimum, to demonstrate to the colonies that they were subordinate to Parliament and so were to be ruled, even if more or less benignly, by it.

Congress rhetorically ponders whether there is a "secret Principle of the Constitution," and then answers itself: "The Government, we have long revered, is not without its Defects, and that while it gives Freedom to a Part, it necessarily enslaves the Remainder of the Empire." Here, Congress pointed to an issue that Whig political theory, largely shared by both sides in this contest of wills, was incapable of answering. Neither side was able to explain how to maintain British freedom and parliamentary supremacy without rendering the American colonists either less free and more dependent on parliamentary beneficence, or totally independent of it (and almost certainly of the Crown as well). Thus, Congress' description of the real flaws in the imperial constitution was recognizable even to those who defended it in Great Britain.

Congress in this address appealed, more frequently than was usual, to the lessons of British history: because the English (later the British) had long defended liberty, "*Britons* can never become the Instruments of Oppression, till they lose the Spirit of Freedom." But for most members of Parliament and many others throughout Britain, defending British freedom was the same as defending parliamentary sovereignty— more evidence of the fundamental disconnection between colonists and mother country. Congress denied again that it was "aiming at Independence" and challenged its British readers to recount "what Measures have we taken that betray a Desire of Independence." Congress gave its own answers: "By the Allegations of your Ministers, not by our Actions . . . We have carried our dutiful Petitions to the Throne. We have applied to your Justice for Relief," and no more.

Congress continued to remind its British audience that in spite of its defensive military response to continued ministerial provocation, the colonists "have not yet lost Sight of the Object we have ever had in View, a Reconciliation with you on constitutional Principles." Congress also reiterates most of the fourth resolution of its earlier Bill of Rights and List of Grievances (see document 13.1), in which it confirmed its continued "submission to the several Acts of Trade and Navigation, passed before the Year 1763," and avowed that the colonists "cheerfully consent to the Operation of such Acts of the *British* Parliament, as shall be restrained to the Regulation of our external Commerce, for the Purpose of securing the commercial Advantages of the whole Empire to the Mother Country, and the commercial Benefits of its respective Members." Reaching back to sentiments first expressed by Massachusetts in 1764 (see documents 2.1, 4.8, and 9.1), Congress reiterated "that the Advantages which Great Britain receives from the Monopoly of our Trade, far exceed our Proportion of the Expense" needed to administer and protect the colonies, and that "should these Advantages be inadequate thereto, let the Restrictions on our Trade be removed, and we will cheerfully contribute such Proportion when constitution- ally required." Such a compromise was finally accepted by Parliament in 1778 (see document 47.1), but by then it was far too late to be accepted by the new states.

Congress, as the representative of twelve colonies—Georgia, after its failure to elect delegates to the First Congress on August 10, 1774, was officially unrepresented until the Second Congress reconvened on September 12, 1775—closed by arguing that Lord North's "Plan of Accommodation" was a hoax to deceive their fellow subjects into believing that the colonists were "unwilling to listen to any Terms of Accommodation." To the contrary, Congress repeated its wish, as it had in its petition to the king, for him "to direct some Mode, by which the united Applications of his faithful Colonists may be improved into a happy and permanent Reconciliation." Of course, those in Britain who knew that Congress had refused to offer a full hearing on Joseph Galloway's thoughtfully designed federal "Plan of Union" and had expunged any record of it from its *Journal,* may have had well-founded doubts concerning Congress' credibility on this matter. Either way, what is left unsaid in the address is that Great Britain and the colonies no longer understood British constitutional principles in the same way.

20.1

 THE TWELVE UNITED COLONIES TO THE
INHABITANTS OF GREAT BRITAIN

Worthington Chauncey Ford et al., eds., *Journals of the Continental Congress, 1774–1789* (Washington, D.C.: Government Printing Office, 1904–37), 2:163–70.

*The Twelve United Colonies, by their Delegates in Congress, to the Inhabitants of Great Britain.*

FRIENDS, COUNTRYMEN, AND BRETHREN!

By these, and by every other Appellation that may designate the Ties, which bind *us* to each other, we entreat your serious Attention to this our second Attempt to prevent their Dissolution. Remembrances of former Friendships, Pride in the glorious Atchievements of our common Ancestors, and Affection for the Heirs of their Virtues, have hitherto preserved our mutual Connexion; but when the Friendship is violated by the grossest Injuries; when the Pride of Ancestry becomes our Reproach, and we are no otherwise allied than as Tyrants and Slaves; when reduced to the melancholy Alternative of renouncing your Favour or our Freedom; can we hesitate about the Choice? Let the Spirit of *Britons* determine.

In a former Address we asserted our Rights, and stated the Injuries we had then received. We hoped, that the mention of our Wrongs would have roused that honest Indignation which has slept too long for your Honor, or the Welfare of the Empire. But we have not been permitted to entertain this pleasing expectation. Every Day brought an accumulation of Injuries, and the Invention of the Ministry has been constantly exercised, in adding to the Calamities of your *American* Brethren.

After the most valuable Right of Legislation was infringed; when the Powers assumed by your Parliament, in which we are not represented, and from our local and other Circumstances cannot properly be represented, rendered our Property precarious; after being denied that mode of Trial, to which we have long been indebted for the safety of our Persons, and the preservation of our Liberties; after being in many instances divested of those Laws, which were transmitted to us by our common Ancestors, and subjected to an arbitrary Code, compiled under the auspices of *Roman* Tyrants; after those Charters, which encouraged our Predecessors to brave Death and Danger in every Shape, on unknown Seas, in Deserts unexplored, amidst barbarous and inhospitable Nations, were annulled; when, without the form of Trial, without a public Accusation, whole Colonies were condemned, their Trade destroyed, their Inhabitants impoverished; when Soldiers were encouraged to embrue their Hands in the Blood of *Americans,* by offers of Impunity; when new modes of Trial were instituted for the ruin of the accused, where the charge carried with it the horrors of conviction; when a despotic Government was established in a neighbouring Province, and its Limits extended to every of our Frontiers; we little imagined that any thing could be added to this black Catalogue of unprovoked Injuries: but we have unhappily been deceived, and the late Measures of the *British* Ministry fully convince us, that their object is the reduction of these Colonies to Slavery and Ruin.

To confirm this Assertion, let us recal your attention to the Affairs of *America,* since our last Address. Let us combat the Calumnies of our Enemies; and let us warn you of the dangers that threaten you in our destruction. Many of your Fellow-Subjects, whose situation deprived them of other Support, drew their Maintenance from the Sea; but the deprivation of our Liberty being insufficient to satisfy the resentment of our Enemies, the horrors of Famine were superadded, and a *British* Parliament, who, in better times, were the Protectors of Innocence and the Patrons of Humanity, have, without distinction of Age or Sex, robbed thousands of the Food which they were accustomed to draw from that inexhaustible Source, placed in their neighbourhood by the benevolent Creator.

Another Act of your Legislature shuts our Ports, and prohibits our Trade with any but those States from whom the great Law of self-preservation renders it absolutely necessary we should at present withhold our Commerce. But this Act (whatever may have been its design) we consider rather as injurious to your Opulence than our Interest. All our Commerce terminates with you; and the Wealth we procure from other Nations, is soon exchanged for your Superfluities. Our remittances must then cease with our trade; and our refinements with our Affluence. We trust, however, that Laws which deprive us of every Blessing but a Soil that teems with the necessaries of Life, and that Liberty which renders the enjoyment of them secure, will not relax our Vigour in their Defence.

We might here observe on the Cruelty and Inconsistency of those, who, while they publicly Brand us with reproachful and unworthy Epithets, endeavour to deprive us of the means of defence, by their Interposition with foreign Powers, and to deliver us to the lawless Ravages of a merciless Soldiery. But happily we are not without Resources; and though the timid and humiliating Applications of a *British* Ministry should prevail with foreign Nations, yet Industry, prompted by necessity, will not leave us without the necessary Supplies.

We could wish to go no further, and, not to wound the Ear of Humanity, leave untold those rigorous Acts of Oppression, which are daily exercised in the Town of *Boston,* did we not hope, that by disclaiming their Deeds and punishing the Perpetrators, you would shortly vindicate the Honour of the *British* Name, and re-establish the violated Laws of Justice.

That once populous, flourishing and commercial Town is now garrisoned by an Army sent not to protect, but to enslave its Inhabitants. The civil Government is overturned, and a military Despotism created upon its Ruins. Without Law, without Right, Powers are assumed unknown to the Constitution. Private Property is unjustly invaded. The Inhabitants, daily subjected to the Licentiousness of the Soldiery, are forbid to remove in Defiance of their natural Rights, in Violation of the most solemn Compacts. Or if, after long and wearisome Solicitation, a Pass is procured, their Effects are detained, and even those who are most favored, have no Alternative but Poverty or Slavery. The Distress of many thousand People, wantonly deprived of the Necessaries of Life, is a Subject, on which we would not wish to enlarge.

Yet, we cannot but observe, that a *British* Fleet (unjustified even by Acts of your Legislature) are daily employed in ruining our Commerce, seizing our Ships, and depriving whole Communities of their daily Bread. Nor will a Regard for your Honour permit us to be silent, while *British* Troops sully your Glory, by Actions, which the most inveterate Enmity will not palliate among civilized Nations, the wanton and unnecessary Destruction of *Charlestown,* a large, ancient, and once populous Town, just before deserted by its Inhabitants, who had fled to avoid the Fury of your Soldiery.

If you still retain those Sentiments of Compassion, by which *Britons* have ever been distinguished, if the Humanity, which tempered the Valour of our common Ancestors, has not degenerated into Cruelty, you will lament the Miseries of their Descendants.

To what are we to attribute this Treatment? If to any secret Principle of the Constitution, let it be mentioned; let us learn, that the Government, we have long revered, is not without its Defects, and that while it gives Freedom to a Part, it necessarily enslaves the Remainder of the Empire. If such a Principle exists, why for Ages has it ceased to operate? Why at this Time is it called into Action? Can no Reason be assigned for this Conduct? Or must it be resolved into the wanton Exercise of arbitrary Power? And shall the Descendants of *Britons* tamely submit to this?—No, Sirs! We never will, while we revere the Memory of our gallant and virtuous Ancestors, we never can surrender those glorious Privileges, for which they fought, bled, and conquered. Admit that your Fleets could destroy our Towns, and ravage our Sea-Coasts; these are inconsiderable Objects, Things of no Moment to Men, whose Bosoms glow with the Ardor of Liberty. We can retire beyond the Reach of your Navy, and, without any sensible Diminution of the Necessaries of Life, enjoy a Luxury, which from that Period you will want—the Luxury of being Free.

We know the Force of your Arms, and was it called forth in the Cause of Justice and your Country, we might dread the Exertion: but will *Britons* fight under the Banners of Tyranny? Will they counteract the Labours, and disgrace the Victories of their Ancestors? Will they forge Chains for their Posterity? If they descend to this unworthy Task, will their Swords retain their Edge, their Arms their accustomed Vigour? *Britons* can never become the Instruments of Oppression, till they lose the Spirit of Freedom, by which alone they are invincible.

Our Enemies charge us with Sedition. In what does it consist? In our Refusal to submit to unwarrantable Acts of Injustice and Cruelty? If so, shew us a Period in your History, in which you have not been equally Seditious.

We are accused of aiming at Independence; but how is this Accusation supported? By the Allegations of your Ministers, not by our Actions. Abused, insulted, and contemned, what Steps have we pursued to obtain Redress? We have carried our dutiful Petitions to the Throne. We have applied to your Justice for Relief. We have retrenched our Luxury, and withheld our Trade.

The Advantages of our Commerce were designed as a Compensation for your Protection: When you ceased to protect, for what were we to compensate?

What has been the Success of our Endeavours? The Clemency of our Sovereign is unhappily diverted; our Petitions are treated with Indignity; our Prayers answered by Insults. Our Application to you remains unnoticed, and leaves us the melancholy Apprehension of your wanting either the Will, or the Power, to assist us.

Even under these Circumstances, what Measures have we taken that betray a Desire of Independence? Have we called in the Aid of those foreign Powers, who are the Rivals of your Grandeur? When your Troops were few and defenceless, did we take Advantage of their Distress and expel them our Towns? Or have we permitted them to fortify, to receive new Aid, and to acquire additional Strength?

Let not *your* Enemies and *ours* persuade you, that in this we were influenced by Fear or any other unworthy Motive. The Lives of *Britons* are still dear to us. They are the Children of our Parents, and an uninterrupted Intercourse of mutual Benefits had knit the Bonds of Friendship. When Hostilities were commenced, when on a late Occasion we were wantonly attacked by your Troops, though we repelled their Assaults and returned their Blows, yet we lamented the Wounds they obliged us to give; nor have we yet learned to rejoice at a Victory over *Englishmen*.

As we wish not to colour our Actions, or disguise our Thoughts, we shall, in the simple Language of Truth, avow the Measures we have pursued, the Motives upon which we have acted, and our future Designs.

When our late Petition to the Throne produced no other Effect than fresh Injuries, and Votes of your Legislature, calculated to justify every Severity; when your Fleets and your Armies were prepared to wrest from us our Property, to rob us of our Liberties or our Lives; when the hostile Attempts of General *Gage* evinced his Designs, we levied Armies for our Security and Defence. When the Powers vested in the Governor of *Canada,* gave us Reason to apprehend Danger from that Quarter; and we had frequent Intimations, that a cruel and savage Enemy was to be let loose upon the defenseless Inhabitants of our Frontiers; we took such Measures as Prudence dictated, as Necessity will justify. We possessed ourselves of *Crown Point* and *Ticonderoga.* Yet give us leave most solemnly to assure you, that we have not yet lost Sight of the Object we have ever had in View, a Reconciliation with you on constitutional Principles, and a Restoration of that friendly Intercourse, which, to the Advantage of both, we till lately maintained.

The Inhabitants of this Country apply themselves chiefly to Agriculture and Commerce. As their Fashions and Manners are similar to yours, your Markets must afford them the Conveniences and Luxuries, for which they exchange the Produce of their Labours. The Wealth of this extended Continent centers with you; and our Trade is so regulated as to be subservient only to your Interest. You are too reasonable to expect, that by Taxes (in Addition to this) we should contribute to your Expence; to believe, after diverting the Fountain, that the Streams can flow with unabated Force.

It has been said, that we refuse to submit to the Restrictions on our Commerce. From whence is this Inference drawn? Not from our Words, we have repeatedly declared the Contrary; and we again profess our Submission to the several Acts of Trade and Navigation, passed before the Year 1763, trusting, nevertheless, in the Equity and Justice of Parliament, that such of them as, upon cool and impartial Consideration, shall appear to have imposed unnecessary or grievous Restrictions, will, at some happier Period, be repealed or altered. And we cheerfully consent to the Operation of such Acts of the *British* Parliament, as shall be restrained to the Regulation of our external Commerce, for the Purpose of securing the commercial Advantages of the whole Empire to the Mother Country, and the commercial Benefits of its respective Members; excluding every Idea of Taxation internal or external, for raising a Revenue on the Subjects in *America,* without their Consent.

It is alledged that we contribute nothing to the common Defence. To this we answer, that the Advantages which *Great Britain* receives from the Monopoly of our Trade, far exceed our Proportion of the Expence necessary for that Purpose. But should these Advantages be inadequate thereto, let the Restrictions on our Trade be removed, and we will cheerfully contribute such Proportion when constitutionally required.

It is a fundamental Principle of the *British* Constitution, that every Man should have at least a Representative Share in the Formation of those Laws, by which he is bound. Were it otherwise, the Regulation of our internal Police by a *British* Parliament, who are and ever will be unacquainted with our local Circumstances, must be always inconvenient, and frequently oppressive, working our wrong, without yielding any possible Advantage to you.

A Plan of Accommodation (as it has been absurdly called) has been proposed by your Ministers to our respective Assemblies. Were this Proposal free from every other Objection, but that which arises from the Time of the Offer, it would not be unexceptionable. Can Men deliberate with the Bayonet at their Breast? Can they treat with Freedom, while their Towns are sacked; when daily Instances of Injustice and Oppression disturb the slower Operations of Reason?

If this Proposal is really such as you would offer and we accept, why was it delayed till the Nation was put to useless expense, and we were reduced to our present melancholy Situation? If it holds forth nothing, why was it proposed? Unless indeed to deceive you into a Belief, that we were unwilling to listen to any Terms of Accommodation. But what is submitted to our Consideration? We contend for the Disposal of our Property. We are told that our Demand is unreasonable, that our Assemblies may indeed collect our Money, but that they must at the same Time offer, not what your Exigencies or ours may require, but so much as shall be deemed sufficient to satisfy the Desires of a Minister and enable him to provide for Favourites and Dependants. A Recurrence to your own Treasury will convince you how little of the Money already extorted from us has been applied to the Relief of your Burthens. To suppose that we would thus grasp the Shadow and give up the Substance, is adding Insult to Injuries.

We have nevertheless again presented an humble and dutiful Petition to our Sovereign, and to remove every imputation of Obstinacy, have requested his Majesty to direct some Mode, by which the united Applications of his faithful Colonists may be improved into a happy and permanent Reconciliation. We are willing to treat on such Terms as can alone render an accommodation lasting, and we flatter ourselves that our pacific Endeavours will be attended with a removal of ministerial Troops, and a repeal of those Laws, of the Operation of which we complain, on the one part, and a disbanding of our Army, and a dissolution of our commercial Associations, on the other.

Yet conclude not from this that we propose to surrender our Property into the Hands of your Ministry, or vest your Parliament with a Power which may terminate in our Destruction. The great Bulwarks of our Constitution we have desired to maintain by every temperate, by every peaceable Means; but your Ministers (equal Foes to *British* and *American* freedom) have added to their former Oppressions an Attempt to reduce us by the Sword to a base and abject submission. On the Sword, therefore, we are compelled to rely for Protection. Should Victory declare in your Favour, yet Men trained to Arms from their Infancy, and animated by the Love of Liberty, will afford neither a cheap or easy Conquest. Of this at least we are assured, that our Struggle will be glorious, our Success certain; since even in Death we shall find that Freedom which in Life you forbid us to enjoy.

Let us now ask what Advantages are to attend our Reduction? the Trade of a ruined and desolate Country is always inconsiderable, its Revenue trifling; the Expence of subjecting and retaining it in subjection certain and inevitable. What then remains but the gratification of an ill-judged Pride, or the hope of rendering us subservient to designs on your Liberty.

Soldiers who have sheathed their Swords in the Bowels of their *American* Brethren, will not draw them with more reluctance against you. When too late you may lament the loss of that freedom, which we exhort you, while still in your Power, to preserve.

On the other hand, should you prove unsuccessful; should that Connexion, which we most ardently wish to maintain, be dissolved; should your Ministers exhaust your Treasures and waste the Blood of your Countrymen in vain Attempts on our Liberty; do they not deliver you, weak and defenseless, to your natural Enemies?

Since then your Liberty must be the price of your Victories; your Ruin, of your Defeat: What blind Fatality can urge you to a pursuit destructive of all that *Britons* hold dear?

If you have no regard to the Connexion that has for Ages subsisted between us; if you have forgot the Wounds we have received fighting by your Side for the extension of the Empire; if our Commerce is not an object below your consideration; if Justice and Humanity have lost their influence on your Hearts; still Motives are not wanting to excite your Indignation at the Measures now pursued; Your Wealth, your Honour, your Liberty are at Stake.

Notwithstanding the Distress to which we are reduced, we sometimes forget our own Afflictions, to anticipate and sympathize in yours. We grieve that rash and inconsiderate Councils should precipitate the destruction of an Empire, which has been the envy and admiration of Ages, and call God to witness! that we would part with our Property, endanger our Lives, and sacrifice every thing but Liberty, to redeem you from ruin.

A Cloud hangs over your Heads and ours; 'ere this reaches you, it may probably burst upon us; let us then (before the remembrance of former Kindness is obliterated) once more repeat those Appellations which are ever grateful in our Ears; let us entreat Heaven to avert our Ruin, and the Destruction that threatens our Friends, Brethren and Countrymen, on the other side of the *Atlantic.*

*Ordered,* That the Address be published and a number of them sent by Mr. Penn to England.

20.2

 CONGRESS TO THE LORD MAYOR OF LONDON
AND THE COLONIAL AGENTS

On July 6, Congress asked the same committee that had been tasked with writing the British people to write "the Lord Mayor, Alderman, and Livery of the city of London, expressing the thanks of this Congress, for their virtuous and spirited opposition to the oppressive and ruinous system of colony administration adopted by the British ministry." In its letter to the lord mayor, Congress confirmed, yet again, that it still wished "most ardently for a lasting connection with Great Britain on terms of just and equal liberty." On July 8, the letter was debated and approved; it was carried to London by Richard Penn, along with the other documents recently approved by Congress.[49] In the colonies, the letter was printed in the *Pennsylvania Packet,* but not until December 11, 1775.

Worthington Chauncey Ford et al., eds., *Journals of the Continental Congress, 1774–1789* (Washington, D.C.: Government Printing Office, 1904–37), 2:170–72.

The Letter to the Lord Mayor, &c., being read again and debated, was approved, and is as follows:

MY LORD,

Permitt the Delegates of the people of twelve antient colonies, to pay yr Lordship, and the very respectable body of which you are head, the just tribute of gratitude and thanks, for the virtuous and unsolicited resentment you have shown to the violated rights of a free people. The city of London, my Lord, having in all ages, approved itself the patron of liberty, and the support of just government, against lawless tyranny and oppression, cannot fail to make us deeply sensible of the powerful aid, our cause must receive from such advocates. A cause, my Lord, worthy the support of the first city in the world, as it involves the fate of a great continent, and threatens to shake the foundations of a flourishing, and, until lately, a happy empire.

North America, my Lord, wishes most ardently for a lasting connection with Great Britain on terms of just and equal liberty; less than which generous minds will not offer, nor brave and free ones be willing to receive.

A cruel war has at length been opened agst us, and whilst we prepare to defend ourselves like the descendants of Britons, we still hope that the mediation of wise and good citizens, will at length prevail over despotism, and restore harmony and peace, on permanent principles, to an oppressed and divided empire.

We have the honor to be, my Lord,

With great esteem, yr Lordship's

Faithful friends and fellow-subjects.

Signed by order of the Congress,

JOHN HANCOCK

*President.*

*Ordered,* That the above Letter be fairly transcribed, and signed by the president, and sent by Mr. Penn.

The Committee appointed to prepare a letter to Mr. Penn and the Colony Agents, brot. in the same, which being read was approved:

GENTLEMEN,

The perseverance of the British ministry in their unjust and cruel system of colony administration, has occasioned the meeting of another Congress.

We have again appealed to the justice of our sovereign for protection agst the destruction which his Ministers meditate for his American subjects. This Petition to his Majesty you will please, Gentlemen, to present to the King with all convenient expedition, after which we desire it may be given to the public. We likewise send you our second application to the equity and interest of our fellow subjects in G B, and also a Declaration setting forth the causes of our taking up arms: Both which we wish may be immediately put to press, and communicated as universally as possible.

The Congress entertain the highest sense of the wise and worthy interposition of the Lord Mayor and Livery of London, in favour of injured America. They have expressed this, their sense, in a letter to his Lordship and the livery, which we desire may be presented in the manner most agreeable to that respectable body.

You will oblige us, Gentlemen, by giving the most early information to the Congress, and to the speakers of our respective assemblies, of your proceeding in this business, and such further intelligence as you may judge to be of importance to America in this great contest.

We are, with great regard, gentlemen, Yr most obedient and very humble servts. By order of the Congress,

[JOHN HANCOCK,

*Pres.*]

*Ordered,* That the above be fairly transcribed, and to be signed by the prest, and then by him sent under cover, with the petition to the King, and address to the Inhabitants of G B, and letter to the Ld Mayor of London to R[ichard] Penn, Esqr. and to request him, in behalf of the Congress, to join with the Colony Agents in presenting the petition to the King.

Order of the day put off, and adjourned till Monday at 9 o'Clock.

## 21. CONGRESS APPEALS TO NATIVE AMERICANS, JULY 13, 1775

This speech was prepared for a meeting in Albany between the Six Nations and a congressional delegation. It was the second high-level meeting between the Six Nations and a multicolony delegation (and more were to come), the first occurring in 1754 at the Albany Congress. The Six Nations, or tribes, of the Iroquois Confederation—the Mohawk, Oneida, Onondaga, Cayuga, Tuscarora, and Seneca—was formed between 1570 and 1600 as a defensive alliance of five upstate New York tribes, with a sixth being added in 1722. On June 16, 1775, Congress chose five members to form a Committee for Indian Affairs and to recommend how best to preserve the friendship, or at least the neutrality, of northern Native American tribes. It was made up of Philip Schuyler, James Duane, and Philip Livingston, all of New York; Patrick Henry of Virginia; and James Wilson of Pennsylvania. On June 26, when the committee offered its recommendations, it was instructed to prepare a speech to deliver to the Six Nations. On July 13, the committee submitted its draft, which was approved that day.[50]

Congress next appointed commissioners for the Northern Indian Department: two wealthy Dutch landowners from New York, Major General Philip Schuyler and Volkert Douw; from Massachusetts, Turbot Francis and a well-connected radical lawyer, Joseph Hawley; and from Connecticut, a prominent lawyer, Oliver Wolcott. These men were to represent Congress in Albany and to present the speech. The conference began on August 25, 1775, with all the commissioners present except Hawley. The speech explains that the conflict between the colonies and Britain "is a family quarrel" and that because the "Indians are not concerned in it," they should "remain at home, and not join on either side."[51] They should consider carefully the consequences of taking part in the fighting, for "if the king's troops take away our property, and destroy us who are of the same blood with themselves, what can you, who are Indians, expect from them afterwards?" Not surprisingly, no mention is made of the colonists' dissatisfaction with the king's proclamation of 1763, in which he attempted to protect Native American hunting grounds and land claims from the same colonists warning them not to side with the British. The speech was first published by the Bradfords in the *Journals of Congress* before being reprinted on December 11, 1775, in the *Pennsylvania Packet*.[52]

In this revealing speech, Congress notes that when their "fathers crossed the great water and came over to this land, the king of England gave them a talk: assuring them that they and their children should be his children." The king's central role in the planting of colonies and his hierarchical relationship with the colonists are clearly indicated. The colonists are portrayed as being of one blood with the people of England, with whom they had remained one people until the present quarrel arose "betwixt the counsellors of king George," proud and wicked men, "and the inhabitants and colonies of America." The king's ministers were responsible for the colonists not knowing "whether they shall be permitted to eat, drink, and wear the fruits of their own labour and industry." The colonists, Congress explains, were committed to an intimate relationship with their English brethren and thus "have often asked them to love us and live in such friendship with us as their fathers did with ours," yet wondered "who hath shut the ears of the king to the cries of his children in America."

Continuing with the family metaphor, Congress compares the colonies to a son who has been being asked to carry an ever-heavier pack, suggesting that the Americans were being ground down by the tax burden imposed on them by British officials. Congress writes that "such a weight would crush him down and kill him." Although Congress' claims were utterly without foundation—by comparison with the British, the colonists were taxed remarkably little[53]—it is Congress' poignant explanation of the king's indifference that is of great interest for what it reveals. According to Congress, the son "entreats the father once more, though so faint he could only lisp out his last humble supplication—waits a while—no voice returns." But even so, the father is not really to blame: "The child concludes the father could not hear—those proud servants had intercepted his supplications, or stopped the ears of the father."

Much here is deeply revealing regarding colonists' seeing themselves as a son whose father favors his other son, that is, his English subjects. This romantic analogy, in an era when families were beginning to be seen in newly affectionate terms, in important but simple ways goes a long way toward explaining the colonial perspective.[54] That the king couldn't constitutionally intercede in Congress' behalf seems to be something that it never came to understand. Congress closes by explaining that "the king's wicked counsellors will not open their ears, and consider our just complaints," and so the colonists "do not take up the hatchet and struggle for honor and conquest; but to maintain our civil constitution and religious privileges, the very same for which our forefathers left their native land and came to this country." Again, from the colonists' perspective, they were not seeking a new government or an end to monarchy in the colonies, but only the restoration of the monarchical plan of government linked with legislative assemblies, which they had brought from England. It was Parliament, according to the colonists, that had sought to change the constitutional arrangement of the colonies.

## 21.1

 A Speech to the Six Confederate Nations

Worthington Chauncey Ford et al., eds., *Journals of the Continental Congress, 1774–1789* (Washington, D.C.: Government Printing Office, 1904–37), 2:178–83.

*A Speech to the Six Confederate Nations, Mohawks, Oneidas, Tuscaroras, Onondagas, Cayugas, Senekas, from the Twelve United Colonies, convened in Council at Philadelphia.*
Brothers, sachems, and warriors,

We, the Delegates from the Twelve United Provinces, viz. New Hampshire, Massachusetts Bay, Rhode Island, Connecticut, New York, New Jersey, Pennsylvania, the three lower counties of New Castle, Kent, and Sussex, on Delaware, Maryland, Virginia, North Carolina, and South Carolina, now sitting in general Congress at Philadelphia, send this talk to you our brothers. We are sixty-five in number, chosen and appointed by the people throughout all these provinces and colonies, to meet and sit together in one great council, to consult together for the common good of the land, and speak and act for them.

Brothers, in our consultation we have judged it proper and necessary to send you this talk, as we are upon the same island, that you may be informed of the reasons of this great council, the situation of our civil constitution, and our disposition towards you our Indian brothers of the Six Nations and their allies.

(*Three Strings, or a small Belt.*)

Brothers and friends, now attend,

When our fathers crossed the great water and came over to this land, the king of England gave them a talk: assuring them that they and their children should be his children, and that if they would leave their native country and make settlements, and live here, and buy, and sell, and trade with their brethren beyond the water, they should still keep hold of the same covenant chain and enjoy peace.—And it was covenanted, that the fields, houses, goods and possessions which our fathers should acquire, should remain to them as their own, and be their children's forever, and at their sole disposal.

Trusting that this covenant should never be broken, our fathers came a great distance beyond the great water, laid out their money here, built houses, cleared fields, raised crops, and through their own labour and industry grew tall and strong.

They have bought, sold and traded with England according to agreement, sending to them such things as they wanted, and taking in exchange such things as were wanted here.

The king of England and his people kept the way open for more than one hundred years, and by our trade became richer, and by a union with us, greater and stronger than the other kings and people who live beyond the water.

All this time they lived in great friendship with us, and we with them; for we are brothers—one blood.

Whenever they were struck, we instantly felt as though the blow had been given to us—their enemies were our enemies.

Whenever they went to war, we sent our men to stand by their side and fight for them, and our money to help them and make them strong.

They thanked us for our love, and sent us good talks, and renewed their promise to be one people forever.

BROTHERS AND FRIENDS, OPEN A KIND EAR!

We will now tell you of the quarrel betwixt the counsellors of king George and the inhabitants and colonies of America.

Many of his counsellors are proud and wicked men.—They persuade the king to break the covenant chain, and not to send us any more good talks. A considerable number have prevailed upon him to enter into a new covenant against us, and have torn asunder and cast behind their backs the good old covenant which their ancestors and ours entered into, and took strong hold of.

They now tell us they will slip their hand into our pocket without asking, as though it were there own; and at their pleasure they will take from us our charters or written civil constitution, which we love as our lives—also our plantations, our houses and goods whenever they please, without asking our leave.—That our vessels may go to this island in the sea, but to this or that particular island we shall not trade any more.—And in case of our non-compliance with these new orders, they shut up our harbours.

Brothers, this is our present situation—thus have many of the king's counsellors and servants dealt with us.—If we submit, or comply with their demands, you can easily perceive to what state we will be reduced.—If our people labour on the field, they will not know who shall enjoy the crop.—If they hunt in the woods, it will be uncertain who shall taste of the meat or have the skins.—If they build houses, they will not know whether they may sit round the fire, with their wives and children. They cannot be sure whether they shall be permitted to eat, drink, and wear the fruits of their own labour and industry.

BROTHERS AND FRIENDS OF THE SIX NATIONS, ATTEND,

We upon this island have often spoke and intreated the king and his servants the counsellors, that peace and harmony might still continue between us—that we cannot part with or lose our hold of the old covenant chain which united our fathers and theirs—that we want to brighten this chain—and keep the way open as our fathers did; that we want to live with them as brothers, labour, trade, travel abroad, eat and drink in peace. We have often asked them to love us and live in such friendship with us as their fathers did with ours.

We told them again that we judged we were exceedingly injured, that they might as well kill us, as take away our property and the necessaries of life.—We have asked why they treat us thus?—What has become of our repeated addresses and supplications to them? Who hath shut the ears of the king to the cries of his children in America? No soft answer—no pleasant voice from beyond the water has yet sounded in our ears.

Brothers, thus stands the matter betwixt old England and America. You Indians know how things are proportioned in a family—between the father and the son—the child carries a little pack—England we regard as the father—this island may be compared to the son.

The father has a numerous family—both at home and upon this island.—He appoints a great number of servants to assist him in the government of his family. In process of time, some of his servants grow proud and ill-natured—they were displeased to see the boy so alert and walk so nimbly with his pack. They tell the father, and advise him to enlarge the child's pack—they prevail—the pack is increased—the child takes it up again—as he thought it might be the father's pleasure—speaks but few words—those very small—for he was loth to offend the father. Those proud and wicked servants finding they had prevailed, laughed to see the boy sweat and stagger under his increased load. By and by, they apply to the father to double the boy's pack, because they heard him complain—and without any reason said they—he is a cross child—correct him if he complains any more.—The boy intreats the father—addresses the great servants in a decent manner, that the pack might be lightened—he could not go any farther—humbly asks, if the old fathers, in any of their records, had described such a pack for the child— after all the tears and entreaties of the child, the pack is redoubled—the child stands a little, while staggering under the weight—ready to fall every moment. However he entreats the father once more, though so faint he could only lisp out his last humble supplication—waits a while—no voice returns. The child concludes the father could not hear—those proud servants had intercepted his supplications, or stopped the ears of the father. He therefore gives one struggle and throws off the pack, and says he cannot take it up again—such a weight would crush him down and kill him—and he can but die if he refuses.

Upon this, those servants are very wroth—and tell the father many false stories respecting the child—they bring a great cudgel to the father, asking him to take it in his hand and strike the child.

This may serve to illustrate the present condition of the king's American subjects or children.

Amidst these oppressions we now and then hear a mollifying and reviving voice from some of the king's wise counsellors, who are our friends and feel for our distresses, when they heard our complaints and our cries, they applied to the king, also told those wicked servants, that this child in America was not a cross boy, it had sufficient reason for crying, and if the cause of its complaint was neglected, it would soon assume the voice of a man, plead for justice like a man, and defend its rights and support the old covenant chain of the fathers.

BROTHERS, LISTEN!

Notwithstanding all our entreaties, we have but little hope the king will send us any more good talks, by reason of his evil counsellors; they have persuaded him to send an army of soldiers and many ships of war, to rob and destroy us. They have shut up many of our harbours, seized and taken into possession many of our vessels: the soldiers have struck the blow, killed some of our people, the blood now runs of the American children: They have also burned our houses and towns, and taken much of our goods.

Brothers! We are now necessitated to rise, and forced to fight, or give up our civil constitution, run away and leave our farms and houses behind us. This must not be. Since the king's wicked counsellors will not open their ears, and consider our just complaints, and the cause of our weeping, and hath given the blow, we are determined to drive away the king's soldiers, and to kill and destroy all those wicked men we find in arms against the peace of the twelve United Colonies upon this island. We think our cause is just; therefore hope God will be on our side. We do not take up the hatchet and struggle for honor and conquest; but to maintain our civil constitution and religious privileges, the very same for which our forefathers left their native land and came to this country.

BROTHERS AND FRIENDS!

We desire you will hear and receive what we have now told you, and that you will open a good ear and listen to what we are now going to say. This is a family quarrel between us and Old England. You Indians are not concerned in it. We don't wish you to take up the hatchet against the king's troops. We desire you to remain at home, and not join on either side, but keep the hatchet buried deep. In the name and in behalf of all our people, we ask and desire you to love peace and maintain it, and to love and sympathise with us in our troubles; that the path may be kept open with all our people and yours, to pass and repass, without molestation.

Brothers! we live upon the same ground with you. The same island is our common birth-place. We desire to sit down under the same tree of peace with you: let us water its roots and cherish its growth, till the large leaves and flourishing branches shall extend to the setting sun, and reach the skies.

BROTHERS, OBSERVE WELL!

What is it we have asked of you? Nothing but peace, notwithstanding our present disturbed situation—and if application should be made to you by any of the king's unwise and wicked ministers to join on their side, we only advise you to deliberate, with great caution, and in your wisdom look forward to the consequences of a compliance. For, if the king's troops take away our property, and destroy us who are of the same blood with themselves, what can you, who are Indians, expect from them afterwards?

Therefore, we say, brothers, take care—hold fast to your covenant chain. You now know our disposition towards you, the Six Nations of Indians, and your allies. Let this our good talk remain at Onondaga, your central council house. We depend upon you to send and acquaint your allies to the northward, the seven tribes on the river St. Lawrence, that you have this talk of ours at the great council fire of the Six Nations. And when they return, we invite your great men to come and converse farther with us at Albany, where we intend to re-kindle the council fire, which your and our ancestors sat round in great friendship.

Brothers and Friends!

We greet you all farewell.

*(The large belt of intelligence and declaration.)*

BROTHERS!

We have said we wish you Indians may continue in peace with one another, and with us the white people. Let us both be cautious in our behaviour towards each other at this critical state of affairs. This island now trembles, the wind whistles from almost every quarter—let us fortify our minds and shut our ears against false rumors—let us be cautious what we receive for truth, unless spoken by wise and good men. If any thing disagreeable should ever fall out between us, the twelve United Colonies, and you, the Six Nations, to wound our peace, let us immediately seek measures for healing the breach. From the present situation of our affairs, we judge it wise and expedient to kindle up a small council fire at Albany, where we may hear each other's voice, and disclose our minds more fully to each other.

*(A small belt.)*

## 22. CONGRESS APPEALS TO THE IRISH, JULY 28, 1775

Britain's treatment of its Irish colony was, in important ways, similar to how it treated its American colonies (or, as commonly, plantations of settlers), and most of the imperial-constitutional issues that divided Americans and Parliament had embroiled the Irish (and some of the West Indian colonies) and the British Parliament in similar disputes.[55] It was not implausible, therefore, to think that the Irish would prove supportive of the colonists. Arthur Lee, from his perch in London, believing that the Irish could be won over to the American side, wrote Samuel Adams recommending that Congress amend the nonimportation agreement passed in the First Continental Congress (document 11.1) by excluding the Irish from it or, at the very least, providing the Irish with an apologetic explanation for including them in the ban.[56] Accordingly, on June 3, 1775, Congress chose James Duane (New York), William Livingston (New Jersey), and Samuel and John Adams (Massachusetts) to write to the people of Ireland. The committee members, apparently preoccupied with other matters, didn't bring in a draft until July 28; Congress debated and approved it on the same day.[57] The Bradfords published the address as a pamphlet, and on August 7, 1775, it appeared in the *Pennsylvania Packet*.[58]

In its address, Congress displays surprisingly little creativity and not much interest in working closely with a people who had suffered as badly as or worse than Americans had under British imperial rule.[59] Instead, Congress covered ground familiar from earlier declarations and petitions written for North American and British audiences. Before listing additional grievances, Congress explained its actions over the past ten months, in particular its banning of Irish products along with those of Great Britain: "It was with the utmost reluctance we could prevail upon ourselves, to cease our commercial connexion with your island. *Your* parliament had done us no wrong. *You* had ever been friendly to the rights of mankind; and we acknowledge, with pleasure and gratitude, that *your* nation has produced patriots, who have nobly distinguished themselves in the cause of humanity and America." The address then offers its fellow religious dissenters in Ireland, namely, Presbyterians, a vision of America as "a safe asylum from poverty, and, in time, from oppression also." When it returns to cataloguing its grievances, it reminds its Irish readers that "the whole country was, moreover, alarmed with the expected horrors of domestic insurrections." What Congress refers to here, as it did in many other documents, including the Declaration of Independence, and always in elliptical language, was the fear that the British would grant the colonists' African slaves their freedom so that they could fight against their former owners.

What is missing in the familiar litany of overwrought grievances, real and exaggerated, is any exploration of the commonalities between the experiences of American and Irish colonists, particularly regarding the British imperial hierarchy and the need for a newly envisioned imperial constitution. The American colonists seemed to have little interest in grouping themselves with the Irish, a conquered people with limited legal protections and rights, at least until 1783, when, following Britain's defeat in the War of Independence, Parliament surrendered the right to legislate for Ireland via the Renunciation Act.[60] Congress preferred to view its relation to Britain as analogous to that of Scotland and England before the joining of the two nations in 1707—that is, as two nations, after James I (James VI of Scotland) acceded to the throne of England in 1603, under a common monarch.[61]

A possible further indication that Congress was narrowly insistent on the equality only of American and British subjects was that it made little effort to raise the larger question of the equality of all the king's peoples, whether in North America, his dominions elsewhere, or Great Britain. In truth, only Joseph Galloway (see document 10.1) and Benjamin Franklin (see document 44.1) did so, and thus it is that lack of outreach here and elsewhere to other of the king's colonists (see documents 14.1 and 14.2) that is of interest in this otherwise pedestrian address. Only one mention here speaks, minimally, to such critical imperial issues: "We know that *you* are not without your grievances. We sympathize with you in your distress, and are pleased to find that the design of subjugating us, has persuaded [the] administration to dispense to Ireland, some vagrant rays of ministerial sunshine." Indeed, Parliament would abundantly do so, but only after the defeat of the British forces at Yorktown in 1781 and the subsequent negotiation of a peace treaty in 1782–83. Most critically, Parliament denied itself, via the Renunciation Act of 1783, the right to legislate for Ireland (though it could not bind future Parliaments); much the same was offered the American colonists by the Carlisle Peace Commission in 1778 (see document 47.1).

22.1

 AN ADDRESS OF THE TWELVE UNITED COLONIES
TO THE PEOPLE OF IRELAND

Worthington Chauncey Ford et al., eds., *Journals of the Continental Congress, 1774–1789* (Washington, D.C.: Government Printing Office, 1904–37), 2:212–18.

*To the people of Ireland. From the Delegates appointed by the United Colonies of New Hampshire, Massachusetts Bay, Rhode Island, and Providence Plantations, Connecticut, New York, New Jersey, Pennsylvania, the Lower Counties on Delaware, Maryland, Virginia, North Carolina, and South Carolina, in General Congress at Philadelphia, the 10th of May, 1775.*

FRIENDS AND FELLOW-SUBJECTS!

As the important contest, into which we have been driven, is now become interesting to every European state, and particularly affects the members of the British Empire, we think it our duty to address you on the subject. We are desirous, as is natural to injured innocence, of possessing the good opinion of the virtuous and humane. We are peculiarly desirous of furnishing *you* with a true state of our motives and objects; the better to enable you to judge of our conduct with accuracy, and determine the merits of the controversy with impartiality and precision.

However incredible it may appear, that, at this enlightned period, the leaders of a nation, which in every age has sacrificed hecatombs of her bravest patriots on the altar of liberty, should presume gravely to assert, and, by force of arms, attempt to establish an arbitrary sway over the lives, liberties, and property of their fellow subjects in America, it is, nevertheless, a most deplorable and indisputable truth.

These colonies have, from the time of their first settlement, for near two centuries, peaceably enjoyed those very rights, of which the Ministry have, for *ten* years past, endeavoured by fraud and by violence, to deprive them. At the conclusion of the last war, the genius of England and the spirit of wisdom, as if offended at the ungrateful treatment of their sons, withdrew from the British councils, and left that nation a prey to a race of ministers, with whom ancient English honesty and benevolence disdained to dwell. From that period, jealousy, discontent, oppression and discord have raged among all his Majesty's subjects; and filled every part of his dominions with distress and complaint.

Not content with our purchasing of Britain, at her own price, cloathing and a thousand other articles used by near three million of people on this vast Continent; not satisfied with the amazing profits arising from the monopoly of our trade, without giving us either time to breathe after a long, though glorious war, or the least credit for the blood and treasure we have expended in it; Notwithstanding the zeal we had manifested for the service of our Sovereign, and the warmest attachment to the constitution of Britain and the people of England, a black and horrid design was formed, to convert us from freemen into slaves, from subjects into vassals, and from friends into enemies.

Taxes, for the first time since we landed on the American shores, were, without our consent, imposed upon us; an unconstitutional edict to compel us to furnish necessaries for a standing army, that we wished to see disbanded, was issued; and the legislature of New York suspended for refusing to comply with it. Our antient and inestimable right of trial by jury was, in many instances, abolished; and the common law of the land made to give place to Admiralty jurisdictions. Judges were rendered, by the tenure of their commissions, entirely dependent on the will of a Minister. New crimes were arbitrarily created: and new courts, unknown to the constitution, instituted. Wicked and insidious Governors have been set over us; and dutiful petitions, for the removal of even the notoriously infamous Governor *Hutchinson,* were branded with the opprobrious appellation of scandalous and defamatory. Hardy attempts have been made, under colour of parliamentary authority, to seize Americans, and carry them to Great Britain to be tried for offences committed in the Colonies. Ancient charters have no longer remained sacred; that of the Massachusetts Bay was violated; and their form of government essentially mutilated and transformed. On pretence of punishing a violation of some private property, committed by a few disguised individuals, the populous and flourishing town of Boston was surrounded by fleets and armies; its trade destroyed; its port blocked up; and thirty thousand citizens subjected to all the miseries attending so sudden a convulsion in their commercial metropolis; and, to remove every obstacle to the rigorous execution of this system of oppression, an act of parliament was passed evidently calculated to indemnify those, who might, in the prosecution of it, even embrue their hands in the blood of the inhabitants.

Tho' pressed by such an accumulation of undeserved injuries, America still remembered her duty to her sovereign. A Congress, consisting of Deputies from Twelve United Colonies, assembled. They, in the most respectful terms, laid their grievances at the foot of the throne; and implored his Majesty's interposition in their behalf. They also agreed to suspend all trade with Great Britain, Ireland, and the West Indies; hopeing, by this peaceable mode of opposition, to obtain that justice from the British Ministry which had been so long solicited in vain. And here permit us to assure you, that it was with the utmost reluctance we could prevail upon ourselves, to cease our commercial connexion with your island. *Your* parliament had done us no wrong. *You* had ever been friendly to the rights of mankind; and we acknowledge, with pleasure and gratitude, that *your* nation has produced patriots, who have nobly distinguished themselves in the cause of humanity and America. On the other hand, we were not ignorant that the labor and manufactures of Ireland, like those of the silk-worm, were of little moment to herself; but served only to give luxury to those who *neither toil nor spin.* We perceived that if we continued our commerce with you, our agreement not to import from Britain would be *fruitless,* and were, therefore, compelled to adopt a measure, to which nothing but absolute necessity would have reconciled us. It gave us, however, some consolation to reflect, that should it occasion much distress, the fertile regions of America would afford you a safe assylum from poverty, and, in time, from oppression also; an assylum, in which many thousands of your countrymen have found hospitality, peace, and affluence, and become united to us by all the ties of consanguinity, mutual interest, and affection. Nor did the Congress stop here: Flattered by a pleasing expectation, that the justice and humanity which had so long characterized the English nation, would, on proper application, afford us relief, they represented their grievances in an affectionate address to their brethren in Britain, and intreated their aid and interposition in behalf of these colonies.

The more fully to evince their respect for their sovereign, the unhappy people of Boston were requested by the Congress to submit with patience to their fate; and all America united in a resolution to abstain from every species of violence. During this period, that devoted town suffered unspeakably. Its inhabitants were insulted and their property violated. Still relying on the clemency and justice of his Majesty and the nation, they permitted a few regiments to take possession of their town, to surround it with fortifications; and to cut off all intercourse between them and their friends in the country.

With anxious expectation did all America wait the event of their petition. All America laments its fate. Their Prince was deaf to their complaints: And vain were all attempts to impress him with a sense of the sufferings of his American subjects, of the cruelty of their *Task Masters,* and of the *many Plagues* which impended over his dominions. Instead of directions for a candid enquiry into our grievances, insult was added to oppression; and our long forbearance rewarded with the imputation of cowardice. Our trade with foreign states was prohibited; and an act of Parliament passed to prevent our even fishing on our own coasts. Our peaceable Assemblies, for the purpose of consulting the common safety, were declared seditious; and our asserting the very rights which placed the Crown of Great Britain on the heads of the three successive Princes of the House of Hanover, stiled rebellion. Orders were given to reinforce the troops in America. The wild and barbarous savages of the wilderness have been solicited, by gifts, to take up the hatchet against us; and instigated to deludge our settlements with the blood of innocent and defenceless women and children. The whole country was, moreover, alarmed with the expected horrors of domestic insurrections. Refinements in parental cruelty, at which the genius of Britain must blush! Refinements which admit not of being even recited without horror, or practised without infamy! We should be happy, were these dark machinations the mere suggestions of suspicion. We are sorry to declare, that we are possessed of the most authentic and indubitable evidence of their reality.

The Ministry, bent on pulling down the pillars of the constitution, endeavoured to erect the standard of despotism in America; and if successful, Britain and Ireland may shudder at the consequences!

Three of their most experienced Generals are sent to wage war with their fellow-subjects: and *America* is amazed to find the name of *Howe* in the catalogue of her enemies: She loved his brother.

Despairing of driving the Colonists to resistance by any other means than actual hostility, a detachment of the army at Boston marched into the country in all the array of war; and, unprovoked, fired upon, and killed several of the inhabitants. The neighbouring farmers suddenly assembled, and repelled the attack. From this, all communication between the town and country was intercepted. The citizens petitioned the General for permission to leave the town, and he promised, on surrendering their arms, to permit them to depart with their other effects. They accordingly surrendered their arms, and the General violated his faith. Under various pretences, passports were delayed and denied; and many thousands of the inhabitants are, at this day, confined in the town, in the utmost wretchedness and want. The lame, the blind, and the sick, have indeed, been turned out into the neighbouring fields; and some, eluding the vigilance of the centries, have escaped from the town, by swimming to the adjacent shores.

The war having thus began on the part of General Gage's troops, the country armed and embodied. The re-inforcements from Ireland soon after arrived; a vigorous attack was then made upon the provincials. In their march, the troops surrounded the town of Charlestown, consisting of about four hundred houses, then recently abandoned to escape the fury of a relentless soldiery. Having plundered the houses, they set fire to the town, and reduced it to ashes. To this wanton waste of property, unknown to civilized nations, they were prompted the better to conceal their approach under cover of the smoak. A shocking mixture of cowardice and cruelty, which then first tarnished the lustre of the British arms, when aimed at a brother's breast! But, blessed be God, they were restrained from committing further ravages, by the loss of a very considerable part of their army, including many of their most experienced officers. The loss of the inhabitants was inconsiderable.

Compelled, therefore, to behold thousands of our Countrymen imprisoned, and men, women and children involved in promiscuous and unmerited misery! When we find all faith at an end, and sacred treaties turned into tricks of state; When we perceive our friends and kinsmen massacred, our habitations plundred, our houses in flames, and their once happy inhabitants fed only by the hand of charity; Who can blame us for endeavouring to restrain the progress of desolation! Who can censure our repeling the attacks of such a barbarous band! Who, in such circumstances, would not obey the great, the universal, the divine law of self-preservation?

Though vilified as wanting spirit, we are determined to behave like men. Though insulted and abused, we wish for reconciliation. Though defamed as seditious, we are ready to obey the laws. And though charged with rebellion, will cheerfully bleed in defence of our Sovereign in a righteous cause. What more can we say? What more can we offer?

But we forbear to trouble you with a tedious detail of the various and fruitless offers and applications we have repeatedly made, not for pensions, for wealth, or for honors, but for the humble boon of being permitted to possess the fruits of honest industry, and to enjoy that degree of Liberty, to which God and the Constitution have given us an undoubted right.

Blessed with an indissoluble union, with a variety of internal resources, and with a firm reliance on the justice of the Supreme Disposer of all human events, we have no doubt of rising superior to all the machinations of evil and abandoned Ministers. We already anticipate the golden period, when liberty, with all the gentle arts of peace and humanity, shall establish her mild dominion in this western world, and erect eternal monuments to the memory of those virtuous patriots and martyrs, who shall have fought and bled and suffered in her cause.

Accept our most grateful acknowledgments for the friendly disposition you have always shewn towards us. We know that *you* are not without your grievances. We sympathize with you in your distress, and are pleased to find that the design of subjugating us, has persuaded administration to dispense to Ireland, some vagrant rays of ministerial sunshine. Even the tender mercies of government have long been cruel towards *you*. In the rich pastures of Ireland, many hungry parricides have fed, and grown strong to labour in its destruction. We hope the patient abiding of the meek may not always be forgotten; and God grant that the iniquitous schemes of extirpating liberty from the British empire may be soon defeated. But we should be wanting to ourselves—we should be perfidious to posterity—we should be unworthy that ancestry from which we derive our descent, should we submit, with folded arms, to military butchery and depredation, to gratify the lordly ambition, or sate the avarice of a British Ministry. In defence of our persons and properties, under actual violation, we have taken up arms; When that violence shall be removed, and hostilities cease on the part of the aggressors, they shall cease on our part also. For the atchievement of this happy event, we confide in the good offices of our fellow-subjects beyond the Atlantic. Of their friendly disposition, we do not yet despond; aware, as they must be, that they have nothing more to expect from the same common enemy, than the humble favour of being last devoured.

By order of the Congress,

JOHN HANCOCK *President*

Philadelphia, July 28, 1775.

### 23. CONGRESS REJECTS PARLIAMENT'S PEACE OVERTURES, JULY 1775

On February 20, 1775, Lord North, the first minister of the British government from 1770 to 1782, put forward for Parliament's consideration an offer of peace and reconciliation to be extended to the colonies. Though it was adopted by the House on February 27 by a vote of 274–88, support among the friends of his administration was tepid.[62] This proposal was Parliament's only gesture toward peace and reconciliation extended to the colonists before they declared independence in 1776 (another proposal arrived a week or so following passage of the Declaration, and another two years later). Certain of its parliamentary supporters may have hoped that, as proved to be the case, Congress would find it inadequate. Some have speculated that North's underlying intent was to split parliamentary opposition so that his administration could more easily move additional coercive legislation, in particular those acts of March and April 1775 that restrained the colonies' trade (see document 18.3).[63] North had been a supporter of the Stamp Act and the Townshend duties, but in April 1770 had repealed all the latter except the tax on tea. His actions, up to his introduction of this proposal, had consistently defended the supremacy of Parliament, but that record doesn't preclude his having acted here in good faith, in particular because the proposal met the most important of the colonists' long-standing concerns: the promise that Parliament would no longer levy taxes on the colonists.[64]

After the proposal was approved on February 27, 1775, Lord Dartmouth, North's stepbrother and secretary of state for the American colonies, sent it on March 3 to the colonial governors to submit to their legislative assemblies for consideration. William Franklin submitted North's proposal on May 20 to the New Jersey Assembly, which resolved to bring the matter before Congress.[65] (Franklin, the natural son and well-traveled companion of his world-renowned father, was appointed royal governor of New Jersey in 1762; unlike his father, he remained loyal to the king.) After receiving similar requests from New Jersey, Pennsylvania, and Virginia, Congress decided to consider the matter, but not immediately. It did not appoint a committee to report on the proposal until midsummer and did not approve its recommendations until July 31, a day before it adjourned. By that time, the Virginia House of Burgesses had, on June 12, already rejected it. Thomas Jefferson, who had written Virginia's response to North's proposal, soon afterward took his seat in Congress.[66] In some ways, his arrival there, along with the increasingly bloody nature of the conflict and the imposition at about the same time of stringent commercial bans by both sides, coincided with a changed sense in Congress in which moderate voices began to lose influence.

On July 22, Congress appointed a radical committee made up of Benjamin Franklin, Thomas Jefferson, John Adams, and Richard Henry Lee to write a report on North's proposal.[67] All of them were known by their colleagues to be strongly opposed to any accommodation of parliamentary intrusion into the internal regulation of the colonies, so their appointment strongly suggests that less than a majority in Congress wished to see the proposal given serious consideration. Jefferson, in drafting Congress' report and participating in the writing of another document during his first five weeks in Congress (see document 18.1), began his career as Congress' new preeminent penman in a grand style. The committee submitted its draft report on July 25, 1775; on July 31 it was debated in Congress and, with small revisions, approved. The report was first published in the *Pennsylvania Packet* on August 7, 1775.[68]

The report begins by objecting to Parliament's role in raising taxes, something no "body of men, extraneous to their constitution" should be able to do. Congress then, as it had done nine months earlier (see document 12.1), again raised concerns regarding the king's prerogative: "This privilege of giving or of withholding our monies, is an important barrier against the undue exertion of prerogative, which, if left altogether without controul, may be exercised to our great oppression." Indeed, no member of Parliament would have objected to that statement. For more than a decade (or longer), Whigs in Parliament and radicals outside it had been fighting to defend Parliament's control over potentially arbitrary monarchical prerogative.[69] Even though this concern was advanced in an earlier congressional state paper, its return to prominence suggests a number of possibilities: the continuing confusion among the colonists of the fundamentals of their own position, a changing view of Congress' relationship to the Crown, or the new preeminence of Jefferson, with his critical perspective on the king and the king's role in the imperial relationship between the colonies and Britain.[70] Given the possibly changing character of the Second Continental Congress' defense of its rights—which almost wholly rests on English and British precedents in the state papers of the Stamp Act Congress and the First Continental Congress but then veers more and more to references to natural rights in the papers of this Congress (see documents 16.1, 16.2, 20.1, and 22.1)—a renewed focus on monarchical prerogative may suggest a shifting focus, if only the beginning of one, toward the king and monarchy itself as eventual targets.

As had been hinted at in 1764, and argued earlier in the month in Congress' address to the people of Great Britain, and even more directly in Franklin's unpublished vindication (see documents 2.1, 20.1, and 23.4), Congress found it doubly unacceptable that the North American "colonies should be required to oblige themselves to other contributions, while Great Britain possesses a monopoly of their trade. . . . If we are to contribute equally with other parts of the empire, let us equally with them enjoy free commerce with the whole world"—either taxation or commercial regulation was acceptable, but not both. Similarly unacceptable to Congress was that Parliament had failed to renounce "the pretended right to tax us" and its right, claimed in 1766, "of legislating for us themselves in all cases whatsoever." The focus in both instances was less on practice than on Parliament's claimed rights. Parliament, at the end of the year, in the American Prohibitory Act (see document 29.2) did much that the report asks here, though the offer was accompanied by deeply offensive threats. Three years later in its instructions to the Carlisle Peace Commission (see document 47.1), Parliament renewed its offer to cease legislating for the colonies—yet even then it did not limit its claimed "right" to do so, and again made its offer alongside a none too subtle threat of total war.

Like other overtures made by Parliament during its history of difficulties with the colonies, North's peace proposal offered the colonists more or less what they had sought for a decade since the imposition of the Sugar and Stamp Acts of 1764–65. Specifically, Parliament agreed that the individual colonial assemblies would be permitted to raise taxes under their own direction and that Parliament would "forbear in respect of such province or colony, to lay any duty, tax, or assessment, or to impose any farther duty, tax, or assessment, except only such duties as it may be expedient to continue to levy or impose, for the regulation of commerce." But those concessions were no longer sufficient, for Congress demanded that Parliament surrender its right to tax and to pass legislation touching the internal life of the colonies; that issue too went back to 1764 (see documents 3.1–3.3). Accordingly, Congress could not accept the proposal's holding that colonial contributions for "the common defence" would be regulated by Parliament or, still more, that colonial "support of the civil government, and the administration of justice in such province or colony" would have to be approved by the king and, far more objectionably, both "Houses of Parliament." The standard of what was acceptable had moved, and the tone of the report reflects this.

Another long-standing issue referred to in North's proposal was the possible creation of a civil list in the colonies, that is, a secure payment schedule for imperial administrators, which would free them from colonial assemblies' threats to cut their annual salaries unless they acted in ways agreeable to the legislature. Congress responded to Parliament's imprecise language—for there is no clear insistence on a civil list in the proposal—with a firm rejection: "We do not mean that our people shall be burthened with oppressive taxes, to provide sinecures for the idle or the wicked, under colour of providing for a civil list. While parliament pursue their plan of civil government within their own jurisdiction, we also hope to pursue ours without molestation." Congress defensively denied Parliament's reasonable request that the colonial legislatures, as they had always done, "make provisions also, for the support of the civil government"—not for the creation of a civil list. (Congress responded similarly to other of its mistaken assumptions about the proposal.) Colonial support for imperial administrators had become a preeminent issue in 1767, with the Townshend Acts' planned use of tax receipts raised in the colonies. But North's conciliatory proposal was not unreasonable in its suggestion regarding the support of civil government; indeed, Parliament was "prepared to accept that the colonies would contribute less than ten per cent of the sums raised in Britain."[71] Nonetheless, after the Townshend Acts had deeply eroded the colonists' trust, they demanded some kind of constitutional guarantee of their right to tax themselves and to govern their internal affairs free from Parliamentary intrusion.

Congress now demanded that Parliament renounce "the pretended right to tax us," that is, repeal the Declaratory Act, by renouncing "the power of suspending our own legislatures, and of legislating for us themselves in all cases whatsoever." But even that wouldn't have satisfied the Second Continental Congress, for it demanded as well that Parliament rescind all the offensive parliamentary legislation passed, on and off, since 1764. In fact, even though all the old issues of parliamentary-imposed legislation, taxation, commercial regulation, and denial of jury trials were essential ones, Congress found now that the constitutional impasse had gone beyond even those: "what is more important" than property, no matter how important it is, and "what in this proposal they [the British] keep out of sight, as if no such point was now in contest between us," are that Parliament claims "a right to alter our charters and established laws, and leave us without, any security for our lives or liberties," the true ends of property. From the colonists' perspective, when another people can legislate for you, nothing of yours can properly be viewed as secure. Ameliorating that threat demanded a change not just to Parliament's practices but also to the imperial constitution and, as importantly, to its claimed rights.

A final matter of significance in this pivotal document is Congress' asking that the world not be deceived into believing "that there was nothing in dispute between us but the *mode* of levying taxes; and that the parliament having now been so good as to give up this, the colonies are unreasonable if not perfectly satisfied." The report makes clear that taxation was no longer a divisive issue, but that shaping international opinion had become essential to the colonies; it insists, moreover, that the world reflect on a long list of ways in which the Americans had been mistreated and that it not "be deceived into an opinion that we are unreasonable" or "hesitate to believe with us, that nothing but our own exertions may defeat the ministerial sentence of death or abject submission." With Jefferson being asked to wield Congress' pen, the nature and direction of the debate changed, and began moving toward the ultimate end.

23.1

 ## Report on Lord North's Peace Proposal, July 31, 1775

Worthington Chauncey Ford et al., eds., *Journals of the Continental Congress, 1774–1789* (Washington, D.C.: Government Printing Office, 1904–37), 2:224–34. *Delenda est Carthago* ("Carthage must be destroyed") were the concluding words of every speech made in the Roman Senate by Cato the Elder (234–149 BC).

MONDAY, JULY 31, 1775

Met according to adjournment.

The Congress took into consideration the report of the committee on the resolve of the house of Commons, and the same being debated by paragraphs, was agreed to as follows:

here insert it

The several Assemblies of New Jersey, Pennsylvania, and Virginia, having referred to the Congress a resolution of the House of Commons of Great Britain, which resolution is in these words:

*Lunæ, 20° Die Feb. 1775.*

*The House in a Committee on the American papers. Motion made, and question proposed:*

*That it is the opinion of this Committee, that when the General Council and Assembly, or General Court of any of his Majesty's provinces, or colonies in America, shall propose to make provision, according to the condition, circumstance, or situation of such province or colony, for contributing their proportion to the common defence (such proportion to be raised under the authority of the General Court, or General Assembly of such province or colony, and disposable by Parliament) and shall engage to make provision also, for the support of the civil government, and the administration of justice in such province or colony, it will be proper, if such proposal shall be approved by his Majesty, and the two Houses of Parliament, and for so long as such provision shall be made accordingly, to forbear in respect of such province or colony, to lay any duty, tax, or assessment, or to impose any farther duty, tax, or assessment, except only such duties as it may be expedient to continue to levy or impose, for the regulation of commerce; the net produce or the duties last mentioned to be carried to the account of such province or colony respectively.*

### Report on Lord North's Motion

The Congress took the said resolution into consideration, and are thereupon, of opinion,

That the colonies of America are entitled to the sole and exclusive privilege of giving and granting their own money: that this involves a right of deliberating whether they will make any gift, for what purposes it shall be made, and what shall be its amount; and that it is a high breach of this privilege for any body of men, extraneous to their constitutions, to prescribe the purposes for which money shall be levied on them, to take to themselves the authority of judging of their conditions, circumstances, and situations, and of determining the amount of the contribution to be levied.

That as the colonies possess a right of appropriating their gifts, so are they entitled at all times to enquire into their application, to see that they be not wasted among the venal and corrupt for the purpose of undermining the civil rights of the givers, nor yet be diverted to the support of standing armies, inconsistent with their freedom and subversive of their quiet. To propose, therefore, as this resolution does, that the monies given by the colonies shall be subject to the disposal of parliament alone, is to propose that they shall relinquish this right of inquiry, and put it in the power of others to render their gifts ruinous, in proportion as they are liberal.

That this privilege of giving or of withholding our monies, is an important barrier against the undue exertion of prerogative, which, if left altogether without controul, may be exercised to our great oppression; and all history shews how efficacious is its intercession for redress of grievances and re-establishment of rights, and how improvident it would be to part with so powerful a mediator.

We are of opinion that the proposition contained in this resolution is unreasonable and insidious: Unreasonable, because, if we declare we accede to it, we declare, without reservation, we will purchase the favor of parliament, not knowing at the same time at what price they will please to estimate their favor; it is insidious, because, individual colonies, having bid and bidden again, till they find the avidity of the seller too great for all their powers to satisfy; are then to return into opposition, divided from their sister colonies whom the minister will have previously detached by a grant of easier terms, or by an artful procrastination of a definitive answer.

That the suspension of the exercise of their pretended power of taxation being expressly made commensurate with the continuance of our gifts, these must be perpetual to make that so. Whereas no experience has shewn that a gift of perpetual revenue secures a perpetual return of duty or of kind disposition. On the contrary, the parliament itself, wisely attentive to this observation, are in the established practice of granting their supplies from year to year only.

Desirous and determined, as we are, to consider, in the most dispassionate view, every seeming advance towards a reconciliation made by the British parliament, let our brethren of Britain reflect, what would have been the sacrifice to men of free spirits, had even fair terms been proffered, as these insidious proposals were with circumstances of insult and defiance. A proposition to give our money, accompanied with large fleets and armies, seems addressed to our fears rather than to our freedom. With what patience would Britons have received articles of treaty from any power on earth when borne on the point of the bayonet by military plenipotentiaries?

We think the attempt unnecessary to raise upon us by force or by threats, our proportional contributions to the common defence, when all know, and themselves acknowledge, we have fully contributed, whenever called upon to do so in the character of freemen.

We are of opinion it is not just that the colonies should be required to oblige themselves to other contributions, while Great Britain possesses a monopoly of their trade. This of itself lays them under heavy contribution. To demand, therefore, additional aids in the form of a tax, is to demand the double of their equal proportion: if we are to contribute equally with the other parts of the empire, let us equally with them enjoy free commerce with the whole world. But while the restrictions on our trade shut to us the resources of wealth, is it just we should bear all other burthens equally with those to whom every resource is open?

We conceive that the British parliament has no right to intermeddle with our provisions for the support of civil government, or administration of justice. The provisions we have made, are such as please ourselves, and are agreeable to our own circumstances: they answer the substantial purposes of government and of justice, and other purposes than these should not be answered. We do not mean that our people shall be burthened with oppressive taxes, to provide sinecures for the idle or the wicked, under colour of providing for a civil list. While parliament pursue their plan of civil government within their own jurisdiction, we also hope to pursue ours without molestation.

We are of opinion the proposition is altogether unsatisfactory, because it imports only a suspension of the mode, not a renunciation of the pretended right to tax us: because, too, it does not propose to repeal the several Acts of Parliament passed for the purposes of restraining the trade, and altering the form of government of one of our colonies: extending the boundaries and changing the government of Quebec; enlarging the jurisdiction of the courts of Admiralty and vice-Admiralty; taking from us the rights of trial by a jury of the vicinage, in cases affecting both life and property; transporting us into other countries to be tried for criminal offences; exempting, by mock-trial, the murderers of colonists from punishment; and quartering soldiers on us in times of profound peace. Nor do they renounce the power of suspending our own legislatures, and of legislating for us themselves in all cases whatsoever. On the contrary, to shew they mean no discontinuance of injury, they pass acts, at the very time of holding out this proposition, for restraining the commerce and fisheries of the provinces of New England, and for interdicting the trade of other colonies with all foreign nations, and with each other. This proves, unequivocally, they mean not to relinquish the exercise of indiscriminate legislation over us.

Upon the whole, this proposition seems to have been held up to the world, to deceive it into a belief that there was nothing in dispute between us but the *mode* of levying taxes; and that the parliament having now been so good as to give up this, the colonies are unreasonable if not perfectly satisfied: Whereas, in truth, our adversaries still claim a right of demanding *ad libitum,* and of taxing us themselves to the full amount of their demand, if we do not comply with it. This leaves us without any thing we can call property. But, what is of more importance, and what in this proposal they keep out of sight, as if no such point was now in contest between us, they claim a right to alter our charters and established laws, and leave us without any security for our lives or liberties. The proposition seems also to have been calculated more particularly to lull into fatal security, our well-affected fellow subjects on the other side the water, till time should be given for the operation of those arms, which a British minister pronounced would instantaneously reduce the "cowardly" sons of America to unreserved submission. But, when the world reflects how inadequate to justice are these vaunted terms; when it attends to the rapid and bold succession of injuries, which, during the course of eleven years, have been aimed at these colonies; when it reviews the pacific and respectful expostulations, which, during that whole time, were the sole arms we opposed to them; when it observes that our complaints were either not heard at all, or were answered with new and accumulated injury; when it recollects that the minister himself, on an early occasion, declared "that he would never treat with America, till he had brought her to his feet," and that an avowed partisan of ministry has more lately denounced against us the dreadful sentence, "*delenda est Carthago;*" that this was done in the presence of a British senate, and being unreproved by them, must be taken to be their own sentiment, (especially as the purpose has already in part been carried into execution, by their treatment of Boston and burning of Charles-Town;) when it considers the great armaments with which they have invaded us, and the circumstances of cruelty with which these have commenced and prosecuted hostilities; when these things, we say, are laid together and attentively considered, can the world be deceived into an opinion that we are unreasonable, or can it hesitate to believe with us, that nothing but our own exertions may defeat the ministerial sentence of death or abject submission.

*By order of the* C<small>ONGRESS</small>,
John Hancock,
P<small>RESIDENT</small>
*Philadelphia, July 31, 1775.*

## 23.2

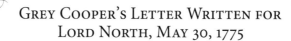

GREY COOPER'S LETTER WRITTEN FOR
LORD NORTH, MAY 30, 1775

Grey (spelled in this document "Gray") Cooper was a loyal British civil servant who served the Rockingham, Grafton, and North administrations as an undersecretary of the treasury. This letter, believed to have been written at the behest of the first minister, Lord North, whose peace proposal was under discussion, was delivered to Thomas Willing, one of the most successful merchants in the colonies and the business partner of Robert Morris. He voted against independence before dropping out of public life for the duration of much of the Revolutionary War. In 1781, though, he became the first president of the Bank of North America. In the letter, Cooper (or North) assures Congress "that these terms are honourable for Great Britain, and safe for the colonies . . . that if the colonies are not blinded by faction, these terms will remove every grievance relative to taxation, and be the basis of a compact between the colonies, and the mother country." Cooper emphasizes that the outstanding taxation issue could, in practice, be resolved by North's proposal and, additionally, that Parliament viewed the acceptance of the proposal as the starting point of a more permanent constitutional arrangement between the colonies and Britain—potentially meeting another of Congress' outstanding and still more difficult to resolve demands. The world in the summer of 1775, though, was a different one from that in the fall of 1774.

After the conciliatory words, Cooper warns the colonies that it would be very much in their best interest to approve North's offer because the British "are perfectly united in opinion and determined to pursue the most effectual measures, and to use the whole force of the Kingdom, if it be found necessary, to reduce the rebellious and refractory provinces and colonies." The British people, as proved true, would even "bear the temporary distresses of a stoppage of the American trade" to achieve that end. Ironically, it was the consensus that the British government should coerce the colonists into obedience—if North's largely reasonable proposal were rejected—that led the Americans to do what the British public and government most feared and against which they would fight so hard and tragically. The unwillingness of Britain to offer truly constitutional concessions to the colonies led to their breaking away and to Britain's (mistaken) fear of losing valuable commercial advantages.[72]

Worthington Chauncey Ford et al., eds., *Journals of the Continental Congress, 1774–1789* (Washington, D.C.: Government Printing Office, 1904–37), 2:71–72.

TUESDAY, MAY 30, 1775

The Congress met according to adjournment.

Mr. [Thomas] Willing, one of the delegates for Pennsylvania, informed the Congress, that a gentleman was just arrived from London, who had brought with him a paper, which he says he recd from Lord North, and which was written, at the desire of his Lordship, by Mr. Gray Cooper, Under-Secy of the Treasury; and he understood it to be his Lordship's desire that it shod be communicated to the Congress. He had for that purpose put it into his hands. Mr. Willing observed, that he had shewn the paper to Dr. Franklin, who was well acquainted with the hand writing of Mr. Cooper, and that he verily believed the paper brought by the gentleman was written by Mr. Cooper.

The paper being read is as follows:

That it is earnestly hoped by all the real friends of the Americans, that the terms expressed in the resolution of the 20th of February last, will be accepted by all the colonies, who have the least affection for their King and country, or a just sense of their own interest.

That these terms are honourable for Great Britain, and safe for the colonies.

That if the colonies are not blinded by faction, these terms will remove every grievance relative to taxation, and be the basis of a compact between the colonies, and the mother country.

That the people in America ought, on every consideration to be satisfied with them.

That no further relaxation can be admitted.

The temper and spirit of the Nation are so much against concessions, that if it were the intention of administration, they could not carry the Question.

But administration have no such intention, as they are fully and firmly persuaded, that further concessions would be injurious to the colonies as well as to Great-Britain.

That there is not the least probability of a change of administration.

That they are perfectly united in opinion and determined to pursue the most effectual measures, and to use the whole force of the Kingdom, if it be found necessary, to reduce the rebellious and refractory provinces and colonies.

There is so great a spirit in the nation against the Congress, that the people will bear the temporary distresses of a stoppage of the American trade.

They may depend on this to be true.

‖*Ordered,* To lie on the table.‖

23.3

 THE EARL OF CHATHAM, BILL FOR SETTLING
THE TROUBLES IN AMERICA, FEBRUARY 1, 1775

William Pitt the elder, a colossus of eighteenth-century British politics, was the
minister most directly responsible for the British military successes that led to
Britain's worldwide preeminence at the end of the Seven Years' War. As Lord
Chatham (from 1766), and though no longer head of the British government (after
1768), he remained a leading member of Parliament and opponent of Parliament's
claimed right to tax the colonies and to send British troops to coerce the colonists
into submission.[73] Accordingly, a day after the First Continental Congress' late-
October Bill of Rights and first petition to the king were laid before Parliament on
January 19, 1775, Chatham "moved an address from the Lords to the king requesting
immediate removal of troops in Boston but was defeated by a 3–1 margin."[74] A few
weeks later he introduced his plan for settling the troubles in America. In it,
Chatham declared "that the Colonies of America have been, are, and of right ought
to be, dependent upon the Imperial Crown of Great-Britain, and subordinate unto
the British Parliament" and that Parliament has the "full power and authority to
make laws and statutes of sufficient force and validity to bind the people of the
British Colonies in America, in all matters touching the general weal of the whole
dominion of the Imperial Crown of Great Britain." Like almost all members of
Parliament, including such friends of the colonies as Rockingham and Burke,
Chatham and his followers were committed imperialists who refused, along with
North in his peace proposal, to question parliamentary supremacy over the empire.

Similarly, Chatham argued that the right to send the army anywhere in the
empire for legitimate purposes belonged without reserve to Parliament and that such
power "cannot be rendered dependent upon the consent of a Provincial Assembly in
the Colonies." And like North in his conciliatory proposal, Chatham insisted that
Congress recognize "the supreme legislative authority and superintending power of
the Parliament" over the colonies, and that congressional requisitions to the king
and his ministers be "subject to the disposition of the British Parliament" (see
document 7.1, Benjamin Franklin's testimony before the House of Commons).

Like almost every member of Parliament, Chatham adhered to the powerful Whig
ideology that placed Parliament in a position of supremacy over the Crown and the
colonies. That superiority, along with the commercial advantages that followed from
it, dissuaded members from questioning their right to legislate for the dominions—
even if in so doing they awkwardly denied colonists the concomitant British right of
self-government.[75] Chatham's proposed bill abandons Parliament's claimed right to
tax the colonies: "No tallage, tax, or other charge for his Majesty's revenue, shall be

commanded or levied, from British freemen in America, without common consent, by act of Provincial Assembly." That same bit of parliamentary renunciation was intentionally left out of the Declaratory Act (1766; document 8.2), but appeared in Galloway's "Plan of Union" (1774; document 10.1), North's peace proposal (1775; see document 23.1), the Howe's peace commission (1776; see documents 35.1 and 36.1), and the Carlisle peace commission (1778; see document 47.1). Chatham even urged that a putatively illegal body, Congress, be recognized as an official legislative body for the colonies and, as such, be permitted to manage colonial taxation.

In the most direct sense, parliamentary taxation from this point forward was no longer an issue dividing the colonies and Parliament.[76] And unlike North's relatively limited conciliatory proposal, Chatham's bill would have gone further in meeting most, though not all, of Congress' concerns (with the central constitutional question remaining unaddressed and unresolved). The bill would have ended all judicial irregularities in the colonies by, most importantly, returning admiralty courts to "their ancient limits" and by restoring "the Trial by Jury, in all civil cases, where the same may be abolished." Additionally, the bill would have, as Congress insisted, repealed all the Coercive Acts. Finally, it met even longer-standing colonial executive grievances concerning the appointment of judges and the status of provincial charters, making the former removable only for misconduct (rather than at will) and the latter safe from revocation except on "legal grounds of forfeiture," with cause needing to be proved in court. Despite being supported by "longtime allies Camden and Shelburne," and Rockingham as well, the bill failed to pass, by a nearly two-to-one margin.[77] Moreover, by July 1775 it doubtless would have proved unacceptable to the newly intransigent Congress, which seems likely to have demanded that Parliament "specifically abandon the Declaratory Act." Chatham had failed to recognize that for "the colonists the real issue was . . . [no longer] taxation but *sovereignty*";[78] in this, of course, he was not alone. In sum, "those areas of local autonomy, as laid down by Chatham, were too large to be approved in Great Britain and too small to satisfy American leaders."[79]

When describing the necessity of his proposed legislation, Chatham "offered it as a *basis* for averting the dangers which now threatened the British Empire," and insisted that acting as expeditiously as possible was necessary so that reconciliation could be achieved.[80] Knowing how thinly the British military forces were spread around the world, he understood that a war with the American colonies, supported as they likely would be by France and Spain (and eventually were by Holland and Russia too), would be more difficult to wage than was often assumed in an already overextended and deeply indebted Britain.[81] His concerns proved prescient. Nonetheless, the Earl of Sandwich led the charge against Chatham's bill, and the Duke of Grafton, the Earl of Gower, and the Earl of Hillsborough joined them in defeating it.[82]

Max Beloff, ed., *The Debate on the American Revolution, 1761–1785* (Dobbs Ferry, N.Y.: Sheridan House, 1989), 195–202. Paragraph breaks have been added for ease of reading.

WHEREAS by an act 6 Geo. III it is declared, that Parliament has full power and authority to make laws and statutes to bind the people of the Colonies, in all cases whatsoever; and whereas reiterated complaints and most dangerous disorders have grown, touching the right of taxation claimed and exercised over America, to the disturbance of peace and good order there, and to the actual interruption of the due intercourse from Great Britain and Ireland to the Colonies, deeply affecting the navigation, trade, and manufactures of this kingdom and of Ireland, and announcing farther an interruption of all exports from the said Colonies to Great Britain, Ireland, and the British Islands in America: Now, for prevention of these ruinous mischiefs, and in order to an equitable, honourable, and lasting settlement of claims not sufficiently ascertained and curcumscribed, May it please your most Excellent Majesty, that it may be declared, and be it declared by the King's most Excellent Majesty, by and with the advice and consent of the Lords Spiritual and Temporal and Commons in this present Parliament assembled, and by the authority of the same, that the Colonies of America have been, are, and of right ought to be, dependent upon the Imperial Crown of Great-Britain, and subordinate unto the British Parliament, and that the King's most Excellent Majesty, by and with the advice and consent of the Lords Spiritual and Temporal and Commons in Parliament Assembled, had, hath, and of right ought to have, full power and authority to make laws and statutes of sufficient force and validity to bind the people of the British Colonies in America, in all matters touching the general weal of the whole dominion of the Imperial Crown of Great Britain, and beyond the competency of the local representative of a distinct colony; and most especially an indubitable and indispensable right to make and ordain laws for regulating navigation and trade throughout the complicated system of British commerce; the deep policy of such prudent acts upholding the guardian navy of the whole British empire; and that all subjects in the Colonies are bound in duty and allegiance duly to recognize and obey (and they are hereby required so to do) the supreme legislative authority and superintending power of the Parliament of Great Britain, as aforesaid.

And whereas, in a petition from America to his Majesty, it has been represented, that the keeping a standing army within any of the Colonies, in time of peace, without consent of the respective Provincial Assembly there, is against law: Be it declared by the King's most Excellent Majesty, by and with the consent of the Lords Spiritual and Temporal and Commons in the present Parliament assembled, that the Declaration of Right, at the ever-glorious Revolution, namely, "That the raising and keeping a standing army within the kingdom, in time of peace, unless it be by the consent of the Parliament, is against law," having reference only to the consent of the Parliament of Great Britain, the legal, constitutional, and hitherto unquestioned prerogative of the Crown, to send any part of such army, so lawfully kept, to any of the British dominions and possessions, whether in America or elsewhere, as his Majesty, in due care of his subjects, may judge necessary for the security and protection of the same, cannot be rendered dependent upon the consent of a Provincial Assembly in the Colonies, without a most dangerous innovation, and derogation from the dignity of the Imperial Crown of Great Britain. Nevertheless, in order to quiet and dispel groundless jealousies and fears, be it hereby declared, That no military force, however raised, and kept according to law, can ever be lawfully employed to violate and destroy the just rights of the people.

Moreover, in order to remove for ever all causes of pernicious discord, and in due contemplation of the vast increase of possessions and population in the Colonies; and having a heart to render the condition of so great a body of industrious subjects there more and more happy, by the sacredness of property and of personal liberty, of more extensive and lasting utility to the parent kingdom, by indissoluble ties of mutual affection, confidence, trade and reciprocal benefits, Be it declared and enacted, by the King's most Excellent Majesty, by and with the advice and consent of the Lords Spiritual and Temporal and Commons in this present Parliament assembled, and it is hereby declared and enacted by the authority of the same, That no tallage, tax, or other charge for his Majesty's revenue, shall be commanded or levied, from British freemen in America, without common consent, by act of Provincial Assembly there, duly convened for that purpose.

And it is hereby further declared and enacted, by the King's most Excellent Majesty, by and with the advice and consent of the Lords Spiritual and Temporal and Commons in the present Parliament asembled, and by the authority of the same, That it shall and may be lawful for delegates from the respective provinces, lately assembled at Philadelphia, to meet in general Congress at the said city of Philadelphia, on the 9th day of May next ensuing, in order then and there to take into consideration the making due recognition of the supreme legislative authority and superintending power of Parliament over the Colonies as aforesaid.

And moreover, may it please your most Excellent Majesty, that the said Delegates, to be in Congress assembled in manner aforesaid, may be required, and the same are hereby required, by the King's Majesty sitting in his Parliament, to take into consideration (over and above the usual charge for support of civil government in the respective Colonies) the making of a free grant to the King, his heirs, and successors, of a certain perpetual revenue, subject to the disposition of the British Parliament, to be by them appropriated as they in their wisdom shall judge fit, to the alleviation of the national debt: no doubt being had but this just, free aid, will be in such honourable proportion as may seem meet and becoming from great and flourishing colonies towards a parent country labouring under the heaviest burdens, which, in no inconsiderable part, have been willingly taken upon ourselves and posterity, for the defence, extension, and prosperity of the Colonies.

And to this great end, be it farther hereby declared and enacted, that the general Congress (to meet at Philadelphia as aforesaid) shall be, and is hereby authorized and empowered (the Delegates composing the same being first sufficiently furnished with powers from their respective provinces for this purpose) to adjust and fix the proportions and quotas of the several charges to be borne by each province respectively, towards the general contributory supply; and this in such fair and equitable measure, as may best suit the abilities and due convenience of all: Provided always, that the powers for fixing the said quotas, hereby given to the delegates from the old provinces now composing the Congress, shall not extend to the new provinces of East and West Florida, Georgia, Nova Scotia, St. John's, and Canada; the circumstances and abilities of the said provinces being reserved for the wisdom of Parliament in their due time. And in order to afford necessary time for mature deliberation in America, be it hereby declared, That the provisions for ascertaining and fixing the exercise of the right of taxation in the Colonies, as agreed and expressed by this present act, shall not be in force, or have any operation, until the delegates to be in Congress assembled, sufficiently authorized and empowered by their respective provinces to this end, shall, as an indispensable condition, have duly recognised the supreme legislative authority and superintending power of the Parliament of Great Britain over the Colonies aforesaid: Always understood, That the free grant of an aid, as heretofore required and expected from the Colonies, is not to be considered as a condition of redress, but as a just testimony of their affection.

And whereas, divers acts of Parliament have been humbly represented, in a petition to his Majesty from America, to have been found grievous, in whole or in part, to the subjects of the Colonies, be it hereby declared by the King's most Excellent Majesty, by and with the advice and consent of the Lords Spiritual and Temporal and the commons in this present Parliament assembled, and by the authority of the same, That the powers of Admiralty and Vice-Admiralty Courts in America shall be restrained within their ancient limits, and the Trial by Jury, in all civil cases, where the same may be abolished, restored: And that no subject in America shall, in capital cases, be liable to be indicted and tried for the same, in any place out of the province where such offence shall be alleged to have been committed, nor be deprived of a trial by his peers of the vicinage; nor shall it be lawful to send persons indicted for murder in any province of America, to another colony, or to Great Britain, for trial.

And be it hereby declared and enacted, by the authority aforesaid, That all and every the said acts, or so much thereof as are represented to have been found grievous, namely, the several acts of the 4th Geo. III. ch. 15. and ch. 34.—5th Geo. III. ch. 25.—6th Geo. III. ch. 52.—7th Geo. III. ch. 41. and ch. 46.—8th Geo. III. ch. 22.—12th Geo. III. ch. 24.—with the three acts for stopping the port and blocking up the harbour of Boston; for altering the character and government of Massachusetts Bay; and that entitled, An act for the better administration of justice, &c., also the act for regulating the government of Quebec, and the act passed in the same session relating to the quarters of soldiers, shall be, and are hereby suspended, and not to have effect or execution, from the date of this act. And be it moreover hereby declared and enacted, by the authority aforesaid, That all and every the before-recited acts, or the parts thereof complained of, shall be and are, in virtue of this present act, finally repealed and annulled, from the day that the new recognition of the supreme legislative authority and superintending power of Parliament over the Colonies shall have been made on the part of the said Colonies.

And for the better securing due and impartial administration of justice in the Colonies, be it declared and enacted by the King's most Excellent Majesty, by and with the advice and consent of the Lords Spiritual and Temporal and Commons in this present Parliament assembled, That his Majesty's Judges in Courts of Law in the Colonies of America, to be appointed with salaries by the Crown, shall hold their offices and salaries as his Majesty's Judges in England, *quamdiu se bene gesserint*. And it is hereby further declared, by the authority aforesaid, that the Colonies in America are justly entitled to the privileges, franchises, and immunities granted by their several Charters or Constitutions: and that the said Charters or Constitutions ought not to be invaded or resumed, unless for misuser, or some legal ground of forfeiture. So shall true reconcilement avert impending calamities, and this solemn national accord between Great Britain and her colonies stand an everlasting monument of clemency and magnanimity in the benignant father of his people, of wisdom and moderation in this great nation, famed for humanity as for valour, and of fidelity and grateful affection from brave and loyal Colonies to their parent kingdom, which will ever protect and cherish them.

## 23.4

### Benjamin Franklin, Vindication, June–July(?) 1775

Franklin, who returned to Philadelphia on May 5, 1775, after a decade in London, had witnessed the debates in Parliament concerning the matters touched on in Chatham's bill.[83] Such exchanges prepared him to respond with well-earned insight to North's conciliatory proposal.[84] Although Franklin's vindication seems to have been written in response to North's proposal, the date of its composition remains uncertain. It is likely, though, that he drafted it before July 20, 1775, since it refers to "the twelve colonies" and Georgia notified Congress on July 20 that it would soon be sending delegates to Congress. Paul Smith suggests that the vindication's intended audience may have been either American or British: it "may have been stimulated by fears that Lord North's conciliatory proposal . . . would find a favorable reception in the colonies," or conversely, Franklin may have felt the need to defend the colonists against those in Britain who questioned their commitment to "reciprocal obligations within the empire" and who believed that Americans "were dishonest traders, and [had] evaded the legitimate costs of their defense."[85]

The likely intended audience being British seems in accord with Franklin's own description of the vindication as responding to "the enemies of America in the Parliament of Great Britain," who wished "to render us odious to the nation" and to others in Europe by castigating Americans as unjust and ungrateful for British sacrifices made in settling or defending the colonies and by accusing the colonists falsely of aiming "at independence" or intending to abolish "the Navigation Acts." If his intent was to rebut such slanderous charges before a British audience, Franklin likely hoped to have the vindication accompany the congressional documents sent to England with Richard Penn on July 9, 1775, for publication there. Maybe he didn't finish in time and thus left the essay unpublished.[86]

In this systematic essay, Franklin considers and responds to five charges that he believes were unfairly leveled against the colonists. He begins by examining, in brief, the history of the colonies in order to demonstrate that, with the exception of New York, Georgia, and Nova Scotia—the last two not being part of the confederacy— "these colonies had been planted and established *without any expense to the [British] state.*" Next, he reports that the colonies had grown, until most recently, without the military support of Britain and that on their own they had fought wars against "the Indian natives, sustained by our infant settlements for a century after our first arrival." Reflecting on the help of Britain in the most recent war, Franklin writes that "as we are daily growing stronger . . . we should with pleasure embrace the first opportunity of showing our gratitude by returning the favor in kind" by helping protect Great Britain as the relationship between colonies and Britain becomes "proportionably mutual." Third, he denies, with little corroboration and too much boldness, that the colonies had ever refused "*to contribute to our protection.*"

Like Congress, though with far more precision, Franklin offers to pay for the discontinuation of British maritime and trade legislation that hampered colonial trade and manufacturing: "Whenever she shall think fit to abolish her monopoly, and give us the same privileges of trade as Scotland received at the union, and allow us a free commerce with all the rest of the world; we shall willingly agree (and we doubt not it will be ratified by our constituents) to *give and pay* into the sinking fund [one hundred thousand pounds] sterling per annum for the term of one hundred years." But if Britain refused to accept the offer, Franklin had another with which he hoped "to remove her groundless jealousies, *that we aim at independence, and an abolition of the Navigation Act.*" In regard to independence, he claims without equivocation that it "hath in truth never been our intention." And he points out that if his friend Galloway's earlier, more comprehensive, and demanding "Plan of Union" or his own Albany Plan of 1754 had been adopted, that might have gone a long way toward settling many of the outstanding issues between Parliament and the colonies.

Indeed, the plans set out in Franklin's unpublished vindication, in Chatham's defeated bill, and even in North's parliamentary-approved proposal help emphasize that the impasse between the colonies and Britain, ultimately, was not about taxation, which these measures and the one proposed by Parliament in 1778 would have resolved. Rather it was about the nature of the constitutional relationship between Parliament and colonies, and implicitly about the one between king and Parliament (at least as understood by the colonists). Franklin ends his remarks by dismissing the fifth charge, that the colonists "*are dishonest traders, and aim at defrauding . . . [their] creditors in Britain,*" by paying perhaps too little attention to the indebted planters of Virginia.[87] In the main, even when Franklin's lines of argument are possibly exaggerated, his desire to present his case to a British audience, even to a wider European one, suggests the importance he, and likely his colleagues in Congress, attached to a "decent Respect to the Opinions of Mankind."

Paul H. Smith, ed., *Letters of Delegates to Congress, 1774–1789* (Washington, D.C.: Library of Congress, 1976–93), 1:561–66.

Forasmuch as the enemies of America in the Parliament of Great Britain, to render us odious to the nation, and give an ill impression of us in the minds of other European powers, have represented us as unjust and ungrateful in the highest degree; asserting, on every occasion, that the colonies were settled at the expense of Britain; that they were, at the expense of the same, protected in their infancy; that they now ungratefully and unjustly refuse to contribute to their own protection, and the common defence of the nation; that they aim at independence; that they intend an abolition of the Navigation Acts; and that they are fraudulent in their commercial dealings, and purpose to cheat their creditors in Britain, by avoiding the payment of their just debts;

And, as by frequent repetition these groundless assertions and malicious calumnies may, if not contradicted and refuted, obtain further credit, and be injurious throughout Europe to the reputation and interest of the confederate colonies, it seems proper and necessary to examine them in our own just vindication.

With regard to the first, *that the colonies were settled at the expense of Britain,* it is a known fact, that none of the twelve united colonies were settled, or even discovered, at the expense of England. Henry the Seventh, indeed, granted Commission to Sebastian Cabot, a Venetian, and his sons, to sail into the western seas for the discovery of new countries; but it was to be "*suis eorum propriis sumptibus et expensis,*" at their *own* costs and charges. They discovered, but soon slighted and neglected these northern territories; which were, after more than a hundred years' dereliction, purchased of the natives, and settled at the charge and by the labor of private men and bodies of men, our ancestors, who came over hither for that purpose. But our adversaries have never been able to produce any record, that ever the Parliament or government of England was at the smallest expense on these accounts; on the contrary, there exists on the journals of Parliament a solemn declaration in 1642, (only twenty-two years after the first settlement of the Massachusetts, when, if such expense had ever been incurred, some of the members must have known and remembered it,) "That these colonies had been planted and established *without any expense to the state.*"

New York is the only colony in the founding of which England can pretend to have been at any expense; and that was only the charge of a small armament to take it from the Dutch, who planted it. But to retain this colony at the peace, another at that time full as valuable, planted by private countrymen of *ours,* was given up by the crown to the Dutch in exchange, viz. Surinam, now a wealthy sugar colony in Guiana, and which, but for that cession, might still have remained in our possession. Of late, indeed, Britain has been at some expense in planting two colonies, Georgia and Nova Scotia; but those are not in our confederacy; and the expense she has been at in their name has chiefly been in grants of sums unnecessarily large, by way of salaries to officers sent from England, and in jobs to friends, whereby dependants might be provided for; those excessive grants not being requisite to the welfare and good government of the colonies, which good government (as experience in many instances of other colonies has taught us) may be much more frugally, and full as effectually, provided for and supported.

With regard to the second assertion, *that these colonies were protected in their infant state by England,* it is a notorious fact, that, in none of the many wars with the Indian natives, sustained by our infant settlements for a century after our first arrival, were ever any troops or forces of any kind sent from England to assist us; nor were any forts built at her expense, to secure our seaports from foreign invaders; nor any ships of war sent to protect our trade, till many years after our first settlement, when our commerce became an object of revenue, or of advantage to British merchants; and then it was thought necessary to have a frigate in some of our ports, during peace, to give weight to the authority of custom-house officers, who were to restrain that commerce for the benefit of England. Our own arms, with our poverty, and the care of a kind Providence, were all this time our only protection; while we were neglected by the English government; which either thought us not worth its care, or, having no good will to some of us, on account of our different sentiments in religion and politics, was indifferent what became of us.

On the other hand, the colonies have not been wanting to do what they could in every war for annoying the enemies of Britain. They formerly assisted her in the conquest of Nova Scotia. In the war before last they took Louisburg and put it into her hands. She made her peace with that strong fortress, by restoring it to France, greatly to their detriment. In the last war, it is true, Britain sent a fleet and army, who acted with an equal army of ours, in the reduction of Canada; and perhaps thereby did more for us, than we in the preceding wars had done for her. Let it be remembered, however, that she rejected the plan we formed in the Congress at Albany, in 1754, for our own defence, by a union of the colonies; a union she was jealous of, and therefore chose to send her own forces; otherwise her aid to protect us was not wanted. And from our first settlement to that time, her military operations in our favor were small, compared with the advantages she drew from her exclusive commerce with us. We are, however, willing to give full weight to this obligation; and, as we are daily growing stronger, and our assistance to her becomes of more importance, we should with pleasure embrace the first opportunity of showing our gratitude by returning the favor in kind.

But, when Britain values herself as affording us protection, we desire it may be considered, that we have followed her in all her wars, and joined with her at our own expense against all she thought fit to quarrel with. This she has required of us; and would never permit us to keep peace with any power she declared her enemy; though by separate treaties we might well have done it. Under such circumstances, when at her instance we made nations our enemies, whom we might otherwise have retained our friends, we submit it to the common sense of mankind, whether her protection of us in these wars was not our *just due,* and to be claimed of *right,* instead of being received as a *favor?* And whether, when all the parts of an empire exert themselves to the utmost in their common defence, and in annoying the common enemy, it is not as well the *parts* that protect the *whole,* as the *whole* that protects the *parts?* The protection then has been proportionably mutual. And, whenever the time shall come, that our abilities may as far exceed hers, as hers have exceeded ours, we hope we shall be reasonable enough to rest satisfied with her proportionable exertions, and not think we do too much for a part of the empire, when that part does as much as it can for the whole.

The charge against us, *that we refuse to contribute to our own protection,* appears from the above to be groundless; but we farther declare it to be absolutely false; for it is well known, that we ever held it as our duty to grant aids to the crown, upon requisition, towards carrying on its wars; which duty we have cheerfully complied with, to the utmost of our abilities; insomuch that frequent and grateful acknowledgements thereof, by King and Parliament, appear on the records. But, as Britain has enjoyed a most gainful monopoly of our commerce; the same, with our maintaining the dignity of the King's representative in each colony, and all our own separate establishments of government, civil and military; has ever hitherto been deemed an equivalent for such aids as might otherwise be expected from us in time of peace. And we hereby declare, that on a reconciliation with Britain, we shall not only continue to grant aids in time of war, as aforesaid; but, whenever she shall think fit to abolish her monopoly, and give us the same privileges of trade as Scotland received at the union, and allow us a free commerce with all the rest of the world; we shall willingly agree (and we doubt not it will be ratified by our constituents) *to give and pay* into the sinking fund [one hundred thousand pounds] sterling per annum for the term of one hundred years; which duly, faithfully, and inviolably applied to that purpose, is demonstrably more than sufficient to extinguish *all her present national* debt; since it will in that time amount, at legal British interest, to more than [two hundred and thirty millions of pounds.]

But if Britain does not think fit to accept this proposition, we, in order to remove her groundless jealousies, *that we aim at independence, and an abolition of the Navigation Act,* (which hath in truth never been our intention,) and to avoid all future disputes about the right of making that and other acts of regulating our commerce, do hereby declare ourselves ready and willing to enter into a *covenant with Britain,* that she shall fully possess, enjoy, and exercise that right, for an hundred years to come; the same being *bonâ fide* used for the common benefit; and, in case of such agreement, that every Assembly be advised by us to confirm it solemnly by laws of their own, which, once made, cannot be repealed without the assent of the crown.

The last charge, *that we are dishonest traders, and aim at defrauding our creditors in Britain,* is sufficiently and authentically refuted by the solemn declarations of the

British merchants to Parliament, (both at the time of the Stamp Act and in the last session,) who bore ample testimony to the general good faith and fair dealing of the Americans, and declared their confidence in our integrity; for which we refer to their petitions on the journals of the House of Commons. And we presume we may safely call on the body of the British tradesmen, who have had experience of both, to say, whether they have not received much more punctual payment from us, than they generally have from the members of their own two Houses of Parliament.

On the whole of the above it appears, that the charge of *ingratitude* towards the mother country, brought with so much confidence against the colonies, is totally without foundation; and that there is much more reason for retorting that charge on Britain, who, not only never contributes any aid, nor affords, by an exclusive commerce, any advantages to Saxony, *her* mother country; but no longer since than in the last war, without the least provocation, subsidized the King of Prussia while he ravaged that *mother country,* and carried fire and sword into its capital, the fine city of Dresden! An example we hope no provocation will induce us to imitate.

## 24. PLANS FOR NEW COLONIAL GOVERNMENTS, NOVEMBER–DECEMBER 1775

On October 18, 1775, as had occurred earlier in the year with Massachusetts (see document 17.1), New Hampshire sought to "obtain the advice and direction of the Congress, with respect to a method for our administering Justice, and regulating our civil police"; that is, it turned to Congress to request an invitation to set up a new government. Congress planned to appoint a committee to consider this request on the following Monday, October 23.[88] On that day, though, Congress suspended action on all matters to honor the first and third president of the Continental Congress, Peyton Randolph of Virginia, who had died. It was on October 26 that a committee consisting of John Rutledge, John Adams, Samuel Ward of Rhode Island, Richard Henry Lee, and Roger Sherman was formed to respond to New Hampshire's request.[89] According to Adams, "this committee was entirely composed of members as well disposed to encourage the enterprise [of forming new governments] as could have been found in Congress." They included Sherman, the son of a farmer, a shopkeeper, and a lawyer, who has the unique status of being the only person whose age and good timing allowed him to sign the Continental Association, the Declaration of Independence, the Articles of Confederation, and the Constitution. Rutledge, like his younger brother, Edward (or Ned), possibly was still hoping that some form of a just reconciliation could be arranged with Britain, but in the excerpt from Adams' autobiography below (document 24.2), he describes Rutledge as "now completely with us in our desire of revolutionizing all the governments." Rutledge's support for the same accommodation being recommended for his state, in fact, seems to bolster Adams' case.[90]

Congress's brief instructions were approved on November 3. They included directions to state representatives to form a government that would "best produce the happiness of the people, and most effectually secure peace and good order in the province." Unlike the instructions offered to Massachusetts in June, New Hampshire's were not linked to the colony returning to an earlier, monarchical government. Still, to Adams' dismay, the instructions suggested that the provisional government, like that of Massachusetts, was to endure only "during the continuance of the present dispute between G[reat] Britain and the colonies."

At the same time that Congress approved instructions to New Hampshire, a new committee of five was appointed to take into consideration, at the behest of the previous committee's chairman, John Rutledge, a similar request from his own colony of South Carolina.[91] The delegates appointed to the new committee were Benjamin Harrison of Virginia, Archibald Bulloch of Georgia, William Hooper of North Carolina, Samuel Chase of Maryland, and Samuel Adams.[92] It is easy to imagine that Bulloch, a lawyer originally from South Carolina, a correspondent of Franklin, and a radical leader in otherwise conservative Georgia; Chase, a lawyer and a member of the Sons of Liberty; and Samuel Adams would support this move. Likely less enthusiastic was Harrison, a wealthy planter, a frequent Speaker of the House of Burgesses, a master of conviviality in Philadelphia, and one of the more conservative members of the Virginia delegation.[93] Similarly, Hooper, a lawyer originally from Boston who, in spite of having trained with James Otis, Jr., and having helped organize the extralegal provincial Congress in North Carolina, was viewed with suspicion by Jefferson, who claimed "there was no greater Tory in Congress than Hooper."[94]

Congress, on its own initiative, invited Virginia to form a new government if its Provincial Convention should find it necessary. Accordingly, on November 10, 1775, Congress appointed another five-person committee to offer instructions to Virginia—in effect, Congress took the initiative in accepting responsibility for Virginia's abandoning its legal government and forming a new one. Just in case things went horribly wrong and the colonists were to find themselves facing charges of capital treason, such issues of responsibility might prove to be matters of life or death.[95] The new committee consisted of Samuel Adams (Massachusetts), Thomas Lynch (South Carolina), James Wilson (Pennsylvania), Samuel Ward (Rhode Island), and Thomas Johnson (Maryland).[96] Lynch, a planter who had inherited great wealth and had been a delegate to the Stamp Act Congress, suffered a stroke in 1776, and was replaced in Congress by his son before dying that year. Wilson emigrated from Scotland in 1765 and read law with John Dickinson in Philadelphia before starting his own successful law practice. Although ultimately a supporter of the Declaration of Independence, he opposed it until July 1 and was among the last to switch his vote in favor. Johnson, also a lawyer, served as a general of the Maryland state militia during the war and served as governor until 1779. He later served, like Wilson, on the U. S. Supreme Court.

Congress, on December 4, approved the committee's report, which, like those for New Hampshire, South Carolina, and Massachusetts, cautioned that any provisional accommodation that a colony might make was to continue only during "the present dispute between Great Britain and these colonies."[97] In its longest statement in any of the three reports, Congress condemned the actions of Virginia's governor, Lord Dunmore, for having on November 7, 1775, placed the colony under martial law, "thereby tearing up the foundation of civil authority and government within the said colony," while beginning to raise a loyalist army.[98] Dunmore, born John Murray, was governor of New York in 1770, then Virginia, and finally, in 1786, the Bahamas.

The most remarkable feature of Dunmore's loyalist army was that it included a regiment of former African slaves, the Ethiopian Regiment, to whom, on November 17, Dunmore had by proclamation offered their freedom in return for military service—an early emancipation proclamation, not dissimilar to the ones issued in June 1779 by the commander in chief of the British forces, General Clinton, who promised freedom to "every Negro who shall desert," or the far more famous ones of President Lincoln, most particularly his first, of September 22, 1863. Dunmore's offer of freedom to Virginia's slaves surely lost him any support he may have still enjoyed among the planter class, and figured prominently in later congressional state papers, including the address to the people of Ireland (document 22.1), in which Britain was castigated for inciting domestic enemies, and the Declaration for Independence, in whose final grievance Congress complained of the king "exciting domestic Insurrections amongst us."[99] Dunmore became possibly still more infamous for his burning of Norfolk, Virginia, on January 1, 1776.

Congress concluded by resolving "that in the present situation of affairs, it will be very dangerous to the liberties and welfare of America, if any Colony should separately petition the King or either house of Parliament"; it then appointed a committee of three moderate delegates (John Dickinson, George Wythe of Virginia, and John Jay) to meet "with the Assembly of New Jersey." Congress was clearly concerned that this mid-Atlantic colony, still governed by a loyalist, Benjamin Franklin's son William, might be considering making its own peace with Parliament.

24.1

CONGRESS, RESPONSE TO NEW HAMPSHIRE'S REQUEST FOR INSTRUCTIONS ON FORMING A NEW GOVERNMENT, AND INSTRUCTIONS FOR SOUTH CAROLINA AND VIRGINIA CONCERNING FORMING NEW GOVERNMENTS, NOVEMBER 3, NOVEMBER 4, AND DECEMBER 4, 1775

Worthington Chauncey Ford et al., eds., *Journals of the Continental Congress, 1774–1789* (Washington, D.C.: Government Printing Office, 1904–37), 3:319, 325–27,

403–4. For the instructions to South Carolina, only the ninth and last resolution is printed below.

FRIDAY, NOVEMBER 3, 1775

The Congress, taking into consideration the report of the Com[mitt]ee on the New Hampshire Instructions,

*Resolved,* That it be recommended to the provincial Convention of New Hampshire, to call a full and free representation of the people, and that the representatives, if they think it necessary, establish such a form of government, as, in their judgment, will best produce the happiness of the people, and most effectually secure peace and good order in the province, during the continuance of the present dispute between G[reat] Britain and the colonies.

The Congress then, taking into consideration the state of South Carolina, and sundry papers relative thereto, being read and considered,

*Resolved,* That a com[mitt]ee of 5 be appointed to take the same into consideration, and report what, in their opinion, is necessary to be done.

The Com[mitt]ee chosen, Mr. Lynch, Mr. [Benjamin] Harrison, Mr. [Archibald] Bullock, Mr. [William] Hooper, Mr. J. Rutledge, Mr. [Samuel] Chase, and Mr. Samuel Adams. . . .

[SATURDAY, NOVEMBER 4, 1775]

The Com[mitt]ee appointed to take into Consideration the state of S[outh] Carolina, brought in their report, which being read, . . .

*Resolved,* That if the Convention of South Carolina shall find it necessary to establish a form of government in that colony, it be recommended to that Convention to call a full and free representation of the people, and that the said representatives, if they think it necessary, shall establish such a form of Government as in their judgment will best produce the happiness of the people, and most effectually secure peace and good order in the colony, during the continuance of the present dispute between Great Britain and the colonies. . . .

[MONDAY, DECEMBER 4, 1775]

The Committee appointed on the state of Virginia, to whom were referred the letters received on Saturday, brought in a report, which was read, on which the Congress came to the following resolutions:

*Resolved,* That three companies of the battalions raised in the colony of Pensylvania, immediately march under the command of lieutenant colonel Irvine, into Northampton county, in Virginia, for the protection of the Association in those parts, and for the defence thereof against the designs of the enemies of America.

*Resolved,* That it be and it is hereby recommended to the Inhabitants of the colony of Virginia, to resist to the utmost the arbitrary government intended to be established therein, by their Governor Lord Dunmore, as manifestly appears by the whole tenor of his Lordship's conduct for some months past.

Whereas Lord Dunmore, by his proclamation lately published, has declared his intention to execute martial law, thereby tearing up the foundations of civil authority and government within the said colony:

*Resolved,* Therefore, that if the convention of Virginia shall find it necessary to establish a form of government in that colony, it be recommended to that Convention to call a full and free representation of the people, and that the said representatives, if they think it necessary, establish such form of government as in their judgment will best produce the happiness of the people, and most effectually secure peace and good order in the colony, during the continuance of the present dispute between Great Britain and these colonies.

*Resolved,* That the Committee on the state of Virginia have leave, at their request, to sit again.

On motion, *Resolved, unanimously,* That in the present situation of affairs, it will be very dangerous to the liberties and welfare of America, if any Colony should separately petition the King or either house of Parliament.

*Resolved,* That a Committee of three be appointed to confer with the Assembly of New Jersey.

The members chosen, Mr. [John] Dickinson, Mr. [George] Wythe, and Mr. [John] Jay.

24.2

JOHN ADAMS, AUTOBIOGRAPHY,
OCTOBER 18, 1775

In this extract from his autobiography (left unfinished at his death), Adams describes the debate in Congress concerning New Hampshire's request for instructions on forming a government. During it, he "embraced with joy the opportunity of haranguing on the Subject at large, and of urging Congress to resolve on a general recommendation to all the States to call conventions and institute regular governments," that is, republican-leaning ones not owing allegiance to the king. Adams suggests that the instructions for New Hampshire were likely requested by one of its radical delegates: John Sullivan, John Langdon, or William Whipple; only Langdon and his fellow radical Josiah Bartlett were serving in Congress at this time. Adams' hopes for a general transformation of government in the colonies rested on nine reasons, among them: "the danger of insurrections in some of the most disaffected parts of the Colonies, in favor of the enemy or as they called them, the mother country, an expression that I thought it high time to erase out of our language"; and "foreign nations, particularly France and Spain, would not think us worthy of their attention while we appeared to be deceived by such fallacious hopes of redress of grievances, of pardon for our offences, and of the reconciliation with our enemies." The most essential reason for him may have been that without instituting new governments, "the people of America would never consider our Union as complete." As so often was the case, Adams was ahead of his colleagues in his drive toward American independence, but far less so in the Second Continental Congress than he had been in the First. Still, his wish for a general congressional recommendation for all colonies to adopt new governments didn't come until May 15, 1776, the preamble to which he would write (document 31.1).

Adams describes the general tenor of Congress, which was changing: "Although the opposition was still inveterate, many members of Congress began to hear me with more patience, and some began to ask me civil questions." He records a number of questions raised in discussion, one of which deserves particular attention: "but what plan of a government would you advise" the colonies to institute? To this, Adams responds, "A plan as nearly resembling the governments under which we were born and have lived as the circumstances of the country will admit. Kings we never had among us. Nobles we never had. Nothing hereditary ever existed in the country; nor will the country require or admit of any such thing." If his point of reference, as seems likely, was New England, there is much truth here; his remarks suggest how little the New England colonies had to change in order to move to fully republican government. Most other colonial governments would soon have to move much further.

*The Works of John Adams,* ed. Charles Francis Adams
(Boston: Little, Brown, 1851–65), 3:18–21.

On Wednesday October 18th, the delegates from New Hampshire laid before the Congress a part of the instructions delivered to them by their Colony, in these words:—

"We would have you immediately use your utmost endeavors to obtain the advice and direction of the Congress, with respect to a method for our administering justice, and regulating our civil police. We press you not to delay this matter, as its being done speedily will probably prevent the greatest confusion among us."

This instruction might have been obtained by Mr. Langdon, or Mr. Whipple, but I always supposed it was General Sullivan who suggested this measure, because he left Congress with a stronger impression upon his mind of the importance of it, than I ever observed in either of the others. Be this, however, as it may have been, I embraced with joy the opportunity of haranguing on the subject at large, and of urging Congress to resolve on a general recommendation to all the States to call conventions and institute regular governments. I reasoned from various topics, many of which perhaps I could not now recollect. Some I remember; as,

1. The danger to the morals of the people from the present loose state of things and general relaxation of laws and government through the Union.

2. The danger of insurrections in some of the most disaffected parts of the Colonies, in favor of the enemy or as they called them, the mother country, an expression that I thought it high time to erase out of our language.

3. Communications and intercourse with the enemy, from various parts of the continent could not be wholly prevented, while any of the powers of government remained in the hands of the King's servants.

4. It could not well be considered as a crime to communicate intelligence, or to act as spies or guides to the enemy, without assuming all the powers of government.

5. The people of America would never consider our Union as complete, but our friends would always suspect divisions among us, and our enemies who were scattered in larger or smaller numbers not only in every State and city, but in every village through the whole Union, would forever represent Congress as divided, and ready to break to pieces, and in this way would intimidate and discourage multitudes of our people who wished us well.

6. The absurdity of carrying on war against a king, when so many persons were daily taking oaths and affirmations of allegiance to him.

7. We could not expect that our friends in Great Britain would believe us united and in earnest, or exert themselves very strenuously in our favor, while we acted such a wavering, hesitating part.

8. Foreign nations, particularly France and Spain, would not think us worthy of their attention while we appeared to be deceived by such fallacious hopes of redress of grievances, of pardon for our offences, and of the reconciliation with our enemies.

9. We could not command the natural resources of our own country. We could not establish manufactories of arms, cannon, saltpetre, powder, ships, &c., without the powers of government; and all these and many other preparations ought to be going on in every State or Colony, if you will, in the country.

Although the opposition was still inveterate, many members of Congress began to hear me with more patience, and some began to ask me civil questions. "How can the people institute governments?" My answer was, "By conventions of representatives, freely, fairly, and proportionably chosen." "When the convention has fabricated a government, or a constitution rather, how do we know the people will submit to it?" "If there is any doubt of that, the convention may send out their project of a constitution, to the people in their several towns, counties, or districts, and the people may make the acceptance of it their own act." "But the people know nothing about constitutions." "I believe you are much mistaken in that supposition; if you are not, they will not oppose a plan prepared by their own chosen friends; but I believe that in every considerable portion of the people, there will be found some men, who will understand the subject as well as their representatives, and these will assist in enlightening the rest." "But what plan of a government would you advise?" "A plan as nearly resembling the governments under which we were born and have lived as the circumstances of the country will admit. Kings we never had among us. Nobles we never had. Nothing hereditary ever existed in the country; nor will the country require or admit of any such thing. But governors and councils we have always had as well as representatives. A legislature in three branches ought to be preserved, and independent judges." "Where and how will you get your governors and councils?" "By elections." "How,—who shall elect?" "The representatives of the people in a convention will be the best qualified to contrive a mode."

After all these discussions and interrogations, Congress was not prepared nor disposed to do any thing as yet. They must consider farther.

"*Resolved,* That the Consideration of this matter be referred to Monday next."

Monday arrived and Tuesday and Wednesday passed over, and Congress not yet willing to do any thing.

On Thursday October 26th, the subject again brought on the carpet, and the same discussions repeated; for very little new was produced. After a long discussion, in which Mr. John Rutledge, Mr. Ward, Mr. Lee, Mr. Gadsden, Mr. Sherman, Mr. Dyer, and some others had spoken on the same side with me, Congress resolved that a committee of five members be appointed to take into consideration the instructions given to the delegates of New Hampshire, and report their opinion thereon. The members chosen,—Mr. John Rutledge, Mr. J. Adams, Mr. Ward, Mr. Lee, and Mr. Sherman.

Although this committee was entirely composed of members as well disposed to encourage the enterprise as could have been found in Congress, yet they could not be brought to agree upon a report, and to bring it forward in Congress, till Friday, November 3d, when Congress, taking into consideration the report of the committee on the New Hampshire instructions, after another long deliberation and debate,—

"*Resolved,* That it be recommended to the Provincial Convention of New Hampshire, to call a full and free representation of the people, and that the representatives, if they think it necessary, establish such a form of government, as in their judgment will best produce the happiness of the people, and most effectually secure peace and good order in the Province, during the continuance of the present dispute between Great Britain and the Colonies."

By this time I mortally hated the Words, "Province," "Colonies," and "Mother Country," and strove to get them out of the report. The last was indeed left out, but the other two were retained even by this committee, who were all as high Americans as any in the house, unless Mr. Gadsden should be excepted. Nevertheless, I thought this resolution a triumph, and a most important point gained.

Mr. John Rutledge was now completely with us in our desire of revolutionizing all the governments, and he brought forward immediately some representations from his own State, when

"Congress, then taking into consideration the State of South Carolina, and sundry papers relative thereto being read and considered,

"*Resolved,* that a committee of five be appointed to take the same into consideration, and report what in their opinion is necessary to be done. The members chosen, Mr. Harrison, Mr. Bullock, Mr. Hooper, Mr. Chase, and Mr. S. Adams.

## 24.3

SAMUEL WARD TO HENRY WARD,
NOVEMBER 2, 1775

Samuel Ward, the representative for Rhode Island who sat on the committees considering the instructions for New Hampshire and Virginia, wrote to his brother, Henry. Both men, from at least the years of the Stamp Act Crisis in 1765, when Henry had served as a delegate to the Stamp Act Congress,[100] were active in their opposition to Parliament's measures. Here, Samuel welcomes the late-October arrival of the king's Proclamation for Suppressing Rebellion and Sedition of August 1775 (see document 25.2), for he understands how much it would help "widen the unhappy Breech between G. B. & the Colonies" and push moderates in Congress to adopt a more aggressive stance.[101] He added that this meant the "Southern Colonies no longer entertain Jealousies of the northern, [and] they no longer look back to G. Britain." Given the prominence of southern delegates in the radical ranks, one wonders whether he meant to write that the men of the mid-Atlantic colonies or moderates in various southern delegations had finally begun to look more favorably on a break with Great Britain. His letter makes clear that the king's proclamation had done much to change the atmosphere in Congress: "One of the Gentn. [identified by Smith, the editor, as Samuel Chase] who has been most sanguine for pacific measures & very jealous of the N[ew]. E[ngland]. Colonies addressing Me in the Stile of Bror. Rebel told me he was now ready to join Us heartily. We have got says He a sufficient Answer to our Petition; I want nothing more but am ready to declare Ourselves independent, send Ambassadors &c."

Paul H. Smith, ed., *Letters of Delegates to Congress, 1774–1789* (Washington, D.C.: Library of Congress, 1976–93), 2:290–92.

Dear Bror.                                                Philadelphia 2d Novr. 1775
Your Favour from Cambridge was very acceptable. Poor Newport I have done and offered every thing in my Power to serve them; May Heaven direct them to such Measures as may be for the best.

Your Concern for Powder is very natural. The Quantity wanted must be very great though not so much as you mention, I will however move to have our Orders enlarged tho I was fully satisfied with the Quantity we were directed to contract for until I recd. your Letter. The leaden Mines in Connecticut are opened, proper Buildings are erecting, vast Quantities of Oar are got out & will soon be smelted & the Gentn. of that Colony tell me they can furnish the whole Continent very soon. The other Resolutions recommended by you I shall move in Congress at a convenient Time.

The Evening before last two Ships arrivd from England. The Advices which they bring (amongst which is a Proclamation for suppressing Rebellion & Sedition) are of immense Service to [us]. Our Councils have been hitherto too fluctuating; one Day measures for carrying on the Ware was adopted, the next nothing must be done that would widen the unhappy Breech between G. B. & the Colonies; as these different Ideas have prevailed our Conduct has been directed. Had We at the opening of the Congress in May immediately taken proper Measures for carrying on the War with Vigor We might have been in Possession of all Canada undoubtedly & probably of Boston. Thank God the happy Day which I have long wished for is at length arrived. The southern Colonies no longer entertain Jealousies of the northern, they no longer look back to G. Britain, they are convinced that they have been pursuing a Phantom and that their only Safety is a vigorous determind Defence. One of the Gentn. who has been most sanguine for pacific measures & very jealous of the N.E. Colonies addressing Me in the Stile of Bror. Rebel told me he was now ready to join Us heartily. We have got says He a sufficient Answer to our Petition; I want nothing more but am ready to declare Ourselves independent, send Ambassadors &c & much more which Prudence forbids me to commit to Paper. Our Resolutions will henceforth be spirited, clear and decisive. May the supreme Govr. of the Universe direct & prosper them. The Pleasure which this Unanimity gives Me is inexpressible. I consider it as a sure Presage of Victory, My Anxiety is now at an End. I am no longer worried with contradictory Resolutions but feel a calm chearfull Satisfaction in having one great & just Object in View & the Means of obtaining it certainly by the divine Bl[essing]. . . .

I am Your most affece. Bror.            Sam Ward

## 24.4

 JOHN ADAMS TO JOSEPH HAWLEY, NOVEMBER 25, 1775

In contrast to Samuel Ward's assessment that congressional radicals and moderates had come together, this letter from John Adams to Joseph Hawley of

Northampton, Massachusetts, a lawyer who was a close associate of John and his cousin Samuel, laments that sharp sectional differences continued in Congress between groups of delegations. In this case, the dispute concerned pay in the Continental Army, with "all the Colonies, excepting New England," believing "that the Pay of the Privates is too high and that of the officers too low." New England's populist stance provides Adams with an opportunity to vent on sectional differences: "We cannot Suddenly alter the Temper, Principles, opinions or Prejudices of Men. The Characters of Gentlemen in the four New England Colonies, differ as much from those in the others, as that of the Common People differs, that is as much as several distinct Nations almost. . . . Gentlemen in the other Colonies have large Plantations of slaves, and the common People among them are very ignorant and very poor."

Still, even Adams admits that all differences were not wholly a matter of sectional preferences, for he complains that his Massachusetts colleague Thomas Cushing was little better than a southern delegate and that it was "very hard to be . . . plagued with the opposition of our own Colony to the most necessary Measures, at the same Time that you have all the Monarchical Superstitions and the Aristocratical Domination, of Nine other Colonies to contend with." Here, Adams had in mind not only Cushing but likely also Robert Treat Paine and even John Hancock. Again, the differences between the delegates at the end of 1775 were surely abating, but with the continued reluctance of mid-Atlantic moderates regarding independence, not fast enough for Adams' taste.[102]

Paul H. Smith, ed., *Letters of Delegates to Congress, 1774–1789* (Washington, D.C.: Library of Congress, 1976–93), 2:385–87.

My dear Sir                               Philadelphia Novr. 25. 1775
This afternoon at five O Clock, I received your kind Letter of November the 14 dated at Brookfield, which was the more agreable because such Favours from you short as this is are very rare.

You tell me, Sir, "that We shall have no Winter Army, if our Congress dont give better Encouragement to the Privates than at present is held forth to them" and that "there must be some small Bounty given them, on the Inlistment."

What Encouragement is held forth, or at least has been, I know not, but before this Time no doubt they have been informed of the Ultimatum of the Congress. No Bounty is offered—40 shillings lawfull Money Per Month, after much Altercation, is allowed. It is undoubtedly true, that an opinion prevails among the Gentlemen of the Army from the Southward, and indeed throughout all the Colonies, excepting New England, that the Pay of the Privates is too high and that of the officers too low. So that you may easily conceive the Difficulties We have had to surmount. You may depend upon it, that this has cost many an anxious Day and Night. And the Utmost that could be done has been. We cannot Suddenly alter the Temper, Principles, opinions or Prejudices of Men. The Characters of Gentlemen in the four New England Colonies, differ as much from those in the others, as that of the Common People differs, that is as much as several distinct Nations almost. Gentlemen, Men of Sense, or any Kind of Education in the other Colonies are much fewer in Proportion than in N. England. Gentlemen in the other Colonies have large Plantations of slaves, and the common People among them are very ignorant and very poor. These Gentlemen are accustomed, habituated to higher Notions of themselves and the distinction between them and the common People, than We are. And an instantaneous alteration of the Character of a Colony, and that Temper and those Sentiments which its Inhabitants imbibed with their Mothers Milk, and which have grown with their Growth and strengthened with their Strength, cannot be made without a Miracle. I dread the Consequences of this Disimilitude of Character, and without the Utmost Caution on both sides, and the most considerate Forbearance with one another and prudent Condescention on both sides, they will certainly be fatal. An Alteration of the Southern Constitutions, which must certainly take Place if this War continues will gradually bring all the Continent nearer and nearer to each other in all Respects. But this is the Most Critical Moment, We have yet seen. This Winter will cast the Die. For Gods Sake therefore, reconcile our People to what has been done, for you may depend upon it, that nothing more can be done here—and I should shudder at the Thought of proposing a Bounty. A burnt Child dreads the fire. The Pay of the officers is raised, that of a Captain to 26 dollars and one third per Month, Lts and Ensigns in Proportion— Regimental officers not raised.

You then hint, "that if Congress should repeal or explain away the Res. of 18 July respecting the appointment of military officers, and vest the Council with the sole Power, it would throw the Colony into Confusion and end in the Distruction of the Council."

The Day before Yesterday I wrote a Letter to the Honorable Board in answer from one from their President by order to us upon that Subject, which Letter Revere carried from this City yesterday Morning. Therein I candidly gave my opinion to their Honours that our Resolution was clear and plain, that the Colony might Use their own Discretion, and therefore that they might yield this Point to the House—and that the Point was so plain that I did not see the least occasion for laying the Controversy before Congress. But my dear Friend I must take the Freedom to tell you that the same has happened upon this occasion which has happened on a thousand others, after taking a great deal of Pains with my Colleague your Friend Mr Cushing, I could not get him to agree with the rest of Us in writing a joint Letter, nor could I get him to say what opinion he would give if it was moved in Congress. What he has written I know not. But it is very hard to be linked and yoked eternally, with People who have either no opinions, or opposite Opinions, and to be plagued with the opposition of our own Colony to the most necessary Measures, at the same Time that you have all the Monarchical Superstitions and the Aristocratical Domination, of Nine other Colonies to contend with.

## 24.5

## Congress to Colonial Agents, November 29, 1775

On November 17, 1775, Congress appointed a committee of seven to write to the agents in London representing the interests of one or more colonies.[103] The committee included George Wythe (Virginia), Edward Rutledge (South Carolina), John Adams (Massachusetts), William Livingston (New Jersey), Benjamin Franklin and James Wilson (Pennsylvania), and Thomas Jefferson (Virginia). The committee had more or less radical delegates (Adams and Jefferson), more or less moderate ones (Rutledge, Livingston, and Wilson), and two who, though increasingly radical, still in some senses fell in between (Franklin and Wythe).

The committee submitted a draft letter to Congress on November 29, which explains to the colonial agents the state of things at home, in particular regarding the administration's failed efforts to bring "the Catholics of Canada and the savages of the wilderness" into the war. The letter offers further evidence that many members of Congress, in opposition to John Adams and like-minded colleagues who "mortally hated the Words, 'Province,' 'Colonies,' and 'Mother Country,'" still hoped to reconcile their differences with Parliament and "to restore harmony and peace to the British Empire," for they claim here that "there is nothing more ardently desired by North America than a lasting union with Great Britain on terms of just and equal liberty." And Congress still held only the king's ministers, not monarchy or the king himself, culpable for the "malignant councils, that surround the sovereign and distract the British Empire."

Worthington Chauncey Ford et al., eds., *Journals of the Continental Congress, 1774–1789* (Washington, D.C.: Government Printing Office, 1904–37), 3:391–92.

The Committee appointed to prepare a draught of a letter to the Agents, brought in the same, which was read and agreed to as follows:

Gentlemen,

The manner in which the last dutiful petition to his Majesty was received and the subsequent proclamation are considered by Congress as further proofs of those malignant councils, that surround the sovereign and distract the British Empire. It is however happy for mankind that ministers can form destructive plans with much more facility than they can execute them. The enclosed printed detail of the operations in Canada this campaign will sufficiently evince what little success is likely to attend ministerial exertions for bringing the Catholics of Canada and the savages of the wilderness to war on the defenceless women and children of unoffending America. The Canadians are much too liberal to be made instruments in the black design of enslaving their brethren and the Indians with their usual sagacity have by the firmest treaties accepted and pledged themselves to observe the neutrality which Congress desired.

Neither General Gage nor his successor has yet been able to penetrate into the Country. The British Men of War, indeed, that formerly with so much glory supported the interest and the honor of the nation, have with a wanton barbarity and inhumanity that would disgrace savages, have burned the flourishing but defenceless town of Falmouth in the Colony of Massachusetts bay and have frightened many of the weaker sex with their children from other places on the sea coast. It grieves us exceedingly to see the British arms employed in such a manner and for such purposes; but we hope the spirit and virtue of a sensible nation will soon be exerted to procure justice for the innocent oppressed colonies and to restore harmony and peace to the British Empire. There is nothing more ardently desired by North America than a lasting union with Great Britain on terms of just and equal liberty; but as men and as descendants of Britons the good people of these colonies will rely to the last on heaven, and their own virtuous efforts for security against the abusive system pressed by administration for the ruin of America and which if pursued must end in the destruction of a great Empire.

The intelligence now sent is, Gentlemen, to prevent the nation's being imposed upon by misrepresentations and to guard against mistakes that may probably arise from wanting a true state of facts. We cannot suppose that a brave and sensible people will be prevented by proclamation from furnishing North America with such advice and assistance as the laws permit and justice to an oppressed people demands.

N. B. This and the former letter to the agents in England are in Mr. Hancock's (the president's) letter Book.

*Ordered,* That a fair copy of the above be made, signed by the president and forwarded to the Agents.

## 24.6

## Josiah Bartlett to John Langdon, March 5, 1776

This letter concerns a protest sent to Congress from some in Portsmouth and other towns who opposed Congress' having urged the New Hampshire Provincial Congress to set up a new government. It was written from Congress by Josiah Bartlett, the son of a poor Massachusetts shoemaker. After training with a family relative, he set up a medical practice in Kingston, New Hampshire, before later serving the state on its highest judicial bench and then becoming its first governor. He was an active member of Congress and truly a self-made man. Langdon, though a radical too, was a very successful merchant from Portsmouth who also served his state in numerous capacities. Bartlett defends Congress by reminding Langdon that it sought "not to interfere with internal Govt of any of the Colonies, any further than to recommend to them to adopt such forms, as they shall think best calculated, to promote the quiet and peace of the Society, leaving every Colony to take such govt as is most agreeable to the majority, during the present dispute." Congress, consistent with the instructions provided to each of the colonial delegates and its own limited capacities to legislate, could not legitimately involve itself in the interior concerns of any of its members, any more than it believed Parliament could. Accordingly, some in New Hampshire reasonably thought that Congress had gone too far in its instructions to that colony and had interfered in its internal affairs.

This was not the last time that Congress was accused of going beyond its limited intercolonial or continental set of mandates. Similar concerns were raised in mid-May when Congress, without invitation from any of the colonies, recommended, at John Adams' urging, that they reform their governments along republican lines, whether they needed to or not. Something similar occurred in February 1777 when Congress attempted to control desertion by issuing instructions directly to local committees of safety (see documents 31.1 and 37.1) without seeking the permission or cooperation of putatively sovereign states.

Paul H. Smith, ed., *Letters of Delegates to Congress, 1774–1789* (Washington, D.C.: Library of Congress, 1976–93), 3:333–35.

Dear Sir,                                                          Philadelphia March 5 1776

Yours of the 19th ulto is now before me and am very sorry that any person in New Hampshire could pretend to write and print so ridiculous a piece as that you mention. I had the reading of it, being enclosed to Col Whipple. I think your Committee acted wisely in putting a stop to it, though the chief hurt that will arise from the publishing such trifling, inconsistent and puerile pieces is to make the persons and the place producing them mean and ridiculous to every sensible reader. I am extremely sorry that our Colony, who has hitherto stood high in the esteem of the whole Continent, for their manly and spirited exertions in the cause of liberty should by such productions added to some late manoeuvres of Portsmouth and some other towns in regard to taking up govt. fall to the lowest depth of ignominy and contempt, which unless a stop is put it will certainly be the case. The packet containing the whole of the affairs of taking up civil govt we carried in the evening to the President, who opened it while we were present. After reading the whole to himself for some time, he asked us what was the question the Colony wanted to have put to the Congress for their answer as he said he could not find out by reading the papers, and neither Col Whipple nor I could inform him; for the order of Congress to take up civil Govt. in such a manner as the Colony should think proper nobody can deny and that the Colony had taken up such a form as was most agreeable to majority is not disputed; that a number disliked it and protested against it is set forth, but what the Congress can say in the matter I am at a loss to guess, consistent with their constant declaration not to interfere with internal Govt of any of the Colonies, any further than to recommend to them to adopt such forms, as they shall think best calculated, to promote the quiet and peace of the Society, leaving every Colony to take such govt as is most agreeable to the majority, during the present dispute. However as it was directed to the Congress, it was the next day publicly read together with the petition for a regt to be stationed at Portsmouth; the whole was committed to Dr Franklin, Mr Wythe and Mr Braxton, a new member from Virginia; what or when they will report is uncertain, but for the honor of the Province I wish it had been kept at home.

The protestor's insinuation that it was unfairly obtained, I think (and they are not alone in it) reflects highly on the Congress in general as well as the delegates of New Hampshire, which the whole Congress know is illiberal and unjust. According to the best of my remembrance (as well as of some others that I have asked) not more than one Colony voted against it (if one): however I hope the difficulty will soon subside, and by the future good conduct of the Colony, they will regain their former esteem. Their spirit and activity in raising the regt. for Canada is highly commended. . . .

I am, Sir, your friend,                                                    Josiah Bartlett . . .

## 25. CONGRESS RESPONDS TO THE KING'S CHARGE OF INSURGENCY, DECEMBER 1775

On October 31, 1775, the king's proclamation of August 23 declaring the colonies in rebellion (see immediately below), along with the disturbing news that he had refused to receive the Olive Branch Petition, arrived in North America.[104] Instead of attempting to mollify the rising anger, fear, and distrust of many in the North American colonies, even those numerous moderates who continued to hope for a constitutional and just means for the colonies to remain in the British Empire, the king's proclamation exacerbated tensions by legitimizing the use of military force against the colonists. Step by fatal step, in opposition to the desire of king and Parliament to keep the empire intact and to continue profiting from imperial commercial regulation of the colonies' economic life, and in keeping with their haunting fear of the colonists' seeking independence, Britain effectively worked in concert with a growing number in Congress to push the colonies toward independence.[105]

The playing out of this drama, regardless of the merits of the constitutional issues advanced by either side, has a certain haunting and tragic character. In spite of the charges of rebelliousness and sedition, Congress decided to create a committee on November 13, 1775, "to prepare a declaration, in answer to sundry illegal ministerial proclamations that have lately appeared in America." A mixed group of delegates, including Richard Henry Lee, James Wilson, and William Livingston, were assigned to it. In keeping with the composition of the committee, it produced a document that in denying the king's charge that the colonies were in rebellion and seeking independence, was in some ways still moderate, and in others ways was defensively bold in preparing the way for independence and war.[106]

On December 6, 1775, Congress' answer to the king was read and approved. Congress accepted that under the British Constitution, the colonists' "best inheritance, rights, as well as duties, descend upon us: We cannot violate the latter by defending the former," that is, rights and duties are correlatively linked. The colonists, having never failed to act in accord with their duties, had done nothing to diminish their just rights under the British Constitution. More particularly, the North American colonists had never forgotten to whom they owed allegiance: "What allegiance is it that we forget? Allegiance to Parliament? We never owed—we never owned it. Allegiance to our King? Our words have ever avowed it,—our conduct has ever been consistent with it." Congress discussed the colonists' relationship to the king—something not often done during the most intense phases of the crisis—asking whether it is "objected against us by the most inveterate and the most uncandid of our enemies, that we have opposed any of the just prerogatives of the Crown, or any legal exertion of those prerogatives?" If not, "Why then are we accused of forgetting our allegiance? We have performed our duty."

In response to the charge of supporting an "open and avowed rebellion," Congress not so humbly asked, "In what does this rebellion consist. It is thus described—'Arraying ourselves in hostile manner, to withstand the execution of the law, and traiterously preparing, ordering, and levying war against the King.' We know of no laws binding upon us, but such as have been transmitted to us by our ancestors, and such as have been consented to by ourselves, or our representatives elected for that purpose." Yet in spite of this anything but reticent defense, Congress explained, "We view him [the King] as the Constitution represents him. That tells us he can do no wrong. . . . We will not, on our part, lose the distinction between the King and his Ministers: happy would it have been for some former Princes, had it been always preserved on that part of the Crown." (The "former Prince" alluded to is Charles I, executed in 1649.) Congress in its answer was torn between, on the one hand, a lingering loyalty to the king and, at least for some delegates, the hope of some form of reconciliation, and on the other, an open and bold defense of its actions while preparing for more open warfare, a rejection of monarchy and an embrace of republicanism, and a permanent rupture in the British Empire.

Congress ridiculed one of the principal aims of the king's proclamation, to cut off the lively correspondence between rebellious colonists and radical correspondents in Britain. Congress questioned the constitutionality of the law: "How shall he ascertain who are in rebellion, and who are not?" But if the constitution, in the end, proved inadequate in controlling this measure, Congress promised to turn to another law, that of retaliation, so "that whatever punishment shall be inflicted upon any persons in the power of our enemies for favouring, aiding, or abetting the cause of American liberty, shall be retaliated in the same kind, and the same degree upon those in our power." Nearly a year earlier, the county of Suffolk, Massachusetts, had supported such retaliatory measures, as had John Adams (see documents 9.1 and 11.3); seven months later, the source of oppression was no longer only the king's ministers, Parliament, and their colonial supporters, but the beginning claims against the king himself, and those to be met with retaliation were all North American subjects remaining loyal to him.

25.1

Congress, Answer to the King's
Proclamation for Suppressing Rebellion and
Sedition, December 6, 1775

Worthington Chauncey Ford et al., eds., *Journals of the Continental Congress, 1774–1789* (Washington, D.C.: Government Printing Office, 1904–37), 3:409–12.

The Congress resumed the consideration of the report of the committee on proclamations, which being debated by paragraphs, was agreed to as follows:

*Ordered,* That it be published.

Here insert it

We, the Delegates of the thirteen United Colonies in North America, have taken into our most serious consideration, a Proclamation issued from the Court of St. James's on the Twenty-Third day of August last. The name of Majesty is used to give it a sanction and influence; and, on that account, it becomes a matter of importance to wipe off, in the name of the people of these United Colonies, the aspersions which it is calculated to throw upon our cause; and to prevent, as far as possible, the undeserved punishments, which it is designed to prepare, for our friends. We are accused of "forgetting the allegiance which we owe to the power that has protected and sustained us." Why all this ambiguity and obscurity in what ought to be so plain and obvious, as that he who runs may read it? What allegiance is it that we forget? Allegiance to Parliament? We never owed—we never owned it. Allegiance to our King? Our words have ever avowed it,—our conduct has ever been consistent with it. We condemn, and with arms in our hands,—a resource which Freemen will never part with,—we oppose the claim and exercise of unconstitutional powers, to which neither the Crown nor Parliament were ever entitled. By the British Constitution, our best inheritance, rights, as well as duties, descend upon us: We cannot violate the latter by defending the former: We should act in diametrical opposition to both, if we permitted the claims of the British Parliament to be established, and the measures pursued in consequence of those claims to be carried into execution among us. Our sagacious ancestors provided mounds against the inundation of tyranny and lawless power on one side, as well as against that of faction and licentiousness on the other. On which side has the breach been made? Is it objected against us by the most inveterate and the most uncandid of our enemies, that we have opposed any of the just prerogatives of the Crown, or any legal exertion of those prerogatives? Why then are we accused of forgetting our allegiance? We have performed our duty: We have resisted in those cases, in which the right to resist is stipulated as expressly on our part, as the right to govern is, in other cases, stipulated on the part of the Crown. The breach of allegiance is removed from our resistance as far as tyranny is removed from legal government. It is alledged, that "we have proceeded to an open and avowed rebellion." In what does this rebellion consist. It is thus described—"Arraying ourselves in hostile manner, to withstand the execution of the law, and traiterously preparing, ordering, and levying war against the King." We know of no laws binding upon us, but such as have been transmitted to us by our ancestors, and such as have been consented to by ourselves, or our representatives elected for that purpose. What laws, stampt with these characters, have we withstood? We have indeed defended them; and we will risque every thing, do every thing, and suffer every thing in their defence. To support our laws, and our liberties established by our laws, we have prepared, ordered, and levied war: But is this traiterously, or against the King? We view him as the Constitution represents him. That tells us he can do no wrong. The cruel and illegal attacks, which we oppose, have no foundation in the royal authority. We will not, on our part, lose the distinction between the King and his Ministers:

happy would it have been for some former Princes, had it been always preserved on that part of the Crown.

Besides all this, we observe, on this part of the proclamation, that "rebellion" is a term undefined and unknown in the law; it might have been expected that a proclamation, which by the British constitution has no other operation than merely that of enforcing what is already law, would have had a known legal basis to have rested upon. A correspondence between the inhabitants of Great Britain and their brethren in America, produced, in better times, much satisfaction to individuals, and much advantage to the public. By what criterion shall one, who is unwilling to break off this correspondence, and is, at the same time, anxious not to expose himself to the dreadful consequences threatened in this proclamation—by what criterion shall he regulate his conduct? He is admonished not to carry on correspondence with the persons now in rebellion in the colonies. How shall he ascertain who are in rebellion, and who are not? He consults the law to learn the nature of the supposed crime: the law is silent upon the subject. This, in a country where it has been often said, and formerly with justice, that the government is by law, and not by men, might render him perfectly easy. But proclamations have been sometimes dangerous engines in the hands of those in power; Information is commanded to be given to one of the Secretaries of State, of all persons "who shall be found carrying on correspondence with the persons in rebellion, in order to bring to condign punishment the authors, perpetrators, or abettors, of such dangerous designs." Let us suppose, for a moment, that some persons in the colonies are in rebellion, and that those who carry on correspondence with them, might learn by some rule, which Britons are bound to know, how to discriminate them; Does it follow that all correspondence with them deserves to be punished? It might have been intended to apprize them of their danger, and to reclaim them from their crimes. By what law does a correspondence with a criminal transfer or communicate his guilt? We know that those who aid and adhere to the King's enemies, and those who correspond with them in order to enable them to carry their designs into effect, are criminal in the eye of the law. But the law goes no farther. Can proclamations, according to the principles of reason and justice, and the constitution, go farther than the law?

But, perhaps the principles of reason and justice, and the constitution will not prevail: Experience suggests to us the doubt: If they should not, we must resort to arguments drawn from a very different source. We, therefore, in the name of the people of these United Colonies, and by authority, according to the purest maxims of representation, derived from them, declare, that whatever punishment shall be inflicted upon any persons in the power of our enemies for favouring, aiding, or abetting the cause of American liberty, shall be retaliated in the same kind, and the same degree upon those in our power, who have favoured, aided, or abetted, or shall favour, aid, or abet the system of ministerial oppression. The essential difference between our cause, and that of our enemies, might justify a severer punishment: The law of retaliation will unquestionably warrant one equally severe.

We mean not, however, by this declaration, to occasion or to multiply punishments; Our sole view is to prevent them. In this unhappy and unnatural controversy, in which Britons fight against Britons, and the descendants of Britons, let the calamities immediately incident to a civil war suffice. We hope additions will not from wantonness be made to them on one side: We shall regret the necessity, if laid under the necessity, of making them on the other.

*Extract from the Minutes,*

CHARLES THOMSON, *Sec.*

25.2

 GEORGE III, PROCLAMATION FOR SUPPRESSING
REBELLION AND SEDITION, AUGUST 23, 1775

On August 18, 1775, upon receiving from General Haldimand a report on the increasing violence in the North American colonies, King George III condemned the colonists before issuing on the twenty-third a proclamation for suppressing the rebellion.[107] The colonists, believed to have been "misled by dangerous and ill-designing men," had "at length proceeded to an open and avowed rebellion by arraying themselves in hostile manner to withstand the execution of the law, and traitorously preparing, ordering, and levying war against us." In the proclamation, much of the king's attention is directed against "divers wicked and desperate persons within this realm" who were believed to have "promoted and encouraged" through "traitorous correspondence, counsels, and comfort . . . an open and avowed rebellion." Accordingly, the proclamation asks the king's subjects in Great Britain "to disclose and make known all treasons and traitorous conspiracies which they shall know to be against us, our Crown and dignity . . . in order to bring to condign punishment the authors, perpetrators and abettors of such traitorous designs." It seems that the king and his "friends" in Parliament were as concerned with rooting out and suppressing opposition to the administration in Parliament and in Great Britain generally as in suppressing rebellion in the North American colonies against the Crown's policies.

Merrill Jensen, ed., *English Historical Documents: American Colonial Documents to 1776*
(New York: Oxford University Press, 1969), 9:850–51.

Whereas many of our subjects in divers parts of our colonies and plantations in North America, misled by dangerous and ill-designing men, and forgetting the allegiance which they owe to the power that has protected and sustained them, after various disorderly acts committed in disturbance of the public peace, to the obstruction of lawful commerce and to the oppression of our loyal subjects carrying on the same, have at length proceeded to an open and avowed rebellion by arraying themselves in hostile manner to withstand the execution of the law, and traitorously preparing, ordering, and levying war against us; and whereas there is reason to apprehend that such rebellion hath been much promoted and encouraged by the traitorous correspondence, counsels, and comfort of divers wicked and desperate persons within this realm; to the end therefore that none of our subjects may neglect or violate their duty through ignorance thereof, or through any doubts of the protection which the law will afford to their loyalty and zeal; we have thought fit, by and with the advice of our Privy Council, to issue this our royal proclamation, hereby declaring that not only all our officers, civil and military, are obliged to exert their utmost endeavours to suppress such rebellion and to bring the traitors to justice; but that all our subjects of this realm and the dominions thereunto belonging are bound by law to be aiding and assisting in the suppression of such rebellion, and to disclose and make known all traitorous conspiracies and attempts against us, our Crown, and dignity; and we do accordingly strictly charge and command all our officers, as well civil as military, and all other our obedient and loyal subjects, to use their utmost endeavours to withstand and suppress such rebellion, and to disclose and make known all treasons and traitorous conspiracies which they shall know to be against us, our Crown and dignity; and for that purpose, that they transmit to one of our principal secretaries of state, or other proper officer, due and full information of all persons who shall be found carrying on correspondence with, or in any manner or degree aiding or abetting the persons now in open arms and rebellion against our government within any of our colonies and plantations in North America, in order to bring to condign punishment the authors, perpetrators and abettors of such traitorous designs.

Given at our court at St. James the twenty-third day of August, one thousand seven hundred and seventy-five, in the fifteenth year of our reign.

## 25.3

 EDWARD RUTLEDGE TO RALPH IZARD, DECEMBER 8, 1775

Two days after the colonies sent off their answer to the king's proclamation, the younger of the Rutledge brothers wrote to a fellow South Carolinian, Ralph Izard, then living in London. Izard had spent much of his adolescence there before moving to Paris in 1776. The next year, he was named America's commissioner to the Court of Tuscany, but given its refusal to meet with the colonies' representative, Izard remained in Paris and aided Arthur Lee. Izard was recalled from Paris in 1779 because of his deteriorating relations with Benjamin Franklin and Silas Deane, who was, in turn, recalled from his mission because of accusations of corruption leveled against him by Izard's ally, the ever-troublesome Arthur Lee.[108]

In this letter, Rutledge offers additional evidence that the actions of Parliament and the British administration were driving colonists toward independence. In particular, he believed that Lord Dunmore's proclamation offering freedom to slaves in Virginia had more effectively worked for "an eternal separation between Great Britain and the Colonies, than any other expedient, which could possibly have been thought of" and that, by necessity, that separation seemed "to be not very far distant—if the Administration, continue their wicked projects." He asks Izard about "the sentiments of the English Nation" and whether "the people of that Country [are] determined to force us, into Independence." If perspectives like Rutledge's were widespread, as seems likely, since less than a third of congressional delegates were yet willing to endorse independence, then Americans' move toward declaring independence in 1776 can be attributed as much to the British administration's loosening of the ties that bound the colonists to the empire as to the intrigues of a minority of radicals in the colonies and Congress—and possibly more.[109]

Unlike many of the men of New England who welcomed a change in government and, as John Adams noted, had lived their lives under substantially republican arrangements, the well-born Rutledge viewed the upcoming experiment in republican government with trepidation. As he describes it, the colonists were to be cast "into an unknown Ocean—and engage in a Business to which we are strangers." Clearly, the most radical New England delegates saw the future differently from many of the delegates from the other colonies. Of course, there were others, particularly in the Virginia delegation, who shared with the New Englanders a hunger for a republican future.

Rutledge nonetheless was mindful of the increasing insults suffered by the colonists and of how their experience was pushing them ever closer toward independence. Thus, he asks Izard whether the British "expect that after our Towns have been destroyed—our Liberties repeatedly invaded—our women and children, driven from their Habitations—our nearest Relatives sacrificed at the Altar of Tyranny, our Slaves emancipated for the express purpose of massacring their Masters . . . that we shall return to our former connection with a forgiving, and cordial Disposition." Indeed, even Rutledge, with his strong commitment to the British Constitution, expressed deep bitterness toward the administration: "I feel such high Resentment for the unmerited—and indiscriminate cruelties committed against the Inhabitants of this Country—that I do not believe I shall ever forget—or forgive them." Still, he estimated that not all was yet lost and that Parliament had one last opportunity before "they may loose forever their American Colonies." As we know, Parliament did not, indeed possibly could not, take advantage of this opportunity to keep the empire together.

Paul H. Smith, ed., *Letters of Delegates to Congress, 1774–1789* (Washington, D.C.: Library of Congress, 1976–93), 2:462–64. Bracketed ellipses are those present in the source text.

My Dear Sir:                                                    Philadelphia, December 8, 1775.

I should have wrote you frequently, and fully, had I had the least reason, to imagine that you would have been in England at this day. But your own letters, and general report induced me to believe, that immediately upon your return to London, you would have prepared for a voyage to your Native Country—to act, and suffer in the Common Cause.

Let this then be my apology for silence—unmerited entirely on your part, and far from intentional offence on mine. Permit me to add further, that your residing abroad, at least for a time, will, in my opinion, be of more service than returning to America.

You will receive by this conveyance a proclamation issued by Lord Dunmore—tending in my judgment, more effectually to work an eternal separation between Great Britain and the Colonies, than any other expedient, which could possibly have been thought of.

Indeed my Friend, however chimerical such an Event may appear, to the feeble understanding of a deluded people, it seems to be not very far distant—if the Administration, continue their wicked projects, nor in itself is it at all impracticable.

I cannot, however, without much anxiety look forward. If all connection with your Island, shall but once be put an end to, we must bid adieu, at least for a number of years, to Ease, and Happiness. We launch as it were into an unknown Ocean—and engage in a Business to which we are entire strangers.

If, on the other hand, we fondly continue our Connection—at a time when every Engine of Oppression is raised against us—our Executive will be so weak—foreign Powers, will be so unwilling to assist us—the Demon of Anarchy, will lay such fast hold upon us—that we may at last fall a prey to those sons of Darkness on your side of the Atlantic.

Tell me then, I beseech you, (before it is too late) what are the sentiments of the English Nation—are the people of that Country determined to force us, into Independence? Or do they really imagine, that we are so void of the Feelings of Humanity, and so insensible to the calls of Reason as willingly to submit to every Insult—to every Injury? Do they expect that after our Towns have been destroyed—our Liberties repeatedly invaded—our women and children, driven from their Habitations—our nearest Relatives sacrificed at the Altar of Tyranny, our Slaves emancipated for the express purpose of massacring their Masters—can they, I say, after all their injuries, expect that we shall return to our former connection with a forgiving, and cordial Disposition.

Surely if the Administration had consulted their friends, the Bishops, they could have informed them, that Christian charity—however strongly enjoined in Holy Writ—has seldom, if ever, extended so far in practice. Speaking for myself, I freely confess, that I feel such high Resentment for the unmerited—and indiscriminate cruelties committed against the Inhabitants of this Country—that I do not believe I shall ever forget—or ever forgive them; and so determined am I on being free that I will even quit my Native Country without a sigh—if the Genius of Liberty shall loose her Influence. That, however, I trust will never be the case.

America, indeed, appears to be the natural clime, for Freedom—and she seems to spread her powers still wider and wider [ . . . ]

How truly vain must be the expectations of those, who wish to subjugate us, when we consider, that wanting every sinew of War, we have been able to resist—and baffle—their wicked attacks.

Let them reflect that America engaged in this contest, without Arms—Ammunition—Officers—or money. We shall, however, soon have a sufficient quantity of the two first articles—to do Mr. Howe's business for him—in the course of the winter [ . . . ]

This session may determine the Fate, of a great Kingdom—unless the Parliament improve the opportunity now offered them, they may loose forever their American Colonies. May God grant them Wisdom to discover—and Virtue to pursue such measures—as may best tend to the Establishment of Peace, and Happiness [ . . . ]

You must take this as I write it, for we are so closely engaged in Business, that we have hardly time to eat and drink, what with attention in the House, and committees.

I shall write to A[rthur] L[ee] in a few days. With much sincerity and affection, I am, my dear sir, Your friend.

## 25.4

 BENJAMIN FRANKLIN TO CHARLES WILLIAM
FREDERIC DUMAS, DECEMBER 9, 1775

In 1768, after meeting two years earlier in the Netherlands, Benjamin Franklin and Charles Dumas began a trans-Atlantic correspondence that lasted until Franklin's death. Dumas, who lived in The Hague, was born to French parents in present-day Germany. He was a writer, tutor, and translator who served the American cause in Europe, first by reporting on European affairs and then as an irregularly compensated (in spite of Franklin's promise) American agent to the Dutch Republic; in the latter role, he did much to help with the outfitting of American ships. Franklin here writes to thank Dumas for sending him Vattel's *Law of Nations,* then seeks his assistance in ascertaining, among the European powers resident in The Hague, "whether any one of them, from principles of humanity, is disposed magnanimously to step in for the relief of an oppressed people; or whether, if, as it seems likely to happen, we should be obliged to break off all connexion with Britain, and declare ourselves an independent people, there is any state or power in Europe, who would be willing to enter into an alliance with us for the benefit of our commerce." At the end of 1775, for Franklin and most likely for other delegates, the probability that the colonies would soon seek independence was no longer a frightening phantom.

But the colonists were short of almost every manner of war-fighting material. As Franklin explains, "Our artificers are also everywhere busy in fabricating small arms, casting cannon, &c.; yet both arms and ammunition are much wanted. Any merchants, who would venture to send ships laden with those articles, might make great profit." The colonies badly needed not only supplies and money but also, and possibly even more, the military assistance of European powers, especially in helping harass stretched British supply lines. Indeed, by the end of the Revolutionary War, the French army and navy had played a significant, indeed vital, role in the young country's final military success. At the Battle of Yorktown, in October 1781, of the 16,650 allied soldiers engaged against the British forces, 7,800 were French. And the French navy under Admiral de Grasse, with his tens of thousands of sailors and twenty-eight ships of the line—considerably more than the British could devote to the North American theatre—blockaded the sea-lanes off the coast of Yorktown against British warships and ferried allied troops to the battle.[110]

Paul H. Smith, ed., *Letters of Delegates to Congress, 1774–1789* (Washington, D.C.: Library of Congress, 1976–93), 2:465–68.

Dear Sir,                                         Philadelphia, 9 December, 1775.

I received your several favors, of May 18th, June 30th, and July 8th, by Messrs. Vaillant and Pochard; whom if I could serve upon your recommendation, it would give me great pleasure. Their total want of English is at present an obstruction to their getting any employment among us; but I hope they will soon obtain some knowledge of it. This is a good country for artificers or farmers; but gentlemen of mere science in *les belles lettres* cannot so easily subsist here, there being little demand for their assistance among an industrious people, who, as yet, have not much leisure for studies of that kind.

I am much obliged by the kind present you have made us of your edition of Vattel. It came to us in good season, when the circumstances of a rising state make it necessary frequently to consult the law of nations. Accordingly that copy, which I kept, (after depositing one in our own public library here, and sending the other to the College of Massachusetts Bay, as you directed,) has been continually in the hands of the members of our Congress, now sitting, who are much pleased with your notes and preface, and have entertained a high and just esteem for their author. Your manuscript "*Idee sur le Gouvernement et la Royaute*" is also well relished, and may, in time, have its effect. I thank you, likewise, for the other smaller pieces, which accompanied Vattel. "*Le court Expose de ce qui s'est passe entre la Cour Britannique et les Colonies*," &c. being a very concise and clear statement of facts, will be reprinted here for the use of our new friends in Canada. The translations of the proceedings of our Congress are very acceptable. I send you herewith what of them has been farther published here, together with a few newspapers, containing accounts of some of the successes Providence has favored us with. We are threatened from England with a very powerful force, to come next year against us. We are making all the provision in our power here to oppose that force, and we hope we shall be able to defend ourselves. But, as the events of war are always uncertain, possibly, after another campaign, we may find it necessary to ask the aid of some foreign power.

It gives us great pleasure to learn from you, that *toute l'Europe nous souhaite le plus heureux succès pour le maintien de nos libertés.* But we wish to know, whether any one of them, from principles of humanity, is disposed magnanimously to step in for the relief of an oppressed people; or whether, if, as it seems likely to happen, we should be obliged to break off all connexion with Britain, and declare ourselves an independent people, there is any state or power in Europe, who would be willing to enter into an alliance with us for the benefit of our commerce, which amounted, before the war, to near seven millions sterling per annum, and must continually increase, as our people increase most rapidly. Confiding, my dear friend, in your good will to us and to our cause, and in your sagacity and abilities for business, the committee of Congress, appointed for the purpose of establishing and conducting a correspondence with our friends in Europe, of which committee I have the honor to be a member, have directed me to request of you, that, as you are situated at the Hague, where ambassadors from all the courts reside, you would make use of the opportunity that situation affords you, of discovering, if possible, the disposition of the several courts with respect to such assistance or alliance, if we should apply for the one, or propose the other. As it may possibly be necessary, in particular instances, that you should, for this purpose, confer directly with some great ministers, and show them this letter as your credential, we only recommend it to your discretion, that you proceed therein with such caution, as to keep the same from the knowledge of the English ambassador, and prevent any public appearance, at present, of your being employed in any such business; as thereby we imagine many inconveniences may be avoided, and your means of rendering us service increased.

That you may be better able to answer some questions, which will probably be put to you, concerning our present situation, we inform you, that the whole continent is very firmly united, the party for the measures of the British ministry being very small, and much dispersed; that we have had on foot, the last campaign, an army of near twenty-five thousand men, wherewith we have been able, not only to block up the King's army in Boston, but to spare considerable detachments for the invasion of Canada, where we have met with great success, as the printed papers sent herewith will inform you, and have now reason to expect the whole province may be soon in our possession; that we purpose greatly to increase our force for the ensuing year, and thereby we hope, with the assistance of a well disciplined militia, to be able to defend our coast, nothwithstanding its great extent; that we have already a small squadron of armed vessels to protect our coasting trade, who have had some success in taking several of the enemy's cruisers, and some of their transport vessels and store ships. This little naval force we are about to augment, and expect it may be more considerable in the next summer.

We have hitherto applied to no foreign power. We are using the utmost industry in endeavouring to make saltpetre, and with daily increasing success. Our artificers are also everywhere busy in fabricating small arms, casting cannon, &c.; yet both arms and ammunition are much wanted. Any merchants, who would venture to send ships laden with those articles, might make great profit; such is the demand in every colony, and such generous prices are and will be given; of which, and of the manner of conducting such a voyage, the bearer, Mr. Story, can more fully inform you; and whoever brings in those articles is allowed to carry off the value in provisions, to our West Indies, where they will probably fetch a very high price, the general exportation from North America being stopped. This you will see more particularly in a printed resolution of the Congress.

We are in great want of good engineers, and wish you could engage and send us two able ones, in time for the next campaign, one acquainted with field service, sieges, &c., and the other with fortifying of seaports. They will, if well recommended, be made very welcome, and have honorable appointments, besides the expenses of their voyage hither, in which Mr. Story can also advise them. As what we now request of you, besides taking up your time, may put you to some expense, we send you for the present, enclosed, a bill for one hundred pounds sterling, to defray such expenses, and desire you to be assured that your services will be considered, and honorably rewarded, by the Congress.

We desire, also, that you would take the trouble of receiving from Arthur Lee, agent for the Congress in England, such letters as may be sent by him to your care, and of forwarding them to us with your despatches. When you have occasion to write to him to inform him of any thing, which it may be of importance that our friends there should be acquainted with, please to send your letters to him, under cover, directed to Mr. Alderman Lee, merchant, on Tower Hill, London; and do not send it by post, but by some trusty shipper, or other prudent person, who will deliver it with his own hand. And when you send to us, if you have not a direct safe opportunity, we recommend sending by way of St. Eustatia, to the care of Messrs. Robert and Cornelius Stevenson, merchants there, who will forward your despatches to me. With sincere and great esteem and respect, I am, Sir, &c.

B. Franklin.

Philad. Dec. 12.1775.

[P. S.] We the underwritten, appointed by the American Congress a Committee of Foreign Correspondence, having perused the above Letter, written at our Request, do approve and confirm the same.

Was signed

John Dickinson

John Jay

25.5

 **ROBERT MORRIS TO AN UNKNOWN**
**CORRESPONDENT, DECEMBER 9, 1775**

Robert Morris of Pennsylvania was born in Liverpool, England, and came to be known as the financier of the American Revolution.[111] Morris, a partner with Thomas Willing in one of the leading mercantile firms in the colonies, during the war used his own substantial resources to maintain the value of the rapidly depreciating Continental dollar and to keep the Continental Army in the field. Later, he chose to serve as a U. S. senator rather than accept the post of secretary of the treasury, but by the late 1790s, like a number of his colleagues, he was deeply in debt, largely because of failed land speculations, and sent to debtor's prison. He died penniless.[112]

Morris, in spite of his bleak assessment that "nothing is done towards peace & reconciliation but on the contrary every thing breaths Warr & Bloodshed," still believed at the end of 1775 "that nobody wish[es] for Independance on Great Britain; the People all call out for reconciliation on Constitutional Terms, & they do not act against Great Britain untill drove to it by some apparent necessity." And he believed the colonists continued to demand, as they had for the past ten years, that the British "consider Us as Brothers entitled to the same freedom, the same priviledges themselves enjoy." Morris, a man who genuinely abhorred "the Name & Idea of a Rebel" and neither wanted nor wished "a Change of King or Constitution," closed by writing that in spite of the harsh treatment that had been meted out to the colonists, he would continue to make every possible exertion "in favour of every measure that has a tendency to procure Accomodation on terms consistant with our just Claims & if I thought there was any thing ask'd on this side not founded in the Constitution in Reason & Justice I wou'd oppose it."

Thus, the year ended with the Second Continental Congress less divided than the First had been. Still, nearly half the delegates expressed a measure of loyalty to the king, some still hoping against hope to remain part of his empire. Others were looking forward, with newly gained confidence, to instituting independent republican governments in the not too distant future. In the first month of the new year, the colonies moved ever closer, though still with considerable opposition in the mid-Atlantic region, toward independence.

Paul H. Smith, ed., *Letters of Delegates to Congress, 1774–1789* (Washington, D.C.: Library of Congress, 1976–93), 2:470–71.

Philadelphia 9th Decr. 1775

Herewith you'l receive some prints by which you'll be much surprized to find the Americans have not only kept the English army pent up in Boston but at the same time have wrested all Canada out of their possession, in short I am unhappy to tell You that as yet nothing is done towards peace & reconciliation but on the contrary every thing breaths Warr & Bloodshed. On this side it seems absolutely necessary to provide for a vigorous defence seeing that every Account we receive from England threatens nothing but destruction. These threats will prove vain whilst the Americans continue united & there is every appearance that the Union will be preserved & grow stronger the longer we are oppress'd. It is but doing bare Justice to assert that nobody wish for Independance on Great Britain; the People all call out for reconciliation on Constitutional Terms, & they do not act against Great Britain untill drove to it by some apparent necessity. From this Cause they attack'd the Ministerial Army at Lexington, defended their Lines at Bankers hill & have kept them there ever since. From Necessity they have taken possession of Canada as it was notorious that the Ministry depended on that Country & its Inhabitants to pierce Us in the Rear, & get Us between two fires, in short it is meer necessity that ever induc'd Us to take up arms, & that now forces Us to depend on them. We love the people of England. We wanted no other Friends, no other Allys, but alas if they cannot be content to Consider Us as Brothers entitled to the same freedom, the same priviledges themselves enjoy, they cannot expect a people descended from their own flesh & blood, long Used to & well acquainted with the blessings of freedom, to sit down tamely & see themselves stripd of all they hold dear. For my part I abhor the Name & Idea of a Rebel, I neither want or wish a Change of King or Constitution, & do not conceive myself to act against either when I join America in defence of

Constitutional Liberty. I am now a Member of the Continental Congress & if I have any influence or shoud hereafter gain any it shall be exerted in favour of every measure that has a tendancy to procure Accomodation on terms consistant with our just Claims & if I thought there was any thing ask'd on this side not founded in the Constitution in Reason & Justice I wou'd oppose it. This subject is so Important that it's ever uppermost & you must excuse me for running into it. I will finish with sincerely praying that a Speedy end may be put to the Unhappy Contest.

# ACT IV

## TOWARD INDEPENDENCE, 1776

The fateful year 1776 began with a flurry of news reaching Congress that only exacerbated the impetus of congressional radicals toward independence—Adams later claimed that it was in December 1775 or January 1776 that he and like-minded colleagues, unlike the more timid majority, first came to view independence as an absolute necessity (see document 33.6). On January 7, news reached Philadelphia that Lord Dunmore, the governor of Virginia, had burned Norfolk on January 1. On January 8, news arrived that the king, in his speech to Parliament on October 26, 1775, had declared the colonies to be in open rebellion and seeking to establish "an independent empire." And, with especially good timing, on the day after the king's disheartening speech arrived, one of the first and by far the most successful of the attacks on monarchy written in the colonies, *Common Sense,* by the English radical Thomas Paine, was published in Philadelphia. On January 17, Congress learned of General Montgomery's failed effort on December 31, 1775, to capture Quebec; he was killed in the attack, and four hundred troops, most from New England, were killed, wounded, or captured. War was anticipated in the South, and before the end of the month, Congress dispatched a committee to New York to make plans "respecting the immediate defence of the said city."

In late January and early February, Congress frequently discussed the seemingly ever-more disastrous campaign in Canada—which proceeded from bad to worse until abandoned in the summer—and the need, while still operating as an intergovernmental legislative body, to serve as an executive agency in supplying an army and running a war. It also considered issuing an Address to the Inhabitants of These Colonies, something of a sequel to its Memorial to the Inhabitants of British America of the preceding October. The address, which was not published, is of particular interest, for its tabling on February 13 demonstrated that the moderates lacked sufficient strength to see a resolution or address through Congress. From that point on, congressional moderates were on the defensive, able only to delay or temper measures. The tabling of the address, written by a respected committee of delegates, was also the beginning of Congress', and no doubt the colonies', inevitable move toward independence. On February 26, Congress received a copy of the Prohibitory Act issued by Parliament on December 22, 1775, which removed the North American colonists from the king's protection, thus releasing them from their reciprocal duty of allegiance and loyalty. The act, along with earlier monarchical statements and a later one that arrived at the beginning of June, worked wonders in convincing moderates in Congress that reconciliation was ever less likely. A steady procession of events over the next five months led to the colonists' delegates declaring independence on July 2.

On March 1, the French foreign minister, Count Vergennes, wrote to the Spanish foreign minister asking whether Spain might be willing to help Britain's rebellious colonists. Spain was willing to do so. On March 2, the Committee of Secret Correspondence, unaware that this correspondence had already begun between Spain and France, appointed Silas Deane as its agent to conduct business, commercial and political, in France. Before his departure, Louis XVI had already ordered a sizable quantity of arms and gunpowder be shipped to the North American colonists through a fictitious company, Roderigue Hortalez et Cie. Spain's Charles III made similar arrangements, and the colonists early on received most of their war-fighting materials from one or the other of those two countries.

On March 17, under threat of bombardment from the cannons and mortars that the colonists had removed from Fort Ticonderoga and then arduously hauled across three colonies, the British forces occupying Boston decided to evacuate. Congress issued its Declaration on Armed Vessels on March 23, which allowed Americans to seize and sell British shipping and small armed vessels, the profits to be kept by the owners of the ship, the sailors, and sponsoring polity (see document 29.1). For some in Congress, that declaration, along with one made the following month, signified independence.

On April 6, discussions that had begun in January culminated in Congress' opening the North American colonial ports to the shipping of all countries except that of Britain, Ireland, and the British West Indies (see document 30.1). It is hard to overestimate the impact of this act in Britain, since so many of Parliament's actions over the previous twelve years were driven by its wish for British merchants and manufacturers to continue enjoying unique commercial advantages in its North American colonies. After the colonies declared themselves free of commercial regulation by Parliament, Britain would have to fight to regain control. On April 12 the North Carolina Convention instructed its congressional delegation to vote, along with other colonies, for independence. On the sixteenth, in trying to put additional pressure on the mid-Atlantic colonies, Congress requested that the Maryland Council of Safety arrest the colony's proprietary governor, William Eden. In an attempt to make something positive of the colonists' attack on Quebec, Congress on April 23 sent commissioners to publish a friendly "Address to the People of Canada" even as it was preparing an expedition against the northwestern outpost Fort Detroit.

Rhode Island, on May 4, formally disavowed its allegiance to the king—the first colony to do so after Mecklenburg County, North Carolina, did so provisionally on May 31, 1775—in Rhode Island's case, without conditions. On May 6, after being queried by Washington, Congress postponed the divisive issue of writing formal procedures on how to receive the British peace commissioners believed to be en route to the colonies. By an extraordinary coincidence, on that same day the king appointed the commissioners. On May 10, Congress recommended, without controversy and much as it had done in late 1775, that all colonies, where needed, "adopt such government as shall . . . best conduce to the happiness and safety of their constituents." Far more controversially, on May 15, in a preamble to the resolution on establishing new republican colonial governments, Congress explicitly declared the necessity of colonial governments suppressing "the exercise of every kind of authority under the British crown" (see document 31.1). What more was needed for independence? In an explicit answer, Virginia representatives, meeting in convention, on the same day instructed their congressional delegates "to propose to that respectable body to declare the United Colonies free and independent States" (see document 32.2).

On May 21, Congress received the frightening and infuriating news that the king had succeeded in hiring nearly seventeen thousand German mercenaries to fight in the American theatre of what soon became, like the antecedent Seven Years' War, an international war with military engagements taking place around the world. Congress on May 25 resolved "to engage the Indians in the service of the United Colonies"—a departure from Congress' earlier call for Indian neutrality. Later in May, after British reinforcements had reached Quebec and relieved the city, the Americans were forced into a retreat that the British and Canadians soon turned into something approaching a rout. That reversal led, in June, to Congress persistently trying to improve the colonies' military fortunes in Canada while also preparing for what the delegates rightly believed would be a pivotal battle and the first true test of the Continental Army, the Battle of Long Island.

On June 4, Congress received what some delegates described as the last straw in the conflict: a rejection by the king of a petition for reconciliation placed before him by the City of London on March 22 (see document 32.3). Each of the king's significant speeches and the acts of Parliament concerning the colonies received in North America from the end of 1775 had done much to alienate those colonists still committed to monarchy, king, and Empire. On June 7, Richard Henry Lee placed before

Congress three resolutions, the most memorable and controversial one declaring the colonies to be independent states. On June 10, Congress, meeting as a committee of the whole, agreed on the uncontroversial second and third resolutions, which concerned some plan of colonial or state confederation and sought to form alliances with foreign powers, but decided that "consideration of the first resolution," on independence, "would be postponed to this day, three weeks," that is, July 1 (see document 32.1).

Given the strong possibility that all three resolutions would be approved, Congress decided to appoint a committee to prepare a declaration concerning independence, along with another to outline a plan of confederation and a third to present a plan for treaties with foreign powers. It made appointments to the three committees on June 11 and 12. Additionally, Congress created a fourth permanent committee, the Board of War and Ordnance, and on the 13th elected its members. On June 19, Congress recommended that the New Jersey Provincial Congress arrest and detain its royal governor, William Franklin. At nearly the same time, Admiral Richard Howe, who had arrived in Halifax with hundreds of ships of war and supply, thirty thousand soldiers, and ten thousand sailors, issued an open declaration to the colonies, offering "free and general pardons to all those who . . . may have deviated from their just allegiance, and who are willing, by a speedy return to their duty, to reap the benefits of the Royal favour" (see document 35.3). The committee writing a declaration of independence, chaired by Thomas Jefferson, laid before Congress on June 28 a draft document, during the preparation of which Jefferson claimed to have "turned to neither book nor pamphlet." The longest section of the document by far was a detailed indictment of the king's actions that borrowed much from Jefferson's preamble to the Virginia Constitution of June 29, 1776.

As planned, Congress resolved itself into a committee of the whole on July 1 to consider Lee's resolution recommending independence, as well as the accompanying explanatory statement submitted by Jefferson's committee. Congress approved Lee's resolution. The colonial delegations voted on July 1 9–2 in favor, with 1 delegation divided and 1 abstaining. At the request of one of the colonies in opposition, South Carolina, the final vote was postponed until July 2. On that day, Congress, again with one delegation abstaining, voted unanimously in support of Lee's resolution. The South Carolina delegates, for the sake of unanimity, changed their votes; two of Pennsylvania's delegates were absent, allowing the delegation to vote yes; and a third Delaware delegate had ridden overnight by post to break that colony's tie vote in favor of the resolution. On July 2, the colonies declared their independence and terminated their allegiance to the king of Great Britain.

Congress, meeting again as a committee of the whole, began debating the Jefferson committee's draft Declaration on the same day, July 2. It met until the morning of July 4, when the committee chairman, Benjamin Harrison, reported to Congress "that the committee of the whole Congress have agreed to a Declaration, which he delivered in." After another reading, the Declaration was approved by all colonies voting, with New

York abstaining. Congress ordered that the Declaration be authenticated and printed and that copies be sent "to the several assemblies, conventions and committees, or councils of safety, and to the several commanding officers of the continental troops; that it be proclaimed in each of the United States, and at the head of the army."

Almost at the same time as the Declaration was approved, on July 7, Silas Deane reached France on a mission to entreat King Louis XVI to supply the colonies, by then the states, with war-fighting materials and money with which to defeat France's nemesis, Great Britain, which had recently defeated France and taken so much of its territory around the world. On July 12, Admiral Richard Howe—eight or ten days too late—arrived off the coast of Staten Island with much of his enormous flotilla of warships, transports, soldiers and sailors, and material. He posted letters to former governors and others he considered still to be on friendly terms with Britain, to publicize his declaration offering pardons to all those returning to loyalty to the king.

Also on July 12, the Dickinson committee, which had prepared articles of confederation, even though its chair had left Congress after the July 2 or 4 vote because of his disagreement with Congress' declaring the colonies independent states, "brought in a draught, which was read," before eighty copies were ordered printed, with one copy to be given to each member (see document 34.1). On July 15, Congress received New York's concurrence with the arguments advanced for independence, so the vote in favor became unanimous. The committee asked to write a draft plan for treaties with foreign powers brought in a report on July 18 that was read and ordered to lie on the table. The final congressional act directly linked to the colonies' declaring independence came on July 19, when Congress ordered "that the Declaration passed on the 4th, be fairly engrossed on parchment, with the title and stile of 'the unanimous declaration of the thirteen United States of America,' and that the same, when engrossed, be signed by every member of Congress." The process of signing the Declaration began on August 2; Congress ordered the printing of it, for the first time with delegates' signatures, on January 18, 1777.

## DOCUMENT SUMMARY

The readings for 1776 begin with the fourth congressional resolution from a set agreed to on January 2 that sought to explain "the Origin, Nature, and Extent of the Present Controversy." It bases the colonies' grievances on inherited British rights rather than on natural-rights claims, and in terms more conciliatory than those in Congress' answer to the king's Proclamation for Suppressing Rebellion and Sedition of August 23, 1775. In this resolution, Congress hoped to correct misconceptions regarding its goals and, more broadly, the colonial cause. Congress claimed to have consistently acted in a pursuit of "reconciliation and [a] redress of grievances" and in defense of "those very rights, liberties and estates, which we and our forefathers had so long enjoyed unmolested in the reigns of his present Majesty's predecessors." Congress' justification of its actions, as John Jay's essay (document 26.3) clarifies, was facilitated by the publication on December 11, 1775, of the *Journal* of the first three months of the Second Continental Congress. Significantly, the resolutions from January 2, with their defense of reconciliation and inherited British political rights, were written a few days before the publication of Paine's *Common Sense* and before the receipt on January 8 of the king's speech to Parliament on October 26, 1775 (document 26.2), in which he announced that he had found mercenaries to fight in the colonies and accused the colonists of seeking independence.

The next principal reading, a congressional address to the colonies of February 13, offers a useful marker for a shift in congressional sentiment; indeed, it might be viewed as demarcating the end of the Imperial Crisis as a constitutional struggle between Parliament and colonists, well before the actual declaration of independence almost five months later. This unpublished address, still couched in the language of British liberty, defends the right of colonial assemblies and the king to rule in the colonies, resting the colonists' case, in a fashion typical of the years 1764–74, wholly on English historical and legal precedents, the common law, and the British Constitution. The colonists had turned to British laws, for they knew "too well their happy Tendency to diffuse Freedom, Prosperity and Peace wherever they prevail, to desire an independent Empire."

The address argues strenuously that the king in his speech to Parliament the previous October had been misled by his ministers into thinking that the colonies intended to seek independence—a common trope in congressional documents before the Declaration. It then appeals again for him to intercede and proposes a constitutional remedy, possibly something along the lines of that suggested by Joseph Galloway in 1774. In conclusion, its authors reminded their fellow subjects that they had fought for twelve years for "THE RE-ESTABLISHMENT AND SECURITY OF THEIR CONSTITUTIONAL RIGHTS." The essay, by the time it was considered in mid-February, no longer accurately captured the sentiment in Congress. The moderate delegates responsible for the address would completely lose control of Congress within a month, if they had not already. Accordingly, this last of the moderate congressional state papers was never published; instead, it was tabled and all but forgotten.

The third set of documents involves a second Proclamation for a Day of Humiliation, Fasting, and Prayer, which was approved on March 16, 1776. It set aside May 17 as a day of observance for "Christians of all denominations" to fast and pray for God's forgiveness. As in the first proclamation of a year earlier (see document 17.2), the delegates ask that their fellow colonists, "with united hearts, confess and bewail our manifold sins and transgressions, and, by a sincere repentance and amendment of life, appease his righteous displeasure, and, through the merits and mediation of Jesus Christ, obtain his pardon and forgiveness." The plea for Christ's intercession had not changed; what had changed was Congress' failure to ask God's blessing on George III, instead seeking it only for "our civil rulers, and the representatives of the people, in their several assemblies and conventions." In response to Lord Dunmore's effort to free Virginia's slaves at the end of 1775, Congress included a condemnation of the

British ministry for trying "to subvert our invaluable rights and priviledges, and to reduce us by fire and sword, by the savages of the wilderness [Native Americans], and our own domestics [African slaves], to the most abject and ignominious bondage"— this became a common refrain in 1776.

As can be seen in an accompanying document, the British king too implored God to intercede in his behalf, "to open the Eyes of those who have been deluded by specious Falsehoods, into Acts of Treason and Rebellion, to turn the Hearts of the Authors of these Calamities, and finally to restore Our People in those distracted Provinces and Colonies to the happy Condition of being free Subjects of a free State." Both sides believed themselves to be acting in the right and therefore justified in appealing to God for his righteous aid.

In the fourth principal document, the Declaration on Armed Vessels of March 23, Congress authorized American ships to prey on British commercial shipping in order to sell the seized ships and their goods before courts of admiralty or those specially designed for this purpose, with the proceeds, in the main, going to the officers and crews of the privateers. Congress defended its actions by arguing that that the declaration was retaliation for Parliament's recent passage of the American Prohibitory Act, which, as of March 1, had made American shipping subject to confiscation and its sailors to forced service, under penalty of death, in the Royal Navy. Congress complained again of the British having encouraged Native Americans to oppose the colonists and of having freed slaves in order to have them join loyalists in opposing patriot forces. This declaration, it should be noted, was the first in which Congress considered holding the king, not Parliament, accountable for the actions of the administration. This change in the target of Congress' ire became explicit only in its recommendations to the colonies of May 15. Warfare by privateering, which effectively was legalized piracy, was exciting and lucrative, and proved far more popular than land warfare among seagoing New Englanders. This declaration, along with those to follow soon after in early April and May, rendered the colonies all but independent.

In the fifth document, the declaration opening American ports to non-British trade of April 6, Congress went still further toward declaring the colonies to be independent states, by allowing only non-British goods and ships to enter American ports. The resolutions had been under heated discussion since January 17, 1776, for the members of Congress knew that as of March 1 their own export ban would expire and that more stringent British ones, stemming from the American Prohibitory Act, would take effect. The delegates understood the significance of making this decision. Here they focused on the actions of the "King of Great Britain" without explicitly blaming him for the accumulated grievances. In the course of a prolonged discussion, Richard Smith reported that a procedural vote took place on February 16, 1776, on whether to entertain the question of independence; at the time, seven colonies agreed that it should be discussed and five disagreed. Congress still could not settle on the substance of the question in February. In April, however, a majority of members, even if not yet ready to declare independence, were in favor of opening American ports to non-British shipping—something approaching a necessity with the importation of war-fighting materials from France soon to begin.

As independence inched closer, discussions in the colonies began in earnest regarding the nature of the political institutions that would follow separation from Britain. No doubt the new governments would be republican, as this was the only viable alternative, but how popular they would be became an ever-more divisive question. In ways some of the congressional radicals may not have anticipated or even understood, arguments made against Parliament, in tandem with the ensuing movement toward independence, had produced changing expectations among men of modest means and lowly birth, including men far more radical than those in Congress, regarding their political participation. Words and ideas had consequences. Some men, such as John Adams, found that the ancillary demands of classical republican government—primarily, selflessness and limited interest in commercial life—were standards that Americans would likely be unable to meet and, thus the new states would need to avoid establishing overly popular governments.

The sixth principal document, Congress' Recommendation to the United Colonies, Where Needed, to Adopt New Governments, something like the Declaration of Independence, consisted of a relatively simple resolution passed on May 10, preceded by a more provocative and lengthier preamble written by John Adams, which was approved on May 15. In the resolution, Congress invited all colonies, where appropriate, to institute new governments. It was similar to resolutions passed in 1775 for Massachusetts and, still more so, for three other colonies the previous fall (see documents 17.1 and 24.1). But whereas the earlier resolutions had been requested by the colonies or their representatives and had issued instructions as temporary measures—and in the case of Massachusetts, had sought to return its government to that formed by its royal charter—none of those things were true this time. Still, many moderate members of Congress found this resolution not significantly different from the earlier ones.

What they did find strikingly dissimilar and what, accordingly, led to heated debate, was the preamble, which held that because "his Britannic Majesty, in conjunction with the lords and commons of Great Britain, has, by a late act of Parliament, excluded the inhabitants of these United Colonies from the protection of his crown . . . it is necessary that the exercise of every kind of authority under the said crown should be totally suppressed, and all the powers of government exerted, under the authority of the people of the colonies." In short, since the king had removed his North American subjects from his protection, they no longer owed him their allegiance.

This was yet another effective declaration of independence. Six colonies were in favor—those of New England along with Virginia and South Carolina; four were opposed—all from the mid-Atlantic colonies; two abstained, Pennsylvania and Maryland; and Georgia likely was not represented or did not vote. No one in Congress was confused as to the preamble's meaning—an open avowal of "Independence &

Separation." In fact, after passage of the recommendation, most of the Maryland delegation, in opposition, withdrew for a week from Congress. Carter Braxton of Virginia accused Congress, in particular the New England delegates, of forcing the issue of independence on the mid-Atlantic colonies and their inhabitants before they were ready to separate from the king; he alleged misrepresentation, too, if not dishonesty, in how they characterized British plans. If true, it wouldn't be the first time that Congress was guilty of doing that.

On June 4, yet another rejection by the king of a petition for peace—this one having been laid before him on March 22, 1776, by the City of London—arrived in the colonies. The king stated that his "Subjects in America have brought [this suffering] upon themselves by an unjustifiable Resistance to the Constitutional Authority of this Kingdom," and that he would be happy to alleviate it "whenever that Authority [that is, the king and Parliament] shall be established, and the now existing Rebellion [brought] to an End." For many in Congress still opposed to independence, the king's response helped bring to an end the hope that a just reconciliation could be found. As Jefferson observed, "The people of the middle colonies (Maryland, Delaware, Pennsylva., the Jersies & N. York) were not yet ripe for bidding adieu to [their] British connection but that they were fast ripening & in a short time would join in the general voice of America." On June 7, Richard Henry Lee introduced in Congress Three Resolutions Respecting Independency, which, when the most important and eponymous one was finally approved by Congress on July 2, 1776, proclaimed the American colonies to be independent states.

The final documents of this section contain Congress' unanimous (with one abstention) approval on July 2 of a brief Resolution Proclaiming the Colonies to Be Independent States, and the far more famous Declaration of [Its Reasons for] Independence of July 4; the earlier resolution was appended to this longer explanation and defense of congressional action. The resolution approved was Lee's first of June 7, and the Declaration was that submitted on June 28 by the committee chaired by Thomas Jefferson. Congress debated and marked up the explanatory document (see document 45.1 for the changes made in Congress) for most of three days. As approved (see document 33.1), it begins with an introductory paragraph explaining the need for the document, that is, clarifying that the colonies, now states, were acting out of "a decent respect to the opinions of mankind," most especially the powerful and rich nations of Europe.

Next, the Declaration puts forth the most famous paragraph in all early congressional state papers. In it, Congress provides a theoretical defense of its right to declare independence and a brief summary of the necessity of its doing so. The Declaration provides a rich philosophical description of republican political theory, one at variance with the constitutional-monarchical principles and political institutions that three earlier Congresses had defended over a twelve-year span up to May 1776. Congress proclaimed that the rights that the king had violated were inalienable natural ones rather than, as had been the norm, British constitutional or civil ones. Similarly, in a manner largely absent from earlier congressional state papers and wholly so from thousands of pages of delegates' correspondence, Jefferson wrote of individual English rights to life and liberty, not those that Congress had claimed for the previous twelve years—the corporate rights to self-government and taxation exercised by property-holding heads of household standing in vehement opposition to Parliament's claimed sovereign right to rule. In short, in this paragraph, Congress turned to a heretofore more or less peripheral republicanism and natural-rights theorizing in making its case for the colonies to be internationally recognized as independent and sovereign states before the informal court of world opinion.[1]

The rest of the document, largely framed as a legal brief,[2] divides its indictment of the king into four lines of argument. It begins with charges leveled against the Crown as an executive agency, grievances that had been relatively absent over the past twelve years, since the colonists' focus was then on parliamentary overreach, but that had been common in the political squabbling between colonial legislatures and the Crown in the decades preceding the Imperial Crisis. Since Congress was severing its relation to the king, it made sense to highlight long-unresolved executive issues. Next comes a series of grievances leveled against Parliament, though without open acknowledgment of its being the culprit, for having asserted its claimed constitutional right to legislate for and tax the colonies, and for acts passed in 1764–65, 1767, and 1774 to tax and punish the colonists. Among the laws most resented was Parliament's still offensive and not yet repealed Declaratory Act of 1766.

Third are issues advanced in late-1775 and early-1776 congressional documents in which the king alone is faulted for his conduct of the war against the colonies. The list of charges includes the burning of several towns (sometimes inadvertently or defensively), the much-resented hiring of mercenaries, the impressment of American sailors, and, as frequently noted in a number of late congressional documents, the exciting of "domestic Insurrections amongst us," that is, the freeing of slaves in Virginia. Fourth and last, Congress reminded its projected, mostly international audience that at "every stage of these Oppressions we have Petitioned for Redress in the most humble Terms," concluding that "a Prince, whose Character is thus marked by every act which may define a Tyrant, is unfit to be the Ruler of a free People." As John Adams objected, George III never had acted like a tyrant, but rather had been "deceived by his courtiers on both sides of the Atlantic." More accurately still, the constitutional conundrum that the colonists and Britain proved unable to resolve resulted from George III refusing to rule outside the constitutional norms of the eighteenth-century British Constitution (that is, as a tyrant), which demanded co-sovereignty, at least, with Parliament in his governing of the realm and the Crown's dominions.

## THEORETICAL ISSUES

After the receipt on January 8, 1776, of the king's speech to Parliament of the previous October 26, in which he declared the colonists to be in rebellion and seeking independence, and announced the hiring of mercenaries to fight in the colonies; after the publication of Paine's *Common Sense;* and after the tabling on February 13 of the second, unpublished address to the colonies, a fateful step-by-step movement toward independence—even if lacking a controlling agency—emerged. In comparison with congressional papers from earlier periods in the previous twelve years of the Crisis, those from March to July focus less on grievances—though new ones related to the war were still being added—and the colonial rights violated by Parliament, and more on actions that would lead the colonists away from monarchy and their allegiance to the king and toward republicanism and independence. The majority in Congress only with regret ended its efforts to win the king over to its constitutional position of being under his continued rule but independent of Parliament. By May, moderates could no longer prevent Congress from holding the king personally culpable, for the first time, for American suffering and therefore viewing him as an enemy.

For many moderate delegates, receipt of Parliament's American Prohibitory Act of December 22, 1775 (see document 29.2) led to the lasting rupture between the king and his North American subjects, since in it he removed them from his protection. For those still committed to reconciliation, however, it was not until early June 1776, with the receipt of yet another rejection by the king of a petition for peace, one placed before him by the City of London on March 22, 1776 (see document 32.3), that they dropped their opposition to declaring independence. Yet a sizable number of delegates, mainly those from the mid-Atlantic colonies, no matter how dire the prospects for reconciliation seemed, still weren't ready, even then, to separate—they wanted a number of institutional changes to be made while they waited to see what the king's commissioners might offer in support of reconciliation. But by then a minority, they were unable to prevent the declaring of independence on July 2. Accordingly, when Lord Howe, one of the two commissioners (and brothers) empowered by the Crown to grant pardons, finally arrived off Staten Island on July 12, 1776, he discovered that he had come too late and with far too little authority to settle long-standing constitutional issues. As one of the congressional delegates mused in a letter, the door to reconciliation had been shut ten days earlier by Congress' declaring independence on July 2.

As the documents collected below show, Congress continued to list new grievances while hoping to persuade distinct constituencies of the justice of its position. One of these new laments, which appeared as early as March 16 (see document 28.1), concerned Lord Dunmore's having emancipated, in November 1775, Virginia slaves willing to fight with loyalist forces. Another concern began to appear in April, mostly in private correspondence (see documents 30.4–30.6). There was an enhanced preoccupation with who would rule at home in the new states. Here, even erstwhile congressional radicals like John Adams began moving in a conservative direction as they worried that some of the "new men" helping shape politics in the new states might have, well, revolutionary ends in mind.[3] With this new specter before Adams and others, the protean language of natural rights introduced in congressional papers in 1775 was already, for some, and soon became for many more, a cause for concern.[4]

By March, after the tabling in mid-February of the second address to the colonies—the last congressional document produced by the moderates—a slim consensus had emerged that reconciliation was ever less likely. In response, the ends of the struggle that had begun in 1764 shifted over the next four months from finding a means to heal the rift between two of the king's peoples to declaring independence, forming republican provincial and central governments, and forming alliances with foreign powers. Resolution after resolution in March, April, May, and June led to or was the product of a steady march toward independence and republican government.

Even as a newfound consensus emerged, relations in Congress deteriorated as each side failed to treat the other "with that decency and respect that was observed heretofore." For congressional radicals from the New England colonies and a majority of the delegates from the South, independence had become the all-encompassing goal, never to be deviated from. Moderates, mostly delegates from the mid-Atlantic colonies and some from North and South Carolina, had a more complex view of independence, to the degree they accepted it as inevitable—and still many did not. For them, independence was to be declared, if at all, only after creating an intercolonial or continental confederation and signing treaties with foreign powers, and the explicit approbation of their constituents. Of Lee's three seminal resolutions, only the one concerning independence was opposed by them; the other two, regarding the possibility of forming foreign alliances and creating some manner of central government, were accepted without debate by all the delegates, with or without a consideration of independence.

Most famously, John Dickinson, as late as July 1, came to accept the need to declare independence, but only after a confederation had been formed and the colonies had won assurances from foreign powers of their willingness to conclude commercial and military alliances (see document 33.7). Importantly, too, moderates such as Dickinson believed that independence should only be declared after the arrival of the promised British commissioners, just in case they had the power to resolve the decade-old constitutional impasse between Parliament and the colonies, and after the will of their constituents had been accurately canvassed.

By Carter Braxton's estimation, the radicals' haste was uncalled for: independence should be declared not only if the commissioners disappointed colonial expectations, but also after the numerous land disputes, setting colony against colony, were resolved (see documents 30.5 and 31.3). Moreover, he believed that the New England delegates were pushing for a quick resolution because they were afraid that the commissioners might be able to bring peace and that, as a result, the New Englanders' republican plans and alluring land deals in what would become the Northwest Territories (in 1776 still ceded to Native Americans) might come to naught. He therefore thought, wrongly, that any "Assertion of Independence is far off." And moderate delegates—often the very same men so insistent on hearing first from "the people" regarding independence—were uncertain not only of the wisdom of declaring independence, but also (and still more) of the desirability of moving toward a republican future and greater popular participation in political life. As Adams noted, "the Barons of the South, and the Proprietary interests of the Middle Colonies" viewed "popular Principles and Maxims" with abhorrence. For most moderates, hostility toward independence was joined to a similar antipathy to greater popular participation. Many congressional radicals came to agree with them.

As should be clear at this point, and as a number of the letters presented along with the Declaration make evident, a war of ideas had been going on for much of the past decade in the colonies. The minority view for most of that time was the protorepublicanism of New England and Virginia, though the two areas likely approached the matter from different viewpoints, Reformed Protestant and secular-enlightened, respectively. Besides opposing Parliament's pretensions, those colonists sought to change the underpinnings of the relationship between the king and his North American subjects. The majority view defended constitutional monarchy; outside of a few population centers, colonists in the mid-Atlantic region in particular were desperate to find a British constitutional solution to the impasse with Parliament so that the colonies could remain subject to the king and members of the British Empire.

In the end, those previously in the minority emerged victorious after successfully working to replace, often in ways inconsistent with Congress' long-proclaimed respect for the internal political lives of its member colonies, mid-Atlantic provincial governments and delegations in late June 1776. In some cases, though, delegates changed their votes or declined to vote so that the congressional vote for independence would be unanimous, as the vote on July 1 by the committee of the whole had not been.

One form of the division between republicans and monarchists ended with the Declaration of Independence. But in important new ways, it carried over into the different views of how to shape the new continental government, a draft of which was written eight or ten days after Congress declared independence. The divisions between sectional groupings of the newly independent and sovereign states—there wasn't a unitary nation in July 1776—did not end with the Articles of Confederation and Perpetual Union. They continued well into the nineteenth century, even though the question of republicanism versus constitutional monarchy was no longer at issue.

## 26. THE STATE OF AFFAIRS IN AMERICA BEFORE AND AFTER PAINE, JANUARY 1776

On December 8, 1775, Congress assigned John Jay (New York), James Wilson (Pennsylvania), and William Livingston (New Jersey) to respond to a series of letters from Colonel William Alexander, who had taken the title Lord Stirling.[5] This committee was made up of mid-Atlantic moderates who only reluctantly supported independence some months later in July. Their report of January 2 was used by Congress in framing the nine resolutions that followed. They were printed in the *Pennsylvania Evening Post,* January 4, 1776, and in the *Pennsylvania Gazette,* January 11, 1776.

The goal of the third resolution, which is reproduced here, was to correct misconceptions regarding Congress' goals and, more broadly, the colonial cause so that all parties would recognize that Congress had consistently acted in a pursuit of "reconciliation and redress of grievances." Congress wrote, "The more our right to the enjoyment of our ancient liberties and privileges is examined, the more just and necessary our present opposition to ministerial tyranny will appear." Strikingly, in its first address of the new year, Congress reverted to the particularistic language of ancient liberties and privileges, even if not clearly designated as British, rather than the most recently adapted abstract terms of universal rights. With this "educational" purpose in mind, Congress invited "all conventions and assemblies in these colonies, liberally to distribute among the people, the proceedings of this and the former Congress, the late speeches of the great patriots in both houses of parliament relative to American grievances, and such other pamphlets and papers as tend to elucidate the merits of the American cause."

26.1

### "The Origin, Nature, and Extent of the Present Controversy," January 2, 1776

Worthington Chauncey Ford et al., eds., *Journals of the Continental Congress, 1774–1789* (Washington, D.C.: Government Printing Office, 1904–37), 4:18–19.

Whereas it has been represented to this Congress, that divers honest and well-meaning, but uninformed people in these colonies, have, by the art and address of ministerial agents, been deceived and drawn into erroneous opinions respecting the American cause, and the probable issue of the present contest:

*Resolved,* That it be recommended to the different committees, and other friends to American liberty, in the said colonies, to treat all such persons with kindness and attention; to consider them as the inhabitants of a country determined to be free, and to view their errors as proceeding rather from want of information than want of virtue or public spirit; to explain to them the origin, nature and extent of the present controversy; to acquaint them with the fate of the numerous petitions presented to his Majesty, as well by assemblies as Congresses, for reconciliation and redress of grievances: and that the last from this Congress, humbly requesting the single favour of being heard, like all the others, has proved unsuccessful; to unfold to them the various arts of administration to ensnare and enslave us, and the manner in which we have been cruelly driven to defend, by arms, those very rights, liberties and estates, which we and our forefathers had so long enjoyed unmolested in the reigns of his present Majesty's predecessors. And it is hereby recommended to all conventions and assemblies in these colonies, liberally to distribute among the people, the proceedings of this and the former Congress, the late speeches of the great patriots in both houses of parliament relative to American grievances, and such other pamphlets and papers as tend to elucidate the merits of the American cause, the Congress being fully persuaded that the more our right to the enjoyment of our ancient liberties and privileges is examined, the more just and necessary our present opposition to ministerial tyranny will appear. . . .

## 26.2

### GEORGE III, SPEECH TO PARLIAMENT, OCTOBER 26, 1775

King George's speech of October 26 arrived in Philadelphia on January 8, 1776. In his address, he notes that the colonists had come to understand their relationship to Parliament in a way "repugnant to the true constitution of the colonies, and to their subordinate relation to Great Britain," before accusing them, as he had in his Proclamation of August 23, 1775 (see document 25.2) of "openly avow[ing] their revolt, hostility, and rebellion." More damning still, the king accused the colonists of being consistently disingenuous: "They meant only to amuse by vague expressions of attachment to the parent state and the strongest protestations of loyalty to me, whilst they were preparing for a general revolt." After elaborating on his pacific intentions, the king remarks that he had hoped that his subjects "in America would have discerned the traitorous views of their leaders and have been convinced that to be a subject of Great Britain, with all its consequences, is to be the freest member of any civil society in the known world."

Going further than he had in his August 23 Proclamation, the king charged that "the rebellious war now levied is become more general and is manifestly carried on for the purpose of establishing an independent empire," which, if successful, would lead to grievous effects on British economic well-being. Accordingly, he found that "the object is too important, the spirit of the British nation too high . . . to give up so many colonies which she has planted with great industry," without a fight. Regarding the impending war, the king proudly announced that he would augment his land forces in the manner "least burdensome to my kingdoms" upon receiving "the most friendly offers of foreign assistance." Thus were the colonists introduced to the frightening prospect of the king hiring non-English-speaking foreign mercenaries to kill them, his subjects. That action, of enormous significance at the time, went far in undermining support of monarchy and loyalty to the king in the colonies. Only on May 21, 1776, however, did the colonists receive confirmation of these fateful negotiations.

Finally, in the limpest possible move toward a reconciliation resting on novel constitutional grounds, the king announced that he would be sending peace commissioners with the power "to grant general or particular pardons and indemnities, in such manner and to such persons as they shall think fit, and to receive the submission of any province or colony which shall be disposed to return to its allegiance." As Merrill Jensen observed, this speech "declared that Americans were fighting for independence before the Americans officially admitted it themselves. It also made plain that Britain would take every measure to defeat them. The promise that commissioners would be sent to grant pardons and receive submissions gave hope to Americans who were opposed to independence but had little effect except to delay an open declaration of independence for a time."[6] In a manner to be repeated over and over again in a desperate quest to preserve its commercial advantages, Britain refused to address the constitutional issues at the heart of the Imperial Crisis, instead making conciliatory offers that were consistently too little and too late.[7]

Merrill Jensen, ed., *English Historical Documents: American Colonial Documents to 1776* (New York: Oxford University Press, 1969), 9:851–52.

The present situation of America, and my constant desire to have your advice, concurrence, and assistance on every important occasion, have determined me to call you thus early together.

Those who have long too successfully laboured to inflame my people in America by gross misrepresentations and to infuse into their minds a system of opinions repugnant to the true constitution of the colonies, and to their subordinate relation to Great Britain, now openly avow their revolt, hostility, and rebellion. They have raised troops, and are collecting a naval force; they have seized the public revenue, and assumed to themselves legislative, executive, and judicial powers, which they already exercise in the most arbitrary manner over the persons and properties of their fellow subjects; and although many of these unhappy people may still retain their loyalty and may be too wise not to see the fatal consequence of this usurpation, and wish to resist it; yet the torrent of violence has been strong enough to compel their acquiescence till a sufficient force shall appear to support them.

The authors and promoters of this desperate conspiracy have in the conduct of it derived great advantage from the difference of our intentions and theirs. They meant only to amuse by vague expressions of attachment to the parent state and the strongest protestations of loyalty to me, whilst they were preparing for a general revolt. On our part, though it was declared in your last session that a rebellion existed within the province of the Massachusetts Bay, yet even that province we wished rather to reclaim than to subdue. The resolutions of Parliament breathed a spirit of moderation and forbearance; conciliatory propositions accompanied the measures taken to enforce authority, and the coercive acts were adapted to cases of criminal combinations amongst subjects not then in arms. I have acted with the same temper; anxious to prevent, if it had been possible, the effusion of the blood of my subjects and the calamities which are inseparable from a state of war; still hoping that my people in America would have discerned the traitorous views of their leaders and have been convinced that to be a subject of Great Britain, with all its consequences, is to be the freest member of any civil society in the known world.

The rebellious war now levied is become more general and is manifestly carried on for the purpose of establishing an independent empire. I need not dwell upon the fatal effects of the success of such a plan. The object is too important, the spirit of the British nation too high, the resources with which God hath blessed her too numerous, to give up so many colonies which she has planted with great industry, nursed with great tenderness, encouraged with many commercial advantages, and protected and defended at much expense of blood and treasure.

It is now become the part of wisdom, and (in its effects) of clemency, to put a speedy end to these disorders by the most decisive exertions. For this purpose I have increased my naval establishment, and greatly augmented my land forces, but in such a manner as may be the least burdensome to my kingdoms.

I have also the satisfaction to inform you that I have received the most friendly offers of foreign assistance; and if I shall make any treaties in consequence thereof, they shall be laid before you. And I have, in testimony of my affection for my people who can have no cause in which I am not equally interested, sent to the garrisons of Gibraltar and Port Mahon a part of my Electoral troops in order that a larger number of the established forces of this kingdom may be applied to the maintenance of its authority; and the national militia, planned and regulated with equal regard to the rights, safety, and protection of my Crown and people, may give a farther extent and activity to our military operations.

When the unhappy and deluded multitude against whom this force will be directed shall become sensible of their error, I shall be ready to receive the misled with tenderness and mercy; and in order to prevent the inconveniences which may arise from the great distance of their situation, and to remove as soon as possible the calamities which they suffer, I shall give authority to certain persons upon the spot to grant general or particular pardons and indemnities, in such manner and to such persons as they shall think fit, and to receive the submission of any province or colony which shall be disposed to return to its allegiance. It may be also proper to authorize the persons so commissioned to restore such province or colony so returning to its allegiance to the free exercise of its trade and commerce and to the same protection and security as if such province or colony had never revolted.

Gentlemen of the House of Commons:

I have ordered the proper estimates for the ensuing year to be laid before you; and I rely on your affection to me and your resolution to maintain the just rights of this country, for such supplies as the present circumstances of our affairs require. Among the many unavoidable ill consequences of this rebellion none affects me more sensibly than the extraordinary burden which it must create to my faithful subjects.

My Lords and Gentlemen:

I have fully opened to you my views and intentions. The constant employment of my thoughts, and the most earnest wishes of my heart tend wholly to the safety and happiness of all my people, and to the re-establishment of order and tranquility through the several parts of my dominions, in a close connection and constitutional dependence. You see the tendency of the present disorders and I have stated to you the measures which I mean to pursue for suppressing them. Whatever remains to be done that may farther contribute to this end, I commit to your wisdom. And I am happy to add that as well from the assurances I have received as from the general appearance of affairs in Europe, I see no probability that the measures which you may adopt will be interrupted by disputes with any foreign power.

26.3

JOHN JAY, "ESSAY ON CONGRESS
AND INDEPENDENCE," JANUARY 1776

This essay was written by John Jay, the moderate New York delegate who was negotiating with Lord Drummond to see whether some manner of reconciliation between the colonies and Great Britain might be achieved. Lord Drummond had served as an unofficial British representative in the colonies from 1768 to 1774. He returned to Britain, then came back to the colonies in 1775 with a plan of accommodation. In Drummond's notes, written around January 14, 1776, Jay is mentioned as a possible congressional emissary to England to serve in a "peace delegation." Drummond contends that Congress had consciously decided against appointing radical members, such as the two Adamses or Silas Deane, to serve on this proposed mission.[8] Jay's intention here, in keeping with Congress' answer to the king of December 6, 1775 (document 25.1), was to demonstrate that those accusing the colonists of seeking independence were slandering them and grossly misrepresenting their words, goals, and actions. In the main, Jay's principal audience included those who were suspicious that their congressional delegates had been surreptitiously working to achieve independence rather than seeking a constitutionally acceptable plan of reconciliation, as they had been instructed to do. As he points out, Congress' enemies, including agents of the British ministry, had spared no pains "to traduce that respectable Assembly and misrepresent their Designs and actions" by suggesting that it had worked in search of independence. Such a charge was viewed by Jay still as slanderous.

In support of his position, Jay went through the first three months of the Second Continental Congress' record, which amply demonstrated that accusing Congress of aiming at independence was "an ungenerous & groundless Charge," for it had consistently sought to restore the colonists' constitutional relationship with Britain by means of a just reconciliation—and no more. Thus, among many examples, Jay reminds his readers that Congress advised Massachusetts (see document 17.1) that its "Assembly or Council exercise the Powers of Government *until a Governor of his Majestys Appointment* will consent *to govern the Colony according to its Charter*" and that the delegates had written to assure their British Protestant brethren "that *we mean not to dissolve that Union which has so long & so happily subsisted between us, and which we sincerely wish to see restored*" (see document 20.1), while solemnly assuring them "*that we have not yet lost Sight of the Object we have ever had in View, a Reconciliation with you on constitutional Principles.*" For Jay, the case against the colonies for having sought independence in the summer of 1775, much less during the First Continental Congress, was an easy one to disprove.

Jay's efforts to exonerate Congress from such charges were greatly aided by the publication on December 11, 1775, of the *Journal of the Proceedings of the Congress, held at Philadelphia; May 10, 1775*. Also important in making sense of and quickly dating his remarks was a rapid succession of January events that had done much, by early spring, to transform congressional and colonial sentiment further and make reconciliation all but impossible. On January 7, news of Lord Dunmore's burning of Norfolk on January 1, 1776, arrived in Philadelphia. Next, on January 8, the king's speech to Parliament from the previous October reached the colonies. Of possibly the greatest significance in providing a background against which to read Jay's comments was the publication on January 9 of *Common Sense,* by the English radical Thomas Paine.[9] The pamphlet, which became the best-selling colonial publication, is credibly viewed as having done much to change colonial attitudes toward monarchical government, republicanism, and the colonies' continued membership in the British Empire.[10] Finally, on January 17, Congress learned of General Montgomery's defeat in Canada on December 31.

Given all that happened in January 1776, it is unlikely that Jay would have written his essay defending Congress against the king's charges of seeking independence much later than the end of that month or early February. By March, the colonists had spent twelve years opposing what they believed was Parliament's unconstitutional legislation and seeking the active intercession of the king in support of them, his North American subjects, but their commitment to those objectives was coming to an end.

Paul H. Smith, ed., *Letters of Delegates to Congress, 1774–1789* (Washington, D.C.: Library of Congress, 1976–93), 3:175–78.

It has long been the Art of the Enemies of America to sow the seeds of Dissentions among us and thereby weaken that Union on which our Salvation from Tyranny depends. For this Purpose Jealousies have been endeavoured to be excited, and false Reports, wicked Slanders and insidious misrepresentations industriously formed and propagated.

Well knowing that while the People reposed Confidence in the Congress, the Designs of the Ministry would probably be frustrated no Pains have been spared to traduce that respectable Assembly and misrepresent their Designs and actions.

Among other aspersions cast upon them, is an ungenerous & groundless Charge of their aiming at Independence, or a total Separation from G. Britain.

Whoever will be at the Trouble of reviewing their Journal will find ample Testimony against this accusation, and for the sake of those who may not have either Leisure or Opportunity to peruse it, I have selected the following Paragraphs which abundantly prove the Malice and falsity of such a Charge.

Page 59. The Congress in giving orders for securing the Stores taken at Crown Point & Ticonderoga direct "That an Exact Inventory be taken of all such Cannon and Stores, in order that they may be safely returned, *when the Restoration of the former Harmony between Great Britain & these Colonies, so ardently wished for by the latter* shall render it prudent and consistent with the *over-ruling Law of self Preservation.*"

Page 63. The Congress after resolving that the Colonies ought to be put in a State of Defence, thus proceed unanimously. "But as *we most ardently wish for a Restoration of the Harmony* formerly subsisting between our Mother Country and these Colonies, the Interruption of which must, at all Events be exceedingly injurious to both Countries, *that with a sincere Design of contributing by all the Means in our Power,* (not incompatible with a just Regard for the undoubted Rights and true Interests of these Colonies) *to the Promotion of this most desireable Reconciliation,* an humble and dutiful Petition be presented to his Majesty. Resolved that *measures be entered into for opening a negotiation, in order to accommodate the unhappy disputes subsisting between Great Britain and these Colonies,* and that *this* be made *a Part of the Petition to the King.*"

Page 64. The Congress recommend to the Convention of New York "to persevere the more vigorously in preparing for their Defence, as it is very uncertain whether *the earnest Endeavours of the Congress to accommodate the unhappy Differences between Great Britain and the Colonies, by conciliatory Measures, will be successful.*"

Page 84. The Congress in order to rescue the Province of Massachusetts Bay from Anarchy, advise that their "Assembly or Council exercise the Powers of Government *until a Governor of his Majestys Appointment will consent to govern the Colony according to its Charter.*"

Page 87. The Congress in their vote for a general Fast recommend that we should "offer up our joint Supplications to the all wise, omnipotent & merciful Disposer of all Events (among other Things) *to bless our rightful Sovereign King George the Third,* that *a speedy End* may be put to the *civil Discord between Great Britain and the American Colonies* without further Effusion of Blood." "And that all America may soon behold a gracious Interposition of Heaven for the Redress of her many Grievances, the Restoration of her invaded Rights, *a Reconciliation with the parent State on Terms constitutional and honorable to both.*"

Page 149. The Congress after declaring the Reasons which compelled them to recur to Arms, thus express themselves—"Lest this Declaration should disquiet the Minds of our Friends & Fellow Subjects in any Part of the Empire, we assure them that *we mean not to dissolve that Union which has so long & so happily subsisted between us,* and which we *sincerely wish to see restored. Necessity* has not yet *driven* us into that *desperate* Measure, or induced us to excite any other nation to War against them. We *have not* raised Armies *with ambitious Designs of separating from Great Britain, and establishing independent States.*"

[Page] 150. "We most humbly implore the divine Goodness *to dispose our Adversaries to Reconciliation on reasonable Terms.*"

Page 155. In the Petition to the King, every Line of which breaths affection for his Majesty & Great Britain, are these remarkable Sentences.

"Attached to your Majestys Person, Family & Government, with all the Devotion that Principle & Affection can inspire, *connected with Great Britain by the strongest Ties that can unite Societies,* and *deploring every Event* that tends in *any Degree* to *weaken* them, we *solemnly assure* your Majesty, that we not only *most ardently desire* the former *Harmony* between her and these Colonies may be *restored,* but that a Concord may be *established between them* upon so *firm a Basis* as to perpetuate its Blessings uninterrupted *by any future Dissentions to succeeding Generations in both Countries.*" "We beg Leave further to assure your Majesty that notwithstanding the *Sufferings* of your loyal Colonists during the Course of this present Controversey our Breasts retain *too tender a Regard for the Kingdom from which we derive our origin,* to request such a Reconciliation as might in *any Manner be inconsistent with her Dignity or Welfare.*"

Page 163. In the last Address of the Congress to the People of Great Britain are the following Passages.

"*We are accused of aiming at Independence;* but *how* is this accusation *supported?* By the *Allegations* of your *Ministers* not by *our Actions. Abused, insulted [and] contemned what steps have we pursued to obtain Redress? We have carried our dutiful Petitions to the Throne. We have applied to your Justice for Relief.*"

Page 165. "Give us Leave most solemnly to assure you, *that we have not yet lost Sight of the Object we have ever had in View, a Reconciliation with you on constitutional Principles, and a Restoration of that friendly Intercourse which to the Advantage of both, we till lately maintained.*"

Page 172. In the Address of the Congress to the Lord Mayor, Aldermen and Livery of London, there is this Paragraph vizt.

"*North America* My Lord! *wishes most ardently for a lasting connection with Great Britain on Terms of just and equal Liberty.*"

From these testimonies it appears extremely evident that to charge the Congress with aiming at a Separation of these Colonies from Great Britain is to charge them falsely and without a single Spark of Evidence to support the accusation.

Many other Passages in their Journal might be mentioned, but as that would exceed the Limits of this Paper, I shall reserve them for some future Publication.

It is much to be wished that People would read the Proceedings of the Congress and consult their own judgments, and not suffer themselves to be *duped by Men who are paid for decieving them.*

26.4

JOSIAH BARTLETT TO JOHN LANGDON,
JANUARY 13, 1776

In this letter from one of New Hampshire's radical delegates to another, one begins to comprehend the widespread impact created by Paine's *Common Sense.* Josiah Bartlett was a doctor who was elected to New Hampshire's General Court in 1765. John Langdon was a merchant who served, among a number of offices, as Speaker of the New Hampshire Assembly and as a U.S. Senator. Bartlett writes disdainfully that the majority of his constituents in Portsmouth, New Hampshire, were "very much afraid of the idea conveyed by the frightful word *Independence,*" but he believes that a remedy for this may be at hand: "This week a pamphlet on that Subject was printed here, and greedily bought up and read by all ranks of people. I shall send you one of them, which you will please to lend round to the people; perhaps on consideration there may not appear any thing so terrible in that thought as they might at first apprehend, if Britain should force us to break off all connections with her." Even, then, in parts of New England, as Jay argued above, independence was still viewed by moderates with trepidation.

Paul H. Smith, ed., *Letters of Delegates to Congress, 1774–1789* (Washington, D.C.: Library of Congress, 1976–93), 3:87–88.

Sir,                                                                Philadelphia Jany 13th 1776.

I wrote you 9th inst per post informing you of a contract for importing goods for the use of the Army to the amount of ten thousand dollars which the Secret Committee are willing to make with you which letter I hope will come safe to your hands, and that you will answer it as soon as may be.

Last evening the draughts of the several ships of war were laid before the Marine Committee and approved of; and they have ordered one for each of the Contractors to be forthwith made out. But it is so large I know not how to send it to you; it cannot be sent in a letter and what other way to contrive I know not, but will do the best I can as soon as I can procure it.

This morning I see in the newspaper (which by the way is almost the only way I hear from our Colony) that Portsmouth had appointed Messrs Cutts, Sherburne and Long, to represent that town in Provincial Convention, and by the Instructions I find the town is very much afraid of the idea conveyed by the frightful word *Independence!* This week a pamphlet on that Subject was printed here, and greedily bought up and read by all ranks of people. I shall send you one of them, which you will please to lend round to the people; perhaps on consideration there may not appear any thing so terrible in that thought as they might at first apprehend, if Britain should force us to break off all connections with her. Give my compliments to Col Whipple who I see is left out by the Town in their choice of Delegates for the Provincial Convention.

I am Sir your friend and servt,                                Josiah Bartlett

[P.S.] The 57 tons of Salt petre which arrived here last week was this day by order of Congress purchased by the Secret Committee for the use of the Continent and three tons of powder this day arrived here from the Jersies.                      J. B.

Pray write me a full account of our affairs and don't forget to put the Colony in mind to send Delegates here as soon as may be that I may return to my family.

## 26.5

## JOHN HANCOCK TO THOMAS CUSHING, JANUARY 17, 1776

John Hancock of Massachusetts, president of the Continental Congress from May 1775 until 1777, was believed to be the wealthiest merchant in Boston. Nonetheless, like many other wealthy merchants, he was an early supporter of colonial resistance to parliamentary impositions and was, therefore, linked to popular forces in Boston, as well as to Samuel Adams. Indeed, along with Adams, Hancock was a focus of Britain's efforts to suppress Boston's radicals. Here he writes to his friend and former ally in Congress, Thomas Cushing, who was a prosperous Boston merchant and lawyer, an early leader of the colonial resistance movement, and a delegate from Massachusetts during the First Continental Congress and early months of the Second. Cushing, because he was unable to support independence, was replaced in a January 1776 election by Elbridge Gerry, who took his seat in

Congress on February 9. This change helped shift the balance of power in the Massachusetts delegation in a still more radical direction and, in turn, to steer Congress in the same direction.[11]

Although reticent about the increasingly radical direction of the opposition in Congress, Hancock wrote to Cushing of the efforts of John and Samuel Adams to stir up "Jealousies & Animosities." He claimed that they had practiced "undue Methods" to undermine the political influence of the three other, more moderate members of the Massachusetts delegation, including Hancock and Robert Treat Paine.[12] Like Bartlett (see above), Hancock also mentions Paine's wildly popular pamphlet, though with less enthusiasm: "I send it for your and Friend's Amusement." It is clear that divisions still existed in Congress between colonial delegations, in particular those from different regions, but also within delegations, including the otherwise generally radical New England delegations.

Paul H. Smith, ed., *Letters of Delegates to Congress, 1774–1789* (Washington, D.C.: Library of Congress, 1976–93), 3:104–6.

Dear Sir                                                                     Philadelphia Januy. 17th. 1776

Your favr. from Milford I duly Rec'd, and thank you for it. Your observations respectg. the Conduct of the Merchts. of New York as to Remittances is very just, and I think with you that those Sums could & ought to be improv'd here for much better purposes. I am much oblig'd for your trouble in Calling upon my Aunt. I hope this will find you safe arriv'd & in the Enjoyment of Domestick Ease & happiness, that you found all your particular Connections well, & not Destitute of many Friends, altho' some would gladly have it thought that you are totally deserted, but by no means, My Good Friend, let the Circumstance of the Election Discourage you from the Noble pursuit in which you are Engaged, your Cause is just, and I am Confident your Conscience will Acquit you. I can tell you for a truth that you have left in Congress many who are peculiarly friendly to you, & who, had they a Suspicion that you would not have Return'd soon to Congress, would have given you many Expressions of their Friendship previous to your Departure. I never Flatter, but shall ever in future unbosom my self to you, & write freely, in Confidence that I can Rely on your Friendship, & from a Conviction that you are Deserving of the Esteem I have for you, & I shall ever feel a pleasure in doing any thing that can Contribute to your Ease or Reputation, as I must Say I have Reason to think Endeavours have been made to Disturb both, & which I will not let pass over unnotic'd, for it may Operate further & be the means of Stirring up Jealousies & Animosities which had better be nipt in the Bud, of wch. more in my next.

Severall Members of Congress have mention'd to me the Desire they have to Establish you in that Agreeable point of light which your Conduct in their Estimation merits. For that purpose they are framing a Letter to you, to be made such use of as you think best, to be Sign'd by a number of them, as they have some how an opinion that undue Methods have been practic'd which have Operated to your Disadvantage in the late Election. They are very sanguine in this matter, and I assure you that you are mention'd by Respectable Members in the most Advantagious & Agreeable Light, & you may Rely I do not throw any Contradictory Strokes in the way; of this more in my next. As I did not Expect to be able to write you a Line by this, you must Excuse my not being more Explicit, having ever since your Departure been exceeding ill, my Cold brought on a Fever, & much Affected one of my Eyes, that I have, & still do, suffer greatly, I hope by next oppory. to be able to write you more fully.

With Respect to the Ships, I must Beg you will set the Wheels in Motion; Money & particular Instructions shall come by next as I am now unable to Compleat what I intended. The whole Conduct of these Ships I Submit to you. Pray be Expeditious in setting forward the work, & let me hear from you.

South Carolina have Authoriz'd Mr. Lynch & Rutlidge to Act, & have sent for Mr. Gadsden home, who Departs by water tomorrow. We have this Day rec'd disagreeable Accotts. from Canada, poor Montgomery & severall officers kill'd, Arnold Wounded &c. We have Agreed to have Nine Battalions in Canada, I now Send this Express, to have one Rais'd in N. Hampshire, one in Connecticutt &c. I fear for the Defection of New York, the Spring will open before we are Ready, however we must bestir ourselves. I hope in my next to Send you a good Accott. of a little Expedition order'd, which is now Executing, but I am under injunction &c. Intercepted Letters from Gov. Franklin & the Speaker of the Jersey Assembly Mr Skinner have been Read in Congress, their Contents I can't mention. Gov. Franklin is under Guard, & Skinner gone on board the Asia.

I inclose you a pamphlet which makes much Talk here, said to be wrote by an English Gentleman Resident here by the name of Paine, & I believe him the Author, I Send it for your and Friend's Amusement.

The Inclos'd Letters I Return you having Rec'd them since your Departure.

I shall Look on you as a stated friendly Correspondent, I make offers of sincere Attachment & Friendship to you, & wish for a Return of yours, & you may Rely on every Service in my power, & that I am totally undisguis'd, & beg that our friendly Correspondence may continue, I will Give you every thing from hence, both in & out Doors, that I consistently can, & pray write me every Occurrence with you, by every Post, omitt no Oppor[tunitie]s. For a very particular Reason do send me the State of the late Election of members for Congress, Number of Votes &c Candidates &c what is the Assembly about. I have Rec'd no orders to Remain here, we know nothing of the Election but by the News papers. Give me all news, & by every Oppory. I shall Send your Letters always under Cover to the General.

Mrs. Hancock Joines me in best Complimts. to you & Lady & Family. Do Tell Mrs. Cushing when I See her I shall use friendly Freedoms more than ever & shall not look upon her as a Stranger, & would not be so thought by her. I shall give her your history.

I am with Real Esteem, My Good Friend, Yours without Reserve,

John Hancock

[P.S.] How goes on the militia matters in assembly; am I to be notic'd in the appointment of officers.

### 27. CONGRESSIONAL MODERATES' UNPUBLISHED LAST DEFENSE OF EMPIRE AND RECONCILIATION, FEBRUARY 1776

On January 24, 1776, a committee of five delegates, consisting of Robert Alexander (Maryland), John Dickinson and James Wilson (Pennsylvania), William Hooper (North Carolina), and James Duane (New York), was instructed "to prepare an address to the inhabitants of the United Colonies," in particular, at the urging of Wilson, to respond to the king's speech to Parliament of October 26, 1775.[13] This was an unusually moderate group, all staunch opponents of independence and supporters of reconciliation. Alexander chose to remain loyal to the king and departed the colonies after independence, leaving behind his family and fortune. Dickinson refused to vote for the Declaration of Independence. Hooper was considered a Tory by the radical members of the Congress. Wilson opposed independence until the last minute in early July.[14]

Wilson had begun in mid-January to organize support in Congress for a rebuttal of the king's allegations. When a draft was brought before Congress on February 13, as Richard Smith records below (document 27.3), it was tabled and never referred to again; it was never published. The time for a document that appeared "full against Independence," whatever Wilson's intentions, was passing. Contributing to this was the changing membership in Congress. Samuel Huntington and Oliver Wolcott of Connecticut were added on January 16, Samuel Chase of Maryland arrived on February 3, and, of particular consequence, Elbridge Gerry joined the Massachusetts delegation (along with John Adams' return after a month's break) on February 9.[15] As Merrill Jensen notes, "The failure to adopt the address marked the end of the conservative control of Congress. From that day on, step by step, the radicals adopted measures calculated to establish independence of the colonies. Nevertheless, the conservatives remained a powerful restraining influence, not in preventing independence but in delaying its final declaration."[16] Indeed, as is clear in Dickinson's remarks below and in those of Jay and others who were working with Lord Drummond in search of a plan of conciliation, the moderates in Congress continued to resist independence until the summer of 1776.

Wilson here puts forward, as he would far more famously in Philadelphia at the Constitutional Convention and afterward in defense of the new Constitution, a theory of popular sovereignty that he claimed was embodied in the English Constitution. According to Wilson, "that all Power was originally in the People—that all the

Powers of Government are derived from them . . . are Maxims of the English Constitution." More interestingly, he defends the idea that the people's ultimate sovereignty can be divided between different governmental bodies, in this case between that "share of Power, which the King derives from the People," which "is the same in *Great Britain* and in the Colonies," and the share that the House of Commons enjoys in Britain but is "entrusted by the Colonies to their Assemblies in the Several Provinces." The role of the Crown, accordingly, was the same in both the realm and the dominions. But the power of Parliament outside the realm did not overlap with the power of the colonial assemblies in their proper domain. For Wilson and all his colleagues, "the *House of Commons* neither has nor can have any Power deriv'd from the *Inhabitants of these Colonies,*" so Parliament could have no legitimate authority to legislate for or to tax the colonists. His claims were extensions of those that the colonists began to make in 1765–67.

The address next defends the right of colonial delegations to come together in a congress, resting its case entirely on antecedent English historical analogies. Wilson defends the colonists, as had Jay before him, against the king's charge that their expressions of loyalty were disingenuous: their "protestations of Loyalty and Expressions of Attachment ought, by every Rule of Candour, to be presumed to be sincere." He adds that all their military preparations had been consistently defensive in nature and legitimately *"cloathed with the sacred Authority of the People, from* WHOM *all* LEGITIMATE AUTHORITY proceeds." Although colonists had been "accused of carrying on the war "for the Purpose of establishing an independent Empire," they had consistently aimed only at *"the Defence and the Re-establishment of the constitutional Rights of the Colonies."* Note, he defends constitutional corporate rights, harking back again to arguments that had been made consistently for a decade.

Indeed, according to Wilson, the colonists had only ever sought the "re-establishment of their Rights," and nothing in their behavior could lead to any other conclusion. In support of this, again like Jay, he turns to the words of the Declaration on Taking Arms, the Olive Branch Petition, and the Address to the People of Great Britain from October 1774. In particular, quoting from the last, he repeats that the colonists sought "most solemnly to assure you, that we have not yet lost Sight of the Object we have ever had in View, a Reconciliation with you on constitutional Principles." He then rhetorically asks why, if independence were the goal pursued by Congress, had the colonists made such efforts to maintain a strong connection with their "fellow-Subjects in Great Britain."

Finding that no plan of accommodation had been offered to the colonists—no mention is made of Lord North's of February 1775—Wilson suggested that "some salutary System" was needed for general ends, one that would give voice to the will of both the colonists and "the Inhabitants of Great Britain." The suggestion brings to mind Joseph Galloway's "Plan of Union" (document 10.1). What Wilson, and perhaps those he represented in Congress, was unwilling to do was to set American politics adrift without a continuing link to, at best, the British king and the empire, but at minimum to the colonies' English legal and constitutional inheritance. As Wilson writes, "We are too much attached to the English Laws and Constitution, and know too well their happy Tendency to diffuse Freedom, Prosperity and Peace wherever they prevail, to desire an independent Empire." If, in February, this was still the view of a bare majority of delegates in Congress, it was not one that endured for long.

The source of the problem, for Wilson, wasn't Britain writ large or even the king, but rather, as had been the case for the past decade, the "House of Commons." He reminds the colonists that the Commons "have undertaken to *give* and *grant* your Money" and presumed "from a supposed virtual Representation in *their* House . . . that *you* ought to be bound by the Acts of the British Parliament in all Cases whatever." Driving his point home in a manner that left little to clarify—even if it suggested the confused mixture of Tory and Whig elements in colonial opposition thought—Wilson explains that "the same Principles, which directed *your Ancestors* to oppose the exorbitant and dangerous Pretensions of the Crown" and that led to the rise of Parliament as the custodian of such rights, "should direct *you* to oppose the no less exorbitant and dangerous Claims of the House of Commons." Of course it was this juxtaposition of roles that had left committed Whigs in Parliament and in America so uncertain of their roles.[17]

What was not a matter of confusion for Wilson (or for most in Congress) was the goal of both securing the colonists' rights, if possible, under the British Constitution and keeping America within the empire. If doing so proved impossible, then more universal and abstract approaches would need to be considered. Wilson ends by reminding his fellow subjects that he and, he believes, most of British North America hope that "the Colonies may continue connected, as they have been, with Britain," but that this "is our second Wish: Our first is—THAT AMERICA MAY BE FREE."

Although this doesn't sound like a clarion call for independence, Wilson claimed otherwise. As James Madison reports, Wilson thought he was leading "the public mind into the idea of Independence, of which the necessity was plainly foreseen in Congress."[18] His colleagues, though, believed him to be arguing against independence (see document 27.3). Even Wilson admitted that "the language" in the address was "evidently short of the subsisting maturity" regarding independence, and "the address was in consequence dropped."[19] No matter what his intention, this draft address enjoys an important role in the history of Congress, the final stage of the Crisis, and the onrushing war—it is the last state paper, though unpublished, that outlines the long-held position of the congressional moderates. This was, though, their last hurrah.

27.1

 ADDRESS TO THE INHABITANTS OF THE
COLONIES, FEBRUARY 13, 1776

Worthington Chauncey Ford et al., eds., *Journals of the Continental Congress, 1774–1789* (Washington, D.C.: Government Printing Office, 1904–37), 4:134–46. The essay has been edited for excessive repetition and length.

*To the Inhabitants of the Colonies of New Hampshire, Massachusetts Bay, Rhode Island and Providence Plantations, Connecticut, New York, New Jersey, Pennsylvania, the Counties of New Castle, Kent and Sussex on Delaware, Maryland, Virginia, North Carolina, South Carolina and Georgia, from their Delegates in Congress.*

FRIENDS AND COUNTRYMEN.

History, we believe, cannot furnish an Example of a Trust, higher and more important than that, which we have received from your Hands. It comprehends in it every Thing that can rouse the Attention and interest the Passions of a People, who will not reflect Disgrace upon their Ancestors nor degrade themselves, nor transmit Infamy to their Descendants. It is committed to us at a Time when every Thing dear and valuable to *such* a People is in imminent Danger. This Danger arises from those, whom we have been accustomed to consider as our Friends; who really were so, while they continued friendly to themselves; and who will again be so, when they shall return to a just Sense of their own Interests. The Calamities, which threaten us, would be attended with the total Loss of those Constitutions, formed upon the venerable Model of British Liberty, which have been long our Pride and Felicity. To avert those *Calamities* we are under the disagreeable Necessity of making temporary Deviations from those *Constitutions*.

Such is the Trust reposed in us. Much does it import you and us, that it be executed with Skill and with Fidelity. That we have discharged it with Fidelity, we enjoy the Testimony of a good Conscience. How far we have discharged it with Skill must be determined by you, who are our Principals and Judges, to whom we esteem it our Duty to render an Account of our Conduct. To enable you to judge of it, as we would wish you to do, it is necessary that you should be made acquainted with the *Situation,* in which your Affairs have been placed; the *Principles,* on which we have acted; and the *Ends,* which we have kept and still keep in View.

*That all Power was originally in the People—that all the Powers of Government are derived from them—that all Power, which they have not disposed of, still continues theirs—* are Maxims of the *English* Constitution, which, we presume, will not be disputed. The Share of Power, which the King derives from the People, or, in other Words, the Prerogative of the Crown, is well known and precisely ascertained: It is the same in *Great Britain* and in the Colonies. The Share of Power, which the House of Commons derives from the People, is likewise well known: The Manner in which it is conveyed is by Election. But the House of Commons is not elected by the Colonists; and therefore, from *them* that Body can derive no Authority.

Besides; the Powers, which the House of Commons receives from its Constituents, are entrusted by the Colonies to their Assemblies in the several Provinces. Those Assemblies have Authority to propose and assent to Laws for the Government of their Electors, in the same Manner as the House of Commons has Authority to propose and assent to Laws for the Government of the Inhabitants of *Great Britain*. Now the same collective Body cannot delegate the same Powers to distinct representative Bodies. The undeniable Result is, that the *House of Commons* neither has nor can have any Power deriv'd from the *Inhabitants of these Colonies*. . . .

The Colonies, wearied with presenting fruitless Supplications and Petitions *separately;* or prevented, by arbitrary and abrupt Dissolutions of their Assemblies, from using even those fruitless Expedients for Redress, determined to *join* their Counsels and their Efforts. Many of the Injuries flowing from the unconstitutional and ill-advised Acts of the British Legislature, affected all the Provinces equally; and even in these Cases, in which the Injuries were confined, by the Acts, to one or to a few, the *Principles,* on which they were made, extended to all. If common Rights, common Interests, common Dangers and common Sufferings are Principles of Union, what could be more natural than the Union of the Colonies?

Delegates authorised by the several Provinces from Nova Scotia to Georgia to represent them and act in their Behalf, met in GENERAL CONGRESS.

It has been objected, that this Measure was unknown to the Constitution; that the Congress was, of Consequence, an illegal Body; and that its Proceedings could not, in any Manner, be recognised by the Government of Britain. To those, who offer this Objection, and have attempted to vindicate, by its supposed Validity, the Neglect and Contempt, with which the Petition of that Congress to his Majesty was treated by the Ministry, we beg Leave, in our Turn, to propose, that they would explain the Principles of the Constitution, which warranted the *Assembly of the Barons at* RUNNINGMEDE, when MAGNA CHARTA was signed, the *Convention-Parliament* that recalled Charles 2d, and the *Convention of Lords and Commons* that placed King William on the Throne. When they shall have done this, we shall perhaps, be able to apply their Principles to prove the Necessity and Propriety of a Congress.

But the Objections of those, who have done so much and aimed so much against the Liberties of America, are not confined to the *Meeting* and the *Authority* of the Congress: They are urged with equal Warmth against the *Views* and *Inclinations* of those who composed it. We are told, in the Name of Majesty itself, "that the Authors and Promoters of this *desperate Conspiracy,*" as those who framed his Majesty's Speech are pleased to term our *laudable Resistance;* "have, in the Conduct of it, derived great Advantage from the Difference of his Majesty's Intentions and theirs. That they meant only to amuse by vague Expressions of Attachment to the Parent State, and the strongest Protestations of

Loyalty to the King, whilst they were preparing for a general Revolt. That on the Part of his Majesty and the Parliament, the Wish was rather to reclaim than to subdue." It affords us some Pleasure to find that the Protestations of Loyalty to his Majesty, which have been made, are allowed to be strong; and that Attachment to the Parent State is owned to be expressed. Those Protestations of Loyalty and Expressions of Attachment ought, by every Rule of Candour, to be presumed to be sincere, unless Proofs evincing their Insincerity can be drawn from the Conduct of those who used them.

In examining the Conduct of those who directed the Affairs of the Colonies at the Time when, it is said, they were preparing for a general Revolt, we find it an easy Undertaking to shew, that they merited no Reproach from the British Ministry by making any Preparations *for that Purpose.* We wish it were as easy to shew, that they merited no Reproach from their Constituents, by neglecting the necessary Provisions *for their Security.* Has a single Preparation been made, which has not been found requisite for our Defense? Have we not been attacked in Places where fatal Experience taught us, we were not sufficiently prepared for a successful Opposition? On which Side of this unnatural Controversy was the *ominous Intimation* first given, that it must be decided by Force? Were Arms and Ammunition imported into *America,* before the Importation of them was prohibited? What Reason can be assigned for this Prohibition, unless it be this, that those who made it had determined upon such a System of Oppression, as they knew, would *force* the Colonies into Resistance? And yet, they "wished only to reclaim!" . . .

In our present Situation, in which we are called to oppose an Attack upon your Liberties, made under bold Pretensions of Authority from that Power, to which the executive Part of Government is, in the ordinary Course of Affairs, committed—in this Situation, every Mode of Resistance, though directed by Necessity and by Prudence, and authorised by the Spirit of the Constitution, will be exposed to plausible Objections drawn from its Forms. Concerning such Objections, and the Weight that may be allowed to them, we are little solicitous. It will not discourage us to find ourselves represented as "labouring to enflame the Minds of the People in America, and openly avowing Revolt, Hostility and Rebellion." We deem it an Honour to "have raised Troops, and collected a naval Force"; and, *cloathed with the sacred Authority of the People, from* WHOM *all* LEGITIMATE AUTHORITY *proceeds* "to have exercised legislative, executive and judicial Powers." For what Purposes were those Powers instituted? For your Safety and Happiness. You and the World will judge whether those Purposes have been best promoted by us; or by those who claim the Powers, which they charge us with assuming.

But while we feel no Mortification at being misrepresented with Regard to the *Measures* employed by us for accomplishing the great Ends, which you have appointed us to pursue; we cannot sit easy under an Accusation, which charges us with laying aside those *Ends,* and endeavouring to accomplish *such as are very different.* We are accused of carrying on the War "for the Purpose of establishing an independent Empire."

We disavow the Intention. We declare, that what we aim at, and what we are entrusted by ~~our Constituents~~ you to pursue, *is the Defence and the Re-establishment of the constitutional Rights of the Colonies.* Whoever gives impartial Attention to the Facts, we have already stated, and to the Observations we have already made, must be fully convinced that all the Steps, which have been taken by us in this unfortunate Struggle, can be accounted for as rationally and as satisfactorily by supposing that the Defence and Reestablishment of their Rights were the Objects which the Colonists and their Representatives had in View; as by supposing that an independent Empire was their Aim. Nay, we may safely go farther and affirm, without the most distant Apprehension of being refuted, that many of those Steps can be accounted for rationally and satisfactorily only upon the former Supposition, and cannot be accounted for, in that Manner, upon the latter. The numerous Expedients that were tried, though fruitlessly, for avoiding Hostilities: The visible and unfeigned Reluctance and Horrour, with which we entered into them: The Caution and Reserve, with which we have carried them on: The Attempts we have made by petitioning the Throne and by every other Method, which might probably, or could possibly be of any Avail for procuring an Accommodation—These are not surely the usual Characteristics of Ambition. . . .

Is no regard to be had to the Professions and Protestations made by us, on so many different Occasions, of Attachment to Great Britain of Allegiance to his Majesty; and of Submission to his Government upon the Terms, on which the Constitution points it out as a Duty, and on which alone a *British Sovereign* has a Right to demand it?

When the Hostilities commenced by the ministerial Forces in Massachusetts Bay, and the imminent Dangers threatening the other Colonies rendered it absolutely necessary that they should be put into a State of Defence—even on that Occasion, we did not forget our Duty to his Majesty, and our Regard for our fellow Subjects in Britain. Our Words are these: "But as we most ardently wish for a Restoration of the Harmony formerly subsisting between our Mother-Country and these Colonies, the Interruption of which must at all Events, be exceedingly injurious to both Countries: Resolved, that with a sincere Design of contributing, by all Means in our Power, not incompatible with a just Regard for the undoubted Rights and true Interests of these Colonies, to the Promotion of this most desirable Reconciliation, an humble and dutiful Address be presented to his Majesty."

If Purposes of establishing an independent Empire has lurked in our Breasts, no fitter Occasion could have been found for giving Intimations of them, than in our Declaration setting forth the Causes and Necessity of our taking up Arms. Yet even there no Pretence can be found for fixing such an Imputation on us. "Lest this Declaration should disquiet the Minds of our Friends and fellow Subjects in any Part of the Empire, we assure them that we mean not to dissolve that Union, which has so long and so happily subsisted between us, and which we sincerely wish to see restored. Necessity has not yet driven us into that desperate Measure, or induced us to excite any other Nation to war against them. We have not raised Armies with the ambitious Designs of separating from Great Britain, and establishing independent States." Our Petition to the King has the following Asseveration: "By such Arrangements as your Majesty's Wisdom can form for collecting the united Sense of your American People, we are convinced your Majesty would receive such satisfactory Proofs of the Disposition of the Colonists towards their Sovereign and the Parent State, that the wished for Opportunity would be soon restored to them, of evincing the Sincerity of their Professions by every Testimony of Devotion becoming the most dutiful Subjects and the most affectionate Colonists." In our Address to the Inhabitants of Great Britain, we say: "We are accused of aiming at Independence: But how is this Accusation supported? By the Allegations of your Ministers, not by our Actions. Give us Leave, most solemnly to assure you, that we have not yet lost Sight of the Object we have ever had in View, a Reconciliation with you on constitutional Principles, and a Restoration of that friendly Intercourse, which to the Advantage of both we till lately maintained."

If we wished to detach you from your Allegiance to his Majesty, and to wean your Affections from a Connexion with your fellow-Subjects in Great Britain, is it likely that we would take so much Pains, upon every proper Occasion, to place those Objects before you in the most agreeable Points of View?

If any equitable Terms of Accommodation had been offered us, and we had rejected them, there would have been some Foundation for the Charge that we endeavoured to establish an independent Empire. But no Means have been used either by Parliament or by Administration for the Purpose of bringing this Contest to a Conclusion besides Penalties directed by Statutes, or Devastations occasioned by War. Alas! how long will Britons forget that Kindred-Blood flows in your Veins? How long will they strive, with hostile Fury to sluice it out from Bosoms that have already bled in their Cause; and, in their Cause, would still be willing to pour out what remains, to the last precious Drop?

We are far from being insensible of the Advantages, which have resulted to the Colonies as well as to Britain from the Connexion which has hitherto subsisted between them: We are far from denying them, or wishing to lessen the Ideas of their Importance. But the Nature of this Connexion, and the Principles, on which it was originally formed and on which alone it can be maintained, seem unhappily to have been misunderstood or disregarded by those, who laid and conducted the late destructive Plan of Colony-Administration. It is a Connexion founded upon mutual Benefits; upon Religion, Laws, Manners, Customs and Habits common to both Countries. Arbitrary Exertions of Power on the Part of Britain, and servile Submission on the [part of the] Colonies, if the Colonies should ever become degenerate enough to [accept] it, would immediately rend every generous Bond asunder. An intimate Connexion between Freemen and Slaves cannot be continued without Danger and, at last, Destruction to the former. Should your Enemies be able to reduce you to Slavery, the baneful Contagion would spread over the whole Empire. We verily believe that the Freedom, Happiness, and Glory of Great Britain, and the Prosperity of his Majesty and his Family depend upon the Success of your Resistance. You are now expending your Blood, and your Treasure in promoting the Welfare and true Interests of your Sovereign and your fellow-Subjects in Britain, in Opposition to the most dangerous Attacks that have been ever made against them. . . .

Britain and these Colonies have been Blessings to each other. Sure we are, that they might continue to be so. Some salutary System might certainly be devised, which would remove from both Sides, Jealousies that are ill-founded, and the Causes of Jealousies that are well-founded; which would restore to both Countries those important Benefits that Nature seems to have intended them reciprocally to confer and to receive; and which would secure the Continuance and the Encrease of those Benefits to numerous succeeding Generations. That such a System may be formed is our ardent Wish.

But as such a System must affect the Interest of the Colonies as much as that of the Mother-Country, why should the Colonies be excluded from a Voice in it? Should not, to say the least upon this Subject, their Consent be asked and obtained as to the *general Ends,* which it ought to be calculated to answer? Why should not its Validity depend upon us as well as upon the Inhabitants of Great Britain? No Disadvantage will result to them: An important Advantage will result to [us]. We shall be affected by no Laws, the Authority of which, as far as they regard us, is not *founded on our own Consent.* This Consent may be expressed as well by a solemn Compact, as if the Colonists, by their Representatives, had an immediate Voice in passing the Laws. In a Compact we would *concede* liberally to Parliament: For the *Bounds* of our Concessions would be known.

We are too much attached to the English Laws and Constitution, and know too well their happy Tendency to diffuse Freedom, Prosperity and Peace wherever they prevail, to desire an independent Empire. If one Part of the Constitution be pulled down, it is impossible to foretell whether the other Parts of it may not be shaken, and, perhaps overthrown. It is a Part of our Constitution to be under Allegiance to the Crown, Limited and ascertained as the Prerogative is, the Position—*that a King can do no wrong*—may be founded in *Fact* as well as in *Law,* if you are not wanting to yourselves.

We trace your Calamities to the House of Commons. *They* have undertaken to *give* and *grant* your Money. From a supposed virtual Representation in *their* House it is argued, that *you* ought to be bound by the Acts of the British Parliament in all Cases whatever. This is no Part of the Constitution. This is the Doctrine, to which we will never subscribe our Assent: This is the Claim, to which we adjure you, as you tender your own Freedom and Happiness, and the Freedom and Happiness of your Posterity, never to submit. The same Principles, which directed *your Ancestors* to oppose the exorbitant and dangerous Pretensions of the Crown, should direct *you* to oppose the no less exorbitant and dangerous Claims of the House of Commons.

Let all Communication of despotic Power through that Channel be cut off, and your Liberties will be safe.

Let neither our Enemies nor our Friends make improper Inferences from the Solicitude, which we have discovered to remove the Imputation of aiming to establish an independent Empire. Though an independent Empire is not our *Wish;* it may—let your Oppressors attend—it may be the Fate of our Countrymen and ourselves. It is in the Power of your Enemies to render Independency or Slavery your and our Alternative. Should we—will you, in such an Event, hesitate a Moment about the Choice? Let those, who drive us to it, answer to their King and to their Country for the Consequences. We are *desirous* to continue Subjects: But we are *determined* to continue Freemen. We shall deem ourselves bound to renounce; and, we hope, you will follow our Example in renouncing the *former* Character whenever it shall become incompatible with the *latter*.

While we shall be continued by you in the very important Trust, which you have committed to us, we shall keep our Eyes constantly and steadily fixed upon the Grand Object of the Union of the Colonies—THE RE-ESTABLISHMENT AND SECURITY OF THEIR CONSTITUTIONAL RIGHTS. Every Measure that we employ shall be directed to the Attainment of this great End: No Measure, necessary, in our Opinion, for attaining it, shall be declined. If any such Measure should, against our principal Intention, draw the Colonies into Engagements that may suspend or dissolve their Union with their fellow-Subjects in Great Britain, we shall lament the Effect; but shall hold ourselves justified in adopting the Measure. That the Colonies may continue connected, as they have been, with Britain, is our second Wish: Our first is—THAT AMERICA MAY BE FREE.

‖*Ordered,* To lie on the table.‖

27.2

 JOHN DICKINSON, PROPOSED RESOLUTIONS ON A PETITION TO THE KING, JANUARY 9–24(?), 1776

John Dickinson was among the most prominent members of Congress; he had served as the principal author of the primary document of the Stamp Act Congress in 1765, the most celebrated pamphlet of the late 1760s, and most of the congressional state papers in 1774 and 1775, as well as the first draft in 1776 of the Articles of Confederation. Although a longtime critic of Parliament's actions, he persistently opposed independence and, in the end, refused to vote for it. Accordingly, in response to the king's speech to Parliament of October 26, 1775, in which he accused the colonists of seeking independence, Dickinson, along with other moderates in Congress, hoped to convince the king that his faithful subjects in America were not "contending for Empire & Independence" and that he was "misinform'd concerning the Intentions of his faithful subjects in America"; the proposed resolutions again asked him to "point out some Mode for terminating the present unhappy Differences by a mutually beneficial Accommodation." In early February it may well have been still true, if only barely, that, with the exception of most of the New England delegates and some Virginians, "the 'violents' were a minority," but they were known to "try all schemes in all shapes, act in concert, and thereby have a considerable advantage over the others, who are by no means so closely united."[20] For these reasons or, at least as likely, the king's continued intransigence and

Parliament's inflammatory policies, Dickinson's hoped-for third petition to the king was never issued by Congress.

Paul H. Smith, ed., *Letters of Delegates to Congress, 1774–1789* (Washington, D.C.: Library of Congress, 1976–93), 3:63. The blank spaces in the resolution are present in the original text.

1. That an humble & dutiful Petition be presented to his Majesty, expressing the deep Affliction with which the Inhabitants of these Colonies, perceive by his Majesty's late speech to Parliament, that his Majesty apprehends, We are contending for Empire & Independence—to assure his Majesty that he is misinform'd concerning the Intentions of his faithful subjects in America, and repeating our former supplications, that his Majesty will point out some Mode for terminating the present unhappy Differences by a mutually beneficial Accommodation.

2. That       or more Delegates Members of this Congress be appointed to present this Petition—to confer         to mention some terms.

## 27.3

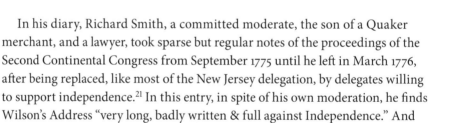

RICHARD SMITH, DIARY ENTRY,
FEBRUARY 13, 1776

In his diary, Richard Smith, a committed moderate, the son of a Quaker merchant, and a lawyer, took sparse but regular notes of the proceedings of the Second Continental Congress from September 1775 until he left in March 1776, after being replaced, like most of the New Jersey delegation, by delegates willing to support independence.[21] In this entry, in spite of his own moderation, he finds Wilson's Address "very long, badly written & full against Independence." And because the tide of opinion in Congress had swung from reconciliation to separation and independence when the address was tabled in mid-February, Smith noted that Wilson never thought again of advancing it.

Paul H. Smith, ed., *Letters of Delegates to Congress, 1774–1789* (Washington, D.C.: Library of Congress, 1976–93), 3:252.

Tuesday 13. Votes read. The Question Whether the 3 Battals. in Virginia shall be taken into Continental Service passed in the Negative 8 Colonies to 3, & one divided. It was agreed to pay the Two first Battals. there from Novr. last. 30,000 Dollars advanced for the Troops in Virginia and the Field Officers of the 6 Battalions there, were now elected by Ballot which is our Customary Method. A Major Gen. & Adjutant General were asked for by the Virgians and a Comee. of 5 chosen to consider of a Southern Military Department. Letters from the Jersey Convention & from the Field Officers of Daytons Regt. were read and comd. to myself, Bartlett & S. Adams. 600 Dollars advanced to Fairlamb the Commissary in Chester County, & several large sums ordered for sundry Uses. Wilson brought in the Draught of an Address to our Constituents which was very long, badly written & full against Independency. (Wilson percieving the Majority did not relish his Address & Doctrine never thought fit to stir it again.) Chase gave Notice that he would move tomorrow for Orders to Admiral Hopkins to seize all Ships of Great Britain & to recommend to all the Colonies to fit out Privateers. A Direction given that McKean should request the City Comee. to delay publishing the Sellers of Tea in the Papers till further Order. Some Money advanced for Gen Lee's Troops in New York & for Col. John Dickinsons who goes on Thursday with a Detachment of Associators from hence to that City. Agreed to continue the Pay of Capt. Bernard Romans during his Stay in Philada. on public Business.

## 28. AMERICAN AND BRITISH CALLS FOR FASTING, MARCH AND OCTOBER 1776

On March 13, William Livingston, a wealthy Presbyterian and moderate lawyer from New York and New Jersey, and the father-in-law of John Jay, placed before his colleagues a request that he be allowed "to bring in a resolution for appointing a fast," which he did three days later, on March 16. Congress on the same day approved his resolution, and it was published on March 20 in the *Pennsylvania Gazette*.[22] His proclamation was similar to the one of the same type issued June 12, 1775 (see document 17.2); a dozen or so followed Livingston's.[23] Although no committee was appointed to join Livingston in its production, most of what was stated differed little from others penned by congressional committees. Livingston laments the "warlike preparations of the British ministry . . . to reduce us by fire and sword, by the savages of the wilderness, and our own domestics [slaves], to the most abject and ignominious bondage." That the colonists were busily engaged in offensive military operations in their aggressive campaign in Canada, or that the British freeing of slaves might be viewed as defensible, was no more part of Livingston's religious meditation than of anyone else's.

Livingston asks that Congress "do earnestly recommend, that Friday, the Seventeenth day of May next, be observed by the said colonies as a day of humiliation, fasting, and prayer; that we may . . . through the merits and mediation of Jesus Christ, obtain his pardon and forgiveness." Such language and a commitment to corporate repentance were to be expected in colonies deeply shaped by Reformed Protestant religiosity, which had done much to influence the contours of most colonies' political institutions.[24] Besides fasting and praying, it was "recommended to Christians of all denominations, to assemble for public worship, and abstain from servile labour on the said day." What was noticeably different from the first proclamation was that Livingston's did not beseech God to bless George III, nor did he pray for a just reconciliation.[25] Americans' Christocentric political theology had not changed in eight months, but Congress' conciliatory politics had.

28.1

## Second Proclamation for a Day of Humiliation, Fasting, and Prayer, March 16, 1776

Worthington Chauncey Ford et al., eds., *Journals of the Continental Congress, 1774–1789* (Washington, D.C.: Government Printing Office, 1904–37), 4:208–9.

Mr. W[illiam] Livingston, pursuant to leave granted, brought in a resolution for appointing a fast, which ‖being taken into consideration,‖ was agreed to as follows:

In times of impending calamity and distress; when the liberties of America are imminently endangered by the secret machinations and open assaults of an insidious and vindictive administration, it becomes the indispensable duty of these hitherto free and happy colonies, with true penitence of heart, and the most reverent devotion, publickly to acknowledge the over ruling providence of God; to confess and deplore our offences against him; and to supplicate his interposition for averting the threatened danger, and prospering our strenuous efforts in the cause of freedom, virtue, and posterity.

The Congress, therefore, considering the warlike preparations of the British Ministry to subvert our invaluable rights and priviledges, and to reduce us by fire and sword, by the savages of the wilderness, and our own domestics, to the most abject and ignominious bondage: Desirous, at the same time, to have people of all ranks and degrees duly impressed with a solemn sense of God's superintending providence, and of their duty, devoutly to rely, in all their lawful enterprizes, on his aid and direction, Do earnestly recommend, that Friday, the Seventeenth day of May next, be observed by the said colonies as a day of humiliation, fasting, and prayer; that we may, with united hearts, confess and bewail our manifold sins and transgressions, and, by a sincere repentance and amendment of life, appease his righteous displeasure, and, through the merits and mediation of Jesus Christ, obtain his pardon and forgiveness; humbly imploring his assistance to frustrate the cruel purposes of our unnatural enemies; and by inclining their hearts to justice and benevolence, prevent the further effusion of kindred blood. But if, continuing deaf to the voice of reason and humanity, and inflexibly bent, on desolation and war, they constrain us to repel their hostile invasions by open resistance, that it may please the Lord of Hosts, the God of Armies, to animate our officers and soldiers with invincible fortitude, to guard and protect them in the day of battle, and to crown the continental arms, by sea and land, with victory and success: Earnestly beseeching him to bless our civil rulers, and the representatives of the people, in their several assemblies and conventions; to preserve and strengthen their union, to inspire them with an ardent, disinterested love of their country; to give wisdom and stability to their counsels; and direct them to the most efficacious measures for establishing the rights of America on the most honourable and permanent basis—That he would be graciously pleased to bless all his people in these colonies with health and plenty, and grant that a spirit of incorruptible patriotism, and of pure undefiled religion, may universally prevail; and this continent be speedily restored to the blessings of peace and liberty, and enabled to transmit them inviolate to the latest posterity. And it is recommended to Christians of all denominations, to assemble for public worship, and abstain from servile labour on the said day.

*Resolved,* That the foregoing resolve be published.

## 28.2

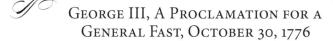 

## GEORGE III, A PROCLAMATION FOR A GENERAL FAST, OCTOBER 30, 1776

The colonists were not alone in seeking forgiveness of their sins and divine intervention and blessing. King George III likewise linked the calamities confronting his people with the need for public worship and greater religious devotion as he set aside five more days during the war years, 1778 to 1782, for "fasting and humiliation."[26] Throughout England and Scotland, public worship services were held "so both We and Our People may humble Ourselves before Almighty God, in order to obtain Pardon of Our Sins." Continuing, the king asks God "speedily to deliver Our loyal Subjects within Our Colonies and Provinces in North America from the Violence, Injustice, and Tyranny of those daring Rebels who have assumed to themselves the Exercise of Arbitrary Power." Catholic and Jewish as well as Anglican services were performed so that all the king's subjects in the realm could come together to confess their sins publicly during a time when the British people were at war with their American brethren in the colonies, and soon would be with three of the major powers of Europe as well.[27]

Clarence S. A. M. Brigham, ed., *British Royal Proclamations Relating to America, 1603–1783* (Worcester, Mass.: American Antiquarian Society, 1911), 234–35.

GEORGE R.

We, taking into Our most serious Consideration the just and necessary Measures of Force which We are obliged to use against Our rebellious Subjects in Our Colonies and Provinces in North America; and putting Our Trust in Almighty God, that he will vouchsafe a Special Blessing on Our Arms, both by Sea and Land, have resolved, and do, by and with the Advice of Our Privy Council, hereby command, That a Publick Fast and Humiliation be observed throughout that Part of Our Kingdom of Great Britain called England, Our Dominion of Wales, and Town of Berwick upon Tweed, upon Friday the Thirteenth Day of December next; that so both We and Our People may humble Ourselves before Almighty God, in order to obtain Pardon of Our Sins; and may, in the most devout and solemn Manner, send up Our Prayers and Supplications to the Divine Majesty, for averting those heavy Judgements, which Our manifold Sins and Provocations have most justly deserved, and for imploring his Intervention and Blessing speedily to deliver Our loyal Subjects within Our Colonies and Provinces in North America from the Violence, Injustice, and Tyranny of those daring Rebels who have assumed to themselves the Exercise of Arbitrary Power, to open the Eyes of those who have been deluded by specious Falshoods, into Acts of Treason and Rebellion, to turn the Hearts of the Authors of these Calamities, and finally to restore Our People in those distracted Provinces and Colonies to the happy Condition of being free Subjects of a free State; under which heretofore they flourished so long and prospered so much: And We do strictly charge and command, that the said Publick Fast be referently and devoutly observed by all Our loving Subjects in England, Our Dominion of Wales, and Town of Berwick upon Tweed, as they tender the Favour of Almighty God, and would avoid his Wrath and Indignation; and upon Pain of such Punishment, as We may justly inflict upon all such as contemn and neglect the Performance of so religious a Duty. And for the better and more orderly solemnizing the same, We have given Directions to the most Reverend the Archbishops, and the Right Reverend the Bishops of England to compose a Form of Prayer suitable to this Occasion, to be used in all Churches, Chapels, and Places of Publick Worship; and to take Care the same be timely dispersed throughout their respective Dioceses.

Given at Our Court at St. James's, the Thirtieth Day of October, One thousand seven hundred and seventy-six, in the Seventeenth Year of Our Reign.

GOD SAVE THE KING.

## 29. CONGRESS AND PARLIAMENT DECLARE A TRADE WAR—THE COLONIES' FIRST STEP TOWARD INDEPENDENCE, MARCH 1776

Following a vote on March 18, 1776, in which "the four New England colonies, New York, Virginia, and North Carolina voted for granting letters to privateers while Pennsylvania and Maryland voted against it,"[28] Congress on March 19 appointed George

Wythe (Virginia), John Jay (New York), and James Wilson (Pennsylvania) to draft this declaration in response to Parliament's American Prohibitory Act of December 22, 1775 (document 29.2). That act prohibited, as of March 1, 1776, all external colonial commercial activity, including colonial shipping to British ports. Congress' ban on most exports also was to come to end on March 1.[29] The committee had two moderate members, Jay and Wilson, and a radical one, Wythe, the likely author of the declaration's preamble, who was a legal scholar and close ally of Jefferson (see Richard Smith's diary entry for March 22—document 29.5). The committee's makeup and Wythe's authorship of the preamble suggest that even moderates in Congress were ready to approve ever-more aggressive military and commercial challenges to British interests while simultaneously continuing to support Congress' long-standing offensive policies in Canada. The declaration was printed on March 27 in the *Pennsylvania Gazette*.

The colonies had very limited naval capacities—although Congress had, on December 13, 1775, authorized the construction of thirteen warships for the fledgling Continental navy—but a relatively large commercial fleet, and this declaration made it possible to use American commercial ships for military purposes as armed privateers under grants of marque and reprisal. American sailors were to become publicly and internationally sanctioned pirates whose goal was to disrupt British shipping and to bring smaller armed vessels, cargo ships, and their holdings into port, where they would be sold before a "prize" court, the proceeds to be split between the privateers' owners (in effect, their investors), their officers and crews, and the sanctioning governmental body, either colonial or congressional. Such activities, along with the enormous naval commitment of ships of the line provided by the Spanish and French navies, helped balance the stark disparity in naval power between the colonies and Britain. Given the profitable, even if risky, nature of the enterprise, serving on a privateer was highly popular.[30]

In the preamble, which was warmly debated in Congress, the actions of Parliament are held up for condemnation, in particular those that had led to open warfare in the colonies and to Britain's prosecuting the war "in a cruel manner; wasting, spoiling, and destroying the country." Also subject to criticism are Britain's having invited Native Americans to participate in the war; yet again, Britain's having instigated "negroes to murder their masters" by freeing them; and, most recently, Parliament's passage of the American Prohibitory Act, which declared the colonists' "property, wherever found upon the water, liable to seizure and confiscation" (see document 29.2). Congress asked too that its friends in Great Britain forgive the colonists for any consequent loss of property and that they hold accountable "the authors of our common calamities." Congress, for the first time seriously, even considered holding the king responsible for Parliament's actions. Doing so was defended by Wythe and Lee, but such a momentous change—one that would have effectively ended all hopes of reconciliation—was successfully opposed by Jay, Wilson, and Thomas Johnson (Maryland). Accordingly, Congress went no further than to write of "the royal authority" while defending Congress' stance as justified by "the laws of nature and the English Constitution"—in effect, giving voice to both factions in Congress.

The declaration itself boldly asserts that "ships and other vessels, their tackle, and furniture, and all goods, wares of merchandizes, belonging to any inhabitant or inhabitants of Great Britain . . . shall be deemed and adjudged to be lawful prize." Shipping owned by other nationals, along with "any vessel bringing settlers arms, ammunition or warlike stores to and for the use of these colonies," was not to be treated as enemy property. However one might understand the repeated colonial attacks on Canadian targets and on the king's troops in Boston, this declaration came very close to announcing independence.

At this time, European opinion of the colonies' standing was in flux. Congress, unaware of the change, on March 3 had sent Silas Deane to Europe with the hope of obtaining needed military supplies. His mission, seen in conjunction with this declaration and the Continental forces having on March 17 forced the British to evacuate Boston, was a sign that the colonies were moving closer to a formal a declaration of independence. Yet as the accompanying letters (documents 29.4–29.6) suggest, divisions persisted among the delegates; only seven colonies, mostly from New England and the South, supported the declaration, and a sizable minority of colonial delegations still refused, even in the midst of an increasingly violent war, to hold the king accountable and thereby foreclose all possibilities for reconciliation.

29.1

### Declaration on Armed Vessels, March 23, 1776

Worthington Chauncey Ford et al., eds., *Journals of the Continental Congress, 1774–1789* (Washington, D.C.: Government Printing Office, 1904–37), 4:229–32.

The Congress resumed the consideration of the declaration, which was agreed to as follows:

Whereas the petitions of the United Colonies to the King, for the redress of great and manifest grievances, have not only been rejected, but treated with scorn and contempt, and the opposition to designs evidently formed to reduce them to a state of servile subjection, and their necessary defence against hostile forces actually employed to subdue them, declared rebellion; And whereas an unjust war hath been commenced against them, which the commanders of the British fleets and armies have prosecuted, and still continue to prosecute, with their utmost vigour, and in a cruel manner; wasting, spoiling, and destroying the country, burning houses and defenceless towns, and exposing the helpless inhabitants to every misery, from the inclemency of the winter; and not only urging savages to invade the country, but instigating negroes to murder their masters; And whereas the parliament of Great Britain hath lately passed an Act, affirming these colonies to be in open rebellion, forbidding all trade and commerce with the inhabitants thereof, until they shall accept pardons, and submit to despotic rule, declaring their property, wherever found upon the water, liable to seizure and confiscation; and enacting, that what had been done there by virtue of the royal authority, were just and lawful acts, and shall be so deemed; from all which it is manifest, that the iniquitous scheme, concerted to deprive them of the liberty they have a right to by the laws of nature and the English constitution, will be pertinaciously pursued. It being therefore necessary to provide for their defence and security, and justifiable to make reprisals upon their enemies, and otherwise to annoy them, according to the laws and usages of Nations, the Congress, trusting that such of their friends in Great Britain (of whom it is confessed there are many entitled to applause and gratitude for their patriotism and benevolence, and in whose favour a discrimination of property cannot be made) as shall suffer by captures, will impute it to the authors of our common calamities, Do Declare and Resolve, as followeth, to wit:

*Resolved,* That the inhabitants of these colonies be permitted to fit out armed vessels to cruize on the enemies of these United Colonies.

*Resolved,* That all ships and other vessels, their tackle, apparel, and furniture, and all goods, wares, and merchandizes, belonging to any inhabitant or inhabitants of Great Britain, taken on the high seas, or between high and low water mark, by any armed vessel, fitted out by any private person or persons, and to whom commissions shall be granted, and being libelled and prosecuted in any court erected for the trial of maritime affairs, in any of these colonies, shall be deemed and adjudged to be lawful prize; and after deducting and paying the wages of the seamen and mariners on board of such captures, as are merchant ships and vessels, shall be entitled to, according to the terms of their contracts, until the time of the adjudication, shall be condemned to and for the use of the owner or owners, and the officers, marines, and mariners of such armed vessel, according to such rules and proportions as they shall agree on: Provided always, that this resolution shall not extend to any vessel bringing settlers arms, ammunition or warlike stores to and for the use of these colonies, or any of the inhabitants thereof, who are friends to the American cause, or to such war-like stores, or to the effects of such settlers.

*Resolved,* That all ships or vessels, with their tackle, apparel, and furniture, goods, wares, and merchandizes, belonging to any inhabitant of Great Britain as aforesaid, which shall be taken by any of the vessels of war of these United Colonies, shall be deemed forfeited; one third, after deducting and paying the wages of seamen and mariners as aforesaid, to the officers and men on board, and two thirds to the use of the United Colonies.

*Resolved,* That all ships or vessels, with their tackle, apparel, and furniture, goods, wares, and merchandises, belonging to any inhabitants of Great Britain as aforesaid, which shall be taken by any vessel of war fitted out by and at the expence of any of the United Colonies, shall be deemed forfeited, and divided, after deducting and paying the wages of seamen and mariners, as aforesaid, in such manner and proportions as the assembly or convention of such colony shall direct.

*Resolved,* That all vessels, with their tackle, apparel, and furniture, and cargoes, belonging to the inhabitants of Great Britain, as aforesaid, and all vessels which may be employed in carrying supplies to the ministerial armies, which shall happen to be taken near the shores of any of these colonies, by the people of the country, or detachments from the army, shall be deemed lawful prize; and the court of admiralty within the said colony is required, on condemnation thereof, to adjudge that all charges and expences which may attend the capture and trial, be first paid out of the monies arising from the sales of the prize, and the remainder equally divided among all those, who shall have been actually engaged and employed in taking the said prize. Provided, that where any detachments of the army shall have been employed as aforesaid, their part of the prize money shall be distributed among them in proportion to the pay of the officers and soldiers so employed.

*Ordered,* That the foregoing resolution be published.

## 29.2

 AMERICAN PROHIBITORY ACT, DECEMBER 22, 1775

Replacing the Restraining Acts of March 30 and April 13, 1775 (for the former, see document 18.3), which had proscribed trade between the colonies and all nations other than Britain, Ireland, and the British West Indies, the American Prohibitory Act was intended to end "all manner of American colonial trade and commerce," even coastal intercolonial trade, from March 1, 1776. Parliament, following its consideration of the Olive Branch Petition (document 19.1) in early November 1775, defeated motions in each house, by 2–1 and 3–1 margins, that found the petition—as Richard Howe later contended—an adequate basis from which to negotiate reconciliation. Although there remained strong opposition in the House of Lords to further aggravating the situation, the American Prohibitory Act, when amended, was passed, and on December 22 was signed by the king.[31] The reasons given by Parliament for its actions were simple enough: the colonists had defied "the just and legal authority of the king and parliament of Great Britain"; they had "assembled together an armed force, engaged his Majesty's troops, and attacked his forts"; and they had "usurped the powers of government, and prohibited all trade and commerce with this kingdom and the other parts of his Majesty's dominions." None of these charges, although surely subject to multiple interpretations, could be denied by Congress.

The act, by cutting off "all trade and commerce with this kingdom and the other parts of his Majesty's dominions," exceeded in severity earlier legislation, but its significance went well beyond that. In Parliament's declaring "that all ships and vessels of or belonging to the inhabitants of the said colonies, together with their cargoes, apparel, and furniture . . . shall become forfeited to his Majesty, as if the same were the ships and effects of open enemies," the king signaled the withdrawal of his protection from his American subjects and thus terminated the reciprocal relationship between royal protection and subject loyalty. Of particular offense to Americans was that the act permitted the capturing of North American sailors, who would then be forced to serve in the British navy and "to be as much in the service on board his Majesty, to all intents and purposes, as if the said mariners and crews had entered themselves voluntarily to serve on board his Majesty's said ships and vessels." This meant that for them, unlike British sailors "pressed" into service, attempted desertion was punishable by death.[32]

With this act, Parliament and the king implicitly declared the colonists to be no longer, in a certain moral sense, the king's subjects owing him their loyalty. Although Lord North offered, in conjunction with the act, "to repeal all the Coercive Acts of 1774 and to 'suspend every exercise of the right of taxation, if the colonies would point out any mode by which they would bear their share of the burden and give their aid to the common defence,'" this legislation was a decisive event that tilted the table, finally and unmistakably, in the favor of congressional radicals.[33] As Merrill Jensen observed, the act had "in effect declared them to be outlaws." He added that its likely impact on congressional delegates was not lost on forward-looking MPs: "A member of the opposition in Parliament said that the Bill answered all the purposes of the most violent Americans and that its title should be altered to fit its purpose and be called 'a Bill for carrying more effectively into execution the resolves of Congress.' Its effect was precisely that."[34] Once again, an act of Parliament or a proclamation by the king did much to help the cause of radicals in Congress by pushing the majority of otherwise reluctant delegates toward separation and independence. Overreaction seemingly has been the response of almost all regimes confronting a successful independence movement—few strategies are appropriately demanding without going too far, and Britain, clearly, did not find one this time.[35]

Danby Pickering, ed., *The Statutes at Large from the Magna Charta to the End of the Eleventh Parliament of Great Britain* (Cambridge: John Archdeacon, 1775), 31:135.

WHEREAS *many Persons in the Colonies* of New Hampshire, Massachusetts Bay, Rhode Island, Connecticut, New York, New Jersey, Pennsylvania, *the three lower counties on* Delaware, Maryland, Virginia, North Carolina, South Carolina, *and* Georgia, *have set themselves in open rebellion and defiance to the just and legal authority of the king and parliament of* Great Britain, *to which they ever have been and of right ought to be, subject; and have assembled together an armed force, engaged his Majesty's troops, and attacked his forts; have usurped the powers of government, and prohibited all trade and commerce with this kingdom and the other parts of his Majesty's dominions: for the more speedily and effectually suppressing such wicked and daring designs, and for preventing any aid, supply, or assistance, being sent thither during the continuance of the said rebellious and treasonable commotions,* be it therefore declared and enacted by the King's most excellent majesty, by and with the advice and consent of the lords spiritual and temporal, and commons, in this present parliament assembled, and by the authority of the same, That all Manner of Trade and Commerce is and shall be prohibited with the Colonies of *New Hampshire, Massachusetts Bay, Rhode Island, Connecticut, New York, New Jersey, Pennsylvania,* the three lower counties on *Delaware, Maryland, Virginia, North Carolina, South Carolina,* and *Georgia;* and that all ships and vessels of or belonging to the inhabitants of the said colonies, together with their cargoes, apparel, and furniture, and all other ships and vessels whatsoever, together with their cargoes, apparel, and furniture which shall be found trading in any port or place of the said colonies, or going to trade, or coming from trading, in any such port or place, shall become forfeited to his Majesty, as if the same were the ships and effects of open enemies, and shall be so adjudged, deemed, and taken in all courts of admiralty, and in all other courts whatsoever. . . .

III. *And, for the encouragement of the officers and seamen of his Majesty's ships of war,* be it further enacted, That the flag-officers, captains, commanders, and other commissioned officers in his Majesty's pay, and also the seamen, marines, and soldiers on board, shall have the sole interest and property of and in all and every such ship, vessel, goods, and merchandise, which they shall seize and take, (being first adjudged lawful prize in any of his Majesty's courts of admiralty) to be divided in such proportions, and after such manner, as his Majesty shall think fit to order and direct by proclamation or proclamations hereafter to be issued for those purposes.

IV. And be it further enacted by the authority aforesaid, That it shall and may be lawful to and for the said flag officers, captains, and commanders respectively, to cause to be taken, or put on board any of His Majesty's ships or vessels of war, or on board any other ships or vessels, all and every the masters, crews, and other persons, who shall be found on board such ship and ships as shall be seized and taken as prize as aforesaid; and also to enter the names of such of the said mariners and crews, upon the book or books of his Majesty's said ships or vessels, as they, the said flag officers, captains, and commanders, shall respectively think fit; from the time and times of which said entries respectively, the said mariners and crews shall be considered, and they are hereby declared to belong to, and to be as much in the service of his Majesty, to all intents and purposes, as if the said mariners and crews had entered themselves voluntarily to serve on board his Majesty's said ships and vessels respectively . . .

XLIV. Provided always nevertheless, and it is hereby enacted by the authority aforesaid, That in order to encourage all well affected Persons in any of the said colonies to exert themselves in suppressing the rebellion therein, and to afford a speedy protection to those who are disposed to return to their duty, it shall and may be lawful to and for any person or persons, appointed and authorized by his Majesty to grant a pardon or pardons to any number or description of persons, by proclamation, in his Majesty's name, to declare any colony or province, colonies or provinces, or any county, town, port, district, or place, in any colony or province, to be at the peace of his Majesty; and from and after the issuing of any such proclamation in any of the aforesaid colonies or provinces, or if his Majesty shall be graciously pleased to signify the same by his royal proclamation, then, from and after the issuing of such proclamation, this act, with respect to such colony or province, colonies or provinces, county, town, port, district, or place, shall cease, determine, and be utterly void; and if any captures shall be made, after the date and issuing of such Proclamations, of any ships or vessels, and their cargoes, belonging to the inhabitants of any such colony or province, colonies or provinces, county, town, port, district, or place, or of any ships trading to or from such colony or province, colonies or provinces respectively, the same shall be restored to the owners of such ships or vessels, upon claim being entered, and due proof made of their property therein, and the captors shall not be liable to any action for seizing or detaining the said ships or vessels, or their cargoes, without proof being made that they had actual notice of such proclamations having been issued.

XLV. Provided always, That such proclamation or proclamations shall not discharge or suspend any proceeding upon any capture of any such ship or vessel made before the date and issuing thereof.

29.3

 RICHARD SMITH, DIARY ENTRY,
MARCH 18, 1776

Richard Smith records in his diary that the vote in Congress regarding the Declaration on Armed Vessels was actively debated and, in the end, was supported by seven colonies (all of New England, where service on privateers proved richly rewarding and thus far more popular than land warfare; two southern colonies; and, more surprisingly, New York), with two mid-Atlantic colonies opposed and four others not sufficiently represented to vote. Absence from Congress was a ploy often used by delegates to avoid taking sides on a controversial measure—in this case, voting to approve a declaration that many rightly feared constituted a clear act of treason, a capital offense. Smith also notes that he and Samuel Chase (Maryland) had unsuccessfully sought to extend, after the Irish Parliament in November had voted to approve the king's request to transfer four thousand troops from Ireland to the colonies, the ability of American privateers to prey on shipping belonging to others, including the Irish and other subjects in the British Dominions.

Paul H. Smith, ed., *Letters of Delegates to Congress, 1774–1789*
(Washington, D.C.: Library of Congress, 1976–93), 3:397–98.

Monday 18 March [1776]

The Votes read. 20,000 Dollars advanced to Commissary Mease. Some Promotions made in One of the Virginia Regts. in Consequence of Col. Henry's Resignation. The Congress was again in Comee. on the privateering Business, several Resoluts. were come to after an able Debate. By the first, Leave is to be given to commission Privateers and Letters of Marque to cruize on British Property. The Vote stood thus, For the Resolution New Hampshire, Massachusetts, Rhode Island, Connecticut, N York, Virginia and North Carolina, against it Pennsa. and Maryland, the other Colonies not sufficiently represented to vote. Ireland was excepted & the other British Domins. with the Consent of all but Chase & myself (it appearing to me very absurd to make War upon Part only of the Subjects & especially after the Irish Parlt. had declared decisively agt. Us). Leave for the Comee. to sit again on the same Affair. R H Lee moved to take Monsr. Arundel and another Frenchman into the Southern Departmt. which was opposed by Dr. Franklin and referred to our Comee. for considerg. the Application of Foreigners.

## 29.4

 JOSEPH HEWES TO SAMUEL JOHNSTON,
MARCH 20, 1776

Joseph Hewes, a moderate delegate from North Carolina, wrote to Samuel Johnston, the president of the North Carolina Provincial Congress and a man deeply distrustful of democratic leveling, that the American Prohibitory Act "will make the Breach between the two Countries so wide as never more to be reconciled." Hewes, although not looking forward to the colonists' declaring independence, had little confidence in the ability of the proposed British peace commissioners to bring about a reconciliation, since, as described in the closing section of the American Prohibitory Act, they would have power only "to receive submissions and grant pardons." Thus, he assumed, there was nothing "left now but to fight it out." But the colonies were not in the best shape to prosecute a war. They were bereft of war-fighting materials, and according to Hewes, tensions in Congress had gotten worse: "We do not treat each other with that decency and respect that was observed heretofore. Jealousies, ill natured observations and recriminations take [the] place of reason and Argument." And although "some among us urge strongly for Independency and eternal separation, others wish to wait a little longer and to have the opinion of their Constituents on that subject."

It is evident, though, that the tide had shifted and the question of independence was less one of if than of when. Indeed, this letter was written only a few weeks before the Halifax resolves, a motion adopted by all eighty-three legislators of the North Carolina Provincial Congress on April 12, 1776, directing their congressional delegation to vote, when supported by other colonies, for independence. Surprisingly again, as with the Mecklenburg County resolves of May 1775, it was North Carolina, not Massachusetts or Virginia, leading the way.[36]

Paul H. Smith, ed., *Letters of Delegates to Congress, 1774–1789* (Washington, D.C.: Library of Congress, 1976–93), 3:416–17.

Dear Sir,                                                              Philadelphia 20th March 1776.

I have received your favour of the 23rd of Feb'y, and also one from Mr. Hogg at Hillsborough of the 20th, I am exceedingly anxious for the safety of our Province. We sent an express to you about five weeks ago, since which I have not heard anything of him, I wait his return with impatience. The act of Parliament prohibiting all Trade & Commerce between Great Britain and the Colonies has been lately brought here by a Mr. Temple from London, it makes all American property found on the Sea liable to Seizure & confiscation and I fear it will make the Breach between the two Countries so wide as never more to be reconciled. We have heard much talk of Commissioners to be sent to treat with us, I do not expect any, the act of Parliament empowers the King to appoint Commissioners to receive submissions and grant pardons but no futher. Doctor Franklin told me last evening he had a Letter from London dated the 25th December, no Commissioners were then appointed, parliament was prorogued to 25th of January. I see no prospect of a reconciliation, nothing is left now but to fight it out, and for this we are not well provided, having but little ammunition, no Arms no money, nor are we unanimous in our Councils. We do not treat each other with that decency and respect that was observed heretofore. Jealousies, ill natured observations and recriminations take place of reason and Argument, our Tempers are sound, some among us urge strongly for Independency and eternal separation, others wish to wait a little longer and to have the opinion of their Constituents on that subject, you must give us the sentiment of your province when your Convention meets. Several Merchants and others have petitioned the Congress for leave to fit out privatiers to Cruize against British Vessels, it was granted yesterday, the Restrictions are not yet completed or I would have sent you a copy of them. I send you the last News paper enclosed to which refer for news.

My Compliments to all. I am Sir, Your most obedt Servt.

Jos. Hewes.

29.5

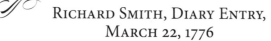 RICHARD SMITH, DIARY ENTRY,
MARCH 22, 1776

Here, Smith recounts additional elements of the congressional debate over the Declaration on Armed Vessels while taking note of the division in Congress regarding whether to make the king "the author of our Miseries instead of the Ministry." According to his records, the radical position was opposed by the majority, on the supposition enacting it would effectively "severe the King from Us forever." Arguing for holding the king accountable (in effect, declaring independence) were Benjamin Harrison, George Wythe, and R. H. Lee (all of Virginia), Samuel Chase (Maryland), and Jonathan Dickinson Sergeant (New Jersey). The radicalism of the men of Virginia—Harrison and Braxton excepted—was, by then, no longer a surprise. Samuel Chase, though, was unusual in his radicalism for a delegate from Maryland. He became notorious for trying to corner the flour market while in Congress and ending up disgraced, and later for being the only Supreme Court justice to be impeached, although he was acquitted by the Senate. Jonathan Dickinson Sergeant was forceful in bringing New Jersey into the pro-independence camp and later became infamous for his vengeful prosecution of loyalists. Arrayed against them, in a debate that lasted four hours, were John Jay (New York), Thomas Johnson (Maryland), and James Wilson (Pennsylvania).

Paul H. Smith, ed., *Letters of Delegates to Congress, 1774–1789* (Washington, D.C.: Library of Congress, 1976–93), 3:426–27. "Ferriage" refers to the fee charged for passage on a ferry.

Friday 22 March [1776]
Votes read & Letters from Gen Washn., Ld. Stirling and others.
Dr. Franklin moved that 750 Doll[ar]s be advanced to the Baron de Woedtke out of his Pay & this was agreed to, he moved also to present the Baron with 250 Dollars to bear his Expences in coming over Sea & to buy Horses &c. Lee and others supported the Motion which was opposed by Duane & al. & carried in the Negative. Wyth reported

the Preamble about Privateering, he and Lee moved an Amendt. wherein the King was made the Author of our Miseries instead of the Ministry, was opposed on Supposition that this was effectually severing the King from Us forever and ably debated for 4 Hours when Maryland interposed its Veto and put it off till Tomorrow, Chief Speakers for the Amendt. Lee, Chase, Serjeant, Harrison, against it Jay, Wilson, Johnson. Willing presented Heard's Accounts and asked Whether Congress would allow Pay to the Minute Men who went on the late Expedition to Queens County, this was denied and the Accot. amounting to £2300 and upwards docked to £800 and odd, the Feriages being above £60 were allowed, Willing moved for a Standing Rule that only Half Ferriage shall be hereafter taken for Soldiers, but other Business intervened. A Petition from a Sufferer in the Disputes at Wyoming was committed to 3, after Objection that it was improper for our Cognizance. Agreed to grant Commissions to Capt. Wm. Shippen & his Officers who are about to cruize in a Privateer on or out of Chesapeak Bay, agreed also to sell Him lb 300 of Powder.

29.6

JOHN ADAMS TO HORATIO GATES,
MARCH 23, 1776

Adams here writes to General Gates of the prospect of an evacuation of British forces from Boston (it had in fact taken place six days earlier), of the Declaration on Armed Vessels, and of the forthcoming declaration opening American ports to non-British trade. Gates, a former major in the British army and a combatant in the Seven Years' War in the colonies, played a formative role in the creation of the Continental Army and, possibly, a still more active part in its politics. In a particularly nasty rift between New England and New York, he was championed by the New Englanders. In July 1780, Gates lost much of his stature for his cowardice at a battle in Camden, South Carolina, in which he deserted his troops and fled.

As he had done for months, Adams ridiculed those in Congress not yet willing to cut off relations with Great Britain: "In Politicks the Middle Way is none at all." Similarly, he found contemptible those for whom "Independency is an Hobgoblin, of so frightful Mein, that it would throw a delicate Person into Fits to look it in the Face." But he writes with relish regarding the American Prohibitory Act, believing that it should be called "the Act of Independency, for King, Lords and Commons have united in Sundering this Country and that I think forever. It is a compleat Dismemberment of the British Empire." The provocative nature of Parliamentary acts and Crown proclamations were valued by radicals in Congress for the essential role they played in moving moderate colonists toward independence. Accordingly, Adams found it "fortunate that the Act of Independency should come from the

British Parliament, rather than the American Congress," meaning, implicitly, the men of Massachusetts who had done so much to move the colonies toward independence. Still, he was dismayed that "Americans should hesitate at accepting Such a Gift from them."

More pointedly, according to Adams, why were some delegates still refusing to commit to independence? Adams had no doubts—it resulted from "the Reluctance of the Southern Colonies to Republican Government," that is, wholly popular government, not the partial kind found in most colonies with royal governors. Here, the southern colonies meant everything south of New England, including the mid-Atlantic colonies and, erroneously, Virginians, who had worked so closely with New Englanders in advancing the separatist cause. Sectional differences meant that "the success of this War depends upon a Skillfull Steerage of the political vessel." Adams finally succeeded in having Congress direct that "each Colony should establish its own Government, and then a League should be formed, between them all." He had fought for this at least since the winter of 1775 (see document 24.2). He insisted that the change could "be done only on popular Principles and Maxims," which Adams believed were "so abhorrent to the Inclinations of the Barons of the South, and the Proprietary Interests in the Middle Colonies" that he dreaded the consequences of the transformation.

Land issues, as much as anything else, divided the colonies. According to Adams, it was speculation, "that avarice of Land[,] which has made upon this Continent so many Votaries to Mammon." It was land issues, discussed by Smith above when referring to "the Disputes at Wyoming," that prevented the Articles of Confederation and Perpetual Union, drafted in 1777, from being ratified until March 1, 1781.[37] Adams, here as so often before, drew attention to the differences between the delegates from the New England colonies and those to their south regarding customs, politics, religion, and manner of right living. As noted previously, even when working in tandem for independence and republican governments, New England and Virginia delegates almost certainly continued to differ on other issues, including but not only slavery.

Paul H. Smith, ed., *Letters of Delegates to Congress, 1774–1789* (Washington, D.C.: Library of Congress, 1976–93), 3:429–32.

Dear Sir                                                                                   Philadelphia March 23. 1776
I had the Pleasure, a few days ago, of your Favour of 8th Instant, for which I esteem myself under great obligations to you.

We rejoice here at the Prospect there is of your driving the Enemy from Boston. If you should Succeed in this I hope effectual Measures will be taken to fortify the Harbour, that the Navy may never enter it again. I think the Narrows may be so obstructed that large Ships will not be able to pass—and the Channell between Long Island and the Moon may be commanded by Batteries upon each of these Islands in such a manner that Boston may be Safe from Men of War. I hope my Countrymen will hesitate at no Expence to attain this End, if in order to accomplish it, they should be obliged to remove the rocky Mountains of my Town of Braintree into the Harbour.

But I cannot yet clearly Satisfy myself that they will leave Boston. It will be a greater Disgrace to the British Arms than to be taken Prisoners in the Town in a Body. If they should abandon the Persons and Property of their dear Friends the Tories in Boston, will any other Tories in any other Part of the Continent ever trust to their Protection? It will be considered as such Impotence, or such Infidelity that I am inclined to think few Professors of Toryism would ever afterwards be found anywhere.

I agree with you, that in Politicks the Middle Way is none at all. If we finally fail in this great and glorious Contest, it will be by bewildering ourselves in groping after this middle way. We have hitherto conducted half a War, acted upon the Line of Defence &c &c. But you will See by tomorrows Paper, that for the future We are likely to wage three Quarters of a War. The Continental ships of War, and Provincial ships of War, and Letters of Mark and Privateers are permitted to cruise upon British Property, wherever found on the Ocean. This is not Independency you know, nothing like it.

If a Post or two more should bring you unlimited Latitude of Trade to all Nations, and a polite Invitation to all Nations to trade with you, take care that you dont call it, or think it Independency. No such Matter. Independency is an Hobgoblin, of so frightful Mein, that it would throw a delicate Person into Fits to look it in the Face.

I know not whether you have seen the Act of Parliament called the restraining Act, or prohibitory Act, or piratical Act, or plundering Act, or Act of Independency, for by all these Titles is it called. I think the most apposite is the Act of Independency, for King, Lords and Commons have united in Sundering this Country and that I think forever. It is a compleat Dismemberment of the British Empire. It throws thirteen Colonies out of the Royal Protection, levels all Distinctions and makes us independent in Spight of all our supplications and Entreaties.

It may be fortunate that the Act of Independency should come from the British Parliament, rather than the American Congress: But it is very odd that Americans should hesitate at accepting Such a Gift from them.

However, my dear Friend Gates, all our Misfortunes arise from a Single Source, the Reluctance of the Southern Colonies to Republican Government. The success of this War depends upon a Skillfull Steerage of the political vessel. The Difficulty lies in forming Constitutions for particular Colonies, and a Continental Constitution for the whole. Each Colony should establish its own Government, and then a League should be formed, between them all. This can be done only on popular Principles and Maxims which are so abhorrent to the Inclinations of the Barons of the South, and the Proprietary Interests in the Middle Colonies, as well as to that avarice of Land, which has made upon this Continent so many Votaries to Mammon that I Sometimes dread the Consequences. However Patience, Fortitude and Perseverance, with the Help of Time will get us over these obstructions.

Thirteen Colonies under Such a Form of Government as that of Connecticutt, or one not quite so popular leagued together in a faithfull Confederacy might bid Defiance to all the Potentates of Europe if united against them.

Pray continue to make me happy with your Favours, accept of my most cordial Wishes for your safety, Happiness and Honour, make my most respectful Compliments to the General and the Ladies, and the whole Family, and believe me to be with great Respect your affectionate Friend & servant,              John Adams

## 30. CONGRESS INTENSIFIES THE TRADE WAR—A BOLDER STEP TOWARD INDEPENDENCE, APRIL 1776

On April 4, 1776, as a result of discussions held in Congress while it sat as a committee of the whole, Benjamin Harrison (Virginia), its moderate chairman and a longtime supporter of reconciliation, reported that it had taken "into consideration the trade of the United Colonies . . . and had come to sundry resolutions, which he was ordered to deliver." Having read the committee report, it was "*Ordered,* To lie on the table." It did so for two days—April 5 being Good Friday—until April 6, when the report to open American ports to non-British shipping was approved. In addition to opening the ports to shipping from all countries "not subject to the King of Great Britain," Congress took this opportunity to ban "East India Tea" and the importation of slaves "into any of the thirteen United Colonies." The explosive declaration was printed in the *Pennsylvania Gazette* on April 10.

These resolutions had been under discussion in Congress since Wednesday, January 17, 1776, when "Congress resolved itself into a committee of the whole, to take into consideration the propriety of opening the ports after the 1 March next"; after that date, unless some action was taken, the ports would, under the terms of the Association as amended on November 1, 1775, be opened and trade with Great Britain, at least before the passage of the American Prohibitory Act, would have been possible. "Mr. [Samuel] Ward reported that the Committee had taken into consideration the matter to them referred, and had come to a resolution, which he read in his place, and delivered in." It was resolved that "a committee of five be appointed . . . the members chosen, [were] Mr. [Benjamin] Harrison [of Virginia], Mr. [Robert] Morris [of Pennsylvania], Mr. [Thomas] Lynch [of South Carolina], Mr. [Samuel] Adams, and Mr. [Roger] Sherman [of Connecticut]." The select committee's report was brought in on February 6, when it "was read, and referred to Thursday next, to a committee of the whole."[38]

There is no mention of the report until February 15, when Congress, after considering it, resolved that it "will, to morrow Morning, resolve itself into a committee of the
whole, to take into consideration the propriety of opening the ports, and the restrictions and regulations of the trade of these colonies after the first of March next." On
February 16 and 17, Congress met in a committee of the whole to discuss the report.
From that point forward until April 4, the *Journal* makes no further mention of the
matter and then only of the committee of the whole and not of the earlier committee's
report.[39]

This series of unusual delays suggests that the opening of the ports met with
exceptionally high levels of opposition and excited heated debate. John Adams
reported as much: "The measure, of opening the ports, etc. labored exceedingly,
because it was considered as a bold step to independence. Indeed, I urged it expressly
with that view, and as connected with the institution of government in all the States,
and a declaration of national independence. The party against me had art and influence as yet, to evade, retard, and delay every motion that we made." As Adams
explained, little of this is visible in the *Journals:* "Many motions were made, and
argued at great length, and with great spirit on both sides, which are not to be found
in the Journals. When motions were made and debates ensued in a committee of the
whole House, no record of them was made by the secretary, unless the motion prevailed and was reported to Congress, and there adopted."[40] For Adams, the opening of
the ports was of a piece with Congress' recommendation to the colonies on May 15 to
institute new governments (see document 31.1), and Congress declaring on July 2 the
colonies independent (see documents 32.1 and 33.1).

In Adams' eyes, congressional opposition to the opening of the ports—the declaration was "far short of what had been moved by members from Massachusetts,"
Virginia, and, surprisingly, Maryland—and the momentous step toward independence
that it represented greatly delayed the taking of that final step.[41] But even if moderates'
opposition could no longer prevent the consideration of independence, it remained
strong enough to prevent the success of such motions (and anything approaching
unanimity). They could not, however, prevent from being included in this declaration,
as they had done a few weeks earlier in the Declaration on Armed Vessels, the epoch-
changing emphasis placed by Congress on the king as the colonists' primary foe. It
was no longer the king's ministers or Parliament with whom they were at war, but the
king himself. In this declaration, the king is named four times, as if in an indictment,
as the sovereign of the subjects with whom the North American colonists would no
longer trade.

The question of being in revolt, given the implicit attack on monarchical prerogative,
no longer was debatable. It is not too much to claim that these accusations changed the
nature of the twelve-year colonial resistance movement. The colonists were no longer
interested in changing the British Constitution. Instead of seeking to strengthen colonial

monarchical government and bring about reconciliation through the king's intercession in behalf of his loyal American subjects, they wanted independence.[42] And as such a transformation became highly likely, concerns regarding who was eligible to govern took on a new relevance, as can be seen in the especially rich and thoughtful correspondence reproduced below.

30.1

 DECLARATION OPENING AMERICAN PORTS
TO NON-BRITISH TRADE, APRIL 6, 1776

Worthington Chauncey Ford et al., eds., *Journals of the Continental Congress, 1774–1789* (Washington, D.C.: Government Printing Office, 1904–37), 4:257–59.

The Congress resumed the consideration of the report from the committee of the whole; and the same being twice read, and debated by paragraphs, was agreed to as follows:

*Resolved,* That any goods, wares, and merchandise, except staves and empty casks, other than shaken or knocked down casks for molasses, may be exported from the thirteen United Colonies, by the inhabitants thereof, and by the people of all such countries as are not subject to the King of Great Britain, to any parts of the world which are not under the dominion of the said King; provided, that no vessel be permitted to export any greater number of shaken or knocked down molasses casks, than the same vessel is capable of carrying when they shall be filled with Molasses.

*Resolved,* That any goods, wares, and merchandise, except such as are of the growth, production, or manufacture of, or brought from any country under the dominion of the King of Great Britain, and except East India Tea, may be imported from any other parts of the world to the thirteen United Colonies, by the inhabitants thereof, and by the people of all such countries as are not subject to the said King; liable, however, to all such duties and impositions as now are, or may hereafter be laid by any of the said colonies.

*Resolved,* That nothing herein contained shall be understood to prevent such future commercial regulations as shall be thought just and necessary by these United Colonies, or their respective legislatures.

*Resolved,* That no slaves be imported into any of the thirteen United Colonies.

*Resolved,* That it be recommended to the assemblies and conventions in the several colonies, to appoint proper officers, at convenient places in their respective colonies, to take bonds, in adequate penalties, for observing the regulations made by the Congress, or assemblies, or conventions, concerning trade, and for securing the observation of such parts of the association as are not inconsistent therewith; and that the obligor shall, within eighteen months after the departure of the vessel, produce to such officers a certificate, under the hands and seals of three or more reputable merchants, residing at the port or place where the cargo shall be delivered, that the same was there unladed, and take manifests upon oath, of the cargoes exported and imported, and keep fair accounts and entries thereof, give bills of health when desired, grant registers shewing the property of the vessels cleared out, and sign certificates that the requisites for qualifying vessels to trade have been complied with: And that the fees of the said officers be stated by the respective assemblies or conventions: Provided always, that no prosecution upon any of the said bonds shall be commenced but within three years after the date thereof.

*Resolved,* That all goods, wares, and merchandise, except such as are made prize of, which shall be imported directly or indirectly from Great Britain or Ireland, into any of these United Colonies, contrary to the regulations established by Congress, shall be forfeited and disposed of, agreeable to such rules as shall be made by the several assemblies or conventions, and shall be liable to prosecution and condemnation in any court erected, or to be erected, for the determination of maritime affairs, in the colony where the seizure shall be made.

*Ordered,* That the above resolutions be published.

30.2

## RICHARD SMITH, DIARY ENTRY, FEBRUARY 16, 1776

Richard Smith records in his diary for February 16, 1776, as did John Adams, the outline of one of the first discussions in Congress, meeting as a committee of the whole, of the select committee's report on the opening of American ports, which was finally agreed to on April 6. He notes that the debate lasted four to five hours and that one of the central points of contention was whether, as part of the delegates' discussion, they should consider "a Right to contract Alliances with Foreign Powers," with "an Objection being offered that this was Independency." On the question whether to consider such a proposal, "it was carried in the Affirmative 7 Colonies to 5." Still, Congress could not come to an agreement on anything approaching independence and so postponed the question, as occurred as well with the antecedent question of opening American ports to foreign trade; both were left to be determined at a later date.

It is worth noting that this debate was not, as might have been expected, between New England delegates and those of the mid-Atlantic colonies, with the southern colonies divided. Indeed, John Adams records in his diary that the moderate

James Wilson took issue with a member of the Massachusetts delegation who had spoken in opposition to opening the ports, at least "for all Things and to all Places," with Wilson holding that "trade ought in War to be carried on with greater Vigour."[43] Wilson was joined, as Smith reports, by Edward Rutledge of South Carolina, who rarely sided with the likes of Roger Sherman on controversial issues. Adams, writing retrospectively, helped clear this up when he recalled that in early 1776, in matters regarding foreign alliances, the opening of American ports, and independence, he had "received little Assistance from my Colleagues in all these Contests: three of them [Cushing, Paine and Hancock], were either inclined to lean towards Mr. Dickinsons System, or at least chose to be silent, and the fourth [Samuel Adams] spoke but rarely in Congress, and never entered into any extensive Arguments."[44] But when Elbridge Gerry replaced Thomas Cushing in the Massachusetts delegation on February 9, Adams finally had a reliable majority (both Adamses and Gerry) in the Massachusetts delegation, which allowed him to move forward the opening of American ports and other independence leaning measures.

Paul H. Smith, ed., *Letters of Delegates to Congress, 1774–1789* (Washington, D.C.: Library of Congress, 1976–93), 3:267.

Friday 16 Feb. [1776]

After various Subjects were discussed & decided upon 4 or 5 Hours were spent in Grand Comee. on Trade, Harrison offered some Propositions in Lieu of the Report heretofore delivered in from a Comee. on the necessary Regulations, Wyth also offered Propositions whereof the first was that the Colonies have a Right to contract Alliances with Foreign Powers, an Objection being offered that this was Independency there ensued much Argument upon that Ground, a leading Question was given Whether this Proposn. shall be considered by the Comee. it was carried in the Affirmative 7 Colonies to 5. Then it was debated and postponed, afterwards the Regulations of the Trade were handled & finally whether it shall be opened or not and when, upon this Head Chase spoke largely against carrying on Trade at present and Harrison and E Rutledge vehemently for it. There was no Determination.

## 30.3

# ABIGAIL ADAMS TO JOHN ADAMS, MARCH 31, 1776

In this letter, Abigail Adams, John's justly celebrated wife, discusses her views on Virginians, the British evacuation of Boston on March 17, her consequent retaking possession of their Boston townhouse, and the hoped-for standing of women in the world to follow independence. Abigail was a woman with a keen interest in politics and strong views—she abhorred slavery, defended a new vision of family life based on sentiment rather than patriarchal control, and advocated a certain sense of women's rights, with a particular emphasis on female education. She begins by writing of the stark, by New England standards, differences between rich and poor in Virginia and then comments on the "savage and even Blood thirsty" character of Virginia riflemen. At the time, the main infantry forces—colonial, British, French, and German—all used smoothbore muskets. Each also had auxiliary forces that used "rifled" firearms, which were accurate at much greater distances and could be fired from behind defensive positions and even at officers in the rear.[45] In the colonies, many of the riflemen lived along the frontier and used the guns in hunting. She not only had doubts about the civilized character of these southern frontiersmen, but also questioned the moral principles of southern gentlemen because of their support of slavery.

More famous were Abigail's views on the kinds of changes in gender relationships and family dynamics that she hoped to see develop along with colonial independence. She hoped for the advent of a more loving and egalitarian family that would also be less hierarchical and authoritarian.[46] She reminded her husband that the new codes of laws should not repeat the mistakes of older, monarchical ones: "I desire you would Remember the Ladies, and be more generous and favourable to them than your ancestors. Do not put such unlimited power into the hands of the Husbands. Remember all Men would be tyrants if they could. If perticuliar care and attention is not paid to the Laidies we are determined to foment a Rebellion." Although her tone is playful, the issue of who would be permitted to participate in the new republican political project soon became a serious and hotly contested one.

*The Book of Abigail and John: Selected Letters of the Adams Family, 1762–1784*, ed. L. H. Butterfield, Marc Friedlander, and Mary-Jo Kline (Cambridge, Mass: Harvard University Press, 1975), 120–21.

Braintree March 31, 1776

I wish you would ever write me a Letter half as long as I write you; and tell me if you may where your Fleet are gone? What sort of Defence Virginia can make against our common Enemy? Whether it is so situated as to make an able Defence? Are not the Gentery Lords and the common people vassals, are they not like the uncivilized Natives Brittain represents us to be? I hope their Riffel Men who have shewen themselves very savage and even Blood thirsty; are not a specimen of the Generality of the people.

I [illegible] am willing to allow the Colony great merrit for having produced a Washington but they have been shamefully duped by a Dunmore.

I have sometimes been ready to think that the passion for Liberty cannot be Eaquelly Strong in the Breasts of those who have been accustomed to deprive their fellow Creatures of theirs. Of this I am certain that it is not founded upon that generous and christian principal of doing to others as we would that others should do unto us.

Do not you want to see Boston; I am fearfull of the small pox, or I should have been in before this time. I got Mr. Crane to go to our House and see what state it was in. I find it has been occupied by one of the Doctors of a Regiment, very dirty, but no other damage has been done to it. The few things which were left in it are all gone. Cranch has the key which he never deliverd up. I have wrote to him for it and am determined to get it cleand as soon as possible and shut it up. I look upon it a new acquisition of property, a property which one month ago I did not value at a single Shilling, and could with pleasure have seen it in flames.

The Town in General is left in a better state than we expected, more oweing to a percipitate flight than any Regard to the inhabitants, tho some individuals discoverd a sense of honour and justice and have left the rent of the Houses in which they were, for the owners and the furniture unhurt, or if damaged sufficent to make it good.

Others have committed abominable Ravages. The Mansion House of your President is safe and the furniture unhurt whilst both the House and Furniture of the Solisiter General have fallen a prey to their own merciless party. Surely the very Fiends feel a Reverential awe for Virtue and patriotism, whilst they Detest the paricide and traitor.

I feel very differently at the approach of spring to what I did a month ago. We knew not then whether we could plant or sow with safety, whether when we had toild we could reap the fruits of our own industery, whether we could rest in our own Cottages, or whether we should not be driven from the sea coasts to seek shelter in the wilderness, but now we feel as if we might sit under our own vine and eat the good of the land.

I feel a gaieti de Coar to which before I was a stranger. I think the Sun looks brighter, the Birds sing more melodiously, and Nature puts on a more chearfull countanance. We feel a temporary peace, and the poor fugitives are returning to their deserted habitations.

Tho we felicitate ourselves, we sympathize with those who are trembling least the Lot of Boston should be theirs. But they cannot be in similar circumstances unless pusilanimity and cowardise should take possession of them. They have time and warning given them to see the Evil and shun it.—I long to hear that you have declared an independency—and by the way in the new Code of Laws which I suppose it will be necessary for you to make I desire you would Remember the Ladies, and be more generous and favourable to them than your ancestors. Do not put such unlimited power into the hands of the Husbands. Remember all Men would be tyrants if they could. If perticuliar care and attention is not paid to the Laidies we are determined to foment a Rebelion, and will not hold ourselves bound by any Laws in which we have no voice, or Representation.

That your Sex are Naturally Tyrannical is a Truth so thoroughly established as to admit of no dispute, but such of you as wish to be happy willingly give up the harsh title of Master for the more tender and endearing one of Friend. Why then, not put it out of the power of the vicious and the Lawless to use us with cruelty and indignity with impunity. Men of Sense in all Ages abhor those customs which treat us only as the vassals of your Sex. Regard us then as Beings placed by providence under your protection and in immitation of the Supreem Being make use of that power only for our happiness.

## 30.4

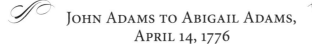

JOHN ADAMS TO ABIGAIL ADAMS,
APRIL 14, 1776

Responding to his wife's letter of March 31, Adams comments on many of the issues she brought up, including her criticism of the Virginians. He agrees with her about the gulf between the social classes there: "The Gentry are very rich, and the common People very poor. This Inequality of Property, gives an Aristocratical Turn to all their Proceedings, and occasions a strong Aversion in their Patricians, to Common Sense." In commenting on Virginians' relation to their former governor, he takes the opportunity to attack the foolishness of waiting for royal peace commissioners, with whom a constitutional settlement might be negotiated: "All the Colonies are duped, more or less, at one Time and another. A more egregious Bubble was never blown up, than the Story of Commissioners coming to treat with the Congress." As he predicted, when Lord Richard Howe arrived on July 12 off the coast of Staten Island, he and his brother enjoyed too limited a discretion to effect easily any sort of just reconciliation. Of course, further complicating matters, Howe arrived a week or so after the Declaration of Independence's passage (see documents 35.1–36.5).

Of greater moment, however, is John's response to Abigail's provocative challenge to include some measure of political rights for women in the codes of laws to be formed by the new republican governments. In a largely dismissive, though possibly teasing manner, Adams writes that he "cannot but laugh" regarding his wife's proposal for women to be granted political rights. He admits that others had been warning of the dangerous consequences of the colonies' struggles, which had "loosened the bands of Government every where . . . [so that] Children and Apprentices were disobedient" and Indians now "slighted their Guardians and Negroes grew insolent to their Masters." But he fails to respond to these general concerns and dismisses his wife's plea by suggesting that such changes as she proposed "would completely subject Us to the Despotism of the Peticoat." He seems not to have fully anticipated the revolutionary consequences that his quest for independence and the uncoupling of rights and duties in the Declaration of Independence would create. He concludes—again, most likely in jest—by suggesting that the rise of women in search of their just rights, as with Tories, Canadians, Indians, Hessians, Russians, Negroes, Irish Roman Catholics, and Scotch renegades, was somehow a product of the British ministry's efforts to disrupt colonial life. What he failed to consider was that such changes would follow from the very arguments that colonials within the past year had begun to advance in opposition to the British administration and its surprisingly more inclusive policies.[47]

Paul H. Smith, ed., *Letters of Delegates to Congress, 1774–1789* (Washington, D.C.: Library of Congress, 1976–93), 3:519–20.

Ap. 14. 1776

You justly complain of my short Letters, but the critical State of Things and the Multiplicity of Avocations must plead my Excuse. You ask where the Fleet is. The inclosed Papers will inform you. You ask what Sort of Defence Virginia can make. I believe they will make an able Defence. Their Militia and minute Men have been some time employed in training them selves, and they have Nine Battallions of regulars as they call them, maintained among them, under good Officers, at the Continental Expence. They have set up a Number of Manufactories of Fire Arms, which are busily employed. They are tolerably supplied with Powder, and are successfull and assiduous, in making Salt Petre. Their neighbouring Sister or rather Daughter Colony of North Carolina, which is a warlike Colony, and has several Battallions at the Continental Expence, as well as a pretty good Militia, are ready to assist them, and they are in very good Spirits, and seem determined to make a brave Resistance. The Gentry are very rich, and the common People very poor. This Inequality of Property, gives an Aristocratical Turn to all their Proceedings, and occasions a strong Aversion in their Patricians, to Common Sense. But the Spirit of these Barons, is coming down, and it must submit.

It is very true, as you observe they have been duped by Dunmore. But this is a Common Case. All the Colonies are duped, more or less, at one Time and another. A more egregious Bubble was never blown up, than the Story of Commissioners coming to treat with the Congress. Yet it has gained Credit like a Charm, not only without but against the clearest Evidence. I never shall forget the Delusion, which seized our best and most sagacious Friends the dear Inhabitants of Boston, the Winter before last. Credulity and the Want of Foresight, are Imperfections in the human Character, that no Politician can sufficiently guard against.

You have given me some Pleasure, by your Account of a certain House in Queen Street. I had burned it, long ago, in Imagination. It rises now to my View like a Phoenix. What shall I say of the Solicitor General? I pity his pretty Children, I pity his Father, and his sisters. I wish I could be clear that it is no moral Evil to pity him and his Lady. Upon Repentance they will certainly have a large Share in the Compassions of many. But let Us take Warning and give it to our Children. Whenever Vanity, and Gaiety, a Love of Pomp and Dress, Furniture, Equipage, Buildings, great Company, expensive Diversions, and elegant Entertainments get the better of the Principles and Judgments of Men or Women there is no knowing where they will stop, nor into what Evils, natural, moral, or political, they will lead us.

Your Description of your own Gaiety de Coeur, charms me. Thanks be to God you have just Cause to rejoice—and may the bright Prospect be obscured by no Cloud.

As to Declarations of Independency, be patient. Read our Privateering Laws, and our Commercial Laws. What signifies a Word.

As to your extraordinary Code of Laws, I cannot but laugh. We have been told that our Struggle has loosened the bands of Government every where. That Children and Apprentices were disobedient—that schools and Colledges were grown turbulent—that Indians slighted their Guardians and Negroes grew insolent to their Masters. But your Letter was the first Intimation that another Tribe more numerous and powerfull than all the rest were grown discontented. This is rather too coarse a Compliment but you are so saucy, I wont blot it out.

Depend upon it, We know better than to repeal our Masculine systems. Altho they are in full Force, you know they are little more than Theory. We dare not exert our Power in its full Latitude. We are obliged to go fair, and softly, and in Practice you know We are the subjects. We have only the Name of Masters, and rather than give up this, which would compleatly subject Us to the Despotism of the Peticoat, I hope General Washington, and all our brave Heroes would fight. I am sure every good Politician would plot, as long as he would against Despotism, Empire, Monarchy, Aristocracy, Oligarchy, or Ochlocracy. A fine Story indeed. I begin to think the Ministry as deep as they are wicked. After stirring up Tories, Landjobbers, Trimmers, Bigots, Canadians, Indians, Negroes, Hanoverians, Hessians, Russians, Irish Roman Catholicks, Scotch Renegadoes, at last they have stimulated the        to demand new Priviledges and threaten to rebell.

## 30.5

 CARTER BRAXTON TO LANDON CARTER,
APRIL 14, 1776

Carter Braxton, born to a wealthy and politically well-connected planter family in Virginia, was appointed to complete the congressional term of the deceased Peyton Randolph. Braxton, with his deeply skeptical and antipopulist politics, was not reelected, but returned nonetheless to the Virginia legislature. His letter is to Landon Carter, his maternal uncle, a well-known diarist who canvassed the political and intellectual atmosphere of Virginia over a twenty-five-year period, 1752–68; he was the son of Robert "King" Carter, a landowner of great wealth and influence and one of the most powerful figures in Virginia political life of the time. Robert Carter used his power in the colony to procure for his sons political appointments, such as council seats and military positions.[48] Landon Carter's extensive diaries have proved especially useful in providing a window into the political and cultural landscape of colonial Virginia.

Here Braxton describes Congress as enmeshed in a consuming debate concerning independence. Although he is supportive of it, if "it can be obtained with Safety & Honor," he outlines his ongoing opposition to a premature declaration of independence. He rested his case on three concerns: a reconciliation might be achieved through the British peace commissioners; a treaty should be concluded first with a naval power; and outstanding intercolonial land issues had to be resolved before independence could be safely declared.

Braxton writes with penetration regarding the peace commissioners: "There are some who are affraid to await the Arrival of Commissioners, lest the dispute should be accomodated much agt their Will even upon the Admission of our own terms. For however strange it may appear I am satisfied that the eastern Colonies do not mean to have a Reconciliation and in this I am justified by publick & private Reasons." As he further explains, the New England colonies were desperate to declare independence before the Howe commission finally arrived, because "two of the new England Colonies enjoy a Government purely democratical the Nature & Principle of which both civil & religious are so totally incompatible with Monarchy that they have ever lived in a restless State under it." Thus, their delegates viewed the Imperial Crisis as a welcome opportunity "to throw off all Subjection & embrace their darling Democracy." If true, that perspective could help explain much of what had taken place in Congress over the past two years, possibly the past decade, and the sense of urgency voiced by some in Congress for independence. His thoughts about why the New Englanders were in such a hurry to declare independence is reinforced by the insistence of the committee that met with Lord Howe in early

September that since independence had been declared a week earlier, they no longer were at liberty to negotiate a plan of reconciliation.

The other issue to which much of his letter is devoted was the ongoing land disputes among the colonies, in particular that between Connecticut and Pennsylvania over the Wyoming Valley, which, Braxton suggests, may be another reason why the New England colonies were so anxious to declare independence. The territory in question was Pennsylvania land that the Connecticut Susquehanna Company had sold to Connecticut settlers and that, subsequently, came to be claimed by both colonies. As Braxton explains, it was only the intercession of Congress—and before it, Parliament—that kept the two colonies from militarily contesting for control over the territory.[49] Similarly, he draws attention to the land claims of residents of the New Hampshire Grants, which would become Vermont, on land claimed by New York (see document 39.1), and the ongoing disputes between Virginia, Maryland, and Pennsylvania that did much to delay ratification of the Articles of Confederation. Based on these conflicts—"the secret movements of Men & things"—Braxton wrongly predicted that "the Assertion of Independence is far off." He wrongly predicted as well that if independence "was to be now asserted, the Continent would be torn in pieces by intestine Wars & Convulsions." Indeed, even though among those least supportive of immediate American independence, believing that first "all disputes must be healed & Harmony prevail," he voted for it three months later and signed the Declaration of Independence.

Paul H. Smith, ed., *Letters of Delegates to Congress, 1774–1789*
(Washington, D.C.: Library of Congress, 1976–93), 3:520–23. Braxton refers
to Virginia when he writes "my country."


Dear Sir,                                                      Philada April 14 1776.

In this much elevated Station to which I fear I was improperly called by my Country, it has been my desire to seek the Advice and opinions of my friends that I might with better Judgment determine on the important matters that daily occur. In this number Nature gave me a right to rank you, & my knowledge taught me to expect your Wisdom & Experience would be a luminary in the present maze of Politicks, the intricacies and windings of which I own often puzzles my Understanding. To assist in finding a Clue by which my Country may be safely & honourably directed thro this labyrinth shall be my peculiar Study & Attention. If in this pursuit I differ in Sentiment with some of my Countrymen I flatter my self their Charity will prevent any injurious imputations on the motives that influence my Actions.

Independency & total Seperation from Great Britain are the interesting Subjects of all ranks of Men & often agitate our Body. It is in truth a delusive Bait which Men inconsiderately catch at without knowing the hook to which it is affixed. It is an Object to be wished for by every American; when it can be obtained with Safety & Honor. That this is not the moment I will prove by Arguments that to me are decisive & which exist with certainty. Your refined notion of our publick Honor being engaged to await the terms to be offered by Commissioners operates strongly with me & many others & makes the first reason I would offer. My next is that America is in too defenseless a State for the declaration having no Alliance with a naval Power nor as yet any Fleet of Consequence of her own to protect that trade which is so essential to the prosecution of the War & without which I know we cannot go on much longer. It is said by the Advocates for Seperation that France will undoubtedly assist us after we have asserted the State, and therefore they urge us to make the experiment.

Would such a blind, precipitate measure as this be justified by Prudence, first to throw off our Connection with G. Britain and then give ourselves up to the Arms of France. Would not this Court so famous for Intrigues & Deception avail herself of our Situation & from it exact much severer terms than if we were to treat with *her* before hand & settle the terms of any future alliance. Surely she would, but the truth of the matter is, there are some who are affraid to await the Arrival of Commissioners, lest the dispute should be accomodated much agt their Will even upon the Admission of our own terms. For however strange it may appear I am satisfied that the eastern Colonies do not mean to have a Reconciliation and in this I am justified by publick & private Reasons.

To illustrate my Opinion I will beg leave to mention them. Two of the new England Colonies enjoy a Government purely democratical the Nature & Principle of which both civil & religious are so totally incompatible with Monarchy that they have ever lived in a restless State under it. The other two tho not so popular in their frame bordered so near upon it that Monarchical Influence hung very heavy on them. The best opportunity in the World being now offered them to throw off all Subjection & embrace their darling Democracy, they are determined to accept it.

These are aided by those of a private Nature but not less cogent. The Colonies of Massachusetts & Connecticut who rule the other two have Claims on the Province of Pensylvania in the whole for near one third of the Land within their Provincial Bounds & indeed the Claim extended to its full extent comes within four Miles of this City. This dispute was carried to the King & Council & with them it now lies. The eastern Colonies unwilling they should now be the Arbiters have exerted their Claim by force & have at this time eight hundred Men in Arms upon the upper part of this Land called Wyoming, where they are peaceble at present only thro the Influence of the Congress. There naturally then arises a heart burning & Jealousy between these People & they must have two very different Objects in View.

The Province of New York is not without her Fears & apprehensions from the Temper of her Neighbours, their great Swarms & small Territory.

Even Virginia is not free from Claims on Pennsylvania nor Maryland from those on Virginia.

Some of the delegates from our Colony carry their Ideas of right to Lands so far to the eastward that the middle Colonies dread their being swallowed up between the

Claims of them & those from the East. And yet without any Adjustment of their disputes & a variety of other matters, some are for lugging us into Independence. But so long as these remain unsettled & Men act upon the Principles they ever have done, you may rely no such thing will be generally agreed on. Upon viewing the secret movements of Men & things I am convinced the Assertion of Independence is far off. If it was to be now asserted, the Continent would be torn in pieces by intestine Wars & Convulsions.

Previous to Independence all disputes must be healed & Harmony prevail. A grand Continental League must be formed & a superintending Power also. When these necessary Steps are taken & I see a Coalition formed sufficient to withstand the Power of Britain or any other, then am I for an independent State & all its Consequences, as then I think they will produce Happiness to America. It is a true saying of a Wit—We must hang together or seperately. I will not beg yr pardon for intruding this long Letter upon yr old age which I judged necessary in my Situation & to conclude by assuring you I am with great regard, your affect Nephew,                    Carter Braxton

*[P.S.]* If any of our News papers will be agreeable say so in yr next.

## 30.6

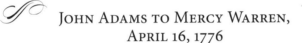

 JOHN ADAMS TO MERCY WARREN,
APRIL 16, 1776

Adams responded to a letter of March 10 from the outspoken and highly accomplished poet, historian, and essayist Mercy Otis Warren, who was the daughter of Colonel James Otis; the sister of the eccentric Massachusetts lawyer, Stamp Act activist, and pamphleteer James Otis, Jr.; and the wife of James Warren, a ubiquitous figure in Massachusetts politics but of somewhat less stature than the war hero with whom he might be confused, Dr. Joseph Warren. Notable as well was the Warrens' friendship with Catharine Macaulay, one of the most accomplished historians of her time and one of only a handful of admitted eighteenth-century radical republicans writing in Great Britain.[50] Warren was, in short, a radical's radical and well placed to record and comment, in predictably provocative ways, on the history of the period as it unfolded.

Adams writes to Warren concerning the traditional subject matter of political philosophy—"the best Forms of Government"—especially appropriate once the colonies were on the verge of declaring their independence. As he notes, the time was "approaching, when the Colonies will find themselves under a Necessity of engaging in Earnest in this great and indispensible Work" of forming new governments. He did not underestimate the arduousness of the task: "I have ever Thought it the most difficult and dangerous Part of the Business Americans have to do . . . to glide insensibly, from under the old Government, into a peaceable and contented Submission to new ones." In opposition to Warren's more radical views, Adams argues the inappropriateness of traditional or, better said, classical republican government for the soon to be independent colonies. In a manner fully consistent with the inherited tradition of republican and commonwealth political thought,[51] Adams points out the necessary conditions for successful republicanism: "Such a Government is only to be supported by pure Religion, or Austere Morals. Public Virtue cannot exist in a Nation without private [Virtue], and public Virtue is the only Foundation of Republics. . . . Men must be ready, they must pride themselves, and be happy to sacrifice their private Pleasures, Passions, and Interests, nay their private Friendships and dearest Connections, when they Stand in Competition with the Right of Society." Although New Englanders believed that they possessed more of this love of the public than any other Americans, stemming from their Reformed Protestant inheritance, Adams did not believe that they had enough, for he insisted "there are no more" nations or peoples capable of this kind of virtue.

In particular, "the Spirit of Commerce" made republican government inappropriate for the American colonies, since it was "incompatible with that purity of Heart, and Greatness of soul which is necessary for an happy Republic." His own region was not exempt from this stricture: "This Same Spirit of Commerce is as rampant in New England as in any Part of the World," and thus "there is great Danger that a Republican Government would be very factious and turbulent there." Such a form of government would be practical, Adams argues, in opposition to Warren, only if every man were to "set himself to root out his Passions, Prejudices and Attachments, and to get the better of his private Interest." Accordingly, although Adams for almost a year had argued openly that Britain's constrained form of constitutional monarchy did not deserve colonial support, he found traditional republicanism equally unsuitable for the colonies—even New England—because of its too-powerful commercial interests.[52] Not surprisingly, when opposing a New England republican stalwart, Roger Sherman, in 1789, Adams asked, in trying to find a middle ground, "whether any other name can with propriety be given it [our constitution], than that of a monarchical republic, or if you will, a limited monarchy."[53]

Paul H. Smith, ed., *Letters of Delegates to Congress, 1774–1789* (Washington, D.C.: Library of Congress, 1976–93), 3:537–39.

Madam                                                                                     April 16. 1776

Not until Yesterdays Post, did your agreable Favour of March the Tenth, come to my Hands. It gave me great Pleasure and altho in the distracted Kind of Life, I am obliged to lead, I cannot promise to deserve a Continuance of so excellent a Correspondence yet I am determined by Scribbling Something or other, be it what it may, to provoke it.

The Ladies I think are the greatest Politicians, that I have the Honour to be acquainted with, not only because they act upon the Sublimest of all the Principles of Policy, vizt the [that] Honesty is the best Policy, but because they consider Questions more coolly, than those who are heated with Party Zeal, and inflamed with the bitter Contentions of active public Life.

I know of no Researches in any of the sciences more ingenious than those which have been made after the best Forms of Government nor can there be a more agreable Employment to a benevolent Heart. The Time is now approaching, when the Colonies will find themselves under a Necessity of engaging in Earnest in this great and indispensible Work. I have ever Thought it the most difficult and dangerous Part of the Business Americans have to do, in this mighty Contest, to continue some Method for the Colonies to glide insensibly, from under the old Government, into a peaceable and contented Submission to new ones. It is a long Time since this opinion was conceivd, and it has never been out of my Mind, my constant Endeavour has been to convince Gentlemen of the Necessity of turning their Thoughts to these Subjects. At present the sense of this Necessity seems to be general, and Measures are taking which must terminate in a compleat Revolution. There is Danger of Convulsions. But I hope, not great ones.

The Form of Government, which you admire, when its Principles are pure is admirable indeed. It is productive of every Thing, which is great and excellent among Men. But its Principles are as easily destroyed, as human Nature is corrupted. Such a Government is only to be supported by pure Religion, or Austere Morals. Public Virtue cannot exist in a Nation without private, and public Virtue is the only Foundation of Republics. There must be a possitive Passion for the public good, the public Interest, Honour, Power, and Glory, established in the Minds of the People, or there can be no Republican Government, nor any real Liberty. And this public Passion must be superiour to all private Passions. Men must be ready, they must pride themselves, and be happy to sacrifice their private Pleasures, Passions, and Interests, nay their private Friendships and dearest Connections, when they Stand in Competition with the Right of Society.

Is there in the World a Nation, which deserves this Character. There have been several, but they are no more. Our dear Americans perhaps have as much of it as any Nation now existing, and New England perhaps has more than the rest of America. But I have seen all along my Life, Such Selfishness, and Littleness even in New England, that I sometimes tremble to think that, altho We are engaged in the best Cause that ever employed the Human Heart, yet the Prospect of success is doubtfull not for Want of Power or of Wisdom, but of Virtue.

The Spirit of Commerce, Madam, which even insinuates itself into Families, and influences holy Matrimony, and thereby corrupts the Morals of Families as well as destroys their Happiness, it is much to be feared is incompatible with that purity of Heart, and Greatness of soul which is necessary for an happy Republic. This Same Spirit of Commerce is as rampant in New England as in any Part of the World. Trade is as well understood and as passionately loved there as any where. Even the Farmers, and Tradesmen are addicted to Commerce. And it is too true, that Property is generally the standard of Respect there as much as any where. While this is the Case there is great Danger that a Republican Government would be very factious and turbulent there. Divisions in Elections are much to be dreaded. Every Man must sincerely set himself to root out his Passions, Prejudices and Attachments, and to get the better of his private Interest. The only reputable Principle and Doctrine must be that all Things must give Way to the public.

This is very grave and Solemn Discourse to a Lady. True, and I thank God, that his Providence has made me Acquainted with two Ladies at least, who can bear it.

I think Madam, that the Union of the Colonies, will continue and be more firmly cemented. But We must move slowly. Patience, Patience, Patience! I am obliged to invoke this every Morning of my Life, every Noon, and every Evening.

It is Surprising to me that any among you should flatter themselves with an Accommodation. Every Appearance is against it, to an Attentive observer. The Story of Commissioners is a Bubble. Their real Errant is an Insult. But popular Passions and Fancies will have their Course, you may as well reason down a Gale of Wind.

You expect, if a certain Bargain Should be complied with, to be made acquainted with noble and Royal Characters. But in this you will be disappointed. Your Correspondent has neither Principles, nor Address, nor Abilities, for such Scenes. And others are as sensible of it, I assure you as he is. They must be Persons of more Complaisance and Ductility of Temper as well as better Accomplishments for such great Things.

He wishes for nothing less. He wishes for nothing more than to retire from all public Stages, and public Characters, great and Small, to his Farm and his Attorneys office. And to both these he must return.

## 31. MORE PLANS FOR NEW COLONIAL GOVERNMENTS—ALMOST INDEPENDENCE, MAY 1776

In May 1776, a majority in Congress, having given up on reconciliation with the Crown and having realized the likely necessity of achieving independence outside the empire, began to search for means with which to accomplish the latter. Most particularly, this demanded an effort to undercut the legitimacy of the (frequently legally elected) governments of the still-recalcitrant mid-Atlantic colonies, three of them proprietary.[54] In the spring, Congress, sitting as a committee of the whole, began to consider anew "the state of the United Colonies" and, in particular, the continuance of monarchical government in them. On May 9, 1776, a resolution was ready to be reported, but "at the request of a colony, [the report] was postponed till tomorrow." On May 10, Congress again considered the report and agreed to its sole resolution, which urged colonial bodies, where no regular government existed, "to adopt such government as shall, in the opinion of the representatives of the people, best conduce to the happiness and safety of their constituents." This was effectively the same language that Congress had used in the winter of 1775 when responding to requests for instructions on forming new governments from three colonies, all of them royal (see document 24.1).

Unlike those earlier statements, the new instructions were not issued at the invitation of particular colonies, nor did they limit the duration of the proposed replacement governments, where needed, to the end of the dispute with Britain. Most critically, Congress extended this recommendation to all colonial governments, including most of the mid-Atlantic colonies, which remained opposed to independence and to changing their legally elected provincial governments, that is, where regular government continued to exist. Indeed, this was the goal of the resolution's supporters in Congress: to do whatever they could to bring down the legally constituted mid-Atlantic colonial governments and to lead to their replacement by ones friendlier to independence. It is essential to keep in mind that "the contest for independence in its later stages, that is just before July 4, 1776, in Pennsylvania, New Jersey, North and South Carolina, and to almost an equal extent, in New York, Delaware, and Maryland, became virtually not less one between the people and the aristocrats for control, than one between the United Colonies and Great Britain for the establishment of a separate government."[55] This was especially true of the government of Pennsylvania, which understood the congressional resolution to be directed in particular at it, with the goal of undermining its recently confirmed legal authority—as well it did.[56] Yet, the language of the resolution was sufficiently moderate, lacking, for instance, a concrete denunciation of the king or any reference to a direct break with Great Britain, and slyly recommending change only in those colonies "where no government sufficient to the exigencies of their affairs have been hitherto established," that moderate delegates could, and did, freely support it.[57]

On May 10, Congress appointed a committee of three to prepare a preamble "to the foregoing resolution" and elected Edward Rutledge, Richard Henry Lee, and John Adams. Adams, rightfully, given his long-term commitment to this goal, was chosen as its chair.[58] On May 13, 1776, the draft preamble, penned by Adams, was submitted to Congress; after it was read, further action was postponed, originally, for one day.[59] On May 15, Congress again "took into consideration the draught of the preamble brought in by the committee, which was agreed to" and ordered published in the *Pennsylvania Gazette;* that occurred on May 22, 1776.[60] If there was considerable ambiguity in the original resolution concerning the colonies' troubled relation to the king and Great Britain, there was none in the preamble, in which Adams was finally able, with congressional support, to renounce monarchy and the colonies' allegiance to George III and to the British empire. This renunciation of allegiance to the king, some twelve years from the beginning of the Imperial Crisis, was foreshadowed on April 6 in Congress' declaration opening American ports, but here it is unequivocally clear.

Adams writes, accurately but with little appreciation of constitutional constraints, that the king had forced the colonies into taking this action, for it was his Britannic

Majesty who had "excluded the inhabitants of these United Colonies from the protection of his crown," had refused to respond to "the humble petitions of the colonies for redress of grievances and reconciliation with Great Britain," and had directed against the colonists "the whole force of that kingdom, aided by foreign mercenaries." Indeed, on May 10 it was reported (and confirmed on May 21) that 12,000–17,000 German mercenaries had been hired and were on their way to fight in the colonies; this did much to destroy any lingering loyalty to the king among moderates in Congress.[61] With such acts in mind, Adams held it unreasonable "for the people of these colonies now to take the oaths and affirmations necessary for the support of any government under the crown of Great Britain"; instead, "it is necessary that . . . all the powers of government [be] exerted, under the authority of the people of the colonies." In effect, like James II after he left Great Britain for France in 1688, George III had, according to Adams, "unkinged" himself in his most prominent North American colonies. In response to James Duane (New York), who described the preamble as " 'a machine for the fabrication of independence,' " Adams observed that, indeed, "it was independence itself."[62]

In between Congress' initial consideration of the preamble and the final approval of it on May 15, Congress on May 14 accepted and read the newly adopted credentials for the two Rhode Island delegates, Stephen Hopkins and William Ellery. Their certification included language drawn from Rhode Island's bold measure of May 4 in which the assembly, in the Act of Renunciation, repealed an earlier law pledging the allegiance of the colonists of Rhode Island to the king, thereby altering the formulas used in all judicial writs and processes, commissions, and oaths. As the Rhode Island Assembly noted, "Protection and Allegiance are reciprocal, the latter being only due in Consequence of the former." Since the king had withdrawn his protection from the colonists and was actively waging war on them, the residents of Rhode Island no longer, under well-accepted international moral and legal standards, owed him their allegiance and loyalty. The assembly therefore ordered that "wherever the Name and Authority of the said King is made Use of the same shall be omitted and in the Room thereof the Name and Authority of the Governor and Company of this Colony shall be substituted."[63] Thus, indirectly, began the colonies' experiments in republican government; for Rhode Island and Connecticut, however, little changed in practice.[64]

In the credentials for Hopkins and Ellery, passed the same day as the Act of Renunciation, the Rhode Island Assembly authorized its delegates to combine with others in Congress to secure "to the said Colonies their Rights and Liberties, both civil and religious," while remembering "to secure to this Colony, in the strongest and most perfect Manner, its present established Form, and all the Powers of Government, so far as it relates to its internal Police [Power] and Conduct of our Affairs, civil and religious."[65] Its delegates, while preserving inviolate Rhode Island's civil and religious rights and its control over its internal affairs, were to work with other delegates in forming "the strictest Union and Confederation" and in seeking to form treaties with foreign powers. Rhode Island and most of the other colonies, soon to be states, were no more interested in permitting an intercolonial or continental American government to intervene in their internal affairs than they had been in permitting Parliament to do so. One of the primary constitutional issues, the relationship between subordinate and superordinate governmental units, that had undergirded the imperial difficulties would be no closer to being solved after independence, at least until the ratification of the Articles of Confederation in 1781, if then, than it had been before.

## 31.1

### CONGRESSIONAL RECOMMENDATION TO THE UNITED COLONIES, WHERE NEEDED, TO ADOPT NEW GOVERNMENTS, MAY 10 AND 15, 1776

Worthington Chauncey Ford et al., eds., *Journals of the Continental Congress, 1774–1789* (Washington, D.C.: Government Printing Office, 1904–37), 4:342, 357–58.

[FRIDAY, MAY 10, 1776]

The Congress then resumed the consideration of the report from the committee of the whole, which being read was agreed to as follows:

*Resolved,* That it be recommended to the respective assemblies and conventions of the United Colonies, where no government sufficient to the exigencies of their affairs have been hitherto established, to adopt such government as shall, in the opinion of the representatives of the people, best conduce to the happiness and safety of their constituents in particular, and America in general.

*Resolved,* That a committee of three be appointed to prepare a preamble to the foregoing resolution:

The members chosen, Mr. J[ohn] Adams, Mr. [Edward] Rutledge, and Mr. R[ichard] H[enry] Lee. . . .

[WEDNESDAY, MAY 15, 1776]

The Congress took into consideration the draught of the preamble brought in by the committee, which was agreed to as follows:

Whereas his Britannic Majesty, in conjunction with the lords and commons of Great Britain, has, by a late act of Parliament, excluded the inhabitants of these United Colonies from the protection of his crown; And whereas, no answer, whatever, to the humble petitions of the colonies for redress of grievances and reconciliation with Great Britain, has been or is likely to be given; but, the whole force of that kingdom, aided by foreign mercenaries, is to be exerted for the destruction of the good people of these colonies; And whereas, it appears absolutely irreconcileable to reason and good Conscience, for the people of these colonies now to take the oaths and affirmations necessary for the support of any government under the crown of Great Britain, and it is necessary that the exercise of every kind of authority under the said crown should be totally suppressed, and all the powers of government exerted, under the authority of the people of the colonies, for the preservation of internal peace, virtue, and good order, as well as for the defence of their lives, liberties, and properties, against the hostile invasions and cruel depredations of their enemies; therefore, resolved, &c.

*Ordered,* That the said preamble, with the resolution passed the 10th instant, be published.

31.2

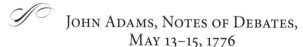 JOHN ADAMS, NOTES OF DEBATES,
MAY 13–15, 1776

In his diary, John Adams records the outlines of a heated debate that took place over several days in Congress while it met in a committee of the whole (and thus without any record of the same being entered into the *Journals*). The topic under discussion was Adams' proposed preamble to Congress' recommendation to the United Colonies. The moderate delegate from New York, James Duane, began the recorded discussion by reading from New York's delegate credentials of 1775, which included an instruction to seek a means of restoring harmony between Great Britain and the colonies. Moreover, as had been argued by some New Hampshire residents the previous fall (see document 24.6), he denied that a congress of colonial delegates had any more right to pass a recommendation that interfered in the internal governance of autonomous colonies than did Parliament—which, all agreed, it did not. Next, without waiting for anyone to respond to his challenge, he questioned the need for "all the haste" in moving forward the independence agenda.

Samuel Adams, following the logic of the preamble and Rhode Island's Act of Renunciation, pointed out in a rare congressional statement that Duane in good conscience could support the preamble, because "the King has thrown us out of his Protection." James Wilson rightly reminded his colleagues that the congressional recommendation of May 10 differed little from the instructions offered in 1775 to Massachusetts, New Hampshire, South Carolina, and Virginia, which he had helped author, but that the preamble was a different matter. More particularly, he opposed it for fear that the consequence of its passage would be "an immediate Dissolution of every Kind of Authority" in Pennsylvania. His rhetoric turned briefly Hobbesian: "The People will be instantly in a State of Nature," that is, engulfed in a civil war, so "Why then precipitate this Measure"? Wilson's concerns were justified, but in fact it was Philadelphia radicals, working with like-minded delegates in Congress, who had pushed for this measure, specifically in order to bring down the legally elected proprietary Pennsylvania government and see it replaced with a popular one more positively disposed to a declaration of independence.[66] In addition, the haste by some radicals in Congress, according to Braxton (see documents 30.5 and 31.3), reflected their impatience to achieve colonial independence before the royal peace commissioners arrived.

Adams' preamble was approved on May 15, 6–4, with 2 abstentions. As Paul Smith observes, "If Braxton's recollection is correct, the alignment of the colonies on the motion was probably: New Hampshire, Massachusetts, Rhode Island, Connecticut, Virginia, and South Carolina in favor; New York, New Jersey, Delaware, and North Carolina opposed; and Pennsylvania and Maryland abstaining."[67] In general, the mid-Atlantic colonies steadfastly remained the least convinced that they needed to replace their provincial monarchical governments with republican ones, and the most hesitant to declare their independence from Britain.[68]

Paul H. Smith, ed., *Letters of Delegates to Congress, 1774–1789* (Washington, D.C.: Library of Congress, 1976–93), 3:668–70.

Mr. Duane moves that the Delegation from N. York might be read.

When We were invited by Mass. Bay to the first Congress an Objection was made to binding ourselves by Votes of Congress.

Congress ought not to determine a Point of this Sort, about instituting Government. What is it to Congress, how Justice is administered. You have no Right to pass the Resolution—any more than Parliament has.

How does it appear that no favourable Answer is likely to be given to our Petitions? Every Account of foreign Aid, is accompanied with an Account of Commissioners.

Why all this Haste? Why this Urging? Why this driving? Disputes about Independence are in all the Colonies. What is this owing to, but our Indiscretion?

I shall take the Liberty of informing my Constituents that I have not been guilty of a Breach of Trust. I do protest vs. this Piece of Mechanism, this Preamble.

If the Facts in this Preamble should prove to be true, there will not be one Voice vs. Independence.

I suppose the Votes have been numbered and there is to be a Majority.

McKean. Construes the Instructions from N. York as Mr. Sherman does, and thinks this Measure the best to produce Harmony with G. Britain. There are now 2 Governments in direct Opposition to each other. Dont doubt that foreign Mercenaries are coming to destroy Us. I do think We shall loose our Liberties, Properties and Lives too, if We do not take this Step.

S. Adams. We have been favoured with a Reading of the Instructions from N. York. I am glad of it. The first Object of that Colony is no doubt the Establishment of their Rights. Our Petitions have not been heard—yet answered with Fleets and Armies and are to be answered with Mirmidons from abroad. The Gentleman from N. York, Mr. Duane, has not objected to the Preamble, but this—he has not a Right to vote for it. We cant go upon stronger Reasons, than that the King has thrown us out of his Protection. Why should We support Governments under his Authority? I wonder the People have conducted so well as they have.

Mr. Wilson. Was not present in Congress when the Resolution pass'd, to which this Preamble is proposed. I was present and one of the Committee, who reported the Advice to Mass. Bay. New Hampshire, Carolina and Virginia, had the same Advice, and with my hearty Concurrence.

The Claims of Parliament will meet with Resistance to the last Extremity. Those Colonies were Royal Governments. They could not subsist without some Government.

A Maxim, that all Government originates from the People. We are the Servants of the People sent here to act under a delegated Authority. If we exceed it, voluntarily, We deserve neither Excuse nor Justification.

Some have been put under Restraints by their Constituents. They cannot vote, without transgressing this Line. Suppose they should hereafter be called to an Account for it. This Province has not by any public Act, authorized us to vote upon this Question. This Province has done much and asked little from this Congress. The Assembly, largely increased, will [not] meet till next Monday. Will the Cause suffer much, if this Preamble is not published at this Time? If the Resolve is published without the Preamble. The Preamble contains a Reflection upon the Conduct of some People in America. It was equally irreconcileable to good Conscience Nine Months ago, to take the Oaths of Allegiance, as it is now. Two respectable Members last February, took the Oath of Allegiance in our Assembly. Why should We expose any Gentlemen to such an invidious Reflection?

In Magna Charta, there is a Clause, which authorises the People to seize the K[ing]'s Castles, and opposes his Arms when he exceeds his duty.

In this Province if that Preamble passes there will be an immediate Dissolution of every Kind of Authority. The People will be instantly in a State of Nature. Why then precipitate this Measure. Before We are prepared to build the new House, why should We pull down the old one, and expose ourselves to all the Inclemencies of the Season.

R. H. Lee. Most of the Arguments apply to the Resolve and not to the Preamble.

31.3

CARTER BRAXTON TO LANDON CARTER,
MAY 17, 1776

Carter Braxton of Virginia, again writing to his maternal uncle, offers further evidence that many moderates in Congress, men like James Wilson, supported the congressional recommendation—"the Assumption of Governt. was necessary & to that resolution little Objection was made"—but not Adams' preamble: "When the Preamble was reported much heat and debate did ensue for two or three days." Indeed, the Maryland delegates who had abstained from voting for the preamble even went so far as to withdraw from Congress for a week after it was adopted—two never returned. Braxton felt that Congress had acted with undue haste and that a number of colonial delegations were moving well beyond what their instructions permitted. For this, he blamed "the wise Men of the East [that is, from New England] & some from the *South*," who thought that waiting for peace commissioners was "a reprehensible delay which might give a turn to their favourite plan & defeat those pursuits they had so nearly compleated and the plan for which they had so wisely & so long laid down in their own Minds."

Moreover, he was among those who objected to the distorted nature of congressional state papers, in which one side of a story was represented, and even then often exaggerated. He faulted Adams' preamble for being "not altogether candid nor true": "For it is well known & has even been in print . . . that twenty seven Commissioners were coming over at the same time . . . [and] that the Persons appointed would undoubtedly make Peace. To suppress this & insert the other in my Judgmt. was not candid. Nor was it right to insert the worst part of an act without giving the substance of the whole." Of course, the tactic observed by Braxton was one that Congress had long and consistently employed in its state papers in an effort to shape domestic and world opinion. The same can be seen in the Declaration of Independence most particularly.

Yet even Braxton, possibly the least supportive of the congressional delegates of immediate independence, admitted, "That a Separation will take place seems almost evident." He was not alone in that assessment; indeed, most of the delegates in Congress still opposed to independence were no longer concerned with whether it would occur, but when. He thus found, as he had in a letter to his uncle the previous month, that "a number of Precautions should precede" independence. In particular, two associations needed to be formed: a naval alliance, and "a Union of the Colonies" in which the larger and richer states had proportionately greater representation. He thought the need for the latter self-evident: "Justice has long since called forth for equal [that is, proportional] Representation here that the Wealth of the great Colonies might not be disposed of by Men who represent scarcely any Colony at all." The question of appropriate representation became a matter of ever-increasing concern and disagreement as plans for federation came soon to be discussed with greater urgency.

Paul H. Smith, ed., *Letters of Delegates to Congress, 1774–1789* (Washington, D.C.: Library of Congress, 1976–93), 4:18–21.

Philaa May 17 1776.

Dr Sir.

I did myself the Honor to write to you & my friend Bob about six weeks since in answer to your two friendly Letters & directed them Via Hobs Hole; but from a hint sent me by Coll Frank you had not recd them. For this accident I am truly sorry because I had written with freedom for your private Inspection upon some facts not intended or proper for the publick Eye, and as that Letter would serve as a Key to my future ones. Unwilling farther to trust your host I have postponed writing again untill Mr Glascock should return from hence, where by the bye he has staid much longer than was expected. However he has waited to convey you a very important declaration & recommendation from the Congress, which you will say falls little short of Independence. It was not so understood by Congress but I find those out of doors on both sides the question construe it in that manner. The Assumption of Governt. was necessary & to that resolution little Objection was made, but when the Preamble was reported much heat and debate did ensue for two or three Days. At length I think by 6 to 4 it was determined to be accepted & accordingly published. Maryland withdrew after having desired in vain a Copy of the proceedings & their dissent; and gave us to understand they should not return nor deem our farther Resolutions obligatory, untill they had transmitted an Acct. of their Proceedings to their Convention & had their Instructions how to act or conduct themselves upon this alarming Occasion. This Event is waited for with Impatience and while it is in agitation the Assembly of this Province will meet and it is not impossible but they may join in this extraordinary proceeding. What then will be the Consequence God only knows.

It will surely have this effect if *some Men* were capable of Conviction, to convince them of the great danger of Rashness & precipitancy.

It was seen & known that these & other Colonies could not consistent with their Instructions come into this measure and all knew that they would be recalled if Commissioners did not soon arrive or if when arrived their terms were not free & honourable. In this Case America with one united Voice would have joined hand in hand to repell the haughty Invaders & to have rejected with disdain their future Superiority. But the wise Men of the East & some from the *South* thought it a reprehensible delay which might give a turn to their favourite plan & defeat those pursuits they had so nearly compleated and the plan for which they had so wisely & so long laid down in their own Minds. It may and I presume will be objected to the Preamble that it is not altogether candid nor true. For it is well known & has even been in print, that the same Captain who brought an Acct. of the twelve thousand Hessians going to Boston with the other Armaments for different parts of America also said that twenty seven Commissioners were coming over at the same time and that the People of England had expressed great Uneasiness at the Number of Forces coming over agt. us which nothing could satisfy but an Assurance that the Persons appointed would undoubtedly make Peace. To suppress this & insert the other in my Judgmt. was not candid. Nor was it right to insert the worst part of an act without giving the substance of the whole, which I own is bad enough but not so bad as the part handed out to the People.

Deception is what at all events we should avoid, as we are about to determine the fate & fortunes of Millions who have placed the most implicit Confidence in us. That a Separation will take place seems almost evident.

But in my Judgment there are a number of Precautions which should precede it. A Naval Alliance to protect our trade must be requisite, yet this is not obtained, nor do we know what friends we can procure. Our own Fleet is trifling as yet & before it will increase I fear some of them will fall into the Enemys Hands, as they are every where sought after & if seen will be taken. A Continental League was surely indispensable, & so was a Union of the Colonies. Justice has long since called forth for equal Representation here that the Wealth of the great Colonies might not be disposed of by Men who represent scarcely any Colony at all & who with all the pedantic Impudence will harangue us for Hours upon their Importance.

These with a variety of other things seemed absolutely necessary to me.

As I had long foreseen the Necessity of taking up Governt. in our Colony particularly, I had thrown my thoughts together on that Subject for yr Convention a Pamphlett containing which I send you & beg your opinion of it. As it is the first Essay of a poor Genius unassisted by a good Education you will shew it all the Indulgence in yr Power & allow much for the Zeal of the Author, who wishes nothing so ardently as to see his Country happy & flourishing. We have no certain Accts. from Canada nor any of the arrival of Troops to the Northward tho daily expected. I fear you will say that tho you meant to get a Letter now & then from me you did not expect to have your patience tryed by such long Letters. Therefore I will appologize for this & be done when I have asured you of my regard for yr Family & my desire that you will make it known to them & that with all respect I am Sir, your affece Nephew,

Carter Braxton

[P.S.] Mrs. Braxton begs me to add her Respects to you & Family.

## 31.4

 JAMES DUANE TO JOHN JAY, MAY 18, 1776

James Duane wrote to his fellow New Yorker, John Jay, of the proceedings in Congress and the opposition among the delegates from New York, New Jersey, Pennsylvania, Maryland, and possibly Delaware to the recently approved recommendation and "the preamble of which so openly avows Independence & Separation." He notes, perhaps surprisingly, that "the orators of Virginia with Col. Henry at their Head are against a Change of Government," most likely for the reason suggested by Duane in the debate recorded by Adams above: Congress enjoyed no more right to interfere in the internal affairs of its member colonies, even if they were represented in that body, than did Parliament. Duane argues against New York being "too precipitate in changing the present mode of Government" until the colonists themselves could be heard on the subject: "I woud wish first to be well assured of the Opinion of the Inhabitants at large." Whether genuinely concerned about popular opinion or not, Duane, along with other moderates, hoped to delay Congress' precipitous march toward declaring the colonies independent.

Paul H. Smith, ed., *Letters of Delegates to Congress, 1774–1789*
(Washington, D.C.: Library of Congress, 1976–93), 4:34–35.

Philad 18 May 1776

I wrote you, my dear Sir, a hasty Scrawl by the post on a most important Subject. You know the Maryland Instructions and those of Pennsylvania. I am greatly in doubt whether either of their Assemblies or Conventions will listen to a Recommendation the preamble of which so openly avows Independance & Seperation. The lower Counties will probably adhere to Pensylvania. New Jersey you can form a good Judgment of from the Reception this important Resolution has met with. The orators of Virginia with Col. Henry at their Head are against a Change of Government. The Body of the People, Col. Nelson, on whose Authority you Hint, thinks are for it. The late Election of Deputies for the Convention of New York sufficiently proves that those who assumed clandestine power & gave Laws even to the Convention & Committees were unsupported by the people. There seems therefore no Reason that our Colony shou'd be too precipitate in changing the present mode of Government. I woud wish first to be well assured of the Opinion of the Inhabitants at large. Let them be rather followed than driven on an Occasion of such momentuous Concern. But, above all, let us see the Conduct of the middle Colonies before we come to a Decision. It cannot injure us to wait a few weeks: the Advantage will be great, for this trying Question will clearly discover the true principles & the Extent of the Union of the Colonies. This, my dear Sir, is a delicate Subject on which

I cannot enlarge at present. If I coud be relievd I woud immediately set out and give you a meeting. Pray hasten the Return of one of the Gentlemen: I know *you ought* to be at the Convention who are too uninform'd of the State and Temper of their Neighbours, & want, at least in this Respect, some Assistance.

I am pleasd with the Situation Mr Livingston has fixd for your Saturday's Retreat on the Banks of the Shammony. Nothing coud have been more convenient. Present my Compliments to Mrs Jay and believe me to be with great Regard, Dr Sir, Your Affection-ate & most Obed Sevt,                                                  Jas. Duane

## 31.5

 John Adams to James Warren, May 20, 1776

Here Adams writes to James Warren of Boston, the husband of Mercy Otis Warren and an ally of the Adams cousins, with whom he worked closely in moving Congress toward independence. Adams begins by describing those colonies that provided their delegates with instructions to vote for independence, and he notes, correctly, that by the date of his letter all the southern colonies had done so, and none of the mid-Atlantic ones had—but possibly with too great a confidence, he believed that "they are very near it." Indeed, the earliest one to change, New Jersey, did not provide its delegates with new instructions until June 23, a week or so before Congress' momentous votes on July 1 and 2. The last of the mid-Atlantic colonies to change its instructions was New York, on July 9, not Maryland (which had switched on June 18), as Adams feared. Adams proudly describes how the congressional recommendation of May 15, with his preamble, had helped radicals in Philadelphia outmaneuver the Pennsylvania Assembly. On the very day he was writing, they moved to have the legally elected body replaced by an extralegal provincial assem-bly that would support the independence movement.

Adams concludes in celebration: "What do you think must be my sensations, when I see the Congress now daily passing Resolutions, which I most earnestly pressed for against Wind and Tide, Twelve Months ago? and which I have not omitted to labour for, a Month together from that Time to this?" It was, in fact, almost exactly a year earlier that the Second Continental Congress had met and issued four resolutions, including one describing Parliament's violation "of the natural and civil rights of the colonists," and a second that put the colonies immediately into a state of defense (see document 16.2). Adams' claims regarding John Dickinson's newfound agreement with him, however, proved inaccurate (see document 33.7). What is curiously absent from Adams' account is his failure to mention that the New England colonies, except for Rhode Island, had not yet sent positive instructions to their delegates in Congress to support independence. They did not do so until mid-June or later.[69] They may have believed such instructions unnecessary, or internal dissension may have prevented some of them from acting sooner.

Paul H. Smith, ed., *Letters of Delegates to Congress, 1774–1789* (Washington, D.C.: Library of Congress, 1976–93), 4:40–42. "The Farmer" refers to John Dickinson, author of *Letters from a Farmer in Pennsylvania.*

My Dear Sir                                                           May 20. 1776

Every Post and every Day rolls in upon Us Independance like a Torrent. The Delegates from Georgia made their Appearance, this Day, in Congress, with unlimited Powers, and these Gentlemen themselves are very firm. South Carolina has erected her Government and given her Delegates ample Powers, and they are firm enough. North Carolina have given theirs full Powers after repealing an Instruction given last August against Confederation and Independence. This Days Post has brought a Multitude of Letters from Virginia, all of which breath the same Spirit. They agree they shall institute a Government—all are agreed in this they say. Here are four Colonies to the Southward, who are perfectly agreed now with the four to the Northward. Five in the Middle are not yet quite so ripe. But they are very near it. I expect that New York will come to a fresh Election of Delegates in the Course of this Week, give them full Powers, and determine to institute a Government.

The Convention of New Jersey, is about Meeting, and will assume a Government.

Pensylvania Assembly meets this Day and it is Said will repeal their Instruction to their Delegates which has made them So exceeding obnoxious to America in general, and their own Constituents in particular.

We have had an entertaining Maneuvre, this Morning in the State House Yard. The Committee of the City Summoned a Meeting at Nine O Clock in the State House Yard, to consider of the Resolve of Congress of the fifteenth instant. The Weather was very rainy, and the Meeting was in the open Air, like the Comitia of the Romans. A Stage was erected, extempore for the Moderator, and the few orators to ascend. Coll Roberdeau was the Moderator. Coll McKean, Coll Cadwallader and Coll Matlack the principal orators. It was the very first Town Meeting, I ever Saw in Philadelphia and it was conducted with great order, Decency and Propriety.

The first Step taken was this: the Moderator produced the Resolve of Congress of the 15th inst, and read it with a loud Stentorean Voice that might be heard a Quarter of a Mile "Whereas his Britannic Majesty &c." As soon as this was read, the Multitude, several Thousands, some say, tho so wett, rended the Welkin with three Cheers, Hatts flying as usual &c.

Then a Number of Resolutions were produced and moved & determined, with great Unanimity. These Resolutions I will send you, as soon as published. The Drift of the whole was that the assembly was not a Body properly constituted, authorized and qualified to carry the Resolve for instituting a new Government into Execution and therefore that a Convention should be called, and at last they voted to support and defend the Measure of a Convention, at the utmost Hazard, and at all Events &c.

The Delaware Government, generally is of the Same opinion with the best Americans, very orthodox in their Faith and very exemplary in their Practice. Maryland remains to be mentioned. That is so excentric a Colony—some times so hot, sometimes so cold—now so high, then so low—that I know not what to say about it or to expect from it. I have often wished it could exchange Places with Hallifax. When they get agoing I expect some wild extravagant Flight or other from it. To be sure they must go beyond every body else, when they begin to go.

Thus I have rambled through the Continent, and you will perceive by this state of it, that We cant be very remote from the most decisive Measures and the most critical Event.

What do you think must be my sensations, when I see the Congress now daily passing Resolutions, which I most earnestly pressed for against Wind and Tide, Twelve Months ago? and which I have not omitted to labour for, a Month together from that Time to this? What do you think must be my Reflections when I see the Farmer himself, now confessing the Falshood of all his Prophecies and the Truth of mine, and confessing himself, now for instituting Governments, forming a Continental Constitution, making alliances with foreigners, opening Ports and all that—and confessing that the Defence of the Colonies, and Preparations for defence have been neglected, in Consequence of fond delusive hopes and deceitfull Expectations?

I assure you this is no Gratification of my Vanity. The gloomy Prospect of Carnage and Devastation that now presents itself in every Part of the Continent and which has been in the most express and decisive nay dogmatical Terms foretold by me a thousand Times is too affecting to give me Pleasure. It moves my keenest Indignation—yet I dare not hint at these Things for I hate to give Pain to Gentlemen whom I believe sufficiently punished by their own Reflections.

## 31.6

 THOMAS STONE TO JAMES HOLLYDAY(?),
MAY 20, 1776

Thomas Stone was a lawyer, who, like most in the Maryland delegation, Samuel Chase and Charles Carroll of Carrollton being the exceptions, was not an enthusiastic supporter of independence. James Hollyday, also a lawyer, was a member of the provincial convention and the Maryland council of safety. The Maryland congressional delegates had written on May 15 to the Maryland Convention, immediately after the vote on the preamble, to provide them with copies of Congress' recommendations of May 10 and 15, which Stone discusses here and which were received on the same day as his letter was written, May 20, 1776. The convention created a committee to consider the recommendations, and it, in turn, submitted a report on the same day. On May 21, the convention agreed to the report, which concluded that "it was not necessary that all authority of the Crown should be suppressed in Maryland." In fact, the convention had "resolved unanimously that a reunion 'on constitutional principles would most effectually secure the rights and liberties, and increase the strength and promote the happiness of the whole empire.'" Therefore, the delegates were to follow "the instructions against independence which had been adopted on 11 January."[70] Finally, though, after the congressional debate on June 10 (see document 32.1), the Maryland Convention met again and on June 28 rescinded its previous, month-old instructions against independence.

The views expressed in the report were in keeping with those of the Maryland delegation; as Stone wrote: "Never was a fairer Cause, with more promising appearances of final Success ruined by the rash and precipitate Councils of a few men. In a very short Time we should have been restored to our rights & have enjoyed Peace if the Ministry are in Earnest in promoting a Negotiation with a Design to do Justice to America." That outcome even he doubted, but the charade of the peace commissioners was necessary nonetheless: "Upon their deceitfull Shew of reconciliation being detected, laid open & exposed, the General & almost unanimous Voice of America would have been for separation." His condemnation of the congressional resolution just passed was unsparing: "To strike a decisive Stroke & at once when the Minds of Men are not prepared for such an Event, to cut the only Bond which held the discordant Members of the Empire together, appears to me the most weak and ill judged Measure I ever met with in a State which had the least Pretention to wisdom or Knowledge in the Affairs of Men." Given the delegates' personal feelings, in keeping with their instructions, "we conceived ourselves bound to withdraw from Congress immediately on the Vote upon the Preamble, & have not voted since." Most of the delegates returned a week later, although two, Robert Alexander and Robert Goldsborough, never returned, and Stone did not until 1784.

What most troubled Stone was the "great change in the declared End of the war." Maryland, due to the rashness of others, was confronted with two equally unpalatable choices: destroying the unity of colonial opposition to unconstitutional parliamentary measures, or fighting for independence and the creation of new republican governments—"either of which are dangerous Extremes." Like John Adams, Stone described the revolutionary changes taking place on May 20 in Philadelphia—but with much less enthusiasm than Adams (see document 31.6). He closes the part of the letter reproduced below by describing how little credence should be given to the British peace commissioners and by expressing doubts whether, on either side, the spirit for reconciliation still existed. He feared that "the Ministry are strongly attached to their Sistem, perhaps from Principle," and distrusted whether a just constitutional plan, no matter how fair, "would be accepted by the present haughty Temper of America." Given, for example, Congress' rapid rejection of North's conciliatory peace proposal the previous July (see document 23.1), his pessimism seems to have been well grounded. Principled constitutional differences on both sides, along with the regularly occurring bouts of pride and arrogance that do so much to deform the policies of states, made it unlikely that a solution would be arrived at without much more bloodshed.

Paul H. Smith, ed., *Letters of Delegates to Congress, 1774–1789* (Washington, D.C.: Library of Congress, 1976–93), 4:46–54. Paragraph breaks have been added, and matters unrelated to congressional business deleted.

Dr. Sir.                                                       Phila. May 20. 1776

I am very much obliged by the Intelligence communicated in yours of the 17th and am much pleased by the Temper shewn in the Convention—tho I fear it can now be of little Service in the general Scale of American Politicks. The Dye is cast. The fatal Stab is given to any future Connection between this Country & Britain: except in the relation of Conqueror & vanquished, which I can't think of without Horror & Indignation. Never was a fairer Cause, with more promising appearances of final Success ruined by the rash and precipitate Councils of a few men. In a very short Time we should have been restored to our rights & have enjoyed Peace if the Ministry are in Earnest in promoting a Negotiation with a Design to do Justice to America, which however I very much doubt, or upon their deceitfull Shew of reconciliation being detected, laid open & exposed, the General & almost unanimous Voice of America would have been for separation, but just at the Time when anxious Expectations are raised & not satisfied one way or the other, to strike a decisive Stroke & at once when the Minds of Men are not prepared for such an Event, to cut the only Bond which held the discordant Members of the Empire together, appears to me the most weak and ill judged Measure I ever met with in a State which had the least Pretention to wisdom or Knowledge in the Affairs of Men.

I think it probable You will before this reaches you have taken some decisive Measures in Consequence of the joint Letter of your Deputies in Congress. It gave me exceeding Pain, that the Convention should be necessitated to take one or other of the perplexing alternatives suggested by the Preamble & Resolve sent you & our Conduct in Consequence thereof, but it could not be avoided. We postponed the Question somedays, and did every thing to prevent that destructive Precipitancy which seems so agreable to the Genius of some. Further delay could not be obtain[ed] Altho there was the strongest reason for it. Two Colonies being unrepresented & a representation shortly expected, it was in vain to reason or expostulate. The Majority of Colonies attending was known to be for the Proposition & the opportunity not to be let slip. We conceived ourselves bound to withdraw from Congress immediately on the Vote upon the Preamble, & have not voted since. Having once determined in our Judgments against the Propriety of the Measure and of its Tendency, it became us not to hesitate obeying the Instructions of our constituents which in all Cases with me (& I am persuaded with my Brother Delegates) are sacred. The Vox Populi must in great measure influence your Determination of the part to be taken by the Province upon this great change in the *declared* End of the war—and I am strongly inclined to wish it could be well known before any decisive Step is taken in Convention and for this End, a little Time & delay might be profitably used. You must I presume either declare explicitly that you will go all Lengths with the majority of Congress or that you will not join in a War to be carried on for the purposes of Independency & new Establishments, and will break the Union or rather not enter into one for these Ends, either of which are dangerous Extremes. But in whatever is determined it will be wise and prudent to have the Concurrence of the People. . . . The People of this Province are thrown into the most violent Convulsions by the resolve of Congress sent you, the result of which it is impossible to foresee.

A considerable number of People met this morning in Consequence of an hand Bill for that purpose, & determined that Government ought to be assumed, the Assembly suppressed, the Instructions to the Delegates rescinded & a Convention called for the purpose of judging of the Propriety of forming a new Government, & to form the same. This Meeting as I am informed consisted of the people only who are of one side, & that all their Determinations were very unanimous. The County Committee I hear met yesterday and determined by a great majority only two dissenting, to support the assembly under the present form of Government. We have not heard from the out counties. The [Pennsylvania] assembly was to have met this day, but I believe there were not members enough to make an House. . . .

We hear of a considerable British Force having arrived in N Carolina, & that Genl. Lee is gone to oppose their Landing. A person who was taken in Canada with Allen is I am told just arrived in Town Via Hallifax. He was carried to England and examined as he said before the Council & was discharged. He said he was treated in a most friendly manner, was found every thing he wanted. The people of England talk much of Settlement with America. No foreign Troops arrived in England the 24 of March. He brings Papers as low as the 20th but I have not seen them. He also brings Letters, as I am told, to several Gent. in Town & to the congress—reports that it is said 30 or 40 thousands Troops will be sent to America, 10000 for the South, 10000 for Canada, the rest for the Northern Provinces. He left How & his Troops at Hallifax in bad Condition, no Troops arrived to the Eastward. The person who gave me this relation did not hear any thing mentioned of Commissioners or forgot what he heard as he is averse to beleiving any thing of their coming over. I shall probably hear more of this affair in the morning and will subjoin the Intelligence if worth communicating. I think it very probably Commissioners will be sent with the Troops, tho I very much doubt of the Sincerity of administration to offer just & reasonable Terms to us. I do not form this opinion upon the Circumstance of Troops being sent for I think they will naturally suppose if Commissioners are sent without support we must dictate the Terms of Accomodation & they may also readily conceive they will not be of the most moderate kind. But I fear the Ministry are strongly attached to their Sistem, perhaps from Principle, that they have discovered the strong Inclination to Peace in many Colonies & are in hopes, by offering something like reasonable Terms at a Time when the Distresses of war are painted strongly upon the minds of those who have not been irritated & enraged by feeling them in reality, to create Divisions & Dissentions through the Country. The last act of Parliament seems to have been produced under the influence of this Idea, & is calculated to ansr. the purpose. I wish I may be mistaken; However should the most reasonable Terms be offered preserving the subordinate relation of this Country to Britain I much question if they would be accepted by the present haughty Temper of America. . . .

### 31.7

 John Adams to James Sullivan, May 26, 1776

John Adams is here responding to two earlier May letters from James Sullivan, a prosperous attorney, an active figure in Massachusetts politics, a justice on the Massachusetts Superior Court of Judicature, and a future member of Congress. In keeping with the reassessment in the spring of 1776 of all things political that the anticipated break with Britain created, Sullivan had considered "the Principles of Representation and Legislation" and defended a rapid liberalization of "the qualifications of Voters." In response, Adams stood firm against any change to Massachusetts law to widen the franchise. According to Adams, although "in Theory . . . the only moral Foundation of Government is the Consent of the People," certainly not all the people could be permitted to vote. In particular, if men without property were permitted to vote, Adams asks, upon what convincing ground could society prevent women and children from voting, "for generally Speaking, Women and Children have as good Judgment, and as independent Minds as those Men who are wholly destitute of Property." He reduced the question to political fundamentals: "Whence arises the Right of the Majority to govern, and the obligation of the Minority to obey? From Necessity, you will Say, because there can be no other Rule. But why exclude Women?"

For Adams, economic dependence and a lack of leisure to attend to affairs of state rendered propertyless men, women, and children all similarly incapable of voting freely and responsibly: "Harrington has Shewn that Power always follows Property. This I believe to be as infallible a Maxim, in Politics." (James Harrington was a prominent seventeenth-century English political theorist of a republican bent.) One need only remember that representation in the colonial legislatures, which, as had been argued for a decade, were the only entities that could legitimately tax the colonists, was for property holders and, one might add, in almost all instances adult males of European extraction.

In arguing against extending the franchise for free men without property, Adams draws attention to the admittedly arbitrary nature of those rules that allow someone age twenty-one to vote, but not someone a few days younger: "The Reason is you must fix upon Some Period in Life, when the Understanding and Will of Men in general is fit to be trusted by the Public. Will not the Same Reason justify the State in fixing upon Some certain Quantity of Property, as a Qualification." Adams summarizes his case defending property as a qualification for the vote by retreating from specifics to abstraction: "Society can be governed only by general Rules. Government cannot accommodate itself to every particular Case, as it happens, nor to the Circumstances of particular Persons." Without a trace of irony or, seemingly, self-awareness, and in contrast to his radical sentiments of the past eighteen months, when he viewed anything approaching moderation as anathema, Adams here advises "that Wisdom and Policy would dictate in these times, to be very cautious of making Alterations."

Adams' remarks were offered only a few weeks after he wrote the preamble to Congress' recommendation of May 15, which included the claim that "all the powers of government [must be] exerted, under the authority of the people of the colonies." It seems that for Adams (most likely for Sullivan as well), his decade-long struggle had not been to change the nature of government in the colonies, and most certainly not in Massachusetts, but, more straightforwardly, to change the nature of the colonies' constitutional relationship to Britain. As William Hogeland recently argued, "The Pennsylvania radicals demolished, for a short time, and in one place, the basic assumption of Whig politics, sacred to men like the Adamses: property as the basis of representation, bulwark against tyranny . . . [Later] the Adamses and others like them devoted their energies to ensuring that political power in America remained in the hands of elites."[71] In ways that Adams may not have intended or even understood (see documents 30.4 and 30.6), the struggle for independence led to a revolution in values and political norms, creating a newly popular culture and stringently republican politics.[72] With independence and a new spirit of political self-examination and openness fast approaching, and a breakdown of the linkage between rights and duties, a different and more conservative Adams began to emerge.

Paul H. Smith, ed., *Letters of Delegates to Congress, 1774–1789* (Washington, D.C.: Library of Congress, 1976–93), 4:72–75.

Dear Sir.                                                    Philadelphia May 26. 1776

Your Favours of May 9th and 17th are now before me; and I consider them as the Commencement of a Correspondence, which will not only give me Pleasure, but may be of Service to the public, as, in my present Station I Stand in need of the best Intelligence, and the Advice of every Gentlemen of Abilities and public Principles, in the Colony which has seen fit to place me here.

Our worthy Friend, Mr Gerry has put into my Hand, a Letter from you, of the Sixth of May, in which you consider the Principles of Representation and Legislation, and give us Hints of Some Alterations, which you Seem to think necessary, in the Qualification of Voters.

I wish, Sir, I could possibly find Time, to accompany you, in your Investigation of the Principles upon which a Representative assembly Stands and ought to Stand, and in your Examination whether the Practice of our Colony, has been conformable to those Principles. But alass! Sir, my Time is so incessantly engrossed by the Business before me that I cannot Spare enough, to go through so large a Field: and as to Books, it is not easy to obtain them here, nor could I find a Moment to look into them, if I had them.

It is certain in Theory, that the only moral Foundation of Government is the Consent of the People. But to what an Extent Shall We carry this Principle? Shall We Say, that every Individual of the Community, old and young, male and female, as well as rich and poor, must consent, expressly to every Act of Legislation? No, you will Say, this is impossible. How then does the Right arise in the Majority to govern the Minority, against their Will? Whence arises the Right of the Men to govern Women, without their Consent? Whence the Right of the old to bind the Young, without theirs?

But let us first Suppose, that the whole Community of every Age, Rank, Sex, and Condition, has a Right to vote. This Community is assembled—a Motion is made and carried by a Majority of one Voice. The Minority will not agree to this. Whence arises the Right of the Majority to govern, and the obligation of the Minority to obey? From Necessity, you will Say, because there can be no other Rule. But why exclude Women? You will Say, because their Delicacy renders them unfit for Practice and Experience, in the great Businesses of Life, and the hardy Enterprises of War, as well as the arduous Cares of State. Besides, their attention is so much engaged with the necessary Nurture of their Children, that Nature has made them fittest for domestic Cares. And Children have not Judgment or Will of their own. True. But will not these Reasons apply to others? Is it not equally true, that Men in general in every Society, who are wholly destitute of Property, are also too little acquainted with public affairs to form a Right Judgment, and too dependent upon other Men to have a Will of their own? If this is a Fact, if you give to every Man, who has no Property, a Vote, will you not make a fine encouraging Provision for Corruption by your fundamental Law? Such is the Frailty of the human Heart, that very few Men, who have no Property, have any Judgment of their own. They talk and vote as they are directed by Some Man of Property, who has attached their Minds to his Interest.

Upon my Word, Sir, I have long thought an Army a Piece of Clock Work and to be governed only by Principles and Maxims, as fixed as any in Mechanicks and by all that I have read in the History of Mankind, and in Authors, who have Speculated upon Society and Government, I am much inclined to think, a Government must manage a Society in the Same manner; and that this is Machinery too.

Harrington has Shewn that Power always follows Property. This I believe to be as infallible a Maxim, in Politicks, as, that Action and Reaction are equal, is in Mechanicks. Nay I believe We may advance one Step farther and affirm that the Ballance of Power in a Society, accompanies the Ballance of Property in Land. The only possible Way then of preserving the Ballance of Power on the side of equal Liberty and public Virtue, is to make the Acquisition of Land easy to every Member of Society: to make a Division of the Land into Small Quantities, so that the Multitude may be possessed of landed Estates. If the Multitude is possessed of the Ballance of real Estate, the Multitude will have the Ballance of Power, and in that Case the Multitude will take Care of the Liberty, Virtue, and Interest of the Multitude in all Acts of Government.

I believe these Principles have been felt, if not understood in the Massachusetts Bay, from the Beginning: and therefore I Should think that Wisdom and Policy would dictate in these times, to be very cautious of making Alterations. Our People have never been very rigid in Scrutinising into the Qualifications of Voters, and I presume they will not now begin to be so. But I would not advise them to make any alteration in the Laws, at present, respecting the Qualifications of Voters.

Your Idea, that those Laws, which affect the Lives and personal Liberty of all, or which inflict corporal Punishment, affect those, who are not qualified to vote, as well as those who are, is just. But, so they do Women, as well as Men, Children as well as Adults. What Reason Should there be, for excluding a Man of Twenty Years, Eleven Months and Twenty seven days old, from a Vote when you admit one who is twenty one? The Reason is you must fix upon Some Period in Life, when the Understanding and Will of Men in general is fit to be trusted by the Public. Will not the Same Reason justify the State in fixing upon Some certain Quantity of Property, as a Qualification.

The Same Reasoning, which will induce you to admit all Men, who have no Property, to vote, with those who have, for those Laws, which affect the Person will prove that you ought to admit Women and Children: for generally Speaking, Women and Children have as good Judgment, and as independent Minds as those Men who are wholly destitute of Property: these last being to all Intents and Purposes as much dependent upon others, who will please to feed, cloath, and employ them, as Women are upon their Husbands, or Children on their Parents.

As to your Idea of proportioning the Votes of Men in Money Matters, to the Property they hold, it is utterly impracticable. There is no possible Way of ascertaining, at any one Time, how much every Man in a Community, is worth; and if there was, so fluctuating is Trade and Property, that this State of it, would change in half an Hour. The Property of the whole Community, is Shifting every Hour, and no Record can be kept of the Changes.

Society can be governed only by general Rules. Government can not accommodate itself to every particular Case, as it happens, nor to the Circumstances of particular Persons. It must establish general, comprehensive Regulations for Cases and Persons. The only Question is, which general Rule will accommodate most Cases and most Persons.

Depend upon it, Sir, it is dangerous to open so fruitfull a Source of Controversy and altercation; as would be opened by attempting to alter the Qualifications of Voters. There will be no End of it. New Claims will arise. Women will demand a Vote. Lads from 12 to 21 will think their Rights not enough attended to, and every Man, who has not a Farthing, will demand an equal Voice with any other in all Acts of State. It tends to confound and destroy all Distinctions, and prostrate all Ranks, to one common Levell. I am &c

## 32. PRELUDE TO THE DECLARATION AND INDEPENDENCE, JUNE 1776

Although Rhode Island on May 4 was the first colony to disavow its allegiance to the king,[73] Virginia, on May 15, working in close collaboration with its delegates in Congress, went a step further and "instructed" its congressional delegates "to propose to that respectable body to declare the United Colonies free and independent States, absolved from all allegiance to, or dependence upon, the Crown or Parliament of Great Britain" (see document 32.2). Accordingly, on June 7, Richard Henry Lee of Virginia introduced in Congress three resolutions, which were seconded— appropriately enough—by John Adams: one for independence, using the language of Virginia's instructions; another "for forming foreign Alliances"; and a third for drafting "a plan of confederation [to] be prepared and transmitted to the respective Colonies for their consideration and approbation." On May 7 or 8, Congress, on a close procedural vote, agreed to consider Lee's resolutions. Meeting as a committee of the whole on the eighth, Congress was unable to come to agreement concerning the first, and most controversial resolution, regarding independence, and decided to meet again on the following Monday for "further consideration [of] the resolutions referred to them."

On Monday, June 10, Congress again met as a committee of the whole and, after a number of votes, decided "that the consideration of the first resolution be postponed to this day, three weeks [July 1], and in the mean while, that no time be lost, in case the Congress agree thereto, that a committee be appointed to prepare a declaration to the effect of the said first resolution," that is, that the American colonies were henceforth to be free and independent states. Congress, seemingly, agreed with little, if any debate, to the second and third resolutions, concerning the forming of foreign alliances and creating a plan of confederation. Committees to prepare the appropriate documents were appointed on June 12.[74]

The radicals had come a long way. Their cause had made progress by the beginning of 1776, but ultimate success was far from certain, especially after the mid-Atlantic colonies renewed their delegates' instructions to vote against independence.[75] Then on June 4, Congress received a final denial by the king that he would work for reconciliation (see document 32.3). This was the proverbial last straw for many, and the radicals in and out of Congress were well on their way to achieving their goal, American independence. Over the preceding six months, their cause had received considerable help from an intransigent Parliament, a diligent and conscientious but unimaginative king,[76] a wildly popular pamphlet by a British republican radical, and a feared invasion by German mercenaries. Still, at the insistence of the mid-Atlantic delegates, Congress agreed to delay for three weeks its almost inevitable declaration of independence of the colonies.

Because there was little doubt as to the final outcome to be reached on July 1—though in fact the vote for independence came on July 2—Congress named five delegates on June 11 to serve on the committee to draft a declaration of independence. Its chair was Thomas Jefferson, and the other members were John Adams, Benjamin Franklin, Roger Sherman (Connecticut), and Robert R. Livingston (New York). With the exception of Livingston, who likely thought the time for independence was not yet ripe (in the end, he did not support or sign the document), the committee members were vocal supporters of American independence. On the same day, June 11, Congress resolved to appoint committees to act on Lee's other two resolutions of June 7, "to prepare and digest the form of a confederation" and "to prepare a plan of treaties to be proposed to foreign powers."[77]

The next day, June 12, Congress created, after protracted delays and indecision, a new executive body, the Board of War and Ordnance, to manage the conflict that it viewed as critical to the colonies' survival. The next day, June 13, Congress appointed delegates to the Board of War: John Adams, Sherman, Harrison, James Wilson, and Edward Rutledge, who served on the confederation committee also.[78] Among the committee members drafting a declaration of independence, only Jefferson did not serve on one of the three other most significant committees: Adams, Franklin, and Livingston each sat on two, and the irreplaceable Sherman, who later did much to broker a compromise at the Constitutional Convention, sat on three.

Also on June 12, Congress decided that the committee to draft a plan of confederation should consist of a member from each colony. It was to include Sherman and Livingston from the declaration committee and, most importantly, John Dickinson, the heretofore dominant penman of Congress, who, though unwilling to support independence, was chosen to chair the committee and write the first draft of the Articles of Confederation. It seems that in the minds of the delegates, these were independent activities with separable goals. Similarly, Congress elected five members to serve on the committee charged with preparing a plan of treaties to be proposed to foreign powers: Dickinson, Franklin, John Adams, and two more moderates, Benjamin Harrison (Virginia) and Robert Morris (Pennsylvania).

## 32.1

### RICHARD HENRY LEE, THREE RESOLUTIONS RESPECTING INDEPENDENCY, JUNE 7, 8, 10, AND 11, 1776

Worthington Chauncey Ford et al., eds., *Journals of the Continental Congress, 1774–1789* (Washington, D.C.: Government Printing Office, 1904–37), 5:425–31.

[FRIDAY, JUNE 7, 1776]

Certain resolutions ‖respecting independency‖ being moved and seconded,

*Resolved,* That these United Colonies are, and of right ought to be, free and independent States, that they are absolved from all allegiance to the British Crown, and that all political connection between them and the State of Great Britain is, and ought to be, totally dissolved.

That it is expedient forthwith to take the most effectual measures for forming foreign Alliances.

That a plan of confederation be prepared and transmitted to the respective Colonies for their consideration and approbation.

*Resolved,* That the consideration of them be referred till to morrow morning; and, that the members be enjoined to attend punctually at 10 o'Clock, in order to take the same into consideration. . . .

SATURDAY, JUNE 8, 1776

The Congress took into consideration the resolutions moved yesterday:

*Resolved,* That they be referred to a committee of the whole [Congress.] Whereupon,

The Congress resolved itself into a committee of the whole to take into consideration the resolutions referred to them; and, after some time spent thereon, the president resumed the chair, and Mr. [Benjamin] Harrison reported, that the committee have taken into consideration the matter to them referred, but not having come to any resolution thereon, desired leave to sit again on Monday next.

*Resolved,* That this Congress will, on Monday next, at 10 o'Clock, resolve itself into a committee of the whole, to take into their farther consideration the resolutions referred to them. . . .

[MONDAY, JUNE 10, 1776]

Agreeable to order, the Congress resolved itself into a committee of the whole, to take into their farther consideration the resolutions to them referred; and, after some time spent thereon, the president resumed the chair, and Mr. [Benjamin] Harrison reported, that the committee have had under consideration the resolutions to them referred, and have come to a resolution, which he read.

The Congress took into consideration the report from the Committee of the whole: Whereupon,

*Resolved,* That the consideration of the first resolution be postponed to this day, three weeks [July 1], and in the mean while, that no time be lost, in case the Congress agree thereto, that a committee be appointed to prepare a declaration to the effect of the said first resolution, which is in these words: "That these United Colonies are, and of right ought to be, free and independent states; that they are absolved from all allegiance to the British Crown: and that all political connexion between them and the state of Great Britain is, and ought to be, totally dissolved."

*Resolved,* That the committee be discharged.

The several matters to this day referred, being postponed,

Adjourned to 9 o'Clock to Morrow.

[TUESDAY, JUNE 11, 1776]

*Resolved,* That a committee be appointed to prepare and digest the form of a confederation to be entered into between these colonies:

*Resolved,* That a committee be appointed to prepare a plan of treaties to be proposed to foreign powers.

## 32.2

 RESOLUTIONS OF THE VIRGINIA CONVENTION,
MAY 15, 1776

On May 7, 1776, the Virginia Convention met as a committee of the whole to consider the state of the colony. By May 15, it had proposed a number of resolutions, the most famous of which was offered by President Edmund Pendleton in response to a stream of petitions pouring in "from county after county" and to which the 112 men present unanimously agreed.[79] One of its congressional delegates was to put before that body a resolution calling for a declaration of independence.[80] Congressional delegates, including Richard Henry Lee and Thomas Jefferson, were in attendance.

In this resolution, Virginia points out that "by the most decent representations and petitions to the king and Parliament of Great Britain," the colonies had attempted "to restore peace and security to America under the British government and a reunion with that people upon just and liberal terms," which "instead of a redress of grievances, have produced from an imperious and vindictive administration increased insult, oppression, and a vigorous attempt to effect our total destruction." Like the Rhode Island Assembly, the Virginia Convention complained Parliament had declared "our properties subjected to confiscation, our people, when captivated, compelled to join in the murder and plunder of their relations and countrymen." As well, the Virginians condemned the British administration, as had Congress any number of times, for freeing Virginia's slaves and "training and employing them against their masters." Accordingly, Virginia had "no alternative left but an abject subjection to the will of those overbearing tyrants, or a total separation from the Crown and government of Great Britain." The convention closed by expressing Virginia's "desire to preserve the connection with that nation," but it was "driven from that inclination by their wicked councils and the eternal law of self-preservation." Even Virginia, then, claimed to have been driven to take the extreme measure of separating from the British Empire by the actions of the British administration rather than by intention or design.

Just as Massachusetts and its radical faction, both in and out of Congress, had opened debate in the First Continental Congress with the Suffolk resolves (see document 9.1), Virginia and its radical members, working both in and out of Congress—for it sent its resolution to the other colonies as well—led Congress and the colonies toward a declaration of independence.[81] Like Rhode Island in its instructions, Virginia reminded its delegates "that the power of forming government for, and the regulations of the internal concerns of each colony be left to the respective colonial legislatures." Although such strictures were ubiquitous, Carter Braxton and James Duane had noted previously (see documents 31.3 and 31.4) that concern for congressional interference in the internal affairs of the colonies had been abrogated in Congress' recommendation of May 15 urging the colonies to adopt new governments (they would be again in February 1777; see document 37.1).

Still more significant for Virginia was the final resolution it passed on May 15, ordering that "a committee be appointed to prepare a declaration of rights, and such a plan of government as will be most likely to maintain peace and order in this colony, and secure substantial and equal liberty to the people." George Mason—who took his seat in the Virginia Convention two days after these resolutions had been agreed to—completed the first of these tasks, a bill of rights, on May 27. The convention agreed to it on June 12. The convention chose a committee of twenty-eight, including Mason, Patrick Henry, and James Madison, to draft a constitution. Mason again took a lead role. His draft, with Jefferson's preamble, which included many of the grievances he later listed in the Declaration, was adopted by the convention on June 29, a few days before Congress formally declared independence on July 2.

Merrill Jensen, ed., *English Historical Documents: American Colonial Documents to 1776* (New York: Oxford University Press, 1969), 9:866–67.

Forasmuch as all the endeavours of the united colonies by the most decent representations and petitions to the king and Parliament of Great Britain to restore peace and security to America under the British government and a reunion with that people upon just and liberal terms, instead of a redress of grievances, have produced from an imperious and vindictive administration increased insult, oppression, and a vigorous attempt to effect our total destruction. By a late Act, all these colonies are declared to be in rebellion and out of the protection of the British Crown, our properties subjected to confiscation, our people, when captivated, compelled to join in the murder and plunder of their relations and countrymen, and all former rapine and oppression of Americans declared legal and just. Fleets and armies are raised, and the aid of foreign troops engaged to assist these destructive purposes. The king's representative in this colony has not only withheld all the powers of government from operating for our safety, but, having retired on board an armed ship, is carrying on a piratical and savage war against us, tempting our slaves by every artifice to resort to him, and training and employing them against their masters. In this state of extreme danger we have no alternative left but an abject submission to the will of those overbearing tyrants, or a total separation from the Crown and government of Great Britain, uniting and exerting the strength of all America for defence, and forming alliances with foreign powers for commerce and aid in war. Wherefore, appealing to the Searcher of hearts for the sincerity of former declarations, expressing our desire to preserve the connection with that nation, and that we are driven from that inclination by their wicked councils and the eternal law of self-preservation:

Resolved, unanimously. That the delegates appointed to represent this colony in general congress be instructed to propose to that respectable body to declare the united colonies free and independent states, absolved from all allegiance to, or dependence upon, the Crown or Parliament of Great Britain; and that they give the assent of this colony to such declaration, and to whatever measures may be thought proper and necessary by the congress for forming foreign alliances, and a confederation of the colonies, at such time, and in the manner, as to them shall seem best. Provided, that the power of forming government for, and the regulations of the internal concerns of each colony be left to the respective colonial legislatures.

Resolved, unanimously. That a committee be appointed to prepare a declaration of rights, and such a plan of government as will be most likely to maintain peace and order in this colony, and secure substantial and equal liberty to the people.

32.3

 ADDRESS AND PETITION OF THE LORD MAYOR,
ALDERMEN, AND COMMONS OF LONDON TO THE
KING, AND HIS ANSWER, MARCH 22–23, 1776

In this petition to the king, he is beseeched by the elected officials of London to make a strenuous effort at reconciliation with the colonies before proceeding with "the dreadful Operations of your Armament," for with remarkable insight and accuracy, they believed that the consequences of such a war would be the "Dismemberment of the Empire; that Increase of the National Debt, and of burthensome Taxes; that Loss of our most valuable Resources; those Distresses of our Merchants and Manufacturers; those Deficiencies of the Revenue; that Effusion of the Blood of our Countrymen and Brethren." Besides fearing the consequences of the impending war, the Londoners believed that their fellow subjects in North America, following passage of the American Prohibitory Act of December 22, 1775 (see document 29.2), were in the right: "No People can be bound to surrender their Rights and Liberties as a Return for Protection."

The petitioners pointed out that remarkably, "even now, driven to open Hostilities in their own Defence, they [the North American colonists] are willing (their Charters being inviolably secured) to continue to us all those Advantages of a regular and exclusive Commerce, to which we have long owed our Opulence and Prosperity." In other words, as any number of congressional state papers had declared, the colonists were willing to continue in a dependent commercial relationship with Britain and to allow its economic advantages to persist. Some, like Benjamin Franklin, had even been willing to guarantee these advantages in a new constitutional arrangement (see document 23.4).

Of course, as it had been from the beginning, it was the constitutional arrangements that Parliament and a dutiful but constrained king were unwilling to modify. Thus, the king responded yet again that his subjects in America had brought all the miseries they were suffering "upon themselves by an unjustifiable Resistance to the Constitutional Authority of this Kingdom." The governing constitutional arrangement was the king in Parliament circa 1770—not the pre-1649 English Constitution with the king as head of his personal or Crown dominions, nor the relation of the king to some minor and small Dominions. Robert Morris describes (immediately below) the news of the king's rejection of this petition on the day after it had reached the colonies on June 4 as being, depressingly, the last straw that destroyed, even for the most loyal moderates "all hope of Reconciliation." This was yet another royal document, then, that did so much to move recalcitrant mid-Atlantic moderate delegates, men like the English-born Morris, to accept the need to declare independence from Britain despite all the dangers that a republican government was believed to entail.

*Daily Advertiser* (London), Saturday, March 23, 1776, issue 14,122.

[FRIDAY, MARCH 22, 1776]

To the KING's most excellent Majesty.

Most gracious Soveign,

WE, the Lord Mayor, Aldermen, and Commons of the City of London, in Common Council assembled, beg Leave to approach your Throne, and to intreat your Majesty's Royal Attention, whilst, with the Humility of dutiful Subjects, we lay before your Majesty, what at present most immediately affects us in the Spirit and Tendency of the publick Measures now depending; and the Anxiety we feel at the naked and exposed State in which this Country will be left, by draining it of the national Troops, as well as at the Danger and Disgrace attending the late Treaties for foreign Mercenaries, whose Latitude is such, as to provide the Means of introducing a foreign Army into this Realm.

We cannot, Sir, without Horror, look forward to that Dismemberment of the Empire; that Increase of the National Debt, and of burthensome Taxes; that Loss of our most valuable Resources; those Distresses of our Merchants and Manufacturers; those Deficiencies of the Revenue; that Effusion of the Blood of our Countrymen and Brethren; that Failure of publick Credit, and those dreadful Calamities and Convulsions which must follow a Civil War so begun and pursued, whose Extent no Wisdom can foresee.

We humbly conceive, that no People can be bound to surrender their Rights and Liberties as a Return for Protection. The Colonies have fought our Battles with us; and in the last War, they so far exceeded their Abilities, that this Nation thought it just and necessary to make them an annual Compensation; and even now, driven to open Hostilities in their own Defence, they are willing (their Charters being inviolably secured) to continue to us all those Advantages of a regular and exclusive Commerce, to which we have long owed our Opulence and Prosperity. And we have every Assurance which Men in their Situation can safely give, that, if asked as Freemen, they are willing to go farther, and to afford to the exhausted State of the Revenue of this Country, such reasonable voluntary Aid as their Abilities permit, provided that their Contributions are unalienably applied to relieve that Distress, which is the only fair and politick Foundation of requiring them, and that neither their Aids, nor our own Sinking Funds, shall be any longer perverted from a publick Benefit, and misapplied to the Purpose of Corruption, instead of redeeming the Debts of the Nation, according to the first wise and just Institution.

Indulge but, most gracious Sovereign, the Humanity and Benignity of your own Royal Disposition, and our Prayers will be granted. We implore the Extension of your Majesty's Justice and Mercy towards that Continent which, when Arbiter of the Terms of Peace, it was your Majesty's own Determination to prefer to every other Compensation, for all the Expences of the last War.

We humbly and earnestly beseech your Majesty, that the most solemn, clear, distinct and unambiguous Specification, of those just and honourable Terms, which your Majesty, with both Houses of Parliament, mean to grant to the Colonies, may precede the dreadful Operations of your Armament. Every Colour and Suspicion of Injustice and Oppression will then be removed from the Proceedings of the Mother Country; and, if those just and honourable Terms are not submitted to, your Majesty will undoubtedly be enabled to meet, what will then be Rebellion, with the zealous Hearts and Hands of a determined, loyal, and united People.

His Majesty was pleased to return an Answer to the following Purport:

I deplore, with the deepest Concern, the Miseries which a great Part of my Subjects in America have brought upon themselves by an unjustifiable Resistance to the Constitutional Authority of this Kingdom; and I shall be ready and happy to alleviate those Miseries by Acts of Mercy and Clemency, whenever that Authority shall be established, and the now existing Rebellion at an End: To obtain these salutary Purposes, I will invariably pursue the most proper and effectual Means.

## 32.4

 ROBERT MORRIS TO SILAS DEANE, JUNE 5, 1776

Silas Deane, a former Connecticut congressional delegate who was sent to Paris in March to serve as an American agent, wrote from Bermuda on April 26, 1776, recommending that the colonies send privateers to Bermuda to disrupt the British West Indian trade. He wrote to Robert Morris of Pennsylvania, who was a member of the Secret Committee, Secret Correspondence Committee, and Marine Committee. Little, ultimately, came from his suggestion.[82] Morris gently rebuked Deane for including in the same letter business and political matters—although Morris probably knew better than most that in practice they were hard to separate—before turning to politics. He noted that the divisions in Congress and Pennsylvania were as deep as ever, but that "the King has put an effectual stop to those divisions by his Answer to an Address of the Ld Mayor & Aldermen &c the [22] of March, as His Majesty has there totally destroyed all hope of Reconciliation." News of that had arrived only the day before. He pointed out that the colonies had finally been pushed too far: "Great Britain may thank herself for this Event, for whatever might have been the original designs of some Men in promoting the present Contest I am sure that America in general never set out with any View or desire of establishing an Independant Empire. They have been drove into it step by step." Morris was not alone in believing that the majority of the delegates in Congress had never wanted the colonies to separate from the British king and Empire, but had been driven to it by the ever-more aggressive and ill-advised policies of the Crown and Parliament.

Indeed, the actions of the king, Morris argued, had also shaped the struggles inside the colonies regarding who would rule at home. He reminded Deane that the upcoming political fight would concern the new provincial governments: "The necessity of assuming new Governments has been pretty evident for sometime and the Contest is who shall form them & who upon such a Change shall come in for the Power. The divisions woud probably have run very high particularly in this Province, had not His Majesty determined so peremptorily that there can be no reconciliation but through the door of abject Submission."

Also of significance was the importance that Americans attached to the king's hiring of mercenaries—"the Numerous hosts of Foes that are coming to Slaughter us, especially your Hessians, Hanoverians, Waldeckers &c." That perceived betrayal alienated even as conservative a man as Morris, who refused, on July 2, to vote for independence and absented himself on July 4 from the vote on what effectively was the Declaration's preamble. Morris, though, unlike Dickinson, did decide to sign the Declaration of Independence sometime after August 2, 1776, when the engrossed (that is, the final certified) version was first available for signing.[83]

Paul H. Smith, ed., *Letters of Delegates to Congress, 1774–1789* (Washington, D.C.: Library of Congress, 1976–93), 4:146–49.

Dr. Sir, Philada. June 5th. 1776

I had great satisfaction in receiving your favours of the 26th April & 3d May from B[ermuda] as I think there was little risque in the rest of your Voyage & I flatter myself you have arrived safe previous to this date.

I extracted from your letter of the 26th all the parts that related to the Public & laid them before Congress. Those extracts are Committed but no report is yet brought in. I am on the Committee and we are to meet tomorrow morning but whether they will determine to benefit by your usefull hints or not I cannot yet tell.

You have mixed business & Politics in your letter which is a bad example and I must try to avoid it, therefore this letter must be Confined to the latter.

This goes by Wm Bingham Esqr. a Young Gentln who has for sometime acted as Secretary to the Committee of Secret Correspondence. He carrys with him triplicates of your Credentials & instructions, the Duplicates went by another Conveyance and each of these as well as yourself having an exceeding good Chance to arrive safe I think it needless to send you any more. Mr Bingham now goes out to Martinico in order to procure some Arms from the Governor & with another view that I need not mention as he will write to you. You can send advices under Cover to him but you'l remember he is a *Young* tho' a Worthy Young Man. The papers he carrys will give you the Public News, the worst part of which is an appearance of great division amongst ourselves especially in this Province; however I believe the King has put an effectual stop to those divisions by his Answer to an Address of the Ld Mayor & Aldermen &c the [22] of March, as His Majesty has there totally destroyed all hope of Reconciliation. I confess I never lost hopes of reconciliation untill I saw this Answer which in my opinion breaths nothing but Death & Destruction. Every body see it in the same light and it will bring us all to one way of thinking, so that you may soon expect to hear of New Governments in every Colony and in Conclusion a declaration of Independancy by Congress. I see this step is inevitable and you may depend it will soon take place. Great Britain may thank herself for this Event, for whatever might have been the original designs of some Men in promoting the present Contest I am sure that America in general never set out with any View or desire of establishing an Independant Empire. They have been drove into it step by step with a reluctance on their part that has been manifested in all their proceedings, & yet I dare say our Enemies will assert that it was planned from the first movements. The Dogs of Warr are now fairly let loose upon us. We are not dismayed but expect to give a good Account of the Numerous hosts of Foes that are coming to Slaughter us, especially your Hessians, Hanoverians, Waldeckers &c. Our Climates will most probably handle them pretty severely before they get seasoned and our Troops are pretty well prepared for their reception but the Fortune of Warr being ever uncertain God only knows what may be the Event.

Our affairs in Canada have been badly managed by Your Countryman Genl Worster but I hope Genl. Thomas & your Friend Arnold will invigorate them. However I dont think we have any occasion to hold that Country, if we maintain the passes on the Lakes it is sufficient for our purposes and the Garrison that defend those passes will always be ready to rush into Canada if the Enemy quit it, so that a good Force well posted for this purpose may keep Mr. Burgoyne with his 10,000 men uselessly employed the whole year without any expence of ammunition or loss of Men on our side unless they attack exceedingly to their own disadvantage. Genl. Washington has taken post at New York. He has lately been here attended by Genl. Gates & Genl. Mifflin and the plan of operations has been fully settled in several Conferences between them & a Committee of Congress appointed for that purpose & in Consequence of the arrangements made we shall have not less than 30,000 men ready to take the Field, so divided & posted as to oppose the Enemys attacks wherever made.

Genl. Lee commands to the Southward and I fancy that department will be well defended. We are to have a flying Camp of 10,000 men here the Commander of which is not yet named. Genl. Washington at New York, Gates at Boston, Thomas in Canada & each of these are well supported by able General officers and we hope a Sufficient number of Troops. We are better supplyd with Powder than formerly; our Mills make it fast & some of the Colonies have had great success in making Salt Petre. Arms we are most in Want of, but our manufactorys of them improve & increase daily. In short it appears to me We shall be able to baffle all attempts of our Enemy, if we do but preserve Union amongst ourselves. I dont mean the Union of the Colonies, but union in each Colony. The former is safely fixed on a broad & firm basis, the latter had been greatly threatned. The necessity of assuming new Governments has been pretty evident for sometime and the Contest is who shall form them & who upon such a Change shall come in for the Power. The divisions woud probably have run very high particularly in this Province, had not His Majesty determined so peremptorily that there can be no reconciliation but through the door of abject Submission. This seems to bend all mens minds one way and I have no doubt but Harmony will be restored & our united efforts exerted to defend our Country & its freedom in which God grant Success to an injured & oppressed People. . . .

## 32.5

 EDWARD RUTLEDGE TO JOHN JAY, JUNE 8, 1776

Edward Rutledge, the young (at twenty-seven, the youngest to sign the Declaration, whose passage he tried so hard to confound), wealthy, and influential lawyer from South Carolina, had, surprisingly, found a group in Congress with whom he found himself at ease and with whom he shared political principles—the moderate, wealthy, and mostly young lawyers, landowners, and merchants of the New York delegation. Thus, we find Rutledge writing here to one of the most prominent members of that group, John Jay, who, like Rutledge, little supported independence, yet went on to become, among a number of posts, the first chief justice of the U.S. Supreme Court. His letter focuses on the debate in Congress on whether to approve Richard Henry Lee's three proposals respecting independence.

In Rutledge's opinion, "the Sensible part of the House opposed the [first] Motion": "They saw no Wisdom in a *Declaration* of Independence, nor any other Purpose to be answer'd by it, but placing ourselves in the Power of those with whom we mean to treat . . . [and] rendering ourselves ridiculous in the Eyes of foreign Powers." The second and third resolutions were unobjectionable: "They had no Objection to forming a Scheme of a Treaty which they would send to France by proper Persons, & a uniting this Continent by a Confederacy."

In case there was any confusion regarding whom Rutledge did not include among Congress's sensible members, he made the distinction explicit: "A Man must have the Impudence of a New Englander to propose in our present disjointed State any Treaty (honourable to us) to a Nation now at Peace. No Reason culd be assigned for pressing into this Measure, but the Reason of every Madman, a Shew of our Spirit." Along with other men of moderation—James Wilson, Robert R. Livingston, and John Dickinson—Rutledge was able to delay the vote on Lee's resolutions until Monday, June 10, when the vote was postponed for another three weeks. Not surprisingly, pushing against any delay were "the Powers of all N. England, Virginia & Georgia."

Georgia's emergence as one of the pro-independence factions in this debate deserves some comment. Its two delegates in attendance at the time, Button Gwinnett and Lyman Hall, had arrived to take their seats in Congress only a few weeks earlier, on May 20, 1776. Three other delegates had departed in November 1775, leaving Georgia without representation in the Second Continental Congress for nearly six months. Because of widespread opposition in the colony to those support-ing the actions of Congress, Georgia had not sent an official delegation to any of the proceedings of the First Continental Congress in the fall of 1774. One of the new delegates, Gwinnett, was born in England and had traded with the American colonies before emigrating in the mid-1760s. His commercial ventures were almost all failures, but he was successful in representing, along with Hall, a large number of transplanted New Englanders living in Georgia.[84] That partiality, however, greatly limited his political success elsewhere in the colony.

Hall too was a man with a troubled past and ties to New England. A minister and physician from Connecticut who had been dismissed by his congregation on charges of immorality, he moved to South Carolina to live among a group of New Englanders before settling in a New England enclave in Sunbury, Georgia, in St. John's Parish. That group elected him in March 1775 its unofficial delegate to Congress. He was, thus, an observer in Congress for much of the summer of 1775. When Georgia was finally persuaded, during the same summer, to join the other twelve continental colonies in opposing Great Britain's policies, Hall was elected one of its official delegates. He returned to Congress with Gwinnett on May 20. With their strong New England ties and a measure of English radicalism, Hall and Gwinnett supported Congress' move toward independence, while most in the colony were far more reluctant to do so.[85]

Paul H. Smith, ed., *Letters of Delegates to Congress, 1774–1789* (Washington, D.C.: Library of Congress, 1976–93), 4:174–75.

My dear Jay                                    Saturday Evg 10 o'clock [June 8, 1776]

I am much obliged to you for your Introduction of Mr. Merckle—he will tell you what has been done in Consequence of it. I have shown him all the Civility in my Power. I fear in the present Situation of Affairs we will not be able to give the Dutch much Security as will induce so cautious a Power to part with that which they consider the first Blessing. The Congress sat till 7 o'clock this Evening in Consequence of a Mo-tion of R. H. Lee's resolving ourselves free & independent States. The Sensible part of the House opposed the Motion. They had no Objection to forming a Scheme of a

Treaty which they would send to France by proper Persons, & a uniting this Continent by a Confederacy. They saw no Wisdom in a *Declaration* of Independence, nor any other Purpose to be answer'd by it, but placing ourselves in the Power of those with whom we mean to treat, giving our Enemy Notice of our Intentions before we had taken any Steps to execute them & there by enabling them to counteract us in our Intentions & rendering ourselves ridiculous in the Eyes of foreign Powers by attempting to bring them into an Union with us before we had united with each other. For daily experience evinces that the Inhabitants of every Colony consider themselves at Liberty to do as they please upon almost every occasion. And a Man must have the Impudence of a New Englander to propose in our present disjointed State any Treaty (honourable to us) to a Nation now at Peace. No Reason culd be assigned for pressing into this Measure, but the Reason of every Madman, a Shew of our Spirit. The Event however was that the Question was postponed. It is to be renewed on Monday when I mean to move that it should be postponed for 3 Weeks or a Month. In the mean Time the plan of Confederation & the Scheme of Treaty may go on. I don't know whether I shall suceed in this Motion; *I think not,* it is at least Doubtful. However I must do what is right in my own Eyes & Consequences must take Care of themselves. I wish you had been here. The whole Argument was sustained on one side by R. Livingston, Wilson, Dickenson & myself, & by the Powers of all N. England, Virginia & Georgia on the other. Remember me to Morris affectionately. I wuld have wrote to him, but did not know of this Conveyance until a few Minutes ago, & am as you will see by this incorrect Letter too fatigued to hold my Pen any longer than whilst I tell you how sir truely I esteem & love you. Yours Affect,

E. Rutledge

32.6

 THE MARYLAND DELEGATES TO THE MARYLAND
COUNCIL OF SAFETY, JUNE 11, 1776

Here, Thomas Stone writes on behalf of the Maryland delegation then present in Congress, which included John Rogers and Matthew Tilghman. Stone and Rogers were both lawyers who only reluctantly came to support independence, while Tilghman, born into a wealthy planter family, withdrew from Congress three days after signing this letter and did not return. The three of them had withdrawn from Congress on May 16 in protest against the preamble to Congress' recommendation of May 10, returning only on May 24. Three other delegates, Robert Alexander, Robert Goldsborough, and Thomas Johnson, had withdrawn from Congress on May 15 or 16, and only Johnson returned, but not until September 16.

In early June, Maryland's most radical delegate, Samuel Chase, was on a congressional mission of inquiry to Canada, which stretched from March 25 to June 11. Upon his return, after a few days in Congress, he traveled around Maryland with William Paca and Charles Carroll (a Roman Catholic from Carrollton) to build support for Congress' present and future actions. William Paca, as part of Maryland's changing congressional delegation, took his seat on June 15, as Carroll did on July 17. Paca was a successful British-trained lawyer and a fervent defender of colonial rights. Interestingly, Carroll, a lawyer, landowner, and planter, was likely one of the wealthiest men in the colonies, and in spite of Maryland's long-standing (but now overlooked) prohibition against Catholics holding political office, served in Congress and signed the Declaration of Independence—in fact, he was the only Catholic to do so.

When the Maryland Convention issued instructions on June 28 allowing its delegates to vote for independence, it did so because its members were "far more worried about threats to the internal stability of the colony than they were about the implications of independence from Britain." They had reason to be: "The convention spent most of 28 June, not in debating independence but in making plans to send troops to the eastern shore to suppress a threatened rebellion against the planters by poor whites, slaves, and loyalists."[86] Clearly, as recognized by proponents and opponents, the congressional recommendation (with preamble) of May 15 and Lee's first resolution had, as the radicals intended, forced moderates' attention from concerns about British rule to who was to rule at home.[87]

Stone explains that the final vote on independence was delayed for three weeks so that "the Delegates from those Colonies, which had not as yet given Authority to adopt this decisive Measure, [could] consult their Constituents"; Maryland was in that group. By mid-May, all the southern colonies had either positively instructed their delegates to vote with the others for independence or, as in the case of Georgia, had left their delegates (upon their return to Congress on May 20) free to act as they saw fit.[88] Possibly reflecting difficult-to-uncover divisions in the New England colonies, only tiny Rhode Island had committed its delegates by the time of Stone's writing to voting for independence.[89] Of much greater concern, none of the mid-Atlantic colonies had by the time of his writing either withdrawn instructions to vote against independence or issued new instructions to vote for it. Much, however, changed in the next five or six weeks. The first of the mid-Atlantic colonies to act was Pennsylvania, which withdrew on June 14 its April 6 instructions against voting for independence. Maryland changed its delegates' instructions on June 28. By July 1, the rest, with the exception of New York, had changed their instructions and their delegations.

Stone, in advance of this change, laments that the much-anticipated British peace commissioners were unlikely, whenever they arrived, to be able to end the conflict. Still, with such hopes in mind, the Maryland delegates had been instructed, as late as May 21, not to vote for independence. Only the congressional vote on June 10 and the pending one on July 1 forced the Maryland Convention, in an effort to keep control of its own provincial political affairs, to rescind its earlier instructions and allow its delegates to vote for independence.

We learn from Stone that the question whether to postpone the vote on independence "was carried seven Colonies against five"—with New England and Virginia likely being the colonies voting against any delay. By then, the only weapon that the moderate delegates of New York, New Jersey, Pennsylvania, Delaware, Maryland, and South Carolina had left was the threat of walking out of Congress, as Maryland's delegates had done on May 16.[90]

Paul H. Smith, ed., *Letters of Delegates to Congress, 1774–1789* (Washington, D.C.: Library of Congress, 1976–93), 4:192–94.

Gentlemen.                                                                Phila. June 11th. 1776. Tuesday
... The Proposition from the Delegates of Virginia to declare the Colonies independent was yesterday after much Debate postponed for three Weeks, then to be resumed, and a Committee is appointed to draw up a Declaration to prevent Loss of time in Case the Congress should agree to the Proposition at the day fixed for resuming it. This postpone was made to give an Oppertunity to the Delegates from those Colonies, which had not as yet given Authority to adopt this decisive Measure, to consult their Constituents; it will be necessary that the Convention of Maryland should meet as soon as possible to give the explicit Sense of the Province on this Point. And we hope you will accordingly exercise your Power of convening them at such Time as you think the members can be brought together. We wish to have the fair and uninfluenced Sense of the People we have the Honour to represent in this most important and interesting Affair And think it would be well if the Delegates to Convention were desired to endeavour to collect the opinion of the people at large in some Manner or other previous to the Meeting of Convention. We shall attend the Convention whenever it meets if it is thought proper we should do so. The approaching Harvest will perhaps render it very inconvenient to many Gentlemen to attend the Convention; This however must not be regarded when matters of such momentous Concern demand their deliberation. We beg you will inform Us as soon as may be of the Time you fix for the Convention to meet, and We should also be very glad to receive the Proceedings of the last session. We see with the deepest Concern the Attempts from various Quarters to throw the Province into a State of Confusion, Division & Disorder but trust the Exertions of those who are the true friends of Virtue & the American Cause will be adequate to the surrounding Difficulties & Dangers. From every Account and Appearance the King and his Ministers seem determined to hazard every thing upon the Success of the Sword; with out offering any Terms to America which she ought to accept. That Peace & Security which every virtu-

ous man in this Country has so earnestly desired seems not attainable in the present disposition of the ruling powers of Britain. We wish we had any reason to suppose there was any foundation for what Mr Smith reports to have been told him by Capt Hammond & Ld Dunmore, but all Circumstances strongly oppose the Supposition of Commissioners, as Messengers of Peace. However we know not more of this matter than you & the publick do and it is impossible to speak certainly upon this or any other Subject without more full Information than we have. We will send the Gun Carriage, Instruments & paper by Mr Steward who informs us he has sundry Articles for the Province to be sent from hence. We begg to be informed frequently of the State of the Province and of your Proceedings: And assure you of our readiness to attend your Commands. Our hurry and necessary Attendance in Congress must apologize for this Scrawl. The Question for postponing the Declaration of Independence was carried by seven Colonies against five. We are with great Respect, Gent., Yr most Obt Sevts.

Mat. Tilghman

T. Stone

J. Rogers

## 32.7

 THOMAS JEFFERSON, NOTES OF PROCEEDINGS IN CONGRESS, JUNE 7–28, 1776

Thomas Jefferson, having returned to Congress on May 14, provided rich notes of the June and July congressional debates on independence (see as well documents 33.5 and 34.2).[91] As had been the case since the beginning of the First Continental Congress in September 1774, the delegates remained split, in the main, between moderates from the mid-Atlantic colonies and most of the South Carolina delegation, and radical delegates from New England and Virginia. Jefferson records on June 8 that James Wilson of Pennsylvania, Robert R. Livingston of New York, Edward Rutledge of South Carolina, and John Dickinson of Pennsylvania were the principal speakers against independence, for although "they were friends to the measures themselves, and saw the impossibility that we should ever again be united with Gr. Britain, yet they were against adopting them at this time." John Adams of Massachusetts, with Richard Henry Lee and George Wythe of Virginia, argued for an immediate declaration of independence. They forcefully pointed out "that no gentleman had argued against the policy or the right of separation from Britain, nor had supposed it possible we should ever renew our connection: that they had only opposed it's being now declared."

The opponents of declaring independence argued, accurately, that "the people of the middle colonies (Maryland, Delaware, Pennsylva., the Jersies & N. York) were not yet ripe for bidding adieu to British connection but that they were fast ripening & . . . that the resolution entered into by this house on the 15th of May for suppressing the exercise of all powers derived from the crown, had shewn . . . that they had not yet accomodated their minds to a separation from the mother country." They made clear, too, that as of June 7 none of the mid-Atlantic delegations had been permitted by their provincial assemblies to vote for independence, and if forced to do so before receiving new instructions, "these delegates must (*now*) retire & possibly their colonies might secede from the Union." Finally, these men were less sanguine than their opponents about the salutary consequences of forming alliances with France and Spain. Congressional moderates imagined that unless great care were exercised, France and Spain might look as favorably on partitioning North America with the British as on supporting the colonies in their rebellion.

Those impatient to declare independence, however, were not easily dissuaded. They reminded their colleagues that as for the "parliament of England, we had alwais been independant of them, their restraints on our trade deriving efficacy from our acquiescence only," and "that as to the king, we had been bound to him by allegiance, but that this bond was now dissolved by his assent to the late act of parliament, by which he declares us out of his protection . . . [with] it being a certain position in law that allegiance & protection are reciprocal, the one ceasing when the other is withdrawn." Thus, the colonists, somewhat like the people of England under James II, who had never declared "the people of England out of his protection yet his actions proved it," were now freed from their duty of allegiance. Offering sobering testimony of the king's intransigence was, again, his response of March 22 to the lord mayor of London, "which had come to hand four days ago," that is, June 4. Those arguing for independence were confident that the average residents of the middle colonies, in contrast with their congressional delegates and provincial governments, were ready to declare independence, and even if they weren't, "the people wait for us to lead the way." The continued hostility of the people of Pennsylvania, Delaware, and Maryland to continental goals, and the lack of support they provided the Continental Army—for example, during its encampment in Valley Forge during the winter of 1777–78—suggest that Jefferson and his independence-favoring colleagues may have too sanguine in their expectations.

Possibly the most important question and matter of debate was whether, without the colonies first declaring independence, European powers would provide them with support. Unbeknownst to the delegates in Congress, on May 2 the French had decided to support the colonists in their drive toward independence. In the end, the advocates for a quick declaration of independence believed "that the colonies of N. York, New Jersey, Pennsylvania, Delaware, Maryland & South Carolina were not yet matured for falling from the parent stem, but that they were fast advancing to that state, it was thought most prudent to wait a while for them, and to postpone the final decision to July 1." Jefferson closes by recording that on the last day of his notes, June 28, he laid before Congress the committee's draft Declaration of Independence.

Paul H. Smith, ed., *Letters of Delegates to Congress, 1774–1789* (Washington, D.C.: Library of Congress, 1976–93), 4:158–65. Material in parentheses was crossed out in the manuscript version but later restored.

In Congress. [June 7–28, 1776]

Friday June 7. 1776. The Delegates from Virginia moved in obedience to instructions from their constituents that the Congress should declare that these United colonies are & of right ought to be free & independant states, that they are absolved from all allegiance to the British crown, and that all political connection between them and the state of Great Britain is & ought to be totally dissolved; that measures should be immediately taken for procuring the assistance of foreign powers, and a Confederation be formed to bind the colonies more closely together.

The house being obliged to attend at that time to some other business, the proposition was referred to the next day when the members were ordered to attend punctually at ten o'clock.

Saturday June 8. They proceeded to take it into consideration and referred it to a committee of the whole, into which they immediately resolved themselves, and passed that day & Monday the 10th in debating on the subject.

It was argued by Wilson, Robert R. Livingston, E. Rutlege, Dickinson and others

That tho' they were friends to the measures themselves, and saw the impossibility that we should ever again be united with Gr. Britain, yet they were against adopting them at this time:

That the conduct we had formerly observed was wise & proper now, of deferring to take any capital step till the voice of the people drove us into it:

That they were our power, & without them our declarations could not be carried into effect:

That the people of the middle colonies (Maryland, Delaware, Pennsylva., the Jersies & N. York) were not yet ripe for bidding adieu to British connection but that they were fast ripening & in a short time would join in the general voice of America:

That the resolution entered into by this house on the 15th of May for suppressing the exercise of all powers derived from the crown, had shewn, by the ferment into which it had thrown these middle colonies, that they had not yet accomodated their minds to a separation from the mother country:

That some of them had expressly forbidden their delegates to consent to such a declaration, and others had given no instructions, & consequently no powers to give such consent:

That if the delegates of any particular colony had no power to declare such colony independant, certain they were the others could not declare it for them; the colonies being as yet perfectly independant of each other:

That the assembly of Pennsylvania was now sitting above stairs, their convention would sit within a few days, the convention of New York was now sitting, & those of the Jersies & Delaware counties would meet on the Monday following & it was probable these bodies would take up the question of Independance & would declare to their delegates the voice of their state:

That if such a declaration should now be agreed to, these delegates must (*now*) retire & possibly their colonies might secede from the Union:

That such a secession would weaken us more than could be compensated by any foreign alliance:

That in the event of such a division, foreign powers would either refuse to join themselves to our fortunes, or having us so much in their power as that desperate declaration would place us, they would insist on terms proportionably more hard & prejudicial:

That we had little reason to expect an alliance with those to whom alone as yet we had cast our eyes:

That France & Spain had reason to be jealous of that rising power which would one day certainly strip them of all their American possessions:

That it was more likely they should form a connection with the British court, who, if they should find themselves unable otherwise to extricate themselves from their difficulties, would agree to a partition of our territories, restoring Canada to France, & the Floridas to Spain, to accomplish for themselves a recovery of these colonies:

That it would not be long before we should receive certain information of the disposition of the French court, from the agent whom we had sent to Paris for that purpose:

That if this disposition should be favourable, by waiting the event of the present campaign, which we all hoped would be succesful, we should have reason to expect an alliance on better terms:

That this would in fact work no delay of any effectual aid from such ally, as, from the advance of the season & distance of our situation, it was impossible we could receive any assistance during this campaign:

That it was prudent to fix among ourselves the terms on which we would form alliance, before we declared we would form one at all events:

And that if these were agreed on & our Declaration of Independence ready by the time our Ambassadour should be prepared to sail, it would be as well, as to go into that Declaration at this day.

On the other side it was urged by J. Adams, Lee, Wythe and others

That no gentleman had argued against the policy or the right of separation from Britain, nor had supposed it possible we should ever renew our connection: that they had only opposed it's being now declared:

That the question was not whether, by a declaration of independance, we should make ourselves what we are not; but whether we should declare a fact which already exists:

That as to the people or parliament of England, we had alwais been independant of them, their restraints on our trade deriving efficacy from our acquiescence only & not from any rights they possessed of imposing them, & that so far our connection had been federal only, & was now dissolved by the commencement of hostilities:

That as to the king, we had been bound to him by allegiance, but that this bond was now dissolved by his assent to the late act of parliament, by which he declares us out of his protection, and by his levying war on us, a fact which had long ago proved us out of his protection; it being a certain position in law that allegiance & protection are reciprocal, the one ceasing when the other is withdrawn:

That James the IId never declared the people of England out of his protection yet his actions proved it & the parliament declared it:

No delegates then can be denied, or ever want, a power of declaring an existent truth:

That the delegates from the Delaware counties having declared their constituents ready to join, there are only two colonies Pennsylvania & Maryland whose delegates are absolutely tied up, and that these had by their instructions only reserved a right of confirming or rejecting the measure:

That the instructions from Pennsylvania might be accounted for from the times in which they were drawn, near a twelvemonth ago, since which the face of affairs has totally changed:

That within that time it had become apparent that Britain was determined to accept nothing less than a carte blanche, and that the king's answer to the Lord Mayor, Aldermen & common council of London, which had come to hand four days ago, must have satisfied every one of this point:

That the people wait for us to lead the way (*in this step*):

That *they* are in favour of the measure, tho' the instructions given by some of their *representatives* are not:

That the voice of the representatives is not alwais consonant with the voice of the people, and that this is remarkeably the case in these middle colonies:

That the effect of the resolution of the 15th of May has proved this, which, raising the murmurs of some in the colonies of Pennsylvania & Maryland, called forth the opposing voice of the freer part of the people, & proved them to be the majority, even in these colonies:

That the backwardness of these two colonies might be ascribed partly to the influence of proprietary power & connections, & partly to their having not yet been attacked by the enemy:

That these causes were not likely to be soon removed, as there seemed no probability that the enemy would make either of these the seat of this summer's war:

That it would be vain to wait either weeks or months for perfect unanimity, since it was impossible that all men should ever become of one sentiment on any question:

That the conduct of some colonies from the beginning of this contest, had given reason to suspect it was their settled policy to keep in the rear of the confederacy, that their particular prospect might be better even in the worst event:

That therefore it was necessary for those colonies who had thrown themselves forward & hazarded all from the beginning, to come forward now also, and put all again to their own hazard:

That the history of the Dutch revolution, of whom three states only confederated at first proved that a secession of some colonies would not be so dangerous as some apprehended:

That a declaration of Independence alone could render it consistent with European delicacy for European powers to treat with us, or even to receive an Ambassador from us:

That till this they would not receive our vessels into their ports, nor acknowlege the adjudications of our courts of Admiralty to be legitimate, in cases of capture of British vessels:

That tho' France & Spain may be jealous of our rising power, they must think it will be much more formidable with the addition of Great Britain; and will therefore see it their interest to prevent a coalition; but should they refuse, we shall be but where we are; whereas without trying we shall never know whether they will aid us or not:

That the present campaign may be unsuccessful, & therefore we had better propose an alliance while our affairs wear a hopeful aspect:

That to wait the event of this campaign will certainly work delay, because during this summer France may assist us effectually by cutting off those supplies of provisions from England & Ireland on which the enemy's armies here are to depend; or by setting in motion the great power they have collected in the West Indies, & calling our enemy to the defence of the possessions they have there:

That it would be idle to lose time in settling the terms of alliance, till we had first determined we would enter into alliance:

That it is necessary to lose no time in opening a trade for our people, who will want clothes, and will want money too for the paiment of taxes:

And that the only misfortune is that we did not enter into alliance with France six months sooner, as besides opening their ports for the vent of our last year's produce, they might have marched an army into Germany and prevented the petty princes there from selling their unhappy subjects to subdue us.

It appearing in the course of these debates that the colonies of N. York, New Jersey, Pennsylvania, Delaware, Maryland & South Carolina were not yet matured for falling from the parent stem, but that they were fast advancing to that state, it was thought most prudent to wait a while for them, and to postpone the final decision to July 1. but that this might occasion as little delay as possible, a committee was appointed to prepare a declaration of independence. the Commee. were J. Adams, Dr. Franklin, Roger Sherman, Robert R. Livingston & myself. committees were also appointed at the same time to prepare a plan of confederation for the colonies, and to state the terms proper to be proposed for foreign alliance. the committee for drawing the Declaration of Independance desired me to do it. (*I did so*) it was accordingly done and being approved by them, I reported it to the house on Friday the 28th of June when it was read and ordered to lie on the table.

## 33. INDEPENDENCE IS DECLARED, JULY 1776

On June 8, Pennsylvania withdrew its earlier instructions against voting for independence and replaced them on June 14 with a positive decree to do so, becoming the first mid-Atlantic colony to make this change. The reversal took place against a background in which the legally elected government of May 1 had been effectively overthrown by Philadelphia radicals with the considerable support of congressional ones, in particular the Adams cousins.[92] Delaware agreed on June 15 to allow its delegates to work with others in promoting "'the liberty, safety, and interests of America,'" without ever mentioning the word "independence." New Jersey acted next, on June 23. The election of a new provincial congress there on June 10 led to the eviction of the colony's royal governor, William Franklin, and then, on June 21, to his arrest. Afterward, a new slate of congressional delegates was elected and given fresh instructions to vote for independence. Next to act was Maryland. It changed its delegates' instructions on June 28. The last colony to do so was New York; its convention waited until July 9. These momentous changes all took place within a span of five weeks. During that time, all the mid-Atlantic governments had been challenged domestically (in ways often orchestrated or supported by congressional separatists) in ways that pushed them toward, in many cases, a grudging endorsement of independence.

Thus, on July 1, Congress read a resolution of June 28 from the Maryland Convention, instructing its delegates "to concur with the other United Colonies, or a Majority of them, in declaring the United Colonies free and independent States," yet also reminding Congress, as every colony had done, that "the sole and exclusive Right of regulating the internal Government and Police of this Colony be reserved to the People thereof." Congress then resolved "itself into a committee of the whole, to take into consideration the resolution respecting independency," and while so sitting, was read a letter of June 11 from the Provincial Congress of New York in which it explained that its delegates were not permitted to vote for independence. Next, the drafting committee's June 28 declaration of independence—this refers to Jefferson's celebrated explanatory preamble, not Lee's resolution declaring independence—was "referred to said committee," that is, the committee of the whole, which then began consideration of the resolution concerning independence and Jefferson's much longer draft statement of explanation.[93]

Congress, while sitting as a committee of the whole on July 1, considered Lee's first resolution, which declared the colonies independent of Great Britain. The committee's chairman, Benjamin Harrison, reported that it had "agreed to the resolution, which they ordered him to report." As John Adams notes, in the committee of the whole "the Question was carried in the affirmative, and reported to the House."[94] More exactly, Lee's resolution regarding independence was supported by nine colonies and opposed by two, Pennsylvania and South Carolina; Delaware was divided (McKean yes, Read no); and the New York delegation abstained because of its instructions. At the request of South Carolina's Edward Rutledge, a final vote in Congress meeting in regular session (with more formal and restrictive rules of voting, debate, and recording in the *Journal* than occurred when the body met as a committee of the whole) on the resolution was postponed, but only for one day: "He and his colleagues of the South Carolina delegation were opposed to Lee's resolution, but he believed that they 'would join in it for the sake of unanimity.'"[95]

On July 2, Congress voted 12–0 in favor of Lee's resolution declaring the American colonies independent states. South Carolina changed its vote to yes; a third Delaware delegate, Caesar Rodney, suffering from cancer of the face, had ridden overnight by post to break the tie in that three-person delegation; and the Pennsylvania delegation, with the last-minute decision of Wilson to support independence and with two of its members, John Dickinson and Robert Morris, either physically absent or abstaining— the few accounts that exist differ about the date(s) on which they failed to vote on particular measures—voted 3–2 for independence.[96] Congress then resolved again to sit as a committee of the whole in order "to take into their farther consideration" the measure referred to it the day before, that is, the Declaration of Independence. As Congress had done with its recommendation to the United Colonies of May 10 and 15, 1776 (see document 31.1), it debated then placed an explanatory preamble at the head of Lee's resolution for independence.

On July 3 and 4, Congress sat in a committee of the whole to consider Jefferson's draft Declaration of June 28. It did so until the committee chairman, the moderate Virginian Benjamin Harrison, reported to Congress sitting in normal session "that the committee of the whole Congress have agreed to a Declaration, which he delivered in." After one last reading, the Declaration was agreed to by twelve colonies, with none opposing and New York again abstaining. With its passage, Congress "solved" one of the two fundamental constitutional challenges that had confronted the colonies since the beginning of the Imperial Crisis in 1764, namely, the nature of their constitutional relationship to Great Britain: there would be none.

The second constitutional quandary, the proper relationship between the new states and a continent-level government, was being debated in another committee appointed on June 12. The document that tried to define and describe that relationship was the Articles of Confederation and Perpetual Union. A draft written by John Dickinson, who had left Congress after failing to delay passage of the Declaration of Independence, was delivered on July 12 (see document 34.1). On November 15, 1777, some sixteen months later, Congress finally approved the first plan of government, which—when ratified—created a United States of America rather than united states in Congress. The articles were sent to the states for ratification, which occurred nearly four years later on March 1, 1781. This first federal plan of union, at least in the minds of many, did not really resolve the second constitutional issue—its resolution had to wait until 1787, or even 1865.

On July 15, Congress received notice from the New York Convention that on July 9 it had decided "that the reasons assigned by the Continental Congress for declaring the United Colonies Free and Independent States are cogent and conclusive; and, that while we lament the cruel necessity which has rendered that measure unavoidable, we approve of the same." Accordingly, on July 19, Congress ordered the now unanimously approved Declaration be put on parchment, and then, on August 2, "the declaration of independence being engrossed and compared at the table was signed [by the members]."[97] Some number of delegates signed that day, including many who had not been present on July 4 to vote for it—for "a fourth of the members whose names appear [on the signed Declaration] were not present on that day, some of them not even being members at that time."[98] One delegate, George Read of Delaware, voted against the Declaration of Independence but was later allowed to sign it (others who absented themselves in order to avoid voting against it also later signed it).[99] More delegates added their names during the fall, and "finally, on January 18, 1777, the Continental Congress authorized the printing of the Declaration of Independence, this time with the names of the signers included, although the fifty-sixth signature, that of Thomas McKean, had not yet been affixed by that date and would be added later," sometime in 1781.[100]

The Declaration begins by explaining the reason for its existence: one people had dissolved "the Political Bands which have connected them with another,"[101] in order "to assume, among the Powers of the earth, the separate and equal station to which the Laws of Nature and of Nature's God entitle them."[102] The break was necessary, Congress explains, because no other means had proved successful in achieving the end for which they had been contending from the beginning of the crisis in 1764: an equal status for the American people with the king's subjects in his realm. Congress was making this news public because "a decent respect to the opinions of mankind requires that they should declare the causes which impel them to the separation." With the new states' great need for financial and military support, what passed for world public opinion—mainly the views of wealthy or powerful European nations—obviously mattered.

In the Declaration's most famous paragraph, the second, Congress offers a powerful and eloquent defense of the natural right of a people to revolution, a right resting on popular consent; that grounding was absent from continental congressional state papers during the first decade of the Imperial Crisis and only irregularly present during the past year.[103] This is not surprising. In the minds of most eighteenth-century Britons—including British colonists—a revolutionary rhetoric of rights was closely connected with regicide, civil war, Oliver Cromwell, the Commonwealth, and all the perceived disasters of the Interregnum.[104] In fact, with the notable exception of this theory-laden paragraph, Congress avoided making such claims in its state papers,[105] focusing instead on the particular misdeeds first of Parliament and the king's ministers, and then finally, in the spring of 1776, of the king himself, something that this body, almost half of whom were lawyers, was more comfortable (and eminently capable of) doing.[106]

This is not to claim that such language was unusual among radical British political and religious dissenters, men such as Thomas Paine, or among similarly minded colonists.[107] Indeed, radical-leaning language is to be found in this collection in the resolves of a few of the colonies in opposition to the Stamp Act, in statements of New England Sons of Liberty, and in the Suffolk resolves (documents 4.1–4.11, 6.1–6.5, and 9.1). Congress too, mostly in the summer of 1775, made references to natural rights in lieu of British constitutional ones (documents 16.1, 18.1, 20.1, and 22.1). And, of course, in the pamphlet literature, sermons, and newspaper editorials, absolute defenses of the sufficiency of popular consent for legitimate government are common, though not to the extent often reported.[108] What is remarkable, though, given the wide dissemination of such conceptions, is their near-total absence from the declarations and resolutions of the Stamp Act Congress and the First Continental Congress, and the sparse use made early on of them by the Second Continental Congress, which had to manage active hostilities with Britain, something akin to a civil war in Massachusetts and New York,[109] and severe economic dislocations brought on by the restraints on commercial life and shipping.

If Congress had declared much earlier that "all men are created equal, that they are endowed by their Creator with certain unalienable Rights," and "that to secure these rights, Governments are instituted among Men, deriving their just Powers from the consent of the governed," it might have found itself irrecoverably out of phase with a political system founded on the inherited dynastic prerogative rights of a monarch.[110] Such claims of active popular consent, particularly of a variety that even John Locke, much less John Adams (see documents 30.6 and 31.7), might have found too unregulated,[111] were more in keeping with a classic republic than with the kind of stable constitutional monarchy found in the colonies before the difficulties of 1764–76.

Similarly, colonists trying to reform an imperial government by appealing to its constitutional monarch to intercede in their behalf would be extremely unlikely to declare "that, whenever any form of Government becomes destructive of these ends, it is the Right of the People to alter or to abolish it, and to institute new Government, laying its foundation on such Principles, and organizing its Powers in such form, as to them shall seem most likely to effect their Safety and Happiness." Nor, as Congress soon made clear in its response to radical upstarts in Vermont seeking its support, was the absolute theory of popular consent all that helpful in a new nation where disparate populations were trying to exploit a difficult-to-contain language of natural rights (see document 39.1). Language that proved helpful in defending an independence movement, even one with less than truly radical goals regarding basic political and economic entitlement, would, not too surprisingly, prove wonderfully useful to similar movements, in the eighteenth century and beyond, with truly revolutionary goals of upsetting received social and political practices.[112]

This celebrated paragraph, then, generally marks a discontinuity with the broad contours of congressional state papers of the previous twelve years. This rupture is not surprising when one remembers that the Congresses' preeminent goal during those years was the strengthening of the colonies' ties to the British monarchy as a means of reconciling them with the empire. Also in this paragraph, one encounters Congress' abrupt and still more epochal departure from a traditional world in which inalienable rights were derived from antecedent perfect duties to one in which stand-alone rights would be defended without necessarily being linked to correlative duties. Given the colonists' abandonment of arguments resting on constitutional and domestic law under a common sovereign, the Declaration's main line of argument was necessarily couched in the language not of civil or constitutional rights, but of international law. Only such a defense was suitable for an environment bereft of a common sovereign, and thus it was formulated in the language of natural law and rights.[113] The reliance on natural law explains too why Congress listed, along with the demanded natural rights of life and liberty, that of the pursuit of happiness, and not the civil or adventitious right of property.[114] As Thomas Burke of North Carolina observed in 1777, with independence, Americans were no longer bound by British domestic law, "only the laws of Nature and Nations"; although "it was the proper policy of Britain still to regard the Americans as subjects, and to insist on the execution of the municipal laws," it could do so only by "the Law of Nations."[115]

After endorsing a republican theory of government previously associated most closely with Reformed Protestant New Englanders, progressive Virginia delegates, and "out of doors" publicists in Britain and the colonies,[116] Congress settled down to the more lawyerly and well-practiced business of laying out its case against the British king, who had so grievously disappointed the once-loyal colonists.

The indictment begins with three long-standing executive-level grievances that were mostly absent from congressional documents, which instead had focused on Parliament's putative trespasses, but not from earlier colonial legislative ones. Accordingly, these grievances look back beyond 1763 to the incessant, though largely predictable, strife between colonial legislatures and Crown officials. Necessarily, this traditional set of concerns targeted the king and his servants rather than Parliament.[117] In particular, Jefferson had in mind the king's Privy Council's regular vacating of colonial laws limiting the slave trade, the issuing of fiat currency, etc.,[118] the king's demand that his governors veto any legislation lacking "a clause suspending its action until transmitted to England for consideration," and the king's insistence on his right to issue "writs of representation."

These grievances not only looked back to a period before the eruption of the Imperial Crisis, but also condemned fundamental aspects of the imperial relationship that had gone unremarked upon in most of the past twelve years of congressional declarations, resolves, and petitions.[119] In fact, one of the only other complaints regarding something similar is found in the only other congressional document written by Jefferson, the report on Lord North's peace proposal, which was approved on July 31, 1775 (document 23.1). Jefferson, particularly when in opposition, had never put aside the traditional Whig understanding of a tension-ridden executive-legislative relationship.[120]

The next three charges concern the difficult imperial relations that, in the wake of the Stamp Act, prompted colonial governors to prorogue, dissolve, or refuse to call colonial assemblies that actively opposed Parliament's insistence that it enjoyed the sovereign right to legislate for and tax the colonists. The seventh charge, which concerns naturalization and land grants, arose as an issue after the end of the Seven Years' War in 1763 with the king's proclamation and plans to protect Native American hunting grounds, to restrict disruptive land speculation that exploited Native American landholding patterns,[121] and to limit colonial charter claims that stretched, effectively, to the Pacific Ocean (the South Seas).

The eighth through twelfth charges, in the main, continue to focus on executive matters. The eighth concerns a standoff in 1768 between the North Carolina Assembly and its royal governor. The ninth was a persistent colonial grievance concerning the appointment of colonial judges, their salaries, and the nature of their tenures; the matter had exploded in Massachusetts in 1773, and was raised by Congress in its Bill of Rights and List of Grievances of 1774 (see document 13.1). The tenth charge was something of a hybrid in that it attacked the king for permitting Parliament to create a new, more efficient, and less corrupt customs agency, which it did in an effort both to raise revenues in the colonies (to help support its administration and fund its extremely expensive defense in the newly acquired lands in North America) and to prevent persistent colonial smuggling and breaches of imperial maritime and commercial regulations. The focus then returns to the beginning of the Imperial Crisis in the Sugar and Stamp Acts of 1764–65 and the Townshend duties of 1767.[122] The final two charges of the first set of indictments allude to Parliament's Quartering Acts of 1765–66 and the appointment of General Gage as governor of Massachusetts in 1774 while he was commander in chief of the king's armed forces in the colonies.

As Donald Lutz, one of the two or three political scientists most familiar with these materials, explains, "the thirteenth charge is in certain respects what the Declaration is all about" or, at least, what had been at the center of the Imperial Crisis for the past twelve years.[123] But the Declaration frames the issue in a novel way: it holds the king, not Parliament, guilty of having acted unconstitutionally by subjecting the colonies "to a jurisdiction," that is, Parliament, "foreign to our constitution, and unacknowledged by our laws; [and for] giving his Assent to their Acts of pretended Legislation." Of course, this, rather than the executive concerns raised earlier, was the core issue that had divided colonists and Parliament: did Parliament have the sovereign right to legislate for the colonies? As should be clear by now, this proved to be a far simpler question to state than to solve, particularly when met by intransigence from two sides with divergent understandings of the British Constitution.

Having stated the core issue, Congress rehearsed grievances regularly raised over the past twelve years, including those against the Sugar and Stamp Acts, punitive parliamentary measures passed between 1765 and 1774, the Restraining Acts, the Tea Acts of 1770 and 1773, and the Quebec Act of 1774, before ending with a fundamental objection to Parliament's "declaring themselves invested with Power to legislate for us in all cases whatsoever," the words of the Declaratory Act of 1766, which suspended the Imperial Crisis, with this Declaration being its true end.[124]

In its final list of grievances, Congress indicts the king alone for a series of failings, consistent with its constitutional theory that it was with him and not Parliament that the colonies had a constitutional bond and that he, by acting tyrannically, had forced them to cut their ties to him.[125] It forensically begins by accusing him of having "abdicated Government here, by declaring us out of his protection, and waging War against us," effectively removing his North American subjects from their duty of loyalty and allegiance to him. Indeed, many moderates in Congress had viewed the American Prohibitory Act of December 22, 1775 (document 29.2) as marking the end of their allegiance to the king and their obligations of loyalty to him. For others, it was the king's response to the petition of the lord mayor of London on March 22 that ended all hope of reconciliation with the British Crown and cut the colonists' ties (see documents 32.3, 32.4, and 32.7).

Following this essential charge are four highly emotional and likely effective ones related to the king's conduct of the war over the previous sixteen months: his troops burning of the towns of Falmouth, Charlestown, Norfolk, and Charleston; his engaging foreign mercenaries; his abducting colonial sailors to serve in the Royal Navy and against their fellow subjects, and treating them as if they had volunteered so that they could be hung for desertion; and his fomenting "domestic insurrections amongst us," that is, freeing slaves willing to fight against their former masters. Jefferson—with his usual vivid coloration and slanting of historical detail—in his draft described this last point as the king "exciting those very people to rise in arms among us, and to purchase that liberty of which he has deprived them, by murdering the people on whom he also obtruded them" (document 45.1). Ironically, at least one of Jefferson's slaves was among those departing with the British forces at the end of the war in 1783. Continuing, Congress indicts the king for bringing "on the inhabitants of our frontiers, the merciless Indian Savages," a charge that could have just as well been leveled against the colonists during the Seven Years' War.[126]

Keeping with themes from earlier congressional documents, Congress reminds its readers that it had "Petitioned for Redress, in the most humble terms: Our repeated Petitions, have been answered only by repeated injury," and that it had not "been wanting in attentions to our Brittish brethren": "We have warned them from time to time of attempts by their legislature to extend an unwarrantable jurisdiction over us."

The latter point is comparable to complaints issued by British radicals against Parliament.[127] Fittingly, Congress then appends Richard Henry Lee's resolution declaring independence, which had been approved two days earlier. Congress closes by returning to the central theme of the first paragraph, explaining that the new international rights enjoyed by the former colonies "as FREE and INDEPENDENT STATES," including the capability to conduct war, "conclude peace, contract alliances, [and] establish Commerce" with other nations unencumbered by British maritime legislation. Finally, the delegates pledge to each other their lives, fortunes, and sacred honor at a time when some would lose their lives, and many more their fortunes, and when all were at considerable risk of losing all three if the new states were defeated in the war.

## 33.1

## RESOLUTIONS DECLARING INDEPENDENCE, AND THE DECLARATION OF THE THIRTEEN UNITED STATES OF AMERICA, JUNE 28, JULY 1–4, AND JULY 19, 1776

Worthington Chauncey Ford et al., eds., *Journals of the Continental Congress, 1774–1789* (Washington, D.C.: Government Printing Office, 1904–37), 5:491, 504–15, 590–91. Two drafts of the Declaration of Independence, the "First Draft" and the "Reported Draft," appear on pages 491–502 of the *Journal.*

[FRIDAY, JUNE 28, 1776]

The committee appointed to prepare a declaration, &c. brought in a draught, which was read:

*Ordered,* To lie on the table. . . .

[MONDAY, JULY 1, 1776]

A resolution of the convention of Maryland, of the 28 June, was also laid before Congress and read, wherein it is resolved:

IN CONVENTION, *28 June 1776.*

*Resolved, Unanimously,* That the Instructions given by the Convention December last, (and renewed by the Convention in May,) to the Deputies of this Colony in Congress, be recalled, and the Restrictions therein contained, removed; and that the Deputies of this Colony, attending in Congress, or a Majority of them or of any three or more of them, be authorized and empowered to concur with the other United Colonies, or a Majority of them, in declaring the United Colonies free and independent States; in forming such further Compact and Confederation between them; in making foreign Alliances, and in adopting such other Measures as shall be adjudged necessary for securing the Liberties of America; and this Colony will hold itself bound, by the Resolutions of a Majority of the

United Colonies, in the Premises; Provided, the sole and exclusive Right of regulating the internal Government and Police of this Colony be reserved to the People thereof.

Extract from the Minutes,

G. DUVALL,
*Clerk.*

The order of the day being read,

*Resolved,* That this Congress will resolve itself into a committee of the whole, to take into consideration the resolution respecting independency:

*Resolved,* That the Declaration be referred to said committee.

The Congress resolved itself into a committee of the whole. ‖After some time,‖ the president resumed the chair. Mr. [Benjamin] Harrison reported, that the committee have had under consideration the matters referred to them, and have agreed to the resolution, which they ordered him to report, and desired him to move for leave to sit again.

The resolution agreed to by committee of the whole being read, the determination thereof was postponed, at the request of a colony, till to morrow. . . .

[TUESDAY, JULY 2, 1776]

The Congress resumed the consideration of the resolution agreed to by and reported from the committee of the whole; and the same being read, was agreed to as follows:

*Resolved,* That these United Colonies are, and, of right, ought to be, Free and Independent States; that they are absolved from all allegiance to the British crown, and that all political connexion between them, and the state of Great Britain, is, and ought to be, totally dissolved.

Agreeable to the order of the day, the Congress resolved itself into a committee of the whole; ‖and, after some time,‖ the president resumed the chair. Mr. [Benjamin] Harrison reported, that the committee have had under consideration the declaration to them referred; but, not having had time to go through ‖the same,‖ desired leave to sit again:

*Resolved,* That this Congress will, to morrow, again resolve itself into a committee of the whole, to take into their farther consideration the declaration on independence. . . .

[WEDNESDAY, JULY 3, 1776]

Agreeable to the order of the day, the Congress resolved itself into a committee of the whole, to take into their farther consideration, the Declaration; ‖and, after some time, ‖ the president resumed the chair, and Mr. [Benjamin] Harrison reported, that the committee, not having finished, desired leave to sit again.

*Resolved,* That this Congress will, to morrow, resolve itself into a committee of the whole, to take into their farther consideration, the Declaration.

Adjourned to 9 o'Clock to Morrow.

[THURSDAY, JULY 4, 1776]

Agreeable to the order of the day, the Congress resolved itself into a committee of the whole, to take into their farther consideration, the declaration; ‖and, after some time, ‖ the president resumed the chair. Mr. [Benjamin] Harrison reported, that the committee of the whole Congress have agreed to a Declaration, which he delivered in.

The Declaration being again read, was agreed to as follows:

*The unanimous Declaration of the thirteen United States of America.*

WHEN, in the Course of human events, it becomes necessary for one people to dissolve the political bands which have connected them with another, and to assume, among the Powers of the earth, the separate and equal station to which the Laws of Nature and of Nature's God entitle them, a decent respect to the opinions of mankind requires that they should declare the causes which impel them to the separation.

We hold these truths to be self-evident, that all men are created equal, that they are endowed by their Creator with certain unalienable Rights, that among these, are Life, Liberty, and the pursuit of Happiness. That, to secure these rights, Governments are instituted among Men, deriving their just Powers from the consent of the governed. That, whenever any form of Government becomes destructive of these ends, it is the Right of the People to alter or to abolish it, and to institute new Government, laying its foundation on such Principles, and organizing its Powers in such form, as to them shall seem most likely to effect their Safety and Happiness. Prudence, indeed, will dictate that Governments long established should not be changed for light and transient causes; and, accordingly, all experience hath shewn, that mankind are more disposed to suffer, while evils are sufferable, than to right themselves by abolishing the forms to which they are accustomed. But, when a long train of abuses and usurpations, pursuing invariably the same Object, evinces a design to reduce them under absolute Despotism, it is their right, it is their duty, to throw off such Government, and to provide new Guards for their future Security. Such has been the patient sufferance of these Colonies; and such is now the necessity which constrains them to alter their former Systems of Government. The history of the present King of Great Britain is a history of repeated injuries and usurpations, all having in direct object the establishment of an absolute Tyranny over these States. To prove this, let Facts be submitted to a candid world.

He has refused his Assent to Laws the most wholesome and necessary for the public good.

He has forbidden his Governors to pass Laws of immediate and pressing importance, unless suspended in their operation till his Assent should be obtained; and when so suspended, he has utterly neglected to attend to them.

He has refused to pass other Laws for the accommodation of large districts of People, unless those People would relinquish the right of Representation in the legislature; a right inestimable to them and formidable to tyrants only.

He has called together legislative bodies at places unusual, uncomfortable, and distant from the depository of their Public Records, for the sole Purpose of fatiguing them into compliance with his measures.

He has dissolved Representative Houses repeatedly, for opposing, with manly firmness, his invasions on the rights of the People.

He has refused for a long time, after such dissolutions, to cause others to be elected; whereby the Legislative Powers, incapable of Annihilation, have returned to the People at large for their exercise; the State remaining in the mean time exposed to all the dangers of invasion from without, and convulsions within.

He has endeavoured to prevent the Population of these States; for that purpose obstructing the Laws for Naturalization of Foreigners; refusing to pass others to encourage their migrations hither, and raising the conditions of new Appropriations of Lands.

He has obstructed the Administration of Justice, by refusing his Assent to Laws for establishing Judiciary Powers.

He has made Judges dependent on his Will alone, for the tenure of their offices, and the amount and payment of their salaries.

He has erected a multitude of New Offices, and sent hither swarms of Officers to harrass our People, and eat out their substance.

He has kept among us, in times of Peace, Standing Armies, without the Consent of our legislatures.

He has affected to render the Military independent of and superior to the Civil Power.

He has combined with others to subject us to a jurisdiction foreign to our constitution, and unacknowledged by our laws; giving his Assent to their Acts of pretended Legislation:

For quartering large bodies of armed troops among us:

For protecting them, by a mock Trial, from Punishment for any Murders which they should commit on the Inhabitants of these States:

For cutting off our Trade with all parts of the world:

For imposing Taxes on us without our Consent:

For depriving us, in many cases, of the benefits of Trial by Jury:

For transporting us beyond Seas to be tried for pretended offences:

For abolishing the free System of English Laws in a neighbouring province, establishing therein an Arbitrary government, and enlarging its Boundaries, so as to render it at once an example and fit instrument for introducing the same absolute rule into these Colonies:

For taking away our Charters, abolishing our most valuable Laws, and altering fundamentally the Forms of our Governments:

For suspending our own Legislatures, and declaring themselves invested with Power to legislate for us in all cases whatsoever.

He has abdicated Government here, by declaring us out of his protection, and waging War against us.

He has plundered our seas, ravaged our Coasts, burnt our towns, and destroyed the Lives of our People.

He is at this time transporting large Armies of foreign Mercenaries to compleat the works of death, desolation and tyranny, already begun with circumstances of Cruelty and perfidy scarcely paralleled in the most barbarous ages, and totally unworthy the Head of a civilized nation.

He has constrained our fellow Citizens, taken Captive on the high Seas, to bear Arms against their Country, to become the executioners of their friends and Brethren, or to fall themselves by their Hands.

He has excited domestic insurrections amongst us, and has endeavoured to bring on the inhabitants of our frontiers, the merciless Indian Savages, whose known rule of warfare, is an undistinguished destruction of all ages, sexes and conditions.

In every stage of these Oppressions, We have Petitioned for Redress, in the most humble terms: Our repeated Petitions, have been answered only by repeated injury. A Prince, whose character is thus marked by every act which may define a Tyrant, is unfit to be the ruler of a free People.

Nor have We been wanting in attentions to our Brittish brethren. We have warned them from time to time of attempts by their legislature to extend an unwarrantable jurisdiction over us. We have reminded them of the circumstances of our emigration and settlement here. We have appealed to their native justice and magnanimity, and we have conjured them by the ties of our common kindred, to disavow these usurpations, which, would inevitably interrupt our connexions and correspondence. They too have been deaf to the voice of justice and of consanguinity. We must, therefore, acquiesce in the necessity, which denounces our Separation, and hold them, as we hold the rest of mankind, Enemies in War, in Peace Friends.

WE, THEREFORE, the Representatives of the UNITED STATES OF AMERICA, in GENERAL CONGRESS assembled, appealing to the Supreme Judge of the World for the rectitude of our intentions, DO, in the Name, and by Authority of the good People of these Colonies, solemnly PUBLISH and DECLARE, That these United Colonies are, and of Right, ought to be FREE AND INDEPENDENT STATES; that they are Absolved from all Allegiance to the British Crown, and that all political connexion between them and the State of Great Britain, is and ought to be totally dissolved; and that, as FREE and INDEPENDENT STATES, they have full Power to levy War, conclude Peace, contract Alliances, establish Commerce, and to do all other Acts and Things which INDEPENDENT STATES may of right do. AND for the support of this Declaration, with a firm reliance on the protection of divine Providence, we mutually pledge to each other our Lives, our Fortunes, and our sacred Honour.

‖The foregoing declaration was, by order of Congress, engrossed, and signed by the following members:‖

JOHN HANCOCK.

| JOSIAH BARTLETT. | GEO. TAYLOR. |
| WM WHIPPLE. | JAMES WILSON. |
| SAML ADAMS. | GEO. ROSS. |

John Adams.

Robt Treat Paine.

Elbridge Gerry.

Steph. Hopkins.

William Ellery.

Roger Sherman.

Samel Huntington.

Wm Williams.

Oliver Wolcott.

Matthew Thornton.

Wm Floyd.

Phil Livingston.

Frans Lewis.

Lewis Morris.

Richd Stockton.

Jno Witherspoon.

Fras Hopkinson.

John Hart.

Abra Clark.

Robt Morris.

Benjamin Rush.

Benja Franklin.

John Morton.

Geo Clymer.

Jas Smith.

Cæsar Rodney.

Geo Read.

Thos M: Kean.

Samuel Chase.

Wm Paca.

Thos Stone.

Charles Carroll of
   Carrollton.

George Wythe.

Richard Henry Lee.

Th. Jefferson.

Benja Harrison.

Thos Nelson, Jr.

Francis Lightfoot Lee.

Carter Braxton.

Wm Hooper.

Joseph Hewes.

John Penn.

Edward Rutledge.

Thos Heyward, Junr.

Thomas Lynch, Junr.

Arthur Middleton.

Button Gwinnett.

Lyman Hall.

Geo Walton.

[FRIDAY, JULY 19, 1776]

*Resolved,* That the Declaration passed on the 4th, be fairly engrossed on parchment, with the title and stile of "The unanimous declaration of the thirteen United States of America," and that the same, when engrossed, be signed by every member of Congress.

## 33.2

 JOHN ADAMS TO TIMOTHY PICKERING,
AUGUST 6, 1822

Although Jefferson, at thirty-three, was the most junior and least accomplished member of the committee that prepared a draft Declaration for Congress' consideration, he was its chair, a decision made "out of doors," for he was the least objectionable of the Virginia delegation and already well known for possessing an eloquent pen.[128] Additionally, he was the least occupied of the five men; each of the other four members sat on two or three of the four most important congressional committees. Thus, it made sense for him to draft the committee's report to Congress. As John Adams observes in his autobiography, "The committee had several meetings, in which were proposed the articles of which the declaration was to consist, and minutes made of them. The committee then appointed Mr. Jefferson and me to draw them up in form, and clothe them in proper dress. The sub-committee met, and considered the minutes, making such observations on them as then occurred, when Mr. Jefferson desired me to take them to my lodgings, and make the draught. This I declined, and gave several reasons for declining. 1. That he was a Virginian, and I a Massachusettensian. 2. That he was a southern man, and I a northern one. 3. That I had been so obnoxious for my early and constant zeal in promoting the measure, that any draught of mine would undergo a more severe scrutiny and criticism in Congress, than one of his composition. 4. And lastly . . . I had a great opinion of the elegance of his pen."[129]

Forty-seven years after the Declaration was issued, Adams recalled its drafting in a letter to Timothy Pickering, a lawyer from Essex County, Massachusetts, who served in the war as a general and on the Board of War, and later as a Hamiltonian secretary of state. Still later, he was a U.S. senator who worked with others, as part of the "Essex Junto," to organize a New England secession movement in protest against the policies of Jefferson and Madison. Concerning the writing of the draft Declaration, Adams stated, "I do not remember that Franklin or Sherman criticized any thing. We were all in haste. Congress was impatient, and the instrument was reported, as I believe, in Jefferson's handwriting, as he first drew it. Congress cut off about a quarter of it, as I expected they would." Adams famously explained that "there is not an idea in it but what had been hackneyed in Congress for two years before," but if so, more likely because of Adams and the delegates of Massachusetts and Virginia rather than the majority of delegates of the mid-Atlantic colonies. This was one of the reasons Adams believed himself so unpopular. He noted of the Declaration that "the substance of it is contained in the declaration of rights and the violation of those rights," that is, the Bill of Rights and List of Grievances issued by Congress in 1774 (see document 13.1), and in an early pamphlet by James Otis, Jr., apparently written in opposition to the Sugar or Stamp Act.

The claim that the Declaration merely reiterated long-standing charges may have been true, but not in regard to the major line of argument presented by the majority of congressional state papers from 1764 until the spring of 1776. Most critically, it was not true regarding the primary target of colonial complaint—Parliament, not the king. Even Adams found Jefferson's castigation of the king as a tyrant over-wrought; Adams "never believed George to be a tyrant in disposition and in nature; I believed him to be deceived by his courtiers on both sides of the Atlantic, and in his official capacity only, cruel." Adams here seems to be taking a milder stance than he did in 1776; indeed, it is one that would have been more congenial to his moderate congressional opponents than to his earlier, radical self. What is remarkable is that Adams still did not take fully into account how little leeway the king had to respond to colonial demands, constrained as his powers were by the parliamentary supremacy enshrined in the eighteenth-century British Constitution.[130]

*The Works of John Adams,* ed. Charles Francis Adams (Boston: Little, Brown, 1851–65), 2:513–14. The first five paragraphs of the letter are omitted below. According to Benjamin Rush, "soon" in the first sentence refers to 1775, when Adams was the "object of nearly universal scorn and detestation" in Philadelphia.

It soon became rumored about the city that John Adams was for independence. The Quakers and proprietary gentlemen took the alarm; represented me as the worst of men; the true-blue sons of liberty pitied me; all put me under a kind of conventry. I was avoided, like a man infected with the leprosy. I walked the streets of Philadelphia in solitude, borne down by the weight of care and unpopularity. But every ship, for the ensuing year, brought us fresh proof of the truth of my prophecies, and one after another became convinced of the necessity of independence. I did not sink under my discouragements. I had before experienced enough of the wantonness of popularity, in the trial of Preston and the soldiers, in Boston.

You inquire why so young a man as Mr. Jefferson was placed at the head of the Committee for preparing a Declaration of Independence? I answer; It was the Frankfort advice, to place Virginia at the head of everything. Mr. Richard Henry Lee might be gone to Virginia, to his sick family, for aught I know, but that was not the reason of Mr. Jefferson's appointment. There were three committees appointed at the same time. One for the Declaration of Independence, another for preparing articles of Confederation, and another for preparing a treaty to be proposed to France. Mr. Lee was chosen for the Committee of Confederation, and it was not thought convenient that the same person should be upon both. Mr. Jefferson came into Congress, in June, 1775, and brought with him a reputation for literature, science, and a happy talent of composition. Writings of his were handed about, remarkable for the peculiar felicity of expression. Though a silent member in Congress, he was so prompt, frank, explicit, and decisive upon committees and in conversation, not even Samuel Adams was more so, that he soon seized upon my heart; and upon this occasion I gave him my vote, and did all in my power to procure the votes of others. I think he had one more vote than any other, and that placed him at the head of the committee. I had the next highest number, and that placed me the second. The committee met, discussed the subject, and the appointed Mr. Jefferson and me to make the draught, I suppose because we were the two first on the list.

The sub-committee met. Jefferson proposed to me to make the draught. I said, "I will not." "You should do it." "Oh! no." "Why will you not? You ought to do it." "I will not." "Why?" "Reasons enough." "What can be your reasons?" "Reason first—You are a Virginian, and a Virginian ought to appear at the head of this business. Reason second—I am obnoxious, suspected, and unpopular. You are very much otherwise. Reason third—You can write ten times better than I can." "Well," said Jefferson, "if you are decided, I will do as well as I can." "Very well. When you have drawn it up, we will have a meeting."

A meeting was accordingly had, and conned the paper over. I was delighted with its high tone and the flights of oratory with which it abounded, especially that concerning negro slavery, which, though I knew his Southern brethren would never suffer to pass in Congress, I certainly never would oppose. There were other expressions which I would not have inserted, if I had drawn it up, particularly that which called the King tyrant. I thought this too personal; for I never believed George to be a tyrant in disposition and in nature; I believed him to be deceived by his courtiers on both sides of the Atlantic, and in his official capacity only, cruel. I thought the expression too passionate, and too much like scolding, for so grave and solemn a document; but as Franklin and Sherman were to inspect it afterwards, I thought it would not become me to strike it out. I consented to report it, and do not now remember that I made or suggested a single alteration.

We reported it to the committee of five. It was read, and I do not remember that Franklin or Sherman criticized any thing. We were all in haste. Congress was impatient, and the instrument was reported, as I believe, in Jefferson's handwriting, as he first drew it. Congress cut off about a quarter of it, as I expected they would; but they obliterated some of the best of it, and left all that was exceptionable, if any thing in it was. I have long wondered that the original draught has not been published. I suppose the reason is, the vehement philippic against negro slavery.

As you justly observe, there is not an idea in it but what had been hackneyed in Congress for two years before. The substance of it is contained in the declaration of rights and the violation of those rights, in the Journals of Congress, in 1774. Indeed, the essence of it is contained in a pamphlet, voted and printed by the town of Boston, before the first Congress met, composed by James Otis, as I suppose, in one of his lucid intervals, and pruned and polished by Samuel Adams. Your friend and humble servant.

## 33.3

 ELBRIDGE GERRY TO JAMES WARREN, JUNE 25, 1776

Both Elbridge Gerry and James Warren were among the more outspoken Boston advocates of independence. Gerry replaced a more moderate Massachusetts delegate, Thomas Cushing, in Congress on February 9, 1776, thereby changing the balance within the Massachusetts delegation. The addition of Samuel Chase to the Maryland delegation helped do the same in Congress as a whole.[131] In this letter, Gerry confirms that the mid-Atlantic colonies, with the exception of Maryland and New York, were moving toward independence. He also reiterates, like others from the

New England colonies, that "the New-England delegates have been in a continual war with the advocates of proprietary interests [Pennsylvania, Maryland, and Delaware] in congress . . . These are they who are most in the way of the measures we have proposed, but I think the contest is pretty nearly at an end," for the people of the mid-Atlantic colonies, whatever may be true of their delegates, "now more confide in the politics of the New-England colonies than they ever did in those of their hitherto unequal governments."

Indeed, he clarifies that something of a civil war of ideas occurred in Congress and in the colonies themselves, alongside one of bloodshed between loyalists and patriots throughout the colonies, while the war for political supremacy between the colonies and Great Britain raged in the background. It is unclear whether, after the immediate victory won by the New England delegates, any of these wars would immediately subside, for many of the same divisions and issues remained as the colonies (now as states) began organizing their politics anew and Congress completed work on a draft Articles of Confederation, which it debated intermittently over the next sixteen months.

Paul H. Smith, ed., *Letters of Delegates to Congress, 1774–1789* (Washington, D.C.: Library of Congress, 1976–93), 4:316–17.

My Dear Sir,                                                                    Philadelphia, June 25, 1776

I am favoured with your very agreeable letter of 10th June, and am in hopes congress will soon render it unnecessary to take further measures preparatory to the declaration of independence. New-Jersey has appointed five new delegates, and instructed them to vote in favour of the question, and it appears to me there is not even a doubt of any colony on the continent except New-York and Maryland. These will not impede us a moment. I do not affirm that either of these are of the neuter gender, but on the other hand am persuaded the people are in favour of a total and final separation, and will support the measure, even if the conventions and delegates of those colonies vote against it.

Since my first arrival in this city the New-England delegates have been in a continual war with the advocates of proprietary interests in congress and this colony. These are they who are most in the way of the measures we have proposed, but I think the contest is pretty nearly at an end, and am persuaded that the people of this and the middle colonies have a clearer view of their interest, and will use their endeavours to eradicate the ministerial influence of governours, proprietors and jacobites, and that they now more confide in the politics of the New-England colonies than they ever did in those of their hitherto unequal governments.

Your's as ever,                                                                                    E. Gerry.

33.4

 EDWARD RUTLEDGE TO JOHN JAY, JUNE 29, 1776

Edward Rutledge found John Jay, Robert R. Livingston, and Gouverneur Morris, all of New York, kindred spirits. He here implores Jay to return to Congress, for he foresees that on July 1, a declaration of independence, a plan of confederation, and a plan for foreign treaties will be under consideration, and he hopes to have as many "Honest and sensible" members in attendance as possible in order "effectually to oppose the first, and infuse Wisdom into the" other two. His focus was not on what we think of as the "Declaration of Independence," submitted the day before—it isn't even mentioned—what concerned him was whether Lee's resolution on independence could be blocked and whether the plan for confederation and for treaties could be improved upon. Jefferson's explanatory "Declaration" was apparently of insufficient importance to warrant discussing with Jay. Lee's resolution on independence was first voted on July 1, Jefferson's Declaration was discussed over the next three days, and the drafts of the other two documents were introduced over the next two weeks, that of the Articles of Confederation on July 12 and that of the Plan for Foreign Treaties on July 18.

Rutledge comments on Dickinson's draft of the Articles of Confederation, and besides criticizing its style, he objects to its overly centralizing tendencies, which, if accepted as proposed, would have resulted in "nothing less than Ruin to some Colonies." The heart of Rutledge's concern was "the Idea of destroying all Provincial Distinctions and making every thing of the most minute kind bend to what they call the good of the whole." Under that sort of plan, the nation would be "subject to the Government of the Eastern Provinces," that is, New England. He worries not because of their force of arms, which he holds in contempt, but because of their "over-ruling Influence in Council." Moreover, he dreads "their low Cunning, and those levelling Principles which Men without Character and without Fortune in general Possess, which are so captivating to the lower Class of Mankind"—in effect, he fears New Englanders' almost innate populism, republicanism, and religious piety. Moderates like Dickinson and Wilson of Pennsylvania differed from those like Rutledge in what they considered the danger of social and political "leveling," that is, democracy. Accordingly, as a member of the committee preparing the Articles, Rutledge hoped "to vest the Congress with no more Power than what is absolutely necessary, and to use a familiar Expression to keep the Staff in our own Hands, for I am confident if surrendered into the Hands of others a most pernicious use will be made of it."

His concerns over the creation of a strong centralizing intercolonial or continental government, at least in the short term, did not come to pass, thanks to the intervention of Thomas Burke, the North Carolina delegate who successfully fought Dickinson's centralizing draft and ensured that the Articles of Confederation became more state-centered before being adopted by Congress. A delegate's understanding of the dangers or benefits of a strong central government seemingly was as much shaped by local circumstances as by any overarching political philosophy. This was seen too in the wrangles in Congress over Joseph Galloway's "Plan of Union" (document 10.1) and Franklin's draft Articles (document 44.1).

Rutledge was more fearful of the populist politics of New Englanders working at the national level than of the leveling aspirations of the small number of poor whites in preponderantly slave-populated South Carolina. Those in other colonies, soon states, might have viewed a strong central government, as they had the British colonial government, as a bulwark against social and political leveling, and thus might have supported such government. James Wilson, for example, did so, and helped develop and push the idea of a largely fictitious sovereign national people. Of course, as conditions changed, the attractiveness of one option or another could change as well. Merrill Jensen's classic neo-Progressive work on the Articles of Confederation and his treatment of this issue demands continued close attention.[132]

Paul H. Smith, ed., *Letters of Delegates to Congress, 1774–1789* (Washington, D.C.: Library of Congress, 1976–93), 4:337–39.

My dear Jay             Philadelphia, June 29, 1776

I write this for the express Purpose of requesting that if possible you will give your Attendance in Congress on Monday next. I know full well that your Presence must be useful at New York, but I am sincerely convinced that it will be absolutely necessary in this City during the whole of the ensuing Week. A Declaration of Independence, the Form of a Confederation of these Colonies, and a Scheme for a Treaty with foreign Powers will be laid before the House on Monday. Whether we shall be able effectually to oppose the first, and infuse Wisdom into the others will depend in a great Measure upon the Exertions of the Honest and sensible part of the Members. I trust you will contribute in a considerable degree to effect the Business and therefore I wish you to be with us. Recollect the manner in which your Colony is at this Time represented. Clinton has Abilities but is silent in general, and wants (when he does speak) that Influence to which he is intitled. Floyd, Wisner, Lewis and Alsop though good Men, never quit their Chairs. You must know the Importance of these Questions too well not to wish to [be] present whilst they are debating and therefore I shall say no more upon the Subject.

I have been much engaged lately upon a plan of a Confederation which Dickenson has drawn. It has the Vice of all his Productions to a considerable Degree; I mean the Vice of Refining too much. Unless it is greatly curtailed it never can pass, as it is to be submitted to Men in the respective Provinces who will not be led or rather driven into Measures which may lay the Foundation of their Ruin. If the Plan now proposed should be adopted nothing less than Ruin to some Colonies will be the Consequence of it. The Idea of destroying all Provincial Distinctions and making every thing of the most minute kind bend to what they call the good of the whole, is in other Terms to say that these Colonies must be subject to the Government of the Eastern Provinces. The Force of their Arms I hold exceeding Cheap, but I confess I dread their over-ruling Influence in Council, I dread their low Cunning, and those levelling Principles which Men without Character and without Fortune in general Possess, which are so captivating to the lower Class of Mankind, and which will occasion such a fluctuation of Property as to introduce the greatest disorder. I am resolved to vest the Congress with no more Power than what is absolutely necessary, and to use a familiar Expression to keep the Staff in our own Hands, for I am confident if surrendered into the Hands of others a most pernicious use will be made of it.

If you can't come let me hear from you by the Return of the Post. Compliments to Livingston and G. Morris. God bless you.

With Esteem and affection, Yours,

E. Rutledge

33.5

 Thomas Jefferson, Notes of Proceedings
in Congress, July 1–4, 1776

Here in an abbreviated form (document 45.1, the final section of Jefferson's notes, presents the committee's draft of the Declaration of Independence as marked up by the delegates in Congress) Thomas Jefferson presents his account, composed sometime between August 1776 and June 1783, of congressional actions in early July relating to independence. He describes the July 1 vote of the committee of the whole on Lee's resolution on independence, which nine colonies supported. At the urging of Edward Rutledge, a final vote on independence was postponed for a day. Jefferson reports that after a change in South Carolina's and Pennsylvania's votes, and the addition of a deciding vote in the Delaware delegation, all colonies authorized to vote supported Lee's resolution regarding independence on July 2.

Jefferson reports that Congress went back into a committee of the whole on the second "to consider the declaration of Independance, which had been reported & laid on the table the Friday preceding [June 28], and on Monday referred to a commee. of the whole." To Jefferson's dismay, considerable portions of his Declaration were cut and other parts edited, in his mind, because "the pusillanimous idea that we had friends in England worth keeping terms with, still haunted the minds of many." Accordingly, "those passages which conveyed censures on the people of England were struck out, lest they should give them offence." In addition, a long section "reprobating the enslaving the inhabitants of Africa, was struck out in complaisance to South Carolina & Georgia, who had never attempted to restrain the importation of slaves . . . Our Northern brethren also I believe felt a little tender under those censures; for tho' their people have very few slaves themselves yet they had been pretty considerable carriers of them to others."[133] Thus, the debate on the wording of Congress' Declaration, after the resolution for independence had passed, took up the rest of the second, much of the third, and some of the fourth until it was "reported by the commee., agreed to by the house, and signed by every member present except Mr. Dickinson." It is now well known that Jefferson was likely confused about the whereabouts of Dickinson on the fourth, and also about the day the signing of the Declaration of Independence began, which was August 2.[134]

Paul H. Smith, ed., *Letters of Delegates to Congress, 1774–1789* (Washington, D.C.: Library of Congress, 1976–93), 4:358–65.

On Monday the 1st of July the house resolved itself into a commee. of the whole & resumed the consideration of the original motion made by the delegates of Virginia, which being again debated through the day, was carried in the affirmative by the votes of N. Hampshire, Connecticut, Massachusets, Rhode island, N. Jersey, Maryland, Virginia, N. Carolina, & Georgia. S. Carolina and Pennsylvania voted against it. Delaware having but two members present, they were divided: the delegates for New York declared they were for it themselves, & were assured their constituents were for it, but that their instructions having been drawn near a twelvemonth before, when reconciliation was still the general object, they were enjoined by them to do nothing which should impede that object. They therefore thought themselves not justifiable in voting on either side, and asked leave to withdraw from the question, which was given them. The Commee. rose & reported their resolution to the house. Mr. Rutlege of S. Carolina then requested the determination might be put off to the next day, as he believed his collegues, tho' they disapproved of the resolution, would then join in it for the sake of unanimity. The ultimate question whether the house would agree to the resolution of the committee was accordingly postponed to the next day, when it was again moved and S. Carolina concurred in voting for it. In the mean time a third member had come post from the Delaware counties and turned the vote of that colony in favour of the resolution. Members of a different sentiment attending that morning from Pennsylvania also, their vote was changed, so that the whole 12 colonies, who were authorized to vote at all, gave their voices for it; and within a few days the convention of N. York approved of it and thus supplied the void occasioned by the withdrawing of their delegates from the vote.

Congress proceeded the same day to consider the declaration of Independance, which had been reported & laid on the table the Friday preceding, and on Monday referred to a commee. of the whole. The pusillanimous idea that we had friends in England worth keeping terms with, still haunted the minds of many. For this reason those passages which conveyed censures on the people of England were struck out, lest they should give them offence. The clause too, reprobating the enslaving the inhabitants of Africa, was struck out in complaisance to South Carolina & Georgia, who had never attempted to restrain the importation of slaves, and who on the contrary still wished to continue it. Our Northern brethren also I believe felt a little tender under those censures; for tho' their people have very few slaves themselves yet they had been pretty considerable carriers of them to others. The debates having taken up the greater parts of the 2d 3d & 4th days of July were, in the evening of the last closed. The declaration was reported by the commee., agreed to by the house, and signed by every member present except Mr. Dickinson. . . .

## 33.6

 JOHN ADAMS, DIARY ENTRIES, JUNE 28, JULY 1,
AND JULY 4, 1776

John Adams describes the debate on July 1 in the committee of the whole regarding Lee's "Resolution respecting Independency" as taking place principally between the champion of the moderates, John Dickinson, and that of the congressional radicals, Adams himself. According to Adams, such a conversation was unnecessary, for "the Subject had been in Contemplation for more than a Year and frequent discussions had been had concerning it." Dickinson thought otherwise. Adams reports that he spoke first, whereas other accounts have Dickinson responding to Adams.[135] He claims that, in spite of Dickinson's eloquence (see document 33.7), he "had confidence enough in the plain Understanding and common Sense that had been given me, to believe that I could answer to the Satisfaction of the House all the Arguments which had been produced."

Adams made a special and noticeable effort to mention that John Jay, James Duane, and William Livingston "were not present [on July 1]. But they all acquiesced in the Declaration and steadily supported it ever afterwards." In his remarks for June 28, however, he reported that "Mr. William Livingston and all others [in the New Jersey delegation] who had hitherto resisted Independence were left out." All three men had consistently opposed the radicals in Congress, and none were likely in attendance for the critical votes on July 2 or 4—nor did any of them return to Congress in 1776. Finally, Adams' very brief entry for July 4 might reflect his widely reported vanity, suggesting that he focused only on issues with which he was intimately involved, or it might reflect a lack of attention in Congress itself to the Declaration of Independence.

*Diary and Autobiography of John Adams,* ed. L. H. Butterfield (Cambridge, Mass.: Harvard University Press, 1961), 3:395–98.

Fryday June 28. 1776 a new Delegation appeared from New Jersey. Mr. William Livingston and all others who had hitherto resisted Independence were left out. Richard Stockton, Francis Hopkinson and Dr. John Witherspoon were new Members.

Monday July. 1 1776 A Resolution of the Convention of Maryland, passed the 28th. of June was laid before Congress and read: as follows: That the Instructions given to their Deputies in December last, be recalled, and the restrictions therein contained, removed, and that their Deputies be authorised to concur with the other Colonies, or a Majority of them, in declaring the United Colonies free and independent States: in forming a Compact between them; and in making foreign Alliances &c.

Resolved that Congress will resolve itself into a Committee of the whole to take into Consideration the Resolution respecting Independency.

That the Declaration be referred to said Committee.

The Congress resolved itself into a Committee of the whole. After some time The President resumed the Chair and Mr. Harrison reported, that the Committee had come to a Resolution, which they desired him to report and to move for leave to sit again.

The Resolution agreed to by the Committee of the whole being read, the determination thereof, was at the Request of a Colony postponed till tomorrow.

I am not able to recollect, whether it was on this, or some preceeding day, that the greatest and most solemn debate was had on the question of Independence. The Subject had been in Contemplation for more than a Year and frequent discussions had been had concerning it. At one time and another, all the Arguments for it and against it had been exhausted and were become familiar. I expected no more would be said in public but that the question would be put and decided. Mr. Dickinson however was determined to bear his Testimony against it with more formality. He had prepared himself apparently with great Labour and ardent Zeal, and in a Speech of great Length, and all his Eloquence, he combined together all that had before been said in Pamphlets and News papers and all that had from time to time been said in Congress by himself and others. He conducted the debate, not only with great Ingenuity and Eloquence, but with equal Politeness and Candour: and was answered in the same Spirit.

No Member rose to answer him: and after waiting some time, in hopes that some one less obnoxious than myself, who had been all along for a Year before, and still was represented and believed to be the Author of all the Mischief, I determined to speak.

It has been said by some of our Historians, that I began by an Invocation to the God of Eloquence. This is a Misrepresentation. Nothing so puerile as this fell from me. I began by saying that this was the first time of my Life that I had ever wished for the Talents and Eloquence of the ancient Orators of Greece and Rome, for I was very sure that none of them ever had before him a question of more Importance to his Country and to the

World. They would probably upon less Occasions than this have begun by solemn Invocations to their Divinities for Assistance but the Question before me appeared so simple, that I had confidence enough in the plain Understanding and common Sense that had been given me, to believe that I could answer to the Satisfaction of the House all the Arguments which had been produced, notwithstanding the Abilities which had been displayed and the Eloquence with which they had been enforced. Mr. Dickinson, some years afterwards published his Speech. I had made no Preparation beforehand and never committed any minutes of mine to writing. But if I had a Copy of Mr. Dickinsons before me I would now after Nine and twenty Years have elapsed, endeavour to recollect mine.

Before the final Question was put, the new Delegates from New Jersey came in, and Mr. Stockton, Dr. Witherspoon and Mr. Hopkinson, very respectable Characters, expressed a great desire to hear the Arguments. All was Silence: No one would speak: all Eyes were turned upon me. Mr. Edward Rutledge came to me and said laughing, Nobody will speak but you, upon this Subject. You have all the Topicks so ready, that you must satisfy the Gentlemen from New Jersey. I answered him laughing, that it had so much the Air of exhibiting like an Actor or Gladiator for the Entertainment of the Audience, that I was ashamed to repeat what I had said twenty times before, and I thought nothing new could be advanced by me. The New Jersey Gentlemen however still insisting on hearing at least a Recapitulation of the Arguments and no other Gentleman being willing to speak, I summed up the Reasons, Objections and Answers, in as concise a manner as I could, till at length the Jersey Gentlemen said they were fully satisfied and ready for the Question, which was then put and determined in the Affirmative.

Mr. Jay, Mr. Duane and Mr. William Livingston of New Jersey were not present. But they all acquiesced in the Declaration and steadily supported it ever afterwards.

July [4]. 1776. Resolved that Dr. Franklin, Mr. J. Adams and Mr. Jefferson be a Committee to prepare a device for a Seal for the United States of America.

## 33.7

### John Dickinson, Notes for a Speech in Congress, July 1, 1776

In the sections of the long speech copied below, which marked John Dickinson's last stand in Congress against independence, he argues that declaring independence could have two immediate benefits—animating the populace domestically and encouraging financial and military support internationally. The first he dismissed as unnecessary, and the second as better served by battlefield victories than by mere words. In particular, to declare independence before consulting France would be "totally slighting their sentiments." Moreover, Dickinson predicted that "when We have bound ourselves to an eternal Quarrel with G. B. by a Declaration of Independence, France has nothing to do but to hold back & intimidate G. B. till Canada is put into her Hands, then to intimidate Us into a most disadvantageous Grant of our Trade."

In arguing against an immediate declaration, Dickinson pointed out that it could further unite a divided Britain and lead to a more vicious policy of war, and would be unlikely to help unify the colonies. He, along with many other moderates, urged that Congress complete the confederation and outline a treaty with France before declaring independence. Because little in the speech puts him in opposition to the substance of independence—that issue, as Adams fairly reported, seems close to having been decided—the only remaining matter under discussion was timing.

Still, since the peace commissioners arrived on Staten Island a week later, timing turned out to be anything but a trivial matter, and a postponement, even for a month, might have resulted in a rather different outcome. Dickinson makes an impressive case that "G. B. after one or more unsuccessful Campaigns may be endued to offer Us such a share of Commerce as would satisfy Us—to appoint Councillors during good Behaviour—to withdraw her armies—in short to redress all the Grievances complained of in our first Petition—to protect our Commerce—Establish our Militias." There was still, then, something in him that believed some manner of reconciliation was possible. He suggested, accordingly, that Congress wait to learn the terms to be offered by France: "Let Us know, if We can get Terms from France that will be more beneficial than these. If We can, let Us declare Independance. If We cannot, let Us at least withhold that Declaration, till We obtain Terms that are tolerable." Carter Braxton, it might be remembered, believed that he had discovered the cause of the impatience in Congress, that is, the fear among radical delegates that Britain might actually offer just terms for reconciling the colonies to it. And, indeed, if it had done so, "the moderates in Congress—and much of public opinion 'out-of-doors'—would have leapt at the offer."[136]

With the seemingly inexplicable haste of some in Congress in mind, Dickinson was amazed that some delegates had secretly supported independence for up to a year while declaring the opposite in private and public speeches. Adams, in his diary (see above), admits as much. Dickinson hints that in twenty or thirty years, America might grow too large to remain a unified single country, and if that happened, "Hudson's River [may] be a proper Boundary for a separate Commonwealth to the Northward," adding, "I have a strong Impression on my Mind that this will take place." The distrust of the New England delegates by those of mid-Atlantic colonies, in spite of the recent and rapid changes in the latter's delegations and reports to the contrary, remained little changed from the first days of the First Continental Congress. Back then, in the fall of 1774, the men of New England admitted that they needed to be secretive if they were to accomplish their political goals, and that remained the case during the ensuing twenty months, even on the day before the Second Continental Congress declared the colonies independent states.

Paul H. Smith, ed., *Letters of Delegates to Congress, 1774–1789* (Washington, D.C.: Library of Congress, 1976–93), 4:351–57. "Masserano" refers to Felipe Ferrero de Fiesco, prince of Masserano, who was the Spanish ambassador to Britain.

Arguments against the Independance of these Colonies—In Congress. . . .

What Advantages? 2. 1. Animate People. 2. Convince foreign Powers of our Strength & Unanimity, & aid in consequence thereof.

As to 1st—Unnecessary. Life, Liberty & Property sufficient Motive. General Spirit of America.

As to 2d—foreign Powers will not rely on Words.

The Event of the Campaign will be the best Evidence. This properly the first Campaign. Who has received Intelligence that such a Proof of our Strength & daring Spirit will be agreeable to France? What must she expect from a People that begin their Empire in so high a stile, when on the Point of being invaded by the whole Power of G.B. aided by [formidable foreign?] aid—unconnected with foreign Power? She & Spain must perceive the imminent Danger of their Colonies lying at our Doors. Their Seat of Empire in another world. Masserano. Intelligence from Cadiz.

More respectful to act in Conformity to the views of France. Take advantage of their Pride, Give them Reason to believe that We confide in them, desire to act in conjunction with their Policies & Interests. Know how they will regard this (*new Star*) Stranger in the States of the world. People fond of what they have attained in producing. Regard it as a Child—A Cement of affection. Allow them the glory of appearing the vindicators of Liberty. It will please them.

It is treating them with Contempt to act otherwise. Especially after the application made to France which by this time has reach'd them. Bermuda 5 May. Abilities of the person sent. What will they think, if now so quickly after without waiting for their Determination—Totally slighting their sentiments on such a prodigous [ . . . ]—We haughtily pursue our own Measures? May they not say to Us, Gentlemen You falsely pretended to consult Us, & disrespectfully proceeded without waiting our Resolution. You must abide the Consequences. We are not ready for a Rupture. You should have negotiated till We were. We will not be hurried by your Impetuosity. We know it is our Interest to support You. But we shall be in no haste about it. Try your own strength & Resources in which you have such Confidence. We know now you dare not look back. Reconciliation is impossible without declaring Yourselves the most rash & at the same Time the most contemptible Thrasos that ever existed on Earth. Suppose on this Event G.B. should offer Canada to France & Florida to Spain with an Extension of the old Limits. Would not France & Spain accept them? Gentlemen say the Trade of all America is more valuable to France than Canada. I grant it but suppose she may get both. If she is politic, & none doubts that, I averr she has the easiest Game to play for attaining both, that ever presented itself to a Nation.

When We have bound ourselves to an eternal Quarrel with G.B. by a Declaration of Independence, France has nothing to do but to hold back & intimidate G.B. till Canada is put into her Hands, then to intimidate Us into a most disadvantageous Grant of our Trade. It is my firm opinion these Events will take Place—& arise naturally from our declaring Independance.

As to Aid from foreign Powers. Our Declaration can procure Us none this Campaign tho made today. It is impossible.

Now consider if all the advantages expected from foreign Powers cannot be attained in a more unexceptionable manner. Is there no way of giving Notice of a Nation's Resolutions than by proclaiming it to all the world? Let Us in the most solemn Manner inform the House of Bourbon, at least France, that we wait only for her Determination to declare an Independence. We must not talk generally of foreign Powers but of those We expect to favor Us. Let Us assure Spain that we never will give any assistance to her Colonies. Let France become Guarantee. Form arrangements of this Kind.

Besides, first Establish our governments & take the Regular Form of a State. These preventive Measures will shew Deliberation, wisdom, Caution & Unanimity.

Our Interest to keep G.B. in Opinion that We mean Reunion as long as possible. Disadvantage to administration from Opposition. Her Union from our Declaration. Wealth of London &c pour'd into Treasury. The whole Nation ardent against us. We oblige her to persevere. Her Spirit. See last petition of London. Suppose We shall ruin her. France must rise on her Ruins. Her Ambition. Her Religion. Our Danger from thence. We shall weep at our victories. Overwhelm'd with Debt. Compute that Debt 6 Millions of Pa. Money a Year.

The War will be carried on with more Severity. Burning Towns. Letting Loose Indians on our Frontiers. Not yet done. Boston might have been burnt. What advantages to be expected from a Declaration? 1. Animating our Troops. Answer, Unnecessary. 2. Union of Colonies. Answer, Also unnecessary. It may weaken that Union—when the People find themselves engaged in a [*war*] rendered more cruel by such a Declaration without prospect of End to their Calamities by a Continuation of the War. People changeable. In Bitterness of Soul they may complain against our Rashness & ask why We did not apply first to foreign Powers. Why We did not settle all Differences among ourselves. Take Care to secure unsettled Lands for easing their Burthens instead of leaving them to particular Colonies. Why not wait till better prepar'd. Till We had made an Experiment of our Strength. This [probably?] the first Campaign.

3. Proof of our strength & Spirit. France & Spain may be alarm'd & provoked. Masserano. Insult to France. Not the least Evidence of her granting Us favorable Terms. Her probable Conditions. The Glory of recovering Canada. She will get that & then dictate Terms to Us.

A *Partition* of these Colonies will take Place if G.B. cant conquer Us. Destroying a House before We have got another. In Winter with a small Family. Then asking a Neighbor to take Us in. He unprepared.

4th. The Spirit of the Colonies calls for such a Declaration. Answer, not to be relied on. Not only Treaties with foreign powers but among Ourselves should precede this Declaration. We should know on what Grounds We are to stand with Regard to one another.

Declaration of Virginia about Colonies in *their Limits*.

The Committee on Confederation dispute almost every Article—some of Us totally despair of any reasonable Terms of Confederation.

We cannot look back. Men generally sell their Goods to most Advantage when they have several Chapmen. We have but two to rely on. We exclude one by this Declaration without knowing What the other will give.

G.B. after one or more unsuccessful Campaigns may be endued to offer Us such a share of Commerce as would satisfy Us—to appoint Councillors during good Behaviour—to withdraw her armies—in short to redress all the Grievances complained of in our first Petition—to protect our Commerce—Establish our Militias. Let Us know, if We can get Terms from France that will be more beneficial than these. If We can, let Us declare Independence. If We cannot, let Us at least withhold that Declaration, till We obtain Terms that are tolerable.

We have many Points of the utmost moment to settle with France—Canada, Acadia, Cape Breton. What will Content her? Trade or Territory? What Conditions of Trade? Barbary Pirates. Spain. Portugal. Will she demand an Exclusive Trade as a Compensation or grant Us protection against piratical States only for a share of our Commerce?

When our Enemies are pressing us so vigorously, When We are in so wretched a State of preparation, When the Sentiments & Designs of our expected Friends are so unknown to Us, I am alarm'd at this Declaration being so vehemently prest. A worthy Gentleman told Us, that people in this House have had different Views for more than a 12 month. Amazing after what they have so repeatedly declared in this House & private Conversations—that they meant only Reconciliation. But since they can conceal their Views so dextrously I should be glad to read a little more in the Doomsday Book of America—Not all—that like the Book of Fate might be too dreadful.

I should be glad to know whether in 20 or 30 Years this Commonwealth of Colonies may not be thought too unwieldy—& Hudson's River be a proper Boundary for a separate Commonwealth to the Northward. I have a strong Impression on my Mind that this will take place.

## 33.8

JOHN ADAMS TO ABIGAIL ADAMS, JULY 3, 1776

John Adams wrote his wife the day after Congress had voted on and approved Lee's resolution declaring the colonies independent states. In his letter, he continues to lament that "many Gentlemen in high Stations and of great Influence have been duped," no doubt with Dickinson and other moderates in mind, "by the ministerial Bubble of Commissioners." Because of the delay insisted on by those hoping for the best from the peace commissioners, Adams believed the colonies failed in their quest to conquer Canada: many in Congress were "slow and languid, in promoting Measures for the Reduction of that Province." He adds that smallpox, not stiff military resistance, was still more likely the cause of their failure there.

Though the delay in declaring independence may have contributed to the colonies' failure to conquer Canada, it nonetheless yielded substantial benefits, one in particular: "The Hopes of Reconciliation, which were fondly entertained by Multitudes of honest and well meaning tho weak and mistaken People, have been gradually and at last totally extinguished. Time has been given for the whole People, maturely to consider the great Question of Independence and to ripen their Judgments." One can only wonder whether it would have made any difference, in the judgment of Adams or those he belittled for hoping for reconciliation with Britain, if the peace commissioners had arrived off the coast of Staten Island a few weeks before the vote on July 2.

Adams writes with intoxication of the importance of the vote that day: "The Second Day of July 1776, will be the most memorable Epocha, in the History of America. I am apt to believe that it will be celebrated, by succeeding Generations, as the great anniversary Festival. It ought to be commemorated, as the Day of Deliverance by solemn Acts of Devotion to God Almighty." The following year, to Adams' great surprise, Americans began celebrating, whether by accident, design, or both, the fourth of July, not the second or the ninth, as the day upon which thirteen North American British colonies finally declared their independence from the British king and Empire.

Paul H. Smith, ed., *Letters of Delegates to Congress, 1774–1789* (Washington, D.C.: Library of Congress, 1976–93), 4:375–76.

Philadelphia July 3d. 1776

Had a Declaration of Independency been made seven Months ago, it would have been attended with many great and glorious Effects. [ ... ] We might before this Hour, have formed Alliances with foreign States. We should have mastered Quebec and been in Possession of Canada. [ ... ] You will perhaps wonder, how such a Declaration would have influenced our Affairs, in Canada, but if I could write with Freedom I could easily convince you, that it would, and explain to you the manner how. Many Gentlemen in high Stations and of great Influence have been duped, by the ministerial Bubble of Commissioners to treat. [ ... ] And in real, sincere Expectation of this Event, which they so fondly wished, they have been slow and languid, in promoting Measures for the Reduction of that Province. Others there are in the Colonies who really wished that our

Enterprise in Canada would be defeated, that the Colonies might be brought into Danger and Distress between two Fires, and be thus induced to submit. Others really wished to defeat the Expedition to Canada, lest the Conquest of it, should elevate the Minds of the People too much to hearken to those Terms of Reconciliation which they believed would be offered Us. These jarring Views, Wishes and Designs, occasioned an opposition to many salutary Measures, which were proposed for the Support of that Expedition, and caused Obstructions, Embarrassments and studied Delays, which have finally, lost Us the Province.

All these Causes however in Conjunction would not have disappointed Us, if it had not been for a Misfortune, which could not be foreseen, and perhaps could not have been prevented, I mean the Prevalence of the small Pox among our Troops. [ ... ] This fatal Pestilence compleated our Destruction. It is a Frown of Providence upon Us, which We ought to lay to heart.

But on the other Hand, the Delay of this Declaration to this Time, has many great Advantages attending it. The Hopes of Reconciliation, which were fondly entertained by Multitudes of honest and well meaning tho weak and mistaken People, have been gradually and at last totally extinguished. Time has been given for the whole People, maturely to consider the great Question of Independence and to ripen their Judgments, dissipate their Fears, and allure their Hopes, by discussing it in News Papers and Pamphletts, by debating it, in Assemblies, Conventions, Committees of Safety and Inspection, in Town and County Meetings, as well as in private Conversations, so that the whole People in every Colony of the 13, have now adopted it, as their own Act. This will cement the Union, and avoid those Heats and perhaps Convulsions which might have been occasioned, by such a Declaration Six Months ago.

But the Day is past. The Second Day of July 1776, will be the most memorable Epocha, in the History of America. I am apt to believe that it will be celebrated, by succeeding Generations, as the great anniversary Festival. It ought to be commemorated, as the Day of Deliverance by solemn Acts of Devotion to God Almighty. It ought to be solemnized with Pomp and Parade, with Shews, Games, Sports, Guns, Bells, Bonfires and Illuminations from one End of this Continent to the other from this Time forward forever more.

You will think me transported with Enthusiasm but I am not. I am well aware of the Toil and Blood and Treasure, that it will cost Us to maintain this Declaration, and support and defend these States. Yet through all the Gloom I can see the Rays of ravishing Light and Glory. I can see that the End is more than worth all the Means. And that Posterity will tryumph in that Days Transaction, even altho We should rue it, which I trust in God We shall not.

# ACT V

## NEW NATIONS, 1776–1777

The spring of 1776 proved a busy one for the delegates to Congress. While directing a war with northern, southern, and internal fronts and simultaneously trying to encourage France, Spain, and Holland to grant the colonies financial aid and military assistance, Congress drafted a plan for future treaties, which was completed on July 18. Additionally, it drafted a plan for a central government that would unite the colonies, which legally were separate republics. In early summer, of course, Congress rushed to declare the colonies independent. Congress then prepared for the arrival of the British peace commissioners, for debates on the draft Articles of Confederation, and for a new escalation in the war. Congress had begun preparing for the arrival of the peace commissioners on April 2, 1776, when it took under consideration a letter of March 24 from General Washington, asking how Congress wished him to receive them. After delaying some, and rejecting reports written by two committees, Congress finally agreed on May 6 on a brief resolution regarding the proper treatment of the commissioners.

Coincidentally, that was the same day the king confirmed that Admiral Lord Richard Howe and his brother General William Howe had three days earlier been appointed commissioners to travel to the colonies with powers to pardon and offer protection to those colonists willing to return to their allegiance to the king; they would also be there as commanders of the king's naval and army forces. The Howes were not empowered to negotiate directly with what the Crown viewed as an extralegal body, Congress. Admiral Howe, while sailing down the coast from Halifax, on June 20 wrote a "Declaration and Circular Letter" for distribution upon his arrival near Staten Island on July 12. On July 19, the same day that Congress ordered the Declaration of Independence be engrossed on parchment, it directed the publication of Lord Howe's circular letter, accompanied by its own introductory statement.

Earlier, on July 12, a draft of the Articles of Confederation and Perpetual Union composed by a committee chaired and guided by John Dickinson was laid before Congress. Eighty copies were printed under tight security. On July 22, Congress began three weeks of intermittent debate on the Articles, ending on August 8. Then, on August 20, the chairman of the committee of the whole, John Morton of Pennsylvania, reported out a revised draft of the Articles of Confederation, and eighty copies were again printed, under strict secrecy, for further consideration by congressional delegates. The most controversial issues were how the states were to vote in the new Congress, equally or proportionally; how national expenses were to be apportioned among the states, that is, by population or by some other measure of wealth; and whether Congress should have the power to decide land disputes between the states, in particular concerning undistributed western lands.

There was a pressing need for an intergovernmental body to bind the states in a legal framework. Congress was at best a makeshift body, exercising oversight only over the Continental Army, the navy, foreign relations, and a currency. Yet it was unable to complete a plan of government quickly because of the demands of executive functions—in the main, managing, funding, and supplying the needs of a war—and its own survival, being forced, while under military threat, to relocate to Baltimore and then back to Philadelphia. There was also a lack of enthusiasm among a number of delegates toward any plan of central government, for like many of their constituents, they were content with running their sovereign and wholly independent "nations" without the intervention of an outside body, be it Parliament or a national government in America. Accordingly, in spite of Congress' intention to return immediately to completing the Articles of Confederation, it did not do so for another eight months, until April 21, 1777, and even then for only, at best, two days a week. Congress did not focus intensely again on the Articles of Confederation and Perpetual Union, in preparation for sending it out to the states for consideration and ratification, until the fall of 1777.

On July 2, the day that the colonies declared their independence, General William Howe landed on Staten Island with the 10,000-man army that he had evacuated from Boston earlier in the spring. Ten days later, Admiral Lord Richard Howe arrived with a fleet of warships and 150 transports, with more on the way. This was the largest expeditionary force ever gathered by the British. By late August, General Howe had under his command approximately "32,000 men, about 9,000 of whom were German mercenaries." Before August 25, "he landed about 20,000 troops on Long Island . . . On the morning of the 27th Howe fell upon the rear" of the Americans' position and routed them. He took the American in command, General Sullivan, prisoner and inflicted "1,500 casualties upon an American force of about 5,000 at a cost of less than 400 of his own men." Unknown to the British, "Washington during the night of 29–30 Aug. skillfully withdrew" his forces from Long Island to Manhattan.[1]

After the overwhelming British victory, the Howes hoped that the king's former colonists might be more willing to consider his offer of pardons for those willing to return to their allegiance to him. Accordingly, they broke off offensive operations and sent the captured General Sullivan, under parole, to Congress to propose that a peace conference be held before any additional lives were lost. After obtaining permission from General Washington, Sullivan traveled to Philadelphia and on September 2 delivered to Congress Lord Howe's request that a peace conference be held, not formally with Congress, but with "some of the members, whom he would Consider . . . as private Gentlemen" (see document 36.1). Congress agonized over the propriety of sending a delegation to meet with the Howes, but on September 5 decided to send a committee, instructing Sullivan to communicate the same to Howe. On September 6, Congress chose a committee of three, which on September 11 met with Lord Howe on Staten Island.

On September 17, the committee members reported on their meeting with Howe. He had made clear that nothing could be accomplished until Congress rescinded the Declaration of Independence. Similarly, little could be done, at least in the short term, until delegates were willing to continue to confer with Howe outside their roles as members of Congress, which, in British eyes, was an illegal gathering of colonial delegates that threatened Britain's imperial supremacy (see documents 36.4 and 36.5). The declaring of independence, Congress responded, was not something that it had the power to undo unless the independent states first instructed it to act.

Given the failure of their peace efforts, the Howe brothers returned to offensive operations. On September 15, British forces routed the remaining Continental forces on lower Manhattan before occupying New York City. Six days later, a devastating fire swept through the city, destroying almost three hundred buildings. In Congress, on September 17, the plan of treaties with foreign nations for commerce and friendship, which had been drafted on July 18, was, after amending, adopted. On September 26, Congress appointed three of its members to negotiate with European powers: Silas Deane, who had remained in France after Congress sent him there the previous spring; Benjamin Franklin, who had returned from Europe a little over a year earlier; and Thomas Jefferson, who declined the appointment. In his place, a close confidant of Samuel Adams, Arthur Lee of Virginia, who was already in Europe, was chosen on October 22. The commissioners were instructed to arrange for the purchase in France of eight ships of the line. In December, Franklin joined Deane and Lee in Paris; a month later, he was temporarily appointed American commissioner to the Court of Spain also.

From October 1776 through February 1777, Congress and the states in the northern mid-Atlantic region were consumed with planning for and fighting the war. On October 11 and 13, 1776, at the Battles of Valcour Bay and Split Rock, the small Continental fleet on Lake Champlain was nearly destroyed. On October 28, immediately north of Manhattan in White Plains, New York, the British army defeated the Continental forces under General Washington and on November 16 returned to Fort Washington and took it, along with 2,818 American prisoners. In the same campaign, Howe sent General Cornwallis across the Hudson on November 18 to take Fort Lee, which General Greene was forced to evacuate, leaving behind much-needed military stores. Generals Greene and Washington retreated southward toward the Delaware River. On December 1, under orders from a Congress fearful of a British attack on Philadelphia, Washington crossed back into Pennsylvania with his troops.

Congress on December 9 appointed committees to prepare a new Address to the Inhabitants of America and "a recommendation to the several states, to appoint a day of fasting, humiliation, and prayer." On December 10 and 11, the committees produced, and Congress approved, an Address to the People of the United States and a recommendation, on a day to be chosen by the states, for a day of fasting and humiliation, most especially among Continental troops, whose officers were enjoined to encourage "repentance and reformation" and to forbid "profane swearing, and all immorality" among their troops. By December 12, Congress feared an imminent British attack on Philadelphia and the loss of needed "quiet and uninterrupted attention . . . which ever should prevail in the great continental council." So it adjourned to "Baltimore, in the state of Maryland, to meet on the 20th instant," and vested General Washington, not for the last time, with near-dictatorial powers "to order and direct all things relative to the department, and to the operations of war."[2]

On December 21, 1776, after reconvening in Baltimore, Congress appointed an executive committee of three "to execute such continental business as may be proper and necessary to be done in Philadelphia" during its absences. On the twenty-sixth, Congress made the momentous decision to appoint a committee to prepare a plan "for better conducting the executive business of Congress, by boards composed of persons, not members of Congress."[3] Finally, after nearly sixteen months of managing a war and all manner of ancillary executive duties, Congress began creating permanent national-level executive bodies.

On the same day, Washington and 2,400 troops famously crossed the ice-choked Delaware River from Pennsylvania and surprised and routed the unprepared Hessian garrison of 1,400 men in Trenton, New Jersey. Nearly 1,000 of the Hessians were taken prisoner, while Washington's Continental troops suffered only 5 casualties. On the last day of the year, Congress received news of this much-needed victory. Within days, on January 3, 1777, Washington had another victory to report, this time in Princeton, New Jersey, against British regulars. Washington repulsed their attempt to regain Trenton and drove the British, with substantial losses, back toward New Brunswick. Those two victories in New Jersey did much to restore a measure of confidence in Congress and to a people badly shaken by recent defeats and the forced evacuation of Congress.

In one of its last acts of 1776, Congress resolved on December 30 to send commissioners "to the Courts of *Vienna*, Spain, Prussia, *and the grand Duke of Tuscany*" to persuade them that "Congress and the inhabitants of these states" were determined "at all events to maintain their independence"; if possible, the commissioners were to encourage those governments to attack "*the Electorate of Hanover, or any part of the dominions of Great Britain in Europe,* [and] *the East or West Indies.*"[4] Throughout most of January and February 1777, Congress, still in Baltimore, was occupied with war-related matters: appointing a commissary to ensure the proper treatment of American prisoners held in fire-ravaged New York City; finding ways to support the value of the Continental dollar; meeting the threat of loyalist insurrections in New Jersey, New York, Delaware, and Maryland;[5] and helping Washington staff his army at the highest levels.

On February 12, in response to persistent losses in the ranks from desertion, Congress chose a committee of three "to consider the most effectual means of discouraging and preventing desertions." The next day, it brought in a report whose final amended paragraph fostered considerable controversy. It permitted Congress to authorize, without the states' involvement, local committees of safety or inspection to apprehend, without legal protections, suspected deserters and turn them over to "the nearest Continental officer." The officers, in turn, were "directed to receive and secure such deserters that they may be safely delivered to their respective Regiments, and brought to a speedy trial and exemplary punishment" (see document 37.1). For many in Congress, most particularly Thomas Burke of North Carolina, the amendment was an unprecedented and illegal extension of congressional power and an abuse of the civil rights of the states' citizens. Nonetheless, Congress approved the measure on February 25. The repercussions of this debate on the Articles of Confederation and their previously nationalist bent, though, may have made this victory a Pyrrhic one for the nationalists.

On February 15, Congress endorsed the general outlines of the recommendations adopted by the December–January conference held in New England regarding wage and price inflation, and suggested that similar conferences be held in the middle states in March, and in the southern states in May. The conferees had recommended measures to "be taken for preventing the depreciation of their currency" and "for regulating the price of labour, of manufactures and of internal produce within those States," in other words, wage and price controls. Congress went on to recommend as well that all other states "adopt such measures, as they shall think most expedient to remedy the evils occasioned by the present fluctuating and exorbitant prices."[6] None of the states carried through with the recommendations.

On February 27, Congress adjourned "to ten o'clock on Wednesday next [March 5], to meet at the State House in Philadelphia." In Britain, on February 28, General John Burgoyne submitted to Lord George Germain, a hard-liner serving as secretary of state for the colonies (since November 1775), a three-pronged plan of attack on New York State to isolate New England from the states to the south. Germain approved it, and Burgoyne was given command of the main component, which was to push southward from Lake Champlain and down the Mohawk Valley. While in Philadel-phia, with new war plans afoot, Congress couldn't muster a quorum when scheduled to reconvene; it implored Delaware and New York immediately to send their delegates. Though Congress reconvened on March 12, it had difficulty mustering a quorum of nine states on March 17–18, so business was again postponed.

On April 8, Congress resolved to resume debate on "the report of the committee of the whole house, on the articles of confederation." But it didn't begin debating the Articles again until the twenty-first. Before doing so, on April 17, Congress changed the name of the Committee of Secret Correspondence to the Committee of Foreign Affairs and appointed a secretary, the celebrated, controversial Thomas Paine. Some-time before April 29 and while meeting as a committee of the whole (so there is no record of the proceedings), Congress, at the urging of Thomas Burke, fundamentally transformed Dickinson's Articles of Confederation, in which the states, while enjoying limited and enumerated powers, were to be subordinate to a sovereign central govern-ment. In what has come to be called Burke's amendment—in truth, one of two or more—the confederated central government would be limited to enumerated powers, and the states would continue to enjoy sovereign and undefined powers (see docu-ments 38.1 and 38.2). The government for unifying the states had been transformed. On April 30, Congress appointed yet another committee of three, including James Wilson, William Duer of New York, and Thomas Burke, to draft an address to "the inhabitants of the thirteen United States, on the present situation of public affairs," which was submitted by James Wilson to Congress for its consideration on May 29. Like Wilson's address of February 13 (document 27.1), it was left unpublished.

In May 1777, Congress continued meeting intermittently as a committee of the whole to consider the draft Articles of Confederation; on May 13, Congress resolved "that the further consideration be postponed." Following up on a resolution made at the end of December 1776, it appointed commissioners to European courts: to Spain, Arthur Lee; to Tuscany, Ralph Izard of South Carolina; and to Berlin and Vienna, William Lee, the inept and scheming Lee brother who was a former sheriff of London. Congress also appointed a committee to consider whether Portugal had breached "the laws and customs of Nations respecting neutrality" by refusing to allow American vessels to enter Portuguese ports. Intriguingly, Congress on May 9 had written to each of the thirteen states, asking them "to transmit to Congress" all state papers sent to king or Parliament, with all responses received, from January 1764 to September 1774.[7]

On June 10, Congress resolved to "carry into execution the law of retaliation" regarding British prisoners in Continental hands, treating them, "as nearly similar as circumstances will admit," as the British treated American prisoners of war.[8] On the twelfth, Congress had to adjudicate a challenge to a duel issued by one member to another for words spoken "in the course of debate in Congress," and on the fourteenth it adopted a flag for a yet-to-be-created new nation, the United States, which was still without a plan of government or a constitution. On June 17, with a force of almost eight thousand troops—British, German, Canadians, and Indians—General "Gentle-man Johnny" Burgoyne left St. Johns, Quebec, with heavy artillery, reaching Fort Ticonderoga on June 20. On July 5, after Burgoyne had seized the heights overlooking the fort and had hauled cannons to the top, the American forces evacuated overnight, leaving behind desperately needed war materials. On June 20, Congress resolved again "that Monday next be assigned for considering the articles of confederation."

On June 23, a delegate from New York laid before Congress "a printed paper" signed by Dr. Thomas Young of Philadelphia and addressed to the inhabitants of Vermont, which was then called the New Hampshire Grants (document 39.2). Congress referred the matter to the committee of the whole and scheduled it for consideration on the twenty-fifth. The question was whether residents of the area, still legally part of New York State, by appealing to the language of Congress' recommendation for colonies needing to adopt new governments (May 15, 1776) and the Declaration for Independence, could proclaim their independence from "oppressive and tyrannical" New York. On June 30, Congress vehemently denied their right to do so, writing that the residents of the grants could "derive no countenance or justification from the act of Congress declaring the United Colonies to be independent of the crown of Great Britain," and repudiating the idea that Congress in the Declaration of Independence had defended the right of individuals or groups subordinate to the states, lacking such freedom, to govern themselves. Congress made clear that such a conclusion was "unwarrantable in itself, and highly dangerous in its Consequence" (document 39.1). In explaining that its proclamations during the summer of 1776 were meant to serve only the thirteen colonies that it represented, Congress was already attempting to rein in the explosive natural-rights language that it had used then so proudly to undermine the legitimacy of first mid-Atlantic colonial governance and then of king and empire.

From July through October, the war raged on two fronts. In the North, General Burgoyne's progress south toward Albany was slowed by the densely forested terrain and a growing shortage of supplies. In a number of decisive battles throughout the summer and early fall, Burgoyne's forces suffered repeated defeats. Finally, in what certainly was the most consequential event of the war, Burgoyne, surrounded by a force three times larger than his own, surrendered on October 13 in Saratoga, New York. On October 17, according to the terms of the Convention of Saratoga, his remaining troops, nearly six thousand men, were required to lay down their arms before being transported back to Great Britain, never to reenter the war (the repatriation did not take place as planned).[9] The victory at Saratoga, when news of it reached Europe, sometime in early December, did much to change the character of the war and Britain's posture.

Continental forces did not enjoy the same success on a second front. General Howe left New York City on July 23 with 15,000 men and sailed up the Chesapeake Bay, landing on August 25. At Brandywine Creek in southeastern Pennsylvania, on September 11, Washington's 10,000-man army suffered a difficult defeat. Consequently,

Congress was forced to flee to Lancaster on September 18, and then to York-Town on the twenty-first. General Howe occupied Philadelphia on September 26.

During this time, as one might imagine, Congress was predominantly consumed with managing the war, foreign affairs, and economic matters, as best it could. On July 5, the Secret Committee was replaced by the Committee of Commerce. On July 7, Congress took into consideration an appeal from three pastors concerned about the difficulty of importing British products, including Bibles, for Congress to support the printing of an English-language Bible. Congress, on September 11, decided against publication but ordered the new Committee of Commerce to import twenty thousand Bibles (how ironic that this was one of the first activities of a commerce committee). Because of the chaos attending Congress' move from Philadelphia, and likely for other reasons as well, nothing immediately came of this. More momentously for the future, Congress resolved on August 2 to begin recording roll-call votes, "if required by any State," and did so for the first time on August 8.[10] In August, too, Congress concerned itself with an ongoing struggle between Pennsylvania officials and prominent Quaker dissidents. On September 3, without compelling evidence of any wrongdoing, or any regard for the civil or procedural rights of the accused, Congress approved "of the Quaker prisoners being sent to Virginia."[11]

On October 2, Congress resolved to begin, on the following morning, considering anew the Articles of Confederation. By October 15, 1777, it had hammered out an agreement concerning the three most contentious issues: voting in Congress, apportioning the expenses of the proposed central government, and adjudicating land disputes between states while controlling the distribution of western lands. Throughout the rest of the month and into the first half of November, Congress refined these agreements while completing the Articles of Confederation.

The defeat of the American forces at the Battle of Germantown, on October 4, provided the British, by the end of November, with unlimited access for its ships traveling up the Delaware River. On October 17, in its move toward greater executive efficiency, Congress momentously resolved to create a Board of War that would include "three persons not members of Congress." On the twenty-first, Congress officially learned of Burgoyne's capitulation and the surrender of his army at Saratoga, receiving the Convention of Saratoga, that is, the terms of surrender, on the thirty-first. On the same day, Congress appointed a committee to prepare what would be America's first national day of thanksgiving, to honor the Continental forces' decisive victory over Burgoyne at Saratoga. It was reported the next day, November 1, and scheduled for celebration on Thursday, December 18 (see document 40.1). On November 1, with John Hancock's departure from Congress, Henry Laurens of South Carolina was elected as Congress' fifth president.

In early November, Congress held its final debates on the Articles; it appointed a committee on November 10 to study "sundry propositions" that Congress would consider over the following four days. Finally, on November 15, the completed text of the Articles of Confederation and Perpetual Union was approved. On November 17, the Articles were sent out, along with a circular letter (document 42.1) explaining the long delays in coming to agreement on the much-needed plan of government—substantial differences between the independent states were blamed—that would create the United States rather than united states. During the rest of the month and into December, Congress returned to issues relating to the war—most critically, supplying the troops with adequate food and clothing—and the colonies' foreign affairs and fiscal woes— issues that were interstate in focus and, thus, congressional. On December 3, Congress agreed to another speech to be delivered to the Six Nations confederation.

Of preeminent concern throughout December 1777 was the lack of supplies for the Continental Army, then in winter quarters at Valley Forge, Pennsylvania. On December 30, Congress reauthorized General Washington—who had been awarded similar authority on September 17, October 8, November 14, and December 10—to seize food, clothing, and other goods from farmers within a seventy-mile radius of his encampment (see document 43.1). That power was "extended from the last day of the present month to the 10th day of April next, unless sooner revoked by Congress."[12] Washington's troops were to provide farmers with a promissory note of payment, the amount paid to be determined at a future date in New Haven, Connecticut, in depreciated Continental currency. As one might imagine, this population, not altogether sympathetic to the American cause in any case, was not won over by such intrusive actions, which resulted from their lack of voluntary compliance.

News of the defeat of Burgoyne at Saratoga arrived in Europe in early December. Lord North began working on a new offer of reconciliation, one that he hoped would woo the Americans back to their former dependent relationship and prevent them from building a closer one with the French. Worried that the British might be successful in those efforts, and buoyed by the news of the British defeat at Saratoga, the French informed the American envoys on December 17, 1777, that Louis XVI had decided to recognize the independence of the United States; on January 8, 1778, France indicated its willingness to enter into an alliance, both commercial and military, with the United States. Hoping to prevent this, Lord North introduced a series of bills in Parliament on February 17, 1778, that he hoped would lead to reconciliation with the North American states. The Earl of Carlisle was selected to head a new peace commission, which was to include William Eden, George Johnstone, and, again, the Howe brothers. Instructions provided to the Carlisle Commission (document 47.1) empowered it to negotiate with Congress, to offer to repeal offensive legislation from the period 1764–1775, to promise, like Lord North's peace proposal (see document 23.1), that Parliament would not impose taxes for revenue on the North American colonies, and to normalize any other outstanding issues.

After arriving in early June 1778, the commission members learned that Congress on April 22, 1778, had resolved not to meet with them and to brand anyone coming to terms with them a traitor. In desperation, the commission members appealed directly

to the American people on October 3 via a manifesto and proclamation that threatened a war of greater destructiveness if America did not abandon its newly found
French allies and return to the British Empire. Receiving no response, the commissioners left New York on November 27, having utterly failed in their peace mission.
Meanwhile, Louis XVI officially received the three American agents on March 20,
1778, and soon afterward, at about the same time that the Carlisle Commission arrived
in Philadelphia, war broke out between France and Great Britain. On May 4, 1778,
Congress ratified two treaties with France, and in September elected Franklin to be
the first minister to France. The new states never returned to their dependent relationship with Great Britain, and on March 1, 1781, with the ratification of the Articles of
Confederation and Perpetual Union they became unified in a new nation.

## DOCUMENT SUMMARY

The first document reproduces parts of five articles from the draft of the Articles of
Confederation presented to Congress on July 12, 1776. Four major issues pitted the
congressional delegations one against another: how states would vote in Congress,
equally or in proportion to some standard, either wealth or population (Article XVII);
how much sovereignty each state was to retain (Articles III and XX); how taxes for
national expenses would be apportioned among the states (Article XI); and how much
authority Congress would exercise in deciding land disputes among states and in
allocating western lands. In regard to voting in Congress, the Articles between July 1776
and November 1777 changed little, that is, all States, as was true in the Stamp Act
Congress and both Continental Congresses, would continue to enjoy an equal vote.
Regarding the other issues, the Articles were changed substantially during sixteen
months of intermittent debate and revision. Possibly the most critical change, and the
least contested, involved state sovereignty, for the Articles moved, without great fanfare,
from being a document weighted toward central governmental authority, in the draft
produced by the Dickinson committee, to a more localist and state-centered one, as
amended by Thomas Burke, approved by Congress, and sent out for ratification.

Compromises on apportioning tax burdens among the states, including assessing
them by population and counting every two slaves as the equivalent of one free
laborer, were rejected as each delegation consistently adhered to its state's particular
interests. As would be true in the Constitutional Convention, most delegates compe-
tently represented their state's interest as a large state or a small one, rather than
taking what one might view as a more disinterested or principled stance. Finally, in
regard to land claims, the standard to be employed, only a month after the colonies
declared their independence from Britain, was not natural reason or natural law, but
the language of English royal charters and the principles of the English common law.

The second set of readings is concerned with the long-anticipated British peace
commission, which finally arrived off the coast of Staten Island on July 12. The primary documents are Lord Howe's declaration and circular letter of June 20, and

Congress' Resolution of July 19 to publish them. Two conclusions can readily be drawn from these and associated documents: the Howe brothers had grossly insufficient authority to settle the constitutional issues dividing the colonies and Great Britain—merely offering pardons was entirely inadequate; and the congressional radicals' rush to declare independence in advance of the commissioners' arrival was a shrewd move, since both independence and Britain's view of Congress as an illegal assembly proved to be insurmountable obstacles to any meaningful negotiations.

The third set of readings focus on the meeting between Lord Howe and three congressional delegates on September 11. That meeting followed the crushing defeat of Continental forces at the Battle of Long Island on August 27, an outcome that the Howes believed, wrongly, might lead to a spirit of accommodation on the American side. Both sides understood that the real issues separating them reached back to 1764: whether Parliament had the right to tax or legislate for the former colonies, and how Britain could maintain its commercial advantages if Parliament ceded any ground on the first issue. These readings corroborate the sense of action and counteraction—Parliament and king versus Congress—that runs throughout the earlier sections. Congress' Olive Branch Petition of July 1775 (see document 19.1) was met by Parliament's American Prohibitory Act of December 1775 (see document 29.2), which removed the colonists from the king's protection; those two documents are shown to bookend the final stage of the Imperial Crisis.

During the meeting with Howe, the delegates represented Congress as unable to "undo" the Declaration of Independence, for each state was, as a result of it, a fully independent and separate polity. The legal authority of Congress to intrude into the internal life of the states, even in pursuit of agreed-upon aims such as matters relating to the Continental Army, is the focus of the next principal reading, the congressional Report on the Discouraging and Preventing of Desertions of February 13 and 25, 1777. The goal of the resolution, to return deserters to their units and, as needed, duly punish them, was not disputed, and so the body of the text was not subject to close consideration. But the paragraph appended in conclusion, which became operative only if a state legislature was out of session, produced strong opposition. In it, Congress requested that "the committees of observation or inspection in these United States . . . cause diligent enquiry to be made, in their respective Counties or Districts, for all Deserters that may be lurking and harboured therein, and cause such, whenever found, to be immediately secured, and conveyed to the nearest Continental officer."

Here, Congress was instructing local committees, without the concurrence of their state governments, to secure suspected deserters and remand them to the custody of a Continental officer, not a local or state official. The suspects were denied the due process rights enjoyed by a state's citizens and then whisked away to parts unknown. The same substantive issue was replayed seventy-five years later in the Fugitive Slave Act of 1850, but by then Congress' authority was far greater. In 1777, opposition to this part of the resolution was led by the irrepressible and difficult Thomas Burke. He claimed that the majority in Congress supported him in his opposition, yet for reasons not fully explained, the resolutions, including the last paragraph, were approved on February 25. Burke's assessment of the stance taken by the majority in Congress, that it supported his defense of what can only be described as states' rights, even if unhelpful in explaining the approval of this resolution, was fully confirmed in Congress' almost unanimous support of his amending of the Articles of Confederation as described in the next set of documents.

The fifth set of readings compares Article III in the July 12, 1776, version of the Articles of Confederation to the final November 15, 1777, version, Article 2 (Congress changed, and would change again, its method of enumerating them), and both to Burke's "Plan for a Bicameral Central Government with Enumerated Powers" of May 5, 1777. This amendment to the Articles failed; however, in proposing that they endorse a bicameral legislature with one body having equal state representation and the other proportional, he anticipated the solution to the large state–small state dilemma that was adopted by the Constitutional Convention. With far greater success, in a letter to Richard Caswell on April 29, Burke explains that he managed to shift, by a 11–1 vote, the center of gravity of the Articles of Confederation from a central-government-dominant plan to one in which the states would continue to have the upper hand. In so doing, he defeated in debate two congressional stalwarts, James Wilson and R. H. Lee. Burke's amending of the draft Articles generated little debate or controversy even though it fundamentally reshaped the Articles approved in November 1777 and sent out to the states.

The sixth set of readings, related to Congress' response to the petition of the inhabitants of the New Hampshire Grants for independence on June 30, 1777, suggests that Congress may have had something less than universal goals in mind when promulgating its recommendation for colonies needing to adopt new governments (May 15, 1776) and the Declaration of Independence. The inhabitants of what had been part of New York State declared their independence on January 15, 1777, and petitioned Congress for recognition and representation in that body. In their declaration and in associated documents, the residents claimed that, based on Congress' earlier pronouncements, they were duly entitled to self-government and to separate from oppressive New York in pursuit of their happiness. Although Congress, in the end, did little to put an end to the matter—its resources in that part of New York and Vermont, with General Burgoyne marching down from Canada along the border between the two, were stretched far too thin—its language of denunciation was unequivocal.

The next principal reading is America's first national thanksgiving proclamation, offered by Congress on November 1, 1777, in celebration of General Burgoyne's defeat at Saratoga on October 13 at the hands of Continental forces. Unlike earlier congressional proclamations for fasting, humiliation, and prayer, this one was for thanksgiving. An unlike still earlier ones in New England, this was a national, not a provincial, day of celebration. In it, Congress recommends that the states set aside Thursday, December 18, for a day of "solemn thanksgiving and praise" and that "through the merits of Jesus

Christ," in spite of "their manifold sins," the Continental Army had been victorious. It seems clear that the power of Reformed Protestantism, which had done so much to guide New Englanders in their opposition to Britain's intrusive legislation and had sustained their long-festering discomfort with monarchical institutions, was still alive and well in independent America. This was not a celebration that can be readily described as fostering some manner of secular civil religiosity.[13]

The eighth principal reading is a speech by one of the colonists' longtime parliamentary allies, the Earl of Chatham. Desperately seeking a reconciliation between Britain and the colonies before the latter formed an alliance with France, Chatham was reduced to a species of wishful thinking, speculating that the more moderate middle and southern colonies could be won back, one by one, from their year-old embrace of independence. It was a well-intentioned but vain attempt, since by late 1777 there was little chance of anyone on either side of the Atlantic crafting a solution that would allow for divided sovereignty within an imperial federal system that simultaneously maintained Parliament's ultimate superiority, something that even America's Whig admirers in Parliament refused to concede.

The next set of readings leads off with Congress' circular letter that accompanied the Articles of Confederation sent to the states. In this apologetic letter, Congress describes the purpose of the proposed new government—"securing the freedom, sovereignty, and independence of the United States"—then explains why the drafting of the Articles had taken so long, about sixteen months. In the main, it was the need to compromise between sovereign and independent States "differing in habits, produce, commerce, and internal police." Given these hurdles, Congress believed that the current plan was "the best which could be adapted to the circumstances of all; and as that alone which affords any tolerable prospect of a general ratification." Congress reminded the states "of the difficulty of combining in one general system the various sentiments and interests of a continent divided into so many sovereign and independent communities." In closing, Congress hoped for an expeditious ratification by the states of the new plan of government, one that would bind them together to form a new nation, help defeat enemies domestic and foreign, support the public credit, "and add weight and respect to our councils at home, and to our treaties abroad."

In a series of final votes on contested issues, the colonies most responsible for the drive toward independence, Virginia and those of New England, did not always have their way, even in a less conservative Congress. Regarding the mode of voting to be followed in the proposed Confederation Congress, only Virginia voted in opposition to equal representation. Similarly, regarding the apportionment of national expenses among the states, all the New England delegates opposed the idea of basing them on the value of surveyed land. They lost that critical vote. The close partnership between New England and Virginia congressional radicals, exemplified in a letter from Richard Henry Lee of Virginia to Roger Sherman of Connecticut (document 42.5), no longer enjoyed its earlier salience as issues other than the movement toward independence and republican government took center stage.

The last set of documents focuses on Congress' resolutions on supplying the needs of the Continental Army and an accompanying circular letter. In the resolutions, Congress encourages state officials to seize clothing and other necessities "suitable for the army" and to offer certificates for property taken. Curiously, only state citizens were subject to having their property confiscated. The request was issued in conjunction with those made to General Washington, on December 10 and 30, and to a committee of Congress, each empowered to do the same. Additionally, Congress encouraged the states to make every effort to control price gouging. It lamented the need for such actions, but "certain persons, devoid of . . . every principle of public virtue and . . . instigated by the lust of avarice, are, in each State, assiduously endeavouring, by every means of oppression, sharping, and extortion, to accumulate enormous gain to themselves." Congress seemed to fear a falling away among the people of the selfless version of republican public virtue that outspoken radicals had long defended.[14]

This same theme is emphasized still more in the accompanying circular letter, in which Congress explains that it feels "constrained to recommend measures which the virtue of all classes of men rendered not long since unnecessary, and which a scrupulous regard for security of property to every citizen of these states has hitherto restrained from adopting." Unfortunately, "laws unworthy the character of infant republics are become necessary to supply the defect of public virtue." As one of the accompanying letters explains, none of this should have been surprising, since "two thirds of the State of Delaware are Notoriously known in their Hearts to be with our Enemys." Such accounts, seen against the deprivation experienced in the winter of 1777 by the Continental Army at Valley Forge, bring back to mind how little the mid-Atlantic colonies supported the hurried move in 1776 toward independence. Furthermore, the seizing of property by state officials, a congressional committee, and Washington's troops was certain to "give Umbrage to the Inhabitants." In sum, the theoretical expansiveness of the second paragraph of the Declaration of Independence no more described the reasoning or outlook of three continental congresses over a twelve-year span than it explained the actions of Congress during the year immediately following its promulgation.

## THEORETICAL ISSUES

The documents in the fifth and final section of this collection were created immediately following the Declaration of Independence and extend until the end of 1777 and the completion in November of the Articles of Confederation. The preeminent concern of Congress over those difficult eighteen months was the management of truly continental concerns: the war, foreign affairs, and currency and financial issues. Possibly still more pressing, though, was its constitutional focus on the Articles and the three related issues that so divided the states—voting in Congress, the apportionment of national taxes, and the western lands. A monumental fourth one was decided with little controversy: would the states enjoy sovereignty and the central government be limited to strictly enumerated powers, or vice versa. Congress wrestled with that constitutional question for more than thirty years, from at least 1754 to 1787. Also of considerable importance to Congress during this period, as is evident from the number of resolutions relating to it, was how to respond to the arrival of the Howes' peace commission. Surprisingly, when Lord Howe arrived off Staten Island on July 12, his commission's offer of pardons fostered remarkably little division in Congress, perhaps because of the weakness of his mandate.

Protection of the internal police powers of each colony (state), although at times ignored (see document 31.1), continued to enjoy strong support. Yet concern over this matter may have become pressing when Congress exercised new continental powers such as authorizing local agents, freed from the need to obtain state authorization or observe due process rights, to apprehend citizens suspected of deserting the Continental Army (see document 37.1). The granting of New York lands to settlers who eventually formed the state of Vermont provides an unusually helpful lens with which to view the limited goals, at least as viewed in 1777 by Congress, of the Declaration of Independence, goals that are at some distance from what the expansive language of its second paragraph might otherwise suggest.

The Declaration appears, then, to express not necessarily something new in the colonies, though in important ways it did that too, so much as the failure of the colonists and their British supporters and opponents to solve the problem of how constitutionally to conceptualize, within a predominantly Whig political theory, multiple federally arranged parliaments. When the colonists needed to find a political theory to replace their long-held commitment to constitutional monarchy, they turned out of necessity to a largely inherited seventeenth-century British republican theory that placed an absolute emphasis on popular consent, and they couched that transition in the internationally acceptable and diplomatic language of eighteenth-century natural law and natural rights. Much of the radicalism of the Declaration's second paragraph, as this documentary history makes evident, was something that continued to be contested well into 1776 and beyond. In short, the documents, debates, proclamations, resolutions, and delegates' letters leading up to and surrounding the Declaration of Independence describe a history little supportive of a visionary, confident, successful, and republican-theory-driven view of the colonies;[15] more accurately, they describe a halting, confused, messy, often inadvertent, constitutionally monarchical, and persistently divisive history of thirteen colonies in the process of creating thirteen nations and a confederated government while successfully exiting from the British Empire.

## 34. FIRST DRAFT OF A PLAN FOR A NATIONAL GOVERNMENT—THE FOUR PRINCIPAL ISSUES OF CONCERN, JULY 1776

Congress on June 10, 1776, while awaiting approval of R. H. Lee's resolution on independence whose consideration had been postponed until July 1, approved in a committee of the whole "that a plan of confederation be prepared and transmitted to the respective Colonies for their consideration and approbation." Accordingly, the next day, Congress appointed the committee to prepare a declaration of independence and one "to prepare and digest the form of a confederation to be entered into between these colonies."[16] On June 12, Congress decided that this committee should "consist of a member from each Colony." It included Roger Sherman of Connecticut and Robert R. Livingston of New York from the Declaration committee and, most importantly, John Dickinson of Pennsylvania, the penman of Congress, who, though unwilling to support independence, was asked to chair the committee and author the first draft of the Articles of Confederation. He completed the work before departing Congress in early July and being formally removed from the Pennsylvania delegation on July 20.[17] Like many in Congress, Dickinson, "had at length been converted to the doctrine of confederation, even if he was not yet prepared to embrace the gospel of independence."[18]

Also on the confederation committee were Josiah Bartlett of New Hampshire, Samuel Adams of Massachusetts, Stephen Hopkins of Rhode Island, Thomas McKean of Delaware, Thomas Stone of Maryland, Thomas Nelson of Virginia, Joseph Hewes of North Carolina, Edward Rutledge of South Carolina, and Button Gwinnett of Georgia. Francis Hopkinson of New Jersey was added on June 28. The committee was of mixed membership. Five prominent delegates were unenthusiastic or opposed to declaring independence: Dickinson, Livingston, Stone, Hewes, and Rutledge; five were outspoken congressional radicals: Sherman, Adams, Hopkins, McKean, and Nelson; and the rest were of relatively middling views.[19] The moderates benefited from the nature of the task before them—constructing a plan of confederation rather than dismantling one—and so prevailed in committee while drafting the Articles. On July 12, the committee's revised draft of Dickinson's original,[20] was laid before Congress, and "eighty copies, and no more," under the strictest secrecy, were ordered printed.[21]

On July 22, Congress, meeting as a committee of the whole, debated the committee's draft and did so each day it was in session until August 2, when delegates began signing the Declaration of Independence, before returning to the Articles on August 6–8. The chairman was John Morton of Pennsylvania, a farmer and surveyor of Swedish-Finnish descent and one of the delegates to the Stamp Act Congress in 1765. His moderate politics allowed him to join, unenthusiastically, with Franklin and Wilson in support of separation from Britain; that stance didn't, however, prevent him from powerfully opposing Pennsylvania's new, radically democratic constitution, which was ratified in the fall of 1776.[22] On August 20, 1776, he reported that, meeting as a committee of the whole, Congress had gone through the Articles and "agreed to sundry," "which he was ordered to submit to Congress." As with Dickinson's draft, eighty copies of the revised Articles (see document 38.1) were ordered printed under absolute secrecy.[23] Not all delegates felt the need for a central government, so in spite of Congress' intentions to return immediately to debating and completing the Articles, it did not do so for another eight months, until April 21, 1777, and, even then for only two days a week at best. Congress did not focus intensely on completing the Articles of Confederation and Perpetual Union, in preparation for sending the document out to the states for consideration, until the fall of 1777.

As shown in the following excerpt, there were three major issues of contention, all of which proved difficult to resolve. First was how to apportion taxes among the states in order to supply the needs of the central government. Use the value of developed land or use population, either including or excluding slaves, as a proxy for a state's assessed wealth? Article XI below indicates that it would be "in Proportion to the Number of Inhabitants of every Age, Sex and Quality, except Indians not paying Taxes," including, controversially, chattel slaves. Second was how the states were to vote in Congress. Equally or proportionally? If proportionally, according to population or wealth? Article XVII stipulated that, as in the Continental Congress, "each Colony shall have one Vote."

The third problem was, from contemporary perspectives, the most unexpected but nonetheless the most intractable. According to John Adams, it was "whether Congress shall have Authority to limit the Dimensions of each Colony, to prevent those, which claim, by Charter, or Proclamation, or Commission, to [extend to] the South Sea, from growing too great and powerfull, so as to be dangerous to the rest" (in a letter to Abigail; see document 34.4). In Dickinson's draft of Article XVIII, "the United States assembled shall have the sole and exclusive Right and Power of . . . Limiting the Bounds of those Colonies, which by Charter or Proclamation, or under any Pretence, are said to extend to the South Sea, and . . . Assigning Territories for new Colonies, either in Lands to be thus separated from Colonies and heretofore purchased or obtained by the Crown of Great-Britain." In other words, all interstate land issues were to be determined by Congress. This feature changed greatly before Congress, in October and November 1777, finally agreed on reducing its own future power over such issues.

In addition, though, there was possibly an even more significant matter, one of the two ongoing constitutional issues that looked back to the beginning of the First Continental Congress and Joseph Galloway's "Plan of Union." Seemingly unnoticed by many members of Congress was the problem of how sovereignty was to be federally divided between the states and the proposed central government. This was not overlooked by Thomas Burke of North Carolina, an Irish physician and lawyer, a man easily irritated (and readily irritating to others) and one of the great defenders in 1777 of Revolutionary-era states'-rights localism.[24]

In the Dickinson committee's draft Article III, each colony is to exercise control over its internal legislation "in all matters that shall not interfere with the Articles of this Confederation." In Article XVIII, the United States was proscribed from interfering "in the internal Police of any Colony, any further than such Police may be affected by the Articles of this Confederation." As seen in documents 38.1 and 42.1, a comparison of the draft wording of Articles III and XVIII in July 1776 with the final wording of the corresponding articles, 2 and 9, from November 1777 (Congress inconveniently switched from roman to arabic numerals before again finally returning to roman) shows that the relationship between national and state sovereignty was reversed.

What Burke successfully demanded when Congress returned at the end of April 1777 was for the delegates to consider "the vast field of undefined and unenumerated powers" that in Dickinson's draft fell within the purview of the central government. Burke sought to have those powers retained by the states so that "Congress could function only within an area of precisely delegated and carefully limited authority."[25] The contest over this issue ended fairly rapidly—at least compared with the protracted battles over other parts of the Articles. The passage of Burke's "amendment," shortly before April 29, provided a quick victory for him and most of his anticentralizing colleagues in Congress (see document 38.2). They went on to transform the Articles of Confederation and Perpetual Union from being a centralizing national document as envisioned by Dickinson, as would be true of the 1787 U. S. Constitution, to one that was state-centered and localist in character.

The Articles of Confederation came to be a "constitutional expression of this [democratic-localist] movement and the embodiment in governmental form of the philosophy of the Declaration of Independence."[26] The ascendancy of this ethos at the continental level, however, endured unchallenged for only another thirteen years. Many of those who had been the most uncertain regarding the urgent need for independence became determined to see the Declaration and the philosophy of its localist supporters replaced nationally by a different document with a different philosophy.

34.1

 JOHN DICKINSON'S COMMITTEE, DRAFT OF THE
ARTICLES OF CONFEDERATION, JULY 12, 1776

Worthington Chauncey Ford et al., eds., *Journals of the Continental Congress, 1774–1789* (Washington, D.C.: Government Printing Office, 1904–37), 5:547–54.

ART. III. Each Colony shall retain and enjoy as much of its present Laws, Rights and Customs, as it may think fit, and reserves to itself the sole and exclusive Regulation and Government of its internal police, in all matters that shall not interfere with the Articles of this Confederation. . . .

ART. XI. All Charges of Wars and all other Expences that shall be incurred for the common Defence, or general Welfare, and allowed by the United States in General Congress assembled, shall be defrayed out of a common Treasury, which shall be supplied by the several Colonies in Proportion to the Number of Inhabitants of every Age, Sex and Quality, except Indians not paying Taxes, in each Colony, a true Account of which, distinguishing the white Inhabitants who are not slaves, shall be triennially taken and transmitted to ~~Congress~~ the Assembly of the United States. The Taxes for paying that Proportion shall be laid and levied by the Authority and Direction of the Legislatures of the several Colonies, within the Time agreed upon by United States assembled. . . .

Art. XVII. In determining Questions ~~in Congress~~ each Colony shall have one Vote.

Art. XVIII. The United States assembled shall have the sole and exclusive Right and Power of . . . Limiting the Bounds of those Colonies, which by Charter or Proclamation, or under any Pretence, are said to extend to the South Sea, and ascertaining those Bounds of any other Colony that appear to be indeterminate—Assigning Territories for new Colonies, either in Lands to be thus separated from Colonies and heretofore purchased or obtained by the Crown of Great-Britain from the Indians, or hereafter to be purchased or obtained from them—Disposing of all such Lands for the general Benefit of all the United Colonies—Ascertaining Boundaries to such new Colonies, within which Forms of Government are to be established on the Principles of Liberty . . .

Art. XX. . . . These Articles shall be proposed to the Legislatures of all the United Colonies, to be by them considered, and if approved by them, they are advised to authorize their Delegates to ratify the same in Assembly of the United States, which being done, the ~~foregoing~~ Articles of this Confederation shall inviolably be observed by every Colony, and the Union is to be perpetual. . . .

## 34.2

 Thomas Jefferson, Notes of Proceedings in Congress, July 12–August 1, 1776

These notes, a continuation of those from July 1–4 (see document 33.5), were composed sometime between August 1776 and June 1783, at which time Jefferson gave them to James Madison. According to Jefferson, they describe "voting in Congress, and the Quotas of money to be required from the states."[27] There was general agreement in Congress to support the Dickinson committee's proposal that each state's portion of the central-governmental tax burden should be in proportion to "the wealth of the state" and that the population of a state was the most readily obtainable proxy for its wealth. John Witherspoon was the only dissenting vote from the proposition that population was a reliable proxy for wealth, believing instead "that the value of lands & houses was the best estimate of the wealth of a nation, and that it was practicable to obtain such a valuation." Although his proposal was ignored in July 1776, in the end, despite vehement opposition from the New England states, it became the method of apportionment approved in the final version of the Articles (see document 42.2).

There was an even sharper division between delegates from states with large slave populations and those with significantly smaller ones on whether slaves should be counted in this assessment. As might be expected, southern delegates argued against slaves being counted for taxation. Samuel Chase of Maryland—before independence, generally viewed as a mid-Atlantic colony—found that there was no more reason "for taxing the Southern states on the farmer's head, & on his slave's head, than the Northern ones on their farmer's heads & the heads of their cattle." Delegates from northern states, such as John Adams, defended the idea that slaves were to be equally counted along with white residents in apportioning the tax burdens of each state. As he noted in debate, "Certainly 500 freemen produce no more profits, no greater surplus for the paiment of taxes than 500 slaves. Therefore the state in which are the labourers called freemen should be taxed no more than that in which are those called slaves . . . It is the number of labourers which produce the surplus for taxation, and numbers therefore indiscriminately are the fair index of wealth."

Also under discussion was a compromise measure proposed by Benjamin Harrison of Virginia. A forerunner of the Article I, Section 2 clause of the U.S. Constitution in which the number of slaves in a state would be counted as three-fifths of their total for purposes of representation and taxation, it would have, for tax-apportionment purposes only, counted two slaves for every one freeman. The assumption underlying this (and the later) proposal was that slave labor was approximately half as economically productive as free labor. On a vote in which all the New England and northern mid-Atlantic states voted together against all the southern states except Georgia—with one of its two present delegates, Lyman Hall, being from Connecticut—which was split, the amendment to count slaves dispro-portionally in the apportionment of a state's national tax burden was rejected. If any commonly held higher moral principles regarding human equality or inalienable natural rights of the kind often associated with the soaring rhetoric of the Declaration of Independence were at work, it is far from obvious in the self-interested pattern of state voting, in which each one voted in accord with its economic interests and seemingly little else.

The next issue of interest reported by Jefferson was Article XVII, which concerned how the states would vote in Congress after the ratification of the Articles. This was an issue that similarly divided the delegates to the Constitutional Convention. During both periods, the issue would come close to splitting the assemblies and the Union. As Samuel Chase observed of the earlier moment in 1776, "The larger colonies had threatened they would not confederate at all if their weight in congress should not be equal to the numbers of people they added to the confederacy; while the smaller ones declared against an union if they did not retain an equal vote for the protection of their rights." Chase, a large man from a small state, offered a compromise in which "votes relating to money" would be decided by each state voting in proportion to its population, and those on all other matters "concerning life or liberty" by each state enjoying an equal vote. No other delegate, however, came forward to support his compromise.

Again, delegates represented the perceived interests of their states. Delegates from populous ones (Benjamin Franklin, Benjamin Rush, and James Wilson from Pennsylvania, and John Adams from Massachusetts) defended proportional representation. This was often confusingly described as "equality of representation" based on the number of state residents. Small-state delegates (John Witherspoon from New Jersey and Stephen Hopkins from Rhode Island) also defended "equal representation," but they meant equal state representation. Both Franklin and Wilson were willing to extend to the smaller states equal voting rights in Congress, but only if they were willing to pay an equal share of the national tax burden. Many of the arguments advanced here, most particularly the claim by large-state delegates that the diversity of their states' interests would prevent them from acting in concert, were repeated at the Constitutional Convention and, in many cases, by the same men.

Although most of the arguments advanced in debate rested on historical analogies regarding the practices and experiences of earlier amalgamations of nations (Scotland and England) or confederations (the Dutch Republic, and German and Belgic confederations), one discussion of particular theoretical interest concerned how best to understand the nature of the proposed union. Was it made up of states, the component pieces of traditional confederations, or of individuals, who were more often seen as components of unitary national states than confederations? This particular debate endured for at least another decade. The otherwise progressive-leaning Witherspoon argued, "The colonies should in fact be considered as individuals; and that as such in all disputes they should have an equal vote . . . Nothing relating to individuals could ever come before Congress; nothing but what would respect colonies."

Opposing Witherspoon, the erstwhile radical but increasingly moderate John Adams defended proportional representation of the states and showed that he knew his Hume: "Reason, justice, & equity never had weight enough on the face of the earth to govern the councils of men. It is interest alone which does it, and it is interest alone which can be trusted. That therefore the interests within doors should be the mathematical representatives of the interests without doors. That the individuality of the colonies is a mere sound." Wilson, the leading proponent of the idea of a national people, continued by noting that "the objects of it's [Congress'] care are all the individuals of the states. . . . As to those matters which are referred to Congress, we are not so many states; we are one large state. We lay aside our [state] individuality whenever we come here." He concluded that what was being complained of by the opposite side was that "the minority will be in danger from the majority." This may have been unavoidably so: "And is there an assembly on earth where this danger may not be equally pretended?" Notwithstanding the truth of his charge, Congress supported the draft position of having states vote equally, not proportionally.

In this debate, elevated principles, even majority rule, regularly lost to the interests of the states as corporate bodies. And like good lawyers—nearly half of the congressional delegates were lawyers (62 out of 130 serving from 1774 to 1777), and still more were trained in the law—the delegates defended the interests of their clients: the colonial assemblies or conventions that had sent them to Congress. Accordingly, irrespective of former alliances, political alliances, and previously commonly held positions vis-à-vis Britain, the delegates defended their clients' interests. Thus, we find Virginia, its interests no longer aligned with those of New England, voting in opposition to its former allies. State and delegate political alignments in Congress were taking on new configurations.[28] The dominant position— that Congress represented not individuals, but states—was driven home dramatically in Congress' curt response a year later to a petition from the future residents of Vermont. It declared that in 1776 Congress had represented the thirteen colonies breaking away from Great Britain—not the individuals of those colonies— and that the Declaration of Independence was not a catchall document, but rather one reflecting the will of those thirteen colonies (and no others) in declaring them independent of Great Britain (see document 39.1).

Paul H. Smith, ed., *Letters of Delegates to Congress, 1774–1789* (Washington, D.C.: Library of Congress, 1976–93), 4:438–45. The Latin phrase *jus trium liberorum* ("the right of three children") refers to a Roman law that granted legal immunities and exemptions to those who produced three or more offspring. Material in parentheses and italics was crossed out in the manuscript version but later restored.

On Friday July 12 the Committee appointed to draw the articles of confederation reported them and on the 22d the house resolved themselves into a committee to take them into consideration. On the 30th and 31st of that month & 1st of the ensuing, those articles were debated which determined the (*manner of voting in Congress, & that of fixing the*) proportion or quota(*s*) of money which each state should furnish to the common treasury, and the manner of voting in Congress. The first of these articles was expressed in the original draught in these words. 'Art. XI. All charges of war & all other expenses that shall be incurred for the common defence, or general welfare, and allowed by the United states assembled, shall be defrayed out of a common treasury, which shall be supplied by the several colonies in proportion to the number of inhabitants of every age, sex & quality, except Indians not paying taxes, in each colony, a true account of which, distinguishing the white inhabitants, shall be triennially taken & transmitted to the assembly of the United states.'

Mr. Chase moved that the quotas should be fixed, not by the number of inhabitants of every condition, but by that of the 'white inhabitants.' He admitted that taxation should be alwais in proportion to property; that this was in theory the true rule, but that from a variety of difficulties it was a rule which could never be adopted in practice. The value of the property in every state could never be estimated justly & equally. Some other measure for the wealth of the state must therefore be devised, some (*measure of wealth must be*) standard referred to which would be more simple. He considered the number of inhabitants as a tolerably good criterion of property, and that this might alwais be obtained. (*yet numbers simply would not*) he therefore thought it the best mode which we could adopt, with (*some*) one exception(*s*) only. He observed that negroes are property, and as such cannot be distinguished from the lands or personalties held in those states where there are few slaves. That the surplus of profit which a Northern farmer is able to lay by, he invests in (*lands*) cattle, horses &c. whereas a Southern farmer lays out that same surplus in slaves. There is no more reason therefore for taxing the Southern states on the farmer's head, & on his slave's head, than the Northern ones on their farmer's heads & the heads of their cattle. That the method proposed would therefore tax the Southern states according to their numbers & their wealth conjunctly, while the Northern would be taxed on numbers only: that Negroes in fact should not be considered as members of the state more than cattle & that they have no more interest in it.

Mr. John Adams observed that the numbers of people were taken by this article as an index of the wealth of the state & not as subjects of taxation. That as to this matter it was of no consequence by what name you called your people, whether by that of freemen or of slaves. That in some countries the labouring poor were called freemen, in others they were called slaves; but that the difference as to the state was imaginary only. What matters it whether a landlord employing ten labourers in his farm, gives them annually as much money as will buy them the necessaries of life, or gives them those necessaries at short hand. The ten labourers add as much wealth annually to the state, increase it's exports as much in the one case as the other. Certainly 500 freemen produce no more profits, no greater surplus for the paiment of taxes than 500 slaves. Therefore the state in which are the labourers called freemen should be taxed no more than that in which are those called slaves. Suppose by any extraordinary operation of nature or of law one half the labourers of a state could in the course of one night be transformed into slaves: would the state be made the poorer or the less able to pay taxes? That the condition of the labouring poor in most countries, that of the fishermen particularly of the Northern states is as abject as that of slaves. It is the number of labourers which produce the surplus for taxation, and numbers therefore indiscriminately are the fair index of wealth. That it is the use of the word 'property' here, & it's application to some of the people of the state, which produces the fallacy. How does the Southern farmer procure slaves? Either by importation or by purchase from his neighbor. If he imports a slave, he adds one to the number of labourers in his country, and proportionably to it's profits & abilities to pay taxes. If he buys from his neighbor, it is only a transfer of a labourer from one farm to another, which does not change the annual produce of the state, & therefore should not change it's tax. That if a Northern farmer works ten labourers on his farm, he can, it is true, invest the surplus of ten men's labour in cattle: but so may the Southern farmer working ten slaves. That a state of 100,000 freemen can maintain no more cattle than one of 100,000 slaves. Therefore they have no more of that kind of property. That a slave may indeed from the custom of speech be more properly called the wealth of his master, than the free labourer might be called the wealth of his employer: but as to the state both were equally it's wealth, and should therefore equally add to the quota of it's tax.

Mr. Harrison proposed a compromise, that two slaves should be counted as one freeman. He affirmed that slaves did not do so much work as freemen, and doubted if two effected more than one. that this was proved by the price of labor, the hire of a labourer in the Southern colonies being from 8 to £12, while in the Northern it was generally £24.

Mr. Wilson said that if this amendment should take place the Southern colonies would have all the benefit of slaves, whilst the Northern ones would bear the burthen. That slaves increase the profits of a state, which the Southern states mean to take to themselves; that they also increase the burthen of defense, which would of course fall so much the heavier on the Northern. That slaves occupy the places of freemen and eat their food. Dismiss your slaves & freemen will take their places. It is our duty to lay every discouragement on the importation of slaves; but this amendment would give the *jus trium liberorum* to him who would import slaves. That other kinds of property were pretty equally distributed thro' all the colonies: there were as many cattle, horses, & sheep in the North as the South, & South as the North: but not so as to slaves. That experience has shewn that those colonies have been alwais able to pay most which have the most (*males*) inhabitants, whether they be black or white. And the practice of the Southern colonies has alwais been to make every farmer pay poll taxes upon all his labourers whether they be black or white. He acknoleges indeed that freemen work the most; but they consume the most also. They do not produce a greater surplus for taxation. The slave is neither fed nor clothed so expensively as a freeman. Again white women are exempted from labour generally, which negro women are not. In this then the Southern states have an advantage as the article now stands. It has sometimes been said that slavery is necessary because the commodities they raise would be too dear for market if cultivated by freemen; but now it is said that the labor of the slave is the dearest.

Mr. Payne urged the original resolution of Congress, to proportion the quotas of the states to the number of souls.

Dr. Witherspoon was of opinion that the value of lands & houses was the best estimate of the wealth of a nation, and that it was practicable to obtain such a valuation. This is the true barometer of wealth. The one now proposed is imperfect in itself, and unequal between the states. It has been objected that negroes eat the food of freemen & therefore should be taxed. Horses also eat the food of freemen; therefore they also should be taxed. It has been said too that in carrying slaves into the estimate of the taxes the state is to pay, we do no more than those states themselves do, who alwais take slaves into the estimate of the taxes the individual is to pay. But the cases are not parallel. In the Southern colonies slaves pervade the whole colony; but they do not pervade the whole continent. That as to the original resolution of Congress to proportion the quotas according to the souls, it was temporary only, & related to the monies heretofore emitted: whereas we are now entering into a new compact and therefore stand on original ground.

Aug. 1. The question being put the amendment proposed was rejected by the votes of N. Hampshire, Massachusets, Rhode Island, Connecticut, N. York, N. Jersey, & Pennsylvania, against those of Delaware, Maryland, Virginia, North & South Carolina. Georgia was divided.

The other article was in these words. 'Art. XVII. In determining questions each colony shall have one vote.'

July 30. 31. Aug. 1. Present 41 members. Mr. Chase observed that this article was the most likely to divide us of any one proposed in the draught then under consideration. That the larger colonies had threatened they would not confederate at all if their weight in congress should not be equal to the numbers of people they added to the confederacy; while the smaller ones declared against an union if they did not retain an equal vote for the protection of their rights. That it was of the utmost consequence to bring the parties together, as should we sever from each other, either no foreign power will ally with us at all, or the different states will form different alliances, and thus increase the horrors of those scenes of civil war and bloodshed which in such a state of separation & independance would render us a miserable people. That our importance, our interests, our peace required that we should confederate, and that mutual sacrifices should be made to effect a compromise of this difficult question. He was of opinion the smaller colonies would lose their rights, if they were not in some instances allowed an equal vote; and therefore that a discrimination should take place among the questions which would come before Congress. (*He therefore proposed*) that the smaller states should be secured in all questions concerning life or liberty & the greater ones in all respecting property. He therefore proposed that in votes relating to money, the voice of each colony should be proportioned to the number of it's inhabitants.

Dr. Franklin (*seconded the proposition*) thought that the votes should be so proportioned in all cases. He took notice that the Delaware counties had bound up their Delegates to disagree to this article. He thought it a very extraordinary language to be held by any state, that they would not confederate with us unless we would let them dispose of our money. Certainly if we vote equally we ought to pay equally: but the smaller states will hardly purchase the privilege at this price. That had he lived in a state where the representation, originally equal, had become unequal by time & accident he might have submitted rather than disturb government: but that we should be very wrong to set out in this practice when it is in our power to establish what is right. That at the time of the Union between England and Scotland the latter had made the objection which the smaller states now do. But experience had proved that no unfairness had ever been shewn them. That their advocates had prognosticated that it would again happen as in times of old that the whale would swallow Jonas, but he thought the prediction reversed in event and that Jonas had swallowed the whale, for the Scotch had in fact got possession of the government and gave laws to the English. He reprobated the original agreement of Congress to vote by colonies, and therefore was for their voting in all cases according to the number of taxables (*so far going beyond Mr. Chase's proposition*).

Dr. Witherspoon opposed every alteration of the article. All men admit that a confederacy is necessary. Should the idea get abroad that there is likely to be no union among us, it will damp the minds of the people, diminish the glory of our struggle, & lessen it's importance, because it will open to our view future prospects of war & dissension among ourselves. If an equal vote be refused, the smaller states will become vassals to the larger; & all experience has shewn that the vassals & subjects of free states are the most enslaved. He instanced the Helots of Sparta & the provinces of Rome. He observed that foreign powers discovering this blemish would make it a handle for disengaging the smaller states from so unequal a confederacy. That the colonies should in fact be considered as individuals; and that as such in all disputes they should have an equal vote. That they are now collected as individuals making a bargain with each other, & of course had a right to vote as individuals. That in the East India company they voted by persons, & not by their proportion of stock. That the Belgic confederacy voted by provinces. That in questions of war the smaller states were as much interested as the larger, & therefore should vote equally; and indeed that the larger states were more likely to bring war on the confederacy, in proportion as their frontier was more extensive. He admitted that equality of representation was an excellent principle, but then it must be of things which are co-ordinate; that is, of things similar & of the same nature: that nothing relating to individuals could ever come before Congress; nothing but what would respect colonies. He distinguished between an incorporating & a federal union. The union of England was an incorporating one; yet Scotland had suffered by that union: for that it's inhabitants were drawn from it by the hopes of places & employments. Nor was it an instance of equality of representation; because while Scotland was allowed nearly a thirteenth of representation, they were to pay only one fortieth of the land tax. He expressed his hopes that in the present enlightened state of men's minds we might expect a lasting confederacy, if it was founded on fair principles.

John Adams advocated the voting in proportion to numbers. He said that we stand here as the representatives of the people. That in some states the people are many, in others they are few; that therefore their vote here should be proportioned to the numbers from whom it comes. Reason, justice, & equity never had weight enough on the face of the earth to govern the councils of men. It is interest alone which does it, and it is interest alone which can be trusted. That therefore the interests within doors should be the mathematical representatives of the interests without doors. That the individuality of the colonies is a mere sound. Does the individuality of a colony increase it's wealth or numbers? If it does; pay equally. If it does not add weight in the scale of the confederacy, it cannot add to their rights, nor weight in arguments. A. has £50. B. £500. C. £1000 in partnership. Is it just they should equally dispose of the monies of the partnership? It has been said we are independant individuals making a bargain together. The question is not what we are now, but what we ought to be when our bargain shall be made. The confederacy is to make us one individual only; it is to form us, like separate parcels of metal, into one common mass. We shall no longer retain our separate individuality, but become a single individual as to all questions submitted to the Confederacy. Therefore all those reasons which prove the justice & expediency of equal representation in other assemblies, hold good here. It has been objected that a proportional vote will endanger the smaller states. We answer that an equal vote will endanger the larger. Virginia, Pennsylvania, & Massachusets are the three greater colonies. Consider their distance, their difference of produce, of interests, & of manners, & it is apparent they can never have an interest or inclination to combine for the oppression of the smaller. That the smaller will naturally divide on all questions with the larger. Rhode Isld. from it's relation, similarity & intercourse will generally pursue the same objects with Massachusets; Jersey, Delaware & Maryland with Pennsylvania.

Dr. Rush took notice that the decay of the liberties of the Dutch republic proceeded from three causes. 1. The perfect unanimity requisite on all occasions. 2. Their obligation to consult their constituents. 3. Their voting by provinces. This last destroyed the equality of representation, and the liberties of Great Britain also are sinking from the same defect. That a part of our rights is deposited in the hands of our legislatures. There it was admitted there should be an equality of representation. Another part of our rights is deposited in the hands of Congress: why is it not equally necessary there should be an equal representation there? Were it possible to collect the whole body of the people together, they would determine the questions submitted to them by their majority. Why should not the same majority decide when voting here by their representatives? The larger colonies are so providentially divided in situation as to render every fear of their combining visionary. Their interests are different, & their circumstances dissimilar. It is more probable they will become rivals & leave it in the power of the smaller states to give preponderance to any scale they please. The voting by the number of free inhabitants will have one excellent effect, that of inducing the colonies to discourage slavery & to encourage the increase of their free inhabitants.

Mr. Hopkins observed there were 4 larger, 4 smaller & 4 middlesized colonies. That the 4 largest would contain more than half the inhabitants of the Confederating states, & therefore would govern the others as they should please. That history affords no instance of such a thing as equal representation. The Germanic body votes by states. The Helvetic body does the same; & so does the Belgic confederacy. That too little is known of the antient confederations to say what was their practice.

Mr. Wilson thought that taxation should be in proportion to wealth, but the representation should accord with the number of freemen. That government is a collection or result of the wills of all. That if any government could speak the will of all it would be perfect; and that so far as it departs from this it becomes imperfect. It has been said that

Congress is a representation of states; not of individuals. I say that the objects of it's care are all the individuals of the states. It is strange that annexing the name of 'State' to ten thousand men, should give them an equal right with forty thousand. This must be the effect of magic, not of reason. As to those matters which are referred to Congress, we are not so many states; we are one large state. We lay aside our individuality whenever we come here. The Germanic body is a burlesque on government: and their practice on any point is a sufficient authority & proof that it is wrong. The greatest imperfection in the constitution of the Belgic confederacy is their voting by provinces. The interest of the whole is constantly sacrificed to that of the small states. The history of the war in the reign of Q. Anne sufficiently proves this. It is asked Shall nine colonies put it into the power of four to govern them as they please? I invert the question and ask Shall two millions of people put it in the power of one million to govern them as they please? It is pretended too that the smaller colonies will be in danger from the greater. Speak in honest language & say the minority will be in danger from the majority. And is there an assembly on earth where this danger may not be equally pretended? The truth is that our proceedings will then be consentaneous with the interests of the majority and so they ought to be. The probability is much greater that the larger states will disagree than that they will combine. I defy the wit of man to invent a possible case or to suggest any one thing on earth which shall be for the interests of Virginia, Pennsylvania & Massachusets, and which will not also be for the interest of the other states.

34.3

 JOSEPH HEWES TO SAMUEL JOHNSTON,
JULY 28, 1776

Joseph Hewes, a successful and politically moderate merchant from North Carolina, writes here to the Scottish-born lawyer, man of conservative sensibilities, and longtime prominent figure in North Carolina politics Samuel Johnston. Hewes was concerned that, before declaring independence, Congress ought to have agreed upon a plan of confederation and negotiated foreign alliances. He feared that divisions concerning one of those issues could lead to dissolution of the fragile coalition of states represented in Congress into multiple unions. A confederation agreed to before independence would have created a truly legal union and government and, quite likely, a heightened capacity to pursue common purposes. Thus, with or without a continuing relationship with Great Britain, such a union would have decreased the urgency of independence. That may have been why, in fact, those most urgent to declare independence had not placed greater emphasis on first framing a plan of central government.

Paul H. Smith, ed., *Letters of Delegates to Congress, 1774–1789* (Washington, D.C.: Library of Congress, 1976–93), 4:555–56.

Dear Sir                                                    Philadelphia 28th July 1776

Since my last by Mr. Wyatt I have seen Mr Gibson and should have paid him but looking over the Account I found you had not mentioned what currency it was, and as Mr. Gibsons Books are in the Country where his Family resides the matter is suspended till he examines the Acct. with his Books. I wish you had said whether it is Proc. or currency of this Province.

Much of our time is taken up in forming and debating a Confederation for the united States, what we shall make of it God only knows, I am inclined to think we shall never modell it so as to be agreed to by all the Colonies. A plan for foreign Alliances is also formed and I expect will be the subject of much debate before it is agreed to. These two Capital points ought to have been setled before our declaration of Independance went forth to the world, this was my opinion long ago and every days experience serves to confirm me in that opinion. I think it probable that we may Split on these great points. If so our mighty Colossus falls to pieces when (as our old friend Mr Gordon used to say) we shall be in a whimsical Situation.

I have enclosed to R Smith a news paper which contains a state of what passed at the interview between Genl. Washington and the Adjutant General of Howes Army. We have no news from any quarter.

I am with best Compliments to your family, Dear Sir, Your mo. Obed Serv,

Joseph Hewes

34.4

 JOHN ADAMS TO ABIGAIL ADAMS, JULY 29, 1776

In this letter to his wife, who was recovering in Boston from a smallpox variolation (a form of inoculation in which a smallpox scab was placed under the skin of a healthy person; true vaccinations were still some twenty years off), John Adams highlights two of the overriding issues dividing Congress in forming a confederation: how states were to vote in Congress, equally or in proportion to a measure such as population, wealth, or exports and imports; and "whether Congress shall have Authority to limit the Dimensions of each Colony . . . from growing too great and powerfull, so as to be dangerous to the rest."

Paul H. Smith, ed., *Letters of Delegates to Congress, 1774–1789* (Washington, D.C.: Library of Congress, 1976–93), 4:556–57.

Philadelphia July 29. 1776

How are you all this morning? Sick, weak, faint, in Pain; or pretty well recovered? By this Time, you are well acquainted with the Small Pox. Pray how do you like it?

We have no News. It is very hard that half a dozen or half a Score Armies cant supply Us, with News. We have a Famine, a perfect Dearth of this necessary Article.

I am at this present Writing perplexed and plagued with two knotty Problems in Politicks. You love to pick a political Bone, so I will even throw it to you.

If a Confederation should take Place, one great Question is how We shall vote. Whether each Colony shall count one? or whether each shall have a Weight in Proportion to its Numbers, or Wealth, or Exports and Imports, or a compound Ratio of all?

Another is whether Congress shall have Authority to limit the Dimensions of each Colony, to prevent those which claim, by Charter, or Proclamation, or Commission, to the South Sea, from growing too great and powerfull, so as to be dangerous to the rest.

Shall I write you a Sheet upon each of these Questions. When you are well enough to read, and I can find Leisure enough to write, perhaps I may.

Gerry carried with him a Cannister for you. But he is an old Batchelor, and what is worse a Politician, and what is worse still a kind of Soldier, so that I suppose he will have so much Curiosity to see Armies and Fortifications and Assemblies, that you will loose many a fine Breakfast at a Time when you want them most.

Tell Betcy that this same Gerry is such another as herself, Sex excepted. How is my Brother and Friend Cranch. How is his other Self, and their little Selves. And ours. Dont be in the Dumps, above all Things. I am hard put to it, to keep out of them when I look at home. But I will be gay, if I can.

Adieu.

34.5

 JOHN ADAMS, NOTES OF DEBATES, AUGUST 2, 1776

John Adams recorded part of the debate in Congress (meeting as a committee of the whole) concerning the Dickinson committee's Article XVIII, which awarded Congress control over the allocation and use of western lands. Again, the delegates who believed that their states possessed additional lands—in this case, Connecticut and Virginia—opposed giving Congress the power to adjudicate land disputes. Curiously, a month after Congress' celebrated rejection of British law and its appeal to natural law and natural rights in the Declaration of Independence, the disputants faithfully recurred to the former colonies' English charter rights and the common law in this matter, not universal or abstract natural principles.

According to Samuel Huntington, a lawyer at the center of Connecticut political life and president of Congress from 1779 to 1781, "We all unite against mutilating Charters . . . The Q[uestion] of Right must be determined by the Principles of the common Law." After protesting that Congress had no right to make determinations regarding Virginia's charter-derived land claims extending to the Pacific Ocean, Jefferson magnanimously noted that Virginia "has released all Claims to the Lands settled by Maryland," lands on which Maryland residents had long lived.

Paul H. Smith, ed., *Letters of Delegates to Congress, 1774–1789* (Washington, D.C.: Library of Congress, 1976–93), 4:603–4.

Aug. 2d. [1776]

Limiting the Bounds of States which by Charter &c. extend to the South Sea.

Sherman thinks the Bounds ought to be settled. A Majority of States have no Claim to the South Sea. Moves this Amendment, to be subsituted in Place of this Clause and also instead of the 15th Article.

No Lands to be seperated from any State, which are already settled, or become private Property.

Chase denys that any Colony has a Right, to go to the South Sea. [ . . . ]

Harrison. How came Maryland by its Land? but by its Charter: By its Charter Virginia owns to the South Sea. Gentlemen shall not pare away the Colony of Virginia. R. Island has more Generosity, than to wish the Massachusetts pared away. Delaware does not wish to pare away Pensilvania.

Huntington. Admit there is danger, from Virginia, does it follow that Congress has a Right to limit her Bounds? The Consequence is not to enter into Confederation. But as to the Question of Right, We all unite against mutilating Charters. I cant agree to the Principle. We are a Spectacle to all Europe. I am not so much alarmed at the Danger, from Virginia, as some are. My fears are not alarmed. They have acted as noble a Part as any. I doubt not the Wisdom of Virginia will limit themselves. A Mans Right does not cease to be a Right because it is large. The Q[uestion] of Right must be determined by the Principles of the common Law.

Stone. This Argument is taken up upon very wrong Ground. It is considered as if We were voting away the Territory of particular Colonies, and Gentlemen work themselves up into Warmth, upon that Supposition. Suppose Virginia should. The small Colonies have a Right to Happiness and Security. They would have no Safety if the great Colonies were not limited. We shall grant Lands in small Quantities, without Rent, or Tribute, or purchase Money. It is said that Virginia is attacked on every Side. Is it meant that Virginia shall sell the Lands for their own Emolument?

All the Colonies have defended these Lands vs. the K. of G.B., and at the Expence of all. Does Virginia intend to establish Quitrents?

I dont mean that the united States shall sell them to get Money by them.

Jefferson. I protest vs. the Right of Congress to decide, upon the Right of Virginia. Virginia has released all Claims to the Lands settled by Maryland &c.

## 35. A MEAGER OFFER OF PEACE FROM THE KING, JULY 1776

On July 18, 1776, Congress appointed a committee to examine sundry intercepted letters of a public nature from Lord Richard Howe to former colonial governors, along with some more private ones.[29] Thomas Jefferson (Virginia), Robert Treat Paine (Massachusetts), and Charles Carroll (Maryland) were chosen for the committee.[30] Howe was the commander in chief of the king's North American naval forces; he and his brother, General William Howe, the commander in chief of the king's land forces, were the long-awaited commissioners appointed by the king to "restore peace to his Colonies." En route from Halifax to Staten Island, Lord Howe wrote, on June 20, the declaration found below and a circular letter that was to be posted immediately after his arrival.

The circular letter was addressed to Lord John Dunmore, until June 1775 the controversial governor of Virginia; Josiah Martin, until July 1775 the governor of North Carolina; Sir James Wright, until January 1776 the governor of South Carolina; William Franklin, until June 1776 the governor of New Jersey; Sir Robert Eden, until June 1776 the governor of Maryland; and John Penn, the last proprietor and, until September 1776, lieutenant governor of Pennsylvania. Howe hoped that "within ten days of his arrival he would be able to consummate a peace, and he was therefore grievously disappointed that he had not come in time to try his persuasive powers before the adoption of the Declaration of Independence." In truth, as noted previously, "there is good reason for believing that the proponents of independence had pushed that measure all the more vigorously for the very purpose of forestalling the possibility of reconciliation."[31]

A day later, on July 19, Congress recommended that "the Declaration passed on the 4th, be fairly engrossed . . . [and] signed by every member of Congress"—a time aptly chosen by congressional separatists, while commissioners were offering to negotiate for peace.[32] In addition, Congress resolved, in order "to reinforce its reputation for virtue and unanimity,"[33] to publish in various newspapers Lord Howe's circular letter, which empowered him to grant "*pardons* to such of his [the King's] subjects therein as shall be *duly solicitous* to benefit that effect of his gracious indulgence." Congress did so in the hope of influencing those in the new mid-Atlantic states still undecided about the wisdom of Congress' declaring independence. Howe announced in his declaration, following a long citation from the American Prohibitory Act of December 22, 1775, outlining his authority to grant pardons, that the king "hath been graciously pleased . . . [to grant] his free and general pardons to all those who in the tumult of and disorder of the times may have deviated from their just allegiance, and who are willing, by a speedy return to their duty, to reap the benefits of the Royal favour." This limited offer of pardons, no doubt, was not what those anxiously waiting the commissioners' arrival, had hoped to read.

Congress believed that by demonstrating just how limited the commissioners' powers truly were and by showing the colonists that "the insidious court of Britain has endeavoured to amuse and disarm them," it could convince those "who still remain suspended by a hope founded either in the justice or moderation of their late King" that "the valour alone of their country is to save its liberties." The erstwhile radicals in Congress believed such evidence would finally put an end to the long-held hope of the onetime majority in Congress for some manner of constitutional reconciliation that could allow the colonies to remain loyal to the king and in the British Empire. The circular letter and declaration of Lord Howe first appeared on July 24, 1776, in the *Pennsylvania Gazette.*

<br>

35.1

## RESOLUTION TO PUBLISH LORD HOWE'S CIRCULAR LETTER AND DECLARATION, JULY 19, 1776

Worthington Chauncey Ford et al., eds., *Journals of the Continental Congress, 1774–1789* (Washington, D.C.: Government Printing Office, 1904–37), 5:592–93.

The committee, to whom the letters from Lord Howe to Mr. [William] Franklin, &c. ||were referred||, brought in a report, which was taken into consideration: Whereupon,

*Resolved,* That a copy of the circular letters, and of the declarations they enclosed from Lord Howe to Mr. W[illiam] Franklin, Mr. Penn, Mr. Eden, Lord Dunmore, Mr. Martin, and Sir James Wright, late governors, which were sent to Amboy, by a flag, and forwarded to Congress by General Washington, be published in the several gazettes, that the good people of these United States may be informed of what nature are the commissioners, and what the terms, with the expectation of which, the insidious court of Britain has endeavoured to amuse and disarm them, and that the few, who still remain suspended by a hope founded either in the justice or moderation of their late King, may now, at length, be convinced, that the valour alone of their country is to save its liberties.

35.2

 LORD HOWE, CIRCULAR LETTER, JUNE 20, 1776

Peter Force, *American Archives,* 4th series (Washington, D.C.: M. St. Clair Clarke and Peter Force, 1839), 6:1001.

LORD HOWE'S CIRCULAR TO THE GOVERNOURS OF THE COLONIES.

Eagle, off the Coast of the Province of Massachusetts-Bay, June 20, 1776.

SIR: Being appointed Commander-in-Chief of the ships and vessels of his Majesty's Fleet employed in *North-America,* and having the honour to be, by his Majesty, constituted one of the Commissioners for restoring peace to his Colonies, and for granting pardons to such of his subjects therein as shall be duly solicitous to benefit by that effect of his gracious indulgence, I embrace this opportunity to inform you of my arrival on the *American* coast, where my first object will be an early meeting with General *Howe,* whom his Majesty hath been pleased to join with me in the said Commission.

In the mean time I have judged it expedient to issue the enclosed Declaration, in order that all persons may have immediate information of his Majesty's most gracious intentions; and I desire you will be pleased forthwith to cause the said Declaration to be promulgated, in such manner and at such places in the Colony of *Connecticut* as well render the same of the most publick notoriety.

Assured of being favoured with your assistance in every measure for the speedy and effectual restoration of the publick tranquillity, I am to request you will communicate from time to time such information as you may think will facilitate the attainment of that important object in the Colony over which you preside.

I have the honour to be, with great respect and consideration, your most obedient, humble servant,

HOWE.

35.3

 LORD HOWE, DECLARATION, JUNE 20, 1776

Peter Force, *American Archives,* 4th series (Washington, D.C.: M. St. Clair Clarke and Peter Force, 1839), 6:1001–2.

*By* RICHARD *Viscount* HOWE, *of the Kingdom of* IRELAND, *one of the King's Commissioners for restoring peace to his Majesty's Colonies and Plantations in* NORTH-AMERICA, *&c., &c., &c.*

DECLARATION.

Whereas, by an act passed in the last session of Parliament to prohibit all trade and intercourse with the Colonies of *New-Hampshire, Massachusetts-Bay, Rhode-Island, Connecticut, New-York, New-Jersey, Pennsylvania,* the three lower Counties on *Delaware, Maryland, Virginia, North Carolina, South Carolina,* and *Georgia,* and for other purposes therein mentioned, it is enacted, that "it shall and may be lawful to and for any person or persons, appointed and authorized by his Majesty, to grant a pardon or pardons to any number or description of persons, by Proclamation, in his Majesty's name; to declare any Colony or Province, Colonies or Provinces, to be at the peace of his Majesty; and that from and after the issuing of any such Proclamation in any of the aforesaid Colonies or Provinces, or if his Majesty shall be graciously pleased to signify the same by his Royal Proclamation, then, and from and after the issuing of such Proclamation, the said act, with respect to such Colony or Province, Colonies or Provinces, County, Town, Port, District, or place, shall cease, determine, and be utterly void."

And whereas the King, desirous to deliver all his subject from the calamities of war, and other oppressions which they now undergo, and to restore the said Colonies to his protection and peace, as soon as the constitutional authority of Government therein may be replaced, hath been graciously pleased, by letters patent under the great seal, dated the 6th of *May,* in the sixteenth year of his Majesty's reign, to nominate and appoint me, *Richard* Viscount *Howe,* of the Kingdom of *Ireland,* and *William Howe,* Esq., General of his Forces in *North-America,* and each of us, jointly and severally, to be his Majesty's Commissioner and Commissioners for granting his free and general pardons to all those who in the tumult of and disorder of the times may have deviated from their just allegiance, and who are willing, by a speedy return to their duty, to reap the benefits of the Royal favour, and also for declaring, in his Majesty's name, any Colony, Province, County, Town, Port, District, or place, to be at the peace of his Majesty;—I do, therefore, hereby declare that due consideration shall be had to the meritorious service of all persons who shall aid and assist in restoring the publick tranquility in the said Colonies, or in any part or parts thereof; that pardons shall be granted, dutiful representations received, and every suitable encouragement given for promoting such measures as shall be conducive to the establishment of legal Government and peace, in pursuance of his Majesty's most gracious purposes aforesaid.

Given on board his Majesty's ship the *Eagle,* off the coast of the Province of *Massachusetts-Bay,* the 20th day of *June,* 1776.

HOWE.

## 35.4

 CONGRESSIONAL RESOLUTION ON THE HOWE PEACE COMMISSION, MAY 6, 1776

Congress had been preparing for the arrival of the peace commissioners since at least April 2, 1776, when a letter from George Washington, dated March 24, was laid before Congress. Washington inquired how Congress wanted him to receive the commissioners upon their arrival. On the following day, Washington's letter and related papers were referred to a committee of three moderate mid-Atlantic delegates. Thomas Johnson, John Jay, and James Wilson were lawyers, and none were supportive of a quick move toward independence. On April 12, Congress considered taking up the committee's report, but did not do so until April 30, when it again postponed consideration of it. On May 2, Congress ordered the report revised by a new committee comprising John Dickinson, William Livingston, and Edward Rutledge, another three delegates without any enthusiasm for independence.

The new committee brought in its report on May 3. Congress briefly took it into consideration the next day, then finally gave full consideration to the report and agreed to it on May 6.[34] But Congress' agreement amounted to a recommendation that, when needed, it would "direct the proper measures for the reception of such commissioners."

No doubt, what appear as simple delays in the record of the *Journals* resulted from heated and prolonged debate when Congress was meeting as a committee of the whole—and thus not recording its debates. John Adams confirmed this: "It will be observed how long this trifling business had been depending, but it cannot be known from the Journal how much debate it had occasioned. It was one of those delusive contrivances, by which the party in opposition to us endeavored, by lulling people with idle hopes of reconciliation into security, to turn their heads and thoughts from independence."[35] By May, indeed, probably by the end of March, the radical delegates in Congress had the upper hand, but too easily overlooked is the continued resistance offered them by a not insignificant number of delegates— that is, the delegates of five or six colonies, especially the mid-Atlantic ones, to the radicals' seven or eight. It was with particular irony that "on the same May 6 on which Congress had adopted its tentative resolve the British monarch had put his seal to the appointment of Lord Howe and General Howe as 'Commissioners for restoring peace to his Majesty's Colonies and Plantations in North America, and for granting pardons to such as his Majesty's subjects there, now in rebellion, as shall deserve the Royal mercy.' "[36]

Worthington Chauncey Ford et al., eds., *Journals of the Continental Congress, 1774–1789* (Washington, D.C.: Government Printing Office, 1904–37), 4:328.

Congress resumed the consideration of the report on General Washington's letter of the 24 of March; and, thereupon, came to the following resolution:

[Whereas] General Washington having requested directions concerning the conduct that should be observed towards commissioners, said to be coming from Great Britain to America,

*Resolved,* That General Washington be informed, that the Congress suppose, if commissioners are intended to be sent from Great Britain to treat of peace, that the practice usual in such cases will be observed, by making previous application for the necessary passports or safe conduct, and on such application being made, Congress will then direct the proper measures for the reception of such commissioners.

35.5

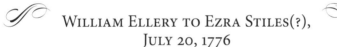

WILLIAM ELLERY TO EZRA STILES(?),
JULY 20, 1776

William Ellery of Rhode Island, an undistinguished lawyer from an affluent merchant family, feared that signing the Declaration of Independence would be like signing his own death warrant. He had been chosen in 1776 to replace the influential former governor Samuel Ward after the latter's death from smallpox. Here, Ellery is likely writing to Ezra Stiles, a Congregational clergyman and scholar, pastor of the Second Congregational Church in Newport, Rhode Island, and future president of Yale, who was living in Massachusetts at the time. Ellery describes the circumstances under which General Washington, on a matter of punctilio, had rejected Howe's letter until it was properly addressed to him before forwarding it, along with others, to Congress for its consideration.

Ellery's assessment is that the colonies had been driven to declare independence and that there was no longer any possibility of reconciliation between them and Great Britain. After the Declaration of Independence was issued, "the Door is shut, & it would now be in vain, to talk of any sort of Alliance with Britain but a Commercial One. We have been driven into a Declara of Independency & must forget our former Love for our British Brethren." Britain, after driving the colonies to seek independence and a separate life outside the empire, could not do much beyond either fighting a war to maintain their commercial privileges or suing for peace and building a new commercial relationship. It ended up doing both.

Paul H. Smith, ed., *Letters of Delegates to Congress, 1774–1789* (Washington, D.C.: Library of Congress, 1976–93), 4:497–98. The "Farmer" referred to is John Dickinson. The Latin phrase *Odi Danaös, etiam Dona ferentes* should be *Timeo Danaös et dona ferentes* (*Aeneid,* bk. 2, l. 49), literally "I fear the Greeks even when they bring gifts," but usually translated as "Beware of Greeks bearing gifts."

Ld. Howe is arrived in the Eagle Man o'War. The Reinforcmt is not arrived & I hope will never arrive. His Ldship sent a Flag o' truce a few days ago with Letters to Gen. Washington directed "to George Washington Esq." which were not received because his proper Title was not given him: since that some others have been sent to him with a similar Superscription & were for the same Reason not received. After this a flag was sent to Amboy with Letters to all the late Governors So. of N. York inclosg written Declarations containing his & his Brother's (Genl Howe) appointmt as Commissioners to receive the Submission of the Colonies or private Persons & grant Pardons agreeable to the late act of the Brit. Parliament, and a number of Letters principally from *Friends* in London to *Friends* here placing the Character of the Howes in the most amiable point of View, & recommending Reconciliation with G. Britain. These Letters were all sent by the commanding Officer at Amboy to G. Washington, & were transmitted by him to Congress, and were opened & read, that part of them, I mean which related to our Affairs. Among the Letters were some to Dr Franklin, one to the Farmer, and one to Mr Stockton. Dr Franklin was not in Congress when the Letters were bro't in, but was sent for. When he entered, his Letters were delivered to him sealed. He opened them, looked over them, and handed them to the President desiring him to read them. They were accordingly read to Congress & contained much the same Sentiments with those to *Friends,* as did that to Mr Stockton, who is a Member of Congress, and who was treated and behaved in the same manner that Dr Franklin did. As the *Farmer* is in the Jersey at the Head of his Battalion, his Letter is kept sealed by the President until he shall return & receive it in Congress. The Letters to the late Governors & the Declarations are ordered to be printed to let the People see upon what Terms Reconciliation is proposed to them: Odi Danaös, etiam Dona ferentes: but when what some People, Tories, may call the Olive-plant is handed to us at the point of the Bayonet, or is hurled to us from the Mouths of Canon, if possible I should more than hate it. The Truth is the Door is shut, & it would now be in vain, to talk of any sort of Alliance with Britain but a Commercial One. We have been driven into a Declara of Independency & must forget our former Love for our British Brethren. The Sword must Determine our Quarrel. Our Repulse from Canada is disagreeable, but we must expect repeated Defeats. The *Road to Liberty, like the Road to Heaven is strewed with Thorns. Virtue lives in Exertion.* But thank Providence, altho' our Northern Army hath been unsuccessful, our Southern Forces under Gen. Lee have been successful. A Letter which Congress this day received by Express from him dated at Charlesto[n] July 2d gives us a very agreeable acco[unt] of a severe Repulse given to the fleet under Capt Parker by our fort on Sullivans Island &c.

## 35.6

 BENJAMIN FRANKLIN TO LORD HOWE,
JULY 20, 1776

Benjamin Franklin, in emotionally charged terms, responded to Howe by castigating British wartime measures, ones that Jefferson had similarly emphasized in the Declaration of Independence—burning towns, engaging Native Americans to fight, freeing the colonists' slaves, and hiring mercenaries. Franklin correctly predicted that Howe's offer of mere pardons would have "no other Effect than that of increasing our Resentment." Indeed, Franklin thought that a close-knit commercial alliance between the newly independent states and Britain would not be possible until Britain first punished the states' former governors, rebuilt their burnt towns, and worked to make amends for other mischief. But he was convinced of the small likelihood of any of those things happening: "I know too well her abounding Pride and deficient Wisdom, to believe she will ever take such Salutary Measures. Her Fondness for Conquest as a Warlike Nation, her Lust of Dominion as an Ambitious one, and her Thirst for a gainful Monopoly as a Commercial one (none of them legitimate Causes of War) will all join to hide from her Eyes every View of her true Interests."

According to Howe, the overriding cause of the war was "the Necessity of preventing the American Trade from passing into foreign Channels." Franklin responded that war over trade was unjustified: "It seems that neither the obtaining or retaining of any Trade, how valuable soever, is an Object for which Men may justly Spill each others Blood, [and] that the true and sure means of extending and securing Commerce is the goodness and cheapness of Commodities." He concluded that "this War against us therefore, is both unjust, and unwise."[37] Whatever faults were attributable to the American side, and no doubt there were many, Franklin's profile of the British is a pretty fair character-ization and not far removed from one offered at about the same time by Adam Smith in describing Britain's imperial motivation and actions in the North American colonies. Although, as he noted, "under the present system of man-agement . . . Great Britain derives nothing but loss from the dominion which she assumes over her colonies," it was impossible to imagine proposing that Britain abandon the colonies, for such actions "are always mortifying to the pride of every nation . . . always contrary to the private interest of the governing part of it."[38]

Franklin also emphasized how hard he had fought against the breakup of the empire: "Long did I endeavour with unfeigned and unwearied Zeal, to preserve from breaking, that fine & noble China Vase the British Empire . . . Your Lordship may possibly remember the Tears of joy that wet my Cheek, when, at your good Sister's in London, you once gave me Expectations that a Reconciliation might soon take place." Like many of the more moderate defenders of independence, which he was not, Franklin had held to a consistent belief in the benefits once enjoyed by both sides. His words were not those of a man committed to a precocious attachment to republicanism, but rather one who in 1765 had sought to have the Crown revoke Pennsylvania's proprietary charter and replace it with a royal one directly under the king, but who by July 1775 had come to accept and regret the necessity of a forced separation of the British from their North American colonies.[39]

Paul H. Smith, ed., *Letters of Delegates to Congress, 1774–1789* (Washington, D.C.: Library of Congress, 1976–93), 4:498–501.

My Lord,                                                             Philada. July 20th. 1776.

I received safe the Letters your Lordship so kindly forwarded to me, and beg you to accept my Thanks.

The Official Dispatches to which you refer me, contain nothing more than what we had seen in the Act of Parliament, viz. Offers of Pardon upon Submission; which I was sorry to find, as it must give your Lordship Pain to be sent so far on so hopeless a Business.

Directing Pardons to be offered the Colonies, who are the very Parties injured, expresses indeed that Opinion of our Ignorance, Baseness, & Insensibility which your uninform'd and proud Nation has long been pleased to entertain of us; but it can have no other Effect than that of increasing our Resentment. It is impossible we should think of Submission to a Government, that has with the most wanton Barbarity and Cruelty, burnt our defenceless Towns in the midst of Winter, excited the Savages to massacre our Farmers, and our Slaves to murder their Masters, and is even now bringing foreign Mercenaries to deluge our Settlements with Blood. These atrocious Injuries have extinguished every remaining Spark of Affection for that Parent Country we once held so dear. But were it possible for *us* to forget and forgive them, it is not possible for *you* (I mean the British Nation) to forgive the People you have so heavily injured; you can never confide again in those as Fellow Subjects, & permit them to enjoy equal Freedom, to whom you know you have given such just Cause of lasting Enmity. And this must impel you, were we again under your Government, to endeavour the breaking our Spirit by the severest Tyranny, & obstructing by every means in your Power our growing Strength and Prosperity.

But your Lordship mentions "the Kings paternal Solicitude for promoting the Establishment of lasting *Peace* and Union with the Colonies." If by *Peace* is here meant, a Peace to be entered into between Britain and America as distinct States now at War, and his Majesty has given your Lordship Powers to treat with us of such a Peace, I may venture to say, tho' without Authority, that I think a Treaty for that purpose not yet quite impracticable, before we enter into Foreign Alliances. But I am persuaded you have no such Powers. Your Nation, tho' by punishing those American Governors who have created & fomented the Discord, rebuilding our burnt Towns, & repairing as far as possible the Mischiefs done us, She might yet recover a great Share of our Regard & the greatest part of our growing Commerce, with all the Advantage of that additional Strength to be derived from a Friendship with us; I know too well her abounding Pride and deficient Wisdom, to believe she will ever take such Salutary Measures. Her Fondness for Conquest as a Warlike Nation, her Lust of Dominion as an Ambitious one, and her Thirst for a gainful Monopoly as a Commercial one (none of them legitimate Causes of War) will all join to hide from her Eyes every View of her true Interests; and continually goad her on in these ruinous distant Expeditions, so destructive both of Lives and Treasure, that must prove as pernicious to her in the End as the Croisades formerly were to most of the Nations of Europe.

I have not the Vanity, my Lord, to think of intimidating by thus predicting the Effects of this War; for I know it will in England have the Fate of all my former Predictions, not to be believed till the Event shall verify it.

Long did I endeavour with unfeigned and unwearied Zeal, to preserve from breaking, that fine & noble China Vase the British Empire: for I knew that being once broken, the separate Parts could not retain even their Share of the Strength or Value that existed in the Whole, and that a perfect Re-Union of those Parts could scarce even be hoped for. Your Lordship may possibly remember the Tears of joy that wet my Cheek, when, at your good Sister's in London, you once gave me Expectations that a Reconciliation might soon take place. I had the Misfortune to find those Expectations disappointed, & to be treated as the Cause of the Mischief I was labouring to prevent. My Consolation under that groundless and malevolent Treatment was, that I retained the Friendship of many Wise & Good Men in that Country, and among the rest some I have in the Regard of Lord Howe.

The well founded Esteem, and permit me to say Affection, which I shall always have for your Lordship; makes it painful to me to see you engag'd in conducting a War, the great Ground of which, as expressed in your Letter, is, "the Necessity of preventing the American Trade from passing into foreign Channels." To me it seems that neither the obtaining or retaining of any Trade, how valuable soever, is an Object for which Men may justly Spill each others Blood, that the true and sure means of extending and securing Commerce is the goodness and cheapness of Commodities, & that the profits of no Trade can ever be equal to the Expence of compelling it, and of holding it, by Fleets and Armies. I consider this War against us therefore, as both unjust, and unwise; and I am persuaded cool dispassionate Posterity will condemn to Infamy those who advised it; and that even Success will not save from some degree of Dishonour, those who voluntarily engag'd to conduct it. I know your great Motive in coming hither was the Hope of being instrumental in a Reconciliation; and I believe when you find *that* impossible on any Terms given you to propose, you will relinquish so odious a Command, and return to a more honourable private Station.

With the greatest and most sincere Respect, I have the honour to be; My Lord, Your Lordships most obedient humble Servt.

B. Franklin

35.7

 ROBERT MORRIS TO JOSEPH REED, JULY 21, 1776

Because of his financial acumen, resources, and commercial connections, Robert Morris was a man as critical as any other to the success of the war and the states' continued independence. He did not support, however, the break with Great Britain, and so refused to vote for independence. Still, the newly radicalized Pennsylvania Assembly on July 20 reappointed him to Congress (unlike his fellow holdout, Dickinson). Here, he writes to Joseph Reed, an English-trained Philadelphia lawyer who had also been slow to endorse independence. He had, however, come around earlier than Morris and was serving as Washington's chief staff officer. As such, he served as an American military envoy to Lord Howe for the conference on Staten Island.

Unlike Franklin, Morris was still troubled by those dogmatically opposed to reconciliation with Britain, those who could not "bear the thought of reconciliation on any terms." Although "to these men all propositions of the kind sound like high Treason against the States," Morris believed "that if the Commissioners have any propositions to make" or any "powers different from what we immagine them to be Vested with, and an inclination to imploy those powers favourably for America, it is our duty to attend to such." Morris, though he was soon to be superintendent of finances for the United States, considered independence, even after its declaration, a live issue: "If they can offer Peace on admissible terms I believe the great majority of America wou'd still be for accepting it." But like Franklin and most others, Morris understood that if the Howe brothers "can only offer *Pardons* & that is fully ascertained it will firmly Unite all America in their exertions to support the Independency they have declared." Moreover, according to Morris, the new states needed whatever help was available to unite them.

In a rare remark about the principles (rather than the political differences) behind the drive for self-government, Morris erroneously notes that declaring independence "will neither promote the interest or redound to the honor of America, for it has caused division when we wanted Union, and will be ascribed to very different principles than those which ought to give rise to such an Important measure." As for which principles he had in mind, he leaves readers guessing. He closes his letter by going over the failures of American forces in Canada, a remarkably frequent topic of conversation, debate, and commissions in Congress. That campaign, indeed, may well have been America's first military defeat.

Paul H. Smith, ed., *Letters of Delegates to Congress, 1774–1789* (Washington, D.C.: Library of Congress, 1976–93), 4:510–13.

Dear sir                                     From the Hills of Schuylkill July 21st. 1776

I received your obliging letter of the 18th yesterday in Congress, and shou'd have been tempted to have laid the enclosure immediately before the House, had not a letter from the same person on the same Subject & in a similar stile addressed to J. Kinsey Esqr. of New Jersey been read in Congress the day before. The Temper of the House was plain and you may judge what it was, when I tell you the only enquiry that letter produced was how it got to Mr. Kinseys hands.

I am sorry to say there are some amongst us that cannot bear the thought of reconciliation on any terms. To these men all propositions of the kind sound like high Treason against the States and I really believe they wou'd sooner punish a Man for this Crime than for bearing arms against us.

I cannot help Condemning this disposition as it must be founded in keen resentment or on interested Views where we ought to have the Interest of our Country and the Good of Mankind to Act as the main Spring in all our Public Conduct. I think with you that if the Commissioners have any propositions to make they ought to be heard. Shou'd they disclose powers different from what we immagine them to be Vested with, and an inclination to imploy those powers favourably for America, it is our duty to attend to such offers, weigh well the Consequences of every determination we come to and in short to lay aside all prejudices, resentments and sanguine Notions of our own Strength in order that reason may influence and Wisdom guide our Concils. If the admiral & General are really desirous of a Conference I think & hope they will address our General properly. This may be expected if they have powers beyond granting pardons. If they have not it is Idle for them to solicit any intercourse as no good can possibly arise to them or their Cause from it, but on our parts I think good Policy requires that we shou'd hear all they have to say. I am not for making any Sacrifice of Dignity, but still I woud hear them if possible, because if they can offer Peace on admissible terms I believe the great majority of America wou'd still be for accepting it. If they can only offer *Pardons* & that is fully ascertained it will firmly Unite all America in their exertions to support the Independency they have declared and it must be obvious to every body that our *United Efforts* will be absolutely necessary. This being the case why should we fear to Treat of Peace or to hear the Commissioners on that Subject. If they can offer terms that are advantageous & honorable for this Country, let us meet them. If they cannot We are not in a situation or temper to ask or receive pardons & all who dont mean to stoop to this Ignominious submission will consequently take up their Arms with a determination to Conquer or die. If they offer or desire a Conference & we reject it, those who are already dissatisfyed will become more so and others will follow their example & we may expect daily greater disunion & defection in every part of these States. At least such are my apprehensions on this Subject. I have uniformly Voted against & opposed the declaration of Independance because in my poor oppinion it was an improper time and will neither promote the interest or redound to the honor of America, for it has caused division when we wanted Union, and will be ascribed to very different principles than those which ought to give rise to such an Important measure. I did expect my Conduct in this great Question woud have procured my dismission from the great Council but find myself disapointed for the Convention have thought proper to return me in the New Delegation, and altho my interest & inclination prompt me to decline the Service yet I cannot depart from one point that first induced me to enter in the Public Line. I mean an oppinion that it is the duty of every Individual to Act his part in whatever Station his Country may Call him to, in times of difficulty, danger & distress. Whilst I think this a duty I must submit, altho the Councils of America have taken a different course from my Judgements & wishes. I think an individual that declines the Service of his Country because its Councils are not conformable to his Ideas, makes but a bad Subject; a good one will follow if he cannot lead.

Untill the good News from Carolina raised our Spirits, they were constantly depressed by every Account We received from the Northern Army. Such scenes of mismanagement, misconduct and Ill success as have been exhibited in that quarter ever since the loss of the Brave Montgomery have no paralel. There is a Committee of Congress appointed to inquire into the Causes of our Ill Success in Canada. Probably it may be no difficulty to ascertain the cause in a general point of light, but it may not be easy to saddle individuals with their just share of reproach for it seems to me that every officer & other person that has been connected with our operations in that Country have on their return given different & contradictory Accounts, some blaming one party, some another, but all Complaining of mismanagement in every department.

I don't know Genl. Schuyler personally but he holds an able pen and his clear intelligent manner of writing, with an apparent Anxiety expressed in all his letters for the good of the Service had gained my entire Confidence and I cannot help feeling a reluctance to receive unfavourable impressions, yet if that Man is sacrificing the interest of America to his ambition or avarice he must be a Wretch indeed. I hope this will not prove to be his Case, but at any rate as he is more of a Commissary & Quarter Master than a General, it may probably be best to shift his Station that Gates may be left at liberty to put our affairs at the Lakes in the best posture that can be.

I hope you are or will be properly Strengthened and Supported at New York. For my own part I dont like your situation there, but think you had better give up that City to the Enemy than let them get behind & pen you in there, as they were cooped in Boston last year. However, I dont pretend to any Judgement in this matter nor to have Considered the Subject. My Confidence in the abilities of Genl. Washington is entire. His Life is the most Valuable in America & whenever an engagement happens I sincerely hope he will think how much depends on it and guard it accordingly. The Public papers will Anounce to you the New appointments & Changes here, and as I have not much unemployed time I am always ready to spare the use of my pen. This being Sunday morning & in the Country I have spun out this letter to a length not common with me nowadays.

I beg my Compts to the Genl. I dined in Company with Mrs. Washington yesterday at Colo Harrisons & expect her here at dinner to day. Remember me to Genl. Mifflin, Col Shee & Moylan and believe me to be very Sincerely, sir, Your obedt hble servt.

Robt Morris

[P.S.] I will lay the London Letter before Congress tomorrow.

## 36. THE HOWE PEACE COMMISSION, SEPTEMBER 1776

On August 27, at the Battle of Long Island, General Howe, with his largest army of the war—over thirty thousand men, of whom nine thousand or so were German mercenaries—defeated the American forces and captured more than a thousand, including their commander, General John Sullivan.[40] Howe believed that this humiliating defeat would lead to increased openness in Congress regarding peace negotiations. Accordingly, the Howes discontinued offensive operations and sent the captured General Sullivan on parole to meet with Congress. He arrived on September 2 and delivered Lord Howe's message, "which he was desired to reduce to writing, and withdrew." The next day, he supplied

Congress with a written version of the message as well as his correspondence with Lord Howe.

Howe explained that he could not meet with Congress as the official representative body of the states, but still hoped to meet with some of its members, "whom he would Consider for the present only as private Gentlemen." Because Howe desired "to Compromise the Dispute between Great Britain and America, upon Terms advantageous to both," he was troubled that his obtaining such powers had "Delayed him near Two months in England, and prevented his arrival at this place before the Declaration of Independency took place." In spite of his inability to accept Congress' authority, he sweetened his offer by writing that if some form of accommodation were achieved, then "the authority of Congress must be afterwards Acknowledged." This proposal was Britain's second effort to negotiate some kind settlement, the first being Lord North's somewhat more detailed conciliatory peace proposal of twenty months earlier (see document 23.1); another, the Carlisle Peace Commission, was made two years later (see document 47.1). Each effort consistently proved to be far too little, too late.

On September 4, Congress approved of Lord Howe's offer to exchange General Sullivan and the self-styled "Lord Stirling," General William Alexander, for two British generals in American custody, Richard Prescott and Donald McDonald.[41] On September 5, Congress, acting on a report from the Board of War, decided that while acting as "representatives of the free and independent states of America," it couldn't "with propriety, send any of its members to confer with his lordship in their private characters." Still, and in tension with that holding, Congress, "ever desirous of establishing peace on reasonable terms," decided to "send a committee of their body to know whether he has any authority to treat with persons authorized by Congress for that purpose." The next day, Congress unanimously chose Benjamin Franklin and John Adams to meet with Lord Howe; in the voting for the third delegate, Edward Rutledge tied with Richard Henry Lee. But as Josiah Bartlett of New Hampshire observed, "As Mr Lee had opposed the measure he declined being voted for, as he said he could not accept [the appointment]. The votes then were for Stogden [Stockton of New Jersey] and Rutledge and the latter carried it."[42] Adams, too, had requested to be excused, but was asked to reconsider overnight, and on the following day he accepted the appointment.

## 36.1

### AN EXCHANGE OF LETTERS PREPARATORY TO ARRANGING A MEETING ON STATEN ISLAND BETWEEN LORD HOWE AND A COMMITTEE OF THREE CONGRESSIONAL DELEGATES, SEPTEMBER 3, 5, AND 6, 1776

Worthington Chauncey Ford et al., eds., *Journals of the Continental Congress, 1774–1789* (Washington, D.C.: Government Printing Office, 1904–37), 5:730–31, 737–38.

[TUESDAY, SEPTEMBER 3, 1776]

General Sullivan having reduced to writing the verbal message from Lord Howe, the same was laid before Congress, and read as follows:

The following is the purport of the message from Lord Howe to Congress, by General Sullivan:

That, though he could not at present Treat with Congress as such, yet he was very Desirous of having a Conference with some of The members, whom he would Consider for the present only as private Gentlemen, and meet them himself as such, at such place as they should appoint:

That he, in Conjunction with General Howe, had full powers to Compromise the Dispute between Great Britain and America, upon Terms advantageous to both; the obtaining of which Delayed him near Two months in England, and prevented his arrival at this place before the Declaration of Independency took place:

That he wished a Compact might be Settled at this time, when no Decisive Blow was struck, and neither party could say, that they were Compelled to enter into such agreement:

That, in Case Congress were Disposed to Treat, many things, which they had not as yet asked, might and ought to be granted Them; and That if, upon the Conference, They found any probable Ground of an Accommodation, The authority of Congress must be afterwards Acknowledged, otherwise The Compact would not be Compleat.

*Copy of General Sullivan's Letter to Lord Howe*

NEW YORK, *30th of August, 1776*

MY LORD.—agreeable to your Lordships Request I have Conversed with General Washington, who says that he has no power to Treat upon the Subject your Lordship mentioned, but has not the least objection to my going to Philadelphia to Inform Congress of what your Lordship has been pleased to Communicate to me upon the Subject. I shall wait your Lordships further Direction, and am with much esteem, your

Lordships most obedient Servant,

JNO SULLIVAN

The Right Honble Lord Viscount Howe

*His Lordship's Answer:*

EAGLE, 30 August, 1776
SIR,

Understanding by your Letter That the only Doubt of the propriety of your going to Philadelphia is, by your Conversation with General Washington, Removed, I do not see occasion to give you further Trouble but to Recommend the prosecuting of your Journey, as you were pleased on that Condition to propose. I am Sir, your most obedt Humble Servt,

HOWE

General SULLIVAN. . . .

[THURSDAY, SEPTEMBER 5, 1776]

The Congress then resumed the consideration of the report of the Board of War; and thereupon,

*Resolved,* That General Sullivan be requested to inform Lord Howe, that this Congress, being the representatives of the free and independent states of America, cannot, with propriety, send any of its members to confer with his lordship in their private characters; but that, ever desirous of establishing peace on reasonable terms, they will send a committee of their body to know whether he has any authority to treat with persons authorized by Congress for that purpose, in behalf of America, and what that authority is, and to hear such propositions as he shall think fit to make respecting the same:

That the president be desired to write to General Washington, and acquaint him that it is the opinion of Congress, that no proposals for making peace between Great Britain and the United States of America ought to be received or attended to, unless the same be made in writing, and addressed to the representatives of the said states in Congress, or persons authorized by them: And, if application be made to him by any of the commanders of the British forces on that subject, that he inform them that these United States, who entered into the war only for the defence of their lives and liberties, will cheerfully agree to peace on reasonable terms, whenever such shall be proposed to them in manner aforesaid.

*Ordered,* That a copy of the first of the two foregoing resolutions be delivered to General Sullivan, and that he be directed immediately to repair to Lord Howe.

*Resolved,* That to Morrow be assigned for electing the committee:

The several matters to this day referred, being postponed,

Adjourned to 10 o'Clock to Morrow.

FRIDAY, SEPTEMBER 6, 1776

*Resolved,* That General Sullivan be requested to deliver to Lord Howe the copy of the resolution delivered to him.

*Resolved,* That the committee, "to be sent to know whether Lord Howe has any authority to treat with persons authorized by Congress for that purpose, in behalf of America, and what that authority is, and to hear such propositions as he shall think fit to make respecting the same," consist of three:

Congress then proceeded to the election, when the following gentlemen were elected: Mr. [Benjamin] Franklin, Mr. J[ohn] Adams, and Mr. [Edward] Rutledge.

~~Mr. J. Adams requesting to be excused, the question whether he shall be excused from this service was postponed till to morrow.~~

---

## 36.2

BENJAMIN RUSH, RECORD OF CONGRESS
DEBATING ITS RESPONSE TO HOWE, SEPTEMBER 5, 1776(?)

Benjamin Rush, one of the country's best-educated physicians, persistent political intriguers, and fervent opponents of George Washington, was elected to Congress from Pennsylvania on July 20. As is apparent from his remarks here, Rush, a friend of Thomas Paine, joined with other congressional radicals in working to consolidate America's independence and thwarting any possibility of reconciliation with Great Britain. In trying to minimize the seriousness of the Continental Army's Long Island defeat and to prevent Congress from sending a delegation to meet with Lord Howe, Rush wrote dramatically that even if all the states were eventually defeated, he wished that the country would "not survive her precious birthright, but in yielding to superiour force, let her last breath be spent in uttering the word *Independance.*" He was opposed by more moderate and pragmatic delegates from Maryland and South Carolina, one of whom who countered that "he would much rather live with *dependance* than die with *independance* upon his lips." Rush too later had second thoughts about such utterances and his radical affiliations.[43] Even with independence declared, the split in Congress between radicals and moderates, though it began to change and take on new contours, did not fully dissipate. Britain's failure to invest the Howes with substantial powers to negotiate made the moderate position still more difficult to defend going forward.[44]

*The Autobiography of Benjamin Rush,* ed. George W. Corner (Princeton, N.J.: Princeton University Press for the American Philosophical Society, 1948), 119–20.

I took part in several debates; the first or second time I spoke was against a motion for a committee of Congress to meet Lord Howe in their private capacity to confer upon peace with Great Britain. On the same side of the question Jno. Adams, Dr. Witherspoon, and George Ross spoke with uncommon eloquence. The last of those gentlemen began his speech by asking what the conduct of George the 3rd would be, had Congress proposed to negociate with him as Elector of Hanover instead of King of Great Britain. He would spurn, and very properly spurn the insulting proposal. "Let the American States," said he, "act in the same manner. We are bound to cherish the honor of our country which is now committed to our care. Nothing could dishonour the Sovereign of Britain that would not in equal circumstances dishonour us." In the conclusion of my speech, I said that "our country was far from being in a condition to make it necessary for us to humble ourselves at the feet of Great Britain. We had lost a battle, and a small island, but the city and State of New York were still in possession of their independance. But suppose that State had been conquered; suppose half the States in the Union had been conquered; nay, suppose all the States in the Union except one had been conquered, still let that one not renounce her independance; but I will go further: should this solitary state, the last repository of our freedom, be invaded, let her not survive her precious birthright, but in yielding to superiour force, let her last breath be spent in uttering the word *Independance*." The speakers in favor of the motion were Ed. Rutledge, Thos. Lynch, Jno. Stone, and several others. One of them, in answer to the concluding sentence of my speech, said "he would much rather live with *dependance* than die with *independance* upon his lips." The motion was carried with some modification.

36.3

## BENJAMIN FRANKLIN TO LORD HOWE, SEPTEMBER 8, 1776

In this letter to Lord Howe, Franklin alerts him that Congress has appointed a delegation to meet with him. On September 11 they would arrive in Amboy, New Jersey, where they hoped to receive directions regarding Howe's preferred time and place to meet.

Paul H. Smith, ed., *Letters of Delegates to Congress, 1774–1789* (Washington, D.C.: Library of Congress, 1976–93), 5:123.

My Lord                                                              Philada. Sept. 8. 1776

I received your Favour of the 16th past. I did not immediately answer it, because I found that my Corresponding with your Lordship was dislik'd by some Members of

Congress. I hope now soon to have an Opportunity of discussing with you, vivâ voce, the Matters mention'd in it; as I am with Mr Adams & Mr Rutledge appointed to wait on your Lordship in consequence of a Desire you expresd in some Conversation with Gen. Sullivan, and of a Resolution of Congress made thereupon, which that Gentleman has probably before this time communicated to you. We purpose to set out on our Journey to-morrow Morning, and to be at Amboy on Wednesday about 9 oClock, where we should be glad to meet a Line from your Lordship, appointing the Time and Place of Meeting. If it would be agreable to your Lordship, we apprehend that either at the House on Staten Island opposite to Amboy, or at the Governor's House in Amboy, we might be accommodated with a Room for the purpose. With the greatest Esteem & Respect, I have the Honour to be, My Lord, &c

## 36.4

 HENRY STRACHEY, NOTES ON LORD HOWE'S
MEETING WITH A COMMITTEE OF CONGRESS,
SEPTEMBER 11, 1776

Henry Strachey, a longtime member of Parliament who had served in India as a private secretary to Robert Clive, then as secretary to the Howe brothers' peace commission from 1776 to 1778, recorded the meeting between the congressional delegation and Lord Howe—General Howe was unable to attend—on Staten Island opposite Amboy, New Jersey. Howe began by suggesting that the congressional petition to the king of July 8, 1775, known as the Olive Branch Petition (document 19.1), had been viewed by many in the House of Lords as a proper foundation for reconciliation. Howe thought that the petition provided "a sufficient Basis to confer upon—that it contained Matter, which, with Candour & Discussion might be wrought into a Plan of Permanency." The address to the people of Great Britain (document 20.1) that had accompanied the petition, he believed, had had the opposite effect.

In the intervening fourteen months, the colonists "themselves had changed the ground . . . by their Declaration of Independency, which, if it could not be got over, precluded him from all Treaty." Howe reiterated later "that their Declaration of Independency had since rendered him the more cautious of opening himself—that it was absolutely impossible for him to treat, or confer, upon that Ground, or to admit the Idea in the smallest degree." Insistence on maintaining their status as independent states outside the British Empire, and on demanding that the three men meeting with Howe be recognized as representatives of a body unacknowledged by the king, that is, Congress, Howe made clear, would result in the end of their conversation and, in truth, his peace mission. Howe next pointed out that, in all honesty, the British commitment to an imperial relationship with the former colonies had little to do with advantages gained from taxation, a point that Franklin highlighted in emphasizing that the colonies had never refused to contribute when the king had sought proper requisitions from the colonies through the king's governors. As Howe noted at the meeting and in an earlier letter to Franklin (see document 35.6), it was America's "Commerce, her Strength, her Men, that we chiefly wanted."

In return, Franklin reminded Howe that Britain's response to the Olive Branch Petition had been Parliament's American Prohibitory Act of December 22, 1775 (document 29.2), which removed Americans from the king's protection and made them and their property subject to predatory and confiscatory attacks. For Franklin and so many other delegates, congressional and parliamentary acts were linked in a tragic drama of action and reaction. Accordingly, Franklin's assessment was that "all former Attachment was *obliterated*—that America could not return again to the Domination of Great Britain." Both Adams and Rutledge made it difficult for Howe to misunderstand that the former dependent relationship between the colonies and Great Britain was no longer one that they would accept; as Rutledge claimed, "The People [of South Carolina] were now settled and happy under that Government and would not (even if they, the Congress could desire it) return to the King's Government." Nonetheless, Rutledge cleverly suggested that many of the same commercial benefits that Britain had previously enjoyed might still be available if the two countries were able to conclude mutually beneficial commercial treaties "before any thing is settled with other foreign powers," with a hard-to-miss reference to ongoing congressional discussions with France.

Although not noted here, Adams reported that "Mr R[utledge] mentioned to his Lordship, what G[eneral] Sullivan had said, that his Lordship told him he would set the Act of Parliament wholly aside, and that Parliament had no Right to tax America, or meddle with her internal Polity. His Lordship answered Mr R. that G. Sullivan had misunderstood him, and extended his Words much beyond their import."[45] Here, in Strachey's notes, Howe speaks to this point by claiming "that His Majesty's most earnest desire was to make his American Subjects happy, to cause a Reform in whatever affected the Freedom of their Legislation, and to concur with his Parliament in the Redress of any real Grievances." Of course, the sticking point for twelve years had been the king's well-intended adherence to the British Constitution, which demanded that he concur in Parliament's commitment to play an active role in governing the colonies. The issue that had led to the beginning of the Crisis in 1764—the constitutionality of Parliament's sovereign legislating for and taxing the colonies—was still not, in the minds of those in government, open to negotiation. It was evident also that congressional radicals' tactic of forcing the decision on independence to be taken before the arrival of the peace commissioners helped prevent any backsliding toward reconciliation or any serious negotiating between Great Britain and the new states.

Paul H. Smith, ed., *Letters of Delegates to Congress, 1774–1789* (Washington, D.C.: Library of Congress, 1976–93), 5:137–44. Italicized material in parentheses was crossed out in the manuscript version and later restored.

11th Septr 1776

Lord Howe received the Gentlemen on the Beach. Dr. Franklin introduced Mr. Adams and Mr. Rutledge. Lord Howe very politely expressed the Sense he entertained of the Confidence they had placed in him, by thus putting themselves in his hands.

A general and immaterial Conversation from the Beach to the House—The Hessian Guard saluted, as they passed.

A cold dinner was on the Table—dined—the Hessian Colonel present—Immediately after dinner he retired.

Lord Howe informed them it was long since he had entertained an opinion that the Differences between the two Countries might be accommodated to the Satisfaction of both—that he was known to be a Well Wisher to America—particularly to the Province of Massachusetts Bay, which had endeared itself to him by the very high Honors it had bestowed upon the Memory of his eldest Brother—that his going out as Commissioner from the King had been early mentioned, but that afterwards for some time, he had heard no more of it—That an Idea had then arisen of sending several Commissioners, to which he had objected—that his Wish was to go out singly and with a Civil Commission only, in which case, his Plan was to have gone immediately to Philadelphia, that he had even objected to his Brother's being in the Commission, from the Delicacy of the Situation and his desire to take upon himself all the Reproach that might be the Consequence of it—that it was however thought necessary that the General should be joined in the Commission (for reasons which he explained) having their hands upon the Two Services—and that he, Lord Howe, should also have the naval Command, in which he had acquiesced—that he had hoped to reach America before the Army had moved, and did not doubt but if their Disposition had been the same as expressed in their Petition to the King, he should have been able to have brought about an Accomodation to the Satisfaction of both Countries—that he thought the Petition was a sufficient Basis to confer upon—that it contained Matter, which, with Candour & Discussion might be wrought into a Plan of Permanency—that the Address to the People, which accompanied the Petition to His Majesty, tended to destroy the good Effects that might otherwise have been hoped for from the Petition—that he had however still flattered himself that upon the Grounds of the Petition, he should be able to do some good—that they themselves had changed the ground since he left England by their Declaration of Independency, which, if it could not be got over, precluded him from all Treaty, as they must know, and he had explicitly said so in his Letter to Dr. Franklin, that he had not, nor did he expect ever to

563

have, Powers to consider the Colonies in the light of Independent States—that they must also be sensible, that he could not confer with them as a Congress—that he could not acknowledge that Body which was not acknowledged by the King, whose Delegate he was, neither, for the same reason, could he confer with these Gentlemen as a Committee of the Congress—that if they would not lay aside that Distinction, it would be improper for him to proceed—that he thought it an unessential Form, which might for the present lie dormant—that they must give him leave to consider them merely as Gentlemen of great Ability, and Influence in the Country—and that they were now met to converse together (*upon the Subject of Differences*) and to try if any Outline could be drawn to put a stop to the Calamities of War, and to bring forward some Plan that might be satisfactory both to America and to England. He desired them to consider the Delicacy of his Situation—the Reproach he was liable to, if he should be understood by any step of his, to acknowledge, or to treat with, the Congress—that he hoped they would not by any Implication commit him upon that Point—that he was rather going beyond his Powers in the present Meeting—[Dr. Franklin said You may depend upon our taking care of that, my Lord] That he thought the Idea of a Congress might easily be thrown out of the Question at present, for that if Matters could be so settled that the King's Government should be reestablished, the Congress would of course cease to exist, and if they meant such Accommodation, they must see how unnecessary & useless it was to stand upon that Form which they knew they were to give up upon the Restoration of legal Government.

Dr. Franklin said that His Lordship might consider the Gentlemen present in any view he thought proper—that they were also at liberty to consider themselves in their real Character—that there was no necessity on this occasion to distinguish between the Congress and Individuals—and that the Conversation might be held as amongst friends.

The Two other Gentlemen assented, in very few Words, to what the Doctor had said.

Lord Howe then proceeded—that on his Arrival in this Country he had thought it expedient to issue a Declaration, which they had done him the honor to comment upon—that he had endeavored to couch it in such Terms as would be the least exceptionable—that he had concluded they must have judged he had not expressed in it all he had to say, though enough, he thought, to bring on a Discussion which might lead the way to Accommodation—that their Declaration of Independency had since rendered him the more cautious of opening himself—that it was absolutely impossible for him to treat, or confer, upon that Ground, or to admit the Idea in the smallest degree—that he flattered himself if That were given up, their was still room for him to effect the King's Purposes—that His Majesty's most earnest desire was to make his American Subjects happy, to cause a Reform in whatever affected the Freedom of their Legislation, and to concur with his Parliament in the Redress of any real Grievances—that his Powers were, generally, to restore Peace and grant Pardons, to attend to Complaints & Representations, and to confer upon Means of establishing a Re-Union upon Terms honorable & advantageous to the

Colonies as well as to Great Britain—that they knew We expected Aid from America—that the Dispute seemed to be only concerning the Mode of obtaining it.

[Doctor Franklin here said, *That* we never refused, upon *Requisition*.]

Lord Howe continued—that their Money was the smallest Consideration—that America could produce more solid Advantages to Great Britain—that it was her Commerce, her Strength, her Men, that we chiefly wanted.

[Here Dr. Franklin said with rather a sneering Laugh, Ay, my Lord, we have a pretty considerable Manufactory of *Men*—alluding as it should seem to their numerous Army.]

Lord Howe continued—it is desirable to put a stop to these ruinous Extremities, as well for the sake of our Country, as yours. When an American falls, England feels it. Is there no way of treading back this Step of Independency, and opening the door to a full discussion?

Lord Howe concluded with saying that having thus opened to them the general Purport of the Commission, and the King's Disposition to a permanent Peace, he must stop to hear what they might chuse to observe.

Dr. Franklin said he supposed His Lordship had seen the Resolution of the Congress which had sent them hither—that the Resolution contained the whole of their Commission—that if this Conversation was productive of no immediate good Effect, it might be of Service at a future time—that America had considered the Prohibitory Act as the Answer to her Petition to the King—Forces had been sent out, and Towns destroyed—that they could not expect Happiness now under the *Domination* of Great Britain—that all former Attachment was *obliterated*—that America could not return again to the Domination of Great Britain, and therefore imagined that Great Britain meant to rest it upon Force. The other Gentlemen will deliver their Sentiments.

Mr. Adams said that he had no objection to Lord Howe's considering him, on the present Occasion, merely as a private Gentleman, or in any Character except that of a British Subject—that the Resolution of the Congress to declare the Independency was not taken up upon their own Authority—that they had been instructed so to do, by *all* the Colonies—and that it was not in their power to treat otherwise than as independent States. He mentioned warmly his own Determination not to depart from the Idea of Independency, and spoke in the common way of the Power of the Crown, which was comprehended in the Ideal Power of Lords & Commons.

Mr. Rutledge began by saying he had been one of the oldest Members of the Congress—that he had been one from the beginning—that he thought it was worth the Consideration of Great Britain whether she would not receive greater Advantages by an Alliance with the Colonies as independent States, than she had ever hitherto done—that she might still enjoy a *great Share* of the Commerce—that she would have their raw Materials for her Manufactures—that they could protect the West India Islands much more effectually and more easily than she can—that they could assist her in the Newfoundland Trade—that he was glad this Conversation had happened, as it would be the occasion of opening to Great Britain the Consideration of the Advantages she might derive from America by an Alliance with her as an independent State, before any thing is settled with other foreign Powers—that it was impossible the People should consent to come again under the English Government. He could answer for South Carolina—that Government had been very oppressive—that the Crown Officers had claimed Privilege and confined People upon pretence of a breach of Privilege—that they had at last taken the Government into their own hands—that the People were now settled and happy under that Government and would not (even if they, the Congress could desire it) return to the King's Government—

Mr. Rutledge mentioned (by way of Answer to Lord Howe's Remark upon that point) that their Petition to the King contained all which they thought was proper to be addressed to His Majesty,—that the other Matters which could not come under the head of a Petition and therefore could not with Propriety be inserted, were put into the Address to the People, which was only calculated to shew them the Importance of America to Great Britain—and that the Petition to King was by all of them meant to be respectful.

Lord Howe said, that if such were their Sentiments, he could only lament it was not in his Power to bring about the Accommodation he wished—that he had not Authority, nor did he expect he ever should have, to treat with the Colonies as States independent of the Crown of Great Britain—and that he was sorry the Gentlemen had had the trouble of coming so far, to so little purpose—that if the Colonies would not give up the System of Independency, it was impossible for him to enter into any Negociation.

Dr. Franklin observed that it would take as much time for them to refer to, and get an answer from their Constituents, as it would the Commissioners to get fresh Instructions from home, which he supposed might be done in about 3 Months.

Lord Howe replied it was in vain to think of his receiving Instructions to treat upon that ground.

After a little Pause, Dr. Franklin suddenly said, well my Lord, as America is to expect nothing but upon (*total*) unconditional Submission, and Your Lordship has no Proposition to make us, give me leave to ask whether, if *we* should make Propositions to Great Britain (not that I know, or am authorized to say we shall) You would receive and transmit them.

Lord Howe interrupted the Doctor at the Word Submission—said that Great Britain did not require unconditional Submission, that he thought what he had already said to them, proved the contrary, and desired the Gentlemen would not go away with such an Idea.

Memdn. Perhaps Dr. Franklin meant Submission to the Crown, in opposition to their Principle of Independency.

Lord Howe said he did not know that he could avoid receiving any Papers that might be put into his hands—seemed rather doubtful about the Propriety of transmitting home, but did not say that he would decline it.

## 36.5

### REPORT OF THE COMMITTEE APPOINTED TO CONFER WITH LORD HOWE, SEPTEMBER 17, 1776

On September 13, the congressional delegates who met with Lord Howe offered Congress an oral account of the meeting, and were "directed to make a report in writing, as soon as conveniently they can." The delegation reported back to Congress on September 17, and its report was printed in the *Pennsylvania Gazette* on September 18, 1776.[46]

The delegation reported that Lord Howe's sole proposition for peace had been that "the colonies should return to their allegiance and obedience to the government of Great Britain." In response, the committee members had offered their opinion "that a return to the domination of Great Britain was not now to be expected." They added, as Congress had so often done before, "that it was not till the last act of parliament which denounced war against us, and put us out of the king's protection, that we declared our independence"; once independence had been declared, "it was not in the power of the Congress to agree for them, that they should return to their former dependent state." Congress, it should be kept in mind, wasn't truly a central government but something closer to an alliance of separate nations fighting a war in common, and thus it really did not enjoy such power. Instead, the delegates had smartly suggested that it might be more convenient for Lord Howe to "obtain fresh powers from" Britain to negotiate with them as independent states than it would be for Congress to obtain new powers "from the several colonies, to consent to a submission."

Finally, the members of the committee accurately speculated that even if the states had not declared independence before the meeting, there was no guarantee that the administration would "propose in Parliament, any amendment of the Acts complained of." Thus there was no reason for Congress to trust that the Howes could deliver whatever was promised. The committee members reasonably concluded that "any expectation from the effect of such a power would have been too uncertain and precarious to be relied on by America." They might have added, too, that even if Parliament were to annul intrusive or punitive legislation, without a fundamental and entrenched constitutional change between the colonies and Parliament, there would be nothing to prevent a later Parliament from reenacting similar legislation. For the congressional delegates, declaring independence had indeed altered the grounds upon which peace could be negotiated. Yet even if the colonies had delayed the declaration and managed to reconcile with Britain, the fundamental constitutional issue that led to the Imperial Crisis would likely have remained. The issue of constitutional right—that of Parliament versus that of the

colonies—once raised, was difficult to resolve. As noted by many, and most famously by Edmund Burke, the question of right would have much better been left
unexamined.[47]

Worthington Chauncey Ford et al., eds., *Journals of the Continental Congress, 1774–1789*
(Washington, D.C.: Government Printing Office, 1904–37), 5:765–66.

The committee appointed to confer with Lord Howe, agreeable to order, brought in a
report in writing, which was read as follows:

In Obedience to the order of Congress, we have had a meeting with Lord Howe. It
was on Wednesday last, upon Staten island, opposite to Amboy, where his lordship received and entertained us with the utmost politeness.

His lordship opened the conversation, by acquainting us, that, though he could not
treat with us as a committee of Congress, yet, as his powers enabled him to confer and
consult with any private gentlemen of influence in the colonies, on the means of restoring peace between the two countries, he was glad of this opportunity of conferring with
us on that subject, if we thought ourselves at liberty to enter into a conference with him
in that character. We observed to his Lordship, that, as our business was to hear, he might
consider us in what light he pleased, and communicate to us any propositions he might
be authorized to make for the purpose mentioned; but that we could consider ourselves
in no other character than that in which we were placed, by the order of Congress. His
Lordship then entered into a discourse of considerable length, which contained no explicit proposition of peace, except one, namely, That the colonies should return to their
allegiance and obedience to the government of Great Britain. The rest consisted principally of assurances, that there was an exceeding good disposition in the king and his
ministers to make that government easy to us, with intimations, that, in case of our
submission, they would cause the offensive acts of parliament to be revised, and the
instructions to governors to be reconsidered; that so, if any just causes of complaint
were found in the acts, or any errors in government were perceived to have crept into
the instructions, they might be amended or withdrawn.

We gave it as our Opinion to his lordship, that a return to the domination of Great
Britain was not now to be expected. We mentioned the repeated humble petitions of the
colonies to the king and parliament, which had been treated with contempt, and answered only by additional injuries; the unexampled patience we had shown under their
tyrannical government, and that it was not till the last act of parliament which denounced war against us, and put us out of the king's protection, that we declared our
independence; that this declaration had been called for by the people of the colonies in
general; that every colony had approved of it, when made, and all now considered themselves as independent states, and were settling, or had settled, their governments accordingly; so that it was not in the power of the Congress to agree for them, that they

should return to their former dependent state; that there was no doubt of their inclination to peace, and their willingness to enter into a treaty with Great Britain, that might be advantageous to both countries; that though his lordship had, at present, no power to treat with them as independent states, he might, if there was the same good disposition in Britain, much sooner obtain fresh powers from thence, for that purpose, than powers could be obtained by Congress, from the several colonies, to consent to a submission.

His Lordship then saying, that he was sorry to find, that no accommodation was like to take place, put an end to the conference.

Upon the whole, it did not appear to your committee, that his Lordship's commission contained any other authority of importance than what is expressed in the act of parliament, namely, that of granting pardons, with such exceptions as the commissioners shall think proper to make, and of declaring America, or any part of it, to be in the king's peace, upon submission; For, as to the power of enquiring into the state of America, which his Lordship mentioned to us, and of conferring and consulting with any persons the commissioners might think proper, and representing the result of such conversations to the ministry, who, (provided the colonies would subject themselves,) might, after all, or might not, at their pleasure, make any alterations in the former instructions to governors, or propose in Parliament, any amendment of the Acts complained of, we apprehended any expectation from the effect of such a power would have been too uncertain and precarious to be relyed on by America, had she still continued in her state of Dependence.

*Ordered,* That the foregoing report, and also the message from Lord Howe, as delivered by General Sullivan, and the resolution of Congress in consequence thereof, be published by the committee who brought in the foregoing report.

## 37. DIFFICULTIES IN OVERSEEING THE CONTINENTAL ARMY—STATES VERSUS CONGRESSIONAL AUTHORITIES, FEBRUARY 1777

Following Lord Howe's meeting with the congressional delegation, the British forces returned to the offensive and on September 15 occupied New York City. Then, on October 11 and 13, part of America's minuscule naval fleet suffered crippling losses at the Battles of Valcour Bay and Split Rock, which effectively destroyed it as a fighting force. Washington's forces were defeated on October 28 at the Battle of White Plains, and the British on November 16 and 18 successively took Fort Washington (with nearly three thousand Americans taken prisoner) and Fort Lee. After vesting Washington with something close to dictatorial powers, Congress fled Philadelphia on December 12 and reconvened on December 20 in Baltimore, where it remained until February 27, 1777. Congress returned again to Philadelphia and, after finding a quorum, went back to work on March 12, 1777.[48] Although the American forces on December 26, 1776, and January 3, 1777, enjoyed dramatic, even essential, victories at Trenton and Princeton, which did much to restore morale, some of the optimism, even bravado, in Congress following the Declaration of Independence seemed to have evaporated.[49] The Continental Army was experiencing severe problems in recruiting and retaining troops, and whole militia units sometimes departed without informing the commanding officer.[50] American forces were also experiencing grievous losses due to desertions.[51]

Accordingly, on February 12, 1777, after deciding to inoculate (by means of variolation) Continental troops against smallpox, Congress chose a committee of three "to consider the most effectual means of discouraging and preventing desertions from the army." The members were Richard Henry Lee, Samuel Chase, and Jonathan Dickinson Sergeant, a young lawyer from New Jersey who was a fervent opponent of the British and came to be known for not attending too carefully to the niceties of the law when proscribing the activities of loyalists and seizing their property.[52] The next day the committee brought in a report that was read in Congress; the final consideration, in particular regarding an amended last paragraph, was postponed. The report was again debated on February 25, the long delay being a sure sign of the report having encountered substantial opposition.

The final paragraph of the original report caused controversy. In it, Congress directly authorized, without going through the states, local committees of observation or inspection, which were a product of the Continental Association (see document 11.2), to seize suspected deserters and to turn them over, without due process protections or state approval, to Continental Army officers. Despite being intrusive and high-handed, the language, after a long delay and reconsideration, was approved. The resolutions regarding deserters were distributed, along with other articles of war, to Continental officers and printed nearly a month later, on March 18, in the *Pennsylvania Packet* after Congress had returned to Philadelphia.

The two resolutions approved on February 13 requested state legislatures "to provide as soon as possible by Law . . . for any constable, freeholder, or Keeper of any public ferry within any of the United States, to apprehend or cause to be apprehended" deserters. Local magistrates were to follow accepted legal procedures, and safeguards were to be maintained that protected the rights of the accused. Congress held that accused deserters were "to be brought before any Justice of the peace, living in or near the place where such person shall be taken," and there examined. In short, Congress acted through the states and their local agents. Penalties associated with "harboring deserters, and the purchasing from them their arms, or cloathes" were assigned. Important legal remedies for the mistaken search and apprehension of someone wrongly believed to be a deserter were put in place: "if any commissioned officer, constable, or other person shall break open any dwelling House" errantly, then he "shall forfeit twenty Dollars."

On February 25, Congress approved the resolution to communicate directly, over the heads of the sovereign states, with "the committees of observation or inspection in these United States." The committees were instructed to "cause diligent enquiry to be made, in their respective Counties or Districts, for all Deserters that may be lurking and harboured therein, and cause such, whenever found, to be immediately secured and conveyed." Such men, however, were not to be surrendered to duly authorized local or state officials, but to be handed over, without regard to the accused deserter's common-law due process rights, "to the nearest continental officer; and all such officers are hereby directed to receive and secure such deserters, that they may be safely delivered to their respective regiments, and brought to a speedy trial and exemplary punishment."

Although Congress had directly communicated with committees of inspection or safety almost for the entire period of its existence and had even incorporated the relationship into earlier legislation, in particular the Continental Association, such practices as those confirmed in the resolution of February 25 became a matter of controversy—thus, the postponement and delay of its consideration—in light of the still-unresolved constitutional question of how sovereignty between the states and the impending central government was to be distributed. Congress' power to act with impunity, questionable legality, and without regard to either the sensibilities of the sovereign states or due process protections—the very things three congresses had complained of for twelve years when applying to Parliament for relief—soon came to an end.[53]

The spokesmen for each side of this issue, here and more broadly in Congress at this time, were two British immigrants from its peripheries, Thomas Burke and James Wilson. Merrill Jensen describes them thus: "Early in 1777, Dr. Thomas Burke came to Congress as a delegate from North Carolina. In the controversy which followed, this Irish doctor [and lawyer], trained at Dublin University, led the forces of radicalism; James Wilson, a Scotch lawyer trained in Scottish universities, led the remnants of the conservative forces."[54] What was of greatest significance in this debate was not the immediate issue—the devastating desertions suffered by the Continental Army—nor even the abrogation of due process rights, but the continued controversy regarding the apportionment of sovereignty, one of the two fundamental constitutional questions that had stymied all efforts to construct intercolonial or continental government during the Imperial Crisis.

The primary issue was the proper relationship between the colonies and Parliament, which had been effectively mooted when Congress voted for independence. But the second, still-unresolved question continued to fester. The implicit issue of divided sovereignty had been a concern in 1754 at the Albany Congress and in 1774 at the meeting of the First Continental Congress and its rejection of Galloway's "Plan of Union"; it would roil the Constitutional Convention in 1787. As is evident in the congressional debate over the Articles of Confederation (see documents 34.1, 34.2, 38.1, and 42.1), the matter of how sovereignty was to be divided was no closer to being resolved now than it had been twenty years earlier.[55]

37.1

  REPORT ON THE DISCOURAGING AND PREVENTING
OF DESERTIONS FROM THE CONTINENTAL ARMY,
FEBRUARY 13 AND 25, 1777

Worthington Chauncey Ford et al., eds., *Journals of the Continental Congress, 1774–1789*
(Washington, D.C.: Government Printing Office, 1904–37), 7:115–18, 154–55.

[THURSDAY, FEBRUARY 13, 1777]
The Committee on Deserters, brought in a report, which was read.

Whereas several Soldiers and Mariners duly enlisted in the service of the United States do afterwards desert, and are often found wandering, or otherwise absenting themselves illegally from the service.

*Resolved* that it be recommended to the Legislatures of the several States to provide as soon as possible by Law, that it shall and may be lawful to and for any constable, free-holder, or Keeper of any public ferry within any of the United States, to apprehend or cause to be apprehended, any person ~~suspected of~~ being a deserter, and cause such person to be brought before any Justice of the peace, living in or near the place where such person shall be taken, who shall have power to examine such ~~suspected~~ person, and if by his confession, or the testimony of one or more credible witness or witnesses, upon oath, or by the knowledge of such Justice it shall appear, that such ~~suspected~~ person is an enlisted soldier, or mariner, and ought to be with the company, troop, crew, or vessel, to which he belongs, such Justice shall forthwith cause him to be conveyed to any the nearest commissioned officer, of the Land or Sea Service, as the case may be, or to the public Goal of the County or place, where such deserter shall be apprehended, and shall immediately transmit an account thereof to the Secretary of War, for the time being, and to the Commanding officer of such Deserter, and for the better encouragement of any person or persons to apprehend and secure such deserter, that such Justice shall give to the person who shall apprehend and bring such Deserter, after Conviction, a certificate expressing the service and the distance such deserter shall be brought, which certificate shall entitle the Bearer to the reward of five Dollars for the apprehending such deserter, and twelve ninetieths of a Dollar for every mile therein expressed, and any person who shall convey and deliver such deserter to the Officer, or goal as afore-said, shall also receive the same mileage; and the said reward, and mileage shall be paid by the officer, sheriff or goaler to whom such deserter shall be delivered, and the Sheriff or goaler shall be reimbursed the money by him paid by his State, together with the expence of advertising such Deserter, and one fifth of a Dollar per day for his mainte-nance, to be charged to the Continent; and the Sheriff or goaler shall immediately publish the name of the deserter and the company, Regiment, or vessel to which he belongs in some one of the newspapers of his State for four successive weeks.

Whereas the mode heretofore recommended to prevent the harboring deserters, and the purchasing from them their arms, or cloathes hath not proved effectual to abolish so pernicious a practice:

*Resolved,* that it be recommended to the Legislatures of the several States to provide as soon as possible, by law, That if any person shall harbor conceal or assist any deserter from the land or Sea Service, knowing him to be such, the person so offending shall forfeit for every such offence, ten dollars, or if any person shall knowingly detain, buy or exchange, or otherwise receive, any arms, horse, cloaths or other furniture, belonging to the United States, from any soldier, trooper, mariner, deserter, or any other person, under any pretence, or shall cause the colour of such clothes to be changed, or the mark or brand, of such horse to be altered, the person so offending shall forfeit, for every such offence, ten dollars, and upon conviction, by the oath of one or more credible witness or witnesses, before any one justice of the peace of the City, County, Town or place, where the offence shall be committed, the said respective penalties shall be levied by warrant from the Justice, to any constable, by distress and sale of the goods and chattels of the offender, one moiety of the penalty to be paid to the informer, and the residue to the officer to whom any such Deserter, soldier, trooper, or mariner did belong, and where no informer, the whole thereof to the officer, and if any such offender, convicted as aforesaid, shall not have sufficient goods and chattles whereon distress may be made for the penalty, or shall not pay the same within four days after such conviction, in such case such justice may and shall, by warrant, either commit such offender to the common goal there to remain without bail not exceeding three months, or may cause such offender to be publicly whipt, not exceeding thirty nine stripes, at the discretion of such justice; and that if any commissioned officer, constable, or other person shall break open any dwelling House, or outhouse under pretence to search for deserters, without warrant from a Justice of the peace, which such Justice shall grant, such offender, if no deserter shall be found therein, shall forfeit twenty Dollars, to be awarded by any Justice, and levied on the offenders person, goods, or chattels.

Whereas it may be some time before adequate laws, for the apprehending deserters, and punishing persons concealing them, can be framed, arising from the recess of some Legislatures, and the distance of others: To the end, that the most speedy stop may be put to the pernicious and unsoldierly practice of deserting, and that such offenders who receive the public money for services that they design not to perform, may be certainly and speedily carried back to the corps they have deserted from, It is earnestly recommended to the committees of observation or inspection in these United States, that they cause diligent enquiry to be made, in their respective Counties or Districts, for all Deserters that may be lurking and harboured therein, and cause such, whenever found, to be immediately secured, and conveyed to the nearest Continental officer; and all such officers are hereby directed to receive and secure such deserters, that they may be safely delivered to their respective Regiments, and brought to a speedy trial and exemplary punishment. . . .

[TUESDAY, FEBRUARY 25, 1777]

Congress took into consideration the report of the Committee on Deserters; and, thereupon, came to the following resolution:

To the end, that the most speedy stop may be put to the pernicious and unsoldierly practice of deserting, and that such offenders who receive the public money for services that they design not to perform, may be certainly and speedily carried back to the corps they have deserted from, it is earnestly recommended to the committees of observation or inspection in these united States, that they cause diligent enquiry to be made, in their respective counties or districts, for all deserters that may be lurking and harboured therein, and cause such, whenever found, to be immediately secured, and conveyed to the nearest continental officer; and all such officers are hereby directed to receive and secure such deserters, that they may be safely delivered to their respective regiments, and brought to a speedy trial and exemplary punishment; and farther, to pay to the persons delivering such deserters, eight dollars for each deserter so brought and delivered, and twelve ninetieths of a dollar in lieu of expences for every mile from the place where the deserter was taken up to the place where he is delivered to the officer.

*Ordered,* That the foregoing resolve, and the 1st, 2d, and 3d articles of the 6th section of the articles of war, be published in the several news papers for six months, and also that 300 copies be printed in hand bills, and sent to camp, to be distributed among the officers.

37.2

 JOHN ADAMS TO HENRY KNOX, SEPTEMBER 29, 1776

John Adams wrote to Henry Knox, the Bostonian commander of the Continental artillery, a future commandant at West Point, and a future secretary of war, to complain of the poor performance of New England militia and troops at the Battle of Long Island on August 27 and the fighting around New York City on September 15, during which the men of New England were reported to have fled under relatively light fire. Adams, a man with no military experience, pompously suggested that he could "almost" agree to imposing the Roman law of decimation: "The Legion which run away, had the Name of every Man in it, put into a Box and then drawn out, and every tenth Man was put to death." Most dismaying to Adams was the possibility that it was only New England troops that had performed poorly, while those from the South had acted the part of courageous heroes. Similarly

irritating, and supporting the hostility of some in Congress toward New Englanders, was that General Washington "gives too much occasion for these Reports
by his Letters, in which he (*is eternally throwing some slur or other upon*) often
mentions things to the Disadvantage of some Part of New England, but (*never one
Word*) Seldom any Thing of the Kind about any other Part of the Continent."
Washington, as was well known, had his difficulties and differences with the overly
familiar, democratic, slovenly, and quixotic New England soldiers.[56]

Paul H. Smith, ed., *Letters of Delegates to Congress, 1774–1789*
(Washington, D.C.: Library of Congress, 1976–93), 5:260–61. Italicized material in
parentheses was crossed out in the manuscript version and later restored.

Dear Sir.                                                              Philadelphia Septr. 29. 1776
This Evening I had the Pleasure of yours of the 25th. I have only to ask you whether it
would be agreable to you to have Austin made your Lt Coll.? Let me know sincerely, for
I will never propose it without your Approbation.

I agree with you that there is nothing of the vast in the Characters of the Enemies
General, or Admiral. But I differ in opinion from you, when you think, that if there had
been, they would have annihilated your Army. It is very true that a Silly Panick has
been spread in your Army, and from thence come to Philadelphia. But Hannibal spread
as great a Panick once at Rome, without daring to attempt to take advantage of it. If he
had his own Army would have been annihilated—and he knew it. A Panic, in an Army,
when pushed to Desperation becomes Heroism.

However, I despise that Panic and those who have been infected with it, and I could
almost consent that the good old Roman fashion of Decimation should be Introduced.
The Legion which run away, had the Name of every Man in it, put into a Box and then
drawn out, and every tenth Man was put to death. The Terror of this Uncertainty whose
Lot it would be to die, restrained the whole in the Time of danger from indulging their
Fears.

Pray tell me, Coll Knox, does every Man to the Southward of Hudsons River behave
like an Hero and every Man to the Northward of it like a Poltroon or not. The Rumours,
Reports, and Letters which come here upon every occasion represent the New England
Troops as Cowards running away perpetually, and the Southern Troops as standing
bravely. I wish I could know whether it is true. I want to know for the Government of my
own Conduct, because if the New Englandmen are a Pack of Cowards, I would resign my
Place in Congress where I should not choose to represent Poltroons and remove to some
Southern Colony, where I could enjoy the Society of Heroes, and have a Chance of learning
Sometime or other, to be Part of an Hero myself. I must say that your *amiable* General
gives too much occasion for these Reports by his Letters, in which he (*is eternally throwing
some slur or other upon*) often mentions things to the Disadvantage of some Part of New

England, but (*never one Word*) Seldom any Thing of the Kind about any other Part of the Continent.

You complain of the popular Plan of raising the new Army. But if you make the Plan, as unpopular as you please, you will not mend the Matter. If you leave the appointment of officers to the General, or to the Congress, it will not be so well done, as if left to the assemblies. The true Cause of the Want of good officers in the Army is not because the appointment is left to the assemblies, but because such officers in sufficient Numbers are not in America. Without Materials the best Workman can do nothing. Time, Study and Experience alone must make a sufficient Number of able officers.

I wish We had a military Accademy, and should be obliged to you for a plan of such an Institution. The Expence would be a Trifle, no object at all with me.
Oct. 1. This day I had the Honour of making a Motion for the appointment of a Committee to consider of a Plan for the Establishment of a military Academy in the Army. The Comtee was appointed and your ser[van]t was one. Write me your sentiments upon the subject.

37.3

 THOMAS BURKE, NOTES OF DEBATES, SHORT FORM,
FEBRUARY 25, 1777

As Burke of North Carolina notes below, the central issue before Congress in the debate ostensibly over desertion was in fact the jurisdictions "of Congress & the States." The wrangling this time served as a warm-up bout for the one to follow concerning how the Articles of Confederation would define the relationship and balance of power between Congress and the states. According to Burke, most of the delegates in Congress supported him in his motion to reconsider the final amended paragraph of the original report, which, after debate and a delay of almost two weeks, was passed on February 25. For reasons not fully explained, "it was not deemed prudent to decide" to remove the contested passage.

Paul H. Smith, ed., *Letters of Delegates to Congress, 1774–1789*
(Washington, D.C.: Library of Congress, 1976–93), 6:356.

Feb'y. 25th. [1777]
This day there was a very interesting debate on some amendments proposed to a report of a Committee, appointed to consider of some means for preventing desertion; but the main question was concerning the jurisdiction of Congress & the States. The decision was postponed. The debate lay chiefly between Mr. Wilson, of Pennsylvania, and

the Delegate from North Carolina. The opinion of a great majority was with the latter; but it was not deemed prudent to decide. N.B. This is all that I can now transmit: but as you know the opinion of your Delegate on such questions, you can judge the opinion of Congress: & for this reason it is that I mention that a majority was in his favour.

## 37.4

 THOMAS BURKE, NOTES OF DEBATES, LONG FORM,
FEBRUARY 25, 1777

Burke at great length detailed his case—not of all of which is reproduced below—against Congress' final approval of the amended resolution on deserters. His main interlocutor was James Wilson, who argued that continental concerns, most importantly the Continental Army, were subject to continental oversight and ought to "be carried into execution by Continental authority." Moreover, Wilson added that "Congress had always directed their resolves to be put in Execution by Committees of Inspection and it was never denied that they had [such] Power." Burke admitted that "Continental objects were subjects of Continental Councils— but denied that the provisions made by Continental Councils were to be enforced by Continental authority." If continental councils were so empowered, he reminded his fellow delegates, "it would be giving Congress a Power to prostrate all the Laws and Constitutions of the states because they might create a Power within each that mush act entirely Independent of them, and might act directly Contrary to them."[57]

Burke also drew attention to due process concerns: "It appeared to him that Congress was herein assuming a Power to give authority from themselves to persons within the States to seize and Imprison the persons of the Citizens, and thereby to endanger the personal Liberty of every man in America." In keeping with the philosophy of popular consent articulated in the Declaration of Independence, Burke noted that "the subject of every state was entitled to the Protection of that particular state, and subject to the Laws of that alone, because to them alone did he give his Consent." Accordingly, "the states alone had Power to act Coercively against their Citizens, and therefore were the only Power Competent to carry into execution any Provisions whether Continental or Municipal."

Burke next reminded his eminent opponents in Congress "that his fellow Citizens were struggling against unlawful exertions of Power, and they would submit to them from no Authority," including an American central government. Even representative bodies should not have "the Power to appoint any Person to decide" someone's guilt without due process. If Congress did have such power, then it had "power unlimited over the Lives and Liberties of all men in America and the Provisions so anxiously made by the respective States to Secure them, at Once Vanish before this Tremendous Authority." Burke offered quite possibly the rarest and most stirring defense of individual due process rights by any congressional delegate in three years of recorded debate and correspondence—though, in this instance, in a losing effort.

Burke was opposed not only by Wilson, but also by two of Congress' most eminent and outspokenly radical delegates: R. H. Lee, who noted, seemingly with reference to Burke, that "it was a Misfortune to be too learned"; and John Adams, who came to agree that "the articles of War must be enacted into Laws in the several States," as he had argued for the past decade concerning parliamentary legislation. To each of them, Burke responded devastatingly. In response to Wilson, he defended the necessity of habeas corpus, an essential safeguard absent from the dangerous amendment approved by Congress: "Every Individual who might be Apprehended had a right to call for the Interposion of the state where he was Apprehended to Enquire whether he was a person liable to suspicion and whether the restraint of his Liberty was lawful or not." To Lee, he answered that the "difference is certainly very perceptable between offering reward to any Individual who shall apprehend Deserters and Subject . . . [and] Impowering persons in the States to decide this Question, and to Imprison and remove out of the State in Consequence of such decision." To Adams, he riposted that enacting the articles of war in the states would amount to the imposition of martial law; persons consenting to be governed by articles of war—soldiers and sailors—give up significant personal rights, and only those directly concerned, not their representatives, could take such action. An obscure Irish doctor and lawyer had bested Congress' bright stars, both radical and moderate, and, in so doing, had moved to close its brief window of largely unobstructed power.

Paul H. Smith, ed., *Letters of Delegates to Congress, 1774–1789* (Washington, D.C.: Library of Congress, 1976–93), 6:356–63.

Feby 25th 1777

The Question of Interest was again debated and postponed. A Report was taken up relative to Deserters. It stood Originally a recommendation of Congress to the several states to Enact Laws Empowering all Constables, Ferry keepers and Freeholders to take up persons suspected of being Deserters and Carry them before any Justice of the Peace. An Amendment was moved the purport of which was that the Power should go Immediately from Congress without the Intervention of the States. Many Gentlemen were inattentive and it passed. The Delegate from North Carolina desired to be informed if he might enter his Protest against it. He was informed by the Chair that he could not, he then desired to have his dissent entered on the Journal declaring he was not Apprehensive of any Injury from it in the State he represented because he knew it would never be there observed, the People too well knowing the Maxims of their Government, but that as it was as much as his Life was worth to Consent to the Congress exercising such a Power, he desired that he might be able to prove from the Journals that he did not. He said it appeared to him that Congress was herein assuming a Power to give authority from themselves to persons within the States to seize and Imprison the persons of the Citizens, and thereby to endanger the personal Liberty of every man in America. A motion was now made for reconsidering. On the reconsideration the Debate lay chiefly between Mr Wilson of Pensylvania, and the North Carolina Delegate. Mr. Wilson argued that every object of Continental Concern was the subject of Continental Councils. That all Provisions made by the Continental Councils must be carried into execution by Continental authority. That the Army was certainly a Continental object, and preventing Desertion in it was certainly as necessary an object as the raising of it. That nothing could be more necessary to prevent Desertion than to take Effectual Measures for apprehending deserters, that this Power must necessarily be in the Congress, and that they certainly had Power to authorise any persons in the States to put them in Execution. That the Power of taking up deserters was in every Soldier and officer of the army, and that the Congress might make any Justice of Peace in any state such an officer and thereby give him that Power, and if by making him an officer they Could give him that Power, they surely could without. That the officers and soldiers of the army were certainly not subject to Laws of the states. That this was no more than what was every day done in appointing Commissioners to purchase provisions and other things under the resolves of Congress. That the Congress had always directed their resolves to be put in Execution by Committees of Inspection and it was never denied that they had Power.

The Delegate of North Carolina answered that he admitted Continental objects were subjects of Continental Councils—but denied that the provisions made by Continental Councils were to be enforced by Continental authority. That it would be giving Congress a Power to prostrate all the Laws and Constitutions of the states because they might create a Power within each that mush act entirely Independent of them, and might act directly Contrary to them. That they might by virtue of this Power render Ineffectual all the Bariers Provided in the states for the Security of the Rights of the Citizens for if they gave a Power to act Coercively it must be against the Subject of some State, and the subject of every state was entitled to the Protection of that particular state, and subject to the Laws of that alone, because to them alone did he give his Consent. That he hoped the Gentleman would not Insist on this Principle which in its nature was so very Extensive and alarming. That the states alone had Power to act Coercively against their Citizens, and therefore were the only Power Competent to carry into execution any Provisions whether Continental or Municipal. That he was well satisfied no Power on Earth would ever obtain Authority to act Coercively against any of the Citizens of the state he represented except under their own Legislature; unless it was obtained by Violence. That his fellow Citizens were struggling against unlawful exertions of Power, and they would submit to them from no Authority. That he admitted the army to be a proper object to be governed and directed by Continental Councils, and that it is proper the Congress should provide for punishing Desertion, and that Desertion was a very [great] evil, but that who is a deserter or who is not is a Question that must be determined previous to any Punishment, and who ever can determine it has a Power over the Life and Liberty of the Citizens for as much as any man may be accused of Desertion but every one accused may not be Guilty. That if the Congress has the Power to appoint any Person to decide this Question the Congress has power unlimited over the Lives and Liberties of all men in America and the Provisions so anxiously made by the respective States to Secure them, at Once Vanish before this Tremendous Authority. However proper it might be for Congress to punish Desertion it was Necessary for the states to prevent arbitrary and unjust punishments and Imprisonments of their Citizens, and unless some mode were provided for trying the above Question every man was liable to be imprisoned at the Discretion of Officers and servants of the Congress. No power could be Competent to this but such as is created by the Legislature of each state, and if any Question related to the internal Polity of a state it certainly was this which Involved all the Rights of the Citizens personal Freedom. He would not speak for other states, but for his own he would declare that the Constitution had anxiously provided that no man should be Imprisoned or in any Degree Injured in his Person or Property but under the authority of the Laws of the state. It was a fundamental Maxim well understood there that no Magisterial Authority could be given but by the Legislature, and none could be exercised beyond what was expressly laid down in the Laws. The Congress certainly could not give a Power within any State to hear and Determine offences or to seize and Imprison the Persons of the Citizens. Yet most assuredly the Power Contended for was no less, unless every Deserter was branded in the Face so that it could be determined without [doubt] who was Deserter and who was not. He was sorry to hear the Gentleman Say that the Officers and Soldiers of the Army were not Subject to the Laws of the States, and hoped the Gentleman would retract it, for assuredly the army must always be in some State and might be in every State, and if they were not Subject to the Laws of the respective States, it would follow that a powerful Body of men within any State might violate with Impunity all the Rights of the Citizens and Subject them to the worst of Oppressions. This being Contrary to all the purposes for which men enter into Society, the admission of it must dissolve all Society and Government, and being peculiarly detested by the Americans who were struggling at the risque of Life and property against Oppression, it never could take place among them, until they lost al[l] Common Sense, and all Love of Freedom. That the Power of taking up deserters if it was in every officer and soldier it did not follow that every officer and soldier might call whom he pleased a deserter and Imprison and punish him as such, that there must be a Power to determine whether deserters or not, and the Congress could give no such Power without giving authority to some Individuals within the states to exercise Magisterial Discretion and subject the Citizens to that discretion. He could not conceive a State Independant if any Power could do this except their Internal Legislature who had their authority for that purpose from the People. He would declare firmly it could not be done in North Carolina by any other, if their Bill of Rights and Constitution were of any Effect, and not meer waste paper, for they provided that no freeman within the state should be in any way or Degree restrained of his Liberty or damaged in his Property except under the Laws of the state to which his Consent must be given, because every freeman had a Voice [in his?] Legislature. . . .

Mr. Wilson in reply admitted that he laid down the Principle too largely, and that when he said the officers and soldiers were not subject to the Laws of the States he meant only that in their Military duty they were subject only to the Congress. He did not directly answer the arguments from North Carolina but argued ab inconveniente that the Power was Necessary. He said if the States alone were competent to this Power it would follow that no deserter could be punished or apprehended but in the State where he inlisted, and Consequently by keeping out of that State he was sure of Impurity. That this was in Effect declaring that desertion could not be punished and consequently that the army might be immediately disbanded. That he did not Contend for giving the Power to Justices of the Peace &c. as such but as Individuals proper to execute the resolution. He moved to amend by taking out the words suspected of being, which would leave it deserters which he hoped would remove all objections.

Mr R. H. Lee from Virginia said it was a Misfortune to be too learned, that he could see no more in it than he saw every day in the Newspaper which was advertising and offering a Reward for Deserters and this was certainly exercising no Magisterial Power.

Mr J Adams from Massachusetts confessed the motion passed him without his attention, that he was inclined to think from what passed that the articles of War must be enacted into Laws in the several States, and he believed the officers thought so or they would proceed with greater vigor.

The Delegate from North Carolina rejoined to all three. To Mr Wilson. That Necessity was never to be admitted as an argument for assuming a Dangerous and improper Power tho it might be admitted as an Excuse for some particular unlawful exercise of authority and then the Necessity might appear striking and Inevitable to the Power which Judges and Excuses the act. That otherwise the Plea of Necessity would Subvert all restraints laid on persons instrusted with [power and] authority, and always had been used by Tyrants for [that] Purpose. Instance Ship money, dispensations, and the present oppressive Proceeding of Britain. But even that Plea had no foundation here. The States were Competent to enact Laws for the apprehending deserters, and there surely was no reason to doubt but that they would on a recommendation for that purpose. That the Inconvenience the Gentleman mentioned was Imaginary. It would not follow that desertion could not be prevented or punished altho it should be admitted that the states alone were Competent to give the Power of arresting suspected persons, and trying the Question deserter or not. Nor could it be concluded from this that deserters could be apprehended nowhere but in the states where they enlisted. That desertion was a Crime and like all other Crimes to be punished wherever it should be Committed, and by the Power who had Competent Jurisdiction. That the Crime Once Committed the offender might be apprehended in any state and removed to the Jurisdiction who had power to punish, but every Individual who might be Apprehended had a right to call for the Interposion of the state where he was Apprehended to Enquire whether he was a person liable to suspicion and whether the restraint of his Liberty was lawful or not, but the Power to Interpose in this manner could only be derived from the Internal Legislature [so?] the Power to arrest must be derived from the same source, or it would follow that the Citizens of each state might be restrained of their Liberty by an Authority not derived from themselves which could not subsist with freedom and Independance. Tis plain from these Considerations that desertion was no more secure of Impunity than Murder, for in both the offender must be arrested by Virtue of an authority derived from the state where found, and each must be tried by the Competent Jurisdiction and punished according to the Laws of the Community against which he offended. . . . . .

To Mr. Lee. The Difference is certainly very perceptable between offering reward to any Individual who shall apprehend Deserters and Subject them to the proper tribunals for deciding Concerning Guilt or Innocence (for the advertisements could have no other Effect) and Impowering persons in the States to decide this Question, and to Imprison and remove out of the State in Consequence of such decision. The One was no more than Inviting people to run the hazard of an action for being mistaken, and to be dilligent in looking out for deserters by hopes of the reward, but the other was giving Power to Exercise discretion in deciding Guilt or Innocence, and Consequently of freedom and Imprisomnent, and Eventually Life and Death. That in the latter case no remedy could be had for the Injury, if the Congress could give the Power because the Magistrate must decide Judicially, and must be subject to no punishment for being Mistaken because every Judge undertook to use his best endeavors to discover Truth, but did not promise to be Infallible but the states would undoubtedly punish the Magistrate for acting without Jurisdiction, which would prove they did not admit the Power of Congress.

To Mr. Adams. The Congress was Impowered by the several States to levy an Army, and to conduct the War and the Government of the Army was Incident to that Power. The army could not be governed without rules and such rules were the articles of War which the Congress undoubtedly had a right to make, and every Soldier was particularly bound to submit to them, because he Consents to be governed by them, and tried and punished by them not by representatives merely but by actual person Consent, for they are read to him at the time of Inlistment. But the Power of Congress could not extend to subject any other but such as enlisted and personally consented to the articles War, and it was the Duty of the states to Interpose whenever the Question arose whether Soldier or not, because otherwise their Citizens might be subjected to Martial Law against their Consent—and whenever any soldier apprehended the Courts martial exceeded their Jurisdiction he had a right to bring the matter before the Civil Tribunal of the state where he was because other wise the Military might become absolute and Independant of the Civil Authority. . . . .

## 38. DEBATING STATE SOVEREIGNTY AND A BICAMERAL NATIONAL LEGISLATURE—THOMAS BURKE'S AMENDMENTS TO THE ARTICLES OF CONFEDERATION, MAY 1777

After three weeks of debate, from July 22 to August 8, 1776, Congress on August 20 ordered eighty copies printed of the newly amended draft Articles of Confederation.[58] Yet because of a press of business and possibly a lack of interest among some of the delegates, the Articles were not to be regularly discussed again for another eight months. It was decided on April 8, 1777, that they be considered "on Monday next, and that two days in each week be employed" for that purpose until the Article "shall be ||wholly|| discussed in Congress."[59] It would not be until April 21 that Congress resumed debate on the Articles, and on May 13 it postponed "further consideration."[60] Immediately before April 29, Thomas Burke ensured that Dickinson's draft Articles were transformed into a plan of government more in keeping with the spirit that had led to the Declaration of Independence and that he had defended in opposing the congressional resolution on deserters, shortly after taking his congressional seat on February 4 (document 37.1). The Declaration's most dogged opponent in Congress, Dickinson, had, by Burke's lights, crafted a central plan of government little in keeping with the ascendant localist and populist spirit.

What Burke successfully demanded was that the Articles reflect the state-centered constitutionalism that had dominated Congress since its inception and that had led, in part, to the defeat of Galloway's "Plan of Union" in 1774 (document 10.1) and Franklin's Articles of Confederation of 1775 (document 44.1). As Edmund Burnett notes, "Most members of Congress, so it would seem, were scarcely aware of whither they were being led. It fell to the lot of Thomas Burke to sound the alarm and call the errant statesmen of Congress back to their fundamental faith."[61] Eleven states, in fact, voted in support of what has come to be called "Burke's amendment," in truth, one of two or more. By changing Article III of the draft of July 12, 1776 (and Article 3 of that of August 20), Burke changed the proposed plan of government from one in which the states, while enjoying limited and enumerated powers, were subordinate to a sovereign central government, to the one described in Article 2 of the final Articles (of November 1777), in which the confederated central government was limited to enumerated powers, while the states enjoyed sovereign and undefined powers. The lopsided vote in support of his amendment suggests that congressional delegates were not yet ready to move toward a stronger central government of the kind so long resisted by Congress— whether it was located in Britain or somewhere in North America.

Perhaps less expected was Burke's proposing, around May 5, amendments to the Articles, with a plan for a bicameral central government similar to that ultimately created in 1787. His proposal called for a General Council and a Council of States. Representation would be proportional (by either wealth or population, the basis to be determined by the states) in the first and equal in the second. And in keeping with his overall privileging of the states and his insistence on strictly limiting central-governmental powers to only those enumerated, Burke stipulated that "every act, Edict and ordinance So assented to Shall be binding on all and Every of the United States: Provided, the Same Shall be within the Powers hereafter Expressly given to the United States in Congress assembled."

The confederated central government's power was to be further limited, for in declaring and waging an aggressive war of choice, which required supermajorities in both chambers, "every State dissenting from Such War Shall be no further bound thereby than to refuse any aid or protection to the Enemy with whom the other States may be at War, which Dissent every State Shall be at liberty to make by her delegate in the Council of State, and every Such State Shall be Excluded from all Benefits resulting from Such War, and Exempted from all Expences attending the Same." These amendments, if adopted, would have greatly limited the reach of ever-more powerful American central governments.

Burke's intriguing proposal for a bicameral federal legislature was, however, rejected. In his notes, Burke suggests several possible reasons for that outcome: a bicameral body would have delayed the execution of laws—recall that the Continental and Confederation Congresses exercised both executive and legislative responsibilities in a unicameral body; somehow in this format, the legislature resembled a too-dominant executive, approaching a king; combining the two forms of representation would not work; and the amended plan resembled too much the one promulgated by the British Constitution.[62] In rejecting Burke's motion, Congress failed, yet again, to consider seriously the still-challenging question of how constitutionally to integrate the needs and demands of large and small states and, more broadly, how to distribute sovereignty between the states and a central government.

38.1

## Debating the Articles of Confederation and Thomas Burke's Failed Amendment, May 5, 1777

Worthington Chauncey Ford et al., eds., *Journals of the Continental Congress, 1774–1789* (Washington, D.C.: Government Printing Office, 1904–37), 5:547, 9:908, 7:328–29.

[FRIDAY, JULY 12, 1776]

ART. III. Each Colony shall retain and enjoy as much of its present Laws, Rights and Customs, as it may think fit, and reserves to itself the sole and exclusive Regulation and Government of its internal police, in all matters that shall not interfere with the Articles of this Confederation.

[SATURDAY, NOVEMBER 15, 1777]

ART. 2. Each State retains its sovereignty, freedom and independence, and every power, jurisdiction, and right, which is not by this confederation expressly delegated to the united states, in Congress assembled.

[MONDAY, MAY 5, 1777]

Agreeable to the order of the day, Congress resumed the consideration of the report from the Committee of the whole on the articles of confederation; and, after some time spent thereon,

*Resolved,* That the further consideration thereof be deferred till to morrow.


[BURKE'S AMENDMENT FOR A BICAMERAL LEGISLATURE]

For the better managing the Interests of the United States, Shall be Instituted a General Council and Council of State to form a Congress.

The General Council Shall consist of Delegates chosen by the Several States in Such manner as is or Shall be provided by their respective Laws and Constitutions in the following proportions.

The Council of State Shall consist of one Delegate from every State to be chosen in manner provided by their respective Laws and Constitutions.

Every act Edict and ordinance Shall be first moved in the General Council and read three times and three times assented to by a majority of all the voices of which the Council ought to be composed. Every act, Edict and ordinance so assented to Shall also be assented [to] by a majority of all the voices of which the Council of State ought to consist before the Same Shall be binding on the States.

And every act, Edict and ordinance So assented to Shall be binding on all and Every of the United States: Provided, the Same Shall be within the Powers hereafter Expressly given to the United States in Congress assembled. Except in the following cases, that is to say, Where any War is to be waged or acts of hostility commenced, or authorized against any Prince, State or People not having declared War against all or any of the United States, or invaded any of the Same by Acts of Hostility against the Coasts, Ports Fortresses or Dominions of any of the United States: every act, Edict or ordinance declaring Such War Shall be assented to by three fourths at the least of all the voices of which the general Council ought to consist, and of nine voices at the least in the Council of State before the Same Shall be held binding on the United States or any of them, to any intent or purpose, and every State dissenting from Such War Shall be no further bound thereby than to refuse any aid or protection to the Enemy with whom the other States may be at War, which Dissent every State Shall be at liberty to make by her delegate in the Council of State, and every Such State Shall be Excluded from all Benefits resulting from Such War, and Exempted from all Expences attending the Same.

(Endorsement)

Burke's amendments to Confederation proposed on the Qu: Shall the Congress consist of two houses, passed in the Negative. So whole dropt.

1 Delays in Execution
Congress Executive Body resembling King &c:
2. No Combination Except one or the other
Idea of Distinctions resembling British Constitution.

38.2

 THOMAS BURKE TO RICHARD CASWELL, ON BURKE'S
SUCCESSFUL AMENDMENT, APRIL 29, 1777

Writing to Governor Richard Caswell of North Carolina, a former land surveyor, delegate to the First Continental Congress, military hero, and later coward, about the Articles of Confederation, Thomas Burke begins by taking note of one of the issues dividing the delegates in Congress. Once again, New England delegates were pitted against those of New York, in this case regarding the New Hampshire Grants, which were renamed New Connecticut before becoming Vermont. Burke focused primarily on two elements: the article concerned with the relationship of the states to the planned confederation government, and a consideration of how to allot state voting in Congress.

On the first matter, Burke writes that it "occasioned two days debate," most likely immediately before his writing but surely after April 21, when Congress resumed consideration of the Articles of Confederation. As with the proposed resolution concerning deserters, Burke adamantly opposed the committee's report on state versus national sovereignty, for it would have allowed "the future Congress or General Council to explain away every right belonging to the States, and to make their own power as unlimited as they please." Burke "proposed, therefore, an amendment, which held up the principle, that all sovereign Power was in the States separately, and that particular acts of it, which should be expressly enumerated, would be exercised in conjunction, and not otherwise; but that in all things else each State would Exercise all the rights and powers of sovereignty, uncontrolled." Burke's amendment, his first of two, met with great success: "eleven ayes, one no, and one divided. The no was Virginia; the divided, New Hampshire." His second amendment failed.

Given the history of Congress' disputes with Parliament and its own internal debates over the nature of shared sovereignty, it is remarkable that Burke could write that this amendment "was at first so little understood that it was some time before it was seconded." It is striking, too, that it was conservative South Carolina that seconded it—remember, though, its fear that if New England came to dominate national politics, it would institute a strong, populist-oriented central government.[63] Notable also was that "the opposition was made by Mr Wilson of Pennsylvania, and

Mr R. H. Lee of Virginia"—two men often on opposite sides of issues before Congress. This suggests, as Jack Rakove has argued, that "few of Burke's colleagues shared his intense interest in the constitutional principles that the Articles of Confederation were to embody."[64]

Burke and Wilson, an Irishman and a Scot, seemed more willing than most of their colleagues born in the colonies to engage the issue on a sophisticated theoretical level. Rakove notes that the two were exceptional in "their own unusually refined grasp of the central importance of the location of sovereignty."[65] The native-borns' reticence might be explained by the exigencies of conducting a war and the difficulty of grappling with a philosophical or theoretical issue rather than one more suitable to political haggling, the stuff of political life. In addition, the opposition of both Wilson and Lee, and the support of Burke's approved amendment by the conservative New York delegation, make any facile explanation impossible.[66] In the end, Burke wrote that he "was much pleased to find the opinion of accumulating powers to Congress so little supported," and he expected to find his "ideas relative thereto nearly similar to those of most of the States." And, of course, in this matter, he was right.

Looking forward to the debates soon to take place regarding "the structure of the Common Councils," that is, how the states would vote in Congress, equally or proportionally, Burke anticipated "difficulties of the most arduous nature" because of the "inequality of the States." He expected that disparities of physical size, population, and wealth, when joined with the states' insistence on "maintaining their separate independence, will occasion dilemmas almost inextricable." Since the dominant postindependence philosophy was "the doctrine of the sovereignty of the people . . . understood to be *the people organized as states*," it was hard to imagine, much less achieve, in 1777 the transference of sovereignty to a central confederated government, to say nothing of a unitary or national government that would act directly on individual citizens of the states. This was the crux of the debate over the apprehending of deserters. What, in part, made this finally possible in 1787 was the development of James Wilson's idea of a national people rather than the separate people of the individual states. By envisioning a national people as sovereign, a manifestly more powerful central government could be designed without challenging the newly regnant theory of popular sovereignty.[67]

Paul H. Smith, ed., *Letters of Delegates to Congress, 1774–1789*
(Washington, D.C.: Library of Congress, 1976–93), 6:671–74.

Sir                                                                    Philadelphia April 29th 1777

An express going hence to Charlestown gives me an opportunity of writing you a few lines, but without being able to communicate any thing interesting.

We have at present in Congress a representation of all the Colonies, altho' the number of Delegates is not very considerable. New York entertains the most virulent jealousy against her Eastern Neighbours, and it is now heightened by an affair which is something embarrassing. The inhabitants of what is usually called the New Hampshire Grants, have attempted to set up a distinct State, and sent Delegates to Congress to claim a seat. New York remonstrated; the new State (called New Connecticut) seemed to be patronised by the Eastern Delegates; but the Congress laid the papers on the table, and I hope will be wise enough to decline any interposition. I am for my own part clearly against assuming a Judiciary power. Such certainly never was the purpose of our Delegation. As I consider all jealousies as injurious to our common cause and as laying the foundation of future evils, I use my best endeavours to discourage them; and I endeavour as much as possible to keep our attention to the main business, that of subduing our common enemy.

The Confederation comes under consideration two days in every week. On this arduous subject you will easily imagine I want the assistance of my colleagues, and indeed wish it reserved for men more able and experienced than I am. I shall give it however the most attentive consideration, and certainly shall agree to nothing, but on the clearest conviction and most uncontroverted principles. I shall very carefully abstract all the debates of any moment upon it, and every other subject, but particularly upon that, and when I transmit it to you, I will transmit the debates also. At present, nothing but executive business is done, except the Confederation, and on mere executive business there are seldom any debates (and still more seldom any worth remembering). We have agreed to three articles; one containing the name; the second a declaration of the Sovereignty of the States, and an express provision that they be considered as retaining every power not expressly delegated; and the third an agreement mutually to assist each other against every enemy. The first and latter passed without opposition or dissent, the second occasioned two days debate. It stood originally the third article; and expressed only a reservation of the power of regulating internal police, and consequently resigned every other power. It appeared to me that this was not what the States expected, and, I thought, it left it in the power of the future Congress or General Council to explain away every right belonging to the States, and to make their own power as unlimited as they please. I proposed, therefore, an amendment, which held up the principle, that all sovereign Power was in the States separately, and that particular acts of it, which should be expressly enumerated, would be exercised in conjunction, and not otherwise; but that in all things else each State would Exercise all the rights and powers of sovereignty, uncontrolled. This was at first so little understood that it was some time before it was seconded, and South Carolina first took it up. The opposition was made by Mr Wilson of Pennsylvania, and Mr R. H. Lee of Virginia: in the End however the question was carried for my proposition, Eleven ayes, one no, and one divided. The no was Virginia; the divided, New Hampshire. I was much pleased to find the opinion of accumulating powers to Congress so little supported, and I promise myself, in the whole business I shall find my ideas relative thereto nearly similar to those of most of the States. In a word, Sir, I am of opinion the Congress should have power enough to call out and apply the common strength for the common defence: but not for the partial purposes of ambition. We shall next proceed to the structure of the Common Councils; and here, I think, we shall meet with difficulties of the most arduous nature. The inequality of the States, and yet the necessity for maintaining their separate independence, will occasion dilemmas almost inextricable. You shall, Sir, know the whole progress of the matter, if I can conceive and convey it with sufficient clearness.

Maryland has set an exceeding good example to the other States in laying a tax. I hope it will be followed in ours. I mean not in the mode, but the thing. It is the only adequate remedy for the abundance of circulating money, with its consequent depreciation.

I have obtained, from Congress, leave to purchase two hundred gunlocks out of the public stores. I have sent them to Hillsborough, and hope they will very soon be applied to the arms which are there preparing, and that the arms themselves will be put into the hands of soldiers, and sent to their proper places. . . .

I wish I could be informed of the success of my request to be permitted to return in the summer, if the Assembly think proper to command my further attendance in this service: or whether they may not make choice of some more able man to fill the Department. I will detain you, Sir, no longer, only to declare that I am, with the greatest respect & esteem, your Excellency's most obedient Servant,                    Thos Burke

## 39. TESTING THE EXTENT OF POPULAR SOVEREIGNTY—CONGRESS LIMITS THE REACH OF THE DECLARATION'S RIGHTS CLAIMS, JUNE 1777

The long-simmering (1763–91) debate and conflict within and outside Congress regarding the status of the "New-Hampshire Grants" would, after passage of the Declaration of Independence, powerfully test the Declaration's theory of popular sovereignty, the relationship between the states and Congress, and, somewhat more gradually, Congress' power under the Articles of Confederation to adjudicate land disputes between states. The controversy began in 1763 when New Hampshire granted charters to towns west of the Connecticut River in what was then New York. Not surprisingly, New York resented New Hampshire's awarding its territory to settlers without its approval.

In the late 1760s, a group of marauders known as the Green Mountain Boys began a campaign of intimidation, beating, and property destruction intended to drive away surveyors and prevent New York–sanctioned settlers from taking possession of deeded property in the contested area. The group was led by a sometimes larger-than-life figure, Ethan Allen, a heroic man who commanded the forces that took Fort Ticonderoga, but may later have acted traitorously in trying to negotiate with the British a separate peace treaty that would have declared Vermont independent. On April 11,

1775, the inhabitants of the region, in imitation of a decade of boilerplate congressional verbiage—but with here a target rather different from Parliament or the king's ministers—declared themselves "in great danger of having their property unjustly, cruelly, and unconstitutionally taken from them by the arbitrary and designing administration of New York."[68]

On January 15, 1777, a convention of town delegates from the New Hampshire Grants adopted their own declaration of independence and defended their actions by claiming that they were in accord with Congress' recommendation of May 15, 1776, to colonies adopting new governments (see document 31.1). Thus, in keeping with what they reasonably took to be Congress' own words, they asserted that "a just right exists in the people to adopt measures for their own security, not only to enable them to secure their rights against the usurpations of Great Britain, but also against that of New York." The convention further proclaimed, this time relying on the words of Lee's resolution for independence (June 7, 1775) and the Declaration itself (documents 32.1 and 33.1), that the New Hampshire Grants "of right ought to be, and is hereby declared forever hereafter to be considered a separate, free, and independent jurisdiction or State."[69] The language in the convention documents was wonderfully close to that which had been used for much of a decade by congressional delegates to describe the horrific character of Parliament, proclaim the colonists' rights, and declare independence.

Soon to follow, on July 8, 1777, was a constitution and declaration of rights. The language of those documents drew on the guidance, sometimes verbatim, of Dr. Thomas Young, who had been mentored by Samuel Adams and in turn mentored Ethan Allen. The son of immigrant tenant farmers in upstate New York, Young was yet another doctor with a political bent; and like Warren, Rush, Hall, and Burke, he was a radical. Indeed, he was a radical of radicals—with plans for changes that went well beyond those envisioned by congressional radicals. As William Hogeland noted, Young and other like-minded radicals sought "to disconnect rights from property" as part of "a revolution against class privilege in America," thus going considerably further than congressional radicals and the Declaration, which had provocatively begun the process of disconnecting rights from duties—allowing abstract rights to stand alone without historical moorings or ties to correlative duties—although not necessarily from property. [70]

Young had played an active role in organizing the Boston Tea Party and, in June 1776, had worked to replace the elected government of Pennsylvania, before helping write the controversial Pennsylvania state constitution of that year, with its unicameral legislature. Even that document, beloved by French philosophes, was not sufficiently radical for his tastes. So while in Philadelphia, he worked with Allen in shaping the political documents of the nascent, still-more radical state, naming it Vermont. They collaborated too on a radical deist tract that years later would be published as *Reason:*

*The Only Oracle of Man.* Young's deism, economic and political radicalism, and defense of absolute popular sovereignty—for all people, regardless of their property holding, religion, or other qualifications—made it all the easier for Congress to reject his plea for Vermont independence.

The New York convention's letters of January 20 and March 1, 1777, in which the New Yorkers sought Congress' help in recovering their territory, were read in Congress on April 7. The next day, the Grants' declaration of independence and petition were read before Congress.[71] On June 23, 1777, a New York delegate laid before Congress, "a printed paper, signed 'A word to the wise is sufficient,' containing an extract from the minutes of Congress, and a letter signed Thomas Young, to the inhabitants of Vermont, dated 'Philadelphia, April 11, 1777,' which was read."[72] In it, Young urges the residents of the New Hampshire Grants "to organize fairly, and make the experiment, and I will ensure you success at the risque of my reputation, as a man of honor or common sense." He added that Congress could "by no means, refuse you: you have as good a right to choose how you will be governed, and by whom, as they had."[73]

Young's letter, along with other papers, was referred to a committee of the whole. On Monday, June 30, "the report of the committee of the whole ||Congress|| was read, and agreed to."[74] Congress had spent "the greatest part of four days" in discussing what, given the time devoted to it, must have been a controversial issue of some importance. In the end, however, Congress failed to take any meaningful action and wouldn't do so for years.[75] Congress was too consumed with one war and the reported British plans to march down through the disputed territory in an upcoming campaign. Its resources in that part of New York or Vermont were stretched far too thin to take on an intracolonial war or to lose the support of so many well-equipped men along the border with Canada.

There are three copies of the committee's report of June 30. The final one is in the writing of James Wilson; an earlier version is in the handwriting of William Duer of New York, an English immigrant, businessman, and state judge, and another was by the ubiquitous Thomas Burke. In the final report, Congress rejected, in remarkably distinct language, the petition of January 15, 1777, of the residents of the New Hampshire Grants to be admitted as a state, for "Congress is composed of delegates chosen by, and representing the communities . . . as they respectively stood at the time of its first institution," and therefore Congress could not do "any thing injurious to the rights and jurisdictions of the several communities which it represents." Moreover, Congress pointedly advised the petitioners that they could "derive no countenance or justification from the act of Congress declaring the United Colonies to be independent of the crown of Great Britain." Similarly, Congress urged them to ignore Young's recommendation that they take up government, as he claims they had been directed to do by the "resolution of Congress of the 15th May, 1776." Congress, in the report published August 7 in the *Pennsylvania Evening Post,* pointed out that in July 1776, as representative of the colonies that had sent delegates, it had protected those communities and their rights against British-designed usurpations. That protection did not apply to groups of individuals who believed that they were being oppressed by one of Congress' members. Congress couldn't have been much clearer in stating that it had defended select corporate rights in 1776, not the abstract rights of individuals.

It might be observed, too, that Congress on June 4, 1776, in responding to an earlier (January 17, 1776) petition from the residents of the New Hampshire Grants, had been far more conciliatory toward the petitioners. Congress had then urged the petitioners "to submit to the government of New-York, and contribute their assistance, with their countrymen, in the contest between Great-Britain and the United Colonies." Congress' remarks, however, were not to be "construed to affirm or admit the jurisdiction of New-York in and over that country."[76] Surprisingly, then, declaring independence and the right of a people, when dissatisfied, "to alter or to abolish" a previous form of government and "to institute new Government, laying its Foundation on such Principles, and organizing its Powers in such Form, as to them shall seem most likely to effect their Safety and Happiness" had done little to make Congress more open to such claims of universal rights, in this case regarding New York State; indeed, it had become demonstrably less so.

Apparently, it was not the protection of "Americans" or all "individuals," as one might have surmised from the famous language of the Declaration of Independence, that Congress had viewed in 1776 as its principal end. Indeed, in the second resolution of an earlier draft of the committee's report, Congress makes unusually evident that the Declaration of Independence had not extended to the inhabitants of the New Hampshire Grants "a Right to form a Government for themselves," whatever their wishes or beliefs about the oppressive character of the government of New York might be. That Congress was supposedly defending in the Declaration, as argued by Young, the right of any group to govern itself, Congress continued, was "unwarrantable in itself, and highly dangerous in its Consequence since if it should prevail, and be carried into practice, it must inevitably destroy all Order, Stability and good Government, in particular States and entail Disunion, Weakness, and Insecurity on the United States." (Well, yes, but that was what loyalists and a number of moderates had been arguing for two years.) Thus, Congress concluded "that the said Printed Paper, signed Thomas Young, is a false scandalous and malicious Libel, calculated to foment a Spirit of Jealousy, and Distrust betwixt the Congress and the State of New York, and to deceive, and mislead the people to whom it is addressed." This was not the last time that such rights would be claimed by those seeking to establish a new government that, in accord with Congress' resolution of May 15, 1776, and the Declaration, they believed they naturally had the right to enjoy, as defended in those famous, radical-sounding congressional documents.

## 39.1

### CONGRESSIONAL RESPONSE TO THE PETITION OF THE INHABITANTS OF THE NEW HAMPSHIRE GRANTS FOR INDEPENDENCE, JUNE 30, 1777

Worthington Chauncey Ford et al., eds., *Journals of the Continental Congress, 1774–1789* (Washington, D.C.: Government Printing Office, 1904–37), 8:508–13. The drafts of the reports were written by James Wilson (*"first form of this report"*), William Duer (*"extract from the printed paper"*), and Thomas Burke.

Congress resolved itself into a committee of the whole, to take into consideration the letters and papers from the State of New York, the petition from Jonas Fay, &c. and the printed paper referred to them; and, after some time spent thereon, the president resumed the chair, and Mr. [Benjamin] Harrison reported, that the committee have had under consideration the letters and papers to them referred, and have come to sundry resolutions thereupon, which he was ready to report, when the Congress would receive it.

*Ordered,* That it be now received.

The report from the committee on the whole ‖Congress‖ was read, and agreed to, as follows:

*Resolved,* That Congress is composed of delegates chosen by, and representing the communities respectively inhabiting the territories of New Hampshire, Massachusetts bay, Rhode Island and Providence Plantations, Connecticut, New York, New Jersey, Pensylvania, Delaware, Maryland, Virginia, North Carolina, South Carolina, and Georgia, as they respectively stood at the time of its first institution; that it was instituted for the purposes of securing and defending the communities aforesaid against the usurpations, oppressions, and hostile invasions of Great Britain; and that, therefore, it cannot be intended that Congress, by any of its proceedings, would do or recommend or countenance any thing injurious to the rights and jurisdictions of the several communities which it represents.

*Resolved,* That the independent government attempted to be established by the people stiling themselves inhabitants of the New Hampshire Grants, can derive no countenance or justification from the act of Congress declaring the United Colonies to be independent of the crown of Great Britain, nor from any other act or resolution of Congress.

*Resolved,* That the petition of Jonas Fay, Thomas Chittenden, Heman Allen and Reuben Jones, in the name and behalf of the people stiling themselves as aforesaid, praying that "their declaration, that they would consider themselves as a free and independent State may be received; that the district in the said petition described may be ranked among the free and independent States, and that delegates therefrom may be admitted to seats in Congress," be dismissed.

*Resolved,* That Congress, by raising and officering the regiment commanded by Colonel Warner, never meant to give any encouragement to the claim of the people aforesaid, to be considered as an independent State: but that the reason which induced Congress to form that corps was, that many officers of different States, who had served in Canada, and alleged that they could soon raise a regiment, but were then unprovided for, might be reinstated in the service of the United States.

Whereas, a printed paper, addressed to the inhabitants of the district aforesaid, dated Philadelphia, April 11, 1777, and subscribed Thomas Young, was laid before Congress by one of the delegates of New York, to which address is prefixed the resolution of Congress of the 15th May, 1776, and in which are contained the following paragraphs: "I have taken the minds of several of the leading members of the honorable the Continental Congress, and can assure you, that you have nothing to do, but to send attested copies of the recommendation to take up government, to every township in your district, and invite all the freeholders and inhabitants to meet and choose members for a general convention, to meet at an early day to choose delegates for the general Congress and committee of safety, and to form a constitution for yourselves. Your friends here tell me that some are in doubt, whether delegates from your district would be admitted into Congress. I tell you to organize fairly, and make the experiment, and I will ensure you success at the risque of my reputation, as a man of honor or common sense. Indeed, they can by no means, refuse you: you have as good a right to choose how you will be governed, and by whom, as they had."

*Resolved,* That the contents of the said paragraphs are derogatory to the honour of Congress, are a gross misrepresentation of the resolution of Congress therein referred to, and tend to deceive and mislead the people to whom they are addressed.

*First form of this report.*

Whereas certain Persons within the State of New York, stiling themselves Inhabitants of the New Hampshire Grants, have published, and circulated a paper dated the 15th. day of Jany last, in which it is asserted that by the Resolution of Congress of the 4th. day of July last, declaring the United Colonies in America to be free and independent of the Crown of Great Britain the Jurisdiction granted by the Crown to the Government of New York over the Inhabitants of the said Grants is totally dissolved, that they are without Law or Government, and in a State of Nature, and consequently have a Right to form a Government for themselves,

And, Whereas, in persuance of such Declaration a Petition was on the 8th. day of April last presented to Congress signed in behalf of the Inhabitants aforesaid by Jonas Fay and others, and praying that their Declaration of Independence may be received, and the District therein described be rank'd by Congress among the free and Independant States, and Delegates therefrom admitted to Seats in Congress.

And, Whereas, a Representation from the State of New York was on the         day of         presented setting forth among other things that the Convention of that State had contemplated the Misconduct of a Part of its Inhabitants in the District aforesaid with Silent Concern, being restrain'd from giving it suitable Opposition, lest at so critical a Juncture it might weaken their Exertions in the common Cause; that Advantage had been taken of their patient Forbearance, and the Spirit of Disaffection artfully fomented by misconstruing certain Resolutions of Congress into an Approbation of their Proceedings, and by propagating Reports that particular Members had advis'd, and were resolved to justify, and support their Scheme of Separation.

And as under this Delusion some of the said Inhabitants had proceeded so far as to claim the Protection of Congress in their propos'd Independence and a Seat for their Delegates, so on the other hand the State of New York requested Congress, by a public Declaration, to undeceive the said Inhabitants, with respect to any of their Resolutions which had been construed to imply an Approbation of their establishing a Government distinct from the rest of their Fellow Citizens, and independent of the Authority of the State of which they are Members.

[*Here followed the extract from the printed paper.*]

*Resolved*, Therefore, I     That the Seperation from the State of New York and the Independant Government attempted to be establish'd by the said Inhabitants can derive no Countenance, or Justification from the Resolution of Congress, declaring the United Colonies to be free and Independent of the Crown of Great Britain, and that such Separation, and Independence have not been countenanced, or encouraged, or intended to have been countenaced or Encouraged, by any other Act, or Resolution of Congress.

II     *Resolved,* That the Principle upon which such intended Separation is asserted to be grounded (to wit) "That by the Declaration of Independence of the United Colonies the Jurisdiction granted by the Crown of Great Britain to the Government of New York is dissolved, and the said Inhabitants possessed of a Right to form a Government for themselves," is unwarrantable in itself, and highly dangerous in its Consequences; since if it should prevail, and be carried into practice, it must inevitably destroy all Order, Stability and good Government, in particular States and entail Disunion, Weakness, and Insecurity on the United States.

III     *Resolved,* That it be recommended to the aforesaid Inhabitants who have attempted such Separation to desist therefrom, and to Submit themselves quietly and peaceably to the Jurisdiction of New York, to which it appears from their own Representation they were subject before, and at the Time of the Declaration of Independance of the United Colonies.

IV     *Resolved,* That the said Printed Paper, signed Thomas Young, is a false scandalous and malicious Libel, calculated to foment a Spirit of Jealousy, and Distrust betwixt the Congress and the State of New York, and to deceive, and mislead the people to whom it is addressed.

Whereas this Congress ... [ ... not being by their Constituents Invested with the Power or Authority to consider or decide any Disputes relative to the particular Bounds or Jurisdiction of these States, nothing in the Resolutions of Congress contained can be construed to have any Effect upon such Disputes,] therefore

Resolved, That the paper signed        of the following Tenor is a gross Misrepresentation of the Resolution of Congress of the        day of        recommending to each State to form Constitutions of Civil Government for their Internal Police which Misrepresentation tends to mislead many of the Inhabitants of these United States into unwarrantable Separation from and Opposition to the Jurisdiction of the several Communities of which they were Members at the Time when the Congress was first Instituted.

Resolved, That the Contents of the said paper are highly Injurious to the Honour and Dignity of Congress.

39.2

 DECLARATION AND PETITION OF THE INHABITANTS
OF THE NEW HAMPSHIRE GRANTS, JANUARY 15, 1777

The inhabitants of thirty-five towns on the west and east sides of the Green Mountains came together, after fourteen years of legal battles with New York, mob intimidation by the Green Mountain Boys, the burning and destroying of property, and, ultimately, on March 13, 1775, two deaths in the "Westminster Massacre," to declare their independence from New York and to petition Congress to be admitted as a new state. As described above, Congress categorically denied their request and seemed to take offense at the suggestion that any congressional documents could have led the residents of the New Hampshire Grants to such a mistaken conclusion. Nonetheless, after declaring independence on January 15, 1777, and framing, on July 8, a radical constitution fashioned after Pennsylvania's unicameral one, but still more progressive, with an outright prohibition of slavery and a declaration of universal male suffrage, the Republic of Vermont enjoyed an independent status until March 4, 1791, when, after resolving its land disputes with New York (and by then, New Hampshire too), it was admitted as the fourteenth state.

Those most intimately involved in this movement included Ethan Allen and one of his brothers, Captain Heman Allen, both from Litchfield, Connecticut. Besides being a founder of Vermont, Ethan Allen was a war hero and prisoner of war who was transported to Great Britain in late 1775, where he came close to being hanged for treason. In ways that might enjoy contemporary relevance, Allen was legally subject to hanging because he could as easily have been considered a rebel or an "irregular combatant" as an enemy prisoner of war; rebels were guilty of treason, a capital crime, whereas prisoners of war had to be treated in internationally accepted ways. It should be remembered that at the time, Continental soldiers, to say nothing of ancillary forces of backwoods riflemen, were not sanctioned by any country; the American colonies had yet to organize politically, and would not be recognized as an independent entity by another country until December 1777.[77] Allen, from an American perspective, was also likely guilty of treason against the new country when he negotiated in the early 1780s with the British governor of Canada, General Haldimand, for recognition of Vermont as an independent province under the British Crown.

Another important figure and signatory of the New Hampshire Grants' declaration, and also a former Connecticut resident, was Thomas Chittenden. In 1778, he was elected the first governor of the Republic of Vermont and served, except for one year, until his death in 1797. Dr. Jonas Fay, an active partisan born in Massachusetts, was selected in 1772 to petition the New York governor, William Tryon, on behalf of the New Hampshire Grants' settlers. Along with Heman Allen, he was appointed on January 17, 1776, to present Congress with the Grants' petition and remonstrance made against the efforts of New York to regain its land. He later signed Vermont's declaration of independence, and, along with Chittenden and Ethan Allen, was involved in negotiating with the British to make Vermont a British province.

The Grants' declaration of independence follows closely the logic of the Declaration of July 4, 1776, and any number of other congressional documents. It argues that "whenever protection is withheld, no allegiance is due, or can of right be demanded"; "that whenever the lives and properties of a part of a community, have been manifestly aimed at by either the legislature or executive authority of such community, necessity requires a separation"; and that the residents of the Grants had so suffered under the "usurpations of Great Britain" and of New York. The authors not only rested their case on the claims of the Declaration, but also substantially drew too from Congress' recommendation of May 15, 1776, on forming new governments. They concluded that they had acted in accord with that document by forming "such government as shall, in the opinion of the representatives of the people, best conduce to the happiness and safety of their constituents in particular, and of America in general."

Clearly, the residents of the Grants, or at least Thomas Young, had paid close attention to Congress' seminal documents from the summer of 1776.[78] Their claims and Congress' responses thus deserve close attention as indications of the meaning and intention of Congress' celebrated state papers of May 15 and July 4. And Congress—composed of almost the same delegates who had agreed to both documents—unequivocally rejected the broad and universalistic meanings assigned to them by the residents of the New Hampshire Grants.

William Slade, ed., *Vermont State Papers* (Middlebury, Vt.: J. W. Copeland, 1823), 67–73.

On the 15th of January, 1777, the Convention again met, at Westminster; and after much deliberation, came to the important resolution to declare the New-Hampshire grants a free and independent State. The following is a journal of the proceedings.

NEW-HAMPSHIRE GRANTS

Westminister Court-House, *January 15th,* 1777.

Convention opened according to adjournment. . . .

6th. Voted, N. C. D, That the district of land commonly called and known by the name of New-Hampshire grants, be a new and separate state; and for the future conduct themselves as such.

7th. Voted, that Nathan Clark, Esq., Mr. Ebenezer Hosington, Capt. John Burnham, Mr. Jacob Burton, and Col. Thomas Chittenden, be a committee to prepare a draught for a declaration, for a new and separate state; and report to this convention as soon as may be. . . .

Friday morning, convention opened according to adjournment. The committee appointed to bring in a draught of a declaration, setting forth the right of the inhabitants of that district of land, commonly called and known by the name of the New-Hampshire grants, have, to form themselves into a state or independent government, do make the following report to the honorable convention at Westminster, January 15th, A. D. 1777, viz.

"To the honorable convention of representatives from the several towns on the west and east side of the range of Green Mountains, within the New-Hampshire grants, in convention assembled.

Your committee to whom was referred the form of a declaration, setting forth the right the inhabitants of said New-Hampshire grants have, to form themselves into a separate and independent state, or government, beg leave to report, viz.

Right 1. That whenever protection is withheld, no allegiance is due, or can of right be demanded.

2d. That whenever the lives and properties of a part of a community, have been manifestly aimed at by either the legislature or executive authority of such community, necessity requires a separation. Your committee are of opinion that the foregoing has, for many years past, been the conduct of the monopolizing land claimers of the colony of New-York; and that they have been not only countenanced, but encouraged, by both the legislative and executive authorities of the said state or colony. Many overt acts in evidence of this truth, are so fresh in the minds of the members, that would be needless to name them.

And whereas the Congress of the several states, did, in said Congress, on the fifteenth day of May, A. D. 1776, in a similar case, pass the following resolution, viz. "*Resolved,* That it be recommended to the respective assemblies and conventions of the United Colonies, where no government, sufficient to the exigencies of their affairs, has been, heretofore, established, to adopt such government as shall, in the opinion of the representatives of the people, best conduce to the happiness and safety of their constituents in particular, and of America in general."—Your committee, having duly deliberated on the continued conduct of the authority of New-York, before recited, and on the equitableness on which the aforesaid resolution in Congress was founded, and considering that a just right exists in this people to adopt measures for their own security, not only to enable them to secure their rights against the usurpations of Great-Britain, but also against that of New-York, and the several other governments claiming jurisdiction in this territory, do offer the following declaration, viz.

"This convention, whose members are duly chosen by the free voice of their constituents in the several towns, on the New-Hampshire grants, in public meeting assembled, in our own names, and in behalf of our constituents, do hereby proclaim and publicly declare, that the district of territory, comprehending and usually known by the name and description of the New-Hampshire grants, of right ought to be, and is hereby declared forever hereafter to be considered, as a free and independent jurisdiction, or state; by the name, and forever hereafter to be called, known, and distinguished by the name of New-Connecticut, alias Vermont: And that the inhabitants that at present are, or that may hereafter become resident, either by procreation or emigration, within said territory, shall be entitled to the same privileges, immunities, and enfranchisements, as are allowed; and on such condition, and in the same manner, as the present inhabitants, in future, shall or may enjoy; which are, and forever shall be considered to be such privileges and immunities to the free citizens and denizens, as are, or, at any time hereafter, may be allowed, to any such inhabitants of any of the free and independent states of America: And that such privileges and immunities shall be regulated in a bill of rights, and by a form of government, to be established at the next adjourned session of this convention."

10th. Voted, N. C. D. to accept the above declaration.

"To the honorable the chairman and gentlemen of the convention, your committee appointed to take into consideration what is further necessary to be transacted as the present convention, beg leave to report, viz.

That proper information be given to the honorable Continental Congress of the United States of America, of the reasons, why the New-Hampshire grants have been declared a free state, and pray the said Congress to grant said state a representation in Congress; and that agents be appointed to transfer the same to Congress, or the committee be filled up that are already appointed, and that a committee be appointed draw the draught: That a committee of war be appointed on the east side of the mountains, to be in conjunction with the committee of war on the west side of the mountains, to act on all proper occasions: That some suitable measures be taken to govern our internal police for the time being, until more suitable measures can be taken: that some suitable way be taken to raise a sum of money, to defray the expenses of the agents that are to go to Congress; and for printing the proceedings of the convention, which, we are of opinion, ought to be printed. All of which is humbly submitted to the convention, by your committee.

*By order of Committee,*

THOMAS CHANDLER, *Chairman.*"

11th. Voted, N. C. D. to accept the above report.

Having made some other regulations, on January 22d, the convention adjourned to Windsor, to meet on the first Wednesday in June.

*The Declaration and Petition of the Inhabitants of the New-Hampshire Grants, to Congress, announcing the District to be a Free and Independent State.*

TO THE HONORABLE THE CONTINENTAL CONGRESS.

The declaration and petition of that part of North America, situate south of Canada line, west of Connecticut river, north of the Massachusetts Bay, and east of a twenty mile line from Hudson's river, containing about one hundred and forty four townships, of the contents of six miles square, each, granted your petitioners by the authority of New-Hampshire, besides several grants made by the authority of New-York, and a quantity of vacant land, humbly sheweth,

That your petitioners, by virtue of several grants made them by the authority afore-said, have, many years since, with their families, become actual settlers and inhabitants of the said described premises; by which it is now become a respectable frontier to three neighbor states, and is of great importance to our common barrier Tyconderoga; as it has furnished the army there with much provisions, and can muster more than five thousand hardy soldiers, capable of bearing arms in defence of American liberty:

That shortly after your petitioners began their settlements, a party of land-jobbers in the city and state of New-York, began to claim the lands, and took measures to have them declared to be within that jurisdiction:

That on the fourth day of July, 1764, the king of Great-Britain did pass an order in council, extending the jurisdiction of New-York government to Connecticut river, in consequence of a representation made by the late lieutenant governor Colden, that for the convenience of trade, and administration of justice, the inhabitants were desirous of being annexed to that state:

That on this alteration of jurisdiction, the said lieutenant governor Colden did grant several tracts of land in the above described limits, to certain persons living in the state of New-York, which were, at that time, in the actual possession of your petitioners; and under color of the lawful authority of said state, did proceed against your petitioners, as lawless intruders upon the crown lands in their province. This produced an application to the king of Great-Britain from your petitioners, setting forth their claims under the government of New-Hampshire, and the disturbance and interruption they had suf-fered from said post claimants, under New-York. And on the 24th day of July, 1767, an order was passed at St. James's, prohibiting the governors of New-York, for the time be-ing, from granting any part of the described premises, on pain of incurring his Majes-ty's highest displeasure. Nevertheless the same lieutenant governor Colden, governors Dunmore and Tryon, have, each and every of them, in their respective turns of administration, presumed to violate the said royal order, by making several grants of the prohibited premises, and countenancing an actual invasion of your petitioners, by force of arms, to drive them off from their possessions.

The violent proceedings, (with the solemn declaration of the supreme court of New-York, that the charters, conveyances, &c. of your petitioners' lands, were utterly null and void) on which they were founded, reduced your petitioners to the disagreeable necessity of taking up arms, as the only means left for the security of their possessions. The consequence of this step was the passing twelve acts of outlawry, by the legislatute of New-York, on the ninth day of March, 1774; which were not intended for the state in general, but only for part of the counties of Albany and Charlotte, viz. such parts thereof as are covered by the New-Hampshire charters.

Your petitioners having had no representative in that assembly, when these acts were passed, they first came to the knowledge of them by public papers, in which they were inserted. By these, they were informed, that if three or more of them assembled together to oppose what said assembly called legal authority, that such as should be found assembled, to the number of three or more, should be adjudged felons: And that, in case they or any of them, should not surrender himself or themselves to certain officers appointed for the purpose of securing them, after a warning of seventy days, that then it should be lawful for the respective judges of the supreme court of the province of New-York, to award execution of *Death,* the same as though he or they had been attainted before a proper court of judicatory. These laws were evidently calculated to intimidate your petitioners into a tame surrender of their rights, and such a state of vassalage, as would entail misery on their latest posterity.

It appears to your petitioners, that an infringement on their rights, is still meditated by the state of New-York; as we find that in their general convention at Harlem, the second day of August last, it was unanimously voted, "That all quit-rents, formerly due and owing to the crown of great-Britain within this state, are now due and owing to this convention, or such future government as may hereafter be established in this state."

By a submission to the claims of New-York your petitioners would be subjected to the payment of two shillings and six pence sterling on every hundred acres annually; which, compared with the quit-rents of Livingston's Phillips's, and Ransalear's manors, and many other enormous tracts in the best situations in the state, would lay the most disproportionate share of the public expense on your petitioners, in all respects the least able to bear it.

The convention of New-York have now nearly completed a code of laws, for the future government of that state; which, should they be attempted to be put in execution, will subject your petitioners to the fatal necessity of opposing them by every means in their power.

When the declaration of the honorable the Continental Congress, of the fourth of July last past, reached your petitioners, they communicated it throughout the whole of their district; and being properly apprized of the proposed meeting, delegates from the several counties and towns in the district, described in the preamble to this petition, did meet at Westminster in said district, and after several adjournments for the purpose of forming themselves into a distinct and separate state, did make and publish a declaration, "that they would, at all times thereafter, consider themselves as a free and independent state, capable of regulating their own internal police, in all and every respect whatsoever; and that the people, in the said described district, have the sole, exclusive right of governing themselves in such a manner and form, as they, in their wisdom, should choose; not repugnant to any resolves of the honorable the Continental Congress." And for the mutual support of each other in the maintenance of the freedom and independence of said district or separate state, the said delegates did jointly and severally pledge themselves to each other, by all the ties that are held sacred among men, and resolve and declare that they were at all times ready, in conjunction with their brethren of the United States, to contribute their full proportion towards maintaining the present just war against the fleets and armies of Great-Britain.

To convey this declaration and resolution to your honorable body, the grand representative of the United States, were we (your more immediate petitioners) delegated by the united and unanimous voices of the representatives of the whole body of the settlers on the described premises, in whose name and behalf, we humbly pray, that the said declaration may be received, and the district described therein be ranked by your honors, among the free and independent American states, and delegates there-from admitted to seats in the grand Continental Congress; and your petitioners as in duty bound shall ever pray.

*New-Hampshire Grants, Westminster, Jan. 15th, 1777.*

Signed by order, and in behalf of said inhabitants,

JONAS FAY,
THOMAS CHITTENDEN,
HEMAN ALLEN,
REUBEN JONES.

39.3

 THE NEW YORK DELEGATES TO THE NEW YORK
COUNCIL OF SAFETY, JULY 2, 1777

Here New York's delegates in Congress—Philip Livingston, James Duane, and William Duer—address the petition of the residents of the New Hampshire Grants. As Congress did in its report, the New York delegates emphasize that the petitioners' claims "were admitted to be of universal concern to the general confederacy;

and they were considered as particularly odious, from the attempt to confirm them by the grossest misrepresentation of the resolutions of Congress." They noted that Congress clarified its duty "to secure and defend the several communities of which it is composed . . . by totally reprobating the idea that a minority can establish an independence of the community of which they are members." Of course, this was almost the same position taken by the British regarding their North American colonies that chose to declare independence from the rest of the empire. And it was the U.S. stance toward the seceding states some eight-five years later. In July 1776, Congress believed itself to be defending the thirteen colonies' right of self-government, not the right of individuals or minority communities within the colonies to "institute new Government . . . as to them shall seem most likely to effect their Safety and Happiness."

From the perspective of the New York delegates, this issue resulted not only from the meddling of neighboring New England colonies in its affairs, but, in particular, from the claims of the residents of the New Hampshire Grants being championed by one of the longest-serving and hardest-working members of Congress, the pious and self-made delegate from Connecticut, Roger Sherman, "who brought in the petition for these people to Congress, and has all along acted openly as their advocate and patron." The tensions between the New England colonies and those of the mid-Atlantic, in particular New York, clearly had not ended with the colonies' declaring independence. Indeed, the difficulties Congress had with this issue likely resulted not only from the military importance of the disputed territory but also from the continuing tensions between the New England delegates and those to their south.

Paul H. Smith, ed., *Letters of Delegates to Congress, 1774–1789* (Washington, D.C.: Library of Congress, 1976–93), 7:284–86.

Honourable Gentlemen,                                                Philadelphia, 2d July, 1777.

Since our last we have applied to Commissary Trumbull to exchange in the manner directed by Congress the 2,000 bushels of salt which they were pleased to grant for the relief of our State; as soon as we receive his answer you shall know the result. We are endeavouring to purchase further quantities of this necessary article for the use of our fellow citizens, and have a prospect of succeeding.

The manufacturing of salt in the interior parts of our own State is certainly an object most worthy of the attention of the public. The Indians far from being averse to it, seem heartily disposed to favour the design, and by being made partakers of the advantages, might become warmly engaged for its success.

If the war should be prolonged, it is far from being improbable that we may be deprived of all foreign supplies. How necessary then may this expedient prove to our comfortable subsistence and to our internal union and repose?

We hope to hear that the experiments which were directed before we left Kingston have proved favourable, as well as that good progress has been made in the manufacture of lead and flints, and the refining of sulphur. A certain prospect of internal supply of these important articles would give Congress singular satisfaction; and if derived from your researches and exertions, would add highly to the reputation of the State.

We were yesterday honoured with your favour of the　　　and immediately took the necessary steps to procure an account of the State prisoners sent to Philadelphia by our late Convention, and of the manner of their discharge. It shall be transmitted to you by this conveyance, with the reasons which induced the Council of Safety of this Commonwealth to use so little ceremony in a business which had been represented to them as of a very serious nature.

Congress, between this and the 26th of June, have spent the greatest part of four days in considering the claim of some of the inhabitants of our State to a new government, independent of the community, and the letters and remonstrances of our late Convention and your Honourable Council, on that interesting subject. The principles upon which this ambitious project was granted, were admitted to be of universal concern to the general confederacy; and they were considered as particularly odious, from the attempt to confirm them by the grossest misrepresentation of the resolutions of Congress. No debate was ever conducted with more deliberation and solemnity, and the decision was such as, in our judgment, ought, for the present, to be satisfactory; it does not, it is true, come up to the requisition of our State, "that the insurgents should be recommended to a peaceable submission to its jurisdiction by the authority of Congress, and that Warner's regiment should be discharged." But by totally reprobating the idea that a minority can establish an independence of the community of which they are members, by proclaiming the duty of Congress to secure and defend the several communities of which it is composed:

By censuring the supposition that Congress could do, recommend or countenance any thing injurious to the rights and jurisdictions of those communities:

By declaring expressly that the independent government attempted to be established by those misguided people, can derive no countenance or justification from the particular resolution on which it is pretended to be founded, or from any other act or proceeding of Congress:

By the contemptuous rejection of their petition to be received and ranked as a free State, and to be represented by their own Delegates in Congress:

By the apology to the State of New-York for raising Warner's regiment, implied in the explanation of the motives which gave rise to it, and by the severe censure of Doct. Young's address, encouraging those people to persevere in their defection:

By all these different resolutions, we think a substantial foundation, on general and undeniable principles, is laid, either for reclaiming our fellow citizens to their duty and a submission to the laws, by the force of reason and persuasion, and the fears of offending a whole continent; or should they obstinately persevere in their revolt, for a future requisition of the aid of Congress, to be administered in such manner as the opposition of the disaffected, and our own circumstances, may render expedient.

We flatter ourselves, therefore, that we shall meet with your approbation, and that our country will be pleased and benefitted by the measures adopted on this occasion. May we be permitted to suggest the propriety of despatching commissioners, without delay, to explain and enforce, among our too aspiring countrymen, these resolutions of Congress, and to seize the advantage which the first impression of unexpected disappointment and condemnation from the only tribunal they fear, may make on their minds, in order to induce them to a submission of your jurisdiction.

This appears to us to be the more necessary, as Mr. Roger Sherman, of Connecticut, who brought in the petition for these people to Congress, and has all along acted openly as their advocate and patron, and in the last debate plead their cause with a zeal and passion which he never discovered in any other instance, and which, in a judge, between a State and some of its own members, was far from being commendable. This gentleman, we say, immediately on passing the resolutions, procured copies, and having obtained leave of absence, is already set out on his journey to the eastward. What may be his views with respect to our dispute, we know not, but to his enmity and officiousness you ought not to be strangers.

We have the honour to be, with the greatest respect, honourable gentlemen, Your most obedient humble servants,

Phil. Livingston,
Jas. Duane,
Wm. Duer.

## 39.4

 WILLIAM DUER TO ROBERT R. LIVINGSTON,
JULY 9, 1777

William Duer, born in England, was one of New York's young delegates. A wealthy land speculator with extensive holdings in the West Indies, he was a close friend of the even younger Alexander Hamilton (twenty-two at this time). Here he writes to another young delegate, Livingston, a wealthy lawyer, member of one of the two or three great families of New York, law partner of John Jay, and one of the congressional delegates tasked with drafting the Declaration of Independence, with which he disagreed. In Duer's discussion of the ongoing issue of the New Hampshire Grants, the camaraderie in the New York delegation is palpable. Also evident is its continued contempt, a year after declaring independence, for the congressional radicals of New England and

Virginia, in particular R. H. Lee. Duer describes him as riveted "to his Eastern Friends" and as someone who should be held "in that Contemptable Point of View which he really deserves."[79] As in the previous document, New York views the problem of the New Hampshire Grants as one created by the New England states, long supportive of republican principles. Duer describes several days of debate in which "very Warm Opposition was given by some of our Eastern Freinds against the Resolution for dismissing the Petition of Jonas Fay &ca and that censuring Dr. Youngs Incendiary Production." In the not so distant future, when the troublesome residents of Vermont had begun to nibble away at New Hampshire territory and to negotiate with Britain regarding their possible future status within the British Empire, New Hampshire's delegates came to question the wisdom of their earlier generosity in giving away New York territory.

Paul H. Smith, ed., *Letters of Delegates to Congress, 1774–1789* (Washington, D.C.: Library of Congress, 1976–93), 7:327–28.

My dear Friend,                                           Philadelphia July 9th. 1777
That I may not give you Reason to think that your Pardon is bestowed on an Ingrate, I steal a Few Moments from urgent Business to acknowledge the Receipt of yours of the Inst.

I have the Pleasure to inform you that Congress have adopted Sundry Resolutions respecting the Insurgents in the Counties of Gloucester, Cumberland, and Charlotte, which, if our New Legislature acts with Spirit, and Wisdom, will I think be attended with happy Effects. We transmit them by this Opportunity to the Council of Safety.

I beleive no Matter has ever been more solemnly argued in Congress than this. The House were in Committee for three Days, and very Warm Opposition was given by some of our Eastern Freinds against the Resolution for dismissing the Petition of Jonas Fay &ca and that censuring Dr. Youngs Incendiary Production. Mr. Sherman was quite thrown off his Bias, and betrayd a Warmth not usually learnt within the Walls of Yale Colledge. I think it is of the utmost Consequence that these Resolu[tio]ns should be generally throughout the revolted Counties, and that means should be speedily devised by the Legislature of doing Right to such as have really Cause of Complaint from the Iniquities of the old Government. Their Number I think is not many.

I am sorry to inform you that Colo. R. H. Lee is returning to Congress Crownd with Laurels. His Smooth Discourse, and Art of Cabal have blunted the Edge of his Country-mens Resentment, and they have lauded him Encomiums on his Patriotism and Attention to Business, which he modestly says, he is Anxious of deserving. For particulars I refer you to the Pensilvania Papers. I suppose he will return here more rivitted than ever to his Eastern Friends; I assure you they lost in him no Contemptable Ally.

You tell that you hope I have given over Thoughts of returning for some Time. I assure you that I can not with Justice to myself, or indeed with others in our State with whom I have Transactions in Business, stay here long. Since my Letter to you I have made a formal Application to the Council of Safety for Leave of Absence, which I hope will be granted. I entreat your Influence to prevent any Procrastination in this Matter.

At present there are no very great Matters in which our State is particularly interested before Congress; and indeed if they were, Mr. Morris can supply my Place with great Advantage to the Reputation of the State, as well as his own. His Coolness of Temper, and happy Vein of Irony are Qualifications, which would render him a very powerful Antagonist to Mr. R. H. Lee.

I hope you will give him a Hint not to neglect this great Orator. You may depend upon it, he will advance his own Reputation, and be of Advantage to the Public in making the *Person* appear in that Contemptable Point of View which he really deserves.

In Case I have not Time to write to Mr. Jay, I beg you to remember me to him and to Mr Morris. I am very affectionately, Yours,

W. Duer.

## 40. CONGRESS' FIRST "NATIONAL" DAY OF THANKSGIVING AND ITS SUPPORT FOR ORDERING BIBLES, SEPTEMBER AND NOVEMBER 1777

This was a time of trial and then jubilation. On September 18, 1777, Congress began a second round of peregrinations. After being again forced to flee Philadelphia, it reconvened on September 27 in Lancaster before adjourning to York, Pennsylvania, where it met on September 30. Congress remained there until June 27, 1778, then returned to Philadelphia on July 2. Jubilation arrived on October 31, 1777, when the delegates received confirmation that General Gates had defeated General Burgoyne and that, according to the "Convention of Saratoga," Burgoyne's army of nearly six thousand men was to be transported back to Britain with a pledge never to serve again in the war.[80] With that victory, much changed.

Most importantly, in early December 1777 when Lord North, the long-serving British first minister, learned of Burgoyne's defeat, he began preparing a series of bills and a new offer of reconciliation with which he hoped to forestall a Franco-American alliance. Those efforts culminated in the Carlisle Peace Commission of April 1778 (see document 47.1). Similarly, the French, fearful that the Americans might be tempted to come to terms with the British, informed the American envoys in Paris, Benjamin Franklin and Silas Deane, on December 17 that Louis XVI had decided to recognize American independence. On January 8, 1778, the French foreign minister, Count Vergennes, informed Deane and Franklin that France was prepared to enter into an alliance with America, which it did on February 6 with two treaties. Congress ratified them on May 4, 1778, almost immediately upon receipt. By June 17, 1778, the French and British were at war; Spain entered in 1779, and Holland, along with a league of armed neutrals, in 1780. Quickly, by eighteenth-century standards, the new states' prospects for success and international recognition as separate nations and soon, possibly, a unified nation enormously improved after Burgoyne's defeat.

On the same day that Congress learned definitively of America's spectacular victory at Saratoga, a committee of three was appointed "to prepare a recommendation to the several states, to set apart a day of thanksgiving, for the signal success, lately obtained over the enemies of these United States." This, it should be noted, was Congress's first day of thanksgiving rather than, as had been the norm, of fasting, humiliation, and prayer. Also, this was the first "national" day of thanksgiving for the new states. Those members chosen for the committee were Samuel Adams, R. H. Lee, and Daniel Roberdeau, a West Indian–born Pennsylvanian who was a successful merchant in Philadelphia. A day later, on November 1, the committee brought in its report for a day of thanksgiving; it was attributed to Adams, in whose handwriting it was submitted and whose deep religiosity and comfort with the language both of natural rights and Christian piety it reflected.

Congress asked that a Thursday in mid-December be set aside for the citizens of the new states "to acknowledge with gratitude their obligation to him for benefits received," "to implore such farther blessings as they stand in need of," and to ask that God aid Americans "in the prosecution of a just and necessary war, for the defence and establish-ment of our unalienable rights and liberties." Americans were asked once again (see documents 17.2 and 28.1) to confess their sins, "whereby they had forfeited every favour," and to make a "humble and earnest supplication that it may please God, through the merits of Jesus Christ, mercifully to forgive and blot them out of remembrance." In addition, God was asked to inspire leaders "to take schools and seminaries of education, so necessary for cultivating the principles of true liberty, virtue and piety, under his nurturing hand, and to prosper the means of religion for the promotion and enlarge-ment of that kingdom which consisteth 'in righteousness, peace and joy in the Holy Ghost.'" The values of Congress, a year after the Declaration's issue, remained closely linked with the Reformed Protestant religiosity of the vast majority of Americans.[81]

40.1

 ## CONGRESS, THANKSGIVING PROCLAMATION, NOVEMBER 1, 1777

Worthington Chauncey Ford et al., eds., *Journals of the Continental Congress, 1774–1789* (Washington, D.C.: Government Printing Office, 1904–37), 9:854–55. The phrase "in righteousness, peace and joy in the Holy Ghost" comes from Romans 14:17.

The committee appointed to prepare a recommendation to these states, to set apart a day of thanksgiving, brought in a report; which was agreed to as follows:

Forasmuch as it is the indispensable duty of all men to adore the superintending providence of Almighty God; to acknowledge with gratitude their obligation to him for benefits received, and to implore such farther blessings as they stand in need of; and it having pleased him in his abundant mercy not only to continue to us the innumerable bounties of his common providence, but also to smile upon us in the prosecution of a just and necessary war, for the defence and establishment of our unalienable rights and liberties; particularly in that he hath been pleased in so great a measure to prosper the means used for the support of our troops and to crown our arms with most signal success: It is therefore recommended to the legislative or executive powers of these United States, to set apart Thursday, the eighteenth day of December next, for solemn thanksgiving and praise; that with one heart and one voice the good people may express the grateful feelings of their hearts, and consecrate themselves to the service of their divine benefactor; and that together with their sincere acknowledgments and offerings, they may join the penitent confession of their manifold sins, whereby they had forfeited every favour, and their humble and earnest supplication that it may please God, through the merits of Jesus Christ, mercifully to forgive and blot them out of remembrance; that it may please him graciously to afford his blessing on the governments of these states respectively, and prosper the public council of the whole; to inspire our commanders both by land and sea, and all under them, with that wisdom and fortitude which may render them fit instruments, under the providence of Almighty God, to secure for these United States the greatest of all human blessings, independence and peace; that it may please him to prosper the trade and manufactures of the people and the labour of the husbandman, that our land may yet yield its increase; to take schools and seminaries of education, so necessary for cultivating the principles of true liberty, virtue and piety, under his nurturing hand, and to prosper the means of religion for the promotion and enlargement of that kingdom which consisteth "in righteousness, peace and joy in the Holy Ghost."

And it is further recommended, that servile labour, and such recreation as, though at other times innocent, may be unbecoming the purpose of this appointment, be omitted on so solemn an occasion.

## 40.2

## HENRY LAURENS TO THE STATES, NOVEMBER 1, 1777

The day after Congress' fourth president, John Hancock of Massachusetts, retired (he had served since replacing Peyton Randolph, the first and third president), on May 24, 1775, Henry Laurens, one of South Carolina's wealthiest merchants, replaced him (he would serve until December 9, 1778). Laurens wrote the states' executive bodies to inform them that he had become Congress' fifth president and to ask that "Thursday the 18th December next be Set apart to be observed by all Inhabitants throughout these States for a General thanksgiving to Almighty God," since America had "been blessed in the present Campaign with remarkable Success." Laurens, it might be noted, like many in Congress, was "'strict and exemplary' in his performance of religious duties. He 'read the scriptures diligently to his family.'"[82]

Paul H. Smith, ed., *Letters of Delegates to Congress, 1774–1789* (Washington, D.C.: Library of Congress, 1976–93), 8:218.

Sir                                                             York Town 1st November 1777

The Arms of the United States of America having been blessed in the present Campaign with remarkable Success, Congress have Resolved to recommend that one day, Thursday the 18th December next be Set apart to be observed by all Inhabitants throughout these States for a General thanksgiving to Almighty God. And I have it in command to transmit to you the inclosed extract from the minutes of Congress for that purpose.

Your Excellency *or Honour* will be pleased to take the necessary measures for carrying the Resolve into effect in the State in which you preside.

You will likewise find inclosed a Certified Copy of a minute which will Shew your Excellency the Authority under which I have the honour of addressing you.

I am with great Esteem & regard, Sir, Your Excellencys most Obt. Servt.

## 40.3

RESOLUTION AND VOTE OF CONGRESS ON IMPORTING TWENTY THOUSAND PROTESTANT BIBLES, JULY 7 AND SEPTEMBER 11, 1777

Because of Parliament's American Prohibitory Act and Congress' continued embargo on trade with Britain, the United States had, since late 1775, experienced a shortage of English-language Bibles. On July 7, 1777, three Philadelphia pastors placed before Congress a petition seeking the publication of an American version of the King James Bible, though one dedicated to Congress rather than King James. The three men were the Reverend Francis Allison of the First Presbyterian Church of Philadelphia, a leader in establishing the first General Assembly of the Presbyterian Church; the Reverend John Ewing, provost of the University of Pennsylvania;

and the Reverend William Marshall, pastor of the Scots Presbyterian Church. The petition was read and referred to a committee made up of Daniel Roberdeau and Jonathan Bayard Smith, both of Pennsylvania, and John Adams. The committee's report of September 11, issued in Roberdeau's handwriting a week before Congress evacuated Philadelphia, opposes the publication of an American Bible supervised and funded by Congress.

The committee came to its conclusion after two months of research, including cost estimates from at least five Philadelphia printers. They concluded that the costs and difficulties of producing an American Bible were too great at the time, particularly with Howe's army menacing Philadelphia and Congress knowing that it would soon be forced to flee and unable to supervise the work.[83] The committee suggested instead, since "the use of the Bible is so universal, and its importance so great," that Congress consider instructing "the Committee of Commerce to import 20,000 Bibles from Holland, Scotland, or elsewhere into the different ports of the states in the Union." Congress duly "moved, to order the Committee of Commerce to import twenty thousand copies of the Bible."

But Congress was not of one mind on this matter. At least one state requested a recorded vote—a feature of Congress first used on August 8, 1777[84]—which shows that the New England states (still consistently Reformed Protestant or Congregational) uniformly supported the motion, the mid-Atlantic states divided approximately along religious lines (Anglican-dominated New York, Delaware, and Maryland voted no; Presbyterian and Quaker New Jersey and Pennsylvania voted yes), and the Anglican South opposed it. Three southern delegates, however, voted in favor of the measure: Francis Lightfoot Lee of Virginia, President Laurens of South Carolina, and the lone Georgia delegate, Nathan Brownson, yet another Connecticut transplant residing in Savannah. Although the roll-call vote supported the report's instructions to import twenty thousand Bibles, when Congress was asked to "pass a resolution" to support the measure financially, the final consideration of it was "postponed to Saturday next," September 19. Congress did not meet then, for on the day prior it had left Philadelphia for Lancaster.

The next mention made in the *Journals* of the need for Congress to purchase Bibles or to oversee their printing was not until October 26, 1780, when Congress "recommended to such of the States who may think it convenient . . . to procure one or more new and correct editions of the old and new testament to be printed." On January 26, 1781, the saga of Robert Aitken's efforts to print Bibles began. A "Presbyterian elder and congressional printer," he had submitted to the congressional committee exploring the matter in 1777 a thorough estimate of the cost of printing twenty thousand Bibles. On September 12, 1782, during a period in Philadelphia far less tumultuous than 1777, that Congress resolved "that the

United States in Congress assembled, highly approve the pious and laudable undertaking of Mr. Aitken . . . [and] recommend this edition of the Bible to the inhabitants of the United States, and hereby authorize him to publish this recommendation in the manner he shall think proper."[85] Although Congress again made no financial commitment, "the Pennsylvania legislature . . . offered Aitken a one-hundred-fifty-pound, interest-free loan to complete his work, and ten thousand copies of his Bible were printed with an American congressional endorsement."[86]

Worthington Chauncey Ford et al., eds., *Journals of the Continental Congress, 1774–1789* (Washington, D.C.: Government Printing Office, 1904–37), 8:536, 733–35.

[MONDAY, JULY 7, 1777]

A petition from the Rev. F[rancis] Allison, J[ohn] Ewing, and W[illiam] Marshall, was read:

*Ordered,* That it be referred to a committee of three:

The members chosen, Mr. [Daniel] Roberdeau, Mr. J[ohn] Adams, and Mr. J[onathan] B[ayard] Smith. . . .

[THURSDAY, SEPTEMBER 11, 1777]

The committee appointed to consider the memorial of the Rev. Dr. Allison and others, report, "That they have conferred fully with the printers, &c. in this city, and are of the opinion, that the proper types for printing the Bible are not to be had in this country, and that the paper cannot be procured, but with such difficulties and subject to such casualties, as render any dependence on it altogether improper: that to import types for the purpose of setting up an entire edition of the bible, and to strike off 30,000 copies, with paper, binding, &c. will cost £10,272 10, which must be advanced by Congress, to be reimbursed by the sale of the books:

"That, your committee are of opinion, considerable difficulties will attend the procuring the types and paper; that, afterwards, the risque of importing them will considerably enhance the cost, and that the calculations are subject to such uncertainty in the present state of affairs, that Congress cannot much rely on them: that the use of the Bible is so universal, and its importance so great, that your committee refer the above to the consideration of Congress, and if Congress shall not think it expedient to order the importation of types and paper, your committee recommend that Congress will order the Committee of Commerce to import 20,000 Bibles from Holland, Scotland, or elsewhere, into the different ports of the states in the Union:"

Whereupon, the Congress was moved, to order the Committee of Commerce to import twenty thousand copies of the Bible;

The question being put, the house was divided:

| State / Member | Vote | Result |
|---|---|---|
| *New Hampshire,* | | |
| Mr. Folsom, | ay | |
| Frost, | ay | } ay |
| *Massachusetts bay,* | | |
| Mr. S. Adams, | ay | |
| J. Adams, | ay | |
| Gerry, | ay | |
| Lovell, | ay | } ay |
| *Rhode Island,* | | |
| Mr. Merchant, | ay | } ay |
| *Pennsylvania,* | | |
| Mr. Wilson, | ay | |
| Roberdeau, | ay | } ay |
| *Delaware,* | | |
| Mr. Reed, | no | } no |
| *Maryland,* | | |
| Mr. Chase, | no | } * |
| *Virginia,* | | |
| Mr. Harrison, | no | |
| F. L. Lee, | ay | |
| Jones, | no | } no |
| *Connecticut,* | | |
| Mr. Dyer, | ay | |
| Law, | ay | |
| Williams, | ay | } ay |
| *New York,* | | |
| Mr. Duane, | no | } * |
| *New Jersey,* | | |
| Mr. Clark, | ay | |
| Witherspoon, | ay | } ay |
| *North Carolina,* | | |
| Mr. Harnett, | no | } no |
| *South Carolina,* | | |
| Mr. Middleton, | no | |
| Heyward, | no | |
| Laurens, | ay | } no |
| *Georgia,* | | |
| Mr. Brownson, | ay | } ay |

So it was resolved in the affirmative.

The house was moved to pass a resolution, and the same being read,

*Ordered,* The consideration thereof be postponed to Saturday next, to be taken up after reading the public letters.

## 41. ANOTHER INADEQUATE AND UNSUCCESSFUL BRITISH EFFORT AT RECONCILIATION, NOVEMBER 1777

The first Earl of Chatham, formerly William Pitt the elder, was well disposed toward the colonies and widely admired by the colonists. At his death in 1778, he stood in opposition to the North government. At the opening of the new parliamentary session in 1777, Chatham delivered a speech that sought to find some formula for reconciliation with the states before they formed an alliance with France. Definitive news of the surrender of Burgoyne at Saratoga wouldn't arrive in London for another two or three weeks, but the military news from the northern front for some time had not been good.

After beginning his speech with the assertion that "no man wishes for the due dependence of America on this country more than I do," Chatham lambastes

Parliament for driving the colonists toward the "state of independence." He lauds "the Americans, contending for their rights against the arbitrary exactions . . . it is the struggle of free and virtuous patriots." But he could not accept the right to separate from the empire: in their "contending for independency and total disconnection from England, as an Englishman, I cannot wish them success." He wished for a return to the "due constitutional dependency, including the ancient supremacy of this country in regulating their commerce and navigation." He believed it was in that relationship, in which the colonies were "the fountain of our wealth, the nerve of our strength, the nursery and basis of our naval power"—here Chatham echoed Lord Howe's comments to the congressional delegation in September (see document 36.4)—that "the mutual happiness and prosperity both of England and America" consisted. But this nostalgia was for naught, because Chatham was still unable to envision a constitutionally recognized, imperial-federal plan of government. Nor could the North government, as may be seen in the instructions to the Carlisle Peace Commission of 1778 (see document 47.1).

Like many in the North government, Chatham believed, wrongly, that it would be possible to peel off "the sound part of America . . . the middle and southern provinces" and then win over the more radical New Englanders. The colonies would be offered "those immutable rights of nature, and those constitutional liberties, to which they are equally entitled with ourselves . . . but no more." Too often, British officials underestimated just how widespread opposition was in the colonies—even among those opposed to declaring independence, separating from the king, and republican governance—to the actions of Parliament.

In truth, it would have been nearly impossible to craft a constitutional settlement that divided sovereignty, protected North American colonial rights to self-government under the king, and yet satisfied traditional or Old Whigs like Chatham or Edmund Burke, given their inviolable commitment to parliamentary supremacy and sovereignty as essential components of British liberty.[87]

<br>

## 41.1

 # THE EARL OF CHATHAM, SPEECH IN THE HOUSE OF LORDS, NOVEMBER 20, 1777

Max Beloff, ed., *The Debate on the American Revolution, 1761–1785* (Dobbs Ferry, N.Y.: Sheridan House, 1989), 291–93. The following is an excerpt from a much longer speech.

My Lords, no man wishes for the due dependence of America on this country more than I do. To preserve it, and not confirm that state of independence into which *your measures* hitherto have *driven* them, is the object which we ought to unite in attaining.

The Americans, contending for their rights against the arbitrary exactions, I love and admire; it is the struggle of free and virtuous patriots: but contending for independency and total disconnection from England, as an Englishman, I cannot wish them success: for, in a due constitutional dependency, including the ancient supremacy of this country in regulating their commerce and navigation, consists the mutual happiness and prosperity both of England and America. She derived assistance and protection from us; and we reaped from her the most important advantages:—She was, indeed, the fountain of our wealth, the nerve of our strength, the nursery and basis of our naval power. It is our duty, therefore, my Lords, if we wish to save our country, most seriously to endeavour the recovery of these most beneficial subjects: and in this perilous crisis, perhaps the present moment may be the only one in which we can hope for success: for in their negotiations with France, they have, or think they have, reason to complain: though it be notorious that they have received from that power important supplies and assistance of various kinds, yet it is certain they expected it in a more decisive and immediate degree. America is in an ill humour with France, on some points that have not entirely answered her expectations: let us wisely take advantage of every possible moment of reconciliation. Besides, the natural disposition of America herself still leans towards England; to the old habits of connection and mutual interest that united both countries. This *was* the established sentiment of all the Continent; and still, my Lords, in the great and principal part, the sound part of America, this wise and affectionate disposition prevails, and there is a very considerable part of America yet sound—the middle and southern provinces; some parts may be factious and blind to their true interests; but if we express a wise and benevolent disposition to communicate with them those immutable rights of nature, and those constitutional liberties, to which they are equally entitled with ourselves, by a conduct so just and humane, we shall confirm the favourable and conciliate the adverse. I say, my Lords, the rights and liberties to which they are equally entitled, with ourselves, but no more. I would participate to them every enjoyment and freedom which the colonizing subjects of a free state can possess, or wish to possess; and I do not see why they should not enjoy every fundamental right in their property, and every original substantial liberty, which Devonshire or Surrey, or the county I live in, or any other county in England, can claim; reserving always, as the sacred right of the mother country, the due constitutional dependency of the Colonies. The inherent supremacy of the state in regulating and protecting the navigation and commerce of all her subjects, is necessary for the mutual benefit and preservation of every part, to constitute and preserve the prosperous arrangement of the whole empire.

The sound parts of America, of which I have spoken, must be sensible of these great truths, and of their real interests. America is not in that state of desperate and contemptible rebellion, which this country has been deluded to believe. It is not a wild and lawless banditti, who having nothing to lose, might hope to snatch something from public convulsions; many of their leaders and great men have a great stake in this great contest:—the gentleman who conducts their armies, I am told, has an estate of four or five thousand pounds a year: and when I consider these things, I cannot but lament the inconsiderate violence of our penal acts, our declarations of treason and rebellion, with all the fatal effects of attainder and confiscation.

## 42. FINALIZING THE ARTICLES OF CONFEDERATION AND RESOLVING THE FOUR PRINCIPAL ISSUES OF CONCERN, NOVEMBER 1777

In October 1777, after a year of intermittent attention (or, better said, inattention), Congress began, with a new sense of urgency, to review the draft Articles of Confederation. Rather quickly it reached agreement on the three persistently difficult questions that it had wrestled with since July 1776. Regarding state voting in Congress, it decided on October 7 that "each State shall have one vote." On the apportionment of taxes, Congress decided on October 14 that they would be based on each state's surveyed land and "buildings and improvements thereon." On October 27, Congress voted to make itself the final arbiter of disputes between states, a decision tied mostly to the adjudication of western land claims. That matter nonetheless remained a vexing problem, preventing ratification of the Articles by all the states for another four years. The most significant amendment to the draft Articles, that of Thomas Burke shifting sovereignty toward the states and away from the central government, had been decided quickly and with little controversy shortly before April 29 (see document 38.2). "The remaining Articles of the August 1776 draft were reconsidered between October 21 and November 7"; six were approved as written, and two significant changes were made to the article that "detailed the powers and authority of Congress."[88]

On November 10, Congress appointed a committee consisting of Richard Law of Connecticut (a prominent lawyer who in 1784 would work with Roger Sherman in codifying the statutes of the state), R. H. Lee, and James Duane to take into consideration possible further amendments while "not changing or altering any of the articles already agreed on." The next day, the committee reported seven amendments for Congress to consider further; "of these, four were adopted essentially as reported, two were approved with significant amendments, and one authorizing Congress to discipline its own members was rejected."[89]

With this work completed, on November 13, another committee of three was appointed: R. H. Lee, James Duane, and James Lovell of Massachusetts. Lovell was a former Boston schoolteacher and one of the few members of Congress with good command of French (as such, he was assigned to deal with the horde of Frenchmen seeking military appointments). This committee was asked "to revise and arrange the articles of confederation . . . [and] to prepare a circular letter to the respective states to accompany the said articles." After final consideration on November 15, 1777, three hundred copies of the Articles of Confederation and Perpetual Union were ordered printed, and the circular letter was considered and approved on November 17. It was decided to request that the states return their delegates empowered to ratify the Articles on March 10, 1778.[90] That date was wildly unrealistic, for the Articles of Confederation and Perpetual Union, and the new nation to which it legally gave birth, would not come into force until Maryland ratified the plan, which it duly did in Congress on March 1, 1781.

The committee's report, likely the work of its chair, R. H. Lee, explains the goal of the confederacy as "securing the freedom, sovereignty, and independence of the United States." As in many similar congressional state papers, including the Declaration of Independence, it was the sovereignty and freedom of the states that was to be defended in the proposed new nation. The report apologetically tries to explain the yearlong delay in completing the Articles, which resulted from the difficulty of bringing together "in one general system the various sentiments and interests of a continent divided into so many sovereign and independent communities," with their differing "habits, produce, commerce, and internal police." To defend their common liberties, the particular preferences of individual states had to be sacrificed in the pursuit of the good of all. Above all, it was hoped that the ratification of the Articles and the creation of a newly confederated nation would "confound our foreign enemies, defeat the flagitious practices of the disaffected, strengthen and confirm our friends, support our public credit, restore the value of our money, [and] enable us to maintain our fleets and armies." The letter closes by beseeching the states as quickly as possible to vest their delegates with the ability to "subscribe to the articles of confederation and perpetual union of the United States."

42.1

# Circular Letter to the States Accompanying the Final Articles of Confederation, November 17, 1777

Worthington Chauncey Ford et al., eds., *Journals of the Continental Congress, 1774–1789* (Washington, D.C.: Government Printing Office, 1904–37), 9:932–34.

The committee appointed to arrange the articles of confederation, and prepare a circular letter to accompany it to the several states, brought in the following draught:

In Congress, York Town, 17 November, 1777.

Congress having agreed upon a plan of confederacy for securing the freedom, sovereignty, and independence of the United States, authentic copies are now transmitted for the consideration of the respective legislatures.

This business, equally intricate and important, has, in its progress, been attended with uncommon embarrassments and delay, which the most anxious solicitude and persevering diligence could not prevent. To form a permanent union, accommodated to the opinion and wishes of the delegates of so many states, differing in habits, produce, commerce, and internal police, was found to be a work which nothing but time and reflection, conspiring with a disposition to conciliate, could mature and accomplish.

Hardly is it to be expected that any plan, in the variety of provisions essential to our union, should exactly correspond with the maxims and political views of every particular State. Let it be remarked, that, after the most careful enquiry and the fullest information, this is proposed as the best which could be adapted to the circumstances of all; and as that alone which affords any tolerable prospect of a general ratification.

Permit us, then, earnestly to recommend these articles to the immediate and dispassionate attention of the legislatures of the respective states. Let them be candidly reviewed under a sense of the difficulty of combining in one general system the various sentiments and interests of a continent divided into so many sovereign and independent communities, under a conviction of the absolute necessity of uniting all our councils and all our strength, to maintain and defend our common liberties: let them be examined with a liberality becoming brethren and fellow-citizens surrounded by the same imminent dangers, contending for the same illustrious prize, and deeply interested in being forever bound and connected together by ties the most intimate and indissoluble; and finally, let them be adjusted with the temper and magnanimity of wise and patriotic legislators, who, while they are concerned for the prosperity of their own more immediate circle, are capable of rising superior to local attachments, when they may be incompatible with the safety, happiness, and glory of the general Confederacy.

We have reason to regret the time which has elapsed in preparing this plan for consideration: with additional solicitude we look forward to that which must be necessarily spent before it can be ratified. Every motive loudly calls upon us to hasten its conclusion.

More than any other consideration, it will confound our foreign enemies, defeat the flagitious practices of the disaffected, strengthen and confirm our friends, support our public credit, restore the value of our money, enable us to maintain our fleets and armies, and add weight and respect to our councils at home, and to our treaties abroad.

In short, this salutary measure can no longer be deferred. It seems essential to our very existence as a free people, and without it we may soon be constrained to bid adieu to independence, to liberty and safety; blessings which, from the justice of our cause, and the favour of our Almighty Creator visibly manifested in our protection, we have reason to expect, if, in an humble dependence on his divine providence, we strenuously exert the means which are placed in our power.

To conclude, if the legislature of any State shall not be assembled, Congress recommend to the executive authority to convene it without delay; and to each respective legislature it is recommended to invest its delegates with competent powers ultimately in the name and behalf of the state to subscribe articles of confederation and perpetual union of the United States; and to attend Congress for that purpose on or before the          day of          .

## 42.2

FINAL VOTES AND LANGUAGE FOR CONTESTED
SECTIONS OF THE ARTICLES OF CONFEDERATION, OCTOBER 7,
OCTOBER 14, AND NOVEMBER 15, 1777

Here the final language of those sections of the Articles of Confederation most heatedly debated is reproduced so that it can be compared with the language used in the Dickinson committee's draft (see document 34.1). Final Article 2—keep in mind that in the ratified Articles of 1781 the numbering shifted back to roman numerals—reflects Burke's first successful amendment. It reverses the balance of power from Dickinson's Article III, tightly constraining the central government and leaving the states largely autonomous and sovereign. This subtle but important change produced a plan of government much more in keeping with the decentralist philosophy that had led to the Declaration of Independence. Relevant to this issue is the wording in the final version of Article 13. Dickinson had written (in his Article XX) that "the Articles of this Confederation shall inviolably be observed by every Colony, and the Union is to be perpetual." In the final version of Article 13, Congress, while retaining that sentence, preceded it with "every State shall abide by the determinations of the United States, in Congress assembled, on all questions which, by this confederation, are submitted to them." The difference, though small, may have been intended to help compensate for the central government's reduced sovereignty.[91]

Article 5 in the final congressional version, like Article XVII in Dickinson's draft, allocated to each state one vote in Congress. The question had been heatedly debated by delegates of small and large states alike, and it was the most contested issue at the Philadelphia convention in 1787, with slavery a distant second. On the final vote in Congress, reproduced here, every state supported the continuation of equal voting in Congress, except Virginia. It persisted in arguing that the number of votes should be proportional—not to population, as the philosophy of popular sovereignty made famous by Jefferson in the Declaration might have suggested, but to a state's "contribution of money or tax levied."

The final version of Article 8, regarding the apportionment of national taxes to individual states (Article XI in Dickinson's original draft), was decided in Congress on October 14. In the vote, reproduced below, the New England and the southern states voted as opposing blocs, with two of the mid-Atlantic State delegations (New York and Pennsylvania) divided.[92] Accordingly, the deciding vote fell to New Jersey, which voted to apportion taxes based on "the value of all land within each State granted to, or surveyed for any person, as such land, and the buildings and improvements thereon shall be estimated." So, by a 5–4 vote, with Delaware and Georgia not represented, Congress changed the basis for apportioning national taxes to be paid by each state, which initially had been by "the Number of Inhabitants of every Age, Sex, and Quality," including slaves, in the state. This issue, more than any other, divided the New England states from their former allies in Virginia, and was one that Massachusetts, in particular, continued to oppose.

When it came to final state approval, these long-contested issues paled in comparison to the question whether Congress would have the power to control the western lands and settle interstate land disputes. In Dickinson's draft (Article XVIII), Congress was vested with control over this issue. The matter was largely decided on October 15, 1777, when Congress determined to strip its future self, the Confederation Congress, of much of its power in this area, with only Maryland continuing to support Congress' being vested with robust powers to control contested western lands. Congress' greatly diminished role was eventually embodied in final Article 9. Congress relinquished original jurisdiction and became instead "the last resort on appeal on all disputes and differences now subsisting, that hereafter may arise between two or more states concerning boundary" matters. Maryland, which found the language of the Article as approved utterly unacceptable, persisted up to the final vote in Congress on fighting the unbounded land claims of, in particular, Virginia. Maryland continued to insist on Virginia surrendering its land claims before Maryland would ratify the Articles. Virginia refused to do so until January 2, 1781. Once that happened, Maryland agreed to ratify the Articles of Confederation and Perpetual Union, which became the supreme law of the land on March 1, 1781.

The debates over land claims, the voting of states in Congress, and the apportionment of national expenses were far more often driven by the particular interests of individual states than by anything that might be described as highly principled stances. This is not to claim that principled concerns were absent from the minds of the delegates, but only to note again that as representatives of their states and as skilled lawyers, they used principles instrumentally to advance the claims of their states rather than as stand-alone or dominant claims. Accordingly, if a delegate advanced a democratic argument based on the population of a state, that delegate, not surprisingly, was always from a state with a large population. One must be careful in viewing the delegates' claims as being predominantly principled, for when looked at with some care, they may more accurately be understood as regularly advancing purely instrumental views. It is too easy to think that politics then were fundamentally different from politics today.

Worthington Chauncey Ford et al., eds., *Journals of the Continental Congress, 1774–1789*
(Washington, D.C.: Government Printing Office, 1904–37), 9:781, 801–2, 908–25.

[TUESDAY, OCTOBER 7, 1777]

It was then moved [concerning what would become Article 5 in the final version] "That the quantum of representation for each State shall be computed by numbers proportioned according to its contribution of money or tax levied, agreeable to the 9th article of this confederation [Article 8 in the final draft], and paid into the public treasury towards the annual expences necessary for the support of the union;"

And the question being put, and the yeas and nays required:

| | | | | | | | |
|---|---|---|---|---|---|---|---|
| *New Hampshire,* | | | | *Maryland,* | | | |
| Mr. Folsom, | no | } | no | Mr. Chase, | no | | |
| *Massachusetts Bay* | | | | Carroll, | no | } | no |
| Mr. S. Adams, | [no] | | | Smith, | no | | |
| J. Adams | ay | } | no | *Virginia,* | | | |
| Gerry, | no | | | Mr. Harrison, | ay | | |
| *Rhode Island,* | | | | Jones, | ay | | |
| Mr. Marchant, | no | } | no | F. L. Lee, | ay | | ay |
| *Connecticut,* | | | | R. H. Lee, | ay | | |
| Mr. Dyer, | no | | | *North Carolina,* | | | |
| Law, | no | } | no | Mr. Penn, | no | } | no |
| Williams, | no | | | Harnett, | no | | |
| *New York,* | | | | *South Carolina,* | | | |
| Mr. Duane, | no | } | no | Mr. Middleton, | ay | | |
| Duer, | no | | | Heyward, | no | } | no |
| *New Jersey,* | | | | Laurens, | no | | |
| Mr. Witherspoon, | no | } | no | *Georgia,* | | | |
| *Pennsylvania,* | | | | Mr. Walton, | no | } | no |
| Mr. Morris, | no | } | no | Brownson, | no | | no |
| Roberdeau | no | | | | | | |

So it passed in the negative.

The question being put on the article as reported, and the yeas and nays required: . . .

[after a second vote in which the entire Virginia delegation voted no] So it was resolved, That in determining questions each State shall have one vote. . . .

[TUESDAY, OCTOBER 14, 1777]

Congress resumed the consideration of the 9 article of confederation [Article 8 in the final draft], and the amendment moved yesterday, viz. "That the proportion of the public expence incurred by the United States for their common defence and general welfare, to be paid by each State into the treasury, be ascertained by the value of all land within each State granted to, or surveyed for any person, as such land, and the buildings and improvements thereon shall be estimated, according to such mode as Congress shall, from time to time, direct and appoint;"

The yeas and nays being required, and the Question put

| New Hampshire, | | | Pennsylvania, | | |
|---|---|---|---|---|---|
| Mr. Folsom, | no } no | | Mr. Morris, | ay ⎫ div. | |
| Massachusetts Bay, | | | Roberdeau, | no ⎭ | |
| Mr. S. Adams, | no | | Maryland, | | |
| J. Adams, | no | | Mr. Chase, | ay | |
| Gerry, | no ⎬ no | | Smith, | ay ⎬ ay | |
| Lovell, | no | | Carroll, | ay | |
| Rhode Island, | | | Virginia, | | |
| Mr. Marchant, | no } no | | Mr. Jones, | ay | |
| Connecticut, | | | F. L. Lee, | ay ⎬ ay | |
| Mr. Dyer, | no | | R. H. Lee, | ay | |
| Law, | no ⎬ no | | North Carolina, | | |
| Williams, | no | | Mr. Penn, | ay | |
| New York, | | | Burke, | ay ⎬ ay | |
| Mr. Duane, | no ⎫ div. | | Harnett, | ay | |
| Duer, | ay ⎭ | | South Carolina, | | |
| New Jersey, | | | Mr. Middleton, | ay | |
| Mr. Witherspoon, | ay ⎫ | | Heyward, | ay ⎬ ay | |
| Elmer, | ay ⎭ | | Laurens, | ay | |

So it was resolved in the affirmative. . . .

[SATURDAY, NOVEMBER 15, 1777]

ART. 2 [analogous to Article III in the drafts of July 12 and August 20, 1776]. Each State retains its sovereignty, freedom and independence, and every power, jurisdiction, and right, which is not by this confederation expressly delegated to the United States, in Congress assembled. . . .

ART. 5 [Article XVII in the July 12 draft and Article XIII in the August 20 draft, unchanged throughout] . . .

In determining questions in the United States, in Congress assembled, each State shall have one vote. . . .

ART. 8 [Article XI in the July 12 draft and Article IX in the August 20 draft]. All charges of war and all other expences, that shall be incurred for the common defence or general welfare, and allowed by the United States, in Congress assembled, shall be defrayed out of a common treasury, which shall be supplied by the several states, in proportion to the value of all land within each State, granted to or surveyed for any person, as such land and the buildings thereon shall be estimated according to such mode as the United States, in Congress assembled, shall, from time to time, direct and appoint.

The taxes for paying that proportion shall be laid and levied by the authority and direction of the legislatures of the several states, within the time agreed upon by the United States, in Congress assembled.

ART. 9. [Article XVIII in the July 12 draft and Article XIV in the August 20 draft, and then postponed] . . .

The United States, in Congress assembled, shall also be the last resort on appeal in all disputes and differences now subsisting, or that hereafter may arise between two or more states concerning boundary, jurisdiction or any other cause whatever; which authority shall always be exercised in the manner following . . .

ART. 13 [Article XX in the July 12 draft and Article XVI in the August 20 draft]. Every State shall abide by the determinations of the United States, in Congress assembled, on all questions which, by this confederation, are submitted to them. And the articles of this confederation shall be inviolably observed by every State, and the union shall be perpetual; nor shall any alteration at any time hereafter be made in any of them, unless such alteration be agreed to in a Congress of the United States, and be afterwards confirmed by the legislatures of every State.

## 42.3

 CORNELIUS HARNETT TO RICHARD CASWELL,
OCTOBER 10, 1777

Cornelius Harnett, a merchant, was one of the more radical members of the North Carolina delegation. In April 1776, he sponsored the motion in the provincial congress to vote in Congress for independence, which led, ultimately, to his arrest by invading British forces. Here he writes from York to Governor Caswell regarding military matters, in particular the recent defeat on September 11 of Continental forces at the Battle of Brandywine Creek, and renewed congressional focus on the Articles of Confederation. He states that the "method of voting by States was yesterday determined"; since it was in fact decided on the seventh, his letter may have been written a few days earlier than the tenth. He lists, in discussing what would become Article 8 of the Articles of Confederation, the three proposals before Congress on how best to apportion to the states their part of national taxes: by population ("by the Poll"), by the value of lands, or by property in general, which was Harnett's preferred alternative. Congress, in the end, decided on surveyed land as the basis.

He points out that "the Delegates of the several States are exceedingly anxious to finish this business," for it was generally believed "that the very salvation of these States depend upon it," in particular because many of the delegates understood "that none of the European powers will publicly acknowledge them free and independent, until they are confederated." As many of the congressional moderates had counseled well into the spring and summer of 1776, the American colonies' quest for international standing depended more on unifying themselves and achieving victory in battle than it did on simply declaring independence. The necessary legal union of the independent states was four years away, while the needed battlefield victory occurred only three days later.

Paul H. Smith, ed., *Letters of Delegates to Congress, 1774–1789* (Washington, D.C.: Library of Congress, 1976–93), 8:97–98.

Sir,                                                     York Town Pennsylvania Oct. 10th. 1777

I had the honor of receiving your favour of the second of September, two days ago, and I am surprised you have not received four other of my letters since the 11th of August. I fear there is little dependence on our Post office for the safe conveyance of Intelligence. Since mine, soon after the Battle of the Brandywine nothing happened material in the movements of Genl Washington's Army, until the 4th Instant when he attacked the Enemy early in the morning. The particulars you have enclosed in an abstract from the General's letter to Congress. Poor General Nash is since dead of his wound, his thigh being shattered by a Cannon Ball. We lost several other brave officers and many wounded, the latter were all brought off the field. The Enemy as appears from a deserter had Genl Agnew, Col Bird & Col Walcot killed, with several other officers. Also Genl Sir William Erskine wounded in the head & ancle, it is said mortally. The whole loss of the Enemy by several accounts amount to about 800 killed and wounded.

I forwarded your letter to Capt Caswell by express. Our President enclosed it in his letter to the General. I have not the least doubt of his having come off unhurt. God send it may be so.

It gives me pleasure to hear Col Shephards Battalion is in such forwardness, and hope they may arrive here in time to be serviceable. Our affairs to the NorthWard wear a very promising aspect, since the late drawn Battle in that quarter, of which some time ago I gave you information. It is firmly believed Genl Burgouyn must meet with inevitable ruin. It is imagined Genl Washington intends very soon another attack on the Enemy's army. He has since that of the 4th Instant been reinforced by a large body from Virginia and Peeks Kiln. I am rejoiced to hear the Tories have been prevented from carrying their infernal plan to execution. I hope decisive measures will be adopted to bring the Ringleaders to punishment.

Congress have once more began to think of confederation, I could wish to know the sentiments of our General Assembly upon some Capital points. The method of voting by States was yesterday determined viz. that each State should have one vote, no Colony against it but Virginia. The grand point of settling the Quota of Taxes each State is to pay, comes on this afternoon. Three proposals have been made, one to tax by the Poll, another to assess the value of the Lands, and the other to assess property in general. The latter at present I think most equitable, should the confederation be agreed upon Mr Penn and myself will embrace the earliest opportunity of transmitting it to your Excellency, to be laid before the General Assembly. The Delegates of the several States are exceedingly anxious to finish this business, many assert that the very salvation of these States depend upon it; and that none of the European powers will publicly acknowledge them free and independent, until they are confederated. The time of Congress ever since my Arrival has been chiefly taken up with Army matters.

We have as yet no printing press, or Post Office established here. This will be done in a few days. I shall then have it more in my power to communicate to your Excellency every piece of interesting intelligence which comes to hand. At present I can hardly find time to write a letter, Congress sits from morning 'till night, and Committees 'till 10 & 11 Oclock. In fact I am almost tired of my troublesome office, and heartily wish to be with my family. I have not time to enlarge, but have the honor to be with respect, Your Excellency's most Obedt & very huml Servant,                    Cornl Harnett

[*P.S.*] I beg your Excellency will remember me most respectfully to your Council.

## 42.4

 CORNELIUS HARNETT TO THOMAS BURKE, NOVEMBER 13, 1777

Here Cornelius Harnett writes to his fellow North Carolinian and congressional delegate (along with John Penn) Thomas Burke to warn him that he is unlikely to find the final Articles of Confederation to his liking: "you will think it a Monster." Harnett seems skeptical of just how essential confederation is; although favoring it, he notes that "many Carry their Ideas of this Matter so far as to believe Our Affairs must be ruined without it." His words confirm that some, possibly many, in Congress didn't understand completion of the Articles to be a pressing matter. He also highlights that the New England states remained strongly opposed to the method chosen in the end for apportioning national expenses to the states, that is, by assessed land values. In a final, revealing aside, he writes of his weariness of being in Congress: "I have a great inclination to return home & wish to be in future excused from this kind of Service . . . I wish to make way for some Gentm who values his honor *in this way,* at a much higher rate than I do." Such demanding service, he suggests, was for gentlemen interested in their honor and not for men whose primary concerns were their farms, businesses, families, or God. He seems to suggest, too, that there were other men of a different stripe similarly committed to honor, most importantly those willing to risk their lives on the field of battle rather than their reputations on the floor of Congress.

Paul H. Smith, ed., *Letters of Delegates to Congress, 1774–1789* (Washington, D.C.: Library of Congress, 1976–93), 8:254–56.

Dear Sir                                                                    York Pennsylvania Novr. 13. 1777

The Child Congress has been big with these two Years past, is at last brought forth (Confederation). I fear it will by several Legislatures be thought a little deformed, you will think it a Monster. I wish however some kind of Confederation might take place, many Carry their Ideas of this Matter so far as to believe Our Affairs must be ruined without it; Be this as it may it will in a few days be sent to the Legislatures of the several States. Nothing more has been done worth your notice. Our time has been chiefly employed in Army matters and God knows we have had perplexity enough. . . .

. . . Pray let me have your opinion freely & *dispassionately* on the Articles of Confederation. The Mode of Settling the Quota on each State towards defraying the Genl. Expence has taken up much time. Some States were for the Valuation of all the property in each State; Others for fixing it by the Number of inhabitants; Others, on the Value of lands. This Last seemed to come as near the mark as any except a Valuation of all property, however the Value of Lands has taken place, much against the desire of the delegates from the Eastern States.

As I expect you will be directed to return immediately after the rising of Our Assembly, I hope you will take Care to be properly instructed in every Measure they may wish to Accomplish. You ought to be here, no State should have a less number of Delegates than three present in Congress & I hope Our State will Attend Constantly to that rule.

I have a great inclination to return home & wish to be in future excused from this kind of Service. Between you and I we shall be ruined in it, & I wish to make way for some Gentm who values his honor *in this way,* at a much higher rate than I do. I have not time to say one word more than to desire you'll make my Compliments to All my friends in Assembly. I wrote Mr. Hooper & Maclain a few days ago, & shall write them again very soon. No Post or Press as yet established here & when I meet with an Opportunity to write my friends I am obliged to do it in such hurry that I hardly know what I write. Believe me to be with unfeigned Esteem, Dr Sir, Your affect & ob Servt,                                                                    Cornl Harnett

[*P.S.*] Our very worthy friend Mrs. Trist is well at Lancaster. I just now received a line from her. I forwarded a Letter from her to you about a fortnight ago which I hope you have received.

## 42.5

 RICHARD HENRY LEE TO ROGER SHERMAN,
NOVEMBER 24, 1777

Richard Henry Lee begins his letter to Roger Sherman (absent from Congress since September) by writing of military matters, in particular Burgoyne's recent defeat, which was "no doubt of great consequence to our righteous cause." He noted the ever-expanding international character of a war that Americans today are likely to view as having taken place only in the United States and Canada. In India, Britain had experienced a setback: "'twas reported Madrass had been taken by the Natives, which had fallen India Stock." The global scope of the conflict helps explain why such a small portion of Britain's entire military might was devoted to the North American theatre. Additionally, "France, Spain, & England were preparing with all possible dispatch for War," and "five thousand troops were immediately to be sent to Martinique & Guadaloupe additional to those already there." According to Lee, the British ministry, "desperately wicked men," were "setting Europe on fire that the Smoke may cover them from the vengeance of their injured Country."

In regard to the just-finished Articles of Confederation, Lee reminded Sherman that "we must yield a little to each other, and not rigidly insist on having everything correspondent to the partial views of every State." Sherman, like all the New England delegates, was staunchly opposed to using the value of land in assessing state tax quotas and firmly supported using population as the basis instead (as Sherman had argued to Lee in a letter of November 3). Meanwhile, fully in keeping with the view of the southern delegates, Lee noted that "if we take a view of the World, we shall find that [population] numbers are by no means a just criterion to fix the relative riches of States." These different measures were trying to ascertain not anything intrinsically tied to population or some manner of popular or humanistic concern, but rather the relative wealth of each state.

What was striking about this debate was the perfect correlation between delegates of states with relatively well-developed lands and few slaves and those who argued for using population as the best measure of wealth, and between delegates of largely undeveloped states with many slaves and those who argued for using land valuation as the best way to assess wealth. Delegates made generalized arguments in defense of their states' interests but presented them as principled rather than interested. This seems to be a pattern worth keeping in mind when approaching the merits of a delegate's claims, even when made, as here, in a private letter and to someone opposed to the position being advanced.

Paul H. Smith, ed., *Letters of Delegates to Congress, 1774–1789* (Washington, D.C.: Library of Congress, 1976–93), 8:318–20. The Latin phrase *fiat justicia, ruat coelum* (properly, *fiat justitia ruat caelum*) is the legal maxim "Let justice be done though the heavens fall."

Dear Sir                                          York the 24th of November 1777.

I am much obliged to you for your favor of the 3d which I should have answered sooner if I had not been prevented by ill health and very much business.

The surrender of Burgoyne is no doubt of great consequence to our righteous cause, and I could wish it were in my power to entertain hopes of a similar event at Philadelphia. Howe has made his situation very strong by double lines and these strongly fortified. They do also contrive to get provisions up from the fleet in small Vessels by means of a channel between Province Island & Fort Island. The latter of these places having lately fallen into their hands will facilitate this business exceedingly. Yet the better opinion is, that the fleet cannot get up so long as we hold Red Bank, and the Cheveaux de Frize remain covered by the gallies. To reduce the former we hear that Cornwallis lately crossed the Delaware with 3000 men. We are very strong at that place, fully so I hope to give his Lordship a sound drubbing. We every day expect important news from thence.

We have just received a letter from Mr. Bingham at Martinique, covering one from Mr. Carmichael at Paris dated June 25 & July 6. Mr. Bingham's letter is dated the 13th of October. Mr. Carmichael tells us that Dr. Lee is returning from Berlin having finished his business successfully at the Court of Prussia. That the English could get no foreigners to assist making up their last Loan, altho' the terms were higher than usual. That 'twas reported Madrass had been taken by the Natives, which had fallen India Stock. That France, Spain, & England were preparing with all possible dispatch for War, and that he thought it was inevitable. Mr. Bingham says the General of Martinique had just received information from the French Ministry Sept 4 that demand was made upon England for a delivery of all the French Vessels captured by the English without the limits prescribed by treaty for bounding the approach of foreign Vessels to the Shores of British America, and if this demand was not complied with the Ambassador was to leave the Court of London. That the General had orders to put the Island in a posture for immediate war, and to prevent the sailing of all Ships bound to Europe by Embargo least they should fall into the enemies hands. Five thousand troops were immediately to be sent to Martinique & Guadaloupe additional to those already there. Mr. Bingham further informs that the Ministerial Writers in England were endeavouring to raise the National cry for a War with France, meaning to secure personal safety at the risk of National ruin. Thus these desperately wicked men are for setting Europe on fire that the Smoke may cover them from the vengeance of their injured Country. These are good presages for us but yet I cannot help being astonished at the horrid iniquity of these Wretches. We have finished the Confederation and it will go forward to the States in a few days, with strong exhortation to consider and return it quickly. In this great business dear Sir we must yield a little to each other, and not rigidly insist on having every thing correspondent to the partial views of every State. On such terms we can never confederate. If we take a view of the World, we shall find that numbers are by no means a just criterion to fix the relative riches of States. Of old times take Tyre and Scythia, Germany and Carthage. In Modern look at Holland & Poland, England & Germany. But the truth is, that let wealth flow into a Country from whatever source, it will forever reflect value on the lands of that Country and they rise in value in proportion to the influx of wealth. Thus the value of lands in England has doubled & tripled as commerce has brought wealth into the Island. For my own part, I doubt extremely whether Virginia will not pay more by the present Mode than if it had been determinable by numbers. But I am satisfied that the mode now fixt is the most just, and so fiat justicia, ruat coelum. We have recommended extensive taxation, sinking the provincial currencies, and regulating prices. I think that if the States will vigorously execute the recommendations of Congress, we shall, under providence, be a safe and happy people.

My ill state of health will compel me soon to return home for the winter season. I shall be particularly happy to hear from you, as well before as after you get to Congress, and for this purpose you will please direct to me at Chantilly Westmoreland County, to the care of the Post Master at Leeds Town in King George County Virginia. I live at some distance from the line of Post, and therefore propose to send weekly to the Office for such letters as my friends may favour me with.

I am, with sentiments of esteem and regard, Sir your most obedient Servant,

Richard Henry Lee . . .

## 43. CONTINUING DIFFICULTIES IN OVERSEEING THE CONTINENTAL ARMY, DECEMBER 1777

Late in the fall of 1777, General Washington, after being defeated at Germantown, withdrew his army northwestward to take up winter quarters at Valley Forge, Pennsylvania. At about the same time, on December 10, Congress expressed its "deep concern, that the principal supplies for the army under his command have, since the loss of Philadelphia, been drawn from distant quarters, whereby great expence has accrued to the public." Accordingly, Congress ordered Washington to exercise the extraordinary powers granted him earlier in the year—on September 17 and October 8—to obtain food and other supplies for his army from the surrounding countryside and thereby, prevent those same supplies from being sold to the British forces.[93] Washington responded that he had strenuously tried to extract needed materials from those living in proximity to his camp, but as he was to discover ever more starkly over the next several months, "they preferred to sell their provisions for British gold than for depreciated Continental money." The inability to secure stores locally only heightened his concern for his "'naked, and distressed Soldier,'" whom he pitied, but whose condition it was not in his "'power to relieve or prevent.'"[94]

On December 12, 1777, Congress appointed a committee of three to consider a number of letters, including one from Samuel A. Otis, the deputy clothier general. On this committee were William Duer, Francis Lightfoot Lee, and Francis Dana of Massachusetts, a moderate lawyer who had traveled privately to England to negotiate a plan of reconciliation between the colonies and Great Britain. Although less flamboyant than his brother and fellow delegate R. H. Lee, Francis Lightfoot had been no less an ardent supporter of independence. On December 16, the committee brought in a report. The next day, it was considered and recommitted, and a fourth member was added to the committee, Elbridge Gerry of Massachusetts. The group was "instructed to prepare a circular letter to the states to accompany the resolutions of Congress." Finally, on December 20, the recommitted report and accompanying circular letter were "taken into consideration" and approved.[95]

Congress, in its resolutions, requested that the states enact laws "appointing suitable persons to seize and take, for the use of the continental army of the said states, all woollen cloths, blankets, linens, shoes, stockings, hats, and other necessary articles of cloathing, suitable for the army, which may be in the possession of any persons inhabitants of, or residents within, their respective states, for the purpose of sale and not for their own private use or family consumption." The former owners were to be provided "certificates or receipts for the same." This particular resolution did not extend to noncitizens, who were to be protected from having their property seized. The resolution was issued in conjunction with the same authority being given to General Washington on December 10 and later on the thirtieth.

Congress also recommended that the states encourage a greater production of clothing and discourage those "assiduously endeavouring, by every means of oppression, sharping, and extortion, to accumulate enormous gain to themselves." To control such behavior, Congress "most seriously recommended" that the state legislatures "enact laws, limiting the number of retailers of goods . . . and obliging them to take license and enter into bonds for the observance of all laws made for their regulation." Patriotic enthusiasm, it seems, was insufficient motivation.

In a related concern, Congress believed that "emissaries and abettors of General Howe" in America were working "to spread disaffection, intimidate the people by false news, [and] depreciate the currency." "To prevent these mischiefs," Congress encouraged each state's chief executive "to cause all persons whose character and business is not well known and approved of, to be apprehended"; if unable to "give a good and satisfactory account of themselves," they were "to return to their own states, or be confined in gaol." Congress, clearly concerned about the distressing circumstances of the Continental Army at Valley Forge and the violent occurrences in the area known as the "neutral ground"—where patriot and loyalist forces attacked, ransacked, foraged, and spied on each other[96]—was willing to recommend that the states take coercive measures. Private property could be seized, and those suspected of lacking enthusiasm for the American war effort could be detained, expelled, or arrested. Earlier in the summer, Congress had recommended that numerous prominent Quakers, who were well known as pacifists, in and around Philadelphia be sent to Virginia for the duration of the war.[97]

In its circular letter to state executives that was to accompany the resolutions, Congress explains that these measures were necessary because of the "avarice of the times," and that "laws unworthy the character of infant republics are become necessary to supply the defect of public virtue, and to correct the vices of some of her sons." Borrowing language that Britain might have once used, Congress explained that it was "called upon by the grand principle of self preservation, to guard against . . . parricide." The public support that congressional radicals claimed in 1776 to have developed in the mid-Atlantic region had, it seemed, precipitously declined. In fairness to one of the congressional radicals, John Adams had predicted as much in a letter of April 1776 to Mercy Warren (see document 30.6). In a more optimistic vein, Congress hoped "that the wise and spirited laws of the different states, aided by the influence and exertions of the real patriots, will apply effectual remedies to these alarming evils."

The deadly circumstances of the Continental Army at Valley Forge demonstrated both the powerful commitment of those soldiers and officers to the American cause and the lack of any "national" feeling among far too many citizens, who were little willing to make needed sacrifices. As noted by one commentator, "No episode of the history of the Revolution affords a finer example of patriotic sacrifice than the winter's encampment at Valley Forge; but why were the sufferings at Valley Forge encountered? Simply because the country at large, with whatever excuses, did not support the war, and the army which was waging it. . . . Clothes and shoes and blankets and tents were lacking."[98] Remarkably, even those most fervently committed to the emerging nation's struggles, such as Thomas Jefferson, as seen below, seemed distracted at times by purely personal concerns during this time of trial.

43.1

RESOLUTIONS ON SUPPLYING THE NEEDS OF THE
CONTINENTAL ARMY AND AN ACCOMPANYING CIRCULAR
LETTER TO THE STATES, DECEMBER 20, 1777

Worthington Chauncey Ford et al., eds., *Journals of the Continental Congress, 1774–1789* (Washington, D.C.: Government Printing Office, 1904–37), 9:1042–47.

The committee to whom was re-committed the report of the committee on the letters from S. A. Otis, brought in their report, which was taken into consideration; Whereupon,

*Resolved,* 1. That it be most earnestly recommended to the respective legislatures of the United States, forthwith to enact laws, appointing suitable persons to seize and take, for the use of the continental army of the said states, all woollen cloths, blankets, linens, shoes, stockings, hats, and other necessary articles of cloathing, suitable for the army, which may be in the possession of any persons inhabitants of, or residents within, their respective states, for the purpose of sale and not for their own private use or family consumption, giving them certificates or receipts for the same, expressing the quantity and quality of the goods; provided, that such laws do not extend to any goods, wares, or merchandise which are, or shall be, *bona fide,* imported into the respective states on account of any persons not citizens of any of these United States, so long as the same shall continue their property, and no longer: and that they inflict such penalties as may be deemed proper on such persons possessed of any of the above enumerated goods, wares, and merchandise, or other articles of cloathing suitable for the army, who, to evade the good intention of the said laws, shall falsely affirm or declare the same to be the property of persons not citizens of any of the said United States. . . .

5. And whereas, great waste of cloathing has arisen from the want of fidelity or skill in the persons employed to make up the same:

*Resolved,* That it be recommended to the respective states to appoint one or more suitable persons to superintend and direct the tradesmen employed to make up the cloaths to be collected as aforesaid, who shall conform themselves to the instructions of the Board of War relative to the form thereof, provided that no delays be suffered to take place from the want of such instructions.

6. And whereas, the comfortable support of the army of these states may hereafter greatly depend on the supplies which they may be able to draw from their own internal resources; it is therefore most earnestly recommended to the said states, to employ a sufficient number of manufacturers and tradesmen to supply the cloathing wanted for their respective batallions, exempting them, under proper regulations, from military duty; and authorizing suitable persons to collect and supply, at the stipulated prices, cotton, wool, flax, leather, and other articles for carrying on the said manufactures.

7. And whereas, certain persons, devoid of, and in repugnance to every principle of public virtue and humanity, instigated by the lust of avarice, are, in each State, assiduously endeavouring, by every means of oppression, sharping, and extortion, to accumulate enormous gain to themselves, to the great distress of private families in general, and especially of the poorer and more dependent part of the community, as well as to the great injury of the public service. For the effectual suppression of such nefarious practices it is most seriously recommended to the several legislatures aforesaid, forthwith to enact laws, limiting the number of retailers of goods, wares, and merchandise in their several counties, towns, and districts, and obliging them to take license and enter into bonds for the observance of all laws made for their regulation; to make provision in the said laws that no person be allowed to sell by wholesale except the importer, and he only to persons having such licenses, or the certificates hereafter mentioned; and that

such of their inhabitants as are not licensed as aforesaid, be restrained from purchasing a greater quantity of such goods, wares, or merchandise than is requisite for their own private or family's use or consumption. And that it be farther recommended to the several states to prohibit any persons whatever, not citizens of their respective states, to purchase within the same, any articles of cloathing or provision necessary for the use of the army, (unless so much as may be requisite for their own private or family's use or consumption,) excepting only such person or persons as shall produce a certificate, under the seal and sign manual of the supreme executive authority of the respective states, purporting that the said person or persons are employed or permitted to make purchases either on account of the public or for the use or benefit of the inhabitants of the State of which he or they are members; and to inflict such punishment upon all atrocious offenders before described, as shall brand them with indelible infamy.

8. And whereas, there is good reason to apprehend that many of the emissaries and abettors of General Howe are dispersed through the United States, under various pretences of amusement or business, whereby they are enabled to spread disaffection, intimidate the people by false news, depreciate the currency of the United States, and avoid serving in the militia, or paying their fines; to prevent these mischiefs it is most earnestly recommended to the supreme executive power of each State, to take the most effectual measures to cause all persons whose character and business is not well known and approved of, to be apprehended, and if they cannot give a good and satisfactory account of themselves, that they be obliged immediately to return to their own states, or be confined in gaol.

The committee having prepared a circular letter to accompany the foregoing resolutions, submitted it to Congress, and the same being read, and approved, is as follows:

SIR: I am directed by Congress to transmit to your honorable body the enclosed resolutions, which the pressing wants of the army, and the arts and avarice of engrossers and extortioners have rendered indispensably necessary to the general welfare.

It is with deep concern that Congress, after having for some time contemplated, in painful silence, the mischiefs which threatened this extended Continent from the growing avarice of the times, feel themselves constrained to recommend measures which the virtue of all classes of men rendered not long since unnecessary, and which a scrupulous regard for security of property to every citizen of these states has hitherto restrained from adopting. But, unhappy the case of America! laws unworthy the character of infant republics are become necessary to supply the defect of public virtue, and to correct the vices of some of her sons; and she is called upon by the grand principle of self preservation, to guard against the parricide of those whom she has fostered in her own bosom.

To minds whose reflections are employed on the importance of the cause in which we are engaged, and which feel for every circumstance which may affect the honour and safety of these states, it must give the most painful sensations to consider that, at a time when the late signal successes we have been blest with, the reduced numbers of the

enemy, the difficulties they meet with in procuring foreign levies, and the political complexion of affairs in Europe, have deprived Britain of many of those resources on which
she so much depended; when the numbers and improving discipline of our army, the
prodigious augmentation of our military stores, the quantity of provisions with which
this country abounds, and the large supplies of cloathing which have of late been imported by private persons, afford not only the opportunity but the means, under Divine
Providence, of establishing our liberties by a few exertions; this bright prospect should
be clouded over, and this great and glorious event endangered by the languor of too
many, and by the arts and avarice of designing individuals, who, like the British nabobs
of the east, are corrupting the manners of a whole nation, and building vast fortunes on
the destruction of the liberties of the western world.

It is to be hoped, however, that the wise and spirited laws of the different states, aided
by the influence and exertions of the real patriots, will apply effectual remedies to these
alarming evils; that the old and hardened offenders will be punished; that those in
whose bosoms the sparks of public virtue are not yet extinguished, will be reclaimed,
the languid roused from their present apathy; and that all classes of men will unite with
their former spirit and virtue against an enemy whose progress is marked with every
vestige of barbarity, and whose determined object is to establish a tyranny of the most
dangerous and debasing nature over the inhabitants of a vast Continent.

Congress flatter themselves that the resolutions herewith transmitted will tend to accomplish some of these valuable purposes, and they therefore esteem it their duty to
recommend them to the serious consideration of your honorable house, and hope they
will be carried into execution as secretly and expeditiously as possible.

By order of Congress.

43.2

##  JOHN HARVIE TO THOMAS JEFFERSON, DECEMBER 29, 1777

Here John Harvie, a lawyer and Virginia congressional delegate, writes to Thomas
Jefferson, who last attended Congress on September 2, 1776. Jefferson preferred to
remain in Virginia while revising the laws of the state as part of a five-man board in
the House of Delegates. His committee made its recommendations in June 1778; an
impressive one hundred of them were approved. Writing from Congress while in
York, Harvie describes for Jefferson the rampant greed of those in the area surrounding Congress, in southeast Pennsylvania and due west of Valley Forge: "The Avarice
and disaffection of the people here is so great that they refuse any price that we can
give for the Necessary provisions for the Army." Indeed, he claims that avarice

threatens the states "with Inevitable Destruction unless his Carrier is Immediately Check'd by the joint Efforts of the United States."

More generally to be overcome was the continued disaffection of those in the area to the American cause. According to Harvie, Maryland and Delaware deserved the same execration as Pennsylvania: "Two thirds of the State of Delaware are Notoriously known in their Hearts to be with our Enemys. They have not at present the Shadow of Government amongst them and their Representation to Congress has been withdrawn a Considerable time." Maryland had pulled its congressional delegates even earlier. None of this should have been surprising, given the persistent divisions in Congress and the limited support for independence evinced by the mid-Atlantic colonies, "Execrable States" that "Clogg the Operations of the Continent in an Alarming Degree." He wonders whether Congress would be justified "in persueing such Measures as will Eventually save this Continent from perdition?" Yet he can't help worrying about the effects of intrusive congressional measures on states and individuals; like Thomas Burke, he reveres "the Sovereignity of the States and the Civil rights of the people as much as any man living."

Harvie was also concerned about the lack in Congress of men of "the First Characters." Why couldn't such men—including possibly Jefferson—"be prevail'd upon to give their attendance in Congress" for a few months? Against the background of the desperate needs of the Continental Army at Valley Forge and Harvie's concern about self-interested behavior, he awkwardly wrote of his difficulty in finding appropriately skilled workmen who would settle for "moderate compensation" when fulfilling Jefferson's private building needs. Harvie still hoped to find such men among the British prisoners in Maryland or Virginia. Also somewhat in tension with earlier remarks about the need to sacrifice, but reminiscent of Cornelius Harnett's letter to Burke (see document 42.4), Harvie wrote that his own situation in York was disagreeable because of his limited wealth and his need to care for his wife and children: "There is a duty oweing to them as well as to my Country." This tension was neither new nor soon to disappear.

Paul H. Smith, ed., *Letters of Delegates to Congress, 1774–1789* (Washington, D.C.: Library of Congress, 1976–93), 8:493–96.

Dear Sir                                                York Town December the 29th 1777
Your Letter of November the 26th was handed to me by the post before the last. The great Objects of the Assemblys Deliberations are of the most Interesting Nature and I have no Doubt they will bring them to Maturity with their Usual Wisdom. If the late Generous Spirit of Virginia in their Act for Cloathing and Measures for preventing of Forestalling does not Inspire the other States with a Virtuous Emulation the Avarice of

Individuals will be more Fatal to the Liberties of America than the Sword of the Enemy. I have a great while past Shudder'd at the Rapid Strides of this Monster in Society, but lately he has broke through every feeble Fort Opps'd to him, and threatens us with Inevitable Destruction unless his Carrier is Immediately Check'd by the joint Efforts of the United States. In Short the Avarice and disaffection of the people here is so great that they refuse any price that we can give for the Necessary provisions for the Army, and the Generals last Letter Couch'd in terms Strong and pathetic holds out a probability of the Armys Desolveing unless they are more fully and Constantly Supplied. You would Execrate this State if you were in it. The Supporters of this Government are a set of Weak men without any Weight of Character. No kind of Respect is paid by the people either to their Laws or Advice, and instead of Checking they in many Instances Countenance the Exactions of their Constituents being otherwise fearful of looseing their present Shadow of power. Two thirds of the State of Delaware are Notoriously known in their Hearts to be with our Enemys. They have not at present the Shadow of Government amongst them and their Representation to Congress has been withdrawn a Considerable time before I had a Seat in it. From this you must foresee that these Execrable States Clogg the Operations of the Continent in an Alarming Degree. Then what is to be done? Are we with this Conviction upon our Minds to suffer them for the want of Virtue and Vigour in their Governments to Involve the whole in the Worst of Calamitys or will not Congress be Justifyable (from the Necessity of the Case as Guardians to the Sacred rights of the people at large) in persueing such Measures as will Eventually save this Continent from perdition? The feelings of my own Heart tells me they will. Yet I Revere the Sovereignity of the States and the Civil rights of the people as much as any man liveing who is not Capable of more refin'd and deeper reflections than myself, such I acknowledge see things of this Dilicate Nature in a more Enlarged Comprehensive point of View and by such I Ardently wish to be Instructed. Indeed my Honored Friend for such I esteem you, the present State and Condition of this Continent, Oweing to the Alarming disaffection in this Quarter, an Almost Universal discontent in the Army, a Reformation therein Meditated by Congress to Commence and be Carry'd into Effect this Winter with Numberless other Matters that I am not at Liberty to disclose even to you, requires the Wisdom of the first Characters amongst us to give them weight and Efficacy. Then why cant some of those who so fully come under this Description be prevail'd upon to give their attendance in Congress if it was only for a few Months? I am sure you know me two well to Impute this Earnestness to Unworthy Motives. It arises from the purest Intentions for the Interests of my Country. It would be Stupid Vanity in me not to be Sensible of my own lack of Abilitys to Constitute a Member of this August Assembly with Reputation to myself and Service to the publick, and other States in part of their Delegation equally Experience this Misfortune.

Your Supply of Cloathing came very Opportunely to Cover the Shivering Limbs of our poor Naked Soldiers. Thousands of them are now in the Hospitals for the want of even Wrags to keep them from the Cold. We hear Two Hundred thousand pounds worth of Goods (at Exorbitant prices) has been purchased in the Masachusets. We hope they will be soon forwarded to the Army.

There is no late Interesting Intelligence from either of our Army's. General Washingtons is now in Forge Valley about twenty three Miles from Philadelphia where they will probably remain Inactive the greatest part of the Winter. The Waste of the Enemy wherever they move is a Scene of Cruelty and distress. This dreadful Calamity is only Alleviated to the Whig by seeing the Torys property made one Common Ruin with his own, for all their late Ravages is Indiscriminate.

It would take a much wiser man than me to Unravel the Misterious Conduct of the French Court. They have not yet given us any publick Avowal of their patronage. Our Commissioners are never Admitted to publick or private Audiences with their Ministers. What little Business they transact with them is by the Aid of a third person and their Scanty Supplies to us seem to be Conducted with Timidity Caution and Secrecy. Some Weeks past we daily expected to hear that they had taken a dicisive part for us, but our last Letters Advise us Not to be two Sanguine in our Expectations of Foreign Assistance but to place our Security in our own Resources with this only exception that a Capital Advantage over our Enemys in the Feild may give a different Turn to the refin'd politics in Europe and Operate powerfully in our favour. This we have Obtain'd in the Surrender of Burgoyne of which the French Court are now or must Shortly be Acquainted. It is only to you that I Communicate any thing of this Nature that can have the least Tendency to Damp the Ardour or Expectations of our Countrymen.

I have wrote to a gentleman of my Acquaintance in Lancaster to endeavour to find out and procure the Workmen you desire if to be had in that Town, there being none such that will engage in this. I have not received his Answer but have but little expectations from his Enquirys, as a Tradesmans prospects here is not a Moderate Compensation for his Labour. Nothing less than a small Fortune made without Merrit or trouble will Content him. I am told there is amongst the British prisoners in Maryland or Virginia some expert Workmen of the Trades you want. I have written to the Commissary of prisoners to Acquaint me with their Names and the Places of their confinement. My design after Obtaining proper Information is to Get a permission from the Board of War for you to Employ such of them as you think proper, which I shall in due time Inclose you. This I think will be the Cheapest and probably the most Convenient way for you to Carry on your Buildings but of this you are the only proper Judge. Drums for our Militia has been an Object of my Enquirys since I first came here. They are not to be had on any Terms whatever. Our State is at present unrepresented, Mr. Jones having left us a few days ago. Our Assembly was kind to him. I wish they would Confer the same favour on another of their Servants. Indeed my Situation is disagreable here besides you knowing my very Narrow Fortune may Immagine that sometimes the Cares of a Husband and parent tell me there is a duty oweing to them as well as to my Country. I beseech you not to Consider this Sentiment as ariseing from a littleness of Soul or a Sordid Spirit, but I could not be just to the Woman who from much higher Expectations devoted herself to me if I now altogether Neglected the Interests of her and the little pledges she has presented me with. The Complication of this Letter will Convince you of the respect I must have for the man to whom I open my whole Soul without Ceremony, Punctilio or Reserve.

Jno. Harvie

43.3

# Committee on Emergency Provisions to Thomas Wharton, December 30, 1777

On December 26, a committee of three was formed to respond to two letters from General Washington, dated December 22 and 23 and containing sundry enclosed papers, in which Washington graphically described the dire needs of the Continental Army. The committee was made up of William Duer, John Witherspoon, and John Harvie. Three days later, this committee was dismissed and the letters were referred to the Board of War. To its nine members (including Duer, Harvie, and Witherspoon) were added three others: Cornelius Harnett, Elbridge Gerry, and Abraham Clark of New Jersey. This larger committee was "fully empowered to take the necessary measures for supplying the army with provisions and other necessaries."[99] As a result of actions taken by the committee, the immediate needs of the Continental Army were relieved, but not its longer-term ones.[100]

Writing to Thomas Wharton, Jr., of Pennsylvania, a prominent Quaker merchant who was serving as Pennsylvania's first president, the committee looked forward to his cooperation even as it warned that the army would be sending out patrols "to collect such Cattle, Flour & Grain as the Army wants without the least Delay as the Crisis is too alarming to admit of the Business being postponed on any Consideration." Until the government of Pennsylvania showed that it could fulfill such requisitions, the committee would "be obliged to give Orders for the taking, conveying & driving all Cattle, Hogs, Pork, Flour & Grain fit for their Consumption to the Army"; the owners of the commandeered stock and stores would be given certificates for their value.

For a Congress committed to maintaining the sovereignty of the states, this fiat was a remarkable assertion of executive power, one resting on little or no legal or constitutional foundation. Unsurprisingly, more than a few of the farmers in the surrounding area, not known for their commitment to the American cause in the first place, took "umbrage" at the forced sell of their livestock and grain for unspecified prices to be paid in the future in a deeply depreciated Continental currency. This extension of congressional power, difficult to defend in law, was surely no more agreeable to those on the receiving end of its strictures than the threat of less onerous parliamentary taxation had been a decade earlier to outraged American colonists.

Paul H. Smith, ed., *Letters of Delegates to Congress, 1774–1789* (Washington, D.C.: Library of Congress, 1976–93), 8:499–502.

Sir                                                 War Office Decr. 30th. 1777

Congress have received such unexpected & distressing Accounts from the General relative to the Situation of the Army that they have appointed a Comittee to fall upon immediate Methods for Supplying them with Provisions. They are so much in Want of an instant Supply owing to Delays & Embarrassments in the Commissary's Department & other unexpected Causes that however plenty we shall have them in future, at present at least a Removal out of this State must be the immediate Consequence of even a short Continuance of their present Circumstances. An instant Supply must be procured from this State for the Support of the Army until the Supplies expected from the neighbouring States arrive. As it may give Umbrage to the Inhabitants the Committee deplore the Necessity *they* are under of sending Officers with Parties to collect such Cattle, Flour & Grain as the Army wants without the least Delay as the Crisis is too alarming to admit of the Business being postponed on any Consideration. It will be improper to communicate the real Situation of the Army but with the Utmost Prudence & Caution. Your Excellency will therefore judge in what Manner the Concurrence of this State is to be procured as their vigorous Exertions are necessary in Cooperation with those of the Committee who will, at least 'til they see the Business properly conducted as doubtless it will be by the Government of this State, be obliged to give Orders for the taking, conveying & driving all Cattle, Hogs, Pork, Flour & Grain fit for their Consumption to the Army the Persons employed for this Purpose giving Certificates to the Owners expressing as nearly as possible the Weight & Quality of them & agreeing to pay for them at such Prices as shall be settled by the Convention of Committees from the several States who are to meet at New Haven the 15th of Jany next agreeable to a Resolution of Congress of the 22d Novr last.

I have the Honour to be, with great Respect, Your very obed Servt,

Francis Lightfoot Lee, for the Committee

[*P.S.*] The Committee request you will be pleased to inform them whether the Proclamation ordering the Inhabitants of York & Cumberland Counties to thresh out their Grain has been issued.

# APPENDIX

## Four Additional Documents,
## Informative but Off-Stage

This appendix contains four additional documents that readers might find helpful to an understanding of the tragic drama that resulted in Congress' declaration of independence, the creation of thirteen republics, and the ratification on March 1, 1781, of a loosely confederated central plan of government. Though each might have been included in the body of the book, for one reason or another I decided that none was central to the unfolding of the drama, and have therefore placed them here.

Benjamin Franklin's Articles of Confederation (document 44.1) was one of two or three prominent proposed plans for confederating the colonies and/or the states; another was written by Silas Deane of Connecticut, probably a bit later than Franklin's. Neither proposal, however, was ever considered by Congress or seems to have had any influence on John Dickinson's July 1776 Committee draft of the Articles. The copy of the Declaration of Independence (document 45.1), unlike the final product reproduced in document 33, makes visible editorial and substantive changes introduced by Congress to Thomas Jefferson's Committee draft, while document 46.1 contains the full text of the Articles of Confederation and Perpetual Union that Congress agreed to on November 15, 1777, and finally ratified on March 1, 1781. Finally, the Royal Instructions to the Carlisle Peace Commission (document 47.1) represent, following the American victory at Saratoga and the offer of French recognition and a treaty of alliance, the last effort made by the British to preserve their imperial ties to their former colonies. This document is especially illuminating because of what the British were willing to offer as inducements for a return of the colonies to the Empire—almost everything the colonists had asked for, but not all that had led them to separate—and, possibly still more illuminating, for what they were not willing, even while confronting the possibility of defeat, to concede. The last two documents take the reader well beyond the close of the drama described in this volume.

## 44.1

# BENJAMIN FRANKLIN, ARTICLES OF CONFEDERATION, JULY 21, 1775

Worthington Chauncey Ford et al., eds., *Journals of the Continental Congress, 1774–1789* (Washington, D.C.: Government Printing Office, 1904–37), 2:195–99

~~Ordered, That the resolves respecting the militia be immediately published.~~

Agreeable to the standing order, the Congress resolved itself into a Committee of the whole, to take into consideration the state of America, and after some time spent therein, the president resumed the chair, and Mr. [Samuel] Ward reported, that the Committee had come to certain resolutions, which he read, and desired leave to sit again.

*Franklin's Articles of Confederation*

Articles of Confederation and perpetual Union, entred into ~~agre~~ *proposed* by the Delegates of the several Colonies of New Hampshire, &c, in general Congress met at Philadelphia, May 10, 1775.

### ART. I.

The Name of this Confederacy shall henceforth be *The United Colonies of North America.*

### ART. II.

The said United Colonies hereby severally enter into a firm League of Friendship with each other, binding on themselves and their Posterity, for their common Defence ~~and Offence,~~ against their Enemies for the Security of their Liberties and Propertys, the Safety of their Persons and Families, and their ~~common and~~ mutual and general Welfare.

### ART. III.

That each Colony shall enjoy and retain as much as it may think fit of its own present Laws, Customs, Rights, ~~and~~ Privileges, and peculiar Jurisdictions within its own Limits; and may amend its own Constitution as shall seem best to its own Assembly or Convention.

### ART. IV.

That for the more convenient Management of general Interests, Delegates shall be annually elected in each Colony to meet in General Congress at such Time and Place as shall be agreed on in ~~each~~ the next preceding Congress. Only where particular Circumstances do not make a Deviation necessary, it is understood to be a Rule, that each succeeding Congress be held in a different Colony till the whole Number be gone through, and so in perpetual Rotation; and that accordingly the next Congress after the present shall be held ~~in the~~ at Annapolis in Maryland.

## ART V.

That the Power and Duty of the Congress shall extend to the Determining on War and Peace, to sending and receiving ambassadors, and entering into Alliances, [the Reconciliation with Great Britain;] the Settling all Disputes and Differences between Colony and Colony about Limits or any other cause if such should arise; and the Planting of new Colonies when proper.

The Congress shall also make ~~and propose~~ such general ~~Regulations~~ Ordinances as tho' necessary to the General Welfare, particular Assemblies ~~from their local Circum~~ cannot be competent to; viz. ~~such as may relate to~~ those that may relate to our general Commerce; or general Currency; to the Establishment of Posts; and the Regulation of our common Forces. The Congress shall also have the Appointment of all General Officers, civil and military, appertaining to the general Confederacy, such as General Treasurer, Secretary, &c.

## ART. VI.

All Charges of Wars, and all other general Expences to be incurr'd for the common Welfare, shall be defray'd out of a common Treasury, which is to be supply'd by each Colony in proportion to its Number of Male Polls between 16 and 60 Years of Age; the Taxes for paying that proportion are to be laid and levied by the Laws of each Colony. ~~And all Advantages gained at a common Expence.~~

## ART. VII.

The Number of Delegates to be elected and sent to the Congress by each Colony, shall be regulated from time to time by the Number of such Polls return'd; so as that one Delegate be allowed for every [5000] Polls. And the Delegates are to bring with them to every Congress, an authenticated Return of the number of Polls in the respective Provinces which is to be annually triennially taken for the Purposes above mentioned.

## ART. VIII.

At every Meeting of the Congress One half of the Members return'd exclusive of Proxies be necessary to make a Quorum, and Each Delegate at the Congress, shall have a Vote in all Cases; and if necessarily absent, shall be allowed to appoint any other Delegate from the same Colony to be his Proxy, who may vote for him.

## ART. IX.

An executive Council shall be appointed by the Congress out of their own Body, consisting of [12] Persons; of whom in the first Appointment one Third, viz. [4], shall be for one year, [4] for two Years, and [4] for three Years; and as the said Terms expire, the Vacancy shall be filled by Appointments for three Years, whereby One Third of the Members will be changed annually. And each Person who has served the said Term of three Years as Counsellor, shall have a Respite of three Years, before he can be elected again. ~~The Appointments to be determined by Ballot.~~ This Council (of whom two thirds shall be a Quorum,) in the Recess of the Congress, is to execute what shall have been enjoin'd thereby; to manage the general continental Business and Interests to receive Applications from foreign Countries; to prepare Matters for the Consideration of the Congress; to fill up [*Pro tempore*] ~~general~~ continental Offices that fall vacant; and to draw on the General Treasurer for such Monies as may be necessary for general Services, & appropriated by the Congress to such Services.

### Art. X.

No Colony shall engage in an offensive War with any Nation of Indians without the Consent of the Congress, or great Council above mentioned, who are first to consider the Justice and Necessity of such War.

### Art. XI.

A perpetual Alliance offensive and defensive, is to be enter'd into as soon as may be with the Six Nations; their Limits to be ascertain'd and secur'd to them; their Land not to be encroach'd on, nor any private or Colony Purchases made of them hereafter to be held good; nor any Contract for Lands to be made but between the Great Council of the Indians at Onondaga and the General Congress. The Boundaries and Lands of all the other Indians shall also be ascertain'd and secur'd to them in the same manner; and Persons appointed to reside among them in proper Districts, who shall take care to prevent Injustice in the Trade with them, and be enabled at our general Expence by occasional small Supplies, to relieve their personal Wants and Distresses. And all Purchases from them shall be by the ~~General~~ Congress for the General Advantage and Benefit of the United Colonies.

### Art. XII.

As all new Institutions ~~are Subject to~~ may have Imperfections which only Time and Experience can discover, it is agreed, That the general Congress from time to time shall propose such Amendments of this Constitution as ~~they~~ may be found necessary; which being approv'd by a Majority of the Colony Assemblies, shall be equally binding with the rest of the Articles of this Confederation.

### Art. XIII.

Any ~~other~~ and every Colony from Great Britain upon the Continent of North America and not at present engag'd in our Association ~~shall~~ may upon Application and joining the said Association be receiv'd into this Confederation, viz. [Ireland] the West India Islands, Quebec, St. Johns, Nova Scotia, Bermudas, and the East and West Floridas; and shall thereupon be entitled to all the Advantages of our Union, mutual Assistance and Commerce.

These Articles shall be propos'd to the several Provincial Conventions or Assemblies, to be by them consider'd, and if approv'd they are advis'd to impower their Delegates to agree to and ratify the same in the ensuing Congress. After which the *Union* thereby establish'd is to continue firm till the Terms of Reconciliation proposed in the Petition of the last Congress to the King are agreed to; till the Acts since made restraining the American Commerce and Fisheries are repeal'd; till Reparation is made for the Injury done to Boston by shutting up its Port; for the Burning of Charlestown; and for the Expence of this unjust War; and till all the British Troops are withdrawn from America. On the Arrival of these Events the Colonies [shall] return to their former Connection and Friendship with Britain: But on Failure thereof this Confederation is to be perpetual.

45.1

## The Declaration of Independence in Thomas Jefferson's Notes, July 1–4, 1776

Paul H. Smith, ed., *Letters of Delegates to Congress, 1774–1789* (Washington, D.C.: Library of Congress, 1976–93), 4:360–65. Material inserted by Congress into Jefferson's draft is here placed in braces rather than, as Jefferson suggests, in the margin.

As the sentiments of men are known not only by what they receive, but what they reject also, I will state the form of the declaration as originally reported. The parts struck out by Congress shall be distinguished by a black line drawn under them; & those inserted by them shall be placed in the margin or in a concurrent column.

A Declaration by the representatives of the United States of America, in General Congress assembled

When in the course of human events it becomes necessary for one people to dissolve the political bands which have connected them with another, and to assume among the powers of the earth the separate & equal station to which the laws of nature and of nature's god entitle them, a decent respect to the opinions of mankind requires that they should declare the causes which impel them to the separation.

We hold these truths to be self evident: that all men are created equal; that they are endowed by their creator with {certain} inherent and inalienable rights; that among these are life, liberty & the pursuit of happiness: that to secure these rights, governments are instituted among men, deriving their just powers from the consent of the governed; that whenever any form of government becomes destructive of these ends, it is the right of the people to alter or to abolish it, & to institute new government, laying it's foundation on such principles, & organising it's powers in such form, as to them shall seem most likely to effect their safety & happiness. Prudence indeed will dictate that governments long established should not be changed for light & transient causes; and accordingly all experience hath shewn that mankind are more disposed to suffer while evils are sufferable than to right themselves by abolishing the forms to which they are accustomed. But when a long train of abuses & usurpations [begun at a distinguished period and] pursuing invariably the same object, evinces a design to reduce them under absolute despotism it is their right, it is their duty to throw off such government, & to provide new guards for their future security. Such has been the patient sufferance of these colonies; & such is now the necessity which constrains them to {alter} [expunge] their former systems of government. the history of the present king of Great Britain is a history of {repeated} [unremitting] injuries & usurpations, [among which appears no solitary fact to contradict the uniform tenor of the rest but all have] {all having} in direct object the establishment of an absolute tyranny over these states. to prove this let facts be submitted to a candid world [for the truth of which we pledge a faith yet unsullied by falsehood.]

He has refused his assent to laws the most wholsome & necessary for the public good.

He has forbidden his governors to pass laws of immediate & pressing importance, unless suspended in their operation till his assent should be obtained; & when so suspended, he has utterly neglected to attend to them.

He has refused to pass other laws for the accomodation of large districts of people, unless those people would relinquish the right of representation in the legislature, a right inestimable to them, & formidable to tyrants only.

He has called together legislative bodies at places unusual, uncomfortable, and distant from the depository of their public records, for the sole purpose of fatiguing them into compliance with his measures.

He has dissolved representative houses repeatedly [& continually] for opposing with manly firmness his invasions on the rights of the people.

He has refused for a long time after such dissolutions to cause others to be elected, whereby the legislative powers, incapable of annihilation, have returned to the people at large for their exercise, the state remaining in the mean time exposed to all the dangers of invasion from without & convulsions within.

He has endeavored to prevent the population of these states; for that purpose obstructing the laws for naturalization of foreigners, refusing to pass others to encourage their migrations hither, & raising the conditions of new appropriations of lands.

He has {obstructed} [suffered] the administration of justice [totally to cease in some of these states] {by} refusing his assent to laws for establishing judiciary powers.

He has made [our] judges dependant on his will alone, for the tenure of their offices, & the amount & paiment of their salaries.

He has erected a multitude of new offices [by a self assumed power] and sent hither swarms of new officers to harrass our people and eat out their substance.

He has kept among us in times of peace standing armies [and ships of war] without the consent of our legislatures.

He has affected to render the military independant of, & superior to the civil power.

He has combined with others to subject us to a jurisdiction foreign to our constitutions & unacknoleged by our laws, giving his assent to their acts of pretended legislation for quartering large bodies of armed troops among us; for protecting them by a mock-trial from punishment for any murders which they should commit on the inhabitants of these states; for cutting off our trade with all parts of the world; for imposing taxes on us without our consent; for depriving us {in many cases} of the benefits of trial by jury; for transporting us beyond seas to be tried for pretended offenses; for abolishing the free system of English laws in a neighboring province, establishing therein an arbitrary government, and enlarging it's boundaries, so as to render it at once an example and fit instrument for introducing the same absolute rule into these {colonies} [states]; for taking away our charters, abolishing our most valuable laws, and altering fundamentally the forms of our governments; for suspending our own legislatures, & declaring themselves invested with power to legislate for us in all cases whatsoever.

He has abdicated government here {by declaring us out of his protection & waging war against us.} [withdrawing his governors, and declaring us out of his allegiance & protection.]

He has plundered our seas, ravaged our coasts, burnt our towns, & destroyed the lives of our people.

He is at this time transporting large armies of foreign mercenaries to compleat the works of death, desolation & tyranny already begun with circumstances of cruelty and perfidy {scarcely paralleled in the most barbarous ages, & totally} unworthy the head of a civilized nation.

He has constrained our fellow citizens taken captive on the high seas to bear arms against their country, to become the executioners of their friends & brethren, or to fall themselves by their hands.

He has {excited domestic insurrections amongst us, & has} endeavored to bring on the inhabitants of our frontiers the merciless Indian savages, whose known rule of warfare is an undistinguished destruction of all ages, sexes, & conditions [of existence.]

[He has incited treasonable insurrections of our fellow-citizens, with the allurements of forfeiture & confiscation of our property

He has waged cruel war against human nature itself, violating it's most sacred rights of life and liberty in the persons of a distant people who never offended him, captivating & carrying them into slavery in another hemisphere or to incur miserable death in their transportation thither. This piratical warfare, the opprobrium of *infidel* powers, is the warfare of the *Christian* king of Great Britain. Determined to keep open a market where *Men* should be bought & sold, he has prostituted his negative for suppressing every legislative attempt to prohibit or to restrain this execrable commerce. And that this assemblage of horrors might want no fact of distinguished die, he is now exciting those very people to rise in arms among us, and to purchase that liberty of which he has deprived them, by murdering the people on whom he also obtruded them: thus paying off former crimes committed against the *Liberties* of one people, with crimes which he urges them to commit again the *lives* of another.]

In every stage of these oppressions we have petitioned for redress in the most humble terms: our repeated petitions have been answered only by repeated injuries. A prince whose character is thus marked by every act which may define a tyrant is unfit to be the ruler of a {free} people [who mean to be free. Future ages will scarcely believe that the hardiness of one man adventured, within the short compass of twelve years only, to lay a foundation so broad & so undisguised for tyranny over a people fostered & fixed in principles of freedom.]

Nor have we been wanting in attentions to our British brethren. We have warned them from time to time of attempts by their legislature to extend {an unwarrantable} [a]

jurisdiction over {us} [these our states.] We have reminded them of the circumstances of our emigration & settlement here, [no one of which could warrant so strange a pretension: that these were effected at the expence of our own blood & treasure, unassisted by the wealth or the strength of Great Britain: that in constituting indeed our several forms of government, we had adopted one common king, thereby laying a foundation for perpetual league & amity with them: but that submission to their parliament was no part of our constitution, nor ever in idea, if history may be credited: and,] we {have} appealed to their native justice and magnanimity {and we have conjured them by} [as well as to] the ties of our common kindred to disavow these usurpations which {would inevitably} [were likely to] interrupt our connection and correspondence. They too have been deaf to the voice of justice & of consanguinity, [and when occasions have been given them, by the regular course of their laws, of removing from their councils the disturbers of our harmony, they have, by their free election re-established them in power. At this very time too they are permitting their chief magistrate to send over not only souldiers of our common blood, but Scotch & foreign mercenaries to invade & destroy us. These facts have given the last stab to agonizing affection, and manly spirit bids us to renounce for ever these unfeeling brethren. We must endeavor to forget our former love for them, and to hold them as we hold the rest of mankind enemies in war, in peace friends. We might have been a free and a great people together; but a communication of grandeur & of freedom it seems is below their dignity. Be it so, since they will it. The road to happiness & to glory is open to us too. We will tread it apart from them, and] {we must therefore} acquiesce in the necessity which denounces our [eternal] separation {and hold them as we hold the rest of mankind, enemies in war, in peace friends}!

[The committee's draft of the final paragraph] We therefore the representatives of the United States of America in General Congress assembled do in the name, & by the authority of the good people of these [states reject & renounce all allegiance & subjection to the kings of Great Britain & all others who may hereafter claim by, through or under them: we utterly dissolve all political connection which may heretofore have subsisted between us & the people or parliament of Great Britain: & finally we do assert & declare these colonies to be free & independant states,] & that as free & independant states, they have full power to levy war, conclude

[Congress' final paragraph] We therefore the representatives of the United States of America in General Congress assembled, appealing to the supreme judge of the world for the rectitude of our intentions, do in the name, & by the authority of the good people of these colonies, solemnly publish & declare that these United colonies are & of right ought to be free & independant states; that they are absolved from all allegiance to the British crown, and that all political connection between them & the state of Great Britain is, & ought to be, totally dissolved; & that as free & independent states they have full power to levy war, conclude peace, contract alliances, establish commerce & to do all

peace, contract alliances, establish commerce, & to do all other acts & things
which independant states may of right do.
And for the support of this declaration
we mutually pledge to each other
our lives, our fortunes & our sacred
honour.

other acts & things which independant states
may of right do.

And for the support of this declaration,
with a firm reliance on the protection of
divine providence we mutually pledge to
each other our lives, our fortunes & our sacred honour.

## 46.1

 RATIFIED TEXT OF THE ARTICLES OF
CONFEDERATION AND PERPETUAL UNION, MARCH 1, 1781

Worthington Chauncey Ford et al., eds., *Journals of the Continental Congress, 1774–1789*
(Washington, D.C.: Government Printing Office, 1904–37), 19:213–23.

According to the order of the day, the honble John Hanson and Daniel Carroll,
two of the delegates for the State of Maryland, in pursuance of the act of the legislature of that State, entitled "An act to empower the delegates of this State in Congress
to subscribe and ratify the Articles of Confederation," which was read in Congress
the 12 of February last, and a copy thereof entered on the minutes, did, in behalf of
the said State of Maryland, sign and ratify the said articles, by which act the Confederation of the United States of America was completed, each and every of the Thirteen
United States, from New Hampshire to Georgia, both included, having adopted and
confirmed, and by their delegates in Congress, ratified the same, [which is in the words
following:]

To all to whom these Presents shall come, we the under signed Delegates of the States
affixed to our Names, send greeting.

Whereas the Delegates of the United States of America, in Congress assembled,
did, on the 15th day of November, in the Year of our Lord One thousand Seven Hundred and Seventy seven, and in the Second Year of the Independence of America,
agree to certain articles of Confederation and perpetual Union between the States of
New-hampshire, Massachusetts-bay, Rhodeisland and Providence Plantations, Connecticut, New York, New Jersey, Pennsylvania, Delaware, Maryland, Virginia, North-
Carolina, South-Carolina and Georgia in the words following, viz. "Articles of
Confederation and perpetual Union between the states of Newhampshire, Massachusetts-
bay, Rhodeisland and Providence Plantations, Connecticut, New-York, New-Jersey,

Pennsylvania, Delaware, Maryland, Virginia, North-Carolina, South-Carolina and Georgia.

Article I. The Stile of this confederacy shall be "The United States of America."

Article II. Each state retains its sovereignty, freedom, and independence, and every Power, Jurisdiction and right, which is not by this confederation expressly delegated to the United States, in Congress assembled.

Article III. The said states hereby severally enter into a firm league of friendship with each other, for their common defence, the security of their Liberties, and their mutual and general welfare, binding themselves to assist each other, against all force offered to, or attacks made upon them, or any of them, on account of religion, sovereignty, trade, or any other pretence whatsoever.

Article IV. The better to secure and perpetuate mutual friendship and intercourse among the people of the different states in this union, the free inhabitants of each of these states, paupers, vagabonds and fugitives from justice excepted, shall be entitled to all privileges and immunities of free citizens in the several states; and the people of each state shall have free ingress and regress to and from any other state, and shall enjoy therein all the privileges of trade and commerce, subject to the same duties, impositions and restrictions as the inhabitants thereof respectively, provided that such restriction shall not extend so far as to prevent the removal of property imported into any state, to any other state, of which the Owner is an inhabitant; provided also that no imposition, duties or restriction shall be laid by any state, on the property of the united states, or either of them.

If any Person guilty of, or charged with treason, felony, or other high misdemeanor in any state, shall flee from Justice, and be found in any of the united states, he shall, upon demand of the Governor or executive power, of the state from which he fled, be delivered up and removed to the state having jurisdiction of his offence.

Full faith and credit shall he given in each of these states to the records, acts and judicial proceedings of the courts and magistrates of every other state.

Article V. For the more convenient management of the general interests of the united states, delegates shall be annually appointed in such manner as the legislature of each state shall direct, to meet in Congress on the first Monday in November, in every year, with a power reserved to each state, to recal its delegates, or any of them, at any time within the year, and to send others in their stead, for the remainder of the Year.

No state shall be represented in Congress by less than two, nor by more than seven Members; and no person shall be capable of being a delegate for more than three years in any term of six years; nor shall any person, being a delegate, be capable of holding any office under the united states, for which he, or another for his benefit receives any salary, fees or emolument of any kind.

Each state shall maintain its own delegates in a meeting of the states, and while they act as members of the committee of the states.

In determining questions in the united states in Congress assembled, each state shall have one vote.

Freedom of speech and debate in Congress shall not be impeached or questioned in any Court, or place out of Congress, and the members of congress shall be protected in their persons from arrests and imprisonments, during the time of their going to and from, and attendance on congress, except for treason, felony, or breach of the peace.

Article VI. No state, without the Consent of the united states in congress assembled, shall send any embassy to, or receive any embassy from, or enter into any conference, agreement, alliance or treaty with any King prince or state; nor shall any person holding any office of profit or trust under the united states, or any of them, accept of any present, emolument, office or title of any kind whatever from any king, prince or foreign state; nor shall the united states in congress assembled, or any of them, grant any title of nobility.

No two or more states shall enter into any treaty, confederation or alliance whatever between them, without the consent of the united states in congress assembled, specifying accurately the purposes for which the same is to be entered into, and how long it shall continue.

No state shall lay any imposts or duties, which may interfere with any stipulations in treaties, entered into by the united states in congress assembled, with any king, prince or state, in pursuance of any treaties already proposed by congress, to the courts of France and Spain.

No vessels of war shall be kept up in time of peace by any state, except such number only, as shall be deemed necessary by the united states in congress assembled, for the defence of such state, or its trade; nor shall any body of forces be kept up by any state, in time of peace, except such number only, as in the judgment of the united states, in congress assembled, shall be deemed requisite to garrison the forts necessary for the defence of such state; but every state shall always keep up a well regulated and disciplined militia, sufficiently armed and accoutred, and shall provide and constantly have ready for use, in public stores, a due number of field pieces and tents, and a proper quantity of arms, ammunition and camp equipage.

No state shall engage in any war without the consent of the united states in congress assembled, unless such state be actually invaded by enemies, or shall have received certain advice of a resolution being formed by some nation of Indians to invade such state, and the danger is so imminent as not to admit of a delay till the united states in congress assembled can be consulted: nor shall any state grant commissions to any ships or vessels of war, nor letters of marque or reprisal, except it be after a declaration of war by the united states in congress assembled, and then only against the kingdom or state and the subjects thereof, against which war has been so declared, and under such regulations as shall be established by the united states in congress assembled, unless such state be infested by pirates, in which case vessels of war may be fitted out for that occasion, and kept so long as the danger shall continue, or until the united states in congress assembled, shall determine otherwise.

Article VII. When land-forces are raised by any state for the common defence, all officers of or under the rank of colonel, shall be appointed by the legislature of each state respectively, by whom such forces shall be raised, or in such manner as such state shall direct, and all vacancies shall be filled up by the State which first made the appointment.

Article VIII. All charges of war, and all other expences that shall be incurred for the common defence or general welfare, and allowed by the united states in congress assembled, shall be defrayed out of a common treasury, which shall be supplied by the several states in proportion to the value of all land within each state, granted to or surveyed for any Person, as such land and the buildings and improvements thereon shall be estimated according to such mode as the united states in congress assembled, shall from time to time direct and appoint. The taxes for paying that proportion shall be laid and levied by the authority and direction of the legislatures of the several states within the time agreed upon by the united states in congress assembled.

Article IX. The united states in congress assembled, shall have the sole and exclusive right and power of determining on peace and war, except in the cases mentioned in the sixth article—of sending and receiving ambassadors—entering into treaties and alliances, provided that no treaty of commerce shall be made whereby the legislative power of the respective states shall be restrained from imposing such imposts and duties on foreigners, as their own people are subjected to, or from prohibiting the exportation or importation of any species of goods or commodities whatsoever—of establishing rules for deciding in all cases, what captures on land or water shall be legal, and in what manner prizes taken by land or naval forces in the service of the united states shall be divided or appropriated—of granting letters of marque and reprisal in times of peace—appointing courts for the trial of piracies and felonies committed on the high seas and establishing courts for receiving and determining finally appeals in all cases of captures, provided that no member of congress shall be appointed a judge of any of the said courts.

The united states in congress assembled shall also be the last resort on appeal in all disputes and differences now subsisting or that hereafter may arise between two or more states concerning boundary, jurisdiction or any other cause whatever; which authority shall always be exercised in the manner following. Whenever the legislative or executive authority or lawful agent of any state in controversy with another shall present a petition to congress stating the matter in question and praying for a hearing, notice thereof shall be given by order of congress to the legislative or executive authority of the other state in controversy, and a day assigned for the appearance of the parties by their lawful agents, who shall then be directed to appoint by joint consent, commissioners or judges to constitute a court for hearing and determining the matter in question: but if they cannot agree, congress shall name three persons out of each of the united states, and from the list of such persons each party shall alternately strike out one, the petitioners beginning, until the number shall be reduced to thirteen; and from that number not less than seven, nor more than nine names as congress shall direct, shall in the presence of congress be drawn out by lot, and the persons whose names shall be so drawn or any five of them, shall be commissioners or judges, to hear and finally determine the controversy, so always as a major part of the judges who shall hear the cause shall agree in the determination: and if either party shall neglect to attend at the day appointed, without showing reasons, which congress shall judge sufficient, or being present shall refuse to strike, the congress shall proceed to nominate three persons out of each state, and the secretary of congress shall strike in behalf of such party absent or refusing; and the judgment and sentence of the court to be appointed, in the manner before prescribed, shall be final and conclusive; and if any of the parties shall refuse to submit to the authority of such court, or to appear or defend their claim or cause, the court shall nevertheless proceed to pronounce sentence, or judgment, which shall in like manner be final and decisive, the judgment or sentence and other proceedings being in either case transmitted to congress, and lodged among the acts of congress for the security of the parties concerned: provided that every commissioner, before he sits in judgment, shall take an oath to be administered by one of the judges of the supreme or superior court of the state, where the cause shall be tried, "well and truly to hear and determine the matter in question, according to the best of his judgment, without favour, affection or hope of reward:" provided also, that no state shall be deprived of territory for the benefit of the united states.

All controversies concerning the private right of soil claimed under different grants of two or more states, whose jurisdictions as they may respect such lands, and the states which passed such grants are adjusted, the said grants or either of them being at the same time claimed to have originated antecedent to such settlement of jurisdiction, shall on the petition of either party to the congress of the united states, be finally determined as near as may be in the same manner as is before prescribed for deciding disputes respecting territorial jurisdiction between different states.

The united states in congress assembled shall also have the sole and exclusive right and power of regulating the alloy and value of coin struck by their own authority, or by that of the respective states—fixing the standard of weights and measures throughout the united states—regulating the trade and managing all affairs with the Indians, not members of any of the states, provided that the legislative right of any state within its own limits be not infringed or violated—establishing or regulating post-offices from one state to another, throughout all the united states, and exacting such postage on the papers passing thro' the same as may be requisite to defray the expences of the said office—appointing all officers of the land forces, in the service of the united states, excepting regimental officers—appointing all the officers of the naval forces, and commissioning all officers whatever in the service of the united states—making rules for the government and regulation of the said land and naval forces, and directing their operations.

The united states in congress assembled shall have authority to appoint a committee, to sit in the recess of congress, to be denominated "A Committee of the States," and to consist of one delegate from each state; and to appoint such other committees and civil officers as may be necessary for managing the general affairs of the united states under their direction—to appoint one of their number to preside, provided that no person be allowed to serve in the office of president more than one year in any term of three years; to ascertain the necessary sums of Money to be raised for the service of the united states, and to appropriate and apply the same for defraying the public expences—to borrow money, or emit bills on the credit of the united states, transmitting every half year to the respective states an account of the sums of money so borrowed or emitted,—to build and equip a navy—to agree upon the number of land forces, and to make requisitions from each state for its quota, in proportion to the number of white inhabitants in such state; which requisition shall be binding, and thereupon the legislature of each state shall appoint the regimental officers, raise the men and cloath, arm and equip them in a soldier like manner, at the expence of the united states; and the officers and men so cloathed, armed and equipped shall march to the place appointed, and within the time agreed on by the united states in congress assembled: But if the united states in congress assembled shall, on consideration of circumstances judge proper that any state should not raise men, or should raise a smaller number than its quota, and that any other state should raise a greater number of men than the quota thereof, such extra number shall be raised, officered, cloathed, armed and equipped in the same manner as the quota of such state, unless the legislature of such state shall judge that such extra number cannot be safely spared out of the same, in which case they shall raise officer, cloath, arm and equip as many of such extra number as they judge can be sagely spared. And the officers and men so cloathed, armed and equipped, shall march to the place appointed, and within the time agreed on by the united states in congress assembled.

The united states in congress assembled shall never engage in a war, nor grant letters of marque and reprisal in time of peace, nor enter into any treaties or alliances, nor coin money, nor regulate the value thereof, nor ascertain the sums and expences necessary for the defence and welfare of the united states, or any of them, nor emit bills, nor borrow money on the credit of the united states, nor appropriate money, nor agree upon the number of vessels of war, to be built or purchased, or the number of land or sea forces to be raised, nor appoint a commander in chief of the army or navy, unless nine states assent to the same: nor shall a question on any other point, except for adjourning from day to day be determined, unless by the votes of a majority of the united states in congress assembled.

The congress of the united states shall have power to adjourn to any time within the year, and to any place within the united states, so that no period of adjournment be for a longer duration than the space of six Months, and shall publish the Journal of their proceedings monthly, except such parts thereof relating to treaties, alliances or military operations, as in their judgment require secrecy; and the yeas and nays of the delegates of each state on any question shall be entered on the Journal, when it is desired by any delegate; and the delegates of a state, or any of them, at his or their request shall be furnished with a transcript of the said Journal, except such parts as are above excepted, to lay before the legislatures of the several states.

Article X. The committee of the states, or any nine of them, shall be authorized to execute, in the recess of congress, such of the powers of congress as the united states in congress assembled, by the consent of nine states, shall from time to time think expedient to vest them with; provided that no power be delegated to the said committee, for the exercise of which, by the articles of confederation, the voice of nine states in the congress of the united states assembled is requisite.

Article XI. Canada acceding to this confederation, and joining in the measures of the united states, shall be admitted into, and entitled to all the advantages of this union: but no other colony shall be admitted into the same, unless such admission be agreed to by nine states.

Article XII. All bills of credit emitted, monies borrowed and debts contracted by, or under the authority of congress, before the assembling of the united states, in pursuance of the present confederation, shall be deemed and considered as a charge against the united states, for payment and satisfaction whereof the said united states, and the public faith are hereby solemnly pledged.

Article XIII. Every state shall abide by the determinations of the united states in congress assembled, on all questions which by this confederation are submitted to them. And the Articles of this confederation shall be inviolably observed by every state, and the union shall be perpetual; nor shall any alteration at any time hereinafter be made in any of them; unless such alteration be agreed to in a congress of the united states, and be afterwards confirmed by the legislatures of every state.

And Whereas it hath pleased the Great Governor of the World to incline the hearts of the legislatures we respectively represent in congress, to approve of, and to authorize us to ratify the said articles of confederation and perpetual union. Know Ye that we the undersigned delegates; by virtue of the power and authority to us given for that purpose, do by these presents, in the name and in behalf of our respective constituents, fully and entirely ratify and confirm each and every of the said articles of confederation and perpetual union, and all and singular the matters and things therein contained: And we do further solemnly plight and engage the faith of our respective constituents, that they shall abide by the determinations of the united states in congress assembled, on all questions, which by the said confederation are submitted to them. And that the articles thereof shall be inviolably observed by the states we respectively represent, and that the union shall be perpetual. In Witness whereof we have hereunto set our hands in Congress. Done at Philadelphia in the state of Pennsylvania the ninth day of July, in the Year of our Lord one Thousand seven Hundred and Seventy-eight, and in the third year of the independence of America.

Josiah Bartlett,
John Wentworth, junr
   August 8th, 1778
} On the part & behalf of the State of New Hampshire.

John Hancock,
Samuel Adams,
Elbridge Gerry,
Francis Dana,
James Lovell,
Samuel Holten,
} On the part and behalf of the State of Massachusetts Bay.

William Ellery,
Henry Marchant,
John Collins
} On the part and behalf of the State of Rhode-Island and Providence Plantations.

Roger Sherman,
Samuel Huntington,
Oliver Wolcott,
Titus Hosmer,
Andrew Adams,
} On the part and behalf of the State of Connecticut.

Jas Duane,
Fra: Lewis,
Wm Duer,
Gouvr Morris,
} On the part and behalf of the State of New York.

Jno Witherspoon,
Nathl Scudder,
} On the Part and in Behalf of the State of New Jersey, November 26th, 1778.

Robert Morris,
Daniel Roberdeau,
Jon. Bayard Smith,
William Clingar,
Joseph Reed,
   22d July, 1778,
} On the part and behalf of the State of Pennsylvania.

Thos McKean,
   Feby 22d, 1779,
John Dickinson,
   May 5th, 1779,
Nicholas Van Dyke,
} On the part & behalf of the State of Delaware.

John Hanson, March 1, 1781,
Daniel Carroll, do
} On the part and behalf of the State of Maryland.

Richard Henry Lee,
John Banister,
Thomas Adams,
Jno. Harvie,
Francis Lightfoot Lee,
} On the Part and Behalf of the State of Virginia.

| John Penn,<br>    July 21st, 1778,<br>Corns Harnett,<br>Jno. Williams, | On the part and behalf of the State of North Carolina. |

| Henry Laurens,<br>William Henry Drayton,<br>Jno Mathews,<br>Richd Hutson,<br>Thos Heyward, junr. | On the part and on behalf of the State of South Carolina. |

| Jno Walton,<br>    24th July, 1778,<br>Edwd Telfair,<br>Edwd Langworthy, | On the part and behalf of the State of Georgia. |

## 47.1

 ROYAL INSTRUCTIONS TO THE CARLISLE PEACE COMMISSION, APRIL 12, 1778

Samuel Eliot Morison, ed., *Sources and Documents illustrating the American Revolution, 1764–1788, and the Formation of the Federal Constitution,* 2nd ed. (Oxford: Oxford University Press, 1929), 186–203.

ST. JAMES'S, 12 April 1778

GEORGE R.

*Orders and Instructions to be observed by our right trusty and right well-beloved cousin and Councillor,* FREDERICK, EARL OF CARLISLE, *Knight of the most antient Order of the Thistle; our right trusty and wellbeloved cousin and councillor* RICHARD, LORD VISCOUNT HOWE, *of Our Kingdom of Ireland; our trusty and wellbeloved* SIR WILLIAM HOWE, *Knight of the most honourable Order of the Bath, Lieutenant General of our forces, General and Commander-in-Chief of all and singular our forces employed or to be employed within Our Colonies in North America, lying upon the Atlantic Ocean, from Nova Scotia on the north to West Florida on the south, both inclusive;* WILLIAM EDEN, *Esq., one of our Commissioners for Trade and Plantations; and* GEORGE JOHNSTONE, *Esq., Captain in our Royal Navy; being our Commissioners appointed by us with sufficient Powers to treat, consult, and agree upon the means of quieting the disorders now subsisting in certain of our colonies, plantations, and provinces in North America. Given at our Court at St. James's, the twelfth day of April 1778, in the eighteenth year of our reign.*

With these our Instructions, you will receive our commission under the great seal of Great Britain, constituting you, or any three of you, our Commissioners, with certain powers to treat, consult, and agree upon the means of quieting the disorders now subsisting in certain of our colonies, plantations, and provinces in North America. You are therefore to repair, with all convenient speed, to New York, or such other place in North America as you shall judge most proper; and when you shall have arrived in any of them, you are to proceed to the execution of the trust we have reposed in you, and for that purpose you, or any three of you, are to communicate your arrival to the Commander-in-Chief of the American forces, or to any body of men, by whatever name known or distinguished, who may be supposed to represent the different provinces, colonies, and plantations in America.

And you are hereby directed to address them by any style or title which may describe them, and to lay before them a copy of the Act of Parliament by virtue of which we are enabled to appoint Commissioners, together with a copy of our commission; and we do direct you, or any three of you, to express your desire and readiness to receive or meet them or any of them authorized for that purpose, at New York, or any place which shall be mutually agreed upon; and that upon notice of the intention of all or any such persons constituting such body as aforesaid to confer with you, or any three of you, upon the subject of this our commission and these our instructions, you do immediately dispatch safe conduct for them to the place at which it may be agreed to consult and confer.

You may likewise assure them that, as soon as peace is established, they shall thenceforth be protected in the antient course of their trade and commerce by the power of Great Britain; and we authorize you to admit of any claim or title to independency in any description of men, during the time of treaty, and for the purpose of treaty.

If, under pretence of diffidence and distrust, they should decline treating upon the ground that you are not authorized finally to conclude any treaty or agreement, inasmuch as any resolution must be reserved for the future approbation or disapprobation of us and our two Houses of Parliament, after observing that the Legislature might reasonably imagine that the matters to be discussed were of too great concernment to be delegated to individuals, especially as you could not expect to meet with equal and corresponding powers in those persons who might act for and on the behalf of the thirteen revolted colonies, who may remind them that as a proof of the good faith and sincerity of the intentions of Great Britain, to promote a full and permanent reconciliation between Great Britain and the said colonies, the Legislature have spontaneously passed 'An Act for removing all doubts and apprehensions concerning taxation by the Parliament of Great Britain in any of the colonies, provinces, and plantations in North America and the West Indies; and for repealing so much of an Act made in the 7th year of our reign as imposes a duty upon tea imported from Great Britain into any colony or plantation in America, or relates thereto.' And they have also passed 'An Act for repealing an Act passed in the 14th year of our reign, intitled, An Act for the better regulating the Government of the Province of Massachusetts Bay, in New England;' and also the

Act enabling us to vest you, or any three of you, with the powers and authorities with which we have entrusted you and do intrust you, of suspending all Acts passed since 1763, and for other purposes therein mentioned.

And as a further proof of such sincerity, you, or any three of you, are authorized to consent, as you are hereby authorized to consent, to make any propositions that they can offer, and that you shall think reasonable and fit to be entertained, the subject of an immediate reference to us and our two Houses of Parliament, separate from the other points of the treaty, in which the disposition of us and our two said Houses of Parliament to promote, by every proper concession, the restoration of peace and union can with no probability be doubted. You may particularly agree to a proposal that if, in the ensuing treaty, any mode can be settled of providing by provincial forces for the sufficient security and protection of our subjects, no standing army shall be raised or kept within the said Colonies in time of Peace without their consent. And also that none of the antient governments or constitutions in the said colonies shall be changed or varied without the consent or request of such of our respective colonies, signified by their general assemblies.

If this should likewise fail to produce the desired effect of entering into a treaty, it may be proper that such propositions and offers should, in such manner as you shall see fit, be made public and known as generally as possible; and the first appearance of a desire in any Province to revert to the antient form of government must be watched with the utmost attention; but, nevertheless, if an Assembly could be formed under your power of appointing a Governor, in the case in which you are at liberty to enter upon such detached treaty, the good consequences and the extensive effects in the operations of such Assembly are obvious. You are, however, to avoid, giving umbrage or jealousy to the powers with which you are publicly treating, and you are not to make any public appeal to the inhabitants of America at large until you shall be satisfied that such public body of men, and the Commander-in-Chief of the American forces, shall refuse to enter into or proceed in such treaty.

But such caution is not to prevent you, or any three of you, from entering into any correspondence or treaty with particular colonies, bodies of men, or individual persons, to answer the purposes of the commission wherewith we have entrusted you, if your attempt to enter into a treaty, or come to any conclusion, with such representative body of men, as we have before described, should fail or miscarry.

And if you should at length despair of bringing such body or bodies of men to a treaty, or effectually to proceed in such treaty, you are, if you find it proper, finally to set forth a declaration, for the information of our well-disposed subjects at large, in which, after reciting the Act and the commission with which we have thought fit to empower you, or any three of you, you shall, if you think proper, publish a proclamation, containing a declaration of the earnest wishes of us and our Parliament for composing any differences that have unhappily subsisted between Great Britain and our said colonies, and for the re-establishment of peace and union upon firm and lasting foundations, and the means which have been used to obtain such salutary and happy purposes.

The propriety, nature, and extent of a suspension of arms will be best determined upon the spot in conjunction with the commanders-in-chief of our Army and Navy; but in the present apparent situation of things it does not seem to us to be necessary or advantageous that the first overture should come from you; nevertheless you, or any three of you, are to determine on this point as you shall deem most expedient on due deliberation.

If it should be proposed to accede to either a local cessation of hostilities within a certain district round the place of treaty, or in general by land, and on rivers, or entirely by sea and land, with such provisions as are usual or proper for the security and accommodation of the persons assembled and for the facilitating the treaty, you, or any three of you, are at liberty to agree to the same.

The proposals which among others appear to us to deserve your attention, are, as to the operations at land:

That a line of quarters shall be marked out for the respective forces beyond which neither side shall advance during the truce, except with leave given by the respective commanders of the opposite forces.

That there shall be a free and open communication for provisions to the respective quarters, and no persons supplying provisions to be molested in going or returning, except only as to such restrictions as the commanders may think fit to impose in their respective quarters, for the more orderly supply of their forces.

That no new levies shall be made, nor any augmentation to the force of either army, during the truce.

That the militia shall not be called out and trained during that interval.

And that a removal of our troops cannot be required till peace shall be restored; and

That no arrays or drafts shall be made of the militia, or any military works whatever carried on, pending such treaty.

The naval operations cannot be put under similar terms. A cessation of arms supposes no augmentation of force during that period. It would be incongruous with that idea to permit military stores to be imported. The only provision that can be made, consistent with the seizure and detention of such vessels as are employed in carrying military stores is, that you should permit, and you, or any three of you, have hereby our royal authority, to permit all vessels sailing from America to have passes from you, or any three of you, for their protection, and that all vessels under sixty tons burthen shall pass from place to place in North America without interruption, and all other vessels above sixty tons, without passes, or seized and detained as having arms or ammunition on board, shall be restored to the owners, if the accommodation shall take place, otherwise to be proceeded against as prize.

You will also require and insist, as far as circumstances will admit, that after the commencement of any truce, no person shall be molested in any of the provinces for declaring his opinion upon any point of government, or for refusing to sign any test or association, or to take any oath.

That all persons now confined for any of the above causes, shall be restored to their liberty.

That no person shall be punished from the above period, but for some crime, and according to the known laws of the land, or for military offences, if that exception must be admitted.

That all proceedings on forfeitures, sequestrations and confiscations against persons for their attachment to the antient connexion with Great Britain, or against the estates of such persons, should be discontinued during the treaty, and in the progress of the treaty you will make it a condition, that they shall be annulled and revoked.

And you are to agree to the same with regard to any similar proceedings on our part, if any such shall have taken place against any of our revolted American subjects.

You will also insist that all persons may reside freely at their dwelling houses, and remain in quiet possession of their estates.

That all churches and places of legal and tolerated worship shall be opened, and the ministers and congregations protected in the exercise of their religion.

It is our will and pleasure that you should make these demands with due earnestness, even if upon some or all of them there should be found a necessity of relaxing.

It being to be understood that the design expressed by our subjects in America, to return to their condition in 1763, is the principle of the present negotiation, that proposition, in general terms, must be agreed to at once. But the explanation of it will lead into some discussion, and it is very essential not only to evince the good faith of Great Britain, but, for the successful result of the treaty, to proceed by ascertaining in the first place the demands of our subjects in America, and the extent to which we mean to acquiesce, in those demands, reserving the terms to be proposed to them as a subsequent consideration.

If they should require any security that the benefits held out to them by the 11th and 12th ch. of the 18th of our reign, should not be at any future time annulled or revoked, the demand is not to be rejected. But it would be proper to place it in the class of those demands which have been made to us and our two Houses of Parliament for the alteration and improvement of their Constitution, which Great Britain is desirous to consider with the utmost attention; and it will be reasonable to put them upon proposing the security they may require.

As to contribution, it is just and reasonable that you should remind those with whom you treat that you are led to hope they will now make good, in the name and on the part of our subjects in America, their own repeated declarations of their readiness to contribute to the public charge, in common with all our other subjects, seeing they are to enjoy the common privileges of all our other subjects; and they are the rather called upon to exercise this act of justice, as such contribution would now be a mere act of free will.

If they are disposed to consider that idea without prejudice, they will find their advantage in fixing upon a ratio by which the amount of a contribution may be regulated.

The sum required will be moderate. It may be taken upon a ratio of their numbers, their tonnage, or exports. The increase of the payment can only be in proportion to the increase of their abilities; and it becomes the interest of Great Britain to promote the industry, the trade, or the population of our subjects in America. If, however, no such specific measure should be agreed upon, they will probably be easily brought to see that it would be their own interest to maintain some force at their own charge; and as it was granted in the preliminary articles, that no standing army should be raised or kept within the said colonies, except in the cases therein mentioned, you may urge the propriety of providing for the establishment and maintenance of a provincial force, regular or militia, for the defence of the said colonies, the preservation of the public peace, and the protection and security of our subjects.

You will therefore enter into the consideration, and settle the number of troops proper to be kept on foot in each colony, together with all regulations necessary for the raising, exercising, clothing, and paying the same. But they are to be under our command, or under the command of those whom we may think to appoint, and all commissions are to be in our name, and by our authority.

If obstacles should arise to either of the modes in which the point of the contribution to the common defence hath been stated, there is still another mode in which the proposition may be put.

There are duties payable in the colonies under Acts of the Legislature, passed long before 1763, to which they never made any objection: the port duties, postage, the escheats, the forfeited grants of lands, and the quit-rents. These, tho' not considerable in the state of collection which will ever prevail while they are to be accounted for here, would form a very considerable article of revenue, if collected under a vigilant authority upon the spot. In lieu of all these, and upon a cession of them to the respective colonies, let their assemblies grant a certain sum for the service of the public, and for a certain term.

If all these points should fail, you must then propose to let the question rest in oblivion, and to secure them in fact, by concessions upon the repeal of such Acts as you have power to suspend, and such others as they may represent as fit to be repealed. And if the suspension of the Declaratory Act should be urged as a condition on their part, you may propose to supersede the necessity of it by a declaration to be framed upon the close of the whole treaty of the respective rights of Great Britain and America.

These four expedients, in the order in which they are placed, will afford you the means of avoiding the difficulties of settling this important and delicate point. But tho' we have suggested them in this place, you are always to remember that it will be more advantageous to postpone the discussion of them, or at least the decision upon them, to the second part of the treaty, concerning those terms which may be required from our subjects in America.

If, however, they should propose to fall into any other measures for the purpose of contributing to the public charge, in common with all our other subjects, or should entertain a prejudice in favour of the mode adopted by their Articles of Confederation lately proposed in Congress, and signed 'Henry Laurens, President,' you will so frame your discussions upon that matter as to facilitate the same, in such mode as you shall judge most advisable.

But if you find them peremptorily fixed on coming to no resolution favourable to any proposition of contribution at all, you, or any three of you, have hereby our royal authority ultimately to declare your acquiescence.

The preservation of their charters is another article upon which our subjects in America may require some security. It is not to be supposed that they will desire that in no case any alteration shall ever be made in any of their charters, because it is certain that numbers of them wish some charters to be materially altered; but if the example of the repeal of the Act for altering the Government of the Massachusetts Bay, and our royal declaration made, or to be made, in the preliminaries to this treaty, are not sufficient to quiet all their alarms on this head, you may admit, as a stipulation on their part, to be declared by us and our two Houses of Parliament, that no bill for the alteration of any of the constitutions of the colonies shall be brought into Parliament, but upon petition from the Assembly of such colony or colonies, as is declared in the preliminaries above referred to.

It is to be presumed then, that the proposition of restoring our colonies to the same situation in which they stood in the year 1763, may lead to an examination of the several Acts passed since that period, of which they have desired a repeal.

You may therefore consent to the suspension of all or any part of them, in manner hereinafter mentioned. The 15th ch. of the 4th of our reign, and the 52nd ch. of the 6th . . . , and the 2nd ch. of the 7th . . . ; as far as these Acts concern the regulations of trade, they ought to be postponed to the general head of the advantages of commerce to be allowed to America, which advantages must be taken up upon a larger view of things, than merely upon the Acts of our reign passed since 1763. [4 Geo. III, c. 29] is for the benefit of our colonies, and falls under the regulations of trade.

[4 Geo. III, c. 34] regulates and restrains paper bills of credit. It is impossible to agree to so unjust a regulation, as that paper bills of credit should be a legal tender in private payment, nor can it be seriously demanded. If the great extent of paper currency issued since the rupture began, is urged in support of such an Act, it will be competent to you to point out a mode of relief which we will more fully explain, in the course of these our instructions, and which may be adopted for that evil without the injustice of admitting so many creditors to suffer. The Act above mentioned has been varied and explained by ch. 35 of the 10th of our reign, and the 57th ch. of the 13th, . . . which, from their date, have also been stated as grievances, but the restraint now subsisting extends no farther than strict justice requires: bills may be issued, may pass at the treasury of the particular colony in which they are issued, but are not to be legal tender in private payment. Beyond this line it cannot be expected that any further concession should be made, in justice to private rights; but this article need occasion no specific difficulty in the settlement of the treaty. If, on other grounds, the provincial legislatures are finally allowed to have the power of passing Acts of a local nature, the regulation of a paper currency is one of these Acts, and the evils which will arise from an improper exercise of the power in this instance are of a sort to correct themselves.

The next Act is the 18th ch. of the 6th of our reign, for quartering troops. This, which is now expired, and the several Acts continuing it, including the only one that now subsists, are in fact annulled by the rebellion, and it will become matter of new regulation to provide for the military force to be hereafter maintained in America.

[7 Geo. III, c. 41, c. 46, c. 56] may likewise be suspended, as may be the 44th ch. of the 13th of our reign. The 22nd ch. of the 8th of our reign, relating to the courts of admiralty, may be referred to the regulations of trade. The 24th ch. of the 12th of our reign is a general and necessary law, not pointed at America, but that part of it which affects America it may be proposed to repeal. [14 Geo. III, c. 19 and c. 45 are] repealed, [c. 39] is already expired.

[15 Geo. III, c. 10, c. 18; 16 Geo. III, c. 5; 17 Geo. III, c. 7, c. 9, c. 40, are] measures of war, and must be treated as such, and will of course determine on a peace being established. [15 Geo. III, c. 15] is also a measure of war, and is in fact expired. The law subsisting on this subject will cease when the pacification takes place. [c. 31] is a regulation of the trade of the British European dominions. The 4th and 19th sections of it affect America, and you may consent to a suspension, and treat for a repeal of them if necessary.

One of the most important objects of these considerations is the large quantity of paper currency issued since the beginning of these unfortunate disputes.

From the first opening of the negotiation you will have opportunities of pointing out the possibility of an immediate provision for the liquidation and discharge of that debt by various methods.

It may be proposed to erect a corporation in America upon the plan of a bank, composed of a certain number of proprietors, subscribing their shares, to be made in paper currency at a certain rate of depreciation, and converted into the stock of that country; the corporation to receive from each of the British colonies a certain annuity towards the payment of an interest upon this fund, and to have the privilege of a banking company, besides which, any other advantages that they may propose, and that can reasonably be granted.

Another plan may be that each colony shall proceed to a liquidation of the paper bills issued within its district, and after providing a fund to discharge the interest, that the capital ascertained shall be created into a fund, to be charged on the amount of all the American revenues, and to be paid in Great Britain.

Another plan may be to leave to each colony the discharge of its peculiar debt, by creating within itself a particular fund to sink the interest and principal of the debt, and to accomplish the payment by lotteries.

Or it may be more eligible to adopt the plan proposed by themselves, in the Articles of Confederation before referred to by us, by which they are to erect a public treasury, and to assess such sums themselves, in the representative body, as each colony should pay respectively, each colony being to raise such sum in the mode and manner they think most convenient and least burthensome.

The best of the plans seems to be to transfer the fund and the payment to Great Britain, provided it can be done without engaging the credit of this country beyond the application of American duties; and this plan would also be the most lucrative to the holders of the paper.

You are also at liberty to concert with the persons with whom you are to treat, the mode in which the expense, not only already incurred, but which is to be incurred for the public service in America, shall be raised from time to time.

But you are not to consent that the charges of the war, incurred by our colonies in America, should, in any manner whatever, be defrayed by Great Britain, though you may concur in any of the above-named propositions, or in any measures which may be proposed, and which should appear reasonable to you, for securing and discharging the same by the said colonies.

The appointment of Governors being left to you, and the recommendation to other situations in your power, if proper persons occur it would be our royal wish that some of the first and most considerable offices in America should be bestowed on our American subjects. Or otherwise, that such Governors and judicial and ministerial officers, the appointment and nomination of whom was received from us before the troubles broke out, should continue in their respective appointments, but with such variations and regulations, as well in the civil and criminal, as in the courts of admiralty, as you shall think most conducive to the due administration of justice, and to have the best tendency to give all reasonable content and satisfaction to our subjects there.

If it appears to you that no pacification can take place except upon a condition that the office of Governor, which has heretofore in most of the provinces made a part of our royal prerogative, should become elective, even this point may in such case be conceded; but it must always be provided that election shall be approved and the commission to such Governor or Governors issued under our authority. And the same instruction may be understood to extend to the appointment of all or any judicial and civil magistrates.

It is also our will and pleasure, for a further satisfaction to the minds of our subjects in America, that such offices there, as they can show to be burthensome shall be suppressed; and the offices held under us shall be granted under such restrictions as may secure the performance of the duty.

The advantages that may be offered to our subjects of America at large, beyond the renewal of the rights they formerly exercised, and as an improvement of their situation, must in some measure depend upon the terms they are willing, on their part, to yield to Great Britain.

If a proper contribution could be obtained, it is obvious that all laws of revenue would then be reduced into a very small compass. The custom-house officers, though appointed by us, would in truth be officers of the Province, to whose treasury the amount of the duties would be carried; and if they desired the appointment, in such case, to be by their Assemblies, there seems to be no objection to give this testimony of a desire on our part to comply with their wishes.

The admiralty courts may be restrained in such manner as will satisfy our subjects in America, as far as it can be made consistent with a reasonable security, and an impartial administration of justice on the subject matter of such jurisdiction in causes maritime.

An extension of the trade of America would also be an object that might be very fairly put in discussion. The principle of the Act of Navigation, and of the 22nd ch. of the 7th and 8th of King William has been relaxed in favour of many articles of American production, which are allowed to be carried directly to an European market upon condition only of touching at an English port.

It is impossible to foresee the particular demands which may [be] made to you in behalf of particular branches of trade. This only we direct you to observe in general, that no check should be given to any of them. One caution, however, should be attended to, that of all advantages, that of bounties should be the least favoured.

Upon the subject of commercial regulations, the prevailing principle has always been to secure a monopoly of American commerce.

The fetters of custom-house regulations are but a weak security for this monopoly in practice, and it should seem that the most effectual way to insure its continuance would be to lay upon articles of foreign produce, not imported from Great Britain, the amount of the provincial duties, whether collected for general or local purposes. This is a point to be watched in the course of the treaty; and if there is, on the one hand, a relaxation from antient restraints, that new stipulation may reasonably be required on the other. The articles agreed upon by you, under the head of regulations of trade, must necessarily pass into an Act of Parliament, and to avoid the revival of any question upon right and authority, a representation from our colonies may precede the Act.

There are, however, some advantages, unconnected with this subject, which you will have in your power to offer immediately.

The regulation of the judicatures in America is a point in which it would be very easy to improve the condition of our subjects there, but upon which it is very difficult to give pointed instructions. They have objected to the judges holding commissions during good behaviour. If they are disposed to think differently, and also to give an independent provision to the judges, there could be no objection on our part to giving them commissions, if they are to receive their commissions from us, during good behaviour.

You will likewise acquiesce in any just and proper regulations that may be proposed relative to the courts of justice, and the mode of practice there, and to such regulations as you may think proper, to render appeals to us more speedy and less expensive.

If it should be proposed that a general assembly, in nature of the present Congress, or similar thereto, consisting of delegates from the said several colonies, should be constituted or established by authority, to meet in Congress for the better management of the general concerns and interests of the said colonies, you are not to decline entering into the consideration of the said proposal, and to see whether any such plan can be so settled and digested as to contribute to the welfare of our colonies, and preserve and secure their connection with Great Britain. But the greatest attention should be given that, in ascertaining the powers and functions of that Assembly, the sovereignty of the mother country should not be infringed, nor any powers given or ascribed to it that should be capable of being construed into an impeachment of the sovereign rights of His Majesty, and the constitutional control of this country. And if it should appear to you that such a plan may be formed as shall be likely to serve the good purpose of establishing a lasting confidence and reconciliation, yet, after it shall be so digested and matured, as it will make so great an alteration in the Constitution of America, it may be more advisable, if circumstances will admit, to refer the approbation of it to the Legislature of Great Britain, previous to inserting it as a concluded article of the treaty.

If it should be desired that our subjects in America should have any share of representation in our House of Commons, such a proposal may be admitted by you, so far as to refer the same to the consideration of our two Houses of Parliament; and it will be proper that in stating such a proposition, the mode of representation, the number of the representatives, which ought to be very small, and the considerations offered on their part, in return for so great a distinction and benefit, should be precisely and distinctly stated.

You may also offer to our American subjects a release from us of all arrears of quit rents whatever.

And it is our royal intention that a full pardon, without any exception, should be offered to all that have been in rebellion. An amnesty, and also an indemnity, shall follow such pardon.

And finally, as the trial in England of treasons committed abroad, tho' unquestionably legal, has been a matter of complaint to our subjects in America, you may treat of, and agree upon any law to be proposed to us and our two Houses of Parliament, similar to that which has been occasionally made in England, in times of rebellion, authorizing a trial out of the county, where the treason hath been committed, but in some place adjoining, where justice may conveniently be administered.

In return for all you give, you are, if possible, to attain a reasonable contribution and compensation directly from the several provinces.

A duty to be imposed on all articles not British, or sent from Britain.

A duty on the foreign trade of America paid in Europe, if it shall be further extended.

These are all the demands that immediately affect the revenue of Great Britain; but the honour and security of Great Britain require other terms, equally important. For instance:

A restoration of all rights of private property, and a full restitution for all violations of such rights, in the most ample manner, ought to be made good by the said colonies; and perhaps the most eligible method might be of adding the amount of such losses to the debt contracted by the said colonies during the war, and discharged in the same manner, unless some more speedy and advantageous method could be pointed out for discharging the same.

Many particular cases of distress and losses sustained by our British merchants and proprietors of estates, during these commotions, have excited our most serious attention and concern; and you will receive with these instructions several memorials on this head, to which you will give all possible consideration; and throughout the whole progress of this treaty, as far as circumstances will admit, you will anxiously lay hold of every opportunity to exert every means of providing for them that relief which justice requires, and which it is our earnest wish to obtain in their behalf.

It is likewise to be observed that the conduct of the clergy of the Church of England has been so worthy of the profession and principles inculcated by the doctrine which has ever distinguished it amongst all the Reformed Churches, that particular attention must be paid to the care of all established clergymen dispossessed of their benefices, and for the preservation of their just rights, in the respective colonies where there is an established maintenance provided for the clergy. It must, therefore, be your particular care, and we do especially recommend it to you, to attend to every possible occasion of repairing their losses, and establishing their situations in the same condition in which they formerly held them.

It should also be agreed, amongst those points which they should concede to us, that no vessels of war should be kept up but such as shall be employed and commissioned by us.

All forts and fortifications should be delivered up to us, and the command of them should be in such Governors, or officers, as we shall, from time to time, appoint, garrisoned, however, by American troops.

No coin should be struck, or coinage established, but by our orders, and in our name.

All prisoners of war, and persons in custody, should be discharged.

As to the Declaration of Independence dated the 4th of July 1776, and all votes, resolutions, and orders passed since the rupture began, it is not necessary to insist on a formal revocation of them, as such declaration, votes, orders and resolutions, not being legal acts, will be in effect rescinded by the conclusion of the treaty.

Supposing upon the whole that the negociation should fall chiefly into the hands of the Congress, it will still be highly expedient, before the close of the negociation, that the several Assemblies should be called.

The proper time to propose this would be when the material concessions on the part of Great Britain are settled, and when it becomes necessary to fix terms on the part of America. To give sanction and effect to these terms, each Legislature should empower persons to engage on behalf of the colonies, as it is proposed to do by the Articles of Confederation before mentioned.

As it is impossible to foresee and enumerate all the matters which may arise during such an inquiry, you are not to consider these instructions as precluding you from entering into the examination and decision of any matters not contained herein, nor of any additional circumstances relative to such things as are the subject matter of these instructions. But you are at liberty to proceed upon every matter within the compass of your commission, and to give all possible satisfaction to the minds of our subjects in America, consistent with that degree of connection which is essentially necessary for preserving the relation between us and our subjects there.

Lastly. If there should be a reasonable prospect of bringing the treaty to a happy conclusion, you are not to lose so desirable an end, by breaking off the negociation on the adverse party absolutely insisting on some point which you are hereby directed, or which, from your own judgment and discretion, you should be disposed, not to give up or yield to, provided the same be short of open and avowed Independence (except such independence as relates only to the purpose of treaty).

But in such case you will suspend coming to any final resolution till you shall have received our further orders thereupon.

And you are upon all occasions to send unto us, by one of our principal secretaries of state, a particular account of all your proceedings, relative to the great object of these our instructions, and to such other objects as you may think worthy of our royal attention.—G.R.

# NOTES

### NOTE TO THE READER

1. See Shain, "Rights Natural and Civil in the Declaration of Independence."

2. In important ways, this collection builds upon that edited by James H. Hutson, *A Decent Respect to the Opinions of Mankind: Congressional State Papers, 1774–1776,* in which he confines his materials to those produced by two congresses. I have added materials from the earlier congress of 1765, additional debates, and delegates' letters from all three congresses.

3. I look forward to working in the immediate future, again, with a relatively circumscribed universe of materials, the 230 or so political pamphlets published, republished, or responded to in the Colonies between 1764 and 1776. In this work, I will include pamphlets from those years not represented in the current collection. In the pamphlet collection, I will again employ clearly articulated rules for inclusion intended to lessen the dangers of selection bias.

4. What is remarkable is just how few of these letters are theoretically valuable in any political sense. Perhaps not all that surprising, most concern economic or military matters or, still more commonly, familial issues.

### INTRODUCTION

1. Gibson, *Interpreting the Founding.* This is a useful, though flawed, work. Its failure to take note of approaches that emphasize either religious or imperial and monarchical elements in the Revolutionary era is emblematic of the lacunae present in the field. Others, of course, have offered different typologies of the contending literatures. See, for example, LaCroix, *The Ideological Origins of American Federalism,* which, in discussing the origins of federalism, divides the "founding" scholarship into three schools: institutionalists, who build upon the British inheritance; those who emphasize republican theorizing; and those who begin their story with the 1787 Convention in Philadelphia. For LaCroix, a historian and lawyer, the dominant Lockean liberal interpretation emphasized by political theorists barely merits a mention.

2. Gibson, *Interpreting the Founding,* 11.

3. See Colbourn, *The Lamp of Experience,* and Robbins, *The Eighteenth-Century Commonwealthman,* 58–59. Colbourn and Robbins, among the most authoritative authors on this tradition, view John Locke as a member of this community of discourse.

4. Gibson, *Interpreting the Founding,* 22–52.

5. See Gerber, "Whatever Happened to the Declaration of Independence?" In *Interpreting the Founding,* Gibson writes that among the "most conspicuous omissions" in his review of the literature is "the importance of religion—especially Protestantism" (104). Elsewhere, he lists other approaches that he failed to consider, including "British common law and constitutionalism, Protestantism . . . [and] the ideas of Native Americans in the American Founding," with the sense that they are each of comparable importance. See, among those emphasizing the importance of Protestant religiosity in this era, Dreisbach and Hall, *The Sacred Rights of Conscience,* and Hall, *The Genevan Reformation and the American Founding.*

6. See Shain, *The Myth of American Individualism.*

7. See Gibson, *Interpreting the Founding,* 53–63; for the most famous examples, see Kloppenberg, "The Virtues of Liberalism," and R. Smith, *Civic Ideals.* The latter, according to Gibson, concluded unusually "that much of American political thought, including that of the American Founders, is incoherent."

8. For something of an exception to this generalization, see Bilder, *Transatlantic Constitution,* which recounts how British Privy Council officials, until 1774, attempted to balance the claims of divergent constituencies in the empire.

9. See Burrows, *Forgotten Patriots,* 246–47, in which this Pulitzer Prize winner denounces scholars from both the 1930s and today who believe—to his mind, errantly—that it is their responsibility to produce impartial scholarship rather than to celebrate American virtues and decry British vices. Indeed, the pressure to produce pro-patriot history, even among those writing from a politically progressive perspective, is most difficult to overcome. The awards, too, given to those historians and biographers who serve as neo-Whig apologists for the United States should not be overlooked.

10. All these characterizations are readily discoverable in the textualist theories Gibson canvasses. He examines two other traditions, Progressive historiography and social history, that don't share these common traits. On the need for British perspectives and their edifying effect on American parochialism, see Dickinson, "Britain's Imperial Sovereignty: The Ideological Case against the American Colonists," in *Britain and the American Revolution,* 65.

11. See Gibson, *Interpreting the Founding,* 7–13; the most famous works associated with the Progressive school are Beard, *An Economic Interpretation of the Constitution,* and Jensen, *The Articles of Confederation* and *The New Nation.* There are many more recent works, among them Nash, *The Unknown American Revolution,* and McGuire, *To Form a More Perfect Union.*

12. There is an extensive literature, today often forgotten, that deserves renewed attention. Among those works of greatest relevance to this volume (though not all of them are strictly part of the Imperial school) are R. G. Adams, *Political Ideas of the American Revolution,* 1922; McIlwain, *The American Revolution,* 1923; Schuyler, *Parliament and the British Empire,* 1929; Namier, *England in the Age of the American Revolution,* 1930; Coupland, *The American Revolution and the British Empire,* 1930; Clark, *British Opinion and the American Revolution,* 1930; McLaughlin, *The Foundations of American Constitutionalism,* 1932; Brown, *Empire or Independence,* 1941; Ritcheson, *British Politics and the American Revolution,* 1954; and Christie and Labaree, *Empire or Independence,* 1976.

13. See Gibson, *Interpreting the Founding,* 64–85, for his discussion of those social historians most interested in the socially and politically marginalized. He provides no coverage, though, of a somewhat earlier group of social historians predominantly interested in the largest part of the political nation, that is, nonelite Protestant farmers who made up 90-plus percent of the politically

active white male population. For a possibly dated overview of this literature, see Shain, *Myth of American Individualism,* 61–83.

14. See Reid, "The Authority of Rights at the American Founding."

15. Two historians stand out as continuing links to the imperial historiography of the earlier period: Jack P. Greene and John Phillip Reid. For an introduction to their work in this area, see Greene, *The Constitutional Origins of the American Revolution,* and Reid, *Constitutional History of the American Revolution.*

16. McConville, *The King's Three Faces,* 2; he later suggests that to understand colonial society properly we will need "to retell American stories with a uniquely British accent" (165). Among other contemporary authors emphasizing the centrality of empire and monarchy to an understanding of American political institutions and colonial resistance are Marston, *King and Congress;* Gould, *The Persistence of Empire;* Bilder, *Transatlantic Constitution;* Hulsebosch, *Constituting Empire;* and most emphatically, recently, and controversially, Nelson, "Patriot Royalism."

17. Quoted in Guttridge, *English Whiggism and the American Revolution,* 105.

18. Kenyon, "Republicans and Radicalism in the American Revolution," 304. See Maier, *From Resistance to Revolution,* v–xiii, for her retrospective view from 1991 of the challenge raised by students of Bernard Bailyn in the late 1960s and early 1970s to earlier generations of historians. In a certain sense, the new imperial historians are challenging two groups of what might be described as neo-Whigs: that is, the liberals who preceded Maier as well as the defenders of republicanism like Bailyn and Maier. In opposition, see McConville, who writes that these earlier historians have inaccurately filled the colonial world "with protorepublicans, readers of Country pamphlets, rising assemblies, plain-folk Protestants, budding contract theorists . . . in short, future Americans" (*King's Three Faces,* 4), and Marston, who claims that colonists' "vision of legitimate authority of a continental government was based on, not upon a republican model of the future, but upon an idealized British monarchical model of the past" (*King and Congress,* 9).

19. See Black, "The Constitution of Empire."

20. See Fisher, who in 1912 wrote that earlier interpreters of the revolution had failed to "substitute truth and actuality for the mawkish sentimentality and nonsense with which we have been so long nauseated," with the object "to make it appear that the Revolution had been a great spontaneous uprising of the whole American people without faction or disagreements among themselves" ("The Legendary and Myth-Making Process in Histories of the American Revolution," 54–55). He continues, in a way that seems eerily contemporary: "The real Revolution is more useful and interesting than the make believe one. The actual factions, divisions, mistakes, atrocities, if you please, are far more useful to know about" (75). This is most especially true for students of colonial wars of national liberation, who, by including the American case, would have available an eighteenth-century settler community with which to test various models of explanations resting on later African, Asian, and South American movements.

21. Especially valuable in gauging the influence of European authors on colonial and early-national Americans is Lutz, "The Relative Influence of European Writers on Late Eighteenth-Century American Political Thought" (193), which reports that the two most cited authors were Montesquieu (in 8.3 percent of works canvassed) and Blackstone (7.9 percent). These two authors, however, are of little interest to those working in the three dominant, text-based schools of interpretation.

22. For a brief sampling of those working in this tradition, see Baldwin, *The New England Clergy;* Heimert, *Religion and the American Mind;* Bonomi, *Under the Cope of Heaven;* Hutson, *Church and*

*State in America;* and Maloy, *The Colonial Origins of Modern Democratic Thought.* For a sampling of the sermons, see Moore, *Patriot Preachers of the American Revolution;* Sandoz, *Political Sermons of the American Founding Era;* and Thornton, *The Pulpit of the American Revolution.*

23. Gibson, *Interpreting the Founding,* 7–8. McGuire, *To Form a More Perfect Union,* for example, uses a variant of rational choice theory to explore these issues.

24. For a more traditional understanding of colonial and early-national social history than that offered by Gibson, one might begin with Main, *The Social Structure of Revolutionary America,* and Katz and Murrin, *Colonial America.*

25. Again, two authors of prolific output are of unusual importance to the continued standing of this line of thinking: John Phillip Reid and Jack P. Greene. See, for example, Reid, *The Briefs of the American Revolution,* along with many of his other works; and Greene, *Peripheries and Center, Negotiated Authorities,* and *Constitutional Origins of the American Revolution.* Also see Hulsebosch, *Constituting Empire,* and McConville, *King's Three Faces.*

26. See Maier, *American Scripture,* and Armitage, *The Declaration of Independence.*

27. I follow and build upon the work of others who have added greatly to my understanding of these materials and, in the case of Ford, *Journals of the Continental Congress,* and Smith, ed., *Letters of Delegates to Congress,* have made this volume possible. Among my most important other predecessors are Burnett, *The Continental Congress;* Henderson, *Party Politics in the Continental Congress;* Marston, *King and Congress;* Morgan and Morgan, *Stamp Act Crisis;* Jensen, *Articles of Confederation;* Rakove, *The Beginnings of National Politics;* and Hutson, *Decent Respect,* which provided the initial inspiration for this work.

28. See, for example, Zuckert, *The Natural Rights Republic.*

29. On the nature of extended texts in American political thought, see Lutz's most helpful *Preface to American Political Theory.*

30. McIlwain, *American Revolution,* 192, and see Shain, "Rights Natural and Civil in the Declaration of Independence."

31. For his insightful and critical take on this interpretive issue, see Dreisbach, "Founders Famous and Forgotten."

32. As Greene summed up his monumental half century of research into this topic: "The Declaration represented something of a departure from the impressive political tracts and state papers they [the colonists] had been producing over the previous twelve years" (*Constitutional Origins of the American Revolution,* 185).

33. See Marston, *King and Congress;* McConville, *King's Three Faces;* Rozbicki, *Culture and Liberty in the Age of the American Revolution;* and Rakove, *Revolutionaries,* in which he writes that men as different as Robert Morris and Samuel Adams agreed "that British mis-steps, rather than American desires, had brought the colonies to the point of independence" (102).

34. Although too often overlooked, as in Maier, *From Resistance to Revolution,* or underplayed, as in Marston, *King and Congress,* or Rakove, *Revolutionaries,* this is not a new insight. See, most importantly, Henderson, *Party Politics in the Continental Congress* and Jensen, *Articles of Confederation.*

35. See Kenyon, "Republicanism and Radicalism in the American Revolution," 295.

36. McConville, *King's Three Faces,* is once again especially helpful in bringing to light the strength of colonial affection for the British monarchy settled in a Protestant line.

37. The term *moderate* rather than *conservative,* as is used by some scholars to describe the same population of colonists strenuously seeking a path toward reconciliation, is used here so that the more conservative men who remained loyal to the Crown can be distinguished from those

who, while sharing many of the same concerns about the dangers of republican government with their future loyal colleagues, refused to place their fear of republicanism over that of what they viewed to be unconstitutional British parliamentary legislation. See Kenyon, "Republicanism and Radicalism," 296, and Handlin and Handlin, "Radicals and Conservatives in Massachusetts after Independence," 344, for their divisions. Henderson divides the delegates into three groups: "radical Whigs (or simply radicals, Samuel Adams being an example)," moderate Whigs such as John Dickinson, and Tories, who early on joined with the moderates before departing from Congress (*Party Politics in the Continental Congress,* 7–8). In *Revolutionaries,* Rakove also denominates this population as moderates and, along with Marston (*King and Congress*), emphasizes, though insufficiently, the differences between them and the congressional radicals in the First Continental Congress and the early years of the Second. He characterizes moderates thus: "Moderates were not ideologues, as historians might apply that term to Samuel Adams or Richard Henry Lee. They were not inclined to think that the king's ministers were waging a systematic campaign to turn the colonists into docile slaves. . . . Rather, moderates believed that the ministry had badly miscalculated. . . . The heartland of moderation lay in the middle colonies" (75).

38. Especially helpful in understanding the final month of concerted congressional and truly radical action, most importantly in working to overthrow the newly and duly elected government of Pennsylvania, is Hogeland, *Declaration.* As Hogeland makes clear, it is important to discriminate between those whom I am describing as congressional radicals and those who were "true" radicals, men like Thomas Paine or Ethan Allen, who were committed to transforming the fundamental nature of intracolonial life. Congressional radicals like Samuel Adams would—when to their advantage—work with true radicals, as when they brought about the fall of the legitimately elected Pennsylvania government, even while trying to concede to the true radicals as little as possible. Particularly symbolic of this is the long-enduring congressional rejection of the petitions of the radical residents of the New Hampshire Grants.

39. For example, see Webking, *The American Revolution and the Politics of Liberty,* 108–9. Far more extreme than the most exaggerated scholarly works are the perspectives found in any number of websites advancing libertarian or neoconservative perspectives. For a particularly striking one that embodies the characteristics described here, see the entry "Founding Fathers" in the *Ayn Rand Lexicon,* http://aynrandlexicon.com/lexicon/founding_fathers.html.

40. With the New York delegates being of particular interest, see Hulsebosch, *Constituting Empire.*

41. Henderson reports that the average age of the New England leadership in 1779 was forty-seven and that of the middle and southern colonies was thirty-six (*Party Politics in the Continental Congress,* 180).

42. In this interpretive tradition, see, most prominently, Maier, *From Resistance to Revolution,* or Bailyn, *The Ideological Origins of the American Revolution,* and long antedating them but offering a helpful opposing point of view, McIlwain, *American Revolution.*

43. See Becker, *The Declaration of Independence.* Becker, in this 1922 work, is one of the seminal figures in the liberal school of interpretation described by Gibson in *Interpreting the Founding,* but in an earlier 1909 work, *The History of Political Parties in the Province of New York, 1760–1776,* Becker did much to shape the Progressive school of interpretation. The most celebrated work in the liberal tradition is Hartz, *The Liberal Tradition in America.*

44. See Robbins, *Eighteenth-Century Commonwealthman,* 82–83.

45. From 1764 on, the efforts of British imperial officials to protect French Canadians and Native Americans from the exploitation of the older "English" American colonists were a constant

source of tension, as, no doubt, was Dunmore's December 1775 offer of emancipation to Virginia's enslaved African and African American populations, to which the Declaration referred in its final grievance. One of Jefferson's former slaves and three of Washington's, in fact, were among the three thousand former slaves who left New York in 1783 with the evacuation of the British forces; see Allen, *Tories*, 332.

46. See Kenyon, "Republicanism and Radicalism," 302.

47. See Montesquieu, *Spirit of the Laws,* and Lolme, *The Constitution of England.*

48. See Montross, *The Reluctant Rebels.* I also wish to thank George McKenna for his suggestion that this work might be renamed, following that of the majority of congressional delegates, "reluctant revolutionaries."

49. Kenyon writes "that no revolution was intended; the colonists wanted merely a redress of grievances as British subjects and had no plans either for independence or for the formation of republican government" ("Republicanism and Radicalism," 295); according to Colbourn, "In insisting upon rights which their history showed were deeply embedded in antiquity, American Revolutionaries argued that their stand was essentially conservative; it was the corrupted mother country which was pursuing a radical course of action" (*Lamp of Experience,* 191).

50. Dickinson notes that the American Revolution "was a civil war *within* the British Empire caused by an honest failure to reach a consensus" (*British Pamphlets on the American Revolution,* 1:xxxvi).

51. Ritcheson, *British Politics and the American Revolution,* 13; and see Dickinson, "The Eighteenth-Century Debate on the Sovereignty of Parliament," 189.

52. See Schuyler, *Parliament and the British Empire,* 22. According to McIlwain, "Rightly or wrongly Ireland and America were commonly linked together, as 'Dominions of the Crown,' with a common status, different from 'Dominions of the King.' . . . The status which Scotland undeniably had as a mere 'dominion of the King' and not 'of the Crown' was the same as that demanded as of right for Ireland by the Irish and for America by the Congress in 1774" (*American Revolution,* 80–81).

53. Quite possibly, the most compelling defense of the colonial position was made by John Adams in 1773. His argument, along those of others, and Thomas Hutchinson's rebuttal are reprinted in Reid, *Briefs of the American Revolution.*

54. The seminal source and guide to understanding this debate, even if in some measure flawed, is still McIlwain, *American Revolution,* in particular 20–21, and still more importantly, 192. He should be read in tandem with the important but controversial corrective provided by Schuyler, *Parliament and the British Empire.*

55. Among others, see Reid, *Constitutional History of the American Revolution;* Greene, *Constitutional Origins of the American Revolution;* Yirush, *Settlers, Liberty, and Empire;* and Nelson, "Patriot Royalism."

56. See Guttridge, *English Whiggism and the American Revolution,* 11–12. The colonists, as new Americans, embraced this already-dated Whig theory of opposition between king and Parliament and turned to it in forming state and federal governmental structures; this originally monarchical opposition between executive and legislature is institutionally something with which Americans continue to live (possibly unfortunately) even today.

57. See Dickinson, "Debate on the Sovereignty of Parliament," 193–94.

58. McIlwain argues that the American position was neither Whig nor Tory, but increasingly radical: "By 1774, America was no longer Whig. The doctrines of Camden had been exchanged for those of Molyneux . . . [because] the doctrine of the Whigs was really a doctrine of the supremacy

of Parliament. . . . Such a theory imposed no checks on any abuses of Parliament's power. . . . The essential weakness of the Whig doctrine here clearly appears. It offered no more remedy against an oppressive parliament than the theory of divine right had offered against a despotic king" (*American Revolution,* 156–58). See, too, Mill's related observation in 1859: "The notion that the people have no need to limit their power over themselves might seem axiomatic, when a popular government was a thing only dreamed about . . . In time, however, a democratic republic came to occupy a large portion of the earth's surface and . . . elective and responsible government became subject to the observations and criticisms which wait upon a great existing fact. . . . [It was found that the limitation] on the power of government over individuals loses none of its importance when the holders of power are regularly accountable to the community" (*On Liberty,* 3–4). Only, then, by the mid-nineteenth century, and not before, did Mill think that a proper understanding of the need to restrain popular legislatures as well as executives had begun to be accepted.

59. York writes that Franklin's articles "would have tied all of British North America, the West Indies, and Ireland together into a legislative union under the crown, [with] a Continental Congress expanded to include the British Atlantic basin" ("When Words Fail," 372).

60. Colonial political thinkers took into consideration the king's role in governing his ancestral lands in Germany, as well as lands in Ireland, in the Channel Islands, and in Chester and Durham, which were counties palatine; see John Adams, "Novanglus." None of these examples, though, for the reasons suggested below, seem apposite, and of course if such a stature had been achieved, the colonies would have been legally a feudal-like holding of the king, without any of the hard-fought-for constitutional protections resulting from the Glorious Revolution and subsequent Bill of Rights.

61. This position is contested by Greene, *Constitutional Origins of the American Revolution,* and Yirush, *Settlers, Liberty, and Empire,* who find the colonial understanding of the imperial constitution credible and the colonists' defense plausible. Similarly, the colonists' defense was more charitably viewed by R. G. Adams as anticipating the nineteenth-century imperial constitution of the evolving British Commonwealth (*Political Ideas of the American Revolution,* 61). It well may be that how one assesses the colonial position may depend on through which lens one views it: legal, constitutional (English, British, and imperial), or theoretical. The documents offered in this volume will likely not decide this issue. What should be clear, though, is the centrality of British constitutional issues to the twelve-year crisis and not a new, radical, individualistic, and democratic political philosophy frequently associated with John Locke or any other seventeenth- or early eighteenth-century English or continental authors.

62. See Guttridge, *English Whiggism and the American Revolution,* 15, 40–43, and 118, where he discusses "Dunning's Motion," in which, on April 6, 1780, a committee of the whole House declared the king's influence, by a vote of 233–215, to be too great and in need of reduction.

63. In George III's proposed statement of abdication, the king wrote of "his devotion to the British Constitution claiming that all his difficulties in America had arisen from 'his scrupulous attachment to the Rights of Parliament'" (quoted in O'Shaughnessy, "'If Others Will Not Be Active, I Must Drive,'" 43); see also Dickinson, "Debate on the Sovereignty of Parliament," 210.

64. David Hume notes that the "spirit of tyranny, of which nations are as susceptible as individuals, had extremely animated [from 1666 on] the English to exert their superiority over their dependent state" (*The History of England,* 6:231).

65. Edmund Burke wrote of "the imperial rights of Great Britain, and the privileges which the Colonists ought to enjoy under these rights . . . [ought to be] the most reconcilable things in the world" ("Speech on American Taxation," 1:217).

66. See, for example, Cartwright, "American Independence, the Interest and Glory of Great Britain," and York, "Federalism and the Failure of Imperial Reform," 176. Still, while defending the colonials' position and, ultimately, their independence, Cartwright offers little in the way of a novel constitutional institutional arrangement.

67. Greene concludes that the Revolution failed to solve underlying constitutional issues and notes that the "ancient problem of how, in an extended polity, to distribute authority between the center and peripheries, would be the primary concern of American constitutional thought during the 1780s and during the national debate" of 1787–88 (*Constitutional Origins of the American Revolution*, 190).

68. This claim is contra that expressed in LaCroix, *Ideological Origins of American Federalism*.

69. See Hulsebosch, *Constituting Empire*, and Bilder, *Transatlantic Constitution*.

70. See Rozbicki, *Culture and Liberty*, for his insights on the failed assumptions of colonial gentry regarding their status among a "people" limited to property holders; see also King, *The Founding Fathers v. The People*, 16–38, on contrasting eighteenth-century meanings of "the people."

71. Of the 130 delegates who attended the first three years of the first two Continental Congresses, by my account there were 62 lawyers, 22 merchants, and 17 large landowners or planters, that is, around three-fourths were social and economic elites from just three professional groups. See also Montross, *Reluctant Rebels*, 28–42, which interestingly observes that of the 56 initial delegates, 12 "had received most of their schooling in the British Isles . . . [and] leading the list of colleges with seven graduates were the Inns of Court . . . [and] Harvard was represented with five graduates, Yale with three, [and] William and Mary with three" (29).

72. See Shain, *Myth of American Individualism*, 84–115.

73. For the differences between true radicals, who sought to make fundamental changes to American politics, society, and economics, and congressional radicals, who wished principally, though not only, for independence from Britain, see Hogeland, *Declaration*.

74. Greene, *Constitutional Origins of the American Revolution*, xxi.

75. King claims that Americans are exceptional in the enormous reverence with which they hold "the main actors and episodes in their country's political history," which occasionally "borders on ancestor worship" (*Founding Fathers v. the People*, 130). See Rozbicki for his insightful remarks on the nature of rhetoric, then and now, and the master narrative broadly shaping contemporary views of the founding, which is curiously shared by adherents of both the political Left and the Right (*Culture and Liberty*, 21 and throughout).

76. For example, one of the contenders for the 2012 Republican presidential nomination, Representative Michele Bachmann, proudly explained on her website that she was motivated, in part, to leave the Democratic Party and join the Republican after reading an unflattering account of the Founders in Gore Vidal's novel *Burr*. One might have hoped that Americans were now sufficiently self-assured that their public leaders would be able to consider critical accounts without such reactions.

77. Hume offers both a striking challenge to Whig politicized history and a defense of historical accuracy in his brief for political moderation (*History of England*, 6:533–34).

78. For the Supreme Court over much of its early history, the central importance of the Declaration of Independence was in adjudicating international questions regarding when the colonies were legally no longer British, not anything of a more philosophical nature; see Shain, "Declaration of Independence."

ACT I: THE STAMP ACT CRISIS, 1764–1766

1. Morris, *Encyclopedia of American History*, 75. Much of my history here is informed by Morris' summary.

2. Edmund Burke, "Speech on American Taxation," 1:162, 194, 215.

3. The publication of Franklin's testimony was, according to Thomas R. Adams, the eighth most popular political pamphlet in the North American colonies in the years 1764–76 (*American Independence*, xii).

4. Morgan, *Prologue to Revolution*, 3.

5. Weslager, *The Stamp Act Congress*, 81–82.

6. For Smith, see Hulsebosch, *Constituting Empire*, 92.

7. Morgan, *The New York Declaration of 1764*, 3–4.

8. William Blackstone, who offers the most authoritative legal understanding of the time, characterizes all the American colonies as either conquered or ceded territories rather than ones having been unoccupied; thus, by the law of nations, "the common law of England, as such, has no allowance or authority there [that is, in the colonies]; they being no part of the mother country, but distinct (though dependent) dominions. They are subject however to the control of the parliament; though (like Ireland, Man, and the rest) not bound by any acts of parliament, unless particularly named" (*Commentaries on the Laws of England*, 1:104–5). This pronouncement, in spite of Blackstone's extraordinary prominence in the colonies, was rejected by the colonists at every level.

9. McIlwain describes the changes introduced by Parliament's Act Concerning Monopolies (1624) and Parliament's subsequent ability, for cause or not, to overturn royal charters (*American Revolution*, 176, 180). Courts too, with cause, could do so under writs of *scire facias* or *quo warranto*.

10. See Reid, *Constitutional History of the American Revolution*, on the importance of custom and use.

11. Morgan suggests that the petitioners rested their argument on a natural-right foundation ("New York Declaration of 1764," 3); I think Morgan's interpretation, in view of subsequent claims and the grounds used here, exaggerated the importance of natural rights.

12. Knollenberg, *Origin of the American Revolution*, 185.

13. Putney, "Oxenbridge Thacher."

14. Kershaw, "Bowdoin, James."

15. See John Adams, "Novanglus."

16. Kershaw, "Cushing, Thomas."

17. See Blackstone, *Commentaries on the Laws of England*, 1:39–44, and Reid, *Constitutional History of the American Revolution*, 13–14.

18. Pencak, "Otis, James."

19. Kershaw, "Cushing, Thomas."

20. Knollenberg, *Origin of the American Revolution*, 185, 190.

21. John Adams, "Novanglus," 179.

22. Knollenberg, *Origin of the American Revolution*, 199–200.

23. Purcell, *Who Was Who in the American Revolution*, 49, and see Henderson, *Party Politics in the Continental Congress*, 8.

24. Detweiler, "Bland, Richard."

25. Risjord, "Harrison, Benjamin."

26. Konig, "Pendleton, Edmund," and see Henderson, *Party Politics in the Continental Congress*, 46.

27. Selby, "Randolph, Peyton."

28. Greene and Pole, *The Blackwell Encyclopedia of the American Revolution,* 745.

29. Of the fifteen delegates that Virginia sent to the first three years, 1774–77, of the two Continental Congresses, none were merchants. The same could be said only of New Jersey and Delaware.

30. Greene, *Colonies to Nation,* 59.

31. Morgan and Morgan, *Stamp Act Crisis,* 102.

32. Ibid., 102–3.

33. Morgan, "Colonial Ideas of Parliamentary Powers."

34. Morton, *The American Revolution,* 127–28.

35. Thomas R. Adams, *American Independence,* xi.

36. McIlwain, *American Revolution,* 152. Colbourn writes that "Dickinson based his arguments on a total acceptance of God-Given natural rights as substantiated in the English Constitution" (*Lamp of Experience,* 110); McConville notes that, like Paine and Arthur Lee, who had lived long in London, "it was British thinkers who were enthralled with aspects of the radical Enlightenment. As one provincial put it, 'Old England, and not New, must be the land of deists and freethinkers'" (*King's Three Faces,* 138). Others, however, think the influence may have gone the other way. According to H. T. Dickinson: "Appeals to such vague, ill-defined notions as natural rights, natural law, fundamental law or the spirit of the constitution proved ineffective. The American colonists were much more successful . . . [ultimately] in devising means to limit sovereignty in their new state . . . The major exception [in Britain] was Thomas Paine" ("Debate on the Sovereignty of Parliament," 208). In some ways, both sides may in part be right.

37. See Morgan, "Colonial Ideas of Parliamentary Powers."

38. See Shain, "Rights Natural and Civil," where I explain that the breakdown of the distinction between civil and natural rights, along with the loss of the correlative relationship between rights and duties, effectively created a new radical world of rights.

39. *Maryland Gazette,* Thursday, October 3, 1765.

40. Morgan, *Prologue to Revolution,* 54–56.

41. Ibid., 45, 57–62.

42. Weslager, *Stamp Act Congress,* 61, 65.

43. Morgan and Morgan, *Stamp Act Crisis,* 108n42.

44. Pencak, "Ruggles, Timothy"; see also Allen, *Tories.* On Otis, see Knollenberg, *Origin of the American Revolution,* 210, and Morgan and Morgan, *Stamp Act Crisis,* 109.

45. Morgan and Morgan, *Stamp Act Crisis,* 63.

46. Weslager, *Stamp Act Congress,* 123–24.

47. Banner, "Livingston, Robert R."

48. Weir, "Rutledge, John."

49. Weslager, *Stamp Act Congress,* 124. For Bowler, see Purcell, *Who Was Who in the American Revolution,* 55.

50. Farrand, *The Records of the Federal Convention of 1787,* 2:13–15.

51. Tyler, *The Literary History of the American Revolution,* 2:84.

52. Morgan and Morgan, *Stamp Act Crisis,* 113.

53. Shain, "Rights Natural and Civil," 144.

54. Reid, *Constitutional History of the American Revolution,* 4–5, 100–6.

55. Morgan and Morgan, *Stamp Act Crisis,* 114.

56. Coupland, *American Revolution and the British Empire,* 268, and Van Tyne, *England and America,* 183–84.

57. There is a subtle distinction between the traditional English understanding of the laws of nature as embedded over time in the English or British constitutions, as defended here by Johnson, and an emerging understanding of natural rights and law resting on abstract reason and freed from such slow-to-develop historical creations.

58. See Morgan and Morgan, *Stamp Act Crisis,* 116.

59. See York, "The Impact of the American Revolution on Ireland," 231. Barré, apparently, had in turn borrowed the phrase from an Irish pamphleteer, Charles Lucas.

60. See Morgan, *Prologue to Revolution,* 105; York, "When Words Fail," 346–55; and Guttridge, *English Whiggism and the American Revolution.*

61. Morgan and Morgan, *Stamp Act Crisis,* 187–88, 194.

62. Weslager, *Stamp Act Congress,* 39, 43.

63. Weslager writes that "the Act was enforced in Nova Scotia, Bermuda, Granada, and Quebec against varying protests; in Jamaica and Barbados there was some opposition; in the Leeward Islands there was considerable opposition, and the Stamp Act Distributor was forced to resign" (*Stamp Act Congress,* 56).

64. Quoted in Morgan and Morgan, *Stamp Act Crisis,* 207.

65. See Robbins, *Eighteenth-Century Commonwealthman.*

66. Hume points out that "were you to preach, in most parts of the world, that political connexions are founded altogether on voluntary consent or mutual promise, the magistrates would soon imprison you, as seditious, for loosening the ties of obedience; if your friends did not before shut you up as delirious" ("Of the Original Contract," in *Political Essays,* 189).

67. Interestingly, among the large number of congressional state papers and letters reproduced in this volume, the radical republican language in which an absolutist portrait of popular consent to government is developed—in contrast to the ubiquitous presence of the need for a more limited popular consent to government, most particularly, of property holders to taxation—is found only in the Connecticut Statement of the Sons of Liberty and later, in a more muted form, in the Declaration of Independence. The first was a provincial document at the beginning of the crisis and the other a continental or intercolonial one at the end. On this history, see Rodgers, "Rights Consciousness in American History."

68. According to Handlin and Handlin, "There were no moderates in Massachusetts, no Friends of Liberty and Trade to counterbalance the Sons of Liberty. The conservatives knew the potential power of those beneath them in the social scale, feared it, and would have no truck with it" ("Radicals and Conservatives in Massachusetts," 347).

69. Franklin, "Petition to the King," in *The Writings of Benjamin Franklin,* 4:314.

70. Morgan, *Prologue to Revolution,* 127–28.

71. Franklin, *The Papers of Benjamin Franklin;* see also York, "When Words Fail," 364–70, and Valentine, *The British Establishment,* 1:202, 1:385–86, 2:866–67.

72. Thomas R. Adams, *American Independence,* 21–25.

73. Dumbauld writes that "to English ears this must have seemed like a dangerous extension of the powers of the crown" (*The Declaration of Independence and What It Means Today,* 123); according to Dickinson, "The legislature's ultimate control over the raising of revenue ensured that the king would not be able to exercise arbitrary or absolute power" ("Debate on the Sovereignty of Parliament," 200).

74. One of the most interesting discussions of this matter is found in Lolme, *Constitution of England,* 377–79. In particular, he writes of "being with Dr. Franklin at his house in Craven-street, some months before he went back to America" and that he "mentioned to him [that] a few of the

remarks contained in this chapter [about Franklin's 1766 testimony], and, in general, that the claim of the American colonies directly clashed with one of the vital principles of the English constitution. The observation, I remember, struck him very much" (378n). In particular, what was of central importance to Lolme, given that "the constitutional tendency of the claim of the Americans to be a subject [was] not very generally understood," was his "general observations on the right of granting subsidies."

75. See Nelson, "Patriot Royalism," and McConville, *King's Three Faces*, 193–202.

76. Morgan and Morgan, *Stamp Act Crisis*, 104–5.

77. Dickinson writes that "Britain did not pass the legislation that so angered the colonists in order to demonstrate parliament's sovereignty over the empire so much as resort to a defence of parliament's sovereignty over the empire *after* the colonies had argued that this legislation was unconstitutional" ("Britain's Imperial Sovereignty: The Ideological Case against the American Colonists," in *Britain and the American Revolution*, 68).

78. See Guttridge, *English Whiggism and the American Revolution*, 17–58.

79. York notes that Rockingham intentionally removed from the resolution that became the Declaratory Act "the incendiary word 'taxation.'" More particularly, he removed "Charles Yorke's insertion of: 'as well as cases of taxation' before the phrase 'in all cases whatsoever'" ("When Words Fail," 362, 362n75); Greene, following John Phillip Reid, writes that the central issue that "took the constitutional quarrel to the point of armed conflict" was not Parliament's authority to tax but to legislate for the colonies (*Constitutional Origins of the American Revolution*, xviii). For confirmation of the same, see, for example, Edmund Burke, "Speech on American Taxation."

80. York, "Impact of the American Revolution," 209–11. The Irish Declaratory Act of 1719/20, along with the far older Poynings Law, were repealed by the Renunciatory Act of 1782, after Britain's defeat in the war against America and the ensuing general malaise.

81. Purcell, *Who Was Who in the American Revolution*, 6–7.

82. Godbold, *Christopher Gadsden and the American Revolution*, ix, 70.

83. Quoted in Morgan and Morgan, *Stamp Act Crisis*, 113.

## ACT II: RESPONSE TO THE COERCIVE ACTS, 1774

1. Morris, *Encyclopedia of American History*, 78. Much of my history here is informed by Morris' summary.

2. Greene, *Constitutional Origins of the American Revolution*, 113.

3. See Rakove, *Revolutionaries*, 22; for a more variegated account, see Knollenberg, *Growth of the American Revolution*, 77–80.

4. Greene, *Constitutional Origins of the American Revolution*, 106.

5. Ibid., 134.

6. Samuel Adams, "A State of the Rights of the Colonists." This pamphlet led to quite possibly the most sophisticated exchange of constitutional views, between Thomas Hutchinson and John Adams; see Reid, *Briefs of the American Revolution*. Reid draws attention to Samuel Adams' pamphlet being "one of the very few statements of rights issued by American whigs during the prerevolutionary era that relied on the authority of natural law" (2).

7. Ritcheson, *British Politics and the American Revolution*, 156–62.

8. Commager, *Documents of American History*, 71.

9. Greene observes that "one of 'the great fundamental principles of the Government of Great Britain,' the Crown's incapacity to grant any 'dispensation from the laws of the land, and the authority of parliament' without the concurrence of the other two branches of the legislature,

could not be violated, an anonymous pamphleteer insisted, without dissolving the constitution and annihilating the most important foundation of British liberty" (*Constitutional Origins of the American Revolution*, 109).

10. See Henderson, *Party Politics in the Continental Congress*, 46–47, 72–73, for his helpful typologies of the members during the first three years of the first two Continental Congresses.

11. Hyneman and Lutz, *American Political Writing during the Founding Era*, 1:257.

12. Paul H. Smith writes that the manuscript "copy of these resolutions, in the writing of Richard Henry Lee, is among" his papers . . . "It does not, however, follow that he was the framer" (*Letters of Delegates to Congress*, 1:130).

13. See Maloy, *Colonial Origins of Modern Democratic Thought*.

14. Delegates, most particularly those in the radical faction, attempted to steer the Continental Congress in sought-after directions by sponsoring or requesting that particular proclamations or resolves be sent to the congress from colonial assemblies or congresses back home, ones that congressional delegates, in particular Samuel Adams, often had helped produce. Yet Friedenwald writes that at the end of 1774 there was still no sign among any of the delegates "that can rightly be interpreted as indicating a wish for the establishment, even remotely, of an independent government" (*The Declaration of Independence*, 28). It is even questionable whether "avowed radicals as John and Samuel Adams, Jefferson, and Patrick Henry, would have advocated independence in earnest at this time." Others, of course, had begun out of doors to speak loosely of it. Also see Dutcher, "Rise of Republican Government," 206.

15. See Rakove, *Beginnings of National Politics*, 6, and *Revolutionaries*, 17, where he states that "with the possible (and doubtful) exception of Samuel Adams, none of those who took leading roles in the struggle actively set out to foment rebellion or found a republic."

16. See Hawke, *Honorable Treason*, 6–8, and Hogeland, *Declaration*, 185.

17. See Marston, *King and Congress*, 185. Yirush writes that in 1665 "the Bay Colony's intransigence hardened metropolitan attitudes towards chartered autonomy throughout the empire" (*Settlers, Liberty, and Empire*, 57). A hundred years later, little had changed on either side.

18. Thomas R. Adams reports that he published sixteen pamphlets in thirty-one editions (*American Independence*, 256).

19. Commager, *Documents of American History*, 81. York describes Galloway's Plan as "the only significant reform proposal to come out of the First Continental Congress" ("Federalism and Imperial Reform," 164).

20. Lutz, *Colonial Origins of the American Revolution*, 391.

21. Ford records in a note: "'21st. Met, dismissed the plan for a union, &c., (Mr. Hopkins [of Rhode Island] for the plan, I against it).' *Ward.* This probably refers to Galloway's *Plan*" (*Journals of the Continental Congress*, 1:102, citing Samuel Ward of Rhode Island,).

22. Rakove argues that "the fact that his [Galloway's] plan was not reexamined during the following three weeks, when Congress *was* debating proposals for accommodation, suggests that it did not command wide support, and that the vote of the 28th did not reflect an even division of opinion on the proposal's substantive merits" (*Beginnings of National Politics*, 35).

23. See Burnett, *Continental Congress*, 258. Hulsebosch writes that "it took a war and another decade before the American provinces were ready to agree to a constitution that gave substantial authority to a 'grand Wittenagemoot'" (*Constituting Empire*, 141). According to Jensen, "The radical leaders of the opposition to Great Britain after 1765 had consistently denied the authority of any government superior to the legislatures of the several colonies. From 1774 on, the radicals

continued to deny the authority of a superior legislature whether located across the seas or within the American states" (*Articles of Confederation*, 238).

24. Lutz, *Colonial Origins of the American Revolution*, 391–92, and Jensen, *English Historical Documents*, 808.

25. Montross, *Reluctant Rebels*, 85.

26. See York, "Federalism and Imperial Reform," 166.

27. Benjamin Franklin to Galloway, February 25, 1775: "Lord Gower I believe alluded to it, when in the House he censur'd the Congress severely, as first resolving to receive a Plan for uniting the Colonies to the Mother Country, and afterwards rejecting it, and ordering their first Resolution to be eras'd out of their minutes" (in Smith, ed., *Letters of Delegates to Congress*, 1:113).

28. York, "Federalism and Imperial Reform," 174. He believes that there may have been up to a dozen plans, of varying complexity, put forward between 1773 and late 1775 (157).

29. See R. G. Adams, *Political Ideas of the American Revolution*, 71–83. Among the British authors Adams lists are to be found Joshua Steele, John Cartwright, Granville Sharp, William Pulteney, and the anonymous author of *A Plan, or Articles of Perpetual Union* (1780). Pulteney, a member of Parliament, saw his 1778 pamphlet, published the same year as the Carlisle Commission, go through five editions. Adam Smith all too accurately and incisively writes that "to propose that Great Britain should voluntarily give up all authority . . . would be to propose such a measure as never was, and never will be adopted, by any nation in the world. . . . Such sacrifices, though they might frequently be agreeable to the interest, are always mortifying to the pride of every nation, and what is perhaps of still greater consequence, they are always contrary to the private interest of the governing part of it" (*An Inquiry into the Nature and Causes of the Wealth of Nations*, 666).

30. See Henderson, *Party Politics in the Continental Congress*, and Marston, *King and Congress*.

31. See Handlin and Handlin, "Radicals and Conservatives in Massachusetts"; Van Tyne, *England and America*, 55–56.

32. Perry, *Sources of Our Liberties*, 274.

33. See Otis, "The Rights of the British Colonies Asserted and Proved."

34. This was a matter much disputed in the 1760s, and the argument was taken up in the 1920s by McIlwain in *American Revolution* (1923) and by Schuyler in *Parliament and the British Empire* (1929), and more recently by Black in "Constitution of Empire."

35. Governor Thomas Hutchinson, making much the same argument, was similarly anachronistic, while John Adams, in the opposite manner, was as well. See Reid, *Briefs of the American Revolution*.

36. Gipson describes the contempt with which the colonies met the Albany Plan and notes that Franklin had clearly "lost touch with the one group that he was supposed to understand so well—the common people of the colonies" ("Thomas Hutchinson and the Framing of the Albany Plan of Union," 26).

37. Thomas Burke, "The Albany Plan of Union, 1754." Yirush reports on a plan presented to Robert Walpole in 1739 "for a colonial union designed to combat the threat from the Spanish and French" (*Settlers, Liberty, and Empire*, 204, 195). McConville emphasizes at the same time the role of Martin Bladen (*King's Three Faces*, 223).

38. Newbold, *The Albany Congress and Plan of Union of 1754*, 47.

39. Ibid., 38–53.

40. See Gipson, "Hutchinson and the Albany Plan of Union," 25–28.

41. Burke, "Albany Plan of Union," 109–12.

42. See Gipson, "Hutchinson and the Albany Plan of Union," 18.

43. Gipson, "The American Revolution as an Aftermath of the Great War for the Empire," 163.

44. Burke, "Albany Plan of Union," 108, 112.

45. Ford, *Journals of the Continental Congress,* 1:43.

46. Morgan, *Prologue to Revolution,* 104.

47. See Maier, *From Resistance to Revolution,* 113–57.

48. See Guttridge, *English Whiggism and the American Revolution,* 79, and O'Shaughnessy, "'If Others Will Not Be Active,'" 12.

49. Hutson, *Decent Respect,* 10.

50. Kershaw, "Cushing, Thomas"; see also Henderson, *Party Politics in the Continental Congress.*

51. Countryman, "Low, Isaac."

52. Ford, *Journals of the Continental Congress,* 1:62–63, 75.

53. Greene, *Colonies to Nation,* 243.

54. Jensen, *English Historical Documents,* 813.

55. See Shain, *Myth of American Individualism,* 23–48. This restrictive morality, even if predominantly advanced by Reformed Protestants from New England, also was something sought by those influenced by a more secular strain of republican-influenced communalism, particularly among men from the southern colonies. See, too, Potter, *The Liberty We Seek,* 37–38.

56. The conservative commentary came from the "To the Americans," published anonymously in Suffolk County, New York, February 4, 1775; it is quoted in Jensen, *Articles of Confederation,* 74. Additional material is from Potter, *The Liberty We Seek,* 38.

57. Preston, *Documents Illustrative of American History,* 192–93; see also Hutson, *Decent Respect,* 11, citing Powell.

58. Montross, *Reluctant Rebels,* 59. Marston reports that "the process of local committee elections brought fully 7,000 Americans into positions of local resistance leadership" (*King and Congress,* 124).

59. It is not at all clear when something that can be called a unified American state came into existence. The most obvious choices are December 17, 1777, when France recognized American independence; March 1, 1781, when the Articles of Confederation were ratified; October 19, 1781, when the British forces were defeated at Yorktown by an allied American-French force; and September 3, 1783, when the Treaty of Paris was signed. Still, the Association in many ways can be considered the first piece of "national" legislation operating internally in the colonies with little direct oversight by individual colonies or states.

60. Ford, *Journals of the Continental Congress,* 1:56.

61. Ibid., 1:58.

62. Hutson, *Decent Respect,* 22.

63. Prince, "Livingston, William."

64. Ford, *Journals of the Continental Congress,* 1:75, 81, 90.

65. See Robbins, *Eighteenth-Century Commonwealthman.*

66. See Greene, *Constitutional Origins of the American Revolution,* 106.

67. Hutson, *Decent Respect,* 29.

68. Ibid., 34.

69. Ginsberg, "Dickinson, John"; see also Hawke, *Honorable Treason.*

70. Ford, *Journals of the Continental Congress,* 1:26, 28, 41.

71. John Adams, *The Works of John Adams,* 3:309–10.

72. Hutson, *Decent Respect,* 50.

73. Hutson, *Decent Respect*, 50–51. Dickinson wrote three of America's most important early state papers (and others as well): the Stamp Act Declaration (1765), the Bill of Rights of the First Continental Congress (1774), and the initial draft of the Articles of Confederation (1776). Only Jefferson, with his authorship of the Declaration of Independence, ranks ahead of Dickinson for the importance (though perhaps not the quantity) of seminal documents he produced.

74. Jensen writes that the two issues that divided Congress "were the theoretical foundation of colonial rights and the question of the regulation of trade by Parliament": "Although the final declaration represented a compromise of views it was in essence a victory for the popular leaders since it contained most of their ideas, including the 'law of nature' as one basis for colonial rights, and made 'consent' and 'necessity' rather than 'right' the basis for the regulation of trade by Parliament" (*English Historical Documents*, 805).

75. Shain, "Rights Natural and Civil," 138.

76. Interestingly, and possibly in keeping with the almost seventeenth-century constitutionalism of the colonial position, the only three references in the document to "British" elements are derogatory.

77. Friedenwald, *Declaration of Independence*, 36.

78. See Burke, "Speech on American Taxation,"1:217.

79. See Greene, *Constitutional Origins of the American Revolution*, 36–37, 109.

80. John Adams, *The Diary and Autobiography of John Adams*, 3:309.

81. See Robbins, *Eighteenth-Century Commonwealthman*, and Colbourn, *The Lamp of Experience*.

82. Blackstone found that plantations or colonies are of three types: those held by right of occupancy, by conquest, or by treaties. In regard to colonies established by occupation, if "planted by English subjects, all the English laws are immediately there in force. . . . But in conquered or ceded territories they have already laws of their own, [and] the king may indeed alter and change those laws . . . Our American plantations are principally of this latter sort, being obtained in the last century either by right of conquest . . . or by treaties. And therefore the common law of England, as such, has no allowance or authority there; they being no part of the mother country, but distinct (though dependent) dominions. They are subject however to the control of parliament" (*Commentaries*, 1:104–5).

83. Randolph, "Edmund Randolph's Essay on the Revolutionary History of Virginia," 45.

84. See Shain, "Rights Natural and Civil," 116–62. The late eighteenth-century breakdown of the distinction between natural and civil liberty, along with the loss of the close and necessary link between rights and duties, helped foster a radical rights revolution.

85. Ford, *Journals of the Continental Congress*, 1:101.

86. Ibid., 1:103, 105, 122.

87. Hutson, *Decent Respect*, 60.

88. Perry, *Sources of Our Liberties*, 284.

89. On the tensions between corporatism and individualism in common-law juries, see Shain, *Myth of American Individualism*, 260, and Pekelis, *Law and Social Action*, 61–62.

90. See Montross, *Reluctant Rebels*, 54; Coupland, *American Revolution and the British Empire*, 222, 229–30, 239–40; Knollenberg, *Growth of the American Revolution*, 141–47; and Hulsebosch, *Constituting Empire*, 107–8.

91. Ritcheson agrees too that "the [Quebec] act was, then, a sincere attempt to right the wrongs inflicted upon a great body of alien people absorbed into the empire through conquest" (*British Politics and the American Revolution*, 167).

92. See Roeber, "The Limited Horizons of Whig Religious Rights," and Hamburger, *Separation of Church and State.*

93. Ford, *Journals of the Continental Congress,* 1:53, and Henderson, *Party Politics in the Continental Congress.*

94. Ford, *Journals of the Continental Congress,* 1:102–4.

95. See Wolf, "The Authorship of the 1774 Address to the King Restudied."

96. Hutson, *Decent Respect,* 72–74.

97. See Rakove, *Revolutionaries,* 93.

98. Ritcheson, *British Politics and the American Revolution,* 12–13.

99. See Hume, *History of England,* 6:532.

100. See Schuyler, *Parliament and the British Empire,* 143–44.

101. Ford, *Journals of the Continental Congress,* 1:54.

102. See Rakove, *Beginnings of National Politics,* 57.

103. According to Blackstone, "All foreign protestants, and Jews, upon their residing seven years in any of the American colonies, without being absent above two months at a time, are upon taking the oaths naturalized to all intents and purposes, as if they had been born in this kingdom" (*Commentaries,* 1:363). Notwithstanding the colonists' fears, Catholics were excluded from this accommodation.

## ACT III: THE FIGHTING BEGINS, 1775

1. For the various terms, see Allen, who writes that he does not use "'American army' or 'American' for one side or the other because the Revolutionary War was a civil war, and when Loyalists or Tories fought Patriots or Rebels, everyone in the fight was an American" (*Tories,* xxiii).

2. Morris, *Encyclopedia of American History,* 86. Much of my history here is informed by Morris' summary.

3. On the early and continuing violence between the two sides, particularly in New England, see Allen, *Tories.*

4. Tansill, *Documents Illustrative of the Formation of the Union,* 6–9.

5. Ford, *Journals of the Continental Congress,* 2:89–92. In the eighteenth century, those equipped with rifles, firearms with rifled barrels, mostly served as auxiliaries and were used for irregular engagements, most particularly for shooting the enemy from a longer range than was possible with muskets.

6. Morris, *Encyclopedia of American History,* 88.

7. Palmer reports that the annual tax burden in 1765 for subjects in Britain was twenty-six shillings, compared to one shilling in most of the colonies (*Age of the Democratic Revolution,* 1:155).

8. For confirmation of this, see Maier, *From Resistance to Revolution,* 228–70.

9. Ford, *Journals of the Continental Congress,* 2:64.

10. Ibid., 2:70.

11. Lanctot, *Canada and the American Revolution,* 30–31, 46–48.

12. Hutson, *Decent Respect,* 84.

13. Commager, *Documents of American History,* 91.

14. See Shain, "Rights Natural and Civil."

15. Bancroft, *History of the United States,* 4:583.

16. See Gordon Wood, "The History of Rights in Early America."

17. Burnett, *The Continental Congress,* 71.

18. Rafuse, "Warren, Joseph."

19. Dreisbach and Hall, *Sacred Rights of Conscience*, 217, quoting Davis, *Religion and the Continental Congress*, 86.

20. Van Tyne reports that in a study of 274 leaders of the patriot cause whose religious affiliation can be determined, "one hundred and seventy-nine were either Presbyterian or Congregationalist, thirty-six Dissenters of another stripe, and fifty-six Episcopalians, of whom only fourteen came from north of Maryland. Eighty per cent. of the Patriot leaders were therefore Dissenters" (*England and America*, 75–76). See also Henderson, *Party Politics in the Continental Congress*, 179.

21. Hutson, *Religion and the Founding of the American Republic* and *Church and State in America*; Dreisbach and Hall, *Sacred Rights of Conscience*.

22. Greene, *Colonies to Nation*, 260–61.

23. See Shain, *Myth of American Individualism*, 197–209. There and throughout the work, I argue for the overwhelmingly Reformed Protestant nature of American cultural life and political institutions, and for Protestantism's formative role in structuring both.

24. Ford, *Journals of the Continental Congress*, 2:105.

25. Hutson, *Decent Respect*, 90.

26. Ford, *Journals of the Continental Congress*, 2:138–39. Montross writes that Jefferson's contribution was "so inferior in every respect that the editorial judgment of the delegates cannot be questioned" (*Reluctant Rebels*, 80).

27. Perry, *Sources of Our Liberties*, 290.

28. O'Shaughnessy, "'If Others Will Not Be Active,'" 15, and Marston, *King and Congress*, 59.

29. Perry, *Sources of Our Liberties*, 290, and Hutson, *Decent Respect*, 90.

30. Ford, *Journals of the Continental Congress*, 2:129–30. Jensen writes that the moderates in Congress held that "all political authority in the colonies derived from a superior power and not from the people. . . . [Therefore,] the acceptance of the Declaration of Independence meant the establishment of the radical theory of the derivation of political authority. It meant that the people of the individual states rather than the British crown were to be the ultimate theoretical source of power" (*Articles of Confederation*, 167). The moderate (or conservative) James Wilson of Pennsylvania later developed an innovative third possible source of sovereign authority, a national people.

31. See Dickinson, "Britain's Imperial Sovereignty: The Ideological Case against the American Colonists," in *Britain and the American Revolution*, ed. Dickinson, 64–96, for his defense of both Parliament and king, framed against internal British political needs and concerns.

32. For the minutemen, see Frothingham, *Life and Times of Joseph Warren*, 403.

33. Hutson, *Decent Respect*, 98n9.

34. Ford, *Journals of the Continental Congress*, 2:80.

35. Hutson, *Decent Respect*, 127.

36. Ford, *Journals of the Continental Congress*, 2:65, 126–27. Thomas Jefferson wrote in his *Autobiography*: "Congress gave a signal proof of their indulgence to Mr. Dickinson, and of their great desire not to go too fast for any respectable part of our body, in permitting him to draw their second petition to the King according to his own ideas, and passing it with scarcely any amendment" (quoted in Ford, *Journals of the Continental Congress*, 2:158). In contrast, Marston argues that the moderates took this appeal seriously and still had sufficient power "to impose much of their plan," a closely linked strategy of reconciliation and defensive measures, "upon their colleagues" (*King and Congress*, 210). Similarly, Henderson writes that the Olive Branch Petition demonstrated that a still-powerful contingent in Congress "did not want hostilities to lead to independence" (*Party Politics in the Continental Congress*, 49).

37. Hutson, *Decent Respect,* 126.

38. Force, "Penn and Lee to the President of Congress [September 2, 1775]," in *American Archives,* 3:627.

39. See Penn and Lee, "The Olive Branch Petition." Dickinson reminds his readers that the petition's "offer to raise revenue to be paid directly to the King but not to Parliament deeply alarmed opinion in Britain, where it was seen as vital that Parliament could limit royal power by means of its control of the purse strings" (*British Pamphlets on the American Revolution,* 1:xxxiv).

40. Bargar, *Lord Dartmouth and the American Revolution,* 155.

41. Quoted in Jensen, *English Historical Documents,* 847.

42. Burnett, *Continental Congress,* 88.

43. Burnett writes that "Congress was not yet, after six months of weighing and balancing, quite in the mood to slam the door of reconciliation, although its ire was rapidly rising, and ere another half-year had passed would slam shut the door with a bang" (*Continental Congress,* 92).

44. See Perry, *Sources of Our Liberties,* 295.

45. See Henderson, *Party Politics in the Continental Congress,* 15.

46. Ford, *Journals of the Continental Congress,* 2:79–80, 110, 127, 157, 162.

47. Hutson, *Decent Respect,* 100.

48. Bradford Family, "Bradford Family Papers."

49. Ford, *Journals of the Continental Congress,* 2:157, 170.

50. Hutson, *Decent Respect,* 140.

51. Allen reports that ultimately the Six Nations split, with the Oneida and Tuscarora supporting "the Patriots, while the other tribes agreed to become warriors for the British and their Loyalist allies" (*Tories,* 211–12).

52. Hutson, *Decent Respect,* 147.

53. As noted earlier, the colonists were taxed at one shilling a person and the British at twenty-six shillings.

54. See Fliegelman, *Prodigals and Pilgrims;* Greven, *Protestant Temperament;* and seminal to this tradition of thought, Locke, *Some Thoughts Concerning Education.*

55. See Reid, *Constitutional History of the American Revolution,* 44–45, 59–60, 75, 98; Schuyler, *Parliament and the British Empire.* For the effect of the American Revolution on Irish-British relations, see Harlow, *The Founding of the Second British Empire,* 493–557, and York, "Impact of the American Revolution."

56. Maier, *From Resistance to Revolution,* 255, and Ford, *Journals of the Continental Congress,* 2:80, 194.

57. Ford, *Journals of the Continental Congress,* 2:212.

58. Hutson, *Decent Respect,* 110.

59. See McIlwain, *American Revolution,* 29–56, and Reid, *In a Defiant Stance.*

60. Schuyler describes the Renunciation Act as "a complete victory for Ireland" (*Parliament and the British Empire,* 100).

61. See LaCroix, *Ideological Origins of American Federalism,* 24–29, 87–88, 120–24.

62. MacDonald, *Select Charters and Other Documents Illustrative of American History,* 367.

63. Jensen, *English Historical Documents,* 839.

64. Guttridge writes that the "conciliatory proposals may have been entirely sincere, but, if so, their ultimate success was doomed by the impolitic mode of presentation, which insured the utmost suspicion" (*English Whiggism and the American Revolution,* 79–80).

65. Ford, *Journals of the Continental Congress,* 2:61–63.

66. Jefferson, *Papers of Thomas Jefferson,* 1:170–74.

67. Ford, *Journals of the Continental Congress,* 2:202.

68. Ibid., 2:203, 224; Hutson, *Decent Respect,* 118.

69. See Edmund Burke, "Thoughts on the Cause of the Present Discontents," in *Select Works.*

70. See Jefferson, "Summary View of the Rights of British America," 260, 268–69, 273–75, and Colbourn, *Lamp of Experience,* 158–84.

71. Dickinson reports that in 1775 "eight million Britons paid £10 million per annum in taxes, while three million American colonists paid £75,000 per annum. The British therefore contributed about fifty times more tax per head than the Americans, who were not poor by comparison" (*British Pamphlets on the American Revolution,* 1:xxxiii).

72. According to Cannon: "As early as 1784 British exports to America had recovered beyond the level of the last year of peace, and after that the expansion was extraordinary. By the 1790s the liberated Americans were buying twice as much from Britain as they had done as subjects of the empire in the 1760s" ("Loss of America," 246). That outcome had been predicted and defended by, among others, Adam Smith (*Wealth of Nations,* 664–67) and even earlier by Josiah Tucker, who, according to Dickinson "was the first British commentator to take the plunge and to advocate complete independence for the American colonies" (*British Pamphlets on the American Revolution,* 1:xlviii).

73. See Beloff, *The Debate on the American Revolution,* 195, and York, "Federalism and Imperial Reform," 168–76.

74. Morris, *Encyclopedia of American History,* 85.

75. Ritcheson writes that "the Glorious Revolution had established the supremacy of Parliament; that Parliament itself, the guardian of the people's rights and the protector of the empire, might be thought tyrannical was a patent absurdity" (*British Politics and the American Revolution,* 25).

76. As Edmund Burke noted in his much-discussed "Speech on American Taxation" (170–71) the taxation issue had been largely put to rest by 1769 or 1770. Burke cites Lord Hillsborough, then secretary of state for the colonies, in a speech before Parliament in May 1769, noting "'that his Majesty's *present Administration have at no time entertained a design to propose to Parliament to lay any further taxes upon America for the purpose of* RAISING A REVENUE . . . [for] such duties *having been laid* [are] *contrary to the true principles of Commerce.*'"

77. See York, "Federalism and Imperial Reform," 169–70.

78. O'Gorman, "The Parliamentary Opposition to the Government's American Policy," 109.

79. Ritcheson, *British Politics and the American Revolution,* 185.

80. Thackeray, *A History of the Right Honorable William Pitt,* 292.

81. See too, Janus, *The Critical Moment,* for a particularly trenchant and prescient critique of the British military's likely difficulties in trying to pacify the colonies.

82. Beloff, *Debate on the American Revolution,* 195.

83. Benjamin Franklin House, "The London Years."

84. Sparks, *The Works of Benjamin Franklin,* 5:83–90.

85. Smith, ed., *Letters of Delegates to Congress,* 1:566.

86. Ibid.

87. See Henderson, *Party Politics in the Continental Congress,* 322; Hulsebosch, *Constituting Empire,* 192; Van Tyne, *The Loyalists in the American Revolution,* 275–78; and Jensen, *New Nation.*

88. Ford, *Journals of the Continental Congress,* 3:298.

89. John Adams, *Works,* 3:18–21.

90. Jensen writes in confirmation that "when New Hampshire appealed to Congress for advice in October, a committee dominated by radicals was appointed to prepare an answer, and the reply they made was in accord with radical views." Unlike the instructions offered Massachusetts in June, "no mention was made of charter restrictions. . . . In these two letters of advice lies the whole difference between the philosophy of conservatism and the philosophy of radicalism" (*Articles of Confederation*, 96).

91. Burnet, *Continental Congress*, 123.

92. Ford, *Journals of the Continental Congress*, 3:319.

93. See Henderson, *Party Politics in the Continental Congress*, and Hawke, *Honorable Treason*, 38–40.

94. Haywood, "The Genesis of Wake County."

95. Congress' initiative here and with the other three states where similar invitations had been issued might be of interest to those considering later states'-rights debates. The debate in Virginia, in which Congress took the initiative, gives credence to those who view the states as creatures of a still-to-be-born central government. A more telling explanation may be that the colonies, given their monarchical histories, were not yet ready to act solely on the perceived impetus of the people. They seemed still to need, in effect, the warrant of some higher authority to act.

96. Ford, *Journals of the Continental Congress*, 3:344.

97. Ibid., 3:319, 403–4.

98. Burnet, *The Continental Congress*, 124.

99. See Nash, *Unknown American Revolution*, 157–66. He writes that "regardless of the horrible death toll at the hands of smallpox, Dunmore's Proclamation reverberated throughout the colonies and became a major factor in convincing white colonists that reconciliation with the mother country was impossible" (166). Much the same is reported in Allen, *Tories*.

100. Weslager, *Stamp Act Congress*, 124.

101. Friedenwald, *Declaration of Independence*, 41.

102. Ibid., 42–43.

103. Ford lists the colonial agents employed as of October 1774. The agents for Massachusetts were William Bolan, Benjamin Franklin, and Arthur Lee; Paul Wentworth represented New Hampshire; Thomas Life represented Connecticut; Franklin also represented New Jersey and Pennsylvania; Edmund Burke, a member of Parliament, represented New York; Charles Garth, another member of Parliament, served South Carolina (he had also been the agent for Maryland); and none were listed at the time for Rhode Island, Delaware, Maryland, Virginia, and North Carolina (*Journals of the Continental Congress*, 1:122).

104. Frothingham, *The Rise of the Republic of the United States*, 445.

105. Friedenwald, *Declaration of Independence*, 47.

106. Burnett, *Continental Congress*, 117, and Ford, *Journals of the Continental Congress*, 3:353.

107. Frothingham, *Rise of the Republic*, 445.

108. Chaplin, "Izard, Ralph."

109. Friedenwald, *Declaration of Independence*, 50.

110. See Wood, *Battles of the Revolutionary War*, 287. Conway reports that there were about three hundred thousand British soldiers, sailors, militiamen, and volunteers: "In other words, between one in seven and one in eight males of the appropriate age served in some kind of military or naval capacity during the war" ("The Politics of British Military and Naval Mobilization," 1180). Only a fraction of that number, given Britain's vast imperial reach and need to protect the home

islands against French and Spanish warships, could be committed to the North American continental theatre.

111. Greene and Pole, *Blackwell Encyclopedia of the American Revolution,* 757.

112. Purcell, *Who Was Who,* 337.

ACT IV: TOWARD INDEPENDENCE, 1776

1. See Armitage, *Declaration of Independence* and Shain, "Rights Natural and Civil."

2. See Hoffer, "The Declaration of Independence as a Bill in Equity."

3. For a wonderful description of this changing landscape and the differences between congressional and "real" radicals out of doors, particularly in Philadelphia (and later in Vermont), see Hogeland, *Declaration.*

4. See Rodgers, "Rights Consciousness in American History."

5. Ford, *Journals of the Continental Congress,* 3:417.

6. Jensen, *English Historical Documents,* 851.

7. As Adam Smith and Josiah Tucker correctly predicted, from a pro-British commercial perspective, the war to retain the colonies was, in truth, absolutely unnecessary. Nonetheless, pamphlet after pamphlet in Great Britain predicted the opposite. For examples, see Dickinson, *British Pamphlets on the American Revolution.*

8. Lord Drummond, "Lord Drummond's Minutes."

9. There are some who believed that Paine's pamphlet was solicited, possibly by Benjamin Franklin, so as to appear in print at nearly the same time that the king's speech was expected to arrive in the colonies; see Friedenwald, *Declaration of Independence,* 54–55.

10. Hazleton, *The Declaration of Independence,* 90. Hazleton quotes a letter from Francis Lightfoot Lee: "I suppose you have recd a copy of Common sense which I sent you some time ago, if not I now send a parcel to Col Taylor of whome you may have one. Our late King & his Parliament having declared us Rebils & Enemies confiscated our property as far as they were likely to lay hands on it have effectually decided the question for us, whether or no we shall be independent" (93–94). Jensen reports that 120,000 copies of *Common Sense* were sold in the first three months after publication (*Founding of a Nation,* 669).

11. Jensen, *Founding of a Nation,* 652.

12. Allan, *John Hancock.*

13. Ford, *Journals of the Continental Congress,* 4:87.

14. See Jensen, *Founding of a Nation,* 651; Friedenwald, *Declaration of Independence,* 129; Burnett, *Continental Congress,* 183.

15. Friedenwald, *Declaration of Independence,* 58–59.

16. Jensen, *Articles of Confederation,* 88.

17. See, among many others, Thomas, *The Townshend Duties Crisis.*

18. Ford, *Journals of the Continental Congress,* 4:146n.

19. Ibid., 4:146.

20. Edward Tilghman to his father, February 4, 1776, quoted in Jensen, *Founding of a Nation,* 652.

21. Russell, "Smith, Richard."

22. Ford, *Journals of the Continental Congress,* 4:208–9.

23. Hall writes of eight fast-day proclamations and six proclamations for days of thanksgiving issued by Congress between 1775 and 1784 (*Genevan Reformation,* 424–30). According to Hutson, "Congress adopted and preached to the American people the political theology of the national

covenant, settling into a pattern of issuing a fast day proclamation every March and a thanksgiving proclamation every October" (*Church and State in America,* 99). A national covenant, similar to that between God and the Jews or Israel, is a corporate compact with God that binds the entire nation to love and glorify him, with the consequent responsibility of the nation's citizens to ensure that everyone, regardless of personal spiritual condition or beliefs, does so.

24. See Shain, *Myth of American Individualism.*

25. Still, Livingston had created something of a controversy a month earlier when he moved that a vote of thanks be extended by Congress to Dr. William Smith for his sermon honoring General Montgomery, in which Smith boldly defended loyalty and allegiance to the king.

26. See Thomas R. Adams, *American Independence,* 216.

27. Ippel, "Blow the Trumpet, Sanctify the Fast," 45.

28. Jensen, *Founding of a Nation,* 659.

29. Ford, *Journals of the Continental Congress,* 4:214, 3:314.

30. Jameson writes that "the privateering successes of the Revolution quite overshadowed those obtained by the vessels of the federal and state government . . . In the course of the whole war more than five hundred privateers were commissioned by the various states, and probably as many as ninety thousand Americans were, first and last, engaged in these voyages, a number of men almost as great as served in the army, and greater than that of the army in any single year save one" (*The American Revolution Considered as a Social Movement,* 65–66).

31. MacDonald, *Select Charters and Other Documents,* 391.

32. Dumbauld, *Declaration of Independence,* 144–45.

33. Dickinson, *British Pamphlets on the American Revolution,* 1:xxxv.

34. Jensen, *English Historical Documents,* 853.

35. See Thomas, *Townshend Duties Crisis,* 258–64.

36. North Carolina Historical Commission, "Halifax Resolves." Nearly a year earlier, Mecklenburg County, North Carolina, had, on May 31, 1775, adopted a set of resolves that began, "We conceive that all Laws and Commissions confirmed by, or derived from the Authority of the King or Parliament, are annulled and vacated," and concluded with, "These Resolves [shall] be in full Force and Virtue, until Instructions from the General Congress of this Province . . . shall provide otherwise, or the legislative Body of *Great Britain* resign its unjust and arbitrary Pretentions with respect to *America.*" See Tansill, *Formation of the Union,* 6–9; for the fascinating 1819 controversy concerning a fraudulent version, see Hazleton, *Declaration of Independence,* 20–33.

37. Jensen, *Articles of Confederation,* 122. The Wyoming Valley is an area in north-central Pennsylvania that was claimed by Connecticut, which had begun settling it shortly before the sharp rise in imperial difficulties. There were sufficiently frequent clashes between respective groups of settlers to demand congressional attention here and, earlier, on December 20, 1775.

38. Ford, *Journals of the Continental Congress,* 4:62–63, 113.

39. Ibid., 4:153–54, 159, 256.

40. John Adams, *Works,* 3:29.

41. Ibid., 3:39.

42. McIlwain demonstrates that up to April or "May, 1776, then, the American claims were aimed solely at the power of Parliament. About that time they first began to be directed against the Crown. As soon as they were so directed their revolutionary character became obvious. . . . This last phase of the controversy, this defiance of prerogative, however, began very late; in fact, not until many months after the constitutional struggle had turned into a civil war which we call from its final outcome the War of Independence" (*American Revolution,* 7).

43. Smith, ed., *Letters of Delegates to Congress*, 3:260.

44. Ibid., 3:262.

45. Rifles were impractical for close-formation fighting because of the difficulty of quickly loading and reloading them. The rifling in the barrels, which made them deadly accurate at long range, also made it more time consuming to load and clean the barrels.

46. See Fliegelman, *Prodigals and Pilgrims*.

47. On the failure of the gentry to anticipate accurately such changes, see Rozbicki, *Culture and Liberty*, 223–38.

48. Emory G. Evans, "Carter, Robert."

49. Jensen, *Founding of a Nation*, 639.

50. Robbins, *Eighteenth-Century Commonwealthman*, 350–51.

51. See Gordon Wood, *Creation of the American Republic*, 57–64.

52. In "Liberty of the Ancients," Constant persuasively argues that high levels of commercial activity help distinguish liberal polities from republican ones.

53. Montesquieu writes that democratic republics may be "founded on commerce" and "that individuals [may] have great wealth, yet that the mores are not corrupted. This is because the spirit of commerce brings with it the spirit of frugality, economy, moderation, work, wisdom . . . Thus, as long as this spirit continues to exist, the wealth it produces has no bad effect" (*Spirit of the Laws*, 48). In short, Adams appears to have held American colonists to a standard that went beyond the stringent one set by Montesquieu when commenting on something of a confusing hybrid in his own work, commercial republics; see John Adams, *Works*, 6:430.

54. Hogeland describes this process in the most obstreperous and essential colony to the independence movement, Pennsylvania. He writes that the radicals in Philadelphia "would make an actual working-class revolution in Pennsylvania. . . . Only nine weeks after the May 1 election, which determined on reconciliation with England, Samuel Adams's unlikely coalition would turn Pennsylvania, the Congress, and the British government upside down" (*Declaration*, 33–34).

55. Friedenwald, *Declaration of Independence*, 80.

56. Jensen, *Founding of a Nation*, 682–83.

57. Indeed, Marston argues that it was reasonable for many moderates, recognizing the need for established and legitimate government in many of the colonies, to view this resolution as necessary and entirely unthreatening (*King and Congress*, 283).

58. Ford, *Journals of the Continental Congress*, 4:340, 342.

59. John Adams, *Works*, 3:46.

60. Ford, *Journals of the Continental Congress*, 4:351, 353, 357–58.

61. Dumbauld, *Declaration of Independence*, 143. Friedenwald writes that the effect of this information "was, in its intensity, unequaled by any occurrence since the arrival of the King's speech [of October 26, 1775] four months before" (*Declaration of Independence*, 67).

62. John Adams, *Works*, 3:46.

63. Rhode Island General Assembly, Act of Renunciation.

64. Still, the loss of a neutral arbiter between contending colonial factions would be missed and, in a certain sense, not replaced for another decade; see Bilder, *Transatlantic Constitution*, 186–98, and Hulsebosch, *Constituting Empire*.

65. Ford, *Journals of the Continental Congress*, 4:353.

66. Jensen writes that "the preamble John Adams wrote provided the theoretical foundation for revolution which Jefferson was to elaborate in the Declaration of Independence a few weeks

later, but its immediate purpose was to justify Revolution in Pennsylvania" (*Founding of a Nation,* 684); for an account with a greater focus on Philadelphia, see Hogeland, *Declaration.*

67. Smith, ed., *Letters of Delegates to Congress,* 4:20n3.

68. See Henderson, *Party Politics in the Continental Congress,* for a discussion of the continuing divisions in Congress; for detailed voting patterns, see 106–7, 123, 147, 164–68.

69. Jensen explores the internal political and social dynamics in each colony (*Founding of a Nation,* 667–704).

70. Jensen, *Founding of a Nation,* 693. He describes the instructions of the January 11 and 18 conventions as demanding that its delegates withdraw from Congress if independence were declared, and as restating its assessment that "the people of this province . . . [are] the freest members of any civil society in the known world, [and] never did, nor do entertain any views or desires of independency" (642–43).

71. Hogeland, *Declaration,* 185. He notes, too, that "the radicals put in practice a competing idea: government must restrain property, in order to foster fairness and liberate ordinary people."

72. Jensen, *Founding of a Nation,* 662; Wood, *Radicalism of the American Revolution.* Jameson quotes an earlier author, likely Benjamin Rush (and not a South Carolinian), who observes, "There is nothing more common than to confound the terms of the American Revolution with those of the late American war. The American war is over, but this is far from being the case with the American revolution. On the contrary, nothing but the first act of the great drama is closed" (*American Revolution,* 20). Indeed, the war likely had consequences that were far broader, even if wholly unintended, than many of its advocates had envisioned, with repercussions that were worldwide and enduring.

73. As noted above, Mecklenburg County, North Carolina, had done so earlier, though provisionally, on May 31, 1775; see Tansill, *Formation of the Union,* 9.

74. Ford, *Journals of the Continental Congress,* 5:433; see also Elbridge Gerry to James Warren, June 11, 1776: "After a long debate the question of independence was postponed until the first of July, in order to give the assemblies of the middle colonies an opportunity to take off their restrictions and let their delegates unite in the measure. In the interim will go on plans for confederation and foreign alliance" (in Smith, ed., *Letters of Delegates to Congress,* 4:187).

75. Friedenwald, *Declaration of Independence,* 81.

76. Robson, "Why Revolution?," 142–43.

77. Ford, *Journals of the Continental Congress,* 5:431.

78. Ibid., 5:431–38.

79. Burnett, *Continental Congress,* 167.

80. Perry, *Sources of Our Liberties,* 302.

81. Jensen, *Founding of a Nation,* 671–72, 677–79.

82. Ford, *Journals of the Continental Congress,* 4:233, 406, and 5:417, 421, 423–24, 626.

83. Oberholtzer, *Robert Morris,* 17, 21; Hawke, *Honorable Treason,* 158–60, 198; Ford, *Journals of the Continental Congress,* 5:626.

84. Hawke, *Honorable Treason,* 106.

85. Thomas Burke to Governor Caswell, May 23, 1777: "Georgia was of no use in Congress but to vote with Connecticut" (in Ford, *Journals of the Continental Congress,* 7:123).

86. Jensen, *Founding of a Nation,* 694–96.

87. Hazelton, *Declaration of Independence;* in particular regarding New York and Pennsylvania, see 181–92. Becker famously writes that two questions were most important in New York: "The first

was the question of home rule; the second was the question, if we may so put it, of who should rule at home" (*History of Political Parties*, 22). For Rozbicki's partial dissent, see *Culture and Liberty*, 225.

88. According to Jensen, on March 23, South Carolina had freed its delegates to join with the majority to vote for measures "'necessary for the defence, security, interest, or welfare of this colony in particular, and of America in general.'" On April 12, North Carolina was far less equivocal, becoming the first colony to write directly of independence when it "unanimously empowered its delegates to 'concur with the delegates of the other colonies in declaring independence, and forming foreign alliances'" (*Founding of a Nation*, 667–704). Finally and unexpectedly, the last southern colony to act was Virginia, on May 15.

89. Again, Jensen helps situate the state of each colony (*Founding of a Nation*, 667–704). Rhode Island instructed its delegates on May 4 to vote for independence; Connecticut wouldn't until June 14; New Hampshire would do so on June 15; and Massachusetts not until July 3, and in a rather equivocal manner in which the House of Representatives agreed to prepare a letter stating that if Congress should think it appropriate "to declare the colonies independent of the kingdom of Great Britain, this house will approve of the measure." In particular, the sixteen Essex County towns showed so little enthusiasm for the measure that "only one supported independence unequivocally" (677).

90. Jensen, *Founding of a Nation*, 690–91.

91. Paul H. Smith observes that these notes of Jefferson, along with those dated July 1–4 and July 12–August 1, are believed to have been written up sometime between August 1776 and June 1783 (*Letters of Delegates to Congress*, 4:165).

92. Perry, *Sources of Our Liberties*, 324; see also Hogeland, *Declaration*, for his dramatic presentation of the politicking and changes that took place between May 1 and July 4.

93. See Ford, *Journals of the Continental Congress*, 5:491. In the entry for June 28, the *Journal's* editor, Worthington Chauncey Ford, inserted two versions of the Declaration of Independence: a "First Draft," which he describes as "the original form of the paper, but the capitalization is Adams's, not Jefferson's," and a "Reported Draft" containing notes describing differences in various extant manuscripts.

94. Smith, ed. *Letters of Delegates to Congress*, 4:347.

95. Jensen, *Founding of a Nation*, 700.

96. According to Montross: "Accounts as to what took place on the 2nd and 4th of July are meager when not confused and contradictory. This is not surprising when it is considered that the main actors of the drama waited until the next century before ransacking their memories" (*Reluctant Rebels*, 153). Friedenwald writes that "Wilson decided to go with the majority. His decision was all-important, for without his vote Pennsylvania's delegation would have been equally divided," and thus, so far as we know, there were only three individual votes on July 2 "cast against it—those of Willing and Humphreys of Pennsylvania, and Read's of Delaware" (*Declaration of Independence*, 129).

97. Ford, *Journals of the Continental Congress*, 5:491, 504–7, 510–16, 560, 590–91, 626.

98. Friedenwald, *Declaration of Independence*, 136. He finds that "it has been possible to determine definitely that of these forty-nine men" who were delegates to Congress, all but four "were in Philadelphia on July 4 and could have voted for the Declaration" (143). He further reports that "seven of the names that are affixed are those of men who were not members of the Congress of July 4 . . . while exactly the same number were in Congress on that date but never signed at any time—[George] Clinton, [John] Alsop, R. R. Livingston, [Henry] Wisner [all of New York], [and, Charles] Humphreys [of Pennsylvania] and [John] Rogers [of Maryland]" (149). We also know that

some, such as Samuel Chase and Elbridge Gerry, had requested that others serve as proxies in signing their names; see Hazelton, *Declaration of Independence,* 164–65, for his account.

99. See Hawke, *Honorable Treason,* for a discussion of this matter.

100. Lutz, "The Declaration of Independence," 141; Ford, *Journals of the Continental Congress,* 7:48.

101. Of course, as Lind, in *An Answer to the Declaration of the American Congress,* points out, it was anything but clear that the North American colonists were a separate people rather than, as they had been for up to 150 years, an English or British people. In fact, the colonists had, for the past decade and longer, vigorously and emphatically claimed as much.

102. According to Dumbauld: "The equality of states is one of the basic doctrines of international law. . . . The doctrine arose when the 'state of nature' and 'law of nature' concepts were applied to nations and not merely to individuals. It was first formulated by Pufendorf and was popularized by Vattel" (*Declaration of Independence,* 34–35).

103. See Becker, *Declaration of Independence,* and, more recently, among many others, Breen, *The Lockean Moment.* They argue that John Locke, a seventeenth-century English philosopher, was the source of the Declaration's social compact theory. Others—including the two most authoritative sources on this period, Colbourn, *Lamp of Experience,* and Robbins, *Eighteenth-Century Commonwealthman*—convincingly claim that such language was ubiquitous in seventeenth-century English radical political thought. Lutz notes too that "[Algernon] Sidney's essays, written prior to Locke's, had language that is closer to that used in the Declaration than does Locke's. The language in the Declaration resembles that found in half a dozen authors who wrote before or after Locke" ("Declaration of Independence," 142).

104. See Hume, *History of England,* 6:172. McConville writes that the "seventeenth-century disaster was a powerful historical reference point for all political considerations in the provinces up to 1776" (*King's Three Faces,* 93).

105. Friedenwald, *Declaration of Independence,* viii. He notes that not until November 1775 can one see congressional radicals, and even then not publicly, "developing the conscious aim toward independence" (48); and see Dutcher, "Rise of Republican Government."

106. Van Tyne writes that "between 1760 and the close of the Revolution there were forty-seven [lawyers] from South Carolina, twenty-one from Virginia, sixteen from Maryland, eleven from Pennsylvania, [and] five from New York" trained in the Middle Temple in England, and points out that "graduates of the Middle Temple were slow to turn to natural law, shy of revolution and glittering generalities about immutable laws of Nature" (*England and America,* 92–93). See also King, *Founding Fathers v. the People.* Montross writes that "neither the word nor the theory of democracy found much approval in that day" (*Reluctant Rebels,* 27).

107. See, for example, Robbins, *Eighteenth-Century Commonwealthman;* Colbourn, *Lamp of Experience;* Smith, ed., *English Defenders of American Freedom;* Wood, *Creation of the American Republic,* 46–90; Sharp, *A Declaration of the People's Natural Right.* Dickinson reminds us that "many Britons outside of parliament held an older view of the constitution similar to that held by most American colonists. . . . British radicals such as Price and Cartwright even stressed the sovereign authority of the people" (*Britain and the American Revolution,* 12). Other works defending the powerful influence of English radicalism in colonial North America include Bailyn, *Ideological Origins;* Maier, *From Resistance to Revolution;* Nash, *Unknown American Revolution;* Hogeland, *Declaration;* and Rozbicki, *Culture and Liberty.*

108. Hyneman and Lutz, *American Political Writing;* see also Hutson, "The Emergence of the Modern Concept of a Right in America."

109. See Allen, *Tories*.

110. Jensen writes that for a century in the colonies "the people exercised this authority only because they had been allowed to do so by a superior power . . . To this the radicals of the American colonies opposed the ancient doctrine of the sovereignty of the people . . . It was restated in the Declaration of Independence, which was a complete negation of the conservative theory that all authority must proceed in an unbroken legal chain from some superior political power" (*Articles of Confederation*, 164–65).

111. Locke writes "that every man, that hath any possessions, or enjoyment, of any part of the dominions of any government, doth thereby give his *tacit consent,* and is as far forth obliged to obedience to the laws of that government" (*Second Treatise of Government,* 64). Dickinson writes: "Once the political community had been established, then the legislature was sovereign. Locke did not allow the people to recover the original authority unless the social contract was clearly broken and civil society was dissolved," so "while the civil society remained in being, then the people had little active power" ("Debate on the Sovereignty of Parliament," 203). One of Locke's most effective critics, Josiah Tucker, claimed that Locke's endorsement of legislative supremacy did little to prevent colonists from using his ideas for radical ends. Tucker thus asks "whether the *Americans,* in all their Contests for Liberty, have even once made use of Mr. Locke's System for any other Purpose, but that of *pulling down,*" while never using it "to erect a new Edifice of their own" (*Treatise Concerning Civil Government,* 105).

112. See Rodgers, "Rights Consciousness in American History."

113. See Shain, "Rights Natural and Civil."

114. Rousseau explains as well as anyone else writing at the time: "The right of property being only a convention of human institution [that is, adventitious], men may dispose of what they possess as they please: but this is not the case with the essential gifts of nature, such as life and liberty, which every man is permitted to enjoy, and of which it is at least doubtful whether [as inalienable] any have a right to divest themselves" (*The Social Contract and Discourses,* 205).

115. Ford, *Journals of the Continental Congress,* 7:136, citing Burke's *Abstract of Debates in Congress* (1777).

116. It is necessary to keep in mind that the Declaration's second paragraph, even if not representative of a decade of congressional state papers, did accord with an important strand of popular and influential opinion in the colonies that had deep, even if far less immediately influential, roots in Britain.

117. On September 24, 1774, in the first weeks of the First Continental Congress, that body confined itself "to the consideration of such rights only as have been infringed by acts of the British parliament since the year 1763" (Ford, *Journals of the Continental Congress,* 1:42). Clearly, in the grievances listed here, as earlier in Jefferson's "Summary View of the Rights of British America" (1774) and in his "Preamble to the Virginia Constitution" (June 29, 1776), that limitation is not observed (Jefferson, *Papers,* 1:377–86,).

118. See Bilder, *Transatlantic Constitution,* 175–83. Marston reminds readers that the colonists had formerly accepted that the king "was the 'sovereign umpire' who resolved all intra-imperial disputes for the common good" (*King and Congress,* 27).

119. My remarks in what follows were informed by, though they are not necessarily always in agreement with, Friedenwald, *Declaration of Independence,* and Dumbauld, *Declaration of Independence.* To understand the contemporary conservative British perspective on the charges leveled against the king, it is helpful to consult Lind, who writes that "if the Americans insult him by groundless complaints of his government, it is because he *asserted our rights*—if they have

dared to renounce all allegiance to his Crown, it is because he *determined not to give up our rights*" (*Answer to the Declaration,* 9). Almost no attention is paid by Lind, or anyone else in Britain, to the theoretical second paragraph of the Declaration, for he believes that "the opinions of the modern Americans on Government, like those of their good ancestors on witchcraft, would be too ridiculous to deserve any notice, if like them too, contemptible and extravagant as they be, they had not led to the most serious evils" (118).

120. See Guttridge, *English Whiggism and the American Revolution,* and Thomas, *Townshend Duties Crisis,* 2.

121. Gipson writes that "these Indians were assured [by the Crown] that they would be secure in their trans-Appalachian lands as a reward for deserting their allies, the French" ("American Revolution as an Aftermath," 156); see also Thomas, "A Policy for the West, 1767–1773," in *Townshend Duties Crisis,* 51–75.

122. See Friedenwald, *Declaration of Independence,* 230–37.

123. Lutz, "Declaration of Independence," 143.

124. Oddly enough, the identical language, "in all cases whatsoever," was used in 1787 by James Madison in describing his defense of a federal veto, modeled on that of the Privy Council, over state legislatures. In particular, see Madison's letters to Thomas Jefferson on March 19, to Edmund Randolph on April 8, and to George Washington on April 16. See Shain, "Reading *The Federalist,* Looking Backward and Forward," 20–21, and LaCroix, *Ideological Origins of American Federalism,* 263, quoting Larry Kramer, who writes that "Madison could not have picked language more likely to arouse anxiety about centralized authority."

125. O'Shaughnessy writes that "it served the purposes of the revolutionary movement to hold the king personally responsible for the crisis since they held rebellion was only permissible against a tyrant" ("'If Others Will Not Be Active,'" 20).

126. Allen, *Tories,* 210, 332.

127. Robbins, *Eighteenth-Century Commonwealthman,* 313; and see Maier, *From Resistance to Revolution,* and Guttridge, *English Whiggism and the American Revolution.*

128. According to Montross: among the Virginia delegation, which was widely recognized and had to be represented on the committee, "Lee was distrusted because he had been too thick with Sam Adams, while both Harrison and Braxton were considered reactionaries. Jefferson seemed a safe even if unexciting choice" (*Reluctant Rebel,* 146).

129. John Adams, *Works,* 2:510–15. Jefferson found much in Adams' letter to Pickering that he believed was inaccurate. As reported by Hazelton, Jefferson wrote, "In some of the particulars Mr. Adams' memory has led him into unquestioning error. At the age of 88 and 47 years after the transaction of Independence, this is not wonderful" (*Declaration of Independence,* 143). Jefferson, however, was only eight years younger, and given the inaccuracies aggressively advanced in contemporary letters of Jefferson's, his memory was no more perfect.

130. Derry writes that "in a story which was rich in paradox George III had no wish to assert royal prerogatives in the colonial context, seeing his public duty as the vindication of parliament's rights throughout all territories owing allegiance to the British crown" ("Government Policy and the American Crisis," 45). Still, as O'Shaughnessy points out: "The king alone held the jarring elements of the cabinet together and persuaded Lord North to remain in office after 1778. He effectively prolonged the war at least three years" ("'If Others Will Not Be Active,'" 5).

131. Friedenwald writes that "the noticeable stiffening of the attitude of the Congress, which dates from this period, is in large measure due to the influence exerted by these two new delegations,

whose persistency in turn brought about a gradual accession of numbers to their ranks" (*Declaration of Independence*, 59).

132. See Jensen, *Articles of Confederation*.

133. Jameson estimates that by far the largest holder of slaves was Virginia, with two hundred thousand, and South Carolina was next, with one hundred thousand, though part of a far smaller settler population (*American Revolution*, 21–22). New York, with twenty-five thousand, had the most among the mid-Atlantic colonies, and the smallest numbers were found in the New England colonies, each with around five thousand slaves at the time.

134. Although Jefferson writes that the debate ended on the evening of the 4th and that the Declaration was signed then by all members except Dickinson, debate likely terminated in the morning, and the signing of the document did not begin until August 2 (Ford, *Journals of the Continental Congress*, 5:626). It is doubtful that Dickinson and Morris were absent. Jefferson is probably confusing the vote on July 2 on Lee's resolution on independence with the vote on the Declaration on July 4; see Smith, ed., *Letters of Delegates to Congress*, 4:364–65nn4–5. For Jefferson's extended and exaggerated defense of his position in a letter of May 12, 1819, to Samuel Adams Wells, see Hazelton, *Declaration of Independence*, 196–200, and Burnett, *Continental Congress*, 192–97.

135. John Adams, *Works*, 3:55.

136. Rakove, *Revolutionaries*, 101.

## ACT V: NEW NATIONS, 1776–1777

1. Morris, *Encyclopedia of American History*, 93. Much of my history is informed by Morris' summary.

2. Ford, *Journals of the Continental Congress*, 6:1027.

3. Ibid., 6:1041.

4. Ibid., 6:1054–55.

5. Allen describes the savage nature of the war in the so-called neutral ground, where "both sides would fight, not to gain territory but to forage for food and firewood, to demand loyalty oaths, to kill each other in skirmishes—to spy" (*Tories*, 196).

6. Ford, *Journals of the Continental Congress*, 7:124.

7. As far as I can ascertain, this request was never satisfied by the states.

8. Ford, *Journals of the Continental Congress*, 8:450.

9. As Allen notes, "Congress refused to accept Gates's agreement. So the 'Convention Army' eventually was marched from Boston to Charlottesville, Virginia, confined there for a while and then herded elsewhere. In a five-year odyssey of misery and despair, the Convention Army continually lost men to death and desertion" (*Tories*, 233).

10. See Henderson, *Party Politics in the Continental Congress*, for his wonderful use, through block-voting analysis, of these records.

11. Ford, *Journals of the Continental Congress*, 8:708.

12. Ibid., 9:1068.

13. For well-known examples of those defending a civil religion, see Bellah, "The Revolution and the Civil Religion," and Albanese, *Sons of the Fathers*.

14. For his description of the same, see Wood, *Creation of the American Republic*.

15. Dutcher insightfully notes that the new states, "if they were to avoid anarchy and prosecute their own defense, their choices were confined to monarchy, dictatorship or republic. How could there be a monarchy without an available candidate for the throne? . . . The mere statement of the question is sufficient to show that quite apart from any predilection the only possible choice was a republic, first for each colony individually and then for the Union" ("Rise of Republican Government," 207).

16. Ford, *Journals of the Continental Congress*, 5:425, 428–29.

17. Ibid., 5:596.

18. Burnett, *Continental Congress*, 213.

19. Jensen finds that almost all the delegates, even those largely supportive of independence, with the exception of the aged Stephen Hopkins and the largely mute Samuel Adams, were moderate—thus, the reason for the centralizing character of the Dickinson draft (*Articles of Confederation*, 126). Importantly, though, as Jensen further remarks, even some moderates, such as Edward Rutledge, supported a states'-rights position out of fear of the democratic ethos prevalent in New England and the danger that, in a centrally controlled polity, the populous and popular New England states would represent (128).

20. For Dickinson's original draft, along with a copy by Josiah Bartlett, see Paul H. Smith, ed., *Letters of Delegates to Congress*, 4:233–55. Rakove takes note of two additional plans for confederation, in addition to Franklin's earlier plan of July 21, 1775, and concludes that "none of these initial three drafts had a major impact on the seminal text that John Dickinson prepared in June 1776" (*Beginnings of National Politics*, 136–39).

21. Jensen, *Articles of Confederation*, 249.

22. See Hawke, *Honorable Treason*, 62–63.

23. Ford, *Journals of the Continental Congress*, 5:546–55, 600–28, 635–40, 674–89.

24. Montross describes Congress' censuring Burke for "'disorderly and contemptuous'" behavior (*Reluctant Rebels*, 223). Henderson writes that Burke was an unequaled "defender of states' rights when the Articles were given their final modification," but by 1780–81 had become "a strong advocate of executivism when supporting Robert Morris's office of the Superintendent of Finance" (*Party Politics in the Continental Congress*, 132).

25. Jensen, *Articles of Confederation*, 241.

26. Ibid., 15. Jensen writes that "the ascendancy of the radicals of the colonies . . . was of brief duration, but while it lasted an attempt was made to write democratic ideals and theories of government into the laws and constitutions of the American states" (11).

27. Jefferson, *Papers*, 1:327.

28. See Jensen, *Articles of Confederation*, and Henderson, *Party Politics in the Continental Congress*.

29. Ford, *Journals of the Continental Congress*, 5:576–89.

30. Ibid., 5:575.

31. Burnett, *Continental Congress*, 199–200.

32. Ford, *Journals of the Continental Congress*, 5:590–91. Burnett suggests that the timing of the order to engross and, still more significantly, to sign the Declaration of Independence, with British peace commissioners then present in the former colonies, was unlikely to have been coincidental (*Continental Congress*, 201).

33. Rakove, *Beginnings of National Politics*, 114.

34. Ford, *Journals of the Continental Congress*, 4:247, 250, 276, 320–23, 325, 327–28.

35. John Adams, *Works*, 3:43. Adams further notes: "They endeavored to insert in the resolution ideas of reconciliation; we carried our point for inserting peace. They wanted powers to be given to the General to receive the commissioners in ceremony; we ordered nothing to be done till we were solicited for passports. Upon the whole we avoided the snare, and brought the controversy to a close, with some dignity."

36. Burnett, *Continental Congress*, 154.

37. Concerning one matter, though—his prediction of loss of trade as a consequence of the war—Franklin proved to be wrong. As noted previously, Cannon writes that "as early as 1784

British exports to America had recovered beyond the level of the last year of peace. . . . By the 1790s the liberated Americans were buying twice as much from Britain as they had done as subjects of the empire in the 1760s" ("Loss of America," 246).

38. A. Smith, *Wealth of Nations*, 665–66. His view, it might be added, of the motivation of the colonists was no more flattering; see, for example, 672.

39. Hawke cites a British spy in June 1775 as reporting that Franklin remained "'among those who are for moderation, and bringing about reconciliatory measures,'" but by mid-July he had written his ally and former protégé Galloway and his son that he now "favored independence" (*Honorable Treason*, 177).

40. Burrows writes that the British had captured so many Americans that they "had nowhere to put a mass of prisoners other than in the houses and barns of local farmers or the occasional church" (*Forgotten Patriots*, 11). He estimates that by the end of 1776 there were approximately five thousand American prisoners in New York City (316). Adding to this problem was the loss on September 21 of three hundred buildings there as a result of devastating fire.

41. Ford, *Journals of the Continental Congress*, 5:723, 728, 730–31, 735.

42. Josiah Bartlett to William Whipple, September 10, 1776 (Smith, ed., *Letters of Delegates to Congress*, 5:128).

43. See Hogeland, *Declaration*, and Henderson, *Party Politics in the Continental Congress*.

44. Rakove writes that had Lord Howe enjoyed more substantial powers with which to negotiate, "it seems likely that the reverses of late 1776 could well have reopened serious divisions within Congress and exacerbated the existing signs of popular disillusionment" (*Beginnings of National Politics*, 114).

45. John Adams to Samuel Adams, September 14, 1776, (Smith, ed., *Letters of Delegates to Congress*, 5:159–62). John Adams, as was his fashion, described the commission as "a Bubble, an Ambuscade, a mere insidious Manoeuvre, calculated only to decoy and deceive."

46. Ford, *Journals of the Continental Congress*, 5:755, 765–66.

47. See Burke, "Speech on American Taxation," 194–95, 215, 217–18, and Guttridge, *English Whiggism and the American Revolution*.

48. Ford, *Journals of the Continental Congress*, 6:1027. Congress, on leaving Philadelphia, had ordered that "General Washington be possessed of full power to order and direct all things relative to the department, and to the operations of war."

49. Peckham describes the month of November 1776 as Washington's "darkest month of retreat and agonizing disintegration," with desertions cutting deeply into the declining strength "of his dispirited army" (*The War for Independence*, 46).

50. Rosenberg, "Militia, Patriot, and Loyalist," 795.

51. Congress on November 7, 1776, resolved "that General Washington be requested to take proper steps for trying all deserters from his army, and punishing, in the most exemplary manner the articles will admit, all such officers and soldiers who shall be base enough disgracefully to leave the service of their country at this time of trial and danger" (Ford, *Journals of the Continental Congress*, 6:933); see also Van Tyne, *England and America*, 134–35.

52. Ford, *Journals of the Continental Congress*, 7:108–9. Ford records that the vote tallies for membership on this committee were as follows: "Chase, 9; Sergeant, 5; [Thomas] Burke [of North Carolina], 3; R. H. Lee, 5; J. Adams, 2; [Abraham] Clark [of New Jersey], 1."

53. See Friedenwald, *Declaration of Independence*, 31–35, on Congress' peak and subsequently declining power.

54. Jensen, *Articles of Confederation*, 170–72.

55. LaCroix unconvincingly argues that by 1787 the former colonists had made important theoretical and practical strides in resolving this matter (*Ideological Origins of American Federalism*, 126–31, 172–74). Long-developed practice, Dickinson counseled, would guide those in Philadelphia in 1787 rather than any manner of theoretical breakthrough. As he noted, "Experience must be our only guide. Reason may mislead us. It was not Reason that discovered the singular & admirable mechanism of the English Constitution. . . . Accidents probably produced these discoveries, and experience has give a sanction to them" (quoted in Farrand, *Records of the Federal Convention*, 2:278).

56. See Schecter, "New York Campaign."

57. James Madison believed it essential that the national government be able to vacate state laws. He fought to maintain that proposed feature of the Constitution at the Philadelphia Convention and then in the First Congress. Madison argued for a system comparable to the British system, for "nothing could maintain the harmony & subordination of the various parts of the empire, but the prerogative by which the Crown, stifles in the birth every Act of every part tending to discord or encroachment"; such a system entailed the need for "some emanation of the power [of the federal government] into the States" (quoted in Farrand, *Records of the Federal Convention*, 2:28). In a series of letters in March and April 1787 written to Thomas Jefferson, George Washington, and Edmund Randolph, he insisted on the necessity of a Privy Council–like veto "in all cases whatsoever"—which was, remarkably, the exact language used in the hated Declaratory Act of 1766. On the veto and the efforts of Crown officials to balance metropolitan and colonial perspectives in their decisions, see Bilder, *Transatlantic Constitution*.

58. Ford, *Journals of the Continental Congress*, 5:689.

59. Ibid., 7:240.

60. Ibid., 7:351.

61. Burnett, *Continental Congress*, 237.

62. Jensen, *Articles of Confederation*, 179–80.

63. Ibid., 128.

64. Rakove, *Beginnings of National Politics*, 164.

65. Ibid., 183–84.

66. Ibid., 171–72. But see Ford, who draws on Burke's correspondence to show that little love was lost between Burke and Lee (*Journals of the Continental Congress*, 7:122, 136). For example, Burke thought Lee's action "such an instance of contempt and disregard in Virginia, that he could not but receive it with indignation" (7:122).

67. See Jensen, *Articles of Confederation*, 165.

68. Slade, *Vermont State Papers*, 60.

69. Perry, *Sources of Our Liberties*, 359.

70. Hogeland, *Declaration*, 25; see also Maier, *From Resistance to Revolution*, 192–97.

71. Ford, *Journals of the Continental Congress*, 7:230, 239.

72. Ibid., 8:491.

73. Thomas Young, "To the Inhabitants of Vermont," April 11, 1777, quoted in Slade, *Vermont State Papers*, 76.

74. Ford, *Journals of the Continental Congress*, 8:509.

75. Burnett discusses the lengthy and messy history of this matter before Congress (*Continental Congress*, 540–46); for its significance, see Onuf, *The Origins of the Federal Republic*, 127–45, and Marston, *King and Congress*, 243–50.

76. Slade, *Vermont State Papers*, 64.

77. There was no simple, internationally accepted definition of American irregular combatants. They could, when seized, legitimately be described as traitors, tried as spies, and, thus, subjected to summary execution, or, alternatively, they could be treated as prisoners of war with limited but acknowledged rights. The parallel with contemporary Islamic terrorists is unmistakable. See Burrows, *Forgotten Patriots,* and my critical review of his book.

78. For Young's close involvement in both Philadelphia and continental politics in the summer of 1776, see Hogeland, *Declaration.*

79. As Henderson explains, Lee's "opponents in the [Virginia] Assembly charged that he had favored New England to the disadvantage of Virginia." (*Party Politics in the Continental Congress,* 116).

80. Ford, *Journals of the Continental Congress,* 8:754–56, 9:851, 11:662, 671–72. As mentioned in note 6 to this chapter, Congress, unhappy with the Convention of Saratoga, did not observe it.

81. For the meaning of Reformed Protestant theology and ecclesiology, and the breadth of adherence to it among late eighteenth-century Americans, see Ahlstrom, *A Religious History of the American People,* 79–81; Hutson, *Religion and the American Republic;* and Shain, *Myth of American Individualism.*

82. Hutson, *Church and State in America,* 96. Hutson reminds us that Charles Thomson, Congress' permanent secretary, "retired from public life to translate the Scriptures from Greek into English"; that John Dickinson too had "retired from public life to devote himself to religious scholarship"; and that two future presidents of Congress, John Jay (1778–79) and Elias Boudinot (1782–83), served as presidents of the American Bible Society.

83. Gaines, "The Continental Congress Considers the Publication of a Bible, 1777."

84. Ford, *Journals of the Continental Congress,* 8:733–35. On August 2, 1777, Congress resolved that "all questions agitated and determined by Congress, be entered on the journal, and that the yeas and nays of each member, if required by any State, be taken on every question as stated and determined by the house" (8:599). The first recorded roll-call vote, to promote Brigadier General Arnold to major general, was on August 8, 1777, as requested by Rhode Island after the measure's failure (8:624).

85. Ford, *Journals of the Continental Congress,* 18:979–80, 19:91, 22:572–74.

86. Dreisbach and Hall, *Sacred Rights of Conscience,* 231.

87. See Thomas, *Townshend Duties Crisis,* 2.

88. Rakove, *Beginnings of National Politics,* 180.

89. Ibid., 181. Rakove argues that these changes imposed restrictions on the states "similar to those originally proposed by John Dickinson in 1776, and in apparent contradiction with the theory of state sovereignty Thomas Burke had advanced in April 1777. . . . The exercise of these prerogatives of sovereignty was not . . . to be transferred to the union, but simply denied to the states" (ibid). His understanding fails, though, to give sufficient weight to the speed and ease with which Burke's amendment was passed. At the very least, different sentiments regarding this issue were certainly still present in Congress.

90. Ford, *Journals of the Continental Congress,* 9:778–82, 801–2, 806–8, 843, 885–900, 907–25, 928, 932–35, and Jensen, *Articles of Confederation,* 252.

91. Rakove, *Beginnings of National Politics,* 181–82.

92. On the changing constellation of congressional voting that followed independence and the rise of new issues of the greatest saliency, see Henderson, *Party Politics in the Continental Congress.*

93. Ford, *Journals of the Continental Congress,* 9:1013–15.

94. Burnett, *Continental Congress*, 271–73, 276.

95. Ford, *Journals of the Continental Congress*, 9:1022, 1031, 1033, 1042–47.

96. For a description of the unenviable circumstances in this region, the neutral ground lying between New York and New Jersey, see Allen, *Tories*, 184–208.

97. See Ford, *Journals of the Continental Congress*, 8:694–95, regarding Congress' order on August 28, 1777, to arrest and incarcerate Philadelphia Quakers with little or no evidence of individual wrongdoing.

98. Jameson, *American Revolution*, 6.

99. Ford, *Journals of the Continental Congress*, 9:1054, 1064–65.

100. Burnett, *Continental Congress*, 277.

# SELECTED BIBLIOGRAPHY

The works listed here are, in the main, full citations for references found in the Notes of this work. For a fuller listing of background works on the era of the American Revolution, see the bibliography for my *Myth of American Individualism*, listed below.

Adams, John. *Diary and Autobiography of John Adams.* Edited by L. H. Butterfield. 4 vols. Cambridge, Mass.: Harvard University Press, 1961.

———. "Novanglus; or, a History of the Dispute with America, from Its Origin, in 1754, to the Present Time." In *The Revolutionary Writings of John Adams,* edited by C. Bradley Thompson, 147–284. Indianapolis: Liberty Fund, 2000.

———. *The Works of John Adams, Second President of the United States: With a Life of the Author, Notes, and Illustrations.* Edited by Charles Francis Adams. Boston: Little, Brown, 1851–65.

Adams, John, and Abigail Adams. *The Book of Abigail and John: Selected Letters of the Adams Family, 1762–1784.* Edited by L. H. Butterfield, Marc Friedlander, and Mary-Jo Kline. Cambridge, Mass: Harvard University Press, 1975.

Adams, R. G. *Political Ideas of the American Revolution: Britannic-American Contributions to the Problem of Imperial Organization, 1765 to 1775.* 1922. Reprint. New York: Barnes and Noble, 1958.

Adams, Samuel. "A State of the Rights of the Colonists." In *Tracts of the American Revolution, 1763–1766,* edited by Merrill Jensen, 233–55. 1966. Reprint. Indianapolis: Hackett, 2003.

———. *The Writings of Samuel Adams.* Edited by Harry Alonzo Cushing. 4 vols. New York and London: G. P. Putnam's Sons, 1904–8.

Adams, Thomas R. *American Independence: The Growth of an Idea.* Austin, Tex., and New Haven, Conn.: Jenkins and Reese, 1980.

Ahlstrom, Sydney E. *A Religious History of the American People.* New Haven, Conn.: Yale University Press, 1972.

Albanese, Catherine L. *Sons of the Fathers: The Civil Religion of the American Revolution.* Philadelphia: Temple University Press, 1976.

Allan, Herbert S. *John Hancock: Patriot in Purple.* New York: Macmillan, 1948.

Allen, Thomas B. *Tories: Fighting for the King in America's First Civil War.* New York: HarperCollins, 2010.

Armitage, David. *The Declaration of Independence: A Global History*. Cambridge, Mass.: Harvard University Press, 2007.

Armitage, David, and Sanjay Subrahmanyam, eds. *The Age of Revolutions in Global Context, c. 1760–1840*. London: Palgrave Macmillan, 2010.

Avalon Project. "An Act Repealing the Stamp Act; March 18, 1766." New Haven, Conn.: Lillian Goldman Law Library, Yale Law School, 2008. http://avalon.law.yale.edu/18th_century/repeal _stamp_act_1766.asp.

Bailyn, Bernard. *The Ideological Origins of the American Revolution*. Cambridge, Mass.: Harvard University Press, 1967.

Baldwin, Alice. *The New England Clergy and the American Revolution*. Durham, N.C.: Duke University Press, 1928.

Bancroft, George. *History of the United States from the Discovery of the Continent*. 10 vols. Boston: Little, Brown, 1876.

Banner, James M., Jr. "Livingston, Robert R." In *American National Biography Online*. Oxford University Press, 2000. http://www.anb.org/articles/02/02-00214.html.

Bargar, B. D. *Lord Dartmouth and the American Revolution*. Columbia: University of South Carolina Press, 1965.

Beard, Charles A. *An Economic Interpretation of the Constitution of the United States*. 1913. Reprint. New York: Free Press, 1986.

Becker, Carl L. *The Declaration of Independence: A Study in the History of Political Ideas*. 1922. Reprint. New York: Vintage Books, 1958.

———. *The History of Political Parties in the Province of New York, 1760–1776*. 1909. Reprint. Madison: University of Wisconsin Press, 1968

Bellah, Robert N. "The Revolution and the Civil Religion." In *Religion and the American Revolution*, edited by Jerald C. Bauer, 55–73. Philadelphia: Fortress Press, 1976.

Beloff, Max, ed. *The Debate on the American Revolution, 1761–1785*. 1949. Reprint. Dobbs Ferry, N.Y.: Sheridan House, 1989.

Benjamin Franklin House. "The London Years, 1725–1776." Friends of Benjamin Franklin House. http://www.benjaminfranklinhouse.org/site/sections/about_franklin/london_years .html.

Bilder, Mary Sarah. *The Transatlantic Constitution: Colonial Legal Culture and the Empire*. Cambridge, Mass.: Harvard University Press, 2004.

Black, Barbara A. "The Constitution of Empire: The Case for the Colonists." *University of Pennsylvania Law Review* 124 (1976): 1157–1211.

Blackstone, William. *Commentaries on the Laws of England*. 4 vols. 1765. Rev. ed., Chicago: University of Chicago Press, 1979.

Bonomi, Patricia. *Under the Cope of Heaven: Religion, Society, and Politics in Colonial America*. New York: Oxford University Press, 1986.

Bradford, Alden, ed. *Speeches of the Governors of Massachusetts from 1765 to 1775: And the answers of the House of Representatives to the same; With their resolutions and addresses for that period and other public papers relating to the dispute between this country and Great Britain which led to the independence of the United States*. Boston: Russell and Gardner, 1818.

Bradford Family. "Bradford Family Papers." In *Collection 1676* [1620–1906]. Historical Society of Pennsylvania, 2006. http://www.hsp.org.

Breen, T. H. *The Lockean Moment: The Language of Rights on the Eve of the American Revolution*. Oxford: Oxford University Press, 2001.

Brigham, Clarence S. A. M., ed. *British Royal Proclamations Relating to America, 1603–1783.* Worcester, Mass.: American Antiquarian Society, 1911.

Brown, Weldon A. *Empire or Independence: A Study in the Failure of Reconciliation, 1774–1783.* 1941. Reprint. Port Washington, N.Y.: Kennikat, 1966.

Burke, Edmund. "Speech on American Taxation [April 19, 1774]." In *Select Works of Edmund Burke,* edited by E. J. Payne, 1:157–220. 1874–78. Reprint. Indianapolis: Liberty Fund, 1999.

Burke, Thomas E. "The Albany Plan of Union, 1754." In *Roots of the Republic: American Founding Documents Interpreted,* edited by Stephen L. Schechter, 106–13. Madison: Madison House, 1990.

Burnett, Edmund Cody. *The Continental Congress: A Definitive History of the Continental Congress from Its Inception in 1774 to March 1789.* 1941. Reprint. New York: Norton, 1964.

Burrows, Edwin G. *Forgotten Patriots: The Untold Story of the American Prisoners during the Revolutionary War.* New York: Basic Books, 2008.

Calhoon, Robert M. "Johnson, William Samuel." In *American National Biography Online.* Oxford University Press, 2000. http://www.anb.org/articles/01/01-00461.html.

Cannon, John. "Loss of America." In *Britain and the American Revolution,* edited by H. T. Dickinson, 233–58. London and New York: Longman, 1998.

Cartwright, John. "American Independence, the Interest and Glory of Great Britain." In *English Defenders of American Freedoms,* edited by Paul H. Smith, 125–92. Washington, D.C.: Library of Congress, 1972.

Chaplin, Joyce E. "Izard, Ralph." In *American National Biography Online.* Oxford University Press, 2000. http://www.anb.org/articles/02/02-00191.html.

Christie, Ian R., and Benjamin W. Labaree. *Empire or Independence, 1760–1776: A British-American Dialogue on the Coming of the American Revolution.* New York: Norton, 1976.

Clark, Dora Mae. *British Opinion and the American Revolution.* 1930. Reprint. New York: Russell and Russell, 1966.

Colbourn, H. Trevor. *The Lamp of Experience: Whig History and the Intellectual Origins of the American Revolution.* Chapel Hill: University of North Carolina Press, 1965.

Commager, Henry Steele, ed. *Documents of American History.* New York: Appleton-Century-Crofts, 1968.

Constant, Benjamin. "The Liberty of the Ancients Compared with that of the Moderns." In *Political Writings,* translated and edited by Biancamaria Fontana, 307–28. Cambridge: Cambridge University Press, 1988.

Conway, Stephen. "The Politics of British Military and Naval Mobilization, 1775–83." *English Historical Review* 112 (November 1997): 1179–1201.

Countryman, Edward. "Low, Isaac." In *American National Biography Online.* Oxford University Press, 2000. http://www.anb.org/articles/01/01-00540.html.

Coupland, R. *The American Revolution and the British Empire.* 1930. Rev. ed., Cranbury, N.J.: Scholar's Bookshelf, 2005.

Davis, Derek. *Religion and the Continental Congress, 1774–1789.* New York: Oxford University Press, 2000.

Derry, John. "Government Policy and the American Crisis, 1760–1776." In *Britain and the American Revolution,* edited by H. T. Dickinson, 44–63. London and New York: Longman, 1998.

Detweiler, Robert. "Bland, Richard." In *American National Biography Online.* Oxford University Press, 2000. http://www.anb.org/articles/01/01-00077.html.

Dickinson, H. T., ed. *Britain and the American Revolution.* London and New York: Longman, 1998.

————, ed. *British Pamphlets on the American Revolution, 1763–1785*. 8 vols. London: Pickering and Chatto, 2007.

————. "The Eighteenth-Century Debate on the Sovereignty of Parliament." *Transactions of the Royal Historical Society* 26 (1976): 189–210.

————. *Liberty and Property: Political Ideology in Eighteenth-Century Britain*. London: Weidenfeld and Nicolson, 1977.

Dreisbach, Daniel L. "Founders Famous and Forgotten." *Intercollegiate Review* 42 (2007): 3–12.

Dreisbach, Daniel L, and Mark David Hall, eds. *The Sacred Rights of Conscience: Selected Readings on Religious Liberty and Church-State Relations in the American Founding*. Indianapolis: Liberty Fund, 2009.

Dreisbach, Daniel L, Mark Hall, and Jeffry Morrison, eds. *The Founders on Faith and Civil Government*. Lanham, Md.: Rowman and Littlefield, 2004.

Drummond, Thomas Lundin, Lord. "Lord Drummond's Minutes." In *Letters of Delegates to Congress*, edited by Paul H. Smith, 3:92–93. Washington, D.C.: Library of Congress, 1976–93.

Dumbauld, Edward. *The Declaration of Independence and What It Means Today*. Norman: University of Oklahoma Press, 1950.

Dutcher, George M. "The Rise of Republican Government in the United States." *Political Science Quarterly* 55 (June 1940): 199–216.

Evans, Charles. *American Bibliography*. 14 vols. Chicago: Privately printed for the author by the Blakely Press, 1903–59.

Evans, Emory G. "Carter, Robert." In *American National Biography Online*. Oxford University Press, 2000. http://www.anb.org/articles/01/01-00147.html.

Farrand, Max, ed. *The Records of the Federal Convention of 1787*. 4 vols. 1911. Reprint. New Haven, Conn.: Yale University Press, 1966.

Fisher, Sydney G. "The Legendary and Myth-Making Process in Histories of the American Revolution." *Proceedings of the American Philosophical Society* 51 (April–June 1912): 53–75.

Fliegelman, Jay. *Prodigals and Pilgrims: The American Revolution against Patriarchal Authority, 1750–1800*. Cambridge: Cambridge University Press, 1982.

Force, Peter, ed. *American Archives*. 4th ser. Washington, D.C.: M. St. Clair Clarke and Peter Force, 1839.

Ford, Worthington Chauncey, et al., eds. *Journals of the Continental Congress, 1774–1789*. 34 vols. Washington, D.C.: Government Printing Office, 1904–37.

Franklin, Benjamin. *The Papers of Benjamin Franklin*. Vol. 13: *January 1, 1766, through December 31, 1766*. Edited by Leonard W. Labaree, Helen C. Boatfield, and James H. Hutson. New Haven, Conn.: Yale University Press, 1969.

————. *The Writings of Benjamin Franklin*. Edited by Albert Henry Smyth. Vol. 4. New York: Macmillan, 1907.

Friedenwald, Herbert. *The Declaration of Independence: An Interpretation and an Analysis*. 1904. Rev. ed., New York: Da Capo, 1974.

Frothingham, Richard. *Life and Times of Joseph Warren*. Boston: Little, Brown, 1865.

————. *The Rise of the Republic of the United States*. Boston: Little, Brown, 1872.

Gaines, William H., Jr. "The Continental Congress Considers the Publication of a Bible, 1777." *Studies in Bibliography* 3 (1950–51): 275–81.

Gerber, Scott D. "Whatever Happened to the Declaration of Independence? A Commentary on the Republican Revisionism in the Political Thought of the American Revolution." *Polity* 26 (Winter 1993): 207–31.

Gibson, Alan. *Interpreting the Founding: Guide to the Enduring Debates over the Origins and Foundations of the American Republic.* Lawrence: University Press of Kansas, 2006.

Ginsberg, Elaine, K. "Dickinson, John." In *American National Biography Online.* Oxford University Press, 2000. http://www.anb.org/articles/01/01-00218.html.

Gipson, Lawrence Henry. "The American Revolution as an Aftermath of the Great War for the Empire, 1754–1763." 1950. In *The American Revolution: Two Centuries of Interpretation,* edited by Edmund S. Morgan, 147–65. Englewood Cliffs, N.J.: Prentice Hall, 1965.

———. "Thomas Hutchinson and the Framing of the Albany Plan of Union, 1754." *Pennsylvania Magazine of History and Biography* 74 (January 1950): 5–35.

Godbold, E. Stanley. *Christopher Gadsden and the American Revolution.* Knoxville: University of Tennessee Press, 1982.

William Gordon, ed. *The History of the Rise, Progress, and Establishment of the Independence of the United States of America.* 4 vols. London, 1788.

Gould, Eliga H. *The Persistence of Empire: British Political Culture in the Age of the American Revolution.* Chapel Hill: University of North Carolina Press, 2000.

Greene, Jack P., ed. *Colonies to Nation, 1763–1789: A Documentary History of the American Revolution.* 1967. Reprint. New York: Norton, 1975.

———. "Competing Authorities: The Debate over Parliamentary Imperial Jurisdiction, 1763–1776." *Parliamentary History* 14 (1995): 47–63.

———. *The Constitutional Origins of the American Revolution.* New York: Cambridge University Press, 2011.

———. *Negotiated Authorities: Essays in Colonial Political and Constitutional History.* Charlottesville: University Press of Virginia, 1994.

———. *Peripheries and Center: Constitutional Development in the Extended Polities of the British Empire and the United States, 1607–1788.* 1986. Reprint. New York: Norton, 1990.

Greene, Jack P., and J. R. Pole, eds. *The Blackwell Encyclopedia of the American Revolution.* Cambridge: Basil Blackwell, 1991.

Greven, Philip. *Protesant Temperament: Patterns of Child-Rearing, Religious Experience, and the Self in Early America.* New York: New American Library, 1977.

Guttridge, G. H. *English Whiggism and the American Revolution.* 1942. Reprint. Berkeley and Los Angeles: University of California Press, 1963.

Hall, David W. *The Genevan Reformation and the American Founding.* Lanham, Md.: Lexington, 2003.

Hamburger, Philip. *Separation of Church and State.* Cambridge, Mass.: Harvard University Press, 2002.

Handlin, Mary F., and Oscar Handlin. "Radicals and Conservatives in Massachusetts after Independence." *New England Quarterly* 17 (September 1944): 343–55.

Harlow, Vincent T. *The Founding of the Second British Empire, 1763–1793.* Vol. 1: *Discovery and Revolution.* London: Longmans, Green, 1952.

Hartz, Louis. *The Liberal Tradition in America: An Interpretation of American Political Thought since the Revolution.* New York: Harcourt, Brace, and World, 1955.

Hawke, David Freeman. *Honorable Treason: The Declaration of Indepdence and the Men Who Signed It.* New York: Viking, 1976.

Haywood, Marshall DeLancey. "The Genesis of Wake County." *North Carolina Booklet* 5 (1905):61.

Hazleton, John H. *The Declaration of Independence: Its History.* 1906. Rev. ed. New York: Da Capo, 1970.

Heimert, Alan. *Religion and the American Mind: From the Great Awakening to the Revolution.* Cambridge, Mass.: Harvard University Press, 1966.

Henderson, H. James. *Party Politics in the Continental Congress.* 1974. Reprint. Lanham, Md.: University Press of America, 1987.

Hoadly, Charles J., ed. *The Public Records of the Colony of Connecticut from May, 1762, to October, 1767, Inclusive.* Hartford: Case, Lockwood, and Brainard, 1881.

Hoffer, Peter. "The Declaration of Independence as a Bill in Equity." In *The Law in America, 1607–1861,* edited by William Pencak and Wythe Holt, Jr., 186–209. New York: New-York Historical Society, 1989.

Hogeland, William. *Declaration: The Nine Tumultuous Weeks When America Became Independent, May 1–July 4, 1776.* New York: Simon and Schuster, 2010.

Hulsebosch, Daniel J. *Constituting Empire: New York and the Transformation of Constitutionalism in the Atlantic World, 1664–1830.* Chapel Hill: University of North Carolina Press, 2005.

Hume, David. *The History of England from the Invasion of Julius Caesar to the Revolution in 1688.* 6 vols. 1778. Reprint. Indianapolis: Liberty Classics, 1983.

———. *Political Essays.* Edited by Knud Haakonssen. Cambridge: Cambridge University Press, 1994.

Hutson, James. *Church and State in America: The First Two Centuries.* Cambridge: Cambridge University Press, 2008.

———, ed. *A Decent Respect to the Opinions of Mankind: Congressional State Papers, 1774–1776.* Washington, D.C.: Library of Congress, 1975.

———. "The Emergence of the Modern Concept of a Right in America." In *The Nature of Rights at the American Founding and Beyond,* edited by Barry Alan Shain, 25–66. Charlottesville: University of Virginia Press, 2007.

———. *Religion and the Founding of the American Republic.* Washington, D.C.: Library of Congress, 1998.

Hyneman, Charles S., and Donald S. Lutz, eds. *American Political Writing during the Founding Era, 1760–1805.* 2 vols. Indianapolis: Liberty Press, 1983.

Ippel, Henry P. "Blow the Trumpet, Sanctify the Fast." *Huntington Library Quarterly* 44 (1980): 43–60.

Jameson, J. Franklin. *The American Revolution Considered as a Social Movement.* 1926. Reprint. Princeton, N.J.: Princeton University Press, 1967.

Janus [pseud.]. *The Critical Moment, on which the Salvation or Destruction of the British Empire Depends, Containing the Rise, Progress, Present State, and Natural Consequences of Our American Disputes.* London: H. Setchell, 1776.

Jefferson, Thomas. *The Papers of Thomas Jefferson.* Edited by Julian P. Boyd. 25 vols. Princeton, N.J.: Princeton University Press, 1950.

———. "Summary View of the Rights of British America." In *Tracts of the American Revolution 1763–1776,* edited by Merrill Jensen, 256–76. 1966. Reprint. Indianapolis: Hackett, 2003.

Jensen, Merrill, ed. *The Articles of Confederation: An Interpretation of the Social-Constitutional History of the American Revolution, 1774–1781.* 1940. Reprint. Madison: University of Wisconsin Press, 1970.

———, ed. *English Historical Documents: American Colonial Documents to 1776.* New York: Oxford University Press, 1969.

———. *The Founding of a Nation: A History of the American Revolution, 1763–1776.* New York: Oxford University Press, 1968.

———. *The New Nation: A History of the United States during the Confederation, 1781–1789*. 1950. Reprint. Boston: Northeastern University Press, 1981.

———, ed. *Tracts of the American Revolution, 1763–1776*. 1966. Reprint. Indianapolis: Hackett, 2003.

*Journal of the Honourable House of Representatives, at a Great and General Court or Assembly for His Majesty's Province of the Massachusetts-Bay in New-England: Begun and held at Boston, in the County of Suffolk, on Wednesday the Twenty-ninth Day of May, Annoque Domini, 1765*. Boston, 1765.

*Journal of the Votes and Proceedings of the General Assembly of the Colony of New York. Began on the 8th Day of November, 1743; and Ended the 23rd of December, 1765*. 2 vols. New York: Hugh Gaine, 1766.

Katz, Stanley N. and John M. Murrin, ed. *Colonial America: Essays in Politics and Social Development*. 3rd ed. New York: Knopf, 1983.

Kennedy, J. P., ed. *Journals of the House of Burgesses of Virginia, 1761–1765*. Richmond, 1907.

Kenyon, Cecilia M. "Republicanism and Radicalism in the American Revolution: An Old-Fashioned Interpretation." 1960. In *The Reinterpretation of the American Revolution, 1763–1789*, edited by Jack P. Greene, 291–320. New York: Harper and Row, 1968.

Kershaw, Gordon E. "Bowdoin, James." In *American National Biography Online*. Oxford University Press, 2000. http://www.anb.org/articles/01/01-00089.html.

———. "Cushing, Thomas." In *American National Biography Online*. Oxford University Press, 2000. http://www.anb.org/articles/02/02-00104.html.

King, Anthony. *The Founding Fathers v. the People: Paradoxes of American Democracy*. Cambridge, Mass: Harvard University Press, 2012.

Kloppenberg, James T. "The Virtues of Liberalism: Christianity, Republicanism, and Ethics in Early American Political Discourse." *Journal of American History* 74 (June 1987): 9–33.

Knollenberg, Bernard. *Growth of the American Revolution: 1766–1775*. 1975. Reprint. Indianapolis: Liberty Fund, 2003.

———. *Origin of the American Revolution: 1759–1766*. 1961. Reprint. Indianapolis: Liberty Fund, 2002.

Konig, David Thomas. "Pendleton, Edmund." In *American National Biography Online*. Oxford University Press, 2000. http://www.anb.org/articles/01/01-00708.html.

LaCroix, Alison L. *The Ideological Origins of American Federalism*. Cambridge, Mass.: Harvard University Press, 2010.

Lanctot, Gustave. *Canada and the American Revolution, 1774–1783*. Translated by Margaret M. Cameron. Toronto: Clarke, Irwin, 1967.

Lind, Jonathan. *An Answer to the Declaration of the American Congress*. With Jeremy Bentham. London: T. Cadell, 1776.

Locke, John. *Second Treatise of Government*. 1690. Edited by C. B. Macpherson. Indianapolis: Hackett, 1980.

———. *Some Thoughts Concerning Education*, and *Of the Conduct of the Understanding*. 1693 and 1706. Edited by Ruth W. Grant and Nathan Tarcov. Indianapolis: Hackett, 1996.

Lolme, J. L. de. *The Constitution of England; Or, An Account of the English Government*. Rev. ed., 1821, Reprint. Buffalo: Hein, 1999.

Lutz, Donald, S., ed. *Colonial Origins of the American Revolution: A Documentary History*. Indianapolis: Liberty Press, 1998.

———. "The Declaration of Independence." In *Roots of the Republic: American Founding Documents Interpreted*, edited by Stephen L. Schechter, 138–50. Madison: Madison House, 1990.

———. *A Preface to American Political Theory*. Lawrence: University Press of Kansas, 1992.

———. "The Relative Influence of European Writers on Late Eighteenth-Century American Political Thought." *American Political Science Review* 78 (March 1984): 189–97.

MacDonald, William. *Select Charters and Other Documents Illustrative of American History 1606–1775.* London: Macmillan, 1899.

Maier, Pauline. *American Scripture: Making the Declaration of Independence.* New York: Knopf, 1997.

———. *From Resistance to Revolution: Colonial Radicals and the Development of American Opposition to Britain, 1765–1776.* 1972. Reprint. New York: Norton, 1991.

Main, Jackson Turner. *The Social Structure of Revolutionary America.* Princeton, N.J.: Princeton University Press, 1965.

Maloy, J. S. *The Colonial Origins of Modern Democratic Thought.* New York: Cambridge University Press, 2008.

Marston, Jerrilyn Greene. *King and Congress: The Transfer of Political Legitimacy, 1774–1776.* Princeton, N.J.: Princeton University Press, 1987.

*Maryland Gazette.* Issue of Thursday, October 3, 1765. *Maryland Gazette* Collection (October 26, 1758–October 31, 1765). Maryland Archives Online, 2006. http://www.msa.md.gov/megafile /msa/speccol/sc4800/sc4872/001280/html/m1280-1534.html.

McConville, Brendan. *The King's Three Faces: The Rise and Fall of Royal America, 1688–1776.* Chapel Hill: University of North Carolina Press, 2006.

McGuire, Robert. *To Form a More Perfect Union: A New Economic Interpretation of the United States Constitution.* New York: Oxford University Press, 2003.

McIlwain, Charles Howard. *The American Revolution: A Constitutional Interpretation.* 1923. Reprint. Ithaca, N.Y.: Cornell University Press, 1961.

McLaughlin, Andrew. *The Foundations of American Constitutionalism.* New York: New York University Press, 1932.

Mill, John Stuart. *On Liberty.* 1859. Edited by Elizabeth Rapaport. Indianapolis, Hackett, 1978.

Montesquieu, Charles-Louis de Secondat, Baron de La Brède et de. *Spirit of the Laws.* 1748. Edited by Anne M. Cohler, Basia Carolyn Miller, and Harold Samuel Stone. Cambridge: Cambridge University Press, 1989.

Montross, Lynn. *The Reluctant Rebels: The Story of the Continental Congress, 1774–1789.* New York: Harper and Brothers, 1950.

Moore, Frank, ed. *The Patriot Preachers of the American Revolution.* New York: Charles T. Evans, 1862.

Morgan, Edmund S. "Colonial Ideas of Parliamentary Powers, 1764–1766." *William and Mary Quarterly* 5 (1948): 311–41.

———, ed. *The New York Declaration of 1764.* Old South Leaflets, no. 224. Boston: Old South Association, 1948.

———, ed. *Prologue to Revolution: Sources and Documents on the Stamp Act Crisis, 1764–1766.* Chapel Hill: University of North Carolina Press, 1959.

Morgan, Edmund S., and Helen M. Morgan. *The Stamp Act Crisis: Prologue to Revolution.* 3rd ed. Chapel Hill: University of North Carolina Press, 1995.

Morison, Samuel Eliot, ed. *Sources and Documents Illustrating the American Revolution, 1764–1788, and the Formation of the Federal Constitution.* 2nd ed. Oxford: Oxford University Press, 1929.

Morris, Richard B. *Encyclopedia of American History.* 1953. Rev. ed., New York: Harper and Row, 1961.

Morton, Joseph C. *The American Revolution.* Westport, Conn.: Greenwood, 2003.

Namier, Lewis. *England in the Age of the American Revolution.* 1930. Rev. ed., London: St. Martin's, 1970.

Nash, Gary B. *The Unknown American Revolution: The Unruly Birth of Democracy and the Struggle to Create America.* New York: Penguin, 2005.

Nelson, Eric. "Patriot Royalism: The Stuart Monarchy in American Political Thought, 1769." *William and Mary Quarterly* 68 (October 2011): 533–72.

Newbold, Robert C. *The Albany Congress and Plan of Union of 1754.* New York: Vantage, 1955.

North Carolina Historical Commission. "Halifax Resolves." Excerpted from "Historical Miscellanea: An Early History of North Carolina." *The North Carolina Manual* (1991–1992). http://ncpedia.org/history/usrevolution/halifax-resolves.

Oberholtzer, Ellis Paxson. *Robert Morris, Patriot and Financier.* London: Macmillan, 1903.

O'Gorman, Frank. "The Parliamentary Opposition to the Government's American Policy, 1760–1782." In *Britain and the American Revolution,* edited by H. T. Dickinson, 97–123. London and New York: Longman, 1998.

Onuf, Peter S. *The Origins of the Federal Republic: Jurisdictional Controversies in the United States, 1775–1787.* Philadelphia: University of Pennsylvania Press, 1983.

O'Shaughnessy, Andrew Jackson. "'If Others Will Not Be Active, I Must Drive': George III and the American Revolution." *Early American Studies* 2 (Spring 2004): 1–46.

Otis, James. "The Rights of the British Colonies Asserted and Proved." In *Tracts of the American Revolution,* edited by Merrill Jensen, 19–40. 1966. Reprint. Indianapolis: Hackett, 2003.

Palmer, R. R. *The Age of the Democratic Revolution: A Political History of Europe and America, 1760–1800.* Vol. 1: *The Challenge.* Princeton, N.J.: Princeton University Press, 1959.

Peckham, Howard H. *The War for Independence: A Military History.* 1958. Reprint. Chicago: University of Chicago Press, 1979.

Pekelis, Alexander H. *Law and Social Action: Selected Essays.* Ithaca, N.Y.: Cornell University Press, 1950.

Pencak, William. "Otis, James." In *American National Biography Online.* Oxford University Press, 2000. http://www.anb.org/articles/01/01-00690.html.

———. "Ruggles, Timothy." In *American National Biography Online.* Oxford University Press, 2000. http://www.anb.org/articles/01/01-00800.html.

Penn, Rich D., and Arthur Lee. "The Olive Branch Petition: The Humble Petition of Congress, 1775." Karpeles Manuscript Library Museums. http://www.rain.org/~karpeles/olifrm.html.

Perry, Richard L., ed. *Sources of Our Liberties: Documentary Origins of the Individual Liberties in the United States Constitution and Bill of Rights.* 1959. Rev. ed., Buffalo: Hein, 1991.

Pickering, Danby, ed. *The Statutes at Large from the Magna Charta to the End of the Eleventh Parliament of Great Britain.* 35 vols. Cambridge: John Archdeacon, 1775.

Pleasants, J. Hall, ed. *Archives of Maryland 59: Proceedings and Acts of the General Assembly of Maryland, 1764–1765.* Baltimore: Maryland Historical Society, 1942.

Potter, Janice. *The Liberty We Seek: Loyalist Ideology in Colonial New York and Massachusetts.* Cambridge, Mass.: Harvard University Press, 1983.

Preston, Howard W. *Documents Illustrative of American History, 1606–1863.* New York: Putnam's Sons, 1886.

Prince, Carl E. "Livingston, William." In *American National Biography Online.* Oxford University Press, 2000. http://www.anb.org/articles/01/01-00525.html.

Purcell, L. Edward. *Who Was Who in the American Revolution.* New York: Facts on File, 1993.

Putney, Clifford. "Oxenbridge Thacher: Boston Lawyer, Early Patriot." *Historical Journal of Massachusetts* 32 (2004): 90–106.

Rafuse, Ethan S. "Warren, Joseph." In *American National Biography Online*. Oxford University Press, 2000. http://www.anb.org/articles/02/02-00331.html.

Rakove, Jack N. *The Beginnings of National Politics: An Interpretive History of the Continental Congress*. Baltimore: John Hopkins University Press, 1979.

———. *Revolutionaries: A New History of the Invention of America*. Boston and New York: Mariner, 2011.

Randolph, Edmund. "Edmund Randolph's Essay on the Revolutionary History of Virginia, 1774–1782." *Virginia Magazine of History and Biography* 44 (1936): 35–50.

Reid, John Phillip. "The Authority of Rights at the American Founding." In *The Nature of Rights at the American Founding and Beyond*, edited by Barry Alan Shain, 67–115. Charlottesville: University of Virginia, 2007.

———, ed. *The Briefs of the American Revolution: Constitutional Arguments between Thomas Hutchinson, Governor of Massachusetts Bay, and James Bowdoin for the Council and John Adams for the House of Representatives*. New York: New York University Press, 1981.

———. *Constitutional History of the American Revolution*. Abridged ed. Madison: University of Wisconsin Press, 1995.

———. *In a Defiant Stance: The Conditions of Law in Massachusetts Bay, the Irish Comparison, and the Coming of the American Revolution*. University Park: Pennsylvania State University Press, 1977.

Rhode Island General Assembly. Act of Renunciation. Addressed from the Rhode Island General Assembly to King George III, 1776. Rhode Island State Archives, item 68. http://sos.ri.gov/virtualarchives/items/show/68.

Risjord, Norman K. "Harrison, Benjamin." In *American National Biography Online*. Oxford University Press, 2000. http://www.anb.org/articles/01/01-00377.html.

Ritcheson, Charles R. *British Politics and the American Revolution*. Norman: University of Oklahoma Press, 1954.

Robbins, Caroline. *The Eighteenth-Century Commonwealthman: Studies in the Transmission, Development, and Circumstance of English Liberal Thought from the Restoration of Charles II until the War with the Thirteen Colonies*. 1959. Reprint. Indianapolis: Liberty Fund, 2004.

Robson, Eric. "Why Revolution?" In *The American Revolution: Two Centuries of Interpretation*, edited by Edmund S. Morgan, 139–46. Englewood Cliffs, N.J.: Prentice-Hall, 1965.

Rodgers, Daniel T. "Rights Consciousness in American History." In *The Nature of Rights at the American Founding and Beyond*, edited by Barry Alan Shain, 258–79. Charlottesville: University of Virginia Press, 2007.

Roeber, A. Gregg. "The Limited Horizons of Whig Religious Rights." In *The Nature of Rights at the American Founding and Beyond*, edited by Barry Alan Shain, 198–229. Charlottesville: University of Virginia Press, 2007.

Rosenberg, Charles. "Militia, Patriot, and Loyalist." In *The Encyclopedia of the American Revolutionary War: A Political, Social, and Military History*, edited by Gregory Fremont-Barnes and Richard Alan Ryerson, 3:794–97. Santa Barbara, Calif.: ABC-CLIO, 2006.

Rousseau, Jean-Jacques. *The Social Contract and Discourses*. 1750, 1755, 1762. Translated and edited by G. D. H. Cole, 1913. Reprint. London: Everyman, 1993.

Rozbicki, Michal Jan. *Culture and Liberty in the Age of the American Revolution*. Charlottesville: University of Virginia Press, 2011.

Rush, Benjamin. *The Autobiography of Benjamin Rush.* Edited by George W. Corner. Princeton, N.J.: Princeton University Press, 1948.

Russell, Thaddeus. "Smith, Richard." In *American National Biography Online.* Oxford University Press, 2000. http://www.anb.org/articles/01/01-00841.html.

Sandoz, Ellis, ed. *Political Sermons of the American Founding Era, 1730–1805.* Indianapolis: Liberty Fund, 1991.

Schecter, Barnet. "New York Campaign." In *The Encyclopedia of the American Revolution: Library of Military History,* edited by Harold Selesky, 2:828–34. Detroit: Scribner's Sons, 2006.

Schuyler, Robert L. *Parliament and the British Empire: Some Constitutional Controversies concerning Imperial Legislation Jurisdiction.* New York: Columbia University Press, 1929.

Selby, John E. "Randolph, Peyton." In *American National Biography Online.* Oxford University Press, 2000. http://www.anb.org/articles/01/01-00768.html.

Shain, Barry Alan. "Declaration of Independence [in Supreme Court Decisions]." In *Encyclopedia of the Supreme Court of the United States,* edited by David S. Tanenhaus, 2:13–15. Detroit: Macmillan Reference USA, 2009.

———. *The Myth of American Individualism: The Protestant Origins of American Political Thought.* 1994. Reprint. Princeton, N.J.: Princeton University Press, 1996.

———. "Reading *The Federalist,* Looking Backward and Forward: Madison's Creative but Failed Political Theory." Unpublished manuscript.

———. "Review of *Forgotten Patriots: The Untold Story of the American Prisoners during the Revolutionary War,*" by Edwin G. Burrows. *Journal of Presbyterian History* 88 (Fall/Winter 2010): 78–79.

———. "Rights Natural and Civil in the Declaration of Independence." In *The Nature of Rights at the American Founding and Beyond,* edited by Barry Alan Shain, 116–62. Charlottesville: University of Virginia Press, 2007.

Sharp, Granville. *A Declaration of the People's Natural Right to a Share in the Legislature.* London: B. White, 1774.

Slade, William, ed. *Vermont State Papers: Being a Collection of Records and Documents.* Middlebury, Vt.: J. W. Copeland, 1823.

Smith, Adam. *An Inquiry into the Nature and Causes of the Wealth of Nations.* 5th ed., 1789. Reprint. New York: Modern Library, 1994.

Smith, Paul H., ed. *English Defenders of American Freedom, 1774–1778: Six Pamphlets Attacking British Policy.* Washington, D.C.: Library of Congress, 1972.

———, ed. *Letters of Delegates to Congress, 1774–1789.* 25 vols. Washington, D.C.: Library of Congress, 1976–93. http://memory.loc.gov/ammem/amlaw/lwdg.html.

Smith, Rogers. *Civic Ideals: Conflicting Visions of Citizenship in U. S. History.* New Haven, Conn.: Yale University Press, 1997.

Sparks, Jared, ed. *The Works of Benjamin Franklin.* 10 vols. Boston: Hillard, Gray, 1836–40.

Tansill, Charles C., ed. *Documents Illustrative of the Formation of the Union of the American States.* Washington, D.C.: Government Printing Office, 1927.

Thackeray, Francis. *A History of the Right Honorable William Pitt, Earl of Chatham.* London: R. Gilbert, 1827.

Thomas, Peter D. G. *The Townshend Duties Crisis: The Second Phase of the American Revolution, 1767–1773.* Oxford: Clarendon Press, 1987.

Thornton, John Wingate, ed. *The Pulpit of the American Revolution, or the Political Sermons of the Period 1776.* Boston: Gould and Lincoln, 1860.

Tucker, Josiah. *A Treatise Concerning Civil Government.* 1781. Reprint. New York: Kelley, 1967.

Tucker, Robert W., and David C. Hendrickson. *The Fall of the First British Empire: Origins of the War of American Independence.* Baltimore: Johns Hopkins University Press, 1982.

Tyler, Moses Coit. *The Literary History of the American Revolution, 1763–1783.* 2 vols. New York: Putnam's Sons, 1897.

U.S. Continental Congress. *Journals of the Continental Congress, 1774–1789.* Edited by Worthington C. Ford et al. 34 vols. Washington, D.C.: Library of Congress, 1904–37. http://memory.loc.gov/ammem/amlaw/lwjc.html.

Valentine, Alan. *The British Establishment, 1760–1784: An Eighteenth-Century Biographical Dictionary.* 2 vols. Norman: University of Oklahoma Press, 1970.

Van Tyne, Claude H. *England and America: Rivals in the American Revolution.* Cambridge: Cambridge University Press, 1929.

———. *The Loyalists in the American Revolution.* 1902. Reprint. Gloucester, Mass.: Peter Smith, 1959.

Webking, Robert H. *The American Revolution and the Politics of Liberty.* Baton Rouge: Louisiana State University Press, 1988.

Weir, Robert M. "Rutledge, John." In *American National Biography Online.* Oxford University Press, 2000. http://www.anb.org/articles/01/01-00802.html.

Weslager, C. A. *The Stamp Act Congress.* Newark: University of Delaware Press, 1976.

Wolf, Edwin, II. "The Authorship of the 1774 Address to the King Restudied." *William and Mary Quarterly* 22 (April 1965): 189–224.

Wood, Gordon S. *The Creation of the American Republic, 1776–1787.* Chapel Hill: University of North Carolina Press, 1969.

———. "The History of Rights in Early America." In *The Nature of Rights at the American Founding and Beyond,* edited by Barry Alan Shain, 233–57. Charlottesville: University of Virginia Press, 2007.

———. *The Radicalism of the American Revolution: How a Revolution Transformed a Monarchical Society into a Democratic One Unlike Any That Had Ever Existed.* New York: Knopf, 1992.

Wood, W. J. *Battles of the Revolutionary War, 1775–1781.* Chapel Hill, N.C.: Algonquin, 1990.

Yirush, Craig. *Settlers, Liberty, and Empire: The Roots of Early American Political Theory, 1675–1775.* New York: Cambridge University Press, 2011.

York, Neil Longley. "Federalism and the Failure of Imperial Reform, 1774–1775." *History* 86 (2001): 155–79.

———. "The Impact of the American Revolution on Ireland." In *Britain and the American Revolution,* editd by H. T. Dickinson, 205–32. London: Longman, 1998.

———. "When Words Fail: William Pitt, Benjamin Franklin and the Imperial Crisis of 1766." *Parliamentary History* 28 (2009): 341–74.

Zuckert, Michael. *The Natural Rights Republic: Studies in the Foundation of the American Political Tradition.* Notre Dame, Ind.: University of Notre Dame Press, 1996.

# INDEX

*Page numbers in* italics *refer to texts of documents. Letters are listed at the ends of entries.*

INDEX

remittances: colonial trade and, 39, 48, 299, 392; Franklin on, 114, 115

remonstrances, 150, 205, 270, 279; to House of Commons, 59–61

Renunciation Act (1783), 313–14, 689n60

Renunciatory Act (1782), 682n80

representation: of colonists, 210, 212, 357; equal, 85, 446, 447; in New York's assembly, 36; proportional, 85, 156, 15; qualifications to vote and, 455–59; virtual, 95, 100. *See also* nonrepresentation; no taxation without representation

republican government, 17; colonies' experiments in, 440; Congress and, 352; conservatives and, 675n37; democratic project for, 9; as goal of limited minority, 12; no plans for formation of, 676n49; resistance of, 420, 421, 436, 437–38

republicanism, republicans, 2, 3, 673n18; in Congress, 158, 160; in Declaration of Independence, 86, 377–78; language of, 484, 681n67; move toward, 355, 379; New England and, 86, 104, 136, 143, 343, 344–45, 360, 380, 485; popular, 18, 86, 381, 420, 421, 456; reconciliation opposed by, 160; resistance to, 420, 421, 436, 437–38; Sons of Liberty and, 29; in Virginia, 136, 143

resolves and resolutions, 372–73, 693n36; on establishing new state governments, 371, 376–77; of Halifax, N.C., 417; language of, 484; of Massachusetts General Court, 25; of Mecklenberg County, N.C., 255, 371, 417, 695n73; on Stamp Act, 61–89. *See also* Second Continental Congress—resolutions of; Suffolk Resolves

Restraining Acts, 262, 285, 412, 421, 487; condemned by Congress, 296; New England restraining act, 254, 258, 284, *284–87*

retaliation, law of, 357–58

Revere, Paul, 144, 349

Revolutionary War, American. *See* War for Independence, American

Rhode Island, 704n84; Act of Renunciation, 440; Albany Congress and, 174, 175; Assembly of, 463; courts in, 206; disavows allegiance to king, 371, 440, 459; lack of colonial agents, 691n103; as neutral arbiter, 694n64; new state government of, 443; petitions against Sugar and Currency Acts, 33; privateering and, 416; republican government of, 440–41; resolves of, 28, 62; at Stamp Act Congress, 25, 84, 85, 89, 92; states' rights and, 463; supports independence, 450, 473, 501, 696n89

rights: ancient, 46, 141, 208, 209, 226, 229, 232; of assembly, 213; breakdown of, 680n38; British constitutional, 64, 76, 411, 484; of colonists, 25, 28, 29, 43, 56, 57, 70, 210, 215, 233, 676n49; conflict of, 13; corporate, as greater concern for colonists than natural, 5, 12, 13, 15–16, 42, 156–57, 158, 378, 395, 592; defense of, 147; duties and, 354, 686n84; emigration and, 213, 222, 223; of Englishmen, 64, 73, 92, 112, 125; fourfold foundation of, 222; Franklin and, 30; habeas corpus, 141, 229, 232; individual, not as important as corporate, 5, 95, 229; international, 31; to life, liberty, property, 141, 212, 232; loss of, 49; to petition, 80, 86, 89, 213; privileges vs., 27, 52, 62; religious, 92; resting on common law, 216, 218; royal charter, 76, 221, 223; source of, 211; unalienable, 63, 76, 77; universal, 13, 18, 28, 31, 63–64, 87, 262, 382, 592, 698n112. *See also* birthrights, English; British Constitution; civil rights; corporate rights; English Constitution; jury trials, juries; natural rights; Parliament: right of taxation and legislation of; press, freedom of; property: rights of; self-taxation and self-government through colonial legislatures

Ritcheson, Charles R., 13, 230, 239, 672n12, 686n91, 690n75

Robbins, Caroline, 671n3, 697n103

Roberdeau, Daniel: committee service of, 608, 611, 612; in Congress, 613, 621, 622; in Pennsylvania Assembly, 450; as signer of Olive Branch Petition, 656

Robinson, John, as Speaker of House of Burgesses, 55, 61, 66

Rockingham, Charles Watson-Wentworth, Second Marquess of: administration of, 326, 329; Declaratory Act and, 682n79; as friend of colonies, 328, 329; Stamp Act repeal and, 25–26, 30, 33, 110, 126; Whigs and, 155, 192

Rodney, Caesar, 482; on grand committee, 208; signs Continental Association, 186; signs Declaration of Independence, 493; signs Olive Branch Petition, 293; signs petition to king, 243; at Stamp Act Congress, 84

Rogers, John, 472, 475, 696n98

Roman Catholicism, Catholics, 141; British Empire and, 3; Canada and, 241, 249, 350, 351; colonists' denial of rights of, 11, 473; in Congress; naturalization and, 687n103; Protestants and, 236; Quebec Act and, 22, 137–38, 148–49, 180, 209, 214, 238, 241, 249, 251, 264; threat of, 191–92, 198, 230, 264

743